Y0-BIS-571

STRATEGIC MANAGEMENT: AN INTEGRATIVE CONTEXT-SPECIFIC PROCESS

by

Robert J. Mockler
St. John's University

IDEA GROUP PUBLISHING
Harrisburg, U.S.A. • London, U.K.

Published in the United States of America by
Idea Group Publishing
Olde Liberty Square
4811 Jonestown Road, Suite 230
Harrisburg, PA 17109
800-345-4332

and in the United Kingdom by
Idea Group Publishing
3 Henrietta Street
Covent Garden
London WC2E 8LU

Printed in the United States of America

ISBN 1-878289-19-5

ACKNOWLEDGMENTS

I wish to thank my many friends in business who stimulated and guided the development and writing of this book. My late brother and very close friend, Colman Mockler, Jr., to whom this book is dedicated, was CEO of Gillette Corporation for 17 years from 1974 until his death in January 1991. In addition to being an extraordinary human being, he was an extremely successful strategic manager; the example of his own work and his stimulating comments strengthened many areas of this book. His experiences were especially helpful in developing the integrated structured situation/context-specific orientation underlying this book. Colman's strategic management effectiveness came largely from his ability to fully integrate a highly disciplined cognitive approach to management with a very flexible and highly human focus on the needs of individuals, as well as on the ethical concerns of society. The structured context-specific strategic management processes described in this book attempt to reflect this integrated balance.

Other CEOs whose work helped shape the thinking underlying this book include: Gene Sullivan, who headed Borden's and subsequently taught at St. John's University; Warren Buffett, Chairman and CEO of Bershire Hathaway. Inc. and a major investor in Gillette who also headed Salomon Brothers Inc. during the reorganization period after the trading scandal in 1991; the late Sam Walton, founder and former CEO of Walmart; Joseph J. Melone, President and CEO of The Equitable (Equitable Life Assurance Society); and Mike Casper, founder and CEO of Microwave Printed Circuitry, Inc. I am also indebted to the many people who worked with me in building my own companies.

Dozens of people in education and publishing read drafts of material in this book and reviewed and commented on the many articles, earlier books and research monographs, and presentations I did based on material included in this book. They include: Harry Bunn, Lloyd Byars, Justin Carey, Daniel Couger, Dorothy Dologite, David Dykes, Colin Edin, Jim Euchner, Richard Fenton, Bob Flast, Mike Goul, Charles Hofer, Neil Holden, George Huber, David Hunger, Tim Kent, Joseph Latona, Frank Lynch, Ed Mahler, Tom Malone, Larry Mauer, Robert McGlashin, Bill Naumes, William Newman, Jay Nunamaker, John O'Dea, John Pearce, Henry Rhunke, Alan Rowe, Neantro Saavedra-Rivano, George Sawyer, John Seeger, George Steiner, Marilyn Taylor, Julian Vincze, Richard Wohl, and Tom Wheelen. I am especially grateful to the members of the New York Planning Forum's special interest groups of strategic corporate planners who so generously gave of their time in describing their planning experiences.

Many people contributed to the development of the company studies included in the case study section of this book. The 17 original company studies were based in large measure on field research by people working in the industry or working for the company involved in the study. These studies were prepared under the direction of Dr. Robert J. Mockler by the persons listed in parentheses following each case study title. The cases were designed and written especially for readers of this book.

Bio-Reference Laboratories (Narsim Banavara, Gary Gooden, Adrienne T. Palmieri); *CATV Enterprises Inc.* (Chiang-Nan Chao, William Rella, Mark Zarb); *Cooper Tire & Rubber Company* (Dorothy Dologite, Ria Koumouli, Catherine Testani); *Harley Davidson* (Thomas

Sullivan, Larry Boone, John Gluszak); *Hewlett-Packard* (Thomas Goeller, Stephen Persek, Christopher Pryce); *Lumex* (Mary Mirabella, Lawrence de la Haba, Charles Wankel); *Marshall Oil Company* (Michael Caufield, Brenda Massetti, Kamina Singh); *MCA Music Entertainment Group* (William Birmingham, Remo Dello Ioio, Kelly Otter-Cooper); *Mercer's Choice* (Brenda Massetti); *Michael Jewelers* (Kevin Dobbs, Melanie Tanzman Katz, Nancy Ward); *Nordstrom* (Thomas Abraham, Gina Muccioli, Kathleen Tonhazy); *Reebok International Ltd.* (Jairo Jaramillo, William Keffas, Emily Hammond); *The Seven Up Company* (Mark Aune, John T. Becker, Chou Tien-Yao); *Tele-communications Inc.* (Thomas Abraham, Christal Smith, Kathleen Loughran); *Uni-Marts* (Erika Green-Smith, Steven LaSala, Kenneth Nostro); *U.S. Healthcare, Inc.* (John Angelidis, Wayne Bennett, Marion Landesmann, Joanne Solita); *United Parcel Service* (Paul Poppler, Victor Conforti, Javier Caldeiro).

This book also includes two original classic Harvard case studies, *Blakeston and Wilson* and *Superb Biscuits Company*.

Another unique feature of this book is the inclusion of complete prototype expert knowledge-based systems used in business. I wish to thank Cimflex Teknowledge for giving permission to use M.1, an expert system development shell which was used to create and run these systems. I also wish to thank Jay Brownfield of Cimflex for his help in preparing the systems for publication. The following played major roles in developing the knowledge-based systems described in this book and included on the disks accompanying this book: Thomas Abraham, Kenneth Chou and Brenda Massetti (overall strategy formulation); John Angelides, William Holsten and Daniel Popper (new product strategy at a foreign affiliate); John Merseburg (career strategy formulation); Dorothy Dologite, Stephen Persek, and Jane Lamb Morrison (franchise selection); Dagberto Pinol, Thomas Goeller, and Itzak Wirth (production/operations strategy formulation and implementation); Geraldine Denoga, Stephen Persek, and Chistopher Yankana (capital investment planning); John Merseburg, Paul Poppler and Pat Lyons (preliminary screening of systems project); and Chiang-Nan Chao, Irfan Sharif, and Irshad Shiekh (international market entry).

Javier Caldeiro did most of the work involved in preparing the financial analysis and simulation computer support material included on the disks accompanying this book.

Others contributed in structuring decision approaches to specific types of strategic management situations and replicating these approaches in knowledge-based systems. They include John Merseburg, Yuan-I Lin, and Constanza Garrido. In addition, I wish to thank Mark Aune, David Barbieri, Sweelim Chia, Dorothy Dologite, Dane Gobin, Emily Hammond, Helen Ly, Paul Mastrandrea, Kelly Otter-Cooper, Gregory Pizzigno, Cynthia Phillips, Christal Smith, and May-Mei Wong for their extensive help over the past seven years in developing material for the book, preparing the final draft for printing, and obtaining the resources needed to get the job done. Kamina Singh was instrumental in preparing the case studies for publication, and Nancy Ward and Jan Travers did the major work involved in preparing the text for printing. Mehdi Khosprowpour was indispensable in making it all happen.

The material in this book was developed in large part through the research, writing, and case development work of the Strategic Management Research Group.

PREFACE

This book is intended mainly for busy students in undergraduate and MBA school programs. To accommodate them, there is no formal preface. Rather, they can move immediately to Chapter 1 to get acquainted with the subject. For those readers who want an introduction to the ideas behind the book, Appendix C, at the end of the text portion of this book, introduces the concepts underlying this book.

Robert J. Mockler
New York City
November 1992

Dedicated to the late Colman M. Mockler, Jr., former Chief Executive Officer of Gillette, brother and mentor of the author, one of business's truly great leaders, and an extraordinary human being.

OTHER BOOKS AND MONOGRAPHS BY ROBERT J. MOCKLER

- **Strategic Management: A Methodological Approach, 4th Edition** (co-author)
- **Strategic Management: A Research Guide Including Comprehensive Bibliographies**
- **Expert Systems: An Introduction to Knowledge-based Systems** (co-author)
- **Knowledge-based Systems Development Using an Expert System Shell**
- **Strategic Management Cases**
- **Computer Software to Support Strategic Management Decision Making**
- **Contingency Approaches to Strategic Management: Integrating Basic and Applied Research, Research Monograph**
- **Situations Involving Major Social Factors: The Strategic Management Processes, Research Monograph**
- **Entrepreneurial New Venture Situations: The Strategic Management Processes, Research Monograph**
- **Strategic Management for Multinational Operations: The Strategic Management Processes Involved, Research Monograph**
- **Understanding, Doing, and Teaching Strategic Management: Cognitive Modelling and Knowledge-based Systems Applications, Research Monograph**
- **Knowledge-based (Expert) Systems for Strategic Planning**
- **Using Computers** (co-author), 2nd edition
- **Knowledge-based (Expert) Systems for Management Decisions**
- **Using Microcomputers** (co-author), 2nd edition
- **Student Study Guide and Workbook: Using Microcomputers** (co-author)
- **Using Basic: A Structured BASIC Programming Guide** (co-author)
- **A Tutorial for Using EXSYS, an Expert System Shell** (co-author)
- **Business Planning and Policy Formulation**
- **Business and Society**
- **Developing Information Systems for Management**
- **The Business Management Process: A Situational Approach**
- **Management Decision Making and Action in Behavioral Situations**
- **Readings in Business Planning and Policy Formulation** (editor and contributing author)
- **The Management Control Process**
- **Readings in Management Control** (editor and contributing author)
- **New Profit Opportunities in Publishing** (editor and contributing author)
- **Putting Computers to Work More Effectively in Business Publishing** (editor and contributing author)
- **Guidelines for More Effective Planning and Management of Franchise Systems** (co-author)

STRATEGIC MANAGEMENT:
AN INTEGRATIVE CONTEXT-SPECIFIC PROCESS

Table of Contents

CASE STUDY SECTION 471

*Disguised company study

PART ONE

THE NATURE OF STRATEGIC MANAGEMENT

CHAPTER 1

INTRODUCTION

The objective of this introductory chapter is to help readers understand

- The essence of strategic management in business
- Rapidly changing business environments in the 1990s
- The importance of strategic thinking and appropriate organization context to effective strategy implementation
- Who does strategic management
- The wide range of strategic management situations
- Why strategic management is both a structured and an adaptive context-specific management process
- Misconceptions about strategic management

WHAT IS STRATEGIC MANAGEMENT?

Strategic management in business refers to the decisions and actions involved in formulating enterprise-wide strategies and in managing an enterprise's operations in a way that effectively carries these strategies out. Enterprise-wide strategies are longer-term objectives and plans formulated to enable an enterprise to effectively interact with the competitive environment. For this book's purposes, the enterprise being managed may be either an entire business or company, or a major (or strategic) business unit of a firm.

As shown in Figure 1-1 in very general terms, strategic management involves identifying situation context requirements — internal (company) and external (industry and competitive market) factors affecting a specific individual enterprise — and then using that knowledge to formulate and implement enterprise-wide strategies for that specific enterprise. Although it can be structured as shown in Figure 1-1 for discussion purposes, in practice strategic management is a flexible, adaptive context-specific process which can vary substantially in execution from situation to situation.

Formulating company strategies and putting them to work can be exciting and rewarding. The Games Gang Ltd. hit upon the idea of a game called Pictionary — basically a way to play charades on paper. Within two years, the company had annual sales of $125 million. Unlike companies such as Atari (home video games) and Coleco (Cabbage Patch dolls), which had built up fixed costs and then suffered substantial losses when their primary products declined in popularity, The Games Gang paid closer attention to the highly volatile and faddish nature of their own game/toy industry. In 1989 The Games Gang had built no manufacturing plants, owned no distribution unit, had no plush corporate headquarters, had only 25 employees, and was doing little advertising. These were necessary strategic steps in light of the industry's volatile nature and the company's limited resources.

The company's enterprise-wide strategy was simple: find a game already selling well in a local market to reduce research and development costs, check it for "playability" with friends and relatives to test customer usability and acceptance, set up a royalty arrangement with the inventor, farm out the manufacturing to control costs, and let word-of-mouth — supplemented by public relations programs — build sales [Deutsch 1989(A)].

In a highly competitive business environment, a company has to *differentiate* itself from the competition — by doing things differently (for example, new products and services) and better (for example, improved service and quality, or lower costs). The Games Gang gained a competitive edge by formulating and implementing such a differentiated corporate strategy. Top managers at The Games Gang formulated strategies by listening to its customers and the competitive market (their specific situation context) and adapting their strategies to meet the realities of that turbulent market and of their limited available company resources. They did not do it by copying industry leaders.

While the Games Gang is a good example of strategic management at work, formulating enterprise-wide strategies and implementing them is rarely that simple and straightforward.

When asked what he considered an enterprise-wide strategy to be, Colman Mockler, the chief executive officer (CEO) of Gillette from 1974 to his death in January 1991, explained: "I knew exactly what kind of company I envisioned; I just didn't know precisely what it would look like." The rapidly changing competitive market environment led him to define implementation as ultimately "doing whatever was necessary to get the job done, within well-defined moral, legal, ethical, and policy limitations." What specific plans actually looked like, therefore, emerged gradually over a period of time, shaped by Gillette's line managers.

After being promoted to CEO at Gillette, a $4.5 billion multinational company, Mockler spent several years realigning internal business processes to meet changing competitive market requirements and creating an internal company organization context or environment that would enable successful implementation of the company's newly focused strategy. This new strategy involved divesting 21 divisions in order to concentrate on the company's core razor and blade, toiletries, and writing instruments businesses.

Figure 1-1: Strategic Management Process Overview

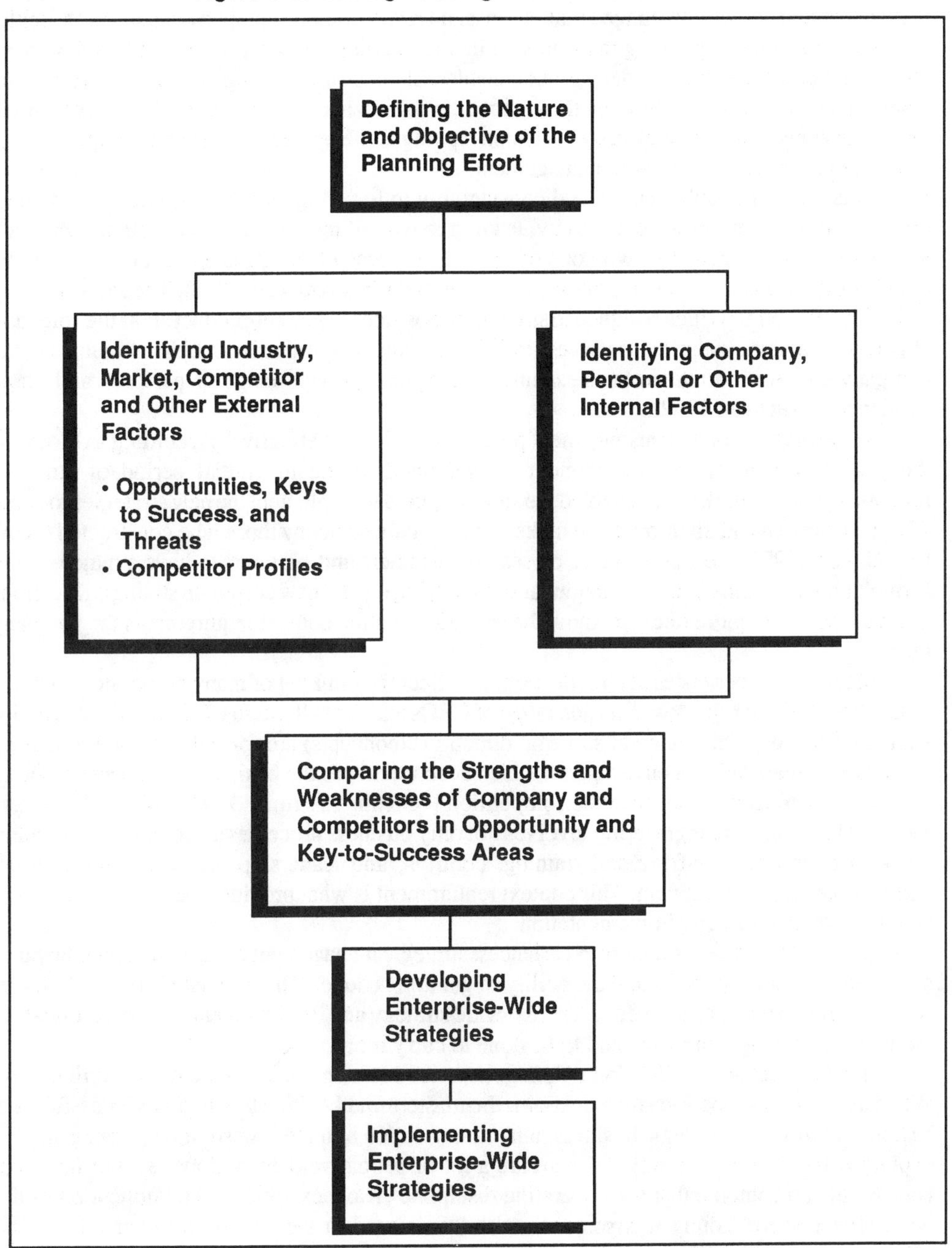

He also created a new organization context by developing an organization with fewer levels of management, which encouraged mutual trust and respect among company managers. Mockler put in dozens of new operating managers while maintaining the company's traditional humane and secure corporate culture, delegating considerable decision making authority, encouraging commitment and strategic thinking throughout the organization. Sophisticated computer information systems allowed for effective decision making at the operating level and for tight control of operating results by corporate management.

This internal realignment helped considerably to lower operating costs and increase new product and product refinement activity, leading to overall reductions in production costs each year and culminating in 1990 with one of the most successful new product introductions in the long history of this mature industry — the Sensor razor [Chakravorty 1991]. The same strategy — highly focused activities designed to strengthen positions in market/product areas the company already dominated — also led to success in Gillette's major subsidiaries, such as Braun A.G., the company's German strategic business unit which made a wide range of personal and home appliances [Protzman 1992].

Why was the strategic management process at Gillette so effective? According to Mockler, the internal organizational realignment he instituted during the initial period of strategic refocusing after he took office enabled the steps required to implement the new strategies to come "from the bottom and up through the ranks" and be "carried out by those who constructed them" [McKibben 1990]. He wanted those closest to customers and suppliers to have a major role in formulating the details of new strategies and in carrying out the new corporate strategic directions because they were more likely to know the specific situation context requirements the company faced.

Mockler's experiences at Gillette seem to reflect the thinking of many corporate managers today, based on interviews with a wide range of CEOs and consultants to CEOs involved in major strategic changes. Once general strategic directions (concepts) are formulated, the focus is on creating an organizational environment which accommodates the business processes needed to serve customer needs better than the competition ["Getting to Prime" 1991; Mills 1991; Peters 1991]. That context reengineering involves not only business processes and company structure, but also appropriate staffing and training, controls, and leadership based on mutual trust, competence, and commitment. This context realignment is what provides the framework which enables effective strategy implementation.

As seen from these company experiences, strategic management requires a special blend of conceptual (visionary) skills and the ability to get things done. This is what Gillette's Mockler was referring to when he defined enterprise-wide strategy and its implementation as formulating the vision and then doing what had to be done to carry it out.

Hewlett Packard's CEO, John Young, described strategic management in a similar way. When asked to describe Richard Hackborn, the mastermind behind HP's highly successful $2.5 billion laser printing strategic business unit, Young called him the "consummate strategist." He explained the term in this way: "There are a lot of people who are visionaries, but he [Dick Hackborn] can combine that with operating discipline" [Pollack 1992]. The implication of the word strategist for Young was someone with "their head in the clouds and their feet on the ground," someone who can deal with general concepts (enterprise-wide strategies and strategic visions) in a way that makes these concepts useful in specific company situation contexts.

Gillette's and The Games Gang's approaches are not the only ones used to formulate and implement strategies in business, however. In some situations, enterprise-wide strategies are formulated and implemented more fully from the top down. At Chase Manhattan's Municipal Bond Division (a strategic business unit of Chase Manhattan Bank) top corporate management formulated a detailed new enterprise-wide strategy for the municipal bond business unit. Subsequently, a new business unit manager was hired from outside the company, and many existing personnel were transferred or released [Doran 1989].

In other situations, strategies are just stumbled on by chance. Two years after he started Alias Research Inc. as a computer animation firm serving the film industry (Alias created the animation software for *Terminator 2*), Alias' president, Stephen Bingham, accidentally stumbled on industrial applications of his computer software. A chance meeting with General Motors' design engineers during a sales call with GM's advertising department led to a change in strategic direction and substantially increased profits for the fledgling company [Farnsworth 1991].

Experience indicates, therefore, that enterprise-wide strategies are not formulated and implemented in the same way at all companies, even though the general process is the structured context-specific process outlined in Figure 1-1. Nor are enterprise-wide strategies always formulated after thorough formal market and company studies. Many studies [Mintzberg 1989; Suchman 1987] of how busy, overworked managers actually make decisions and carry out their jobs show that very often strategies emerge through day-to-day business operations, as at Alias Research. Often in chaotic and stressful business conditions strategies are not even put into writing [Survey, 1986]. In addition, company strategy formulation and implementation can change as the specific situation context changes — as world crises occur, as new competitors and new products appear, and as new information becomes available.

RAPIDLY CHANGING EXTERNAL BUSINESS ENVIRONMENTS

Rapidly changing external business contexts — such as worldwide crises, intensifying competition, changing customer needs, and new information needs and technology — are increasing the need for more disciplined and, at the same time, more adaptive context-specific strategic management.

The Persian Gulf War, a *worldwide crisis* in early 1991, for example, led to sudden disruptions of worldwide oil supplies. Shell Oil Company was able to shift supply sources and continue supplying its customers "without missing a beat" largely because of its sophisticated well-structured strategy management process. For many years, Shell had conducted periodic planning sessions with its operating managers, during which the managers were presented with scenarios of possible world crises, such as wars. These managers then developed plans and action scenarios for responding to such crises. According to Shell's management, these planning sessions enabled the company to handle the Persian Gulf Crisis effectively, although such an approach does not always guarantee success, since Shell encountered a wide range of problems in the early 1990s in its other areas of operation [Knowlton 1991; Solomon 1991].

The brief coup attempt in the USSR on August 18, 1991, and the dissolution of the USSR at the end of 1991, were world crises that affected strategic management by raising serious questions about the volatile situation in Central Europe. Many investment opportunities were created for multinational companies anxious to exploit the major market opportunities created by the breakup of the Soviet Union. At the same time, a very uncertain political and social environment had created enormous risks which could adversely affect those investments [Brady 1992; Engleberg 1992; Johnson 1992; News Roundup 1991].

Competitive rivalries intensified as many industries expanded too rapidly in the 1980s. Eastern Airlines was an early casualty in the airline industry in the 1990s, ceasing operations on January 19, 1991 [Bernstein 1990; Salpukas 1991(A)]. Pan American was the next major airline to falter, first going into bankruptcy, then agreeing to sell almost half of its assets on August 12, 1991, and finally closing down completely on December 4, 1991 [Driscoll 1991; Salpukas 1991(B)]. People's Express, a $2 billion airline, went out of business in the 1980s [Scheier 1989]. Braniff Airlines had gone bankrupt three times prior to 1992 [Collingwood 1991]; in mid-1992, operating as a small niche airline, it went bankrupt again [McDowell 1992(A), 1992(B)]. Midway Airlines went bankrupt in March 1991 and ceased operations on November 13, 1991 [Salpukas 1991(C)]. TWA was taken into bankruptcy in early 1991; it was still struggling to survive in mid-1992 [Salpukas 1992]. In early 1992, the domestic airline industry was one of the world's most competitive and troubled major industries, having shrunk from 27 airlines in 1979 to 7 in 1991 [Uchitelle 1991].

Intensifying competitive rivalries are anticipated in the mid-1990s and beyond. In the late 1980s beer industry growth slowed to a point where individual company growth in the 1990s was expected to come mainly from taking business from competitors [Fisher 1991]. The steel industry, in spite of new technology investments, was being badly hurt by intense foreign competition [Hicks 1991]. In 1992, the TV networks were fighting hard to recover from a substantial drop in market share during the 1980s due to the growth of cable TV and home videos; at the same time, the cable TV industry itself was suffering from substantial oversupply [Auletta 1991; Carter 1991]. Newmark and Lewis was one of many major retailers who went bankrupt after the rapid explosion of retailing in the 1980s — by 1991, 18 square feet of retail space existed for every American — and the intense competitive rivalries that followed [Schwadel 1990; Shapiro 1992(B)]. R.H. Macy & Co.'s department stores [Strom 1992], the 51-year-old 10-store Oklahoma retail chain Street's [Helliker 1991], and McCrory, one of the largest U.S. dime store operators [Shapiro 1992(A), all filed for bankruptcy or went out of business in early 1992. In addition to the above, the casualty list of retailers who filed for bankruptcy between 1988 and 1992 included Federated Department Stores (1990), Allied Stores (1990), Carter Hawley (1991), Revco D.S. (1988), Ames Department Stores (1990), and Hill's DepartmentStores (1991) [Norris 1992].

Changing customer needs, which almost always impact on enterprise-wide strategy formulation, have also intensified pressures on companies to emphasize customer-oriented strategies. In 1992, Cooper Tire & Rubber Co. and Dillard Department Stores were successful in industries with substantial overcapacity and intense competition through differentiating themselves by focusing on better serving changing customer tastes and buying patterns [Hymowitz 1991]. Dillard's strategy was to emphasize convenience, service, and quality at a reasonable price; to stock ample supplies of upscale merchandise; to maintain inventories and reorder merchandise by computer, which enables the company to restock within two weeks; and to reward employees for superior customer service [Barmash 1992].

Cooper also followed a customer-oriented strategy — in its distribution through independent retailers who received high margins and so were encouraged to promote Cooper tires, its low prices which appealed to the growing tire replacement market on which Cooper focused, and its attention to details in servicing its intermediate (retailers) and ultimate (tire purchasers) customers. Banc One grew to be a major superregional bank in the 1980s largely because of its customer orientation: through effective use of advanced computer information systems it reoriented its operations to serve individual customers in its specific area with a variety of accounts and services, something which many major money center banks did not do until ten years later even though the same computer technology was available to them [Keen 1991; Lohr 1991].

The rapidly changing business environment in the 1990s increased the *need for more rapid gathering, analysis, and use of information.* Emerging computer information systems technologies helped to meet these needs. Dillard was able to restock within two weeks because of its computerized cash-register-based sales and inventory system. This important competitive advantage enabled Dillard to profit from sudden unanticipated increases in specific product sales. In the retail industry, bar-code scanners enable tracking what is sold daily or hourly, allowing for quick reordering and restocking. The spreading use of laser scanning and magnetic-strip cards which offer frequent shoppers discounts on many items has enabled stores and manufacturers/vendors to go further. These laser devices enable tracking who buys what products, so that individual stores can stock products to better serve customers and better target promotions (micromarketing). Twelve percent of the grocery chains were offering some sort of electronic-card merchandising program and most chains, and many independents, were studying or testing similar programs in 1991 [Kleinfield 1991].

THE IMPORTANCE OF STRATEGIC THINKING AND APPROPRIATE ADAPTIVE ORGANIZATION CONTEXTS TO MORE EFFECTIVE STRATEGY IMPLEMENTATION

In light of these rapidly changing external business environments, the objective of strategic management in business is not just to do more structured and detailed industry and competitive market analyses, formulate more comprehensive strategies and strategic plans, introduce more effective computer information systems, and deliver them all to operating managers. The ultimate objective is to create an organization context that can on a continuing basis translate strategies and strategic changes into actions which result in improved operations and profitability when operating over a period of time in a rapidly changing external industry and competitive market.

The *strategic thinking* stimulated by the process involved in formulating and implementing strategic plans is often what yields the principal long-term benefits of the process [Robert 1988].

This thinking enables managers, as well as operating personnel, to make decisions and manage operations in a manner that merges long-term strategic viewpoints with day-to-day operating perspectives. In this way, they are better prepared to respond to increasingly turbulent market environments in ways which will help realize top management's strategic vision for the company [Ansoff 1990].

Strategic thinking does not automatically happen, it must be fostered. During the plan formulation and implementation process, several steps can be taken to insure effective implementation and to stimulate strategic thinking among those affected by the plans:

- Encourage strategic business unit managers and key operating managers to participate in the formulation of company strategies
- Ideally allow those carrying out the plans to do as much of the actual planning work as possible
- Communicate the company's strategic directions clearly, simply, and continuously
- Rely, when possible, on oral communications and have an effective integrator, who is either the company's chief executive officer (CEO) or someone aggressively supported by the CEO, to coordinate the planning effort
- Where written communications are used, keep strategy statements as simple and brief as possible
- Provide expert assistance at all levels of planning
- Check results frequently and provide rewards that emphasize the longer-term strategic perspective during control reviews

In addition to these initial *leadership* steps designed to promote strategic thinking, other steps are often needed to *reengineer internal business processes/operations* so that they are more closely aligned with a firm's strategic plan requirements and with customer needs. It is also necessary to create an adaptive *organization culture and structure* based on that realignment, as well as to *staff* the organization with people who can effectively carry out the new strategic direction.

For example, when Louis Gerstner, former president of American Express Company, was brought in to head RJR Nabisco Holdings Inc. in 1989, he had a fairly clear vision of his overall strategy for remaking the company [Anders 1991]. Because his situation differed from Mockler's at Gillette — Gerstner was not well known to his company managers — one of Gerstner's first steps was to establish mutual trust and respect among top managers in the company. A second move was to provide an organization environment that would facilitate movement in new directions. The organization realignments introduced included bringing in new staff, creating a cooperative organization structure that promoted more teamwork and creative thinking and faster decision making, initiating new control and reward systems, and modifying the corporate culture. These same initiatives were also important ones for David Johnson when he took over as president of Campbell Soup Co. in January 1990 [Bevins 1991; Freedman 1991].

The importance of these *organization context* initiatives — involving leadership, business process reengineering, organization culture and structure realignment; making necessary staffing and control changes; and generally taking steps to promote strategic thinking — during the process of formulating and implementing strategies and strategic plans has been demonstrated at many companies. These aspects of strategic management are discussed throughout this book, especially in Chapter 12 and Appendix B. The studies and experiences described there show that the strategic management process is often as important as the strategies and strategic plans formulated.

WHO DOES STRATEGIC MANAGEMENT?

Strategic management is something successful managers do continually, either consciously or intuitively. It is most often not exclusively one person's or department's full-time job.

Decisions about the enterprise-wide strategies for a corporation are ultimately the legal responsibility of the board of directors. This point was reaffirmed by a Delaware court which upheld Time Inc.'s decision to merge with Warner Communications "by affirming the rights of corporate directors to control the fate of their companies" [Fabrikant 1989]. More recently, on April 6, 1992, the General Motors board, frustrated by the pace of change at the loss-plagued company, "radically remade the auto maker's executive suite, taking control of the company's executive committee which in essence runs the company, and effectively demoting the company's chairman and CEO, Robert Stempel" [White 1992]. In mid-1992, the boards of other large companies were taking increasingly active roles in their companies' strategic and operating decision making [Lohr 1992; Treece 1992].

In most situations, a company's CEO is responsible for enterprise-wide strategy formulation. At Gulf and Western Inc. (subsequently named Paramount Communications Inc.), Martin Davis became chairman in 1983 and changed the conglomerate company into a media giant [Stevenson 1989].

Specific planning executives and departments, at the corporate level or within divisions, are often delegated responsibility for strategy formulation and implementation. These departments and executives can do the strategic planning, assist others in doing it, and/or provide support services — such as data gathering and analysis, and coordination with other operating areas. For example, Borden's public relations department helped formulate enterprise-wide safety, quality, and productivity strategic initiatives by working with individual company divisions worldwide. Subsequently, during the early 1990s, the department guided the implementation of this plan in each division by providing technical support, information support, and coordination with other divisions [Deutsch 1989(B); Ventres 1986 and 1989; Mockler 1992(B)]. At other times, a specific corporate officer might be given the job of coordinator of strategic planning, as at Kemper Financial Services, Inc. in the early 1990s [McConahey 1992].

In practice, strategy formulation at large companies is being done increasingly by managers of strategic business units within a company. For example, after David Bryan became president of Fuller Brush, a division of Sara Lee Corporation, he successfully changed the division's character in 1987 by expanding the door-to-door sales company into mail-order selling [Berg 1989]. At other companies strategy formulation is being done by operating managers [Prescott 1989]. This shift to having strategy formulation done by operating managers within a company is based on the feeling that it should be done as much as possible by those who will be carrying out the strategies. This trend is expected to continue throughout the 1990s.

Since all company planning is eventually coordinated within the context of enterprise-wide strategies, it often is a collaborative venture. For this reason, a successful strategic planning coordinator will be someone, either the CEO or another strategic planning champion, who is able to play multiple roles — facilitator, support provider, integrator, coordinator, and at times director. This kind of integrative force is needed to coordinate operations and strategic planning and to use the planning process to promote strategic thinking.

The answer to the question "who does strategic management?" is just about any corporate, strategic business unit, or key operating manager, depending on the specific situation.

A WIDE RANGE OF SITUATIONS

The approach to strategic management will vary by industry situation context. Heavy industries such as steel and wood pulp production are very capital intensive and require fairly long investment cycle planning [Melnbardis 1989]. In contrast, advertising is a service industry, with relatively low capital investment and shorter planning cycles [Rothenberg 1989]. The airline industry is affected by a mix of heavy capital investment and people- and service-related critical factors [Lohr 1989].

Regional and national companies have different situation requirements, because of the size and scope of their operations. Differences in strategic management also exist at companies with limited financial resources, or at companies managed by their owners. Strategic business units (SBU's) of larger companies operate in different contexts than companies that are independently owned and operated, even though these strategic business units may face the same competitive market problems as independently-owned companies. Entrepreneurial companies in emerging industries face situations different from those faced by large companies in mature industries.

While some of the factors influencing success in multinational companies are common in all countries, many of the key-to-success factors vary significantly by country. For example, local cultural and legal factors can affect packaging, advertising, and product composition. Companies operating in highly sensitive social areas — such as those using animals for product testing or those generating toxic waste — are subjected to many special pressures which can complicate strategic management decision making.

The level at which the strategic planning is done within a company can also affect the type and manner of planning done. Planning for a strategic business unit can be quite different from planning for the corporation within which the strategic business unit's planning must be integrated. The capabilities of planners and the organization culture existing in the situation under study will also affect the planning effort.

WHY STRATEGIC MANAGEMENT IS BOTH A STRUCTURED AND ADAPTIVE CONTEXT-SPECIFIC MANAGEMENT PROCESS

Because of the range of possible strategic management situations rather than a one-dimensional approach to strategic management, a *situational management and decision-making approach* to strategic management, which is both context adaptive and at the same time structured, is what most often seems to succeed.

Any effective strategic management process model must focus on situation-specific or domain-specific factors and work from this context to a solution if it is to accurately reflect the way effective business managers work. Such a situation context approach first involves determining and explicitly or implicitly structuring the essential or critical situation elements affecting each specific management situation. This situation context analysis for *strategy formulation* can be broken down into several specific tasks for formal analysis purposes:

- Defining how the business situation (industry, competitive market, and company) works
- Identifying *opportunity areas* (where money will be made), *keys to success* (how money will be made or success achieved), and *possible threats* (special potential problems in the situation)
- Identifying the competition of the company under study, and comparing theirs and the company's strengths and weaknesses in key-to-success and opportunity areas

Such a disciplined structured situation context analysis, provided it is adapted to specific situation needs, can be a useful basis for formulating strategies which best suit the company under study, given its competitors' anticipated strengths and weaknesses in the perceived future competitive market environment [Mockler 1992(C)]. This sometimes involves formulating several alternative strategies and choosing among them. At other times strategies are formulated directly from the situation analysis, as in The Games Gang Ltd. situation described earlier.

Even where done less formally or less explicitly, research has shown that expert managers and planners use similar context-specific approaches to strategic management. Their personal problem structurings may differ somewhat, but their approaches are likely to be based on some kind of structured reconceptualization of the specific situation and competitive market in which they are involved [Adams-Weber 1978; Bannister 1970; Kelly 1955; Mockler 1992(A); Porac and Thomas 1987, 1990].

As discussed in this chapter, strategic management is not only a *thinking* job involving formulation of strategies and plans, it is also a *doing* job which involves carefully planning and managing the *implementation* of the strategies and plans. Depending on the size of the enterprise involved, *implementation* can have two distinct phases:

- Organizing and carrying out the planning effort at all levels of the company involved
- Putting the strategic plans into effect through leadership, business process and organization reengineering, staffing, and control appropriate to the situation

As with strategy formulation, implementation requires recognizing key situation factors, such as the nature of the organization, existing business processes, who is involved in doing and carrying out the plans, the level of planning being done, and many other factors affecting the project being managed. The approach used, however, is adapted to situation needs. For example, Gillette's approach to implementation, described earlier, worked very well for that particular company at that particular time. It is not necessarily a prescription for what every company in every strategic management situation should do.

In contrast, Chase Manhattan Bank's management's formulation of a new strategy for its Municipal Bond strategic business unit in 1989 required substantial changes because the new strategic thrust involved new financial products which would be sold to an entirely different customer market segment. Many existing personnel were transferred or released, and a new division head was hired from outside [Doran 1989]. The extent of the change was substantial, since the skills and experience of many existing personnel were judged incompatible with the kind needed to implement the new strategic direction. In addition, competitive market pressures required fast action, so time was not available for extensive retraining. In corporate management's view, these situational requirements dictated the highly authoritarian and organizationally disruptive approach used.

Implementation situations are unlikely to follow prescribed patterns, but rather more often require tough decisions tailored specifically to the situation at hand. For example, Robert Murphy, senior vice-president for organization and human resources at Rockwell International Corporation, had to formulate policies limiting health payments to injuries and illnesses and excluding "nonessential" medical expenses. He also had to make specific decisions, such as whether or not Rockwell should pay for a doctor-advised operation on a 50-year-old female employee with leukemia when the insurance company said they shouldn't (chances of having a successful operation on a patient in her condition were very slim) [Kramon 1991].

As shown by the company experiences discussed in this chapter, while there is an overall disciplined approach to strategic management [Ansoff 1987, 1990, 1991], the actual steps involved in the strategic management process when making management decisions and taking action in specific situations in business are obviously more complex than any structured outline might suggest [Mintzberg 1989, 1990, 1991]. Although listed sequentially, the tasks shown in Figure 1-1 are not necessarily sequential. The actual strategic management process is an adaptive, dynamic, integrated one, in which the mind moves back and forth through the various phases, testing, retesting, gathering more information, formulating tentative decisions, refining, and redoing continually. New competitive pressures can arise, political and economic crises can occur, and changes in personnel, internal company problems, and unforeseen events can disrupt operations — so that strategies can evolve and change over time. Often, considerable ingenuity and quick action are needed to get things done under chaotic, pressured conditions.

SOME MISCONCEPTIONS ABOUT STRATEGIC MANAGEMENT

One misconception about strategic management is that those who have done it well in one specific kind of situation know how to plan effectively in other situation contexts. *Venture* magazine was advertised in 1979 as a handbook for people starting businesses. In 1989 the company was sold at what was reportedly a "fire sale" for a fraction of what its owner, Arthur Lipper, had invested in it. Lipper's management competency in general was not the problem; he was successful in many other projects [Lipper 1991]. The problem was that he did not strategically manage this particular magazine venture in a way appropriate for achieving success in the periodical publishing industry. In other words, Lipper did not formulate and implement strategies and plans appropriate for the specific competitive market situation and company with which he was involved [Reilly 1990; Scardino 1989].

Another misconception about strategic management is that there is only one way to do it. This idea is encouraged by the fact that texts such as this one outline and model a single strategy formulation and implementation process in their early chapters. Models such as the one shown in Figure 1-1 are needed for strategic management learning purposes. Just as when learning a sport, its components are analyzed and focused on during training. In practice, however, the process is a dynamic, integrated fluid one, whose components may be indistinguishable during execution. While there are some underlying patterns in strategic planning and implementation, the specific way these patterns come into play in each situation depends on that situation's requirements. This is why this book describes a wide range of structured but adaptive situationally-specific strategic management processes in the final sections of each chapter. At the same time the chapters cover a wide range of varying situation applications.

Although useful for a general understanding of strategic management, Figure 1-1 does not capture fully the complexities of strategy formulation and implementation at work. Several of these complexities are discussed in this book:

- Successful strategic management does not rely solely on explicit rational decision processes. It also requires intuitive and creative sensings about possible future events, based on a variety of information sources.
- Changing industry, market, and competitive forces often lead to changes and refinements in strategic plans, so that flexibility and adaptability are important in strategic management.
- Enterprise-wide strategies are not always stated explicitly or formulated in a formal way; in addition, they are often formulated over time.
- Business organizations are dynamic entities, whose individual characteristics affect how strategic planning is done and how strategic plans are carried out in various company situations during different time periods.
- Ultimately, strategic management can vary from situation to situation and so is best understood within a situational management context.
- Effective strategic management depends on oral communications and the organizational behavioral skills of the company executives as much as it does on any written documents or organizational structures.
- Information sources and flows are becoming more varied and complex, as available technology becomes increasingly accessible to non-technical business managers and as the business environment becomes more competitive. This increases the need for some knowledge of information systems technology to do strategic management effectively.
- Carrying out strategies through effective leadership, reengineering of business processes and organization structures, and staffing that creates an enabling context which promotes strategic thinking can be as important to success as formulating effective strategies.

Strategic management then is not a simple set of procedures that can be mastered fully in an 11-to-15-week course. It is a complex management decision-making and human resource management process. In addition, since it deals with the future, the process will necessarily yield uncertain recommendations at the time decisions are made.

REVIEW QUESTIONS

1. What is strategic management and how does the term relate to strategy formulation and implementation?
2. Describe some of the complexities of, and misconceptions about, strategic management.
3. Who is responsible for strategic planning in a company? Describe some of the people who participate in doing it.
4. Describe the skills and knowledge needed to do strategy formulation and implementation effectively.
5. Describe different kinds of strategic management situations which may be encountered in business.
6. Discuss the ways in which strategic management is an adaptive situation- or context-specific process.
7. Describe some of the ways in which strategic management is and is not a structured management process.
8. Describe the essential tasks involved in strategy formulation and implementation.
9. Discuss the ways in which strategic management is an integrative process.
10. Describe what is meant by the terms "strategic thinking" and "appropriate adaptive organization context" and discuss their importance to effective strategic management.

EXERCISES

1. Read recent issues of the periodicals referred to in the references section at the end of the chapter, or other related periodicals of your choice, and find current examples of

    • Effective company strategy formulation and implementation. Write a report on why you think the company was successful. Pay special attention to how the company matched competitive market success requirements in opportunity areas with available company resources, and how it formulated and implemented the strategy in the face of competitors' actions.

    • A strategy that went wrong. Write a report on why you think the company was unsuccessful. Determine whether the problems were caused by changing competitive market conditions during strategy implementation, by incomplete initial diagnosis of competitive market forces, or by ineffective implementation.

• Companies in which the personality of the chief executive officer strongly influenced strategy formulation and implementation. Write a report analyzing the ways the personality of one company's CEO affected strategic management.

2. The disks accompanying this book contain several prototype knowledge-based systems. Using one of the companies you analyzed in Exercise #1, run a consultation using the system named PLANNING.REV by following the directions accompanying the disks.

REFERENCES

Adams-Weber, J. R., *Personal Construct Theory: Concepts and Applications*, Chichester, England: Wiley, 1978.

Anders, George, "Old Flamboyance Is Out as Louis Gerstner Remakes RJR Nabisco," *The Wall Street Journal*, March 21, 1991, pp. A1, A6.

Ansoff, H. Igor, "Critique of Henry Mintzberg's 'The Design School: Reconsidering the Basic Premises of Strategic Management'," *Strategic Management Journal*, September 1991, pp. 449-461.

Ansoff, H. Igor, "The Emerging Paradigm of Strategic Behavior," *Strategic Management Journal*, November-December 1987, pp. 501-516.

Ansoff, H. Igor, *Implementing Strategic Management*, Englewood Cliffs, NJ: Prentice-Hall, 1990.

Bannister, D., editor, *Perspectives in Personal Construct Theory*, New York: Academic Press, 1970.

Barmash, Isadore, "Down the Scale With the Major Store Chains," *The New York Times*, Business Section, February 2, 1992, 5.

Berg, Eric, "At Fuller, a New Way to Get Foot in Door," *The New York Times*, May 18, 1989, pp. D1, D2.

Bernstein, Aaron, *Grounded: Frank Lorenzo and the Destruction of Eastern Airlines*, New York: Simon & Schuster, 1990.

Bevins, Terry, "New CEO Has Campbell Soup Co. Cooking," *Sunday Freeman*, August 25, 1991, pp. 33, 35.

Brady, Rose, Peter Galuska, Richard A. Melcher, and David Greising, "Let's Make a Deal — But a Smaller One," *Business Week*, January 20, 1992, pp. 44, 45.

Carter, Bill, "Cable Networks See Dimmer Future," *The New York Times*, July 22, 1991, pp. D1, D4.

Chakravorty, Subrata, "We Changed the Whole Playing Field: Triumph for Gillette's Colman Mockler — Technology as a Marketing Tool," *Forbes*, February 4, 1991, pp. 82-86.

Collingwood, Harris, "Braniff Goes Under — Again," *Business Week*, August 19, 1991, p. 36.

Deutsch, Claudia, "A Toy Company Finds Life After Pictionary," *The New York Times*, Business Section, July 9, 1989(A), pp. 6, 7.

Deutsch, Claudia, "From Cash Cow to Cash Machine," *The New York Times*, November 12, 1989(B), pp. C1, C10.

Doran, John J., "Ready for the Next Decade: Chase Manhattan Securities Inc. Revamps Its Municipal Banking and Bond Operations," *The Bond Buyer*, April 7, 1989, pp. 1ff.

Driscoll, Lisa, and Michael O'Neal, "When I'm Down and Out, You Owe Me a Drink: Icahn Forces Delta to Sweeten Its Pan Am Bid by $361 in Cash," *Business Week*, August 26, 1991, p. 26.

Engleberg, Stephen, "Eastern Europe Foils All but the Hardiest of Western Investors," *The New York Times*, March 5, 1992, p. A1, D8.

Fabrikant, Geraldine, "A Delaware Court Refuses to Block Time-Warner Merger," *The New York Times*, July 15, 1989, pp. 1-44.

Farnsworth, Clyde H., "Software Star in a Roller Coaster," *The New York Times*, Business Section, September 29, 1991, p. 15.

Fisher, Lawrence M., "Behind All the Bonhomie, the Brewing Industry Gets Tough," *The New York Times*, Business Section, July 21, 1991, p. 4.

Freedman, Alix M., "Campbell Chief Cooks Up Winning Menu," *The Wall Street Journal*, February 15, 1991, pp. B1, B5.

"Getting to Prime," *Inc.*, January 1991, pp. 27-33.

Hicks, Jonathan P., "Steel Hits Hard Times Again," *The New York Times*, August 12, 1991, pp. D1, D6.

Helliker, Kevin, "A Family Retail Chain That Stresses Service Rings Up Its Last Sales," *The Wall Street Journal*, December 4, 1991, pp. A1, A6.

Hymowitz, Carol, and Thomas F. O'Boyle, "Two Disparate Firms Find Keys to Success in Troubled Industries," *The Wall Street Journal*, May 29, 1991, pp. A1, A7.

Johnson, Robert, and Allanna Sullivan, "A Small Joint Venture Is Leading Way in Getting Russian Oil," *The Wall Street Journal*, January 29, 1992, pp. A1, A7.

Keen, Peter G. W., "Redesigning the Organization Through Information Technology," *Planning Review*, May/June 1991, pp. 4-9.

Kelly, George, *The Psychology of Personal Constructs*, Volumes 1 and 2, New York: Norton, 1955.

Kleinfield, N. R., "Targeting the Grocery Shopper," *The New York Times*, Business Section, May 26, 1991, pp. 1, 6.

Knowlton, Christopher, "Shell Gets Rich By Beating Risk," *Fortune*, August 26, 1991, pp. 79-82.

Kramon, Glenn, "Rockwell's Point Man in the Health-Care Campaign," *The New York Times*, Business Section, April 7, 1991, p. 5.

Lipper, Arthur, *Thriving Up and Down the Free Market Food Chain*, New York: HarperBusiness, 1991.

Lohr, Steve, "British Air's Profitable Private Life," *The New York Times*, Business Section, May 7, 1989, p. 4.

Lohr, Steve, "The Best Little Bank in America," *The New York Times*, Business Section, July 7, 1991, pp. 1, 4.

Lohr, Steve, "Pulling Down the Corporate Clubhouse" *The New York Times*, Business Section, April 12, 1992, pp. 1, 5.

McConahey, Steve, Corporate and International Development (Planning Director), Kemper Financial Services, Inc., *The Emerging Role of the Strategic Planner in the 1990s: Key Elements*, New York: Planning Forum's Strategic Planning Special Interest Group, April 8, 1992.

McDowell, Edwin, "A Choppy Ascent for the New Braniff," *The New York Times*, April 23, 1992(A), pp. D1, D7.

McDowell, Edwin, "Braniff Head Expects Others to Close," *The New York Times*, July 9, 1992(B), p. D3.

McKibben, Gordon, "Gillette's Mockler: Going Out on Top," *The Boston Sunday Globe*, Business Section, November 18, 1990, pp. A1, A7.

Melnbardis, Robert, "Wood Pulp Makers Run Expansion Spree," *The Wall Street Journal*, May 27, 1989, p. B8.

Mills, D. Quinn, *Rebirth of the Corporation*, New York: John Wiley & Sons, 1991.

Mintzberg, Henry, "The Design School: Reconsidering the Basic Premises of Strategic Management,"

Strategic Management Journal, April 1990, pp. 171-195.

Mintzberg, Henry, *Mintzberg on Management,* New York: The Free Press, 1989.

Mintzberg, Henry, "Learning 1, Planning 0: Reply to Ansoff," *Strategic Management Journal,* September 1991, pp. 449-461.

Mockler, Robert J., *Contingency Approaches to Strategic Management,* Research Working Paper, New York: Strategic Management Research Group, 1992(A).

Mockler, Robert J., "Implementing Enterprise-Wide Strategies: Innovative Approaches to Managing a Diverse Workforce," Presentation, *Proceedings: International Management Conference,* Charlottesville, VA: April 2-4, 1992(B).

Mockler, Robert J., *Structured Industry/Competitive Market Analysis,* Research Working Paper, New York: Strategic Management Research Group, 1992(C).

News Roundup, "Firms' March on Moscow Bogs Down," *The Wall Street Journal,* August 20, 1991, pp. B1, B5.

Norris, Floyd, "Win or Lose, Buyouts Do It Big," *The New York Times,* January 28, 1992, pp. D1, D8.

Peters, Tom, "Keynote Address," *Strategic Management Society Annual Meeting,* Toronto, Canada: October, 1991.

Pollack, Andrew, "Hewlitt's 'Consummate Strategist'," *The New York Times,* March 10, 1992, pp. D1, D6.

Porac, Joseph F., and Howard Thomas, "Cognitive Taxonomies and Cognitive Systematics," *Paper Presentation,* New Orleans: Academy of Management National Annual Meeting, 1987.

Porac, Joseph F., and Howard Thomas, "Taxonomic Mental Models in Competitor Definition," *Academy of Management Review,* volume 15, number 2, April 1990, pp. 224-240.

Prescott, John E., and Daniel C. Smith, "The Largest Survey of 'Leading Edge' Competitor Intelligence Managers," *Planning Review.* May/June 1989, pp. 6-13.

Protzman, Ferdinand, "Slick Designs, Hefty Profits," *The New York Times,* March 17, 1992, pp. D1, D7.

Reilly, Patrick M., "As Magazine Industry Faces Shakeout, Some Publishers Start to Close the Books," *The Wall Street Journal,* January 31, 1990, pp. B1, B4.

Robert, Michel, *The Strategist CEO,* Westport, Connecticut: Quorum Books, 1988.

Rothenberg, Randall, "With Media Losing Mass, What's Left," *The New York Times,* July 10, 1989, p. D19.

Salpukas, Agis, "Bankruptcy Filing Is Made by T.W.A.," *The New York Times,* February 1, 1992, pp. 1, 48.

Salpukas, Agis, "Eastern Airlines Is Shutting Down and Plans to Liquidate Its Assets," *The New York Times,* January 19, 1991(A), pp. 1, 48.

Salpukas, Agis, "Its Cash Depleted, Pan Am Shuts," *The New York Times,* December 5, 1991(B), pp. D1, D6.

Salpukas, Agis, "Midway Enters Bankruptcy and Obtains a Line of Credit," *The New York Times,* March 21, 1991(C), pp. D1, D5.

Scardino, Albert, "The Magazine That Lost Its Way," *The New York Times,* Business Section, June 18, 1989, pp. 1, 10.

Scheier, Robert L., "Obliterated by the Chip: The Crushing of People's Express," *PC Week,* November 13, 1989, p. 131.

Schwadel, Francine, "Tony Chicago Shopping Area's Struggles Reflect Nationwide Glut of Store Space," *The Wall Street Journal,* December 20, 1990, pp. B1, B7.

Shapiro, Eben, "McCrory Chain Files for Bankruptcy," *The New York Times,* February 27, 1992(A),

p. 5.

Shapiro, Eben, "Newmark & Lewis Stores to Close," *The New York Times*, January 18, 1992(B), pp. 37, 38.

Solomon, Caleb, "Shell, a Fallen Champ of Oil Industry, Tries to Regain Its Footing," *The Wall Street Journal*, August 30, 1991, pp. A1, A2.

Stevenson, Richard W., "Not Just Another Charlie Bluhdorn," *The New York Times*, Business Section, June 11, 1989, pp. 1, 9.

Strom, Stephanie, "Macy's Asks Court to Provide Shield Against Creditors," *The New York Times*, January 28, 1992, pp. A1, A6.

Suchman, Lucy, A., *Plans and Situated Actions*, New York: Cambridge University Press, 1987.

"Survey," *The Wall Street Journal*, October 31, 1986, p. A1.

Treece, James H., "The Board Revolt," *Business Week*, April 20, 1992, pp. 30-36.

Uchitelle, Louis, "Off Course, America's Disappearing Airlines," *The New York Times* Sunday Magazine, September 1, 1991, pp. 12-27.

Ventres, Romeo J., "Speech to the New York Society of Security Analysts," *Company Release*, November 6, 1986.

Ventres, Romeo J., "Speech to the New York Society of Security Analysts," *Company Release*, November 9, 1989.

White, Joseph B., and Paul Ingrassia, "Stunning Shake-Up: Board Ousts Managers at GM, Takes Control of Crucial Committee," *The Wall Street Journal*, April 7, 1992, pp. A1, A8.

CHAPTER 2

TASKS AND GENERAL PROCESSES INVOLVED IN STRATEGIC MANAGEMENT

The objective of this chapter is to help readers understand

- The tasks involved in formulating and implementing strategies
- The integrated adaptive strategic management process
- Why and how the strategic management process is segmented for analysis and learning purposes

This chapter describes the key strategic management tasks and general processes. Chapters 3 through 7 describe in detail how strategies are formulated and Chapters 8 through 12 describe how enterprise-wide strategies are implemented.

Chapter 1 views the strategic management job from the perspective of a busy manager at work in a variety of business situations. Chapter 2 breaks the strategic management job into components, as necessary an introductory training step in learning strategic management as it is in learning to play sports. In strategic management as in golf, for example, such a component-by-component analysis is very useful from a training perspective. It must be remembered, however, that overemphasis on component analysis can lead to poorer performance when actually doing a complex activity, such as managing strategically or playing a sport.

TASKS INVOLVED IN FORMULATING AND IMPLEMENTING STRATEGIES

Figure 2-1 identifies the tasks generally associated with *formulating* enterprise-wide strategies. They include

- Structured situation context analysis, covering such internal and external factors as overall

Figure 2-1: Strategic Management Tasks

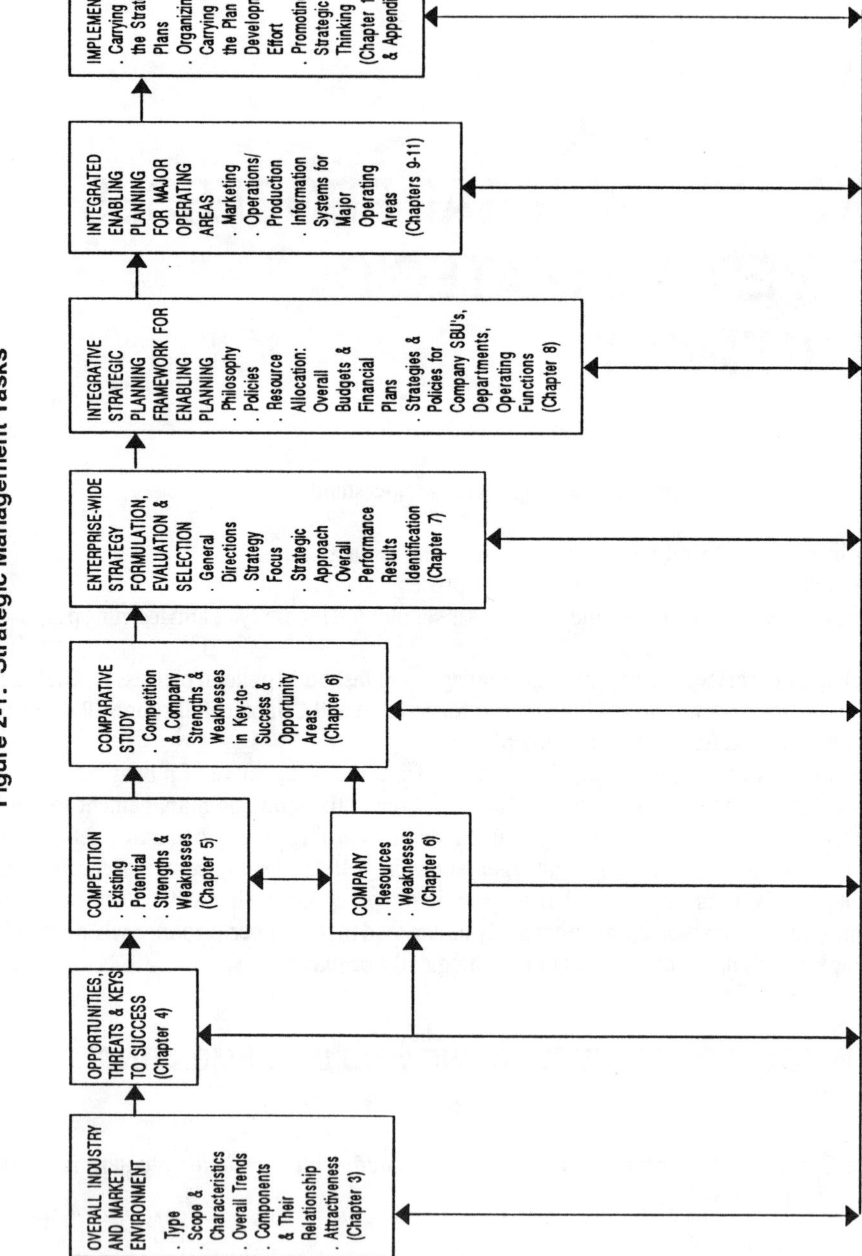

industry and market environment; opportunity areas, possible threats and keys to success; and company strengths and weaknesses in key areas as compared to those of competitors
- Overall company strategy formulation, consisting of general enterprise-wide strategy directions or company mission; strategy focus, concentration or other differentiating characteristics; approaches or thrusts involved in carrying out strategies; and projected financial targets.

Figure 2-1 also shows the tasks generally associated with *amplifying* and *implementing* enterprise-wide strategies. These include

- Formulating an integrative framework for enabling or functional planning
- Integrated enabling strategy formulation and plan development for major operating or functional areas of a business
- Implementing strategies by managing the enabling plan development effort; establishing mutual trust and respect among company managers, reengineering business processes, realigning and creating appropriate organization structures, and, where needed, bringing in new staff and modifying the existing corporate culture; monitoring performance; and effectively using the strategy formulation process to promote strategic thinking throughout the company.

Additionally, there is the preliminary task of planning for strategic management, that is, planning for how the strategy formulation and implementation effort will be carried out. This task is discussed later in this chapter, since it is closely related to implementation.

The arrows at the bottom of Figure 2-1 indicate that these strategic management tasks are not just steps in a procedure. Rather, they are part of an adaptive, dynamic context-specific process and are not necessarily performed separately and sequentially.

INDUSTRY, MARKET, AND COMPANY ANALYSIS

Analyzing the Overall Industry and Market Environment

As data about external industry and internal company factors are collected and analyzed, they can be organized into appropriate categories, including:

- Overall economic environment, as well as the industry's nature and scope, distinguishing characteristics, and estimated probable growth, size, and general future attractiveness
- How the industry works: its components and their interrelationships — that is, its structure — with special emphasis on factors affecting existing and anticipated competitive forces
- Similar information on specific competitive markets in which the company plans to be involved

Scenarios — stories about the way the future might unfold that focus on the logic behind events and are not intended as forecasts — are developed for key trends or events anticipated in such areas as: overall economic forces; technological developments; social, cultural, and demographic climates; government, political, and legal factors; availability of raw materials; other anticipated business developments; general industry and market attractiveness; and competitive market forces. The risk, or likelihood, of the anticipated scenarios or events occurring is also estimated [Knowlton 1991; Schwartz 1990].

Identifying Opportunities, Threats, and Keys to Success

As the industry and market information is collected, sorted, and structured, a planner identifies major opportunity areas and threats, as well as key-to-success factors.

Opportunities and threats. Identifying *general* opportunities is relatively easy in many industries. For example, computer workstations was a recognized growth area in the computer industry in 1992. Recognizing such general opportunity areas is useful in understanding the mood and character of an industry.

Identifying *specific* opportunities is usually more difficult. For smaller companies, this might involve identifying or creating profitable market niches that are not of interest to the major competitors but are large enough for the company under study. For example, Kiamichi Railroad operates profitably ($1.2 million in earnings) as a small ($9.6 million in sales) short-line railroad in a depressed area of Oklahoma [Machalaba 1992]. In the retail food industry, health-food supermarkets filled a niche in that industry in the early 1990s [Burros 1992]. *El Diario-La Prensa*, a Spanish-language newspaper, successfully carved out a market niche by serving New York City's Spanish community; in early 1991 its advertising revenue and circulation rose, while the industry's advertising revenues generally fell [Golden 1991].

Opportunities can be defined in various ways, such as by type, size, profitability, growth potential, or insulation from competition. When defining an opportunity, potential risks and threats associated with each opportunity are identified, often by developing alternative scenarios of what might happen in the future, as was done at Shell Oil Company [Knowlton 1991]. Identifying possible threats is a necessary part of projecting the potential opportunities in an uncertain future environment.

Keys to success. Pinpointing the steps that need to be taken to succeed in a selected opportunity area — a very important phase of strategy formulation — involves developing a profile of the kind of company likely to succeed in the future industry environment. Because the future environment is uncertain, identifying specific success formulas is often very difficult. However, such identification is essential because it provides the structure for subsequent analyses and strategic plan development.

At British Jaguar PLC the identified keys to success were controlling prices and quality, handling militant unions, maintaining brand image while expanding the lower end of the product line, and meeting competitive pressures from Japanese car makers [Lublin 1990; Maremont 1992]. When introducing Pictionary, The Games Gang Ltd.'s success depended on such factors as keeping investments in permanent facilities to a minimum and using word-of-mouth promotions [Deutsch 1989]. Chapter 1 described how Cooper Tire & Rubber Co. and Dillard Department Stores found keys to success in troubled industries [Hymowitz 1991].

Studying Competitor and Company Strengths and Weaknesses in Major Opportunity and Key-to-Success Areas

At some point during the structured industry analysis, the competition is analyzed. This includes identifying their anticipated strengths and weaknesses in major opportunity and related key-to-success areas. Again, scenarios of what competitors are expected to do are developed and risks for the likelihood of different scenarios actually occurring are estimated. Such studies can be extremely important. For example, Borden's formulation of a national brand strategy for its Creamette pasta strategic business unit — Creamette was the nation's largest pasta brand with $195 million in sales in 1990—was a daring departure for a fragmented industry with many ethnic regional brands [Ramirez 1990]. In contrast, for example, Hershey, the second largest U.S. pasta maker, had nine regional pasta brands. Since Borden implemented its strategy on a region-by-region basis and since there was the large number of regional competitors in the industry, a wide range of possible competitor reaction scenarios were developed and studied.

Current and anticipated company strengths and weaknesses in the same areas are also defined and studied.

Comparison of Competitor and Company Strengths and Weaknesses in Major Opportunity and Key-to-Success Areas

In the strategy formulation process, a planner examines the interrelationships of situation elements from various viewpoints. For example, as the strengths and weaknesses of competitors are analyzed, their relation to company strengths and weaknesses is evaluated. This comparative competitive position evaluation helps compare a company's ability to meet key-to-success factors in opportunity areas with the competitors' expected strengths and weaknesses in these areas.

During this comparative analysis, the initial perceptions of what are the key-to-success factors and opportunities will often change and be reformulated or reconceived as new information is obtained or as the competitive market changes. Investments and expansion into China and the Soviet Union appeared to show great promise during the late 1980s. However, as negotiations progressed in the early 1990s, more information was obtained, potential problems were uncovered, and events such as the breakup of the Soviet Union and the riots in Tiananmen Square in China occurred that raised serious questions about investments in China and Central and Eastern Europe [Brady 1992; Clines 1991; Engleberg 1992; Kristof 1992; WuDunn 1991].

KINDS OF ENTERPRISE-WIDE STRATEGIES

The following enterprise-wide strategy, sometimes called an entity-wide or overall-company strategic objective, involves a small candy company —*Blakeston and Wilson Company* — described in the first case study in the Case Study section of this book:

> The strategic objective of the company is to be an aggressively expanding, closely-held regional manufacturer-retailer of a limited line of high-quality, moderately-priced, and distinctively boxed chocolate candies, selling principally through its own retail stores to consumers under its own brand name, but also serving wholesale, chain, and institutional customers or outlets under other brand names to the degree permitted by available production capacity and by the company's ability to raise capital.

This type of objective could be an enterprise-wide strategy for a small independent company or for a small strategic business unit (SBU) of a large company. The objective covers nine areas critical to the company's future success: function performed; customers served; kind of product; breadth of product line; brand; product price, quality, and image; outlets; ownership status; and area of operations.

This comprehensive enterprise-wide strategy statement defines the *kind* of company envisioned in the future. The strategic objective indicates the company's *overall future direction*. In general terms it identifies the way the company is trying to *differentiate* itself from competitors — its *strategic focus* — and what is to be done to achieve that differentiation — its *strategic approach*. Any such statement that defines what kind of company or strategic business unit is desired in the future, including general guidelines on how to get there, is an enterprise-wide strategic objective and business policy statement.

Strategic objectives for smaller companies and for strategic business units within large companies often can be stated in relatively few words, even when sales figures are in the millions. For example, in 1992 New Line Cinema Corporation, the creator of the movie *Teenage Mutant Ninja Turtles*, produced *and* distributed its own films. Initially, the company concentrated on low-budget films for narrow target markets: teenagers, blacks, and children. Subsequently, New Line developed a strategy which enabled the company to expand rapidly through cooperative deals with other film makers which substantially reduced risks. It also expanded its productions to include art films and other niches ignored by major studios. However, the company continued to focus on productions whose low budgets were tailored to the size of the anticipated market. This allowed the company to remain profitable and survive as an independent for over 24 years, a rare achievement in the movie industry. In 1991, the company had sales of $225.7 million (up 70% from sales of $133 million in 1990) and net income of $8.9 million (up 41% from 1990). In contrast, Carolco Pictures Inc. ($145 million in sales in 1990), makers of the *Rambo* films, produced only high-budget, big-star action films and did not handle its distribution in the United States, a strategic focus which caused some major problems for the company during the downturn in the film industry during 1991 [Fabrikant 1990 and 1992; Goldman 1992; Grimes 1991; Grover 1991; Stevenson 1991].

Many companies have considerably longer statements of enterprise-wide strategies than the one given above for the candy company. Figure 2-2 shows the enterprise-wide strategy for a large diversified technology company. This strategy statement covers the components of its strategic objective in considerable detail, as well as additional elements of the company's strategy — such as the company philosophy upon which the strategy is based, and policies which amplify and explain the overall strategy statements.

Figure 2-2: A Company Overall Strategic Planning Statement

The basic objectives and general policies of the company stated below are intended to provide the framework upon which both the long-range and day-to-day operations are to be based. These objectives have developed over a period of time, stemming from the basic philosophy agreed upon by the founders of the Company and have evolved as the Company matured. Changes in objectives must be developed carefully and the objectives should not be neglected for the purpose of everyday expediency.

PREMISES: COMPANY PHILOSOPHY

This statement of objectives is conceived as a mechanism for the examination and appraisal of working policies. The objectives are based on the following five major points:

a. The Company must be operated as a profitable enterprise, and must serve the needs of its customers, shareholders, and employees. It is our responsibility to think of profits in terms of complex responsibilities involving the shareholders (dividends, stock appreciation), employees (salaries, benefits, working conditions), and the customer (quality product, fair price, good service).

b. The Character of the Company is determined by its decision to operate in highly specialized fields, and to carry a large burden of pioneering in new fields of applied science.

c. The rarest commodities in the world are human intelligence and ingenuity. These must not be wasted, neglected, or allowed to stagnate.

d. The best of scientific and engineering talent must be employed and placed in an environment which will facilitate the proper utilization of knowledge, intellect, and skill.

e. The operations of the Company are to be led by a management group which must have the respect of the organization for its business ability, integrity, fairness, and human approach to everyday problems.

Based upon these premises, the basic Company objectives are as follows:

OBJECTIVES

1. *Purpose*

The prime objective is to conduct a strong, well-balanced, stable, well-managed research, engineering, and manufacturing international enterprise organized to return maximum benefits to employees, customers, and stockholders.

2. *Nature of Enterprise*

The Company shall strive to be a highly competent, profit-minded, technically oriented enterprise engaging in research, engineering, and manufacturing to meet the needs of the world markets. The Company shall operate in those fields in which its research and development talents are required for business success. The Company shall endeavor to exploit its talents in establishing new techniques and, through them, new products for commercial, industrial, and defense applications.

3. *Fields of Interest*

The Company shall be engaged in the fields of microwave tubes and components; vacuum systems, instruments, and components; in fields exploiting recent contributions to science, including radio-frequency spectroscopy and instrumentation resulting therefrom; and other fields of science which may produce products useful for industrial, commercial, and defense needs.

4. *Diversification*

In recognition of the usual business cycles, the Company shall develop new products and enter new product areas or activities as may properly diversify, balance, and profitably strengthen the Company's economic position.

The Company shall endeavor to broaden and strengthen its product lines or fields of interest by sponsoring

Adapted from Robert J. Mockler, *Business Planning & Policy Formulation*, New York: D&R Publisher, 1983, pp. 410-414

Figure 2-2: A Company Overall Strategic Planning Statement (continued)

research and engineering programs, by purchase of patent rights, or by acquisition in part or in whole of other companies.

The diversification and growth of the Company shall be tempered with full consideration of its impact upon those who form the Company structure and careful consideration of financial stability and the danger of overextension.

5. *Business Stability*

The Company shall endeavor to optimize profits, stabilize employment, and develop a sound financial position by:

a. Good management practices
b. Long-range planning
c. Product diversification
d. Balanced commercial, industrial, and defense programs
e. Strong research and engineering efforts
f. Strong financial control
g. Efficient, low-cost organization and economical procedures

6. *Planning*

The Company shall prepare management programs looking several years in advance to permit prudent program decisions, and to permit analysis and criticism by the Board of Directors, the management, and others.

7. *Patents*

The Company shall maintain a strong patent position by obtaining patent protection for the inventions made by members of its staff, by acquiring patents from others, and by entering into licensing agreements with others. It shall encourage inventiveness of its employees by financial awards, publication, and other means.

8. *Product Lines*

The Company shall develop a balanced line of profitable products which lend themselves to the company's techniques of engineering, manufacturing, and distribution, and which serve diversified markets having either a continuing profit potential or showing promise of becoming profitable in the future.

In recognition of the importance and obligation of its role in the defense efforts of the United States, the company shall undertake research and development contracts from the government on a larger scale than is needed for the Company's manufacturing programs.

9. *Financial*

The Company shall strive to establish a stable financial structure, tightly controlled, with ample capitalization to operate the business efficiently and to permit necessary expansion and product diversification and to permit the Company to take advantage quickly of changing conditions.

10. *Stock Policy*

The Company shall encourage employee participation in the ownership of the Company.

11. *Organization*

The Company shall establish and maintain a sound structure and plan of organization which is necessary to meet the present and future Company objectives.

The Company shall be organized on a product line basis, with full profit accountability at the product division level. Methods of research, engineering, manufacturing, and marketing shall be adapted to the product areas. Corporate management will be responsible for binding these diverse products into the whole, and corporate staff functions shall supply those services not provided by line functions.

Figure 2-2: A Company Overall Strategic Planning Statement (continued)

Management personnel shall be so developed and guided as to insure able and efficient performance of their duties. It is the Company's policy to hold each execution of its principles and objectives.

The Company shall adopt such principles of personnel administration as will improve the mutual understanding and increase the effectiveness of the staff.

GENERAL POLICIES

In conformance with its objectives, the Company shall adopt general administrative policies, including the following:

I. *Organization*

The Company shall so administer the organization as to make possible and to induce the highest possible productive efforts by:

a. Expecting above-average performance from employees and supervisor.
b. Coupling responsibility with authority, and reaching an understanding with those concerned before changing the scope of any responsibility.
c. Providing that no person shall be given directions by more than one person.
d. Assuring that all directions to an employee come from the immediate supervisor.
e. Assuring that no difference of opinion between supervisors or between employees as to authority or responsibility shall be considered too trivial for prompt and painstaking attention.
f. Assuring that a supervisor will counsel his employees, and will keep them informed on the nature of their performance.

II. *Principles of Supervision*

The Company shall conduct its supervision so as to emphasize respect for the personality and dignity of the individual. The policy of consultation up and down the organization lines of authority and channels of communication shall be encouraged, as well as:

a. Giving consideration to an employee's views before reaching decisions materially affecting his job and interests.
b. Encouraging employees to express their views on matters affecting their jobs and interests.
c. Freely explaining all matters affecting employee relations.
d. Attempting to understand the other person's point of view, and assuming he too wants to do a good job.

III. *Employment*

The Company shall recruit and maintain the highest caliber staff possible to fill all positions, whether scientific, administrative, clerical, or of the skilled trades, and will do so by:

a. Selecting applicants on the basis of character, ability, skill, experience, and training, and without reference to age, sex, race, or creed.
b. Giving careful consideration to the promotion of employees to vacancies which occur, with the understanding that the strength of the Company's organization must be protected.
c. Giving consideration to employees who request job changes, and attempting to place each employee in the work for which he is best suited.
d. Maintaining a planned management development program to assure maximum performance by supervisors.

IV. *Wages and Compensation*

The Company shall establish a balanced compensation program for all employees, clearly related to job requirements of skill, responsibility, education, and experience, as demanded in current job descriptions.

The Company shall pay rates of pay, and establish rate ranges for all jobs, that are at least as good as those prevailing for similar work under similar conditions, and will maintain an equitable program for the granting of merit and promotional salary increases.

Figure 2-2: A Company Overall Strategic Planning Statement (continued)

In recognition of the principle that scientific and technical contributions are as important as those made by management personnel, the Company will make the higher salaries available to top technical personnel without requiring them to shift to management occupations.

V. *Working Conditions*
The Company shall create and maintain working conditions in offices and factories so that they are safe, clean, attractive, and generally conductive of high productive effort.

VI. *Grievances*
The Company shall assure employees that they are free to express themselves and without prejudice as to matters discussed. The Company will also insure that the supervisory staff will try to remove promptly any source of dissatisfaction, and failing prompt and satisfactory adjustment, to provide for submission of the case to the Personnel Office for review and settlement in consultation with management.

VII. *Benefit Plans*
The Company shall make provisions for vacations, sick leave, and holidays with pay; install such insurance plans as will afford financial protection to the individual and his dependents in time of illness, injury, or death; and provide, at the employee's discretion, for the planned accumulation of funds sufficient to assure retirement benefits.

EVALUATION
The Company shall periodically appoint an advisory committee to assess the progress towards achievement of the Objectives and General Policies.

The following is another example of an *enterprise-wide strategic objective* for a large company:

> The objective of the company is to aggressively increase the intrinsic value of its common stock through diversification in industries related to the company's present business lines, in order to build on the company's strengths in efficient asset management.

This strategy is for a company in a single industry — textiles. The company obviously wanted to grow rapidly and become a *conglomerate* or investment-type company, operating in a variety of related industries. Since its focus was on increasing the intrinsic value of its stock, initially it expanded solely through leveraged buyouts which did not involve issuance of common stock. Since it intended to engage in a wide variety of businesses, its enterprise-wide strategy statement was not as detailed as the other strategy statements given above. This is because each distinct strategic business unit (SBU) within the conglomerate had its own, more detailed enterprise-wide strategy. These SBU strategy statements, along with general corporate policy statements, defined the kind of enterprise desired, and gave some sense of its general direction, strategic focus, strategic approach, and performance results anticipated. One of the most successful diversified companies with a wide range of independent SBUs, 166 in mid-1992, is Johnson & Johnson, with annual sales of $12.4 billion; its product lines range from Band-Aids to Tylenol to pharmaceuticals to sanitary pads, all produced and marketed by separate SBUs that have an extraordinary amount of autonomy in formulating their enterprise-wide strategies [Weber 1992].

It is essential for every enterprise-wide strategic plan to define what the enterprise has to do differently or better than the competition (differentiation) to make money or be successful (keys to success) in areas where money can be made (opportunities). In formulating enterprise-wide strategies, therefore, managers strive to find or create differentiation or distinction in order to gain a competitive edge.

Atlantic Richfield Co. succeeded in gaining a competitive edge by "breaking the mold" in a very conservative industry. According to *The Wall Street Journal*: "The nation's eighth largest oil company has flourished by being different....it has emerged as a swift and noisy maverick in a trade dominated by quiet competitors and slow trends.... ARCO has been in the forefront in revamping the filling station, packing in customers with low-priced gasoline. Its AM/PM outlets at stations were some of the first to peddle cheap hamburgers, soft drinks and beer in addition to tires and oil. Costly credit cards were tossed and replaced with a debit card system that takes the payment straight out of the customer's bank account — and makes ARCO money... (The company) recently announced successful tests of low-emission gasoline that other refiners deemed almost impossible to create only months ago." This strategy seemed to work for Atlantic Richfield. Estimates in 1991 were that the company, which also produces natural gas and makes chemicals, would be the nation's most profitable oil company with a five-year average annual return of 21.5 percent of shareholder equity — more than double the industry average [Rose 1991; Wald 1991].

In another situation, J.C. Penney Company changed strategic directions in 1987, moving from a full-line department store to primarily a clothing store. Unlike ARCO, Penney's was having major problems with its new strategy as earnings tumbled in 1990 and 1991. The cause, according to industry reports, was that the company had "no distinct merchandising or pricing identity (distinctive differentiation)," as major a strategic failing in the retail clothing business as it is in most other businesses [Barmash 1991].

An enterprise-wide strategy does not provide a definitive answer as to what will make a company successful in the future. Instead, it allows a company to position or differentiate itself to take advantage of the future environment — that is, to better take advantage of breaks, should they occur, or to minimize problems, if they arise. Strategic management is no guarantee of a company's success; it merely increases the likelihood or chances of success.

While formulating strategies through context-specific analyses has been described so far in this chapter in a sequential, procedural, rational way, that structured description is used mainly for explanation, teaching, and learning purposes. As discussed in Chapter 1, the process of strategy formulation can be no less complex and varied in practice than the process of strategy implementation.

Strategies often emerge over a period of time, frequently during the implementation process. At times they are not even articulated nor need to be articulated. At other times, strategies are stumbled on by chance, as at Alias Research Inc., a computer software animation company, at which the president happened to stumble upon applications of his product to industrial design [Farnsworth 1991]. Mintzberg has done extensive studies of this emergent process [1989, 1990]. Such a fluid emerging discovery process follows from such factors as the diversity of strategic management situations in business, changing competitive markets, new competitors' capabilities and strategies, unexpected political events, economic dislocations, and even the personal values of different persons doing the strategy formulation. It is possible to bring some structure to the strategy formulation process, but only within the context of the somewhat chaotic realities of actual business practices.

FORMULATING AN INTEGRATIVE FRAMEWORK FOR ENABLING OR FUNCTIONAL PLANNING

In the company situations cited earlier, the strategy statements were each supported with

- Specific policy guidelines
- Statements of company philosophy
- Financial plans and budgets
- Financial and other programs, and
- A variety of enabling strategies and plans for key company functions and departments — such as marketing, operations/production, and computer information systems.

Where appropriate to the situation, enterprise-wide strategies and plans for individual strategic business units were also formulated. Strategy formulation, and the strategic thinking arising from it, provides a framework for decision making throughout a company, from marketing to operations/production to public relations to research and development to finance and accounting.

THE IMPORTANCE OF FINANCIAL OBJECTIVES, PLANS, AND BUDGETS

The role of financial planning in strategic management varies widely. In some companies, corporate managers specify financial objectives, such as a specific return on investment (ROI), as part of the enterprise-wide strategic plans. These are referred to as *target or performance results* or *overall quantitative goals*. Frequently, however, these financial objectives are merely aspirations of corporate management, and are therefore treated as planning premises; in such situations, they are only one factor considered, since their feasibility, along with all the items in corporate management's wish list, must be evaluated in light of market realities. For example, one company's owner managers announced a goal of a 15 percent annual increase in sales combined with a 15 percent return on investment. This proved unrealistic and unachievable when market realities and the owners' other requirements, such as limited product expansion and the owner's desire to sell no additional stock in the company to outsiders, were examined.

On the other hand, in many strategic management situations, realistically developed *financial targets* for sales, profits, and return on investment *results* grow out of a carefully structured situation analysis. These can be usefully incorporated into enterprise-wide strategic plans.

Financial factors can be critical to areas supporting strategic management. For example, financial projections are essential in evaluating strategies, since they provide a way to simulate operating results of proposed strategies. Such financial projections in turn become the basis for long- and short-term budgets, and other financial plans — including resource allocation capital budgets — that are developed as the process progresses. These projections provide a useful framework for developing the enabling strategies and plans for key operating areas, including strategic and operational controls, and so are an integral part of strategic plans. In many situations, the projections are the mechanism that *enables* enterprise-wide strategies and plans to be translated into operational plans and operational decision making. When used for control purposes, such benchmark measures are often referred to as *value drivers*.

While strategies are eventually translated into specific budgets and financial plans, and these plans are always evaluated in terms of their impact on company profitability, the financial plans ultimately are only representations of strategies, not the strategies themselves.

The computer disks accompanying this book provide exercises in financial analysis of a company's present position, as well as in using financial simulation to evaluate alternative strategies in ten of the company studies at the end of this book.

INTEGRATED STRATEGIC MANAGEMENT FOR MAJOR FUNCTIONAL AREAS OF A BUSINESS: ENABLING PLANS

In the enterprise-wide strategy examples cited above, in addition to the statements of company philosophy, and specific financial plans and budgets, the strategy statements were supported with other *enabling strategies, plans,* and *programs* — that is, any appropriate strategies and strategic plans and programs for key company strategic business units, divisions, functions, and departments useful in implementing enterprise-wide strategies. These strategies and plans comprise a *strategic plan* which can provide a framework for management decision making throughout a company.

Strategies, policies, and plans can be developed for each major functional or operating area of a company. These areas can include marketing and operations/production, as well as finance, information systems, public relations, legal, research and development, or any other area critical to the long-term success of a company. These plans are called enabling plans because they assist in the carrying out of enterprise-wide company strategies and plans. These plans are also often called functional or operational plans.

At The Games Gang — a small company — company managers developed the enabling plans as the company initially went into business. The plans included detailed strategies for manufacturing, distributing, and promoting Pictionary. At Gillette, a much larger company, operating managers formulated the enabling plans over a relatively long period of time.

IMPLEMENTING STRATEGIES

The effectiveness of a company's strategic management effort depends on how the effort is carried out. In addition to enabling plan development, several aspects of strategy implementation discussed in later chapters of this book are covered in this section.

Leadership can be important in establishing mutual trust and respect among and for top managers in the company and providing an internal environment that encourages the organization to move in new directions. The organization changes or realignment can include bringing in new staff; reengineering organization structure based on realigning existing company business processes; creating a cooperative organization structure that promotes teamwork, creative thinking, and faster decision making; and modifying the corporate culture. In Chapter 1, this was the case when Louis Gerstner, the former president of American Express Company, was brought in to head RJR Nabisco Holdings Inc. [Anders 1991]. These same steps were also important ones for David Johnson when he became president of Campbell Soup Co. in January 1990 [Freeman 1991].

The importance of these initial steps in formulating and implementing strategic plans has been demonstrated at a number of companies ["Getting to Prime" 1991]. Some companies, such as Gillette, go so far as to involve operating managers in formulating enterprise-wide strategies. This both introduces them to the strategic thinking underlying the strategies and obtains their input, as well as helps to give them a proprietary interest in the strategies by letting them help develop (or actually develop) the strategies. These aspects of strategic management are discussed in detail in Chapter 12.

Effectively implementing strategies can require balancing many conflicting forces. For example, the *Los Angeles Times*, like other large city newspapers, was struggling during the early 1990s with the strategic problem of maintaining a unified image of a single paper with a wide range of local, national, and international news. At the same time, the *Times* had to meet competitive pressures from smaller local newspapers to emphasize local news in separate editions of its paper [Jones 1990]. Thomas Murphy, head of Capital Cities Broadcasting, faced similar difficulties when his company took over ABC in January 1986. Only by patiently working through the many problems — business and interpersonal — that arose in balancing the interests of the news and entertainment divisions at ABC did he finally formulate and implement a success strategy. By 1991 he had made ABC a major network competitor again and substantially increased the company's profitability and market value [Auletta 1991].

In addition to meeting competitive pressures on a day-to-day basis through balancing mixed strategies, implementation also involves balancing other conflicting pressures. For example, people's attitudes and organizational inflexibility can create major implementation problems, leading — as they did at Chase Manhattan Bank's Municipal Bond strategic business unit — to major personnel changes [Doran 1989].

In the 1980s, when this author was doing several multimillion dollar real estate coop/condominium conversions, it became apparent that formulating a strategy for doing these conversions was easy, almost common knowledge. Creatively moving the conversions through the problems caused by Attorney General regulators, New York City bureaucrats, tenant and tenant association lawyers, and even hostile newspaper reporters was 95 percent of the job of effectively turning a strategy into several million dollars in profits.

Technology is also having a major impact on strategy implementation. Upon becoming the head of Union Pacific Railroad in the mid-1980s, Michael H. Walsh envisioned a revitalized company that could quickly respond at the lowest organization levels to changing customer requirements. He eliminated six layers of management to facilitate faster decision making. However, it was only when Union Pacific had introduced the most advanced computerized information/communications system in the industry at that time that he was able to fully implement his vision while maintaining the control needed to integrate the movement of equipment across a vast railroad system in a customer efficient and cost efficient way [Hayes 1992; Machalaba 1991; Peters 1991; Salpukas 1991].

In strategic management, finding the balances, making the required compromises, getting specific operating and program jobs done effectively and efficiently, stimulating strategic thinking among employees, creating a supportive internal organization environment, winning managers' trust and respect, and in other ways managing the implementation of strategic plans is often more difficult than formulating the strategic plans themselves. Running day-to-day operations, making the sales, producing high-quality products consistently, solving operating crises as they arise, and responding to competitor moves and changes in the market and political environment, are essential to making a business work. Strategies and related enabling plans provide only a structure for effective managers to work within.

A major benefit of enterprise-wide strategy formulation and implementation is the strategic viewpoint and thinking it instills in those who formulate and implement the strategies. This thinking and viewpoint prepares operating managers and all levels of personnel to deal effectively with rapidly changing environments. Often, a strategy becomes obsolete very quickly because of changing competitive market forces. The process through which strategies are formulated and implemented, therefore, are often more important than the actual strategies themselves [Robert 1988].

DEFINING AND ORGANIZING THE STRATEGIC MANAGEMENT EFFORT

A formal strategy formulation and implementation project, in those companies that have them, needs definition and organization at an early stage to give focus and direction to the project. Ideally, one starts this definition process with an analysis of the existing situation, exploring questions like What kind of planning is presently being done in the company? What are company managers' attitudes towards strategic management and its value? To what degree do formal planning procedures exist? Are there formal strategy statements and how widely are they communicated? Who participates in enterprise-wide strategy formulation now and what is their relative impact on the process? How are strategies presently used and what is their impact on operations and company profitability [Hax 1990]?

Questions are also asked about expectations for the future: What kind of planning is to be done? What outcomes are desired? To what uses will the formulated strategies and implemented plans be put? Which business units and key operating areas will be affected by the strategies and related plans and how are the units interrelated? How formal is the strategic management effort to be? The answers to these questions, as well as information about the time frame of the plans, help to formulate the general direction and parameters of the strategic management effort.

Questions to explore about project organization include What levels of management will be involved in different phases of the effort? How will it be organized and directed? What mechanisms will be used to monitor the project's progress? Is there to be a large department reporting to the CEO? Is the formal strategy formulation to be located at the divisional level, and is it to provide only support services, or is it to be responsible for formulating the actual plans? The answers to such situationally oriented questions will dictate how the strategic management function is formally organized.

As pointed out in Appendix B, many companies that have formal strategy development efforts — such as Atlantic Richfield and Kemper Financial Services [McConahey 1992] — are doing strategic planning at the operating management level, with corporate planning directors providing only coordination, integration, technical support, and encouragement [Prescott 1989].

AN INTEGRATED ADAPTIVE STRATEGIC MANAGEMENT PROCESS

It is important to understand how the different strategic management tasks outlined in Figure 2-1 and discussed in preceding sections are carried out during the formulation and implementation of business strategies. Figure 2-3 and its more detailed extension in Figure 2-4 outline an integrative strategic management process. While it is structured — that is, it is presented in outlined steps — it is not procedural. It is in practice a semi-structured, adaptive, situation context-specific process whose structure focuses on an individual strategic manager's own company strategic management problems.

The process models in Figures 2-3 and 2-4 differ from the task model in Figure 2-1 in that their primary focus and orientation is on the process involved in dealing with an individual planner's own situation. They are in this sense context-specific adaptive situation management processes. In addition, they trace relationships among model components and the reasoning involved in doing strategic management tasks.

The strategic management process shown in Figure 2-3 and 2-4 is useful, based on over thirty years of study and experience with hundreds of business managers. Individual business managers are most interested in solving their own company's specific problems and helping their company succeed in their particular competitive environment. The process shown also has a sound theoretical basis in cognitive psychology, as well as in the management and planning sciences [Mockler 1992 (A,B,C)].

Figures 2-3 and 2-4 are not complete models of the strategic management process, however, nor are they the only way to model or describe it — anymore than there is a single way for all strategic planners to make all their decisions in all strategy formulation and implementation situations. It is a general context-specific structured process model. The purpose of each of the

Figure 2-3: Strategic Management Process Overview

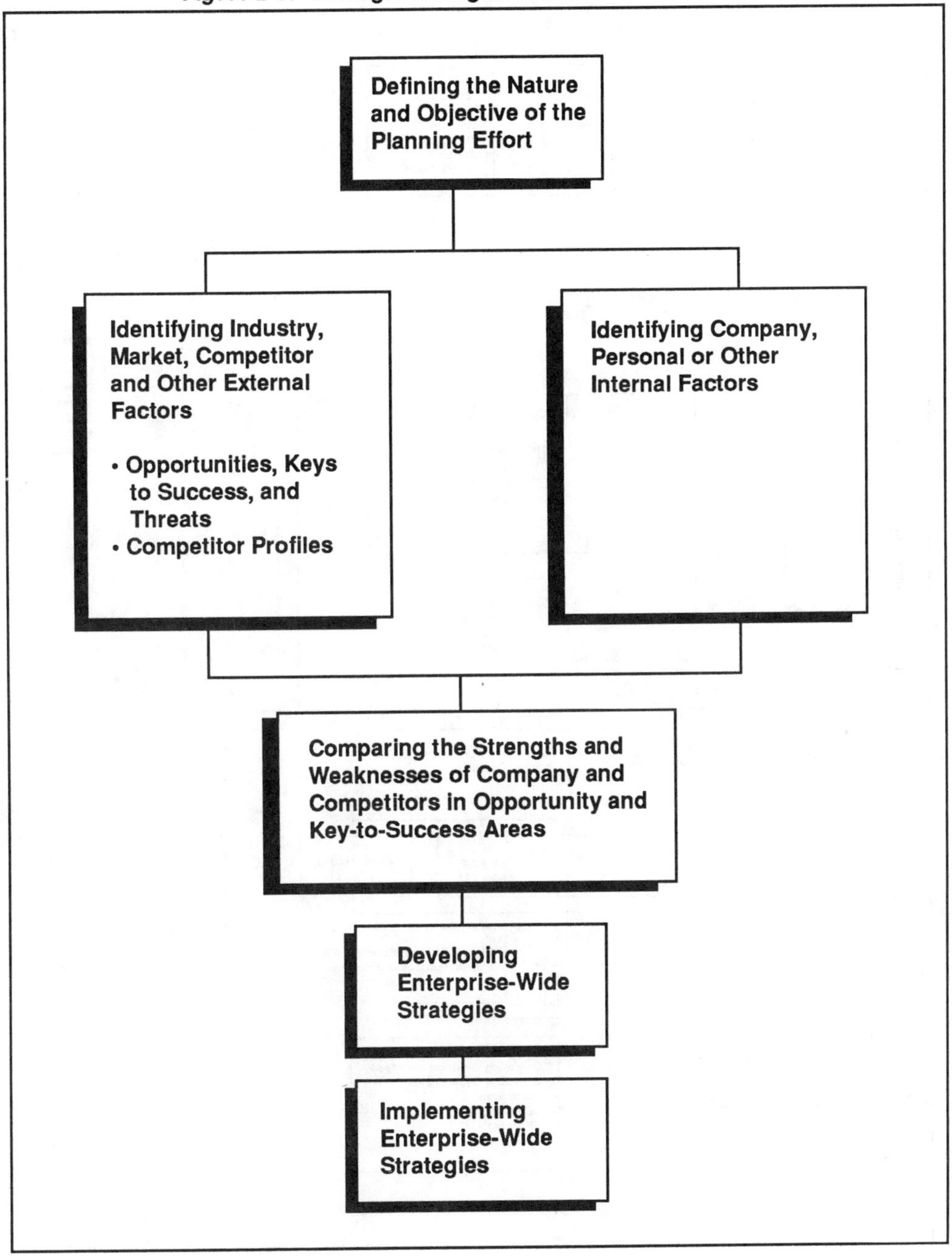

Defining the Nature and Objective of the Planning Effort

Identifying Industry, Market, Competitor and Other External Factors

- Opportunities, Keys to Success, and Threats
- Competitor Profiles

Identifying Company, Personal or Other Internal Factors

Comparing the Strengths and Weaknesses of Company and Competitors in Opportunity and Key-to-Success Areas

Developing Enterprise-Wide Strategies

Implementing Enterprise-Wide Strategies

Figure 2-4: Strategic Management Decision-Making Process

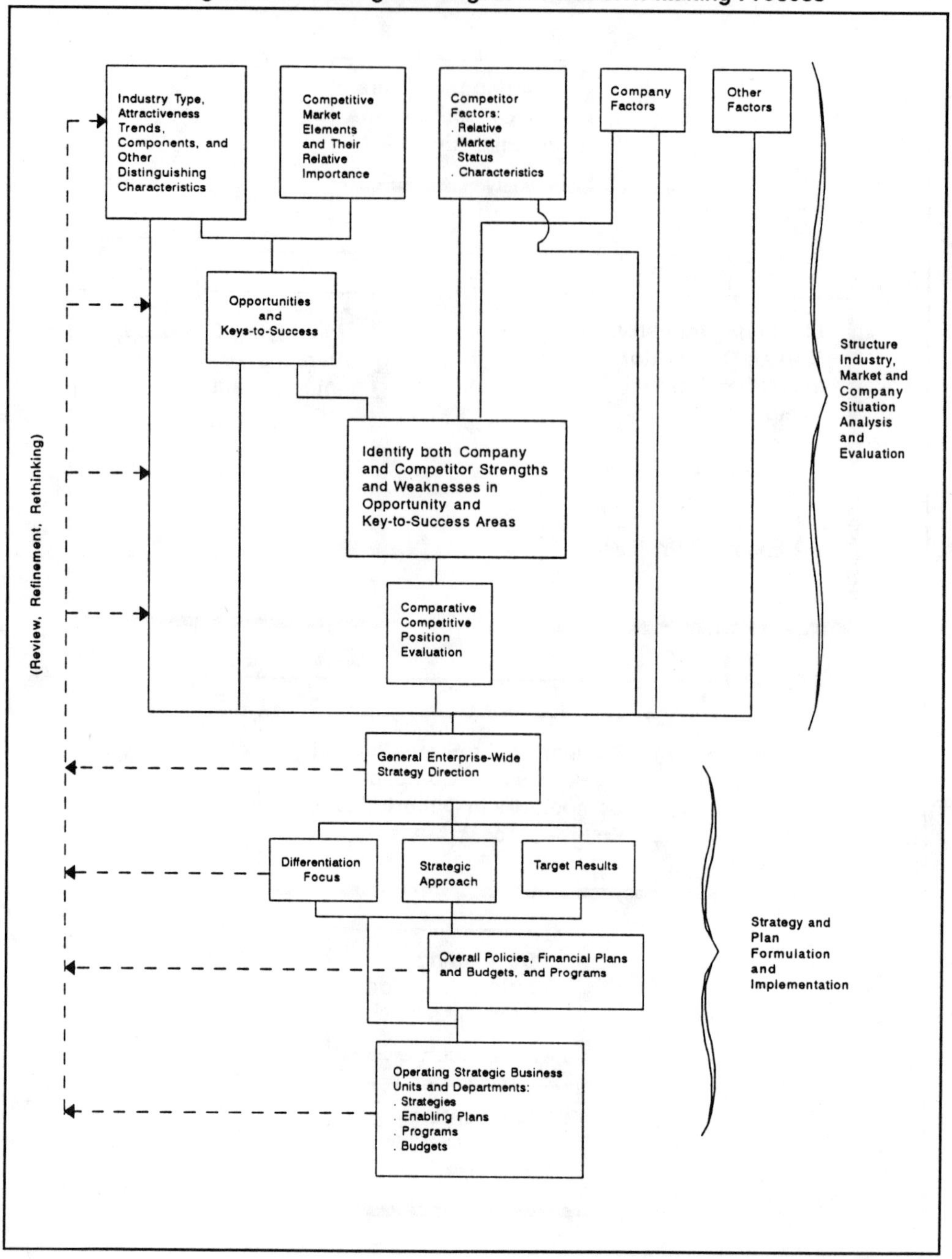

Industry Type, Attractiveness Trends, Components, and Other Distinguishing Characteristics

Competitive Market Elements and Their Relative Importance

Competitor Factors:
. Relative Market Status
. Characteristics

Company Factors

Other Factors

Opportunities and Keys-to-Success

Identify both Company and Competitor Strengths and Weaknesses in Opportunity and Key-to-Success Areas

Comparative Competitive Position Evaluation

Structure Industry, Market and Company Situation Analysis and Evaluation

General Enterprise-Wide Strategy Direction

Differentiation Focus

Strategic Approach

Target Results

Overall Policies, Financial Plans and Budgets, and Programs

Operating Strategic Business Units and Departments:
. Strategies
. Enabling Plans
. Programs
. Budgets

Strategy and Plan Formulation and Implementation

(Review, Refinement, Rethinking)

following chapters' discussions and the company case studies at the end of the book is to explore how this general situationally oriented strategic management process works in different business situations. It is an effort to bring structure to strategic management while still recognizing the dynamic nature of how strategic managers work in action business situations.

The process outlined in Figures 2-3 and 2-4 also provides a useful framework for understanding and learning strategy formulation and strategy implementation.

SEGMENTATION OF THE STRATEGIC MANAGEMENT PROCESS FOR ANALYSIS AND LEARNING PURPOSES

Figure 2-1 identified different tasks involved in the strategic management job. These tasks are discussed in PARTS TWO, THREE, and FOUR of this book.

The enterprise-wide strategy formulation tasks covered in the chapters in PARTS TWO and THREE are

- Structured industry analysis (the arena, the field of play, and its condition — Chapter 3)
- Identifying competitive market opportunities and keys to success (where the money will be made and how the money will be made or success achieved, the rules of the game — Chapter 4)
- The competitors and company analyses (the nature of the competition, scouting the opposing teams and their players — Chapters 5 and 6)
- Comparative competitive position analysis (how we stack up against the competition in areas that affect winning — Chapter 6)
- Enterprise-wide strategy formulation (overall winning strategies, the long-term strategy for building a winning team — Chapter 7)

The chapters in PART FOUR cover various aspects of implementing strategies:

- Formulating detailed policies and philosophy plans, financial plans, and programs (frameworks for translating enterprise-wide strategic plans into enabling strategies and plans for key operating areas, constructing the foundation of a winning team — Chapter 8)
- Developing the enabling strategies and plans (detailed winning strategies, the building blocks — Chapters 9 through 11)
- Implementing the strategies and related enabling plans (playing the game sucessfully — Chapter 12)
- Carrying out the strategic management effort (Appendix B)

While these tasks are discussed separately, they are part of a continuous strategic management process. The discussion of this integrating process begins in Chapter 3 and continues through Appendix B. The chapters in PART FIVE cover two special kinds of strategic management situations: multinational situations and situations involving major social problems.

As in learning a sport, in strategic management it is first necessary to break down the process into discrete tasks or components, and then work on mastering each component. Golf is taught in this way, for example, as one learns the correct grip, stance, body position, and the like. The golfer then perfects these golf-related tasks through practice. Similarly, exercises and explanations for learning strategic management tasks are provided in this book.

As training progresses, for instance, into case studies and the more specific situationally oriented processes given at the end of each chapter, these different aspects of the subject are gradually integrated into actual performance of the strategic management job. The same thing occurs in sports training or playing a sport. While it is important to emphasize each separate component during training, as is done in the chapters in this text, overemphasizing any specific aspect can hurt performance in strategic management, just as thinking too much about the specific hand or head positions during a golf swing can hurt performance on the course.

REVIEW QUESTIONS

1. Discuss the relationship between strategy formulation and implementation, and how they relate to strategic management.
2. Describe different levels of strategies, noting especially the difference among enterprise-wide strategies, strategic business unit strategies, and enabling plans in different functional and operating areas.
3. Describe the tasks involved in strategic management.
4. Discuss the ways in which the structured industry and market analyses — especially the definitions of opportunities, threats, and keys to success — provide a basis for strategy formulation.
5. Describe what is involved in the comparative competitive position evaluation.
6. What is an enterprise-wide strategic objective? Discuss different kinds of such objectives and their scopes and structures.
7. In what ways do enterprise-wide policies and philosophies extend and amplify the enterprise-wide strategic objectives?
8. Describe the importance of financial plans and planning in strategic management.
9. Discuss the role that enabling strategies and plans play in strategic management.
10. What critical tasks are involved in implementing strategies and why are they so important to effective strategic management?
11. Discuss the ways in which strategic management processes are both semi-structured and adaptive context-specific processes.

EXERCISES

1. Read recent issues of the periodicals referred to in the references section at the end of the chapter, or related periodicals of your choice, and find examples of

• Enterprise-wide strategies. Write a report comparing these strategies to those described in this chapter. Pay particular attention to the ways in which the strategies you research are or are not appropriate for the company and competitive market involved.

• A strategy that went wrong. Write a report on why it didn't work. Identify which of the aspects of strategic management described in this chapter appeared to be the cause of the problem.

2. Read the *Blakeston and Wilson Company* study in the Case Study section at the end of this book. Write a report describing the major opportunity areas and critical factors affecting success in the industry involved. In addition, identify the major company strengths and weaknesses.

3. The computer disks accompanying this book contain eight prototype knowledge-based systems involving strategic planning decisions. Follow the directions accompanying the disks to run a consultation using the CAREER.REV system. Should you be thinking about going into business for yourself, this consultation should assist you in estimating your chances of succeeding as an entrepreneur or the steps you might take to improve your chances of success.

REFERENCES

Anders, George, "Old Flamboyance Is Out as Louis Gerstner Remakes RJR Nabisco," *The Wall Street Journal*, March 21, 1991, pp. A1, A6.

Auletta, Ken, *Three Blind Mice: How the TV Networks Lost Their Way*, New York: Random House, 1991.

Barmash, Isadore, "J. C. Penny's Woes Tied to Lack of Identity," *The New York Times*, April 22, 1991, pp. D1, D7.

Brady, Rose, Peter Galuska, Richard A. Melcher, and David Greising, "Let's Make a Deal — But a Small One," *Business Week*, January 20, 1992, pp. 44, 45.

Burros, Marian, "Health-Food Supermarkets? Why Yes, It's Only Natural," *The New York Times*, January 8, 1992, pp. B1, B7.

Clines, Francis, "Soviet-Chevron Oil Venture Mired in Fears of Capitalist Exploitation," *The New York Times*, August 16, 1991, pp. A1, A12.

Deutsch, Claudia,"A Toy Company Finds Life After Pictionary," *The New York Times*, Business Section, July 9, 1989, pp. 6 and 7.

Doran, John J., "Ready for the Next Decade: Chase Manhattan Securities Inc. Revamps Its Municipal Banking and Bond Operations," *The Bond Buyer*, April 7, 1989, p. 1ff.

Engleberg, Stephen, "Eastern Europe Foils All But the Hardiest of Western Investors," *The New York Times*, March 5, 1992, pp. A1, D8.

Fabrikant, Geraldine, "Blitz Hits Small Studio Pix," *The New York Times*, Business Section, July 12, 1992, p. 7.

Fabrikant, Geraldine, "Finding Success in Movie Niches," *The New York Times*, April 4, 1990, pp. D1, D6.

Farnsworth, Clyde H., "Software Star on a Roller Coaster," *The New York Times*, Business Section, September 29, 1990, p. 15.

Freeman, Alix M., "Campbell Chief Cooks Up Winning Menu," *The Wall Street Journal*, February 15, 1991, pp. B1, B5.

"Getting to Prime," *Inc.*, January 1991, pp. 27-33.

Goldman, Kevin, "Hollywood Movie Maker Thrives with Different Script," *The Wall Street Journal*, May 22, 1992, p. B4.

Grimes, William, "A Film Company's Success Story: Low Costs, Narrow Focus, Profits," *The New York Times*, December 2, 1991, pp. C13, C16.

Grover, Ronald, "Nightmares, Turtles — And Profits," *Business Week*, September 30, 1991, pp. 78, 80.

Hax, Arnaldo C., "Redefining the Concept of Strategy and the Strategy Formulation Process," *Planning Review*, May/June 1990, pp. 34-41.

Hayes, Thomas C., "Behind the Iron Hand at Tenneco," *The New York Times*, January 6, 1992, pp. D1, D5.

Hymowitz, Carol, and Thomas F. O'Boyle, "Two Disparate Firms Find Keys to Success in Troubled Industries," *The Wall Street Journal*, May 29, 1991, pp. A1, A7.

Jones, Alex S., "Los Angeles Paper's Rival Visions," *The New York Times*, June 18, 1990, pp. D1. D10.

Knowlton, Christopher, "Shell Gets Rich by Beating Risk," *Fortune*, August 26, 1991, pp. 79-82.

Kristof, Nicholas, "Foreign Investors Pouring into China," *The New York Times*, June 15, 1992, pp. D1, D8.

Lublin, Joann S., "Hayden Is Aiming to Make Jaguar a Roaring Success," *The Wall Street Journal*, June 22, 1990, pp. B1, B4.

Machalaba, Daniel, "The Kiamachi Shows How Small Railroads Can Serve Rural Areas," *The Wall Street Journal*, January 8, 1992, pp. A1, A12.

Machalaba, Daniel, Caleb Solomon, and Robert Johnson, "Tenneco, Recruiting New Chairman, Gets Ready for a Shakeup," *The Wall Street Journal*, August 8, 1991, pp. A1, A4.

Maremont, Mark, Thane Preston, and Lori Bongiorno, "These Repair Jobs Are Taking a Little Longer Than Expected," *Business Week*, April 22, 1992, pp. 117, 121.

McConahey, Steve, Corporate and International Development (Planning Director), Kemper Financial Services, Inc., *The Emerging Role of the Strategic Planner in the 1990s: Key Elements*, New York: Planning Forum's Strategic Planning Special Interest Group, April 8, 1992.

Mintzberg, Henry, "The Design School: Reconsidering the Basic Premises of Strategic Management," *Strategic Management Journal*, April 1990, pp. 171-195.

Mintzberg, Henry, *Mintzberg on Management,* New York: The Free Press, 1989.

Mockler, Robert J., *Business Process Reengineering: A Theoretical and Pracitical Orientation for Managing Organization Change*, Research Working Paper, New York: Strategic Management Research Group, 1992(A).

Mockler, Robert J., *Contingency Approaches to Strategic Management*, Research Working Paper, New York: Strategic Management Research Group, 1992(B).

Mockler, Robert J., *Structured Industry/Competitive Market Analysis*, Research Working Paper, New York: Strategic Management Research Group, 1992(C).

Peters, Tom, "Competitive Strategies and Cooperation," Presentation, 11th Annual Conference, Strategic Management Society, Toronto, CA, October 23-26, 1991.

Prescott, John E., and Daniel C. Smith, "The Largest Survey of 'Leading Edge' Competitor Intelligence Managers," *Planning Review*, May/June 1989, pp. 6-13.

Ramirez, Anthony, "Borden Plan for Profits: One Nation, One Pasta," *The New York Times,* June 21, 1990, pp. D1, D5.

Robert, Michel, *The Strategist CEO*, Westport, CT: Decision Processes International, 1988.

Rose, Frederick, "Atlantic Richfield Co. Is Winning the West by Breaking the Mold," *The Wall Street Journal*, August 7, 1991, pp. A1, A7.

Salpukas, Agis, "Riding Herd on Iron Horses, with Fiber Optics," *The New York Times*, November 27, 1991, p. D5.

Schwartz, Peter, "Accepting the Risk in Forecasting: Multiple Scenarios Allowed Shell to Anticipate the Rise and Then Crash in Oil Prices," *The New York Times*, Business Section, September 4, 1990, p. 13.

Stevenson, Richard W., "Carolco Cuts Staff by 25% and May Scale Back Films," *The New York Times*, December 5, 1991, pp. D1, D8.

Wald, Matthew L., "ARCO Reports New Gasoline That Sharply Cuts Pollutants," *The New York Times*, July 11, 1991, pp. A1, D6.

Weber, Joseph, "A Big Company That Works," *Business Week*, May 4, 1992, pp. 124-132.

WuDunn, Sheryl, "Getting Out of China Harder Than Going In," *The New York Times*, April 25, 1991, pp. D1, D7.

PART TWO

STRUCTURED COMPETITIVE MARKET ANALYSIS

CHAPTER 3

INDUSTRY AND COMPETITIVE MARKET ASSESSMENT: OVERALL CONTEXT ANALYSIS

This chapter discusses the first strategy formulation task identified in Figure 3-1, the overall industry and market analysis. The objective of this initial discussion of structured context analysis is to enable readers to

- Define the overall industry and market context under study
- Identify overall factors affecting the industry's future
- Use environmental forecasting techniques
- Define how the overall business situation works
- Track industry and market information, and be aware of the kinds and sources of information needed to do so
- Do analyses in specific situations

DEFINING THE INDUSTRY

The word "industry" is used here to refer to the overall external situation context or business environment a firm expects to operate within. An industry may be defined by groups of companies, products, outlets, or customers; by territory of operations; or by any combination of these and other appropriate distinguishing characteristics. For instance, some examples of industries are

- The ski equipment and apparel manufacturing industry
- The athletic footwear industry
- The oil exploration services equipment industry

Figure 3-1: Strategic Management Tasks

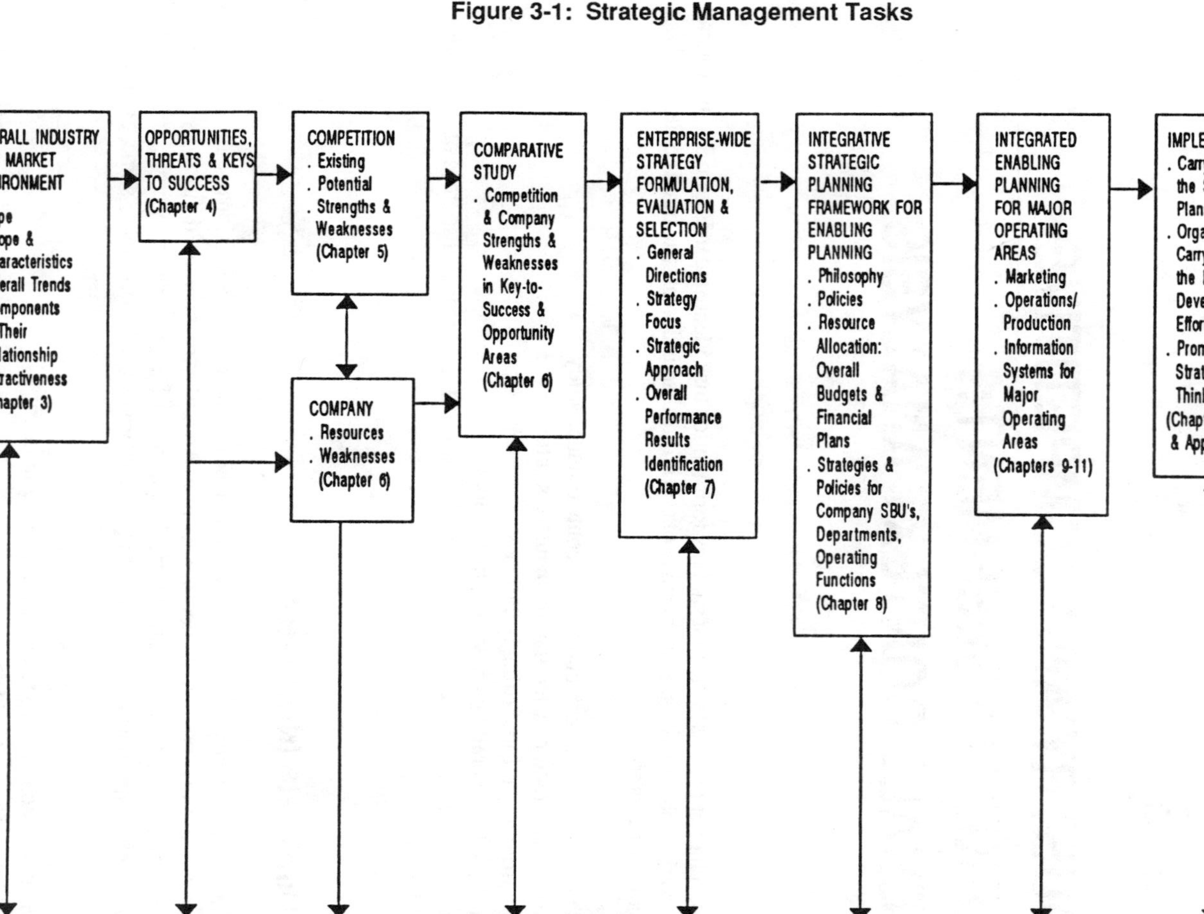

- The mail-order apparel industry
- The home video industry in the United States
- The computer software or hardware industry, or any segment thereof, such as workstations or minicomputers
- The specialty cookie industry, or the broader category, the specialty food industry

The scope of the industry definition and the importance of different industry factors in strategy formulation will vary in different business situations. For example, while world-wide economic factors can have a high impact on General Motors or Gillette, such global factors will often (though not always) have a less direct impact on a local U.S. retailer, unless it sells products from a foreign country. Changes in federal government regulations may have a major impact on the banking industry, but be of very little relevance to a regional candy company.

The objective during this initial phase of strategy formulation is to define the limits or scope of the business situation context in the specific situation under study. This is the *general industry area* in which a planner intends to formulate and explore alternative strategies for his/her company. The industry definition encompasses all the companies which make goods or supply services which may be substituted for one another in areas of possible future interest to the company under study. Precisely identifying industry limits is becoming harder in some industries, since technological advances have led to a blurring of lines between industries. For example, telephone and cable companies are now able technically and legally to compete in each other's markets [McCarroll 1992; Zachery 1992].

Within the general industry context, one or more competitive markets or operating environments may be identified. In studies involving larger companies in major industries which contain distinct larger competitive markets, the competitive market analyses can be distinct. For example, IBM competes in a variety of hardware and software markets within the computer industry. Several of these, such as the computer workstation market, have distinct characteristics and are expected to exceed $20 billion in sales in the early 1990s [Markoff 1990]. In the case of the small regional baked goods company described below, the strategic business situation context is much narrower — both in geographic scope and product line breadth. In that situation, the distinction between the industry and the competitive market is less relevant in formulating enterprise-wide strategies.

In business, the words "market" and "industry" are often interchanged. For example, the periodical publishing industry is, in the view of many, just one market within either the overall publishing industry or the media business.

Whatever the situation under study, it often helps to start with a broad industry definition and then narrow it down to a specific relevant segment. For example, a regional baking goods company's strategy may be to focus specifically on a very limited product line — specialty cookies and high-volume, standard cookies and crackers — in a very limited geographic area — a four-state region. In that situation, the industry analysis might

- first identify characteristics affecting future success in the baked goods industry in general
- then study the specific identified product area and competitive market forces within the

company's region, such as local competition, distribution outlets, and customer tastes.

In this situation, the broader industry context provides a framework for focusing on the specific competitive market segments under study.

When defining critical industry factors, looking at an industry's history can be useful. However, such an historical examination can be unproductive if it locks the mind into thinking patterns related to what has been successful in meeting *past* market needs. Unless future markets are expected to be similar to past ones, future patterns of opportunities and success are likely to be different from past ones.

Defining and redefining the industry scope can also provide new insights. For example, to stimulate the idea generating process, the newspaper industry could be conceptualized as the information communications industry. Dow Jones did this when it expanded beyond newspaper publishing (*The Wall Street Journal* and *Barron's*) and introduced electronic news retrieval and database services in the 1980s. Redefining the stock brokerage industry as the financial services industry helped Merrill Lynch to capture major segments of the financial services market in the late 1970s by introducing such products as integrated or combined customer accounts. On a smaller scale, simply redefining the corner delicatessen as a health food store could lead to restructuring the entire business.

Another way to reconceptualize an industry is by the stage of the industry's growth cycle. Different stages of industry growth have different problems, opportunities, and keys to success. An emerging industry can be forgiving (fast growth covers many mistakes) and very cruel (product obsolescence can be quick and devastating). Both Atari (video games) and Colleco (toys and small computers) enjoyed brief periods of success in the 1980s, but eventually suffered rapid sales declines [Deutsch 1989]. Success in turbulent industries depends on innovation and effective strategy formulation — to create and exploit new opportunities and deal with new threats — as well as creative product innovation.

Success in a mature industry, on the other hand, may depend more on being a low-cost producer or effective marketer than on being an innovative new product developer. For example, in two highly competitive and relatively mature industries that are experiencing overcapacity problems — carpeting and retailing — two small but aggressive newer companies have prospered through price cutting and aggressive marketing. Sales of Shaw Industries Inc., a carpet manufacturer which started operations in the early 1970s, have grown from around $700 million in 1986 to over $1.4 billion in 1990. Shaw has achieved this mainly through low prices and such aggressive marketing moves as handling 96 percent of its distribution, controlling its material supplies, and tracking orders and customers with state-of-the-art computer systems [Ruffenach 1991].

Phar-Mor, the nation's largest and fastest growing discount retail chain in 1991, prospered in an industry estimated to have 20 percent overcapacity and experiencing many bankruptcies and failures [Helliker 1992; Norris 1992; Strom 1992; Wayne 1992]. Phar-Mor utilized selective product stocking, "innovative merchandising, relentless marketing, and bare knuckle negotiating with suppliers," as well as "cut-throat" pricing. Founded only 10 years earlier, company sales were expected to reach $3 billion in 1991 [Hirsch 1991].

OVERALL FACTORS AFFECTING AN INDUSTRY'S FUTURE

Any industry analysis focuses on the future implications of the factors examined. For this reason, this phase of a strategy formulation study would ideally lead to a written statement of the industry trends, forces, and events expected to have a major impact on strategy formulation and strategic plan development, as well as the factors and reasoning underlying these anticipated trends, forces, and events.

Economic Factors

While political events, natural disasters, and individual actions cannot always be anticipated, a planner can attempt to identify possible economic trends and the likelihood of their occurrence.

For example, many experts reasoned that the economy in 1992 was entering an extended period of reduced inflation, which was expected to extend into the late 1990s. In their opinion, the expected abundant availability of capital combined with the relatively stable growth in population supported this viewpoint. While this trend was not certain, it was a reasonable possibility, given the facts cited, and so had be taken into account when formulating enterprise-wide strategies.

Other economic trends that might be examined include interest rates, income distribution by population group, savings rates, credit and capital availability, productivity, wage rates, and disposable income.

Another major trend in the 1980s was the increased internationalization of business and the expected increased global competition arising from the planned 1992 removal of trade barriers between the member countries of the European Economic Community [Truell 1991]. Many companies moved quickly to establish market and manufacturing bases in the newly freed Eastern European block countries, even though there were many potential threats arising from the lack of stability, resources, and infrastructures favorable to business [Hadler 1991].

How trends are taken into account depends on one's estimates of the timing, impact, magnitude, and likelihood of their occurrence. If an analysis concludes that the trend towards lower inflation rates will probably (65 percent certainty) last through the years 2005 to 2010, that it will be sustained and substantial (less than 5 percent annual inflation most years), and that its negative impact will be greatest in the areas that benefited most from high inflation in the past (real estate, for example), then the created strategies will be likely to protect one from these trends or to exploit them.

Since no future economic environment is guaranteed, many experienced planners develop alternative scenarios, and assign probabilities to them in order to estimate risks [Knowlton 1991]. In this way, techniques to reduce risks and increase chances of success are explored.

Planners strive to be risk takers, not gamblers. Gamblers have less than a 50 percent chance of winning, since the house takes a percentage of each bet. Risk takers seek to up the percentages somewhat in their favor, so that the overall likelihood of coming out ahead by a larger margin is increased. Strategic management helps increase chances of success and reduce risks. It does not, however, provide absolute certainty. Shell Oil Company dramatically illustrates this point: while known for its sophisticated scenario writing programs which helped the company deal with the Gulf War in 1991, the company has also suffered substantial losses through unforeseen accidents, such as refinery explosions and oil spills [Knowlton 1991; Solomon 1991].

Studies of overall economic factors are very important to major companies in large industries, such as Volkswagen in the auto industry, whose strategic planning operation is discussed later in this chapter. The impact of economic factors on small companies is more selective.

Technological Developments

The impact of new technology on future opportunities and threats is evident in many industries. The personal computer industry, for example, was barely 10 years old in 1990, and was still experiencing new technological breakthroughs. For example, the development of faster computer chips will likely lead to a whole new generation of super-microcomputers. Computer graphics, communication technology, and information technology are changing entire industries — and even creating new ones, such as desktop publishing, the computer workstation market, and the use of computers for communication.

The costs of research can be high — hundreds of millions of dollars in the case of computer chips and high-resolution television. Such enormous costs have led to many new cooperative arrangements between companies that normally compete in these areas. For example, in a surprise move in mid-1991, two major computer industry competitors, IBM and Apple, signed a letter of intent to jointly develop a new operating system, named "Taligent" [Lewis 1992; Pollack 1991(A)]. Sun Microsystems was also approached to participate in the venture [Markoff 1992].

The impact of technological innovations is felt in many industries. Genetic engineering advances, for example, are creating many new opportunities, as are developments in transportation, medicine, fiber optics, marine biology, micromachines, solar energy, superconductors, and metallurgy [Pollack 1991(B); "The Most Fascinating Ideas" 1991].

In some instances, these developments are market driven. For example, contact lens marketers believed that the aging baby boom generation will be resistant to wearing bifocal eyeglasses or to wearing reading glasses with their distance contacts. For this reason, a major research effort was begun which led in 1989 to the introduction of technologically-advanced, easy-to-use, and reasonably-priced bifocal contact lenses, designed to tap a market estimated to be close to thirty million people in the coming years [Freudenheim 1989].

Technological developments can also threaten existing products. For example, developments expected in high-definition television may disrupt existing television markets while creating opportunities for some companies and major competitive problems for others [Andrews 1991; Elkus 1989; Fantel 1992].

In the 1970s NCR Corp. encountered product problems after it insisted on investing in older cash register technology while competitors turned to computers. RCA Corp., once synonymous with music, continued to produce vinyl albums while Sony Corp. moved into the now ubiquitous compact disk. General Electric has since acquired RCA and sold its record business unit.

But, as Kodak's history shows, predicting the future can be an uncertain business. Early on, for example, Kodak decided not to make 35mm cameras. Now such cameras are the industry standard, and Kodak's Japanese competitors dominate the market while Kodak offers only a few models. More recently, Kodak shied away from camcorders. "[We] missed the opportunity to participate in video," laments Chairman Kay Whitmore. Kodak was hoping to handle the new threat of "filmless" photography more effectively by assuming a product-development leadership role and so gaining a measure of control of its impact on Kodak's core film business [Rigdon 1991]. So-called cardboard (disposable) cameras represented another competitive threat in which Kodak was also taking a leadership approach [Rigdon 1992].

In addition to creating new product opportunities and threats to existing products, technology developments can also affect the way business is done. For example, in the banking business the development of sophisticated computer systems launched 24-hour banking through automated-teller machines. The development of cellular phones allows people to do business while driving or walking and has led to the creation of a billion-dollar industry. Communications technology advances enable companies to communicate policy changes to world-wide employees instantly, as well as to lower the costs (and improve the effectiveness) of employee training [Ozley 1991].

Demographic and Social Factors

The best known, and often the most misinterpreted, demographic trend affecting the future of most industries has been the movement from the baby boom to the baby bust. As shown in Figure 3-2, the baby boom began in 1947, peaked in 1961, and ended between 1964 and 1966. The baby bust, a term used to describe the decline in births after the mid-1960s, ended in 1980. After rising for a decade, births began to fall again in 1991 [Editorial 1991; Barringer 1991].

The baby boom created major opportunities in most markets. Young urban professionals (Yuppies) were a lucrative market to target, as was done by companies ranging from new mail-order ventures such as J. Crew and Land's End [Rudolph 1989] to Levi Strauss with the introduction of Docker's — a $500 million line of clothing [Pollack 1989(B)]. The tastes and needs of the population were changing in the 1990s, however, as baby boomers became conservative and reduced their frivolous buying [Ravo 1992; Schwadel 1991], and as the younger population in the U.S. became less affluent [Bernstein 1991].

Many trends arise from changing demographics, social values, and attitudes. These include family formations (fewer children, singles living together, more divorces, and extended families), environmental concerns, increased use of litigation to settle disputes, and rising crime rates. Such factors create industry threats or opportunities which affect business strategies.

Anticipating changing trends is often difficult. For example, during the early 1990s, there was some feeling the "Yuppie" era was ending and that people were beginning to embrace more traditional values, which in turn would affect not only the amount of their spending but also the kinds of products they purchased [Blackman 1991; Shapiro 1991]. That market was also expected

Figure 3-2: Annual Births in the U.S. (1897-1990)

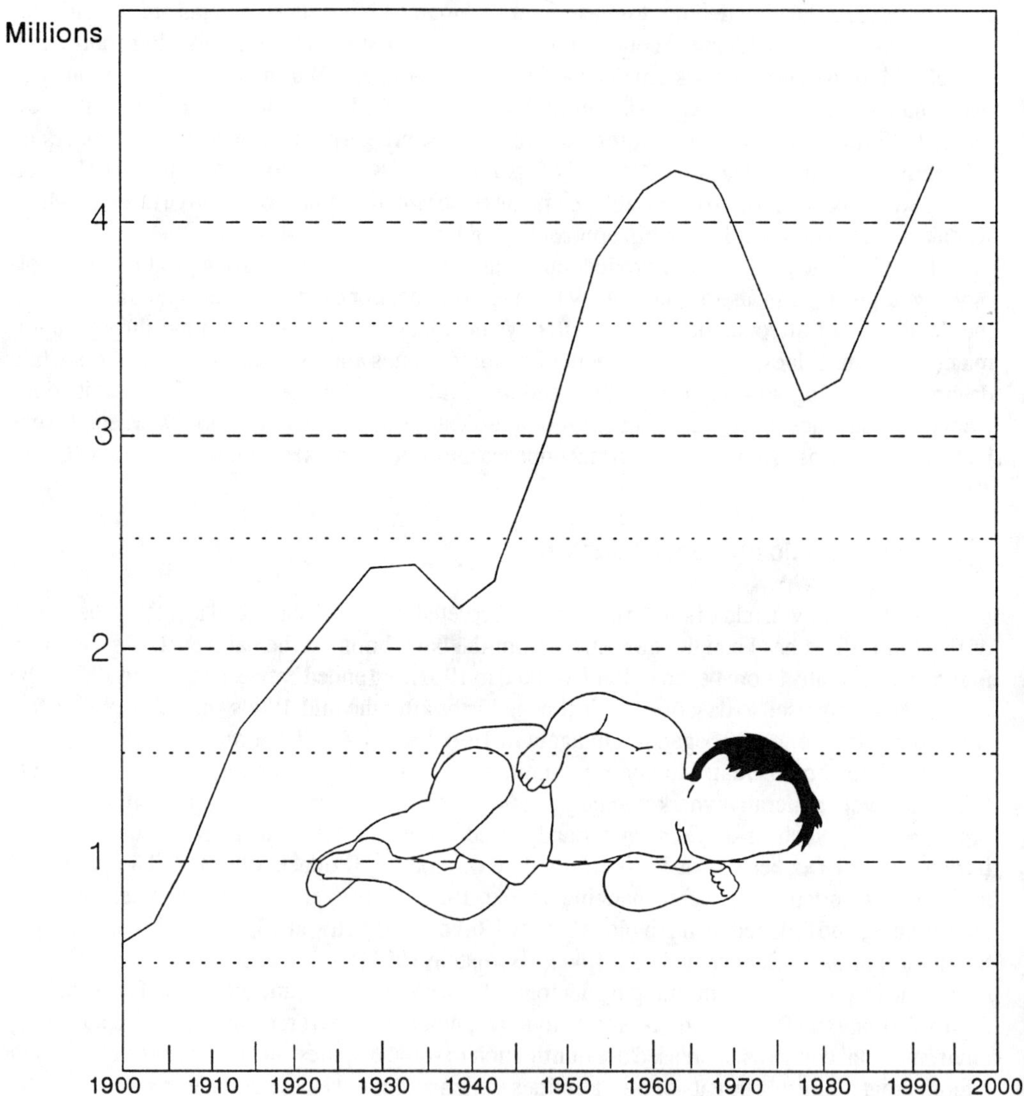

Source: All figures represent births reported by the National Center for Health Statistics

to become even more fragmented. The impact of such shifts was still uncertain in 1992.

Political, Government, and Legal Factors

The actions of local, state, and federal governments can affect the future of all industries. For some groups, such as real estate developers in New York City in the 1970s, strict government regulations created enormous profit opportunities by severely limiting the housing supply. At the same time, for many industries governmental intervention creates potential problems, as when government contracts were reduced in the defense industry in the early 1990s [Borrus 1992; Stevenson 1992].

The new tax laws of 1986 and 1987 were an example of changes in government regulations which substantially affected longer-term success in many industries, such as leasing and real estate. At the same time, other industries were created, especially in the financial services area.

Another example of the opportunities created by political and legal moves occurred in July 1989 when President Bush permanently banned imports of military-style assault rifles. As the headlines announcing the ban, "Gun Import Ban Enriches Small U.S. Arms Makers," indicated, such government actions can create a bonanza for specific companies in an industry [Johnson 1989].

Changes in local laws can also affect a company's strategic moves. When Sears considered moving out of its 110-story Chicago office building, and possibly out of the state, Illinois passed legislation enabling a small Illinois community to issue bonds allowing Sears to purchase a 786-acre site at $100,000 per acre, to be paid off over 20 years instead of property taxes. The state also provided $61 million in subsidies for site preparation [Hwa-Shu 1989].

As for foreign government actions, many multinational companies felt that in spite of the major opportunities in China [Tanzer 1991(B)] the government's attacks on students during the May 1989 demonstrations in Beijing indicated an unfavorable business climate. As a result, a year later few U.S. firms reportedly were pursuing business opportunities in China [Owens 1990] and only few were likely to do so in the future. By 1991, some companies were even trying to abandon projects they had initiated in China [WuDunn 1991], although some companies such as Avon experienced rapid growth in their operations there [Tanzer 1991 (A)], and in 1992 other investors were "pouring" into China [Kristof 1992].

The many international oil crises and resulting fluctuations in oil prices during the 1970s, 1980s, and 1990s are examples of how government actions, such as the Arab oil embargo in the 1970s and Iraq's invasion of Kuwait in 1991, can significantly affect strategic decision making.

The major changes in Central Europe in the late 1980s and early 1990s also affected business strategic planning and performance. On the one hand, opportunities for foreign companies were opened up — especially in Hungary, Czechoslovakia, and Poland [Glasgall 1991; Olsen 1991; Schares 1991]. On the other hand, the changes created a very unstable investment climate. For example, in the U.S.S.R. power struggles led to periodic coup attempts, and eventually the breakup of the Soviet Union [Uchitelle 1992; "News Roundup" 1991]. In addition, the planned large cuts in U.S. defense spending arising from the end of the Cold War with the U.S.S.R. were expected to adversely affect many companies [Borrus 1992; Stevenson 1992].

Availability of Raw Materials

In some industries, supply availability trends can also create opportunities and threats. Energy resources are a classic example, ranging from the politically created shortages in the 1970s to the price plunge generated by lower demand and increased production in the mid-1980s to the price and supply dislocations created by the Gulf War in 1991.

Over the short run, the competitive impact of suppliers' bargaining power on strategic success can be substantial. Over the long run, however, experience shows that capital will flow into areas where supplies are short and in most situations the supply imbalance is corrected eventually.

While substantial money can be lost due to supply imbalances, enormous amounts of money can be made over the short and long runs by anticipating supply imbalances. Where the availability of raw materials has a significant impact on opportunities and threats in an industry, potential supply imbalances will be a critical industry planning factor. For example, the growth and prosperity of the champagne industry is tied directly to the supply of high-quality grapes [Greenhouse 1989].

Estimating Industry Attractiveness

The industry's attractiveness can be viewed from several perspectives. Useful barometers of an industry's state are the number of dominant competitors, the importance of economies of scale, product differentiation, regional dispersion, industry unit sales, product lines, R&D budgets, number of competitors, the state of technology, proportion of new competitors, and proportion of new customers. While present conditions are examined when studying these factors, anticipated trends and estimates of the probable competitive environment in the future are most relevant.

Industry attractiveness can change over time. For example, while the cable TV industry remains attractive during the 1990s, the opportunities will be different from those in the past. In the past, wiring of homes presented the greatest opportunities. With most homes wired by 1990, the ever-present threat of increased government legislation, and the number of cable TV channels increasing, increased competitive rivalries and diminished opportunities were anticipated [Carter 1989 A&B and 1991; Zoglin 1990].

Industry attractiveness also can depend on the relative competitive position of the company under study. What is attractive to one company positioned to exploit new technological developments may not be to another not so well positioned, as shown in Chapter 6.

At this point in the study, then, only a preliminary estimate of industry attractiveness can be made, based on general considerations like the long-term growth prospects (or market demand) for the products produced or services offered, the kinds of trends forecasted for major factors affecting the industry's future, and the overall competitive pressures.

ENVIRONMENTAL FORECASTING TECHNIQUES

Various forecasting techniques are used in an industry analysis. For example, in forecasting inflation, the Center for International Business Cycle Research has developed a so-called *leading indicator for inflation.* The index is based on such factors as the percentage of the working age population employed, the growth rates of debt in private businesses and federal government, the price rate increase of imports and industrial material, and the number of companies experiencing delivery delays on orders from suppliers.

Trend extrapolation is a forecasting technique which assumes that the present trends will continue in the future. It is useful mainly over the short run, since the likelihood of circumstances changing increases as one moves further into the future, reducing the validity of projecting past trends over longer periods of time without adjusting for possible future changes.

Regression analysis is a statistical forecasting method that links dependent and independent variables, and explains variations in the dependent factors by analyzing variations in the independent factors. For example, grade school enrollments, and so demand for grade school textbooks, can be predicted with some degree of accuracy based on analyses of the births. Like trend extrapolation, this method is based on historical data and so is most useful in fairly stable business situations. *Econometric models*, which use *multiple regression methods*, are another statistical method of forecasting. Like regression analysis and trend extrapolation, this forecasting technique is useful mainly in stable industry situations.

Brainstorming involves assembling people reasonably knowledgeable about a situation for which forecasts are being developed. Initially, proposed ideas are not screened or criticized; this stimulates creative thinking and develops a list of possible alternative forecasts that can be evaluated after the brainstorming session ends. Brainstorming is one of the better known *group think* techniques. After the brainstorming session, there can be evaluation sessions in which members of the group act as *devil's advocates*, questioning each proposed forecast and offering contrary opinions.

The *delphi method* involves a panel of experts who independently and anonymously give their opinions on certain future events. Estimates can then be revised based on the anonymous opinions of other panel experts. Like brainstorming, the delphi method can be useful in turbulent, discontinuous industry environments.

Scenario writing — scenarios are simply stories about the way the future might unfold — often involves assessing the business situation, reviewing past events, assuming that different events will occur in the future, describing the logic behind possible future events, and projecting their impact on different aspects of the industry under study. These different aspects might include general monetary, inflation, political, financial, demographic, technological, and social trends, uncertainties, threats, opportunities, and other key-to-success factors under assumed future conditions, as well as competitor reactions to these conditions. The probability of each scenario occurring would be estimated so that the risks involved can be evaluated [Knowlton 1991; *Planning Review* 1992; Schwartz 1990; Ting 1988].

Depending on the planning study's scope and size, the available time and financial resources, and the planner's skills, some combination of the above techniques can be used. The uncertainty of forecasting the future often dictates avoiding overreliance on any one technique.

DEFINING HOW THE OVERALL BUSINESS SITUATION WORKS

As a planner's perception of an industry's character evolves, he or she formulates specific preliminary ideas about how that industry or industry segment works, that is, how money is made or success achieved in the business situation under study. For those who know the industry well, this phase will be almost intuitive. For those unfamiliar with an industry context, such situation studies will be more time-consuming and structured.

In defining how an industry or general business environment works, specific industry components, their interrelationships, the general competitive environment, and the players or competitors (including your own company) in the industry are all identified. This more structured industry analysis provides a framework for studying the specific competitive market environment under study and for formulating strategies.

Analyzing Industry Components

A structured industry analysis can begin by reviewing basic components. These may include products, customers, supply sources, manufacturers or service providers, and distribution outlets or channels.

As with other key strategic planning concepts, the meaning of these terms can differ from industry to industry. Not all industry segments have the same components, nor do the components always function and interrelate in the same way. And the components do not always have the same relative importance to a firm's success in every industry. For example

- In mail-order businesses, products are often sold directly to the public, without the use of retail outlets; on the other hand, in the packaged food industries, supermarket outlets have a major role in the marketing process
- Parts manufacturers in many industries sell almost exclusively to original equipment manufacturers, as do some natural resources companies; other companies sell directly to the public, either by mail or through outlets owned by others
- Some businesses are exclusively retailers to the public and have no involvement in the manufacture of the products sold

Since such concepts as "customer" can mean different things in different industry settings, key concepts must be defined early and carefully in a structured industry analysis. At this point, it often helps those studying strategy formulation for the first time to construct a hierarchical diagram of industry components, such as the one shown in Figure 3-3 for the baked goods industry/ competitive market.

Figure 3-3: Concept Hierarchy of a Baked Goods Company

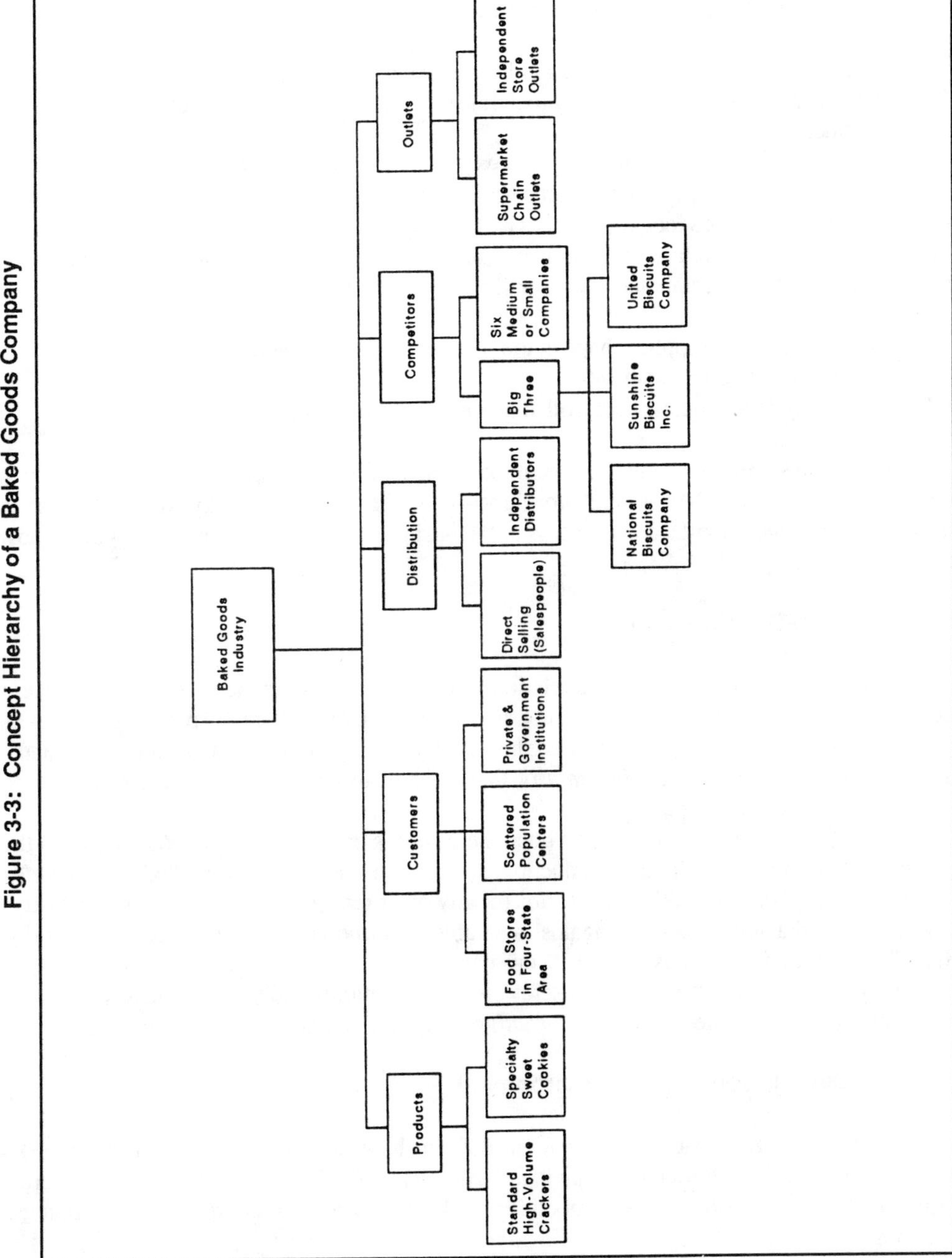

Analyzing Component Interrelationships

Since not all the components in all industries are relevant, have the same importance, nor function in the same way, it is necessary to define how the components interrelate in the specific industry under study.

This study of interrelationships not only examines the way products flow to buyers, but also the impact each component has on the process. For example, outlets can be extremely important to success in the packaged food industry, as in the designer clothing industry. But their affect on the buying decision and relative importance to success in each industry varies. To determine the relative impact of each component, answer such questions as

- How much control do suppliers have in the particular industry under study?
- How much control do buyers have?
- To what degree is the industry controlled by one or two dominant competitors?

These and similar questions explore impacts on success, since the objective is not only to define components and their interrelationships — that is, how the industry works, but also to define their relative importance to success in the business situation under study — that is, how money is made.

Scenario Development

One useful way to study the interrelationships of industry components is through scenario development. The saying is "When in doubt, start with the buyer." Or, pick a point in the business process, preferably the customers, and trace how the buying decision and actual purchase is made. This is called a *competency chain analysis*, that is, an analysis of the competencies needed to succeed, or the keys to success.

Next, focus on another point, and trace the business process flow, for example, from the purchase of raw materials, through production, distribution, and sale. This is called a *value added chain analysis*. Then check these scenarios (or any other reconceptualizations of the industry) against the initial impressions or against available descriptions of how the business works. Surprisingly, they do not always match. At this point, a third scenario might be constructed. Often the newly invented scenario is more useful or accurate than the initial or generally accepted descriptions. This is called the *third alternative approach* in innovative decision making.

The Overall Competitive Environment

Another useful approach in analyzing and defining how the general business situation works is provided in Michael Porter's *Competitive Strategy* [1980, Chapter 2]. In this book, Porter examines five critical forces in the competitive market to determine their impact in any strategic planning study:

- Barriers to entry of new competitors
- Rivalries among competing firms
- The threats of competitive products of companies in other industries
- The bargaining power of suppliers
- The bargaining power of buyers

Such an analysis, which is described in more detail in Chapter 5, is a powerful reconceptualization tool for understanding and defining how the business situation under study works.

A Structured Industry Definition

The ultimate goal of this initial planning phase is to develop a summary definition of how the industry works now and is expected to work in the future.

At a minimum, this summary would list the major components and describe their interrelationships and relative importance. It would also cover the major players in the situation and give a good feeling for how money will be made in the industry. The summary's length could be from a paragraph to a page or two, depending on the situation under study.

In larger studies, the industry definition could be distinct from the description of the specific competitive market under study. For example, IBM is part of the computer industry so any study of that company would require a clear understanding of the overall computer business situation context. Subsequently, more detailed studies of major industry segments, such as the computer workstation market, would be done. These major segments may or may not be considered separate industries, depending on what company or company unit is involved in the study.

Defining an industry can be done in many ways. Two ways were described earlier: the value added chain analysis and the competency chain analysis. At times, the structure of the industry definition is dictated by the kind of industry under study. For example, the definition of an industry such as copper mining might emphasize the raw materials and their movement through the industry. A consumer product industry definition might emphasize the consumer. At other times, the planner's personal preferences might dictate the choice.

The following is the lead paragraph from an early draft of a written business situation definition summary in a baked goods company study which is discussed later in this book:

> The industry and related market consists of large (three major companies), medium (the company under study), and small sized (six companies in our region) manufacturers of cookies, crackers, and other baked goods that distribute (through their own sales force and outside distributors) a variety of cookies and crackers (ranging from competitively-priced mass-produced crackers to special-appeal expensive cookies) to food outlets (ranging from large supermarket chains to small grocery stores) which in turn sell to consumers of all kinds.

In addition to the above summary statement, the overall industry (baked goods) was described, as were its principal characteristics and the major trends affecting it. The study included analyses of

- Each industry/competitive market component, including relative size and characteristics of each segment, past and expected future trends affecting opportunities, factors affecting success, and some indication of the reasons upon which future expectations are based
- Major competitors, including relative size and importance, possible neglected opportunity niches, strengths and weaknesses in opportunity/key-to-success areas, and some indication of the reasoning behind the evaluations

The study's focus, however, was the narrowly-scoped business situation context of a four-state geographic region and of the cookies and crackers segment because those were the strategic limits or focus of the company under study for the foreseeable future.

Since the company under study was relatively small and operated in a limited geographic area, the general industry study was combined with the study of the specific competitive market under study. All of the case studies with actual company names in the Case Study section at the end of this book contain extensive structured industry definitions and analyses.

The lack of such definitions of the industry structure and descriptions of how money is made in an industry and of what is happening in an industry can lead to loss of focus and direction in strategy formulation. Writing structured industry descriptions and definitions often saves considerable time later, since these descriptions and definitions can provide an integrative framework for studying the competitive market in detail [Mockler 1992(B)].

KINDS AND SOURCES OF INDUSTRY AND MARKET INFORMATION

The kind of information needed and the information sources used in tracking the industry and the competitive market depends on the specific industry and company under study.

Information requirements for strategy formulation can be very broad in larger companies. For example, Hohn has described the continuing strategic management information requirements of Volkswagen AG and the systems needed to support those requirements [1986]. These needs included continuing access to quantitative macroeconomic information (from gross national product to trade balances to inflation rates to other figures critical to the planning situation under study) and information on the competitive automobile market sector, as well as qualitative information on political, ecological, and technological factors and trends. This information was obtained from a variety of national and international sources, including the OECD, the EEC, the IMF, national statistical offices, important economic associations, public and private research institutes, data services companies, and consulting firms.

Volkswagen used this information, as well as the strategies and enabling plans formulated using this information, for various internal strategic management reports. These reports provided a basis for the sales forecasts which were used in short and medium term operational planning. The information was also used to develop and evaluate scenarios of possible trends in

- Future product concepts and product range
- Future methods of manufacturing
- International locations of production plants

Information is sometimes gathered to meet a single planning decision situation's requirements. For example, Erkkila and Murphy [1989] describe a study commissioned by a group of companies in the Canadian steel sector on steel imports to the U.S. The study was to provide long-term information, such as information on steel exports from the U.S. to Canada and from Canada to the U.S. The study's results were used to discourage restrictive legislation harmful to Canadian steel exports to the U.S. Such single-purpose strategic studies are often done for proposed new business expansions, mergers and acquisitions, major manufacturing site relocations, and other special-project strategy formulation and implementation decisions.

Sources of the information needed for strategy formulation may be oral or written, manual or computer based, or some combination thereof [Stanat 1989 & 1990]. Computerized on-line databases are probably the most widely used information source for both industry and competitive market intelligence at large companies [McGrane 1987]. A wide array of databases are available from information service companies, government, and other sources. For example, DIALOG offers subscribers access to over 100 databases, and so-called "gateway" companies such as Infomaster provide access to hundreds of independently maintained databases covering all aspects of business. Many large libraries, especially at universities, also provide access to database services. The *Directory of On-Line Services* lists over 4,000 available on-line databases [1992]. These databases are a required resource for students doing exercises and case studies in this book, as they are for executives facing strategy formulation problems at work. Appendix D describes how to use online databases for the kind of market research described in this chapter and in Chapters 4 and 11.

Both text-scanning computers and manual services are used to scan the thousands of periodicals, newspapers, and other government and private written information sources, and to store and disseminate information of all kinds. When stored, this information can be accessed using key words or word combinations [Peters 1989 and Pollack 1989(A)].

Many internal company sources are also used to gather market and industry information. For example, some companies use field sales personnel to gather competitive market information both orally and in writing [Stanat 1989]. Retail grocery stores now gather customer purchase information by computer in order to promote customer loyalty and so reduce customer turnover, as well as to target product stocking and promotions more efficiently [Kleinfield 1991].

In 1992 Reader's Digest Association was developing a customer information management system which would allow the company to target mailings to its 100 million customers worldwide more precisely. The company, which publishes *Reader's Digest* in 41 editions in 17 languages, also publishes condensed books, book series, and specialty magazines and sells books, records and videos. Company management believed that such a massive customer database was essential to the strategic success of its mail-order business; about one-fifth of the company's U.S. employees work in the information systems division [Ambrosio 1992].

Oral sources are also used to gather information. For example, Robert Hudson, director, industry assessment, corporate business research at Kodak in 1989, has described the company's elaborate formal system for gathering information around the world from both personal (oral) contacts and from local periodicals and newspapers, as well as other sources [Hudson 1989]. Markowitz [1987] and Vella [1988] both describe the use of oral information sources in developing competitor profiles and creating effective scenarios.

The gathered information is at times digested and reformulated for planning use by internal company departments, as at Volkswagen [Hohn 1986] and Kodak [Hudson 1989]. At other times this information is used directly by the manager, as at Squibb & Sons. There, Dr. Joe Sonk, director, worldwide business development, directly accessed his external data services and sources both orally and by computer when making merger, acquisition, and licensing decisions [Sonk 1989].

Information service companies also digest data and arrange information to meet a company's specific strategy formulation requirements. For example, Strategic Intelligence Systems in New York provides monthly information reports by market and industry, as well as special studies, to individual companies who do not have internal departments to do this, or who have special situations with which they need assistance [Stanat 1990]. Consulting firms, such as Helicon Group Ltd of Allentown, Pennsylvania, also provide strategic market information collected from a variety of competitive intelligence sources [Vella 1988].

On a more general level, publications such as Washington Research Publishing's *How to Find Information About Companies* and *Understanding the Competition* [1989 and 1984] and Daniels' *Business Information Sources* [1985], offer guidance on searching for industry and competitive intelligence. Also, the Information Industry Association publishes a directory of industry and competitive market information sources and conducts annual conferences on how to gather competitive market intelligence.

DOING ANALYSES IN SPECIFIC SITUATIONS

This chapter has focused on several critical strategic planning tasks that are involved in all kinds of strategic planning situations:

- Developing a written statement defining the industry under study, its scope, and its essential characteristics.
- Identifying the industry trends, forces, and events which are expected to have a major impact on strategy formulation, as well as the underlying factor analysis and reasoning which led to identifying these trends. Examples of such analyses are given in the case studies with actual company names in the final section of this book.
- Defining the major components of the business situation and describing their interrelationships and relative importance. This component-by-component analysis would contain the informa-

tion described in the text; examples of these are given in the original case studies at the end of this book. It would also cover information on the major competitors in the situation. Overall, it should give a good feeling for how money will be made in the industry in the foreseeable future.
- Estimating the general attractiveness of the industry under study and summarizing the situation factor analysis upon which the estimate is based.
- Listing the sources useful for obtaining information on the specific industry and business situation under study.

These structured and semistructured analytical techniques focus on the industry and competitive market in the specific situation under study. They are essentially manual techniques.

Figure 3-4 shows how the decision-making techniques and processes described in this chapter relate to other strategic management decision processes. The phase described in this section involves analyzing and defining the relevant factors in the overall industry situation under study. As shown in the upper-left-hand box in the figure, these factors include

- The type of industry under study
- The attractiveness of the business area
- The major trends anticipated
- The major components of the business area under study and their interrelationships
- The business area's other distinguishing characteristics

All of these industry factors provide necessary background for the strategy formulation tasks that follow. These tasks involve closer scrutiny of a specific competitive marketplace and the opportunities and keys to success within that marketplace, which are discussed in the following chapter, Chapter 4. Identifying the decision-making tasks involved in doing the phase of strategy formulation in this chapter, Chapter 3, is not only helpful in learning how to formulate strategies. It is also useful as a basis for designing knowledge-based systems that do and assist managers in doing and learning to do strategy formulation. Such a knowledge-based system, described in Appendix A, is outlined in Figure 3-5.

In this system, the user is asked a series of questions about the industry under study, including major competitive forces affecting it, major trends, major parameters, and major components. An example of one of these questions is shown in Figure 3-6. These questions cover areas similar to those discussed in the situation analyses described in this chapter. Starting with these type of situation-specific questions explains why such strategic management process models are called "context specific."

Based on the answers to these questions, the system can draw some tentative conclusions useful later in the study, such as about the general attractiveness of the industry, that is, whether it is emerging, mature, or declining, as shown in Figure 3-7. This judgment is based on the answers to questions about the reader's own planning situation. These answers appear in the boxes in the figure (high, decreasing, and the like). The conclusions are in the boxes in the THEN section of the model in Figure 3-6. A prototype version of this system, which is useful as an introductory

Figure 3-4: Strategic Management Decision-Making Process

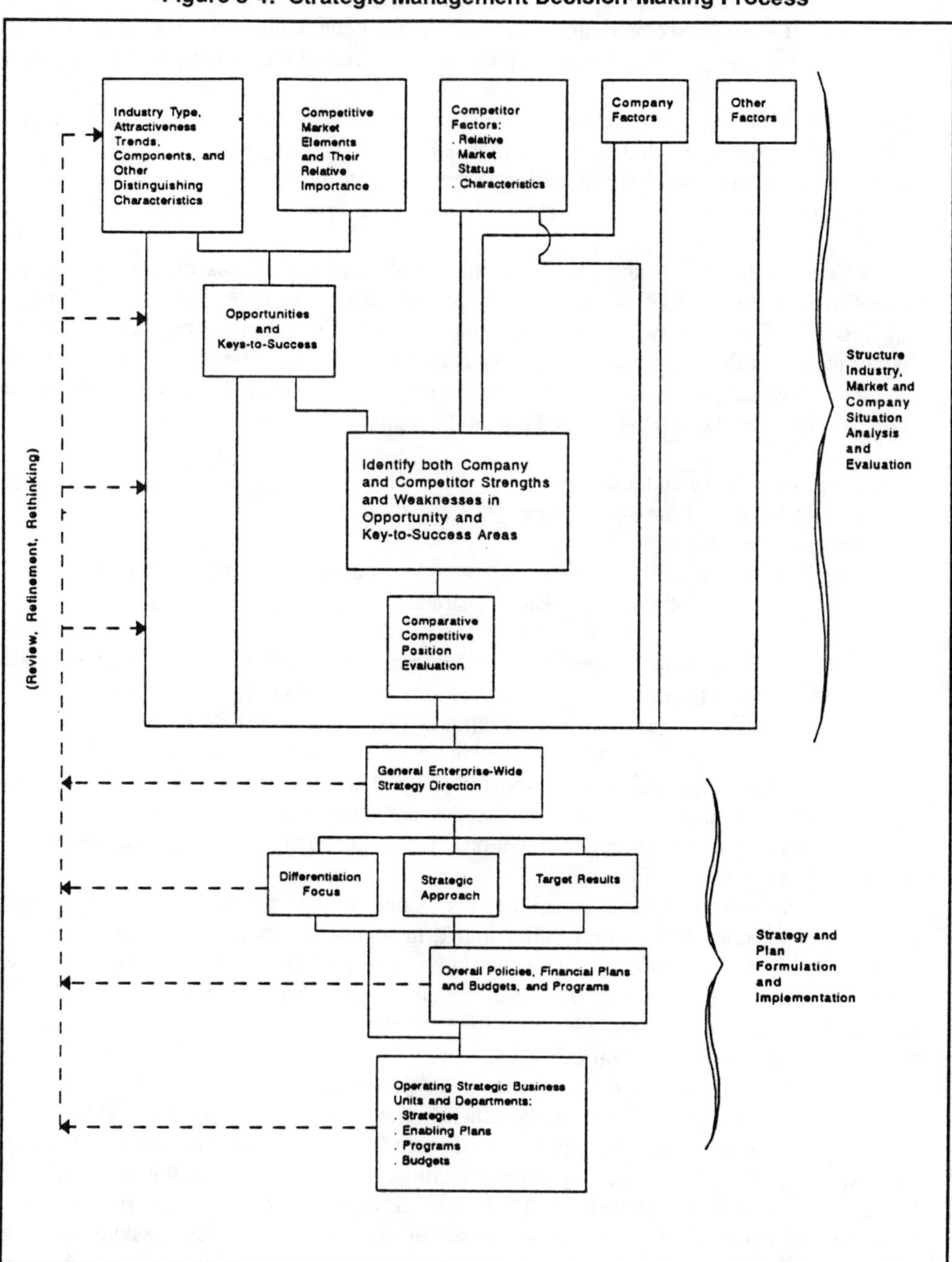

Figure 3-5: Dependency Diagram for Strategy Planning System—General Strategy Directions Subsystem

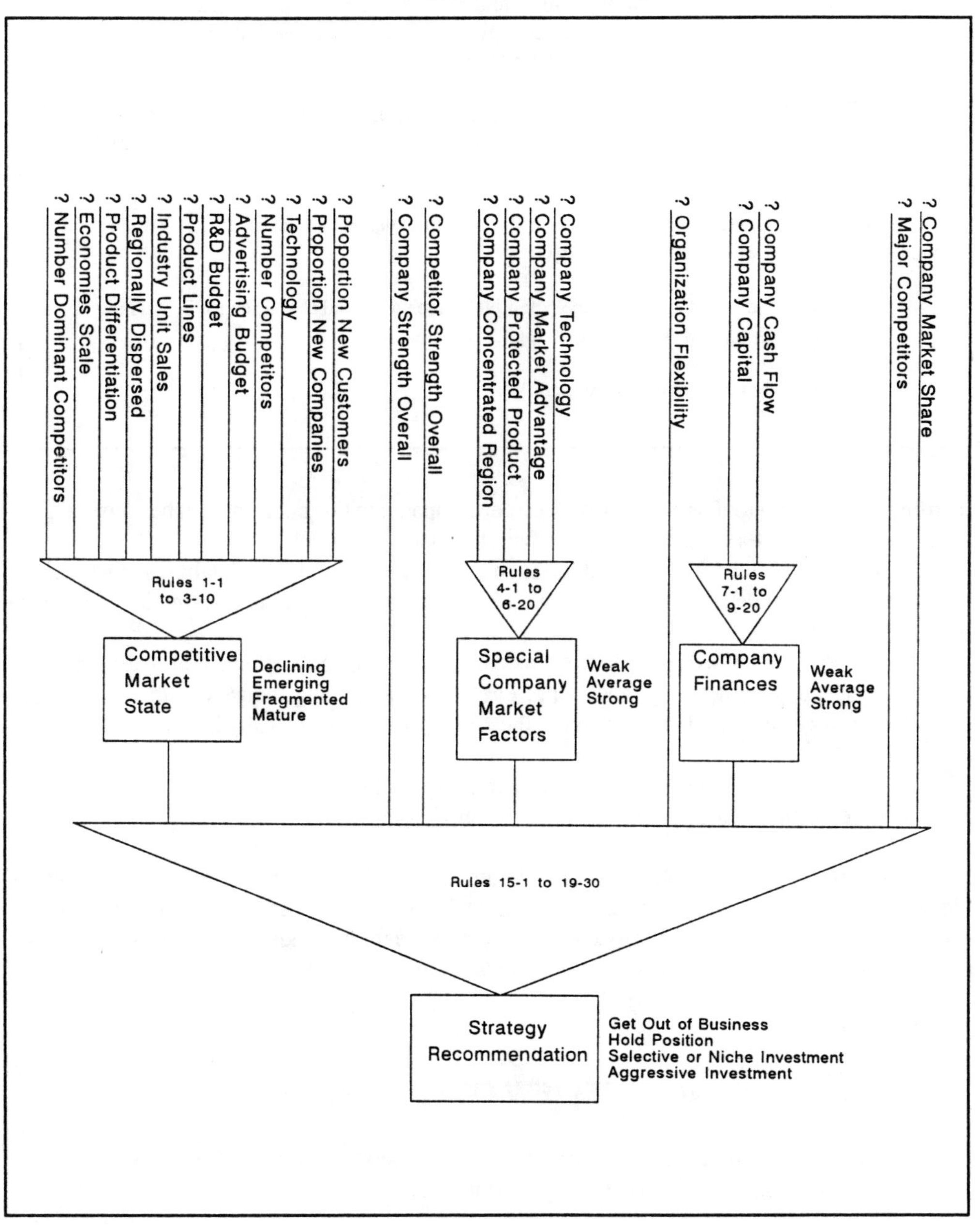

Figure 3-6: Sample Segment of Knowledge-Based Questions and a User Query (Initial Concept Testing Prototype)

question(potential-obsolescence) =	'How would you characterize the potential for technological obsolescence in this industry segment [very low, low, average, high, very high)?'
question(demand-uncertainty) =	'How would you assess the uncertainty of future demand in this industry segment (very low, low, average, high, very high)?'

The first question above, which is stored in the system's knowledge base, causes the system to print the following query on a user's computer screen:

> How would you characterize the potential for technological obsolescence in this industry segment (very low, low, average, high, very high)?
>
> >> (A user types an answer in here.)

learning and teaching tool, is given on the disks accompanying this book and can be consulted by the reader following the instructions given with the disk.

In more advanced versions of the system outlined in Figure 3-5, databases for specific industries have been developed which contain basic competitive market information about the industry.

In addition to knowledge-based systems computer tools, conventional computer tools are useful in collecting, structuring, analyzing, evaluating, and using industry data for strategy formulation. As is discussed in this chapter, these tools are used principally in two critical areas:

- Economic, industry, and market analysis, forecasting, and trend analysis
- Gathering economic, industry, and competitive market intelligence

In addition to the manual, conventional computer, and knowledge-based computer techniques and tools discussed in this chapter, additional ones useful in structured industry analysis for strategy formulation are discussed in Chapter 11 and Appendix D, in the sections on competitive intelligence systems and online databases, and in several useful supplemental studies [Mockler 1992(A); Webster 1989].

REVIEW QUESTIONS

1. How broad should an industry definition be? Describe some ways in which narrowing an industry definition can facilitate strategy formulation.

Figure 3-7: Sample Decision Chart - Competitive Market Situation Defining Type of Industry or Competitive Market Based on Situation Conditions (Initial Concept Testing Prototype)

			RULES			
	PREMISES	1	2	3	4	5
IF	number-dominant competitors	high	med			
	economies-scale	and high	and med			
	product-differentiation	or high	or med			
	regionally-dispersed	or high	or high			
	industry-unit. sales			decreasing	stable	increasing
	product-lines			decreasing	stable	increasing
	r&d budgets			decreasing	stable	increasing
	advertising-budgets			decreasing	stable	increasing
	number-competitors			decreasing	stable	increasing
	technology			mature	mature	emerging
	proportion-new companies			low	average	high
	proportion-new customers			low	average	high
THEN	COMPETITIVE MARKET					
	Fragmented	X	X			
	Declining			X		
	Mature				X	
	Emerging					X

2. When analyzing an industry, what factors are generally examined in order to identify the major trends and forces affecting the business area's future?
3. Describe ways in which these factors are studied to identify major future trends.
4. Examine Figure 3-2. Based on your analysis of the demographic trends evident in the figure, describe some of the major trends which might represent business opportunities. For example, describe the possible effect on different industries of the baby boom generation reaching the ages 25-35? 65-80?
5. In 1987 the first of the so-called baby boomers turned 40. Why do such industries as supermarkets (or any other industry you choose) feel this will be good or bad for their future prospects?
6. Describe some of the ways in which government factors can affect the future prospects of an industry.
7. Name some commonly used forecasting techniques and describe situations in which they may or may not be useful in studying business area trends.
8. Describe the component-by-component approach to understanding and defining how an industry works.
9. In what ways is it useful to identify the general attractiveness of an industry?
10. Describe some of the major information sources and kinds of information useful in analyzing, understanding, and defining how an industry works.
11. How does the structured industry/competitive market context analysis phase of the strategy formulation process relate to the other decision-making phases of the strategic management process?
12. Discuss why estimates of risk are so important in strategy formulation.

EXERCISES

1. Read any one of the company studies in the Case Study section at the end of this book with an actual company's name. From the company study of your choice, write a report which covers the following tasks outlined at the end of the chapter:

- Develop a written statement defining the industry under study, its scope, and its essential characteristics
- Identify the industry trends and forces which are expected to have a major impact on strategy formulation, and the underlying factor analysis and reasoning which led to the identification of these trends and forces
- Describe the major components of the business situation, their interrelationships, and relative importance. Specific information about future opportunities and keys to success, as described in the text, should be included for each component. This analysis should also cover the major players in the situation and give a good feeling for how money will be made in the industry
- Estimate the general attractiveness of the industry under study and summarize the situation factor analysis upon which the estimate is based

• List the information sources useful for the specific industry and business situation under study

2. Read through recent issues of the periodicals referred to in the references section at the end of the chapter, or through other related periodicals of your choice, and find a description of an industry of interest to you. Write a report on that industry covering the same tasks as listed in Exercise #1.

3. Using the computer disks accompanying this book, consult the knowledge-based system with the file PLANNING.REV, using the consultation to study one of the company studies you used in your research for Exercises #1 and #2. To do this follow the instructions given with the disks. While you are using the system, consult the discussion of that system given in the final sections of this chapter (and in Appendix A) and the appropriate accompanying figures. Following the instructions accompanying the disks, you may wish to print out and study the system's knowledge base in order to gain some insights into how basic decisions are made during the industry context analysis.

4. Read Appendix D, "Using Online Databases for Market Research." Discuss ways in which online databases may be used to obtain information useful in doing strategic management tasks described in this chapter.

REFERENCES

Ambrosio, Johanna, "Honing in on Target Customers," *Computerworld*, February 10, 1992, pp. 97, 98.

Andrews, Edmund L., "Six Systems in Search of Approval as HDTV Moves to the Testing Lab," *The New York Times*, Business Section, August 18, 1991, p. 7.

Barringer, Felicity, "Drop in Births Reported, and Recession is Blamed," *The New York Times*, November 3, 1991, pp. 1, 28.

Bernstein, Aaron, David Woodruff, Barbara Buell, Nancy Peacock, and Karen Thurston, "What Happened to the American Dream? The Under-30 Generation May Be Losing the Race for Prosperity," *Business Week*, August 19, 1991, pp. 80-85.

Blackman, Ann, et ala, "The Simple Life: Goodbye to Having It All; Tired of Trendiness and Materialism, Americans Are Rediscovering the Joys of Home Life, Basic Values and Things That Last," *Time*, April 8, 1991, pp. 58-63.

Borrus, Amy, et ala, "It's Kind of Like Bush to Contractors, Drop Dead," *Business Week*, February 10, 1992, pp. 27, 28.

Carter, Bill, "Cable May Face New Regulation," *The New York Times*, July 10, 1989(A), pp. D1 and D7.

Carter, Bill, "Cable Networks See Dimmer Future," *The New York Times*, July 22, 1991, pp. D1, D6.

Carter, Bill, "With American Well Wired, Cable is Changing," *The New York Times*, July 9, 1989(B), pp. 1 and 20.

Daniels, Lorna, *Business Information Sources*, Revised Edition, Berkeley, CA: University of California Press, 1985.

Deutsch, Claudia, "A Toy Company Finds Life After Pictionary," *The New York Times,* Business Section, July 9, 1989, pp. 6 and 7.

Directory of On-Line Services, New York: Cuadra/Elsevier Publishing, 1992.

Editorial, "The Baby Boom Booms," *The New York Times,* April 24, 1991, p. 24.

Elkus, Richard J., "The Fast Track to New Markets," *The New York Times,* Business Section, May 28, 1989, p. 2.

Erkkila, John, and Brendan Murphy, "Strategic Information: An Economic Analysis and Case Study," *Information Management Review*, Winter 1989, pp. 25-36.

Fantel, Hans, "HDTV Faces Its Future," *The New York Times*, February 2, 1992, p. H17.

Freudenheim, Milt, "Race On for Bifocal Contact Lens," *The New York Times*, May 24, 1989, pp. D1 and D6.

Glasgall, William, David Greising, Jonathan Kapstein, and John Templeman, "Eastward, Ho! The Pioneers Plunge In," *Business Week*, April 15, 1991, pp. 51-53.

Greenhouse, Stephen, "Success Has No Kick for Champagne," *The New York Times*, September 18, 1989, pp. D1, D10.

Hadler, Robert, "Born-again Eastern Europe Growing Into a Delinquent," *The Australian* (Sidney), January 7, 1991, p. 9.

Helliker, Kevin, "A Family Retail Chain That Stresses Service Rings Up Its Last Sales," *The Wall Street Journal*, December 4, 1991, pp. A1, A6.

Hirsch, James S., "Brash Phar-Mor Chain Has Uneven Selection, But It's Always Cheap," *The Wall Street Journal*, June 24, 1991, pp. A1, A6.

Hohn, Siegfried, "How Information Is Transforming Corporate Planning," *Long Range Planning,* August 1986, pp. 18-30.

Hudson, Robert, "Foreign Competitive Intelligence Tracking Systems," *A View of the '90s, Forum,* New York: Strategic Intelligence Systems, March 15, 1989.

Hwa-Shu, Long, "What It Took to Keep Sears in Illinois," *The New York Times*, Real Estate Section, July 23, 1989, p. 12.

Johnson, Kirk, "Gun Import Ban Enriches Small U.S. Arms Makers," *The New York Times*, July 14, 1989, pp. A1 and B5.

Kleinfield, N.R., "Targeting the Grocery Shopper," *The New York Times,* Business Section, May 26, 1991, pp. 1, 6.

Knowlton, Christopher, "Shell Gets Rich By Beating Risk," *Fortune*, August 26, 1991, pp. 79-82.

Kristof, Nicholas, "Foreign Investors Pouring into China," *The New York Times*, June 15, 1992, pp. D1, D8.

Lewis, Peter, "Apple IBM Venture, with New Leaders, Searches for Soul," *The New York Times*, Business Section, March 8, 1992, p. 8.

Markoff, John, "A New Battleground for I.B.M.," *The New York Times*, February 9, 1990, pp. D1, D3.

Markoff, John, "Sun Link is Sought by IBM," *The New York Times*, March 13, 1992, pp. D1, D2.

Markowitz, Zane N., "Hidden Sector Competitor Analysis," *Planning Review*, September/October 1987, pp. 20-29.

McCarroll, Thomas, "A Giant Tug-of-Wire: New Technology and Deregulation are Blurring the Lines Between Telephones and Cable TV, Provoking a Battle for America's Homes," *Time*, February 24, 1992, pp. 36-41.

McGrane, James, "Using On-Line Information for Strategic Advantage," *Planning Review,* November/December 1987, pp. 27-30.

Mockler, Robert J., *Computer Software to Support Strategic Management Decision Making,* New York: Macmillan, 1992(A).

Mockler, Robert J., *Structured Industry/Competitive Market Analysis*, Research Working Paper, New York: Strategic Management Research Group, 1992(B).

News Roundup, "Firms' March on Moscow Bogs Down," *The Wall Street Journal,* August 20, 1991, pp. D1, D5.

Norris, Floyd, "Win or Lose, Buyouts Do It Big," *The New York Times*, January 28, 1992, pp. D1, D8.

Olsen, Ken, Lynne Reaves, Gail Schares, and Elizabeth Weiner, "Reawakening: A Market Economy Takes Root in Eastern Europe," *Business Week,* April 15, 1991, pp. 46-50.

Owens, Cynthia, "Few U.S. Firms Are Pursuing China Business," *The Wall Street Journal,* March 12, 1990, p. B6A.

Ozley, Dan, "Reaching People Through Satellite Communications," Conference on Management in the Information Age, Auburn, Alabama: Society for the Advancement of Management, April 4-6, 1991.

Peters, Blair, "Integrating Scanner Data in Marketing Strategies," The Art of Marketing With Information, Conference, New York: Information Industry Association, April 3-5, 1989.

Planning Review, "Special Issues of Scenario Writing and Use," March/April and May/June 1992.

Pollack, Andrew, "A Quirky Loner Goes Mainstrean," *The New York Times,* Business Section, July 14, 1991(A), pp. 1, 6.

Pollack, Andrew, et ala, "Transforming the Decade: 10 Critical Technologies," *The New York Times*, Science Times Section, January 1, 1991(B), pp. 35, 38.

Pollack, Andrew, "Computers That Read and Analyze," *The New York Times*, June 7, 1989(A), pp. D1 and D6.

Pollack, Andrew, "Jeans Fade but Levi Strauss Glows," *The New York Times*, June 26, 1989(B), pp. D1 and D4.

Porter, Michael, *Competitive Strategy,* New York: Macmillan, 1980.

Ravo, Nick, "For the 90's, Lavish Amounts of Stinginess," *The New York Times*, January 15, 1992, pp. C1, C10.

Rigdon, Joan E., "For Cardboard Cameras, Sales Picture Enlarges and Seems Brighter Than Ever," *The Wall Street Journal*, February 11, 1992, pp. B1, B2.

Rigdon, Joan E., "Kodak Tries to Prepare for Filmless Era Without Inviting Demise of Core Business," *The Wall Street Journal*, April 18, 1991, pp. B1, B7.

Rudolph, Barbara, "The Chic Is in the Mail," *Time*, July 17, 1989, pp. 74, 75.

Ruffenach, Glenn, "Shaw Uses Price Cuts to Extend Its Rule Over Carpet Business," *The Wall Street Journal*, June 12, 1991, pp. A1, A8.

Schares, Gail E., "Czechoslovakia: Reluctant Reform," "Poland: The Pain and Gain," and "Hungary: A Giant Step Ahead," *Business Week*, April 15, 1991, pp. 54-58.

Schwadel, Francine, "Turning Conservative, Bay Boomers Reduce Their Frivolous Buying," *The Wall Street Journal,* June 19, 1991, pp. A1, A9.

Schwartz, Peter, "Accepting the Risk in Forecasting: Multiple Scenarios Allowed Shell to Anticipate the Rise and Then Crash in Oil Prices," *The New York Times*, Business Section, September 2, 1990, p. 13.

Shapiro, Walter, "The Birth and — Maybe — Death of Yuppiedom," *Time*, April 8, 1991, p. 65.

Solomon, Caleb, "Shell, a Fallen Champ of Oil Industry, Tries to Regain Its Footing," The *Wall Street Journal*, August 30, 1991, pp. A1, A2.

Sonk, Joe, "The Intelligence Network," *The Ruth Stanat Forum*, New York, Strategic Intelligence Systems, March 15, 1989.

Stanat, Ruth, "Field Sales Intelligence Systems," *Information Management Review*, Winter 1989, pp. 17-24.

Stanat, Ruth, editor, *The Intelligent Corporation*, New York: Amacon, 1990.

Stevenson, Richard W., "Arms Makers Brace for Peace," *The New York Times*, January 30, 1992, pp.

D1, D6.

Strom, Stephanies, "Macy's Asks Court to Provide Shield Against Creditors," *The New York Times*, January 28, 1992, pp. A1, A6.

Tanzer, Andrew, "Ding-Dong, Capitalism Calling," *Forbes*, October 14, 1991(A), pp. 184-86.

Tanzer, Andrew, "The Mountains Are High, the Emperor Is Far Away," *Forbes*, August 5, 1991(B), pp. 70-73.

"The Most Fascinating Ideas for 1991," *Fortune*, January 14, 1991, pp. 30-62.

Ting, Wenlee, *Multinational Risk Assessment and Management*, Westport, CT: Quorum Books, 1988.

Truell, Peter, and Philip Revzin, "A New Era Is at Hand in Global Competition: U.S. vs. United Europe," *The Wall Street Journal*, July 15, 1991, pp. A1, A2.

Uchitelle, Louis, "U.S. Oilmen See Russia's Pitfalls," *The New York Times*, January 30, 1992, pp. D1, D8.

Vella, Carolyn, and John McGonagle, *Improved Business Planning Using Competitive Intelligence*, Westport, CT: Quorum Books, 1988.

Washington Research Publishing, *How to Find Information About Companies*, 2612 P. Street., NW, Washington, DC 20007, 1989.

Washington Research Publishing, *Understanding the Competition: A Practical Guide to Competitive Analysis*, 2612 P. Street., NW, Washington, DC 20007, 1984.

Wayne, Leslie, "Seaman Furniture Files Chapter 11," *The New York Times*, January 4, 1992, pp. 33, 34.

Webster, James L., William E. Reif, and Jeffrey S. Bracker, "The Manager's Guide to Strategic Planning Tools and Techniques," *Planning Review*, November/December 1989, pp. 4-12 and 48.

WuDunn, Sheryl, "Getting Out of China Harder Than Going In," *The New York Times*, April 25, 1991, pp. D1, D7.

Zachery, G. Pascal, "Industries Find Growth of Digital Electronics Brings in Competitors: As Computers, Phones, Video Blend and Overlap, Winners and Losers Will Emerge," *The Wall Street Journal*, February 18, 1992, pp. A1, A4.

Zoglin, Richard, "Cable's Fuzzy Image," *Time*, May 28, 1990, pp. 47, 48.

CHAPTER 4

COMPETITIVE MARKET OPPORTUNITIES AND KEYS TO SUCCESS

The objective of this chapter is to help readers to

- Identify future opportunities: for business enterprises this involves determining where money might be made
- Identify keys to success: for business enterprises this involves determining how money might be made or success achieved
- Make decisions about new avenues to pursue and how to operate more effectively in selected opportunity areas in specific competitive market situations

This chapter discusses the strategy formulation task shown in the second box in Figure 4-1, identifying opportunities and keys to success. The nature of the task, how it is carried out, and its relation to other phases of the strategic management process are described.

As seen in Chapter 3, a sense of business opportunities often emerges during an initial overall industry and competitive market context analysis. For example, scenarios of future events — such as projected technologies, government regulations, ecological concerns, social movements, and overall competitive environment — are developed. Any of these projected events can affect an industry and its competitive markets and be a source of possible opportunities or threats.

This chapter discusses ways to further stimulate emerging ideas, structure them, and refine idea development when searching for future opportunities, threats, and related keys to success during the continuing, detailed structured competitive market analysis. Specific competitive market forces, such as customers, products, distribution, sales and promotion, and suppliers and

Figure 4-1: Strategic Management Tasks

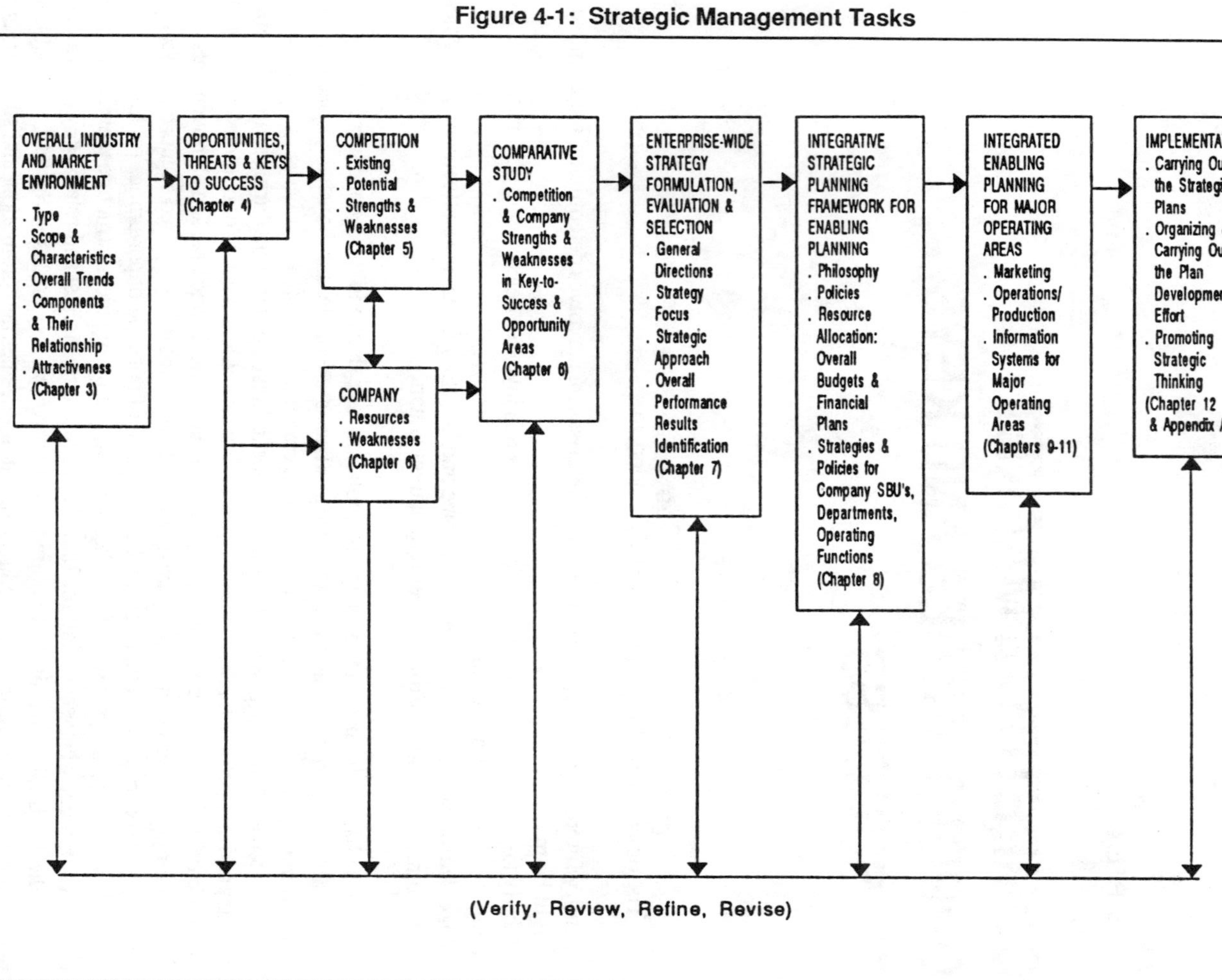

supplies, are covered. The next chapter, Chapter 5, focuses on how competitors and competitive rivalries in the market impact on these perceived opportunities and keys to success.

FUTURE OPPORTUNITIES: WHERE MONEY WILL BE MADE

Identifying Opportunities

Ideas about opportunities may emerge while assessing the general industry or overall market attractiveness, as discussed in Chapter 3. For example, at times identifying industries on the threshold of explosive growth may be possible. LIN Broadcasting did this in 1984 when studying the cellular phone industry. By 1988, the market value of LIN's cellular phone business had grown to over $3 billion [Fabrikant 1989]. With the introduction of "portable" cellular phones small enough to fit into coat pockets and purses, the market was expected to continue to grow in the 1990s [Sims 1990], though problems may arise as major markets are penetrated more heavily. Wayne Huizenga saw the explosive growth potential of video rentals marketed through large retail outlets; between 1987 and 1991 his Blockbuster Entertainment company grew to 20,028 company-owned and franchised stores with combined sales of over $1.5 billion [Sandomir 1991]. As competition from pay-per-view cable increased and the major market became saturated, Blockbuster's strategy included moving into video sales, expanding product lines, expanding overseas, and by hiring executives from such major retail chains as Toy-R-Us and the Limited [Shapiro 1992(A)].

Another common approach to looking for opportunities is to do a detailed analysis of the *competitive market components.* For example, a planner might examine changing market demographics and the resulting *changing customer wants and needs.* The aging of the baby boom generation after the peak in births in the mid-1960s, as shown in Figure 4-2, has led to the development of new products and services [Kerr 1991(B)]. The explosive growth of hiking boots to almost $330 million in annual sales in 1990 was attributed to a renewed interest in the environment and a shift — especially among the aging baby-boom generation — away from vigorous aerobics to the more family-friendly joys of walking [Elsworth 1991]. New products and services have also arisen from satisfying rising consumer concerns with health —from Tom's of Maine and Neutrogena personal care products, to Paul Newman's low-calorie, low-salt, and low-cholesterol microwave popcorn, to Slim-Fast Foods Company's liquid diet meals whose sales doubled to $500 million between 1988 and 1990 [Kerr 1991(A)].

Studying *specific customer segments* can also suggest opportunities. The growing Spanish-language population of New York City created a strong market for the $20 million specialty newspaper *El Diario-La Prensa.* Its advertising revenues grew by 19.7 percent and circulation grew 8 percent in the fiscal year ended September 30, 1990, a period during which advertising revenues in the industry were generally falling [Golden 1991]. Ethnic groups in California have been a major opportunity area for banks, food stores, and telephone companies [Stevenson 1992].

Building on strong *customer/company* ties is often a way to grow. Accounting firms found major opportunities for growth, for example, when they focused on exploring ways to serve

Figure 4-2: Annual Births in the U.S. (1897-1990)

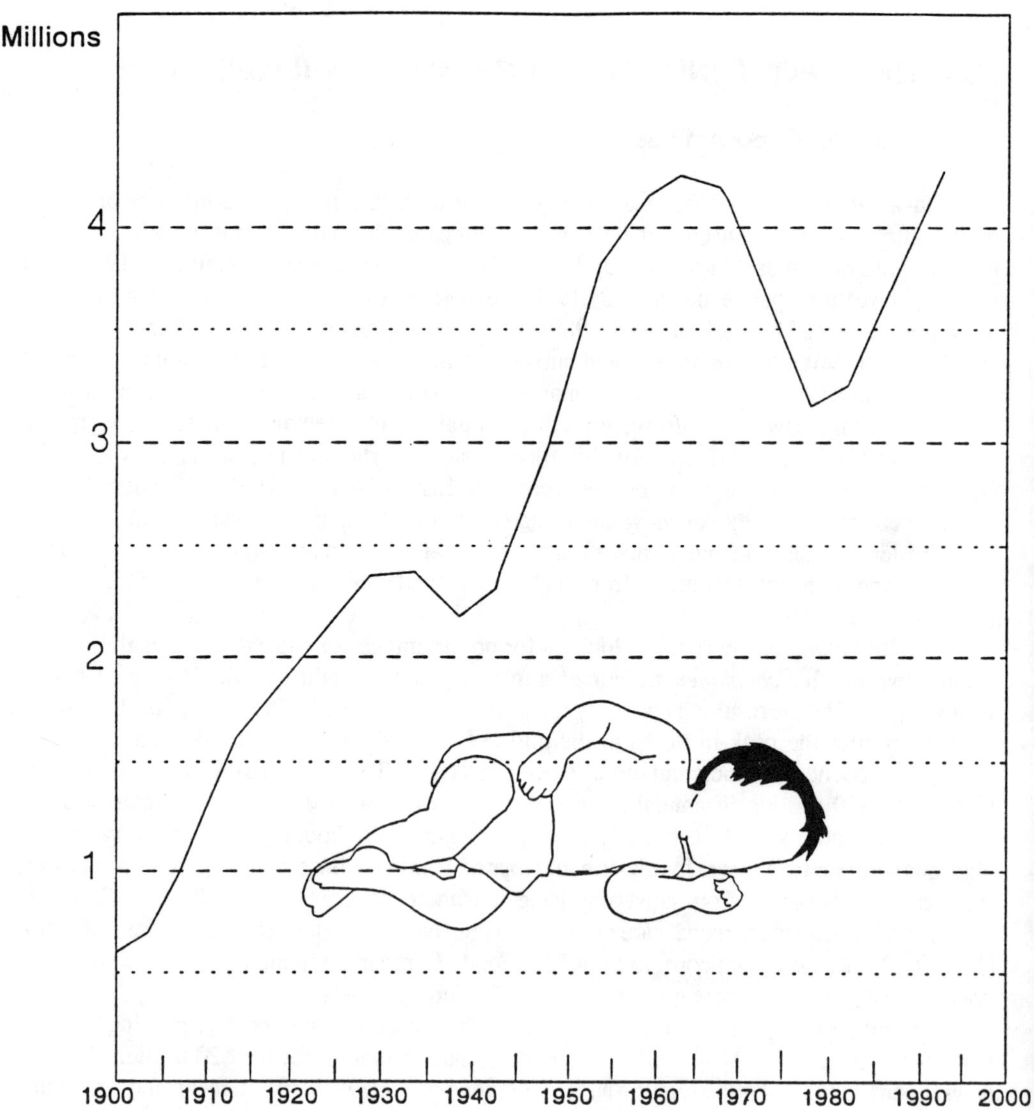

Source: All figures represent births reported by the National Center for Health Statistic

additional needs of their existing auditing and accounting clients. For example, Arthur Andersen, a major accounting and auditing firm, derived most of its income in the early 1990s from information and technology consulting, tax services, and specialty consulting [Cowan 1990].

Ecological and social concerns of customer markets can be a source of new product and service opportunities — even of entire new businesses. Largely because of concern over contaminated drinking water, bottled water sales have increased substantially. Other opportunities arising from ecological and social concerns include waste disposal [Bailey 1991; Feder 1990 and 1991; Sandomir 1991], health-food supermarkets [Burros 1992], fat substitutes [Deveny 1992], low-polluting gasoline [Rose 1991], and battery powered automobiles [Bryant 1991; Wald 1991, 1992]. Just three years after introducing its first Healthy Choice product—with reduced levels of fat and salt—Conagra Inc. expects sales to reach $1 billion for its fiscal year ending in May 1993 [Shapiro 1992(c)].

Examining *existing products and services* can uncover untapped markets. Johnson and Johnson found a large adult market for its baby powder by emphasizing its gentleness. In contrast, Dannon developed a lucrative children's market for its yogurt, essentially an adult product, just as Reebok had done earlier with its Reebok shoes and Calvin Klein with its jeans [Foltz 1992]. Bicycle manufacturers uncovered new opportunities by modifying older models to meet new recreational needs of adults. The mountain bike, for instance, first developed in the late 1970s, accounted for two-thirds of all bikes sold in America in 1990 after being adapted to suit broader market needs [Fisher 1991].

New opportunities for existing products can also be geographic. During the 1980s Coors successfully expanded from a regional beer manufacturer to the third largest beer producer in the country. Coors followed a similar region-by-region growth strategy in introducing its bottled water products [Charlier 1990]. Both Banc One and BankAmerica Corporation have grown substantially through geographic expansion [Lohr 1991; Pollack 1991(B)]. Global expansion was used by McDonald's when opening fast-food stores in Moscow [Maney 1990] and China [Shapiro 1992(B)] and by Avon in China [Tanzer 1991].

Many experts predict that the greatest opportunities during the 1990s will be overseas, where many economies are expected to grow faster than the U.S.'s [Lambert 1990]. The creation of a unified European trade market in 1992 is expected to open up major opportunities, since the new unified European market will probably exceed that of the entire United Sates.

An examination of *distribution and sales channels* can also stimulate thinking about opportunities. Studies of the mail-order business and changing market conditions (such as more working women who were not at home when the salesperson called) led Fuller Brush, a door-to-door sales company, to expand into mail-order in the late 1980s [Berg 1989]. Less than three years later, over 30 percent of the company's business came from mail-order sales and the company was fast losing its strategic identity as a door-to-door selling company. Creative thinking about existing distribution channels in the soft drinks industry led A&W Root Beer to piggyback on established name brand distributors' operations and greatly expand the market for A&W's Root Beer [Deutsch 1989(A)].

An analysis of *suppliers and supplies* often yields potential opportunities. Shaw Industries Inc., a carpet manufacturer whose success was based on a low cost/low selling price strategy, bought its own yarn supply mills in order to lower costs further and so more effectively dominate the market through its low price strategy [Ruffenach 1991].

As discussed above, an analysis of the many different *components of a competitive market* can be a rich source of strategic opportunities. Finding these opportunities in the competitive market, however, is not always easy. One common way is to scan published written material. These sources include business publications, technical journals, industry periodicals and newsletters, conference materials, online databases (as shown in Appendix D), and commercial services, such as Business Trend Analysts, which publishes comprehensive reports on hundreds of industries and competitive markets and their products [for example, Business Trend Analysts 1991; Pollack 1991(C); "The Most Fascinating Ideas" 1991].

Another common way to stimulate thinking about opportunities is to examine different anticipated *trends* within a market *in relation to each other*, that is, by exploring the *associations* among many different situation factors. For instance, during the 1950s a study of *demographic population trends* — including a shift to the suburbs, the increasing birthrate, and a growth in automobile ownership — would have suggested to many the trend towards shopping center and supermarket chain development at that time. As the 1990s progress, new opportunities will emerge, as the baby boomers start entering their 40s and 50s, as medical advances improve the quality of life for older people, as values change, and as younger population segments face increasingly difficult times [Bernstein 1991; Blackman 1991; Nasar 1991; Schwadel 1991; Shapiro 1991; Slater 1992].

Consumers' increased insistence on better service and quality products has led many companies to offer guaranteed service in order to gain a competitive edge [Pearl 1991]. Technological development trends, especially in conventional computer information systems technologies, have helped to meet this trend towards increasing customer service. Airlines now provide personalized service by using global computer databases and satellites to answer customer queries about problems anywhere in the world, regardless of the country in which the reservation was made [Pepper 1991]. Salesforces can offer better service due to computers [Ryan 1991], as can manufacturing companies [Liebs 1991], phone companies [Slater 1992], large grocery chains [Kleinfield 1991; McCarthy 1991], trucking companies [Salpukas 1991], fast-food companies [Radding 1992], restaurant chains [Connolly 1991], and many smaller business, such as video stores, real estate agents, and optometrists [Beal 1991].

Knowledge-based computer systems, samples of which are given on the disks accompanying this book, are another example of how technological development trends can be matched to other industry and market trends to create new opportunities. American Express set no credit limit for its charge card customers in 1990 — a competitive advantage over other credit card companies which had credit limits. This advantage arose in part because American Express developed a knowledge-based system which enabled its phone operators to check up to eight databases quickly when a retailer asked for a purchase approval [Flast 1991; Mockler 1992(C,E)], thus meeting a customer need for faster and better service through advanced technology.

Opportunity searches can lead often to *uncertain conclusions* in today's high-tech environment. For example, the opportunities in high-definition television (HDTV) are not easy to define. Some arguments suggest that the leader in the development of HDTV will have a major competitive advantage in related technology areas, such as cameras, recorders, and computers [Elkus 1989]. Others argue that the major opportunities will be in the fiber optic networks that carry HDTV broadcasting, and since HDTV itself has only one benefit, that of better picture quality, it should be left to someone else to exploit, such as the Japanese [Gilder 1989]. Decisions in this area will be extremely complex, risky, and difficult, due to the expense (hundreds of millions of dollars) and uncertainty of the opportunities in the area [Davis 1990]. In the 1990s, in spite of such uncertainties, Zenith Electronics Corporation, the last U.S. manufacturer of TV sets and the second most popular TV brand, decided to "bet the store" on the HDTV area [Andrews 1991; Fantel 1992; Rose 1992; Shapiro 1990].

Additional Tools and Techniques Useful In Opportunity Identification

Other structured ways to stimulate thinking about new competitive market opportunities exist [Anderson 1991], three of which are discussed here:

- Reconceiving situation elements to stimulate new insights,
- Comparing situation elements (sometimes by visually positioning them next to each other) to stimulate associative reasoning, and
- Contrarian idea exploration

Reconceiving. Figure 4-3 is an example of reconceiving, or reconceptualizing, a situation. It starts with the object in the first column (customer), and first isolates different aspects (attributes) of the object, such as age and income level. Different parts (or values) of each attribute, such as teens and young adults under age, are then specified.

The figure is a basic cognitive model of one of many approaches to reconceiving a situation to stimulate creative opportunity and key-to-success identification. For example, starting with the "Values" column in Figure 4-3, a component such as "young adult" can be reconceived by describing it in conceptual terms, such as "experimental," "growing," or any other word which describes a young adult. The implications of such controlling concepts are then specified, such as "highly fashion conscious," "brand switcher," or whatever other inferences come to mind. These inferences are combined with others, such as "high discretionary income," and translated into action steps useful in formulating strategies.

Reconceiving is a major cognitive tool useful in all areas of strategic management. Its use in overall industry and competitive market analysis was discussed in Chapter 3. Reconceiving is especially useful in competitor and company comparative analysis (Chapters 5 and 6), enterprise-wide strategy alternative development (Chapter 7), and several strategy implementation phases (Chapter 12).

Comparing or juxtapositioning. Figures 4-4 and 4-5 show a competitive market study which allows the characteristics of different situation elements to be compared. Essentially the frames pictured here are structured databases summarizing two aspects of the marketplace — customers and products. Such structured market studies assist in comparing or associating significant aspects of the two frames of knowledge on a conceptual level.

Figure 4-3: Segment of a Knowledge-Based System Worksheet: Identifying Opportunities and Keys to Success

Object	Attributes	Values	Controlling Concept	Implications	Implied Keys to Success or Opportunities
Customer	Age	Infant Teen Young Adult Middle-Age Older	Experimental, Growing, etc.	Fashion conscious Frequent brand changes, etc.	Provide current, even faddish products
	Income	Under $12,000 $12,000 - $24,000 $24,000 - $48,000 etc.	High Disposable	Higher living standard High discretionary income	High-quality product needed Price not a barrier
	Education	High School College Graduate	Well-Educated	Perception of being informed, more sophisticated but sometimes naive	Provide new technology or image of new technology and value
	Sex	M/F			
	Location Other Demographic Information				

Confirmations and Combinations

Provide a product which appears to be high-tech, state-of-the-art, and in vogue or soon to be in vogue

Figure 4-4: Selected Product Database—Consumer Goods

Type of Product:	**Impulse Goods**	**Type of Product:**	**Shopping Goods**
Brief Description:	Goods bought without planning	Brief Description:	Items which are subject to price and style comparisons
Examples:	Toys, inexpensive clothing and food	Examples:	fashion clothes, television sets
		Two types of Shopping Goods:	
		Heterogeneous	Customers compare style and quality for suitability with price relatively unimportant Example: high-priced clothes
		Homogeneous	Customer comparisons of competing merchandise is limited to price Example: television set
Product Characteristics:		**Product Characteristics:**	
Brand Loyalty:	Brand loyalty is low	Brand Loyalty:	Brand loyalty is low
Product Info:	Low information	Product Info:	Requires as much shopping time and information search
Distribution:	Wide geographic distribution/ Mass merchandisers	Distribution:	Specialty/Mass Merchandisers
Performance Risk:	Low	Performance Risk:	High/Medium
Price:	Generally low-priced items	Price:	Medium/High-priced items
Implications:		**Implications:**	
Involvement = Low involvement product		Involvement = High involvement products	
Benefit sought = Convenience		Benefit Sought = a) Fashion/Style & Prestige/Status = Heterogeneous goods b) Economy or Fashion/Style = Homogeneous goods	
Product Info Required = Low info search		Product Info Required = High	
Advertising Requirements= Short duration messages, emphasizing a few key points, visual & sound components are important		Creative Requirements = Media to be used as a shopping medium to compare prices and product offerings	
Media Implications = Requires massive advertising, large media budget			
Target Market = General		Target Market = Selective/General	

Figure 4-4: Selected Product Database—Consumer Goods (contd.)

	Convenience Goods		Specialty Goods
Type of Product:	**Convenience Goods**	**Type of Product:**	**Specialty Goods**
Brief Description:	Nondurable, quickly used and frequently purchased	Brief Description:	Goods for which a customer is willing to make a special purchasing effort
Examples:	Cigarettes, candy, magazines	Examples:	Gourmet foods, Rolls Royce
Product Characteristics:		**Product Characteristics:**	
Brand Loyalty:	Brand loyalty is high	Brand Loyalty:	Brand loyalty is high
Product Info:	Goods bought with a minimum amount of shopping effort, low information search	Product Info:	Product information required is high but customers do not generally compare brands
Distribution:	Wide geographic distribution/ Mass merchandisers	Distribution:	High-image retail outlets/ Specialty stores
Performance Risk:	Low	Performance Risk:	High
Price:	Generally low-priced items	Price:	High priced but customer is usually relatively disinterested in price
Implications:		**Implications:**	
Involvement = Low involvement product		Involvement = High involvement product	
Benefit sought = Convenience		Benefit Sought = Prestige/Fashion Homogeneous goods	
Product Info Required = Low		Product Info Required = High	
Advertising Requirements= Promotion is aimed at brand identification; packaging is important to differentiate product through advertising. Short duration messages, focusing on a few key points.		Advertising Requirements = Selling image and prestige to a market, reinforcing brand name. May need national campaign to reinforce brand name, but use local advertising to inform the the public where products can be purchased.	
Media Implications = Convenience stores require massive selling and large		Editorial content geared toward an upscale market would be good place to advertise	
Target Market = Broad/General		Target Market = Selective	

Figure 4-5: Selected Customer Database Prototype Situation

Customer Category
Family Life Cycle=
teenager/young adult
Fact/Demographics
Age: 12-17
Income:
Education: high school
Sex: M/F
Social Status:
Implied Customer Characteristics
flexible to change
brand switchers
generally buy impulsively
shop in mass merchandisers
media habits= radio, magazine
innovators
other directed
degree of brand loyalty = low
impulsive buying habits
dist. outlets frequently used = mass merchandisers
benefit sought = fashion/style
buyer = irrational buyer

Customer Category
Family Life Cycle=
young/single
Fact/Demographics
Age: 25-34
Income: $21,000-49,000
Education: college grad
Sex: M/F
Social Status:upper middle
Implied Customer Characteristics
socially oriented
fashion opinion leaders
well-educated
appreciate product quality
seek product information/evaluate brands
shop in specialty/department stores
media habits=read magazines more than watch television
innovators
inner directed
brand loyalty = medium/low
planned buying habits
dist. outlets frequently used = dept/specialty stores
benefit sought = fashion/style
buyer = rational

Customer Category
Family Life Cycle=
married no children
Fact/Demographics
Age: 25-34
Income: $50,000 or more
Education: college or higher
Sex: M/F (household)
Social Status:upper middle
Implied Customer Characteristics
affluent (dual income)
high purchase rate of durables
fashion/style conscious
well-educated
career-oriented
media habits=read magazines more than watch television
innovators
inner directed
brand loyalty = medium
planned buying habits
dist. outlets frequently used = dept/specialty stores
benefit sought = status/prestige
buyer = rational

Customer Category
Family Life Cycle=
married/with children
Fact/Demographics
Age: 35-44
Income: $20,000 or less
Education: high school grad
Sex: M/F (household)
Social Status: upper lower class
Implied Customer Characteristics
working class/wage earners
generally do not search for product information
buy standard well-known products
tend to buy lower quality products
media habits= television is an important medium for this group
late adopters
other directed
brand loyalty = high
impulsive buying habits
disc. outlets frequently used = discount stores or mass/merch.
buyer = irrational

Customer Category
Family Life Cycle=
elderly
Fact/Demographics
Age: over 65
Income: $20,000 or less
Education: high school grad
Sex: M/F (household)
Social Status:lower middle
Implied Customer Characteristics
group will pay higher prices to receive service
seek product information
tend to shop in specialty stores
flexibility to change is low
media habits= television is important
late adopters
other directed
tend to be brand loyal
information search is high/low**
(**high/services, low/products)
disc. outlets frequently used = specialty stores
buyer = rational

For example, identifying a company's product as a state-of-the-art or high-tech "Specialty Goods" product and placing that product frame next to a customer profile frame of "married/with children," which specifies customers wanting only a good-enough, well established product, made the decision easy to visualize: that product would be wrong for that market. Such an "associative reasoning" comparison would be made, for instance, when searching for products to sell using specific mailing lists.

The basic idea underlying the above conceptualization and associative reasoning techniques, which are defined and discussed in more detail in Appendix A, is not new. Cognitive scientists have used similar techniques for years to stimulate creative thinking, or, as it is sometimes called, applied imagination. The application of such techniques to strategy formulation and to computer systems supporting strategy formulation is fairly new, however [Mockler 1992(A,B,D)].

Remember that these techniques and the computer systems based on them do not do the creative thinking. They can provide only a framework for guiding and stimulating opportunity analysis in strategy formulation studies.

Contrarian thinking. Opportunities are also sometimes generated by taking contrarian views. For example, Richard E. Rainwater, a consummate contrarian like many investors who have amassed huge fortunes, buys troubled properties and businesses when they are totally out of favor, hoping to cash in when they become more popular. In 1991 he bought Sun Belt hospitals, a depressed business. While eventual success is far from certain, one of his early efforts — with American Medical — yielded him $56 million on an investment of about $26 million [Freudenheim 1991]. In New York City, grocery stores owned by Dominicans who very often opened stores in difficult neighborhoods abandoned by major chains accounted for over $1 billion in grocery sales in 1991 [Myerson 1992]. Ruth Owades did what others said could not be done and sold flowers by mail. Started in 1989, her Sun Petals company sales were $5 million in 1990, $10 million in 1991, and projected to be $13 million in 1992 [Strom 1992].

The Role of Chance or Luck

At times, opportunities are stumbled on accidentally. For example, Alias Research Inc., a young software company, reportedly hit the big money by accident. Originally conceived to provide computer software animation for the movie industry (it worked on movies such as *Terminator 2*), applications of the company's technology to product design were stumbled on by the president during a chance meeting at General Motors. It turned out that Alias's three-dimensional, mathematically accurate images helped engineers to simulate future products and work out bugs more quickly than did the traditional manual methods, such as physical mock-ups [Farnsworth 1991].

In practice, general opportunity areas are fairly easy to identify because so many people are working on them today and so much is written on business opportunities. What is difficult is thinking about specific ways to translate these ideas into profitable programs for a particular company. Doing this is discussed in the following sections of this chapter, as well as in the remaining chapters of the book.

Defining Opportunities More Precisely

As a strategy formulation study continues, there are many ways to define opportunities more precisely.

Quantifying opportunities. In addition to identifying the *kind* of opportunity, it is important to identify the *size* and *growth rate* of the opportunity. In many situations, the size of total market available significantly affects strategy formulation.

At times a total market is so big that large companies cannot be bothered with small segments of only limited potential. This creates niches of opportunity that can represent an opportunity of major proportions for smaller companies. A small retailer of specialty coffee beans, Gloria Jean's Coffee Bean Corporation, grew from a single store in 1979 to 110 franchised stores in 26 states with sales of $32 million in 1990 in part because "big companies like Proctor & Gamble and General Foods have not made substantial investments in the specialty market" [Sharif 1991]. On a much larger scale, Sun Microsystems Inc. established itself in the computer workstation market, an anticipated $20 billion market, largely because IBM hesitated before entering the market aggressively in the 1980s when its future was still unpredictable [Markoff 1989, 1991; Ould 1990]. Until the early 1990s, IBM continued to have a mixture of successes and failures after its late start [Carroll 1991].

Not only size, but also the rate of expected growth can provide a measure of opportunity. For example, both the anticipated size and rapidity of growth of the computer workstation market were significant, as were the size and growth rate of the market for cellular phones [Fabrikant 1989]. In contrast, the growth in regional magazines written for parents was expected to be substantial, but the market was so small — between one and two million dollars annually in any one region — that it was not considered a very significant opportunity area for larger companies [Scardino 1989].

Another quantitative measure of the value of competitive market opportunities is *profitability*. Many opportunities are expected to arise from new clean air legislation [Taylor 1992], but the profitability of many of these opportunities was uncertain [Feder 1989]. The question of profitability is inseparable from expected amount and effectiveness of competition in most situations, since increased competition can create lower prices and less profit. Further competitor studies, such as those described in Chapter 5, are usually needed before the potential profitability of an opportunity can be estimated.

Non-quantitative definitions. Music channels, shopping channels, comedy channels, business news channels, and old movie channels were all being developed and tested in the cable television industry during the 1980s and early 1990s. The problem was defining the specific kind of programming to develop and the best way to market it through the complex cable channel distribution network [Carter 1989; Goldman 1990; Kneale 1990; Turner 1992]. This process of defining an opportunity in more detailed qualitative terms is discussed in the keys-to-success section below. In addition, major potential threats and problems also had to be considered [Carter 1991; Landro 1991].

Evaluating Threats and Reducing Risks

Formulating strategic assumptions about opportunities inevitably leads to an examination of possible threats in the industry and market, since dealing with the future involves a great deal of uncertainty, and so a great deal of risk. The most significant threats can come from competitive rivalries, which is why these are discussed separately in Chapter 5.

Besides competition, the most familiar threats are legal and political. The revised tax laws of 1986 and 1987, for example, greatly reshaped, and in some instances diminished, opportunities in real estate, since they took away major depreciation benefits. Not only were some substantial immediate losses incurred because of the law, but future profits were also curtailed for many whose money was already committed to affected investments.

When Central European countries such as Hungary, Poland, and Czechoslovakia gained their independence from the Soviet Union in the early 1990s, a wealth of opportunities were created for all kinds of businesses, from lightbulbs to automobiles [Glasgall 1991; Olsen 1991; Schares 1991]. However, the uncertain political environment there also created risks [Hadler 1991]. The greater instability in so many foreign countries makes calculating these risks while formulating company strategies especially difficult for multinational companies [Ting 1988]. The problems in China and in Russia, and their implications for American businesses during 1991, were just one example of the difficulty of assessing risks in an international environment [News Roundup 1991; Gupta 1991; Uchitelle 1992; WuDunn 1991]. These kinds of risks, which are often identified during earlier industry studies, were reviewed in Chapter 3.

Major risks are also inherent in possible competitor legal moves. For example, legal action is an often-used strategic weapon, as large companies move to protect their competitive positions. These threats can be very real: Paperback Software was put out of business in the early 1990s as a result of lawsuits initiated by Lotus Development Corporation.

The election of political candidates who favor higher taxes and government spending, versus those who favor lower taxes and spending, is another important continuing risk factor because it can also create and eliminate opportunities.

In addition to calculating the risks posed by these events and other market forces, strategic management involves formulating strategies that reduce these risks. The objective is to formulate strategies for pursuing opportunities that provide a more certain chance of winning, without losing the opportunity. Strategy formulation, therefore, often involves finding low-cost ways of reducing major risks. Entrepreneurs tend to be good at this, probably because successful entrepreneurs generally tend to be conservative and have limited financial resources. They are risk takers rather than gamblers, and generally are adept at balancing opportunities and risks. For example, The Games Gang Ltd., discussed in earlier chapters, took specific steps to reduce risks when they introduced their new game — Pictionary — in the highly volatile, risky, and faddish games market. They kept fixed costs low by contracting out manufacturing, by maintaining no plush corporate headquarters, by having no company distribution system, and by engaging in little expensive advertising [Deutsch 1989(B)].

The books *When Giants Learn to Dance* and *The Knowledge Link: How Firms Compete*

Through Strategic Alliances discuss over one hundred examples of cooperative ventures entered into by large companies, other businesses, and suppliers and labor, in order to exploit new opportunities and to reduce risks [Badaracco 1990; Kanter 1989]. In keeping with this trend, in 1991 IBM and Apple signed a letter of intent to jointly develop a new computer operating system "Taligent" [Pollack 1991(A)]. In 1992 Sun Microsystems added its workstation expertise to the agreement [Lewis 1992; Markoff 1992 (B)]. In mid-1992, IBM signed another cooperative agreement with Toshiba (Japan) and Siemans (Germany), both electronic giants like IBM, to jointly develop computer memory chips that are likely to be the mainstay of computers used in the next century [Markoff 1992(A)]. Ford and Mazda have had a risk-reducing development alliance which has lasted for more than 13 years, an unusual feat in an industry where many cross-national alliances have failed [Treece 1992].

Other ways to reduce risks include moving quickly into an opportunity area on a small scale, or retaining a piece of a more secure business during a transition period to a new venture in order to have something to fall back on if an opportunity does not work out [Reimann 1991]. Because of the high risks involved in entering Russia in the early 1990s, this was the approach being used by many companies there [Brady 1992; Johnson 1992].

IDENTIFYING KEYS TO SUCCESS: HOW MONEY WILL BE MADE OR SUCCESS ACHIEVED

Knowing what it takes to succeed in an opportunity area under consideration gives a company a greater chance of success, or *competitive edge.* This helps determine whether a firm has (or can get) what it takes to make it against the competition in an opportunity area.

Identifying Key-to-Success Factors

Figure 4-6 gives a summary example of keys-to-success definitions based on an analysis of the competencies needed to attract and keep customers at one company. The baked goods company described in the figure operated in a four-state area during the 1950s. Its principal competitors were three major baking companies. Two areas of opportunity were defined based on the industry analysis: products (standardized and specialty cookies and crackers) and outlets (chains and independent food stores).

In this situation, standardized products (sheet cookies, undifferentiated crackers) appeared to have less growth potential than specialized fancier cookies. The anticipated growth rate of specialty cookies was substantially greater both because of the lower sales base specialized products would be starting from and because the growing affluence, life-styles and average age of the consumer was increasing the potential market for higher-priced specialty items.

While the anticipated *growth rate* of specialty cookies was substantial, the ultimate *size* of the potential opportunities in the specialty area was uncertain at the time of study, the 1950s. If the specialty cookie and baked goods area were to remain small in the future, then any strategy emphasizing that area to the exclusion of the standard cookie area would be risky.

Figure 4-6: Medium-Size Baked Goods Company Keys to Success in Major Opportunity Areas

Products:

— *Standardized.* The keys to success are:

1. Substantial capital resources to maintain competitive manufacturing advantage (automation) and so be price competitive.
2. Wide (mass) distribution and strong point-of-sale presence.
3. Wide advertising to insure brand identification and continuing reputation of good quality at a standard price.
4. Maintain present quality.

— *Specialty.* The keys to success are:

1. Strong new product development capability, to be able to develop continuing flow of new products.
2. Good market intelligence, to be able to find out about and quickly copy new products as competitors bring them out.
3. Flexible production processes and organizational flexibility to make quick decisions and to get the products to market quickly.
4. Target market access and point-of-sales visibility, since the products tend to be more impulse items at first.
5. Brand recognition, for producing a high enough quality product to justify a premium product.

Outlets:

— *Chains.* The keys to success are:

1. Strong relationships with individual store managers, through having a strong company-controlled sales force, to obtain shelf space and position (for exposure — many of the products are impulse items), and to maintain freshness of products sold.
2. Strong relationships with chain buyers.
3. Wide line of products.
4. Continuing flow of incentives, point-of-sale promotions, specials and advertising.

— *Independents.* The keys to success are:

1. Keeping distribution costs per unit in line, either through volume or unit pricing.
2. Strong relationships with individual store managers, through having a strong sales force, to obtain shelf space and positions (for exposure — many of the products are impulse items.
3. An appropriate product line for the market.
4. Continuing flow of incentives, point-of-sales promotions and specials.

In retrospect, it is easy to see that the specialty cookie market was an explosive growth area. At the time of the study, however, this outcome was uncertain.

In the same situation, chain stores appeared to be the major growth outlets at the time, largely because of population shifts (from urban to suburban), changing shopping habits, and the price advantage of chain stores. The anticipated sheer size of the chain store market, as well as its growth rate, were dominate measurable characteristics.

Opportunities and keys to success are not always clearly distinguishable. Often keys to success are simply more precise definitions of competitive market opportunities.

Figure 4-3 gives an example of what is involved in doing the inferential reasoning required to identify keys to success in an opportunity area. This shows only one of many such inferential reasoning techniques useful in stimulating and guiding the identification of keys to success while identifying opportunities.

First, the frame or general concept category of knowledge is created. In Figure 4-3 the general category is customer (the object). Customer attributes are specified and analyzed, and the range of possible values within the attribute category are defined in the following columns. The controlling attribute concept in the situation under study was the young adult market (the situation involved specialty sporting goods and the prime market was young adults). So far the reasoning is fairly straightforward and analytical.

Ideas are tested during this phase, in a search for a concept that offers insights into the market's receptivity to the products (sporting goods) under study. Initially, words like "experimental" or "newly wealthy" might be used — words and concepts associated with people just out of school, who are becoming established in their jobs, but do not yet have family responsibilities. Associative reasoning, concept manipulation, and creative imagination are needed during this exploratory phase of strategy formulation.

These concept ("kind of") words in turn suggest or imply other ideas such as "changeable" or "fashion conscious." Tentative strategic assumptions drawn from this might be to provide a stream of new, even faddish products. This particular study involved a sports area — skis — that traditionally had not been noted for rapid change at the time the study was done.

The final step in this situation was to combine this tentative conclusion with others about age and income to develop a key to success:

> provide a continuing flow of new products which appear to be high-tech, state-of-the-art and are appropriately high priced

While each planner and each situation will work differently, observable thinking patterns are involved in manipulating the situation factors:

- An effort is made to analyze or decompose the problem into its keys parts.
- These parts are studied in relation to the characteristics of the subject area (for example, potential customers) and in relation to the problem at hand (for example, product applicability).
- Conceptual thinking is used to reconceive the factors on a more abstract (or "kind of") level to stimulate associative and inferential reasoning within the context of the situation constraints

Figure 4-7

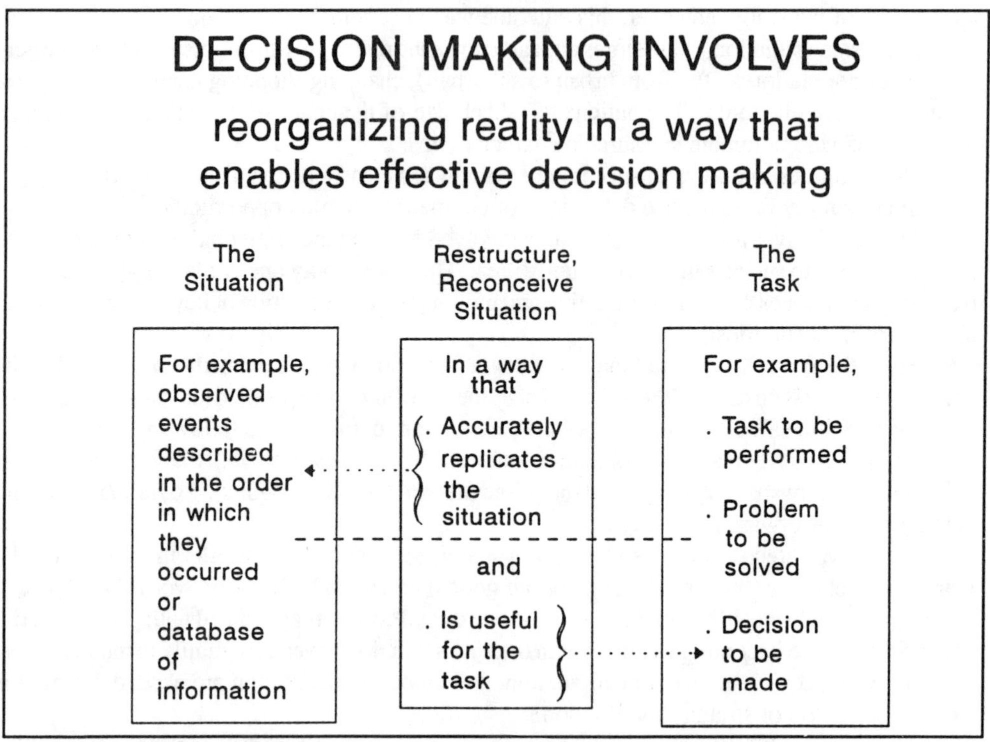

defined in the chart in Figure 4-3.

- Some creative or intuitive thinking is needed.

The systematic approach to inferential reasoning described here and in Figure 4-3 more precisely defines some of the rational and mechanical ways that experts might use at times to identify opportunities and keys to success. The description here and in preceding sections suggests ways to manipulate the factors to help identify keys to success and opportunities. Such an approach is not designed to replace intuitive and creative skills, but rather to help stimulate and guide them in individual situations where they might be appropriate.

The process through which the keys to success in Figure 4-6 were defined for each major opportunity area was similar to that used in Figure 4-3. Creating the list in Figure 4-6, however, required several additional steps, which are discussed in the following section.

The decision situation restructurings or reconceivings shown in Figures 4-3 through 4-6 are examples of the general cognitive process illustrated in Figure 4-7. This process is discussed in more detail in Appendix A, along with other basic cognitive processes involved in strategic management.

Figure 4-8: Comparative Competitive Position Evaluation
Industry Opportunity Area Under Study: ____________________

(1) Industry & Market: Keys to Success	(2) Keys To Success Rethink, Reword, Reorder. Write Down Revised Version in Order of Importance	(3) Give Weight to Each Area (Total = 100)	(4) Our Company's Strengths in Key-to-Success Areas. Use Same Rating Scale as Used in Column (5)	(5) Individual Competitor's or Competitor Group's Strength in Relation to Each Key-To-Success Area (Scale: 1=Weak, 2=Average, 3=Strong)						(6) Competition's Overall Strength Average of Individual Competitor's Strength in Section (5)	(7) Rate Company's Strength Versus Competition's (3 = Greater 2 = Same 1 = Weaker)	(8) Weighted Value = Column (3) Times Column (7) (Highest possible Value = 100 x 3 = 300)
				C-1	C-2	C-3	C-4	C-5	C-6			
1.	1.											
2.	2.											
3.	3.											
4.	4.											
5.	5.											
6.	6.											
8.	8.											
9.	9.											
		Column (3) Total Should Equal 100								Total Score Of Column (8) =		
										Total Score of Column (8) As Percent of 300 =		

Some Tools and Techniques Useful in Determining the Relative Importance of Factors

Deciding on the relative importance of key factors involves

- Determining the relative importance and the interrelationships of key-to-success factors
- Highlighting which aspect of the key-to-success area are important

In constructing the list in Figure 4-6, the key factors had to be ranked by order of importance. A worksheet used to do such comparative evaluations is shown in Figure 4-8. It requires a user to construct a definition of relative importance in moving from Column 1 to Column 2. The user also has room to insert new keys to success that might arise during the study. In this way, the worksheet structures a planner's study of the key success factors while allowing the planner freedom to revise and rethink the wording and conceptualization of the keys to success. Like other strategic management processes described in this book, therefore, it is semi-structured, adaptive, and context-specific.

In examining interrelationships, the importance of each factor is estimated in relation to the others and then placed in order of relative importance in Column 2.

When estimating the relative weight or importance of each factor in Column 3, a user is forced to create a realistic basis for resource allocation later in the study by limiting the total to 100. Company resources are almost always limited. This exercise recognizes those limitations and says in essence, "If you have limited funds, how would you allocate and spend them to make the most of your perceived opportunities?" The remaining columns on this figure are covered in Chapter 6, which describes the comparative competitive evaluation.

Such forms, the cognitive models on which they are based, and the knowledge-based computer systems which use them, are tools which guide and stimulate. They are not a substitute for the intellectual skills of the planner. Some planners will find such semi-structured tools useful; others will find them inhibiting, and develop their own tools which are more suited to their individual work habits and favored reasoning patterns, as well as to their own specific company and competitive market situation.

More complex but less definable reasoning processes are involved in determining which aspects of the key factor areas are critical. For example, in identifying keys to success, it is helpful to concentrate on what a company has to do to succeed rather than on the conditions leading to success. For instance, having shelf space is not a useful key to success in supermarket sales. Maintaining good relations with store managers (which help get shelf space) also is not the most precise definition of the key to success. Rather, it is more useful to couch the key-to-success descriptions in terms useful for determining what a company has to do to succeed: for example, the keys to success in getting shelf space are producing a wide product line, maintaining an aggressive sales force, advertising to achieve and maintain a widely accepted brand image among consumers, having sophisticated computer information systems which shorten the time between customer order placing and delivery, and the like.

Admittedly, such in-depth probing can be endless, and can require considerable judgment.

In business, as in life, the probing is likely to stop after a reasonably good solution is found since deadlines always exist. The same is true in strategy formulation. While in-depth analysis is recommended, continuing the analysis to the point of inaction is not.

MAKING THESE DECISIONS IN SPECIFIC COMPETITIVE MARKET SITUATIONS

Since strategy formulation involves defining opportunities and keys to success, every strategy formulation situation is a possible application of the approaches discussed in this chapter.

Whatever the situation, at minimum a planner would

- Provide a detailed written description of the opportunities and threats in the competitive market under study
- Provide a detailed written description of the keys to success in each major opportunity area, as shown in Figure 4-6
- Identify the situational factors and the reasoning about them that led to these definitions
- Develop a graphic summary of these opportunities and keys to success, either in a form similar to that shown in Figure 4-8, or in a form of their own choosing which will serve as a useful integrative analytical tool in doing the strategy formulation tasks described in the following chapters

Regardless of the nature and scope of the strategy formulation situation under study, the above tasks and manual tools are useful. They provide the background information needed to prepare a strategy formulation summary report. Such a report or one like it is often prepared in strategic management studies to provide information on the recommended strategies and the reasoning involved in arriving at these recommendations.

As seen in Figure 4-9, the decision-making processes described in this chapter relate to other strategy formulation decision areas. When identifying the *industry factors,* one analyzes *competitive market opportunities and threats* and other *competitive market* factors using: literature and other expert source searches; online databases; component-by-component and trend analyses; associative reasoning about the relationships among components, market trends, and forces; and other cognitive tools and techniques such as reconceptualization, inferential reasoning, juxtapositioning, and contrarian reasoning.

In continuing this study of industry type, trends, and other characteristics and of competitive market forces and their relationships, *key-to-success factors* are also identified. These may be for the industry or market in general or for a specific product, customer, or geographic niche in the market. Tools such as the ones shown in Figures 4-3 through 4-8 help develop, define, refine, and rank key-to-success factors.

The tasks performed during this phase, in turn, provide necessary background for other strategy formulation tasks. These involve studying the major players in the competitive market

Figure 4-9: Strategic Management Decision-Making Process

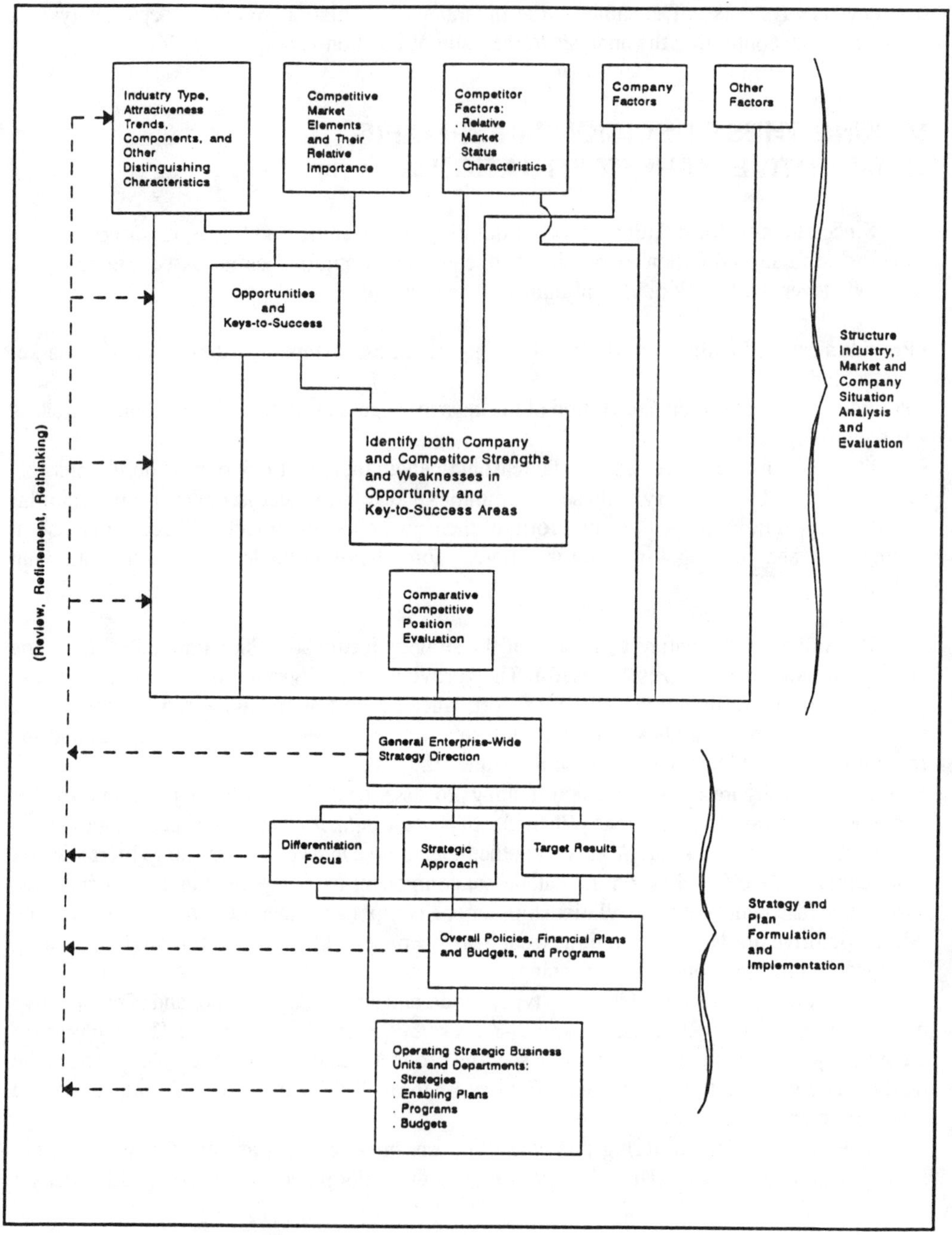

Industry Type, Attractiveness Trends, Components, and Other Distinguishing Characteristics

Competitive Market Elements and Their Relative Importance

Competitor Factors:
. Relative Market Status
. Characteristics

Company Factors

Other Factors

Opportunities and Keys-to-Success

Identify both Company and Competitor Strengths and Weaknesses in Opportunity and Key-to-Success Areas

Comparative Competitive Position Evaluation

Structure Industry, Market and Company Situation Analysis and Evaluation

General Enterprise-Wide Strategy Direction

Differentiation Focus

Strategic Approach

Target Results

Overall Policies, Financial Plans and Budgets, and Programs

Operating Strategic Business Units and Departments:
. Strategies
. Enabling Plans
. Programs
. Budgets

Strategy and Plan Formulation and Implementation

(Review, Refinement, Rethinking)

— both competitors and the company under study — and formulating enterprise-wide strategies within the context of identified situation requirements.

As with the other phases of the strategy formulation process, portions of this phase have been replicated in structured decision-making models. These models, which by no means comprehensively cover the vast array of creative and intuitive processes expert planners follow in finding opportunities, are helpful in learning how to formulate strategies. They also serve as the basis for the knowledge-based system described at the end of Appendix A, which is outlined in Figure 4-9. They also serve as a basis for other manual and computer-based systems which are described throughout this book, that do and assist managers in doing and learning strategy formulation.

Opportunity studies are major components of a wide range of knowledge-based systems developed to support strategy formulation decision making. In a franchising selection system used to advise prospective franchise purchasers, opportunity (*Business Prospects*) analysis is a significant component, as shown in Figure 4-10. The specific analysis of the prospects done in the prototype system is shown in Figure 4-11.

This system guides a user through an analysis of general and specific business prospects and

Figure 4-10: Preliminary Decision Situation Diagram: New Venture Using Franchising (Initial Prototype)

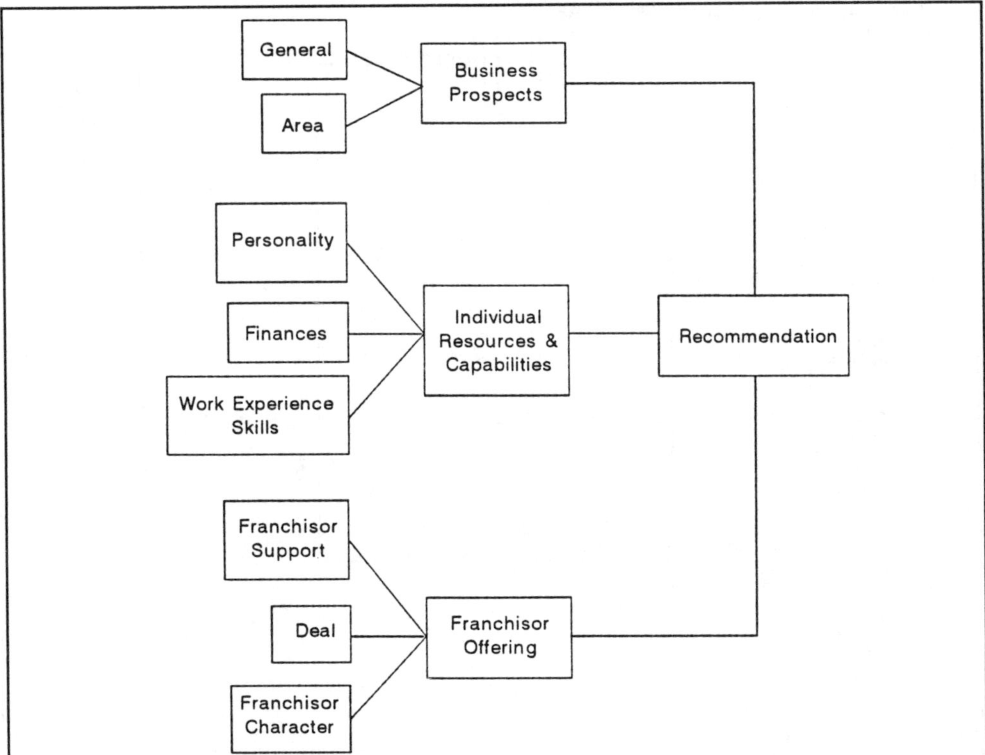

Figure 4-11: Business Prospects Component

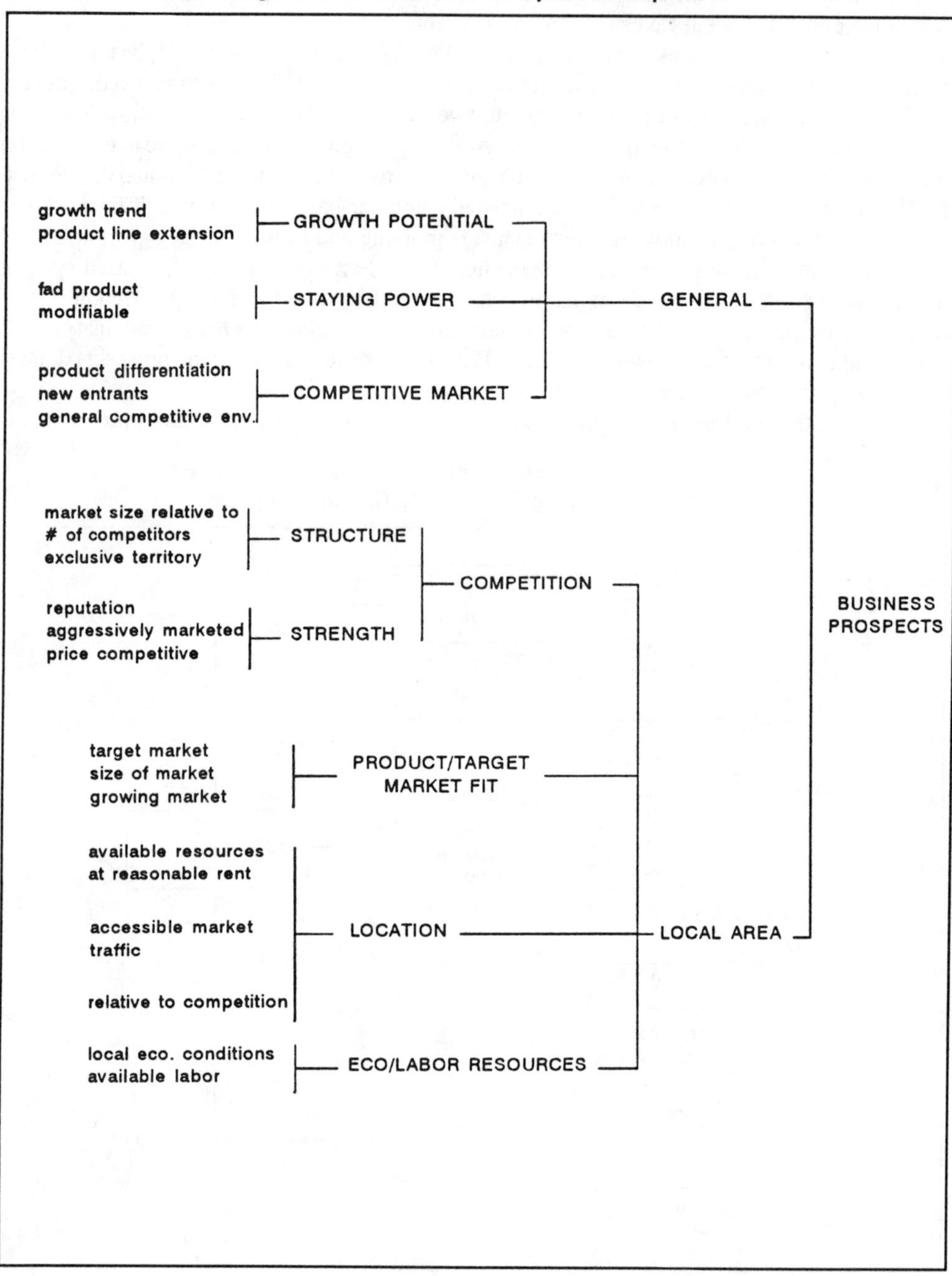

a comparison of an individual's resources to the situation requirements in an effort to make recommendations such as (1) whether or not to go into an opportunity area, and (2) strategies for making the opportunity work. The system is on one of the disks accompanying this book, and so may be analyzed and consulted by readers.

In addition to the knowledge-based systems computer tools, many conventional computer tools are useful in helping managers perform this phase of the strategy formulation process. As is discussed in this chapter, these tools are used principally in four critical areas:

- Gathering competitive market information
- Analyzing trends
- Analyzing the relative importance of key-to-success factors
- Generating and evaluating ideas about opportunities and keys to success

Additional conventional and knowledge-based computer techniques and tools useful in competitive market analysis for strategy formulation are discussed in Chapter 11 and Appendix D in the sections on competitive market intelligence and online databases, and in several supplementary texts [Anacker 1988(A)(B)(C), 1989; Mockler 1992(A); Webster 1989].

A CONTINUING INTEGRATIVE CONTEXT-SPECIFIC PROCESS

This chapter has described only one aspect of making decisions about opportunity and key-to-success identification. Opportunities do not exist in a vacuum. Their accessibility depends on the competition and the company under study's capability to exploit those opportunities in light of the competitive environment.

Essentially, this chapter provides only a preliminary idea of possible opportunities. More analysis is needed to see

- If in fact they really are opportunities when the capabilities of the competing players are taken into account, and
- Whether or not they would be good opportunities for the company under study

For example, while there were major opportunities for growth in the hotel industry in the early 1980s, many companies moved to exploit these opportunities. As a result, by early 1990 a substantial oversupply of rooms existed and companies were losing over $300 per room per year. While financially strong companies were able to weather these problems, and to move into market niches like economy hotels and motels, weaker companies were having difficulty financing such moves or the major refurbishing needed to stay competitive [Foust 1991; Gutis 1990; Hylton 1990]. Such competitor and company aspects of the structured situation analysis are studied in Chapters 5 and 6.

In addition, this chapter, like other chapters, has focused on strategy formulation as an integrative process, not a series of techniques to be learned and used. Most often, while individual planners' strategy formulation processes may resemble those described in this book, the specific techniques they use will be those they have developed to meet the requirements of their own situations and their preferred ways of working.

REVIEW QUESTIONS

1. Discuss the different ways in which opportunities can be identified and how they are developed from situation factors.
2. Define key-to-success factors and discuss how they relate to opportunities, how they are developed from situation factors, and how they are refined to make them more useful in strategy formulation.
3. Describe some of the tools and techniques used to stimulate conceptual, associative, and inferential thinking in the search for business opportunities.
4. Discuss some of the ways generally perceived industry opportunities are translated into specific opportunity definitions for a particular company.
5. Discuss some of the ways opportunities and risks are balanced by business managers, especially entrepreneurs.
6. In the baked goods company situation described in this chapter, was shelf space a major key to success? Describe the ways in which it was and was not.
7. Discuss why it is important to precisely define the keys to success during the early phases of a strategy formulation study.
8. Discuss some of the limitations of using the structured tools and techniques described in this chapter.
9. Discuss the ways in which structured decision situation analysis can generally provide a basis for effective strategy formulation, as illustrated by the material covered in this chapter.

EXERCISES

1. Select and read any one of the company studies in the Case Study section of this book which have actual company names. Using the company study of your choice, write a report which covers the following tasks outlined at the end of the chapter:

   - Provide a detailed written description of the opportunities and threats in the competitive market under study
   - Provide a detailed written description of the keys to success in each major opportunity area, as shown in Figure 4-6
   - Identify the situational factors and the reasoning about them that led to these definitions
   - Develop a graphic summary of these opportunities and keys to success, either in a form similar to that shown in Figure 4-8, or in a form of your own choosing which will serve as a useful

integrative analytical tool in doing the strategy formulation tasks described in the following chapters

2. Read recent issues of the periodicals referred to in the references section at the end of the chapter, or other related periodicals of your choice, and find a description of an industry of interest to you. Write a report on that industry covering the same tasks as listed in Exercise #1.

3. The disks accompanying this book contain several prototype knowledge-based systems. Using one of the company studies you found in your research for Exercises #1 and #2, follow the directions accompanying the disks and run a consultation using the FRNCHISE.REV or PLANNING.REV system. While you are using that system, you may want to consult the discussion of the system given in the final sections of this chapter and in Appendix A and the appropriate accompanying figures. Following the instructions accompanying the disks, you may also wish to print out the system's knowledge base and study it, in order to gain some insights into how basic decisions are made during the structured analysis of the competitive market.

4. Read Appendix D, "Using Online Databases For Market Research." Discuss ways in which online databases may be used to obtain information useful in doing strategic management tasks described in this chapter and in Chapter 3.

REFERENCES

Anacker, Paul, "Decision Support Tools," *PC AI*, July/August 1988(A), pp. 21-25.

Anacker, Paul, "Thinking Tools," *PC AI*, Spring 1988(B), pp. 41-45.

Anacker, Paul, "Thinking Tools: Part III — Creativity Enhancement Tools," *PC AI*, September/October 1988(C), pp. 16-22.

Anacker, Paul, "Thinking Tools Update: Part I," *PC AI*, May/June 1989, pp. 34-49.

Anderson, Duncan Maxwell, editor, "Make Genius Happen: Breakthrough Twists, Tricks, Technologies, and Techniques to Transform Everyday Realities Into Extraordinary Opportunities," *Success*, October 1991, pp. 21-28.

Andrews, Edmund L., "Six Systems in Search of Approval as HDTV Moves to the Testing Lab," *The New York Times*, Business Section, August 18, 1991, p. 7.

Badaracco, Joseph L., *The Knowledge Link: How Companies Compete Through Strategic Alliances*, Boston, MA: Harvard Business School Press, 1990.

Bailey, Jeff, "Economics of Trash," *The Wall Street Journal*, December 3, 1991, pp. A1, A9.

Beal, Reginald, "Achieving Competitive Advantage Using Information Technology: A Viable Strategy for Small Business," Presentation, Annual Meeting, Atlantic City: Association of Management, August 6-9, 1991.

Berg, Eric N., "At Fuller Brush, New Ways to Get Foot in Door," *The New York Times*, May 18, 1989, pp. D1, D2.

Bernstein, Aaron, David Woodruff, Barbara Buell, Nancy Peacock, and Karen Thurston, "What Happened to the American Dream: The Under-30 Generation May Be Losing the Race for Prosperity,"

Business Week, August 19, 1991, pp. 75-80.

Blackman, Ann, Melissa Ludtke, and William McWhirter, "The Simple Life: Tired of Trendiness and Materialism, Americans Are Rediscovering the Joys of Home Life, Basic Values and Things That Last," *Time*, April 8, 1991, pp. 58-63.

Brady, Rose, Peter Galuska, Richard A. Melcher, and David Greising, "Let's Make a Deal — But a Smaller One," *Business Week*, January 20, 1992, pp. 44, 45.

Bryant, Adam, "Faster Recharge Time for Nissan Electric Car," *The New York Times*, August 27, 1991, p. D5.

Burros, Marian, "Health-Food Supermarkets? Why, Yes. It's Only Natural," *The New York Times*, January 8, 1992, pp. B1, B7.

Business Trend Analysts, *Reports*, Commack, New York (2171 Jericho Turnpike): Business Trend Analysts, Inc., 1991.

Carroll, Paul B., "IBM Is Delaying Its Introduction of Workstations," *The Wall Street Journal*, September 20, 1991, pp. B1, B3.

Carter, Bill, "Cable Networks See Dimmer Future," *The New York Times*, July 22, 1991, pp. D1, D6.

Carter, Bill, "With America Well Wired, Cable Is Changing," *The New York Times*, July 9, 1989, pp. 1, 20.

Charlier, Marj, "Coors to Test Bottled Water in Some Markets," *The Wall Street Journal*, February 5, 1990, pp. D1, D4.

Connolly, James, "Restaurant Chain Cooks Up Time Saving IS Strategy," *Computerworld*, March 18, 1991, p. 43.

Cowan, Alison Leigh, "Anderson Breaks the Auditing Mold," *The New York Times*, February 5, 1990, pp. D1, D4.

Davis, Bob, "High Definition TV, Once a Capital Idea, Wanes in Washington," *The Wall Street Journal*, June 6, 1990, pp. A1, A18.

Deutsch, Claudine, "A&W: Prospering By Avoiding the Big Boys," *The New York Times*, Business Section, January 15, 1989(A), pp. 1, 24.

Deutsch, Claudine, "A Toy Company Finds Life After Pictionary," *The New York TImes*, Business Section, July 9, 1989(B), pp. 6, 7.

Deveny, Kathleen, "Unilever Serves Up Fat Substitutes," *The Wall Street Journal*, January 8, 1992, p. B1.

Elkus, Richard J., "The Fast Track to New Markets," *The New York Times*, May 28, 1989, Business Section, p. 2.

Elsworth, Peter C. T., "A Resurgence for Hiking - Make That Strolling - Boots," *The New York Times*, Business Section, April 28, 1991, p. 5.

Fabrikant, Geraldine, "LIN Will Spin Off Its 7 TV Stations," *The New York Times*, May 26, 1989, pp. D1, D17.

Fantel, Hans, "HDTV Faces Its Future," *The New York Times*, February 2, 1992, p. H17.

Farnsworth, Clyde H., "Software Star on a Roller Coaster," *The New York Times*, Money Section, September 29, 1991, p. F15.

Feder, Barnaby, "Profits, and Problems, for Recycler," *The New York Times*, January 8. 1991, pp. D1, D5.

Feder, Barnaby, "Turning Used Oil Into Gold," *The New York Times*, Business Section, October 28, 1990, p. 11.

Feder, Barnaby, "Wringing Profits from Clean Air," *The New York Times*, Business Section, June 18, 1989, pp. 1, 6.

Fisher, Lawrence M., "Boom in Mountain Bikes Revives the U.S. Industry," *The New York Times*, April 1, 1991, pp. A1, D5.

Flast, Robert, "Managing Expert Systems Development," Presentation, Annual Meeting, New York: International Conference on Information Systems (ICIS), December 16-18, 1991.

Foltz, Kim, "Dannon's Bet: Yogurt's 'Just for Kids'," *The New York Times*, May 1, 1992, pp. D1, D9.

Foust, Dean, "Strategies: Marriott is Smoothing Out the Lumps in Its Bed: It's Bouncing Back from Hard Times with Cost-Cutting and Diversification," *Business Week*, April 1, 1991, pp. 74, 75.

Freudenheim, Milt, "Cashing in on Health Care's Troubles," *The New York Times*, Business Section, July 21, 1991, pp. 1, 6.

Gilder, George, "The Technology Wars," *The New York Times*, Business Section, May 28, 1989, p. 2.

Glasgall, William, David Greising, Jonathan Kapstein, and John Templeman, "Eastward, Ho! The Pioneers Plunge In," *Business Week*, April 15, 1991, pp. 51-53.

Golden, Tim, "Hispanic Paper Defies the Ad Slump," *The New York Times*, April 22, 1991, pp. D1, D10.

Goldman, Kevin, "Cable-TV Networks Strive to Stand Out from the Crowd with Original Programs," *The Wall Street Journal*, December 17, 1990, pp. B1, B5.

Gupta, Udayan, "Entrepreneurs Find Risks in East Bloc," *The Wall Street Journal*, August 23, 1991, pp. B1, B2.

Gutis, Phillip S., "After a Decade of Growth, Far Too Much Room at the Inn," *The New York Times*, April 8, 1990, Business Section, p. 8.

Hadler, Robert J., "Born-again Eastern Europe Growing Into a Delinquent," *The Australian* (Sidney), January 7, 1991, p. 9.

Hylton, Richard D., "Hotel Chains' Woes: Just Too Many Rooms," *The New York Times*, March 9, 1990, pp. D1, D2.

Johnson, Robert, and Allanna Sullivan, "A Small Joint Venture Is Leading Way in Getting Russian Oil," *The Wall Street Journal*, January 29, 1992, pp. A1, A7.

Kanter, Rosabeth Moss, *When Giants Learn to Dance*, New York: Simon and Schuster, 1989.

Kerr, Peter, "Casting Hungry Eyes at Dieters," *The New York Times*, August 31, 1991(A), pp. 33, 35.

Kerr, Peter, "Shift for Marketers: Yup to Grump," *The New York Times*, August 27, 1991(B), pp. D1, D6.

Kleinfield, N. R., "Targeting the Grocery Shopper," *The New York Times*, Business Section, May 26, 1991, pp. 1, 6.

Kneale, Dennis, "Two Comedy Channels Make Peace and Merge," *The Wall Street Journal*, December 19, 1990, pp. B1, B7.

Lambert, Craig, "Global Spin," *Harvard Magazine*, January- February, 1990, pp. 17-26.

Landro, Laura, "Despite a Robust Basic Business, Picture Is Flawed for Cable TV," *The Wall Street Journal*, March 21, 1991, pp. B1, B6.

Lewis, Peter, "Apple IBM Venture, with New Leaders, Searches for a Soul," *The New York Times*, Business Section, March 8, 1992, p. 8.

Liebs, Scott, and Mike Fillon, "Why Lithonia MIS Won't Lighten Up," *InformationWeek*, January 14, 1991, pp. 26-30.

Lohr, Steve, "The Best Little Bank in America," *The New York Times*, Business Section, July 7, 1991, pp. 1, 4.

Maney, Kevin, and Dianne Rinehart, "Here Comes the Bolshoi Mac," *The Daily Freeman*, USA Weekend Section, January 26-28, 1990, pp. 4-5.

Markoff, John, "The Niche That I.B.M. Can't Ignore," *The New York Times*, April 23, 1989, Business

Section, pp. 1, 12.

Markoff, John, "The Smart Alecks at Sun Are Regrouping," *The New York Times*, Business Section, April 28, 1991, p. 12.

Markoff, John, "I.B.M. in Chip Deal with Toshiba and Siemans," *The New York Times*, July 13, 1992 (A), pp. D1, D2.

Markoff, John, "Sun Link is Sought by IBM," *The New York Times*, March 13, 1992(B), pp. D1, D2.

McCarthy, Michael J. "Marketers Zero in on Their Customers," *The Wall Street Journal*, March 18, 1991, pp. B1, B8.

Mockler, Robert J., *Computer Software to Support Strategic Management Decision Making*, New York: Macmillan Publishing, 1992(A).

Mockler, Robert J., *Contingency Approaches to Strategic Management*, Research Working Paper, New York: Strategic Management Research Group, 1992(B).

Mockler, Robert J., *Developing Knowledge-based Systems Using an Expert System Shell* (includes 19 sample prototype systems), New York: Macmillan Publishing, 1992(C).

Mockler, Robert J., *Structured Industry/Competitive Market Analysis*, Research Working Paper, New York: Strategic Management Research Group, 1992(D).

Mockler, Robert J., and D.G. Dologite, *Knowledge-based Systems: An Introduction to Expert Systems*, New York: Macmillan, 1992(E).

Myerson, Allan R., "Thriving Where Others Won't Go," *The New York Times*, January 7, 1992, pp. D1, D5.

Nasar, Silvia, "Source of Jobs in 80's Fizzles in 90's," *The New York Times*, August 24, 1990, pp. 39, 42.

News Roundup, "Speedy Reversal of Soviet Coup Makes Some Westerners More Eager to Invest," *The Wall Street Journal*, August 23, 1991, B1, B2.

Olsen, Ken, Lynne Reaves, Gail Schares, and Elizabeth Weiner, "Reawakening: A Market Economy Takes Root in Eastern Europe," *Business Week*, April 15, 1991, pp. 46-50.

Ould, Andrew, "IBM Guns for Sun with New RS/6000s," *PC Week*, June 25, 1990, p. 5.

Pearl, Daniel, "More Firms Pledge Guaranteed Service," *The Wall Street Journal*, July 17, 1991, B1, B4.

Pepper, Jon, "The MIS Battle for the Skies," *InformationWeek*, February 11, 1991, pp. 44-49.

Pollack, Andrew, "A Quirky Loner Goes Mainstream," *The New York Times*, Business Section, July 14, 1991(A), pp. 1, 6.

Pollack, Andrew, "BankAmerica's Foray in the East," *The New York Times*, April 20, 1991(B), pp. 33, 34(A).

Pollack, Andrew, "Transforming the Decade: 10 Critical Technologies," *The New York Times*, Science Times Section, January 1, 1991(C), pp. 35, 38.

Radding, Alan, "GE Answers Call to Evolve 10-Year-Old Help Line," *Computerworld*, January 20, 1992, p. 72.

Reimann, Bernard C., "'Lily Pad' Strategy Leapfrogs Nordson to Enviable Growth," *Planning Forum Network*, April 1991, p. 1.

Rose, Frederick, "Atlantic Richfield Co. Is Winning the West By Breaking the Mold: It Sells Gasoline Dirt Cheap, Peddles Burgers, Concocts New Low-Emission Fuel," *The Wall Street Journal*, August 7, 1991, pp. A1, A7.

Rose, Robert L., "How U.S. Firms Passed Japan in Race to Create Advanced Television," *The Wall Street Journal*, July 20, 1992, pp. A1, A2.

Ruffenach, Glenn, "Shaw Uses Price Cuts to Extend Its Rule Over Carpet Business," *The Wall Street Journal*, June 12, 1991, pp. A1, A8.

Ryan, Alan Jr., "Sales Force Automation: Metamorphosis of the Salesperson," *Computerworld*, April 8, 1991, pp. 59-70.

Salpukas, Agis, "Computers Give Trucker an Edge," *The New York Times*, May 25, 1991, pp. 35, 37.

Sandomir, Richard, "Wayne Huizenga's Growth Complex," *The New York Times,* Business World, June 9, 1991, pp. 22-25.

Scardino, Albert, "The New Baby Boom Spurs Local Magazines for Parents," *The New York Times*, June 26, 1989, pp. D1, D7.

Schares, Gail E., "Czechoslovakia: Reluctant Reform," "Poland: The Pain and Gain," and "Hungary: A Giant Step Ahead," *Business Week,* April 15, 1991, pp. 54-58.

Schwadel, Francine, "Turning Conservative, Baby Boomers Reduce Their Frivolous Buying," *The Wall Street Journal,* June 19, 1991, pp. A1, A9.

Shapiro, Eben, "A Mixed Outlook For Blockbuster," *The New York Times*, February 21, 1992(A), p. D6.

Shapiro, Eben, "Conagra May Be Moving Healthy Choice Too Fast," *The New York Times*, July 13, 1992 (C), pp. D1, D4.

Shapiro, Eben, "Overseas Sizzle for McDonald's," *The New York Times*, April 17, 1992(B), pp. D1, D4.

Shapiro, Eben, "Zenith Bets the Store on New TV," *The New York Times*, March 10, 1990, pp. 31, 37.

Shapiro, Walter, "The Birth and — Maybe — Death of Yuppiedom," *Time*, April 8, 1991, p. 65.

Sharif, Pamela D., "Gloria Jean's Leads the Specialty Coffee Stampede," *The New York Times*, Business Section, August 11, 1991, 11.

Sims, Calvin, "A Gadget That Soon May Become the Latest Necessity," *The New York Times*, Business Section, January 28, 1990, p. 10.

Slater, Derek, "US West Dials Systems Help To Keep Customers Calls Coming," *Computerworld,* January 20, 1992, p. 76.

Stevenson, Richard W., "Catering to Consumers' Ethnic Needs," *The New York Times*, January 23, 1992, pp. D1, D5.

Strom, Stephanie, "In the Mailbox, Roses and Profits," *The New York Times,* February 14, 1992, pp. D1, D5.

Tanzer, Andrew, "The Mountains are High, the Emperor is Far Away," *Forbes,* August 5, 1991, pp. 70-75.

Taylor, Jeffrey, "Smog Swapping: New Rules Harness Power of Free Markets to Curb Air Pollution," *The Wall Street Journal,* April 14, 1992, pp. A1, A12.

"The Most Fascinating Ideas for 1991," *Fortune*, January 14, 1991, pp. 30-62.

Ting, Wenlee, *Multinational Risk Assessment and Management,* Westport, CT: Quorum Books, 1988.

Treece, James B., Karen Lowry Miller, and Richard A. Melcher, "The Partners: Surprise! Ford and Mazda Have Built a Strong Team. Here's How," *Business Week,* February 10, 1992, pp. 102-107.

Turner, Richard, "Nickelodeon's Hip Fare Stretches the Bounds of TV for Youngsters," *The Wall Street Journal,* July 13, 1992, pp. A1, A5.

Uchitelle, Louis, "U.S. Oilmen See Russia's Pitfalls," *The New York Times*, January 30, 1992, pp. D1, D8.

Wald, Matthew L., "A Tough Sell for Electric Cars," *The New York Times*, November 26, 1991, pp. C1, C3.

Wald, Matthew L., "Cars That Whirr and Burn Rubber," *The New York Times,* Business Section, February 2, 1992, p. 10.

Webster, James L., William E. Reif, and Jeffrey S. Bracker, "The Manager's Guide to Strategic Planning Tools and Techniques," *Planning Review*, November/December 1989, pp. 4-12, 48.

WuDunn, Sheryl, "Getting Out of China Harder Than Going In," *The New York Times,* April 25, 1991, pp. D1, D7.

CHAPTER 5

EXISTING AND POTENTIAL COMPETITION

The objective of this chapter is to help readers to

- Analyze the existing competitive environment
- Identify potential new competitors and competition
- Estimate competitors' anticipated capabilities and actions
- Evaluate competitors' anticipated strengths and weaknesses in opportunity and key-to-success areas
- Access sources of information about competitors
- Make decisions in specific competitive market situations

This chapter continues the analysis of the competitive environment described in Chapters 3 and 4. Evaluating competitors and their anticipated actions helps to determine more precisely the attractiveness of competitive market opportunities, the kind and degree of potential threats, and the keys to success. Figure 5-1 shows the strategy formulation tasks involved in analyzing the competition.

Competitive rivalries are intensifying in the 1990s, as industry players expand faster than the markets they serve, as technological developments occur with greater frequency, and as stockholders increase pressures for improved profit performance. In 1991 Eastern Airlines, Midway Airlines, and Pan Am Airlines were three casualties of the intense competitive rivalries in the airline industry. The retailing, beer, steel, real estate, wine, and TV industry are just a few of the many other industries discussed throughout this book that were being plagued by severe

Figure 5-1: Strategic Management Tasks

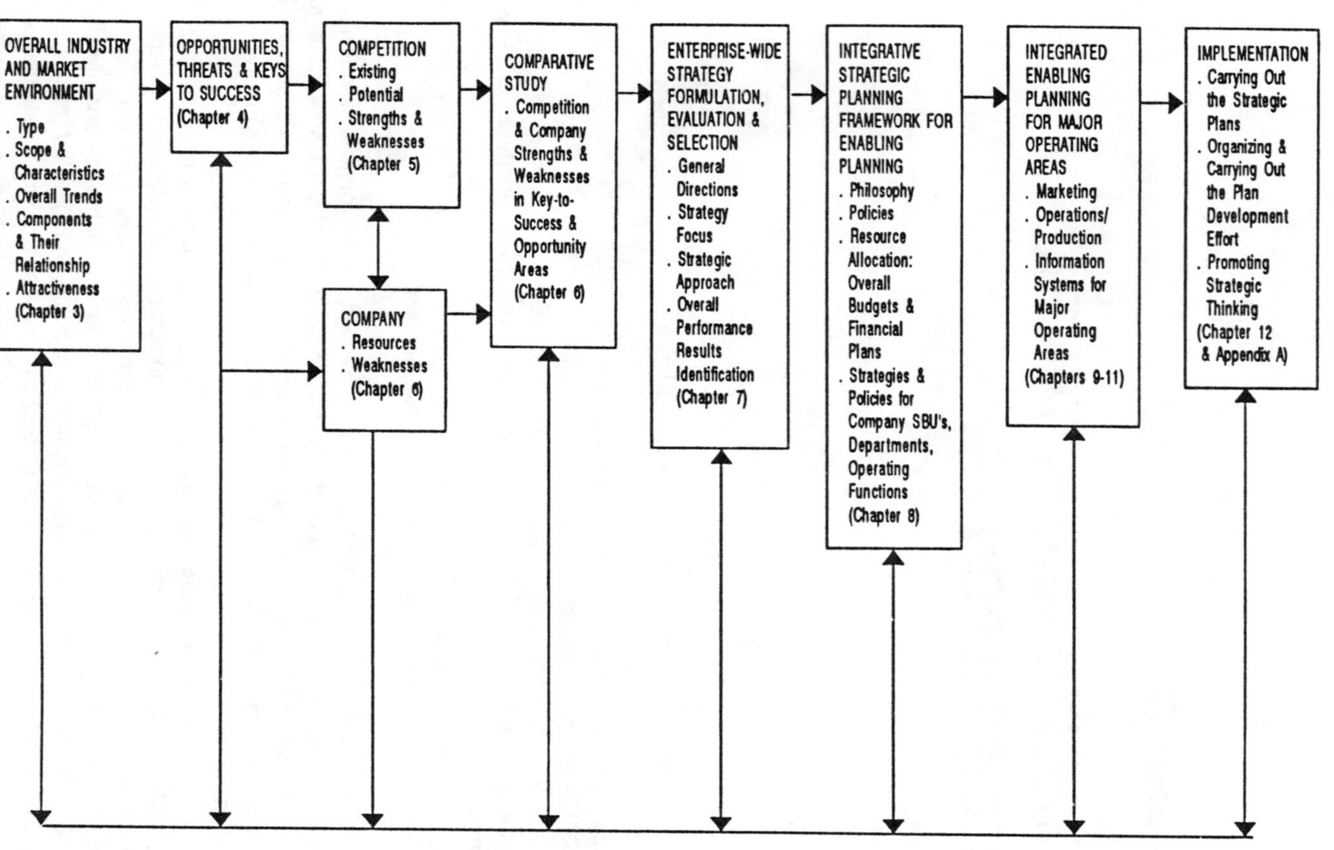

competitive problems and major bankruptcies in 1992.

Even college graduates were affected by intense competition in the early 1990s. By 1992, the number of entry-level jobs for college graduates had declined by almost one-third since the 1989-90 school year. Graduates took longer to find jobs and many were forced to go on to graduate school instead of immediately taking a job [Greenwald 1991; Hinds 1992]. MBA students were facing similar problems in 1992 [Karr and Tomsho 1992; Linden 1992].

Because of the severity of competitive rivalries and the frequency with which they were encountered in so many industries in the early 1990s, an entire chapter is devoted to their discussion.

THE EXISTING COMPETITIVE ENVIRONMENT

Competitors' actions can significantly affect a company's ability to exploit opportunities.

The General Competitive Environment

The initial overall industry and competitive market analysis and the opportunity and key-to-success analyses described in Chapters 3 and 4 help identify the major competitors and the amount of rivalry within an industry and market. For example, do one or two players dominate the market or are there many relatively equal players?

Depending on the situation, studies of overall industry and competitive market structure can lead to identifying niches of opportunity — pockets where the competition may be weak or disinterested or need specialized help. Several of these were described in Chapters 3 and 4. Such studies can also provide clues about potential threats. Most often, however, such analyses simply provide background for more detailed studies of specific competitor factors at work in a competitive environment.

Overall Competitor Groups

Sometimes, for analysis purposes, it is useful to group competitors by category. For example, in the baked goods industry situation described later in this chapter and in the *Superb Biscuits* company study given in the Case Study section of this book, there were three major national companies, one medium-size regional company, and six small regional competitors. The company under study happened to be the one medium-size regional company. Competitive groups necessarily have distinguishing characteristics. When defined, these existing and anticipated competitor characteristics help planners understand competitive strategic pressures to be expected within an industry. In a sense, each major competitor group (like each major competitor) has a *strategic profile* which identifies things they like to do and do well (strengths), and things they are not so good at (weaknesses). The approach described in the following sections for developing individual competitor profiles can be used for doing these group profiles.

Current Individual Competitors

In most strategy formulation situations, a planner studies each major individual competitor. In addition to relative market position, a planner examines each competitor's strategic profile and resources or lack of resources in the management, marketing, production/operations, financial and accounting, and other related areas. From this analysis emerges a picture of each competitor's strengths and weaknesses in major opportunity areas.

Market position. The relative market positions of competitors can provide insights into the competitive market environment. Sara Lee's strategy in the early 1990s was to participate only in markets where its products ranked first or second. Since high market share is related closely to high return on investment in this particular competitive environment — consumer packaged goods — such a strategy was a key to success in this industry for a company with Sara Lee's resources [McGill 1989; "Sara Lee" 1990].

As was shown in the classic Strategic Planning Institute's PIMS analysis, such an approach is effective only in select industries where well-defined industry and company characteristics are present [Woo 1981, 1984]. It is not always necessary to be a market leader to have a high return on investment. Other competitive environments lend themselves to different market share strategies as is seen in the discussions later in this chapter. For example, A&W Root Beer prospered by piggybacking on larger companies' distribution systems because it was too small to be a competitive threat to major competitors.

Figure 5-2 shows summaries of two approaches to competitive market position analyses.

Strategic profile. Companies and competitive groups have distinct strategic profiles. These may involve the way they do business, where they do business, and generally what they will and will not do. Such strategic profiles can affect the competitive market environment. IBM traditionally waited for a market to develop somewhat before entering it. This was the case with software, workstations, and, to some extent, PCs. When IBM failed to move aggressively into the computer workstation market during the 1980s, Sun Microsystems and several other companies were able to establish major positions in the estimated $20 billion market [Markoff 1991; Pollack 1992]. The fact that IBM was unable to respond to the challenges of faster-moving rivals led in mid-1991 to a well-publicized campaign by IBM Chairman John F. Akers to "wake up" IBM employees and to restructure the company [Carroll 1991(A); Lohr 1992; Markoff 1992; McCarroll 1991; Verity 1992].

In industries where the giants intentionally avoid specific niches, opportunities exist for smaller companies to fill these niches. Many small companies have found opportunities by doing jobs that large companies don't want to do or by providing specialized services that big companies need [Selz 1991]. Gloria Jean's Coffee Bean Corporation, a specialty coffee bean importer and retail franchiser with reported $32 million in sales in 1991, used a niche strategy approach. According to industry analysts, the company has prospered "because big companies like Procter & Gamble and General Foods have not made substantial investments in the specialty market" [Sharif 1991]. At times, then, analyzing competitors' strategic profiles can lead to opportunity identification.

Management. In many situations, an analysis of the structures of and changes in competi-

Figure 5-2: Summaries of Competitive Market Positions Analysis Forms

Instructions to user: fill in the total sales and the market share of your company and of each major competitor or competitor group (Comp#1, etc.), both in the industry and in the market segment or opportunity area under study.

A. Market Share Information: Current Year Summary

Industry

Industry Sales ($000)	Yr to Yr Growth %	Market Share as % (current year) Yours	Comp#1	Comp#2	Comp#3	Comp#4	Comp#5	Other
____	____	___%	___%	___%	___%	___%	___%	___%

These should total 100%

Industry Segment
(If Applicable)

Segment Sales ($000)	Yr to Yr Growth %	Market Share as % (current year) Yours	Comp#1	Comp#2	Comp#3	Comp#4	Comp#5	Other
____	____	___%	___%	___%	___%	___%	___%	___%

These should total 100%

B. Market Share Information: Five-Year Projections Summary

Industry

($000)	Industry Sales	Yr to Yr Growth	Market Share as % (current year) Yours	Comp#1	Comp#2	Comp#3	Comp#4	Comp#5	Other
Current Year plus 1 Year	___	____	___%	___%	___%	___%	___%	___%	___%
Current Year plus 2 Years	___	____	___%	___%	___%	___%	___%	___%	___%
Current Year plus 3 Years	___	____	___%	___%	___%	___%	___%	___%	___%
Current Year plus 4 Years	___	____	___%	___%	___%	___%	___%	___%	___%
Current Year plus 5 Years	___	____	___%	___%	___%	___%	___%	___%	___%

These should total 100%

Industry Segment
(If Applicable)

	Segment Sales ($000)	Yr to Yr Growth	Market Share as % (current year) Yours	Comp#1	Comp#2	Comp#3	Comp#4	Comp#5	Other
Current Year plus 1 Year	___	____	___%	___%	___%	___%	___%	___%	___%
Current Year plus 2 Years	___	____	___%	___%	___%	___%	___%	___%	___%
Current Year plus 3 Years	___	____	___%	___%	___%	___%	___%	___%	___%
Current Year plus 4 Years	___	____	___%	___%	___%	___%	___%	___%	___%
Current Year plus 5 Years	___	____	___%	___%	___%	___%	___%	___%	___%

These should total 100%

tors' management can provide insights into how competitors will act in the future. This is especially true when major shifts occur in a competitor's management.

For example, Tenneco Inc, a natural gas, shipbuilding, and manufacturing conglomerate, hired a new chairman and chief executive, Michael H. Walsh, a "brash, innovative cost-cutter and self-described 'organizational architect' who likes to make changes and expects to make waves" [Machalaba 1991]. It was expected that when Walsh took over in October 1991 Tenneco would become a more aggressive competitor in its six major businesses. The possibility was also raised that Tenneco might dispose of some of its divisions, since the break-up value of the company was estimated at over $10 billion compared to its then market value of less than half that amount [Hayes 1992].

Marketing. The marketing audit of a competitive environment covers customers, products and services, pricing, sales, and distribution.

Competitors' relations with the *customer* base in the market can significantly affect strategy formulation. American Hospital Supply created major competitive dislocations when it created computer information systems links with its customer market in the 1980s. American Hospital supplied customers with computers so that they could order directly and conveniently from American Hospital. Similarly, American Airlines provided travel agents with a computerized reservation system that made booking flights easier for travel agents and at the same time initially gave priority treatment to American Airlines. These two companies initially obtained a major competitive advantage from these moves by locking out competitors for a period of time [Mockler 1989, Chapter 15; Wiseman 1988].

Not only is it important to identify as early as possible competitor moves to strengthen relations with customers, it is also important to measure the degree of brand loyalty and other factors which can give a competitor strong ties with its customers.

In the area of *products and services*, a planner determines competitors' present strengths and draws inferences based on them about what competitive moves they are likely to make in the future.

For example, in mid-1989 AT&T was considering entering the credit card business by converting its 40 million phone charge cards into general credit cards — a move that would have far-reaching consequences for the intensely competitive credit card industry [Guyon 1989]. An initial examination of AT&T indicated that it had many of the resources needed to do the job successfully: financial resources, billing experience, a recognized name, and access to major companies that process credit card transactions. The question in 1989 was the likelihood of AT&T actually entering the business, given its ability to do so. That question was answered in 1990 when AT&T introduced its new credit card and rapidly gained a major position in the market [Pae 1992].

In addition to the threat of new *competitors* entering an existing product or service market, new *products* can potentially threaten existing products. In the early 1990s, Kodak was struggling with just such a problem as it tried to develop a strategy to meet the expected competition from filmless cameras, which threatened its core camera film business [Rigdon 1991].

Some companies have dominated an industry by emphasizing *pricing*. Shaw Industries Inc. did this in the carpet industry, forcing all but the smaller specialty manufacturers to emphasize price as a critical success factor [Hymowitz 1991]. Competitive strategies emphasizing low price were a major factor in the rash of bankruptcies in the retailing field [Norris 1992], at the same time that they led to the success of Wal-Mart, K-Mart, the Gap, the Limited, and Dillards in 1992 [Barmesh 1992].

In the *sales* area, information is sought about competitor positions and moves that could be expected to create competitive advantages in this area. For example, Genentech, which had only 300 salespeople, found itself at a disadvantage when competing with Smith, Kline and French, which with its marketing partner Upjohn, had 1,000 salespeople. When introducing the new drug, TPA, therefore, Genentech worked out a cooperative marketing agreement with Boeringher Ingelheim to use Boeringher's 500-person salesforce to help market TPA [Pollack 1990].

An analysis of competitor *distribution* positions can also yield insights into potential opportunities, keys to success, and threats that can affect strategy formulation. For example, in examining the competitive distribution structure in the soft drink industry, A&W Root Beer was faced with close-to-absolute control of distribution to food supermarkets by the major competitors, such as Pepsi, Coca Cola, and Seven-Up. What appeared to be a barrier to entry, however, was in fact an opportunity. A&W reasoned correctly that independent distributors (bottlers) would be willing to carry noncompetitive sodas (they provided the bottlers additional revenues at very little additional cost), such as A&W's root beer, ginger drink, and cream and grapefruit sodas, and so provide an outlet for the company's products [Deutsch 1989].

Operations/production. The competitor audit would also cover the operations/production strengths and weaknesses of competitors. For example, the wood pulp industry was operating at near capacity in 1989 and as a result prices had nearly doubled in three years as growth in demand began to outstrip supply. That attractive supply-demand situation led to plans by wood pulp producers to build over $4 billion in new capacity [Melnbardis 1989]. This caused some industry analysts to predict that prices would fall as new capacity became operational, because of the increased competitive rivalry which they expected would result from overcapacity. Wood pulp makers were convinced, however, that demand would increase substantially because of the information age explosion and that growth would exceed expectations. For this reason, wood pulp producers generally ignored the negative implications of competitor plant building efforts and eventually went ahead with their own facility expansion plans.

Comparing production cost capabilities and cost structures can be especially important competitor considerations in mature markets. Richardson-Sheffield's Bryan Upton identified individual competitor strengths in the production cost area as a threat to his business. Moving ahead of many others in the industry, Upton took steps to remain cost competitive in order to survive and prosper [Lohr 1989].

Information systems. The competitive environment can change significantly due to competitor investments in information systems technology. The regional Banc One has developed computer information systems that draw on all the information the bank has about each customer and presents it in a way that enables branch officers to sell additional products to, and better serve, their customers. Ironically, this increased use of computer technology, through its applications at the branch level, allowed Banc One to maintain more personalized services for customers during an age of increasing business automation. In this way, computer technology helped the company to pursue a strategy of economically serving individual customers and smaller companies, where it can make higher-margined loans. This strategy made Banc One the highest rated bank in the nation in return on assets in the early 1990s [Feder 1989; Lohr 1991].

Such company moves into systems technology can affect the entire competitive environment, since they can force competitors to make similar moves in order to maintain competitive services and control costs.

Finances. Infusions of capital can create shifts in the competitive environment. Many barriers to entry in the U.S. created by high capital costs of entry fell during the late 1980s because of large investments by foreign companies. Many major foreign companies made substantial investments in existing major companies, such as Firestone, National Steel, Inmont, and General Tire, and through these investments transformed once-sluggish operations into truly formidable players in their industries. Although disagreement exists on how serious this new threat of foreign ownership is, there is no question that it is reshaping the competitive dynamics of a number of basic industries — chemical, tire, auto, steel, and building materials in particular [Hicks 1989, 1991].

The extent of the detail of such competitor-by-competitor analyses depends on the ability to obtain information about the competition, as well as on the complexity of the industry and of the strategy formulation project. No matter what the industry and market, however, a planner always makes some effort to gather as much information as possible about significant competitors or competitor groups. Experts use several approaches when profiling competitors. An example of one of these is given in Figure 5-3 [Keiser 1987]. Using available information sources to gather competitive information and develop such profiles is covered later in this chapter and in Chapter 11 and Appendix D.

POTENTIAL NEW COMPETITORS AND COMPETITION

The likelihood of new competition depends on such factors as the general attractiveness of an industry or market, and competitive market forces.

Attractiveness of Industry or Competitive Market

The more attractive a market or industry, the more likely there is to be increased competition in the future. In the 1980s, vodka was an attractive market segment in the stagnant liquor industry. The attractiveness of the $450 million premium vodka market, led by the strong sales of Absolut Vodka, naturally set the stage for increases in competition in 1989, when four major companies — Brown-Forman, Buckingham Wile Company, Schieffelin & Somerset Company, and Seagram — introduced premium vodkas into the market [Freitag 1989]. By 1991, the vodka market was no longer considered an attractive growth market [Freedman 1990].

Emerging industries with perceived profit and growth opportunities almost always experience increased competition. IBM's introduction of its PC in the early 1980s was followed by dozens of new entrants into the field. Many, such as Compaq and Dell, grew into billion-dollar companies.

Figure 5-3: Outline of Competitor Profile and Information Sources

OUTLINE OF A COMPETITOR PROFILE	SELECTED SOURCES OF COMPETITOR INFORMATION
BACKGROUND	
Company identification; location; description; brief history; state of incorporation.	General business directories, in print or online. Industry-specific directories.
Affiliates; How is the company organized? How often has it altered its structure?	Corporate press releases, Business Wire (Nexis), PR Newswire (Nexis, Dialog) D&B America's Corporate Families; Corporate Affiliations database.
Number of stock shares outstanding; ownership (insiders, institutions, major shareholders).	CDA Spectrum reports based on SEC filings; D&B reports.
FINANCE	
Statistics and performance analyses (revenue, earnings, growth); sales by division; profitability by business unit/product line.	SEC filings (disclosure), Compustat, brokerage reports (Investext, Exchange).
Banks/investment banking firms used.	Directories, tombstone ads, SEC filings, D&B reports.
Stock market data; current market value.	Dow Jones News Retrieval.
Ratios and industry comparisons; Do they track, lead or lag the industry?	Prentice-Hall, RMA, D&B, Media General, Investext.
Cash flow analysis assets and return on assets; capitalization; working capital; internal rate of return on investment.	Compustat.
PRODUCTS	
Description of products and services offered (product mix - depth and breadth of product line) and market position by product; product strength and weaknesses (individually and the line as a whole). How committed is the firm to a particular product line?	Directories. Attend trade show and conventions to obtain product literature; send for product catalogs; clip advertisements.
Analysis of new product introductions.	Press releases, new product announcement database (Predicasts); Have your sales force query your customers.
R&D expenditures and apparent interests of technical personnel; an analysis of the company's design and development process.	Scan technical journals for articles authored by employees of competitors.
Patents held/pending; product standards (specs), quality and technical analysis.	World Patent Index (Dialog), Derwent, IFI/Plenum Claims databases. Have your engineers analyze competitors' products.
Pricing policies (Who decides flexibility in pricing levels?); Note special selling arrangements (Are they competing for your customers?)	Note trade discounts offered.
Licensing and joint venture agreements.	Corporate press releases tracked on PR Newswire and Business Wire.

Figure 5-3: Outline of Competitor Profile and Information Sources (contd.)

OUTLINE OF A COMPETITOR PROFILE	SELECTED SOURCES OF COMPETITOR INFORMATION
MARKETS	
Market segmentation and customer analysis; customer base (markets targeted, regional sales analysis, penetration, importance to the firm, dominance of market); profiles of markets/customers (including product mix and sales data by product line); market growth and potential for future growth; market share by product line.	Press release, public documents, industry analyses by investment banking firms or consulting groups (scan Investext, Exchange, FIND/SVP databases or Harfax directories); Check databases for announcements of large customer purchases; Use your sales force to assess customer loyalties.
How does the company view the direction of the industry?	Employment ads in newspapers (What type of positions are they seeking to fill and does this indicate a new direction for the firm?)
Market and geographic area targeted for expansion; marketing tactics.	Check acquisition and divestiture announcements for trends.
Distribution network/channels of distribution.	Press releases by wholesalers and independent reps.
Advertising/marketing/sales efforts including budgets and firms used.	Standard Directory of Advertisers.
Foreign trade analysis. Recent orders; government contracts. Analysis of sales force (experience, compensation); T&E practices.	Trade press, DIOR reports, Commerce Business Daily, DMS.
FACILITIES	
Location, size, domestic vs. foreign.	Directories.
Capacity, capacity utilization, announced capacity expansions.	Check plans for plant expansions and closings (press releases and local press).
Product mix by plant; shipments and profitability data; unit cost/price.	Industry consultants.
Capital investments; equipment purchases; key suppliers.	Press releases.
Number of production lines and shifts.	Business Dateline (Data Courier), local newspapers, Vutext, regional business press (PROMT).
Regulatory issues.	Note investigations by government agencies (Newsnet, Nexis).
PERSONNEL	
Employees - total, management, R&D staffing, engineers - number, education, training, experience.	Directories, public documents.
Biographies of senior management including employment contracts, incentive (bonus) programs and golden parachute agreements.	D&B, S&P directories, public documents.
Description of the members of the board of directors.	D&B, S&P directories, public documents; Who's Who series.

Figure 5-3: Outline of Competitor Profile and Information Sources (contd.)

OUTLINE OF A COMPETITOR PROFILE	SELECTED SOURCES OF COMPETITOR INFORMATION
Consultants used by the firm; Labor union information (relations with management, results of recent negotiations with other firms in the industry, date of next contract renegotiation).	Check labor contract expiration dates and strikes in the trade press.
Detailed corporate structure; Who has P&L responsibility?	Changes in who reports to whom and their responsibilities are often detailed in press releases.
Safety information (accidents) and government/ industry regulations violations.	OSHA, ERISA, EEOC compliance (Nexis, Newsnet).
Management style and flexibility.	General business press, management journal articles.
Fringe benefits and compensation practices.	Use your human resources department's contacts and databases; Do you have any employees who worked for your competitor?
Track managerial changes for indications of disputes in upper management (turnover of personnel).	Listings in business and trade journals: classifieds.
APPARENT STRATEGIC (LONG-RANGE) PLANS	
Detail of acquisition and divestiture strategy.	Dow Jones, Investext.
New products on the horizon (Does it indicate a new for the firm?)	New Product Announcement database, press direction releases.
Statements of plans to enter new markets or improve their market position (increase their share of market).	Presentations to Wall Street analysts.
Apparent strategic objectives; corporate/divisional/ subsidiary company priorities; business unit/segment goals; basic business philosophy/targets.	General business press, letters to the shareholders.
Analysis of company's decision-making process. Overall corporate image and reputation. Assess company's ability to adapt/change; How will the company look/perform in the future? Anti-takeover measures instituted; shareholder actions; Lawsuits pending. What are the firm's key successes and failures? Why have they been successful? Overall corporate attitudes toward risk.	SEC filings, such an exhibits to 10-Ks and proxy statements.

Adapted from Barbie E. Keiser, "Practical Competitor Intelligence," *Planning Review*, September/October 1987, pp. 18-19

The maturity of an industry can also provide clues as to the competitiveness of the industry. The wine industry in California had peaked by 1991 as the number of competitors increased and wine consumption declined nationally, creating a situation where strong wineries were growing largely at the expense of weaker ones [Fisher 1991(B)]. Beer industry sales were rising very slowly in 1991, creating a fiercely competitive environment in that industry [Fisher 1991(A)].

Using competitive market analysis to spot attractive opportunities can be more of an art than a science, and sometimes involves going against the more apparent trends indicated by competitor moves. For example, during the late 1980s Texas financier Gordon Cain began buying nitrogen fertilizer plants and by 1989 had interests in six of them. The fertilizer business is fairly volatile since it is dependent on the farming industry. Thus, many competing companies, like W.R. Grace and USX, took advantage of 1988's recovery to sell their fertilizer plants. In fact, close to half of this country's 50 leading fertilizer plants were taken over by new owners between 1986 (one of the worst years ever for the industry) and 1989.

Gordon Cain, however, viewed this downturn as a long-term opportunity. First, he bought fertilizer plants that were selling for as low as 10 percent of current construction costs. Second, based on his studies of customer markets Cain concluded that the downturn was short-term and the industry was sound over the long-run. Third, he had a very good record of calling such industry turnarounds [Hayes 1989]. Richard E. Rainwater, another experienced buyer of troubled companies in highly competitive industries, bought Sun Belt hospitals in 1991. While eventual success was far from certain, one of his earlier efforts — with American Medical — yielded him $56 million on an investment of about $26 million [Freudenheim 1991]

Attractiveness, then, is not always obvious nor evidenced by increasing sales or profits. In situations where opportunities are clearly visible, however, the attractiveness of an industry or competitive market will be one key indicator of the likelihood of increased competition.

Competitive Market Forces

In his study, *Competitive Strategy* [1980, Chapter 2], Michael Porter identified several competitive forces which can influence future competitiveness in an industry in many strategy formulation situations. Analyzing these factors can help predict the kind of and amount of future rivalry to be expected, and in some situations can provide an effective method for spotting not-so-obvious opportunities.

Barriers to entry of new competitors. Realistically, the harder it is to enter a market, the less likely there is to be an influx of new competitors into a market. Several factors influence the difficulty of entering a market:

Customer brand loyalty and preferences usually occur when products are differentiated sufficiently to create customer attachment to existing brands. In situations where considerable brand loyalty exists, a new entrant may have to spend considerable money and time to overcome this loyalty, by lowering prices, increasing service and quality, and doing more advertising and promotion.

Economies of scale can create barriers to entry, because they may raise initial costs, reduce profits, and generally lead to overcapacity in the market. These economies of scale can involve not only production, but also advertising, distribution, marketing, purchasing, and financing.

Limited access to marketing channels can also create barriers, through increasing costs or slowing growth for a new entrant.

Large capital requirements may limit entrants into a market. However, there are so many large companies with so much capital available today that this restraint usually can be overcome where major opportunities exist [Hicks 1989].

Experience advantages of existing firms may discourage potential competitors, since the accumulated know-how of existing firms may give them significant cost and position advantages.

Cost advantages held by existing firms can create barriers to new entrants. These advantages may include access to lower cost raw material supplies, favorable locations, patent protection, and technological advantages.

Government regulations can create barriers by either limiting or barring competition; this is especially true in foreign countries.

Anticipated reactions of existing firms may limit new entrants. Existing firms may have financial resources to cut prices and create buying incentives. They may defend their market in other ways — by increasing advertising, limiting access to supplies and marketing channels, and taking other steps to hurt new entrant chances of success. This is especially true where it is very costly for existing competitors to abandon a market.

According to Porter, the higher these barriers, the less likely that competitive pressures from outside the industry will exist. Such information is useful in situations where the company in question is affected by such overall market factors. However, the impact on decision making — that is, whether or not these forces create opportunities or threats to individual companies under study in the future — will depend on specific situation characteristics.

Rivalry among competing firms. Porter identifies several conditions which can increase the potential of intense competitive rivalry in a market. Rivalry tends to increase in situations where

- It costs more to get out of a business than to stay in it
- Customer switching costs are low
- The number of competitors is increasing, and they are becoming more equal in size and strength
- It is possible to increase unit volume by using price cuts and other competitive weapons
- The competitors are diverse
- Product demand is growing slowly

A planner analyzes these and other factors to estimate the intensity of competitive rivalry which can be expected in a market in the future.

The threat of competitive products from other industries. Porter considers substitute products from other industries to be potential competition in a market. Beverages are a common example. Alternate beverages can to some degree satisfy the same customer needs, so fruit juices, sodas, and other beverages can be considered competitive products. Since customer switching costs are low in this case, competing products from different areas (the beer, soda, or bottled water industries, for example) are considered part of the competitive environment for any related beverage and so can affect future competition.

The bargaining power of suppliers and of customers. Porter identifies these as two other critical factors affecting competitive conditions in a market or industry. As with the other factors, the influence of these factors on success in the particular market or industry under study is examined and their impact on future competitive conditions assessed. Where there are a large number of suppliers and the products are relatively undifferentiated, the power of suppliers is not likely to be strong. For instance, consolidations in the broiler (chicken) business have increased the bargaining power of customers in that industry. As reported in *The Wall Street Journal,* chicken processors were approaching a monopoly-buyer position, which led to reduced prices and some bankruptcies among chicken farmers in those areas where there is only one major chicken processor buying chickens. [Charlier 1990]. On the other hand, as in the wood pulp industry in 1989, strong demand coupled with limited suppliers led to a near doubling of pulp prices in the mid-1980s and extremely competitive price pressures on paper manufacturers who use pulp [Melnbardis 1989], which were relieved only with subsequent major supplier expansions.

At times, suppliers will even be a new source of competition. Intel Corporation, once just a supplier of computer chips and boards to other manufacturers, began making computers in the late 1980s. By 1990 these computer sales accounted for over 30 percent of total company revenues [Fisher 1990(A)].

The five competitive forces analyzed above provide a structured way to view the competitive environment and the forces at work within it. This, in turn, provides an initial estimate of the kinds and degree of competition to be expected.

It is, however, only one analytical tool, focusing on the characteristics of the situation under study and what these characteristics tell us about the likelihood of new competitors and competition arising from the competitive forces at work within the marketplace. Other factors affect the competition which can be expected in the future: the anticipated capabilities and actions of individual competitors in a market, as discussed in the following section; and the ability of the company under study to take steps to reduce competitive pressures, as is discussed in Chapter 6.

COMPETITORS' ANTICIPATED CAPABILITIES AND ACTIONS

As the analysis continues, estimates are made of competitors' future strengths and weaknesses. Just because a company is *able* to do something does not necessarily mean that the company *will* do it. The answers to three questions can help identify possible risks in this area:

- Is the competitor likely to make the projected move?
- How likely is the competitor to succeed?
- Exactly what will be the specific nature and timing of the anticipated competitive moves?

For example, in 1985 IBM attempted to enter the computer workstation market with very little success. In contrast to other areas where it normally dominates, by 1989 IBM controlled only 2.4 percent of the then $4.1 billion market for computer workstations. In this case, the company had the capabilities, but did not succeed in the market to the degree that it had in other product areas nor to a degree that was threatening to the three major competitors in 1989 [Markoff 1989].

However, in 1990 IBM announced a new line of workstations [Markoff 1990] and cooperative arrangements with Next Inc. to market Next's software, which was needed to support IBM's new workstations [Fisher 1990(B)]. IBM's workstations were referred to as its most significant new product line "ever," with major innovative features and competitive prices. Nonetheless, IBM was expected to have an uphill fight, because competitors were already entrenched in the market, were capable of quickly matching IBM's advanced features at lower prices, could better meet market prices, had stronger software support and products, and did not have to worry as much as IBM about the negative impact on other company products, such as IBM mainframe and high-end PC sales [Carroll 1991(B)].

Developing and reconciling conflicting scenarios of future events is a complex and difficult aspect of the competitive market analysis. Such scenario development involves not only high-level conceptual skills, but also superior inferential, associative, intuitive, and creative reasoning skills. It is also the one aspect of the competitive market analysis with the largest payoff.

Because of the difficulties involved in estimating future competitor capabilities and actions, studies may be needed of different possible reactions of each major competitor. This was necessary, for example, in an oil services company situation, where the company was considering entering a new market. A company-by-company analysis was necessary to develop scenarios for possible competitor reactions to newcomers in the market. A summary of two of these analyses is shown in Figure 5-4.

In that situation, the initial analysis indicated the likelihood of a strong reaction by well-financed large competitors against any newcomer. The subsequent detailed competitor-by-competitor analysis, in contrast, indicated that little incentive existed for competitors to seriously fight a new entrant. The analysis also revealed that competitor reactions might vary over a period of time, and that the timing of the reaction might be slow enough for the company to establish a market position.

Vella and McGonagle discuss various ways to create competitive scenarios, especially in situations where competitor information is difficult to obtain [1987, 1988]. Their approach, referred to as "shadowing markets," is for someone at the firm under study to become an expert in each competitor's way of thinking strategically and then think through management decisions from the competitor's viewpoint. Information sources used to acquire this mental image of the competitor include:

- Monitoring personnel changes affecting any operation of particular interest. This sometimes requires using local newspapers
- Reviewing press releases and speeches as well as stories in the trade press
- Attending trade shows to meet with competitors' personnel and contractors, such as advertising agencies
- Reading corporate documents, ranging from new product brochures to company newsletters

Figure 5-4: Competitive Scenario Analysis and Evaluation: Oil Services Company Situations Most Likely Actions

Competition	What Competitor Might Do	Probability	Reasons for Probability
Competitor A	Try to develop a similar product	75%	- Vast resources - Market leader - Already produces similar products that are well-known in the industry
Competitor B	Try to develop a similar product	70%	- Has extensive engineering services and equipment capabilities - Has 50 years experience
Competitor C	Undecided, will wait to see what happens	70%	- Has only 5 years experience
Competitor D	Will not try to develop a similar product	95%	- 95% of their business is selling a natural resource product.
Competitor E	Try to merge our company	50%	- Small company - High-quality reputation
Competitor F	Can go either way: wait and see what happens, or develop a similar product right away	40%	- Large company - Has power to control prices - Has the engineering and equipment capabilities

Planner B's Analysis

Senarios	Competitor A	Competitor B	Competitor C	Competitor D	Competitor E	Competitor F
Do nothing	3	3	6	3	1	3
Copy/improve new product	6	6	5	1	8	6
Try to buy or merge with us	4	4	1	1	5	7
Dirty tricks	3	5	1	4	1	1
Wait/see	8	8	7	10	3	9
Become our customer	2	8	1	2	8	1

Scale of 1-10
10 = Strong Possibility of Scenario Occurring
1 = Little Possibility of Scenario Occurring

- Following technological developments by tracking papers and articles by key research personnel
- Learning the backgrounds and track records of key executives
- Debriefing new employees who worked for or had contact with the competitors
- Tracking regulatory matters in which competitors are involved
- Questioning current employees, suppliers, and customers, employees who work with employees of competitors on industry and other committees, and dealers who carry competitors' products in addition to your own
- Asking marketing specialists to evaluate the capabilities of competitors' advertising agencies, or other suppliers
- Studying the competitors' track records and prior history to understand their corporate cultures

Many people involved in scenario writing role play in this way — pretending to be competitor decision makers — since it provides valuable and reliable insights into the decisions competitors are likely to make in the future.

COMPETITORS' ANTICIPATED STRENGTHS AND WEAKNESSES IN OPPORTUNITY AND KEY-TO-SUCCESS AREAS

As a study progresses, the focus shifts to the major strategy formulation concern — identifying competitors' and potential competitors' strengths and weaknesses in opportunity and key-to-success areas.

Many of these strengths and weaknesses will have been identified during the analysis of the overall industry competitive structure and the audit of individual competitor strengths and weaknesses. This segment of the analysis goes one step further and relates those strengths and weaknesses to the keys to success in opportunities areas, which were identified in the studies described in Chapter 4.

In the baked goods company situation cited earlier, for example, a planner would cite the ability of the three large national companies to produce standard high-volume cookies cheaply, since the competitors have enormous resources. They also had very wide distribution networks, and good brand identification. These factors would be likely to give them a major competitive (and so strategic) advantage in the standardized product area. An assumption might also be that the competitors' strengths might be a weakness in dealing with the specialized low-volume product area. For example, these competitors might have more difficulty in meeting the production flexibility, local market knowledge, and quick turnaround time requirements needed for success in the speciality cookie area.

In this same study, a look at the future indicated the possibility of critical problems. The major competitive threat was that the large companies, with their enormous resources, would accelerate the rate of production automation (technological change) and increase their price advantage. They would also probably increase their product line, which would pressure store outlets into giving these large competitors more shelf space. These events would increase their competitive advantage in their strongest product areas, standardized high-volume cookies. In addition, the large companies might decentralize and thus increase their ability to compete in the specialized cookie area.

Less information was available about the six small competitors in this study, since they were privately-held companies. In general, however, their size relative to the rest of the competitors (all six combine for less than 15 percent of the total market) indicated they had limited ability to compete in either the standard or specialty cookie areas.

The competitors' ability to meet the keys to success in the major future outlet opportunity area — chain supermarkets — and in the secondary opportunity area — independent food stores — were also identified during this phase of the study.

Figure 5-5 summarizes the results of one phase of these comparative evaluations. It is another example of how situation context information is reformulated in a way useful for strategy formulation decision making.

This analysis is a detailed extension of the analysis described in Figure 4-6. That figure summarized the results of the competitive marketplace analysis leading to the identification of keys to success in the four specific opportunity areas listed in Figure 5-5 — standardized and specialty products, and chain and independent store outlets. The keys to success in each of these four areas are listed in the left-hand column of the figure. Figure 5-5 is one way to summarize the results of the competitor analyses described thus far in this chapter. Individual experienced planners most often develop their own ways to conceptualize and visualize such comparative studies.

Figure 5-5: Competitors' Anticipated Strengths and Weaknesses in Key-to-Success and Opportunity Areas

a. Products	**Big Three**	**Little Six**
Standardized		
1. Resources/price competitive	They have	Probably not
2. Mass market presence	They have	Unlikely
3. Brand/quality reputation	They have	Assumed to some degree
Specialty		
1. New product capability	To some degree	Probably have
2 Market intelligence	To some degree	Probably have
3. Flexible production/org.	Questionable	Probably have
4. Market access/presence	They have	To some extent
5. Brand recognition	They have	Assumed to some degree
b. Outlets		
Chains		
1. Strong store relations	They have	To some extent
2. Chain buyer relations	Assumed they have	Unknown
3. Wide product line	They have	Unlikely
4. Promotional incentives	They have	Assumed they do
Independents		
1. Distribution cost control	They have	Unknown
2. Strong store relations	They have	Assumed to some degree
3. Appropriate product line	To some extent	Assumed to some degree
4. Promotional incentives	They have	Assumed they do

What strategy is formulated in a specific situation will depend to a large extent on assumptions about competitors' increasing strengths in the different opportunity and key-to-success areas. It will also depend on the planner's own company's anticipated future position, as will be discussed in Chapter 6.

SOURCES OF INFORMATION ABOUT COMPETITORS

Several problems may be encountered in gathering competitive information. First, the company under study may compete across several industries. Second, information about competitors is not always readily available. Third, some information sources, such as research firms, can be costly. Each company and industry situation will dictate how these problems are resolved. In all situations legitimate sources of competitive information exist, so some degree of competitive intelligence can always be gathered within the limits of acceptable business practices.

Some sources of competitive intelligence are shown in Figure 5-3 and discussed in Chapter 11. They include

- On-line databases (a very commonly used source) which are described in Appendix D
- Periodicals, newspapers, and other literature reviews
- Internal information sources, such as salespeople
- Industry and market studies, both continually updated ones and *ad hoc* studies for specific strategy formulation projects
- Oral communications with suppliers, consultants, customers, industry associations and other market participants, residents of the local communities in which the competitors operate, local newspapers, and others familiar with the competition [Markowitz 1987]
- Scenario development and role playing

Several sources which offer detailed information on setting up systems for gathering competitive intelligence include

- Stanat: *The Intelligent Corporation* [1990], gives specific directions on developing competitive intelligence systems and contains several dozen instances of how companies have set up competitive intelligence operations
- Vella and McGonagle: *Improved Business Planning Using Competitive Market Intelligence* [1988]
- Washington Research Publishing: *How to Find Information About Companies* [1989] and *Understanding the Competition* [1984]
- Fuld: *Competitor Intelligence: How to Get It; How to Use It* [1985]

In addition, there are two associations dedicated to competitive intelligence — *The Society of Competitor Intelligence Professionals* and *the Information Industry Association* — as well as such journals as *Information Management Review* and *Competitive Intelligence Review*.

Experienced consultants, such as Strategic Intelligence Systems, Inc., The Hellicon Group Ltd, and Barbie E. Keiser Inc., can also be helpful. Keiser has outlined the sources of competitive intelligence information which might be used in developing individual competitor profiles. This outline is given in Figure 5-3 earlier in this chapter.

MAKING THESE DECISIONS IN SPECIFIC COMPETITIVE MARKET SITUATIONS

The strategy formulation processes discussed in this chapter are encountered in a wide range of situations — from those involving billion-dollar multinational giants, to those involving small entrepreneurs undertaking local ventures.

Several critical tasks are involved in strategy formulation situations during this phase. They include

- Identify and list competitors and their relative market position in terms of sales, as shown in Figure 5-2
- Audit competitor resources in major business areas and summarize that audit in the form of a strategic profile of each major competitor or competitor group now operating in the market
- Estimate and prepare a summary of the overall attractiveness of the industry and competitive market under study and its implications for future competitive conditions in the industry and market
- Analyze the five major competitive forces in the market and summarize the conclusions about the amount and nature of competition that might be expected in the future
- Develop scenarios of possible and likely future capabilities of and actions by competitors in the market, including estimates of the likelihood of their occurring, as shown in Figure 5-3
- Prepare a statement of the anticipated strengths and weaknesses of major competitors or competitor groups in opportunity and key-to-success areas, as shown in Figure 5-4
- List appropriate competitive information sources for the situation and outline how these information sources are to be used regularly in the future

Whatever the nature and scope of the situation under study, the above tasks and manual tools will almost always be useful. They provide the background information needed to prepare a summary report. Such a report or one like it is often prepared in strategy formulation studies. It would provide information on the strategy recommendations made and the reasoning that went into arriving at these recommendations.

As seen in Figure 5-6, the decision-making processes described in this chapter relate to other strategic decision-making areas. By analyzing situation factors, such as *competitive market characteristics* and *defined market opportunities and keys to success*, the *anticipated competitor strengths and weaknesses in opportunity and key-to-success areas* are identified.

The tasks performed during this strategy formulation phase provide necessary background for other strategic planning tasks, which involve analyzing the company under study and

Figure 5-6: Strategic Management Decision-Making Process

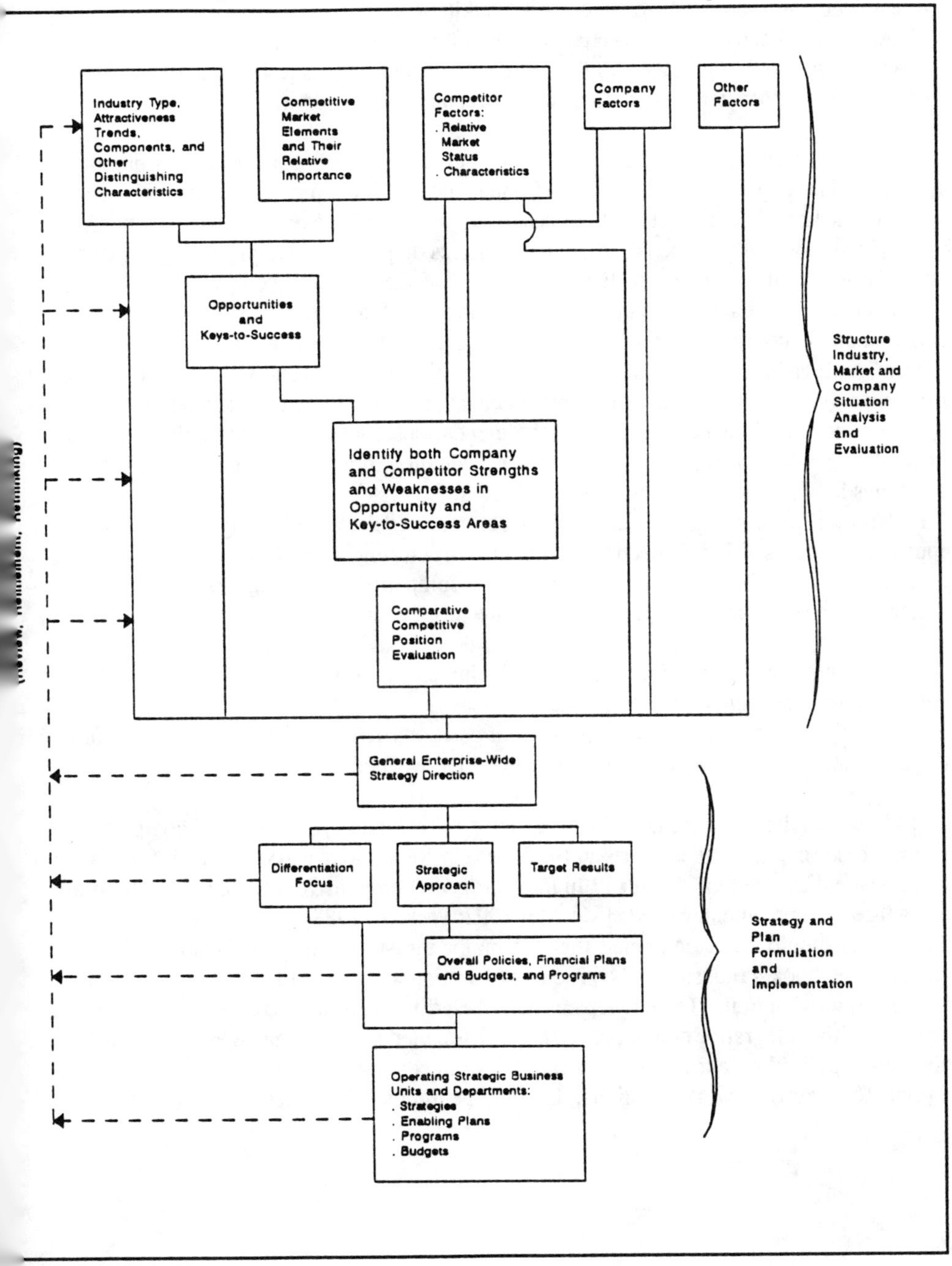

formulating enterprise-wide strategies within the context of identified situation requirements.

Identifying the approaches to the decision making involved in doing this phase of strategy formulation, as has been done in this chapter, is helpful in learning how to formulate strategies. It is also useful in providing a basis for designing and using knowledge-based and other manual and computer-based systems that do and assist managers in doing and learning strategy formulation.

As with the earlier phases of the strategy formulation process, portions of this phase have been replicated in semi-structured decision-making models. These models in turn have served as the basis for the knowledge-based systems described in Appendix A and elsewhere in this book. For example, the system in Appendix A contains a series of questions which guide a user through an analysis of the attractiveness of the industry and of the competitive environment. These questions, many of which explore the competitive market factors identified by Porter, then are used to estimate the competitive conditions expected in the industry and marketplace. In addition, the system guides a user through an analysis of competitor strengths and weaknesses, helps the user organize that information, and then integrates that information with information about the company under study in making strategy recommendations. Screens similar to those shown in Figures 5-2 and 5-4 are part of the system, as are evaluation tools such as the one in Figure 5-7 which shows how the type of industry is identified in the system.

In addition to knowledge-based systems computer tools, a wide range of conventional computer tools are useful in collecting, analyzing, structuring, and using competitive market information for strategy formulation and for creating competitive advantages. As is discussed in this chapter, these tools are used principally in three critical areas:

- Gathering competitive market information, including information on competitor strengths and weaknesses in opportunity and key-to-success areas
- Estimating relative financial and sales competitor positions in the market, now and in the future
- Using computer information systems as a competitive weapon

In addition to the ones discussed in this chapter, other manual, conventional computer, and knowledge-based computer techniques and tools used in competitive market analysis for strategy formulation are discussed in Chapter 11 in the section on competitive intelligence systems and in several useful supplementary texts [Mockler 1992; Webster 1989].

Again, it should be remembered that the major thrust of this book is not on learning techniques. The book's focus is on the process of learning how to develop techniques useful in the reader's own situation. Techniques and task descriptions in this book illustrate working applications of the integrative context-specific process called strategic management, the subject of this book. Individual expert planners have developed a wide range of useful techniques appropriate for their own work situations. It would be impossible to include all of them in one book.

Figure 5-7: Sample Decision Chart—Competitive Market Situation Defining Type of Industry or Competitive Market Based on Situation Condititions (Initial Concept Testing Prototype)

		RULES				
	PREMISES	1	2	3	4	5
IF	number-dominant competitors	high	med			
	economies-scale	and high	and med			
	product-differentiation	or high	or med			
	regionally-dispersed	or high	or high			
	industry-unit. sales			decreasing	stable	increasing
	product-lines			decreasing	stable	increasing
	r&d budgets			decreasing	stable	increasing
	advertising-budgets			decreasing	stable	increasing
	number-competitors			decreasing	stable	increasing
	technology			mature	mature	emerging
	proportion-new companies			low	average	high
	proportion-new customers			low	average	high
THEN	COMPETITIVE MARKET					
	Fragmented	X	X			
	Declining			X		
	Mature				X	
	Emerging					X

REVIEW QUESTIONS

1. Describe the basic business processes and areas examined when analyzing competitors' strengths and weaknesses.
2. Discuss what is involved in auditing existing competitors' resources and developing structured competitor profiles.
3. Describe the usefulness of studying relative competitor market positions. Discuss the situations in which being a major player in a market may or may not be a key to success.
4. In what ways is industry attractiveness indicative of future competitive conditions?
5. What are the five competitive market forces identified by Porter? Discuss ways in which future competitive conditions in a market or industry can be inferred from an analysis of competitive forces.
6. Discuss ways in which scenario development can help in determining what competitive conditions are possible or likely in the future.
7. How does one identify competitors' strengths and weaknesses in opportunity and key-to-success areas? Discuss why making these determinations is so important.
8. Describe ways in which the analysis and evaluation described in this chapter can help to further the exploration of opportunities and keys to success described in Chapter 4.
9. Discuss ways in which the decision making described in this chapter relates to other strategy formulation tasks.

EXERCISES

1. Read one of the company studies in the Case Study section at the end of this book whose title contains the actual company name. Using the company study of your choice, write a report which covers the following tasks outlined at the end of the chapter:

- Identify and list competitors and their relative market position in terms of sales, as shown in Figure 5-2
- Audit competitor resources in major business areas and summarize that audit in the form of a strategic profile of each major competitor or competitor group now operating in the market
- Estimate and prepare a summary of the overall attractiveness of the industry and competitive market under study and its implication for future competitive conditions in the industry and market
- Analyze the five major competitive forces in the market and summarize your conclusions about the amount and nature of competition that might be expected in the future
- Develop scenarios of possible and likely future capabilities of and actions by competitors in the market, including estimates of the likelihood of their occurrence, as shown in Figure 5-4
- Prepare a statement of the anticipated strengths and weaknesses of major competitors or competitor groups in opportunity and key-to-success areas, as shown in Figure 5-4

- List appropriate competitive information sources for your situation and outline how these information sources are to be used regularly in the future

2. Read recent issues of the periodicals referred to in the references section at the end of the chapter, or other related periodicals of your choice, and find a description of an industry of interest to you. Write a report on that industry covering the same tasks as listed in Exercise #1.

3. Read Appendix D, "Using Online Databases For Market Research." Discuss ways in which online databases may be used to obtain information useful in doing strategic management tasks described in this chapter.

REFERENCES

Barmesh, Isadore, "Down the Scale with the Major Store Chains," *The New York Times*, Business Section, February 2, 1992, p. 5.

Carroll, Paul B., "Akers to IBM Employees: Wake Up!", *The Wall Street Journal*, May 29, 1991(A), pp. B1, B2.

Carroll, Paul B., "IBM Is Delaying Its Introduction of Workstation," *The Wall Street Journal*, September 20, 1991(B), pp. B1, B2.

Charlier, Marc, "Chicken Economics: The Broiler Business Consolidates, and That Is Bad News to Farmers," *The Wall Street Journal*, January 4, 1990, pp. A1, A8.

Deutsch, Claudine, "A & W: Prospering By Avoiding the Big Boys," *The New York Times*, Business Section, January 15, 1989, pp. 1, 24.

Feder, Barnaby J., "Getting the Electronics Just Right," *The New York Times*, Business Section, June 4, 1989, pp. 1, 8.

Fisher, Lawrence M., "Behind All the Bonhomie, the Brewing Industry Gets Tough," *The New York Times,* Business Section, July 21, 1991(A), p. 4.

Fisher, Lawrence M., "Dreams Fade in the Wine Country," *The New York Times*, June 16, 1991(B), pp. D1, D5.

Fisher, Lawrence M., "Intel: Supplier Rising as a Big Competitor," *The New York Times,* February 14, 1990(A), pp. D1, D3.

Fisher, Lawrence M., "Work Stations From I.B.M. to Offer Next Inc. Software," *The New York Times*, February 6, 1990(B), pp. D1, D19.

Freedman, Alix M., "With Yuppies Fading, Absolut May Too," *The Wall Street Journal,* December 17, 1990, pp. B1, B4.

Freitag, Michael, "Vodka Import Boom: New Entries Rush In," *The New York Times*, June 6, 1989, pp. D1, D8.

Freudenheim, Milt, "Cashing in on Health Care's Troubles," *The New York Times*, July 21, 1991, Business Section, pp. 1-6.

Fuld, Leonard, *Competitive Intelligence: How to Get It; How to Use It,* New York, Wiley: 1985.

Greenwald, John, "Permanent Pink Slips," *Time*, September 9, 1991, pp. 54-56.

Guyon, Jane, and Robert Guenther, "AT&T Mulls Entering Competitive Credit-Card Field," *The Wall Street Journal,* May 15, 1989, pp. B1, B2.

Hayes, Thomas C., "Behind the Iron Hand at Tenneco," *The New York Times*, January 6, 1992, pp. D1, D5.

Hayes, Thomas C., "Houston Investor's Magic Touch," *The New York Times*, July 1, 1989, pp. 29, 31.

Hicks, Jonathan P., "Steel Hits Hard Times Again," *The New York Times*, August 12, 1991, pp. D1, D6.

Hicks, Jonathan P., "The Takeover of American Industry" and "Foreign Owners Are Shaking Up the Competition," *The New York Times,* May 28, 1989, Business Section, pp. D1, D8, D9.

Hinds, Michael deCourcy, "Graduates Facing Worst Prospects in Last 2 Decades," *The New York Times*, May 12, 1992, pp. A1, A19.

Hymowitz, Carol, and Thomas O'Boyle, "Two Disparate Firms Find Keys to Success in Troubled Industries," *The Wall Street Journal*, May 29, 1991, pp. A1, A7.

Karr, Albert R., and Robert Tomsho, "Business Graduates Scrap for Scarce Jobs," *The Wall Street Journal,* May 19, 1992, p. B1.

Keiser, Barbie E., "Practical Competitor Intelligence," *Planning Review,* September/October 1987, pp. 14-19, 45.

Linden, Dana Wechsler, Jody Brenner, and Randall Lane, "Another Boom Ends," *Forbes,* January 20, 1992, pp. 76-79.

Lohr, Steve, "The Best Little Bank in America," Business Section, *The New York Times*, July 7, 1991, pp. 1, 4.

Lohr, Steve, "Pulling One's Weight at the New I.B.M.," *The New York Times*, Business Section, July 5, 1992, pp. 1-6.

Lohr, Steve, "Sheffield Knife Maker Beats the Odds," *The New York Times,* April 15, 1989, pp. 35, 46. A detailed study of the company's strategic response to competitive market conditions has been done by Baden Fuller at the London Business School.

Machalaba, Daniel, Caleb Solomon, and Robert Johnson, "Tenneco, Recruiting New Chairman, Gets Ready for a Shakeup," *The Wall Street Journal,* August 8, 1991, pp. A1, A4.

Markoff, John, "Slogging Up PC Hill at I.B.M.," *The New York Times,* Business Section, May 10, 1992, pp. 1, 6.

Markoff, John, "A New Battleground For IBM," *The New York Times*, February 9, 1990, pp. D1, D3.

Markoff, John, "The Niche That IBM Can't Ignore," *The New York Times*, Business Section, April 23, 1989, pp. 1, 12.

Markoff, John, "The Smart Alecks at Sun Are Regrouping," *The New York Times*, Business Section, April 28, 1991, p. 4.

Markowitz, Zane N., "Hidden Sector Competitor Analysis," *Planning Review*, September/October 1987, pp. 20-29.

McCarroll, Thomas, "The Humbling of a Computer Colossus," *Time*, May 20, 1991, pp. 40-44.

McGill, Douglas C., "Sara Lee's Success with Brands," *The New York Times*, June 19, 1989, pp. D1, D3.

Melnbardis, Robert, "Wood Pulp Makers Run Expansion Spree," *The Wall Street Journal,* May 27, 1989, p. B8.

Mockler, Robert J., *Computer Software to Support Strategic Management Decision Making,* New York: Macmillan Publishing, 1992.

Mockler, Robert J., *Knowledge-based Systems for Strategic Planning*, Englewood Cliffs, NJ: Prentice Hall, 1989.

Norris, Floyd, "Win or Lose, Buyouts Do It Big," *The New York Times*, January 28, 1992, pp. D1, D8.

Pae, Peter, "Success of AT&T's Universal Card Puts Pressure on Big Banks to Reduce Rates," *The*

Wall Street Journal, February 4, 1992, pp. B1, B2.

Pollack, Andrew,"Doubts Trail Sun Microsystems," *The New York Times,* January 31, 1992, pp. D1, D6.

Pollack, Andrew, "Taking the Crucial Next Step at Genentech," *The New York Times,* Business Section, January 28, 1990, pp. 1, 6.

Porter, Michael, *Competitive Strategy,* New York: Free Press, 1980.

Rigdon, Joan E., "Kodak Tries to Prepare for Filmless Era Without Inviting Demise of Core Business," *The Wall Street Journal,* April 18, 1991, pp. B1, B7.

"Sara Lee CEO Profiles Strategies Behind Their Corporate Growth," *The Planning Forum Network,* January 1990, p. 1.

Selz, Michael, "Small Companies Thrive by Taking Over Some Specialized Tasks for Big Concerns," *The Wall Street Journal,* September 11, 1991, pp. B1, B2.

Sharif, Pamela D., "Gloria Jean's Leads the Specialty Coffee Stampede," *The New York Times,* August 11, 1991, p. 11.

Stanat, Ruth, *The Intelligent Corporation,* New York: Amacon, 1990.

Vella, Carolyn, and John McGonagle, *Improved Business Planning Using Competitive Intelligence,* Westport, CT: Quorum Books, 1988.

Vella, Carolyn, and John McGonagle, "Shadowing Markets: A New Competitive Intelligence Technique," *Planning Review,* September/ October 1987, pp. 36-38.

Verity, John W., "Surprise! The New IBM Really Looks New," *Business Week,* May 18, 1992, pp. 124-26.

Washington Researchers Publishing, *How to Find Information About Companies,* 2612 P Street, NW Washington, DC 20007, 1989.

Washington Researchers Publishing, *Understanding the Competition: A Practical Guide to Competitive Analysis,* 2612 P Street, NW Washington, DC 20007, 1984.

Webster, James L., William E. Reif, and Jeffrey S. Bracker, "The Manager's Guide to Strategic Planning Tools and Techniques," *Planning Review,* November/December 1989, pp. 4-12, 48.

Wiseman, Charles, *Strategic Information Systems,* Homewood, IL: Richard D. Irwin, 1988.

Woo, Carolyn Y., and A.C. Cooper, "Strategies of Effective Low Share Businesses," *Strategic Management Journal,* July/ September 1981, pp. 301-318.

Woo, Carolyn Y., "Market Share Leadership — Not Always So Good," *Harvard Business School,* January/February 1984, pp. 50-65.

PART THREE

FORMULATING STRATEGIES

CHAPTER 6

COMPANY RESOURCES AND COMPARATIVE COMPETITIVE POSITION

The objective of this chapter is to help readers to

- Analyze company resources
- Assess a company's strengths and weaknesses in opportunity and key-to-success areas
- Evaluate a company's comparative competitive position
- Explore the implications of the comparative evaluation
- Make decisions in specific reader situations

This chapter continues the discussion of the strategy formulation tasks outlined in Figure 6-1. This chapter first evaluates a company's resource levels in various management, marketing, manpower, production/operations, research and development, and finance areas. A company's strengths, especially its "core competencies" (what it does or can do very well), are identified along with its major weaknesses [Norkus 1991].

This resource profile is then studied in relation to critical market factors — such as anticipated opportunities and threats, keys to success, and competitor strengths and weaknesses in these same areas. Through this process emerges a sense of what opportunities might best be pursued by the company under study.

In a sense, this chapter merely formalizes and structures something individuals continually do when faced with a competitive situation: they size up their position in relation to their opponents, and then estimate and search for ways to improve their chances of winning.

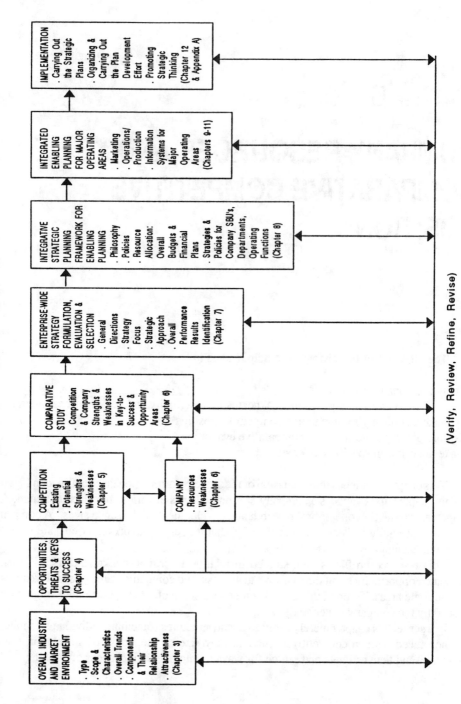

Figure 6-1: Strategic Management Tasks

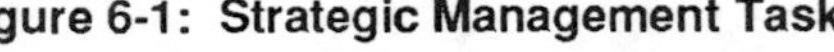

DEFINING THE COMPANY AND ANALYZING ITS RESOURCES

Every company has a strategic profile — some explicit or implicit sense of the kind of company it is, as well as other distinguishing characteristics which affect strategy formulation.

This sensing, which most often is not put into writing ("Survey" 1986), can be the first phase of a company's strategy definition. A company almost always evaluates what will happen if it continues doing what it is doing today in the future. For this reason, the company's current strategy, whether implicitly or explicitly defined, is often one of the alternative strategies evaluated.

Specific company resources in management and organization, marketing, operations/ production, computer information systems, finances, and accounting, as well as the impact of major interest groups which have a stake in a company, also need definition. In addition, other factors which may affect strategy formulation, such as business processes, corporate organization and culture, and owners' wishes, are identified. Company strengths, as well as weaknesses, are identified.

Resource studies are often called "audits," even though they go beyond the traditional accounting meaning of the word. They provide a framework for the study of the company's potential and stimulate thoughts about ways a company's strengths may be exploited strategically. In addition, these audits often suggest ways to improve company efficiency and effectiveness in general, as well as to identify major problems or other areas which relate to the strategic future of the company. The "Company" sections of the company studies in the Case Study section of this book would represent the preliminary fact-gathering phase of such audits in some situations.

Management and Organization

Areas examined when auditing a management situation are listed in Figure 6-2. Planning, organizing, and leadership questions are explored during this phase of the audit. Some of the gathered information may lead to the identification of problems which need to be dealt with regardless of future strategies. For example, low morale, high absenteeism, and poor planning practices can adversely affect any company in any situation. Such was the case at Detroit Diesel in 1987, when it was owned by General Motors and had only 3.2 percent of the heavy truck engine market. When he bought the company in 1988, Roger Penske changed the management philosophy and style by, for example, meeting quickly with employee groups, listening to their complaints, creating new incentive and profit-sharing programs to reduce absenteeism and increase productivity, and working closely with union leaders. These changes had earned Detroit Diesel a 28 percent share of the heavy truck engine market by June 1991 [White 1991].

A similar situation occurred at Salomon Inc., a brokerage firm, when conservative investor Warren Buffet became head of the firm after a trading scandal at the company in mid-1991. Buffet's management skills and conservative style and values changed the character of the firm substantially [Faison 1992].

The skills and values of the owner/managers in small companies will almost always impose limits on the kinds of business strategies possible, and so have an impact on the strategies

Figure 6-2: Sample Management Audit Questions

- How clearly stated are overall organizational goals, objectives, missions, policies, and other strategic plans, and how effectively are they communicated to managers?
- Is there a formal approach to strategic planning in the organization and how effective is it?
- To what degree do those involved in carrying out strategic plans participate in their development?
- How effective are the organization's monitoring of competitor's actions, industry and market changes, and management controls?
- To what degree is decision making authority delegated to operating managers?
- Are there formal organizational structures, with well-defined job descriptions and authority and responsibility relationships? How appropriate are they for perceived needs?
- How much cooperative or integrative decision making is there among managers in related functional areas? How sufficient is it for the perceived business needs?
- What is the status of morale at the management and employee levels?
- What are the turnover and absentee rates?
- How would you characterize the corporate culture and the values of owners and managers?
- Describe what you feel are the strengths and weaknesses of key company or strategic business unit executives.
- What leadership styles are favored by key company or strategic business unit managers?
- Describe the backgrounds and experience of key company or strategic business unit managers.
- What is the average age of the company's top management?
- To what degree are there incentives and rewards for longer term performance in relation to strategic goals?
- Describe the management and employee development and training programs, and estimate their effectiveness.
- Where there are unions, how would you rate union-management relations?

formulated. This was the case at the small candy manufacturer and regional baked goods company described later in this chapter.

The impact of management's attitudes on a company's success was dramatically illustrated at Union Carbide. After the Bhopal disaster in 1984, management turned "cautious and insular (and) reacted defensively to threats and opportunities rather than taking advantage of them." By 1991, internal studies at the company showed that its main chemical operations ranked very low in 9 or 10 critical areas when compared to competitors [McMurray 1992]. One of the major factors that reportedly brought the Bank of New England to the brink of ruin was the "overreaching drive, sloppy management, and hubris" of its CEO, Walter J. Connolly, Jr. [Bacon 1991; Greenwald 1991; Wayne 1990].

These audits will also include an analysis of existing business processes, organization structure and culture, and staffing and control factors. These areas of an audit are covered in depth in Chapter 12 and so are omitted here.

Marketing

Many marketing areas are examined, including customers, products, sales, service, distribution, and planning.

Customers. This analysis begins by defining the customers, their locations, and their key characteristics. The nature of the customer/seller relationship is also an important factor, since brand recognition can be a strength on which to build new strategies. This was the case at the baked goods company described later in this chapter.

At times, customer/seller relationships can force companies to make strategic moves to protect their markets. For example, Chrysler bought three rent-a-car firms at premium prices in 1989 and 1990 to protect its competitive position in the rent-a-car market after other automobile companies had invested in and purchased rent-a-car companies [Levin 1990].

Questions explored during this phase of the audit are listed in Figure 6-3. This checklist, as well as the ones in Figures 6-2, 6-4, and 6-5, simply suggest areas that might be investigated. Not all items apply in all situations, so the lists are used selectively in specific individual situations.

Products. Analyzing a company's products can lead to the identification of strategic opportunities in related product areas. For example, Gillette pursued such a strategy in the 1980s, under Colman Mockler's leadership, when it focused on strengthening its positions in product areas where it had very strong competitive advantages, rather than on expanding into newer product lines [Chakravorty 1991; McKibben 1990]. Faced with a maturing adult market in 1992,

Figure 6-3: Sample Marketing Audit Questions

- How broad is the product line?
- Are there any products which should be phased out?
- How dependent is the company on one or two very profitable products or product lines?
- How vulnerable is the company product line to competing products?
- At what stage of development and maturity is the company's present product line?
- How broad is the customer base?
- How effective and cost efficient is the customer service operation?
- Estimate the degree of brand loyalty.
- Describe customer perceptions of the product line and the company.
- What is the company's pricing strategy and how effective is it?
- How effective is company advertising and promotions?
- Describe the company's distribution system.
- What is the extent of market coverage?
- How adequate and effective are the company's promotions and public relations operations?
- Describe the company's sales force organization and how effective and cost efficient is each of its elements in relation to the competition.
- Does the sales force have high morale? Is the sales force stable and coeffective?
- Does the sales compensation level and structure provide adequate incentive and rewards?
- How effective is the marketing intelligence system in providing accurate, sufficient, and timely information about competitive market developments in relation to customers, products, suppliers, competitors, and distributors?
- Are marketing costs under control?
- Are sales forecasts well-founded, accurate, and used in market planning?
- Are sales quotas realistically developed in light of market conditions?
- How effective is the company's system for generating and screening new product ideas?
- Does the company adequately research and test new products before introducing them?

the Dannon Company, makers of yogurt, began testing children's versions of its product, a market which yogurt companies had had little success in previously [Foltz 1992].

Figure 6-3 shows how this analysis not only identifies strengths or core company competencies to build on, but also identifies weaknesses in existing product lines. These weaknesses, such as poor quality, poor service, or noncompetitive features, may represent opportunities, since correcting these weaknesses will produce benefits no matter what the strategy formulated. Such studies led many companies in the early 1990s to pledge guaranteed service and apply considerable pressure on suppliers to substantially improve their service and quality [Emshwiller 1991; Pearl 1991]. Polaroid, recognizing the declining markets of many of its major products, in 1991 introduced more new products than at any time in the company's history [Rifkin 1991]. Other weaknesses, such as a lack of patent protection and of unique and difficult-to-reproduce product characteristics, may limit what strategies can be pursued, since such weaknesses may affect the ease with which competitors can develop competing or substitute products at lower costs.

Sales. The internal strategic audit also identifies what a company does or does not do well in the selling and promotion area. The strength of the sales force can at times dictate what strategy to pursue. For example, the major resource of the baked goods company studied later on in this chapter was its strong sales force in a four-state area, which called on 85 percent of the food stores in the region. Exploiting this strength or core competency became a key element of the company's strategy.

In 1985 all of Fuller Brush Company's sales came from door-to-door sales. However, with more women working, fewer women were at home for Fuller's salesperson to call on. What had been a sales strength was thus becoming a weakness. In 1987, Fuller introduced its first mail-order catalog and opened its first retail store. In this way, the company built a new strategy around its other two strengths — brand recognition and products — to compensate for its weaknesses in its original area of strength, door-to-door selling. Its sales rose by 17 percent and 25 percent in the two years after it began mail-order and retail store sales, and in 1989 less than 60 percent of the company's sales came from door-to-door sales [Berg 1989].

Service. Service skills and facilities are especially critical in today's economy, where service businesses are growing rapidly and the consumer is demanding more services and personal attention. For example, British Airways encountered major service problems in the early 1980s, and this was reflected in substantial company losses. Under new leadership, in 1983 programs introduced to upgrade service and "put people first" improved profits substantially. In this case, the analysis led not only to new strategic directions for the company, but also to strategies that focused on better meeting critical success factor requirements in the industry [Maremont 1990].

Distribution. Distribution involves getting the product from the company to the customer. A company may have its own distribution system, or use outside wholesalers, retailers, brokers, agents, middlemen, vendors, or other distributors. A company's ability to effectively use and control distribution channels — whether or not they are owned and operated by the company — can have an important impact on long-term success. For example, Atlantic Richfield increased its market position significantly by using the company's existing outlets to sell food and beverages in the early 1990s [Rose 1991].

The purpose of the study of these marketing areas, as of the other functional areas, is to first become familiar with what the company is doing, that is, how the situation works. This analysis often leads to improvements in existing operations areas critical to future success. For instance, based on an analysis of existing operations, Hewlett-Packard reorganized in 1990 — reshuffling sales and regrouping products according to the way they are sold, eliminating excessive layers of management, redesigning advertising, reducing employee costs, and making HP computer products compatible. Industry analysts reported that the reorganization had paid off and revitalized the company [Alster 1991; Yoder 1991]. Hewlett-Packard also provides an outstanding example of how a company built on its strengths in developing a major strategic position in laser printers (almost $3 billion in sales) [Pollack 1992].

Operations/Production

The analysis of a company's strengths and weaknesses in this area (1) provides an understanding of the company's present position, (2) suggests areas for general improvements to operations, and (3) helps in finding ways to compete more effectively.

Pratt & Whitney did such an audit in the early 1990s after it lost ground to its competitors. One of its key steps was to match its major competitor's — General Electric's — lower production costs through layoffs, plant closings, and other internal efficiencies. In addition, the company entered into risk-reducing product development international alliances, and vastly improved its customer service and parts supply inventory [Holusha 1992].

As seen in Figure 6-4, the checklist of questions to explore for the operations/production area includes such factors as facilities, workforce, quality, inventory, supply source, and research and development.

Facilities. Facilities are examined from a number of viewpoints: suitability of location to customers and suppliers; adequacy of capacity and layout; production effectiveness; costs and controls; currency of process technology; and degree of integration of operations/production processes. A profile of the company's effectiveness in the production of goods and services is developed. Depending on the situation, this may lead to major strategic changes.

After examining competitive forces and its existing facilities' ability to compete effectively, Inland Steel invested jointly with Nippon Steel Corporation in two new high-tech steel manufacturing facilities in an effort to remain competitive [Hicks 1991]. In contrast, A.B. Volvo, the Swedish car manufacturer, in mid-1991 was considering abandoning its innovative team facility in Uddevalla, Sweden, where individual cars are built by teams, rather than built on an assembly line. Cars at the Uddevalla facility, which was built in 1988, took 50 man-hours to build, versus the 20 man-hours it took to build a car in Japan [Prokesch 1991].

Workforce. Quality and flexibility of the labor force may also be strategically significant in many situations. For example, to be competitive in the honeycomb ceramic components business, Corning Inc. needed a stable workforce (the training process took about two years) capable of working with flexible production schedules. An analysis of existing facilities indicated that a stable workforce would be difficult to maintain at these facilities. To overcome this problem, Corning opened a new production plant in Blacksburg, Virginia, and negotiated

Figure 6-4: Production/Operations Audit Checklist

- Estimate raw material cost and availability.
- Describe present supplier relationships.
- How dependent is the company on one or two suppliers?
- Where are the facilities located in relation to customers and suppliers?
- What is the average utilization rate of facilities?
- How technically up-to-date and modern are productions and facilities?
- How labor intensive are operations or production?
- How do labor turnover and absentee rates compare with industry averages?
- How do productivity levels compare with others in the industry?
- How would you rate employee morale?
- Estimate the status of labor relations.
- How modern and up-to-date are facilities and their designs?
- How effective and cost efficient are production processes or operations?
- How effective and cost efficient is inventory management, both from a production and marketing viewpoint?
- How effective and cost efficient is the production control system?
- How effective and cost efficient is the quality control system?
- Estimate the adequacy of the product or service and development effort.
- How effective are the mechanisms for getting products or services tested and marketed?
- How effective is research and development planning in relation to company strategic objectives?

separately for the plant with the union [Holusha 1989].

On the other hand, after its first year of operation, a very large experimental Grand Union store in Kingston, New York, reported that turnover at the clerical level (the store clerks wear roller skates because of the size of the store) was close to 100 percent. At the same time, sales and profits were above expectations. In this instance high turnover was not a measure of performance, but a condition of the business — success depended on operating effectively with lower-paid, younger people [Charnow 1989].

Quality. In many industries quality is no longer just a way to distinguish a company from the competition; it is necessary for survival in the marketplace of the 1990s. For example, after examining its production facilities, Kodak opted for an off-site strategy. It assembled an off-site product development team to design a new low-cost microfilmer and then created a new production system whereby one person assembled a complete microfilmer to insure both quality and competitive low cost [Holusha 1989].

Inventory. Since they can affect a company's ability to compete strategically, inventory control and usage are also examined. They can affect a company's ability to meet just-in-time delivery requirements of major customers. Efficient control and usage can also affect a company's ability to compete effectively on a cost basis or to be a full-line supplier to major customers.

Supply sources. Because of its potential impact on strategic positioning in some industries, where appropriate a company audit includes the source of supply. For example, a situation may involve purchasing raw materials or other supplies from a limited number of suppliers, which in turn limits the ability of a company to change suppliers and secure competitive prices. On the other hand, favorable supply contracts might create competitive strengths.

Research and development. In competitive market situations where research and development is a significant factor, such as the drug industry [Freudenheim 1992], capabilities in this area are studied. These studies can lead to innovative strategic moves. For example, Kodak, faced with rapidly changing technology such as the development of the filmless camera which threatened its core business, set up a major research facility in Japan. One of its objectives was to conduct serious research in Japan, and then transfer the Japanese methods back to the United States [Rigdon 1991; Sanger 1991].

Computer Information Systems

Today, computer information systems are included in most company audits because of their importance both to survival and to gaining competitive edges in marketing, operations/production, and finance. In the banking industry, for example, success depends on having advanced computer data processing and information systems, which not only process data quickly and cheaply, but also allow banking at convenient locations and times (24-hour automated teller machines) and more personalized services (coordinated and combined full-service accounts) [Lohr 1991].

According to Donald Burr, former president of People's Express, a $2 billion airline which went bankrupt, the company's failure was due to competitors' powerful computerized reservation systems ("yield pricing" systems). These systems helped American Airlines, for instance, to match People's low fares on seats that otherwise would have gone unsold, while selling other seats at full price. As summed up by Burr, "We were obliterated by the computer chip ...we didn't see the power of the computerized reservation system until it was too late" [Scheier 1989].

Finance and Accounting

A company's past and present financial performance — especially as related to the owners' or managers' perceptions of what that performance should be — are examined to measure how well a company is doing financially. One way to do this is through financial ratio analysis. Figure 6-5 summarizes the most commonly used financial ratios. These ratios give some idea of how a company is performing in such areas as growth, profitability, funds available for expansion, leveraged use of debt, and inventory, accounts receivable, and other asset usage efficiency.

Such analyses are useful in determining the availability of resources — such as funds for potential strategic moves — and in determining the current effectiveness of the company's asset usage. The analyses are also used to evaluate present company performance and to measure the ability of the company to withstand competitive business pressures and economic downturns.

In formulating strategies, it is helpful to view a company from a capital investment perspective, that is, an investment whose value is measured in terms of the present value of its eventual overall return as measured by the financial marketplace [Fahey 1988; Gale 1988]. That return may be any combination of earnings flow or capital gains over the period of the investment or any other measure of value based on the worth of the company as perceived by financial markets.

Figure 6-5: Finance and Accounting Audit Checklist

Ratio	How It Is Calculated Using a Company's Most Recent Performance Results	What It Tells Us About the Company
Growth Ratios		
Sales	Percentage growth in total sales from prior year to current year	Growth rate of company in sales
Income	Percentage growth in profits from prior year to current year	Growth rate of company in profits
Earnings per share	Percentage growth in EPS from prior year to current year	Growth rate of company in EPS
Dividends per share	Percentage growth in dividends per share from prior year to current year	Growth rate of company in dividends per share
Profitability Ratios		
Gross profit margin	Sales less cost of goods sold / Company sales	The total margin available to pay operating expenses and produce a profit
Operating profit margin	Earnings before interest and taxes / Company sales	Profitability without concern for interest and taxes
Net profit margin	Net income / Company sales	After-tax profits per dollar of sales
Return on total assets (ROA)	Net income / Total assets	The net return on the investment in assets
Return on stockholder's equity (ROE)	Net income / Total stockholders' equity	The net return on the stockholders' investment (ROI)
Net earnings per share (EPS)	Net income / # of shares of common stock outstanding	Earnings for each share of common stock
Price-earning ratio	Current market price per share / Net income per share for most current 12-month period	The number of dollars paid by stock buyers for each dollar of annual net earnings
Liquidity Ratios		
Current ratio	Current assets / Current liabilities	The company's ability to meet its short-term obligations
Quick ratio	Current assets - inventory / Current liabilities	The company's ability to meet its short-term obligations without selling its inventories
Leverage Ratios		
Total Debt-to-total-assets ratio	Total debt / Total assets	The percentage of total funds provided by creditors
Total Debt-to-equity ratio	Total debt / Total stockholder's equity	The relation between total debt and equity
Long-term-debt-to-equity ratio	Long-term debt / Total stockholder's equity	The relation between total long-term debt and equity
Times-interest-covered ratio	Profits before interest and taxes / Total interest expenses	The extent that earnings cover annual interest expenses
Activity Ratios		
Inventory turnover	Company sales / Average finished goods inventory	The efficiency of inventory policies - whether a company is carrying excess inventories
Accounts-receivable turnover	Annual credit sales / Average accounts receivable	Whether a company is carrying excessive accounts receivable
Average collection period	Average accounts receivable / Total sales/365 days	The average length of time in days it takes a company to collect on credit sales
Fixed-assets turnover	Company sales / Total fixed assets	Efficiency of asset usage
Total-assets turnover	Company sales / Total company assets	Whether a company's investment in assets is justified by the annual sales they produce

One source of hidden value — that is, value not shown on the company's balance sheet — would be undervalued assets. These assets might be land, buildings, patents, inventory, or any other item whose present market value is greater than the purchase price or depreciated book value of the item. Another unrealized value occurs when a company's book value or the value of its components exceeds the present market value of the common stock. This was the case at Tenneco in 1992 after Michael Walsh took over as CEO [Hayes 1992]. Analyses of these kinds of financial resources are often the basis of leveraged buyouts.

Identifying these and similar financial resources can often suggest ways to improve a company's return on investment and to stimulate new strategic directions, just as similar analyses in the marketing and production areas can lead to operational and strategic improvements in those areas.

For example, while turning back three takeover attempts during the 1980s, Gillette asked itself a simple question: If our company is so valuable to these outsiders, why don't we reexamine our company from their viewpoint and do what they would do to realize greater values for our stockholders? As a result of this analysis, Gillette's management took several strategic operational and strategic steps, including

- Borrowing close to $1 billion
- Reducing capitalization by buying back close to 20 percent of its common stock at market prices, which were considerably higher than per-share book value
- Refocusing on establishing strong positions in products and markets where Gillette had exhibited strengths, and selling off many divisions and eliminating products whose future earnings prospects did not appear to be superior
- Making management realignments at all levels of the company to place more emphasis on entrepreneurial decision making

These steps were possible because

- Gillette's product line consisted largely of high-margin, relatively low-priced personal-care products, giving the company a high cashflow and making it possible to cover additional interest payments on borrowing
- Gillette's main products — razors and related items such as shaving cream — had enormous potential in such areas as Mexico and South American countries where use of blades and shaving cream is at times less than 20 percent (contrasted with over 90 percent penetration of U.S. markets)
- Gillette's business was not capital intensive
- Gillette's brand names had enormous recognition and market position, an inestimable value which does not show on the balance sheet
- Operating earnings were sufficiently high so that full tax benefits would be realized by deducting the increased interest costs from taxable income

This analysis of hidden financial resources in such companies as Gillette is not intended to illustrate specific financial strategies which might be used. Rather, it shows that a careful analysis of the financial situation can lead to imaginative strategy formulation. The specific techniques used are often unique to that situation, having been created to meet specific situation requirements.

In the analysis of the financial situation, the obvious analytical focus is on income statement, balance sheet, and cashflow analysis using financial ratios and other analytical tools. The creative task is to go beyond these ratios and use the financial analysis to identify previously unrecognized resources (and financial weaknesses) and then imaginatively plan ways to strategically exploit them.

Interest Groups

Interest groups with a stake in the company and enough clout to make company management pay attention to them are included in a resource study. These groups would include: owners (shareholders), customers, suppliers, creditors, unions, franchise holders, government agencies, society (local or in general), and company employees.

Stakeholder pressures can create substantial strategic problems for companies. During the 1980s, shareholder pressure forced many companies to sell their operations in South Africa. During Exxon's Alaskan oil spill crisis in 1989, Exxon spent over $1 billion for clean up and encountered major image problems which adversely affected company operations. In addition, other oil companies, such as ARCO, were also subjected to the threat of punitive actions by a variety of governmental, consumer, and shareholder groups because of the publicity generated by Exxon's problems [Stevenson 1989].

Studies of stakeholder relations also can lead to new strategic opportunities. For example, the authors of the books *When Giants Learn to Dance* and *The Knowledge Links: How Firms Compete Through Strategic Alliances*, study several dozen examples of large companies that profited from forming strategic alliances with suppliers and customers by sharing technology, and with unions by wage concessions in exchange for shared ownership [Badaracco 1990; Kanter 1989].

IDENTIFYING A COMPANY'S STRENGTHS AND WEAKNESSES IN OPPORTUNITY AND KEY-TO-SUCCESS AREAS

This section and the following sections continue the internal company analysis by matching the company's strengths and weaknesses with the market opportunities and threats, and with key-to-success factors. Subsequently, these company strengths and weaknesses in opportunity and key-to-success areas are compared with those of competitors.

The ultimate focus of all company resource analyses is on the opportunities and keys to success identified during the competitive market study described in Chapter 4. In the strategy formulation tasks described in this section, a company's strengths and weaknesses are studied in relation to specific competitive market opportunity and key-to-success areas.

For example, in the baked goods situation (the *Superb Biscuits* company study included in the case study section of this book) discussed in Chapters 4 and 5, the company's position in relation to the key success factors in two general opportunity areas —products and outlets — was defined in some detail:

a. *Standardized Products.* The company has a strong brand name in its four-state region of operations, high market penetration (mass distribution) in food outlets in the area, a wide product line, an aggressive personalized sales/distribution system, and good product quality. It does not have costs under control either in manufacturing (with present machinery) or in sales/distribution (with present sales organization and product line) and so may have future problems in maintaining price competitiveness.

b. *Specialty Cookie Products.* The company has a good brand name and a sales/support force which visits most stores in the area. These people live in the region, and as a result are able to track new products introductions immediately and to monitor local tastes. The company has a wide distribution network both to large and small outlets. It has had some limited success in developing new specialized cookies on its own, but the company is weak in that area. It has a relatively flexible production process, and is small enough to respond quickly to market needs. In general, it knows the territory very well and meets many of the requirements for success in this opportunity area.

c. *Supermarket Chain Outlets.* The company has strong relations with both the individual chain store managers and with the chain buyers. It appears to do what is necessary to maintain shelf space and position, by offering sales incentives and maintaining a well-known brand name and wide product line—all keys to success in the supermarket retail area. It also has been price competitive and so able to maintain the volume needed to justify the shelf space. The company's limited financial resources makes its ability to continue to do this in the future questionable.

d. *Independent Store Outlets.* Although the company has contacts with independent store managers/owners, its distribution system is not yet cost effective to these outlets. Its ability to produce a flow of new products appropriate for this market is not yet proven.

In addition, other factors which might be useful in the later stages of strategy formulation were also identified:

a. *Sales Force.* The company's major competitive strength is its sales force, which provides access to and strong relations with almost 85 percent of the food outlets in its four-state area. If another company were to acquire this company, it would likely pay a premium price for this substantial market penetration. This suggests that any strategy which takes advantage of this strength would be a promising one to explore.

b. *BrandName.* The company has excellent brand name recognition in its four-state region. This suggests that strategies which build on that name will be good ones to explore.
c. *Product Line.* The company has a wide line of good quality products. These products are comparable with those of its major competitors.

This evaluation of the strengths and weaknesses of the company in critical areas is summarized in Figure 6-6.

Potential problems are also identified. In the baked goods company, owner/manager goals could be a problem. The young new president (who controlled substantial stock through his family) seemed enamored of automation. He would therefore likely favor any strategy built on expanding in the standardized cookie area, where such automation is a key to success. Balancing this, because he was young and relatively new to the job, he did not yet have full control of company decision making.

A major threat to its present niche strategy, which should also be assessed, is that the company seems unable to maintain its straddle position strategy between the big three and six smaller competitors within its four-state area, a sort of "big fish in a little pond" strategy. This is apparent from the flat sales and profits during the past three years. Competitive pressures from the big three in the future will probably do even greater damage to the company's present strategic position.

Figure 6-6: Company's Strength and Weaknesses in Key-to-Success and Opportunity Areas

a. Products	
Standardized	
1. Resources/price competitive	Fairly limited
2. Mass market presence	They have in their region
3. Brand/quality reputation	They have in their region
Specialty	
1. New product capability	They have some limited proven
2. Market intelligence	They have potential
3. Flexible production/org.	They seem to have
4. Market access/presence	They have in their region
5. Brand recognition	They have in their region
b. Outlets	
Chains	
1. Strong store relations	They have in their region
2. Chain buyer relations	They have in their region
3. Wide product line	They have at present
4. Promotional incentives	They have capability
Independents	
1. Distribution cost control	They have a problem here
2. Strong store relations	They have in their region
3. Appropriate product line	To some extent
4. Promotional incentives	Assumed they do

Another potential problem is that the size and extent of opportunities in the specialty cookie area were unknown at the time of the study.

The above statements, which cover strengths and weaknesses in key-to-success areas (Figure 6-6), and the statement summaries of potential threats are critical assumptions. In every company strategy formulation project, similar summary statements which identify these key assumptions about the future must be prepared from the facts uncovered during the industry and competitive market analyses. These assumptions provide a necessary framework and structure for the remainder of the strategy formulation study.

ASSESSING A COMPANY'S OVERALL POSITION WITHIN THE COMPETITIVE ENVIRONMENT

A company's competitive position within the industry is also studied. Chapter 5 described ways to identify the competitors in the industry.

A planner might first specify which competitive group a company fits into, or its position in relation to other competitive groups. For example, in the baked goods situation, the company under study was positioned between the three big national and six smaller regional companies. An example of such a market position study was given in Figure 5-2.

How the company's relative position in the industry affects strategy formulation can be determined by asking:

- Is the company a dominant player in the market that can control aspects of the market through low-cost raw material supply arrangements?
- Or, is the company one of many equal competitors in the market, and dependent on other strategic variables, such as new product development?
- Or, does the company currently occupy a niche of some sort which is protected by some patent or other distinguishing market strength?

A first step then is to determine a company's position in a competitive market. A dominant position is preferable in many industries, since higher market shares often lead to higher return on investment. Sara Lee, in fact, states that its strategy is not to remain in fields where it does not occupy the number one or two positions [McGill 1989; "Sara Lee" 1990]. Maintaining a dominant position is not always possible, however, nor is it necessarily the only way to successfully position a company strategically.

The many aspects of competitive positioning that occur during the various phases of the company audit have been discussed in this chapter. Such thinking is useful in identifying a company's competitive position in general terms. For example:

- A competitive geographic sales and distribution strength, such as at the baked goods company, which can be exploited strategically in the future
- A competitively weak financial position, which may require a niche strategy in a market where

substantial financial strength is needed to maintain a leadership position, such as at A & W Root Beer

Other competitive market positions which can be identified in general terms during the company audit might include

- Favorable access to supply sources
- Strong ties with government or community buying groups
- Research and development strengths
- Skills or market ties of specific managers
- Patent protection
- Production strengths

THE COMPANY VERSUS THE COMPETITION: COMPARATIVE COMPETITIVE POSITION EVALUATION

While identifying a company's competitive position in general terms can stimulate successful strategy formulation, very often the task is not that simple. More precise studies are needed to provide specific guidelines for the operational planning needed to carry out selected strategies effectively. These studies take into account the major areas covered so far in the structured situation analysis described in PARTS TWO and THREE:

- The special characteristics of your industry
- The opportunities, threats, and keys to success in your competitive market and industry
- The existing and anticipated competitors and their strengths and weaknesses in areas critical to success
- The strengths and weaknesses of the company under study in these same critical success areas

In other words, planners focus on the specific opportunity areas and key-to-success requirements identified and on specific competitors or groups of competitors, and then compare their own company's strengths and weaknesses to competitors' strengths and weaknesses in critical areas affecting success.

The evaluation of relative positions is often reduced to quantitative measures. Figures 6-7 and 6-8 show such a reformulation of the results of a study in the baked goods company situation.

Figure 6-7 reduces the earlier judgments made in Figures 6-3 and 6-6 to three values (weak, good, strong). In the last two columns, the position of the company under study to each competitor group is rated. The rating values are 0 where the company's strength equals the competition's. It is either one or two pluses or minuses for the degree to which the company is stronger or weaker than the competition.

Such evaluations can be taken one step further, using a structured approach like the one shown in Figure 6-8. There the comparative weights are accumulated and a weighted value is

Figure 6-7: Comparative Evaluation of Competitor's and Company's Strengths and Weaknesses in Key-to-Success and Opportunity Areas

	Competitor Groups				
	Company A	**Big Three**	**Little Six**	**Compare Weight* (1)**	**(2)**
a. Products					
Standardized					
1. Resources/price competitive	Weak	Strong	Weak	- -	0
2. Mass market presence	Strong	Strong	None	0	++
3. Brand/quality reputation	Strong	Strong	?	0	+
Specialty					
1. New product capability	Strong	Good	Good	+	0
2. Market intelligence	Strong	Weak	Good	++	+
3. Flexible production/org.	Strong	Weak	Strong	+	+
4. Market access/presence	Strong	Strong	Good	0	+
5. Brand recognition	Strong	Strong	Good	0	+
b. Outlets					
Chains					
1. Strong store relations	Strong	Strong	Good	0	+
2. Chain buyer relations	Strong	Strong	?	0	+
3. Wide product line	Strong	Strong	Weak	0	++
4. Promotional incentives	Strong	Strong	Good	0	+
Independents					
1. Distribution cost control	Weak	Strong	?	-	?
2. Strong store relations	Strong	Strong	Good	0	+
3. Appropriate product line	Good	Good	Good	0	0
4. Promotional incentives	Strong	Strong	Good	0	+

* This is the result of comparing the strength of the company under study with the strength of each competitor group. For example, if the company is rated strong and the competitor weak, the rating would be ++. Where the company is strong and the competitor group strong, the rating would be 0.

assigned to the company's market position in relation to the competition's.

A planner is attempting to do here what is done in most competitive situations — size up his/her chances against the competition. The major difference is that here it is done within a rigorous strategic management framework:

> The keys to success and opportunities controlling outcomes in your own industry situation.

As might be suspected, the *process* is more important than the actual figures. The figures help to measure the differences more precisely and to think about implications of each factor's impact in very specific terms. The figures are not facts, since they are based on judgments; they are merely aids for thinking more precisely about a situation. The tools and the quantifications are only a means to an end. The objective is to build a strategy formulation basis that will offer clues to competitive edges in the market, or help develop ways to better exploit competitive edges a company already has.

These techniques force a detailed review of the specifics. This is tedious; however, it is very

Figure 6-8: Comparative Competitive Position Evaluation
Industry Opportunity Area Under Study: ______________________

(1) Industry & Market: Keys to Success	(2) Keys To Success Rethink, Reword, Reorder. Write Down Revised Version In Order of Importance	(3) Give Weight to Each Area (Total = 100)	(4) Our Company's Strengths in Key-to-Success Areas. Use Same Rating Scale as Used in Column (5)	(5) Individual Competitor's or Competitor Group's Strength in Relation to Each Key-To-Success Area (Scale: 1=Weak, 2=Average, 3=Strong)						(6) Competition's Overall Strength Average of Individual Competitor's Strength in Section (5)	(7) Rate Company's Strength Versus Competition's (3 = Greater 2 = Same 1 = Weaker)	(8) Weighted Value = Column (3) Times Column (7) (Highest possible Value = 100 x 3 = 300)
				C-1	C-2	C-3	C-4	C-5	C-6			
1.	1.											
2.	2.											
3.	3.											
4.	4.											
5.	5.											
6.	6.											
8.	8.											
9.	9.											
		Column (3) Total Should Equal 100								Total Score Of Column (8) =		
										Total Score of Column (8) As Percent of 300 =		

easy to get careless and overlook important aspects of a situation. Structured and systematic approaches such as the ones described in this section can help to overcome that problem.

There are no substitutes for good intuitive and creative thinking. Structured tools and techniques cannot do the study; they can only guide the planner through the study. What is important is what the planners do with the information as they evaluate and synthesize it, and as they manipulate the information through associative reasoning, applied imagination, creative stimulation, and other cognitive processes to draw implications of the information's future relevance.

EXPLORING THE IMPLICATIONS OF THE COMPARATIVE EVALUATION: THE FIRST LOOK

As the situation analysis progresses, the objective is to see what can be learned from the comparative competitive position evaluation results.

This is an exploratory process which involves looking at associations, drawing inferences, making assumptions, searching for tentative conclusions, then retesting and refining them — all in an effort to gain new insights. Here the concern is with the implications of facts, not just the facts themselves. What is described here is done at many stages throughout the strategy formulation process outlined in Figure 6-1.

This phase does not always proceed systematically. Often, paths of investigation lead nowhere. It is important to explore, experiment, test, hypothesize, and juxtapose ideas to stimulate associative reasoning. Any device for doing this, such as the ones shown in Figures 4-3 and 6-8, can help.

Not *all* company strengths or "core competencies" are the basis of strategic plans. And strategies that are built on one or two company strengths at times require strengthening a company's weak areas in order to successfully build a strategy around a company's strengths. For example, a small regional 10-store clothing store chain ceased operations in early 1992 because, even though it was widely known for its superior service and quality, it was not able to compete effectively with low-cost/low-price national chains in its area [Helliker 1991].

The following is a summary of an early attempt in the baked goods company situation to probe the results of the comparative competitive position evaluation and to explore the implications on strategy formulation.

a. *Standard Products*. Looking at the comparative weights, the company would appear to be fairly competitive with the three major competitors, except in the area of production and sales costs. Because the financial resource disadvantage is so great, the company does not appear able (nor does it seem prudent) to concentrate on competing solely in the standard products area, which will be the three major competitors' strongest area in the future.

b. *Specialty Products*. The company has a potential competitive edge over the three big and six small competitors in the specialty cookie area. There is some question about the ability of the three major competitors to overcome the disadvantages in this area in the future, because of their size.

c. *Chain Food Stores.* The company can probably maintain its strong advantage over the six small competitors in the chain food store area (a growth area) if it maintains its sales force, wide product line, strong product/brand recognition and position, and a competitive price level in standard products. It has been able to hold its own against the three major competitors in the past because of its strengths in all these areas, but this advantage could erode in the future under aggressive pressure from competitors in marketing and in production cost efficiencies.

d. *Independent Food Stores.* Currently the company does not appear to have sufficient volume or product variety to support a sales force calling directly on smaller independent food stores. These stores may, however, be good outlets for specialty products.

Several potential problems were also identified during these analyses which would later lead to amplifying and modifying the company's strategy.

a. The potential market for speciality cookies is uncertain. Although in retrospect it is quite clear that the specialty area did in fact grow substantially — both in the specialty cookies and specialty baked goods areas — at the time of the study that future was uncertain.

b. The company will have difficulty competing with the three major competitors in the standard cookie area due to its relatively weak financial resources and the demands of production automation.

c. It is uncertain how the three major competitors will respond to the perceived opportunities in the market. They could decide to become more aggressive in the specialty area. Nothing is known about possible responses of the six small competitors.

d. The company's new president seems to favor putting the company's limited resources into advanced automated production. However, he does not appear to be in absolute control of operations.

e. While the company is involved in the specialty area, its capabilities in this area are not strong.

f. Any tampering with the sales force would have a major impact on the company's competitive position, since the sales force is probably its most valuable asset. This sales force gives the company a strong position in and access to 85 percent of the food markets in its four-state area.

g. The company has been unable to deal on a cost-effective basis with smaller independent food stores.

The amount of exploratory work involved in developing these preliminary ideas will depend on the characteristics and complexity of the situation under study. It may also depend on the way a planner works, or, in some situations, on the amount of time the planner has available.

Whatever the situation to this point, within the context of the structured situation analyses done so far and the thinking upon which they are based, further efforts are needed to explore

Figure 6-9: Strategic Management Decision-Making Process

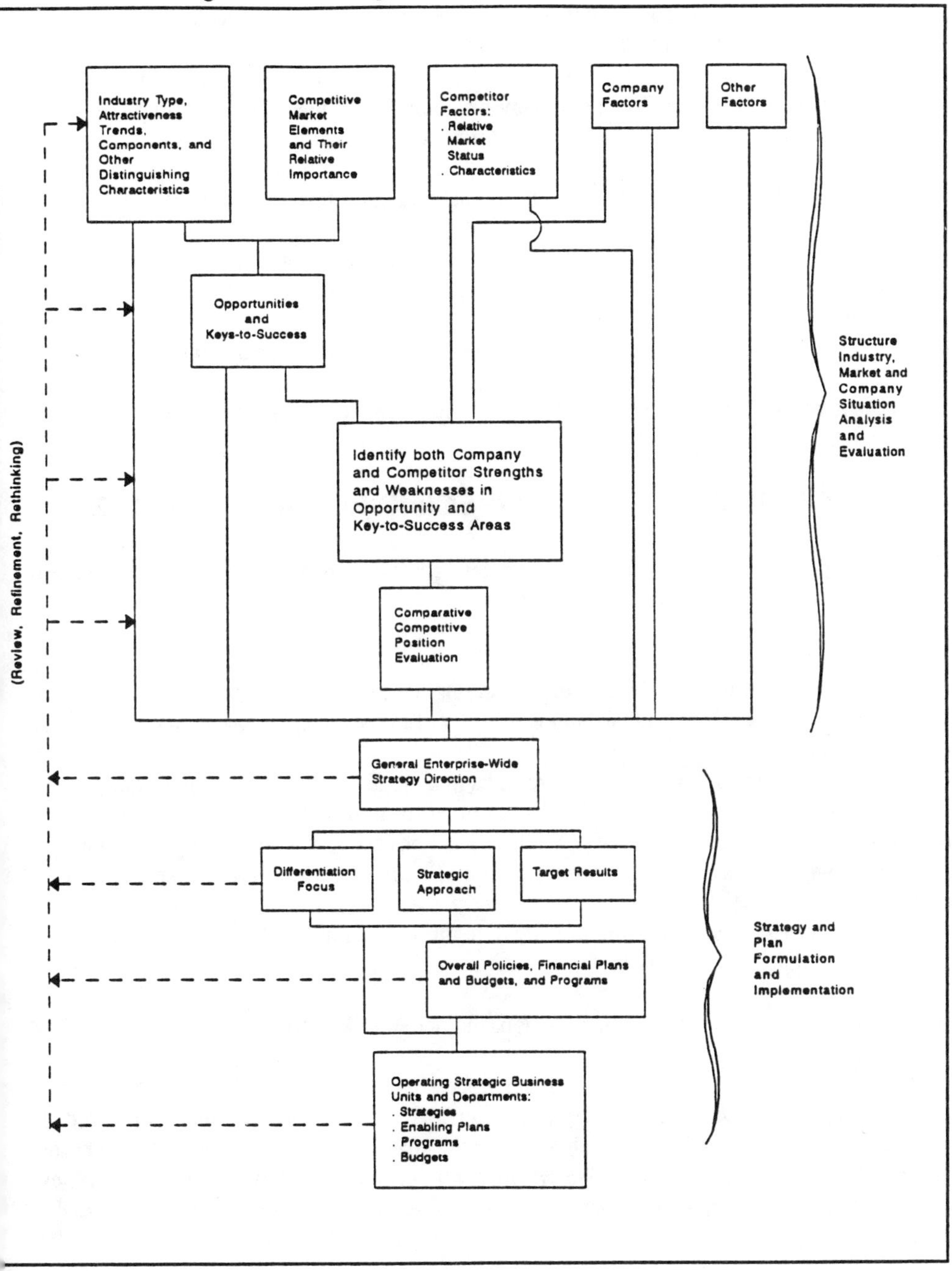

implications. Doing this often requires a planner to break molds, or structured frameworks, to be innovative and creative — to make so-called creative leaps. The focus of these further explorations would be on eventually determining

- Which strategies will best exploit a company's capabilities to meet success criteria
- Which strategies will work best when competition is considered

In other words, a planner is trying to formulate strategies that

- Describe new and innovative ways for a company to gain a competitive edge in the market in light of the company's and competitor's strengths and weaknesses in key-to-success and opportunity areas
- Enable a company to exploit more effectively its existing competitive advantages

These aspects of enterprise-wide strategy formulation are discussed in Chapter 7.

MAKING THESE DECISIONS IN SPECIFIC READER SITUATIONS

This chapter focuses on several critical strategy formulation tasks involved in this phase of the strategy formulation process, They include

- Auditing company resources, using as a guideline such questions as those covered in Figures 6-2 through 6-5, as well as analysis of organizational factors such as those covered in Chapter 12, and preparing a summary of that audit which identifies the company's overall position in the competitive market
- Preparing a summary of a company's strengths and weaknesses in opportunity and key-to-success areas, as shown in Figure 6-6 or in any other form the planner feels comfortable with
- Preparing a comparative competitive position evaluation, such as the one outlined in Figure 6-7
- Completing an analysis such as the one outlined in Figure 6-8, if useful in the situation under study
- Preparing a summary statement of preliminary thoughts on the implications of the company and comparative studies for strategy formulation

Whatever the nature and scope of the situation, the above tasks and manual tools will almost always be useful.

As seen in Figure 6-9, the decision-making processes described in this chapter relate to other strategy formulation areas. A *comparative competitive position evaluation* is prepared by analyzing various situation factors, such as *company strengths and weaknesses* — which are developed from the company audit (*company factors*) — and by studying the relation of these factors to the *competitive market opportunities and keys to success* and *competitor strengths and weaknesses.*

The tasks performed during this phase of the strategy formulation process in turn provide necessary background for other strategic management tasks. These other tasks include formulating enterprise-wide strategies, as well as enabling strategies and plans, within the context of the situation requirements.

Identifying decision-making approaches involved in doing this phase of the strategy formulation process, as has been done in this chapter, is helpful in learning how to formulate strategies. It is also useful in providing a basis for designing and using knowledge-based systems and other manual and computer-based systems that do and assist managers in doing and learning strategy formulation. As with the earlier phases of the strategy formulation process, portions of this phase have been replicated in semi-structured decision-making models. These models in turn have served as the basis for the knowledge-based systems discussed in Appendix A and throughout this book.

REVIEW QUESTIONS

1. Describe the critical business areas that are examined when analyzing a company's strengths and weaknesses.
2. Why is it so important to identify a company's strengths and weaknesses in opportunity and key-to-success areas?
3. Describe what is involved in auditing a company's resources and developing a structured profile of its strengths and weaknesses.
4. Describe some of the ways in which the analysis of a company's strengths and weaknesses in relation to the keys to success stimulates ideas about promising areas of opportunities for the company.
5. Discuss ways in which the analysis of a company's strengths and weaknesses in key-to-success areas can suggest strategic steps a company might take to improve its chances of success.
6. Give some examples of how past strengths might not always be strengths in the future competitive environment.
7. Describe what is done during the comparative competitive position evaluation.
8. Discuss the function of the comparative competitive position evaluation.
9. Describe the ultimate purpose of all the structured and semi-structured situation analyses discussed so far in Chapters 2, 3, 4, and 5 within the context of the strategy formulation process.

EXERCISES

1. Read one of the company studies in the Case Study section of this book whose title contains an actual company. Using this company study, write a report which covers the following tasks outlined at the end of the chapter:

- Audit company resources, using as a guideline such questions as those covered in Figures 6-2 through 6-5. Prepare a summary of that audit which identifies the company's overall position in the competitive market

- Prepare a summary of a company's strengths and weaknesses in opportunity and key-to-success areas, as shown in Figure 6-6 or in any other form with which the planner feels comfortable
- Prepare a comparative competitive position evaluation, such as the one shown in Figure 6-7
- Complete an analysis such as the one shown in Figure 6-8, if useful in the situation under study
- Prepare a summary statement of preliminary thoughts on the implications of the company and comparative studies for strategy formulation

2. Read recent issues of the periodicals referred to in the references section at the end of the chapter, or other related periodicals of your choice, and find a description of an industry of interest to you. Write a report on that industry covering the same tasks as listed in Exercise #1.

3. Read the *Superb Biscuits* company study in the Case Study section of this book. Review the discussions of this study (the "baked goods company") in this chapter, and in Chapters 4 and 5, and suggest ways in which the chapter discussions might be enhanced or modified based on your study of *Superb Biscuits.*

4. The disks accompanying this book contain several prototype KBS. If you have not done so already, follow the directions accompanying the disks to run a consultation using the system with the file name PLANNING.REV or AIMS.REV. If you wish, you might also print out the knowledge base and study it while you are running the system and restudying this chapter, in order to get a detailed picture of how strategy formulation decisions are made.

5. The disks accompanying this book contain basic financial simulation models. Following the guidelines given in the booklet accompanying the disks, choose a case from the nine companies listed in the booklet for which simulations are available and do a financial analysis related to the company study you have chosen.

REFERENCES

"It's Still a Difficult Environment: Thanks to a Hot Line of Workstations and Relatively Lean Staffing, Hewlett- Packard Is Doing Well in a Tough Market," *Forbes*, August 5, 1991, pp. 42-44.

Bacon, Kenneth H., and Ron Suskind, "U.S. Recession Claims Bank of New England as First Big Victim," *The Wall Street Journal*, January 7, 1991, pp. A1, A6.

Badaracco, Joseph L., *The Knowledge Link: How Companies Compete Through Strategic Alliances*, Boston, MA: Harvard Business School Press, 1990.

Berg, Eric N., "At Fuller Brush, New Ways to Get Foot in The Door," *The New York Times*, May 18, 1989, pp. D1, D2.

Chakravorty, Subrata N., "We Changed the Whole Playing Field: Triumph for Gillette's Colman Mockler — Technology as a Marketing Tool," *Forbes*, February 4, 1991, pp. 82-86.

Charnow, Jody, "Grand Stand in Kingston," *Sunday Freeman*, May 14, 1989, p. 39.

Emshwiller, John R., "Suppliers Struggle to Improve Quality as Big Firms Slash Their Vendor Rolls," *The New York Times*, August 16, 1991, pp. B1, B2.

Fahey, Liam, and Sam Felton, "The Bottom Line on Value-Based Planning," *Planning Review*, January/February 1988, pp. 4-5.

Faison, Seth, "Buffet to Leave Top Post at Salomon Soon," *The New York Times*, March 26, 1992, pp. D1, D18.

Foltz, Kim, "Dannon's Bet: Yogurt 'Just for Kids'," *The New York Times*, May 1, 1992, pp. D1, D9.

Freudenheim, Milt, "Keeping the Pipeline Filled at Merck," *The New York Times*, Business Section, February 16, 1992, pp. 1.

Gale, Bradley T., and Donald J. Swire, "Business Strategies That Create Value," *Planning Review*, March/April 1988, pp. 6-13, 47.

Greenwald, John, "Requiem for a Heavyweight," *Time*, January 21, 1991, pp. 54, 55.

Hayes, Thomas C., "Behind the Iron Hand at Tenneco," *The New York Times*, January 6. 1992, pp. D1, D5.

Helliker, Kevin, "A Family Retail Chain That Stresses Service Rings Up Its Last Sales," *The Wall Street Journal*, December 4, 1991, pp. A1, A6.

Hicks, Jonathan, "A Faster Path to Finished Steel," *The New York Times*, Business Section, April 7, 1991, p. 9.

Holusha, John, "Beating Japan at Its Own Game," *The New York Times*, Business Section, July 16, 1989, pp. 1, 8.

Holusha, John, "Pratt & Whitney's Comeback Bid," *The New York Times*, February 4, 1992, pp. D1, D6.

Kanter, Rosabeth Moss, *When Giants Learn to Dance*, New York: Simon and Schuster, 1989.

Levin, Doron P., "Chrysler, in Shift, to Buy Dollar Car Rental," *The New York Times*, June 27, 1990, pp. D1, D2.

Lohr, Steve, "The Best Little Bank in America," *The New York Times*, Business Section, July 7, 1991, pp. 1, 4.

Maremont, Mark, "How British Airways Butters Up the Passenger," *Business Week*, March 12, 1990, p. 94.

McGill, Douglas E., "Sara Lee's Success with Brands," *The New York Times*, June 19, 1989, pp. D1, D3.

McKibben, Gordon, "Gillette's Mockler: Going Out on Top," *The Boston Globe*, November 19, 1990, pp. A1, A7.

McMurray, Scott, "Union Carbide Offers Some Sober Lessons in Crisis Management," *The Wall Street Journal*, January 28, 1992, pp. A1, A9.

Norkus, Michael, President, Alliance Consulting Group, "Core Competencies: The Hidden Source of Competitive Success," Seminar, 60 East Club, New York, NY: The Planning Forum, October 9, 1991.

Pearl, Daniel, "More Firms Pledge Guaranteed Service," *The Wall Street Journal*, July 17, 1991, pp. B1, B4.

Pollack, Andrew W., "Hewlett's 'Consummate Strategist,'" *The New York Times*, March 10, 1992, pp. D1, D6.

Prokesch, Steven, "Edges Fray on Volvo's Brave New Humanistic World," *The New York Times*, Business Section, July 7, 1991, p. 7.

Rifkin, Glenn, "At Polaroid, More Than Snapshots," *The New York Times*, June 11, 1991, pp. D1, D7.

Rigdon, Joan E., "Kodak Tries to Prepare for Filmless Era Without Inviting Demise of Core Business," *The Wall Street Journal*, April 18, 1991, pp. B1, B7.

Rose, Frederick, "Atlantic Richfield C. Is Winning the West By Breaking the Mold," *The Wall Street Journal*, August 7, 1991, pp. A1, A7.

Sanger, David E., "When the Corporate Lab Goes to Japan: Companies Discovering the Wisdom of Doing R.&D. in Japan," *The Wall Street Journal*, Business Section, April 28, 1991, pp. 1-6.

"Sara Lee CEO Profiles Strategies Behind Their Corporate Growth," *The Planning Forum Network*, January 1990, p. 1.

Scheier, Robert L., "Obliterated by the Chip: The Crushing Out of People's Express," *PC Week*, November 13, 1989, p. 131.

Stevenson, Richard W., "Why Exxon's Woes Worry ARCO," *The New York Times*, Business Section, May 14, 1989, p. 1.

"Survey," Wall Street Journal, October 31, 1986, p. 1. Wayne, Leslie, "How One Man's Ego Wrecked a Bank," *The New York Times*, Business Section, March 4, 1990, p. 166.

White, Joseph B., "How Detroit Diesel, Out from Under GM, Turned Around Fast," *The Wall Street Journal*, August 16, 1991, pp. A1, A8.

Yoder, Stephen Kreider, "A 1990 Reorganization at Hewlett-Packard Already Is Paying Off," *The Wall Street Journal*, July 22, 1991, pp. A1, A4.

CHAPTER 7

FORMULATING ENTERPRISE-WIDE STRATEGIES AND STRATEGIC PLANS

The objective of this chapter is to help readers to

- Understand the different kinds and levels of enterprise-wide strategies
- Formulate enterprise-wide general strategic directions
- Identify a specific strategic focus in order to gain a competitive edge or differentiation
- Develop a strategic approach to carrying out enterprise-wide strategic directions and focus
- Anticipate and specify performance results
- Formulate and evaluate alternatives, and make a decision
- Make these decisions in specific situations

This chapter discusses the enterprise-wide strategy formulation, evaluation, and selection task shown in Figure 7-1. The decisions made during this phase are based on the structured situation analyses described in Chapters 3 through 6.

DIFFERENT KINDS AND LEVELS OF ENTERPRISE-WIDE STRATEGIES

Several kinds and levels of enterprise-wide strategies were described in Chapter 2:

1. A *general strategy direction.* This might involve an overall growth-related objective, such as abandon the business, hold one's position, invest selectively, or invest aggressively. Or, it might involve defining the general product or service, geographic location, or other

Figure 7-1: Strategic Management Tasks

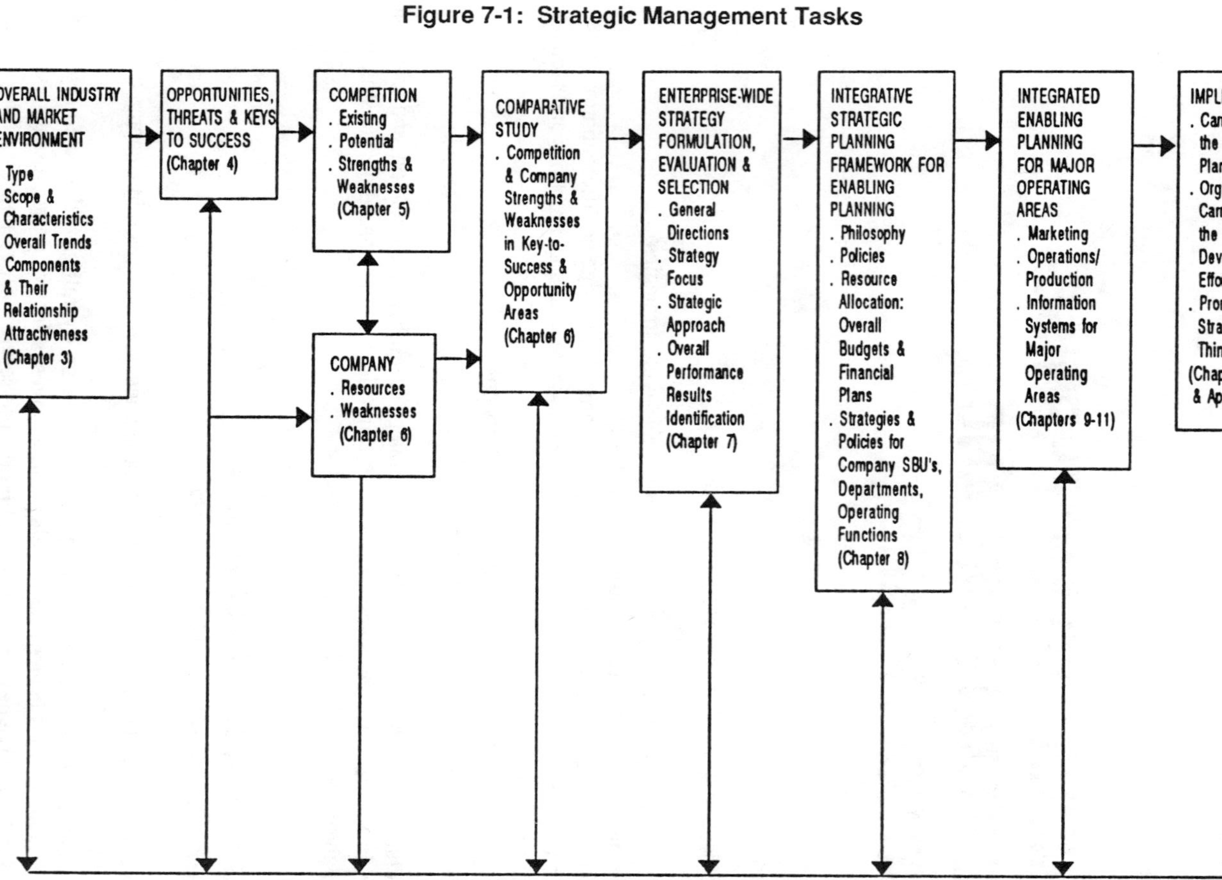

business area in which a company will concentrate. Or, it might involve the general mission of the company, providing that this mission is more than just a "wish list" and instead is based on a thorough situation analysis.

2. An *extension of the general strategy direction, or strategic focus.* This could involve an emphasis on a specific product or resource strength, or on any other area which is likely to differentiate the company from the competition and/or in some way give the company a competitive edge.

3. *Specific definitions of how to achieve strategic enterprise-wide direction and focus.* These are more detailed definitions of enterprise-wide direction and focus, which include some sense of how they will be carried out or achieved. They often deal with how specific key-to-success criteria will be met.

4. *Performance results anticipated.* The results to be achieved, very often in the form of return on investment, sales, or other specific quantitative goals are frequently included in enterprise-wide strategies.

5. *Enabling plans.* These can be company policies and philosophies, financial plans, programs, and other enabling strategies and strategic plans for strategic business units and key operating areas.

This chapter discusses the first four of these kinds and levels of strategies. The chapters in PART FOUR discuss formulating and implementing enabling strategies and plans.

FORMULATING ENTERPRISE-WIDE STRATEGY DIRECTIONS

Strategy formulation involves synthesizing prior planning analyses to formulate enterprise-wide strategies. The first level of these, the general strategy directions, are discussed in this section. Three useful kinds of general strategic directions defined in strategy formulation situations are:

- General growth-related strategies
- General strategies involving product, service, customer, or other business area(s) to be served
- Vision statements

The following discussion of these kinds of general strategies does not comprehensively review all possible strategies in these areas because of the wide range of possible situations — ranging from very large multidivisional, multinational companies to small local entrepreneurial single-retail outlets to strategic business units of large corporations. Instead, the discussion focuses on commonly encountered strategies and on the general decision-making processes involved in formulating strategies appropriate to a specific company situation.

General Growth-related Strategies

It is often useful to formulate and specify overall growth-related strategies for an enterprise. For example, both General Electric and the Boston Consulting Group have defined possible general strategies for multidivisional companies with strategic business units. This approach, often appropriate in diversified companies with many strategic business units, views a corporation as holding investments in different business entities and making decisions about the best ways to maintain a balanced portfolio of investments [Porter 1980, Appendix A].

Four possible enterprise-wide strategies can be identified in these kinds of situations: invest aggressively; invest selectively; hold one's position; or abandon the business. Decisions about which option to choose are based on an analysis of the competitive market, the company's comparative competitive position, and other special company factors. This structured situational analysis, summarized in Figure 7-2, is described in Appendix A of this book.

While the four growth-related strategies mentioned above are useful in some situations, other equally useful and more precise kinds of general growth-related strategies exist [Robert 1989, pp. 8-11]. Such strategies can be classified as stability strategies, growth strategies, and retrenchment strategies.

Stability strategies. Such strategies concentrate on maintaining and improving present products and market positions. Electric utilities, dominant companies in mature industries, and small family-owned and -run businesses often pursue such general strategy directions. Turner Broadcasting, which found itself a maturing industry in the early 1990s, changed from "the most swashbuckling of entrepreneurial enterprises to what is now a stable, even conventional member of the Fortune 500 elite, a company focused less on innovation and more on paring debt and earning a profit" [Fabrikant 1991; Painton 1992; Waldman 1991].

Growth strategies. Growth strategies are by far the most commonly encountered. The most frequently pursued are

- *Concentration* in a single industry, product, service, technology, or market. At times, this is accomplished by vertical integration, such as used by Guiness P.L.C., the British brewer. By 1992, Guiness owned 85 percent of its spirits distributors, up from 20percent in 1987 [Prokesch 1992(A)]. Or concentration can be accomplished through horizontal growth, as when, between 1986 and 1991, Guiness acquired other beer and spirits producers worth over $8.5 billion [Prokesch 1992(A)]. Similarly, Wayne Huizenga built Waste Management — a $6 billion corporation in 1991 — by making acquisitions within the industry [Sandomir 1991; Shapiro 1992].

- *Diversification* into different industries, products, or services. *Conglomerate* diversification occurs when growth is achieved through expansion into areas *unrelated* to a company's current business. For example, Mead Corporation, a pulp and paper company, bought Mead Data General in 1968. Mead Data grew to be a leader in data retrieval by computer, first in the legal area and later expanded to 750 full-text data sources [Caillot 1991]. *Concentric* diversification occurs when growth is achieved through expansion into *related* product areas, such as at Nordson Corporation which pursues a "lily pad" expansion strategy. Like a clever and successful frog which always jumps to the nearest lily pad so that it can see

Figure 7-2: Diagram of Situation to be Prototyped for General Strategy Direction (Initial Prototype)

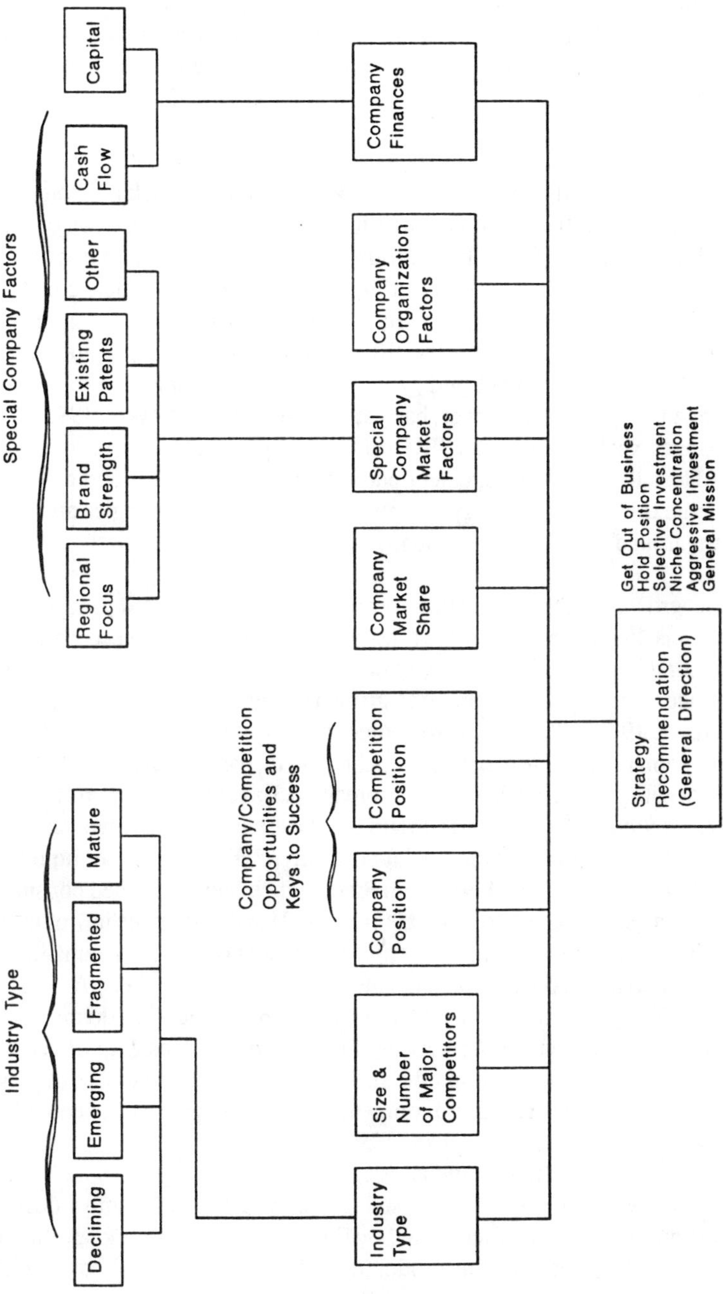

where it is going and still hop back to safety if the new perch starts to sag, Nordson focused on growth into businesses that were "always very close to, or make good use of, its core capabilities" and in this way had achieved a 20 percent annual growth rate since 1960 [Reimann 1991].

• *Entrepreneurial/Spinoff* strategies. One way to stimulate growth of an SBU is through creating a partially public subsidiary (PPS) by selling stock in a company subsidiary to the public. Baxter International, American Express, ARCO, Coca Cola, Disney, Dow, GTE, and Waste Management have all used PPSs; reportedly hundreds more companies were considering them in 1992 [Coles 1992]. Such PPS help stimulate growth for several reasons: a PPS generates low-cost capital; the SBU management and employees are much more motivated to succeed; and the SBU can attract and keep better people and have more flexibility to experiment and grow. The eventual impact on profitability and long-term growth of spinoffs, however, has yet to be documented [Woo 1992]. Other organizational changes, such as moving an SBU to a separate physical location, creating newly independent SBUs, and letting management participate in SBU profits and growth, are other ways to pursue this kind of strategy. Entrepreneurial/Spinoff strategies are often part of efforts to turn around and improve company performance.

The growth-related strategies formulated in each situation depend on that situation's requirements. In the early 1990s, the Marriott Corporation announced it was selling off 20 percent of its existing businesses which were unrelated to its core businesses — hotels and institutional food service — in an effort to focus on a growth strategy concentrated in its core businesses [Foust 1991; Wayne 1990]. Textron, on the other hand, continued to operate successfully in the 1990s as a conglomerate. Such a strategy enabled it to balance cyclical downturns in its defense businesses with growth in other business areas, such as automotive parts in Europe [Harrop 1990].

Retrenchment/turnaround strategies. These strategies involve such approaches as divestment through selling or spinning off a company, SBU or division, liquidation, or turnaround management. In early 1992, Bethlehem Steel, which had retrenched considerably (from 83,000 employees in 1981 to an expected 20,000 in 1993) and had losses in 7 of the 10 prior years, was considering both further retrenchment and divestment of one of its remaining major divisions in the face of increased competition and changing consumer markets. Analysts still questioned in what form, if any, Bethlehem would survive [Milbank 1992]. A dramatic example of a partial liquidation strategy was the proposal by Frank Lorenzo, president of Eastern Airline's parent corporation, to substantially shrink the airline in mid-1989 in response to pressures from unions, creditors, the bankruptcy court, and competitors — a strategy which eventually led to the complete liquidation of the company [Salpukas 1991].

From a public relations viewpoint, a turnaround strategy — which in some situations is a growth strategy and at other times a stability strategy — is the most desirable, since it is not inherently an admission of failure. Playboy Enterprises ran into major problems during the 1970s, as its forays into theatrical film production, recording studios, book publishing, a limousine service, resorts and other services, went awry. In 1982, when Christie Hefner became CEO, the company lost $52 million. Retrenchment steps included closing its famous clubs by 1986, ending its Playboy cable channel, cutting costs and staff, consolidating operations and merging departments, and even selling two paintings for $5.1 million. After this major retrenchment, the company was in the black in 1990, had $30 million in cash, and had turned around sufficiently to begin thinking of growing vigorously again [Cohen 1991].

When David Johnson became president of Campbell Soup Company in January 1990, his turnaround strategy was to transform a company that had pursued revenue growth no matter what the cost — resulting in a somewhat tepid financial performance — into a retrenched downsized company (20 plants sold or closed, workforce cut by 25 percent, unprofitable businesses sold) run strictly for the bottom line. The results yielded a dramatic turnaround in 1991 both in profits (up 36 percent from 1990) and stock market price (almost double) [Bevins 1991; Freedman 1991]. As so often happens when an entrepreneur takes over a stagnating division of a major corporation, Roger Penske turned around Detroit Diesel Corp. after taking it over in 1988. His hands-on entrepreneurial management approach changed the company's corporate culture and raised its share of heavy-truck engine sales from 3.2 percent to 28 percent [White 1991].

General Strategies Involving Product, Service, and Customer Area to Be Served

No matter what the size or type of company, most enterprise-wide strategies define the kind(s) of products or services, and the customer on which a company intends to *concentrate*. A wide range of strategic directions are possible within this area. A company may sell a product or a service to a select group of customers or to large segments of the population. It may operate regionally, nationally, or internationally. The strategic objective defines the product, service, or market area in which the company intends to concentrate. The process of formulating such an enterprise-wide strategy can be an emergent one, which involves becoming more and more specifically focused about general strategic directions.

For a multidivision company with substantial product diversification, this definition necessarily will be fairly general. For example, Reid International P.L.C., a British publishing giant ($2.7 billion in sales in 1991), was originally a paper manufacturer, which first focused on packaging and publishing and then in the mid-1980s on publishing and information [Prokesch 1992(B)]. Gillette similarly refocused in the 1980s, divesting 21 businesses and limiting itself mainly to razors and blades, other personal-care products, and writing instruments [Chakravorty 1991; McKibben 1990].

Smaller companies and strategic business units, on the other hand, can often define this strategic focus very specifically — at times well-defined market niches are identified. The descriptions of the candy and baked goods companies in the following section are examples of such more specific definitions of strategic product, market, and/or customer areas to be served.

Large companies in single-product industries can also at times be defined precisely in enterprise-wide strategy statements. For example, the gas company objectives in Figure 7-3 precisely define product and customer. This is possible in this situation because the company provides a single product/ service in a well-defined geographic area.

Vision Statements

Figure 7-3 also illustrates how the scope of the general strategic direction defined at this level sometimes includes factors such as company self-image, philosophy, social policies, and public posture. Such comprehensive statements — often called "mission" statements — define the fundamental, unique purpose or "vision" that sets a business apart from other firms of its type and identifies its scope of operations in product and market terms. Such expanded strategy definitions of general direction can be useful in situations like the gas company's, where a company operates in an environment dependent on customer goodwill for success.

IDENTIFYING A SPECIFIC STRATEGIC FOCUS: THE COMPETITIVE EDGE

General company strategic directions, such as those described in the preceding section, inevitably need to be defined more precisely as strategies are formulated, as was indicated in the preceding section. The idea of a competitive edge, through some kind of focus within the general product or service area of concentration, is an essential element of an enterprise-wide strategy. Such a definition specifies the way to *differentiate* a company from the competition. This strategic focus is often the result of formulating a strategy based on a company's perceived strengths, or core competencies, and on special market characteristics.

Banc One chose to be a regional bank focusing on serving retail banking customers and smaller businesses [Lohr 1991]. In contrast, after its federal bailout Continental Bank's CEO Thomas Theobald reshaped his company into one of the few major U.S. banks without retail operations and focused on loans to large corporations and wealthy individuals [Fitzgerald 1991; Greising 1991].

John Bryan, chairman of Sara Lee Corporation, discovered early in his career that many companies did not do well because they could not develop a competitive advantage. At Sara Lee, he felt that the company should not be tied behind "strategic fences" that say "food." Rather, he felt that "the main tenant of Sara Lee's diversification strategy was to seek out categories of consumer products where few competitors have used brand marketing — the idea that a product can gain added value through a well-advertised brand name" [McGill 1989; "Sara Lee" 1990]. In 1984 Sara Lee bought Jimmy Dean, a regional sausage company, and made it a nationally known name through advertising. Jimmy Dean held 23 percent of the breakfast sausage meat market by 1989. Such shrewd brand name management had been Sara Lee's differentiating trademark (that is, strategic focus) for more than a decade. In the baking goods situation, the regional company under study had an unusually strong sales force and brand name image in its four-state area — which several possible expansion strategies could exploit.

The source and nature of the differential advantage can vary. For example, the competitive edge may come from becoming the favored supplier to a selected domain. American Hospital did

Figure 7-3: A Major Gas Company (Purposes and Principles)

Basic Purpose: The basic purpose is to perpetuate an investor-owned, free enterprise company, rendering a needed, satisfactory service and earning optimum, long-range profits.

What We Do: The principal business of the Company is the provision of gaseous energy through a pipe system to meet the needs of ultimate consumers. The Company not only will provide the gas itself but also will encourage and help consumers to utilize the gas widely and in the safest, most efficient manager. All such service, research, supply, promotional, market development, financing and similar activities for consumers are regarded as the Company's principal business. In order to accomplish the Company's basic purpose, it may be necessary or desirable for the Company to provide other products or services which supplement, complement and enhance its principal business. Any such activities should be consistent with its responsibilities to its investors, customers, employees and others.

Where We Do It: The utility service area of the Company is shown in the latest Annual Report to stock-holders or in other publications. Service will be offered in this area to everyone who can be served profitably, in accordance with the requirements of the state Commerce Commission. Service will also be offered in this area, subject to state Commerce Commission approval, if indications are that a fair return on the investment will be earned over the long term, or if competitive conditions warrant. The Company will seek to acquire or will construct other gas systems whenever such additions can be made on a basis that promises to be rewarding to the Company's stockholders and can be economically integrated into the Company's existing operations, or whenever competitive conditions warrant. No geographical limitations are imposed upon the acquisition of gas and its transportation to the service area nor upon supplementary and complementary activities into which the Company may enter.

How We Do It: The Company will conduct its business in full recognition of its responsibilities, as set forth hereafter, to the several elements of the community upon which its operations have an impact. The Company believes that in general, over the long run, the interests of all these elements are compatible.

INVESTORS

The Company will:

A. Strive to provide to its owners, the holders of its common stock, a growing per share value, measured in terms of both income and appreciation, and to be the maximum, in the long run, consistent with the Company's responsibilities to its customers, employees and the public.
B. Seek to continue to hold the interest of its broad, diversified, well-balanced and stable family of stockholders, and to attract others who will maintain this balance.
C. Provide for its stock a ready, convenient and technically sound market to ensure optimum flexibility for its owners.
D. Keep present and potential investors in the Company and their representatives well informed about the Company and its prospects, in order that they may make their investment decisions with full knowledge and that the Company's securities are appraised fairly.
E. Keep its books in accordance with accepted accounting principles and practices.
F. Safeguard and soundly employ Company funds and property.
G. Maintain a sound, conservative capital structure to support the quality of all its securities, assure its ability to attract new capital when needed, provide good protection to the investors in its senior securities, and coupled with strong earnings, assure optimum preservation of the investments of both the stockholder and senior security holders.
H. Develop strong earnings. To accomplish this Company will:

    1. Promote aggressively the use of its product through the sale of gas and the sale of appliances and equipment utilizing the product.

Figure 7-3: A Major Gas Company (contd.)
(Purposes and Principles)

2. Maintain a close control over expenses, and constantly seek means to reduce them.
3. Recover, as an operating expense, a realistic allowance for depreciation.
4. Engage in and support research to improve the utilization of gas, develop new uses, provide a substitute when needed, and find better ways to transport, store, deliver, measure, bill and collect for it.
5. Provide capable, well-trained and enthusiastic managers, with adequate replacements ready when needed.
6. Engage in other activities than its principal business which supplement, complement and enhance such business.

I. Pay to the holders of its common stock in dividends a reasonable proportion of earnings, after annual review, bearing in mind the desirability of maintaining dividend stability so far as possible even if economic, regulatory or other developments become adverse.
J. Promote private enterprise and endeavor to minimize municipal or other governmental ownership of business.

CUSTOMERS
The Company will:

A. Deliver to its gas customers, safely and dependably, a gas of uniform heating value that will burn cleanly and efficiently.
B. Provide this gas at a fair and reasonable price, as low as possible consistent with prompt, courteous and dependable service, and consistent with its responsibilities to its investors, employees and the public.
C. Provide an adequate and dependable supply of gas over both the short- and long-range.
D. Provide prompt, courteous, dependable and economical service on customer appliances and equipment, or assure itself that satisfactory service is otherwise available to customers and that they have been so informed.
E. Publicize vigorously the advantages of its product.
F. Respect the right of every customer to use the form of energy which he prefers and, to that end, support energy competition so that a freedom of choice will be available to each customer.
G. See to it that better, even more modern appliances and equipment utilizing its energy are developed and brought to the Customer's attention.
H. Keep abreast of technological change.
I. Seek and utilize innovations and improvements to hold down and reduce costs.
J. Maintain its facilities and equipment well from the viewpoints of both operation and appearance.
K. Provide qualified personnel who are friendly, neat, courteous, well-informed, helpful and promptly attentive in a fair and just manner to the customer's individual problems.

EMPLOYEES
A. *The Company will*, without discrimination as to race, creed, national background, age, sex, or physical handicaps not detrimental to performance or general health:

1. Hire employees with good appearance, attitude, and at least a high school or equivalent education.
2. Fill vacancies above starting levels from within the Company whenever possible.
3. Promote on the basis of ability, performance, and experience, not solely one length of service.
4. Provide job training and educational opportunities to help employees perform better in their jobs and prepare for advancement.

Figure 7-3: A Major Gas Company (contd.)
(Purposes and Principles)

B. *The Company will*, in return for the fulfillment by employees of their responsibilities as outlined later:
1. Pay fair and just compensation comparable to what others are paying for like work.
2. Increase compensation from time to time as merited by improved productivity or performance.

C. *The Company will* provide:
1. Job security to the greatest extent possible, subject to continued satisfactory performance and adherence to Company work rules.
2. A comprehensive, modern benefit program.
3. Safe and, as far as possible, pleasant working conditions and practices. Tools and equipment will be safe and efficient.
4. An opportunity for employees to become stockholders in the business.

D. *The Company will* bargain fairly and realistically with recognized representatives of employees engaged in physical and clerical work.

E. *The Company will* administer discipline to all employees fairly, equitably, and firmly.

F. *The Company will*:

1. Seek to promote a working climate in which all employees understand and accept the Company's objectives and management's decisions, and are motivated to accomplish and implement them in a fully coordinated team effort.
2. Keep employees informed of matters of interest to them pertaining to their jobs, the Company, its product and service.
3. Endeavor to merit the pride of all employees in the Company, its management and policies.
4. Provide good, well-trained supervisors at all levels, with respect both for the individual and the need to get the job done properly, economically, and safely.
5. Provide its managers with a sound organization structure and clearly defined duties.
6. Delegate responsibility and authority as nearly as possible to the point of action.
7. Encourage self-reliance, creativity, initiative and decision-making.
8. Urge supervisors to discuss matters freely with their subordinates and encourage employees to feel free to discuss problems with their supervisors.
9. Encourage the search for new, more efficient ways of conducting its business, in order to reduce costs, increase productivity, and free manpower from the tasks of greatest drudgery to those more challenging and better paying.
10. Strive to utilize every employe on required work to his maximum capability in the long run.
11. Inform each employe what is expected of him and how well he is doing it.

G. *The Company will* expect each employe to:
1. Do a fair day's work for a fair day's pay.
2. Be quick to suggest improvements and be adaptable to change.
3. Uphold the highest standards of integrity.
4. Be loyal, supporting Company objectives and policies.
5. Be a good-will ambassador of the Company, pleasant and courteous in all customer and public contacts.
6. Be enthusiastic about the Company's business and promote it diligently.
7. Use Company-recommended safety equipment properly for his own personal well-being and for that of his fellow employees and of the public generally.
8. Be a good citizen, and participate in community activities of his choice, consistent with Company polices.

PUBLIC

The Company will foster and strive to maintain a sense of public interest. In discharging its responsibility to

Figure 7-3: A Major Gas Company (contd.)
(Purposes and Principles)

the public, it will endeavor to be a good citizen in every way, constantly seeking means to be of service and to deserve and enjoy the highest measure of public confidence and esteem.

The Company will:

A. Keep its properties and equipment in good condition and appearance.
B. Plan ahead so that its operations will be performed with a minimum of public inconvenience.
C. Inform the public of construction to be performed by it and the reasons therefor.
D. Restore property if disturbed.
E. Maintain a safe system.
F. Provide adequate capacity for the present needs of the communities it serves and be ready to meet their growth.
G. Promote the development of the area it serves.
H. Pay its fair share of taxes.
I. Encourage its employees to be leaders in community and civic activities to the extent consistent with Company policies.
J. Contribute to worthwhile community activities, to a reasonable extent considering its public utility status.
K. Keep the public informed of its problems and achievements which affect the public.
L. Be nonpartisan but speak out on issues where interests of the business, its investors, employees or customers are seriously affected.

SUPPLIERS

The Company will:

A. Deal fairly with its suppliers.
B. Place its orders strictly on the basis of ethical and sound business considerations after competitive bidding whenever appropriate.
C. Enter into no agreements with others to apportion business, maintain prices or otherwise restrain trade.
D. Instruct its employees to refuse gifts of immoderate entertainment from present or prospective suppliers.

COMPETITORS

The Company will:

A. Compete vigorously but fairly and ethically.
B. Enter into no agreements with others to apportion business, maintain prices or otherwise restrain trade.

GOVERNMENT

The Company will:

A. Encourage the selection of regulators and other government officials who are able, intelligent, conscientious, experienced and cognizant of the rights of investors as well as consumers.
B. Endeavor through proper channels to keep its regulators and other government officials well informed of the Company's position and problems.
C. Deal with these officials frankly, openly and in good faith.
D. Accept reasonable and farsighted regulation.
E. Make its position known when its interests may be adversely affected.

GAS INDUSTRY

The Company will:

A. Carry its fair share of well-conceived and well-executed gas industry activities.
B. Establish itself as an industry leader and set an outstanding example to others.

this in the 1980s using computer information systems links to their customers, which effectively locked in their customers and raised barriers to entry for competitors for a period of time.

The British publisher Reid International tried to develop a competitive edge by pursuing a niche strategy in its acquisitions, limiting them to niche publications — regional newspapers, specialty business and consumer magazines, and other niche information distribution media. The company felt that advertisers in the 1990s would be looking for media targeted at well-defined, specific markets [Prokesch 1992(B)].

Focusing on specialty products is a common way to strategically develop a competitive edge and carve out a market niche. Examples of such a strategic focus range from Godiva Chocolates, flowers by mail, the *El Diario-La Prensa* Spanish language newspaper, Gloria Jean's specialty coffee beans, and music video cable channels, to tall and short men clothing stores, L.L. Bean's initial focus on the outdoor clothing market, magazines designed for older people, or any of the many businesses serving consumer hobby, sports, or other specialty interests. After World War II, *The Wall Street Journal* significantly expanded its coverage of general business news; it formerly had been a narrowly-focused financial publication. This expanded focus created a new product/market — a unique combination of financial and general business news for both managers and financial professionals — a niche focus which remained unchallenged until the mid-1980s.

A competitive edge can also arise from becoming a high-volume, low-cost/price producer/seller. Phar-Mor used discount prices and rapid expansion to prosper in the retailing industry. In 1991 it was the largest, brashest, and fastest-growing discount retail chain in the U.S. [Hirsch 1991]. Ikea, a large furniture retail chain, which focused on low prices, specified that it would provide very little customer service in order to reinforce its primary low-price competitive focus [Trachtenberg 1991].

The lack of a clear strategic focus can create major problems. According to industry analysts, J.C. Penney Company's 1987 change in strategic direction from being a full-line department store to being primarily a clothing store was in 1991 hurting the company due to a lack of distinct, focused merchandising and pricing identity [Barmesh 1991; Forest 1991].

FORMULATING A STRATEGIC APPROACH TO CARRYING OUT ENTERPRISE-WIDE STRATEGIC COMPANY DIRECTIONS AND FOCUS

Based on market opportunities and keys to success, and on the comparative competitive position analysis, more precise definitions of strategy focus often emerge in stages during strategy formulation as the approach needed to carry out general company strategic directions and focus are studied and defined in more detail.

For example, Shaw Industries' approach to furthering its dominance of the carpet industry through focusing on price-cutting was multifaceted: buy its own yarn mills to control supply costs, establish its own fleet of trucks to ship directly to customers and so cut distribution costs, and use its massive volume to buy supplies more cheaply than smaller competitors [Ruffenach 1991]. The strategic approach developed by Phar-Mor — which was started in the early 1980s and expected to have over $3 billion in sales in 1992 — included innovative merchandising, relentless marketing, bare-knuckle negotiating, rapid expansion to increase volume purchasing discounts, and selective stocking of name brands [Hirsch 1991].

The strategic approach at Banc One relied heavily on computer technology and customer service. One of the first banks to introduce automated teller machines (in 1970), its internal computer information systems enable branch managers to offer a wide array of products and services. Its newer, larger branches — called "financial marketplaces" — often are open on weekends and offer a wide range of products, including travel and real estate services. Banc One also relies heavily on acquisitions and has demonstrated an "uncanny ability to smoothly absorb a steady stream of acquired banks" [Lohr 1991].

Emphasizing research and development leadership is another way to gain a competitive edge. Thus far, Merck and Company has maintained its edge in the pharmaceutical industry by being a leader in research and development. In 1992, it was poised to introduce Proscar, a new drug for treating enlarged prostates, which was expected to produce $1 billion a year in sales [Freudenheim 1992].

A detailed strategy statement for a small candy company described in the *Blakeston and Wilson Company* study at the end of this book is given below. The discussion following it describes how the strategy, and its focus and strategic approach, were formulated.

> The strategic objective of the company is to be an aggressively expanding, closely-held regional manufacturer-retailer of a limited line of high-quality, moderately-priced, and distinctively boxed chocolate candies, selling principally through its own retail stores to consumers under its own brand name, but also serving wholesale, chain, and institutional customers or outlets under other brand names to the degree permitted by available production capacity and by the company's ability to raise capital.

This candy company, a small, well-focused regional candy company with a narrow product line, was developing a geographic niche focus. In addition, it concentrated on a specialized type of product and retail outlet. To further define this focus and how it was to be achieved, the company objective covered five key strategic components. These five components were judged to affect the company's future significantly, based on the company and competitive market analyses. They included: functions performed by the company; product or service offered; market or customer served; ownership of company; and size and scope of operations.

The company was a small but expanding candy manufacturer, which had recently opened its own retail stores. The president held over 50 percent of the company stock. The company sold relatively high-quality, medium-priced, boxed chocolates.

Functions. The first strategic decision to consider was what functions the company should concentrate on in light of its limited resources. Within the past two years, the company had opened its first retail shops. Formerly, it had sold only to wholesalers, chains, and institutions. The opening of retail shops (seven at the time of the study) changed the character of the company — from a manufacturer-wholesaler to a manufacturer-retailer. Since it had limited resources, the company faced a critical strategic decision: should it open more retail stores?

Product. As for the second strategic component, the product offered, the company currently sold a limited line of boxed chocolates under its own brand name. They were considered high-quality, medium-priced chocolates. If the company expanded its retail shops, would it have to expand its product line to include low- and high-priced chocolates, other types of candy, or even related products, such as nuts? As the product analysis continued, it became apparent that four different strategic product decisions had to be made: kinds of products sold; product quality and image; breadth of product line; and product brand name.

Market. A third strategic decision the company faced involved its market or customers. Should it continue to sell to chains and wholesalers, either under its own brand name or under another name? Or, because of its limited production facilities, should the company concentrate on selling directly to consumers only through its retail stores? Based on these analyses, the customer decision was also subdivided into customer and distribution outlets. Answering these questions and doing related analyses were necessary to define the company's strategic focus precisely and to provide a general approach for carrying out that strategic focus.

Ownership. As for the fourth strategic decision significantly affecting the company's future, ownership, the president had indicated he wanted to retain control of the company. He ran the operations personally and made most decisions, and had brought in his daughter and son to work for the company — clearly signalling his intent to have a "family" company. This limited the training and development of managers outside the family, as well as the option of selling stock to raise capital for faster expansion.

Operation size and scope. The owner's desire to have a family-run business also limited the company's potential size and scope, the fifth strategic decision area considered. It also held back expansion of retail stores. Limited management personnel, combined with limited manufacturing and financial resources, severely restricted the company's growth potential. These last two decisions were especially critical ones. If, as seemed likely, retail expansion was continued, then ownership would have to be expanded and greater management resources developed. If ownership and management were not expanded, then expansion objectives would have to be curtailed accordingly.

During this phase, the original five strategic decision components were expanded to nine. The nine areas that emerged from this study included

- Size and scope of operations
- Functions performed by the company
- Breadth of product line
- Product quality and image
- Kinds of product sold
- Product brand name
- Distribution outlets
- Market or customer served
- Ownership of company

Eight of these were identified mainly from earlier comparative studies of the company's and competitors' opportunities and key-to-success factors. One, ownership, arose principally from an analysis of internal company factors: the company was run by the principal stockholder, who wanted to run and control the company in the foreseeable future.

After the war, the market was expanding and the numbers and kinds of competitors expected were as yet unknown. Therefore internal company factors played a significant role in the candy company's strategy decisions. Competitive market factors played a much more important role in the baked goods company's decision situation described in the following paragraphs.

A similar incremental, emerging component-by-component approach was used in the baked goods company situation described in the *Superb Biscuits Company* study in the Case Study section of this book. The strategic components affecting the company's future (based on the defined opportunities and keys to success, comparative competitive position evaluation, and special industry and company factors) were identified during the earlier phases of the situation analysis. The implications of these competitive market analyses were then explored:

a. While the company appears to have major advantages in the specialty cookie area, the future for specialty cookies is uncertain at the time of the study. This suggests the possibility of expanding the concept of "specialty" to include other speciality baked goods, such as cakes and muffins. It also suggests not depending entirely on this area until its potential is clearer.

b. The company's major strengths are its brand recognition and sales force, which gives it access to a very high percentage of the food stores in its area. Therefore, a strategy which exploits these two strengths, such as product line expansion into specialty baked goods (a high margin area), should be promising.

c. The company's strategy must include maintaining a broad line of standard products to maintain shelf position, an important success factor in supermarkets. Maintaining a strong standard cookie line would also help insulate the company from the uncertain future of the specialty cookie area. At the same time, total concentration on the standard cookie line does not appear to be the best strategy for this company. Such a strategy does not exploit the company's strengths relative to competitors', but instead pits them directly against the vast resources of superior competitors—something to be avoided since the company had limited financial resources.

d. The potential threats of large companies expanding in the specialty area suggest that the company should move quickly to establish a strong position in the specialty cookie area. This would require increasing research resources, developing organizational mechanisms to make better use of the company's sales force for product intelligence (to quickly get samples of competitors' new products and also to research local markets for new recipes), and developing more flexible production and new-product-decision processes to quickly exploit newly developed or copied products.

e. The company's limited resources dictate concentrating in its four-state area and using outside distributors for extraterritorial sales. This would be part of its strategic focus, which concentrated on exploiting distribution and brand name strengths in the company's four-state region.

This analysis was followed by a summary of the ideas suggested for changing the company's present strategy and formulating new strategies based on the above implications.

a. Place more emphasis (concentrate resources) on the specialty cookie area and do it quickly.
b. Expand the products offered in the specialty area to include other baked goods.
c. While giving it less emphasis than before, maintain as strong a position in the standard products area as possible given the company's limited resources. While this may cut into profits, it seemed necessary in order to maintain competitive prices in the standard cookie area and retain store shelf positions.
d. The company cannot fully commit to the specialty area until the potential of specialty baked products is more clearly identified. The company should therefore keep current on technological developments in the production automation area.
e. The company cannot fully exploit the specialty cookie area until it has established the brand or name recognition for such high-priced specialty products to differentiate them from competitors. The company might have to create a new brand name for this purpose.

Based on the ideas emerging from such explorations of implications, tentative strategy definitions usually are formulated in stages. At the baked goods company, for example, a summary of the company's present strategic objective was constructed. It initially summarized the company's growth-related direction and defined its strategic focus and approach in more detail:

> To be a rapidly-growing manufacturer/distributor of a wide line of cookies and crackers (both standard and specialty) that are distributed to (and supported with its own sales force) chain and independent food stores (and institutional customers) in a four-state area, with some sales through distributors outside its four-state operating area.

The company had not previously had a formal objective statement. Next, tentative revised company objectives, based on the study, were constructed. Each of the formulated revisions were further evaluated and revised, so that the overall company strategic objective was developed gradually, or incrementally. This evolution, and the significance of the seemingly small changes introduced during it, are discussed in the evaluation section below.

It should be noted that while strategic directions most often identify some new or partially new direction, it is possible that in some situations doing nothing new — that is, not changing anything — will be the best strategy.

PERFORMANCE RESULTS ANTICIPATED

Strategic objectives invariably contain some sense of the results anticipated. These might be defined in terms of

- Company sales projections, both in the aggregate or as a percentage of market share (market position)
- Return on investment targets
- Cashflow goals
- The acceptable risks
- Company ownership and control limitations

Establishing such strategic targets is a key step in translating strategic objectives into enabling or operating plans. At this strategic level, these targets may still be expressed in overall terms, for example, as they are by one very large company in its annual report:

- To preserve stockholders' equity
- To increase earnings an average of 11 percent per year
- To earn a return on book equity of 12 percent to 15 percent per year
- To pay out 30 percent to 40 percent of earnings each year in dividends to stockholders
- To maintain a sound financial position, which would enable the company to borrow on the most favorable terms available in the market
- Where these goals are not met, to meet or exceed the performance of comparable companies in the industry

As seen from this example, strategic targets may be expressed in ranges, as definite figures, or as general goals. As seen in the candy company objective discussed earlier, they may also be defined as ownership limits.

Strategic target creation may require reconciling what is feasible with what is acceptable to company owners and managers. For example, at a life sciences company specializing in animal breeding, the owner/managers' goals of a 15 percent return on investment, with a 15 percent compounded annual growth rate in sales, was unrealistic without diversification into other fields whose risks were unacceptable to the owner/managers. In this situation, the owner/managers' target results had to be modified to take into account the realities of the competitive marketplace and owner's/manager's preferences.

Effective strategic objectives represent realistic and achievable expectations. Any useful strategic performance targets developed would fulfill that criteria.

EVALUATING ALTERNATIVES AND MAKING A DECISION

This section discusses several aspects of strategy evaluation and selection. Some of these involve situations where effective strategic company objectives are formulated and evaluated; in other situations, a strategic objective is formulated incrementally from continuing analyses of situation requirements. Several types of tools and techniques are used to formulate and evaluate company strategies. The first one described here is competitive scenario evaluation.

The Competitor Scenario Evaluation: A Risk Assessment

Competitive scenario evaluation assists in projecting what courses of action the competition might follow and how likely they are to follow them.

For example, in one situation, a small company was considering developing a new product for the oil services industry. Since the company had no significant experience in this industry, it decided to analyze the competitors to see what their response might be to its new product introduction.

A list of major competitors was compiled and the characteristics of each, including strengths and weaknesses, were profiled. A matrix worksheet listing possible actions each competitor might take was initially developed. Probabilities were then assigned to the likelihood of each competitor taking such actions. A summary of two different planners' rough worksheets for such a scenario analysis is given in Figure 7-4.

During the study, the initial perceptions of competitive reactions were found to be inaccurate, after the detailed competitor-by-competitor evaluation was made. The initial assessment made was that several competitors were so large that they were likely to dominate and overpower any new competition, especially if that new competition were relatively small. Specific scenarios were then developed about how each competitor, with its own specific business characteristics, requirements, and management, would view the problem and react. Analysis of these scenarios subsequently indicated that several large competitors might have no interest in the new product because the market for it was so small and the competitive threat was minimal.

Gradually, then, by thoroughly analyzing the situation (for example, through role playing) and imaginatively writing competitor-by-competitor reaction scenarios, the perception of the future competitive environment changed. It soon became apparent that competitors were likely to have several different reactions — first attempting to discredit the new product, then attempting to buy the company making it, and lastly settling for living with the new product — providing of course that the new entrant did nothing out of the ordinary to provoke an aggressive competitor reaction.

Several scenarios were also developed in the baked goods company situation. For example, one major competitor scenario would be for one of the big three competitors to use its resources to buy one of the six smaller competitors. This move seemed unlikely, since it would involve giving up a national name and brand recognition advantage to use a lesser name. At the same time, none of the six smaller companies had a brand name or sales force presence in the market comparable to the company under study. Such scenario development and exploration was used in conjunction with estimates of probability or likelihood, as shown in Figure 7-4.

In using this technique, as in using other quantitative techniques described in this book, it should be clear that the actual figures were not facts but judgments. The process of using figures is designed solely to help a planner think more precisely about the decision.

Figure 7-4: Competitive Scenario Analysis and Evaluation: Oil Services Company Situations Most Likely Actions

Competition	What Competitor Might Do	Probability	Reasons for Probability
Competitor A	Try to develop a similar product	75%	- Vast resources - Market leader - Already produces similar products that are well-known in the industry
Competitor B	Try to develop a similar product	70%	- Has extensive engineering services and equipment capabilities - Has 50 years experience
Competitor C	Undecided, will wait to see what happens	70%	- Has only 5 years experience
Competitor D	Will not try to develop a similar product	95%	- 95% of their business is selling a natural resource product.
Competitor E	Try to merge our company	50%	- Small company - High-quality reputation
Competitor F	Can go either way: wait and see what happens, or develop a similar product right away	40%	- Large company - Has power to control prices - Has the engineering and equipment capabilities

Planner B's Analysis

Senarios	Competitor A	Competitor B	Competitor C	Competitor D	Competitor E	Competitor F
Do nothing	3	3	6	3	1	3
Copy/improve new product	6	6	5	1	8	6
Try to buy or merge with us	4	4	1	1	5	7
Dirty tricks	3	5	1	4	1	1
Wait/see	8	8	7	10	3	9
Become our customer	2	8	1	2	8	1

Scale of 1-10
10 = Strong Possibility of Scenario Occurring
1 = Little Possibility of Scenario Occurring

Building Strategic Objectives Incrementally

At times an enterprise-wide strategy (or alternative strategy to be considered) is formulated by building a good first version of the strategic objective and then gradually modifying it to come up with a final recommendation.

This was done in the baked goods situation, where the original strategy was modified and refined gradually. The following, for example, is a revision of the company's strategic objective given earlier:

> That the company move quickly and aggressively to be a leading manufacturer/distributor of baked goods (a limited line of standard cookies and crackers with increasing emphasis on specialty baked goods of all kinds) that distributed to (and strongly supported with its own detail sales force) chain and independent food stores (and institutional customers) in a four-state area, with some sales through distributors outside its operating area.

The changes made in this version from the preceding version may seem small and insignificant, but the modifications and refinements (such as "increasing emphasis" and moving "quickly") are actually changes in *concepts,* not *words.* While such changes are not always extensive, they can be significant. Cumulatively and individually they can shift management's focus and dictate where the company will concentrate its resources.

Consider the new wording in the baked goods strategic objective: "a limited line of standard cookies and crackers with increasing emphasis on specialty baked goods of all kinds." When a decision arises within the company over an investment in production machinery for standard cookies in the future, company strategy as defined in the revised objective would suggest not making a major capital investment there.

Companies such as Quaker Oats have divested themselves of hundreds of millions of dollars in assets based on strategy changes that were expressed in few words [Phillips 1986]:

> Unless a business is extraordinarily profitable, Quaker Oats will dispose of any division which is not directly related to its primary business — name brand packaged foods — and which does not have a No. 1 or No. 2 market position.

Such divestiture moves were very common during the 1980s, for example at Gillette, in part because many presidents of major corporations were preparing for an expected extended downturn in the U.S. economy in the mid-1990s. Their reasoning was that the best time to dispose of an operating division that is profitable but not a "strategic fit" with the company's main businesses is during a period when stock prices are rising and buyers are spending freely to acquire companies, as during the mid-1980s.

The number of words in the strategy statement, then, does not measure its impact. The strategic concept expressed in the words is what matters. For this reason, the gradually emerging formulation of alternatives in incremental refinement stages can be an effective approach to strategy formulation in many situations.

Evaluating Alternative Strategies

In some situations alternative strategies or strategic objectives will be evaluated during the strategy formulation phase. Such was the case in the candy company situation where this evaluation was both qualitative and quantitative.

Qualitative evaluations. The candy company had developed several alternative strategic objectives which were first examined component by component. For example, the following summary lists alternatives in five of the nine key component areas:

- *Function to be performed.* The company can become a manufacturer-retailer, or go back to being only a manufacturer-wholesaler.
- *Product or service offered.* The company can offer only its present boxed candy line, a wide line of boxed chocolates, a wide line of all types of candies, or a wide line of candies and other confectioneries. It can also offer candy under a variety of brand names. Given the niche focus and the competitive environment, quality is important. As for price, while the company could continue its policy of mid-range pricing of quality boxed candy, it can sell high-priced candy exclusively, or it can sell in a variety of price categories.
- *Market or customers served.* The company can sell to the public solely through its own retail shops; it can sell to wholesalers, chains, and institutions; or it can sell through any combination of the four customer outlets and distribution channels.
- *Ownership.* The president can maintain ownership and operational control, or he can elect to widen stock ownership to grow more rapidly in sales and profits by attracting additional capital and a stronger management group.
- *Scope of operations.* The company can continue to operate within the same geographic area, or it can expand into other regions and eventually sell nationally.

These areas are all related to the decision about retail expansion. A decision to serve both retail and wholesale markets would probably dictate expanding the number of products and/or brands. A decision to double the number of stores would require expanding production facilities, or eliminating some present wholesale and chain accounts, in order to supply candy to the new stores. A decision to maintain the current closely-held ownership control would slow expansion of retail outlets by limiting management and financial resources.

By studying the interrelationships among the areas and the feasibility of the alternatives, a planner can develop comprehensive integrated alternative objectives for the company. The following three alternative strategic company objective statements include the one given earlier plus two others considered in the candy company situation:

1. The strategic objective of the company is to be an aggressively expanding publicly-held national manufacturer-retailer of a wide line of high-quality candies and related products, selling mainly through its own retail stores under its own brand name to all types of customers.

2. The strategic objective of the company is to be an aggressively expanding closely-held regional manufacturer-retailer of a wide line of high-quality candy and related products, selling through its own retail shops (mainly but not exclusively) under its own brand name, and serving other wholesale, institutional, and retail customers with a full line of candy and related products under a variety of company brand names.
3. The strategic objective of the company is to be an aggressively expanding closely-held regional manufacturer-retailer of a limited line of high-quality, moderately-priced, and distinctively boxed chocolate candies, selling principally through its own retail stores under its own brand name to consumers, but also serving wholesale, chain, and institutional customers or outlets under other brand names to the degree permitted by available production capacity and by the company's ability to raise capital.

The following is a summary of the qualitative evaluation of these alternatives. This evaluation was done using the following guidelines:

- Company and competitor strengths and weaknesses are compared in key-to-success and opportunity areas to determine the chances for success
- Reasons are given for each assessment. The reasons are based on earlier industry, market, and company planning assumptions
- Potential problems are identified, where relevant
- Feasible ways around these problems are proposed

The first alternative calls for national expansion. This would appear to be a good idea when the competitive situation is analyzed initially: a world war had recently ended, consumption was expected to increase and competition had only recently begun to increase. However, it requires dilution of ownership control, which seems to be resisted by the present owners. Since selling nationally suggests an extension of the product line, this would theoretically increase volume per store and so compensate for the problems which might arise in a less-controlled national environment. However, one of the keys to success in this industry (especially in light of the competition and demographic trends) is to create a distinct image, preferably through a quality product line, at least when selling a limited line through company-owned outlets. With its limited management, the company would have difficulty maintaining that quality image across a larger product line and many geographically dispersed retail outlets. Broadening the product line and going national would, therefore, be difficult to do in the foreseeable future. This alternative seems to pose many unresolvable problems.

The second alternative has advantages over the first. It limits expansion to a geographic area with which the company is familiar and where it appears to have a competitive edge. This alternative expands the product line, the brand names, and customer base, and so expands the potential for sales volume. The company does not, however, have the production facilities to handle a wider product line. Efforts to overcome this obstacle by subcontracting production of new items to other manufacturers could create quality problems, especially with the limited management resources. While these problems might be overcome over the long run, this strategy has the potential danger of diluting the company's quality image and so preventing the company from excelling in a high-end market niche.

In the third alternative, by concentrating on a limited product line combined with a tightly controlled retail environment and a single brand name in its stores, the company could create a niche at the high end of the market, where it could have competitive edge with its moderate prices. It would sell under another brand name outside of its own stores, so as not to dilute the store image. All elements would work together to support the strategy direction, focus, approach, and ownership target within the situation's financial, production, and management restraints. This base could later be used to extend the product line and geographic scope of company operations, but only if its competitive edge is first established within its region. The third objective, then, seemed to better integrate all the situational factors.

The strategy formulation and evaluation process continued. Further questions were posed in an effort to reevaluate and refine the objective tentatively chosen—the third one. For example, should the objective

- Specify more clearly what is meant by "closely held?" Should it include "closely held" at all, or instead allow for the eventuality of broader ownership control?
- Specify exactly what is meant by "moderately-priced and distinctively boxed chocolate candy?" Or, should it be even more general and say "all types of chocolate candy?"
- Specify the packaging and advertising approaches needed to support the overall quality limited product line niche strategy?
- Specify a different scope of operations? Should the company strive to eventually become a national enterprise through a gradual region by region expansion, or should it remain a regional company? Would the president be willing to give up control eventually, if it were the only means by which to go national?
- Specify what other brands should be produced?
- Allow for selling to non-owned retail outlets or through franchised outlets?

These questions may seem repetitious, but it is important to review basic strategic questions after a tentative objective has been selected. If possible, other experts would be consulted to provide fresh viewpoints and new insights. Such questioning helps either to reaffirm the validity of the tentative initial strategic objective selected or to help refine, revise, and amplify it, or to figure out ways around potential problems.

In this situation, the owner/manager's desire to maintain control will limit retail expansion. Attention, therefore, needs to be paid to the exact limits the owner/manager has placed on allowing lower level managers to participate in profits and ownership. Attention also needs to be paid to what steps might be taken (if any) to convince him to sell some equity in the company to raise expansion capital.

More than a dozen examples of alternative strategy evaluations are given in the *Towards the Future* sections of the comprehensive case studies involving actual companies in the Case Study section of this book.

Quantitative evaluations. In addition to such qualitative evaluations, some quantitative ones are needed. One kind, *assigning probabilities* as scenarios of anticipated competitor reactions to proposed alternative strategies are developed and studied, was discussed earlier in relation to the competitor scenario analysis shown in the scenario development in Figure 7-4.

Another common evaluation involves *financial projections* using financial models. This phase is often referred to as a financial quantification of earlier qualitative assumptions.

At a minimum, in the baked goods company situation, for example, financial projections are needed to assess the impact of a greater volume of specialty cookies on the company's operations and profitability:

- Projections of what profits would be at several levels of sales and under varying assumptions about costs, price, competition, and general business levels
- An estimate of capital requirements, as well as return on investment (ROI), under these various scenarios
- An estimate of cashflows and requirements

In addition, projections are needed of the impact on production, sales operations, and management.

The ultimate goal of the financial evaluation is twofold:

- To determine which alternatives have the greatest rate of return for the company
- To evaluate the feasibility of pursuing a given alternative or set of alternatives in light of available capital inside and outside the company

In order to construct *proforma* financial statements, the assumptions in all areas affecting costs and sales had to be specified. These assumptions covered ranges of anticipated competitor actions, raw material costs, economic conditions, labor and product costs, disposable income, population, market growth projections, and other relevant situation factors. Three projections — optimistic, average, and pessimistic — were made. The worst case scenario was especially needed to estimate the risks of each proposed strategy.

In addition, the kinds of information to be included in the proforma statements had to be defined, as well as their scope and limits. For example, the planner answered such questions as Are the sales projections to be quarterly or monthly? How many years into the future are projections needed? Any other desired financial model specifications are also included.

Various financial software applications are available to assist in doing financial evaluations of strategy alternatives. The computer disks accompanying this book provide examples of some basic financial analysis and simulation tools, as well as the opportunity to use them with nine of the case studies available with this text.

Other *graphic and mathematical* strategy formulation and evaluation approaches are also useful in evaluating alterative strategies. Some of these involve structuring matrices for each strategy in each opportunity area, using a form such as the one shown in Figure 4-8 and reproduced in Figure 7-5.

Using such matrices, weights are assigned to relative company and competitor positions in each area critical to success and a cumulative weight is given to each alternative. An estimate is then made of the relative chances of success against the competition with each strategy. A number of additional readily accessible and understandable graphic and quantitative tools useful in formulating and evaluating alternative strategies are given throughout this book, for example in Figures 6-7 and 7-4, as well as in several useful supplementary texts [Mockler 1992; Webster 1989]. The limitations and possible misuse of such quantitative tools, which are based on value judgments about future events and so are not facts, is covered in other discussions in this book.

Operations research and *management science* provide additional tools for evaluating strategic alternatives [Rosenkranz 1979]. For example, 25 percent of American Airlines' Decision Technologies Group's operations research work involves supporting strategic decision making. One such decision involved creating an operations research analytical tool for evaluating a proposed $1 billion expansion at Dallas/Fort Worth Airport [Cooke 1989]. At Federal Express, operations research tools are used for analysis and evaluation in such strategic decision situations as long-term hub network configurations, staffing, fleet configuration, and facilities requirements [Fisher 1989].

The Place of Reasonable Judgments, Creativity, and Uncertainty

While they are useful and necessary quantitative evaluation tools, the accuracy and usefulness of financial simulations (projections) of the impact of alternative strategies and other quantitative tools varies from situation to situation. First, the financial figures are no better than the assumptions upon which they are built, and competitor and customer actions cannot be anticipated with certainty. For instance, IBM had no way of knowing in 1987 that the market for its new System 2 computers would be so difficult to develop, nor that competitors like Compaq, Dell, and Tandy would continue to expand and develop the traditional PC market so successfully. As another example, union actions, as Eastern Airlines discovered in 1989, can have a high emotional, as well as rational, impact on strategy formulation, and create unforeseen consequences, which in this case led to the liquidation of the entire company.

Second, strategic considerations in some situations can outweigh the conclusions drawn from the financial projections. For example, major technological advances or competitive rivalries may leave a company with no choice but to invest in new technology or new markets in order to survive, in spite of the inherent risks involved, if a strategic decision has been made to stay in business. For example, many companies which did (or wanted to do) business in Europe were forced to invest in plants there at very high prices. New European Economic Community regulations required that by 1992 80 percent of products sold in Europe be made in Europe or heavy tariffs would be imposed on the products [Glasgall 1991; Olsen 1991; Schares 1991].

This does not mean that financial projections should not be made — they are always useful in measuring risk and estimating capital requirements and profitability. It means that financial projections and mathematical analyses are not the only criteria used in evaluating alternative strategies.

At times companies will literally stumble onto strategies. For example, Alias Research Inc. was originally a computer animation company which did movie ("Terminator 2") and television commercial work. In 1985, CEO Stephen Bingham was in Detroit trying to sell animation software to be used in General Motors commercials. During the visit an impromptu meeting with GM engineers led to a $1 million order for automotive design software which gave engineers the

Figure 7-5: Comparative Competitive Position Evaluation

Industry Opportunity Area Under Study: ____________________

(1) Industry & Market: Keys to Success	(2) Keys To Success Rethink, Reword, Reorder. Write Down Revised Version in Order of Importance	(3) Give Weight to Each Area (Total = 100)	(4) Our Company's Strengths in Key-to-Success Areas. Use Same Rating Scale as Used in Column (5)	(5) Individual Competitor's or Competitor Group's Strength in Relation to Each Key-To-Success Area (Scale: 1=Weak, 2=Average, 3=Strong)						(6) Competition's Overall Strength Average of Individual Competitor's Strength in Section (5)	(7) Rate Company's Strength Versus Competition's (3 = Greater 2 = Same 1 = Weaker)	(8) Weighted Value = Column (3) Times Column (7) (Highest possible Value = 100 x 3 = 300)
				C-1	C-2	C-3	C-4	C-5	C-6			
1.	1.											
2.	2.											
3.	3.											
4.	4.											
5.	5.											
6.	6.											
8.	8.											
9.	9.											
		Column (3) Total Should Equal 100								Total Score Of Column (8) =		
										Total Score of Column (8) As Percent of 300 =		

ability to simulate future products and work out bugs more quickly and cheaply than through building and manipulating mock-ups. By 1991, Alias was the world leader in computer-aided industrial-design software [Farnsworth 1991].

For these reasons, quantitative techniques — including financial projections — are almost always combined with qualitative, subjective judgments, as well as creative and intuitive thinking, in formulating strategies. Since the future is uncertain, judgment sometimes ultimately plays some role in strategy formulation and selection. Strategic management can only promise improved chances of success, not the certainty of success.

MAKING THESE DECISIONS IN SPECIFIC COMPANY AND COMPETITIVE MARKET SITUATIONS

This chapter focuses on several critical strategy formulation tasks involved in all kinds of strategic management situations, including:

- Recommend a general strategic direction for the company under study, and identify the situational factors and the evaluation that led to this recommendation
- Recommend a strategy focus for the company under study, and identify the situational factors, such as company strengths, and the evaluation that led to this recommendation
- Recommend a strategic approach for the company under study, and describe the component-by-component evaluation that led to this recommendation
- Recommend strategic targets for the company under study, and describe the evaluation that led to this recommendation
- Outline your competitor-by-competitor analysis and evaluation
- Formulate strategies and explain the evaluation and selection process

As seen in Figure 7-6, the decision-making processes described in this chapter relate to other strategy formulation decision-making areas. During this phase, analyses of such situation factors as *industry type and trends, competitive market elements, competitive factors, company factors, opportunities and keys to success, and the comparative competitive position and related strengths and weaknesses of the company and competition in opportunity and key-to-success areas* are all relevant to decisions made about strategy.

The tasks performed during this phase of the strategy formulation process provide necessary background for other strategic management tasks, which involve developing enabling plans, integrating the planning effort, and implementing the planning effort and plans.

As with the earlier phases of the strategy formulation process, portions of this phase have been replicated in structured decision-making models. These models in turn have served as the basis for the knowledge-based system described at the end of Chapters 3 through 6. As an example of the overall approach, the small concept testing system described in Appendix A and reproduced in Figure 7-7 outlines the initial prototype system used for making the final strategy decision at the general direction level.

In addition to knowledge-based systems computer tools, many conventional computer tools are useful in formulating the overall strategies for a business entity as a whole or for a strategic business unit. As discussed in this chapter, these tools are used principally in three critical areas:

- Evaluating potential competitor moves in response to proposed alternative strategies
- Evaluating financial implications of proposed alternatives
- Formulating and evaluating alternative strategies

A CONTINUING PROCESS

This chapter concludes the discussion in PART THREE of the context-specific decision processes involved in formulating strategies in general, as well as overall or enterprise-wide company strategies in particular. This is referred to by some as the thinking side of strategic management. Further discussions of this topic are included in Appendices A and D of this book.

The chapters in PART FOUR discuss how enterprise-wide strategies are implemented. For this reason, the following chapters are more concerned with activating and getting things done.

While treated separately, strategy formulation and implementation are only on rare occasions two distinct phases in strategic management. Strategy formulation is a continuing, integrative, context-specific process. New knowledge obtained while developing operational plans or implementing strategies can lead to reformulating enterprise-wide strategies. Formulating these strategies is generally an evolving process, during which strategies emerge and take shape gradually and incrementally, as the strategic management process progresses.

In addition, as discussed in Appendix B, the process through which strategies are formulated can have a major impact on the effectiveness of a strategy's implementation.

THE SYSTEMS CONCEPT UNDERLYING STRATEGY FORMULATION AND IMPLEMENTATION

When examining the situation context during strategy formulation and implementation, the focus is on the total business context. That perspective is referred to as the total business process or system involved.

For the enterprise as a whole, this context should be the business system or process that serves the customer—the objective of the process or focus of the business system. Michael Walsh did this at Union Pacific when he studied the customer needs and the business process or system which would most effectively serve those needs. In addition to customer needs, his context study covered the nature of the business, competitive market conditions, company resources, available technology, profitability, and other related factors.

Viewing a business or business segment from a total system context viewpoint, both as an internal system and as a segment of a competitive market system, is not a new concept. Such studies have a long history [Mockler 1977]. Peter Senge [1990] and Larry Hirchhorn and Thomas

Figure 7-6: Strategic Management Decision-Making Process

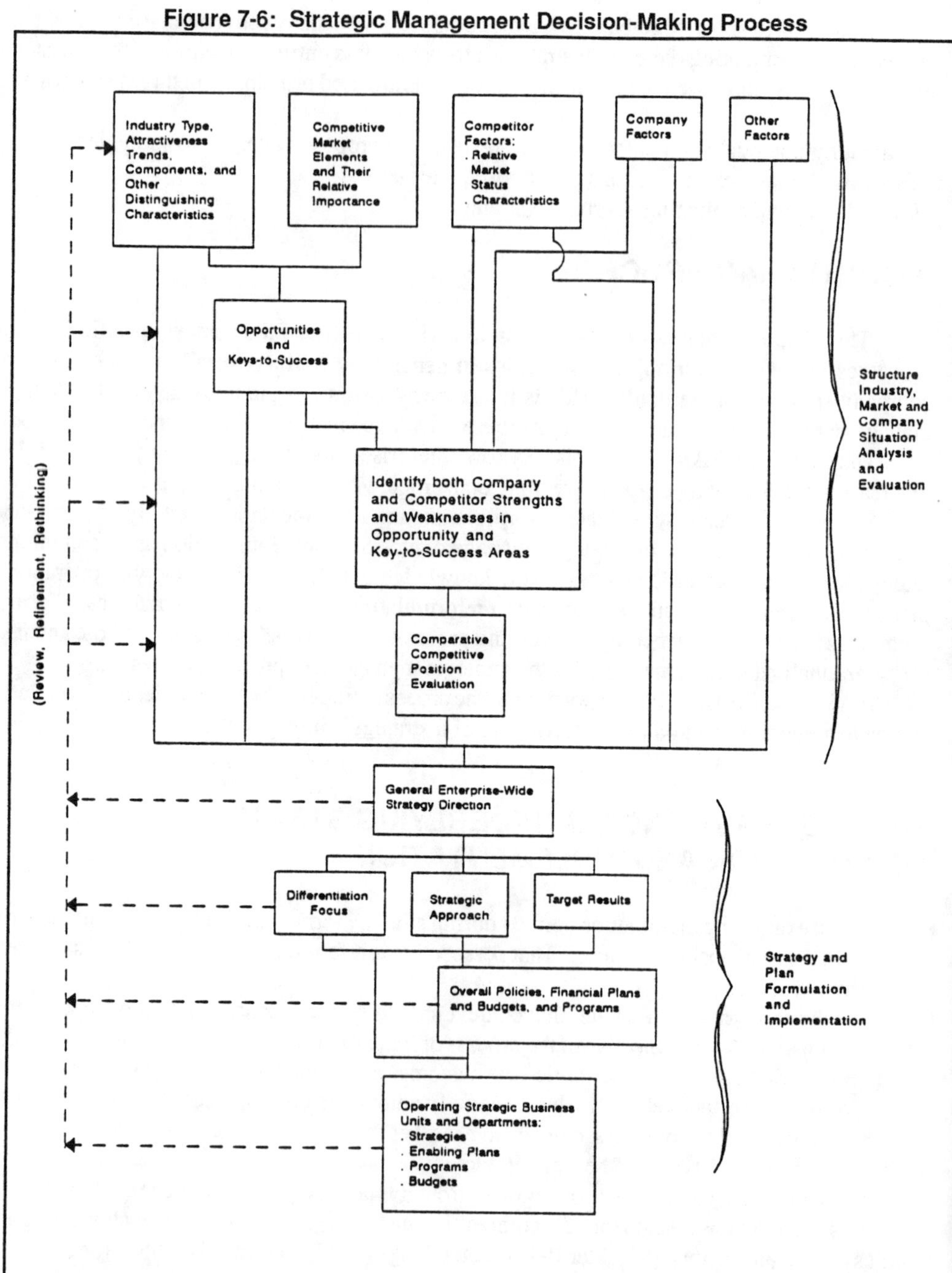

Figure 7-7: Dependency Diagram for Strategy Planning System — General Strategy Directions Subsystem

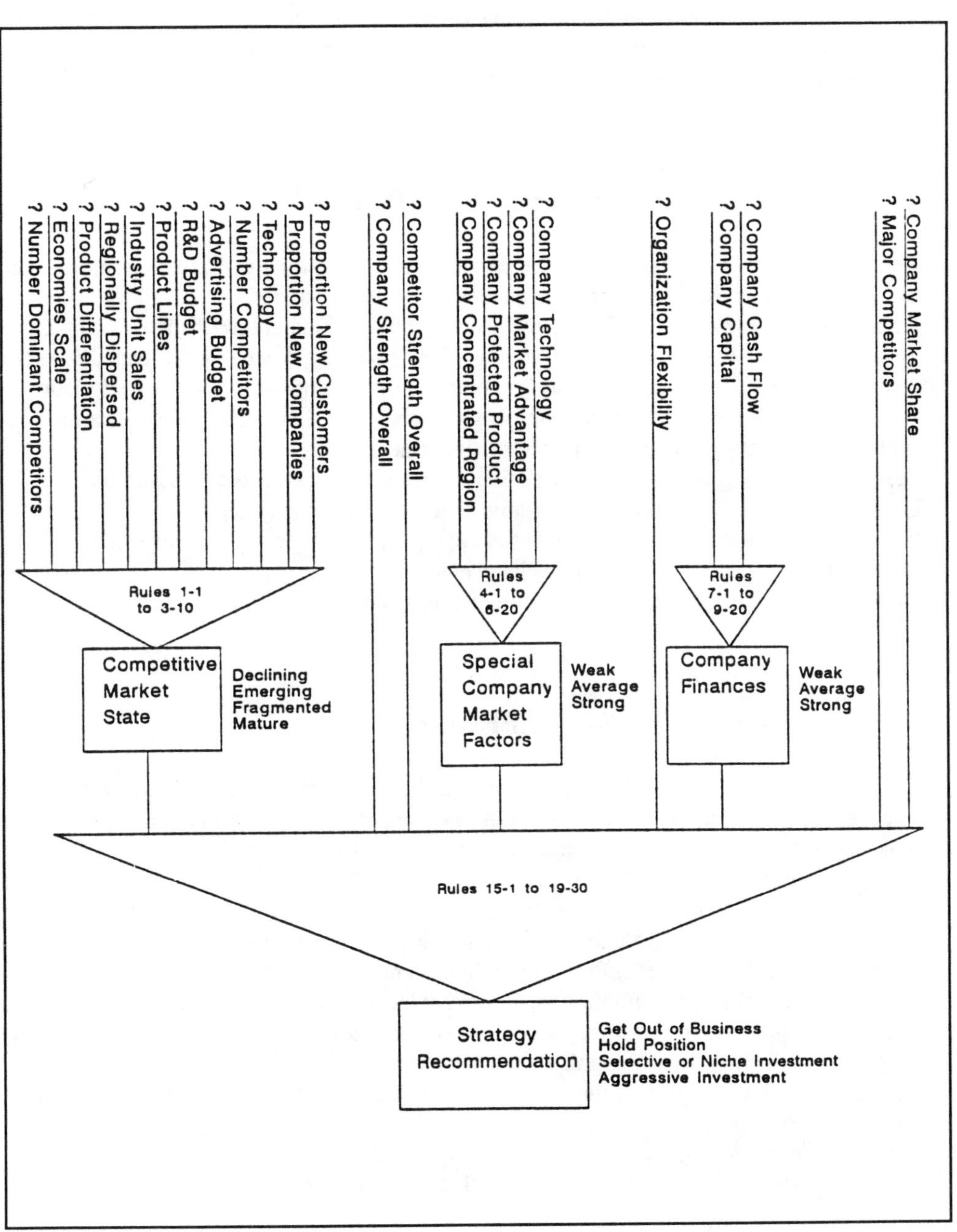

Gilmore [1992] are some of the people who have more recently written on the subject of the total systems thinking approach to business planning and management.

The situation orientation of this text is designed to help readers look at strategy formulation and implemntation decisions from a total context viewpoint. Hopefully, this will enable readers to consider *all* relevant factors, their *interrelationships* to each other, and their impact on alternative development and decision making.

REVIEW QUESTIONS

1. Describe ways in which examining the implications of earlier structured situation analyses and evaluations can be useful in formulating enterprise-wide strategies.
2. Describe the four levels of enterprise-wide strategies identified in this chapter.
3. Describe component-by-component strategy formulation. In what ways can the earlier analyses provide a structure and basis for component-by-component strategy formulation?
4. What is involved in a competitor-by-competitor risk analysis? In what ways is such an analysis useful in formulating and evaluating alternative strategies?
5. Describe different ways in which alternative enterprise- wide strategies are formulated.
6. Describe different ways in which alternative strategies can be evaluated.
7. In what ways can seemingly small changes in a company's strategic objective have a significant impact on a company's operational decision making?
8. Discuss the ways in which strategy formulation is an emerging, continuing process.

EXERCISES

1. Read any one of the company studies in the Case Study section at the end of this book whose title contains the actual company name. Using the company study of your choice, write a report which covers the following tasks outlined at the end of the chapter:

- Recommend a general strategic direction for the company under study, and identify the situational factors and the evaluation that led to this recommendation
- Recommend a strategy focus for the company under study, and identify the situational factors, such as company strengths, and the evaluation that led to this recommendation
- Recommend a strategic approach for the company under study, and describe the component-by-component evaluation that led to this recommendation
- Recommend strategic targets for the company under study, and describe the evaluation that led to this recommendation
- Outline your competitor-by-competitor risk analysis and evaluation
- Formulate strategies, and explain their evaluation and selection

2. Read recent issues of the periodicals referred to in the references section at the end of the chapter, or other related periodicals of your choice, and find a description of a company of interest to you. Write a report on that company covering the same tasks as listed in Exercise #1.

3. The disks accompanying this book contain several prototype KBS. If you have not done so already, follow the directions accompanying the disks to run a consultation using the system with the file name PLANNING.REV or FRNCHISE.REV. If you wish, you might also print out the knowledge base and study it while you are running the system and restudying this chapter, in order to get a detailed picture of how strategy formulation decisions are made.

4. The disk accompanying this book contains basic simulation tools. Following the guidelines given in the booklet accompanying the disk, choose a case from the nine companies listed in the booklet for which simulations are available and do a financial analysis related to the company study you have chosen.

REFERENCES

Barmesh, Isadore, "J.C. Penney's Woes Tied to Lack of Identity," *The New York Times*, April 23, 1991, pp. D1, D7.

Bevins, Terry, "New CEO Has Campbell Soup Co. Cooking," *Sunday Freeman*, August 25, 1991, pp. 33, 35.

Caillot, Jacques J., "Papier Mache: How a Paper Company Built a Leader in High Technology," *The Planning Forum Network*, August 1991, pp. 2, 4, 6.

Chakravorty, Subarte N., "We Changed the Whole Playing Field: Triumph for Gillette's Colman Mockler — Technology as a Marketing Tool," *Forbes*, February 4, 1991, pp. 82-86.

Cohen, Roger, "Ms. Playboy: Christie Hefner May Have Saved Her Father's Company — But Can She Change It?", *The New York Times*, Magazine Section, June 9, 1991, pp. 32, 55-57, 84.

Coles, Carol Bruckner, "A Spinoff Strategy to Ignite Growth," *The New York Times*, Business Section, May 3, 1992, p. 13.

Cooke, Thomas M., "OR/MS: Alive and Flying at American Airlines," *OR/MS Today*, June 1989, pp. 16-20.

Fabrikant, Geraldine, "Turner Broadcasting in Middle-Age Malaise," *The New York Times*, October 12, 1990, pp. D1, D4.

Farnsworth, Clyde H., "Software Star on a Roller Coaster," *The New York Times*, Business (Money) Section, September 29, 1991, F15.

Fisher, Michael, "Operations Research at Federal Express," *OR/MS Today*, June 1989, pp. 20-21.

Fitzgerald, Michael, "Still Searching for the IS Holy Grail," *Computerworld*, August 26, 1991, p. 47.

Forest, Stephanie Anderson, "Trapped Between the Up and Down Escalators: Penney's New Image Is Bringing Problems, and Profits Are Sliding," *Business Week*, August 26, 1991, pp. 49, 50.

Foust, Dean, "Marriott Is Smoothing Out the Lumps in Its Bed," *Business Week*, April 1, 1991, pp. 74-76.

Freedman, Alix M., "Campbell Chief Cooks Up Winning Menu," *The Wall Street Journal*, February 15, 1991, pp. B1, B5.

Freudenheim, Milt, "Keeping the Pipeline Filled at Merck," *The New York Times*, Business Section,

February 16, 1992, pp. 1.

Glasgall, William, David Greising, Jonathan Kapstein, and John Templeman, "Eastward Ho! The Pioneers Plunge In," *Business Week*, April 15, 1991, pp. 51-53.

Harrop, Froma, "The Classic Conglomerate Wades Into the 90's," *The New York Times*, Business Section, February 5, 1990, p.

Hirsch, James S., "Brash Phar-Mor Chain Has Uneven Selection, But It's Always Cheap," *The Wall Street Journal*, June 24, 1991, pp. A1, A6.

Hirschhorn, Larry, and Thomas Gilmore, "The New Boundaries of the 'Boundaryless Company'," *Harvard Business Review*, May/June 1992, pp. 104-114.

Lohr, Steve, "The Best Little Bank in America," *The New York Times*, Business Section, July 7, 1991, pp. 1-4.

McGill, Douglas C., "Sara Lee's Success with Brands," *The New York Times*, June 19, 1989, pp. D1, D3.

McKibben, Gordon, "Gillette's Mockler: Going Out on Top," *The Boston Sunday Globe*, November 18, 1990, pp. A1, A7.

Milbank, Dana, "Bethlehem Steel Takes Steps to Shed Former Identity," *The Wall Street Journal*, February 6, 1992, p. B4.

Mockler, Robert J., *Computer Software to Support Strategic Management Decision Making*, New York: Macmillan Publishing, 1992.

Mockler, Robert J., *Management Information Systems*, Columbus, OH: Merrill, 1977.

Olsen, Ken, Lynne Reaves, Gail Schares, and Elizabeth Weiner, "Reawakening: A Market Economy Takes Root in Eastern Europe," *Business Week*, April 15, 1991, pp. 46-50.

Painton, Priscilla, "The Taming of Ted Turner," *Time*, January 6, 1992, pp. 34-39.

Phillips, Stephen, "Back to Basics at Quaker Oats," *New York Times*, November 26, 1986, p. 37.

Porter, Michael, *Competitive Strategy*, New York: The Free Press, 1980.

Prokesch, Steven, "Guiness Takes a Luxury Tack," *The New York Times*, Business Section, May 10, 1992(A), p. 5.

Prokesch, Steven, "Britain's Low Profile Publishing Giant," *The New York Times*, Business Section, February 9, 1992(B), p. 5.

Reimann, Bernard C., "'Lily Pad' Strategy Leapfrogs Nordson to Enviable Growth," *The Planning Forum Network*, April 1991, pp. 1, 2.

Robert, Michel, *The Strategist CEO*, Westport, CT: Quorum Books, 1988.

Rosenkranz, Friedrich, *An Introduction to Corporate Modelling*, Durham, NC: Duke University Press, 1979.

Ruffenach, Glenn, "Shaw Uses Price Cuts to Extend Carpet Business," *The Wall Street Journal*, June 12, 1991, pp. A1, A8.

Salpukas, Agis, "Eastern Airlines Is Shutting Down and Plans to Liquidate Its Assets," *The New York Times*, January 19, 1991, pp. 1, 48.

Sandomir, Richard, "Wayne Huizenga's Growth Complex," *The New York Times*, The New York Times Magazine, June 9, 1991, pp. 22-25.

"Sara Lee CEO Profiles Strategies Behind Their Corporate Growth," *The Planning Forum Network*, January 1990, p. 1.

Schares, Gail E., "Czechoslovakia: Reluctant Reform," "Poland: The Pain and Gain," and "Hungary: A Giant Step Ahead," *Business Week*, April 15, 1991, pp. 54-58.

Senge, Peter M., *The Fifth Discipline: The Art and Practice of the Learning Organization*, New York: Currency/Doublday, 1990.

Shapiro, Eben, "A Mixed Outlook for Blockbuster," *The New York Times*, February 21, 1992, p. D6.

Trachtenberg, Jeffrey A., "Ikea Furniture Chain Pleases with Its Prices, Not with Its Service," *The Wall Street Journal*, September 17, 1991, pp. A1, A6.

Waldman, Peter, and Michael J. McCarthy, "Derring-Do Fades at Turner's Empire," *The Wall Street Journal*, October 12, 1990, pp. B1, B4.

Wayne, Leslie, "Forging a Global Empire in a Sluggish Market," *The New York Times*, January 21, 1990, Business Section, 5.

Webster, James L., William E. Reif, and Jeffrey S. Bracker, "The Manager's Guide to Strategic Planning Tools and Techniques," *Planning Review*, November/December 1989, pp. 4-12, 48.

White, Joseph B., "How Detroit Diesel, Out from Under GM, Turned Around Fast," *The Wall Street Journal*, August 16, 1991, pp. A1, A8.

Woo, C.Y., J.E. Wilhard, and U.S. Daellenbach, "Spinoff Performance: A Case of Overstated Expectations?" *Strategic Management Journal*, September 1992, pp. 433-448.

PART FOUR

STRATEGY IMPLEMENTATION

CHAPTER 8

CREATING AN INTEGRATED STRATEGIC MANAGEMENT FRAMEWORK

The objective of this chapter is to help readers to

- Extend the scope of enterprise-wide strategies in order to provide an integrated implementation framework through
  - company policies and philosophy
  - financial plans and budgets
  - return-on-investment analysis, policies regarding resource allocation, capital budgeting and management, and capital source identification
  - short- and long-range programming
  - strategy formulation and implementation for major operating departments
- Develop an integrated situational framework for strategy formulation and implementation at the operational level, and for strategy refinement and reformulation as competitive markets change over time

While it is important to have an enterprise-wide strategic vision, it should be clear from the experiences of Colman Mockler at Gillette [Chakravorty 1991], Roger Penske at Detroit Diesel [White 1991], and Michael Walsh at Union Pacific and Tenneco [Hayes 1992] that translating a strategic vision into effective action is not an easy task. Strategy formulation does not automatically lead to strategy implementation. It is often difficult to communicate the strategic thinking underlying enterprise-wide strategies. People often resist new thinking in organizations, and do not always react rationally to change. In addition, judging from the experiences of companies discussed earlier in this text, such as Reid International, the British publisher [Prokesch 1992], success can at times depend on having the flexibility to adapt, modify, clarify and refine, and even reformulate enterprise-wide strategies as new information is obtained, as more people become involved in implementation and as competitive market and company requirements change.

A considerable amount of context-specific management — that is, management appropriate to the specific external and internal situation under study — is therefore required in implementing strategies. For this reason, the final section of this chapter presents an integrated adaptive situational approach to strategy implementation at the departmental levels, where enabling strategies are formulated and carried out.

As a company and its CEO move from vision to reality in strategic management, the vision takes on more specific dimensions. That is, it is gradually translated into specific plans and action.

The chapters in PART FOUR focus on putting enterprise-wide strategies into practice to make money by more precisely defining these strategies and the specific ways they will be carried out, and then carrying them out effectively. This chapter discusses an often encountered early phase in translating enterprise-wide strategies into action — extending the scope of the strategy formulation process to provide a framework for operational (or enabling) planning and plan implementation. The material in this chapter generally covers the strategic management task identified in Figure 8-1 as developing an integrated framework for enabling planning.

Subsequent chapters in PART FOUR discuss the formulation of enabling or operating strategies and plans, as well as the business process reengineering, organization restructuring, leadership, staffing, and control required to effectively implement strategies and related plans. Appendix B discusses approaches to carrying out a company's planning effort in a way that promotes strategic thinking throughout a company.

EXTENDING THE SCOPE OF ENTERPRISE-WIDE STRATEGIES: AN INTEGRATED STRATEGIC MANAGEMENT FRAMEWORK

This section discusses several ways in which the enterprise-wide strategic direction, focus, approach, and performance targets described in Chapter 7 can be extended to help provide an integrated framework for operational planning and plan implementation. Such extension areas include: company policies and philosophies; financial plans and budgets; return-on-investment analyses; resource allocation, capital budgeting and management, and sources of capital; short- and long-range programming; strategy formulation and implementation for strategic business units and for major operating departments.

The examples in this section extend the conceptual patterns of the strategies formulated in Chapter 7 and the earlier competitive market analyses in Chapters 3-6. There a component-by-component pattern of analysis was initiated in the early industry analyses. This same pattern or mental model was continued during the opportunity and key-to-success analyses, and in the later comparative competitive position analyses. As pointed out there, a variety of conceptual patterns can be useful in strategy formulation studies. The choice of one depends on the specific situation

Figure 8-1: Strategic Management Tasks

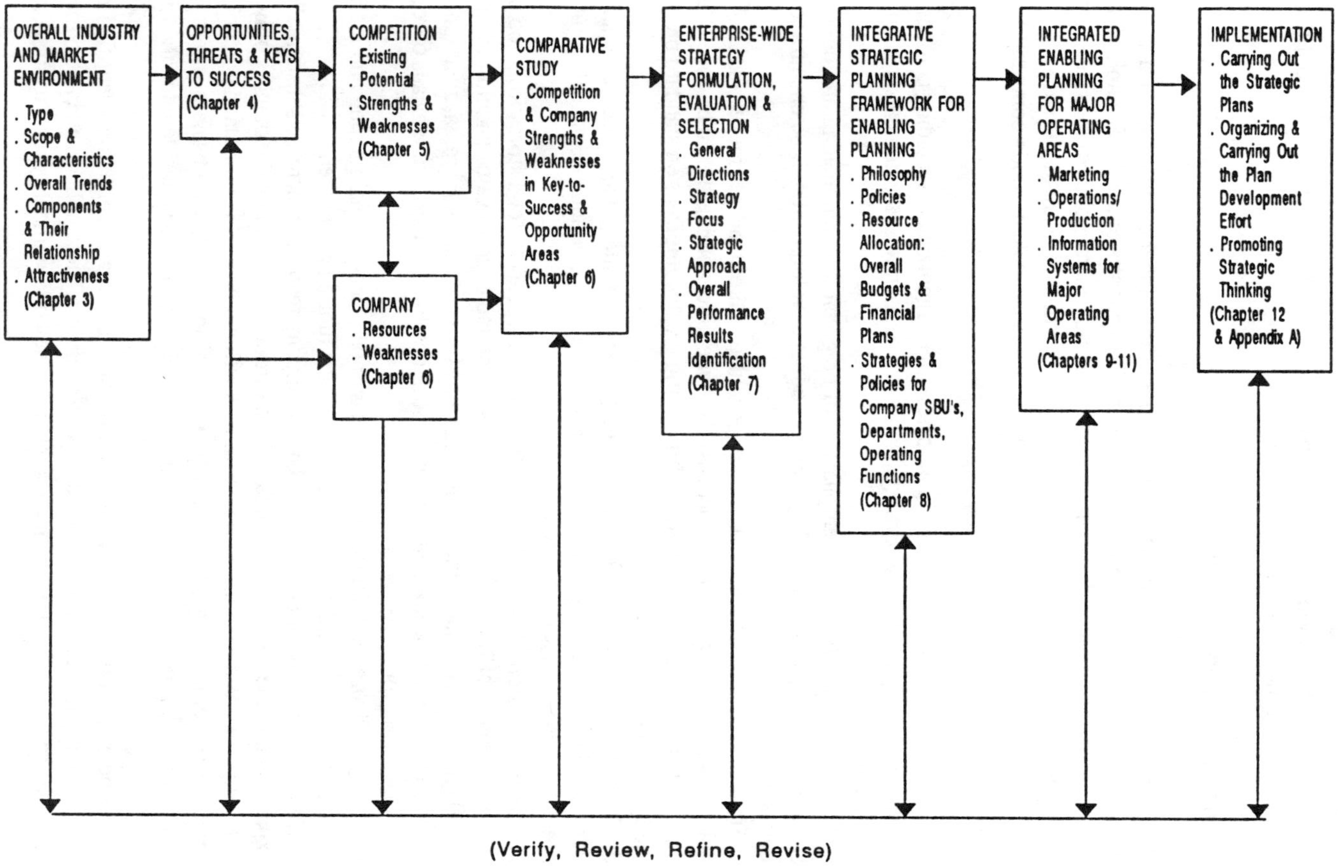

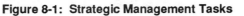

context requirements, including the personal preferences of the one doing the planning [Mockler 1992(A), 1992(B)]. The component-by-component pattern is used here to provide continuity with the discussions in earlier chapters.

Company Policies and Philosophy

Policies can be formulated, where appropriate, for critical components of a company's strategic objective. Policies define and clarify enterprise-wide strategies. An example of how this was done at a large company is shown in Figure 8-2, where general policies covering seven areas are given after eleven aspects of the company's strategic objective are identified.

The following were some policies formulated in the baked goods company situation discussed in Chapters 6 and 7:

a. *Sales Force.* Any major change in the sales force organization, including compensation, will be made only to direct the salesperson's efforts toward strategic goals, not solely for cost-cutting purposes.
b. *Specialty Products.* Special emphasis will be given to strengthening and building the specialty baked goods area, and specialty product development will be encouraged at all levels of the company.
c. *Standard Products.* New products will be added to the standard cracker and cookie line only where they can be cost-justified. At the same time, nothing should be done to alter or cut the standard line which would inhibit placing greater emphasis on standard products in the future, should circumstances warrant it.
d. *Competitor Acquisitions.* Purchasing any existing smaller baked goods competitors is desirable, both to prevent competitor expansion by acquisition and to expand the company's specialty baked goods market base.
e. *Independent Food Stores.* Before cutting any independent food stores from the present outlet list, every effort will be made to determine their future value should the specialty baked goods area expand. While some cuts may be warranted in this area, attention should focus on expanding the specialty product line and volume per store as a means of reducing unit sales costs for these stores.
f. *Chain Food Stores.* Additional emphasis will be placed on maintaining and increasing chain store buyer contacts, as this appears to be a future growth area.
g. *Geographic Scope of Operations.* Until company resources increase substantially, any expansion outside the four-state area will be through independent distributors only.
h. *Production.* While substantial investments will not be made in the standard cookie and cracker area, continuing studies will be made of technological advances in production machinery and processes so that expansion in that area may be considered in the future.

The policies in this situation were based on the planning assumptions identified during earlier industry, competitive market, and company analyses. These policies attempted to clarify and extend the scope of the strategic management framework, without becoming so specific as

Figure 8-2: One Company's Enterprise-Wide Strategic Planning Statement

The basic objectives and general policies of the company stated below are intended to provide the framework upon which both the long-range and day-to-day operations are to be based. These objectives have developed over a period of time, stemming from the basic philosophy agreed upon by the founders of the Company and have evolved as the Company matured. Changes in objectives must be developed carefully and the objectives should not be neglected for the purpose of everyday expediency.

PREMISES: COMPANY PHILOSOPHY

This statement of objectives is conceived as a mechanism for the examination and appraisal of working policies. The objectives are based on the following five major points:

a. The Company must be operated as a profitable enterprise, and must serve the needs of its customers, shareholders, and employees. It is our responsibilities involving the shareholders (dividends, stock appreciation), employees (salaries, benefits, working conditions), and the customer (quality product, fair price, good service).
b. The Character of the Company is determined by its decision to operate in highly specialized fields, and to carry a large burden of pioneering in new fields of applied science.
c. The rarest commodities in the world are human intelligence and ingenuity. These must not be wasted, neglected, or allowed to stagnate.
d. The best of scientific and engineering talent must be employed and placed in an environment which will facilitate the proper utilization of knowledge, intellect, and skill.
e. The operations of the Company are to be led by a management group which must have the respect of the organization for its business ability, integrity, fairness, and human approach to everyday problems.

Based upon these premises, the basic Company objectives are as follows:

OBJECTIVES

1. Purpose
The prime objective is to conduct a strong, well-balanced, stable, well-managed research, engineering, and manufacturing international enterprise organized to return maximum benefits to employees, customers, and stockholders.

2. Nature of Enterprise
The Company shall strive to be a highly competent, profit-minded, technically oriented enterprise engaging in research, engineering, and manufacturing to meet the needs of the world markets. The Company shall operate in those fields in which its research and development talents are required for business success. The Company shall endeavor to exploit its talents in establishing new techniques and, through them, new products for commercial, industrial, and defense applications.

3. Fields of Interest
The Company shall be engaged in the fields of microwave tubes and components; vacuum systems, instruments, and components; in fields exploiting recent contributions to science, including radio-frequency spectroscopy and instrumentation resulting therefrom; and other fields of science which may produce products useful for industrial, commercial, and defense needs.

4. Diversification
In recognition of the usual business cycles, the Company shall develop new products and enter new product areas or activities as may properly diversify, balance, and profitably strengthen the Company's economic position.

Figure 8-2: One Company's Enterprise-Wide Strategic Planning Statement (contd.)

The Company shall endeavor to broaden and strengthen its product lines or fields of interest by sponsoring research and engineering programs, by purchase of patent rights, or by acquisition in part or in whole of other companies. The diversification and growth of the Company shall be tempered with full consideration of its impact upon those who form the Company structure and careful consideration of financial stability and the danger of overextension.

5. Business Stability
The Company shall endeavor to optimize profits, stabilize employment, and develop a sound financial position by:

a. Good management practices
b. Long-range planning
c. Product diversification
d. Balanced commercial, industrial, and defense programs
e. Strong research and engineering efforts
f. Strong financial control
g. Efficient, low-cost organization and economical procedures

6. Planning
The Company shall prepare management programs looking several years in advance to permit prudent program decisions, and to permit analysis and criticism by the Board of Directors, the management, and others.

7. Patents
The Company shall maintain a strong patent position by obtaining patent protection for the inventions made by members of its staff, by acquiring patents from others, and by entering into licensing agreements with others. It shall encourage inventiveness of its employees by financial awards, publication, and other means.

8. Product Lines
The Company shall develop a balanced line of profitable products which lend themselves to the company's techniques of engineering, manufacturing, and distribution, and which serve diversified markets having either a continuing profit potential or showing promise of becoming profitable in the future.

In recognition of the importance and obligation of its role in the defense efforts of the United States, the government on a larger scale than is needed for the Company's manufacturing programs.

9. Financial
The Company shall strive to establish a stable financial structure, tightly controlled, with ample capitalization to operate the business efficiently and to permit necessary expansion and product diversification and to permit the Company to take advantage quickly of changing conditions.

10. Stock Policy
The Company shall encourage employee participation in the ownership of the Company.

11. Organization
The Company shall establish and maintain a sound structure and plan of organization which is necessary to meet the present and future Company objectives.

The Company shall be organized on a product line basis, with full profit accountability at the product division level. Methods of research, engineering, manufacturing, and marketing shall be adapted to the product areas. Corporate management will be responsible for binding these diverse products into the whole, and corporate staff

Figure 8-2: One Company's Enterprise-Wide Strategic Planning Statement (contd.)

functions shall supply those services not provided by line functions.

Management personnel shall be so developed and guided as to insure able and efficient performance of their duties. It is the Company's policy to hold each execution of its principles and objectives.

The Company shall adopt such principles of personnel administration as will improve the mutual understanding and increase the effectiveness of the staff.

GENERAL POLICIES

In conformance with its objectives, the Company shall adopt general administrative policies, including the following:

I. Organization

The Company shall so administer the organization as to make possible and to induce the highest possible productive efforts by:

a. Expecting above-average performance from employees and supervisor.

b. Coupling responsibility with authority, and reaching an understanding with those concerned before changing the scope of any responsibility.

c. Providing that no person shall be given directions by more than one person.

d. Assuring that all directions to an employee come from the immediate supervisor.

e. Assuring that no difference of opinion between supervisors or between employees as to authority or responsibility shall be considered too trivial for prompt and painstaking attention.

f. Assuring that a supervisor will counsel his employees, and will keep them informed on the nature of their performance.

II. Principles of Supervision

The Company shall conduct its supervision so as to emphasize respect for the personality and dignity of the individual. The policy of consultation up and down the organization lines of authority and channels o communication shall be encouraged, as well as:

a. Giving consideration to an employee's views before reaching decisions materially affecting his job and interests.

b. Encouraging employees to express their views on matters affecting their jobs and interests.

c. Freely explaining all matters affecting employee relations.

d. Attempting to understand the other person's point of view, and assuming that he too wants to do a good job.

III. Employment

The Company shall recruit and maintain the highest caliber staff possible to fill all positions, whether scientific, administrative, clerical, or of the skilled trades, and will do so by:

a. Selecting applicants on the basis of character, ability, skill, experience, and training, and without reference to age, sex, race, or creed.

b. Giving careful consideration to the promotion of employees to vacancies which occur, with the understanding that the strength of the Company's organization must be protected.

c. Giving consideration to employees who request job changes, and attempting to place each employee in the work for which he is best suited.

d. Maintaining a planned management development program to assure maximum performance by supervisors.

Figure 8-2: One Company's Enterprise-Wide Strategic Planning Statement (contd.)

IV. Wages and Compensation

The Company shall establish a balanced compensation program for all employees, clearly related to job requirements of skill, responsibility, education, and experience, as demanded in current job descriptions.

The Company shall pay rates of pay, and establish rate ranges for all jobs, that are at least as good as those prevailing for similar work under similar conditions, and will maintain an equitable program for the granting of merit and promotional salary increases.

In recognition of the principle that scientific and technical contributions are as important as those made by management personnel, the Company will make the higher salaries available to top technical personnel without requiring them to shift to management occupations.

V. Working Conditions

The Company shall create and maintain working conditions in offices and factories so that they are safe, clean, attractive, and generally conductive of high productive effort.

VI. Grievances

The Company shall assure employees that they are free to express themselves and without prejudice as to matters discussed. The Company will also insure that the supervisory staff will try to remove promptly any source of dissatisfaction, and failing prompt and satisfactory adjustment, to provide for submission of the case to the Personnel Office for review and settlement in consultation with management.

VII. Benefit Plans

The Company shall make provisions for vacations, sick leave, and holidays with pay; install such insurance plans as will afford financial protection to the individual and his dependents in time of illness, injury, or death; and provide, at the employee's discretion, for the planned accumulation of funds sufficient to assure retirement benefits.

EVALUATION

The Company shall periodically appoint an advisory committee to assess the progress towards achievement of the Objectives and General Policies.

to stifle operational initiative. Depending on the size of the company and other situation factors, many levels of policies and strategies may exist, ranging from general corporate strategic guidelines for all divisions and strategic business units to specific functional or departmental strategic objectives and policies.

Some companies formulate a statement of company philosophy. Such statements articulate the values of the company and its management — a significant strategic management premise or underlying assumption. Figure 8-2 contains an example of a large company's philosophy statement.

Financial Plans and Budgets

Financial planning is the natural extension of, and provides an evaluation tool for, strategy formulation and implementation.

Financial results are one measure of the impact or effectiveness of strategies and strategic plans within a company. Such financial results are the ultimate, and for many the only, measure of survival and success. For this reason, *financial projections* or *proforma* statements are useful measures of the worth of different alternatives. These projections and their use in evaluating alternatives were discussed in Chapter 7. They can include income statements, balance sheets, capital budgets, cashflow statements, and return-on-investment projections. Examples of financial analysis and financial simulation useful in evaluating the impact of strategies on company financial results are given on the disks (and related exercises and examples) accompanying this book.

Financial plans flowing from strategy formulation and strategic plan development can involve both long- and short-range projections. They would include, at a minimum, proforma profit-and-loss, cashflow, capital investment, and return-on-investment projections or budgets. In addition, factory budgets, fixed cost budgets, sales expense budgets, or budgets for any part of a company's business operations may be developed. While the most common type are annual budgets, such projections can be for any time period appropriate to the situation under study. An example of a budget used at one small company is shown in Figure 8-3. There, the budgeted figures are compared with the actual figures.

The financial planning and budgeting discussed here is used to guide and control both operating and capital investment decisions. Since they focus on operating results, financial budgets and plans are a very specific integrative enabling framework for operational planning. For this reason, they are often referred to as "value drivers" of a business and are used as specific benchmarks for control [McConahey 1992].

Return-on-Investment Analysis, Resource Allocation and Capital Budgeting and Management, and Sources of Capital

Enterprise-wide strategies and financial policies often do not specify the exact amounts of capital needed to carry out different strategies, nor in many situations do they specify how the capital will be raised. This is because final versions of such capital budgets are difficult to develop until the specific operating plans and programs have been formulated and because competitive market conditions can change rapidly. For example, when Atlantic Richfield developed a new, lower-polluting gasoline, it was unable to make specific plans to produce and sell it nationwide because of the uncertainty of government regulations, possible competitor moves, and customer resistance to its higher cost [Rose 1991; Wald 1991].

Since planning is not done in isolated phases, capital considerations arise throughout the strategic management process, as the cost of alternatives, return on investment, and availability of capital are evaluated, and as operating plans and financial budgets are formulated.

As planning progresses, more precise estimates of rates of return, capital requirements, and availability of capital are made and alternative strategies are evaluated in light of these estimates. Subsequently, resources are allocated, capital budgets are drawn up, and strategies for obtaining capital are formulated.

Return on investment analysis. Each alternative strategy has an estimated return on investment. In making the estimated *return on investment*, judgment is needed to structure the way the calculations are made. For example, is the calculation to be based on cashflow over the life of the investment, on profits generated before or after taxes, or on both? Each proposal must be evaluated on a consistent and comparable basis.

Some measure of risk normally is associated with different alternatives. Projected returns on investments are, therefore, adjusted for the risks inherent in a proposal. Certain industries inherently carry greater risks than others. For instance, in the periodical publishing industry, the chances of success are historically only 2 out of 10, which makes this a risky business [Freitag 1989; Reilly 1992].

Risks are also related to a company's position in a competitive market. The Chrysler Corporation invested over $1 billion to develop a new line of mid-sized cars. These L/H cars, to be introduced in 1992, were designed to sell for $15,000 to $22,000. Because of Chrysler's small size in relation to the rest of the automobile market, its weakening market position in 1991, and the expected competition from Japanese automakers in the mid-range market, the investment was considered a high-risk one, which Chrysler nonetheless had to make if it was to survive. If the new cars do not sell, overall company sales would be hurt and Chrysler's design and engineering competence would be questioned, which would do long-term damage to the company [Levin 1991, 1992]. In this situation the risks involved in making the investment greatly exceeded the possibility of eventually going out of business if the company did not make the investment.

As seen from the Chrysler example, initial calculations of rates of return have to be adjusted for the risks inherent in each proposal under consideration. For instance, a much higher rate of return would be required for an oil exploration drilling program (a high-risk investment) than for a more stable investment in an apartment building or motel.

When the rate of return adjusted for risk is calculated for each strategic move and associated program, a comparison of alternatives competing for scarce corporate resources can then be made. This is a powerful tool for evaluating alternative company strategies, as well as for capital budgeting.

Resource allocation and capital budgeting and management. At some point in the process, a *capital budget* is prepared formally, and the allocation of resources underlying it are studied in relation to the strategic plans.

Resource allocation is a key way in which strategic management controls the actual direction in which a company moves. In the baking goods company situation, for example, the strategic shift in emphasis from standard to specialty cookies would lead to shifts in the allocation of limited capital among projects. Less investment would be planned for high-volume production machinery, more for marketing support of specialty cookies. Almost every company faces these kinds of strategic choices because capital funds are almost always limited.

The financial figures, such as comparative return on investment of different capital projects to support different strategies, are only one aspect of the comparative study underlying develop-

Figure 8-3: Company Balance Sheet — Actual Versus Budget Comparison

ASSETS:	Actual	Budget	Over (Under)
Current assets:			
Cash on hand and in banks	$229,340	$245,360	($16,020)
Accounts receivable	$358,300	$373,000	($14,700)
Allowance for doubtful accounts	($21,788)	($22,400)	612
Inventories at standard cost:			
Direct materials	$238,600	$219,000	$19,600
Finished parts	$100,400	$100,400	
Work in process	$54,400	$54,400	
Finished product	$559,870	$544,200	$15,670
Prepaid expenses and deferred charges:			
Insurance			
Excess of standard cost in finished product inventory over current standard	$3,150	$3,150	($350)
Deferred advertising	$4,500	$4,500	
Total current assets	$1,526,772	$1,521,960	$4,812
Mixed assets:			
Machinery and equipment	$1,000,000	$1,000,000	
Depreciation taken to date	($210,000)	($210,000)	
Buildings	$800,000	$800,000	
Depreciation taken to date	($102,000)	($102,000)	
Land	$100,000	$100,000	
Total fixed assets	$1,588,000	$1,588,000	
Total assets	$3,114,772	$3,109,960	$4,812
LIABILITIES:			
Current liabilities:			
Accounts payable	$287,500	$271,500	$16,000
Dividends payable			
Accrued sales commissions	$17,682	$18,600	($918)
Federal income tax accrued	$227,995	$233,130	($5,135)
Real estate taxes accrued	$21,300	$21,300	
Accrued interest on mortgage	$5,000	$5,000	
Mortgage payable, current installment	$12,000	$12,000	
Accrued interest on demand note			
Note payable			
Total current liabilities	$571,477	$561,530	$9,947
Long-term debt, mortgage payable	$228,000	$228,000	
Total liabilities	$799,477	$789,530	$9,947
CAPITAL:			
Capital stock, 20,000 shares, common, par $100	$2,000,000	$2,000,000	
Retained earnings	$315,295	$320,430	($5,135)
Total capital	$2,315,295	$2,320,430	($5,135)
Total liabilities and capital	$3,114,772	$3,109,960	$4,812

ment of a capital budget. Strategic considerations can play an even more important role in making these resource allocation decisions.

In choosing among investing in a new business location, expanding an existing location, and refurbishing the present facilities, for example, a retail store owner might weigh the immediate payoffs of the least risky investments (refurbishing and size extension) against the strategic advantages of opening up a new market in a growing part of town and eventually developing a chain of stores. The conclusion may be that, over the long-run, the new location investment is the best one.

In practice, an investment program would probably contain a mix of investments. This was the case at the baked goods company described in the preceding section, where some investment was to be made in the standard cookie line to maintain market position, while the major portion of available funds were to be invested in new product areas.

Overall strategic guidelines can have a major impact on resource allocation in many companies. This was the case at Gillette and Reid International, whose experiences in strategic refocusing were discussed earlier.

Many of the corporate takeovers and buyouts in the 1980s were based on a strategy of maximum utilization of investment capital, the purest form of conglomerate strategy involving financial resource allocation. In many cases, this investment-oriented strategy led to closing down major segments of company operations and substantially reducing the company's size. In some instances, such takeovers led to liquidations of entire divisions of a company. For example, after buying TLC Beatrice International Inc. in 1987, Reginald Lewis sold about half of the company, focusing on building a European food distribution and grocery product company. Along the way, he reduced debt from $600 million to $100 million, and increased sales and profits [Hicks 1991].

Sources of capital. The way money is raised to finance strategic capital needs and the availability of capital are other strategic aspects of financial management. Sources of long-term capital include common and preferred stock, bonds, mortgages, and long-term notes. Sources of short-term capital include commercial bank loans and other short-term borrowing, trade credit, installment payments, leasing, and reduced dividends.

Capital availability and the cost of capital affect strategy formulation since strategies, no matter how attractive they may appear, can be pursued only to the degree that a company has or can raise the money to pursue them. For example, when different ways to finance growth were studied in the candy company study, the strategic limitations arising from the owner/manager's wish not to further dilute his ownership/equity position limited growth objectives. On the other hand, Wayne Huizenga's strategy of expanding only through stock buyouts enabled him to expand Waste Management, and later Blockbuster Entertainment, very rapidly in a fairly short time period [Sandomir 1991].

As enterprise-wide strategies are formulated, enabling financial strategies are developed for a company's capital structure and for ways in which capital is to be raised. Balancing the use of long- and short-term sources of capital requires balancing many situation factors, including

- Keeping capital costs as low as possible

- Making sure the capital needed for strategy implementation is available
- Having capital to meet fluctuating capital requirements
- Satisfying owner/manager requirements, as well as the requirements of shareholders, the financial community, and government agencies

Interest costs depend a great deal on the capital markets' perceptions of a company's financial strength and stability. This strength and stability is related to a company's cashflow position (its ability to meet financial obligations) and to a company's equity position in relation to its borrowing (the lower the borrowing level in relation to the equity, the stronger a company usually is financially).

Financial leveraging — borrowing the maximum amount of money possible and keeping cash reserves as low as possible — is in many situations a very profitable, though risky, strategy which can produce high rates of return. Junk bonds for businesses and high mortgages on real estate properties are examples of this approach. At the same time, these strategies involve substantial risks, as demonstrated dramatically in the early 1990s by the savings and loan problems that cost taxpayers billions of dollars [Hayes 1991; Wayne 1992] and by the rise in defaults of junk bonds issued to high-risk leveraged buyouts.

Strategies covering short-term sources of capital require a similar balancing of risks and rewards, in light of external and internal situation requirements. For example, it is possible to consider leasing versus buying. While buying is normally cheaper over the long run, leasing can have several strategic advantages — reducing risk in turbulent market environments, reducing the need for dilution of ownership, or conserving cash.

Situation requirements may also dictate dividend policies. For example, companies quite often have a no-cash dividend policy in order to place strategic emphasis on long-term future capital appreciation — a key element of many companies' enterprise-wide growth strategies.

Short- and Long-Range Programming

Programs detail how to carry out strategies — what specific tasks are to be done, who is to do them, when they are to be done, and the resources needed to do them. Programs help control strategy implementation since they set intermediate targets that define how to carry out strategies [Anthony 1988].

Programs can be created for specific tasks — for example, introducing a product, opening a territory, or building a facility to meet the demands created by new strategic directions. Programs of strategic concern are those involving large sums of money or those critical to the achievement of a specific strategic objective.

For instance, a program for installing new equipment to improve manufacturing efficiency might not have immediate strategic implications. On the other hand, the program for new product development at the baked goods company discussed in Chapter 7 might be of critical concern, since the new strategic direction of the company is to be based on penetration of that market.

In developing a program, it is necessary to:

- Break the task down into its components. For example, in building a new product program, plans are needed for the acquisition or development, production, promotion, and sale of the product. Each component would in turn be broken down to provide details such as the different kinds of product acquisition or promotional steps needed in the program.
- Identify the interrelationships of the specific program tasks. For example, in some situations, a program may depend on acquiring capital before any tasks are begun.
- Assign responsibility for doing the tasks.
- Identify the jobs to be done in accomplishing each task. For example, in preparing for mail-order promotions, artwork must be prepared, copy written and reviewed, mailing lists screened and evaluated, labels printed, a mailing house hired, printing arranged, envelopes purchased, mailing permits obtained from the post office, and dozens of other detailed jobs must be scheduled and performed.
- Estimate the timing of the jobs, in order to prepare detailed schedules and set target completion dates.

Short-term programs serve a strategic purpose similar to budgets and department operating plans in providing a detailed map of how to carry out the strategic objectives, both at the corporate and operational level. They also serve as control mechanisms for checking on the implementation of strategies and related plans.

Long-term programs involve longer-term plans and are generally less detailed. They can, however, serve as general blueprints for shorter-range programs, operating department strategy formulation, and strategy implementation.

For example, a company planning to start a new regional publication serving the aging baby boomer market outlined a number of critical program steps:

- Conducting demographic studies of different regions in the country, studying the competition in each region, and reviewing the availability of local editorial and production facilities
- Subsequently contracting for printing, for office space rental, for distribution and sales arrangements, and for art support
- Hiring writers
- Renting mailing lists and mailing support services
- Allocating adequate financial resources to complete all the jobs

In this situation, a three-year timetable was developed. Such a general implementation program allowed time to line up suppliers on favorable terms, find rental space at a good price, and give several experienced writers time to readjust their career paths to consider working for smaller ventures such as this one.

Long-term programs, like long-term budgets, can be useful in visualizing, evaluating, facilitating, and controlling strategy formulation and implementation. For example, Bill Gates, chairman of Microsoft Corporation, who is considered an industry visionary, has already spent six years and hundreds of millions of dollars on his "multimedia computing" development program. This computing integrates sound, moving pictures, still pictures, and text — all on the personal computer. Gates envisions multimedia as the ultimate home reference source. Someone writing a term paper on film history, for instance, would be able to call up scenes from particular films, or play voices of given actors from any roles they have ever played — all while reading text about the film's or the actor's place in film history. Gates has already bought reproduction rights to a considerable amount of published and recorded material. In spite of his enormous investment in multimedia computing, his experiences with it have not yet convinced him that it will help make Microsoft — now the world's largest supplier of personal computer operating systems and applications software — an even stronger and more profitable company. His long-term development program in multimedia computing will hopefully help him to clarify and refine his strategic vision and to gather the information needed to make that decision [Bulkeley 1991; Moody 1991; Pollack 1991].

In situations where they are appropriate, long-term programs provide milestones to be checked along the way to insure that strategies are viable and/or are being implemented effectively. They also promote integrative strategic thinking as operating managers are required to think specifically about the most effective way to implement a chosen strategy. For example, Richard Hackborn of Hewlett-Packard Company, who was credited with the phenomenal success of its laser printers in the early 1990s, was considered a "consummate strategist," that is, someone who can combine formulating strategic visions with rigorous operating discipline. Mr. Hackborn was famous for writing long memos containing strategy statements along with detailed explanations of the logic behind them, accompanied by charts, lists, and plans giving the detailed steps necessary to carry out the strategies [Pollack 1992].

Strategy Formulation for Major Business Units

Strategic business units also formulate enterprise-wide strategies and strategic plans. At Hewlett-Packard, Richard Hackborn's were strategic business unit strategies and strategic plans. As another example, Sara Lee has an enterprise-wide strategy which focuses on packaged goods. One of its major strategic business units is the Fuller Brush Company, which had its own detailed strategy and plan for expanding its product line and improving its sales and distribution methods by expanding into retail and mail-order selling and becoming less dependent on door-to-door selling.

Strategy Formulation and Implementation for Major Operating Departments

Overall enterprise-wide strategies and policies provide the structure and the framework for integrated operational planning and plan implementation. For example, companies often publish their enterprise-wide company strategies and policies, as well as strategies and policies for key operating areas, for use as a framework for operational planning and plan implementation.

Such development and integration is rarely a simple process in large companies since additional factors — such as interdepartmental interests, leadership, personal growth objectives, day-to-day business pressures, and other human factors — influence these strategy implementation tasks at the operating level, as is seen in the discussions in the following section.

FORMULATING DEPARTMENTAL ENABLING STRATEGIES IN INDIVIDUAL READER SITUATION CONTEXTS

This section discusses the general adaptive process involved in integrating enterprise-wide and departmental strategies and strategic plans, as well as some tools for overcoming problems often encountered in effectively achieving such integration while implementing enterprise-wide strategies. The discussion is divided into two parts:

- Assessing critical factors in specific company contexts
- Integrating and implementing enterprise-wide strategies and departmental enabling strategies in light of these critical situation factors

The overall adaptive situation-specific process of strategy formulation and implementation is shown in Figure 8-4. This process, adapted and applied to decisions discussed in this section, is outlined in Figure 8-5. The process focuses on the task of integrating strategic plans with operating department requirements. Chapter 12 discusses the broader implementation problems of appropriate leadership and of organization and business process reengineering, staffing, and control. It also presents a context-specific model of the processes involved in those implementation areas, as well as the ones described here.

Assessing Critical Factors

Just because enterprise-wide strategies have been formulated, it cannot be assumed that operational planning and decision making, and plan implementation, will automatically follow these overall patterns. Problems may prevent this, such as: plans being ill-defined, unrealistic, or inappropriate to specific departmental needs; unforeseen roadblocks at the operating level which prevent such integration; and plans not being effectively communicated or cooperatively developed.

In addition to the critical strategic management factors shown in Figure 8-4, many other factors can influence the formulation of operating strategies. These factors, which are shown in Figure 8-5 and discussed in the following paragraphs, can affect how effectively operating strategies and plans are integrated with enterprise-wide strategies. They also can affect how successfully enterprise-wide strategies are carried out. These factors may include

- Department character and functions
- Department external operating environment
- Relationships with other departments
- Managers and other personnel involved
- Enterprise-wide strategies

Department character, culture, functions, and organization. Departmental tasks differ,

Figure 8-4: Strategic Management Decision-Making Process

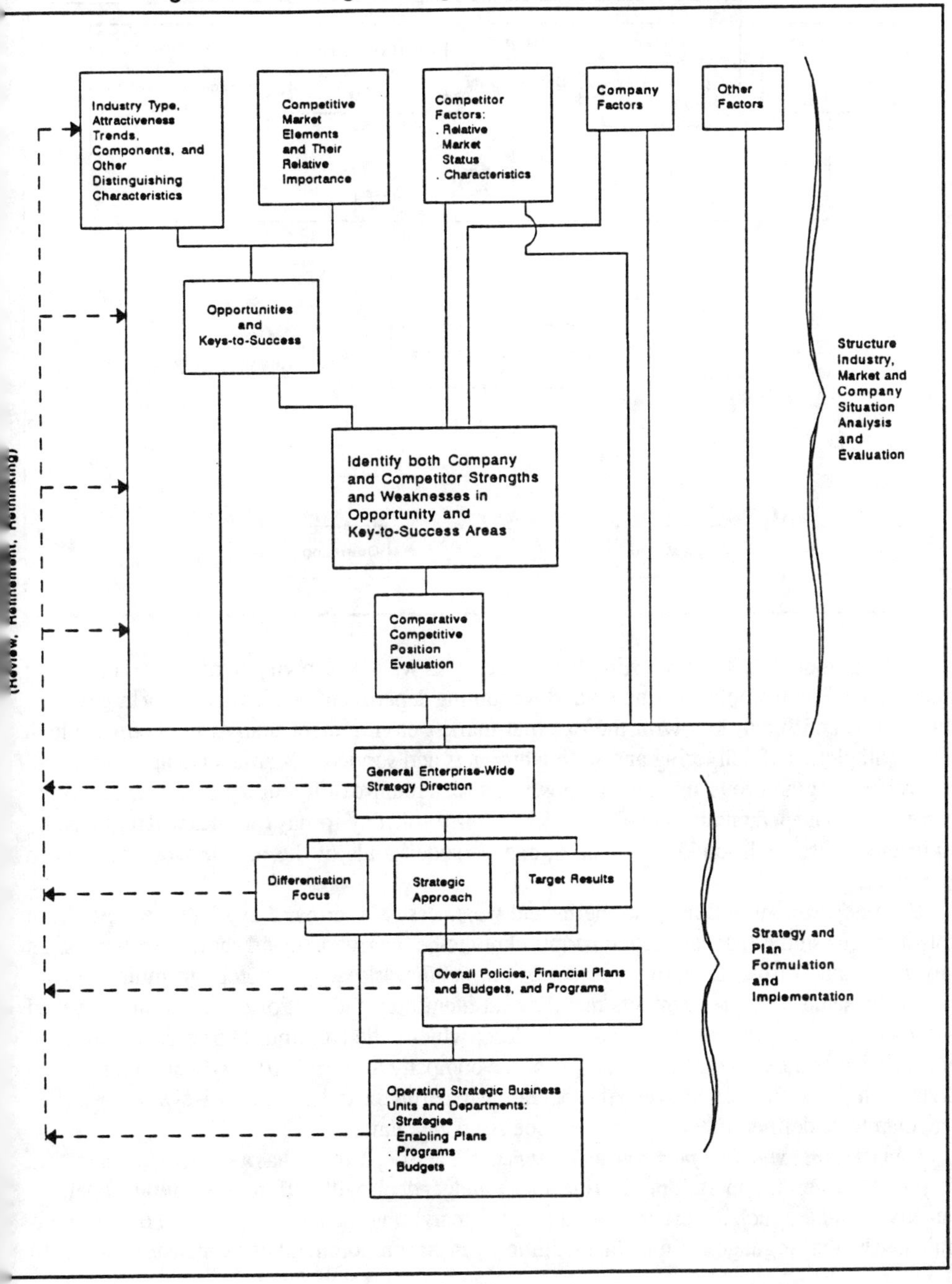

Industry Type, Attractiveness Trends, Components, and Other Distinguishing Characteristics

Competitive Market Elements and Their Relative Importance

Competitor Factors:
. Relative Market Status
. Characteristics

Company Factors

Other Factors

Opportunities and Keys-to-Success

Identify both Company and Competitor Strengths and Weaknesses in Opportunity and Key-to-Success Areas

Comparative Competitive Position Evaluation

Structure Industry, Market and Company Situation Analysis and Evaluation

General Enterprise-Wide Strategy Direction

Differentiation Focus

Strategic Approach

Target Results

Overall Policies, Financial Plans and Budgets, and Programs

Operating Strategic Business Units and Departments:
. Strategies
. Enabling Plans
. Programs
. Budgets

Strategy and Plan Formulation and Implementation

(Review, Refinement, Rethinking)

Figure 8-5: Factors Affecting Integrating Overall and Departmental Strategic Plans

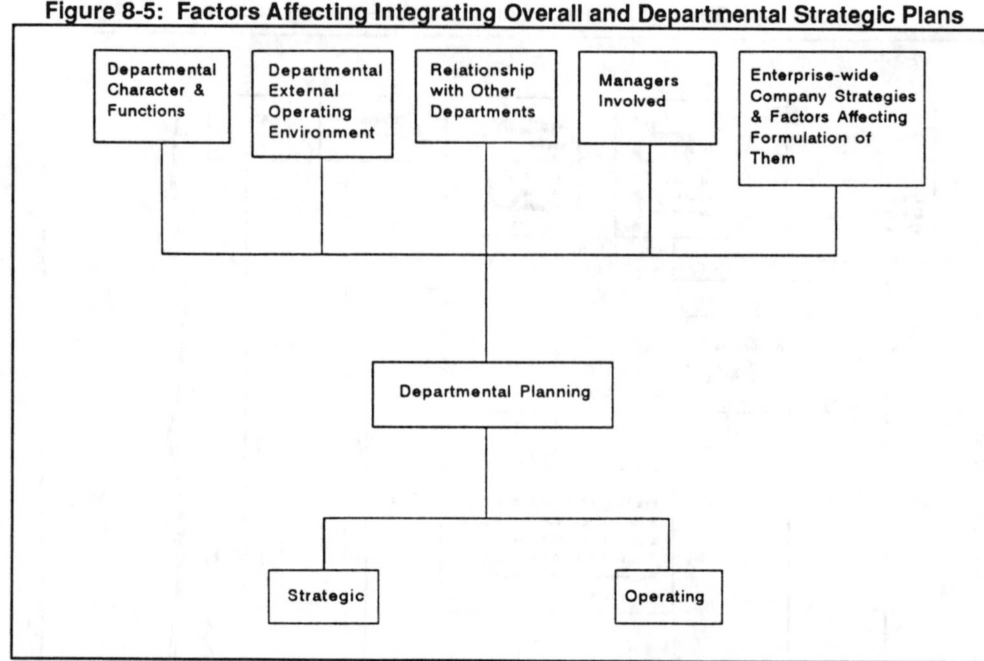

so each department has its own distinctive character, as well as its own personnel and operating requirements. For example, the finance and accounting departments are involved to a large extent with figures, and much less with the external market environment than is marketing, which involves all phases of delivering and selling products and services. Manufacturing, in contrast, can involve less glamorous, more gritty jobs, and so can require different work routines, working environments, and personalities [Milbank 1991]. As a result, day-to-day routines will be different, as will the skills, qualifications, attitudes, and personal goals of the people working in each department.

Each department will have strengths and weaknesses in terms of available resources. In most situations studied, departmental people claim to be overworked and short of resources. In many cases, this is true. Lack of resources can limit enterprise-wide strategy formulation.

At the same time, departments may have strategic strengths. For example, in the baked goods company study the company had a sales force which called on almost 85 percent of the food stores in a four-state region. Major aspects of the company's overall strategy were built around this strength. Specific links between this operating department and the enterprise-wide strategies were, therefore, defined in the enterprise-wide strategic plans.

Department external operating environment. Each department has a set of external factors affecting its successful operation. The financial manager deals with different people and operates in an environment much different from that of the marketing manager. The world of finance is dominated by the language of financial institutions, and its predominant value measures are profit and loss and effective capital utilization. Fulfilling these values may be the key to obtaining financing from external sources, and so is important to getting the financial management job done. In contrast, an advertising manager deals with perceptions, motivations, and feelings. Success in the external marketing environment depends on meeting situation requirements, such as sales volume, ad response, buyer recognition, and the like.

Success in manufacturing also depends on a different environment. Raw material supply availability and fluctuations in prices are of concern to manufacturing managers, as are unit costs, inventory management, and production layout efficiencies.

Each functional department must respond to the needs of its own environment or context to be successful. The measures of professional or business success in the environment may or may not be critical to a company's enterprise-wide strategic plan. For example, industry-wide awards given for excellence in advertising may not be for the advertising which best advances a company's strategy. Similarly, industry recognition for product development does not necessarily recognize the products most profitable to a company. This happens at times in the publishing field, for example, where a major publication such as Manhattan Inc., cited for excellence by professionals in the industry, will not necessarily survive in the marketplace [Carmody 1991; "New England" 1990; Pomper 1990].

A manufacturing department may find that purchasing raw materials efficiently requires purchasing large quantities. On the other hand, a changing market environment and enterprise-wide strategies for responding to rapidly changing consumer tastes may require the department to maintain low inventories in order to have a highly flexible production schedule that can introduce frequent product changes quickly. In this sense, the manufacturing department is suboptimizing its operations — that is, operating at less than ideal cost efficiency. From a corporate viewpoint, however, this may be the optimal way to operate in manufacturing, since production flexibility, even though more costly, may yield competitive market benefits. In this case, the marketing environment would be more critical than the production environment.

Relationships with other departments. Often, a department may want to meet specified goals, but cannot do so without the resources of other departments. For example, production cannot always meet the flexible delivery requirements of marketing and still meet unit cost goals.

Departmental cultures often create obstacles to obtaining needed interdepartment cooperation and integration. For example, production may prefer a stable environment since such an environment allows it to meet cost and quality requirements. On the other hand, marketing often must respond to fluctuating competitor pressures in an unstable and turbulent environment.

Power struggles may exist among departments. Changing strategies can create new centers of power, upgrading the importance of some departments at the expense of others. Information Systems departments have been through several such evolutions. At times, information systems has been a highly centralized function, giving centralized systems development departments considerable power in deciding which systems are developed. With the advent of more powerful microcomputers and networks linking them, systems development has to some degree been transferred to user departments, with the information systems group serving in a support capacity. This move, referred to as "downsizing," is often perceived as a weakening of the centralized systems department's power. The solution often is to have a hybrid structure with a mix of centralization and decentralization, which requires skillfully balancing central Information Systems department requirements with those of the user departments [Drenick 1991; Laplante 1991].

Potential interdepartmental rivalries and other interdepartmental obstacles to integrating enterprise-wide and departmental strategy formulation and implementation can, therefore, have a significant impact on the success of overall-company strategy formulation and implementation.

Manager involvement. Since key departmental managers also impact on effective integration, their attitudes and skills can affect strategy formulation and implementation. For example, the banking industry's strategic moves into computer information systems have depended on management's capabilities in computers and its willingness to learn and use computers in a wide range of operating departments [Hirsch 1990, 1991; Lohr 1991; Quint 1989].

Success in integrating department and enterprise-wide strategy formulation and implementation can also depend on an individual manager's personal agenda. Unlike entrepreneurs, corporate managers often are salaried and dependent on a job. Success in that job may not depend exclusively on performance —it may also depend on the political environment, such as the favor and interest of other high-level executives. If the strategic initiatives proposed are not perceived as furthering an individual manager's career goals, obstacles to these initiatives may be created.

Enterprise-wide strategies. The nature of the enterprise-wide strategies, as well as the factors upon which those strategies are founded, impacts on the integration of strategic management levels. For example, the greater the amount of change inherent in the planned strategies under study, the greater the chance of problems arising within the existing organization. Because of these potential problems Roger Penske met frequently with individual workers and groups of workers, as well as with union representatives, when he purchased Detroit Diesel in 1988 from General Motors. His initial task was to change the entire corporate culture from the massive bureaucratic one at GM to the entrepreneurial one he needed at Detroit Diesel to make the company prosper [White 1991].

Integrating and Implementing Enterprise-wide Strategies and Departmental Enabling Strategies

The approach to integrating various levels of strategic management used depends on the people, plans, and other critical situation requirements. For these reasons, the relevance of the above five situational factors to the specific strategic management situation is examined. As evidenced from research and practice, such a flexible situational decision-making approach is required in strategic management situations [Govindarajan 1988].

In strategy formulation, if the strategies under study

- Involve existing personnel carrying out strategies and related implementation plans through their existing operations;
- Maintain the relative power positions of different operating departments;
- Provide departments with the resources and competencies needed to carry out the plans;
- Realistically take into account the varying requirements of the operating environments involved;

and

- Involve major new strategic directions for operations,

then full participation of key operating managers in the strategy formulation process may be warranted. In such a situation, participation provides an effective means of integrating enterprise-wide and departmental strategies during their formulation. More and more companies are involving operating managers in formulating enterprise-wide strategies, in order to introduce them to the strategic thinking underlying the strategies and obtain their input, as well as to give them a proprietary interest in the strategies. In order to increase management involvement, some companies even have strategic planning departments located in operating divisions [Prescott 1989].

On the other hand, if a new strategic direction involves major power shifts, new people skills and competencies, and strategic directions that extend beyond current operating boundaries in a major way, one would be less inclined to encourage participation of current operating managers in the planning development effort. Even here, however, the requirements of the specific situation context would dictate the exact implementation approach used.

A variety of integrative approaches to formulating enabling strategies and plans in three key operating areas — marketing, operations/production, and computer information systems — in light of the five critical situation factors discussed above are covered in some detail in Chapters 9-11. Specific leadership, organization structure and business process context, control, and staffing considerations involved in implementing strategies and the strategic plan development effort are discussed in Chapter 12 and Appendix B.

STRATEGIC MANAGEMENT: A SEMI-STRUCTURED CONTEXT-SPECIFIC INTEGRATIVE PROCESS

Strategic management involves formulating enterprise-wide strategies and then using whatever management approaches are appropriate to the situation to implement those strategies.

The process outlined in the preceding section is a structured one, which sometimes causes people to mistakenly think it is a procedure. It is not. Rather, it is a flexible, adaptive process model which focuses on specific situation context requirements. These requirements dictate the actual approach used in each situation — the approach is rarely dictated by some theoretical "best" way to do it.

Making strategic management processes work effectively in a specific situation requires obtaining commitments to the company's strategic vision from operating managers. These commitments are obtained through fostering credibility and trust in corporate leadership as plans are formulated. They are important to promoting strategic thinking — thinking which focuses on an enterprise's strategic vision without inhibiting the flexible activities needed to respond to individual company requirements, changing competitive market needs, and the many unforeseen events and sometimes chaotic conditions which can arise in day-to-day business operations. In this sense, the context-specific processes identified above and in other chapters are both semi-structured and adaptive.

While each of the following chapters covers techniques—behavioral and cognitive—which are needed to formulate and implement strategies, the primary focus of these chapters is not on learning techniques. It is on identifying situationally appropriate processes which have proven effective in dealing with specific reader situations.

REVIEW QUESTIONS

1. Describe the ways in which a company's enterprise-wide strategies can be amplified and extended.
2. In what ways can the philosophy and values of company owners and managers influence a company's enterprise-wide strategy formulation?
3. What is the function of company policies in the strategic management process?
4. In what ways can long- and short-range programs be useful in strategy formulation and implementation in a company?
5. Discuss the relationships of financial planning and strategic formulation and implementation.
6. Describe some of the ways enterprise-wide strategies can affect resource allocation within a firm.
7. Describe steps which can be taken to integrate other levels of company planning with enterprise-wide strategy formulation.
8. Why is it so important to have those who will be carrying out strategies and related strategic plans participate in their formulation, when appropriate and possible?
9. Discuss the ways in which strategic management processes are both semi-structured and adaptive situational context-specific processes.

EXERCISES

1. Read one of the ten company studies in the Case Study section of this book for which there is also a financial analysis and simulation model on the computer disk accompanying this book. These companies are listed in the Instruction Booklet accompanying the disks. Use the company study of your choice to write a report which covers the following strategy formulation and implementation tasks discussed in this chapter, after formulating an enterprise-wide strategy for the company:

- Company policies, in whatever areas you feel are appropriate in the situation context under study
- Long- and short-term programs you feel would be appropriate in the situation context under study
- Budgets for the enterprise-wide strategy of your choice
- Financial evaluations of the enterprise-wide strategy you formulated

2. Read recent issues of the periodicals referred to in the references section at the end of the chapter, or other related periodicals of your choice, and find a description of a company of interest to you. Write a report on that company which formulates policies and programs you judge to be useful in carrying out the enterprise-wide strategy.

3. The disks accompanying this book contain several prototype KBS. Follow the directions accompanying the disks to run a consultation using the system with the file name CAP-INV.PLN. If you wish, the knowledge base may also be printed out and studied while you run the system and restudy this chapter in order to get a more detailed picture of how such decisions are made.

REFERENCES

Anthony, Robert N., *The Management Control Function,* Boston, MA: Harvard Business School Press, 1988.

Bulkeley, William M., "Software Industry Loses Start-Up Zest as Big Firms Increase Their Dominance," *The Wall Street Journal,* August 27, 1991, pp. B1, B5.

Carmody, Diedre, "Savvy Woman Magazine Sets Last Issue," *The New York Times,* January 19, 1991, p. 39.

Chakravorty, Subrata, "We Changed the Whole Playing Field: Triumph for Gillette's Colman Mockler — Technology as a Marketing Tool," *Forbes,* February 4, 1991, pp. 82-86.

Drenick, R.F., "The Need to Please," *OR/MS Today,* June 1, 1991, pp. 44-47.

Freitag, Michael, "Wigwag, a Folksy Magazine," *The New York Times,* July 24, 1989, p. D7.

Govindarajan, Vijay, "A Contingency Approach to Strategy Implementation at the Business-Unit Level: Integrating Administrative Mechanisms With Strategy," *Academy of Management Journal,* December 1988, pp. 828-854.

Hayes, Thomas C., "Behind the Iron Hand at Tenneco," *The New York Times,* January 6, 1992, pp. D1, D6.

Hayes, Thomas C., "Casey's Ready as Bailout's Top Gun," *The New York Times,* September 30, 1991, pp. D1, D6.

Hicks, Jonathan P., "The Wall Streeter Who Runs TLC Beatrice," *The New York Times,* Business Section, July 9, 1991, p. 5.

Hirsch, James S., "Banc One Agrees to Buy 4 Ohio Banks Affiliated with PNC for $255 million," *The Wall Street Journal,* January 17, 1991, p. A4.

Hirsch, James S., "Fast-Rising Banc One, Already Big in Texas, Looks at Other Areas," *The Wall Street Journal,* December 20, 1990, pp. A1, A2.

Laplante, Alice, "Here Come the Hybrids," *Computerworld,* June 17, 1991, pp. 57-60.

Levin, Doron, "A Bet Chrysler Can't Afford to Lose," *The New York Times,* August 26, 1991, pp. D1, D3.

Levin, Doron, "Chrysler's New L/H, as in Last Hope," *The New York Times,* Business Section, July 12, 1992, pp. 1,6.

Lewis, Peter, "Laying Down Rules for Workers," *The New York Times,* Business Section, June 11, 1989, p. 12.

Lohr, Steve, "The Best Little Bank in America," *The New York Times*, Business Section, July 7, 1991, pp. 1, 4.

Luther, William, *Strategic Planning Model*, Stanford, CT: Luther Management, 1984.

McConahey, Steve, *Corporate and International Development* (Planning Coordination), Kemper Financial Services Inc. The Emerging Role of the Strategic Planner in the 1990s: Key Elements, New York: Planning Forum's Strategic Planning Special Interest Group, April 8, 1992.

Milbank, Dana, "No Glamour, No Glory, Being a Manufacturer Today Can Take Guts," *The New York Times*, June 3, 1991, pp. A1, A7.

Mockler, Robert J., Contingency Approaches to Strategic Management, Research Working Paper, New York: Strategic Management Research Institute, 1992(A).

Mockler, Robert J., *Computer Software to Support Strategic Management Decision Making*, New York: Macmillan, Publishing 1992(B).

Moody, Fred, "Mr. Software," *The New York Times*, Magazine Section, August 25, 1991, pp. 26-59.

"New England Monthly Closes," *The New York Times*, September 7, 1990, p. D6.

Pollack, Andrew, "One Day, Junior Got Too Big," *The New York Times*, Business Section, August 4, 1991, pp. 1, 6.

Pollack, Andrew, "Hewlett's 'Consummate Strategist'," *The New York Times*, March 10, 1992, pp. D1, D6.

Pomper, Steve, "The Big Shake-out Begins," *Time*, July 2, 1990, p. 50.

Prescott, John E., and Daniel C. Smith, "The Largest Survey of 'Leading Edge' Competitor Intelligence Managers," *Planning Review*, May/June 1989, pp. 6-13.

Prokesch, Steven, "Britain's Low Profile Publishing Giant," *The New York Times*, Business Section, February 9, 1992, p. 5.

Quint, Michael, "A Bank That's Riding Technology to the Top," *The New York Times*, June 30, 1989, pp. D1, D6.

Reilly, Patrick M., "Magazine Launching Moves Timidly," *The Wall Street Journal*, January 20, 1992, pp. B1, B7.

Rose, Frederick, "Atlantic Richfield C. Is Winning the West By Breaking the Mold," *The Wall Street Journal*, August 7, 1991, pp. A1, A7.

Sandomir, Richard, "Wayne Huizenga's Growth Complex," *The New York Times*, Magazine Section, June 9, 1991, pp. 22-25.

Wald, Matthew L., "Arco Reports New Gasoline that Sharply Cuts Pollutants," *The New York Times*, July 11, 1991, pp. A1, D6.

Wayne, Leslie, "Thrift Office's Eager Terminator," *The New York Times*, January 31, 1992, pp. D1, D6.

White, Joseph B., "How Detroit Diesel, Out from Under GM, Turned Around Fast," *The Wall Street Journal*, August 16, 1991, pp. A1, A8.

Chapter 9

MARKETING

The objective of this chapter is to help readers to

- Understand the nature of the marketing function and marketing planning task
- Make marketing strategic planning decisions in specific situation contexts
- Integrate marketing planning with other strategic management areas

The task discussed in this chapter — how to formulate marketing strategies and related enabling plans — is part of the strategic management phase in Figure 9-1 involving integrated planning for key operating areas, a major aspect of implementing enterprise-wide strategies.

THE MARKETING FUNCTION

Marketing generally refers to all the business functions involved in getting a product or service from producer to consumer. These include selecting a product (or service) and market, as well as decisions concerning warehousing, distributing, pricing, selling, advertising, promoting, and servicing. Products — such as soap, automobiles, and refrigerators — are tangible; services — such as health care, financial, and transportation — are intangible, since the consumer does not receive a physical product. The kinds of markets (consumer and industrial) served can also vary, as can the geographic area and the consumer and customer groups within each area.

Since marketing involves a wide range of decision situations, the initial discussion of marketing planning is general, covering the nature of marketing tasks and the kinds of strategies formulated in each task area. Later sections of the chapter discuss specific aspects of how marketing planning decisions are made and implemented in different situations.

Figure 9-1: Strategic Management Tasks

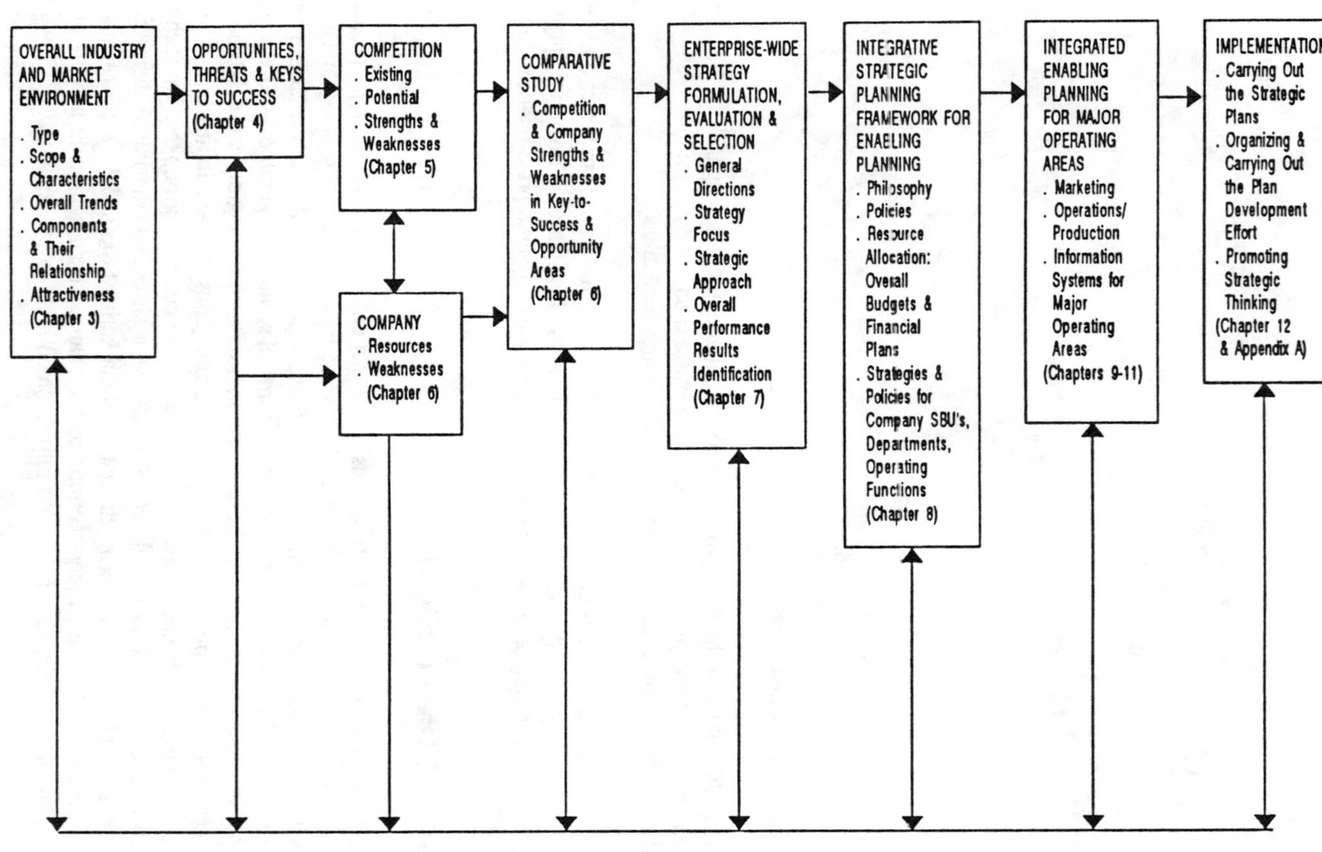

Figure 9-2: Marketing Plans — A General Overview

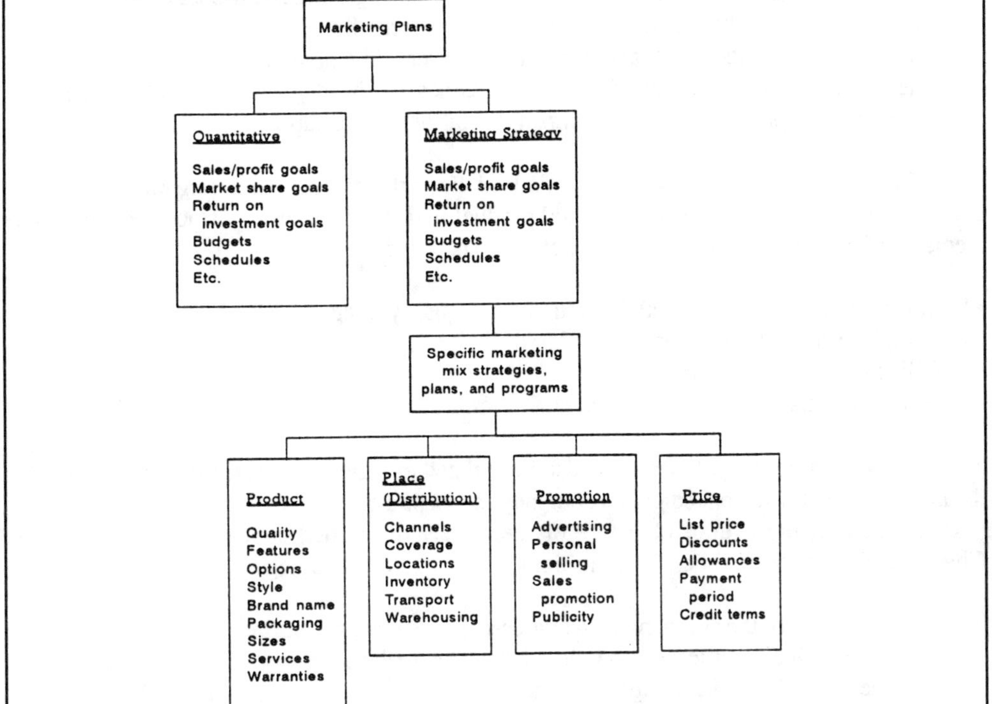

MARKETING PLANNING TASKS

Figure 9-2 gives an overview of the tasks involved in the marketing planning job. Marketing planning involves developing both quantitative plans (budgets and projections) and qualitative plans (including overall strategies and specific operating plans and programs). Marketing strategy decisions, then, are only one segment of marketing planning.

As shown in Figure 9-2, marketing strategy formulation involves defining overall marketing strategy, target markets and the marketing mix of products or services, distribution channels, price, and promotion media for a company. The following sections describe some commonly formulated marketing strategies and the different situations in which they have proven useful.

Overall Marketing Strategy

The discussion of enterprise-wide strategy formulation in Chapter 7 paid considerable attention to the strategy's key marketing components. For example, in the candy company situation, the enterprise-wide strategy was:

> The strategic objective of the company is to be an aggressively expanding closely-held regional manufacturer-retailer of a limited line of high-quality, moderately-priced, and distinctively boxed chocolate candies, selling principally through its own retail stores to consumers under its own brand name, but also serving wholesale, chain, and institutional customers or outlets under other brand names to the degree permitted by available production capacity and by the company's ability to raise capital.

This enterprise-wide strategy essentially defines the *overall marketing strategy* for the company — a small, well-focused limited product regional company — since it contains key elements of the company's marketing strategy. These include

- Product: kinds of products sold, breadth of line, quality image, and brand name
- Geographic scope of operations
- Retailing operations expansion
- Customer and distribution channel identification

Specific marketing policies were also formulated to define the marketing strategy in more detail, as is done for the baked goods company in Chapter 8.

In contrast, the overall objective of the widely diversified conglomerate described in Chapter 2 did not contain specific definitions of the marketing strategy:

> The objective of the company is to aggressively increase the intrinsic value of its common stock through diversification in industries related to the company's present business lines, in order to build on the company strengths in efficient asset management.

In such company studies, where the enterprise-wide strategy is general, strategic business unit strategies are formulated where appropriate. These strategies in turn are likely to contain key elements of the unit's overall marketing strategy.

Whatever the situation, as a study progresses the overall marketing strategy is defined more precisely as the target market is defined and as an appropriate marketing mix of product or service, distribution, price, and promotion is developed.

Target Market

Ultimately, marketing planning is based on an analysis of the buyers and users of the product or service [McCarthy 1991; Phillips 1990]. This is called the *target market*. For example, in the early 1990s Harley-Davidson Inc., the 87-year-old U.S. motorcycle manufacturer, reportedly beat out its Japanese competitors, regained its former U.S. market share, and even invaded the Japanese market, by introducing models tailored to specific customer needs. As a result, staying close to the customer became close to a religion at Harley [Holusha 1990; Rose 1990(B); Stern 1992; Sterngold 1992].

Among the early steps taken after the breakup of the Soviet Union by an American advertising firm was to conduct a market study in order to identify a range of target markets in Russia and define their buying characteristics. This was done even though the firm recognized that it would not represent a significant market for American products for several years [Elliot 1992(B)].

Since the person who uses the product or service (the *consumer*) is not always the person who purchases it (the *customer*), the concept of *target market* includes both user of the product (consumer) and buyer of the product (customer). Where the buyer is not the user, as when a household head buys food for their family, market planning involves studying the characteristics of both the customer and consumer market.

Existing and potential target consumer markets for products and services can be defined according to: size and growth rate; demographic profiles (age, sex, family size, income, occupation, education, religion, race, nationality); psychographic profiles (social class, life-style, personality); behavioral profiles (attitudes, benefits sought, readiness stage, perceived risk, innovativeness, involvement, loyalty status, usage rate, user status); and geographic location (region, city, county, state, international and national segments, density, climate).

An analysis of such factors helps identify the dimensions of the opportunity and the keys to success in selling to each target consumer market identified.

Where industrial buyer markets are involved, a planner identifies such existing and potential customer factors as: overall size; growth rate; size of individual companies; average size of purchases; usage rates; product applications; types of business; source loyalty; locations; purchase status (how long and how frequent); performance (reliability, price, durability, etc.). Key decisions involve determining what target market to serve, and identifying those factors which will affect decisions about what products to sell and how best to serve the market.

Market planning decisions can be made about which target markets best suit existing products, or about which products to sell to selected target markets. For example, during the 1960s and 1970s Levi Strauss thrived by serving the college market with its jeans products. In the mid-1980s its market changed as baby boomers aged, and Levi Strauss developed and introduced a looser fitting product line of pants and related clothing suitable for an older market [Pollack 1989]. Annual sales of this line, called "Dockers," were expected to surpass $500 million in 1991 [Agins 1991].

Overall marketing strategy decisions may also be made to limit the size and location of target markets. In the baked goods company situation discussed in Chapter 7, sales to and through some independent retailers were so small that it made economic sense to consider eliminating many smaller accounts. Because of limited resources and regional company strengths, the company also decided to limit its area of operations to a four-state region.

In looking toward the future, in the early 1990s Reader's Digest Association began a multimillion-dollar database project which would enable it to target mailings with much higher precision to its 100 million customers worldwide [Ambrosio 1992]. This capability to efficiently (cheaply) sell products to well-defined market segments was expected to give Reader's Digest a powerful competitive advantage.

Products or Services

Strategy decisions in the product or service area include defining: the type of product or service; special distinguishing or differentiating features; the breadth of the product or service line; the degree of customizing; brand name emphasis and positioning; what servicing to offer with products; and the frequency of product change.

Type of product or service. The most basic strategy decision is what product or service to sell. Every overall marketing strategy defines the product or service to be offered. For example, Sara Lee focuses on a wide range of consumer packaged *goods* [McGill 1989(B); "Sara Lee" 1990], including food and other packaged goods, such as home-care products. On the other hand, Quaker Oats and Pepsico focus solely on consumer packaged *foods* — a small but critical difference from Sara Lee [McGill 1989(A); Phillips 1986]. These and other aspects of product strategy formulation have been covered extensively in earlier discussions.

Distinguishing features. As planning progresses, distinguishing features that will differentiate a company's products and services from its competitors are developed and emphasized. These features might relate to packaging, product design, quality, innovations, style, sizes, functions, or any other aspect of the product or service. For example, in the candy company study discussed in Chapter 7 the company chose to focus on a very simple and distinctive, yet elegant, white *packaging* for its limited line of boxed chocolates sold through its own stores. In 1991, Pepsi-Cola turned to new packaging to strategically position itself as a more youthful product than its older rival, Coca-Cola [Kerr 1991(B)].

Differentiating features are also common in service businesses. For example, Burger King successfully distinguished itself from McDonalds by offering hamburgers several ways to enable customers to "Have It Your Way." The public's dismay at the lack of personalized customer service in department stores in general enabled Nordstrom's department stores to differentiate its image by offering, advertising, and consistently delivering personalized customer service at all its stores [Faludi 1990; Schwadel 1991; Stevenson 1989]. Differentiation is especially important for small companies seeking a niche in a large market, such as the makers of gourmet ketchups (Uncle Dave's), mustards (Grey Poupon), and salad dressings (Paul Newman's) ["For Specialty Ketchups" 1990].

When a strategy stresses product differentiation, it is important that such features are recognizable by consumers. For example, in the consumer environment of the 1990s, promoting *quality* is almost universally part of any company's marketing strategy. Yet quality is not always recognizable by consumers: consumers cannot see inside a watch to know it works well. Therefore, it is important to take steps both to maintain product quality [Slater 1992] and to make sure that consumers are made aware of quality differences, as Maytag did with its 25-year advertising campaign featuring a lonely repairman [Elliot 1992(A)]. Many companies compete to win nationally recognized quality awards, such as the Malcolm Baldrige National Quality Award given each year by the Commerce Department in an effort to establish their quality image [Bowles 1991; Hillkirk 1991].

Product innovation is another possible product strategy. For example, a product innovation strategy has been essential to the spectacular success of Connor Peripherals. In 1989, its fourth year of business and third year of shipping products, company sales spurted to $705 million, making it the fastest growing start-up company in American history. CEO Finis O'Connor's strategy was to identify and satisfy customer needs faster than the competition. He did this over and over again in making hard disk drives for the computer industry [Pollack 1990].

Apple Computer grew dramatically during the 1980s, largely due to its innovative product line; however, its reputation for innovation began to fade as it emphasized price cutting in the early 1990s [Fisher 1991(A); Markoff 1991]. The introduction of a simple product innovation in the bicycle industry — the mountain bike — revived an entire industry during the 1980s. By 1990 mountain bikes represented nearly two-thirds of all industry sales [Fisher 1991(B)]. U.S. Surgical Corporation, working in a field where new medical procedures are being introduced continually, gained a competitive advantage over its chief rival, J&J's Ethicon division, through product innovation. As a result its sales and profits jumped 50 percent (to $514 million and $46 million) in 1990, with some analysts expecting sales to reach $1 billion in 1992 [Winslow 1991].

The bankruptcy of Wang Laboratories, Inc., a $1.9 billion computer company, in August, 1992 was attributed to the "lack of product innovation" [Bulkeley 1992]. Some companies have a "no-frills" strategy — that is, a strategy which deliberately promotes fewer distinctive features or less service as a trade off for a cheaper price. Many discount stores, such as Phar-Mor, Ikea, and other national chains, have adapted a low-price, less-service strategy [Barnesh 1992; Hirsch 1991; Trachtenberg 1991]. Basic or generic food products companies also often use a low-price, less-features strategy.

Breadth of product or service line. Marketing strategy decisions can also involve breadth of product line. For example, supermarket chains normally carry a wide line of products — in some cases up to 25,000 items — so customers can do *all* their food shopping in one store. For large chains, such a strategy is appropriately competitive. In contrast, Stew Leonard's supermarket in Connecticut, a single store that produces close to $100 million dollars a year in sales (averaging 8 to 10 times more sales per square foot than the average chain supermarket store), carries only several hundred items [Foderaro 1991; Wald 1989].

Other possible breadth of line strategies deal with offering product or service options, or variations from standard offerings, such as allegedly "customized" automobiles. This approach can create the illusion of a company having a broader product line than it actually has. This strategy has been made possible through the use of advanced computer information systems in many high-volume, large company operations. For example, Banc One used computerized integrated customer accounts to enable quick analysis of customers' total financial situation and individually tailored investment advice [Lohr 1991].

Brand name emphasis and positioning. Brand names can also be used to help differentiate and sell products and create a competitive advantage [Mayer 1991]. In the food and packaged goods industries this has been an effective strategy for some large companies, such as Sara Lee. Other companies have successfully built strategies around non-brand or generic names. For example, appliances Sears sold under the Kenmore brand name were manufactured by different suppliers. Many companies pursue a mixed strategy: Richardson-Sheffield sells its quality knives under its own brand name, and also to others who use their own brand name on the knives

[Lohr 1989]. Lack of brand recognition can create problems for smaller companies in highly competitive markets: Royal Crown Cola spent nearly 40 percent of its sales revenue in 1990 on brand promotion in order to maintain its position against widely recognized Coke and Pepsi brands [Pereira 1991]. Ignoring the strength of brand names can also cause problems, as Hardee's discovered when it bought the Roy Rogers restaurant chain and converted its outlets in Washington and Baltimore to Hardee's outlets in a series of overnight changeovers. The subsequent significant sales drop led CEO Purdy Crawford to comment "We didn't pay enough respect to the strength of the Roy Rogers trademark" [Goad 1991].

Servicing. Where appropriate to the situation, marketing strategies can also be developed for the service area. Since servicing can be a major strategic success factor in many situations [Scheuing 1990], an increasing number of firms offer guaranteed service [Pearl 1991]. In many industries, such as automobiles, dealers have their own service facilities, since performance reliability is so important to success. Deere, the maker of farm machinery, found that emphasizing customer service was an effective way to rebuild customer brand loyalty, which had fallen in the 1980s. It was also an effective way to hear what customers wanted and to design new products that met customer needs [Rose 1990(A)]. In contrast, Ikea, a chain of furniture stores, by policy limits its retail services severely in order to maintain its low-price strategy [Trachtenberg 1991].

In other industries, and in many small manufacturing companies, maintaining service facilities in-house—or even having service facilities at all—is not critical. For example, smaller appliance and office equipment manufacturers often have qualified retailers do their servicing, because these manufacturers do not have the resources to maintain in-house service operations. In some product areas, service support has little impact on success and so is not a marketing strategy consideration. In the low-end appliance field it often is more efficient and cost-effective for a customer to throw away a broken radio or cheap watch and buy a new one than have it repaired.

Frequency and speed of change. Distinctive design features are often copied, and product and service differences quickly disappear in many situations. This was true in the baked goods company study discussed in Chapter 7, where new cookies can be copied within weeks. In this situation, tracking competitors' new products by quickly obtaining samples of new products sold was as critical to success as having an in-house research department to develop a continuing flow of original cookies.

In today's market environment, speed and frequency of change can have a major strategic impact on marketing. For example, Sony is a leader in introducing new products and upgrading other products; the company sometimes even makes its own existing products obsolete "quickly," in the words of one top Sony executive [Sanger 1992]. To meet the changing diet habits of the aging population and the competition from Weight Watchers, Slim Fast Food Company, whose principal product was liquid diet meals, brought out over 60 new health-food products within a few months in 1991 [Kerr 1991(A)].

In other situations, a strategy of rapid change is needed not to stay ahead, but to survive. The fashion industry, for example, changes clothing styles annually.

Distribution

Marketing strategies are also formulated for distribution of products or services to consumers. A major strategic decision in this area involves the choice of distribution outlet or channel used: direct to consumers; through exclusive dealerships; through wholesalers; direct to retailers.

Direct to consumers. Service companies generally deliver their services directly to consumers — for example, banks, transportation companies, hotels, and hospitals. For these companies, this is the best way — and in some instances the only way — to deliver their services to the consumer. Mail-order marketing companies effectively use direct distribution to consumers through the mail or through packaged delivery services. A company started in 1989 to sell flowers by mail — considered an impossibility by some experts — was expected to have $13 million in sales in 1992 [Strom 1992]. Direct-to-the-consumer distribution is often necessary with highly technical products, especially at companies servicing larger capital goods industries. In the highly competitive environment of the 1990s, some manufacturers — for example, apparel makers — who have traditionally sold through independent outlets began to sell and distribute directly to customers through their own retail stores or through mail order [Agins 1990].

Exclusive dealerships. Exclusive dealerships are another distribution outlet used both in product and service companies. For example, automobile dealerships are effective in the auto industry, because they combine the advantages of having local entrepreneurs do the selling with the advantages arising from the relatively tight control built into franchise agreements. Service companies, especially in the fast-food industry, also work effectively through exclusive local franchises.

Wholesalers. Wholesalers are often used by smaller companies unable to afford their own distribution system or by larger companies entering new territories. Wholesalers generally buy, store, and deliver manufacturers' products to retailers. They at times assume risks involved in product damage, product obsolescence, and price changes, and also take care of all retailer needs. Wholesalers, usually a fairly expensive distribution method, can sometimes create control problems for a manufacturer.

Direct to retailers. Large companies often deliver directly to retailers. Shaw Industries created its own distribution network as part of its highly successful low-cost, low-selling-price corporate strategy designed to enable the company to dominate the relatively mature carpet industry [Ruffenach 1991].

In some situations, strategic mixes of the above four distribution methods are used. For example, in 1989 Fuller Brush did close to 35 percent of its business through mail order, 5 percent through retail stores, and 60 percent through door-to-door selling [Berg 1989(A)]. Other companies have developed mixed distribution strategies using distribution outlets such as brokers and agents, along with more traditional wholesalers.

In addition to developing channels of distribution strategies, distribution strategies can involve finished goods, inventory levels, geographic locations, levels of penetration and coverage, and transportation strategies.

Pricing

Decisions about price (including mark-ups, discounts, allowances, and terms of sale and service) depend on such factors as existing market practices, production costs, anticipated competitor responses, the impact on volume and demand levels, and strategic marketing objectives. Pricing decisions are important because they have an impact on such things as volume, market penetration, and profits — all strategic concerns. A company has several choices when making strategic pricing decisions.

Above market pricing. Above market pricing is feasible in situations where a genuine product or service differentiation advantage exists. This was the case initially with IBM's personal computer during the early 1980s, when IBM was able to sell at higher prices against untried and unknown competition. Eventually, as competitors' product quality improved and consumers became more sophisticated, IBM encountered price pressures. This strategy is also useful over the short-run to generate a higher cash flow in some situations — a strategy referred to as "skimming" — though over the long run such a pricing strategy can hurt unit sales.

Market leader, pricing below the competition. This strategy assumes that product or service quality is equal to (or perceived to be equal to) the competition, so the price is perceived as a bargain, not as an indication of less service or lower quality. Shaw Industries uses this strategy to dominate the carpet industry, for example [Ruffennach 1991]. Wal-Mart and K-Mart have both grown substantially in the 1990s through leadership in the low-priced merchandise field [Barmash 1992]. This strategy is often used to reinforce a marketing strategy designed to hold or increase product or market penetration in more mature industries.

Temporary price reduction. Deciding whether or not to have a temporary discount sale to get new customers, move specific products, or adjust other imbalances in business operations is generally not a strategic market decision. In the airline industry, however, prior to April 1992 continually adjusting prices in order to fill unsold seats was part of a strategy to increase overall company load factors — the percentage of seats filled throughout the system. Ignoring such strategic price considerations was identified as a major cause of the failure of the $2 billion airline People's Express [Dahl 1991; Scheier 1989].

Pricing designed to meet the competition. This neutral pricing strategy enables companies to compete in other ways, for example, on quality and service. This is one of the most common pricing strategies, as was seen in April 1992, when most major airlines for a time matched the simplified price structure introduced by American Airlines [Salpukas 1992].

Pricing for different classes of customers and services. In many situations permanent price categories — such as quantity discounts and discounts for special groups, such as students or the elderly — are established. These discounts or higher prices might also be used to direct the flow of sales or to take advantage of different sales patterns, as for example when ski resorts charge higher prices on the normally crowded weekends or when transportation and utility companies offer discounts for travelling or using energy during non-peak periods.

Each of these pricing strategies serves a different need and so each is feasible in different situations.

Promotion

Decisions about promotion — the effective communication of product messages (benefits) to the target market — cover personal selling, advertising, sales promotion, and publicity.

Personal selling. Sales force strategies affect the success of companies in different ways. For example, a strategic strength of the baked goods company discussed earlier was its sales force, which called on 85 percent of the food stores in the company's four-state area. The company's strategies tended to both exploit and reinforce this strength, as was discussed in Chapters 7 and 8. Personal selling is especially critical to success in service industries, as evidenced by the growth of Nordstrom's department stores [Stevenson 1989].

Advertising. Strategic decisions about advertising — any paid, nonpersonal presentations of company products and services —are required in many situations. The revival of Chrysler Corporation was attributed largely to the advertising efforts of Lee Iacocca, its president. Decisions to use fictional characters in advertising were major contributors to the success of such products as Charmin bath tissue (Mr. Whipple) and Bartles and James wine coolers. The decision to rely on radio advertising, using the husband and wife comedy team of Jerry Stiller and Ann Meara, was the key strategic move leading to the enormous success of Blue Nun wine in the early 1980s. A two-year campaign advertising Seagram's Extra Dry Gin's "hidden" values was said to be the reason it was the only leading distilled spirit to have a year-to-year sales gain to 1991 [Elliot 1992(C)].

Choosing an advertising approach or theme involves deciding how to position a product in consumers' minds, and how to differentiate a product in the target market's mind. This can be done either by emphasizing product attributes, or by using an endorser or surrogate, such as Kodak and Jello did with Bill Cosby, or as was done with the fictional characters cited above.

Sales promotions. Promotions involving sweepstakes and premium offers are common promotional devices for mail-order companies, while coupons, contests, displays, and premiums are used to promote food company products in stores. In 1990 and 1991, supermarkets began experimenting with using computers to replace coupons, by having computers track customer purchases and offer rebates to regular buyers of certain brands [Kleinfield 1991].

Publicity. Publicity is any unpaid form of nonpersonal presentation of ideas, goods, or services. Publicity strategies can also be important. The Games Gang Ltd.'s use of publicity instead of advertising was a key element of its enterprise-wide strategy. Publicity is especially important to small business owners and professional services, whose success depends on their local reputation since local advertising media is often limited.

MAKING DECISIONS IN SPECIFIC COMPETITIVE MARKET SITUATION CONTEXTS

The discussion in this section goes beyond the descriptions of commonly used marketing strategies in the preceding section, and describes the process of formulating marketing strategies appropriate to the needs of specific business situations. The process described in this section, which is shown in Figure 9-3, is an extension and adaptation of the one described in Chapters 2 through 8 and outlined in Figure 9-4.

Marketing strategy decisions involve defining the overall marketing strategy, target markets, and the appropriate marketing mix for a company. As shown in Figure 9-4, these strategy

Figure 9-3: Developing Enabling Strategy Plans: An Approach to Developing Marketing Strategies

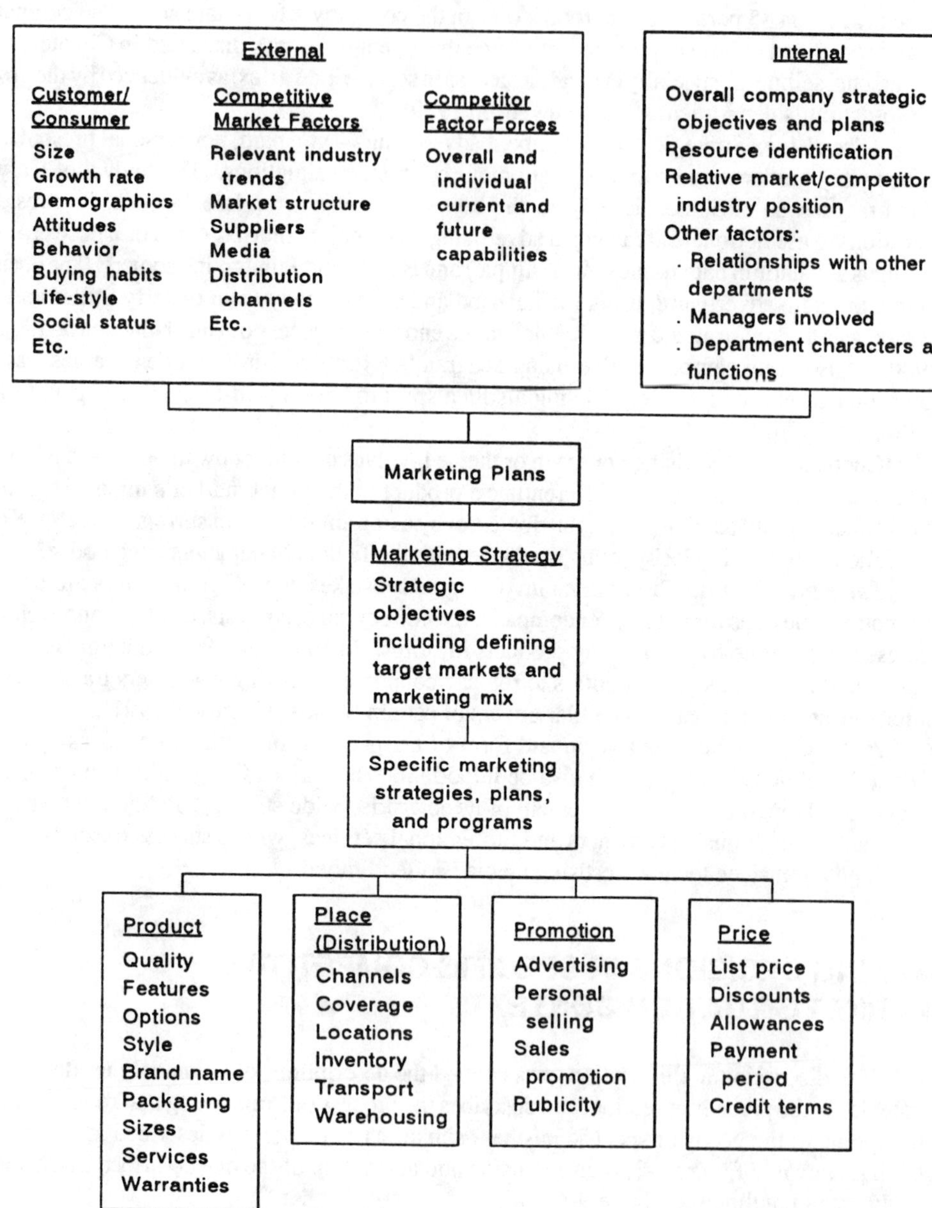

Figure 9-4: Strategic Management Decision-Making Process

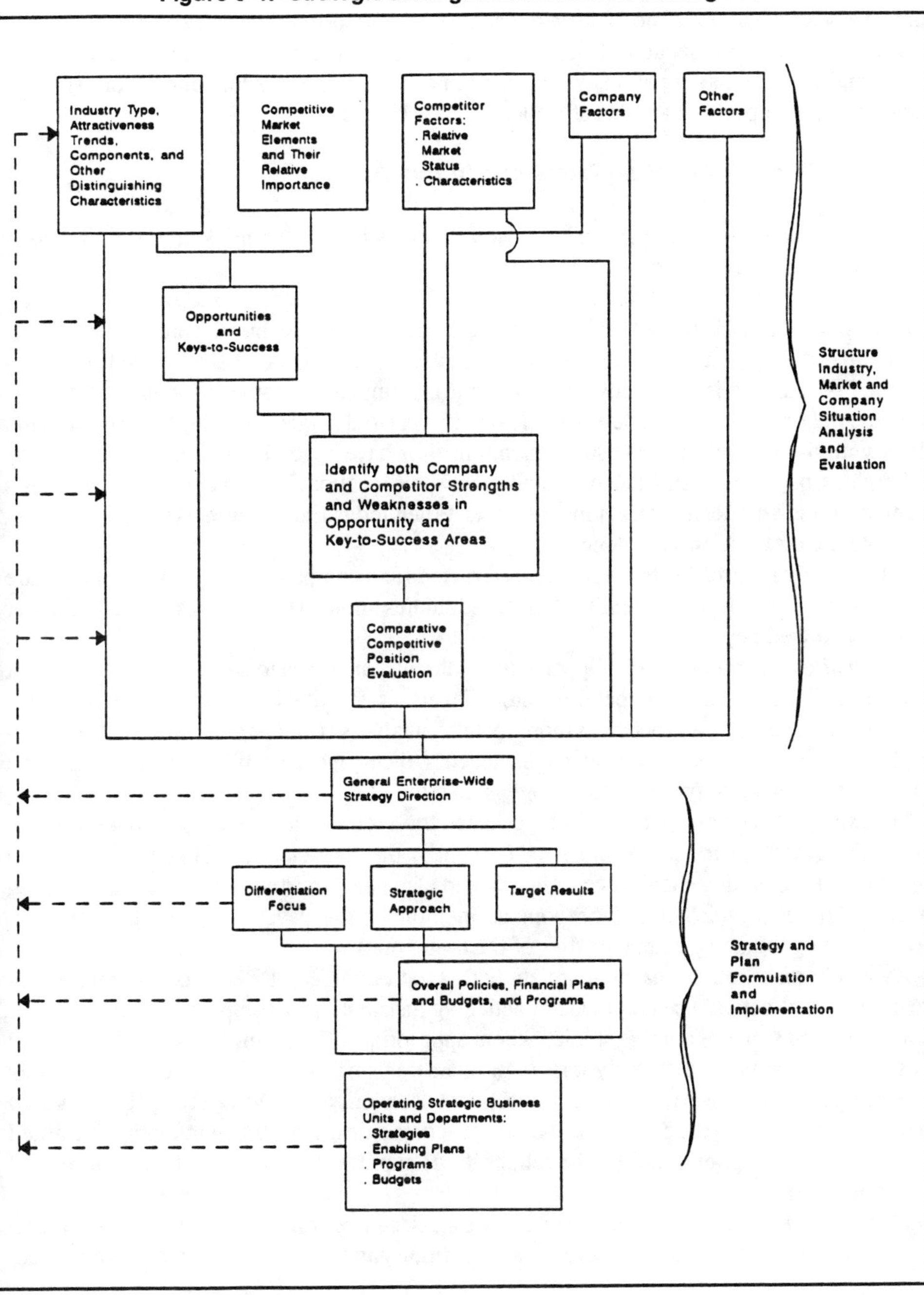

decisions are made within the limitations of the external market factors and internal company factors. They are also formulated within the context of enterprise-wide strategies.

The following two sections discuss generally how these situation context factors are analyzed and used in making strategy decisions in a wide range of situations. More specific applications of the approach are discussed later in this chapter.

Critical Factors Affecting Decisions in this Area

This section discusses the critical situation factors which affect marketing strategy decisions, as outlined in Figure 9-4.

Customer/consumer. All marketing planning is to some degree based on the customer/consumer, since the marketing effort is a failure if the market does not buy the product or service.

Initially, the market under study may be defined in terms of total size, growth rate, and segments. For example, if a company makes skis and is formulating strategies for that competitive market, the major segments of interest are 15- to 35-year-old singles and childless couples and families with young children. Those segments in turn have several subsegments defined by demographics, psychographics, behavior, and geographic location. This analysis provides a basis for later selecting an effective target market mix. When industrial buyer markets are involved, similar total market analyses are done.

As the study progresses, those segments targeted for a company's products or services are identified and defined in greater detail. While these studies build on the ones described in Chapter 4, they also go well beyond them.

Competitive market factors. Opportunities, threats, and keys to success are identified at both the overall industry and competitive market levels, as described in Chapter 3 and 4. As the planning study progresses and becomes more specific, analyses are made of the different channels through which consumers buy, what media reaches them, what suppliers are available and reliable, what the state of product technology is, and the like.

For example, planners involved with packaged foods companies, such as the baking goods company described in earlier chapters, need to identify the characteristics of supermarkets and what factors affect getting shelf space. They would also study existing products in the market, as well as products which might be popular in light of the psychographic, demographic, behavioral, and geographic characteristics of the target market.

Available distribution channels are studied, as at A&W Root Beer, to determine what strategies might effectively be employed in widening distribution of company products. Available suppliers and supplies are also studied where appropriate. For example, the availability and cost of energy sources are extremely important to air transport companies since energy factors affect pricing decisions, as well as capital investment decisions and even survival. Raw material availability is essential to the success of champagne companies, since their production is limited by the availability of grapes and by the reliability of supply sources over a long-term period [Greenhouse 1989].

Competitor factors. Both present and future overall competitor factors, as well as individual competitor strengths and weaknesses in critical opportunity and key-to-success areas, are studied.

Figure 9-5: Outline of Competitor Profile

BACKGROUND:
- company identification
- location
- description
- brief history
- state of incorporation
- affiliates
- how is the company organized?
- how often has it altered its structure?
- number of shares outstanding
- ownership (insiders, institutions, major shareholders)

FINANCE:
- statistics and performance analyses (revenue, earnings, growth)
- sales by division
- profitability by business unit/product line
- banks/investment banking firms used
- stock market data
- current market value
- ratios and industry comparisons
- do they track, lead or lag the industry?
- cash flow analysis
- assets and return on assets
- capitalization
- working capital
- internal rate of return on investment

PRODUCTS:
- description of products and services offered (product mix - depth and breadth of product line) and market position by product
- product strengths and weaknesses (individually and the line as a whole)
- how committed is the firm to a particular product line?
- analysis of new product introductions
- R&D expenditures and apparent interests of technical personnel
- an analysis of the company's design and development process
- patents held/pending
- product standards (specs), quality and technical analysis
- pricing policies (Who decides flexibility in pricing levels?)
- note special selling arrangements (Are they competing for your customers?)
- licensing and joint venture agreements

MARKETS:
- market segmentation and customer analysis
- customer base (markets targeted, regional sales analysis, penetration, importance to the firm, dominance of market)
- profiles of markets/customers (including product mix and sales data by product line)
- market growth and potential for future growth
- market share by product line
- how does the company view the direction of the industry?
- market and geographic area targeted for expansion
- marketing tactics
- distribution network/channels of distribution
- advertising/marketing/sales efforts including budgets and firms used
- foreign trade analysis
- recent orders

Figure 9-5: Outline of Competitor Profile (contd.)

- government contracts
- analysis of sales force (experience, compensation)

FACILITIES:
- location
- size
- domestic vs. foreign
- capacity
- capacity utilization
- announced capacity expansions
- product mix by plant
- shipments and profitability data
- unit cost/price
- capital investments
- equipment purchases
- key suppliers
- number of production lines and shifts
- regulatory issues

PERSONNEL:
- employees - total, management, R&D staffing, engineers - number, education, training, experience
- biographies of senior management including employment contracts, incentive (bonus) programs and golden parachute agreements
- description of the members of the board of directors
- consultants used by the firm
- labor union information (relations with management, results of recent negotiations with other firms in the industry, date of next contract renegotiation)
- detailed corporate structure
- who has profit and loss responsibility?
- safety information (accidents) and government/industry regulations violations
- management style and flexibility
- fringe benefits and compensation practices
- track managerial changes for indications of disputes in upper management (turnover of personnel)

APPARENT STRATEGIC (LONG-RANGE) PLANS:
- detail of acquisition and divestiture strategy
- new products on the horizon (Does it indicate a new direction for the firm?)
- statements of plans to enter new markets or improve their market position (increase their share of market)
- apparent strategic objectives
- corporate/divisional/subsidiary company priorities
- business unit/segment goals
- basic business philosophy/targets
- analysis of company's decision-making process
- overall corporate image and reputation
- assess company's ability to adapt/change
- how will the company look/perform in the future?
- anti-takeover measures instituted
- shareholder actions
- lawsuits pending
- what are the firm's key successes and failures?
- why have they been successful?
- overall corporate strengths and weaknesses
- attitudes toward risk

Adapted from Barbie E. Keiser, "Practical Competitor Intelligence," *Planning Review*, September/October 1987, pp. 18-19

Figure 9-5 illustrates the amount of detail which can be involved in such competitor-by-competitor studies. These studies are described in-depth in Chapters 5 and 11.

Company factors. Existing and potential company resources are examined to define a company's strengths and weaknesses affecting success in identified opportunity areas, and are compared to those of competitors. As discussed in Chapter 6, company resource areas studied include financial, production, marketing, manpower, information systems, and image.

Since marketing strategy formulation is done within the context of enterprise-wide strategies, these strategies and related plans are also studied.

Resource availability affects many marketing strategy decisions since marketing managers rarely have enough money to do everything they would like to do. Other company factors affecting marketing strategy decisions include relationships with other departments, department character and function, and the various personalities and aspirations of the managers involved.

How Decisions Are Made Based on These Critical Situation Factors

Marketing strategies and strategic plans are developed within the context of critical situation factors. For example, the decision-making process involved in formulating *overall market strategies* is similar to that described in Chapter 7. After a structured situation analysis is done, key marketing components are identified. Their relative ranking is established based on both external market and internal company factors. Alternatives are formulated and evaluated in each critical component area, and an initial strategy decision is made. This initial overall marketing strategy would define the marketing strategy in each of the critical component areas.

As for *target market* decisions, in the ski company situation described earlier, the strategic planner identified the market segment with the highest sales potential (high income; young adult — under 35; unmarried; college graduate), as well as the best products to promote to that market (quality, technologically advanced skis in a variety of styles and prices), given the nature of company resources (their experience and existing production capabilities) and the nature of the sport (skiing requires some degree of skill and involves some danger).

The identified target market, along with other critical situation factors, are considered in making strategic *marketing mix* decisions. These decisions can involve a wide range of marketing strategy decision situations, including:

- Designing a product development strategy to meet customer and other market requirements.
- Determining the best positioning strategy for a new product when developing advertising themes.
- Selecting channels of distribution.
- Deciding whether or not to enter a new product area.
- Formulating pricing strategies.
- Formulating a media strategy appropriate to both product and customer.
- Formulating packaging strategies.
- Determining marketing strategies for local foreign affiliates of a multinational company.

The following sections discuss how the general approach described in this section is used in making some of these specific marketing mix strategy decisions.

SPECIFIC PRODUCT STRATEGY DECISIONS

This section describes how expert managers at a local foreign affiliate (SBU) of an international health-care products company evaluate new product proposals generated by the international company headquarters. The alternative strategies considered in this situation are

- Introduce the product (without change to formula): as a new brand, as a line extension to an existing brand, or as a replacement of an existing brand.
- Change one or more elements of the proposed product and introduce it: as a new brand, as a line extension to an existing brand, or as a replacement of an existing brand.
- Reject the proposed product.

In this study, it is assumed that international corporate management has already developed the product formula and recommended overall marketing strategies for the product. These strategies are based on preliminary research in other countries where the product has demonstrated significant international sales potential. International company headquarters normally requests input from the local affiliate manager as to the feasibility and strategic "fit" of the new product in the local manager's country.

The new product proposal received from international headquarters would normally include

- Complete information on the product — its formula and manufacturing (or important) specifications.
- Full details (and necessary supporting documentation) of its medical purpose — that is, what it is designed to do.
- The basic costs of raw materials and manufacturing or of importing the product.
- The product's proposed consumer promise, brand name, and suggested promotional strategy (for local adaptation), an identification of the suggested target market segment(s) for whom the product was designed, and the product's recommended positioning versus competitive products.
- Summaries of experiences (both positive and negative) to date in other international markets, covering: consumers, competitors, and trade reactions; initial levels of product sampling and purchase; likelihood of "me too" copies or generic competition; and regulatory barriers.
- Other information pertinent to local product decisions, such as the strategic importance to the parent company of introducing the product in as many countries and as soon as possible to preempt competition.

The proposal is evaluated in light of key customer, market, competitor, and company factors, as shown in Figure 9-6.

Examining Critical Factors Affecting the Decision

Customer factors. In the local country, it is first determined if there is a sufficiently large,

Figure 9-6: Diagram of Decision Area to Be Prototyped: New Product Strategy for Local Country Product Proposal

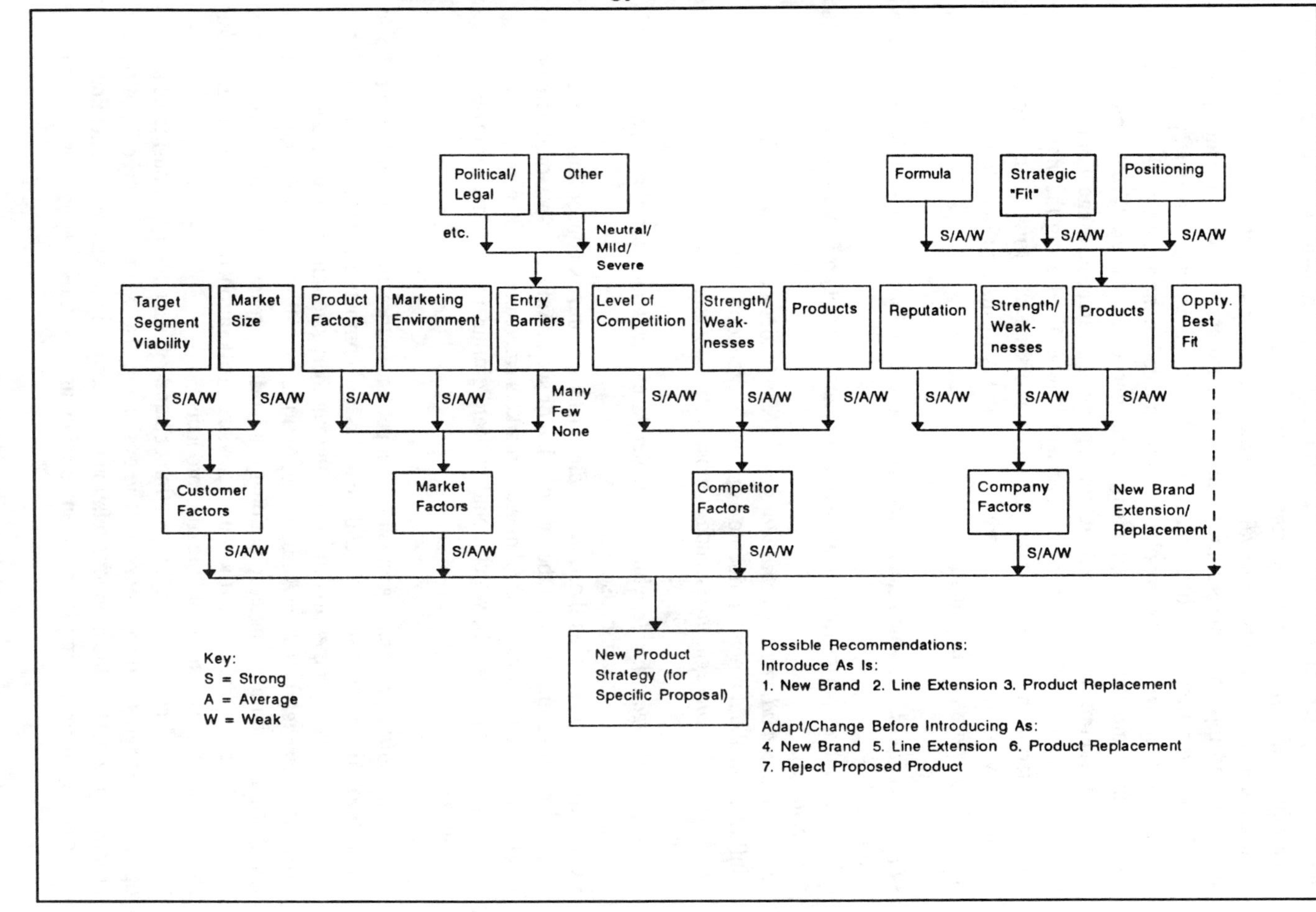

definable, and potentially viable market—or market segment—to which the product can be sold. Determining this involves comparing the target market defined in the proposal with local demographics and conditions. In evaluating the *viability of a target market segment*, such factors as income and appropriateness of the product are considered. A general evaluation of the *market size*, including estimates of total country population and per capita income, is also required.

Market factors. These involve conditions faced in marketing products to customers in a given country and can be grouped into three subcategories. *Product factors* require judgments, based on market research, of such factors as product awareness, usage, brand loyalty, purchase frequency, and overall consumer involvement levels. Evaluating the *marketing environment* involves determining the strengths and weaknesses of the existing marketing structure in the local country. Key considerations here are the availability of distribution channels and advertising media. *Entry barriers* may include:

- *Product regulations*, which can hinder a company's ability to register or distribute a product or formula.
- *Price regulations*, in the form of either price freezes or direct profit constraints on manufacturers or retailers.
- *Promotion and advertising regulations*, which can hinder a company's ability to communicate information about a new product to a specific target population. .
- *Place/distribution regulations,* such as those restricting non-prescription drug sales to pharmacies.
- *Foreign exchange controls*, which can hinder the efficient purchase of raw materials or finished products from international sources.
- *Cultural factors*, such as those in Middle Eastern countries concerning women's dress and behavior, that could prohibit the introduction of such products as personal-care products.
- *Inflation*, which in some Latin American markets can exceed 1000 percent a year.
- *Market saturation levels*, which could indicate diminishing returns for investments in new products.

Competitor factors. Analyzing competitor factors involves examining the level of competition, the specific strengths and weaknesses of competitors in the industry, and competing products. *Level of competition* measures the number, size, and effectiveness of competitors. *Competitor strengths and weaknesses* measure the overall strength of competitors' financial, distribution, manufacturing, promotional, and pricing resources. *Competing products* are examined for their similarity to the product under consideration, their market position, their brand strength, and the likelihood of "me-too" products.

Company factors. A firm's reputation or standing in a country is considered along with its operating strengths and weaknesses. The evaluation also weighs the specific attributes of the proposed product and the product's relation to the company's existing product line. *Reputation* is measured by examining the company's relations with three key groups (the industry trade groups, the medical community, and consumers) and by assessing the strength of the company's sales force. The *company strengths and weaknesses* examined include the firm's distribution, manufacturing, and promotion capabilities, its flexibility in pricing, and the resources available to support a new product introduction. A company's strengths and weaknesses are then compared with competitors'.

Product evaluation involves examining the proposed product's formula and positioning, as described in the new product proposal, and weighing its strategic "fit," both in terms of the local company and its international parent. In evaluating the product, the degree to which the proposed *formula* conforms to locally accepted medical practice is determined, as well as whether or not some aspect of the formula (for example, an ingredient) needs to be changed before the product is introduced. The need for change can arise from regulations, accepted local norms for self-medication treatment, availability of raw materials, and other factors. Whether or not the product can be made in the country or must be imported is also studied. Formula considerations also include estimates of the new product's value to the market: Is it unique? Does it present a significant and valuable improvement over existing product offerings to consumers in the market? The absence of any such advantages would mean that the company is dealing with a "me-too" product — usually a weak competitive position.

Judging *strategic fit* requires evaluating how well a proposed product would blend with or improve a company's existing product mix. It also involves studying a company's worldwide enterprise-wide strategy to determine if this introduction is part of a broader strategy of market penetration or positioning.

Three separate, though related, evaluations are made of a proposed *product's positioning*. These determine whether the positioning, or consumer promise, is: *clear and understandable* to the consumers in a local country; *relevant* to their wants, needs, and life-styles; and *believable* to potential product customers.

Opportunity: Best Fit. A number of other strategic factors, classified under the heading "Opportunity: Best Fit," are considered. For example, if a company has no existing brand in the proposed product category, the product would be introduced as a new brand, if other factors are favorable. If the company already has a strong brand in the category, in most cases it is not advisable to introduce a new brand, but rather to incorporate the new product into the existing product family as a line extension. An example of this was Sterling Drug's introduction of Midol 200, a pain-killing product introduced as a line extension to the existing Midolline, rather than as a new brand. This was a strategically sound move because the company did not have the resources to compete head-on with similar products such as Johnson & Johnson's Tylenol and Medipren.

When a company has a strong existing brand in the new product's category, but that brand is in the declining stage of its lifecycle, it is often advisable to introduce the new product into the market as a new, improved (replacement) version of the existing brand, rather than as an entirely new brand. Where existing brands are weak and declining, introduction as a new brand would be preferable, if other factors are favorable.

Possible Recommendations and How They are Made in Light of the Identified Critical Factors

After evaluating the impact of these major factors, seven possible strategic recommendations can be identified as possible responses a local manager might make to the new product proposal. These decisions can be grouped into three basic categories:

- Introduce the product (without change to formula) as a new brand, as a line extension[1] to an existing brand, or as a replacement[2] of an existing brand.
- Change one or more elements of the proposed product and introduce it: as a new brand; as a line extension[1] to an existing brand; or as a replacement[2] of an existing brand.
- Reject (do not introduce) the proposed product.

The ideal situation is one in which customer, market, and company factors strongly favor the company, and competitor factors are weak. In this case, the final strategy choice is made by combining the appropriate "best-opportunity-fit" values — new brand, line extension, or replacement — with information on whether or not changes are needed. For example, if the best-opportunity-fit analysis concludes that the proposed product should be introduced as a new brand, and that changes in the product are not needed, then the recommendation would be to *introduce the proposed product, as is, as a new brand.* If changes in the formula are needed, the recommendation would be to *adapt/change the proposed product before introducing as a new brand.* If the best-opportunity-fit analysis indicates that the product would be best as a *line extension,* this would be the recommended strategy, depending on whether or not changes were needed. A similar pattern of recommendations occurs when best-opportunity-fit analysis indicates product replacement.

Conditions are, however, rarely so totally favorable. More complex judgments are required in most situations. For example, where customer and market factors are either average or strong (indicating the market could support a new product introduction), but competitor position factors are stronger than company position factors, a new brand's introduction would not be recommended under any circumstances. Instead, assuming the company has a strong existing brand in the category, the recommendation would be to introduce the product as a *line extension.* This strategy relies on the company's existing brands' strengths in otherwise impossible circumstances. If there is no strong existing company brand and no other special strategic corporate considerations, the proposed product would be rejected.

If competitor factors are strong and customer, market, and company factors are weak, the recommendation would be *not to introduce the proposed product* — at least until conditions

[1] A line extension is an additional product, related to an existing one by function and name, yet different in form, flavor, etc.— such as the Children's Tylenol line extensions of tablets, liquids, drops, and syrups.

[2] A replacement/product improvement example would be the replacement (improvement) of a new, alcohol- and sugar-free formula for the syrup version of the same Children's Tylenol product, replacing the old one that contained these two ingredients.

Figure 9-7: Dependency Diagram: New Product Strategy Selection for Local Country Product Proposal (Initial Prototype)

? Life-cycle-stge (Growth/Mature/Decline)
? Str-exist-brands (High/Medium/Low)
? Exist-brand-in-cat. (Yes/No)
22·1 to 22·7
Oppty. Best Fit
New Brand/line extension/replacement

? Positioning-believable (Yes/No)
? Positioning-relevant (Yes/No)
? Positioning-clear (Yes/No)
20·1 to 20·3
Positioning
S/A/W

? International-plans (H/A/L)
? Local-business-fit (Y/N)
? Formula-uniqueness (Yes/No)
21·1 to 21·3
Strategic "fit"
S/A/W

? Finished-goods (Yes/No/Not-applicable)
? Raw-materials (Yes/No/Not-applicable)
? Change-needed (Yes/No)
? Medical-rationale (C/A/NC)
19·1 to 19·5
Formula
S/A/W

18·1 to 18·5
Product
S/A/W

? Resources-available (Strong/Adequate/Not-adequate)
? Promo.-strength (Stronger/Same/Weaker)
? Price-flexibility (Stronger/Same/Weaker)
? Mfgr. strength (Stronger/Weaker/Equal)
? Distrib.-strength (Stronger/Weaker/Equal)
17·1 to 17·15
Str./Weak.
S/A/W

? Consumer-rep. (High/Average/Low)
? Medical-rep. (High/Average/Low)
? Trade-goodwill (High/Average/Low)
? Sales-force (Yes/No)
16·1 to 16·10
Reputation
S/A/W

Rules 5·1 to 5·9
Company factors
S/A/W

? Similarity-product (Strong/Average/Weak)
? Similarity-positioning (Strong/Average/Weak)
? Me-too-likelihood (High/Possible/Not-likely)
? Brands-strength (Strong/Average/Weak)
15·1 to 15·10
Products
S/A/W

? Price-strength (Strong/Average/Weak)
? Promotional-strength (Strong/Average/Weak)
? Mfgr.-strength (Strong/Average/Weak)
? Distrib.-strength (Strong/Average/Weak)
? Finance-strength (Strong/Average/Weak)
14·1 to 14·17
Strengths/Weaknesses
S/A/W

? Capacity-resources (Strong/Average/Weak)
? Int'l.-reputation (Aggressive/Moderate/Conservative)
? Compet.-size (Larger/Equal/Smaller)
? Compet.-number (None/Few/Many)
13·1 to 13·8
Level of Comp.
S/A/W

Rules 4·1 to 4·5
Competitor factors
S/A/W

? Mkt.-saturation-lev. (Low/Medium/High)
? Inflation-level (Low/Medium/High)
? Cultural-factors (Yes/No)
? For.-exchange-cntrls. (Yes/No)
12·1 to 12·5
Other

? Place-regs. (Neutral/Mild/Severe)
? Promo-regs. (Neutral/Mild/Severe)
? Price-regs. (Neutral/Mild/Severe)
? Product-regs. (Neutral/Mild/Severe)
11·1 to 11·10
Political/legal

10·1 to 10·4
N/M/Sv
Entry Barriers
Many
Few
None

? Adv.-media-effect. (Strong/Average/Weak)
? Dist.-channels-avail. (Strong/Average/Weak)
9·1 to 9·4
N/M/Sv
Marketing Envt.
S/A/W

? Involvement-level (High/Medium/Low)
? Purchase-frequency (Frequently/Occasionally/Seldom)
? Brand-loyalty (High/Medium/Low)
? Usage-frequency (Frequently/Occasionally/Seldom)
? Category-awareness (High/Medium/Low)
8·1 to 8·9
Product Factors
S/A/W

Rules 3·1 to 3·10
Market factors
S/A/W

? Market-income-level (Low/Average/High)
? Market-population (Large/Medium/Small)
7·1 to 7·7
Market Size
S/A/W

? Segment-media-target (High/Average/Low)
? Segment-definition (Strong/Average/Weak)
? Segment-value (Yes/No)
? Segment-size (High/Medium/Low)
? Segment-income (High/Medium/Low)
6·1 to 6·12
Target Segment Viability
S/A/W

Rules 2·1 to 2·3
Customer factors
S/A/W

Rules 1·1 to 1·59

New Product Strategy (for Specific Proposal)

Possible Recommendations:
Introduce as is:
1. New brand 2. Line extension 3. Product replacement
Adapt/Change Before Introducing as:
4. New brand 5. Line extension 6. Product replacement
7. Reject proposed product

KEY:
S = Strong
A = Average
W = Weak
N = Neutral
M = Mild
Sv = Severe
H = High
L = Low
Y = Yes
N = No
C = Closely
A = Approximately
NC = Not-closely

changed. Other factors that would also trigger an automatic rejection include the presence of severe political/legal or other entry barriers, weak formula and positioning (in combination), and weak customer and marketing environment factors.

Figure 9-7 outlines a prototype knowledge-based system based on this structured situation analysis. The outline, called a dependency diagram, indicates the knowledge rules used in the system, as well as information contained in the situation diagram in Figure 9-6.

This system is given on the computer disks accompanying this book. The system can be run and its reasoning rules examined in detail by following the instructions accompanying the disks. The file containing the system is named AIMS.REV.

CONTEXT-SPECIFIC PROCESSES INVOLVED IN OTHER MARKETING STRATEGY FORMULATION DECISIONS

Hundreds of marketing strategy decision processes have been structured in a similar way. For example, a diagram of media decision making is given in Figure 9-8 [Mockler, 1989]. The figure lists the factors analyzed in making decisions about which media mix to use for the specific product under study, print (newspapers, magazines), radio, or television.

After the initial screening, the knowledge-based system based on this decision diagram makes recommendations about preferred types of media within each general media category, as is done in actual marketing decision situations.

A complex system developed to make pricing strategy decisions at a major computer hardware manufacturing strategic business unit is replicated in the structured decision diagrams in Figures 9-9 to 9-12. The decision maker (and the knowledge-based system replicating that decision maker's thinking) considers such factors as:

- Product characteristics — type, function, effects on existing products, outside servicing (Figure 9-10)
- Competition — similar products, product characteristics, possible competitors' reactions to the company's planned strategies, strengths and weaknesses (Figure 9-11)
- Financial factors — product forecasts and price sensitivity (Figure 9-12)
- Strategic factors — internal strategy and reputation (Figure 9-12)

This is only a small sampling of the considerable work being done to structure how marketing strategy decisions are made. This structuring is useful in understanding and learning how to do strategy formulation. It is also useful in providing a basis for developing and using knowledge-based systems that replicate these decisions. These systems in turn make and assist managers in making these management decisions. They also allow people to observe in detail how experts go about making such decisions.

In addition to the knowledge-based systems tools, a wide range of conventional computer tools are useful in doing strategic planning for marketing. These conventional computer tools are discussed in several useful supplementary texts [Mockler 1992; Webster 1989].

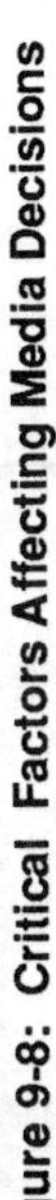

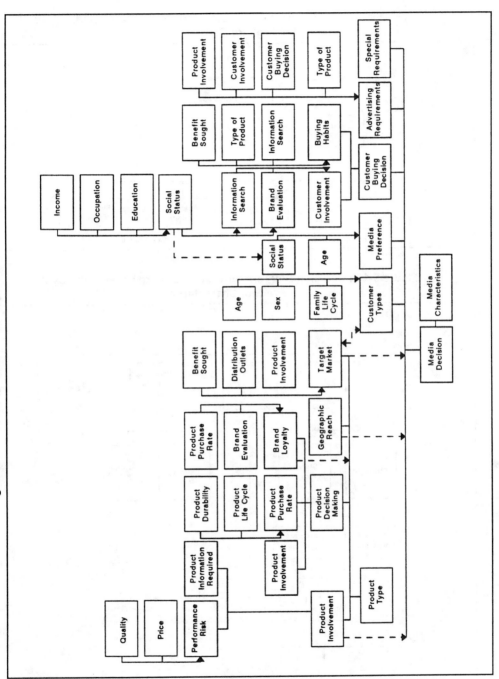

Figure 9-8: Critical Factors Affecting Media Decisions

Figure 9-9: Diagram of Decision Area to Be Prototyped: Pricing Strategy for Computer Hardware

Recommended Markup
Primary Factors
Secondary Factors
Product Characteristics
Competition
Strategic Factors
Financial Factors
(See Figure 9-10)
(See Figure 9-11)
(See Figure 9-12)

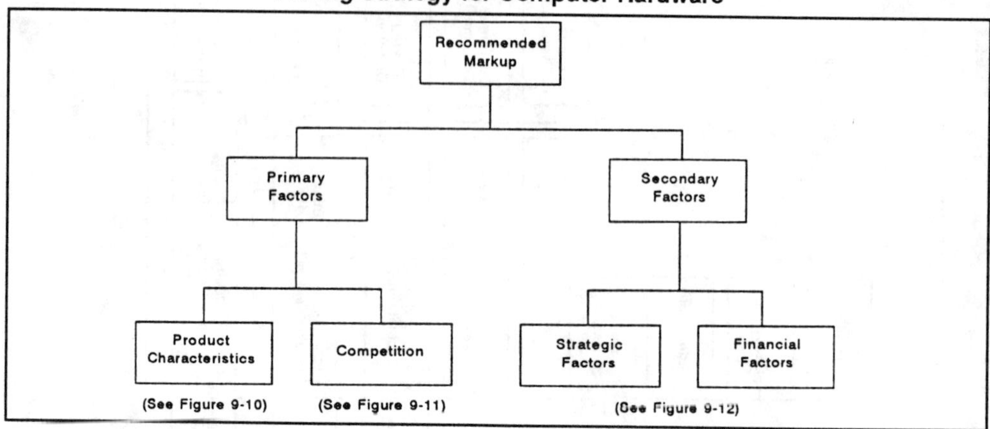

Figure 9-10: Decision Diagram for Computer Hardware Pricing System: Product Characteristics

Product Characteristics
Type
Function
Effects on Existing Products
Outside Sourcing
Strategic
Stand-Alone
Effect Existing Prices
Willing to Change Existing Prices
Software Compatibility
Hardware Compatibility
Amount
High-Tech
New Tech
Ease-of-Use
Capability
Expandable

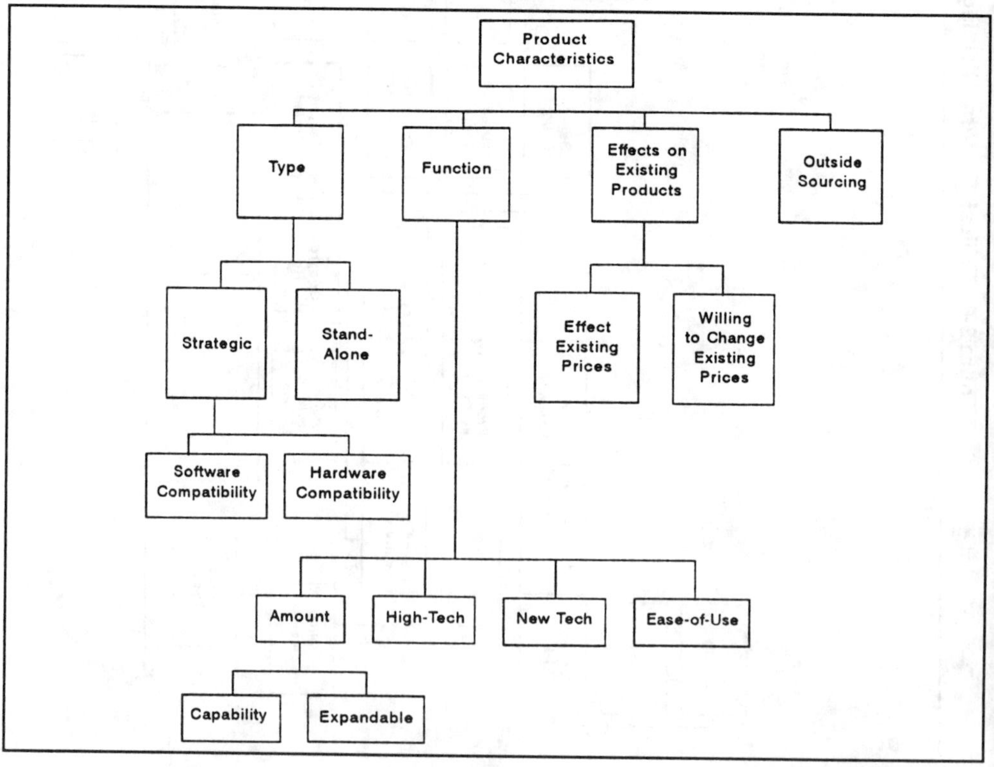

Figure 9-11: Decision Diagram for Computer Hardware Pricing System: Competition Characteristics

Competition
Similar Products
Product Characteristic
Reaction Time
Strengths
Function
Margin or Relative Price
Out-Long
Amount
Outlets
Marketing
Current
Future

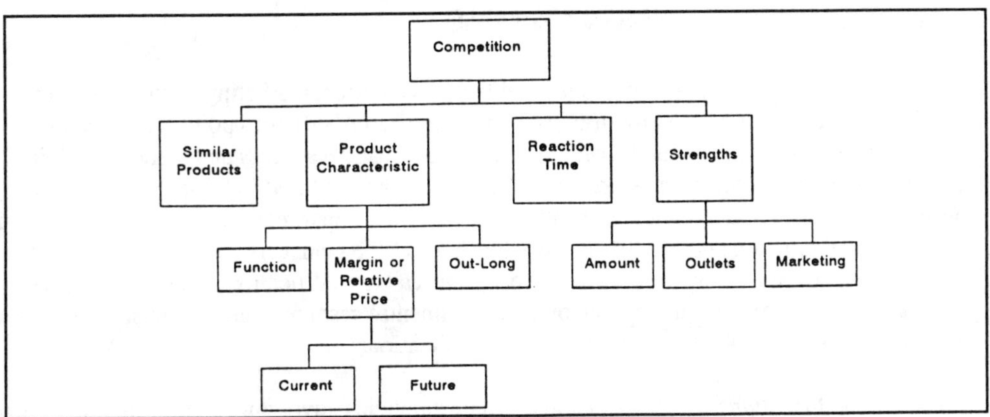

Figure 9-12: Decision Diagram for Computer Hardware Pricing System: Secondary Factors

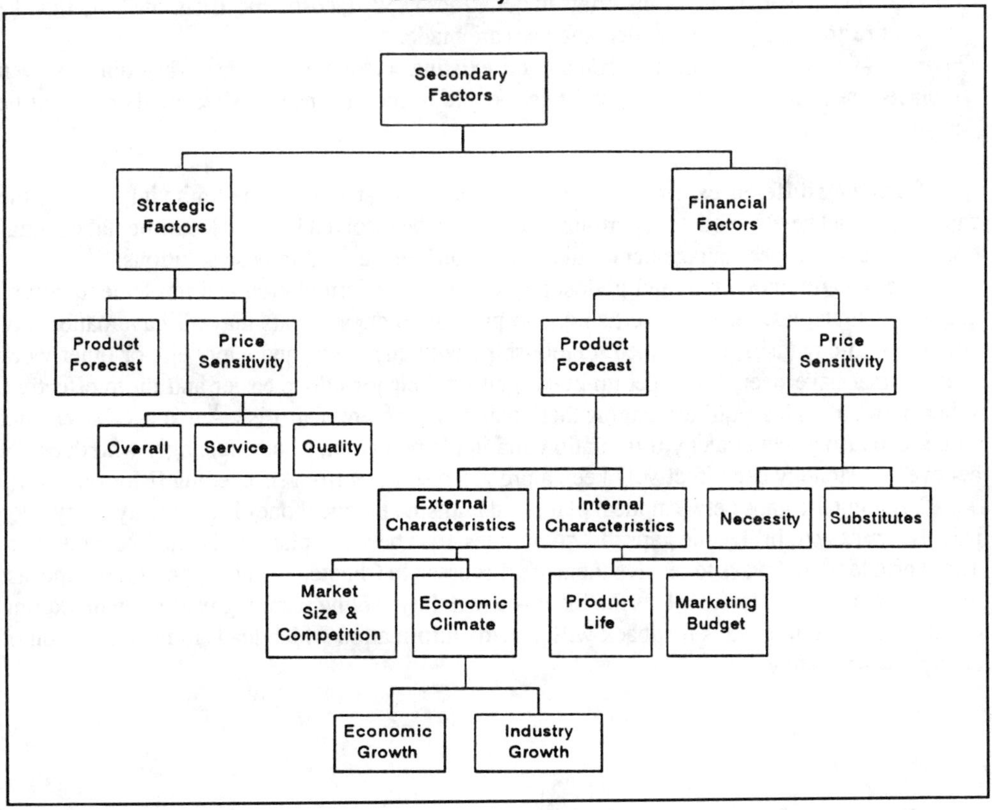

Secondary Factors
Strategic Factors
Financial Factors
Product Forecast
Price Sensitivity
Product Forecast
Price Sensitivity
Overall
Service
Quality
External Characteristics
Internal Characteristics
Necessity
Substitutes
Market Size & Competition
Economic Climate
Product Life
Marketing Budget
Economic Growth
Industry Growth

INTEGRATING MARKETING PLANNING WITH OTHER STRATEGIC MANAGEMENT AREAS

As seen in Figure 9-4, several additional factors can affect marketing strategy decisions.

The initial study of marketing strategy formulation described to this point often creates only "ideal" strategies — what would be best to do given company resources and market conditions. This ideal approach is not always possible. Other factors (identified in Chapter 8, Figure 8-5) considered include: relationships with other departments; department culture, character, and function; and the various personalities and aspirations of the managers involved.

These factors may temper the ideal approach and lead to modifications. For example, in new product strategy formulation, several other departments' resources and interests can affect strategy formulation in different ways in different situations:

- *Production/Operations* — new customers and strategies involving them can mean new processes, schedules, machinery, and the like which production/operations may not be able to deliver exactly as marketing might like within the cost and time estimates.
- *Purchasing* — availability of materials in quantities needed, costs, specifications, and the like may set restraints as more detailed analyses are made.
- *People* — when new strategies are considered, existing personnel may need to be trained or even replaced, as seen in Chapter 12, and new people needed to meet desired goals may not be available.

Resolving differences, which in some situations can arise from the limits imposed by the capabilities and needs of other departments, can often be resolved by interdepartmental negotiations. At times, upper management will arbitrate differences and impose solutions.

The department culture and philosophies may affect formulation and implementation of marketing strategies. Sales, advertising, and promotion departments may all have patterns of doing day-to-day tasks, established relationships with customers and suppliers, or other work routines that have been developed to make getting their jobs done easier and more effective. Where new strategies require changing these patterns, problems can arise. A manager's personal values can also affect strategy formulation and implementation, since a manager who does not believe in a strategy can effectively keep a proposed strategy from succeeding [Morton 1988].

Bridging the gaps between ideal plans and realistic, practical ones is not always easy. Nor is it always easy to bridge the gaps that sometimes arise between plans and actual performance. These problems and ways to resolve them are discussed in Chapter 12 and Appendix B. One last integration consideration involves the feedback that the enabling planning process in marketing can provide. At times, this feedback will provide information which leads to reformulation of enterprise-wide strategies.

REVIEW QUESTIONS

1. Outline the marketing strategy formulation and implementation process. Discuss its relationship to the strategy formulation and implementation processes discussed in Chapters 2 through 8.
2. Discuss the different relationships possible between enterprise-wide strategies and overall marketing strategies in different marketing planning situations.
3. What is a "target market"? Discuss the different ways it can be defined in different marketing situations.
4. Describe some of the different kinds of product strategies which can be formulated in different kinds of marketing situations.
5. What are some of the strategic choices in the distribution area?
6. Describe some ways in which advertising has been used to define the personality and character of a company.
7. Name and describe the critical situation factors which are generally examined in making strategic choices and formulating strategies for the marketing area.
8. Describe some ways in which these critical situation factors affect marketing strategy decisions in several specific situation contexts.
9. Describe some of the interdepartmental problems (and compromises) which may be involved in formulating marketing strategies and related enabling plans.

EXERCISES

1. Read one of the company studies in the Case Study section at the end of this book whose title contains an actual company name. Use the company study of your choice to write reports which cover the following planning tasks:

- Recommend an enterprise-wide strategy for the company under study, and identify the situational factors and the evaluation that led to this recommendation.
- Formulate marketing strategies in areas you feel are important to implementing the enterprise-wide strategy, and give the reasoning upon which they are based.
- Develop marketing plans and programs for implementing enterprise-wide and marketing department strategies.
- Identify any potential integrating problems involving other departments and how you might go about resolving them.

2. Read recent issues of the periodicals referred to in the references section at the end of the chapter, or other related periodicals of your choice, and find a description of a company of interest to you. Write a report on that company covering the same strategic management tasks as listed in Exercise #1.

3. The disks accompanying this book contain several prototype KBS. Follow the directions

accompanying the disks to run a consultation using the system with the file name AIMS.REV. If you wish, you may print out the knowledge base and study it while you are running the system and restudying this chapter, in order to get a more detailed picture of how strategy formulation decisions are made.

4. Read through recent issues of the periodicals mentioned in the References section of this chapter, or any other related publications of your choice. Based on your research and whatever additional research you feel is needed, prepare a company study involving strategy formulation and implementation areas relevant to this chapter's subject matter which you think would be appropriate for use in your class.

REFERENCES

Agins, Teri, "Apparel Makers Increasingly Market Their Clothes Directly to Consumers," *The Wall Street Journal*, February 9, 1990, p. A5.

Agins, Teri, "Once-Hot Lee Jeans Lost Their Allure in a Hipper Market," *The Wall Street Journal*, March 7, 1991, pp. A1, A6.

Ambrosio, Johanna, "Honing in on Target Customers," *Computerworld*, February 10, 1992, pp. 97, 98.

Barmash, Isadore, "Down the Scale with the Major Store Chains," *The New York Times*, Business Section, February 2, 1992, p. 5.

Berg, Eric, "At Fuller Brush, A New Way to Get Foot in the Door," *The New York Times*, May 18, 1989, pp. D1, D2.

Bowles, Jerry, and Joshua Hammond, "Being 'Baldrige Eligible' Isn't Enough," *The New York Times*, Business Section, September 22, 1991, p. 13.

Bulkeley, William M., and John R. Wilke, "Filing in Chapter 11, Wang Sends Warning to High-Tech Circles: Large Size, Customer Base Couldn't Compensate for Lack of Innovation," *The Wall Street Journal*, August 19, 1992, pp. A1, A6.

Dahl, Jonathan, "Agents Rankle Airlines with Fare-Checking Programs," *The Wall Street Journal*, May 20, 1991, pp. B1, B5.

Elliot, Stuart, "Loneliness in a Long-Range Planning Pitch," *The New York Times*, May 15, 1992(A), pp. D1, D7.

Elliot, Stuart, "Sampling Tastes of a Changing Russia," *The New York Times*, April 1, 1992(B), pp. D1, D5.

Elliot, Stuart, "Seagram's Campaign in Hiding Has Conspicuous Results," *The New York Times*, May 1, 1992(C), pp. D15.

Faludi, Susan C., "Sales Job: At Nordstrom Stores, Service Comes First — But at a Big Price," *The Wall Street Journal*, February 20, 1990. pp. A1, A16.

Fisher, Lawrence M., "Apple Pays Price for New Strategy," *The New York Times*, May 20, 1991(A), p. D8.

Fisher, Lawrence M., "Boom in Mountain Bikes Revives the U.S. Industry," *The New York Times*, April 1, 1991(B), pp. A1, D1.

Foderaro, Lisa W., "Store Owner Finds Everybody Likes Him but the I.R.S.," *New York Times*,

September 4, 1991, pp. B1, B5.

"For Specialty Ketchups, A Battle with the Giants," *The New York Times*, March 3, 1990, pp. 31-33.

Goad, G. Pierre, "Trying to Assimilate Roy Rogers Outlets, Hardee's Is Ambushed by Irate Clientele," *The Wall Street Journal,* August 28, 1991, pp. B1, B6.

Greenhouse, Stephen, "Success Has No Kick for Champagne," *The New York Times*, September 18, 1989, pp. D1, D10.

Hillkirk, John, "This Month Will Focus on Quality" and "Award to Honor Individuals, Small Teams," *USA Today*, October 1, 1991, p. 1.

Hirsch, James S., "Brash Phar-Mor Chain Has Uneven Selection, But It's Always Cheaper," *The Wall Street Journal,* June 24, 1991, pp. A1, A6.

Holusha, John, "How Harley Outfoxed Japan with Exports," *The New York Times,* August 12, 1990, p. 5.

Kerr, Peter, "Casting Hungry Eyes at Dieters," *The New York Times*, August 31, 1991(A), pp. 33, 35.

Kerr, Peter, "On a Roll, Pepsi Changes Its Face," *The New York Times*, September 24, 1991(B), pp. D1, D4.

King, Julia, "Coral Lipstick? It Sells Big in Florida," *Computerworld,* May 11, 1992, pp. 117, 118.

Kleinfield, N.R., "Targeting the Grocery Shopper," *The New York Times*, Business Section, May 26, 1991, pp. 1,6.

Lohr, Steve, "Sheffield Knife Maker Beats the Odds," *The New York Times,* April 15, 1989, pp. 35, 46.

Lohr, Steve, "The Best Little Bank in America," *The New York Times*, Business Section, July 7, 1991, pp. 1, 4.

Markoff, John, "Apple Faces Challenge to Its Role as Innovator," *The New York Times,* August 10, 1991, pp. D1, D6.

Mayer, Martin, *Whatever Happened to Madison Avenue?*, New York: Little Brown, 1991.

McCarthy, Michael J., "Marketers Zero in on Their Customers," *The Wall Street Journal,* March 18, 1991, pp. B1, B8.

McGill, Douglas C., "Pepsico, to Aid Europe Sales, Buys 2 British Snack Units," *The New York Times*, July 4, 1989(A), pp. 41-42.

McGill, Douglas C., "Sara Lee's Success with Brands," *The New York Times*, June 18, 1989(B), pp. D1, D3.

Mockler, Robert J., *Computer Software To Support Strategic Management Decision Making,* New York: Macmillan 1992.

Mockler, Robert J., *Knowledge-Based Systems for Management Decisions,* Englewood Cliffs, NJ: Prentice-Hall, 1989.

Morton, S. Morgan, "Whose Plan Is It Anyway?," *Planning Review,* May/June 1988, p. 45.

Pearl, Daniel, "More Firms Pledge Guaranteed Service," *The Wall Street Journal,* July 17, 1991, pp. B1, B4.

Pereira, Joseph, "Name of the Game: Brand Awareness," *The Wall Street Journal,* February 14, 1991, pp. B1, B8.

Phillips, Stephen, "Back to Basics at Quaker Oats," *The New York Times,* November 26, 1986, p. 37.

Phillips, Stephen, "King Customer," *Business Week,* March 12, 1990, pp. 88-94.

Pollack, Andrew, "A Novel Idea: Customer Satisfaction," *The New York Times*, Business Section, May 27, 1990, pp. 1, 6.

Pollack, Andrew, "Jeans Fade but Levi Strauss Glows," *The New York Times*, June 26, 1989, pp. D1, D4.

Rose, Robert L., "Tougher Row: Deere Faces Challenge Just When Farmers Are Shopping Again," *The Wall Street Journal*, February 8, 1990(A), pp. A1, A10.

Rose, Robert L., "After Nearly Stalling, Harley-Davidson Finds New Crowd of Riders," *The Wall Street Journal*, August 31, 1990(B), pp. A1, A10.

Ruffenach, Glenn, "Shaw Uses Price Cuts to Extend Its Rule Over Carpet Business," *The Wall Street Journal*, June 12, 1991, pp. A1, A8.

Salpukas, Agis, "A Call for Discipline in the Airline Industry," *The New York Times*, April 10, 1992, pp. D1, D2.

Sanger, David E., "Stalking the Next Walkman Quickly," *The New York Times*, Business Section, February 23, 1992, pp. 1, 8.

"Sara Lee CEO Profiles Strategies Behind Their Corporate Growth," *The Planning Forum Network*, January 1990, p. 1.

Scheier, Robert L., "Obliterated by the Chip: The Crushing Out of People's Express," *PC Week*, November 13, 1989, p. 131.

Scheuing, Eberhardt, *Customer Service as a Strategic Management Tool*, Oxford, OH: The Planning Forum, 1990.

Schwadel, Francine, "Nordstrom Aim: Midwest Success Amid Recession," *The Wall Street Journal*, April 4, 1991, pp. B1, B8.

Slater, Derek, "IS at Your Service: Increasingly, the Corporate Quest for Happy Customers is Enlisting Technology's Aid," *Computerworld*, January 20, 1992, pp. 72-80.

Stern, Richard L., "The Graying Wild Ones," *Forbes*, January 6, 1992, p. 40.

Sterngold, James, "American Business Starts a Counterattack in Japan," *The New York Times*, February 24, 1992, pp. A1, D4.

Stevenson, Richard W., "Watch Out Macy's, Here Comes Nordstrom," *The New York Times Magazine*, August 27, 1989, pp. 35-40.

Strom, Stephanie, "In the Mailbox, Roses and Profits," *The New York Times*, February 14, 1992, pp. D1, D5.

Trachtenberg, Jeffrey A., "Ikea Furniture Chain Pleases with Its Prices, Not with Its Service," *The Wall Street Journal*, September 17, 1991, pp. A1, A6.

Wald, Matthew, "Stew Leonard's, Believe It or Not," *The New York Times*, May 25, 1989.

Webster, James L., William E. Reif, and Jeffrey S. Bracker, "The Manager's Guide to Strategic Planning Tools and Techniques," *Planning Review*, November/December, 1989, pp. 4-12, 48.

Winslow, Ron, "A Competitive Battle to Sell Surgery Devices Is Spurring Innovations: Fast-Growing U.S. Surgical Takes on J&J in a Field Altered by New Procedures," *The Wall Street Journal*, April 16, 1991, pp. A1, A8.

CHAPTER 10

OPERATIONS/PRODUCTION

The objective of this chapter is to help readers to

- Understand the operations/production function, and the wide range of operations/production tasks and planning decisions
- Make operations/production planning decisions in specific situation contexts
- Apply this context-specific approach to facility planning decisions
- Apply the approach to other operations/production planning decision situations
- Integrate operations/production planning with other functional strategic management areas

This chapter focuses on formulating strategies and related enabling plans for the operations/production area — another strategic management implementation task shown in Figure 10-1.

THE OPERATIONS/PRODUCTION FUNCTION

The operations/production function involves rendering or producing the services or goods offered by a company. As shown in Figure 10-2, this function involves the conversion of *inputs* (personnel, materials, purchased components, facilities, equipment, capital, and information) into *outputs* (goods and services) through a *transformation process. External environmental factors*, such as customer needs and government regulations, can affect the transformation process. The *overall control* function involves measuring actual results, comparing actual and desired results,

Figure 10-1: Strategic Management Tasks

OVERALL INDUSTRY AND MARKET ENVIRONMENT
. Type
. Scope & Characteristics
. Overall Trends
. Components & Their Relationship
. Attractiveness
(Chapter 3)

OPPORTUNITIES, THREATS & KEYS TO SUCCESS
(Chapter 4)

COMPETITION
. Existing
. Potential
. Strengths & Weaknesses
(Chapter 5)

COMPANY
. Resources
. Weaknesses
(Chapter 6)

COMPARATIVE STUDY
. Competition & Company Strengths & Weaknesses in Key-to-Success & Opportunity Areas
(Chapter 6)

ENTERPRISE-WIDE STRATEGY FORMULATION, EVALUATION & SELECTION
. General Directions
. Strategy Focus
. Strategic Approach
. Overall Performance Results Identification
(Chapter 7)

INTEGRATIVE STRATEGIC PLANNING FRAMEWORK FOR ENABLING PLANNING
. Philosophy
. Policies
. Resource Allocation: Overall Budgets & Financial Plans
. Strategies & Policies for Company SBU's, Departments, Operating Functions
(Chapter 8)

INTEGRATED ENABLING PLANNING FOR MAJOR OPERATING AREAS
. Marketing
. Operations/ Production
. Information Systems for Major Operating Areas
(Chapters 9-11)

IMPLEMENTATION
. Carrying Out the Strategic Plans
. Organizing & Carrying Out the Plan Development Effort
. Promoting Strategic Thinking
(Chapter 12 & Appendix A)

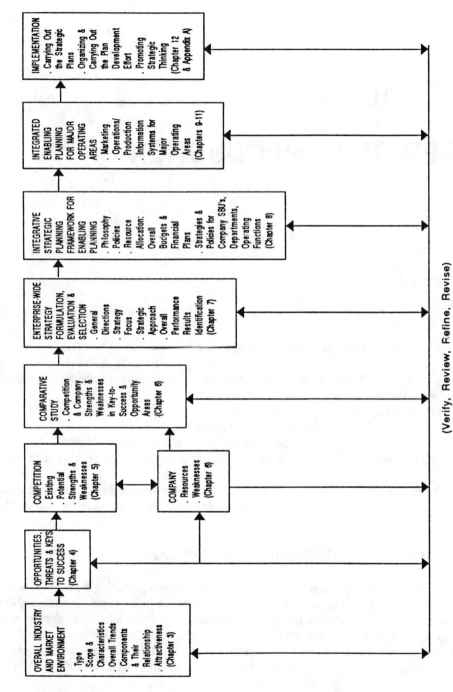

(Verify, Review, Refine, Revise)

and deciding if any changes are needed. *Feedback* is an essential part of the control process.

The transformation process shown in Figure 10-2 can be divided into four areas:

- Developing general planning directions: *formulating overall operations/production strategies*
- Creating the product or service: *product and service design and development*
- Developing facilities to produce the product or render the service: *designing operations/production systems*
- Producing the product or rendering the service: *planning and managing the operations/production function*

The transformation process varies from situation to situation. Producing products, such as television sets, light bulbs, or refrigerators, can involve a continuous production line, where a product's parts and materials move through different assembly stations and processes. Where a product is too large or fragile to move along a production line — such as large aircraft — the labor, materials, components, and equipment are moved to the product worksite. In contrast, drugs and chemicals, for example, may have some common processing, but at the same time have segregated facilities where contamination might occur.

The transformation processes for rendering a service have their own special characteristics. For example, offices that handle large volumes of paperwork, such as insurance claims, may be arranged to move massive amounts of documents through computer-related facilities. In contrast, a cafeteria customer passes from operation to operation — from silverware to salad to entree to dessert to coffee to cashier.

An air transport operation uses computer systems to handle customer queries, ticket purchases, and the like, human service systems to handle the flow of customers, equipment service systems, and the aircraft themselves. On the other hand, people who repair furnaces, handle medical and police emergencies, paint bridges, or deliver flowers must go to a particular location in order to perform their services.

The following section describes the transformation tasks and planning decisions involved in various operations/production situations.

OPERATIONS/PRODUCTION PLANNING

This section discusses some of the operations/production strategies formulated and tasks performed in the four key operations/production transformation task areas shown in Figure 10-2.

Overall Operations/Production Strategies

Five commonly encountered operations/production strategies are examined in this section.

Make or buy. A common strategic operations/production planning decision is whether to make or buy the product or service sold. For example, this book was originally drafted on a microcomputer whose manufacturer bought and assembled components, rather than manufacture

Figure 10-2: The Transformation System

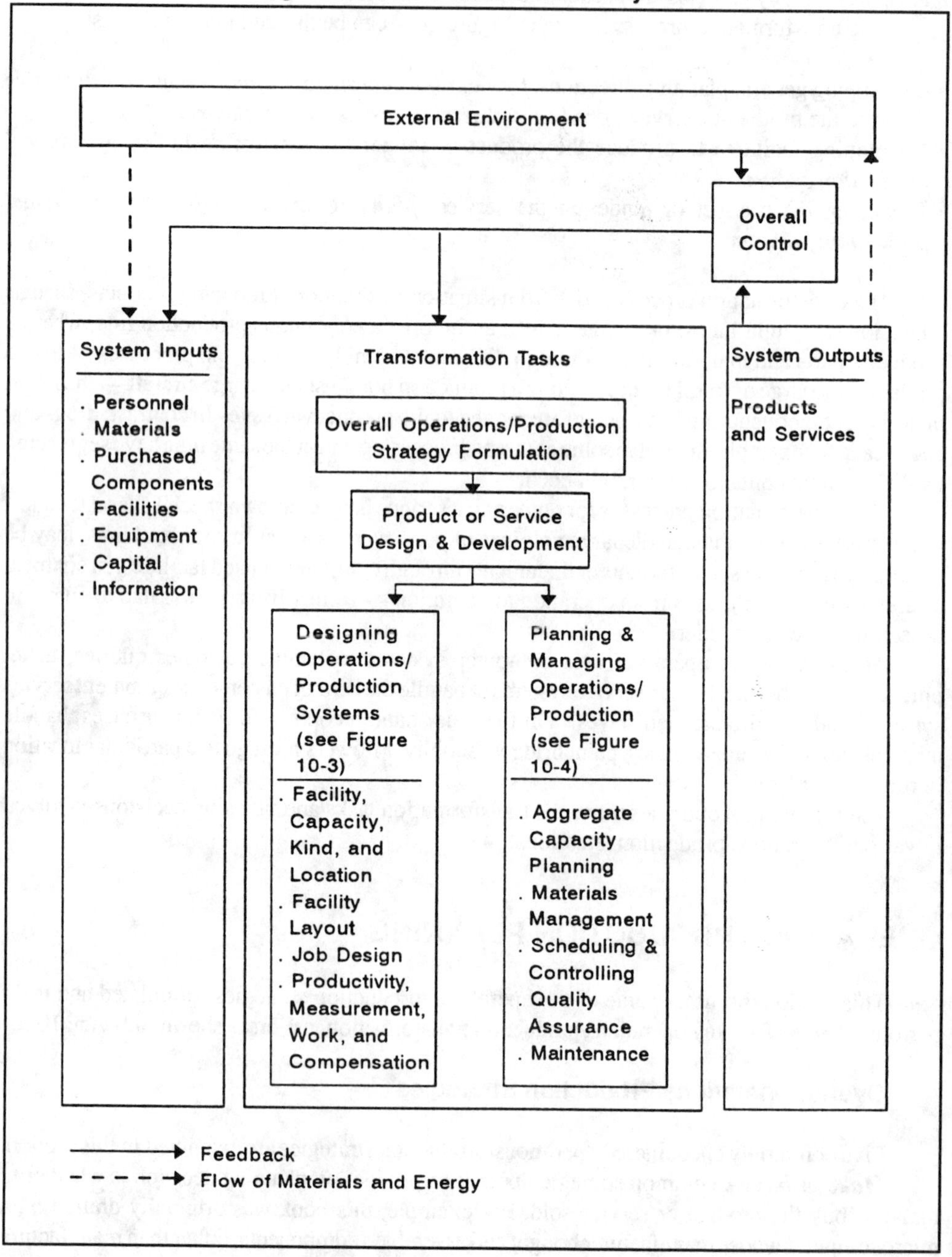

External Environment

Overall Control

System Inputs

- Personnel
- Materials
- Purchased Components
- Facilities
- Equipment
- Capital
- Information

Transformation Tasks

Overall Operations/Production Strategy Formulation

Product or Service Design & Development

Designing Operations/ Production Systems (see Figure 10-3)

- Facility, Capacity, Kind, and Location
- Facility Layout
- Job Design
- Productivity, Measurement, Work, and Compensation

Planning & Managing Operations/ Production (see Figure 10-4)

- Aggregate Capacity Planning
- Materials Management
- Scheduling & Controlling
- Quality Assurance
- Maintenance

System Outputs

Products and Services

———→ Feedback

- - - → Flow of Materials and Energy

the machine itself. A related overall make-or-buy strategy decision involves whether a company will own and operate its supply, service, and other facilities, that is, the degree of vertical integration. Shaw Industries, for example, decided to own its material suppliers and distribution facilities in order to further its overall objective of being a price leader in the carpet industry [Ruffenach 1991].

Low-cost/high-volume. This strategy focuses on using cost efficiency to obtain a strategic advantage. In the retailing industry, both Wal-Mart and K-Mart have become dominant forces through low-cost/high-volume strategies [Barmash 1992]. At times, this strategy requires the use of *high technology* equipment. Competitive pressures from the Japanese motivated Timken, a producer of specialty steel and tapered roller bearings, to modernize its Faircrest factory with a $500 million investment [Holusha 1989]. This step helped Timken to pursue a low-cost/high-volume manufacturing strategy while still maintaining a high level of quality. Inland Steel made similar investments in advanced technology in the early 1990s to revive its sagging fortunes [Hicks 1991].

Quality. Operations/production strategies built around quality can provide a competitive advantage, as was demonstrated through Maytag's lonely repairman advertising campaigns which have lasted over 25 years [Elliot 1992; Garvin 1990]. The strategic importance of quality to corporate success is evidenced by the substantial efforts made by corporations to win the Malcolm Baldridge National Quality Award created in 1987 by the Commerce Department [Hillkirk 1991].

Flexible production/low-volume. This strategic approach emphasizes flexible production and service processes, which are often required to meet specific customer needs. For example, IEC Electronics Corporation, a producer of made-to-order circuit boards in Newark, New York, stressed flexibility because of rapidly changing demand patterns. To serve customers effectively, periodic rearrangement of the shop floor was routine [Breskin 1989].

Hybrid. Some firms combine the above strategies to create a differential advantage. Nissan Motor Company announced in 1991 that it was installing a new *flexible* manufacturing system for its *high-volume* auto body assembly line in its Smyra, Tennessee, plant. The system, controlled by sophisticated computers, was already installed in Nissan's Japanese plants. Nissan claimed that the system decreased the time required for expensive model changeovers from 9-12 months to 2-3 months [Judge 1991].

Lean-Production. An emerging hybrid operations/production strategy in the 1990s, sometimes referred to as "lean-production," is exemplified by the Toyota Motor Corporation auto plant in Georgetown, Kentucky. In 1991, over 2,000 manufacturing executives and production engineers visited the plant to study how mass production is being changed. The strategy combines the high-tech approach used at the Nissan plant with other approaches. It is based on elaborate programs designed to teach workers and supervisors to perform multiple tasks and to provide instant feedback on problems and how to correct them.

For example, workers (often referred to as associates) operate machines, set them up, inspect for quality, perform minor maintenance, clean up, and offer suggestions for improvement. They have access to cords to pull (approximately 3500 times per day) when problems arise. Production is stopped about 7 percent of the time, both to fix problems, and so maintain quality, and to change products to keep work-in-progress inventories of parts and unfinished cars low. Suppliers are generally located nearby to reduce costs and enable just-in-time delivery of more parts and supplies.

Workers are encouraged to study routines and make changes to increase efficiency. This has led to thousands of low-tech improvements — from visual markings and cartoon sketches posted everywhere to prevent factory floor foul-ups, to calculating the number of seconds each movement takes for workers' tasks and then making changes to eliminate wasted motion [Levin 1992].

Product or Service Development and Design

Product or service design involves designing or redesigning a product or service, as well as developing new product or service specifications within the context of overall company and operations/production strategies. Several basic strategies that firms pursue with regard to the design of a product or service are discussed in this section.

Follower or leader. Companies can choose to be followers or leaders in the product development and design field. U.S. Surgical Corp., for example, grew rapidly through being a leader in research in surgical devices in the early 1990s [Winslow 1991]. On the other hand, Sears' Kenmore appliances basically copied and sometimes refined products that more innovative companies had produced. Sun Microsystems Inc. appears to use a mixed strategy: it is a pioneer in the field of new computer chip development, but does not hesitate to use off-the-shelf parts designed by others when necessary [Markoff 1991].

Outside or inside the company. Product development and design, like production, can be done in-house or by an outside company. Most large firms design and develop products in-house. Merck, for example, has a legendary reputation for developing highly profitable new drugs, as does DuPont [Freudenheim 1992]. However, because of cost, time, technology, or the special expertise required, many companies use alternative methods.

Paying someone to do the product development and design, a widely used strategy, can be done by using independent research laboratories or universities, or by purchasing licenses or patents. For example, the Battelle Institute did development work on the Xerox copying machine. Johnson and Johnson used the expertise of the University of Pennsylvania to develop its Retin-A, a drug for acne and wrinkles, and the expertise of Columbia University for photopheresis, a cancer therapy [Weber 1989]. At times, companies purchase *licenses* and *patents* for new products or services. For example, Corning licensed NGK Insulators Ltd., a Japanese firm, to produce and sell its products in Japan [Hammonds 1991; Holusha 1989]. Some companies simply *buy an existing product design*, as Johnson and Johnson did with a Danish manufacturer who developed a way to make disposable contact lenses [Weber 1989]. In some situations, the bulk of product development is done by *suppliers* rather than by the fabricators.

The *government* also does product and service design work useful in business [Broad 1990]. Johnson and Johnson, for example, has sought out partnership arrangements with government labs on projects such as ophthalmological lasers [Weber 1989].

Another way of getting product design done is through *joint ventures*. Johnson and Johnson used such an approach when working with Tate and Lyle PLC on sucralose, a low-calorie sweetener [Weber 1989]. Such design and research joint ventures between Japanese and American companies grew in popularity during the early 1990s [Pollack 1990; Sanger 1990(B)]. Even major competitors, such as Apple and IBM, have at times joined in strategic alliances to do research [Pollack 1991].

Basic or applied research. *Basic research* involves investigating an area or phenomenon without being sure how new knowledge will be used. For example, in 1982 Dow Chemical allocated $500,000 to basic research on ceramic compounds—compounds as strong as steel that weigh half as much. Only years later did the company find uses for that research in such areas as armor for military equipment [Woodruff 1989].

Applied research involves choosing a potential application area based on a factor such as customer need, and devising ways to meet that need. Braun A.G., a Gillette subsidiary which makes kitchen appliances and personal-care products, increased sales from $69 million in 1967 when it was purchased by Gillette to $1.2 billion in 1991 by strategically emphasizing technological innovations, superior design and user functionality, and superior quality — all applied research areas [Protzman 1992]. Japanese skills are especially strong in this area [Murray 1990; Sanger 1992], which is one reason why so many major corporations have set up research facilities in Japan [Sanger 1991].

Some experts expressed concern when U.S. industry spending on research and development declined from $78.63 billion in 1989 to $77.84 billion in 1990 (in constant 1991 dollars) [Broad 1992]. There was some fear that less emphasis on basic research would negatively affect the United States' long-term competitive position in global markets [Diebold 1990; Holusha 1990; Jaroff 1991; Markoff 1990; Sanger 1990(A)]. More recently, semiconductor computer chip manufacturers are one of several U.S. industries that have strengthened their competitive position in the 1990s through superior research [Pollack 1992].

Strategic uses of design and development. Many companies use product design as a strategic competitive tool [Perry 1989]. For example, Ingersoll Rand increased its competitiveness by cutting the product design cycle from three years to one year through employing work-teams which bypassed the existing company bureaucratic structure [Kleinfield 1990]. Product and service design and development in many industries has also changed considerably through the use of computer-aided design (CAD). For example, Navistar truck design now takes two months instead of two years because of computer-aided design [Berg 1989]. New technology is also having an impact on retailing: Second Skin, a seller of custom swimsuits, uses computer-aided design to fit women customers "who are not a perfect 8" [Pike 1989].

Designing Operations/Production Systems

As seen in Figures 10-2 and 10-3, designing operations/ production systems involves four tasks:

Facility type, capacity, and location. Overall decisions in this area are dictated at times by the nature of the business — restaurants, retail clothing, and auto manufacturing, for example, have their own inherent general type and location requirements. In other situations, facility

Figure 10-3: Tasks and Planning Decisions Involved in Designing Operations/Production Systems

Facility Type, Capacity, and Location	Facility Layout	Job Design	Productivity, Work Measurement, and Compensation
. Determining Capacity Needed, Based on Long-Range Demand Forecasts . Evaluating Market Factors, and Tangible and Intangible Cost Factors . Determining Whether New Facilities Should Be Built or Purchased, or Existing Facilities Expanded . Selecting Region, Community, and Site	. Selecting a Materials Handling Method and Support Service . Choosing a Layout . Evaluating Costs of Construction	. Specifying Jobs in the Context of Technical, Economic, and Social Feasibility . Deciding When to Use Machine and/or Human Labor . Managing Machine-Worker Interaction . Motivating Employees . Developing and Improving Work Methods	. Measuring Work . Setting Standards . Selecting and Implementing Compensation Plans

decisions can affect a company's long-term success. For example, Blockbuster Video set an industry trend with its very successful strategy of opening large stores, a *type* of store that was not common in the industry at the time [Sandomir 1991]. Radio Shack is also switching to a strategy of having considerably larger retail stores [Forest 1992]. On the other hand, foreign competition dictated the type of modernized facility to be built in the U. S. steel industry, as described in earlier discussions in this chapter.

When faced with the need to increase *capacity*, a company has several strategic options. *Expanding existing facilities* can be the easiest solution in many situations. Often, however, factors such as the availability of space, raw materials, labor, other support facilities, and customer demand in the surrounding area will create problems that prevent the use of this approach. An alternative is to *buy or lease an existing plant or service facility* from another producer. A problem often encountered here is that existing plants may not have the facilities that a company will need in the future. Also, the facility may be in an undesirable area from a supplier, labor, or customer viewpoint. A third option would be to *build a new facility*. A major obstacle to pursuing this strategy can be financial, since major capital outlays may be involved. The choice of any of these alternative strategies will also depend on the urgency and duration of the increased capacity requirements and on enterprise-wide strategic directions and requirements.

Another strategic facility decision might involve whether to centralize or decentralize facility locations. For example, a firm can have one central plant that produces all company products in the product line. The advantages of this approach include economies of scale, reduced cost per unit, higher equipment utilization rates, and reduced fixed costs per unit. Problems associated with this strategy are the potentially high distribution costs and the risks inherent in having only one plant when emergencies, such as power failures, strikes, and natural disasters, disrupt production at that facility. Another alternative is to have several smaller plants each specializing in one product in the product line or producing the entire line. This reduces the risks of a disaster disrupting the entire company production. At the same time, it can bring production closer to customers. A major problem here is that lower volume may increase unit costs. A third strategy is to have each smaller plant specialize in a particular component or components of the product line. This can reduce production costs by increasing economies of scale. But, at the same time, it will increase shipping costs and create company-wide problems should interruptions in production occur at any one plant.

Facility location decisions, and the factors affecting them, are discussed in detail later in this chapter.

Facility layout. Effective layouts — the arrangement of the various departments, support functions, and equipment within a production or service facility — can help foster improved communication, enable the smooth flow of materials or customers from one area to another within a facility, eliminate bottlenecks, and reduce excess inventory, or customer backlogs, and handling costs.

Five commonly used strategic approaches to layouts are discussed here. The Ford Motor Company uses a *flow line layout* in its factories because of the assembly process required for automobiles [Treece 1989]. *Process layouts,* which allow for flexible production processes, are layouts where all the people or machines performing the same function are grouped together. For example, since IEC Electronics Corporation is in the business of contract manufacturing, which involves meeting a broad range of varying low-and high-volume customer requirements, its Newark, New Jersey, plant is equipped with a process layout that allows for frequent changes in production flows [Breskin 1989].

A third type of layout is the *fixed position layout*. Here, the materials, labor and parts are moved to a specific site. Such a layout exists in the aircraft industry, where the product is too bulky to be moved, or in the computer industry, where products are too fragile to move. A newer type of layout which is becoming popular is the *manufacturing cell*. A manufacturing cell layout groups different equipment into work centers to work on limited product ranges. For example, in 1988 A.B. Volvo built a new manufacturing facility in Udavella, Sweden where a small team of highly skilled workers build an entire car [Prokesch 1991]. Apparently, however, this plant has not been successful. Finally, when combinations of the above four layouts are used the layout is said to be a *hybrid* one.

In addition to decisions about layout type, other decisions involved in facility layout include the selection of materials handling methods and of support services.

Job design and measuring productivity and work. Job design involves developing the formal and informal specifications of an employee's work-related activities, including both structural and interpersonal aspects of the job. *Productivity* refers to the relative efficiency of the operations involved in transforming inputs into outputs. *Measuring work* involves determining the time necessary for a qualified worker to perform a particular task and then using these standards to measure an individual's productivity performance, as well as to determine capacity requirements, work schedules, and cost estimates.

Compensation. Compensation involves decisions as to the most effective amount, schedule, and method of workers' pay. Two basic approaches to compensating workers are time based and incentive pay. *Time based*, as the name suggests, means that the payment schedule is based on an hour, day, month, or some other unit of time. *Incentive plans*, on the other hand, deal with direct relationships between performance and the amount of pay. Some methods of providing wage incentives for individuals include piece-rates, standard-hour plan, gain-sharing, and profit sharing. For example, Cooper Tire & Rubber Company has a strategically significant stock purchase program that has made many of its long-time blue-collar workers millionaires and contributed considerably to the overall success of the company [Hymowitz 1991].

Planning and Managing Production/Operations Function

As shown in Figures 10-2 and 10-4, planning and managing the production/operations function involves tasks dealing with aggregate capacity planning, materials management, scheduling and controlling, quality assurance, and maintenance.

Aggregate capacity planning. This task involves planning the quantity of product to produce in the immediate future, as well as planning the lowest cost method of meeting production requirements. Aggregate planning is usually based on business and marketing plans that are transformed into overall demand forecasts and production plans. The aggregate capacity plan specifies the resource inputs (for example, inventory, material, and labor) to be used in the operations or production process, based on forecasts of demand. Tasks involved in aggregate capacity planning are listed in Figure 10-4.

There are two basic aggregate planning strategies. *Top-down planning* occurs when a desirable overall production plan is developed for periods within a fixed future planning framework. The plan is subsequently broken down into specific feasible production schedules for individual work centers. This approach uses a pseudo-product, that is, a fictitious product with the average characteristics of the entire product line being planned for. *Bottom-up planning*, also known as resource requirements planning, is based on the resources required to meet overall production plans. These two approaches are often used together as overall production plans are refined and developed. Whatever the approach used, the production plan is always coordinated with company marketing and other strategic business plans.

Materials management. Materials management involves all aspects of the flow of materials: the purchase and internal control of raw materials, subassemblies, or parts for production; the planning and control of work in process; and the warehousing, shipping, and distribution of the finished product. Managing a firm's inventories deals with procuring items required for making a product (dependent demand), as well as managing finished products (independent demand).

For independent-demand items several approaches are possible. A *fixed-quantity approach* adds a constant, pre-established amount to inventory each time an item is reordered. A *fixed-*

Figure 10-4: Tasks Involved in Planning and Managing Operations

Aggregate Capacity Planning	Materials Management	Scheduling and Controlling	Quality Assurance	Maintenance
. Forecasting . Balancing Capacity and Demand . Materials and Labor Requirements Planning . Other Resource Requirements Planning . Selecting an Aggregate Planning Time Horizon . Allocating Insufficient Capacity Among Competing Uses . Determining Technical Upgrading Required to Remain Competitive	. Managing Independent Demand Inventory . Managing Dependent Demand Inventory . Purchasing, Traffic Control and Receiving . Production Control . Materials Handling . Packaging . Logistics Management Including Management of Shipping and Warehousing	. Developing and Assigning Specific Dates for the Start and Completion of Tasks . Monitoring Work in Progress . Collecting and Analyzing Data Needed to Measure the Actual Progress of Jobs . Comparing Actual Progress to Plan and Taking Corrective Action	. Ensuring Reliability . Ensuring Product Value . Evaluating Usability . Process Control . Product Screening . Service Assurance . Taking Action to Correct Problems . Deciding Where and When to Inspect	. Procuring Tools and Equipment . Establishing Priorities . Maintaining a Parts Inventory . Forecasting Malfunctions . Scheduling Routine Repairs & Handling Emergency Repairs . Preserving a Company's Investment in Assets & Prolonging the Life of Assets . Minimizing Loss of Productive Time and Cost Due to Malfunctioning Equipment

interval approach to inventory replenishment is based on the passage of time rather than on inventory level. The fixed-interval system results in the placement of very small orders. To prevent uneconomical order sizes, a *minimum-maximum approach* can be used to eliminate the handling of quantities considered too small to be economical. Another approach to managing inventory, *budget allocation*, provides more of a guideline than a set of operating rules. It relies on the discretion of a person familiar with buying patterns, such as the buyer or department manager. Another approach is the *ABC classification*, which provides an initial sorting of items into groups according to the amount of money spent annually on a product.

In managing dependent-demand items, *materials requirement planning* is important because it may be too expensive to stock certain parts for long before using them. Ideally, a company schedules when assemblies will take place and so is in a position to plan and control dependent component ordering in a way that keeps inventories low. The just-in-time (JIT) approach, a popular materials requirement planning approach, can significantly impact on inventory carrying costs. Using this approach, numerous small lots are ordered for production only as they are needed. For example, Proctor and Gamble and other suppliers now work with major retail chains, such as K-Mart and Pay 'n Save, to schedule deliveries on a "just-in-time" basis and provide other services that helps keep inventories low at both the retail and production ends [Feder 1991; Strom 1992].

Scheduling and controlling. Scheduling and controlling refer to planning the timing of specific operations/production with respect to available resources, anticipated backlogs, and production lead times. They also include directing the operations/production processes involved and taking any corrective action required to meet scheduled targets. The scheduling and controlling approach used will depend on a company's type of operation. Three strategic frameworks within which scheduling might be done are: make finished items to stock (sell from finished goods inventory); assemble final products to order and make components, subassemblies, and options to stock; custom design items and make them to order.

Quality assurance. Quality assurance refers to assuring that customers are satisfied with the product or service and that the products or services meet specified company quality objectives and standards. Companies commonly use one, or a combination of two, general strategies when facing a decision on the costs of quality — they can bear the cost either internally or externally. Bearing the cost of quality internally produces costs resulting from scrap, rework, and production seconds. Bearing quality costs externally entails the use of guarantees and customer returns, and the cost of lost future sales resulting from customer dissatisfaction.

Maintenance. Maintenance involves minimizing the cost and loss of productive time due to malfunctioning equipment, determining the most efficient use of maintenance personnel and equipment, and preserving a company's investment in assets by prolonging the life of assets. Key maintenance tasks and planning decisions are listed in Figure 10-4.

MAKING OPERATIONS/PRODUCTION PLANNING DECISIONS IN SPECIFIC SITUATIONS

The decision making discussed in this section extends the context-specific process described in Chapters 2 through 7 and outlined in Figure 10-5. The process involved in making operations/

production planning decisions is shown in Figure 10-6. This section describes how specific external and internal factors involved in operations/production situations are structured and analyzed, and then used in making decisions.

Critical Factors Affecting the Decision

As shown in Figure 10-6 and discussed earlier in this chapter, many external and internal factors can affect strategy formulation and implementation for operations/production.

External factors. These range from customer requirements and competition to technology.

Customer requirements analysis involves considering not only the amount of customer demand, but also the types of products and services needed by customers, the location of customers, when customers need the products or services, the quality needed by customers, customer negotiating power, the seasonality of the demand, and a variety of other special customer requirements.

The impact of *competitive factors* on operations/production strategy formulation in service industries is very apparent at banks and airlines, where strategies affecting service design and delivery are often dictated by competitors' strategic uses of computer information systems technology [Dahl 1991; Lohr 1991]. As for products, competitive factors can affect the kind of products made and their design, where and how they are made, and the overall production strategy used.

Supplies' and suppliers' availability and cost considerations include supplier location, capacity, flexibility, and bargaining power, as well as the cost and types of supplies available. During the early 1990s, for example, computer chip shortages led some computer manufacturers to rethink their manufacturing strategies and to reconsider entering chip manufacturing [Pollack 1992].

Transportation cost and availability can affect facilities location decisions, since locations are often dictated by the availability of transportation facilities that make it possible to meet customer demands in a cost-effective manner. These factors also often affect materials management decisions since they affect materials costs and availability, as well as the ability to meet the demands of just-in-time manufacturing strategies.

Unions and labor market factors also affect operations/ production decisions, especially ones dealing with plant location. For example, firms considering plant location decisions evaluate worker availability, qualifications, wage rates, and composition in the areas close to the site of a proposed plant, as well as the existence and character of unions.

Environmental issues can affect the way many products are made and delivered. These factors are likely to have a continuing major impact on strategic management of operations/production. For example, in early 1989 California considered adopting a sweeping clean-air plan that would eventually affect a wide range of products and services, through such requirements as: reformulating and redesigning everything from hairspray to furniture polish; installing special vents for charcoal broilers at restaurants; buying special equipment at bakeries to reduce emissions from ovens; installing additional pollution control equipment at dry cleaning plants; and converting a high percentage of cars to clean fuels. While many of the proposed regulations

Figure 10-5: Strategic Management Decision-Making Process

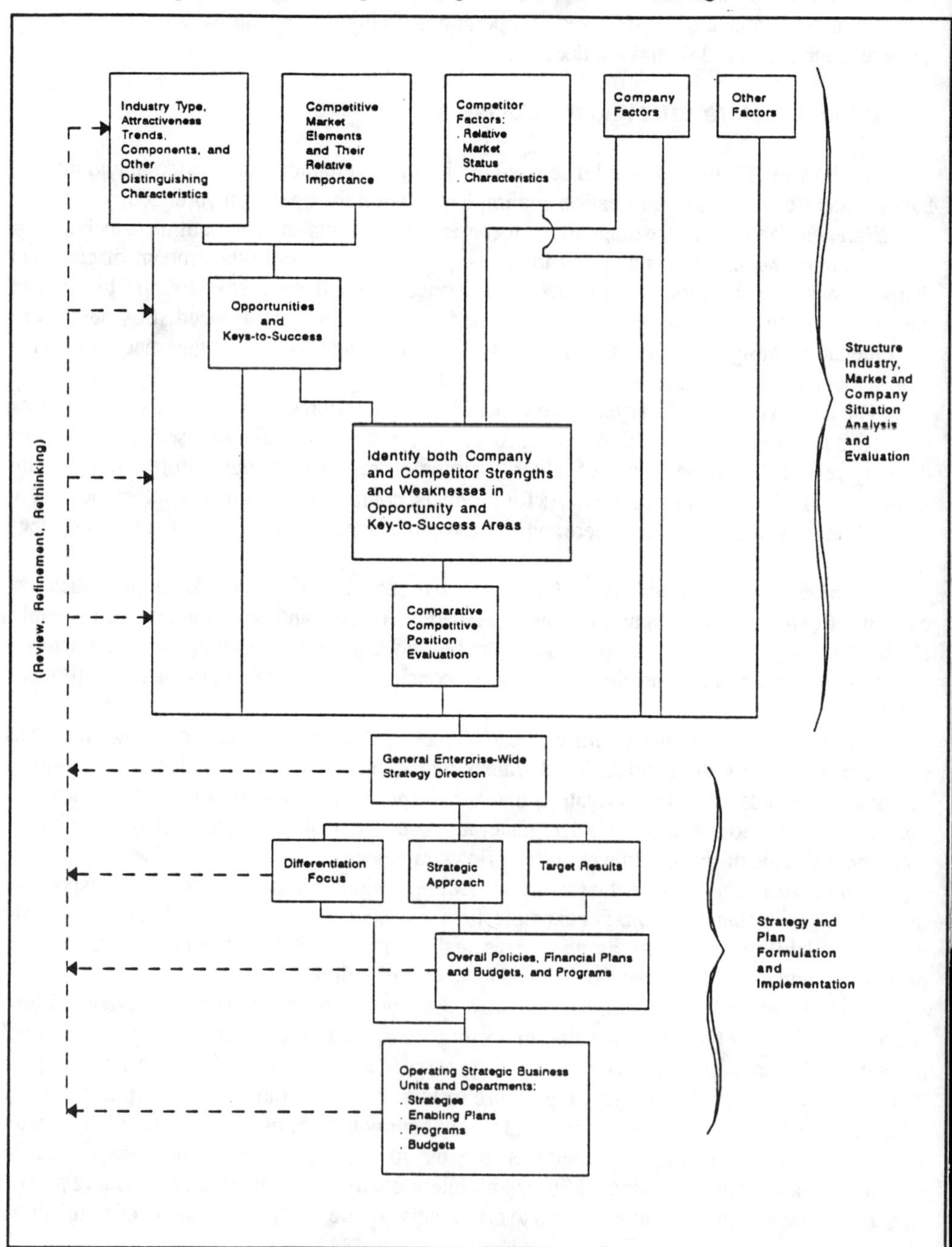

Figure 10-6: Developing Enabling Strategic Plans: An Approach to Making Strategic Planning Decisions

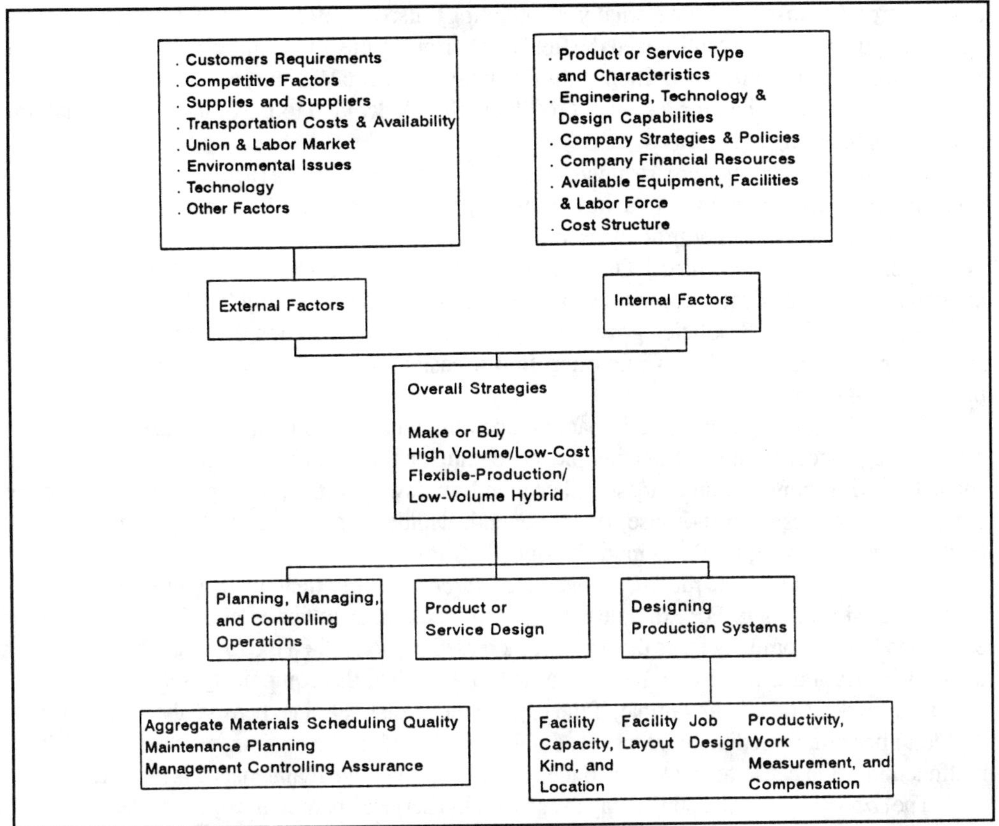

were never adopted, and those that were will take years to introduce, their far-reaching implications are clear for operations/production planning [Stevenson 1989].

Technology availability and cost can influence the design of manufacturing facilities, as at Timkin, and also the ability to deliver services in more innovative and customer-effective ways, as is seen in the many service innovations based on computer information systems technology introduced by banks and airlines.

Other external factors affecting operations/production decision making include the availability of outside sources of financing for production or service facility expansion, cultural climate and educational facilities of communities being considered for new plant location, and proposed and existing government regulations affecting operations/production.

Internal factors. As shown in Figure 10-6, many internal company factors affect operations/production planning decisions.

A company's *product and service type and characteristics* affect a wide range of decisions in operations/production, from overall strategy formulation, to facility design, location, and layout, to quality, maintenance, and materials decisions.

Engineering, technology, and design capabilities affect such decisions as whether a firm designs products in-house or externally. Technology also can affect the strategic use of design since computers have revolutionized the field by shortening the time required to design products. Such factors may also influence whether the company should make or buy a product. For example, when faced with the need for a new microfilmer, Kodak decided to make it since they had the required engineering capabilities.

Enterprise-wide company strategies and policies can influence a firm's operations/production strategic decision making in a variety of ways. For example, a firm may have a policy of innovation, as Intel Corporation does in its approach to being a leader in producing new generations of computer chips. Or, it may simply be a follower, as was Sears with major appliances. At other times, companies have policies governing quality, such as Xerox's zero defects policy. Overall policies governing quality can influence such decisions as whether to make or buy a product, since firms often find it easier to control quality when products are produced in-house.

Financial resources have an impact on operations/production planning, just as they do in other strategy decision areas. For example, depending on the availability of money or borrowing capacity, a firm may decide to lease rather than buy new facilities, have product design done externally as opposed to in-house, or, in general, decide to pursue a strategy of not owning facilities and of having products made by outside firms.

Available equipment, facilities, and labor force are important to operations/productions strategy decision making. For example, when a firm's existing facilities or labor force do not permit expansion but the company faces the need for increased capacity, then the firm may have to satisfy demand by leasing a facility or building a new one. Also, the equipment used will influence maintenance decisions. For example, if the equipment is relatively inexpensive then the firm may decide to perform remedial maintenance. On the other hand, if the equipment is expensive and a malfunction could cause heavy losses to the firm, then preventive maintenance is preferred.

The *cost structure* of existing company production/service operations can affect planning in the operations area. For example, high labor costs may be a major motivating factor in the consideration to modernize facilities, or build new ones, in order to respond to competitive cost pressures.

Making Decisions Based on These Critical Situation Factors

As shown in Figure 10-6, several levels of strategic decisions can be made.

Overall strategies for operations/production. A common overall strategic decision faced by a firm is whether to *make or buy* a product. Such a decision is based on several factors: overall company policies, customer requirements for delivery and quality, facility costs and availability, and company engineering and design capabilities. For example, Kodak was faced with a make-or-buy decision when it needed a new low-priced microfilmer to compete with the Japanese. It chose to produce it for several reasons. The company's policies favored in-house production. The company had cost-effective facilities and labor available, as well the needed engineering and design capabilities. And making it internally would enable Kodak to better meet delivery dates while controlling quality and costs [Holusha 1989].

Another overall strategic decision for operations/production involves volume/cost relationships. Factors affecting this decision are the type of product or service being delivered, the competitive environment, available facilities or financial resources, and available engineering, technology, and design capabilities. The H. J. Heinz Company chose a *high-volume/low-cost* strategy because it is a make-to-stock manufacturer with standardized products requiring volume to achieve economies of scale in order to be competitive. In addition, it had the resources to develop the production capabilities to meet these requirements for production. On the other hand, IEC Electronics Corporation uses a *flexible production/low-volume* strategy because it is a make-to-order manufacturer with product variations that require flexible production processes.

Product and service design strategies. The decision as to whether to be a leader or follower in product design is based on such factors as: company policy, financial resources, engineering capabilities, and technical expertise. Intel Corporation and Merck chose a *leader strategy* because company strategy (based on competitive market analysis) stressed innovation and the companies had adequate financial resources, as well as engineering capabilities and technical expertise [Brandt 1989; Freudenheim 1992].

Strategies for designing operations/production systems. One of the key kinds of *expansion decisions* involves selecting the strategic approach to increasing capacity: for example, build a new facility, expand an existing facility, buy or lease an existing facility, or do not expand and meet demand requirements with some combination of increased use of present facilities and of outside producers. A detailed description of a typical strategy decision made in this area is given in the following section.

As for *layout decisions*, the selection of layout is based on product characteristics (size, weight, and product type), the volume of production, and facility costs. For example, IEC Electronics Corporation chose a *process layout design* because it produced customized products, had low-volume production runs, and facility costs were minimal, since the company had adequate existing depreciated facilities. Most automobile manufacturers, such as The Ford Motor Company, choose *flow line layouts* because the product lends itself to the assembly line process and the products are high volume, even though computers and robots are allowing for more and more flexible product variations along the production line [Judge 1991].

Operations planning, management, and control strategies. These strategy decisions are also made in light of key decision situation factors, such as those discussed in the preceding critical situation factors sections.

Obviously, there is much more to making these decisions than is covered in these brief summaries. This section should, however, introduce the situational context-specific decision process involved in strategic decision making in the operations/production area. In order to explore in more depth the processes involved in making such decisions, the following section discusses in detail the decision process involved in selecting a region for a facility location.

FACILITY PLANNING DECISIONS

This section describes how strategy decisions are made in a specific operations/production planning situation involving production capacity expansion. The alternatives considered are

- Upgrade or expand primary existing facilities by purchasing new equipment
- Use other existing company facilities to meet demand
- Investigate subcontracting production
- Do not invest in new equipment or expand

The facility expansion proposals are evaluated within the context of key situation factors, as outlined in Figure 10-7.

Critical Factors Affecting the Decision

Three critical factors examined in making these decisions are capacity demand requirements, the primary facility's potential for new equipment investment, and the alternative facility's ability to supply any additional forecasted demand.

Capacity demand requirements. In the situation under study, capacity requirements are determined by an in-depth marketing study. This particular market study attempts to establish the change in future demand requirements which is expected to be met by the facility being evaluated for new equipment investment.

By considering such factors as market demand projections, competitive information, and the company's anticipated market share and market share strategy, a marketing manager develops a marketing plan to be met by the manufacturing division. The marketing plan is segmented geographically and is matched against the nearest facility which produces the product being studied. These studies link strategic marketing objectives and operations/production facility expansion decisions.

Primary facility's potential for new equipment investment. The facility initially identified to fulfill the demand requirements is analyzed to

- Determine the current capacity utilization of existing production equipment
- Assess the availability and sources of adequate material inputs to supply proposed new equipment production capacity
- Analyze the general condition of current production equipment
- Assess the restrictions on placing new capital equipment in the facility

Based on this analysis, the primary facility's potential for new equipment investment is strong if the current production equipment is used to capacity, if raw and packing material inputs are available to supply the capacity of proposed new equipment, and if the general condition of existing equipment is determined to be only good to poor. The primary facility's potential for investment is weak if the current production equipment is not being used to capacity and if the general condition of that equipment is determined to be excellent. There is no investment potential if there is substantial idle capacity and the equipment's general condition is excellent. In all situations, if there are site restrictions prohibiting the placement of new equipment in the facility, there is no potential for investment.

Figure 10-7: Decision Situation Diagram: Capacity Expansion Decision

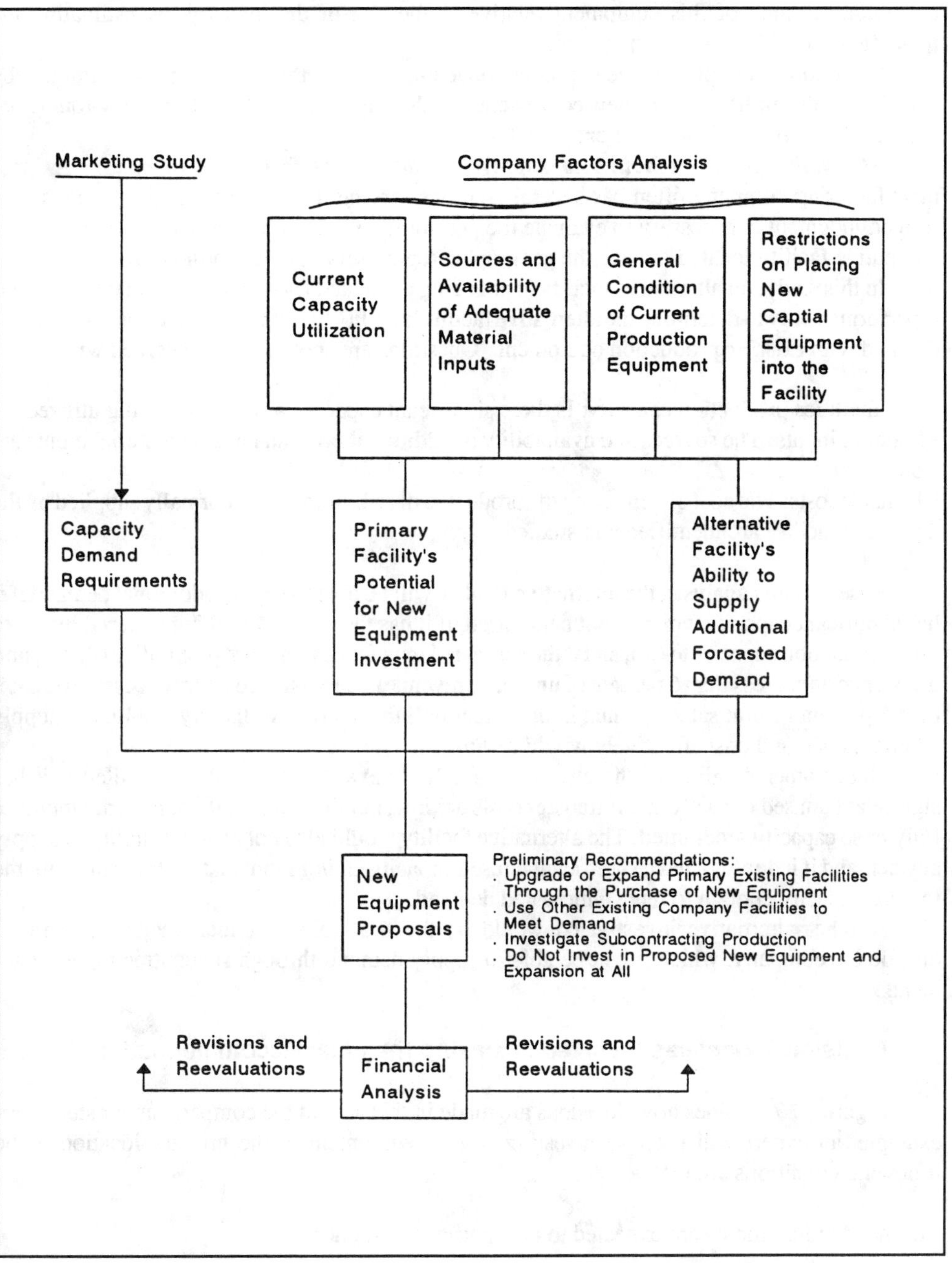

The general condition of current production equipment is analyzed by assessing the technological state of this equipment relative to the rest of the industry, by estimating the remaining useful life of this equipment.

Restrictions on placing new production equipment in the facility are determined by questioning the ability to place new equipment into the physical site. In addition, environmental and health/safety restrictions are examined.

Alternative facility's ability to supply any additional forecasted demand. A large manufacturing company often has several facilities serving different geographic regions. Informed judgment is necessary to evaluate the possibility of allocating production volume to an alternative facility located outside the geographic region served by the primary facility.

In this study, an alternative facility is not being evaluated for capital investment. Analysis is performed only to determine the alternative facility's ability to supply any additional forecasted demand with *existing* production equipment. Questions are specifically concerned with:

- The facilities production capacity: Is there significant capacity which is not being utilized?
- Material inputs: The sources and availability of additional raw and packing material inputs are analyzed.
- Transfer costs: The cost of delivering the product to distribution points normally supplied by the primary facility are identified and studied.

Based on this analysis, the alternative facility will be able to supply additional demand if it has significant capacity which is not being used, if it has the raw and packing material inputs to raise production capacity to full, and if the estimated transfer costs are not prohibitive (that is, unit transfer costs are less than 6 percent of unit sales revenue). If transfer costs are excessive (greater than 6 percent of unit sales revenue in this situation), the alternative facility's ability to supply additional demand cost effectively would be limited.

Under other conditions, the alternative facility's availability would be limited if it has significant unused capacity and if transfer costs are low, but the availability of material inputs to fully raise capacity are limited. The alternative facility would also not have the ability to supply any demand if it does not have significant unused capacity and/or input materials are unavailable to raise capacity enough to meet anticipated demand.

Another alternative investigated would be the availability of manufacturing facilities outside the company, which might be able to supply demand through subcontracting arrangements.

Decision Processes Involved in Making the Final Recommendation

Figure 10-7 outlines how decisions are made in this area at the company under study. For example, an expert will propose investing in new equipment at the primary location if the following conditions are met:

- Demand requirements are expected to be significantly higher

- Current production capacity in the primary facility is limited or is unable to meet a higher demand requirement
- There are no restrictions on placing new equipment in the facility

In this situation, if demand is expected to grow and production capacity in the primary facility is unable to meet a greater demand, then significant sales revenue may be lost, or additional costs may be incurred in using alternative facilities. In all situations, there must not be any site restrictions preventing the placement of new equipment in the facility in order to recommend an investment.

If existing equipment is old or obsolete and a higher demand is expected, then it usually will be necessary to replace that equipment, either because of the higher probability of mechanical failures, or because of the incremental cost of operating inefficient equipment.

An expert is less inclined to recommend investing large amounts of capital in equipment if

- Demand requirements are expected to stabilize or fall
- The primary facility's production capacity is able to meet expected demand
- Existing production equipment is new
- Restrictions make it impossible to place new equipment in the primary facility

In this situation, if demand is expected to be lower, then existing equipment can meet expected demand requirements. It is not necessary to replace the equipment, unless it is old and obsolete. If the equipment is new and technologically advanced, it is practical to replace it only when required to meet a significantly higher forecasted demand.

If demand requirements are expected to be stable or higher, if existing process equipment in the primary facility is unable to meet this demand, and if investment in new production equipment for that facility is not possible because of site restrictions, then an expert will

- Assess the feasibility of meeting the demand with an alternate facility within the corporation
- Investigate subcontracting production

The decision model in Figure 10-7 is a general model of the decisions made prior to the financial analysis. It is referred to as the "strategic front end" of the decision. The financial implications of these strategic recommendations are analyzed before the final decision is made, as seen in Figure 10-7.

The above structured situation analysis was used to create an initial concept testing prototype knowledge-based system to assist in making these kinds of decisions. An outline dependency diagram of the initial system developed is shown in Figure 10-8.

At this point, the critical information and the reasoning paths to be included in the system were deliberately limited to the most important ones. For example, the market analysis segment of the decision is a complex decision area for which an extensive knowledge-based system was developed during later stages of the project. In this initial system, however, only three input questions about the results of the market analysis were included. Although limiting the system in

Figure 10-8: Capacity Expansion Decision Situation Dependency Diagram (Initial Prototype)

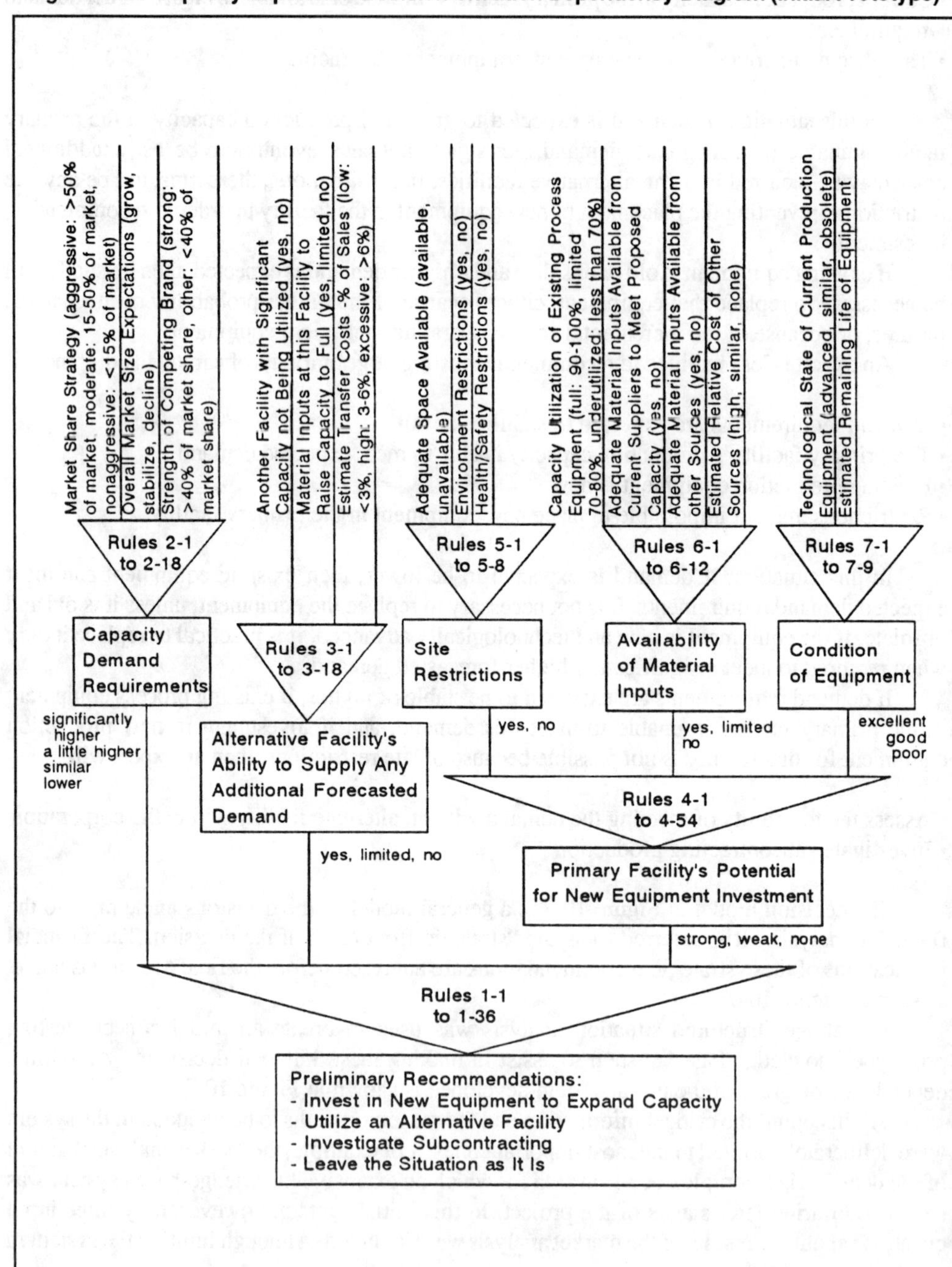

this way created the danger that the system might be trivialized somewhat, such simplification was necessary in testing the concept and structure of the system, and in developing a prototype system.

CONTEXT-SPECIFIC PROCESSES INVOLVED IN OTHER OPERATIONS/ PRODUCTION PLANNING DECISIONS

Hundreds of operations/production planning decision processes have been structured and subsequently replicated in knowledge-based systems. For example, in 1987, Northrop Corporation created a system called *Manufacturing Process Planner* for internal company use. This system aids in planning for the manufacture of the approximately 20,000 components of a fighter plane. The system identifies the operations that need to be performed on a piece of raw material to transform it into a finished item. The plan includes specifications of the equipment to be used on the shop floor, any additional tooling needed, and the sequential routing of the part and its associated material through the factory [Feigenbaum 1988, p. 305]. Frito-Lay has an expert system that automates the production process for tortilla chips and cuts the time required to get the product to market [Garvey 1991]. Navistar, a manufacturer of special-use trucks, has a knowledge-based system for operations/production, *Truck Configuration Expert System*, that allows a Navistar customer to design a truck from different parts to meet particular needs. The system ensures that the designed truck can be manufactured and it plans the manufacturing process, including identification of what parts will be needed at what point in the assembly process [Feigenbaum 1988, p. 312]. Other examples are described in annual innovation expert systems applications conferences run by the American Association of Artificial Intelligence [Rappaport 1991; Schorr 1989; Smith 1991].

In addition to knowledge-based systems, a wide range of conventional computer system tools are useful in strategic and operational planning for operations/production [Kusiak 1990]. For example, *Computerworld* has reviewed over 100 software applications available in all areas affecting planning for manufacturing [Weixel 1989; Briedenback 1989].

As seen in the examples cited in this chapter, *computer-aided manufacturing* is a well-established business concept. During the 1990s, that concept is being extended to cover computer integrated manufacturing. For example, in 1990, Pepperidge Farms built an $181 million plant that integrated computer operations from the manager's office to the factory floor to delivery trucks (via handheld computers). This system allows the company to maintain high freshness standards and exploit more quickly new products with high initial sales — both major competitive advantages [Johnson 1990].

Other conventional computer systems tools useful in the operations/production area are discussed in Chapter 11 and in several supplementary texts [Mockler 1992; Webster 1989].

INTEGRATING OPERATIONS/PRODUCTION PLANNING WITH OTHER STRATEGIC MANAGEMENT AREAS

As in the marketing strategy planning area, integrating operations/production planning with planning in other functional areas requires considering such factors as

- Relationships with other departments
- Individual department culture and character
- Differing personalities and aspirations of the people involved

These factors can lead to modifications in initially developed strategic and operational plans. For example, when developing longer term production plans, marketing needs, purchasing requirements, financial considerations, product design limitations, and people factors can all affect plan development in a variety of ways:

- **Marketing** — Marketers normally have a say in the type of product made since they are responsible for selling it. As a result, in many situations marketing specifications of product variety, cost, delivery, and quality have to be met by the operations department whenever feasible and financially justified. This can lead to modifications of ideally cost-effective operations/production strategies.
- **R&D** — Product design is an important factor since it can affect the way a product is produced and set limits on feasible production strategies. In addition, emerging technologies can affect current production processes, and often impact on strategy formulation in this area.
- **Purchasing** — Availability of materials in quantities needed, costs, specifications, and inventory considerations can all set restraints on operations/production strategy formulation in specific situations.
- **Human Resources** — As new strategies are formulated, the capabilities and availability of production/operations personnel will impact on the possible strategies which can be considered and the effectiveness of their implementation. Unions are often a very critical planning factor in production/operations strategy formulation and implementation.
- **Finance** — Because of the capital requirements so often arising from facility investments, the finance department will very often become involved in operations/production planning, as proposed facilities are evaluated for return on investment and as capital budgets prepared.

Obviously, in some operations/production planning situations conflicts among departments will arise. For example, marketing may need a product designed in a way that may cause problems with the operations/production department or with the R&D department. These conflicts are resolved through interdepartment meetings and negotiations, and through higher level management.

As in the marketing area, personal values of the managers and supervisors can often hamper strategy implementation and formulation [Morton 1988], as can departmental culture. Problems arising from these situational factors and ways to resolve them are discussed in Chapter 12 and Appendix B. As in marketing, the enabling planning process in operations/production can provide feedback which can lead to the reformulation and refinement of enterprise-wide strategies.

REVIEW QUESTIONS

1. Outline the operations/production function. Discuss some of the ways in which it might differ in service companies and in manufacturing companies.

2. Describe the tasks involved in strategically managing and controlling the operations/production function.
3. Describe the tasks involved in designing operations/production systems.
4. Describe the major overall strategies for operations/ production that are generally used in business.
5. List and discuss some of the strategic approaches to product and service design, in regard to both research type and who performs the research.
6. Discuss some of the context-specific strategic questions which arise in facility capacity and location decisions and how they might impact on the decisions.
7. What are some of the strategic choices in the materials management and aggregate planning areas?
8. Name and describe some of the critical situation-specific factors which are generally examined in making strategic choices and formulating strategies in the operations/production area.
9. Describe some ways in which these factors affect operations/production strategy decisions in both manufacturing and service companies.
10. Describe some of the integrating problems which may be involved in formulating and implementing operations/production strategies.

EXERCISES

1. Read one of the company studies in the Case Study section at the end of this book whose title contains an actual company name. Write a report on that case study which covers the following planning tasks:

- Recommend an enterprise-wide strategy for the company under study and identify the situational factors and the evaluation that led to this recommendation.
- Formulate operations/production strategies in areas you feel are important to implementing the enterprise-wide strategy and give the reasoning upon which they are based.
- Develop operations/production plans and programs for implementing enterprise-wide and operations/production department strategies.
- Identify any potential integrating problems involving other departments and how you might go about resolving them.

2. Read recent issues of the periodicals referred to in the references section at the end of the chapter, or other related periodicals of your choice, and find a description of a company of interest to you which is facing or has faced strategic operations/production decisions. Write a report on that company covering the same tasks as listed in Exercise #1.

3. The disks accompanying this book contain several prototype KBS. Follow the directions accompanying the disks to run a consultation using the system with the file name MAKEBUY.REV. If you wish, you might also print out the knowledge base and study it while you are running the system and restudying this chapter in order to get a detailed picture of how

strategy formulation decisions are made.

4. Read recent issues of the periodicals mentioned in the References section of this chapter, or any other related publications of your choice. Based on your research and whatever additional research you feel is needed, prepare a company study involving strategy formulation and implementation areas relevant to this chapter's subject matter which you think would be appropriate for use in your class.

REFERENCES

Barmash, Isadore, "Down the Scale with the Major Store Chains," *The New York Times,* Business Section, February 2, 1992, 5.

Berg, Eric N., "A Slimmer Navistar Puts Stress on Speed," *The New York Times*, July 6, 1989, pp. D1, D7.

Brandt, Richard, "It Takes More Than a Good Idea," *Business Week*, Special Issue, 1989, p. 123.

Breskin, Ira, "Winning Back the Work That Got Away," *Business Week*, Special Issue, 1989, p. 148.

Briedenbach, Susan, "Manufacturers Automate to Fight Foreign Challenge," *Computerworld*, September 18, 1989, pp. 40-52.

Broad, William J., "Research Spending Is Declining in U.S. as It Rises Abroad," *The New York Times*, February 21, 1992, pp. A1, A16.

Broad, William J., "Vast Sums for New Discoveries Pose a Threat to Basic Science," *The New York Times,* May 27, 1990, pp. 1, 20.

Dahl, Jonathan, "Agents Rankle Airlines with Fare-Checking Programs," *The Wall Street Journal*, May 20, 1991, pp. B1, B5.

Diebold, John, *The Innovators*, New York: E.P. Dutton/Truman Talley Books, 1990.

Elliot, Stuart, "Loneliness in a Long-Running Pitch," *The New York Times*, May 15, 1992, pp. D1, D7.

Feder, Barnaby J., "Moving Pampers Faster Cuts Everyone's Costs," *The New York Times,* Business Section, July 14, 1991, p. 5.

Feigenbaum, Edward, Pamela McCorduck, and H. Penny Nii, *The Rise of the Expert Company,* New York: Random House (Times Books), 1988.

Forest, Stephanie Anderson, "Thinking Big--Very Big-- at Tandy," *Business Week*, July 20, 1992, pp. 85, 86.

Freudenheim, Milt, "Keeping the Pipeline Filled at Merck," *The New York Times*, Business Section, February 16, 1992, pp. 1, 6.

Garvey, Martin, "Intelligent Integration," *InformationWeek,* December 2, 1991, pp. 27, 28.

Garvin, David, "Competing Through Quality," *HBS Video Services*, Boston, MA: Harvard Business School Publication Division, 1990.

Hammonds, Keith H., "Corning's Glass Act," *Business Week*, May 13, 1991, pp. 68-76.

Hicks, Jonathan P., "A Faster Path to Finished Steel," *The New York Times*, April 7, 1991, Business Section, p. 9.

Hillkirk, John, "This Month Will Focus on Quality," "Milestones in U. S. Quality," "Award to Honor Individuals, Small Teams" and "Workers Are the Key, Top Firms Find," *USA Today*, October 1, 1991, pp. 27, 28.

Holusha, John, "Are We Eating Our Seed Corn," *The New York Times*, May 13, 1990, Business

Section, pp. 1, 6.

Holusha, John, "Beating Japan at Its Own Game," *The New York Times*, July 16, 1989, pp. 1, 6.

Hymowitz, Carol, and Thomas O'Boyle, "Two Disparate Firms Find Keys to Success in Troubled Industries," *The Wall Street Journal*, May 29, 1991, pp. A1, A7.

Jaroff, Leon, "Crisis in the Labs," *Time*, August 26, 1991, pp. 46-51.

Johnson, Maryfran, "Recipe Calls for Low-Cal Systems," *Computerworld*, March 19, 1990, p. 37.

Judge, Paul C., "Nissan's Flexible, 'Thinking' Line for Auto Body Assembly," *The New York Times*, Business Section, August 25, 1991, p. 11.

Kleinfield, N. R., "How 'Strykeforce' Beat the Clock," *The New York Times*, March 25, 1990, Business Section, pp. 1, 6.

Kusiak, Andrew, *Intelligent Manufacturing Systems*, Englewood Cliffs, NJ: Prentice-Hall, 1990.

Lohr, Steve, "The Best Little Bank in America," *The New York Times*, Business Section, July 7, 1991, pp. 1, 4.

Levin, Doran P., "Toyota Plant in Kentucky Is Font of Ideas for U.S.," *The New York Times*, May 5, 1992, pp. A1, D8.

Markoff, John, "A Corporate Lag in Research Funds Is Causing Worry," *The New York Times*, January 23, 1990, pp. A1, D6.

Markoff, John, "The Smart Alecks at Sun Are Regrouping," *The New York Times*, Business Section, April 28, 1991, p. 4.

Mockler, Robert J., *Computer Software to Support Strategic Management Decisions*, New York: Macmillan Publishing, 1992.

Morton, S. Morgan, "Whose Plan Is It Anyway?," *Planning Review*, May/June 1988, p. 45.

Murray, Alan, and Urban C. Lekner, "Strained Alliances: What US Scientists Discover, the Japanese Convert Into Profit," *The Wall Street Journal*, June 25, 1990, pp. A1, A16.

Perry, Nancy O., "Designed to Compete," *HBS Bulletin*, December 1989, pp. 30-38.

Pike, Helen, "Close to the Customer," *Computerworld Focus on Integration*, October 2, 1989, p. 43.

Pollack, Andrew, "U.S. Chip Manufacturers Stem the Tide in Trade Battles with Japanese," *The New York Times*, April 9, 1992, pp. A1, D6.

Pollack, Andrew, "A Quirky Loner Goes Mainstream," *The New York Times*, Business Section, July 14, 1991, pp. 1, 6.

Pollack, Andrew, "Sony to Share Data at U.S. Plant," *The New York Times*, February 21, 1990, p. D1.

Prokesch, Steven, "Edges Fray on Volvo's Brave New Humanistic World," *The New York Times*, Business Section, July 7, 1991, p. 5.

Protzman, Ferdinand, "Sleek Designs, Hefty Profits," *The New York Times*, March 17, 1992, pp. D1, D7.

Rappaport, Alain, and Reid Smith, editors, *Innovative Applications of Artificial Intelligence 2*, Cambridge, MA: AAAI Press/The MIT Press, 1991.

Ruffenach, Glenn, "Shaw Uses Price Cuts to Extend Its Rule Over Carpet Business," *The Wall Street Journal*, June 12, 1991, pp. A1, A8.

Sandomir, Richard, "Wayne Huizenga's Growth Complex," *The New York Times*, The New York Times Magazine, June 9, 1991, pp. 22-25.

Sanger, David E., "Stalking the Next Walkman Quickly," *The New York Times*, Business Section, February 23, 1992, pp. 1, 8.

Sanger, David E., "Japan's Lead in Computer Research Grows," *The New York Times*, February 21, 1990(A), pp. D1, D4.

Sanger, David E., "U.S. and Japanese Partners in Pact on New Jet Fighter," *The New York Times*, February 21, 1990(B), pp. D1, D4.

Sanger, David E., "When Corporate Lab Goes to Japan," *The New York Times*, Business Section, April 28, 1991, pp. 1, 6.

Schorr, Herbert, and Alain Rappaport, editors, *Innovative Applications of Artificial Intelligence*, Cambridge, MA: AAAI Press/The MIT Press, 1989.

Smith, Reid, and Carlisle Scott, editors, *Innovative Applications of Artificial Intelligence 3*, Cambridge, MA: AAAI Press/The MIT Press, 1991.

Stevenson, Richard W., "Facing Up to a Clean-Air Plan," *The New York Times*, April 3, 1989, pp. D1, D7.

Strom, Stephanie, "More Suppliers Helping Stores Push Goods," *The New York Times*, January 26, 1992, pp. D1, D8.

Treece, James, "How to Teach Old Plants New Tricks," *Business Week*, Special Issue, 1989, p. 130.

Weber, Joseph, "Going Over the Lab Wall in Search of New Ideas," *Business Week*, Special Issue, 1989, p. 132.

Webster, James L., William E. Reif, and Jeffery S. Bracker, "The Manager's Guide to Strategic Planning Tools and Techniques," *Planning Review*, November/December 1989, pp. 4-12, 48.

Weixel, Suzanne, "Manufacturing Technologies," *Computerworld*, May 15, 1989, pp. 55-72.

Winslow, Ron, "A Competitive Battle to Sell Surgical Devices Is Spurring Innovation: Fast-Growing U. S. Surgical Takes on J&J in a Field Altered by New Procedures," *The Wall Street Journal*, April 16, 1991, pp. A1, A5.

Woodruff, David, "Adding Some Spice to an Old Formula," *Business Week*, Special Issue, 1989, p. 134.

CHAPTER 11

COMPETITIVE COMPUTER INFORMATION SYSTEMS (CIS)

The objective of this chapter is to help readers to understand

- The changing role of the computer information systems (CIS) department in a company, the growing strategic importance of CIS, and the different kinds of CIS
- The nature of competitive intelligence systems in supporting strategic management decision making
- How to formulate and implement strategies for the CIS function in specific company and competitive market situations
- Available CIS designed to assist in making strategic planning decisions involving the CIS function

This chapter focuses on the computer information systems function, the last major operating area identified in the strategic management tasks outlined in Figure 11-1.

With few exceptions, computer systems are used in nearly all businesses today. The increased popularity and availability of microcomputers, and their ever-increasing power, has encouraged the use of computer information systems even in small businesses. For example, many local retailers now record customer purchases, manage inventories, and do billing on computers.

Computer systems play various roles in business:

Figure 11-1: Strategic Management Tasks

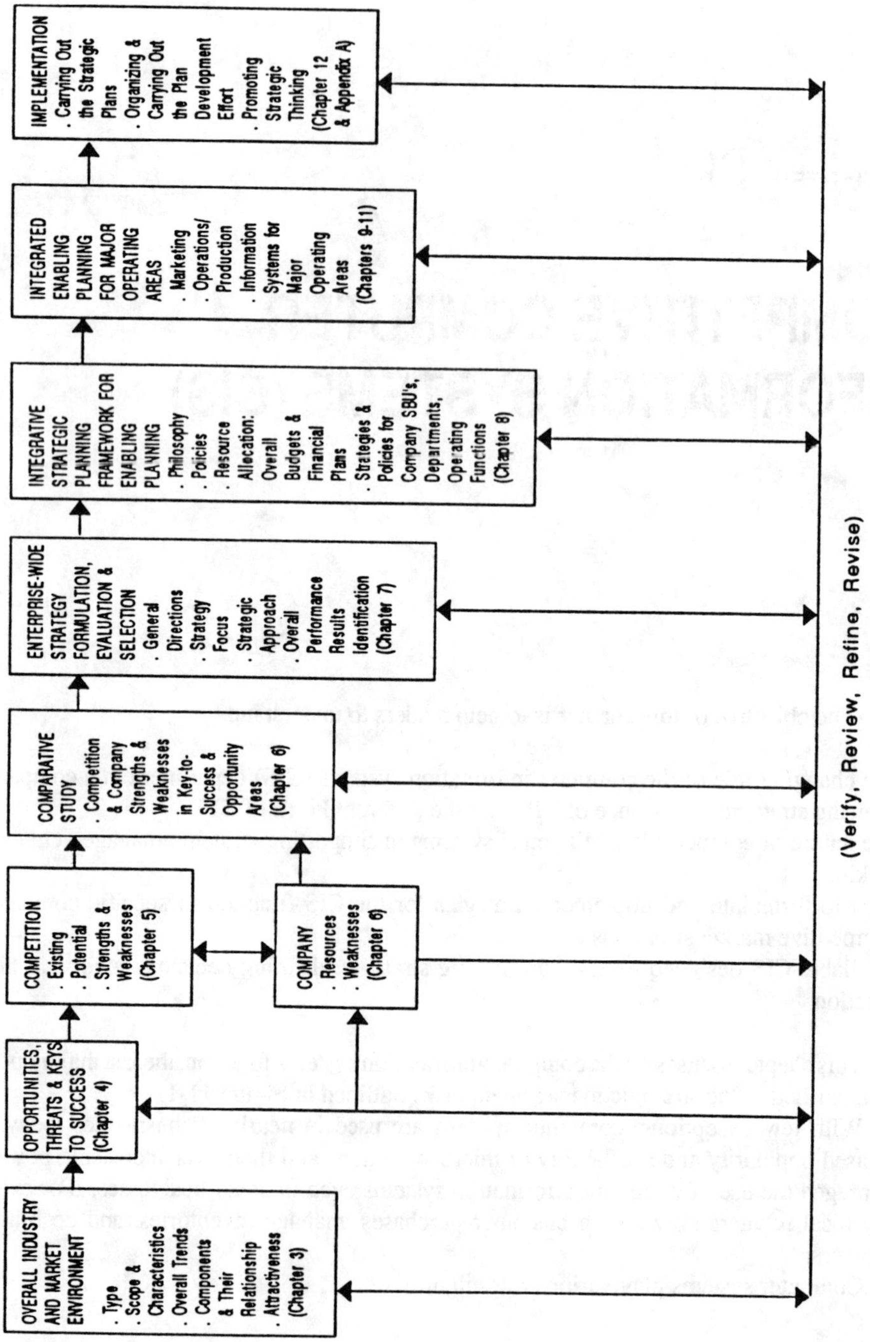

- Gathering, organizing, and storing data
- Providing managers with information needed to make decisions and run the business
- Assisting managers in making decisions
- Performing key business functions
- Making operational and management decisions

This chapter pays particular attention to those computer information systems related to strategic management, that is, systems that give a company a competitive advantage or help prevent it from losing its competitive position, and systems that help to do and actually do planning.

Kennametal Inc., a leading producer of metal working and mining tools, is a good example of how investing heavily in computer information systems technology can help even companies in a stodgy, slow-growing business reverse their market slide, enter the ranks of the nation's largest 500 companies, and stave off powerful foreign competitors. Its computer system can determine within seconds which products are available at Kennametal sites around the country. The system has cut the costs of administering transactions in some instances by 96 percent and considerably speeded up transaction processing. For example, General Electric's tool orders are transmitted electronically to Kennametal's computers. The computers automatically issue notices of when the tools will be shipped and send bills. As a result of the new computer system, Kennametal achieved annual sales per employee of $861,000 in 1991, compared with an industry average of $264,000, while at the same time serving customers more quickly and reducing inventories.

Kennametal's computer information system is also used to offer customers additional services, like tool management support and management of customers' tool storage areas, thus turning customers into partners. In addition, the system enabled the company to enter new businesses, such as distributing industrial products for other companies, and to more effectively control its foreign operations: it doubled its European market share. In 1991, Kennametal's net income was $21 million on sales of $618 million [Feder 1992].

THE CHANGING ROLE OF THE CIS FUNCTION

In a 1986 Arthur Andersen & Co. survey of chief information officers (CIOs) in 120 Fortune 500 companies, the most frequently mentioned concern of CIS managers was keeping current with changing technology. By 1990, the role of CIS was becoming more business oriented. The top issues in 1990 were helping to "reshape business processes through information technology" and in the process translating information technology into a competitive advantage and facilitating/managing end user (business manager) computing [Eskow 1990]. In 1991 the accounting firm of Deloite & Touche surveyed 26 CEOs of companies with revenues between $500 million and $20 billion. These executives indicated that the major focus of CIS executives should be on the firm's customers and suppliers, that is, on the specific dynamics of the markets in which their firms competed [Caldwell 1991; Pepper 1991(B)]. Kennametal's experiences with computer information systems is only one of many examples of this.

As seen from such surveys, CIS managers in the 1990s are emphasizing their business management role, paying special attention to meeting business needs, end user needs, customer and supplier requirements, and competitive pressures. This changing role reflects the growing strategic importance of computer information systems as a major operating department and function in today's business environment. In many companies, especially those in service businesses, such departments are making major contributions to success. As such, they have become a major tool of strategic management.

THE INTELLIGENT ENTERPRISE: THE GROWING STRATEGIC IMPORTANCE OF COMPUTER INFORMATION SYSTEMS (CIS)

The term "Intelligent Enterprise" has been coined to emphasize the growing importance of information, and of the communications systems that convey information, to the successful operation of companies in today's competitive market [Quinn 1992]. For example, Banc One Corporation of Columbus, Ohio, is one of the fastest-growing banks in the country. The exploitation of CIS technology is one of Banc One's central strategies. In 1991, the company's return on assets was the highest of any U.S. bank [Hirsch 1990, 1991; Lohr 1991; Quint 1989].

In using computer technology, Banc One has been both farsighted and skillful. In 1966, at the data processing level, it became the first banking company outside of California to offer BankAmericard (Visa) and within a year was selling its card processing services to other banks. By 1989, it was processing eight million cards, including those issued by 200 other banks and credit unions. In 1971, it was among the first banks to set up automated teller machines, an innovation that was resisted by many banks, but is now commonplace. In 1977, Banc One began handling back office processing for Merrill Lynch's cash management accounts — accounts that combine the features of a checking account, a securities account, and a credit card. In the decision-support area, Banc One has developed computer software that draws on all the information the bank has about each customer and presents it in a way that enables a branch officer to sell additional products and better service customers.

At Pepperidge Farms, CIS were used to strategically refocus the company's operations. The strategic keys to success in Pepperidge's business were judged to be quality, freshness, and the ability to move quickly in an environment with rapidly changing new product turnover. These strategic challenges were met largely through the use of CIS technology. Through integrated computerized order entry (with delivery/ salespeople using handheld computers), production scheduling, and delivery scheduling, the time between order entry and delivery in some instances was reduced from 10 to 3 days, improving freshness and quality. In addition, the company was better able to exploit new products in a market in which competitors very quickly copy and market imitations of any new product placed on store shelves [Forsythe 1989].

New marketing strategies have even been developed based on computer information systems capabilities. For example, computer analyses are now available which give customer/ shopper demographic profiles and buying habits *by store* [Kleinfield 1991]. This has led to "store-specific" marketing strategies. For example, Borden had Market Metrics (a computer-based market research firm) generate a list of the best stores for its Classico pasta sauce based on a specific consumer profile — people earning at least $35,000, living in dual-income households in metropolitan areas, with an interest in gourmet foods. The company then concentrated its sales efforts in those stores. After a similar study, Kraft varied the type of Philadelphia Cream Cheese it stocked in individual stores within a few mile area: for example, stocking extra rows of strawberry-flavored cream cheese in one store, lots of diet cream cheese at another, and mostly 12-ounce cartons of regular cream cheese at another. Sales increased by 147 percent from the prior year at the 30 stores in the test area [King 1992; McCarthy 1991].

Companies that effectively use CIS technology to meet market demands are developing significant competitive advantages. This movement to CIS is discussed in several useful supplementary texts [Mockler 1992(B); Stanat 1990; Wiseman 1988(B)]. Though in general such competitive advantages last only 12 to 18 months [Benjamin 1991; Sullivan-Trainor 1990], advanced CIS have provided some companies, such as Lithonia Lighting, with competitive advantages that have lasted over 10 years [Leibs 1991].

The increasing impact of CIS on strategy formulation and implementation was illustrated dramatically at People's Express, a $2 billion airline which has gone out of business. Donald Burr, the company's former president, attributed the company's failure to competitors' powerful computerized reservation systems ("yield pricing" systems). These systems enabled American Airlines, for instance, to match People's low fares on seats that would otherwise have gone unsold, yet still sell other seats at full price [Scheier 1989].

Computer information systems are changing the way that companies do business to a degree that organizations are being shaped around information and communications technology [Keen 1986, 1988; Penzias 1989; Sol 1992; Sol and Streng 1992]. Because of this, CIS managers are not only studying the ways CIS support and improve existing operations. They are also studying ways in which information technology can help change business processes and create new ways of doing things. Discussions in this chapter have described a few examples of this — at Kennametal, Pepperidge Farms, and Banc One.

Many businesses and business functions have been affected by information technology, from restaurants [Connolly 1991; Mandell 1992; Pepper 1991(A)] to airlines [Pepper 1991 (C)] to drugstores [Henkoff 1992] to sales [Ryan 1991] to customer service [Rudding 1992; Slater 1992] to small businesses [Beal 1991]. This trend seems likely to continue and accelerate though experience has shown that major changes in the way businesses are managed and organized generally must take place before the full benefits of information technology will be realized [Hammer 1993; King 1992; Morton 1991; Rifkins 1992].

TYPES OF COMPUTER INFORMATION SYSTEMS

Computer systems can be divided into five categories: data processing, management information, decision support, knowledge-based, and integrated. These systems are described in this section, as is their use in giving a company a competitive advantage and in helping strategically manage an enterprise.

Data Processing Systems

The original and still major function of computers in business is to collect, organize, and store data, and perform such functions as processing customer accounts and writing employee paychecks. Much of the work in computer systems operations is to maintain and enhance the functioning of these systems. The following discussion of the newer developments in the CIS area is not intended to diminish the value of basic data processing operations to a firm's success. In fact, doing these basic data processing tasks efficiently can often give a company a competitive cost advantage. This is the case at Readers Digest Association which was developing a new database system in 1992 to more precisely target mailings to its 100 million customers worldwide [Ambrosio 1992]. A company can also provide new and improved customer services through the information-generating capabilities made possible by such data processing systems, as described earlier at several banks and other company examples.

Management Information Systems (MIS)

Management information systems (MIS) provide information reports to managers. Once limited to financial and accounting reports and reports on sales and production operations, they now range from systems that provide bank mortgage officers with integrated customer account data to systems that provide production managers with information needed to order inventories on a just-in-time basis. The reports generated by MIS enable

- Corporate managers to measure financial performance against budgets and take corrective action
- Credit managers to manage outstanding accounts receivable
- Factory, inventory, purchasing, and transportation managers to manage operations and production more effectively
- Marketing managers to measure the progress and efficiency of field sales efforts and advertising campaigns
- Bank officers to make decisions about loan applications .
- Mail-order managers to decide which lists to mail which products to
- Investment managers to make stock buy-and-sell decisions
- Hotel managers to assign rooms
- Car rental company managers to make decisions about fleet needs and allocations

At the highest corporate level, such systems are referred to as Executive Support or Executive Information Systems. These are primarily management information reporting systems adapted to top level management needs and work habits [Friend 1989]. Since they often are capable of interacting with other applications, some Executive Support Systems have decision-support capabilities. Sophisticated versions of these systems can cost in excess of $100,000 [Brandel 1991; Sullivan-Trainor 1991; Watson 1991].

MIS enable companies not only to manage their conventional business functions more effectively and efficiently, but also to provide customers with faster and improved services. For this reason, companies that develop new and improved MIS can create strategic opportunities [Wiseman 1988(B)], as did Pepperidge Farms and other companies discussed earlier. Such advantages come from investing in newer software programs, and also from investing in new equipment, such as supercomputers.

MIS can also aid in making strategic decisions by providing reports on, and access to, information needed to formulate, explore, evaluate, and implement strategies, as is shown in the discussion of *competitive intelligence information systems* later in this chapter.

Decision-Support Systems

Decision-support systems go beyond providing managers with information reports and access to records. They enable a manager to interact with a computer system while exploring problems and testing hypotheses, such as by answering "what if?" questions. A decision-support system is usually based on some type of model — a statistical forecasting model, a mathematical model of a business function, a linear programming model, or a spreadsheet model. To the degree that these systems can help a manager be more effective, they can provide a competitive advantage.

These systems can be financial models that allow a manager to explore what will happen to costs at different production levels or to volume and profits at different pricing levels, or to a company's market position under different competitive scenario assumptions. Such financial decision-support systems, using conventional procedural computer software systems, have been in use since the early 1970s and are still commonly used today [Keen 1975; Naylor 1984; Morton 1971; Turban 1990]. The use of such systems in evaluating strategic alternatives and in helping to build related budgetary plans was discussed in Chapters 7 and 8. Some basic examples are given on the disks accompanying this book.

Decision-support systems also use mathematical and statistical models that forecast such things as company sales assuming different economic conditions and the impact of economic changes on industry prospects [Rosenkranz 1979]. Such computer systems also enable evaluation of different alternative economic scenarios by estimating the probability of the different outcomes occurring. For example, at American Airlines the Decision Technologies Group created an operations research/management science tool for evaluating a proposed $1 billion expansion at Dallas/Fort Worth Airport. At Federal Express, operations research management science models are used to deal with such strategic decisions as long-term hub network configurations, staffing, fleet configuration, and facilities requirements [Cooke 1989; Fisher 1989; Homer 1991].

Decision-support systems cover a wide range of situations beyond the financial simulation and forecasting areas, including: providing help in developing personnel policies; training managers and workers through computer simulation games; providing project management assistance; helping in distribution planning and factory and production process layout; and aiding in package design, and other graphics-related decisions.

Specific software applications supporting strategic planning decision making include such systems as

- *Expert Choice*, which enables a manager to compare the value of alternative strategies.
- *Idea Generator*, which assists a manager in generating ideas for new strategies.
- *Business Strategist* and *Compete!*, which enable a planner to identify anticipated planning situation market constraints, formulate and test alternative strategies to deal with them, and forecast probable results.
- *Strategic Planning Model*, which focuses on key-to-success factors in the market and on ways to compare a company's performance with that of competitors. The system enables operating and general managers to define keys to success in each functional area important to their business, refine and rank these, compare a company's strengths to those of competitors, and evaluate the financial impact of alternative strategies. The system also suggests possible future strategies appropriate for the company under study.

An example of a decision-support system designed to help managers do strategic planning for the CIS department, PRISM, is discussed later in this chapter.

Knowledge-Based Systems

Knowledge-based systems, considered by some to be one kind of decision-support system, are actually different from the decision-support computer systems described in the preceding section, which are conventional computer systems based on procedural computer languages and which mainly use numbers. Knowledge-based systems are non-procedural decision-support systems that use artificial intelligence technology. They enable greater flexibility and adaptability to management decision needs than conventional procedural systems by making use of symbols (such as words, instead of numbers) and list processing programming languages. Knowledge-based systems can make decisions, as well as assist managers in making decisions. Knowledge-based systems which provide specific strategic benefits in manufacturing and other business areas are described by Bonnett [1989], O'Brien [1989], Rappaport [1991], Rowan [1989], Schorr [1989], and Smith [1991]. Different knowledge-based systems and their use in assisting in and actually making strategic planning decisions are also described at the end of many chapters in this book. Examples of these systems are included on the disk accompanying this book.

Integrated Systems

Integrated computer systems combine the features and capabilities of different conventional and knowledge-based systems into a single system. They are considered the most promising application of knowledge-based system technology in business [Carr 1992; Garvey 1991; Flast 1991].

STRATEGIC INTELLIGENCE SYSTEMS: COMPETITIVE INTELLIGENCE SYSTEMS TO SUPPORT STRATEGIC MANAGEMENT DECISION MAKING

The use of computers and other types of information systems to support strategic planning has grown substantially during the late 1980s and early 1990s. This section discusses *strategic or competitive intelligence systems*, that is, information systems designed to provide information helpful in making strategic planning decisions. These systems include manual, MIS, conventional decision-support systems, and knowledge-based systems.

The Increasing Importance of Competitive Intelligence Systems

Since the mid-1980s, large companies have made significant investments in competitive information gathering, analysis, dissemination, and use in strategic planning. These moves have been stimulated largely by CIS and telecommunication technology advances, and in part by growing business problems arising from rapidly changing, intensely competitive market environments.

For example, a survey in 1989 [Prescott 1989] indicated that, at the 95 large companies surveyed, on average the competitive intelligence programs were only four years old. Half the programs were devoted to doing strategic planning, half to helping implement strategic plans. Half were project-oriented, half were on-going programs. Half were run by corporate or division planning departments, and almost half by functional departments, such as marketing. Their average annual budget was $550,000. Further supporting this trend, another survey in 1989 showed that the more control of information systems technology user departments had, the more aggressive the company's competitive strategy [Tavakolian 1989].

Different Approaches and Information Sources Used

The most commonly encountered competitive intelligence systems are based on databases, especially external *on-line databases and database services*—such as NEXIS, Dow Jones News/Retrieval, VuText (for local and regional publications), Dialog (which has hundreds of databases), and Infomaster (one of the many gateway services linked to hundreds of independent databases) [McGrane 1987].

Databases exist for just about any kind of information, from competitor financial results to overall economic statistics to competitor sales, and serve a wide range of strategic planning needs. Appendix D describes how to use online databases for the kind of research described in this section and in Chapters 3 and 4.

Periodical and newspaper reviews are another frequently used source of competitive intelligence. Such reviews can be done manually, or through services such as NEXIS and LEXIS that put the articles on computer and highlight article topics with key words. More recently developed computer programs can actually read and analyze articles and messages [Pollack 1989], and then sort and organize the gathered data in ways useful to managers. In 1990, Dow Jones, for example, had two powerful parallel processing computers that could compare many articles at the same time and allow users to ask questions about information in the articles. Such systems are also used to sort and direct incoming wire service news reports at Chase Manhattan Bank.

Internal company information sources can be tapped in a variety of ways. Historically, internal company databases covering all operations have always been useful in strategic management. More imaginative uses of internal resources for competitive information have been developed. For example, Ruth Stanat [1989(A)] developed a daily reporting system for a major consumer products company. The system collects information about competitors from the field sales staff in a coordinated, methodical way, and integrates that information with competitive information gathered from external information sources.

Updated industry and market studies are often available. For example, in 1990 Strategic Intelligence Systems in New York City provided monthly computerized industry updates summarizing significant current events impacting on strategic areas of interest to the company using the reports. In addition to regular industry and market studies, strategic planners use *ad hoc* studies for specific planning problems. For example, one such study done for the Canadian steel industry was intended to help prevent the United States from placing import restrictions on Canada by showing that the trade was a two-way exchange that benefited both parties [Erkkila 1989].

International competitive information gathering presents special problems. Kodak created a worldwide competitive intelligence gathering and analysis information system based mainly on oral communications with company personnel. The system was a formal one, with its own director and extensive networks of oral information sources which were canvassed regularly, mainly through person-to-person contacts [Hudson 1989].

An approach used by several experts [Fuld 1988(A, B); Garsombke 1989; O'Brien 1991] in gathering international intelligence is to

- Study the environment of the overseas market of interest
- Analyze strengths and weaknesses of international competitors
- Assess the firm's competitive position
- Select strategies to compete internationally and globally, taking into account possible competitor reactions

Competitive information on competitors' subsidiaries is usually difficult to acquire and requires somewhat different approaches. In these cases, using person-to-person contacts with each competitor's suppliers and customers to gradually assemble competitor-by-competitor profiles is one expert's recommended approach [Markowitz 1987]. Looking at the community in which competitors' subsidiaries operate and the local publications there, as well as the publications of industry associations most closely linked to competitors' subsidiaries, is another recommended approach [Kight 1989]. In addition, it is sometimes useful to query government regulators who monitor the activities of the competitors' subsidiaries.

Developing Systems to Do It

Setting up competitive intelligence gathering systems and actually doing the job are described in the following:

- Washington Research Publishing: *How to Find Information About Companies* [1989]; *Understanding the Competition* [1984]
- Stanat: *The Intelligent Corporation* [1990], which contains several dozen examples of how companies set up competitive intelligence operations
- Vella and McGonagle: *Improved Business Planning Using Competitive Market Intelligence* [1988]
- Fuld: *Competitor Intelligence: How to Get It; How To Use It* [1985]
- O'Brien and Fuld: "Business Intelligence and the New Europe" [1991]

In addition, two associations are dedicated to competitive intelligence: *The Society of Competitor Intelligence Professionals* and the *Information Industry Association*, as well as a journal, *Information Management Review*. Each of the associations holds an annual conference. Other information sources are cited in the References section of this chapter. Experienced consultants can also be helpful in this area. Several better-known ones are: Strategic Intelligence Systems, Inc.; Competitive Intelligence Inc.; the Hellicon Group Ltd; and Barbie Keiser Inc.

Barbie Keiser describes a general approach to setting up and carrying out a competitive intelligence gathering system which includes the following steps [1987]:

- Identify your competitors
- Determine what you need to know about your competitors. What data and analysis will best illustrate how these companies are performing?
- Identify the specific sources of that information
- Organize the resources of the corporation and devise a strategy for obtaining the information you need but to which you do not have access
- Integrate the information from all sources, analyze the data, and assess your competitors' potential performance versus the forecasts for your own firm
- Monitor your competitors' actions and continuously communicate this information so that management can adjust its operations accordingly

Figure 11-2 outlines in detail a customer profile developed through this process and some of the information sources useful in developing such a profile.

Vella and McGonagle have developed a "role approach" to gathering competitive information which, while less formal, has nonetheless proven effective [1987 and 1988]. This approach, referred to as "shadowing markets," requires someone at the firm under study to become an expert in each competitor's way of thinking strategically and then think through management decisions

Figure 11-2: Outline of Competitor Profile and Information Sources

OUTLINE OF A COMPETITOR PROFILE	SELECTED SOURCES OF COMPETITOR INFORMATION
BACKGROUND	
Company identification; location; description; brief history; state of incorporation.	General business directories, in print or online. Industry-specific directories.
Affiliates; How is the company organized? How often altered its structure?	Corporate press releases, Business Wire (Nexis), PR has it Newswire (Nexis, Dialog) D&B America's Corporate Families; Corporate Affiliations database.
Number of stock shares outstanding; ownership (insiders, institutions, major shareholders).	CDA Spectrum reports based on SEC filings; D&B reports.
FINANCE	
Statistics and performance analyses (revenue, growth); sales by division; profitability by business unit/product line.	SEC filings (disclosure), Compustat, brokerage earnings, reports (Investext, Exchange).
Banks/investment banking firms used.	Directories, tombstone ads, SEC filings, D&B reports.
Stock market data; current market value.	Dow Jones News Retrieval.
Ratios and industry comparisons; Do they track, lead lag the industry?	Prentice-Hall, RMA, D&B, Media General, Investext. or
Cash flow analysis assets and return on assets; capitalization; working capital; internal rate of return on investment.	Compustat.
PRODUCTS	
Description of products and services offered (product mix - depth and breadth of product line) and market position by product; product strength and as a whole). How committed is the firm to a particular product line?	Directories. Attend trade show and conventions to obtain product literature; send for product catalogs; clip advertisements. weaknesses (individually and the line
Analysis of new product introductions.	Press releases, new product announcement database (Predicasts); Have your sales force query your customers.
R&D expenditures and apparent interests of technical an analysis of the company's design and	Scan technical journals for articles authored by personnel; employees of competitors. development process.
Patents held/pending; product standards (specs), and technical analysis.	World Patent Index (Dialog), Derwent, IFI/Plenum quality Claims databases. Have your engineers analyze competitors' products.
Pricing policies (Who decides flexibility in pricing levels?); Note special selling arrangements (Are they competing for your customers?)	Note trade discounts offered.
Licensing and joint venture agreements.	Corporate press releases tracked on PR Newswire and Business Wire.
MARKETS	
Market segmentation and customer analysis; customer base (markets targeted, regional sales	Press release, public documents, industry analyses by investment banking firms or consulting groups

Figure 11-2: Outline of Competitor Profile and Information Sources (contd.)

OUTLINE OF A COMPETITOR PROFILE	SELECTED SOURCES OF COMPETITOR INFORMATION
analysis, penetration, importance to the firm, dominance of market); profiles of markets/customers (including product mix and sales data by product line); market growth and potential for future growth; by product line.	(scan Investext, Exchange, FIND/SVP databases or Harfax directories); Check databases for announcements of large customer purchases; Use your sales force to assess customer loyalties. market share
How does the company view the direction of the industry?	Employment ads in newspapers (What type of positions are they seeking to fill and does this indicate a new direction for the firm?)
Market and geographic area targeted for expansion; marketing tactics.	Check acquisition and divestiture announcements for trends.
Distribution network/channels of distribution.	Press releases by wholesalers and independent reps.
Advertising/marketing/sales efforts including budgets and firms used.	Standard Directory of Advertisers.
Foreign trade analysis. Recent orders; government contracts. Analysis of sales force (experience, compensation); T&E practices.	Trade press, DIOR reports, Commerce Business Daily, DMS.
FACILITIES Location, size, domestic vs. foreign.	Directories.
Capacity, capacity utilization, announced capacity expansions.	Check plans for plant expansions and closings (press releases and local press).
Product mix by plant; shipments and profitability data; unit cost/price.	Industry consultants.
Capital investments; equipment purchases; key suppliers.	Press releases.
Number of production lines and shifts.	Business Dateline (Data Courier), local newspapers, Vutext, regional business press (PROMT).
Regulatory issues.	Note investigations by government agencies (Newsnet, Nexis).
PERSONNEL Employees - total, management, R&D staffing, engineers - number, education, training, experience.	Directories, public documents.
Biographies of senior management including employment contracts, incentive (bonus) programs and golden parachute agreements.	D&B, S&P directories, public documents.
Description of the members of the board of directors.	D&B, S&P directories, public documents; Who's Who series.
Consultants used by the firm; Labor union information (relations with management, results of recent negotiations with other firms in the industry, date of next contract renegotiation).	Check labor contract expiration dates and strikes in the trade press.

Figure 11-2: Outline of Competitor Profile and Information Sources (contd.)

OUTLINE OF A COMPETITOR PROFILE	SELECTED SOURCES OF COMPETITOR INFORMATION
Detailed corporate structure; Who has P&L responsibility?	Changes in who reports to whom and their responsibilities are often detailed in press releases.
Safety information (accidents) and government/ Newsnet). industry regulations violations.	OSHA, ERISA, EEOC compliance (Nexis,
Management style and flexibility. articles.	General business press, management journal
Fringe benefits and compensation practices.	Use your human resources department's contacts and databases; Do you have any employees who worked for your competitor?
Track managerial changes for indications of disputes management (turnover of personnel).	Listings in business and trade journals: in upper classifieds.
APPARENT STRATEGIC (LONG-RANGE) PLANS	
Detail of acquisition and divestiture strategy.	Dow Jones, Investext.
New products on the horizon (Does it indicate a new direction for the firm?)	New Product Announcement database, press releases.
Statements of plans to enter new markets or improve their market position (increase their share of market).	Presentations to Wall Street analysts.
Apparent strategic objectives; corporate/divisional/ subsidiary company priorities; business unit/segment goals; basic business philosophy/targets.	General business press, letters to the shareholders.
Analysis of company's decision-making process. Overall corporate image and reputation. Assess company's ability to adapt/change; How will the company look/perform in the future? Anti-takeover measures instituted; shareholder actions; Lawsuits pending. What are the firm's key successes and failures? Why have they been successful? Overall corporate attitudes toward risk.	SEC filings, such an exhibits to 10-Ks and proxy statements.

Adapted from Barbie E. Keiser, "Practical Competitor Intelligence," *Planning Review*, September/October 1987, pp. 18-19

from the competitor's viewpoint. Information sources used to acquire this mental image of the competitor include

- Monitoring personnel changes affecting any operation of particular interest (this sometimes requires using local newspapers)
- Reviewing press releases and speeches, as well as stories in the trade press
- Attending trade shows to meet with competitors' personnel and contractors, such as ad agencies
- Reading corporate documents, ranging from new technical product brochures to company newsletters .

- Following technological developments by tracking papers and articles by key research personnel
- Learning about the background and track records of key executives
- Debriefing new employees who have had contact with the competitor, either from working for those competing firms or having seen competitors from another angle
- Tracking regulatory matters in which the competitor is involved
- Debriefing current employees, suppliers, and customers, such as salespeople who have lost sales to the competitor, people who work with employees of the competitor on industry and other committees, and dealers who carry competitor's products in addition to your own
- Asking marketing specialists to evaluate the capabilities of the competitor's new advertising agency or other supplier
- Studying the competitor's track record and prior history to understand its personnel's thinking patterns, perspective, and experience

In this way, people involved in scenario writing will be able to provide more valuable and reliable insights into the decisions competitors are likely to make in the future. Such information is gathered in order to tailor the defined competitor information needs to the requirements of the specific company under study ["Tailor Competitor Information" 1990].

Misconceptions About Competitive Intelligence Systems

Several misconceptions about competitive market intelligence are [Smith 1987]:

- Competitive analysis must be comprehensive and uniform from one competitor to the next
- More is better — managers need all the information they ask for
- Competitive analysis is necessary only in highly competitive environments
- Competitive intelligence is costly and appropriate only for major decisions
- Competitive intelligence personnel are primarily information gatherers
- Competitive intelligence is simply marketing research in disguise
- People hoard information for selfish reasons

Understanding the faulty reasoning behind these misconceptions and taking steps to correct them can make a major contribution to the success of a competitive intelligence program.

AN APPROACH TO FORMULATING AND CARRYING OUT STRATEGIES FOR THE CIS FUNCTION IN SPECIFIC COMPANY AND COMPETITIVE MARKET SITUATIONS

This section discusses an approach to strategic planning for the CIS function in light of the business environment of the 1990s. The decision process described here is an extension of the one discussed in earlier chapters and shown in Figure 11-3.

The tasks involved, and their interrelationships when making strategic planning decisions for the CIS function, are outlined in Figure 11-4. The following sections also discuss the formulation

Figure 11-3: Strategic Management Decision-Making Process

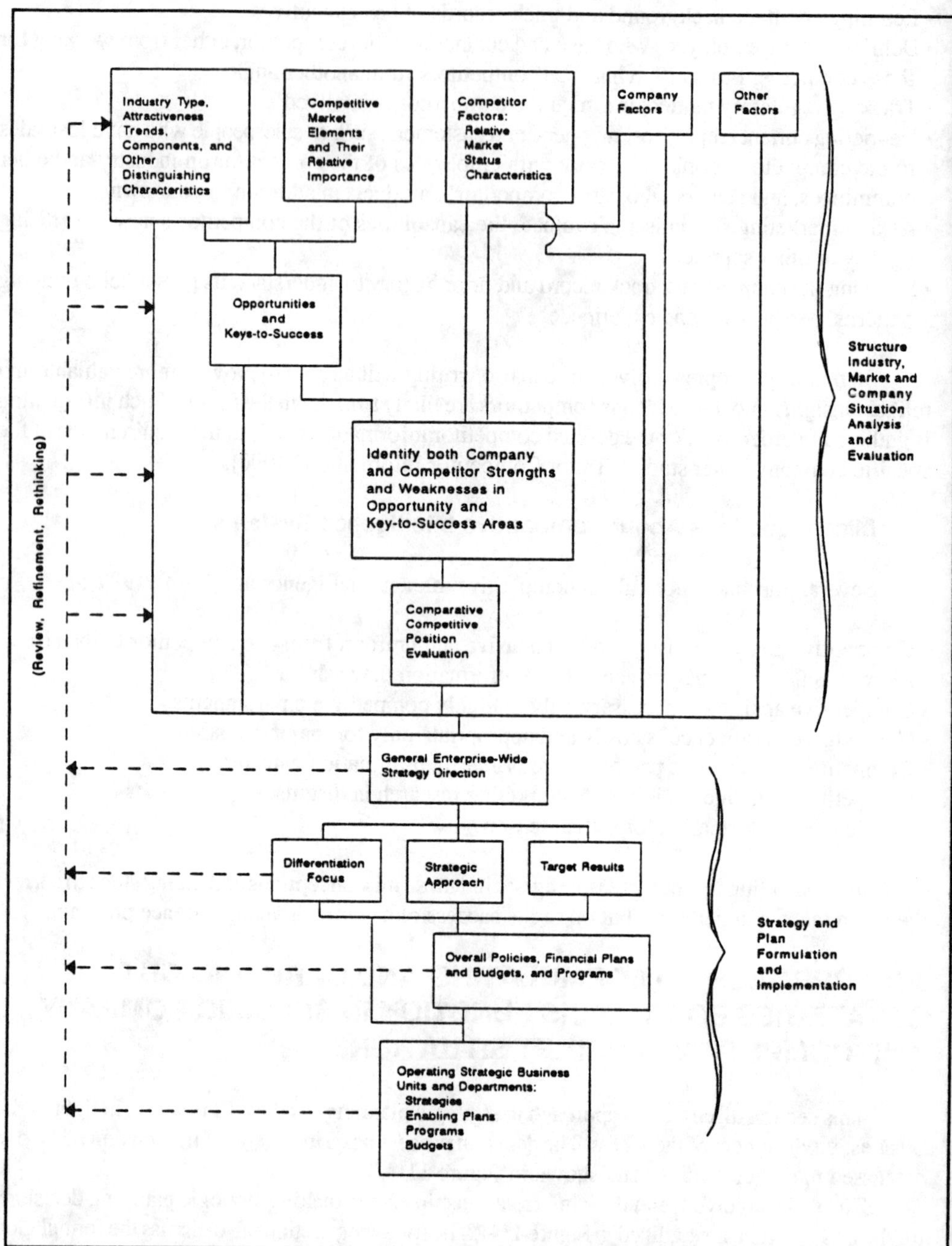

Figure 11-4: An Approach to Making Decisions in Situations Involving Computer Information Systems

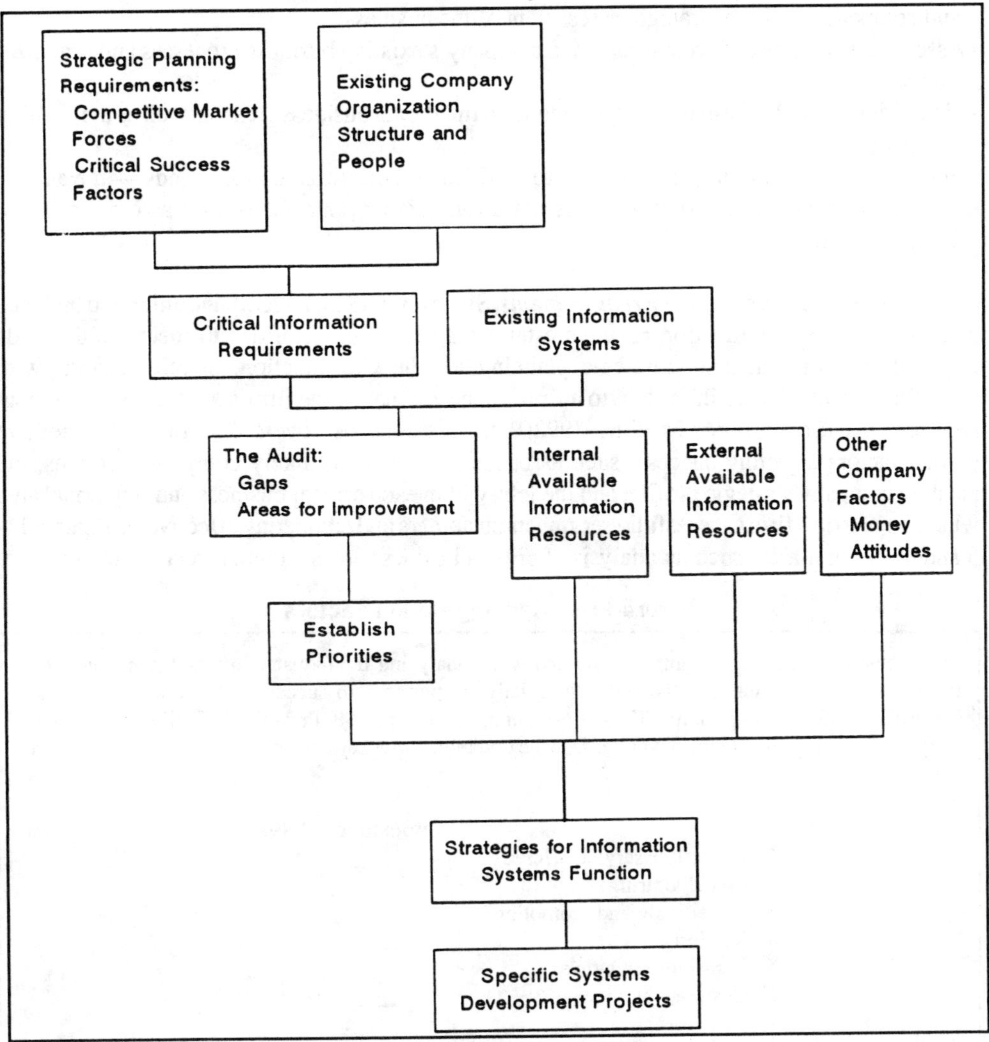

and implementation of CIS strategies in light of the critical situation context-specific factors.

Critical Situation Context Factors Affecting CIS Strategy Decisions

This discussion explores each critical factor affecting strategic management decisions for the CIS function, including

- Identifying critical external opportunity and key-to-success areas, as well as competitive forces and competitors — the strategic assessment of the business
- Assessing strengths and weaknesses of a company's existing business processes and organization
- Identifying critical information requirements in functional business areas, as well as the existing company CIS
- Finding the information gaps that need to be filled and prioritizing those needs — the audit
- Identifying available internal and external information resources, as well as other relevant company factors

Identify strategic planning requirements. Since few CIS managers have unlimited budgets, planning for the CIS function requires establishing strategic priorities to meet the demands imposed by these factors. Strategic planning for the CIS function, therefore, starts with identifying what jobs are important to a firm's success, that is, the firm's strategic management requirements [Tozer 1986; Mockler 1992(B)]. This analysis covers the critical competitive market factors affecting success, such as customer needs and likely competitor actions, the existing company strategic profile, and the jobs within each critical business and functional area which impact on a firm successfully serving its customers and competing effectively. Figures 11-5 and 11-6 summarize such an analysis of critical business areas and their relative importance.

Figure 11-5: Ranking Market Factors

Listed below are 10 areas commonly studied when analyzing the industry in which you compete. Please rate, in the column to the right, the relative importance to success. Use a scale of 0 (not important) to 99 (very important). The entire column should total 100. Press the ENTER key after each entry to move the cursor to the next line. Use the up/down arrow keys to move the cursor up and down the column.

	Importance [0-99]
1. Product or service offered	______
2. Manufacturing	______
3. Advertising and promotion	______
4. Retailing	______
5. Distribution/Outlets	______
6. Customer service	______
7. Sales force	______
8. Research and development	______
9. Human resources	______
10. Finance and management	______
Total	100

Press F10 key here to continue. _

Figure 11-6: Ranking Product or Service Success Factors

Product or Service Offered	Importance to Success [0-99]
product/service-quality.................	____
relative-price-of-product................	____
product-packaging........................	____
company-brand-recognition...............	____
product-ease-of-use......................	____
product-technology-superiorty............	____
product-fashionability..................	____
impulse-buying-motivation...............	____
breadth-of-product-line.................	____
new-product-development.................	____
1.______________________________	____
2.______________________________	____
Total	100

Additions might relate to: frequent product enhancement; product cloning supplementary product/ service support from third parties; patent or copyright protection, import restrictions (e.g. custom duties or quotas), other government policy protections; or any other factors you think are important to success.

Press F10 key to go on. _

Assess strengths and weaknesses of a company's existing business processes and organizations. This area of analysis covers the company's existing business processes, how the functions and jobs within the processes are organized and performed, and who is managing and performing them. Since the CIS function is to help a firm's line and management areas function more effectively and efficiently in running the business, these systems must suit those users' needs. Often during this analysis phase, as is shown in Chapter 12, a company's business processes may be reengineered to better serve customer and market needs. The importance of this preliminary reengineering phase can often outweigh any benefits from new CIS introduced, as seen from the discussions in Chapter 12.

Identify critical information requirements and existing information systems. Based on the analysis of the strategic competitive market and internal business processes, organization, and staff, one identifies information that will be critical to a firm's success. This is information that will have the biggest payoff in terms of meeting competitive market requirements. For example, managing accounts receivable might be a key leverage point for a new small enterprise, while targeting new accounts might be critical for a more mature business. Automating to support the customer service function could be vital to a firm that bases its strategy on superior customer service, but might not be as critical to a company trying to compete based on price.

This phase identifies the type of information and information support needed in the critical business areas identified during the earlier strategic assessments, and analyzes the relative importance of each information need in the specific context under study. This phase would also involve identifying existing information systems serving those needs.

The audit: Find the information gaps that need to be filled and prioritize those needs. This analysis identifies critical information gaps, answering questions of where a company needs better and more information than it is already getting to meet the critical information requirements identified. This audit also identifies ways in which computer technology might enhance access to new and existing information.

Ruth Stanat has described such audits in detail [Stanat 1989(B)]. First the existing information systems are analyzed. Then the effectiveness of those existing systems in meeting the information requirements identified — in terms of sources of information, distribution, and technology used — are examined. In addition, the user department's needs and requirements must also be considered. Figure 11-7 gives a sample questionnaire used by one planner for these audits.

The information obtained from user departments about their perceptions of gaps in present information systems and services, and of future needs obtained from field surveys is then matched and reconciled with the planner's independent perceptions of gaps and potential future needs based on their own strategic assessment of the environment and of the company's existing strengths and weaknesses. Once these gaps and future needs are identified through this reconciliation process, they are ranked in order of strategic importance.

Not all identified opportunities for investment in CIS will have the same value to a company. It is necessary to rate and rank the identified opportunity areas and evaluate their costs in terms of strategic value to a company. One way to do this *prioritizing* in a way that facilitates development and implementation is to focus first on *specific business processes* in critical operating areas.

Every business has multiple processes in each functional area, such as sales, promotion, order processing, manufacturing, distribution, purchasing, personnel, and the like. Key management decision areas — such as capital budgeting, and mergers and acquisition — are also critical, identifiable business processes. Some of these areas will have fully functioning, up-to-date information systems support; others will need improvement.

By identifying information systems priorities that help improve specific business processes, a close relationship between the information systems plan and business operations can be maintained. This is especially helpful when developing and implementing any new or improved information system into the on-going company businesses, since this approach usually involves the business managers who will eventually be using the systems in their development [Onolfo 1989].

This approach can also minimize the tendency to allow love of technology to drive the systems development effort. The focus should not be on developing technology to its fullest potential, but rather on solving business problems and improving business processes [Carr 1992].

Setting implementation priorities also requires trading off opportunities for competitive advantage with technological complexity. The more complex the technical problem, the greater

Figure 11-7: Auditing Existing Systems — Detailed Questionnaire

Date of Interview:________________
Department: ________________
Interviewee: ________________
Interviewer:________________

INFORMATION SOURCES

1) What information source do you use to obtain market intelligence or competititor intelligence?
2) How satisfied are you with these information sources as they pertain to your job function?
3) What is your budget for information sources
4) What publications do you subscribe to? What is the total cost of the subscriptions?
5) What publications that you do not receive should be acquired?
6) What element(s) would make your current information sources more valuable (e.g., more timely information)?

INFORMATION DISTRIBUTION

7) In addition to your department, to what other department(s) do you distribute information?
8) How frequently do you circulate information to other departments?
9) What information sources gathered by your group would be appropriate to input into a shared information network?

CRITICAL INFORMATION ISSUES

10) What type of information would you look for on a systematic or routine basis?
11) How would you like the information indexed (e.g. by competitor, by line of business, or by markets of interest)?
12) What emerging technologies, competitors and/or businesses may threaten the market position of your group or even cause your group to be divested?

TIME FACTORS, EXPECTATIONS, AND FORMAT

13) How often would you like to see the information by updated (e.g. daily, weekly, monthly or quarterly)?
14) What are your initial expectations of a business intelligence network? How would it benefit your role in the organization and your line of business?
15) In what format would you like to see the data of a business intelligence network? Would you rather have summarized abstracts, abstracts with analysis, or full text of a document?
16) How would you like to access this information (e.g. hard copy or floppy disk)?

OTHER

17) What are the future needs of a business intelligence network (e.g. should it focus on regional markets, opportunities overseas, and more competitive policies rather than actual products/services)?
18) What other marketing services would benefit your department and job function (e.g. qualitative research)?
19) Who else would you recommend we interview?

the risk and cost of pursuing the project. A realistic assessment of the technical "risk" of pursuing certain information opportunities is important to a practical, implementable information systems plan. Obviously, the low-risk, high-potential opportunities should receive priority.

A pure cost/benefit approach has to be modified, however, to reflect the external pressures which impact on the strategic value of information. These include

- Competitive pressures which dictate that a company do certain projects simply to remain competitive
- The availability of funding, which is often a function of the overall corporate fiscal health
- The integration of information technologies, specifically the integration of data, text, and graphics which present opportunities for competitive advantage if a company acts quickly
- The opportunities inherent in the explosion of available data, especially in the marketing area, and the ability of technology such as scanners and artificial intelligence (expert knowledge-based systems) to review, identify, and organize that data
- Pressure from top management to identify problems more quickly

Based on the planning process described in this section, General Foods identified several priority opportunity areas where the application of information technology could create strategic competitive advantages in a large consumer goods company [Onolfo 1989]:

- Using advertising and promotions systems where detailed analyses of customer spending patterns and their impact on sales could lead to more cost-effective, finely-tuned advertising and promotion plans and plans for new product development
- Using information technology for package design where integrated graphics and text capabilities could reduce the package design cycle by half and enable marketing to move new products into the market more quickly
- Supply-chain/inventory management, a key area in which improved data processing and management information were needed to maintain competitive positions
- Accessing and manipulating the available competitive intelligence data in order to turn it into useful information for top management
- Taking advantage of newly available scanner data for improved marketing and sales information
- Employing desktop publishing to reduce costs
- Exploring new but not yet clearly defined information systems technology potentials in such areas as expert knowledge-based systems, high-definition television, object-oriented programming techniques and tools, and integrated services data networks (ISDN)

A by-product of this audit can be a reduction in waste. Such a reduction can arise from eliminating duplication of information systems and resources among divisions or departments. For example, in one study two divisions of a company commissioned large research studies of the same problem and regularly obtained reports based on extensive literature searches of the same area [Stanat 1989(B)]. The waste can also arise from obsolete information systems and/or major systems that service areas whose strategic importance has diminished.

Identify available information resources: internal and external. A continuing assessment is required of the existing hardware, software, people, and facilities available within the CIS departments or business units under study. The present allocation of these resources to different new projects and to existing system maintenance and upgrading is also reviewed.

In addition, in some situations external developments in the field will either stimulate or limit what can be done. For example, new software that requires evaluation is constantly being developed. At General Foods, monitoring technological developments led to applications of new design software to possible information needs in the packaging area, a critical area for a consumer packaged goods company. Before new software was developed, it was not possible to consider improved applications in that area. Monitoring new technological developments, therefore, can open windows of opportunities.

At Dow Jones News Service, the development of parallel processing computers, combined with the development of software applications that could read and analyze text, enabled the company to develop ways to more economically and effectively scan, process, organize, and disseminate text data and information — their core business service [Pollack 1989].

The limitations and availability of people can also be critical to the capabilities of CIS departments to exploit new opportunity areas. For example, based on strategic competitive considerations, one bank identified the need for a specific kind of information system in one of its operating departments: the ability to provide credit card customers with copies of signed charge receipts. Computerized imaging technology was available but the bank did not yet have that capability. In this instance, the bank had the necessary resources to provide services now being provided by other credit card companies. However, it did not have the existing people, software, or hardware to develop and deliver such a system. The bank therefore decided to use an outside processing service, even though it would have preferred to develop in-house capabilities.

Other company factors. The budget is usually a primary situational limiting factor. For this reason, when listing priorities for projects it is helpful to make a complete list of projects and assign a value to each, making sure that the total does not exceed 100.

The attitudes of top management is another key internal company factor. Some companies and company managers simply do not have much enthusiasm for CIS, and this will impact on the amount of money and attention devoted to these systems.

Formulating CIS Strategies and Creating and Implementing CIS

Strategies for CIS development are formulated within the context of

- Critical information needs priorities — which CIS are important and how important each is
- Existing systems, available resources, and top management attitudes

The strategy formulation process builds on the prioritizing shown in Figures 11-5 and 11-6, the studies of existing and planner business and CIS needs, and the resource allocations based on such analysis. It can also make use of the elaborate financial "payoff" evaluation systems used by many companies, through which returns on investment are calculated for each major CIS project [Sullivan-Trainor 1989]. At times, these steps are sufficient to justify strategic CIS decisions.

In some situations, however, strategic needs can have an overwhelming impact on the overall strategic mix of CIS. For example, systems designed to create competitive advantages, such as those discussed earlier in this chapter, may be justified for competitive reasons that are difficult to quantify.

Strategic needs may also affect the total amount of corporate resources devoted to CIS. For example, Rockwell International intended to spend $450 million yearly in the early 1990s on CIS because of their strategic importance to the company's business.

Within this overall strategic context, decisions are made about individual systems. Systems discussed in this chapter range from major integrated customer account systems, to systems supporting automated bank teller machines, to sales management systems based on field salespeople's daily reports, to oral information gathering systems, to internal management financial reporting systems, to processing customer queries using parallel processing computers and knowledge-based systems.

The following sections describe several conventional and knowledge-based systems designed to assist in making overall CIS strategy decisions, deciding among individual proposed systems development projects, and evaluating the strategic potential of specific CIS areas for an individual company.

The steps involved in implementing these systems are as important to success as the quality of the systems themselves. Where possible, involving users in the development can facilitate the implementation process. This is not always possible, however. Some people will not adapt to change, nor have the capacity to grow in new directions. Because of the potential problems, studies have shown that in many situations it is best to introduce these systems in stages — initially keeping them small and maintaining parallel systems [Benjamin 1990, p, 293]. The concluding chapter in PART FOUR, Chapter 12, and Appendix B discuss the implementation of strategy planning efforts. Many of the fundamental approaches described there for handling the organization and human resource aspects of decision implementation also apply to CIS implementation.

As discussed in Chapter 12, and earlier in this chapter, a major benefit of computer information studies is that very often substantial improvements are realized through reengineering a firm's existing business processes — before any actual computer systems are installed [Hammer 1993, Rifkin 1992].

COMPUTER INFORMATION SYSTEMS (CIS) DESIGNED TO ASSIST IN MAKING STRATEGIC DECISIONS INVOLVING THE CIS FUNCTION

This section covers conventional and knowledge-based systems used in making strategy decisions for the CIS area.

Figure 11-8: PRISM: The Basic Underlying Models

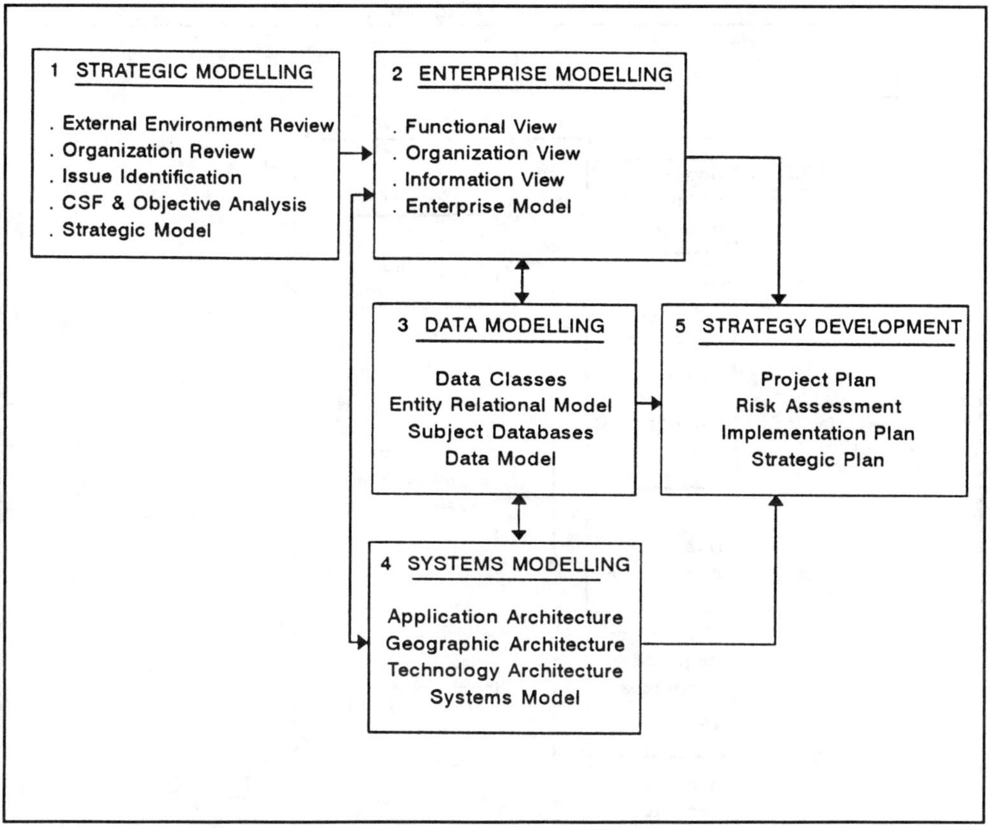

PRISM, a Conventional Computer System That Guides Strategic Planning for the CIS Area

PRISM, a computer software application from Deltacom Incorporated, provides guidance in doing the strategic planning described in the preceding section [George 1988]. This system entails a series of steps, as shown in the Information Systems Strategic Planning (ISSP) Model in Figure 11-8.

The *strategic modelling* phase assesses the competitive market environment and overall company strategic requirements to identify the strategic issues and the critical success factors (CSF). The *enterprise modelling* phase analyzes the decision processes and functions, organization structure and reporting relationships, and organization information (data) requirements. The *strategy development* phase evaluates proposed projects for their feasibility, risks, and benefits in light of other projects, overall-company and business-unit strategic needs, and

Figure 11-9: Decision Situation Under Study—Feasibility or Investigative Studies Decision Diagram

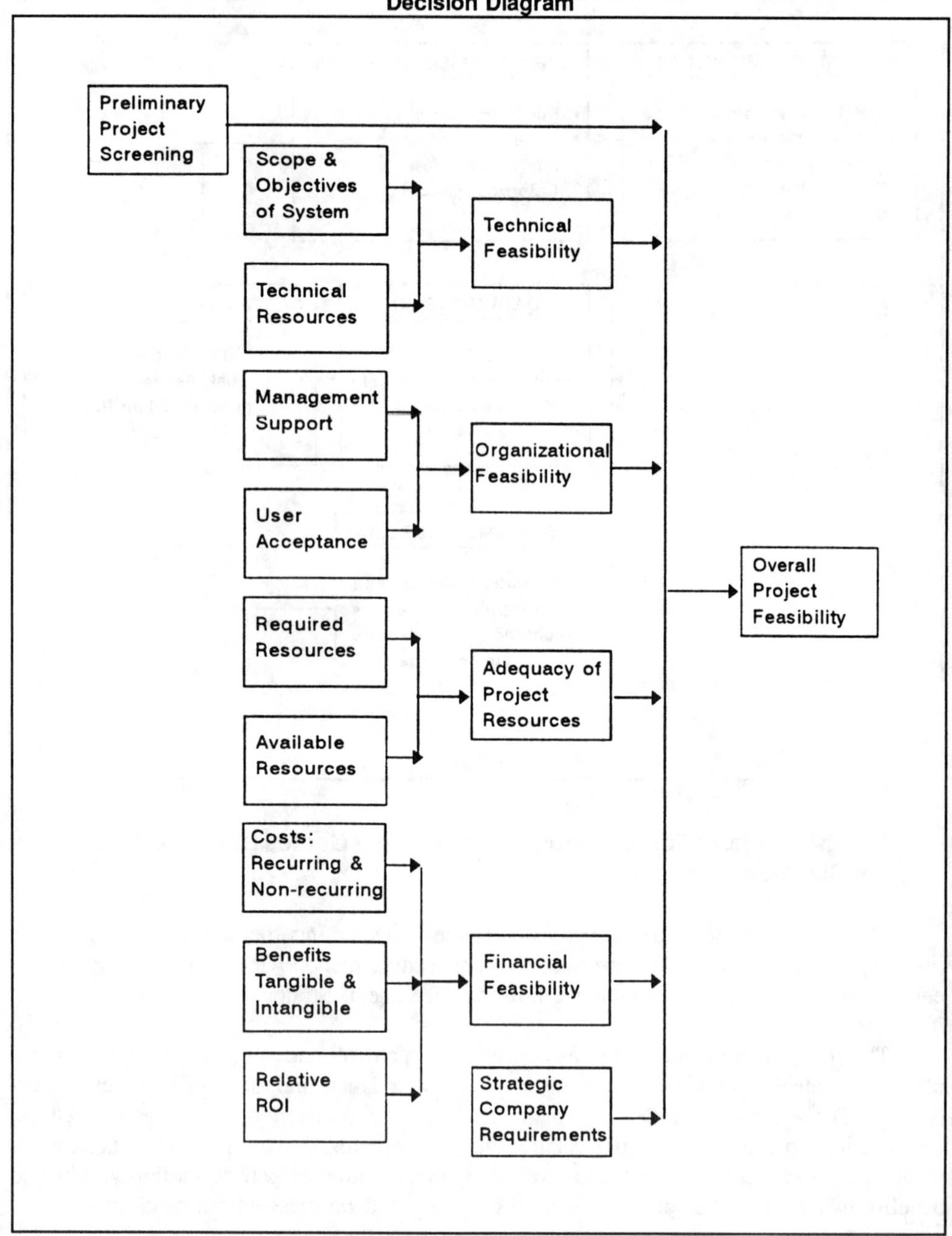

Figure 11-10: Dependency Diagram—Potential for Competitive Advantage Using Computer Information Technology (Initial Prototype)

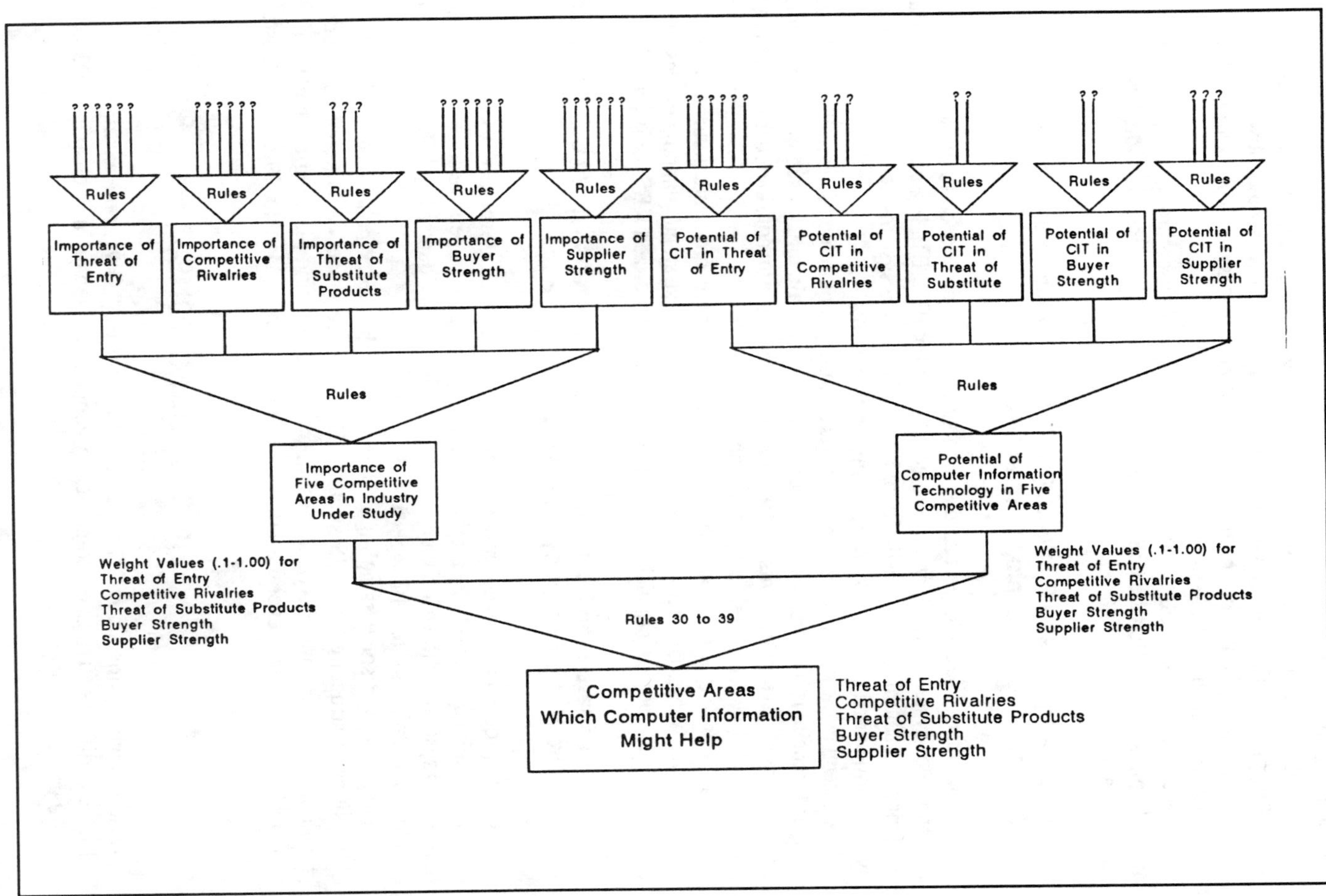

available resources.

Within the context of the internal and external strategic situation requirements, the *data modelling* phase defines the classes of information (data) to be created, how the classes relate to each other, and how the information will be used. The *systems modelling* phase develops specifications for the actual system design.

Systems such as PRISM are useful since they guide a user through the planning involved in formulating strategies for the CIS function, as well as in choosing individual systems development projects.

Knowledge-Based Systems (KBS) for Evaluating the Feasibility of Proposed KBS Development Projects

A number of knowledge-based systems have been developed to guide users through the evaluation of systems development projects [Mockler 1992(B)]. Figure 11-9 outlines a system developed to determine the feasibility of knowledge-based systems development projects. The system is included on the disks accompanying this book.

As seen in the system diagram, strategic company requirements, as well as other factors — such as financial resources, resource requirements and availability, user and other management and organizational requirements, and technical factors — are all considered in evaluating specific proposed KBS development projects. The system helps the user analyze these critical areas through a series of questions, and then makes preliminary recommendations based on the user's answers to the questions. This is another example of how strategic planning process definitions can help guide operating decision making through computerized KBS decision aids.

Knowledge-Based Systems for Identifying Areas Where CIS Technology Can Provide a Company With a Competitive Edge

Other prototype knowledge-based systems have been developed to assist planners in exploring ways CIS technology might be useful in gaining a competitive edge. An overall outline of one such system is shown in Figure 11-10 [Mockler 1989, Chapter 15]. IBM has reportedly also developed a similar system [Gongla 1989].

This is only a small sampling of the considerable work being done in business and at universities to structure how CIS strategy decisions are made. Additional conventional and knowledge-based computer systems useful in doing strategic planning computer information systems are reviewed in several useful supplementary texts [Mockler 1992(A); Webster 1989].

REVIEW QUESTIONS

1. Describe what is meant by "The Intelligent Enterprise." Give some examples.
2. List the different types of computer systems discussed in this chapter. Describe their similarities and differences.

3. What are competitive intelligence systems and how are they used in strategic management?
4. List the different kinds of competitive intelligence systems discussed in this chapter.
5. Discuss some of the information sources used in competitive intelligence systems.
6. Describe how managers of information systems departments formulate and implement strategies for their area.
7. Discuss the questions which are explored while doing a systems audit.
8. Describe how the introduction of computer technology can alter or influence competitive forces strategically.

EXERCISES

1. Read several recent issues of *Infoworld, Computerworld, Marketing, Marketing News, Financial Management, InformationWeek*, or any other related publication of your choice and find a detailed description of recently developed computer information systems which have changed the character of two different companies, or which have given two firms a competitive advantage. Write a report comparing the relative impact of CIS development on each company, in light of the discussions in this chapter.

2. The disks accompanying this book contain several prototype KBS. Follow the directions accompanying the disks to run a consultation using the system named CMP-PRJ.PLN, which guides users in the development of knowledge-based systems (KBS). If you wish, you might also print out the knowledge base and study it while you are running the system and restudying this chapter. Write a report describing how this CIS can be useful to you or to a company in strategy formulation.

3. Read Appendix D, "Using Online Databases for Market Research." Discuss ways in which online databases may be used to obtain information useful in doing strategic management tasks described in this book.

REFERENCES

Ambrosio, Johanna, "Honing in on Target Customers," *Computerworld*, February 10, 1992, pp. 97, 98.

Beal, Reginald M., "Achieving Competitive Advantage Using Information Technology: A Viable Strategy for Small Businesses," Presentation, Annual Meeting, Atlantic City, NJ: Association of Management, August 6-9, 1991.

Benjamin, Robert I., David W. de Long, and Michael S. Scott Morton, "Electronic Data Interchange: How Much Competitive Advantage?," *Long Range Planning*, February 1990, pp. 29-40.

Bonnett, Kendra R., "From Grassroots to Grand Plan," *AI Expert*, August 1989, pp. 54-60.

Brandel, Mary, "Executive Information Systems," *Computerworld*, July 22, 1991, pp. 67-71.

Caldwell, Bruce, "CIOs and CEOs: A Case of Double Vision?", *InformationWeek*, May 6, 1991. p. 42.

Carr, Clay, "Performance Support Systems: A New Horizon for Expert Systems," *AI Expert,* May 1992, pp. 45-49.

Connolly, James, "Restaurant Chain Cooks Up Time Saving IS Strategy," *Computerworld,* March 18, 1991, p. 43.

Cooke, Thomas M., "OR/MS: Alive and Flying at American Airlines," *OR/MS Today*, June 1989, pp. 16-20.

Erkkila, John, and Brendan Murphy, "Strategic Information: An Economic Analysis and Case Study," *Information Management Review,* Winter 1989, pp. 25-36.

Eskow, Dennis, "IS Chiefs Seek to Revamp Business Processes," *PC Week,* February 12, 1990, p. 12.

Feder, Barnaby J., "Kennametal Finds the Right Tools," *The New York Times,* May 6, 1992, pp. D1, D7.

Fisher, Michael. "Operations Research at Federal Express," *OR/MS Today*, June 1989, pp. 20-21.

Flast, Robert, "Managing Expert Systems Development," Presentation, Annual Meeting, New York: International Conference on Information Systems (ICIS), December 16-18, 1991.

Forsythe, Jason, "Systems Give Pepperidge Farm Freshness," *InformationWeek*, March 20, 1989, 29-31.

Friend, David, "Benefits of an Executive Information System," *Information Management Review*, Winter 1989, pp. 7-16.

Fuld, Leonard, *Competitor Intelligence: How to Get It; How to Use It*, New York: Wiley, 1985.

Fuld, Leonard, "How to Gather Foreign Intelligence Without Leaving Home," *Marketing News,* January 4, 1988(A).

Fuld, Leonard, *Monitoring the Competition: Finding Out What's Really Going on Over There,* New York: Wiley, 1988(B).

Garsombke, Diane J., "International Competitor Analysis," *Planning Review*, May/June 1989, pp. 42-47.

Garvey, Martin, "Intelligent Integration: Expert Systems Become More Usable as They Merge Into Existing Technologies," *InformationWeek*, September 3, 1991, pp. 27-28.

George, Ivan T., *PC PRISM (Registered) Professional Planning Series,* Feasterville, PA: Deltacom Incorporated, 1975-1988.

Gongla, P., et ala, "S*P*A*R*K," *IBM Systems Journal*, vol. 28, No. 4, 1989, pp. 628-637.

Hammer, Michael, and James Champy, *Reengineering Work*, New York: Warner Books, 1993.

Henkoff, Ronald, "Walgreen: A High-Tech Rx for Profits," *Fortune*, March 23, 1992, pp. 106-107.

Hirsch, James S., "Banc One Agrees to Buy 4 Ohio Banks Affiliated with PNC for $225 Million," *The Wall Street Journal,* January 17, 1991, p. A4

Hirsch, James, "Fast-Rising Banc One, Already Big in Texas, Looks at Other Areas," *The Wall Street Journal*, December 20, 1990, pp. A1, A2.

Homer, Peter, "Eyes on the Prize" and "The Best in MS," *OR/MS Today,* August 1991, pp. 34-43.

Hudson, Robert O., "Foreign Intelligence Tracking Systems," *Ruth Stanat Forum*, New York: Strategic Intelligence Systems, Inc., March 15, 1989.

Keen, Peter, ed., *The Implementation of Computer-Based Decision Aids*, Cambridge., MA: Proceedings of a Conference Sponsored by the Center for Information Systems Research, M.I.T., April 3-5 1975.

Keen, Peter, *Business Without Bounds: Telecommunications and Business Strategy,* Hagerstown, MD: Ballinger Publishing, 1986.

Keen, Peter, *Computing in Time: Using Telecommunications For Competitive Advantage,* Cambridge, MA: Ballinger Publishing, 1988.

Keiser, Barbie E., "Practical Competitor Intelligence," *Planning Review*, September/October 1987, pp. 14-19, 45.

Kight, Leila, "The Search for Intelligence on Divisions and Subsidiaries," *Planning Review,* May/June

1989, pp. 40-41.

King, Julia, "Coral Lipstick? It Sells Big in Florida," *Computerworld*, May 11, 1992, pp. 117, 118.

Kleinfield, N.R., "Targeting the Grocery Shopper," *The New York Times*, Business Section, May 26, 1991, pp. 1, 6.

Leibs, Scott, and Mike Fillon, "Why Lithonia MIS Won't Lighten Up," *InformationWeek*, January 14, 1991, pp. 26-30.

Lohr, Steve, "The Best Little Bank in America," *The New York Times*, Business Section, July 7, 1991, pp. 1, 4.

Mandell, Mel, "Domino's: How Was Your Pizza, Ma'am?," *Computerworld*, January 20, 1992.

Markowitz, Zane N., "Hidden Sector Competitor Analysis," *Planning Review*, September/October 1987, pp. 20-29.

McCarthy, Michael J., "Marketers Zero in on Their Customers," *The Wall Street Journal*, March 18, 1991, pp. B1, B8.

McGrane, James, "Using On-Line Information for Strategic Advantage," *Planning Review*, November/December 1987, pp. 27-30.

Mockler, Robert J., *Computer Software to Support Strategic Planning Decision Making*, New York: Macmillan, 1992(A).

Mockler, Robert J., *Developing Knowledge-Based Systems*, New York: Macmillan, 1992(B).

Mockler, Robert J., *Developing Knowledge-Based Systems for Strategic Planning*, Englewood Cliffs, NJ: Prentice-Hall, 1989.

Morton, Michael Scott, *Management Decision Systems: Computer-Based Support for Decision Making*, Cambridge, MA: Division of Research, Harvard, 1971.

Morton, Michael Scott, *The Corporation of the 1990s*, New York: Oxford University Press, 1991.

Naylor, Thomas, and Michele H. Mann, eds., *Computer-Based Planning Systems*, Oxford, OH: The Planning Forum, 1982.

O'Brien, John, Wayne P. Johnson, and Richard Woodhead, "The Ford Motor Company DLMS," *AI Expert*, August 1989, pp. 42-53.

O'Brien, Virginia, and Leonard M. Fuld, "Business Intelligence and the New Europe," *Planning Review*, July/August 1991, pp. 29-34.

Onolfo, John, "Strategic Information Planning," *Ruth Stanat Forum*, New York: Strategic Intelligence Systems, March 15, 1989.

Penzias, Arno, *Ideas and Information*, W.W. Norton, 1989.

Pepper, Jon, "A Whopper of a POS," *InformationWeek*, March 18, 1991(A), pp. 28-31.

Pepper, Jon, "Getting Along with the CEO," *InformationWeek*, May 6, 1991(B), pp. 38-45.

Pepper, Jon, "The MIS Battle for the Skies," *InformationWeek*, February 11, 1991(C), pp. 44-49.

Pollack, Andrew, "Computers That Read and Analyze," *The New York Times*, June 7, 1989, pp. D1, D6.

Prescott, John, and Daniel Smith, "The Largest Survey of 'Leading-Edge' Competitor Intelligence Managers," *Planning Review*, May/June 1989, pp. 6-13.

Quinn, James Brian, *The Intelligent Enterprise*, New York: The Free Press, 1992.

Quint, Michael, "A Bank That's Riding Technology to the Top," *The New York Times*, June 30, 1989, pp. D1, D6.

Rapport, Alain, and Reid Smith, editors, *Innovative Applications of Artificial Intelligence 2*, Cambridge, MA: AAAI Press/MIT Press, 1991.

Rifkin, Glenn, "Ardent Preacher of Radical Change," *The New York Times*, April 18, 1992, pp. 33, 36.

Rosenkranz, Frederick, *An Introduction to Corporate Modelling*, Durham, NC: Duke University Press, 1979.

Rowan, Duncan A., "On-Line Expert Systems in Process Industries," *AI Expert*, August 1989, pp. 30-

41.

Rudding, Alan, "GE Answers Call to Evolve 10-Year-Old Help Line," *Computerworld,* January 20, 1992, p. 72.

Ryan, Alan J., "Sales Force Automation: Metamorphosis of the Salesperson," *Computerworld,* April 8, 1991, pp. 59-70.

Scheier, Robert L., "Obliterated by the Chip: The Crushing of People Express," *PC Week,* November 13, 1989, p. 131.

Schorr, Herbert, and Alain Rappaport, editors, *Innovative Applications of Artificial Intelligence,* Cambridge, MA: AAAI Press/MIT Press, 1989.

Slater, Derek, "IS at Your Service," *Computerworld,* January 20, 1992, pp. 72-80.

Smith, Daniel, and John E. Prescott, "Demystifying Competitive Analysis," *Planning Review,* September/October 1987, pp. 8-13.

Smith, Reid, and Carlisle Scott, editors, *Innovative Applications of Artificial Intelligence 3,* Cambridge, MA: AAAI Press/MIT Press, 1991.

Sol, Henk, "Dynamics in Information Intensive Organizations," and with Robert J. Streng, "A Dynamic Modelling Approach to Analyze Chain Dynamics on the Inter-Organizational Level," Research Project, Delft University of Technology (Belgium), presented at *Hawaii International Conference on Systems Sciences (HICSS), 25th Annual Meeting*, Kauai, Hawaii, January 7-10, 1992.

Stanat, Ruth, ed., *The Intelligent Corporation,* New York: Amacom, 1990.

Stanat, Ruth, "Field Sales Intelligence Systems," *Information Management Review*, Winter 1989(A), pp. 17-24.

Stanat, Ruth, "The Strategic Information Audit," *Ruth Stanat Forum*, New York: Strategic Intelligence Systems, March 15, 1989(B).

Sullivan-Trainor, Michael, "Command Center Rates First in EIS Face-off," *Computerworld*, July 22, 1991, pp. 72-76.

Sullivan-Trainor, Michael, and Joseph Maglitta, "Competitive Advantage Fleeting," *Computerworld,* October 8, 1990, pp. 1, 4.

Sullivan-Trainor, Michael, "The Push for Proof of Information Systems Payoff," *Computerworld,* April 3, 1989, pp. 55-61.

"Tailor Competitor Information to Needs of Organization," *The Planning Forum Network,* February 1990, pp. 1, 5.

Tavakolian, Hamid, "Linking the Information Technology Structure with Organizational Competitive Strategy: A Survey," *MIS Quarterly,* September 1989, pp. 309-317.

Tozer, Edwin E., *Planning for Business Information Systems,* Oxford, England: Pergamon Books, 1986.

Turban, Efraim, *Decision Support and Expert Systems,* 2nd Edition, New York: Macmillan Company, 1990.

Vella, Carolyn, and John McGonagle, *Improved Business Planning Using Competitive Intelligence,* Westport, CT: Quorum Books, 1988.

Vella, Carolyn, and John McGonagle, "Shadowing Markets: A New Competitive Intelligence Technique," *Planning Review,* September/October 1987, pp. 39-38.

Washington Researchers Publishing, *How to Find Information About Companies,* 2612 P Street, NW, Washington, DC 20007, 1989.

Washington Researchers Publishing, *Understanding the Competition: A Practical Guide to Competitive Analysis,* 2612 P Street, NW, Washington, DC 20007, 1984.

Watson, Hugh, "Expensive to Implement, Costly to Develop and Maintain," *Computerworld,* July 22, 1991, pp. 70-71.

Webster, James L., William E. Reif, and Jeffrey S. Bracker, "The Manager's Guide to Strategic Planning Tools and Techniques," *Planning Review,* November/December 1989, pp. 4-12, 48.

Wiseman, Charles, "Attack & Counterattack: The New Game in Information Technology," *Planning Review,* September/October 1988(A), pp. 6-12.

Wiseman, Charles, *Strategic Information Systems,* Homewood, ILL: Irwin, 1988(B).

CHAPTER 12

LEADERSHIP, ORGANIZATION, STAFFING, AND CONTROL

This chapter's objective is to help readers effectively implement strategies and related enabling plans by

- Analyzing and evaluating situation requirements
- Formulating situationally appropriate business process and organization realignments, and creating internal business contexts that promote long-term strategic thinking
- Understanding and acquiring the skills needed to direct, staff, control, and acquire resources

While shown as a separate task in Figure 12-1 and described in a separate chapter, in most situations this phase of strategic management is not a discrete task. Nor is it a one-time project. Implementation considerations covered in this chapter affect all phases of strategic management, from the organization and management of the planning effort (Appendix B), to the formulation of enterprise-wide strategies (Chapters 2 through 7 and Appendix A), to the creation and implementation of enabling strategies and plans at all operating levels (Chapters 8 through 11).

The tasks discussed in this chapter are important because they enable formulating and carrying out strategies and related enabling plans. If done well, they can serve as a mechanism for realigning a company's entire infrastructure — its internal business processes and related organizational context. This creates an environment which promotes strategic thinking throughout a firm and so enables managers at all levels to formulate and implement new strategies and to initiate strategically integrated action as new competitive challenges arise. Michael Walsh reportedly established such an environment at Union Pacific before he left to head Tenneco in

Figure 12-1: Strategic Management Tasks

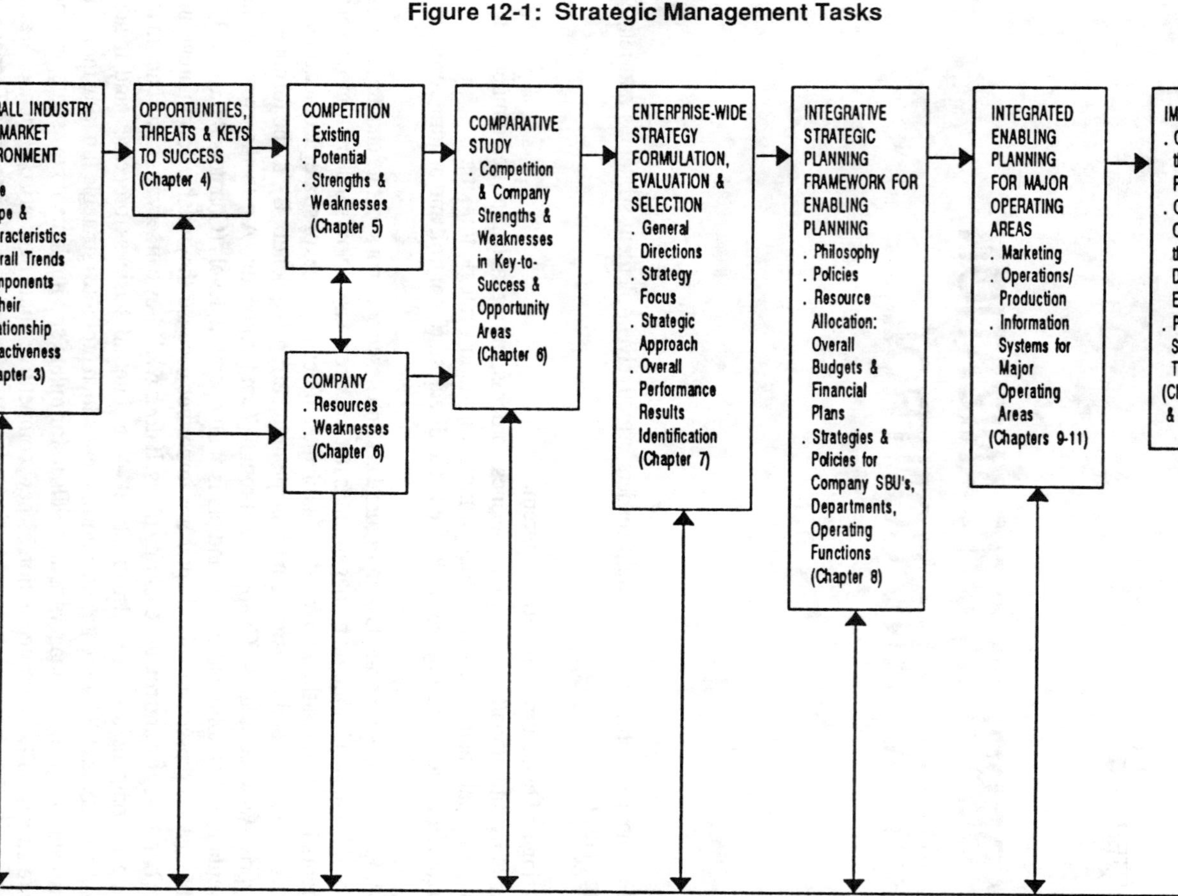

1991. According to one analyst, "Mr. Walsh transformed the Union Pacific Railroad into a hungry, aggressive company" with three instead of nine layers of management, a company whose profits rose 46 percent during the four years prior to 1991 [Hayes 1992; Machalaba 1991].

IMPLEMENTATION VARIES BY SITUATION

Success in management essentially involves doing whatever is necessary in a particular situation to get a job done, within legitimate legal, ethical, and moral restraints. Strategy implementation, therefore, will depend on individual situation factors. For example, Gillette's Colman Mockler used a *bottoms-up* approach, allowing those affected by the enterprise-wide strategic changes to plan and carry out their implementation [Chakravorty 1991; McKibben 1990]. In contrast, when CEO Tom Dolan ran into hard times at Westcon Inc, a small computer parts company, he employed a *top-down* approach — what he called the "Norman Schwarzkopf approach" to motivating employees. First he simply ordered employees to meet the competition head on by paying greater attention to customer demands; Dolan then reinforced his orders daily [Stern 1991]. While this approach appears to have worked at Westcon, it is generally considered out of step with the workplace culture in this country ["Autocratic Leaders," 1991].

An Adaptive Strategic Change Process

Corporate CEOs studied seem to follow an adaptive situational process such as the one outlined in Figure 12-2 to meet the needs of changing competitive markets and diverse internal business environments. The following sections review briefly those critical situation factors identified in Figure 12-2 which might affect implementation decisions and how decisions are made and implemented based on these factors.

The factors covered include

- Nature and size of the company, the industry, and the competitive market place — especially changing external competitive market pressures
- The strategies themselves, to the degree that they may require changes in existing strategic business processes, organization culture and structure, leadership styles, staffing, and controls
- How the strategies were developed, since this process has an impact not only on the quality of the strategies formulated, but also on strategic thinking throughout an organization and so the degree of cooperation obtained later during the implementation
- Existing internal business processes, including the way marketing and production interrelate in product companies and the way services are delivered to customers in service companies
- Existing organization culture, since culture can create major barriers, as well as provide effective enabling mechanisms for strategy implementation
- Existing organization structure, since it has to be used, modified, or changed in implementing strategies

Figure 12-2: Strategy Implementation

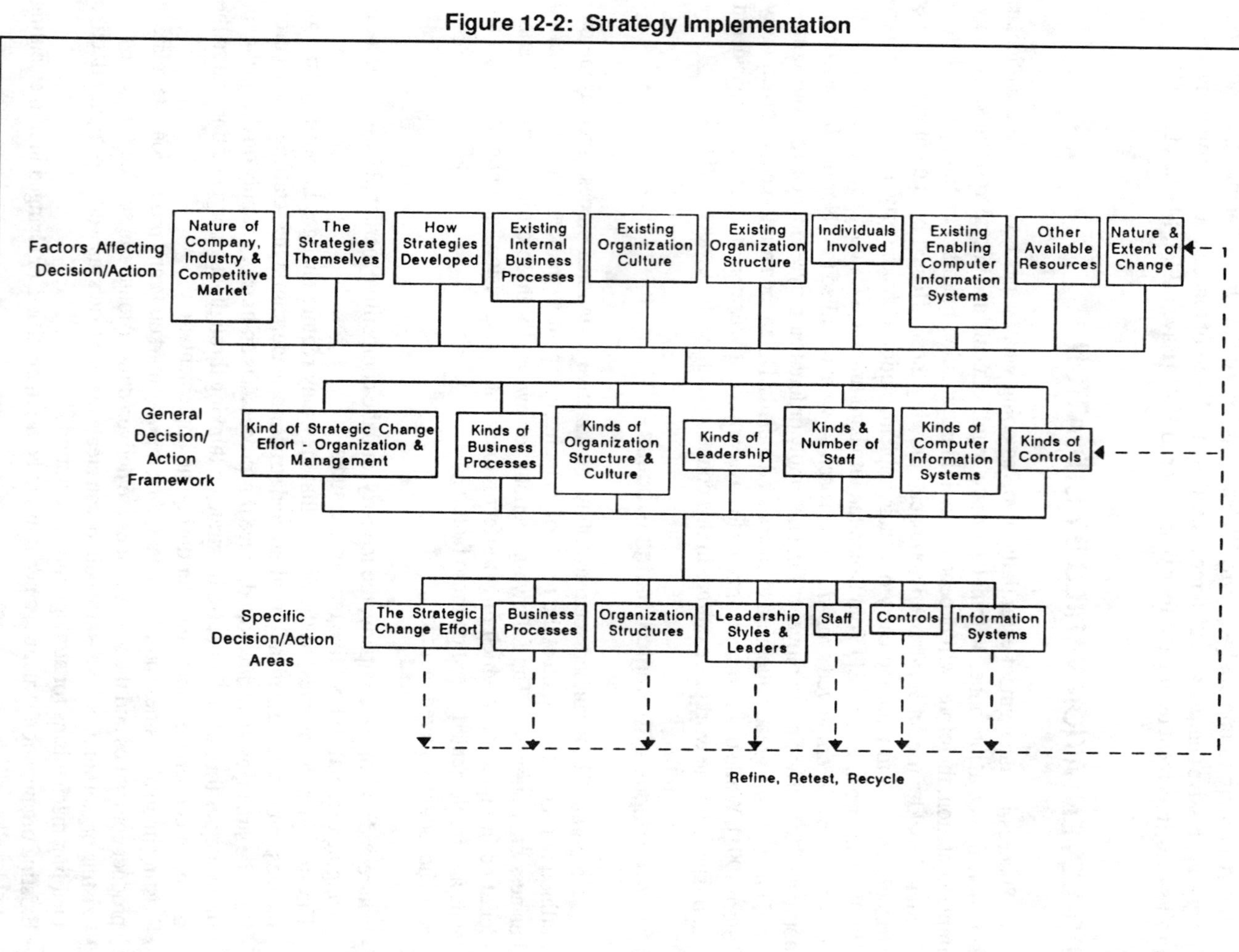

- Individuals who might be involved, since they will be carrying out the strategies and strategic plans
- Existing enabling information systems
- Other resources available, including existing controls and potentially available computer information systems
- The nature and extent of change, and its timing

The analysis of these factors leads to *general* decision and action frameworks, such as:

- The kind of strategic change effort required
- Business processes required to meet strategic requirements
- Kinds of organization structure and changes in organization culture required
- Kinds of leadership required
- Kinds and numbers of staff required
- Kinds of computer information systems and controls required

This is an intermediate conceptualization phase through which specific detailed solutions often emerge in stages.

Decisions, plans, and actions are also needed as to the *specific* management and organization of the strategy formulation and implementation effort, business processes and organization structures, leaders and leadership styles, staff, and controls and information systems. During this formulation and implementation process, the general solution concepts (frameworks) are continually revised, as are the detailed plans and actions formulated within those frameworks. Essentially, the process focuses on the individual manager's situation — the primary focus of this book. Its model in Figure 12-2 is designed to help prompt and guide managers within a firm continue to listening to what the competitive market, the organization, and the people involved are saying, and then continue to adapt to that changing environment. In this sense, the process in Figure 12-2 is not a procedure, but an adaptive, semi-structured general framework for continuing action — just like the other strategic management process models in this text.

The Process at Work

The impact of the situation factors on strategic change implementation varies by situation. For example, after Roger Penske purchased Detroit Diesel from General Motors in 1988, the company became an independent entrepreneurial enterprise which was no longer run as a division of a large company. His industry was industrial products, not consumer products (like Gillette) or railroads (like Union Pacific). In light of these and other situation factors, Penske's personal leadership was needed to change the corporate culture from a traditionally-structured large bureaucratic organization to an entrepreneurial one able to meet changing competitive market pressures. The many specific changes he made — keeping skilled hourly workers while substantially reducing middle management, creating new incentives and rewards, continually interacting with workers — all signalled to workers his interest in retaining his highly specialized, skilled workforce which was so important to the success of his company in the diesel engine market. The implementation in this instance was managed mainly by a single charismatic leader who was a recognized expert in the field as well as an experienced and successful entrepreneur [White 1991].

The situational factors at Chase Manhattan's Municipal Bond strategic business unit (SBU) were very different. The strategic change introduced into the SBU in 1988 was major — a whole new approach to the municipal bond market. The timing was critical — because of competitive initiatives speed was required. Since the existing staff was trained in business patterns and processes different from those required by the new strategic approach, considerable time would have been needed to retrain them. Since the organizational culture was typical of an authoritarian hierarchical old-line financial institution in which changes were very often dictated from the top, the strategy was decided by top management and no tinkering was to be allowed to accommodate individuals. Adequate resources were available to implement desired changes quickly. In light of these specific situation circumstances, the change was managed in a direct authoritarian way: a new leader was hired, key new staff were also brought in from the outside, and the existing staff for the most part left Chase for other brokerage firms [Doran 1991].

Gillette faced yet another set of situation factors and as a result implemented strategic changes differently. In the 1970s, Gillette was a multinational company with over $2 billion in sales in the consumer products field. While the initial vision of the company formulated by newly appointed CEO Colman Mockler — to refocus on three major product areas — came from Mockler and the Board of Directors, the detailed strategic plans were formulated with the participation of those implementing them. He was able to do this because in his words he "knew precisely the kind of company Gillette should be to succeed over the long run; he just didn't know exactly what that envisioned future company would look like."

The business processes were generally stable at Gillette, as was the organization culture and structure, and staff. In implementing the vision, Mockler focused on the people both because of situation factors (such as a more paternalistic corporate culture) and because of his personal values and leadership style. For these reasons, the change process focused on the retraining, retention, and reassignment of existing personnel [Chakravorty 1991; McKibben 1990]. As in the situations studied above, however, Gillette followed no pre-existing formula in its entirety in implementing change. Rather, the solution was to creatively meet specific company requirements by adapting familiar tools drawn from the experiences of others and from behavioral theory, as well as by creating new approaches tailored specifically to Gillette's special needs [Chakravorty 1991; McKibben 1990].

David Johnson took similar steps when he became president of Campbell Soup Co. in January 1990 [Freedman 1991], as did Louis Gerstner, the former head of American Express Company, when he was brought in to head RJR Nabisco Holdings Inc. in 1989 [Anders 1991].

Each management change studied followed the general patterns modelled in Figure 12-2: appropriate factor areas were examined, and in light of them appropriate general decisions or decision and action frameworks were formulated. Specific plans were developed and implemented within these general strategic action frameworks as the situation progressed and evolved.

Each particular corporation, however, had unique problems and methods for dealing with the problems of realignment. At times, wholesale replacement or firing of individuals was dictated (Chase, Westcon). At other times, existing personnel were retrained and reassigned rather than let go (Gillette). In other situations, the corporate structure and culture were changed, along with a balance of other types of staffing changes (Detroit Diesel, RJR Nabisco, Union Pacific).

These examples show that key managers in many ways most often go beyond contingency guidelines or situational management approaches such as the one outlined in Figure 12-2. Considerable creative management and leadership was required — to effect changes, handle differing people and personalties, infer needed adjustments, deal with emergencies, and the like. This suggests that strategy implementation is as much an art as it is a discipline. While systematically organized bodies of reasoning and action are useful, it is equally important to go beyond them when implementing strategies. The ability to analyze specific situations and to tailor general approaches to these requirements, as well as to integrate more rational approaches within the art of creative leadership and management, appears to have been the ultimate keys to success in the companies studied.

ORGANIZATION PLANNING FOR STRATEGY IMPLEMENTATION

Organization structures used to meet varying business strategy needs can range from traditional, hierarchical structures — such as functional, divisional, and strategic business units — to collaborative ones — such as matrix, network, systems, and team/group structures, and strategic alliances.

Traditional Hierarchical Structures

Simple structures. Individual entrepreneurs initially have a direct relationship with employees, as shown in Figure 12-3. Such a structure is adequate for small and highly focused companies.

Functional structures. Under a *functional organization structure*, a company is organized by tasks or activities, such as marketing, production/operations, finance/accounting, and research

Figure 12-3: Simplest Organization Structure

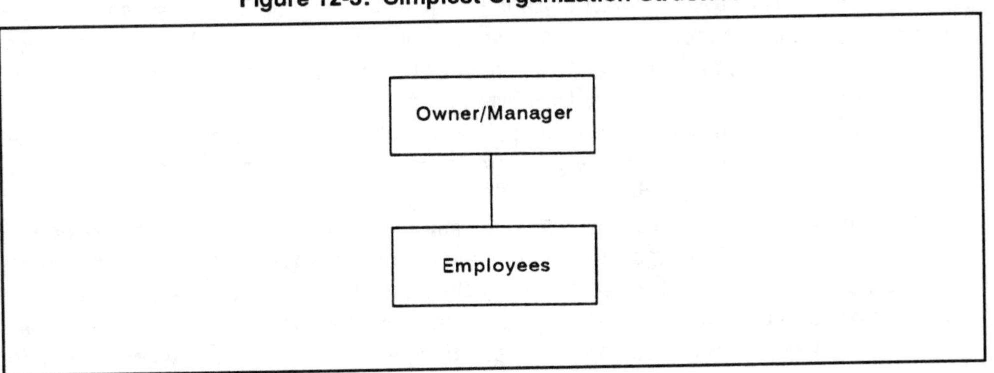

Figure 12-4: Functional Organization Structure

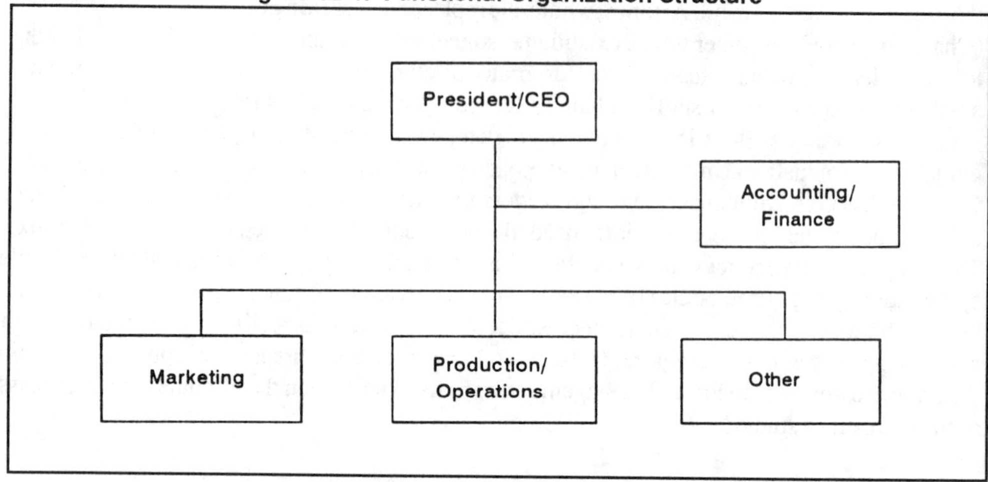

and development or other appropriate categories, as shown in Figure 12-4. This type of organization structure can increase efficiency in functional specialties, simplify functional decision making, and enable top management to maintain strategic control of company operations. Some of its disadvantages are that it can increase difficulties in coordinating and decision making between functional areas, limit training and development of general managers, and create interdepartment rivalries which make implementation of enterprise-wide changes more difficult. Such a structure usually works best with businesses that have limited product/service lines and markets, such as the regional baked goods company discussed in Chapter 7.

Divisional structure. As a business grows, it often diversifies. Diversification can involve products or services, geographic scope, channels of distribution, or customers. At some point, the functional organization structure often becomes inadequate and *divisional organizations*, such as those shown in Figure 12-5, become more appropriate. Major automobile companies have product divisions, international companies often have geographic divisions, and companies serving both industrial and consumer markets often organize by customer category.

Advantages of such an organization structure are that it can enable business segments to be run and evaluated as profit centers encourage the development of more broadly trained managers, promote faster response to market needs, and permit strategy formulation at management levels closer to the competitive environment. Disadvantages are that it can lead to a duplication of staff services, create difficulties in coordinating policy formulation, lessen top management control of operations, create competition for scarce corporate resources, and increase the need for strategic management and thinking.

Strategic business units (SBUs). As companies grow and divisional structures become unwieldy, companies often organize around strategic business groupings, such as products, territories, or other divisional areas. Such structures, shown in Figure 12-6, are useful for managing operations with distinct strategic concerns and competitive market environments. When the pulp and paper company Mead Corporation purchased a small computer information

Figure 12-5: Divisional Organization Structure

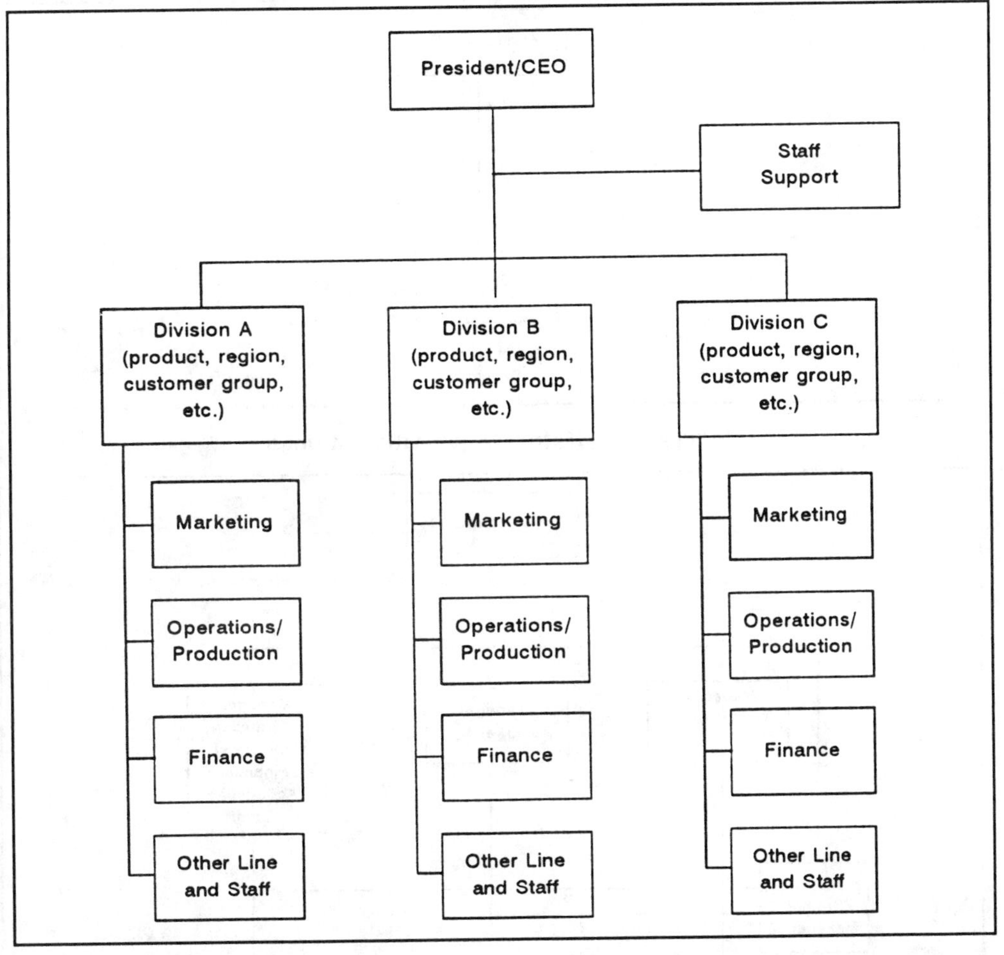

company in 1968, it set it up as a separate strategic business unit, to enable it to respond to changing competitive market needs that were very different from Mead's. That SBU, now known as Mead Data Central, provides such computer information services as LEXIS and NEXIS (legal, business, and news information services). Its sales, which have averaged more than 30 percent annual growth since 1976, approached half a billion dollars in 1991 [Caillot 1991].

Collaborative Structures

Matrix organization structure. Business complexities often dictate crossways organization structures, such as the one shown in Figure 12-7. More than 30 years ago, Procter & Gamble used product or brand managers to coordinate marketing management of product lines which were

Figure 12-6: SBU Organization Structure

President/CEO
SBU A
SBU B
SBU C
Divisions
Divisions
Divisions

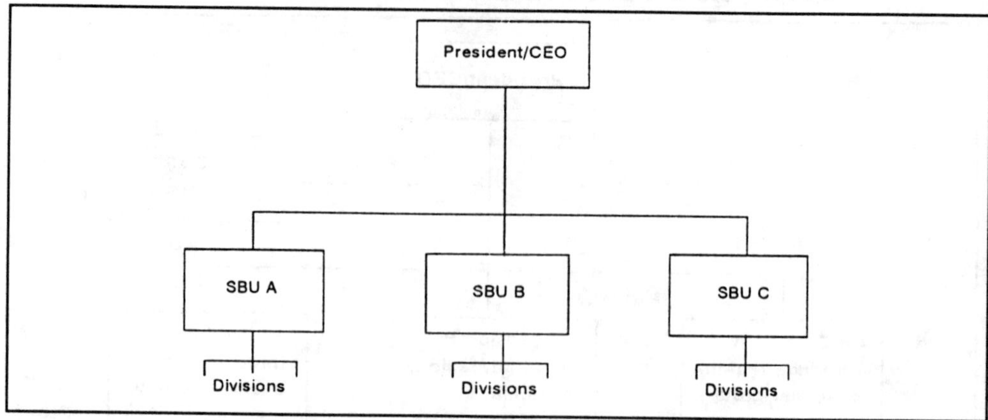

Figure 12-7: Matrix Organization Structure

President/CEO
Manager Operations/ Production
Manager Marketing
Manager Information Systems/ Finance Accounting Other
Brand/ Project Manager A
Brand/ Project Manager B
Brand/ Project Manager C

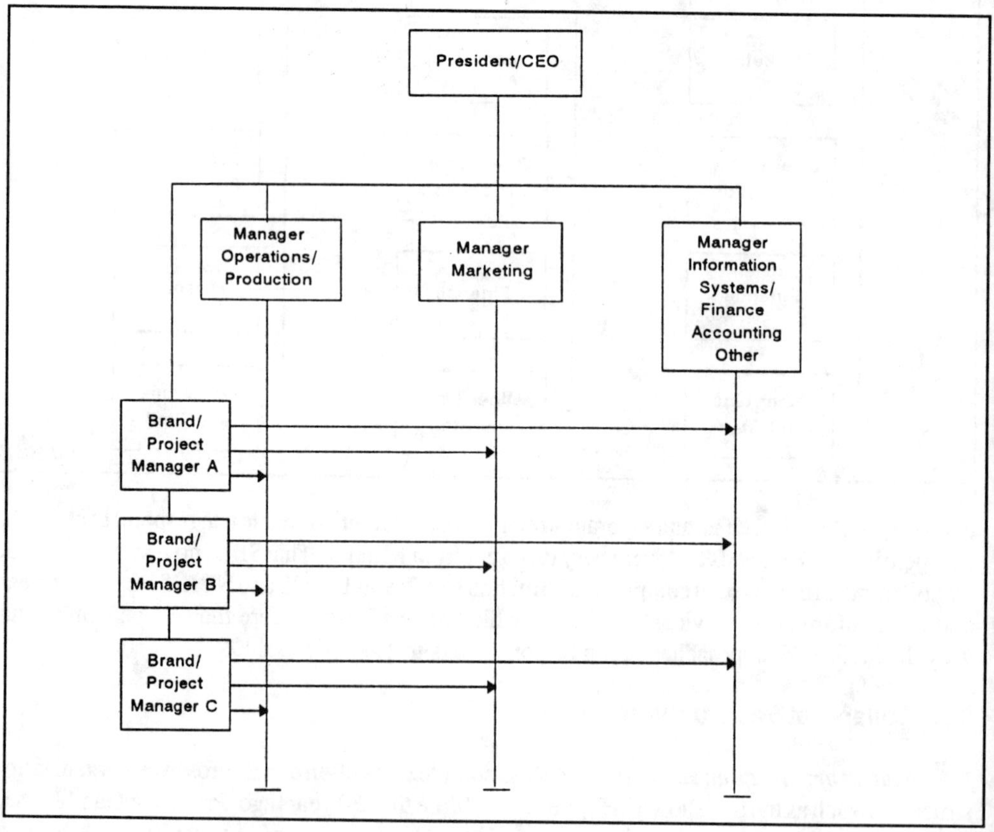

serviced by functional operations such as manufacturing and sales. In this way, each product line's special marketing needs were emphasized, while the efficiencies associated with functional specialization were retained.

Newer collaborative organization structures. The growing need for cooperative work groups to meet competitive market requirements, advances in telecommunications, the information explosion, and the growing complexity of many markets has led to a search for new organization structures which allow for greater *collaboration* among diverse business units and which go beyond the two-dimensional matrix organization structures described in the preceding section. The need for information and the ability to acquire and exchange information electronically has contributed significantly to the growth of such collaborative organization structures [Keen 1986, 1988, 1989; Stanat 1990].

Collaborative organization structures at lower management levels may be permanently organized teams or groups for continuing exploitation of some strategic opportunity area. They may also be temporary (or *ad hoc*) teams or groups, as at several global construction companies, where project group members are located worldwide, yet work together on a single project. Such temporary organization structures are often referred to as *adhocracy* types of organization [Huber 1992].

At higher management levels, information or system network hubs or management groups have developed. Such collaborative organization structures are referred to as *network*, or *systems-based*, organizations. A hub is a small group of people responsible for the strategic focus of the company and for control of company assets [Kilmann 1989; Houghton 1989; Stanat 1990]. Like many lower-level collaborative groups, they can be physically located together or linked by computer and/or communications mechanisms. At the same time they may be electronically linked with those working outside the hub through telecommunications and computer networks. The tendency towards this kind of core management group organization at the corporate level is partially evidenced by the major reductions in corporate staff which occurred during the late 1980s and early 1990s [Greenwald 1991]. While these groups may use hierarchical titles such as "president" and "vice presidents of...," working relationships often are not organized in a traditional organizational hierarchy but instead are organized around several nontraditional functions or processes, such as setting strategic goals and monitoring the results, collecting strategic information, identifying customer needs, attracting resources, delivering new services to operating units, and managing, coordinating, and controlling the network.

These strategic management groups function to facilitate and coordinate business processes, negotiate conflicts, generate ideas, and perform other collaborative tasks. To some degree these new organization structures were made possible by telecommunications and computer information systems technology advances, since they rely heavily on these technologies [Chismar 1991; Keen 1991; Malone 1992].

The organization below and outside the hub or core can be a hybrid. These organizations, therefore, can use any organization form appropriate to their needs, ranging from hierarchical structures to newer collaborative ones, such as the "cluster" organization —groups of people drawn from different disciplines who work together on a semipermanent basis in clusters or self-contained units within an organization [Mills 1991].

Collaborative structures are especially needed where the environment is turbulent, technology is emerging and developing rapidly, the business is highly diversified and geographically dispersed, and competition is aggressive. They are often found in high-tech and financial services companies, and in professional organizations of lawyers, accountants, doctors, and consultants.

Many domestic U.S. corporations, as well as global firms, are finding that collaborative arrangements between firms can be effective. For example, Corning Inc.'s fiber, fiber-optic, and fiber cable businesses serving the telecommunications industry have collaborative alliances both in the United States and abroad [Hammond 1991; Houghton 1989]. Ford and Mazda have an alliance that has lasted over ten years [Treece 1992]. Many such *strategic alliances,* both successes and failures, are described by Badaracco [1990] and Kanter [1989]. They are often referred to as *symbiotic* organizations or *semipermanent symbiosis* [Huber 1992].

Such crossways, collaborative, team organization structures are not always easy to initiate or maintain. They require additional coordination, are difficult for many people to work under, and demand shared authority and responsibility. For these reasons, they sometimes require many years to install, reduce efficiency and increase costs over the short run, and often require changing the entire work environment/context, including compensation, plant layouts, worker attitudes, supervisory practices, and hiring and decision-making processes. Monsanto Corporation was undergoing such a transition to a team organization structure in 1991 at its huge chemical and nylon complex in Pensacola, Florida. At that time, management felt it would take three more years to complete the changeover [Cohen 1991]. At AT&T's Clark, New Jersey, plant it took less than two years to organize the plant's 318-employee workforce into 14 cross-functional, vertically integrated teams whose combined efforts reduced costs 30 percent on the plant's only product (an underwater fiber-optic repeater) and saved the plant from closing [Noble 1992].

Collaborative team organization structures are not suitable for every business. In 1988 Volvo designed a car assembly plant in Sweden that abandoned the traditional assembly line and instead had teams of highly skilled workers build an entire car. Contrary to the high hopes for this experiment in humanistic manufacturing, the team approach doubled the labor costs for assembling a car and management was considering ending the approach in 1992 [Prokesch 1991].

In spite of the difficulties, business in general is moving towards having more adaptive organization structures, that is, more flexible organizations able to meet continually changing competitive market pressures [Lublin 1992]. Some approaches to developing adaptive organization designs and examples of them are discussed in the following section.

Reengineering a Company's Business Processes: An Adaptive Situational Process of Organization Design

The business organization process involved in redesigning or reengineering the internal business processes and then reorganizing operations to meet the needs of these newly designed processes is not new [Hammer 1992]. In the early days of computer systems development in business in the early 1960s, for example, there were methods analysts whose job was to study work flows and recommend changes in the business process to improve efficiency and effectiveness as a first step in developing and introducing computer information systems. The author worked on such business systems engineering efforts. The common wisdom then was that the major benefits of any computer systems development effort was not in the computer's contribution, but in the improvements in operations which arose from the business processes study. In fact, the improvements from the study were sometimes put into place without the introduction of computer systems.

Many business process reengineering studies being done today, while often more complex and elaborate, are fundamentally the same as those encountered 30 years ago. For example, Henk Sol of Delft University (Belgium) describes how, when working on a computer systems project, the preliminary business process analysis done in 1991 for Heineken Breweries led to major improvements in the transportation system itself at the port of Rotterdam. This major benefit (half a million dollars per year cost saving) resulted from the preliminary study and business process changes made based on it, prior to any benefits which came from the installation of any new computer systems [Sol 1992; Sol and Streng 1992].

AT&T Credit, American Telephone & Telegraph Corp.'s financing subsidiary (strategic business unit), which has $2.5 billion in assets and 300,000 customer accounts, provides another business process reengineering example, one unrelated to computer information systems design studies.

AT&T Credit's business consists mainly of providing financing for computer system sales by American Telephone and Telegraph's sales force. When initially formed in 1985, the business processes at AT&T Credit were organized based on two premises: large companies would buy large AT&T equipment and systems and require complicated financing, while small companies would buy smaller systems and accept standard forms of financing. Working with these assumed customer needs, AT&T Credit had one group of employees process national accounts and large transactions individually, while a white-collar assembly line processed purchases made by small companies.

The processes set up for handling credit applications from the AT&T sales force were not effective. Large accounts wanted speedier approval service, while small accounts wanted more flexible financing and personal service. By 1989, things were chaotic: there were long delays, lost paperwork, generally poor customer service, and low worker morale. AT&T Credit decided to let the division personnel reengineer its own business processes — a "bottoms-up" approach. First, it chose ten AT&T Credit employees, trained them in team building and organization design, and allowed them to devote 50 percent of their time to redesigning a merged and reenergized customer-service process. Second, the team interviewed customers, AT&T equipment and system salespeople, and division employees to determine customer and service needs. Third, the team sifted through all the information gathered and did a business process analysis — a work flow analysis tracing what happened from the time a customer application was submitted, through approving it, and later servicing it and collecting the final payment. The team then spent five days at a resort where it at last developed a new organization structure, new job descriptions, and new information systems which matched the work flow analysis with the internal available resources.

The new organization was set up geographically, with 20 regions, each handling all customers in its area. Customers were assigned to portfolio managers who were responsible for managing all aspects of each account. Bonuses were based on the performance of the entire geographic unit. In essence, the internal business process and organization were reengineered around individual customer needs. Once the organization was redesigned based on the reengineering of the business process, existing personnel had to apply for the newly designed jobs, with the screening and selection being handled by an employee group [Deutsch 1991].

The change process at AT&T Credit was a situational one, like the one shown in Figure 12-2. Situation factors were first studied. The extent of the change in internal business processes was to be substantial, but the timing (no imminent competitive threats) and nature of the business (almost entirely in-house financial services) permitted full involvement of existing staff. It was also necessary to examine the strategic business unit's purpose and overall strategy — serve specific types of customers in a specific way to meet those customers' specific needs in order to enable as many of them as possible to buy AT&T equipment and still be able to collect the stream of payments. Economies of processing were not the dominant consideration; customer convenience and satisfaction were.

In light of the new strategic objectives, the business process was restudied and reengineered to create a more effective customer-service operation — one that met actual customer needs, not those imagined by AT&T Credit management or dictated by the existing organization structure. Management did not start by reorganizing jobs or tasks or people. They started with identifying the business processes required to better serve customers. The business process was what was first redesigned. Only later were the detailed conventional organization, staffing, and information systems steps taken, as the needed changes in work routines, organization, staff assignments, and information systems were put in place to enable the new process to function. Implementation was aided considerably by having those affected by the change plan and carry out the change.

Leadership here was cooperative, which helped move the corporate culture away from a hierarchical one towards a more team-oriented one. This facilitated a balanced approach to organization realignments: the staff itself administered the organization structure changes and staffing reassignments needed to implement new strategies. Finally, it was recognized that fine tuning would be needed and that the group should be prepared to continually refine and readjust as customer needs evolved, new people entered the organization, and new ways to improve operations were developed [Deutsch 1991].

What might be overlooked in analyzing this situation was that the major long-term benefit arising from this reengineering process was not the substantially new organization created for the unit. The major long-term benefit was that in the process of reengineering the division an adaptive internal organization — prepared to keep changing in the future — was created. In place were market-oriented teams that were trained to be responsive to changing customer needs. In place was an adaptive organization that was seeped in strategic thinking and ready to continue adapting as necessary.

Not an Isolated Example

AT&T's experience is not an isolated one. Over 20 companies studied have over the past few years moved towards having more adaptive organizations. One of the better known examples is Union Pacific Railroad.

When Michael Walsh became head of Union Pacific Railroad in 1986, he quickly established an overall vision of customer accommodation to meet the competitive requirements in the turbulent domestic transportation industry. In keeping with this vision, success depended on the company's ability to respond more quickly to customers' changing shipping needs at the yard level. This was almost impossible under the existing organization, since decisions passed through many layers of management and could not be made quickly. In addition, Walsh faced an intransigent bureaucracy which was not prepared for change.

Confronted with these problems, Walsh immediately changed the corporate structure by reducing the layers of management from nine to three. This both simplified and speeded up decision making and sent out a signal that change was coming, with or without the cooperation of middle managers, whose positions would be by-passed and eventually eliminated if they couldn't facilitate change. A new computerized information system was also introduced to enable operating personnel at the customer decision level to get a quick response to proposed scheduling changes from a computerized, integrated, company-wide traffic control center [Hayes 1992; Machalaba 1991]. In this situation, the enabling change agents included Walsh's leadership, changes in the organization context, and the introduction of new computer information systems technology.

By using new enabling computer information systems, Pepperidge Farms was able to integrate its order processing and production scheduling operations and reduce reorder time by over two-thirds. This major business process change helped maintain freshness and enabled faster exploitation of new product trends, two keys to business success [Forsythe 1989]. New computer systems technology also enabled Banc One [Lohr 1991; Quint 1989] and most airlines [Pepper 1991] to implement business process changes which helped improve performance. Chapter 11 discussed many other examples of how using computer systems led to major changes in organization environments that made them more responsive to changing market needs, that is, changes that made the organizations more adaptive.

DIRECTING, STAFFING, AND ACQUIRING RESOURCES

Organization structures initially exist only on paper. The effectiveness of those structures in putting strategies to work in a business to make profits depends, to a large extent, on skillfully directing and staffing the implementation.

Directing

Managers can affect the success of strategy implementation in several key areas.

Leadership style. Different leadership styles can be appropriate for different strategy implementation situations.

One of the major reasons cited for the successful rebirth and turnaround of Salomon Brothers brokerage firm after the 1991 trading scandal was the appointment of Warren Buffet as CEO. Buffet, an Omaha investor noted for his conservative management style and philosophy, implanted a very conservative, risk-aversive culture at Salomon and so enabled it to regain customer confidence. This was the same style Buffet exhibited in successfully managing Berkshire Hathaway Inc., another of his investments [Faison 1992; Norris 1991]. It was a style that enabled him to win the trust of managers at Salomon, an important leadership success factor.

At Chase Manhattan's Municipal Bond Division, where major changes were required by a new strategy and key division personnel were not to be involved in the new organization, a cooperative approach did not initially seem appropriate. Rather, changes were instituted from the top, many existing personnel were transferred or released, and a new, "brash" authoritarian division head was hired from outside Chase [Doran 1989].

Andrew Grove faced a different situation at Intel where leading in technological product development was a strategic company goal ["Breaking" 1983]. In a highly technical field, newer and younger employees are usually better informed about the latest technology. In this situation, therefore, situation requirements dictated a more collaborative and people-oriented leadership style and organization structure, since highly-skilled professionals generally do not do their best work in a highly-structured authoritarian environment.

Determining which leadership style or combination of styles might be most effective in a reader's specific situation will depend on situation factors such as those shown in Figure 12-2 and discussed earlier. An analysis of these factors may lead to the conclusion that a single leadership style will best suit the situation under study, or that a combination of leadership styles is more appropriate. For example, Thomas Murphy and Daniel Burke, who were credited with turning the merged Capital Cities and ABC Communications Company into a money machine, used a mixed style characterized as "prudence, management autonomy, and meddling when it is called for" [Auletta 1991; Kneale 1990].

At other times, the leadership style needed will change over time as situation requirements change. For example, at AM International a tough analytical leadership style was needed initially to take the company out of bankruptcy; subsequently a style oriented towards people and strategic thinking was needed [Johnson 1987]. Alan Rowe has developed tests to determine what balance of leadership styles an individual possesses, and which ones seem to be appropriate for specific management situations under study [Rowe 1987].

Communication and corporate culture. While all types of communication are useful in implementing strategies, oral communication is especially important to implementing enterprise-wide strategies and carrying out the planning effort [Povejsil 1989; Reimann 1990]. Oral communication, used in conjunction with other forms of communication, affects strategy implementation directly through its impact on the individuals involved in implementation. It encourages participation in strategy formation, refinement, and implementation as well as enables direct communication of corporate strategies once formulated. By indicating upper management's involvement and belief in the strategic vision, it can create enthusiasm and motivate personnel. Over the long term, it affects implementation through its impact on creating or redirecting the corporate culture.

Corporate culture refers to the shared values, beliefs, expectations, and norms within a specific company. This culture develops over time based on a variety of occurrences. It provides a framework for action, and so can be an important factor in furthering the strategic thinking needed for effective implementation. An organization culture, like individual attitudes and behavior, can be influenced in various ways.

Organization culture development techniques are built on a central premise: what people working in a company think is important is derived from their perception of what their leaders think is important. What their leaders think is important is revealed as much by these leaders' actions as by their formal written pronouncements. Leaders can communicate their basic strategic thinking through a mixture of oral, written, and physical approaches, such as:

- What they pay attention to, measure, and control during oral communication at meetings and while talking informally with company personnel.
- Their reactions to crises and emergencies and other critical incidents. For example, many companies, such as Gillette, are known for not laying off workers during economic downturns and so are perceived as having a more humane attitude towards employees and as being interested in employees' commitments to strategic goals.
- The examples they set. For example, Intel's chairman Andrew Grove refused to fly first class and did not use a limousine to reinforce his belief in the importance of his employees' participation on an equal basis in many decisions involving their technical expertise.
- The kind of coaching they provide and their reward and punishment system.
- Their criteria for recruitment, selection, and promotion. One of the clearest measures of what kind of strategy company managers believe in is the kind of people they hire.
- Stories and legends. Peters cites several legendary stories [1985 pp. 278-279], such as the one about a new manager at Procter & Gamble who drove three hundred miles one night in order to take care of a problem with a bar of soap. This story was designed to impress on all who heard it how important maintaining product quality was to success at Procter & Gamble.
- Organization design. For example, using a collaborative or network organization structure helps foster integrative decision making and strategic thinking, as shown in several company situations described earlier in this chapter.
- Design and condition of physical facilities. For example, at Intel, office space was uniform for all employees, a design which reinforced the company's integrative decision-making processes.
- Formal statements of company policy, creeds, and philosophy. While necessary in most larger companies, by themselves they have only minor influence on corporate culture formulation.

The way corporate culture can have a major impact on strategy implementation was evident at General Motors. The strong corporate culture at its older Pontiac 6000 plant was credited with the plant's outstanding quality record, while GM's newer Orion, Michigan plant — which was equipped with 170 robots and did not have as cohesive and favorable a corporate culture — had major product quality problems [Patterson 1991]. Because of its impact on success, corporate culture is a key situation factor to be considered in making implementation decisions such as what organization structures, leadership styles, communication techniques, incentives, staffing, and controls to use.

Motivation. Motivation is a key to obtaining the necessary commitment from those carrying out the strategies and related enabling plans. An enabling corporate culture, aligned with enterprise-wide strategic directions, and strong leadership help sustain motivation over the years. The many examples of participative management and decision making discussed in this book present useful motivators. Several other examples of the wide range of ways to motivate people in business are cited by Peters [1982]:

- Brand managers at Procter & Gamble were expected to compete fiercely, with the winners being considered something akin to war heroes
- Inspirational meetings are held regularly for the salesforces at Tupperware, Electrolux, and Mary Kay Cosmetics
- Employees meet regularly to sing company songs and hear speeches at many Japanese companies

More than psychic rewards, inspirational speeches, peer pressure, and participation in decision making are needed over the long run to make a strategy work. People also respond in large measure to monetary rewards. One of the keys to the very supportive corporate culture at Cooper Tire & Rubber Company reportedly is the firm's generous stock purchase program which has made many long-term employees millionaires [Hymowitz 1991]. In fact, monetary rewards are often used to overcome other organization and leadership steps that might at first seem to discourage employee commitment to a specified strategy. At Chase Manhattan's Municipal Bond Division, employees working in the new organization were given major stakes in income generated by the new division [Doran 1989]. Such moves can in certain situations overcome potential internal organization and people problems.

Very often, strategy implementation cannot be measured and so rewarded in relation to current earnings. Strategies often take years to implement and can reduce earnings during the early years of implementation. Several approaches have been developed for relating rewards for long-term strategy implementation to benchmarks other than short-term profits. For example, Stonich has described a system that combines three approaches [1984]:

- *Weighted factors method.* This method assigns weights to key factors affecting strategic goals — such as market share, sales growth, or progress in meeting the success criteria significant in a market. Or, in situations involving more stable markets, cash generation or return on investment (ROI) might be given more weight. Any combination of these suitable to the situation might be used. The weight given each critical benchmark measure is used in determining the bonus or salary increase.
- *Long-term evaluation method.* This method measures performance over a longer period of time. For example, the period may be three to five years, and the reward may be linked to meeting an earnings or profit goal at the end of the designated period.
- *Strategic funds method.* This method designates and tracks those funds spent for achieving strategic goals and separates them from those required for shorter-term operations. In this way, current performance can be judged separately and the manager is not burdened with the negative impact that working towards long-range goals can have on current performance.

Such approaches are suggested mainly for situations involving SBUs within a major company, though the basic tools used are adaptable to other incentive award situations.

These and other incentive reward systems useful in implementing strategies attempt to relate rewards to achievement of strategic goals over the long run, or to the accomplishment of the tasks necessary to achieve those strategic goals over a shorter run. For example, the awards at AT&T Credit were given to the entire unit, in order to focus attention on the group effort. As is seen in the discussion of controls later in this chapter, these shorter-term goals can also go beyond financial budgetary goals and involve strategic program goals and goals related directly to strategic keys to success.

Commitment. Effective implementation requires the commitment of managers and other company personnel to a company's strategic vision. A common way to obtain commitment is to have those affected by any change participate in designing the change, as was done at Gillette. It was also done at AT&T Credit, American Telephone & Telegraph's Corp.'s financing division: every aspect of its new structure, from the description of the president's job to the decor, was designed by employees. As reported, the project's success showed that the Japanese process of bottoms-up consensus management did work to obtain commitment in at least one U.S. corporate culture [Deutsch 1991]. Another key to success is obtaining and maintaining credibility and trust since commitment is difficult to sustain without both. Corporate management must have a reputation of doing what it promises to do and of being trusted to act in the best interests of employees within the limits of business demands.

No matter how effectively change is managed, a problem often encountered is that people, no matter how well-intentioned, motivated, or directed, often are unable to change, at least to the degree or in the way required for a planned strategy. In these situations, the question to be solved is finding or developing people who can do the job — a staffing issue.

Staffing

As a picture emerges of the kind of people needed, based on an analysis of the organization plans developed to meet strategic management requirements, staffing decisions are made.

Top management. Depending on how the strategy was formulated and the nature of the strategy being implemented, the board of directors may decide that a new chief executive officer (CEO) is needed. This may occur for several reasons.

First, the *leadership skills* of the present CEO or division manager may not match the skills required by a new strategy. For example, one of the reasons given for the abrupt termination of Peter Cohen in early 1990 as chairman and chief executive of Shearson Lehman Hutton, a major brokerage firm, was that he seemed to lack the "personal touch" needed to create a "new identity for the firm in the 1990s" [Rustin 1990].

Second, the *strategic beliefs* of CEOs can affect the kind of strategy implemented. For this reason, a company may seek out a new CEO who shares its vision of the company's future, as the board at Salomon Brothers did in 1991 when they brought in Warren Buffet after the government securities trading scandal. Not only did Buffet have the reputation for integrity needed to save the company, his personal values and leadership style were extremely conservative, something needed to convince investors that the firm could change and survive the scandal's bad publicity, and possible customer defections [Faison 1992; Norris 1991].

Third, the *personality* of the CEO can be a factor in strategic implementation staffing decisions [Conger 1988; Zaleznik 1989]. Chrysler's Lee Iaccoca is an outstanding example of how a charismatic president can make a critical difference in a company's turnaround strategy implementation. Many of the problems encountered in trying to merge Time Inc. and Warner Communications were attributed to the personality differences between Steven Ross of Warner and other key executives designated to eventually succeed him. These problems were resolved only when one key executive was forced to resign and Ross, who was ill with cancer, eventually took a leave of absence [Cohen 1992].

The staffing choice may involve no changes in top management personnel when major strategic changes occur. At A&W Root Beer a change in strategy occurred when the company was taken private by the existing managers in 1986. With this change in corporate ownership, the existing top managers were able to make major strides in instituting their new strategies [Deutsch 1989]. The staffing choice, therefore, may be to continue with existing management, especially in those situations where the existing CEO initiated the new strategic direction or where the strategic change is incremental or not substantial.

Other management levels. Staffing is not limited to selecting a CEO to implement planned strategic changes. Many other levels of management can be involved. At Chase Manhattan, for example, many existing personnel left or were transferred when new strategies were introduced [Doran 1989]. New top managers frequently bring in people they have worked with elsewhere.

Wholesale changes in personnel are not, however, always possible or desirable. Management development and training is another alternative in situations where more than just leadership and motivation skills are needed to make necessary transitions. Decisions about whether or not to keep existing staff or replace them, and about whether or not and what kind of training will be most effective, depend on the key situation factors shown at the top of Figure 12-2.

When decisions are made to use existing personnel and where existing personnel may need training to meet the new strategic needs, these key factors would be used to develop training programs. This was the case at British Airways in 1983 when new strategic directions emphasizing personalized service were introduced. Developing extensive and continuing training programs for existing personnel, at both the operating and management level, was stressed in order to ensure that the strategic thinking of top management permeated the entire organization [Lohr 1989].

Acquiring Needed Resources

In addition to finding and training staff, other resources will be needed to successfully implement strategies and related enabling plans.

Acquiring resources can often be a major problem for new ventures. For instance, Orbital Sciences Corporation had formulated its strategic plans for creating new ways to launch satellites, established working relationships with Martin Marietta Corporation and NASA, and obtained initial financing of several million dollars from a private investor by late 1983. The feasibility of the venture at that point depended on raising an additional $50 million. The founders decided to raise the money by selling limited partnership units. According to the financing agreement, all the shares or units had to be sold by the end of 1983 or the entire deal would be called off. They were not sold, but further negotiations permitted the remainder to be sold in 1984 and the new venture proceeded [Perry 1989]. While resource needs normally are defined as strategies and related enabling plans are developed and as resource acquisition is planned, therefore, in some situations the implementation of an enterprise-wide strategy can require considerable effort and ingenuity in order to obtain the needed resources.

CONTROL

Management control has been defined as "the process by which managers influence other members of an organization to implement the organization's strategy" [Anthony 1989]. In this general sense, management control encompasses much of what has already been covered in this chapter. More specifically, control of implementation involves developing standards or measures, tracking performance, measuring performance against standards, highlighting deviations, and taking corrective action [Mockler 1972].

Since the idea underlying control is to measure performance against a standard and since the standard is the strategy and its enabling planning extensions, strategic plans serve as the basis for management control. Three aspects of strategy formulation discussed in earlier chapters are covered here: financial budgets and other financial control tools; short- and long-range programming; and critical success factors.

Financial Budgets and Other Financial Control Tools

Financial budgets that are extensions of strategic plans and that are used to provide a framework for departmental planning and budgeting are useful for integrated strategic management control purposes. Financial budgets can range from less than a year to more than 10 years, depending on specific company requirements. The most common kinds of budgets are for sales/revenue, expenses/outlays, profits, capital outlays, cash-flow, and return on investment (ROI).

Sales budgets measure the potential market acceptance of a company's products or services, and so can serve as a useful measure of one key aspect of strategic management — success in the marketplace.

Expense budgets can be especially useful in strategic situations where low-cost production has a major impact on success. This was the case at Shaw Industries, the carpet manufacturer, and the Phar-Mor discount retail chain, where success depends on keeping costs and selling prices low [Hirsch 1991; Ruffenach 1991].

Capital outlay budgets are used to control allocation of resources to strategically important areas of a company's operations. When combined with profit and loss figures, they provide measures of return on investment (ROI), the acid test of the success of any company in a capitalistic environment. Return on investment measures are significant control tools for owners of a company, since they measure their return on investment in the company, and ultimately the value of their capital.

Cash-flow budgets help to plan and subsequently control the flow of funds in and out of the company, and so the company's ability to meet operating expenses and capital outlay needs.

Performance variations from financial budget standards are measured in dollars and percentages. When these variations exceed predetermined limits, control action is considered. Unfortunately, for strategic management purposes this kind of control has limited value. While such controls help keep operations in line with plans on an interim basis, they provide information after the results are in — long after the strategic moves have been made.

In publicly-held companies, the financial controls can go one step further and incorporate stockholder value. Since stock represents the owners' equity in a company, this is another way of analyzing return on investment — from the stockholders' viewpoint. The actual price of the stock, its earnings per share, or the net worth per share are several measures of stock value. Less obvious, though equally important, is the intrinsic value of the common stock — a value which ultimately affects future market value. This value may be based on a company's value when it is broken up into individual parts, or on potential earnings per share, or on any of the factors affecting earnings potential ["Shareholder Value" January/February and March/April 1988]. Such so-called "value-based" analyses have relevance for strategic management, since the success of many companies is judged by such criteria. Therefore, part of any control system developed today would include consideration of its impact on underlying stock or asset or company sale values from the owners' point of view. And the progress of any strategy would be monitored by such value-based criteria as net breakup value of a company, where the company situation warrants it.

Short- and Long-Range Programming

As noted in Chapter 8, programs are detailed maps of how to carry out planned actions. On a simple operational level, they may be no more than project schedules designed to control a planned project's execution. Where they involve major programs directly affecting the implementation of strategic plans, they are of concern to company management since they can serve as a strategic control tool.

Both short- and long-term programs are useful where they provide points from which to measure the progress of specific actions leading to effective strategy implementation. For example, the long-term strategic success of a new publication may require penetration of specific demographic markets, such as the 25- to 40-year-old age group. To do this, certain sales promotions must be scheduled and carried out over a specified period of time and specific editorial themes emphasized in the publication's articles. Using these two scheduled promotional and editorial programs as benchmark criteria, the results of specific promotions and editorial policies can be studied to see if the company's strategy is working over the short run.

For example, over an initial six-month period, the percentage of orders obtained from mailings of introductory offers to subscribe to the new publication (measured as a percentage of orders received per 1000 pieces of mail sent) can be tracked to measure initial consumer response to the new publication. Subsequently, the subscription renewal rate of consumers who ordered introductory trial subscriptions are tracked to measure the interest these readers have shown in the new publication's editorial material. At the same time, newsstand sales are tracked as another measure of reader interest in the publication.

A favorable reading in these areas of measurement would provide a basis for continuing the new publication as initially conceived. Unfavorable results would dictate either abandoning the venture or modifying its strategic editorial profile.

Short-term programs are likely to be more precise and provide specific measures of variation. Long-term programs tend to be less precise and rely more on measuring results against general strategic key-to-success criteria.

Critical Success Factors: Key Control Points

As discussed in Chapter 4, strategic management is based on meeting key-to-success requirements in the opportunity areas targeted by a company. These success factors can in turn be the basis for measuring and controlling progress towards strategic goals. To do this, the general statements of strategic success requirements are translated into specific yardsticks. For example, a company may identify product quality as critical to succeeding in a selected market. This general statement might be more precisely defined by such product quality measurements as: number of customer complaints expressed as a percentage of total shipments; percentage of substandard units found by quality control or percentage of returned products; and range of deviations from specifications.

According to Lee Iacocca, Chrysler's turnaround strategy during the early 1980s used such strategic control factors, including [Iacocca 1983]:

- Cutting wage and salary costs substantially — Chrysler received major wage concessions from the union and reduced its labor costs by half
- Cutting the number of parts by one-third — which it did by a comfortable margin
- Improving product quality — which it did as evidenced by substantially lower warranty costs and scheduled maintenance costs
- Improving capital structure — which it did by converting bank debt into preferred and common stock
- Reducing fixed costs by $4 billion — which it pursued through major plant closings and modernization programs
- Improving product development — which it was doing through fuel economy and new technology leadership

In this instance, not meeting particular strategic subgoals in any critical area would probably have led to taking corrective action to meet these goals.

These critical control measures are often referred to as "value drivers." They are very often financial in nature, appropriate for the specific context under study, and are used as a basis for measuring individual manager performance and granting raises and promotions [McConahey

1992].

At times, the inability to meet success requirements can lead to a change in strategic plans. For example, when four large Japanese securities firms attempted to enter the Wall Street securities market, the results of their first five years in the market convinced them to make major modifications to their initial strategies. What started out as a "headlong rush" to seize a major share of traditional securities markets — a strategy similar in concept to that used by Japanese companies in the semiconductor and automobile markets — turned out to be far too expensive and futile in the securities business. During 1989, the firms scaled back operations considerably and shifted to selective niche strategies [Sterngold 1989].

Strategic control also involves monitoring key external economic and industry variables which might affect future success. Such factors can include changes in government attitudes and regulations, economic cycles, interest rates, and any of the many industry and competitive market factors covered in Chapters 3, 4, and 5. For example, many companies were forced to rethink their strategic moves into China during mid-1989, after the crackdown on student demonstrators, and into Russia, after the breakup of the Soviet Union in late 1991. These companies closely followed events during that period for indications of what the future might hold for foreign businesses.

While some attention has been paid to the kinds of control action that might possibly be taken based on the output of the strategic control system, control action is too situation- dependent to be discussed in detail here.

THE NEED FOR FLEXIBILITY

While it is possible to develop contingency plans for potential problems, not all problems can be anticipated. Considerable flexibility, therefore, is needed in implementing strategies and related enabling plans. Ideally when problems arise steps would be taken to bring operations more into line with planned goals, but this is not always possible.

Sometimes it is necessary to modify or even abandon plans. In these cases, the implementation process recycles information back through the initial phases of the process, since it provides information on changing industry and market trends, new opportunities and keys to success, and competitor moves. In this sense, the strategic management process is a continuing iterative process which requires monitoring and modification as the market changes and as competitors develop new initiatives.

REVIEW QUESTIONS

1. List and describe kinds of hierarchical organization structures found in business firms.
2. List and describe kinds of collaborative organization structures found in business, and discuss some of the changing business forces that have led to their development and use.
3. Describe the adaptive, semi-structured situational approach to making decisions in strategy implementation situations discussed in this chapter.

4. Discuss the importance of aligning organization structures with internal business processes, and the impact of computer information systems technology on organization structure.
5. Describe some of the leadership styles useful in implementing strategies and related enabling plans and the situations in which they may or may not be effective.
6. Discuss the importance of oral communications in strategy implementation.
7. Define corporate culture and its impact on implementation. Discuss some of the ways it can be influenced and molded.
8. Discuss some problems involved in measuring performance while implementing strategies and related enabling plans.
9. Discuss some of the problems involved in staffing for implementation.
10. Describe management control's relationship to strategic management and the use of key success factor analysis in establishing management controls for strategy implementation.

EXERCISES

1. Read recent issues of *Business Week, The New York Times,* or any other related management publication of your choice and find detailed descriptions of leadership's impact on a firm's success or failure. Write a report analyzing one of these companies and describing the ways the company situation does or does not illustrate points made in this chapter.

2. Do similar research and report on control's impact on a firm's strategic success or failure.

3. Several of the case studies in the section at the end of this book, including *Superb Biscuits, Blakeston and Wilson, Nordstrom, Cooper Tire and Rubber,* and *Michael Jewelers,* raise interesting questions about the impact of leadership, communications, staffing, corporate culture, and control on a firm's strategic success. Write a report on the impact of any or all of these on the strategy formulation and implementation in one of the company studies in the case study section.

4. Do further research on one of the companies identified in exercises 1, 2, or 3, and write a case study similar to those given in the case study section of this that you feel would be useful in furthering the learning goals of the strategic management course you are now taking.

REFERENCES

Anders, George, "Old Flamboyance Is Out as Louis Gerstner Remakes RJR Nabisco," *The Wall Street Journal,* March 21, 1991, pp. A1, A6.

Anthony, Robert N., *The Management Control Function,* Boston, MA: Harvard Business School Press, 1989.

Auletta, Ken, *Three Blind Mice: How the TV Networks Lost Their Way,* New York: Random House,

1991.

"Autocratic Leaders Now Out of Step," *USA Today*, December 9, 1991, pp. 1B, 2B.

Badaracco, Joseph L., *The Knowledge Link: How Companies Compete Through Strategic Alliances*, Boston, MA: Harvard Business School Press, 1990.

"Breaking Chains of Command," *Newsweek*, October 3, 1983, p. 23.

Caillot, Jacques, "Papier Mache: How a Paper Company Built a Leader in High Technology," *The Planning Forum Network*, August 1991, pp. 2, 4, 6.

Chakravorty, Subrata, "We Changed the Whole Playing Field: Triumph for Gillette's Colman Mockler — Technology as a Marketing Tool," *Forbes*, February 4, 1991, pp. 82-86.

Chismar, William, "Role of Information Technology in Structuring Multinational Corporations," *Hawaii International Conference on Systems Sciences (HICSS)*, 25th Annual Meeting, Kauai, Hawaii, January 7-10, 1992.

Cohen, Roger, "A Divorce in the Executive Suite: When Styles Clash, Time Warner's Rupture," *The New York Times*, February 24, 1992, pp. D1, D9.

Conger, Jay A., and Rabindra N. Kanungo, *Charismatic Leadership*, San Francisco, CA: Jossey-Bass, 1988.

Deutsch, Claudia H., "A&W: Prospering by Avoiding the Big Boys," *The New York Times*, Business Section, January 15, 1989, pp. 1, 10.

Deutsch, Claudia H., "Workers Get to Redesign Organization's Structure," *International Herald Tribune*, July 4, 1991, p. 11.

Doran, John J., "Ready for the Next Decade: Chase Manhattan Securities Inc. Revamps Its Municipal Banking and Bond Operations," *The Bond Buyer*, April 7, 1989, pp. 1ff.

Faison, Seth, "At Salomon, New Focus, New Attitude," *The New York Times*, February 15, 1992, pp. 37, 50.

Freedman, Alix M., "Campbell Chief Cooks Up Winning Menu," *The Wall Street Journal*, February 15, 1991, pp. B1, B5.

Forsythe, Jason, "Systems Give Pepperidge Farm Freshness," *InformationWeek*, March 20, 1989, pp. 29-31.

Greenwald, John, "Permanent Pink Slips," *Time*, September 9, 1991, pp. 54-55.

Hammer, Michael, *Re-Engineering Work*, New York: Warner Books, 1992.

Hammond, Keith H., "Corning's Class Act," *Business Week*, May 13, 1991, pp. 68-76.

Hayes, Thomas C., "Behind the Iron Hand at Tenneco," *The New York Times*, January 6, 1992, pp. D1, D5.

Hirsch, James S., "Brash Phar-Mor Chain Has Uneven Selection, But It's Always Cheap," *The Wall Street Journal*, June 24, 1991, pp. A1, A6.

Houghton, James R, "The Age of Hierarchy Is Over," *New York Times*, Business Section, September 25, 1989, p. 3.

Huber, George, "New Organizational Forms From New Information Technology," *Hawaii International Conference on Systems Sciences (HICSS)*, 25th Annual Meeting, Kauai, Hawaii, January 7-10, 1992.

Hymowitz, Carol, and Thomas O'Boyle, "Two Disparate Firms Find Keys to Success in Troubled Industries," *The Wall Street Journal*, May 29, 1991, pp. A1, A7.

Iacocca, Lee, "The Rescue and Resuscitation of Chrysler," *Journal of Business Strategy*, Summer 1983, pp. 67-69.

Johnson, Robert, "AM International's Ex-Chief Freeman Tells How His Success Got Him Fired," *The Wall Street Journal*, August 24, 1987, p. 21.

Kanter, Rosabeth Moss, *When Giants Learn to Dance*, New York: Simon and Schuster, 1989.

Keen, Peter G.W., *Business Without Bounds: Telecommunications and Business Strategy*, Hagerstown, MD: Ballinger Publishing, 1986.

Keen, Peter G.W., *Computing in Time: Using Telecommunications for Competitive Advantage*, Cambridge, MA: Ballinger Publishing Company, 1988.

Keen, Peter G.W., "Interview," *Information Management Review*, Winter 1989, pp. 65-75.

Keen, Peter W., "Redesigning the Organization Through Information Technology," *Planning Review*, May/June 1991, pp. 4-9.

Kilmann, Ralph H., "Tommorrow's Company Won't Have Walls," *The New York Times*, Business Section, June 18, 1989, p. 3.

Kneale, Dennis, "Murphy and Burke: Duo at Capital Cities Scores a Hit, but Can Network Be Part of It?", *The Wall Street Journal*, February 2, 1990, pp. A1, A6.

Lohr, Steve, "British Air's Profitable Private Life," *The New York Times*, Business Section, May 7, 1989, p. 4.

Lohr, Steve, "The Best Little Bank in America," *The New York Times*, Business Section, July 7, 1991, pp. 1, 4.

Lublin, Joann S., "Trying to Increase Worker Productivity, More Employers Alter Management Style," *The Wall Street Journal*, February 13, 1992, pp. B1, B3.

Machalaba, Daniel, "Tenneco, Recruiting New Chairman, Gets Ready for a Shakeup," *The Wall Street Journal*, August 8, 1991, pp. A1, A4.

Malone, Tom, and John Rockart, "Information Technology and the New Organization," *Hawaii International Conference on Systems Sciences (HICSS)*, 25th Annual Meeting, Kauai, Hawaii, January 7-10, 1992.

McConahey, Steve, Corporate and International Development (Planning Coordination), Kemper Financial Services Inc. *The Emerging Role of the Strategic Planner in the 1990's: Key Elements*, New York: Planning Forum's Strategic Planning Special Interest Group, April 8, 1992.

McKibben, Gordon, "Gillette's Mockler: Going Out at the Top," *The Boston Sunday Globe*, Business Section, November 18, 1990, pp. A1, A7.

Mills, D. Quinn, *Rebirth of the Corporation*, New York: Wiley. 1991.

Mockler, Robert J., *The Management Control Process*, Englewood Cliffs, NJ: Prentice-Hall, 1972.

Noble, Barbara Presley, "An Approach with Staying Power," *The New York Times*, Business Section, March 8, 1992, p. 23.

Norris, Floyd, "Forcing Salomon Into Buffett's Conservative Mold," *The New York Times*, Business Section, September 29, 1991, 8.

Patterson, Gregory A., "Two GM Auto Plants Illustrate Major Role of Workers' Attitudes: New Factory Lags in Quality, But an Older One Makes Cars With Few Defects," *The Wall Street Journal*, August 29, 1991, pp. A1, A5.

Pepper, Jon, "The MIS Battle for the Skies," *InformationWeek*, February 11, 1991, pp. 44-49.

Perry, Nancy O, "Shooting for the Stars," *HBS Bulletin*, June 1989, pp. 47-55.

Peters, Tom, and Nancy Austin, *A Passion for Excellence*, New York: Random House, 1985.

Peters, Tom, and Robert H. Waterman, *In Search of Excellence*, New York: Harper and Row, 1982, pp. 212, 276, 285.

Povejsil, Donald J., *Setting Strategic Direction: The Design of a Business Vision*, Seminar, New York: The Planning Forum, February 8, 1989.

Prokesch, Steven, "Edges Fray on Volvo's Brave New Humanistic World," *The New York Times*, Business Section, July 7, 1991, p. 5.

Quint, Michael, "A Bank That's Riding Technology to the Top," *The New York Times*, June 30, 1989, pp. D1, D6.

Reimann, Bernard C., "Getting Value From Strategic Planning," The Conference Board's 1990 Strategic Planning Conference, *Planning Review,* March/April 1990, pp. 28-33, 48.

Rowe, Alan, and Richard O. Mason, *Managing With Style*, San Francisco: Jossey-Bass, 1987.

Ruffenach, Glenn, "Shaw Uses Price Cuts to Extend Its Rule Over Carpet Business," *The Wall Street Journal,* June 12, 1991, pp. A1, A8.

Rustin, Richard E., "Fallen Star: How Grand Ambitions Proved the Undoing of Shearson Chairman," *The Wall Street Journal,* January 31, 1990, pp. A1, A8.

"Shareholder Value: The Alchemy of the 80's," *Planning Review*, Special Issue, January/February 1988.

"Shareholder Value: The Key to Better Strategies," *Planning Review,* Special Issue, March/April 1988.

Sol, Henk, "Dynamics in Information Intensive Organizations," and with Robert J. Streng, "A Dynamic Modelling Approach to Analyze Chain Dynamics on the Inter-Organizational Level," Research Project, Delft University of Technology (Belgium), presented at *Hawaii International Conference on Systems Sciences (HICSS)*, 25th Annual Meeting, Kauai, Hawaii, January 7-10, 1992.

Stanat, Ruth, *The Intelligent Corporation,* New York: Amacom, 1990.

Stern, Gabriella, "As the Going Gets Tougher, More Bosses Are Getting Tough with Their Workers," *The Wall Street Journal*, June 18, 1991, pp. B1, B12.

Sterngold, James, "Japan's Washout on Wall Street," *The New York Times*, Business Section, June 11, 1989, pp. 1, 6.

Stonich, Paul J., "The Performance Measurement and Reward System: Critical to Strategic Management," *Organizational Dynamics,* Winter 1984, pp. 45-57.

Treece, James B., et al., "The Partners," *Business Week,* February 10, 1992, pp. 102-107.

White, Joseph B., "How Detroit Diesel, Out from Under GM, Turned Around Fast," The *Wall Street Journal*, August 16, 1991, pp. A1, A8.

Zaleznik, Abraham, *The Managerial Mystique*, New York: Harper and Row, 1989.

PART FIVE

SITUATIONS WITH SPECIAL STRATEGY FORMULATION AND IMPLEMENTATION REQUIREMENTS

CHAPTER 13

MULTINATIONAL SITUATIONS

The objective of this chapter is to help readers to

- Understand the nature of multinational operations and of the tasks involved in multinational strategic management
- Formulate and implement strategies for multinational operations in specific reader situation contexts

THE NATURE OF MULTINATIONAL OPERATIONS

The United Nations has defined *multinational companies* as "enterprises which own or control production or service facilities outside the country in which they are based." The primary difference between multinational and domestic businesses is the environment in which they operate — in several countries instead of one.

Each country in which a multinational company operates can have its own special economic, cultural, legal, political, industry, and competitive market context, so each can have special strategic management requirements. Since each of these separate country situations is part of a single multinational company with an enterprise-wide strategy, these situations present strategic management integration problems.

The creation of an integrated unified European market in 1992 and the anticipated economic growth in third-world countries and in countries in the so-called Pacific Rim has increased activity and interest in multinational businesses. This activity and interest is expected to grow at an increasing pace during the 1990s. For example:

- In 1991 more than 80 percent of Coca-Cola Company's operating income came from outside the United States. This was expected to rise to 90 percent by the year 2000. The words "domestic" and "foreign" have been banished from the corporate vocabulary to bolster the image of a single global company [Cohen 1991].
- Overcoming the difficulties caused by the break-up of the Soviet Union [Bohlen 1991], Polaroid operated one of the few successful manufacturing plants in Russia — turning out 70,000 circuit boards a month. Because of the turbulent environment there, Polaroid wisely started out small to test the waters and build a base for expanding later if and when the Russian economy grew in a way that favored foreign firms [Greenhouse 1991].
- Even smaller firms can succeed in difficult overseas markets, such as Japan. For example, Aflaco Inc. (American Family Corporation) of Columbus, Georgia, a leading supplier of cancer insurance, used its niche product strategy successfully in Japan: 75 percent of its $3.5 billion in revenues came from Japan in 1991. It took the company four years to initially get a license to sell its insurance in Japan, but once licensed the company received the favorable treatment afforded other Japanese companies [Lohr 1992].
- Over the years Stanley Works has developed a mixed strategy for its multinational operations, which varied by product and market depending on situation requirements. For example, products requiring sophisticated or precision manufacturing — such as hydraulic tools made at Stanley's Portland, Oregon, plant — were most effectively shipped throughout the world from a U.S. plant for quality and production efficiency reasons as well as for tax and tariff considerations. Other products — such as wood planes made in Sheffield, England — were supplied to the world market from that plant because Europe has the largest market for wood planes. Stanley's Taiwan plant served the U.S. market with wrenches, partially because of the lower labor costs there [Uchitelle 1989(A) and 1989(B)].
- In 1989, Waste Management Incorporated (the largest waste disposal company in the U.S.) had an opportunity to acquire one of the largest state-owned waste disposal companies in France. However, because of a change in governmental policies and/or pressure from local competition, the company was taken off the market. Waste Management persisted nonetheless and by 1991 had four companies in Western Europe. Its revenues from international operations rose from $100 million in 1985 to over $300 million in 1990.
- 3M went through a transition in anticipation of the 1992 unification of European markets. In the 1980s, it brought together representatives of its 23 plants and 40 divisions in Europe, formed teams, and developed plans to consolidate European operations. One of its first moves was to beef up research and development. Advertising was to be coordinated, as were other marketing programs. Production was also consolidated. The result was a new coordinated European effort. For instance, a new product — the Soft Scour cleaning sponge — was developed at 3M's French consumer products laboratory, manufactured in its Spanish plant, and marketed across Europe by its British subsidiary. At the same time, local tastes were still accommodated [Murray 1989; Rose 1991].

Overall, the importance of international operations to U.S. companies is enormous: during the early 1990s over 16 percent of the total assets of nonfinancial U.S. companies — $700 billion — was held overseas. In addition, companies such as IBM, Ford Motor Company, NCR, Motorola, Colgate-Palmolive, and Stanley Works collected over 30 percent of their revenues from production outside the country. McDonald's planned to open more stores overseas (including one in Beijing, China) in 1992 than in the United States and reported in 1991 that its operating income per store from overseas outlets was, with the exception of Asia, considerably greater than that from U.S. outlets [Shapiro 1992].

The rapid globalization of markets has resulted in part from advances in telecommunications. Ted Turner's Cable News Network (CNN) has brought information on worldwide events to individuals in all countries. CNN was one of the most important contributing factors to the massive changes occurring in Eastern European countries in late 1989, since it gave the average citizen a heretofore inaccessible window on the world of democratic opportunities, benefits, and current events ["World View" 1990; Henry 1992].

Strategy formulation and implementation in this diverse, multinational environment requires considering a large number of political, economic, legal, customs, culture, language, and other social situational factors. For example, Procter & Gamble has battled political meddling, price controls, high inflation, kidnaps and murders of business leaders by leftist terrorists, massive poverty, and poor transportation facilities in Latin America, where the company has subsidiaries in nine countries and sells in ten others through distributors. Yet, in spite of these problems, P&G's Latin American division was a $1 billion business which expected to double its sales between 1990 and 1995 [Swasy 1990]. Despite the difficulties, therefore, opportunities for business growth appear to exist in Latin America [Baker 1992].

THE TASKS INVOLVED IN MULTINATIONAL STRATEGIC MANAGEMENT

Companies without overseas operations who are exploring going international, as well as multinational companies considering further overseas expansion, face several major initial enterprise-wide strategic decisions. As shown in Figure 13-1, a number of decision areas and tasks critical to success can be identified. The following sections discuss ten of these critical task areas.

Selecting a Marketing Area

A wide range of potential overseas markets exist. The unified European market expected in 1992 could eventually exceed the United States in both actual and potential opportunities [Prokesch 1990; Wright 1990]. In anticipation of this, Pepsico Inc. announced in late 1991 that it would invest over $1 billion in Spain to build soft drink plants, open fast-food restaurants, and set up an elaborate computerized system to track snack food sales. In the prior three years Pepsico

Figure 13-1: Multinational Planning Tasks

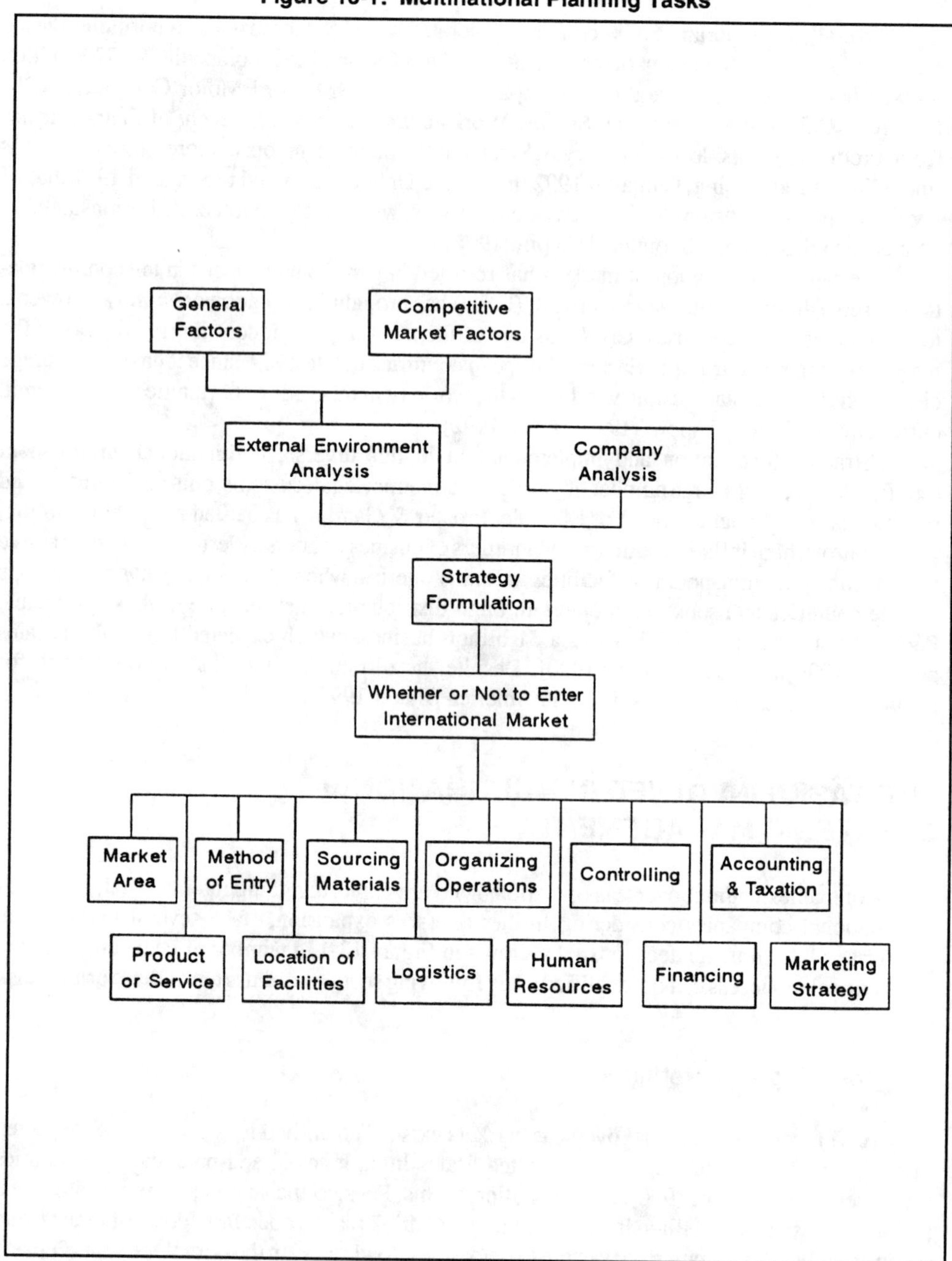

spent $4 billion to expand its presence in Europe [Shapiro 1991].

Newly-freed Eastern Bloc countries, such as Hungary and Poland, are also becoming major market opportunities. For example, Fiat S.p.A., the second largest European automaker, planned to build its new Fiat mini-car in 1992 in a plant in southern Poland [Cowell 1991].

Markets in Japan, Australia, and other countries in the Pacific Rim also appear to have considerable potential for companies in the United States and Europe. Though unstable politically, China should eventually be a major opportunity area, as Avon proved in the early 1990s after it successfully began doing business in Guangdong in the Canton province [Tanzer 1991].

For foreign countries, the United States presents major international opportunities. As of 1988, foreign companies had a total direct investment in the U.S. of over $300 billion [Hicks 1989]. The huge amount of Japanese money pouring into investments in the United States (for example, Sony's $7 billion investment in Columbia Pictures) has led to fears that the U.S. is being "sold" to the Japanese and will soon become overly dependent on Japan [Lehner 1990: Robinson 1991]. As with U.S. companies, not all of these expansions have been successful. For example, the purchase of Pebble Beach resort in California led to close to a third of a billion dollar loss for its Japanese investor [Carlton 1992; Montague 1992] and Bridgestone, a Japanese tire company, suffered major losses in the early 1990s at its recently purchased Firestone tire-making subsidiary [O'Boyle 1991].

Another growth area of the 1990s and twenty-first century is expected to be the former Soviet Union. After its breakup in late 1991, however, serious questions were raised as to when and how that potential might be realized. In addition to the political unrest, two key problems were a lack of contract protection and of guarantees that the U.S. companies would be able to repatriate their profits in dollars from the republics there. When Gillette was negotiating in 1990 to build a $50 million plant in Russia, for example, the outcome hinged on Russia's willingness to allow Gillette (the major shareholder in the new company) to take profits out in hard currency ["Gillette" 1991; Ramirez 1990]. As might be expected, such uncertainties led many companies in early 1992 to pursue a strategy of thinking small when entering that market [Brady 1992; Johnson 1992].

Extensive decision situation analyses are required in making a decision to go overseas and selecting a market area to serve. The situation factors analyzed range from such general country, area, or region factors as the political climate, national economy, exchange rates, and cultural climate to competitive market and internal company resource factors. The decision as to what area to enter often is related to and made simultaneously with decisions as to what products to offer and what entry method to use.

Identifying the Products or Services to be Offered

There are several strategic approaches to identifying and marketing existing, new, or redesigned products, when entering international markets.

When conditions permit, many companies choose a *global* marketing approach to product design, selection, distribution, pricing, packaging, and promotion. This strategy involves using the same products and/or marketing strategies in all countries served. For example, Coca-Cola uses the same brand name, product design, and advertising worldwide [Cohen 1991].

A *multinational* or *market-by-market* approach is required by local circumstances in many situations. For example, accommodating local tastes was a problem for Scott Paper Company, since England, France, and Mediterranean countries each required different products. In Scott's case, therefore, there was much greater concentration on local differentiation in each of the European countries, although there was considerable regional coordination as well [Lampert 1989].

The overseas experience of Federal Express illustrates the problems involved in trying to use U.S. marketing and management approaches in other countries. In trying to gain a foothold overseas, Federal Express initially attempted to duplicate the services and operations which had made it successful in the United States. Only after investing more than $1.5 billion did Federal Express begin to adapt its approach to local overseas conditions [Pearl 1991]. Eventually, the company substantially cut back European operations to reduce its massive losses there [Hawkins 1992].

Very often a *mixed strategy,* which combines some aspects of the global approach with whatever modifications are necessary to meet local requirements, is used. A company marketing decaffinated coffee, for example, might use a global company name, such as Nestle, but modify the formula somewhat country by country to meet local tastes and government regulations. A wide range of modifications are often necessary because, while it is ideal to think globally, necessity often requires a company to act locally and take into account both general environment and competitive market factors when planning for products.

Method of Entry

Four of the major strategies used to enter an overseas market are discussed in this section. The specific approach used in individual situations will depend on situation requirements, as in other strategy formulation and implementation situations.

Buying an existing company or a percentage interest in an existing company. This is the entry method chosen by several automobile companies. For example, Honda purchased a 20 percent interest in the English automaker Rover Group P.L.C. [Sanger 1991]. Also in 1989, Pepsico bought two English snack food companies for $1.35 billion [McGill 1989; Shapiro 1991]. While expensive, this method establishes a market presence quickly.

Setting up a wholly-owned subsidiary. This was the entry method chosen by Compaq in 1984 when it built a plant in Scotland [Lohr 1989] and by both Toyota and Nissan when they built automobile plants in England in the late 1980s [Sanger 1989]. In Compaq's case, this method appeared best, since the products and their technology were relatively new. Toyota and Nissan believed it would be easier and cheaper to start from scratch, since few English automobile manufacturers were available for purchase.

Entering into cooperative arrangements. Many arrangements, such as co-development consortiums, licensing, agency agreements, and other contractual agreements are common in a wide range of industries [Kanter 1989; Lewis 1990]. Often referred to by their Japanese name, Keiretsu, such cooperative arrangements among manufacturers, suppliers, and finance companies also are growing in popularity in the United States, in part because of the successful experiences of some companies in countries such as Japan [Kelly 1992; Strom 1992; Treece 1992].

Exporting products to a country. This entry strategy is often favored by smaller companies which are exploring going overseas. More established companies also find it useful in some situations. For example, Hurco Companies, a machine tool maker, fought its way back to solvency in large measure by increasing overseas sales [Lohr 1991]. Overall, American-manufactured exports rose 10 percent in 1990 to $316 billion and jumped 80 percent from 1985 to 1990, with most of the increase coming from mid-sized companies in the $50 million to under $1 billion range [Rose 1991].

Location of Facilities

Another primary multinational strategic management decision involves the location of facilities, or sources of the product or service to be sold, in a chosen international location.

For example, in 1984 Compaq located a plant in Scotland — to serve the Great Britain market — because of its lower labor rates and high unemployment rate. Another factor affecting the decision was the infrastructure for the computer industry (technical schools and electronics companies) that Scotland provided. This location has proven to be an especially wise choice with the formation of the European Community in 1992, since it gives Compaq entry to the entire European market.

At other times, companies relocate offices as local circumstances change. For many years, General Motors' Opel AG subsidiary in West Germany coordinated its European operations. However, in 1986, GM moved its headquarters to Zurich and established a European headquarters there, not only because it felt a more centralized location would have better control of operations, but mainly because West German law required companies headquartered in Germany to have 50 percent of board membership filled by employees.

Sourcing Materials

Sourcing refers to how a company obtains the raw materials, subcontracted components, and other goods and materials needed to produce goods and services. Basically, firms have two alternatives when sourcing: sourcing from the country in which they produce (*domestic sourcing*) or sourcing from foreign countries (*outsourcing*).

As the definition implies, outsourcing is an import strategy and, like most import strategies, is influenced by the length of supply lines, production costs, production quality, inventory levels, local import and tariff regulations, and currency fluctuations. General Motors has found outsourcing to be very profitable. The company has agreements with Japan's Suzuki Motors, Isuzu Motors Ltd., and Toyota, and with Korea's Daewoo Corp., to procure parts and components for production in its U.S. plants.

However, outsourcing has some disadvantages. IEC Electronics found that sourcing its circuit boards from offshore suppliers created quality problems, with rejects from outside suppliers being substantially higher than from internal production. In addition, since IEC sometimes makes design changes in less than 24 hours, six to eight weeks of circuit boards would have to be thrown out by the time engineering changes worked their way through a trans-Pacific supply line [Breskin 1989].

Logistics

International *logistics* involves the design and management of a system that controls the flow of materials into, through, and out of the international corporation. There are two major phases of material movement that are important to managers: materials management (the movement of raw materials, parts, and supplies through the firm) and physical distribution (the movement of the finished product to the customer).

An international logistics manager considers several factors: transportation (transit time, cost, government regulations); inventory (order cycle time, customer service levels, strategic needs of the firm, such as protection against inflation and devaluation); packaging (size, weight, customer specifications); and storage issues (available space within each country or area, cost, location).

Organizing

Companies employ several general organization strategies in managing international operations. The organization approaches used by firms are discussed in Chapter 12, as are the factors affecting organization design decisions.

Human Resources

A primary strategic decision in multinational strategic management is the degree to which individual multinational operations will be staffed by people native to the area of operations. For example, in 1984 Compaq decided to have nationals manage its new computer plant in Scotland [Lohr 1989]. Using nationals to manage local multinational operations avoids many problems arising from cultural, legal, and market factors unique to each operation. In addition, in some countries nationals dislike being supervised by expatriates. Local nationals have a working knowledge of the customs, beliefs, and attitudes of the people and so are in a better position to handle human resource problems. This is especially true in collective bargaining situations.

In contrast, Stanley Works staffed its overseas management positions with Americans [Uchitelle 1989 (A)]. While this strategy creates some problems, it has one key advantage: easier communication and control for the multinational company.

Finance, Accounting, Taxation, and Control

Strategies in the key areas of finance, accounting, taxation, and control affect almost all multinational operations.

Finance. In many instances, basic financial strategies are dictated by the entry method, which can involve shared ownership, as well as by a company's financial condition and its policy regarding financing expansion through long-term debt, equity, retained earnings, or short-term borrowing. Decisions are also made on financing through local sources, such as government loans and banks, or financing outside the overseas area under study.

Accounting and Taxation. One of the problems faced by multinational companies is that accounting standards differ from country to country, making it more complex for a firm to prepare financial statements consistent with the generally accepted accounting principles in the home country. At least once a year, for example, under normal circumstances, a U.S. firm must produce a consolidated statement of earnings showing all the operations of the firm quoted in United States dollars at current exchange rates.

In addition to exchange rates, several other factors affect the development of accounting strategies. These include: the accounting objectives of the firm, the nature of the enterprise (corporation, proprietorship, or partnership), the internal and external users of information (management, employees, investors, and creditors), the government (responsible for establishing practices), local environmental characteristics (cultural attitudes, the nature and state of the economy), and international influences, such as accounting profession standards and auditing practices.

Controlling. Several factors make the control process more complex on an international level. Geographic distances, for example, inevitably lead to increased time, expense, and the possibility of error in international communications. *Diversity* also creates control difficulties. Since international firms have interests in several multinational locations, they often encounter markets, competition, products, labor costs, currencies, and other conditions that vary. As a result, the task of evaluating performance or setting standards to correct or improve business functions can be extremely complicated. The *degree of uncertainty* also can affect control; in many overseas situations, political and economic conditions are subject to rapid change.

Marketing Strategy

Marketing strategy decisions for multinational operations require the same kinds of external market, competitive environment, and internal company analyses as those described in Chapter 9. The second half of that chapter discusses a marketing decision encountered by foreign affiliates of a major health-care products company. That discussion covers the factors examined in such situations and some of the possible strategy recommendations.

FORMULATING AND IMPLEMENTING MULTINATIONAL STRATEGIES IN SPECIFIC READER SITUATION CONTEXTS

The preceding sections described some of the tasks and strategic decisions involved in managing multinational operations. This section describes the process involved in making decisions in these key strategic management task areas. The overall decision-making process involved in making strategy formulation decisions — shown in Figure 13-2 — is described in Chapter 2. The process involved in making multinational strategic management decisions, which extends that overall process, is shown in Figure 13-3.

Figure 13-2: Strategic Management Decision-Making Process

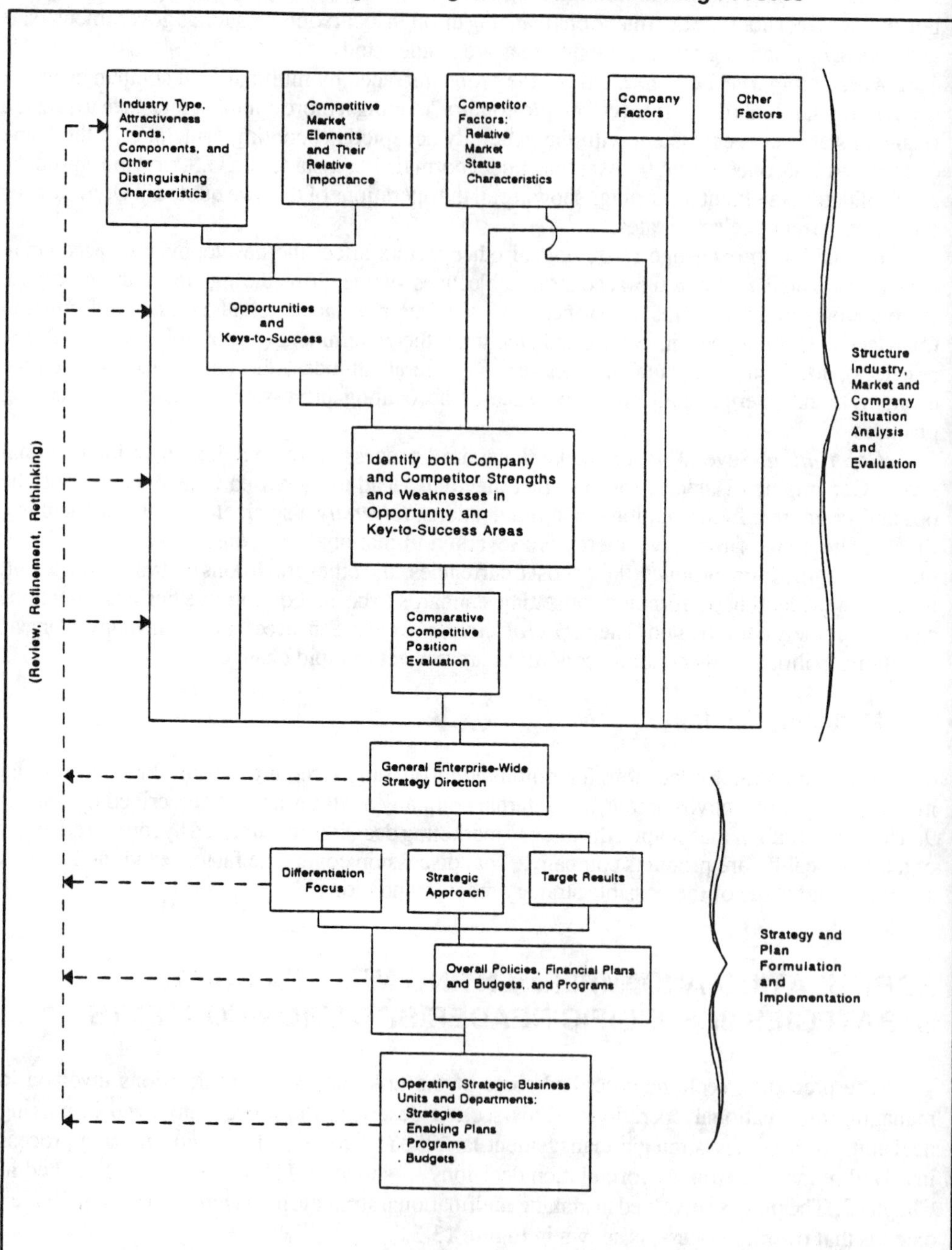

Figure 13-3: Multinational Operations Overall Approach to Making Strategic Management Decisions

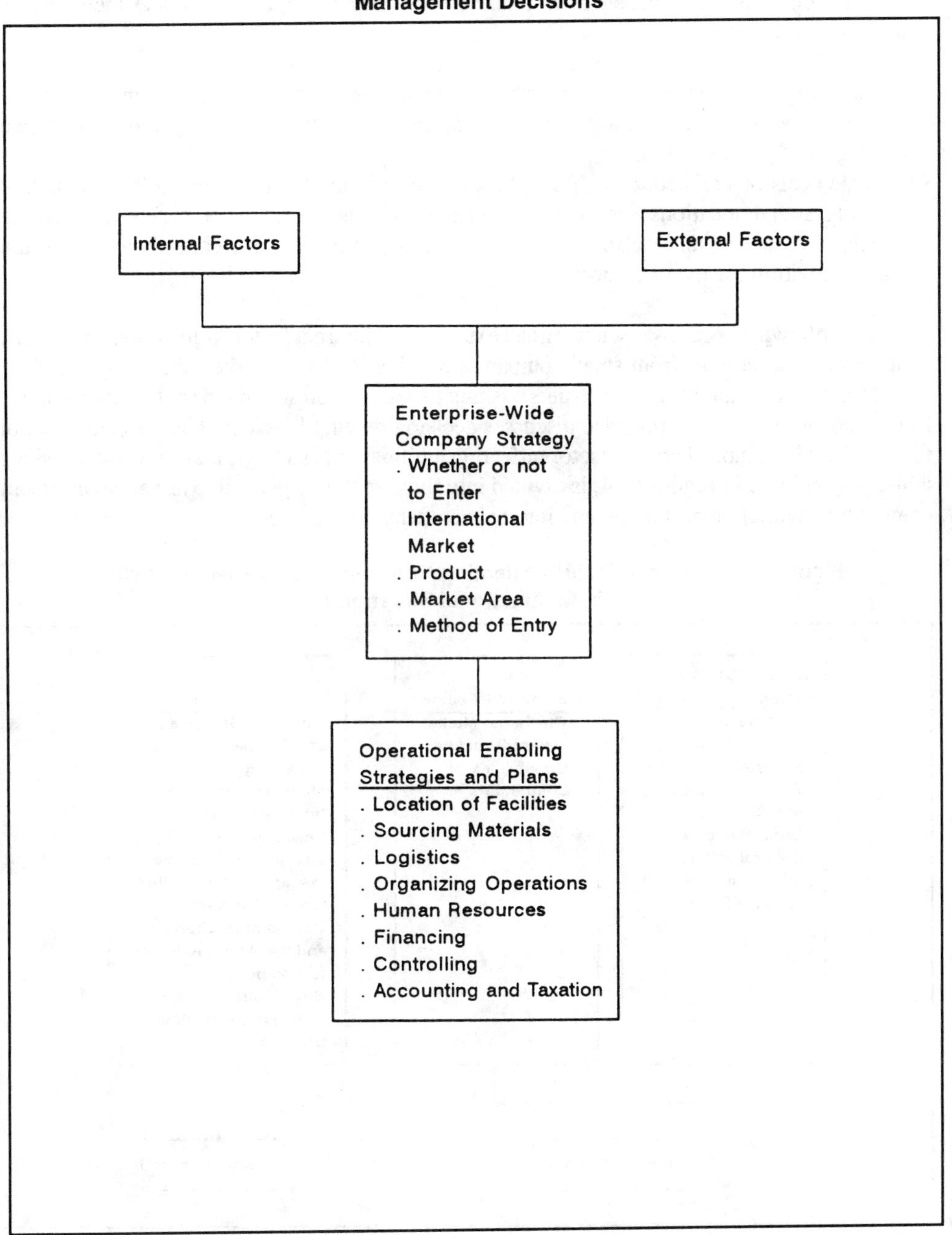

This section describes how the specific external and internal situation factors encountered in multinational strategic management situations are structured, analyzed, and then used, in making such decisions as

- Overall-company strategies, including whether or not to go international, in which international markets to operate, overall strategies for entering and serving these markets, products to market and degree of globalization.
- Strategic decisions related to enabling plans for specific multinational operations, including: choosing actual locations for plants, offices, warehouses, and other facilities; sourcing; logistics; organizing and staffing; finance, accounting, taxation, and control; and marketing strategies within the overseas operation.

The following sections discuss critical external and internal factors affecting decisions in a wide range of situations, from small companies seeking overseas markets for a single product through export consultants to large banks wishing to extend their worldwide network of banks in foreign countries. The section also discusses decision making based on these critical situation factors. The discussion of critical factors affecting multinational strategic management decisions, which are outlined in Figure 13-4, is divided into three sections: general external environment, competitive market environment, and internal company environment.

Figure 13-4: Critical Factors Affecting Strategic Management Decisions in Multinational Situations

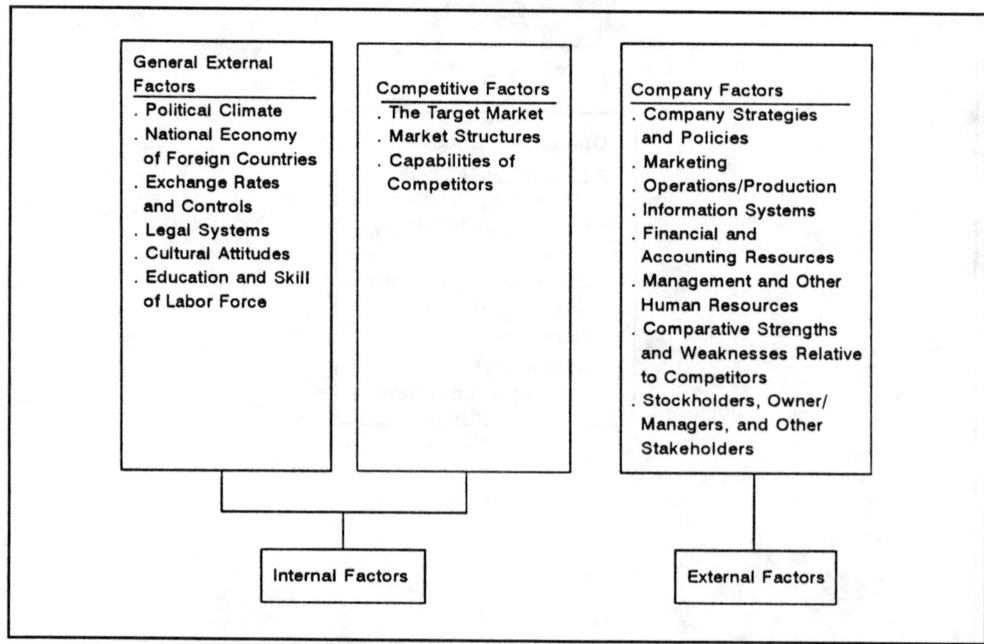

Critical Factors Affecting Decisions in this Area: General External Environment

Six general external environment situation factors are discussed in this section.

Political climate. Political climate refers to the systems and methods affecting government in a country. In Sweden, for example, the political climate is calm and stable, since the population seldom gets overly excited about political matters and the government often seeks national referenda before instituting major policy changes. At the other extreme is a country like Lebanon, where mob rule, terrorism, and anarchy are the norm.

In most countries, various government approvals are needed to do business. In some countries, such as England, this process is well-established and can be pursued in an orderly fashion. In other countries, especially developing ones, the process of obtaining approval can be less straightforward and clear, and often requires considerable knowledge of local customs and the people involved, as well as payoffs to politically well-positioned people. In addition, officials in some countries have a reputation for failing to honor contracts.

National economy of foreign countries. Just as in the United States, the levels of inflation, unemployment, government spending, total economic growth, and the like have significant impacts on any country's business activities. For example, countries with low per capita income, such as Guyana and Rumania, present different opportunities than those countries, such as West Germany, where income levels are closer to or higher than those in the United States. Inflation in countries such as Brazil, where the 1991 inflation rate exceeded 1200 percent, affects how money is invested in a country, since in areas of high inflation local borrowing is preferred as a hedge against inflation. One reason Compaq Computers decided to open a plant in Scotland was that the high unemployment rate there suggested that labor would be plentiful and that labor costs would be more controllable.

Exchange rates and controls. As inflation fluctuates, so do exchange rates. For companies who report their income in the United States based on current exchange rates this can cause considerable variations in reported income. It can in many instances also lead to extraordinary income gains and losses. In countries noted for widely fluctuating exchange rates, strategic planning often requires particular attention to steps, such as dealing in currency futures, which are designed to minimize the potential losses incurred from such fluctuations.

Many countries also have restrictions on how much money can be taken out of the country.

Legal systems. Since practically all business activity involves explicit or implied contracts, understanding the differences in legal systems is critical to doing business successfully in foreign countries. Most countries base their laws on civil law, as opposed to the common law basis of the U.S. legal system. In some countries, for instance, who registered a brand name first (civil law) is more important under the law than who used the name first (common law), as it is in the United States. Labor laws can also be significant multinational planning factors, since many countries have strict laws governing such matters as the hiring and firing of workers, which can severely limit management flexibility.

Cultural attitudes. Cultural attitudes refer to customs, values, beliefs, and the behavior of a people. Such attitudes can affect a wide range of business decisions, from the colors used in advertising, the handles designed for tools, and the texture of toilet paper, to the distribution systems used in a foreign country, to the way employees are compensated, to the ways business meetings and negotiations are conducted.

In the employee relations area in West Germany, status symbols can be so important that at times an employee may accept a lower-paying job if it offers a private office, a company car, or a chauffeur. In France, the respect given a manager often depends on the university at which the manager studied or ancestral family links to nobility rather than on specific organizational chart relationships. In India, the caste system dictates to some degree who can give orders to whom.

If specific stereotypes are important in the society of the foreign country under study, then a company needs to be aware of them to be able to conform to them and so operate effectively in that environment. For example, throughout the Muslim world, and specifically on the Arabian Peninsula, women do not yet have a recognized place in business activity. For this reason, many Saudi-Arabian merchants would be unwilling to deal with a female representative from an overseas exporter.

Education and skill of the labor force. The education and skills of a country's workforce can range from superior in Japan to very low in developing countries like Bangladesh. Where computer manufacturing is planned, the strategic choice would in large measure be dictated by this factor, because a skilled labor force is needed. In situations where the planned entry involves the manufacture or delivery of noncomplex products and services, such as McDonald's hamburgers or 3M's Soft Scour cleaning sponge, the labor skills requirement may be much less critical.

Critical Factors Affecting Decisions in this Area: Competitive Market Environment

The structured decision situation analysis of competitive market forces involves studying external market factors as outlined in Figure 13-4. These factors were discussed in Chapters 4, 5, and 6, as well as in Chapter 10. They include the target market, market structures, and capabilities of competitors.

Target market. The study of the target market covers not only the total number of customers, but also the amount of purchases expected and the present market penetration. For example, Gillette calculates that over 95 percent of American males shave, making this a relatively saturated market; as little as 20 percent shave in some less-developed countries. Identifying the different purchasing patterns and customer characteristics is also important. One of the first steps taken by a major U.S. advertising firm after the 1992 breakup of the Soviet Union was to conduct a study of the range of target markets in Russia and their buying patterns [Elliot 1992].

Geographic location can also affect decision making because of distribution problems and costs. Other decisions, such as controls to establish, location of facilities, entry method to select, size of product, packaging, and even whether or not to enter a market, may be based on geographic factors. In many situations, climate will be a geographic factor affecting multinational strategic planning.

Market structures. As when studying domestic markets, a wide range of other market factors are analyzed, including: available distribution and sales channels, media, and suppliers and supplies, including parts and raw materials; pricing practices; available equipment and technology; supporting services, such as electricity, gas, transportation, communications, and housing; existing manufacturing facilities; and competing products.

Capabilities of competitors. Potential and existing local and international competitors are studied in all multinational strategic planning situations, in much the same way that domestic competition is identified and analyzed.

An important consideration for firms entering overseas markets is that local competition will almost always have some advantages, since it is more familiar with the market. In addition, firms already operating in the market often pressure the government to protect local business, as was the case with Waste Disposal Incorporated when it tried to enter the French market [Bremner 1989]. Local competitors may also benefit from protectionist trade measures [Garsombke 1989]. These factors can create substantial competitive market entry barriers.

Critical Factors Affecting Decisions in this Area: Internal Company Environment

In multinational planning situations, the internal analysis includes the consideration of a variety of factors, involving both the home company and the multinational division operating in the overseas country under study. Eight of these factors, listed in Figure 13-4, are discussed here.

Company strategies and policies. Overall-company strategies, as well as specific strategies affecting multinational operations, are studied. For example, a company may have a policy of always owning subsidiaries 100 percent, but local circumstances may dictate that a joint venture is preferable. Such a conflict must be reconciled.

Marketing. Such factors as existing customers, products, sales, service, and distribution of the home company, as well as existing overseas operations, are studied. In the case of Ford's proposed entry into the Soviet Union, the company first considered its existing product line and built its initial entry strategy around importing a product it already was making — its Scorpio model [Galuszka 1989].

Operations/production. The review of operations/production capabilities covers factors such as facilities, workforce, quality, flexibility, inventory management, and research and development. For example, Stanley decided that the production know-how required to produce some of its precision tools dictated manufacturing them in a single facility and supplying the worldwide market from that facility.

Information systems. Information systems are likely to be included in most company audits today because of their importance to both survival and gaining competitive edges in marketing, production/operations, management decision making, and finance. Their strategic impact appears to be particularly great in service industries, as shown in the discussions in Chapter 11. In multinational corporations in general, telecommunications and related computer information systems are important due to the problems involved in managing geographically dispersed and diversified organizations.

Financial and accounting resources. In analyzing a company's financial situation, the obvious and necessary factors examined are the income statement, balance sheet, and cash-flow, using financial ratios, computer simulations of projected scenarios, and other analytical tools. These analyses provide a basis for estimating financial resources available for overseas operations — overall, country by country, or target market by target market. The more creative task is to go beyond these ratios and tools to uncover hidden resources and opportunities. Imaginative financing arrangements, preferably involving local money sources, are especially important in countries with high inflation rates.

Management and other human resources. Availability of experienced personnel in international operations is critical to success, since international operations can be quite different from domestic operations. This knowledge and experience is needed not only to deal with the many special local factors affecting success, including special political, legal, custom, and attitude factors. This experience is also needed to establish the contacts needed to open up and exploit opportunities in target markets.

Comparative strengths and weaknesses relative to competitors. A key element of the structured industry analysis is how the capabilities of the company under study compare with competitors' capabilities in the targeted market. This comparative evaluation process was discussed in detail in Chapter 6. Figure 13-5 shows a comparative competitive analysis summary for a U.S. specialty seafood firm's position in the Malaysian market [Garsombke 1989].

Stockholders, owner/managers, and other company stakeholders. Interest groups which impact on multinational strategic management include: owners (stockholders), customers, suppliers, creditors and lending institutions, unions, franchise holders, government agencies, society (local or in general), and company managers, professional staff, and hourly workers. Interest groups can impact on company strategy, as was shown by the number of companies that sold their South African operations or their stock in South African companies as a result of shareholder pressure.

Studies of stakeholder relations also can lead to finding new strategic opportunities. For example, *When Giants Learn to Dance* [Kanter 1989] studies a number of multinational companies that benefited from forming international alliances, not only with other firms operating in overseas markets, but also with unions, customers, and suppliers.

Making Decisions Based on These Critical Situation Factors

Decisions made based on these critical situation factors, as shown in Figure 13-3, include

- Overall enterprise-wide company strategies
- Strategic decisions related to enabling plans for specific multinational operations

Overall enterprise-wide strategy decisions. For purely domestic companies, the decision of *whether to go international* for the first time is often very difficult, since it means committing resources to an area about which the company may know very little. However, stagnant domestic markets, the lure of huge foreign markets, the fear of losing a competitive edge, the increasing threat of foreign competition, and the need to satisfy shareholders will often make it necessary to seriously consider entering overseas markets. For example, Stanley Works, once a purely

Figure 13-5: A U.S. Firm Compared with its International Competitors in Malaysian Market

Comparison Criteria	A (U.S. MNC)	B (Korean MNC)	C (Local Malaysian Firm)	D (Japanese MNC)	E (Local Malaysian Firm)
Marketing Capability	0	0	0	0	-
Manufacturing Capability	0	+	0	0	0
R&D Capability	0	0	0	-	0
HRM Capability	0	0	0	0	0
Financial Capability	+	-	0	0	-
Future Growth of Resources	+	0	-	0	-
Quickness	-	0	+	-	0
Flexibility/Adaptability	0	+	+	0	0
Sustainability	+	0	0	0	-

Key:
+ = Firm is better than competition
0 = Firm is same as competition
- = Firm is poorer than competition

domestic company, began thinking internationally when competition from foreigners increased. This was coupled with the very real danger of losing its competitive edge, since many firms were benefiting from reduced manufacturing costs abroad. Compaq saw a similar opportunity in Europe for its products when it opened its Scotland plant. Hurco Companies looked overseas as a way to move out bankruptcy [Lohr 1991]

Decisions about *market choice* concern the selection of markets to enter, covering regions of the world, countries, and the areas and population segments within the country. Since markets invariably overlap, this decision often defines general direction rather than precise site locations. For example, Pepsico obviously had decided that the European market after 1992 would be ideal for its soft drinks, snack foods, and fast-foods products and services before choosing in which countries to place $4 billion plus investments in the late 1980s and early 1990s. Additional factors affect the selection of the actual country or area chosen for entry. For example, Aflaco had a product — cancer insurance — which did not sell well in the U.S. (individual sickness policies are not popular in the U.S.). In Japan, however, where there were worries about cancer and regular insurance policies paid minimal cancer benefits, the market and culture were favorable. However, Aflaco spent four years overcoming the difficulties involved in obtaining a license [Lohr 1992].

When deciding *how to serve selected markets*, a firm has several options available. Depending on market factors, labor availability and costs, available local infrastructure, and government regulations of the country, as well as on internal company factors, a firm can choose to satisfy the market by exporting from the home country, by setting up foreign production facilities through a directed investment, or by licensing or other collaborative agreements. A more detailed example of this kind of strategic decision is given later in this chapter.

Products to market and degree of globalization. Where a company has products available that are appropriate for local markets, and the local overseas market's government regulations permit it, a global approach to multinational product strategy is possible. This is Coca-Cola's approach [Cohen 1991]. Where local attitudes and cultural differences exist from country to country, on the other hand, a market-by-market strategy would be more appropriate. This was the case with Scott Paper Company in serving various European markets with its paper products [Lampert 1989].

Specific operational planning decisions. Strategic decisions related to specific operations can include: choosing actual locations for plants, offices, warehouses, and other facilities; sourcing; logistics; organizing and staffing; finance, accounting, taxation, and control; and marketing strategies within the overseas operation. An example of such a specific marketing operations decision for an overseas affiliate of a U.S. multinational company is given in detail in Chapter 9. In that case, overall the company preferred a global product strategy. The company recognized, however, that frequently local government regulations, customer preferences, media availability, and individual competitor factors dictated some adaptation of a product to local factors. Such a detailed analysis of specific market conditions in overseas target markets is required in all operating areas when developing enabling plans for carrying out enterprise-wide multinational strategies.

To further explore the processes involved in making such decisions, the following sections discuss a detailed approach to making decisions when selecting an entry strategy, as well as decision-making approaches to other multinational strategic management decision situations.

MULTINATIONAL DECISIONS INVOLVING SELECTION OF AN ENTRY STRATEGY

This section discusses one of the early decisions made in multinational strategy formulation — choosing an entry strategy. For this introductory discussion, the possible decisions have been limited to three: export, contractual agreement, and direct investment.

As shown in Figure 13-6, a range of situation factors are examined in making these decisions. The discussion here, which follows the outline in Figure 13-6, covers factors affecting the decision, as well as possible recommendations and how they are made.

Factors Affecting the Decision

As shown in Figure 13-6, an initial idea of an appropriate entry strategy can be determined

Figure 13-6: Decision Situation Diagram
Entry Strategy—International Market Overview Diagram

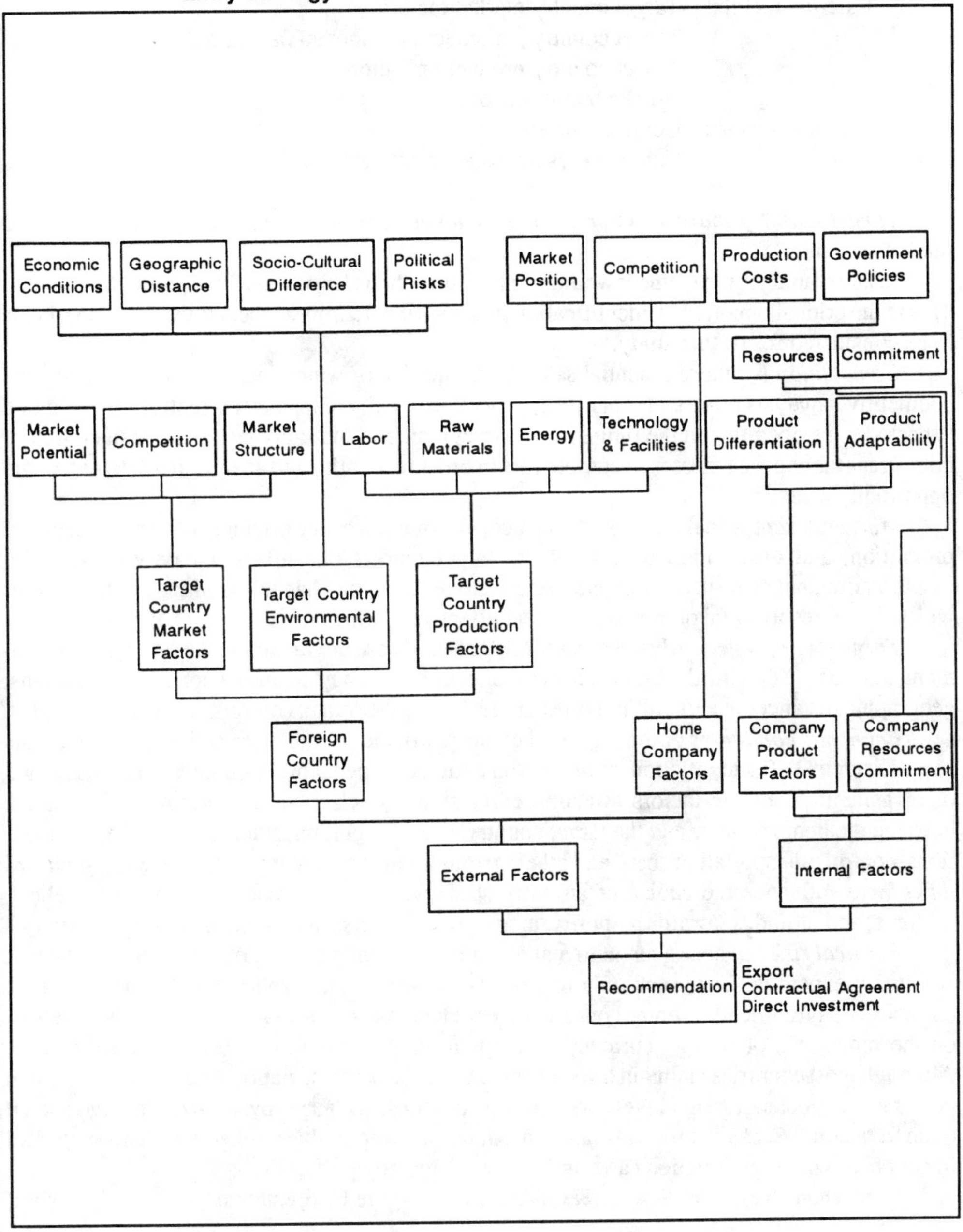

Economic Conditions
Geographic Distance
Socio-Cultural Difference
Political Risks
Market Position
Competition
Production Costs
Government Policies
Resources
Commitment
Market Potential
Competition
Market Structure
Labor
Raw Materials
Energy
Technology & Facilities
Product Differentiation
Product Adaptability
Target Country Market Factors
Target Country Environmental Factors
Target Country Production Factors
Foreign Country Factors
Home Company Factors
Company Product Factors
Company Resources Commitment
External Factors
Internal Factors
Recommendation
Export
Contractual Agreement
Direct Investment

by studying six factors:

External factors:	Target country market factors
	Target country general environmental factors
	Target country production factors
	Home country factors
Internal factors:	Company product factors
	Company resources /commitment factors

Target country market factors. Target market factors include sales, competition, and market structure.

In any country, management would want to know the *sales potential* of a particular product. This is the critical opportunity identification phase — it determines whether the target market is to be considered for further study.

Competition for those potential sales is another factor which interests management. The competitive analysis covers international, as well as local, companies currently operating and expected to be operating in the future in the target market. The study includes consideration of both strengths and weaknesses of competitors in order to identify and analyze market niches and opportunity areas.

Market structure analysis provides critical information on the pricing, product, advertising, promotion, and distribution aspects of the target market that affect not only opportunity identification, but also success factors. Access to distribution channels is often a critical factor which, if not resolved favorably, can prevent effective market entry.

Target country general environmental factors. These are factors in the external environment that affect the firm's future chances of success. They include economic conditions, geographic distances, socio-cultural differences, political climate, controls, and exchange rates.

Economic conditions of the proposed country provide overall information on such factors as anticipated GNP and inflation, as well as on anticipated per capita income, interest rates, and other general economic factors affecting entry strategy selection. The *geographic distance* between the home country and the target country is also important, since it affects communications, control, transportation costs, and other operations areas. In many instances, *socio-cultural differences* influence the choice of an entry strategy, since differences in language, beliefs, customs, and attitudes towards authority, among other things, can create major entry barriers.

Political risk can pose a threat to market entry, especially in developing countries where it is felt that expatriate firms seek only to strip the country of its resources and transfer foreign currency to pay dividends to home country shareholders. As a result, many countries have *controls* on the remittance of foreign currency. Perhaps more of a threat is possible nationalization. Although most countries maintain laws that give them the power to nationalize, very few use that power since it deters foreign investment. Some countries, such as Libya, however, have used it quite frequently. *Exchange rates* are also important, since rapid adverse changes in currency rates in countries with high inflation can eliminate any company profits.

Target country production factors. As shown in Figure 13-6, external factors such as labor, raw materials (including components), energy, technology, and facilities can impact on entry strategy decisions.

Home country factors. These are external factors in the home country of the multinational company which is considering overseas expansion. Considerations such as competition, production costs, and the company's general strategic market position in its home territory, as well as government policies affecting technology transfer, impact on entry strategy decisions, as shown in Figure 13-6.

Internal company factors. *Company product factors*, such as product differentiation and product adaptability, are examined — especially in relation to the possibility of exporting products currently made by a company. *Company resource and commitment factors* are also identified, since these factors define the resources available to the company and the company's commitment to international expansion.

Possible Decisions and How They Are Made

Once the above factors are evaluated in the decision situation under study, an entry strategy is selected.

When recommending a *direct investment* entry strategy, it is important that the firm have financial resources available to establish a production or service facility. Regardless of the favorable position of other factors — such as good sales potential, the availability of high technical skills, a medium or low level of political risk, or even favorable responses by the foreign government — a lack of financial resources will limit use of a direct investment strategy.

On the other hand, available financial resources do not necessarily mean a direct investment strategy would be recommended. For example, in the target market or country under study, political conditions may be unstable, market infrastructure may be unsatisfactory, or labor costs may be excessive. In this situation, if it is clearly desirable for other reasons that a company enter this market, *contractual agreements*, such as a joint venture with a local firm, would be considered. Contractual agreements would also be considered a possible entry strategy if management is unsure as to the sales potential of the target market, product differentiation is high, product adaptation is high, political climate is unstable, and the firm's level of international expertise is only average. Contractual agreements are very often used to limit a company's exposure to risk in entering a new and unfamiliar market.

An *exports* entry strategy is considered a minimum risk approach. In contractual agreements, such as a joint venture, the company may have to fund a part of the project or give up a substantial portion of ownership of the venture. An export strategy eliminates these costs and associated risks. For example, if the sales potential for the target market is high, the estimated production costs are lower at home than in the foreign location, product adaptability requirements are low, import and export restrictions are favorable, raw materials are relatively more expensive abroad, the political climate abroad is unstable, and the firm has limited financial resources, then exporting is considered the recommended strategy.

A prototype knowledge-based system has been developed to replicate this somewhat abbreviated version of how decisions are made regarding entry strategy development. This system

Figure 13-7: Decision Situation Under Study International Lending Decision of Commercial Bank

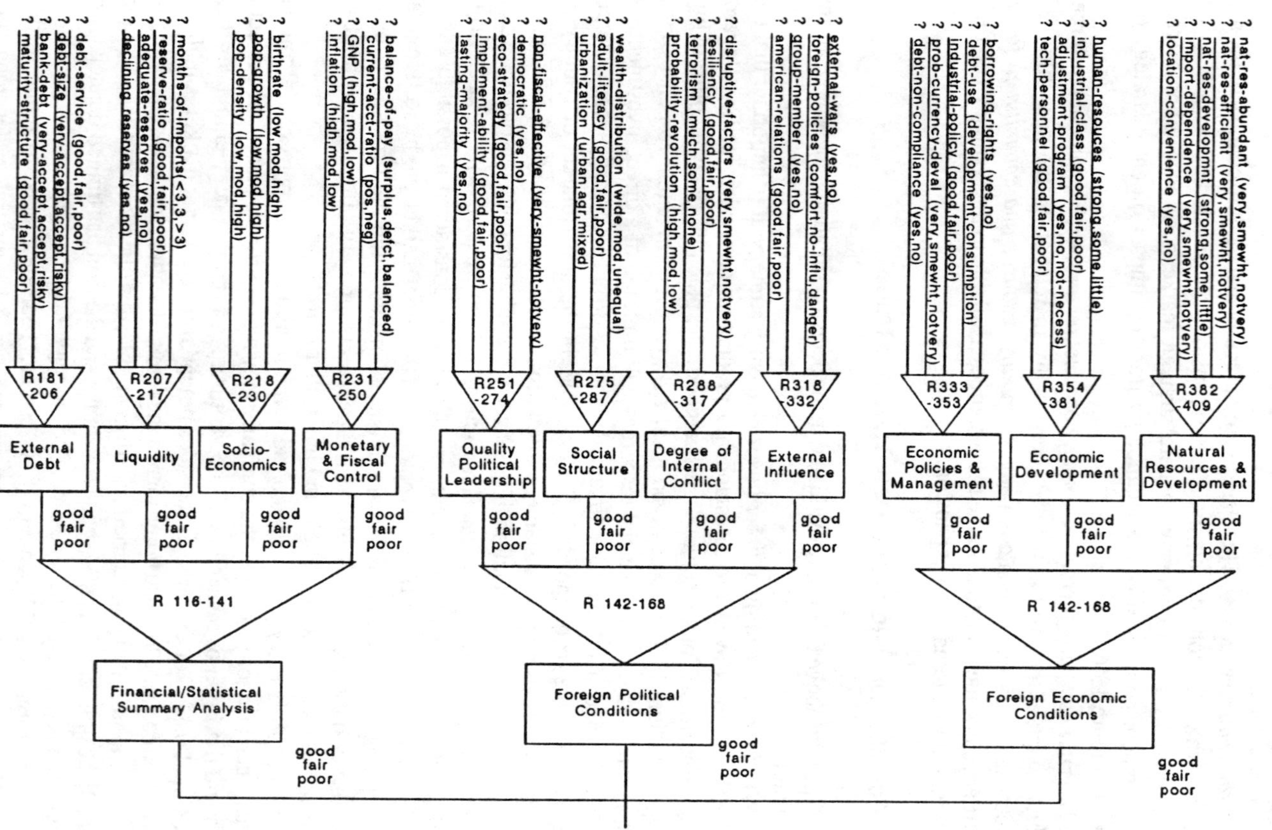

Figure 13-7: Decision Situation Under Study
International Lending Decision of Commercial Bank (contd.)

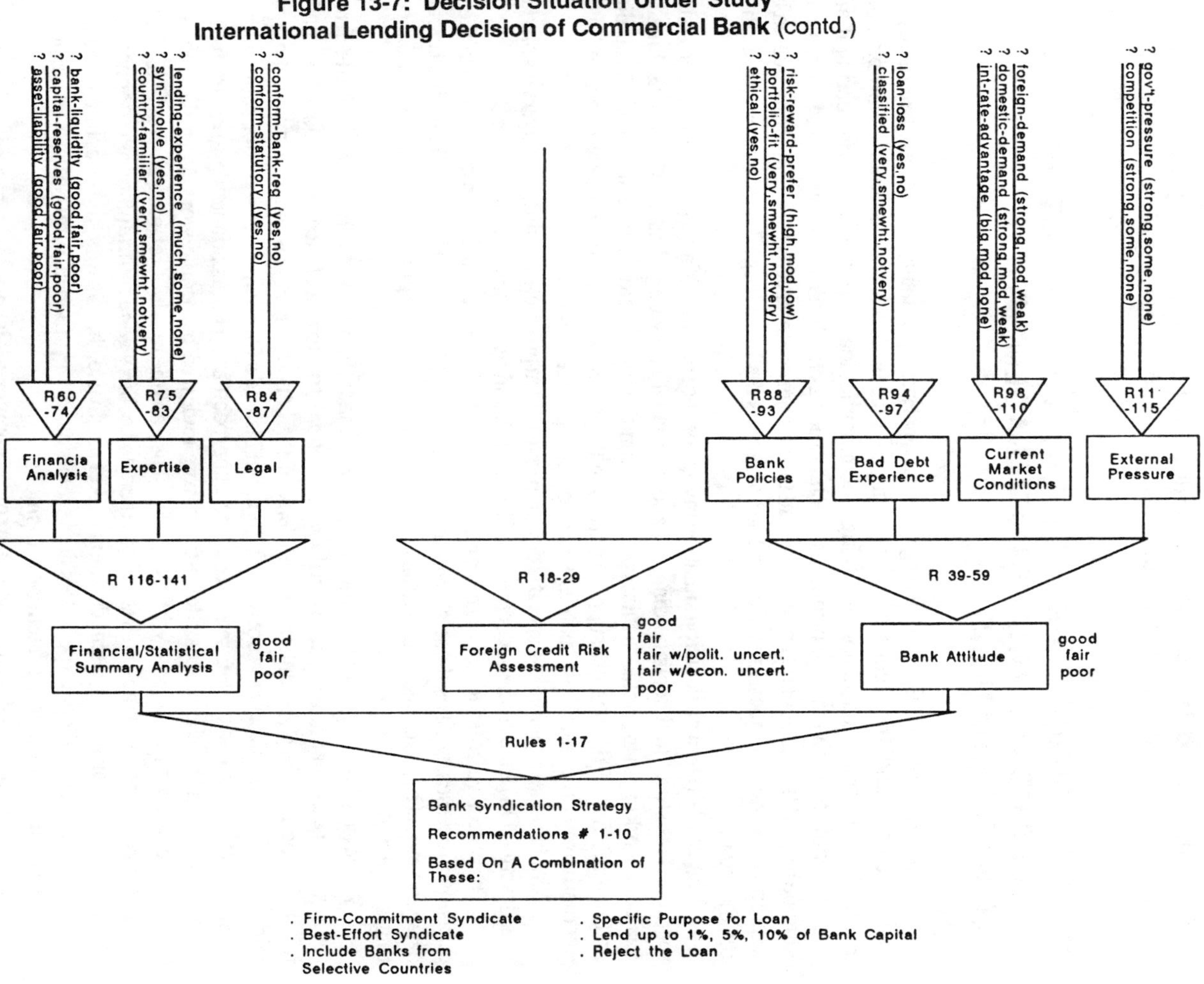

is given on the disks accompanying this book. Instructions for consulting the system are given in the instructor's booklet accompanying the disks. Later versions of the system include a much wider range of possible recommendations and more in-depth probing of situation factors.

CONTEXT-SPECIFIC PROCESSES INVOLVED IN OTHER MULTINATIONAL STRATEGIC MANAGEMENT DECISION SITUATIONS

Other decision situations involving multinational strategic management have been analyzed and structured, and knowledge-based systems have been developed for them. For example, Figure 13-7 diagrams a decision involving a commercial loan officer who is considering if and how to handle foreign loan opportunities. Factors such as the bank's ability to make the loan, its attitude toward the particular type of loan, and the foreign credit-risk assessment are evaluated by exploring a variety of questions. Figure 13-7 diagrams the knowledge-based system replicating the decision.

Figure 13-8 shows a decision situation involving the selection of a supply source for an Asian market. This structured decision diagram and its related knowledge-based system was done by someone working in the field. In this type of decision situation, factors concerning the availability and favorability of the nearest supply sources in the Asian market are first examined, and then alternatives in other markets, such as Brazil or Europe, are examined.

An additional example of a specific decision involved in product planning in an overseas market was described in detail in the second half of Chapter 9, and was diagramed in Figure 9-7.

The objective in defining how experts make such decisions and in drawing diagrams of these decision processes, such as those shown in Figures 13-3, 13-4, 13-6, 13-7, and 13-8, is to create a general model of the decision situation. The models function as a guideline (or expert guidance) to assist in making this kind of decision.

While they are models of how the decisions are made, however, the diagrams in the decision figures in this chapter are not necessarily *prescriptions* for how such decisions should be made in all situations. They are rather *descriptions* of the general process a fairly competent expert might use. Since the process is not a procedure, but instead a framework whose application varies by situation, it is an adaptive, semi-structured approach and is thus adaptable to an individual manager's situation. The process definitions were reviewed by people working in the field and by strategic planners associated with the study. They are the result of refining and revising many earlier rough drafts, until the experts judged them to be *fairly good* reformulations or replications of the approach a fairly competent decision maker might use. In this way, the structured situation analysis, based on typical expert decision scenarios, also provided semi-structured, adaptive models useful for prototype system development.

In addition to knowledge-based systems computer tools, a wide range of conventional computer tools are useful in doing strategy formulation for multinational operations. These tools and the mathematical and diagrammatic techniques underlying them are discussed in several useful supplemental texts [Mockler 1992; Webster 1989].

Figure 13-8: Decision Situation Under Study: Logistics Planning—Determining Supply Source Asian Market

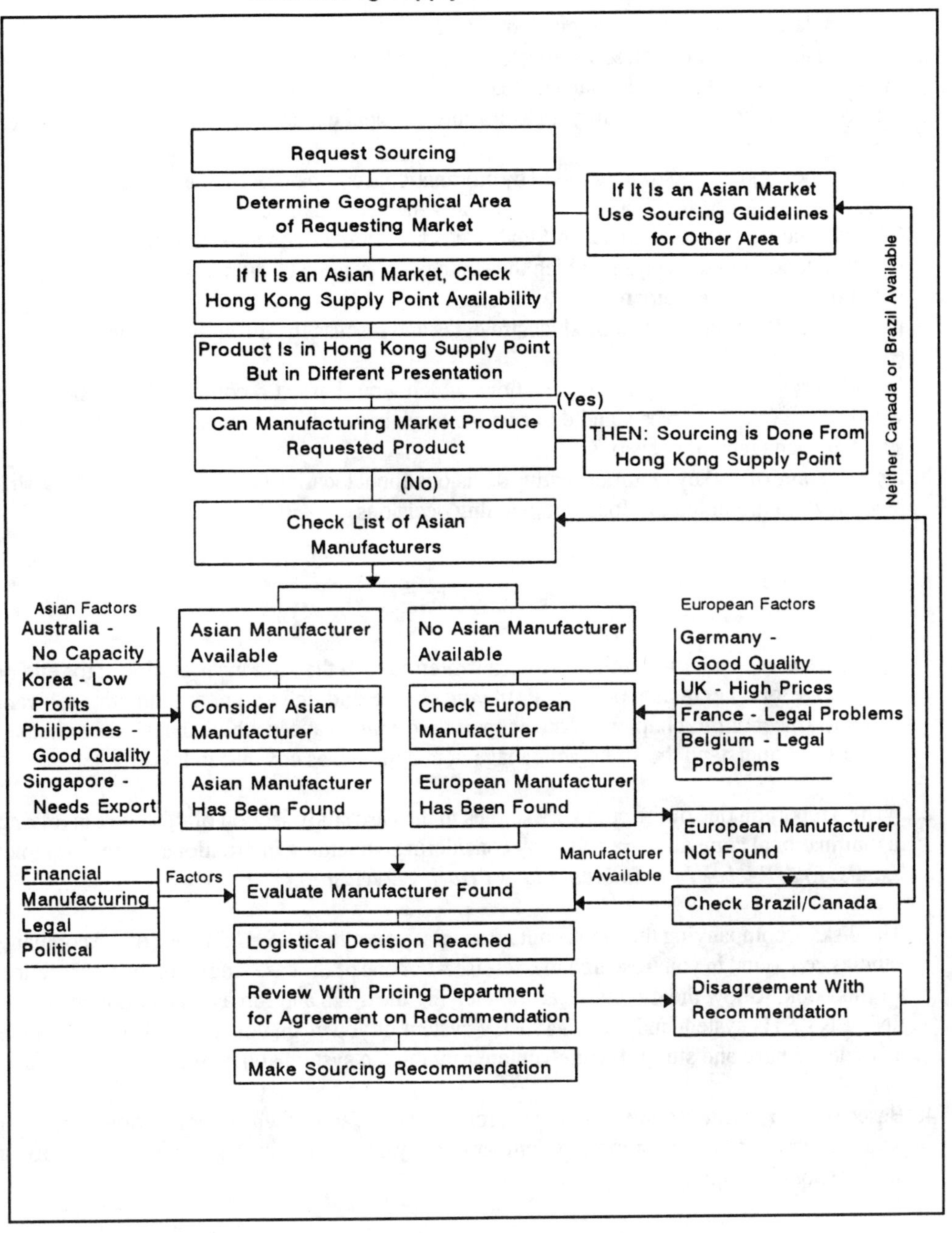

REVIEW QUESTIONS

1. List and describe some multinational companies.
2. Describe the major political, economic, legal, cultural, language, and other social factors which affect multinational strategic management.
3. Describe some major opportunity areas for international expansion, and discuss their differences.
4. Identify the major entry strategies used by multinational companies. Discuss the characteristics of each and describe the kinds of situations in which each can be effective.
5. Compare the entry strategies used by Stanley Works, Compaq, and Waste Management, paying special attention to the ways in which the strategy chosen did or did not suit each company's situation context requirements.
6. Describe major multinational product strategies and discuss the different situations in which each can be useful.
7. Describe some of the major considerations which would affect a company's decision as to whether to expand overseas, and describe the ways in which these considerations can affect strategic management decisions.
8. Identify some of the key factors affecting decisions about locating facilities overseas. Describe how they can affect facility location planning decisions.

EXERCISES

1. Read several recent issues of the periodicals referred to in the references section at the end of the chapter, or other related periodicals of your choice, and find a company situation relevant to some aspect of this chapter. Write a report describing ways in which that situation helped you better understand the strategic management approaches covered in this chapter.

2. Write a report on one of the company studies in the case study section of this book involving a multinational company or a company considering expanding internationally (for example, *Lands' End, Reebok International Ltd.*, or *Harley Davidson*).

3. The disks accompanying this book contain several prototype KBS. Using one of the company studies you found in your research in Exercise #1 or one of the case studies in the final section of this book, follow the directions accompanying the disks and run a consultation using the INT-ENT.STG system and the AIMS.REV system. If you wish, you might also print out the knowledge base and study it while you are running the system and restudying this chapter.

4. Based on your research done as part of exercise #1 above and on whatever additional research you feel is appropriate, prepare a company study involving strategic management for a multinational company.

REFERENCES

Baker, Stephen, et al., "Latin America: The Big Move to Free Markets," "Multinationals Step Lively to the Free-Trade Bossa Nova," and "Brave New Financial World," *Business Week*, June 15, 1992, pp. 50-62.

Bohlen, Celestine, "The Union Buried. What's Being Born," *The New York Times*, December 9, 1991, pp. A1, A9.

Brady, Rose, Peter Galuska, Richard A. Melcher, and David Greising, "Let's Make A Deal — But a Smaller One," *Business Week*, January 20, 1992, pp. 44, 45.

Bremner, Brian, "Europe's Garbage Smells Sweet to Waste Management," *Business Week*, May 29, 1989, p. 33.

Breskin, Ira, "Winning Back the Work That Got Away," *Business Week*, Innovation Issue, 1989, p. 148.

Carlton, Jim, and Neil Barsky, "Japanese Purchases of U.S. Real Estate Fall on Hard Times," *The Wall Street Journal*, February 21, 1992, pp. A1, A4.

Cohen, Roger, "For Coke, World Is Its Oyster," *The New York Times*, November 21, 1991, pp. D1, D5.

Cowell, Alan, "New Fiat from Poland Draws on Old Mystique," *The New York Times*, December 10, 1991, pp. D1, D9.

Elliot, Stuart, "Sampling Tastes of a Changing Russia," *The New York Times*, April 1, 1992, pp. D1, D5.

Galuszka, Peter, "The Deal of the Decade May Get Done in Moscow," *Business Week*, February 5th, 1989, pp. 54-55.

Garsombke, Diane J., "International Competitor Analysis," *Planning Review*, May/June 1989, pp. 42-47.

"Gillette Sets Soviet Venture with Terms for Currency," *The Wall Street Journal*, March 5, 1991, p. A13.

Greenhouse, Steven, "Polaroid's Russian Success Story," *The New York Times*, Business Section, November 24, 1991, pp. 1, 6.

Hawkins, Chuck, "Fedex: Europe Nearly Killed the Messenger," *Business Week*, May 25, 1992, pp. 124-126.

Henry III, William A., "History as It Happens," *Time*, January 6, 1992, pp. 24-27.

Hicks, Jonathan P., "The Takeover of American Industry," *The New York Times*, Business Section, May 28, 1989, pp. 1, 8.

Johnson, Robert, and Allanna Sullivan, "A Small Joint Venture Is Leading the Way in Getting Russian Oil," *The Wall Street Journal*, January 29, 1992, pp. A1, A7.

Kanter, Rosabeth Moss, *When Giants Learn To Dance*, New York: Simon and Schuster, 1989.

Kelly, Kevin, Otis Port, James Treece, Gail DeGeorge, and Zachery Schiller, "Learning from Japan," *Business Week*, January 27, 1992, pp. 52-60.

Lampert, Hope, "Marketing to Local Tastes," *Business Month*, August 1989, pp. 37-41.

Lehner, Urban C., and Alan Murray, "Strained Alliance: 'Selling of America' to Japanese Touches Some Very Raw Nerves," *The Wall Street Journal*, June 19, 1990, pp. A1, A14.

Lewis, Jordan D., *Crafting Strategic Alliances: Corporate Partnerships for Growth and Profit*, New York: Free Press, 1990.

Lohr, Steve, "Compaq's Conquests in Europe," *The New York Times*, Business Section, July 9, 1989, p. 4.

Lohr, Steve, "Under the Wing of Japan Inc., a Fledging Enterprise Soared," *The New York Times,* January 15, 1992, pp. A1, D5.

Lohr, Steve, "U.S. Industry's New Global Power," *The New York Times,* March 4, 1991, pp. D1, D3.

McGill, Douglas C., "Pepsico, to Aid Europe Sales, Buys 2 British Snack Units," *The New York Times,* July 4, 1989, pp. 41-42.

Mockler, Robert J., *Computer Software to Support Strategic Management Decision Making,* New York: Macmillan, 1992.

Montague, Bill, "Huge Deals Now Look Like Big Mistakes," *USA Today,* March 30, 1992, pp. 1B, 2B.

Murray, Tom, "From European to Pan-European," *Business Month,* August 1989, pp. 35-37.

O'Boyle, Thomas F., "Bridgestone Discovers Purchase of U.S. Firm Creates Big Problems," *The Wall Street Journal,* April 1, 1991, pp. A1, A4.

Pearl, Daniel, "Federal Express Finds Its Pioneering Falls Flat Overseas," *The Wall Street Journal,* April 15, 1991, pp. A1, A8.

Prokesch, Steven, "Europe Taking a Lead in Growth," *The New York Times,* January 15, 1990, pp. D1, D2.

Ramirez, Anthony,"Gillette Is Planning to Open a Plant in the Soviet Union," *The New York Times,* February 2, 1990, pp. D1, D2.

Robinson, Phillip, Garth Alexander, and Andrew Davidson, "Sony's Hollywood Nightmare," *The Sunday Times* (London), Business Section, October 13, 1991, p. 9.

Rose, Robert L., "How 3M, by Tiptoeing Into Foreign Markets, Became a Big Exporter," *The Wall Street Journal,* March 29, 1991, pp. A1, A5.

Sanger, David E., "Honda Raises Its Stake in Europe," *The New York Times,* July 14, 1989, pp. D1, D4.

Shapiro, Eben, "Pepsico Sets Its Sights on Spain," *The New York Times,* November 7, 1991, pp. D1, D24.

Shapiro, Eben, "Overseas Sizzles for McDonald's," *The New York Times,* April 17, 1992, D1, D4.

Strom, Stephanie, "More Suppliers Are Helping Stores Push Merchandise," *The New York Times,* January 20, 1992, D1, D8.

Swasy, Alecia, "Foreign Formula: Proctor & Gamble Fixes Aim on Tough Market: The Latin Americans," *The Wall Street Journal,* June 15, 1990, pp. A1, A4.

Tanzer, Andrew, "Ding-dong, Capitalism Calling," *Forbes,* October 14, 1991, pp. 184-186.

Treece, James B., Karen Lowry Miller, and Richard A. Melcher, "The Partners: Surprise! Ford and Mazda Have Built a Strong Team, Here's How," *Business Week,* February 10, 1992, pp. 102-107.

Uchitelle, Louis, "The Stanley Works Goes Global" *The New York Times,* Business Section, July 23, 1989(A), pp. 1, 10.

Uchitelle, Louis, "U.S. Businesses Loosen Link to Mother Country," *The New York Times,* May 21, 1989(B), pp. 1, 30.

Webster, James L., William E. Reif, and Jeffrey S. Bracker, "The Manager's Guide to Strategic Planning Tools and Techniques," *Planning Review,* November/December, 1989, pp. 4-12, 48.

"World View: Ted Turner's CNN Global Gains Influence," *The Wall Street Journal,* February 1, 1990, pp. A1, A6.

Wright, Diana, and Richard Woods, "Investors See Europe as Best Market in 1990s," *The Sunday Times* (London), January 10, 1990, p. E10.

CHAPTER 14

STRATEGIC MANAGEMENT IN SITUATIONS INVOLVING MAJOR SOCIAL FACTORS

The objective of this chapter is to help readers to:

- Understand the nature of the diverse and changing social environment, as well as some critical social issues affecting strategic management
- Make general strategic management decisions in situations involving critical social factors
- This overall context-specific process at work in specific situation contexts

Making strategic management decisions in business is not always just a matter of studying business and market factors and reaching a recommendation based on them. These decisions not only have to make sense for the markets involved, they also must make sense for society in general. This chapter concerns strategy formulation and implementation in situations involving critical social factors.

This chapter begins by reviewing relevant social changes which have occurred during the last three decades and by describing the diverse society facing business in the 1990s. The critical social issues and the interest groups through which these issues impact on business decision making are discussed. The actual impact on business decision making and some of the strategic opportunities, threats, and key-to-success factors flowing from them, as well as some of the strategies developed by business to cope with and take advantage of them, are covered. The second half of the chapter discusses the general process involved in making strategic management decisions in light of these social factors, as well as ways this general process works in specific situations.

A DIVERSE AND CHANGING SOCIAL ENVIRONMENT

Society in this country is diverse and dynamic. The nature and concept of the family is changing. Today substantial numbers of mothers work, and although previously declining birth rates have stabilized recently, annual birth rates are still below the peak numbers recorded during the baby-boom years. The number of unmarried couples living together has increased dramatically, and in July 1989 New York City even formally redefined the concept of a family to include couples of the same sex living together.

Life-styles have been influenced by technological advances. Developments in transportation, communications, information processing, genetic engineering, and many other areas have changed the way we talk to each other, travel, and do business. For example, people can now work at home, in motels, or anywhere they have access to a telephone and a computer. People are also better informed worldwide. Satellite cable news broadcasts can enable people in an apartment in Czechoslovakia or China to observe riots in America or even in their own country and hear objective reports on what is actually happening — not just the tales spun by government opinion molders. This satellite service is an outstanding example of how technology has stimulated major social and political changes, most profoundly in the breakup and freeing of the Soviet Union and Central Europe [Henry 1992].

In spite of the increasing wealth in this country in the 1980s, the savings rate in the United States in 1990 was only 3 percent, compared with 5 percent in Japan and 12 percent in Germany. This is an example of one of the ways in which the United States society's attitudes towards the traditional conservative value of saving had changed to one of spending to support new life styles. Predictions for the 1990s are that the next generation will shift back to being a saving generation [Ravo 1992].

Crime and related drug problems have become a major concern of society, especially in urban areas where crime rates are high and in some instances still rising. Increasing interest in issues related to maintaining law and order, including security for people and property, is an outgrowth of this.

Health concerns have mounted, ranging from radon in the ground to ozone in the air — dangerous levels of which have been measured and publicized. This concern has led to additional changes in life styles — where people live, the products they buy, where they dine. Even where people vacation, the kinds of vacations they take, and what they wear can be affected by health concerns. Advances in medicine have suggested ways to improve the quality of life as one ages, and perhaps even to increase longevity. This has led to changes in the way we eat, the foods we buy, and the steps we take to stay fit — all of which have created new business opportunities. These changes and movements are accentuated, and perhaps distorted to some degree, by an omnipresent media whose power has grown substantially, even to the point of influencing the outcomes of national elections.

These changes have led to the emergence of identifiable social values and attitudes that have an impact on business:

- A rising social conscience that emphasizes ethical behavioral for both government and business
- Concern for the protection of the environment
- Concern for health-related matters
- Changing family values and greater concern for the individual
- A more balanced view of discrimination — one that favors no segment of society over another, regardless of gender, creed, color, or country of origin
- A concern for issues affecting law and order
- Changing life styles

The above is only a sampling of the many changes occurring in society that impact on strategic management in business. These changes have raised many important issues to business managers.

SOME CRITICAL SOCIAL ISSUES AFFECTING STRATEGIC MANAGEMENT IN BUSINESS

This section discusses critical social issues in such areas as consumerism, ecology, health and safety, and civil rights.

Consumerism

Consumerism is defined as any set of activities by any group (government, public and private organizations, or businesses) designed to protect the interests of consumers. The term refers to a broad movement which was given substantial impetus by Ralph Nader and the publication of his book *Unsafe at Any Speed* [1965]. This book pointed out that General Motors knew that its Corvair automobile was unsafe, yet continued to promote and sell it. The movement covers a wide range of areas: truth in advertising and lending, competitive pricing, and deceptive trade practices; food and drug product safety, effectiveness, and labeling; motor vehicle safety standards and automobile fuel economy standards; and meat, poultry, and egg inspection and labeling.

Consumer protection legislation is not a new phenomenon. The Pure Food and Drug Act (1906), the Meat Inspection Act (1906), and the creation of the Federal Trade Commission in 1914 are early examples of such legislation. The 1960s and 1970s saw such consumer protection laws as the Hazardous Substances Labeling Act (1960), Fair Packaging and Labeling Act (1966), Consumer Credit Protection Act (1968), Child Protection and Toy Safety Act (1969), Consumer Product Safety Act (1972), Magnuson-Moss Warranty Act (1975), and Equal Credit Opportunity Act (1977). The consumer movement peaked during the late 1970s and, while strongly enforced, did not expand greatly during Reagan's presidency, primarily because many major problems already had been covered by earlier legislation.

Ecology

Ecological issues deal with the interaction of plants and animals in the environment. The issues most relevant to strategic management involve those situations where waste produced by businesses pollutes the land, water, and air. Concern for the environment was given considerable impetus by the publication of Rachel Carson's book *Silent Spring* (1962), in which she argued forcefully that steps be taken to protect our environment. The ecological movement, which gained momentum during the 1960s and 1970s, is concerned with such areas as water and air quality, noise pollution, toxic substances and hazardous wastes, radiation, pesticides and herbicides, solid wastes, food contamination, and land restoration.

Federal legislation passed to protect the environment includes: National Environment Policy Act (1969), Clean Air Act (1970 and 1977), Noise Pollution and Control Act (1972), Water Pollution Control Act (1972), Pesticide Control Act (1972), Hazardous Materials Transport Act (1974), and Comprehensive Environmental Response, Compensation, and Liability Act — "Superfund" (1980 and 1986). States such as California also have strict legislation covering pollution, as do local communities.

Various private nonprofit and government agencies oversee the enforcement of this legislation and promote a wide range of public concerns about the environment.

Health and Safety

The government established the Occupational Safety and Health Administration (OSHA) in 1970 to ensure that workplaces are free from recognized hazards that cause, or are likely to cause, death or serious injury. It was given broad powers to inspect, fine, and, at times, ask that employers found to be in violation of certain regulations be jailed. In addition to OSHA, many states have laws and regulatory agencies to monitor worker health and safety.

In addition to those heath and safety areas covered by government regulations and control, some segments of society feel that businesses have an obligation to assist in solving broader social health problems, for example, through programs for treating drug abuse and alcoholism and preventing AIDS. A problem frequently encountered here is that the laws governing such actions are not clear. An individual's rights to privacy often must be balanced with the rights of fellow workers to know of the existence of diseases or substance abuse in the workplace.

Civil Rights

Civil rights issues focus on getting businesses to take affirmative action to overcome job discrimination so that equal employment opportunities will be available to all people, regardless of age, race, color, creed, physical or mental handicap, sex, sexual orientation, or country of origin. As with consumerism and ecology, attention to the civil rights movement increased dramatically during the 1960s and 1970s, especially through the works of the late Martin Luther King, Jr., and the publication of books by feminists such as Betty Frieden [1963 and 1983].

Federal legislation passed to deal with job discrimination includes the Equal Pay Act (1963), Civil Rights Act (1964), Age Discrimination in Employment Act (1967), Equal Employment Opportunity Act (1972), Vocational Rehabilitation Act (1973), and the Americans with Disabilities Act (1990). In addition, executive orders have been issued, and a wide range of state and local laws have been passed.

Principal approaches to solving job discrimination problems in the past have been passive nondiscrimination (hiring and promotion decisions made without regard to race, sex, or other factors covered by law), affirmative action (making efforts to attract minorities, women, and others covered by the law), affirmative action with preferential hiring, and employment quotas.

INTEREST GROUPS

The impact of these social issues and of the changes occurring in society is felt by business through a variety of interest groups, who freely use a powerful media and active legislators to push their causes. Such social activism has had and will continue to have a major role on strategic management in business during the 1990s.

Pluralism, that is, the existence of groups among which there is a relative balance of power and variety of allegiances, is basic to this country's notion of democracy. It is the principle upon which the division of power among three branches of government is based. Business and government bodies, while very powerful, are only two of many groups in society that impact on strategic management.

Consumer Interest Groups

Some of the federal agencies which deal with consumer protection are the Federal Trade Commission, Food and Drug Administration, Consumer Product Safety Commission, and National Highway Traffic Safety Administration. State, county and city departments of consumer affairs also exist.

In addition to government agencies, a large number of private organizations promote consumer protection. For example, the Consumer Federation of America brings together hundreds of nonprofit consumer groups, representing some 30-million Americans. Consumers' Research and Consumers' Union test consumer products and publish magazines giving the results of those tests. Ralph Nader and his associates have formed a number of groups advocating consumer interests, including Health Research Group, Citizen Action Group, Litigation Group, Tax Reform Research, Congress Watch, and Public Citizen. Community groups, television consumer advocates, and consumer cooperatives also work to protect consumer interests.

Environmentalists

The primary government agency dealing with the protection of the environment is the Environmental Protection Agency (EPA), which was created in 1970 to coordinate most of the federal government's efforts in this area. Other agencies whose efforts the EPA might coordinate include the Interior Department, Labor Department, Health and Human Resources Department, Energy Department, Transportation Department, Nuclear Regulatory Commission, and Agriculture Department. Government controls are applied by setting and enforcing standards, giving incentives for improvement, bringing pollution charges, and issuing pollution rights that can be sold.

Many private groups also serve as watchdogs over pollution. These include the Sierra Club's Foundation and Legal Defense Fund, the National Wildlife Federation, and the Environmental Defense Fund and Natural Resources Defense Council. Local groups are quite active in this area because pollution is often a community problem.

Civil Rights Activists

Federal government agencies that deal with equal opportunity laws are the Equal Employment Opportunity Commission (EEOC), the Office of Federal Contract Compliance Programs (OFCCP) in the Department of Labor, and the Department of Education. Many state and local agencies exist to enforce state and local equal opportunity laws.

Well-known private groups working for civil rights are the National Association for the Advancement of Colored People (NAACP), the Congress for Racial Equality (CORE), the National Organization for Women (NOW), and the Women's Equity Action League (WEAL).

Labor Unions

Unions have had varying degrees of impact on business, from the early consolidated efforts of Maine fishermen to protest wages in 1636, to the formation of craft unions in the 1790s, to the strike of the Professional Air Traffic Controllers Organization strike during President Reagan's administration which represented a major setback for unions.

While their effectiveness varies from situation to situation, unions are still a potent force in society, as was witnessed at Eastern Airlines in 1989 when a union strike reduced the airline's size and eventually put it out of business [Salpukas 1991].

Individual Employee Rights

Individual employee rights were given more attention during the 1980s. For example, the rights of individuals to some control of their personnel records, to nondisclosure of medical problems, to complain about illegal acts to outside agencies without recrimination, and to certain types of information affecting their health and well-being, have all been raised as issues. While laws covering these issues are still not widespread, such issues can be raised by individual employees and have an impact on a company. For example, both Epson America and Nissan Motors Corporation U.S.A. are being sued over issues related to the privacy of an individual's electronic mail [Rifkin 1991].

Stockholders and Other Company Stakeholders

Stockholders, suppliers, creditors, and distributors all have a clear interest in a company's decisions. Their influence can vary from instituting lawsuits over mergers, as at Time Inc. in 1989, to pressuring companies to divest interests in companies that do business in South Africa, to attacking CEO compensation [Cowan 1992], to simply voting their interests at annual meetings.

All of the groups covered in this section have at one time had some impact on strategic management in business. This influence can be exerted through direct contact with management, initiating lawsuits, pressuring customers not to buy, influencing legislators to propose and pass new laws, and especially through the *media*—one of the major groups affecting business decision making in today's society.

THE IMPACT OF THESE ISSUES AND INTEREST GROUPS ON BUSINESS STRATEGIC MANAGEMENT

Social issues and the interest groups advocating them have a wide and varying impact on different business situations.

Protection of the Environment

Environmental concerns are a source of opportunities and threats for strategic planners. For example, industries have been created to treat waste, clean the air, and help industry fight pollution problems.

New consumer product opportunities are being developed in response to environmental needs. For example, automakers both in the U.S. and abroad are developing electric-powered cars ["Stand By" 1991; Wald 1992], organic wines are growing in popularity [Fisher 1991], Corning Inc. sells over $200 million annually of catalytic converters used to control automobile exhaust emissions [Appleman 1992], and windmills are generating power in California and Hawaii [Wald 1991]. A market even seems to be developing for the sale of pollution rights [Stevenson 1992; Taylor 1992].

The 1989 oil spill from an Exxon tanker in the waters off Alaska dramatically demonstrated the threats to a company arising in the ecological area. Not only Exxon, but the entire industry, was threatened with additional legislation and regulation [Stevenson 1989(B)].

Several factors influence company decisions in the ecological area. The cost of complying with pollution controls can be overwhelming. For example, President Bush's proposed amendments to the Clean Air Act in 1989 were estimated to cost industry between $14 and $18 billion. In addition, competitive pressures exist; overseas industries often operate at lower costs because they do not have to meet the pollution control requirements that firms do.

Balancing the public's need for protection with the public's need for a healthy economy and reasonably priced products is part of the decision process in many situations involving social issues (as seen in the following sections). In many instances, this need has led to a cooperative negotiating atmosphere, in contrast to the earlier confrontational atmosphere, between companies and interest groups in resolving ecological problems by reaching compromises.

Consumer Protection

Business feels the impact of the consumer protection movement from a variety of sources and responds in different ways. For example, banks are feeling pressures arising from complaints about discrimination against groups and individuals in making loans. In one instance, ACORN, a consumer protection group, forced Chemical Bank and Manufacturers Hanover Trust Company to agree to make more such loans ($750 million over five years) by threatening to file a lawsuit which would have held up the proposed merger of the two banks [Quint 1991].

Other threats have arisen in the cable television and insurance industries, where the public exerts continual pressure for reduced rates. In broadcasting, ABC canceled a show and Fox Network modified the content of several of its shows during 1989 because of pressure put on advertisers by individuals and consumer organizations.

Consumers' perception of what is fair and reasonable has for many companies become a critical success factor—when designing products, creating advertising strategies, and even hiring salespeople. In the consumer area, as in other social issue areas, businesses have been active in having legislation modified to be more reasonable and equitable from their viewpoint. This is clearly a viable option in many situations involving critical social issues.

Business Ethics

Ethics is a word used commonly for actions that violate some arbitrary standard (such as an industry or professional association code of ethics — for example, it used to be unethical for a lawyer to advertise). Although considered incorrect usage by some, the term "ethics" is also often used to describe actions that are immoral (lying, cheating, or stealing), illegal, or just something we do not like (for example, when a company has a rigid defective product return policy).

Paying attention to ethical standards and concerns, however they are defined in individual situations, can have a major strategic impact on a company. For example, in the 1980s, product tampering of Johnson and Johnson's Tylenol led to customer deaths. The company swiftly recalled its products and redesigned the product and packaging to make tampering more difficult. This swift and decisive action, while costly, overcame consumer fears and eventually saved one of the company's most profitable product lines ["Tylenol" 1986].

When problems involving sensitive social issues arise, such as at Johnson and Johnson, experience suggests that the strategy to consider first is to admit the problems quickly and take immediate action to solve them, where possible. Dow Corning Corporation did not follow such a policy, and only gradually disclosed its prior knowledge of problems with its silicone breast implants, opening the company to accusations of moral evasion [Fink 1992]. Union Carbide acted similarly in ignoring warnings about problems at its Bhopal, India plant, and was still suffering in 1992 from the mishandling of those warnings and the subsequent disaster that occurred when the plant exploded in 1984 [McMurray 1992].

Strategies of denial and hesitation often backfire. In 1986, when the financial services firm of E.F. Hutton was accused of handling its banking transactions illegally, the company at first denied the charges. The company later admitted to these fraudulent actions when documents showed that company managers knew of the transactions in question. Eventually, the company pleaded guilty to several thousand counts of mail fraud, paid fines of several million dollars, lost customers and employees, and received a great deal of bad publicity in a business that depends on customer confidence [Feloni 1989; Sterngold 1990]. In contrast, when the brokerage firm Salomon Inc. encountered fraudulent trading problems, they brought in Warren Buffet, a conservative, well-respected private investor/manager, as CEO. He changed the corporate culture at Salomon and successfully led the firm through its crisis [Faison 1992]. Phar-Mor Inc., a rapidly growing discount pharmacy chain discussed earlier in this book, took a $350 million charge against earnings and filed for bankruptcy in 1992, after two top executives were accused of embezzlement ["Phar-Mor...," 1992].

Taking steps to prevent incidents such as those at E.F. Hutton, Phar-Mor, and Dow Corning from happening, incorporating ethical policies into strategic plans, and enforcing those policies are important first steps towards minimizing future ethical problems and promoting good public relations. Several examples of such policies are cited later in this chapter.

Health and Safety

The impact of employee health and safety on business decision making in this area is felt most often through government regulations and pressure groups. Not complying with regulations can lead to fines; however, the fines are sometimes minimal and the required inspections under OSHA regulations are at times infrequent. For this reason, some companies find the risks of fines a cheaper alternative than the cost of maintaining the required paperwork and complying with regulations.

Pressures from groups concerned with health, such as the American Cancer Society and the Women vs. Smoking Network, forced J. Reynolds Tobacco to withdraw its new cigarette, Uptown. According to experts, this was a dramatic example of the power of concerned "consumers" and their substantial impact on new product success [Schiffman 1990].

After years of insisting that safety features did not sell cars, automakers changed advertising strategies in the 1990s in response to the public's concern for health and safety. Chrysler, Volvo, Ford, BMW, and General Motors all were running ads emphasizing safety in the early 1990s [Judge 1990]. Consumer concerns about health problems from excessive fat and cholesterol in fried foods have affected products offered by and profits of fast-food companies, supermarket chains, and major food companies.

In other health and safety areas, some companies have established new policies for dealing with such social problems as drug and alcohol abuse. Figure 14-1 gives one institution's policies concerning drugs.

Many companies, such as Grace Specialty Chemicals, have moved aggressively to make health and safety concerns an inherent part of their strategic plans. In 1989, the company had 113 full-time employees working in safety, health, and environmental areas in its various plants worldwide because of the importance of these social concerns to the company's success [Fowler 1989].

Figure 14-1: Enterprise Drug Policy

TO: All Administrators
FROM:
DATE: June 20, 1990
RE: Drug-Free Workplace

The following is self-explanatory and is issued at this time in response to federal requirements. Our company is committed to the maintenance of a drug-free workplace and is committed both to rigorous enforcement of applicable laws and policies and to support for those trying to cope with drug-related problems.

1. Our company is committed to maintaining a drug-free workplace in compliance with applicable laws. The unlawful possession, use, distribution, dispensing, sale or manufacture of controlled substances is prohibited on company premises. Violation of this policy may result in termination of employment or the imposition of other employment discipline as defined by existing company policies, employment contracts and/or labor agreements. All company employees must abide by this policy. At the discretion of the company, and after following appropriate procedures, any employee convicted of a drug offense involving the workplace shall be subject to employee discipline and/or required to satisfactorily complete a drug rehabilitation program as a condition of continued employment.
2. The illegal use of controlled substance can seriously injure the health of employees; adversely impair the performance of their responsibilities; and endanger the safety and well-being of fellow employees and members of the general public. Therefore, the company urges employees engaged in the illegal use of controlled substances to seek professional advice and treatment. Anyone who is employed at this company who has a drug problem is invited to participate in the Substance Abuse Prevention Program (copy attached). Employees engaged in contracts with the U.S. Department of Defense are additionally subject to D.O.D. requirements and may be required to submit to tests for the illegal use of controlled substances.
3. In order to comply with federal law, this company requires that an employee notify the Executive Vice President, Company Substance Abuse Prevention Program, of any criminal drug statute conviction for a violation occurring in the workplace no later than 5 days after such conviction. The company must notify any federal contracting agency within 10 days of having received notice that an employee engaged in the performance of such contract has had any criminal drug conviction for a violation occurring in the workplace. After following appropriate procedures, the company will impose a sanction on, or require the satisfactory participation in a drug abuse assistance or rehabilitation program by, any employee who is so convicted.
4. This statement and its requirements are promulgated in accordance with the requirements of the Drug-Free Workplace Act of 1988 enacted by the United States Congress. The company will continue its efforts to maintain a drug-free environment by adhering to the above policy and by providing on-going drug awareness programs, such as those contained in and envisioned by the company's Substance Abuse Prevention Program.

____
Executive Vice President

Society's concern with health has also opened up a wide range of opportunities for business, from health-food companies to health club chains to major magazine publishers.

Equal Opportunity Employment

In the past, business has felt the impact of civil rights concerns most dramatically through the courts. During the 1970s and 1980s, for example, General Motors and AT&T were involved in lawsuits over alleged job discrimination. The resulting judgments cost the companies tens of millions of dollars. Because of potential threats in this area, many companies welcome the government regulations covering equal employment opportunities, which provide the companies with an objective basis for measuring their progress or position in the area of affirmative action.

Concerns in the 1990s are shifting to women and minority penetration of higher paying jobs in companies [White 1991]. This is the direction from which new threats, and perhaps new opportunities, may arise. For example, on July 11, 1989, Chrysler Corporation announced it had reached an agreement with the NAACP to double to 20 percent the number of women and members of minorities in management roles. Chrysler was the 62nd American company to sign such an agreement ["Chrysler" 1989]. At some larger firms, specific open-door policies and programs have been introduced to promote the hiring of blacks and women and to help them advance into higher management positions [Fowler 1990; Kilborn 1990]. Some firms also have programs which offer part-time professionals the same career advancement opportunities as full-time workers [Deutsch 1990].

Publishing companies often have specific guidelines as to what illustrations in children's books must include. One company required a single illustration to contain black and white twins, an overweight Oriental boy, an American Indian girl, a handicapped Caucasian, a female Irish setter, and a senior citizen jogging [Chira 1990].

In early 1992, the most sweeping anti-discrimination law since the Civil Rights Act of 1964 — the Americans with Disabilities Act — took affect. To meet the new law's specifications, banks might possibly have to lower some automatic teller machines so they could be reached by people in wheelchairs, restaurants might have to provide braille menus or have waiters read menus aloud for the blind, and theaters might have to provide space for people in wheelchairs and their companions [Holmes 1992].

The dangers of not having nondiscriminatory promotion and pay policies in place was illustrated again in 1992 when a woman passed over for a promotion at American Airlines was awarded $7.1 million as compensative and punitive damages based on sex, age, and disability discrimination [Lewin 1992].

MAKING STRATEGIC MANAGEMENT DECISIONS IN SPECIFIC READER SITUATIONS

As seen in Figure 14-2, the decision-making processes described in this chapter relate to other strategic management areas. Figure 14-3, an extension of the general process outlined in

Figure 14-2: Strategic Management Decision-Making Process

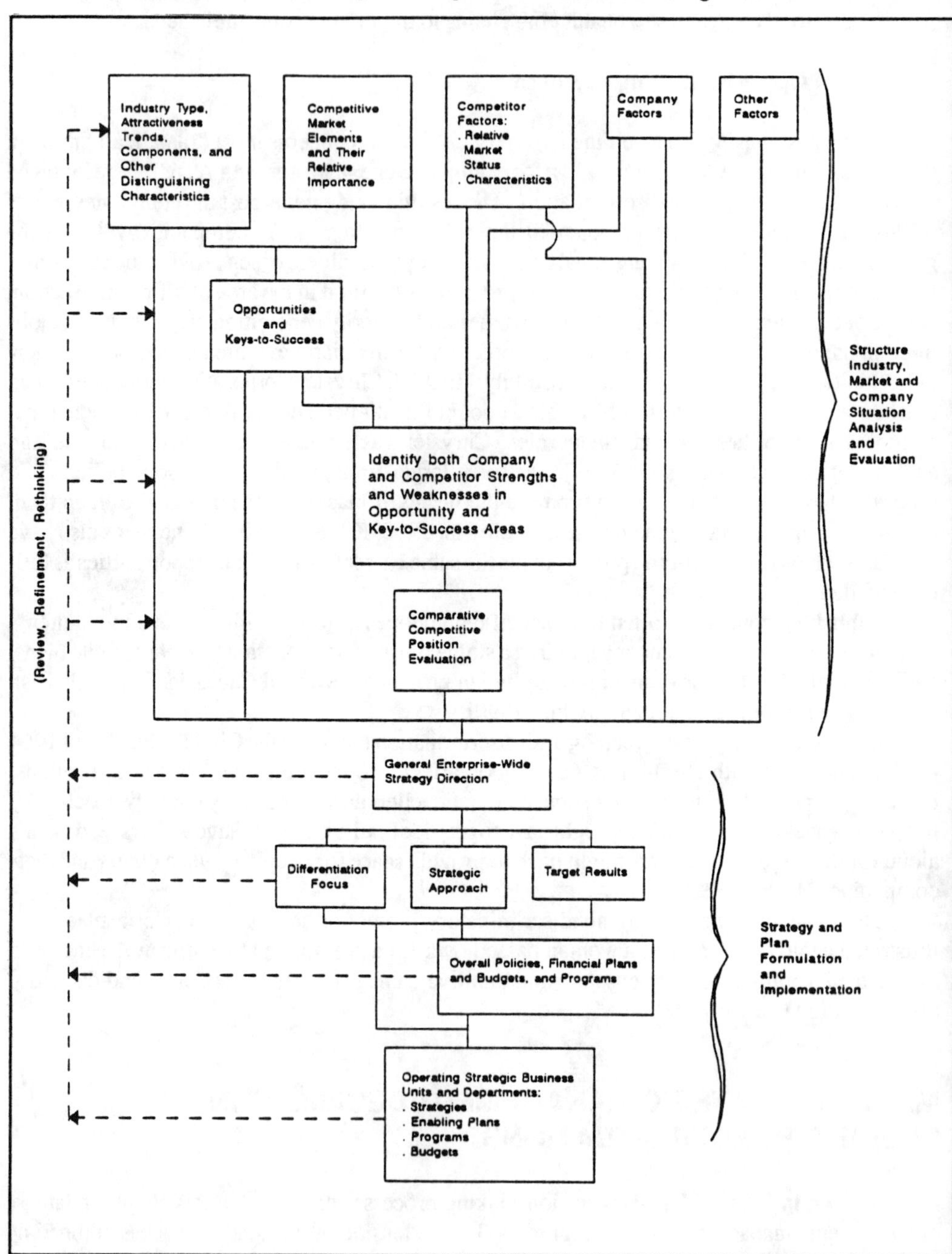

Figure 14-3: An Approach to Developing Strategies in Situations Involving Critical Social Factors

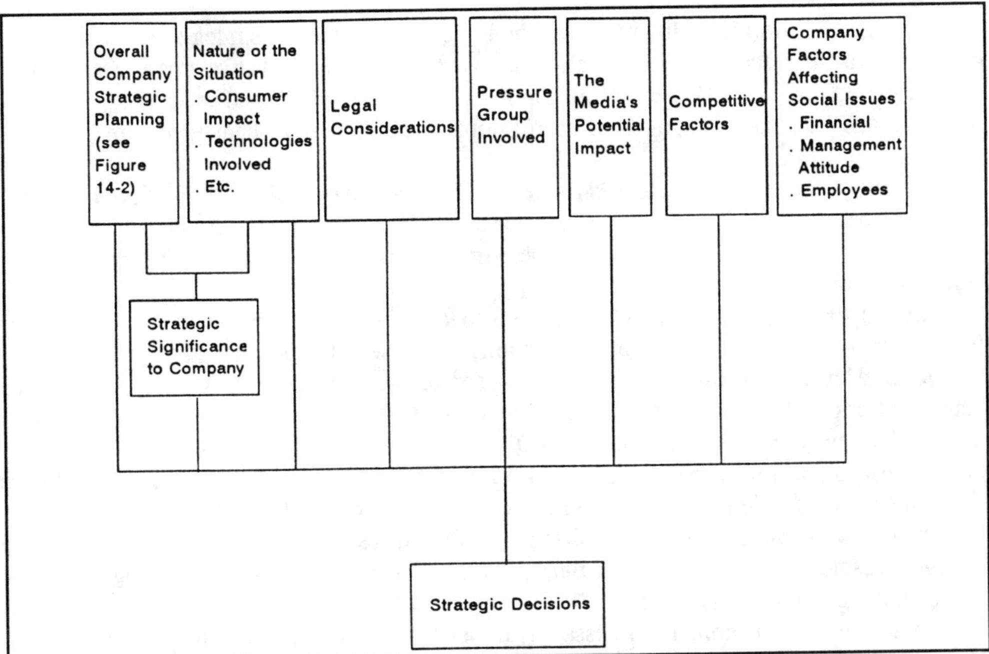

varies from situation to situation. In light of the variety of possible situations, not all the factors identified in the diagram in Figure 14-3 are applicable in every situation. The diagram does, however, serve as a useful model of the basic strategic management process involved in these situations.

Critical Factors Affecting Decisions in This Area

The factors discussed in this section include overall-company strategy and strategic plans; the actual situation, legal considerations, pressure groups involved, the media's potential impact, competitive factors, and company factors.

Overall-company strategic factors. The overall strategic management context is one reference point used to determine the relative importance of social issues. For example, a supermarket depends on consumer goodwill and acceptance for success. In situations of this kind, the perception of protecting customers' rights (especially in regards to health and safety) and of being honest in dealings with customers (especially in regards to pricing) are critical social concerns of today's consumers and so affect a supermarket's long-term strategic success. For this reason, in this industry these specific social issues would have a major impact on strategy formulation.

concerns of today's consumers and so affect a supermarket's long-term strategic success. For this reason, in this industry these specific social issues would have a major impact on strategy formulation.

The actual situation. In situations involving social issues of strategic importance to a company, it is first necessary to obtain all the relevant facts. This is not always as easy as it might seem. For example, days elapsed before Union Carbide management had an accurate picture of what had and was happening at its plant in Bhopal, India, due to inadequate communications facilities.

In emergency situations, such as Exxon's 1989 Alaskan oil spill, such facts are necessary since the first step is to take action to contain the emergency and minimize the damage. They are also necessary to determine the extent of the problems, as well as the available technology for correcting them.

In less dramatic situations, a planner needs to identify the issues involved and any relevant facts. This is often difficult in pollution situations, since the pollution source is often unclear. In addition, the levels of health dangers existing are sometimes uncertain. For instance, many foods contain traces of dangerous chemicals, but acceptable levels of such traces exist. These permissible levels can change as new scientific evidence becomes available and as pressure groups push for lowering the levels considered safe [Reinhold 1990]. Further, in the future companies will be able to buy pollution rights — that is, the right to exceed pollution levels [Hershey 1989; Stevenson 1992]. Establishing the facts in a situation, then, at times may require conducting scientific tests. At other times, it may require reconciling conflicting results of ambiguous tests and data analyses.

Whatever the situation, it is necessary to define the problem, and determine what information is factual, what is speculative, and areas in which more information is needed.

Legal considerations. In many situations, the precise legal restrictions and regulations applying to a situation will affect the decisions made and strategies developed — at times they may even dictate courses of action. For example, government regulations specify the exact wording and positioning of warnings required on cigarette packages and in cigarette advertisements.

Laws and regulations are not always clear, however, as evidenced by the number of lawsuits filed each year. While equal employment opportunities are required by law, the exact measurements of successful compliance are not always clear. In many situations, negotiation is required, as during the hiring of a workforce to build the Alaskan pipeline described below. At other times, the courts must decide, as in the many preferential hiring programs established by the courts during the 1980s.

Sometimes laws and regulations only partially define situation requirements, as with the AIDS issue. Companies, therefore, often initiate legislation in order to avoid uncertainty. In undefined situations, a company might even go so far as to take on a precedent-setting lawsuit. In these instances, estimates are needed of the chances of winning, since the impact of the case may have industry-wide implications and create problems instead of solving them. This happened in New York City when a simple eviction case under existing laws led to a court's redefinition of what constituted a family. The 1989 ruling said that unmarried people living together for a specific length of time could be considered a family. This meant that rent-controlled apartments could be passed on to friends as well as family members when someone left, preventing landlords from getting substantial rent increases allowed when apartments change hands.

Pressure groups involved. Since the groups, individuals, and government agencies involved in a situation can impact on its outcome, identifying these interested parties and their history, power, way of acting, willingness to compromise, tendency towards militancy, or other characteristics which might provide insights on how to develop effective strategies for dealing with a situation can be critical.

Estimating relative strengths of groups is not always easy to do. For example, President Reagan correctly estimated that the Air Traffic Controllers Union could be broken, and he set a precedent for the 1980s in restaffing the air controllers network with nonunion people. Frank Lorenzo did the same thing through effective use of bankruptcy laws during the strike at Continental Airlines in the early 1980s. He was not as successful in 1989, however, when Eastern Airlines pilots struck. Lorenzo ended up with a much-reduced company at Eastern which eventually was sold and went out of business in 1991 because of the union's tenacity and changes in competitive market conditions.

Similar estimates can be made of other interest groups involved, such as government agencies. For example, it was fairly common knowledge that OSHA inspections were few and far between during its early years because of staffing problems, and fines were very often minimal. Consumer interest groups and minority and women's rights groups also have varying degrees of power and influence which can be estimated to some degree based on past experience and an analysis of the people currently involved.

Determining a final position is not always possible during early planning stages in many situations. For example, when staffing the Alaskan pipeline workforce, initial negotiating positions with the government were altered as facts about the available workforce from different population groups were uncovered and as circumstances changed. Many situations involve dynamic environments which change as the situation unfolds. In these kinds of situations, strategic planning provides only a framework for solutions.

The media's potential involvement. Pressure groups make every effort to engage the media's interest in their cause, for example by

- Staging rallies in time for the six o'clock television news
- Inviting newspaper, magazine, and television reporters to demonstrations to photograph and film exciting confrontations
- Using television stations' consumer hotlines to force businesses to honor customer complaints

Situation circumstances will dictate how and what information about the media involved is obtained and the steps taken to influence and use the media. In turn, the media will often be a major influencing factor in determining strategies for handling the situation under study.

Competitive factors. Where appropriate, the impact of competitive forces is studied. Sometimes competitors attempt to take advantage of problem situations, as when competing newspapers woo readers during strikes at other newspapers. In other situations, competitors may find it in their common interest to band together to fight legislation. This occurs often at the federal, state, and local levels, when industry groups — such as banking, airline, oil, steel, retailing, textile, or other industries — vigorously fight to defeat or amend proposed legislation.

Where appropriate, then, both the possible competitor response to social factors and the possibility of cooperative ventures with competitors are explored.

Company factors. Factors such as the available financial resources, management attitudes, and other resource strengths and weaknesses can have an impact on strategic decisions involving social factors. For example, in considering closing down its Shoreham nuclear power plant in Long Island, New York, Lilco (Long Island Power & Light Company) did not have the financial resources to do so without rate relief from state agencies. The situation, therefore, was resolved through political and legal processes.

The changes suggested in an air pollution control plan proposal in early 1989 for Southern California provide an extensive example of how company factors interrelate with social factors in making strategic decisions. The proposed regulations were to take effect over a 20-year period: automobile manufacturers would have to develop and sell vehicles that used electricity or alternative fuels; aerosol spray can restrictions would force changes in the composition and packaging of everything from hairspray to furniture polish; paints would have to be reformulated; and alternative engines designed for gasoline lawn mowers. Strategies for meeting all of these challenges involve studying a company's dependency on these products, the present design of these products, the availability of existing technology both within and outside the company, the company's capacity and financial and human resources for developing new technologies, and management's general determination and capacity to fight to have the regulations modified or abandoned [Stevenson 1989(A)].

While the Southern California case is extreme, it highlights some of the long-term impacts social and company factors can have on strategic management in business. Even in the most contained situations, meeting the requirements of perceived social responsibilities draws on scarce company resources and so affects many areas of company operations.

Making Decisions Based on These Critical Factors

A variety of decisions are possible because of the range of situations in which social factors have an impact and the different ways they can impact on strategic management.

As seen from the examples cited earlier in this chapter, strategies can range from doing nothing or outright denial, to positive actions to cure problems, to actions designed both to prevent problems from occurring in the future and to take advantage of the opportunities presented by emerging social issues.

The following discussions illustrate the basic process outlined in Figure 14-2 at work in making strategic management decisions in situations involving critical social factors.

DECISION MAKING IN DIFFERENT TYPES OF SITUATION CONTEXTS

The following discussion describes how companies made decisions in six situations involving critical social factors.

1. Determining the significance of specific social factors to the long-term success of the business and deciding how to incorporate those factors into overall-company strategic management

W.R. Grace & Company's largest unit, the Grace Specialty Chemicals Company, is involved in various businesses that involve *social issues* related to safety, health, and other environmental factors. The company has to comply with safety and health *laws* and *regulations* throughout the world at its highly decentralized plant locations. The people performing these tasks include a medical doctor who specializes in toxicology, hygienists, environment compliance officers, safety experts, an environmental manager, and senior safety/hygiene/health experts. Experience has shown that mistakes in areas related to chemicals, such as Union Carbide's in Bhopal, India, involve a host of *pressure groups* and unfavorable *media* exposure, as well as enormous costs.

Rather than waiting for a crisis of strategic proportions to occur, Grace incorporated these situation requirements into its overall-company strategy. Grace Specialty Chemicals established a centralized environmental affairs department at its United States headquarters to oversee safety, health, and environmental affairs. Most of the 113 full-time employees in that department report directly to division managers, since the problems were mostly community-related and so decision making must be made at the local level. In addition, Grace hired former New York governor Hugh Carey to head an office of environmental policy and have company-wide oversight of environmental issues. His unit consisted of 60 professionals who dealt mainly with Congress and state legislators.

The analysis of the nature of the company's business and keys to success led to identification of the social issues which were significant factors affecting success, including legal issues, pressure groups (such as legislators and community groups), potential media exposure, and internal cost and organizational factors. This analysis led Grace to develop its environmental affairs department at the highest possible corporate level. Its strategic mission was to anticipate the impact of, avoid problems with, and make skillful use of, relevant social issues affecting success [Fowler 1989].

2. Determining whether or not to go into a business related to a social factor under study

During the early 1980s, Westinghouse began formulating ideas about the opportunities existing in the toxic waste disposal business. These opportunities were enormous, since by 1995 the market for treating hazardous waste materials was expected to be between $3 billion and $5 billion annually.

The particular problem addressed by Westinghouse was the danger and difficulty of transporting both solid and liquid waste to a centralized disposal site. The Environmental Protection Agency insisted that these wastes be disposed of in a safe manner, and Congress had established a Superfund to pay for waste cleanup, which was supposed to begin in earnest in 1992.

The problem and the opportunity was to develop *on-site* hazardous waste disposal technology and delivery. Westinghouse addressed the problem in two ways in the early 1980s. First, since this was a new technology, the company spent the 1980s attracting and educating the people needed by building a development division within the company. Next, they developed the technology. For *liquid waste disposal* they used the technology underlying arc welders and plasma torches. The arc welder and associated equipment is small enough to fit into a trailer that can move from site to site to dispose of liquid waste. Through this planning and development, Westinghouse strategically placed itself to exploit a major opportunity area of the 1990s.

The strategic plan for entering the waste disposal field also made sense from an internal viewpoint since the basic technologies were familiar to Westinghouse and the company had products in related fields, such as nuclear energy, and had the financial resources for such a venture.

The examination of the waste problem, the market potential of hazardous waste disposal, the state of the technology, the legislation affecting the area, and the company resources led the company to devise its entry strategy [Holusha 1989].

3. Determining how to handle a strategically significant decision situation involving an important social issue

Lilco (Long Island Lighting Company of New York) faced a problem involving a single investment, its Shoreham Nuclear Power Plant, which had been in construction for over a decade, had not yet received an operating license, and was in danger of being closed down. In this case, the need for energy in the Long Island area and the promise of nuclear power had originally led the company to undertake the project. This project was of strategic importance, since it involved billions of dollars and the company's ability to meet electricity requirements of its service area.

Several critical situation factors were involved. Local consumers were split between those who did not want the rate increases which would result from the closing of Shoreham or who were not bothered by potential nuclear power dangers, and those who wanted the plant shut down. The county and state legislatures wavered between the two viewpoints, but eventually supported the anti-Shoreham group. The conflict went on for many years, with the county declaring evacuation plans unacceptable and taking legal moves to close the plant. In addition, the state Public Service Commission, New York Power Authority, and Long Island Power Authority supported the plant's closing. At the same time, the Nuclear Regulatory Agency in Washington supported the opening of the plant and issued successively broader operating permits to Lilco.

Management was caught in the middle, especially after New York Governor Cuomo devised a plan which gave Lilco adequate rate increases to help compensate for the cost of abandoning Shoreham. Management represented the stockholders of the company and eventually negotiated to let the stockholders vote on the matter. The stockholders voted to close the plant in mid-1989. That did not end the matter, however. The Federal Nuclear Power Authority persisted in trying to open the plant, in light of the forecasted power needs of the Northeast and the foreseeable energy sources available. Groups supporting the plant began using the same delaying legal tactics that had been employed earlier by groups opposing the plant, delaying the final shutdown and dismantling of the plant for several years [Gilpin 1989].

4. Determining the impact of a social force on a company's strategy

Many examples of these kinds of strategic decisions have been covered in this book. For example, Fuller Brush Company changed the character of its door-to-door selling strategic profile to one of mixed-selling strategies, including heavy reliance on mail-order, in response to the increasing number of working women in the United States and changing family life styles [Berg 1989].

5. Deciding how to handle a specific social problem in a strategically critical business segment

A major construction company faced the problem of filling traditionally male-dominated construction jobs with female workers in order to meet federally-imposed affirmative action guidelines for a $2 billion Alaskan Pipeline Service Company project. The company estimated that it would need a total of 5,540 workers to complete the project on time. Its successful completion had the strategic potential of establishing the company as a leader in the construction industry on a national scale. Until this time, the company's reputation had been based largely on its foreign ventures.

The union with which the company worked indicated that only a small percentage of construction workers needed by the company were women, and it was unlikely that more than 1.5 percent of the needed workers could be found among the union's female members. Even if they could find the women initially, it appeared that working conditions were too severe for most women: twelve-hour shifts, temperatures 65 to 70 degrees below zero, and long absences from home. In addition, living facilities had to be shared with the men, most of the work tools were designed for men, and sexual harassment was commonplace.

Because of these difficulties, the company first presented an affirmative action report detailing its conclusions to the Office of Federal Contract Compliance Programs (OFCCP). The OFCCP rejected the report, saying that it was not enough to allege that qualified women were not available. The company met with the union, who, when it learned that the OFCCP required an effort to recruit women before funding the contract, agreed to allow the company to advertise for nonunion women. Through using various women actions groups, the company was able to hire 201 female construction workers, or 3.5 percent of the workforce. The OFCCP accepted the company's revised affirmative action report.

Implementation — introducing the women into the workforce — required having suppliers design new work clothes, training the women to use the special tools and techniques required, and conducting orientation sessions in which women were given help in integrating with the largely male workforce. The project was successful and completed on time, and the women's performance equalled that of the men.

As seen in this situation, while it is important to build solutions based on a careful situation analysis, these situations are often dynamic ones, in which solutions are frequently developed through interactive negotiations among the parties involved. In addition, the effective implementation of the plan can be as important as the quality of the plan itself.

6. Deciding how to handle an operating planning decision involving social issues in a critical area which might impact on the way the company organizes to do or does business in the future

An example of this kind of situation is discussed later in this chapter.

As indicated by these six examples and those discussed earlier and later in this chapter, past experience is a good place to start the search for effective strategies in situations involving critical social factors. Consultants can provide guidance in handling the special problems created by emerging social issues until a company has gained the experience needed to handle these situations on its own.

Company managers have learned from experiences such as those at E.F. Hutton that the best way to handle bad news often is to be the first to break the news to the public, along with information on what the company intends to do to minimize the resulting problems. Effective strategies for reducing the power of unions through alternative hiring of nonunion people for striking workers took years to develop. This kind of experience, for instance, was helpful as Nissan Motors campaigned against unions at its new Tennessee manufacturing plant and eventually won [Levin 1989]. Years of experience in handling employee alcohol and drug problems were also needed before model approaches were developed.

These discussions of company experiences and approaches to decision making are designed to help managers think about and approach situations involving critical social factors. They can aid in understanding what is involved, in becoming familiar with solutions that might work, and in making judgments about the competence of experts hired to solve problems and develop plans. These discussions can also be useful in determining whether or not the experiences of others will be appropriate guides for handling a specific situation. In some instances, these discussions may be sufficient to guide someone in solving problems on their own. They are not, however, meant to substitute for the lessons learned from first-hand experience at the company under study.

CONTEXT-SPECIFIC PROCESSES INVOLVED IN OTHER STRATEGIC MANAGEMENT SITUATIONS INVOLVING CRITICAL SOCIAL ISSUES

A number of decisions involving the development of company strategies in light of critical social issues have been structured and subsequently replicated in knowledge-based systems. Because of the varied nature of these decisions, the often ill-defined legal context, and the negotiations sometimes required to develop recommendations, the systems developed are necessarily either general in nature or related to narrowly-defined situations.

For example, a fairly common problem faced by owners of commercial and multifamily buildings today involves asbestos. Government regulations are gradually requiring the removal of asbestos in all situations where it creates a health hazard. A small prototype was developed for helping make decisions about asbestos removal — a major cost for many building owners. Figures 14-4A to 14-4D show the initial outline of this decision.

In this decision situation, strategic and operational business factors, such as owner/ management philosophy, customer relationships (where a management firm is working for a

Figure 14-4A: Asbestos Removal Decision: Commercial and Multifamily Buildings—Overall Dependency Diagram (Initial Prototype)

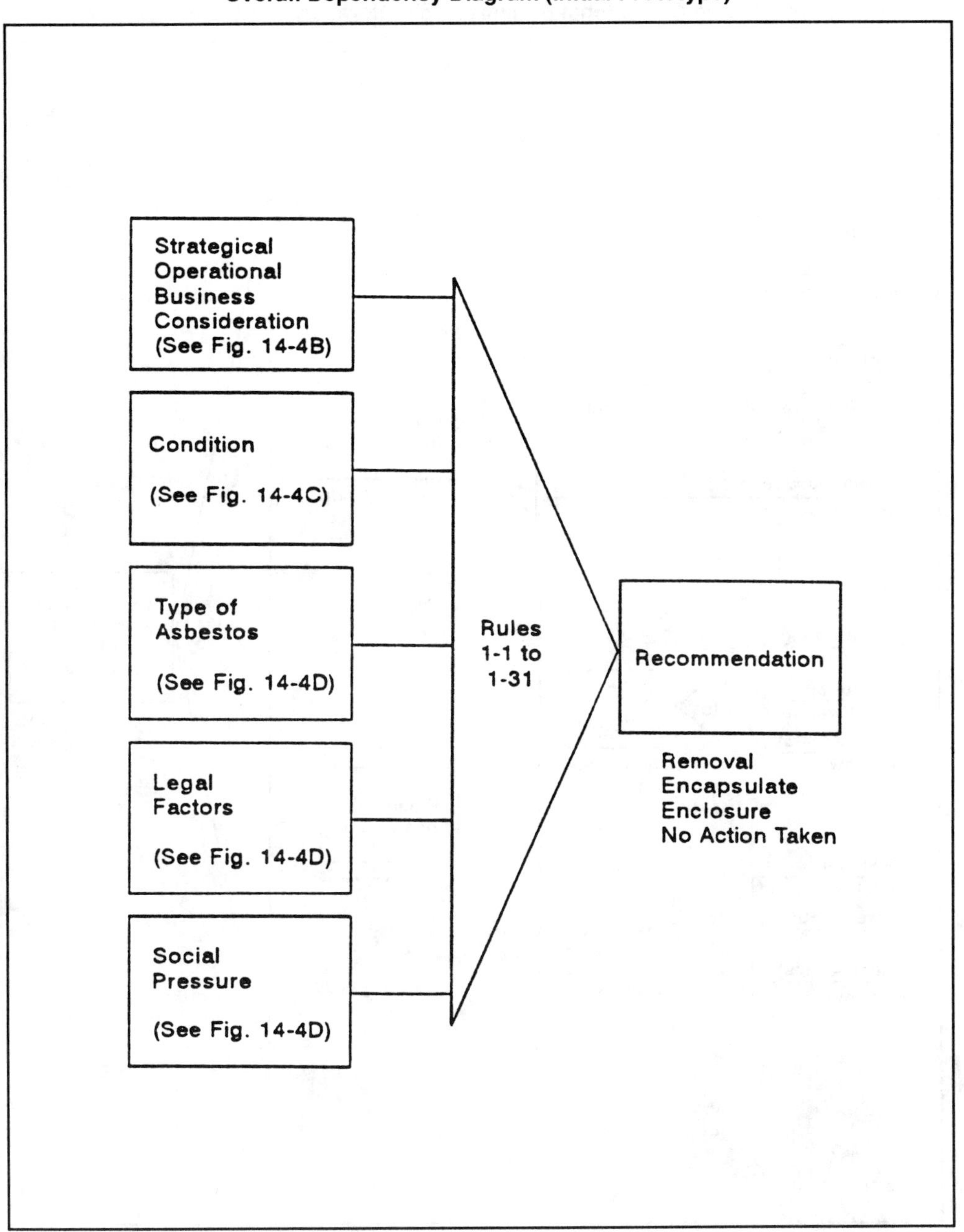

Figure 14-4B: Asbestos Removal Decision: Commercial and Multifamily Buildings—Detailed Dependency Diagram
Strategic and Operational Business Considerations (Initial Prototype)

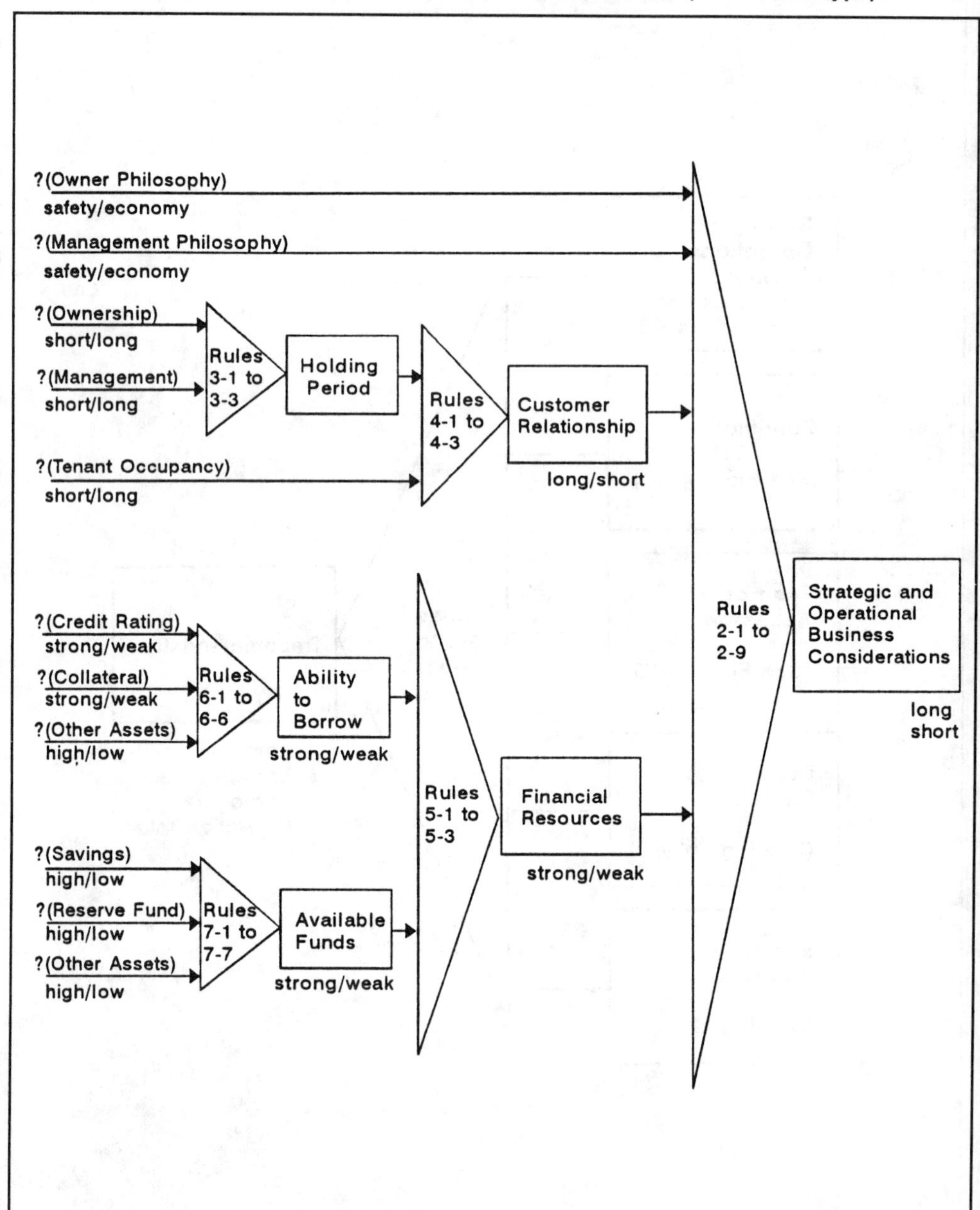

Figure 14-4C: Asbestos Removal Decision: Detailed Dependency Diagram-Condition (Initial Prototype)

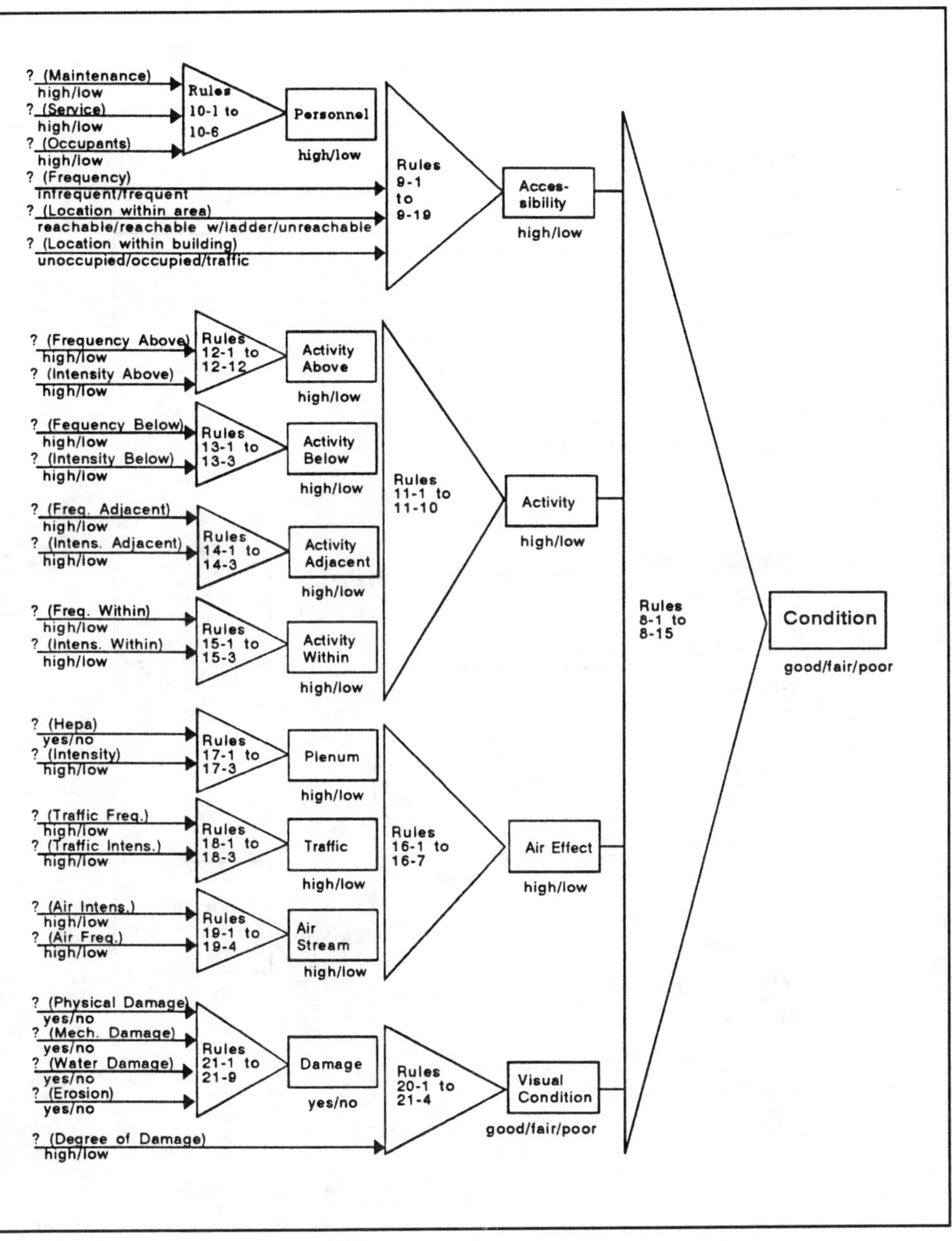

Figure 14-4D: Asbestos Removal Decision: Commercial and Multifamily Buildings—Type of Asbestos, Legal Factors, Social Factors (Initial Prototype)

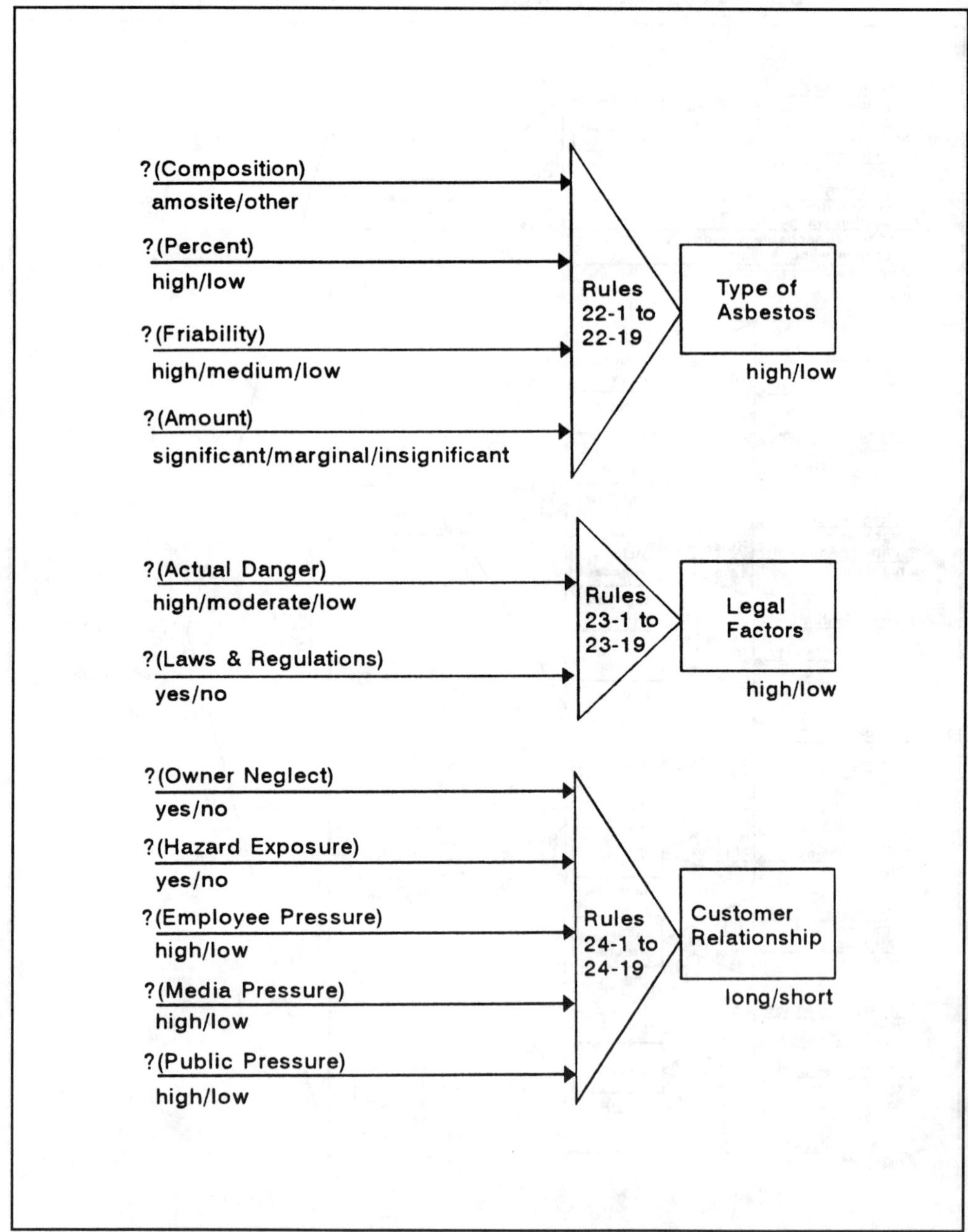

building owner), relationships with building tenants, and the financial resources of the owner, are examined. The technical questions involve the type of asbestos and its accessibility, as well as its impact on such working environment conditions as air flow, surrounding type of work activity, and visibility. Legal factors and various pressure groups involved are also examined. In this prototype situation, the possible recommendations which could be made were removal, encapsulation, enclosure, or no action.

This is only a small sampling of the considerable work being done both in business and at universities to structure how strategy decisions are made in different situations involving critical social factors.

In addition to knowledge-based systems computer tools, a wide range of conventional computer tools are useful in strategic management in the kind of situations described in this chapter. These tools and the mathematical and diagrammatic techniques underlying them are discussed in several useful supplemental texts [Mockler 1992; Webster 1989], as well as throughout this book.

REVIEW QUESTIONS

1. Describe some of the changes in society that have led to new values and attitudes which can be expected to prevail in the social environment of this country in the 1990s.
2. List and describe some of these values and attitudes.
3. Name and describe several critical social issues that have in the past and can be expected in the future to affect strategic management in business.
4. Name and describe the major interest groups concerned with social issues that can be expected to have an impact on strategic management.
5. Discuss the impact of ecological issues and interest groups on strategic management in different kinds of situations.
6. In the health and safety area, describe some of the opportunities and threats which might be found in situations involving health and safety factors.
7. Describe how equal employment opportunity issues in the future may differ from those encountered in the past.
8. In developing strategies in decision situations involving social issues, describe circumstances in which experience is a source of guidance.
9. When confronted with potential legislation, what are some of the possible strategic approaches a manager might use in different kinds of situations?

EXERCISES

1. Read recent issues of the periodicals referred to in the References section which follows, or other related periodicals of your choice, and find a company situation relevant to some aspect

of this chapter. Write a report describing ways in which that situation helped you to better understand the strategic management approaches covered in this chapter.

2. Write a report on one of the company studies in the Case Study section of this book involving some of the social issues covered in this chapter (for example, *Marshall Oil Company* and *Mercer's Choice*).

3. Based on your research done as part of exercise #1 and on whatever additional research you feel is appropriate, prepare a company study involving strategic management in a situation involving major social factors.

REFERENCES

Berg, Eric N., "At Fuller Brush, New Ways to Get Foot in Door," *The New York Times*, May 18, 1989, pp. D1, D2.

Carson, Rachel, *The Silent Spring*, Boston, MA: Houghton Mifflin, 1962.

Chira, Susan, "Writing Children's Textbooks: Too Many Cooks?", *The New York Times*, January 17, 1990, p. B8.

"Chrysler Agrees to Promotions for Minorities," *The New York Times*, July 13, 1989, p. A17.

Cowan, Alison Leigh, "The Gadfly C.E.O.'s Want to Swat," *The New York Times*, Business Section, February 2, 1992, pp. 1, 6.

Deutsch, Claudia H., "Saying No the 'Mommy Track'," *The New York Times*, Business Section, January 28, 1990, p. 29.

Faison, Seth, "At Salomon, New Focus, New Attitude," *The New York Times*, February 15, 1992, pp. 37, 50.

Feloni, John, and Donna Sammons, *The Fall of the House of Hutton*, Markham, Ontario, Canada: Henry Holt, 1989.

Fink, Steven, "Dow Corning's Moral Evasion," *The New York Times*, Business Section, February 16, 1992, p. 13.

Fisher, Lawrence M., "Organic Wines Enter the Mainstream," *The New York Times*, November 19, 1991, pp. D1, D8.

Fowler, Elizabeth M., "Environmental Experts in Short Supply," *The New York Times*, July 11, 1989, D9.

Fowler, Elizabeth M., "'Open Door' for Women Managers," *The New York Times*, January 2, 1990, p. D3.

Frieden, Betty, *The Feminine Mystique*, New York: Norton Publishers, 1963, 1983.

Gilpin, Kenneth N., "In Lilco's Debt Sale, Signs of a New Vigor," *The New York Times*, April 11, 1989, pp. D1, D6.

Henry III, William A., "History as It Happens," *Time*, January 6, 1992, pp. 24-27.

Hershey, Robert D., "New Market for Trading 'Pollution Rights'," *The New York Times*, June 14, 1989, pp. D1, D6.

Holmes, Steven A., "Sweeping U.S. Law to Help Disabled Goes Into Effect: Statute May Force Businesses to Alter Buildings and Offer Specialized Services," *The New York Times*, January 27, 1992.

Holusha, John, "Plastic Trash: 'Silk Pursues' Sought," *The New York Times*, May 3, 1989, pp. D1, D9.

Judge, Paul C., "Selling Autos by Selling Safety," *The New York Times*, January 26, 1990, pp. D1, D3.

Kilborn, Peter L., "A Company Recasts Itself to Erase Bias on the Job," *The New York Times*, October

4, 1990, pp. 1, D21.

Levin, Doron P., "U.A.W. Bid to Organize Nissan Plant Is Rejected," *The New York Times*, July 28, 1989, pp. A1, A6.

Lewin, Tamar, "Woman Gets $7 Million in Airline Discrimination Suit," *The New York Times*, January 25, 1992, p. 27.

McMurray, Scott, "Wounded Giant: Union Carbide Offers Some Sober Lessons in Crisis Management," *The Wall Street Journal*, January 28, 1992, pp. A1, A9.

Mockler, Robert J., *Computer Software to Support Strategic Management Decision Making*, New York: Macmillan, 1992.

Nader, Ralph, *Unsafe at Any Speed*, New York: Grossman Publishers, 1965.

Quint, Michael, "Chemical and Hanover Reach Accord with Community Group," *The New York Times*, November 21, 1991, p. D3.

Reinhold, Robert, "Citing Medical Evidence on Smog, California Lowers Threshold for Its Health Alerts," *The New York Times National*, September 14, 1990, p. A14.

Rifkin, Glenn, "Do Employees Have a Right to Electronic Privacy," *The New York Times*, Business Section, December 8, 1991, 8.

Ravo, Nick, "For the 90's, Lavish Amounts of Stinginess," *The New York Times*, January 15, 1992, pp. C1, C10.

Salpukas, Agis, "Eastern Airlines Is Shutting Down and Plans to Liquidate Its Assets," *The New York Times*, January 19, 1991, pp. 1, 48.

Schiffman, James R., "After Uptown, Are Some Niches Out?", *The Wall Street Journal*, January 20, 1990, p. B1.

"Stand by for the Charge of the Battery Brigade," *The Sunday Times* (London), Style Section, November 17, 1991, p. 4.

Sterngold, James, *Burning Down the House: How Greed, Deceit, and Bitter Revenge Destroyed E. F. Hutton*, New York: Summit Books, 1990.

Stevenson, Richard W., "California Proposal Would Let Industry Sell Pollution Rights," *The New York Times*, January 30, 1992, pp. 1, D7.

Stevenson, Richard W., "Facing Up to a Clean Air Plan," *The New York Times*, April 3, 1989(A), pp. D1, D7.

Stevenson, Richard W., "Why Exxon's Woes Worry ARCO," *The New York Times*, Business Section, May 14, 1989(B), pp. 1, 25.

Taylor, Jeffery, "Smog Swapping: New Rules Harness Power of Free Market to Curb Our Pollution," *The Wall Street Journal*, April 14, 1992, pp. A1, A12.

"The Tylenol Rescue," *Newsweek*, March 3, 1986, pp. 52-53.

Wald, Matthew L., "Cars That Whirr and Burn Rubber," *The New York Times*, Business Section, February 2, 1992, p. 10.

Wald, Matthew L., "Putting Windmills Where It's Windy," *The New York Times*, November 14, 1991, pp. D1, D22.

Webster, James L., William E. Reif, and Jeffrey S. Bracker, "The Manager's Guide to Strategic Planning Tools and Techniques," *Planning Review*, November/December 1989, pp. 4-12, 48.

White, James A., "Minorities and Women Gain a Bigger Role in Money Management," *The Wall Street Journal*, March 13, 1991, pp. A1, A4.

APPENDICES:

RELATED TOPICS

Appendix A

SPECIFIC STRATEGY FORMULATION REASONING PROCESSES

The objective of Appendix A is to help readers better understand

- Strategic management reasoning processes
- Some basic thinking processes and skills involved in strategy formulation
- Qualitative, quantitative, systems, and computer techniques and tools useful in strategy formulation
- Limitations of strategic management reasoning process models

Chapter 2 described the strategic management tasks outlined in Figure A-1 and the general strategic management processes outlined in Figures A-2 and A-3. Chapters 2 through 12 further discussed these tasks and processes. As seen in these discussions, many specific processes and skills (involving both reasoning and interpersonal interaction) are involved in doing these tasks and processes.

This Appendix covers specific *reasoning* or *thinking* processes and skills involved in strategic management. Often referred to as *cognitive* processes and skills, they are involved in all phases of strategic management — from enterprise-wide strategy formulation, to other strategic management tasks such as policy formulation, financial planning and budgeting, program development, and enabling strategy formulation and implementation at the strategic business unit (SBU) and operating department levels.

Figure A-1: Strategic Management Tasks

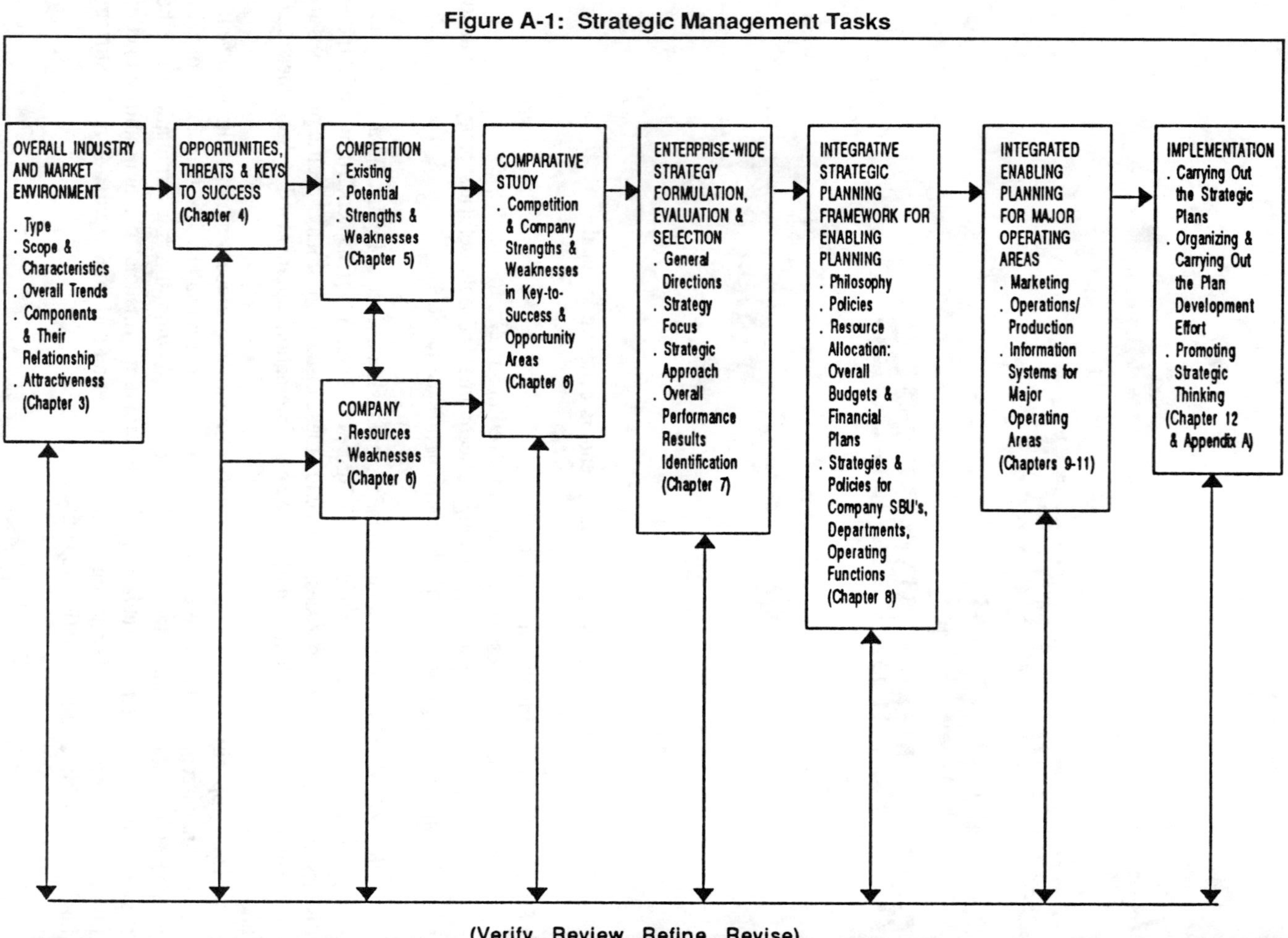

Figure A-2: Strategic Management Decision-Making Process

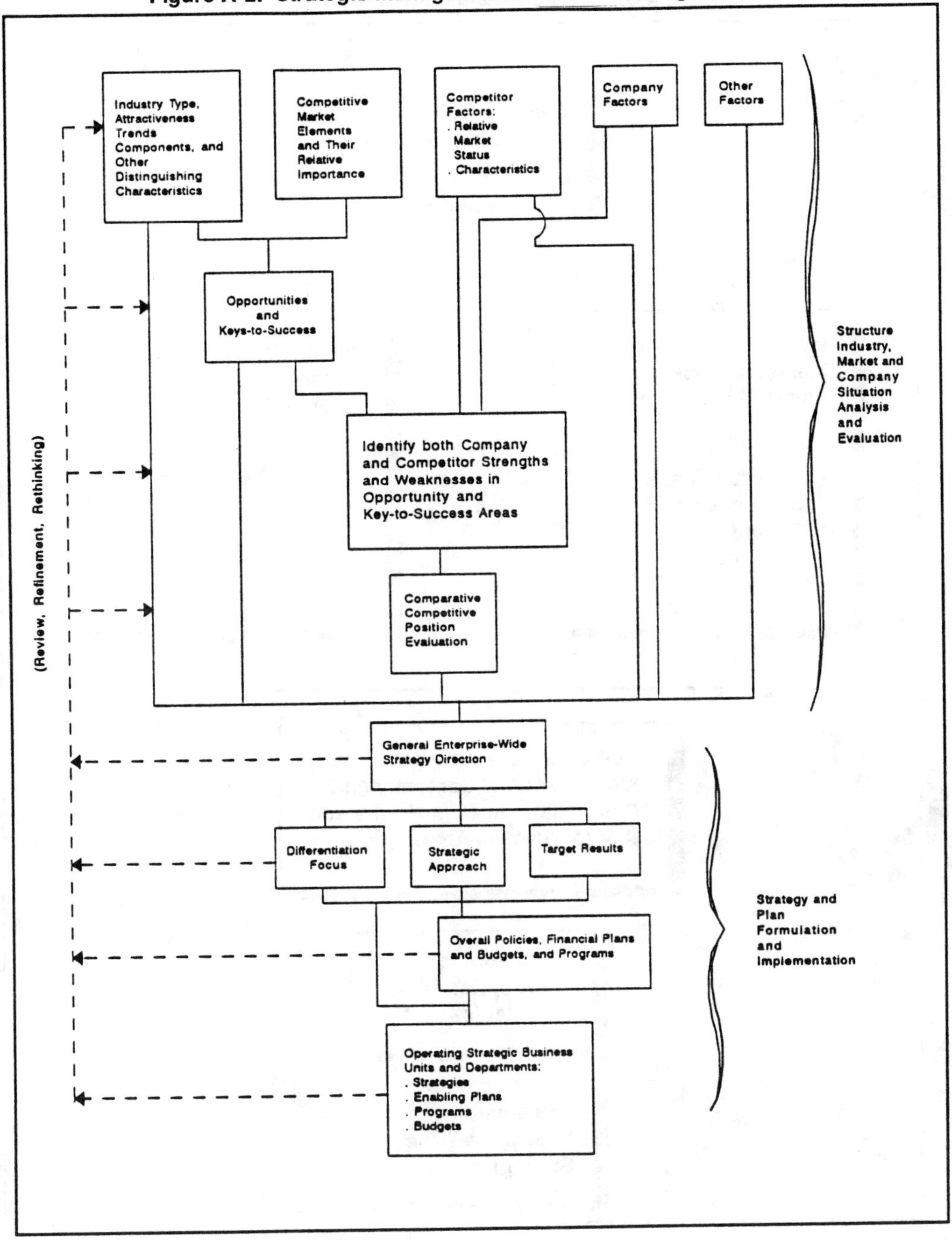

Industry Type, Attractiveness Trends Components, and Other Distinguishing Characteristics

Competitive Market Elements and Their Relative Importance

Competitor Factors:
. Relative Market Status
. Characteristics

Company Factors

Other Factors

Opportunities and Keys-to-Success

Identify both Company and Competitor Strengths and Weaknesses in Opportunity and Key-to-Success Areas

Comparative Competitive Position Evaluation

Structure Industry, Market and Company Situation Analysis and Evaluation

General Enterprise-Wide Strategy Direction

Differentiation Focus

Strategic Approach

Target Results

Overall Policies, Financial Plans and Budgets, and Programs

Operating Strategic Business Units and Departments:
. Strategies
. Enabling Plans
. Programs
. Budgets

Strategy and Plan Formulation and Implementation

(Review, Refinement, Rethinking)

Figure A-3: Strategic Management Process Overview

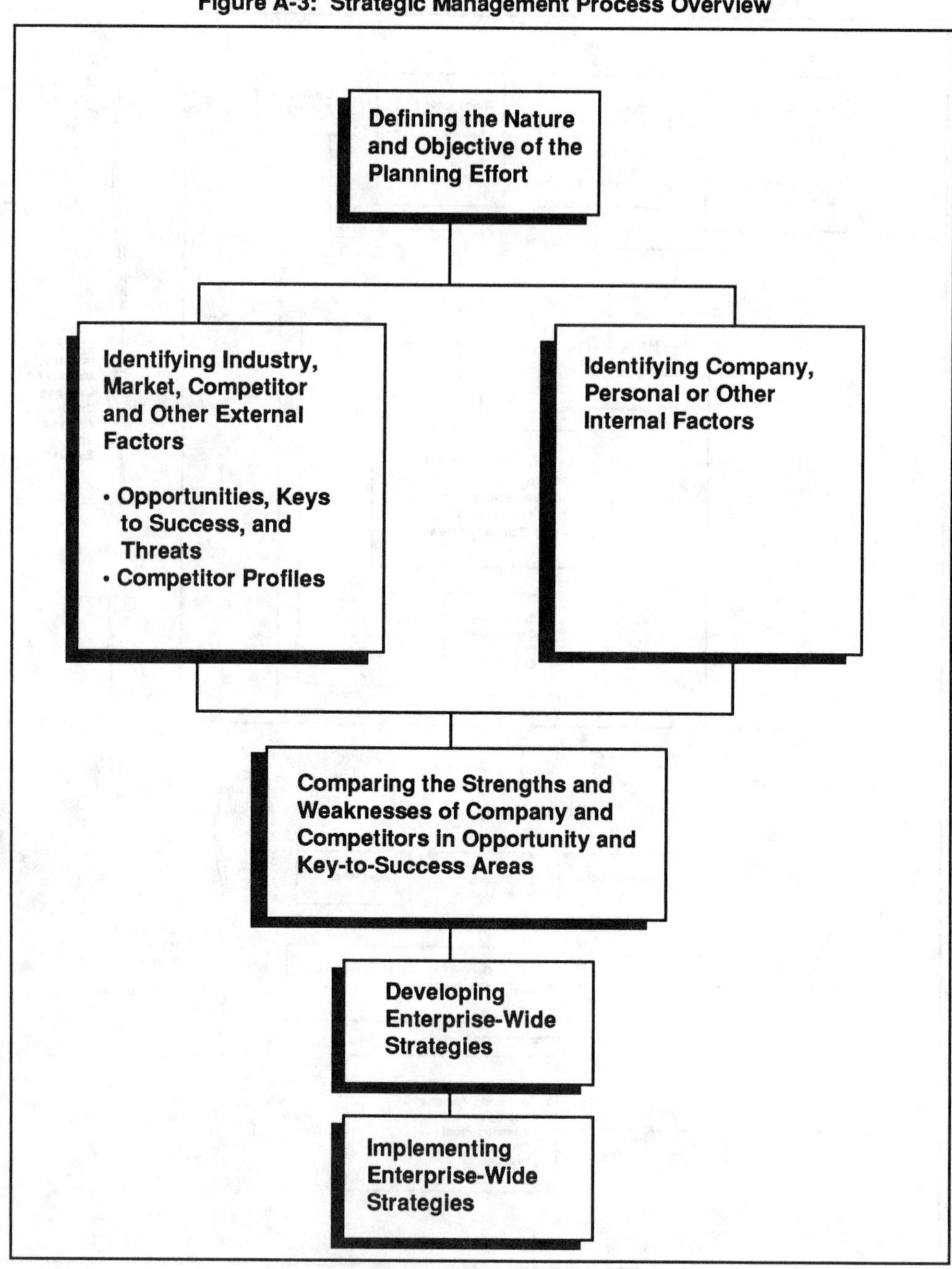

STRATEGIC MANAGEMENT REASONING PROCESSES: CONTEXT-SPECIFIC PROCESSES

When faced with a problem or task, an effective manager instinctively develops some kind of approach for dealing with it — an approach or conceptual mental model appropriate both for the task to be done or problem to be solved, as well as for the situation factors. This general cognitive conceptualization process is outlined in Figure A-4.

For example, on his first visit to a bank to borrow money an entrepreneur was told to return with some evidence that he would be able to repay the money and meet interest payments. Given that *task*, which involved demonstrating he could meet *monthly payments* of interest over a five-year period, plus *periodic loan repayments*, the entrepreneur then studied the *situation* — his projected business activities and the *cash income* they would generate, and the *cash payments* that would be required to cover the costs of these activities. To meet the task requirements, he prepared a monthly summary of cash received and cash paid, a portion of which is shown in Figure A-5, something he later learned was called a *cash-flow statement.*

No prior knowledge of cash-flow techniques was needed to produce such a statement. A tool such as a cash-flow statement is produced merely by restructuring or reconceiving a situation to meet task requirements, as shown in Figure A-4.

Figure A-4

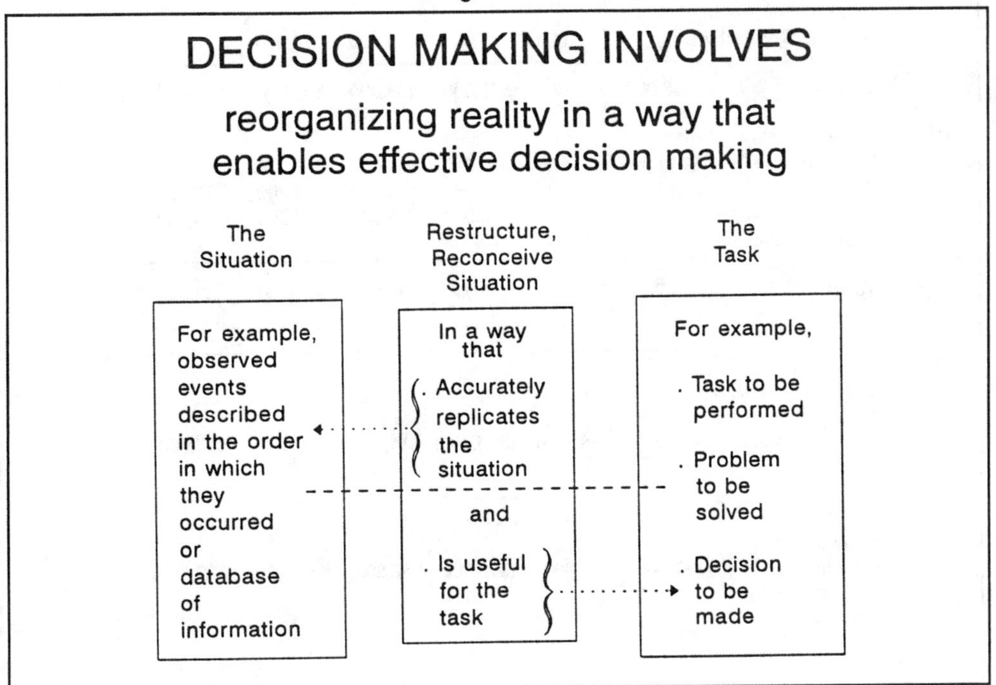

Strategic planners often work in a similar way, creating approaches (sometimes called mental models) to meet varying task and situation requirements. It is very difficult in all but the simplest strategy formulation situations to do an exhaustive search of all situation factors — for instance, all the possible industry trends, all possible competitor moves, all company strengths and weaknesses, and all possible strategies. For this reason, a strategic planner often uses selective mental models of reasoning processes. Some of these reconceptualizations or mental models may be of their own invention, as in the cash-flow example above. Others may be adaptations of those observed in use by other expert planners. Some will have been developed through years of experience. Still other processes may involve simply using recommended approaches. Many of these are highly individualistic, creative, and intuitive; many are structured and rational. Almost every chapter in this book discusses such reconceptualizations and generally summarizes them at the end of the chapter in which they appear.

Figure A-5: Projected Cash-Flow Statement or Cash Budget

	Jan	Feb	Mar	Apr	May	June
Sales	$20,000	$30,000	$40,000	$60,000	$50,000	$30,000
Inflows						
Cash Sales	18,000	24,000	30,000	45,000	42,000	26,000
Collection of Accounts Receivable		3,000	5,000	8,000	10,000	8,000
Total	$18,000	$27,000	$35,000	$53,000	$52,000	$34,000
Outflows						
Inventory	$24,000	$28,000	$40,000	$28,000	$15,000	
Salaries	3,000	3,800	4,000	4,500	4,200	$3,800
Other Expenses	2,800	4,000	5,000	5,500	4,500	4,000
Equipment Purchase		30,000	10,000			
Total	$29,000	$65,800	$59,000	$38,000	$23,700	$7,800
Net Monthly cash gain or loss at en*d of the month	($11,000)	($38,800)	($24,000)	$15,000	$28,300	$27,000
Cumulative cash gain or loss at end of month	($11,000)	($49,800)	($73,800)	($58,800)	($30,500)	($3,500)

A substantial body of research documents and explores this mental modelling process [Mockler 1992(B)]. This Appendix discusses several of the more commonly identified reasoning processes which have proved useful in doing and learning how to do strategic management.

For discussion purposes the topic is divided into five sections:

- Strategic management contingency (context-specific) processes and models
- Basic IF-THEN reasoning processes
- More complex contingency reasoning processes
- Pattern matching processes
- Other reasoning processes

Strategic Management Contingency (Context-Specific) Processes and Models: A General Introduction

The kinds of mental processes and related models of them formulated by expert strategic planners are generally referred to as situation-specific contingency processes and models.

"Contingency" means that the processes and models take into account (that is, are contingent on) the specific situation under study. For example, like the cognitive models underlying the eight knowledge-based systems on the disk accompanying this book, they seek information and ask questions about the reader's specific strategy formulation problem. One example — given in Chapter 9 — is shown in Figure A-6.

Many of these processes have been described throughout this text, especially in the final sections of Chapters 8 through 14. They are models of strategic management contingency reasoning processes which focus on an individual manager's needs. They are in this sense context-specific, and represent what a large body of research has demonstrated is one way strategic managers work either explicitly or implicitly. Additional examples of such context-specific processes, many of which were defined through knowledge-based systems studies, are given in other works [Mockler 1989(A & B)]. These processes differ considerably from the contingency-oriented process models found in most strategic management research today, which explain in industry-wide (macro) terms how businesses work in general but have only limited immediate value to individual working managers [Mockler 1992(B)].

The many processes and models discussed in the chapters on industry and competitive market analysis are also examples of such contingency processes and models. These included:

- The structured component-by-component competitive market analysis
- The comparative competitive position analysis, and its related key factor analyses
- The inferential reasoning analysis for identifying keys to success
- The competitor response scenario analysis

The discussions in Chapters 3 through 7 give some sense of how these processes work in practice. Further discussions of the theories underlying structured competitive market analysis are found in other studies by the author [Mockler 1992(D)].

Figure A-6: Dependency Diagram: New Product Strategy Selection for Local Country Product Proposal (Initial Prototype)

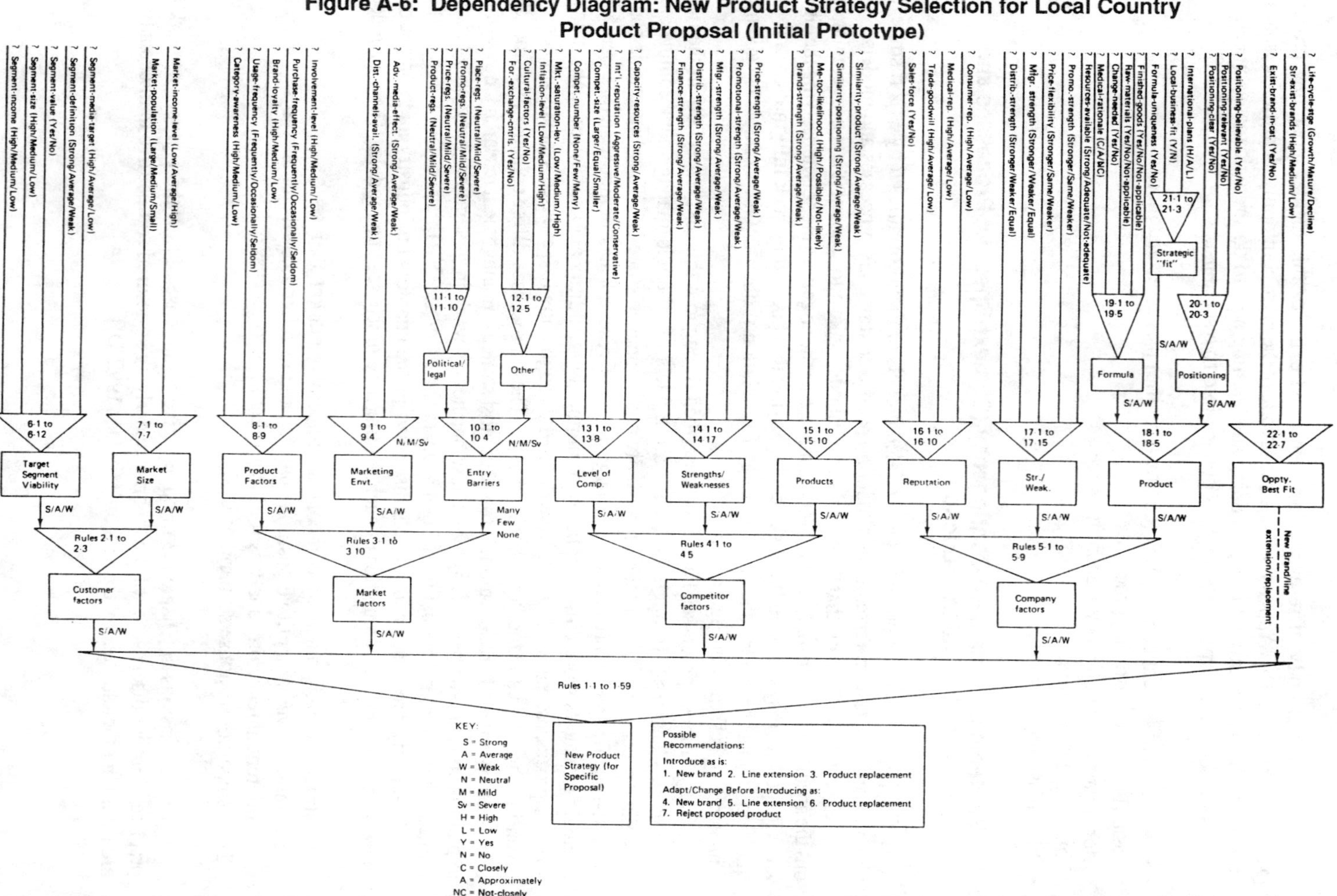

Figure A-7: Strategy Implementation

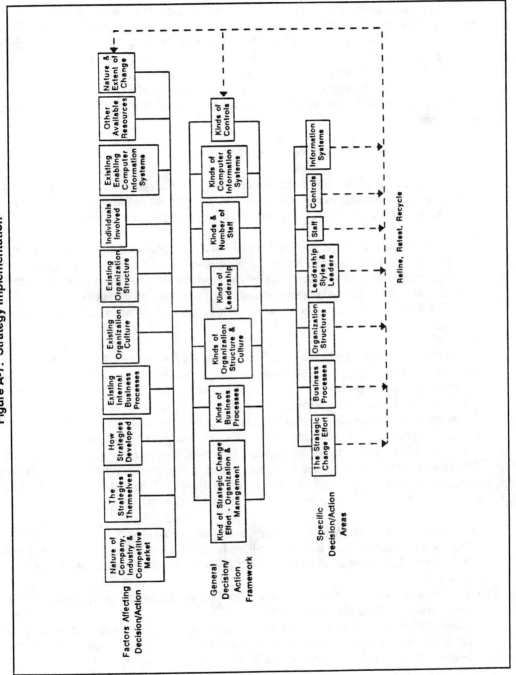

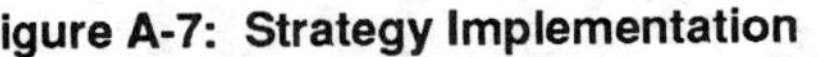

The general process models shown in Figures A-1, A-2, and A-3 are additional examples of contingency process models developed to aid in learning and guiding strategy formulation and implementation. Several models useful in the organization design and staffing areas are given in Chapter 12; an example is shown in Figure A-7. Since all of these require information about one's specific planning situation, they are all adaptive situation-specific contingency models.

The following discussions cover several general and specific strategic management processes and their related contingency models, which were not explored in detail in the chapter discussions.

Basic IF-THEN Reasoning Processes

Planners often use decision guidelines involving *IF-THEN* type statements, which are used as rules of thumb in making decisions. Such rules of thumb are called *heuristics*. In a strategy formulation situation, for instance, a planner might call upon past experience, with such thoughts as:

> IF the industry or competitive market under study is fragmented and growing (emerging), the company market share is low, major competitors are many and only average in size and market strength, the company has or can develop a distinctive product or marketing capability, has a flexible organization and adequate financial resources,
> THEN one possible strategy to consider would be to selectively invest in an attractive market niche.

This strategy was appropriate for the candy company discussed in Chapter 2, because it was in an industry which was growing and thus attractive—retail speciality candy stores. In addition, its competition was fragmented. With no dominant competitors in its region, the company had several product and marketing advantages, such as high quality combined with medium price and distinctive brand and packaging, although its market share was low. Further, the company had a flexible organization and adequate finances for its limited area of operations.

The following is a more detailed description of the heuristic processes involved in formulating a general strategic direction for a company during the initial phases of a fairly simple enterprise-wide strategy formulation situation. For illustration purposes, the possible strategy recommendations made during this initial phase were limited to four:

- ***Get out of the business.*** With this strategy, a company would consider one of several options: Liquidate the business (sell the assets), sell the business as a going entity, or harvest ("milk") the business (run the business without further investment to extract profits until it goes out of business).
- ***Hold position.*** With this strategy, a company would consider investing only enough to produce some earnings to keep the business going.
- ***Selective investment.*** With this strategy, a company has strength in an industry or competitive market segment which has profit potential. It would concentrate its resources in that selective industry or competitive market segment (niche).

- ***Aggressive investment.*** With this strategy, a company has strength in a promising growth area, and so would invest aggressively in that area.

A great deal of work has been done on building structured cognitive models or guidelines for formulating general company strategy directions [Porter 1980, 1985; Hamermesh 1986]. Figure A-8 diagrams one simplified process involved in formulating general strategy directions.

Figure A-8 is a decision model that goes beyond just defining tasks as Figure A-1 did; it attempts to show relationships. As shown in Figure A-8, various factors may be analyzed in strategic management situations:

- The competitive market situation
- Competitors' size and number
- Company market share
- Comparative company and competitor positions relative to the opportunity areas and key-to-success factors
- Special company market, organization, and financial factors

Based on this analysis of the factors identified in Figure A-8, a planner gradually formulates a recommendation for a general strategy direction to pursue.

Figure A-9 gives one of the IF-THEN rules developed as part of this model. It is the rule that was used by the planner in the above candy company example when selecting a niche or considering a selective investment general strategy direction for the company.

Many strategic planners follow such a general process in formulating strategies during the initial stages of a project. For example, Eastern Airlines initially opted for *partial liquidation* after it was struck by its unions in 1989, since it was in a highly competitive stable industry, willing buyers existed for its undervalued assets, it was short of cash, and its competitors were much stronger in most of the markets it served [Bernstein 1990; Weiner 1990].

In another situation, Fuller Brush formulated a strategy of *holding its position* in the door-to-door selling market in the mid-1980s, based on an analysis of the situation factors noted in Chapters 1 and 3. At the same time, the company formulated a secondary strategy based on its product strength. This strategy involved *aggressively investing* in the speciality mail-order and retail selling areas. This strategy was initially successful, since during the mid-1980s Fuller's competition in the specialty mail-order areas was fragmented, the industry was growing, and Fuller had major brand recognition and superior products [Kleinfield 1990; Berg 1989]. During the 1980s, the company's character changed, from being a door-to-door sales company to being a broad-based marketer of home-care products.

A complete listing of all the rules in the decision process modelled in Figure A-8 — more than 300 — is given on the computer disks accompanying this book. The exercises at the end of this Appendix explain how to use this model to make general strategy direction decisions, as well as how to print out the rules on the disk in order to study how they are used to make these decisions.

Figure A-10 gives another example of a rule set in this general strategy direction formulation decision process. Instead of the format used in Figure A-9, in Figure A-10 the rules are listed in

Figure A-8: Diagram of Situation to be Prototyped for General Strategy Direction (Initial Prototype)

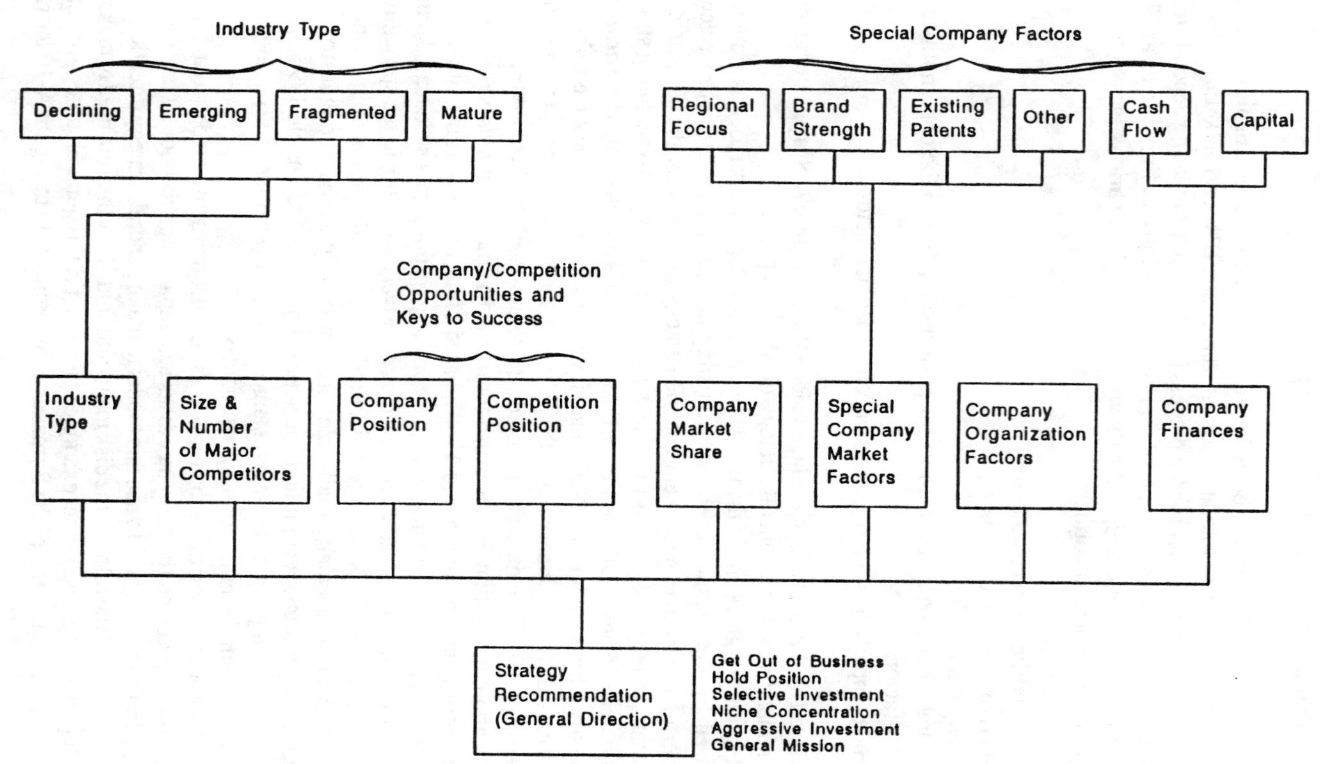

Figure A-9: Sample If-Then Rule
General Strategy Direction Decision Situation (Initial Concept Testing Prototype)

goal = strategy

Rule-7:
If competitive-market = decline, and
  company market-share = average or low
  competitors-size-number = low
  company-strength-overall = strong and
  competition-strength-overall = average or weak and
  company-market-advantage = and
  company-organization-flexibility = high
  company-finance average or strong
Then strategy-1 = Selective-investment

Rule-95:
If potential-obsolescence = high or very high and
  demand-uncertainty = high or very high and
  etc.
Then industry-type = declining.

columns. For example, the first rule in the column indicates that the expert whose reasoning process is replicated in this rule felt that in the industry or competitive market under study [Porter 1980]:

IF the number of competitors = high and
  economies of scale = highly important or
  product differentiation = highly important or
  the dispersion of the market = high
THEN the competitive market = fragmentary

Descriptive cognitive contingency models, such as those in Figures A-8, A-9, and A-10, admittedly are over simplified. This is because they are designed only to illustrate that it is possible to define in detail some of the many thought processes used by experienced planners as they take the information gathered from the planner's specific situation, apply the heuristics contained in the IF-THEN rules to reach a decision, and then recommend a course of action. In most company situations, enterprise-wide strategy formulation involves much more than just specifying a general strategic direction, such as "phased withdrawal" or "selective or niche investment," as is demonstrated at length in Chapter 7.

Such general contingency models are, however, a useful starting point in helping a planner formulate a focused direction for the more detailed strategy formulation studies that follow. In addition, such models are useful for understanding how strategy formulation decisions are made and for teaching strategic management, as well as for providing a basis for developing computer systems that replicate these kinds of decisions. Many strategic management situations involve

Figure A-10: Sample Decision Chart - Competitive Market Situation Defining Type of Industry or Competitive Market Based on Situation Conditions (Initial Concept Testing Prototype)

		RULES				
	PREMISES	1	2	3	4	5
IF	number-dominant competitors	high	med			
	economies-scale	and high	and med			
	product-differentiation	or high	or med			
	regionally-dispersed	or high	or high			
	industry-unit. sales			decreasing	stable	increasing
	product-lines			decreasing	stable	increasing
	r&d budgets			decreasing	stable	increasing
	advertising-budgets			decreasing	stable	increasing
	number-competitors			decreasing	stable	increasing
	technology			mature	mature	emerging
	proportion-new companies			low	average	high
	proportion-new customers			low	average	high
THEN	COMPETITIVE MARKET					
	Fragmented	X	X			
	Declining			X		
	Mature				X	
	Emerging					X

more complex decision-making processes. As pointed out in Chapter 1 and elsewhere in this book, many decisions emerge gradually. They may be made in stages or be stumbled on accidentally. In addition, many expert strategic managers have developed their own contingency approaches to strategic management decision making.

More Complex Contingency Reasoning Processes

The process diagrammed in Figure A-7, which was discussed in Chapter 12, models emergent strategic management decision processes involved in implementation. As shown in this contingency model, the decision process builds on the situation characteristics outlined at the top of the figure.

The intermediate phase involves a gradually emerging picture of the kind of solution desired, many of which may be hypotheses of possible solutions which are tested, rejected, or refined on the way to a solution. A manager's ideas of how to structure a company's organization may emerge in this way, for example.

A CEO's initial strategic vision for a company may start in this same way, as a general concept. As more information is gathered and time passes, the vision is defined more and more precisely and the details of how it will be implemented are sketched in.

This process model recognizes that in strategic management solutions do not always emerge through as simple and direct IF-THEN reasoning processes as outlined in Figures A-8, A-9, and A-10. Creative thinking about the future needs time for ideas to incubate and be discovered, elaborated upon, and validated after the preparatory thinking phase. This is the way the creative process works, through invention to innovation [Couger 1990]. Solutions first appear in general concept outline forms that gradually are refined or rejected, and are made more specific. Only rarely does a solution appear instantly in its final form in complex strategic management situations.

Many of the strategic management decision processes modelled in this text require this kind of intermediate reconceptualization and rethinking stage when at work in more complex management situations.

While in practice many strategic management decision situations have this level of complexity, the simpler contingency process models described earlier in this Appendix are useful and appropriate for an introductory book such as this one. They explain the basic contingency processes involved in simpler strategic management situations. They are useful learning tools, in that they can be examined in detail and so make basic cognitive processes visible to those learning the subject.

Pattern Matching Processes

Another reasoning process commonly used in strategy formulation is the matching of information from two or more sources, or information categories, to reason to a conclusion.

For example, in those competitive markets where there are many significantly different

Figure A-11: Strategic Competitive Success Profiles Within a Competitive Market (Concepts)

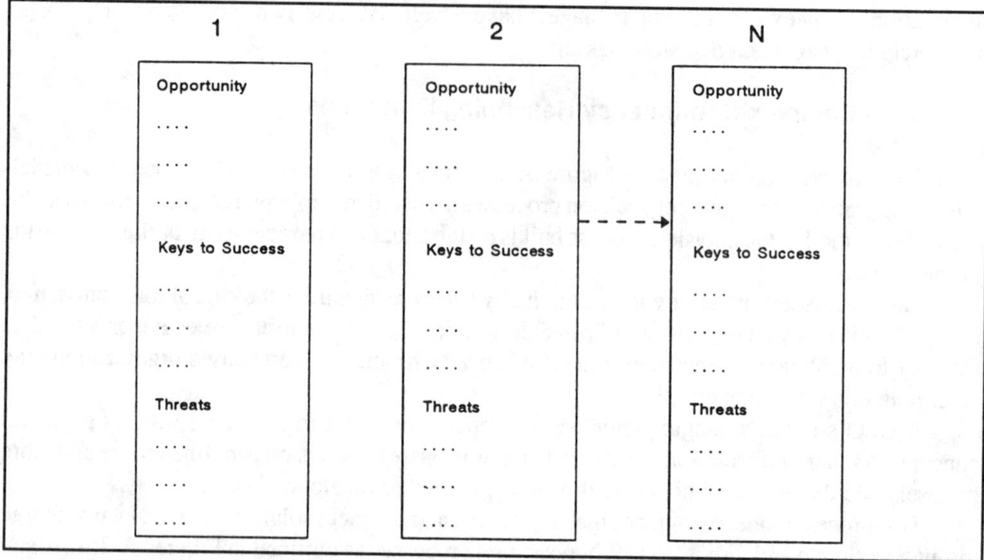

ways to make money, it is often useful to formulate *strategic competitive success profiles* of each of these ways, as shown in Figure A-11. The process differs somewhat from the processes involved in enterprise-wide strategy formulation and implementation shown in Figure A-1 (outline of the basic tasks) and Figures A-8, A-9, and A-10 (IF-THEN rules). The process shown in Figure A-11 adds a new dimension to the competitive analysis — a more structured analysis of competitive ways of making money in the market — which in many situations can provide the basis for more detailed strategies and strategic plan formulation [Mockler 1991].

In a baking goods situation described in Chapters 5 through 8, three competitive groups were initially identified. The following is a brief summary of each.

Major national competitors. Such competitors are characterized by their national brand recognition, broad product lines (and brands) which aggressively emphasize mass-produced standard items, their large volumes (which are needed to advertise nationally and achieve production and distribution efficiencies), significant research and development capabilities, national (mass) distribution, public ownership of the company, and production facilities located throughout the country. Generally, this competitive market segment can sustain four or more major players.

Major regional competitors. Such competitors are characterized by their brand recognition within their own region, their ability to react quickly to competitive moves based on price and product development, their flexibility to be aggressively competitive in the specialized product area, their intimate knowledge of and contact with their regional areas of operation, their ability to control costs, their distribution through most major outlets in their region, and their limited ownership and research capabilities. Generally, the market will support only one or two of these companies.

Regional specialty bakers. Companies in this segment would have fairly limited specialty product lines, local brand recognition, and limited production, distribution, sales, financial, and research capabilities. Any number of companies could compete at this level.

As the study progressed, the initial profiles of competitive groups were expanded. These expanded definitions of opportunities, keys to success, threats, and individual competitors were particularly useful in developing detailed plans. How this was done is described throughout the chapters in PARTS TWO and THREE.

In addition, a search was made for new competitive profiles — that is, new ways to create primary differentiation in the market. For example, in the baked goods study, it was fairly easy to set up a fourth strategic competitive success profile after the first three were juxtaposed in a diagram (actually it was done on a computer software outliner program which used windows, but it can be done manually as well). The fourth major success profile was of a national specialty or premium baked goods company. While today such a company is an obvious alternative — Pepperidge Farms (the largest premium national bread and cookie baker in the U.S.) is an outstanding example (Forsythe 1989), it was not so obvious an alternative to everyone at the time

Figure A-12: Basis for a New Business Entrepreneurial

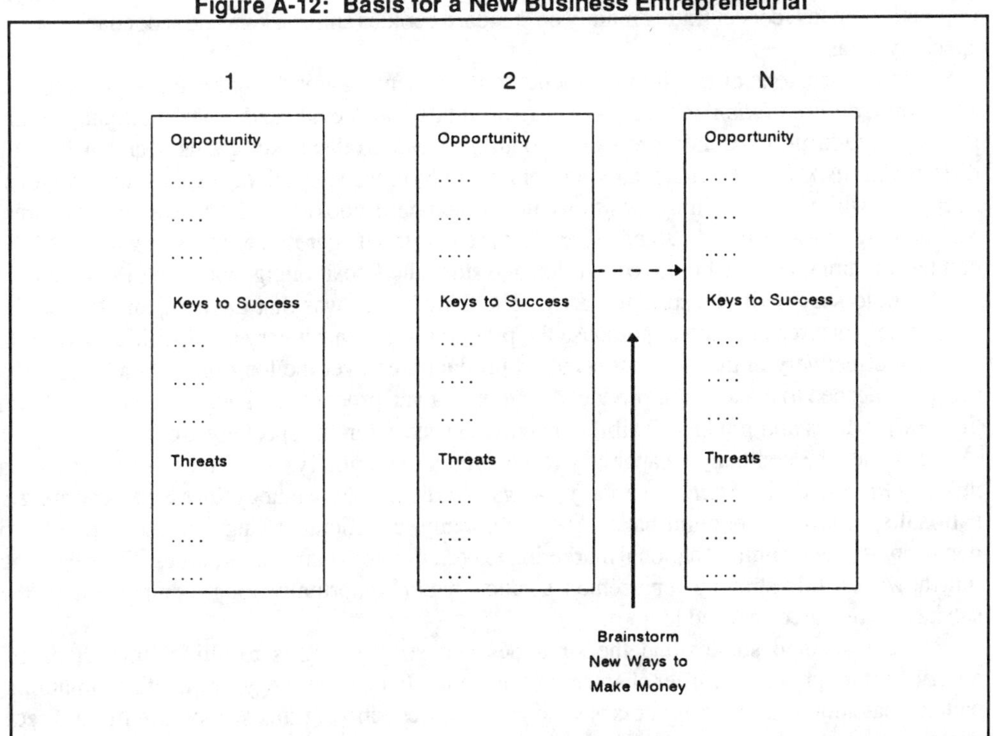

time of the baked goods company study in the late 1950s.

This phase of the study is essentially entrepreneurial — a search for a *primary differentiation* strategy — as shown in Figure A-12. It involves first studying the patterns initially identified and then attempting to develop any *substantially different* patterns or ways to do business which might be effective ways to make money — that is, think of significantly new general approaches (or significantly new variations on existing general patterns) not now used and so not identified earlier. These new approaches might be substantial market niches or be significantly different strategic ways of doing business. This study might involve looking for new technologies and products or processes needed — but not yet invented or commercialized. This process might also require further research into customer needs not yet fulfilled.

Once identified and described, each new entrepreneurial strategic competitive success profile is evaluated in regard to the opportunities created or exploited in them, keys to success, degree of competition, and any other anticipated threats. This would be the basis for forming a new company or SBU — clearly the most exciting way to go, if feasible, since it should produce the greatest rewards in spite of the greater risks.

In addition to using competitive success profiles entrepreneurially, this process also involves studying a company's existing resources, strategies, and operations in relation to the strategic competitive success profiles identified, as shown in Figure A-13.

In the baked goods company situation, the company under study was currently a major regional company, concentrating mainly on standard cookies and crackers and secondarily on the specialty areas.

First, extensions of and improvements in its present way of doing business — including *secondary differentiation* moves — were formulated and evaluated. The company could realistically add more specialty products — both cookies and other baked goods — and in this way differentiate itself from the major national companies by more aggressively exploiting its regional strengths, while still retaining positions in the standard cookies and cracker product area. Maintaining a presence in the standard product areas without aggressively pursuing it helped the company maintain strong brand recognition and store shelf positioning, which in turn were very important to success in the specialty area. The danger here was that the company lacked the substantial resources needed to purchase the production run machinery and facilities needed to compete effectively in the low-cost standard product area over the long run. In addition, the company needed to make major product development and production changes in order to obtain the new products and product flexibility needed to succeed in the specialty area.

Second, the company's capability to become an essentially new kind of company — a *primary market differentiation strategy* — was studied. This strategy involved becoming a national specialty or premium baked goods company, a difficult strategy for the company to pursue in light of its limited national marketing experience and financial resources. Over the long run, however, this strategy represented a much better opportunity for a company with the substantial resources needed to do it.

These detailed studies and the strategies and strategic plans resulting from them are described throughout the earlier chapters of this book. In many strategy formulation situations, pattern matching reasoning processes such as those described in this section are more direct,

Figure A-13: Using the Profiles to Improve a Company's Comparative Competitive Position

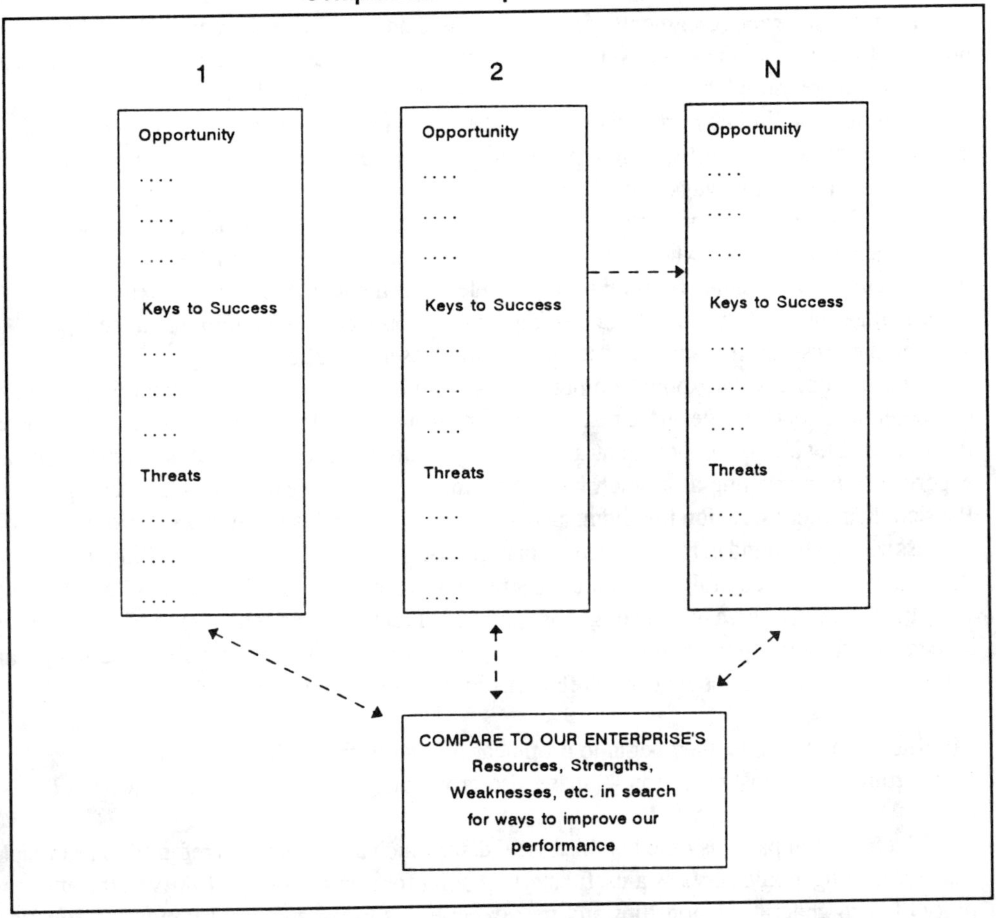

efficient, and effective reasoning processes than IF-THEN rules. In addition, such contingency process models can provide the basis for very specific strategic plan development.

Other Reasoning Processes

Other contingency reasoning processes useful in strategic management have been identified and modelled.

Estimating risks is essential in all decision making involving the future. One common way to do this is to identify the *component factors* affecting outcomes, such as possible actions by competitors, and estimate the *quantitative risk* (for instance a value between 0 and 100 percent) of each possible event occurring. By assigning risks to possible future events, alternatives can often be compared more objectively.

Another common process, mentioned in the pattern matching discussion above, involves *drawing inferences* about segments of a problem based on observable characteristics. This would be done, for example, in Figure A-14 when drawing the implications about customers (such as young adults are more fashion conscious and make frequent brand changes).

During a preliminary analysis of a situation, planners also *review past experiences* in a search for similar patterns that might be useful in the present situation. Such a process helps in thinking about possible ways to deal with the decision at hand.

In reviewing a situation, a planner might observe, for instance, that the situation under study involves a mature industry where several large competitors are dominant in the market, and where the company being planned for is relatively small. A planner would review any experiences with other mature industries to search for *analogous* situation factors which might suggest possible solution patterns useful to making decisions in the present situation.

For example, when Apple Computer grew from being a leader in the emerging personal computer industry to a large, more mature company in an increasingly stable industry, it removed its founder Steve Jobs as president and brought in John Scully, who could draw upon his experiences in marketing at a much larger and more mature consumer products company — Pepsico. In another situation involving an even more mature industry, Stew Leonard drew upon success strategies found in the amusement park industry and in the specialty retailing industry to develop his very successful and distinctive supermarket in Norwalk, Connecticut [Wald 1989].

In other situations, a planner might use patterns of relationships generally true in an industry as a starting point for approaching a strategy formulation problem under study. For example, Alan Rowe [1989] has studied the general relationship to a product's lifecycle of

- Profits — for example, they begin to drop near the end of the cycle
- Opportunities for cost reduction — these also grow fewer as the lifecycle matures

Such general patterns based on historical data, which are sometimes referred to as model-based reasoning, could serve as a useful starting point for investigation. However, the applicability of such general relationships and past experiences to the strategy formulation situation under study would have to be tested, since the present situation may have requirements and characteristics different from those previously encountered.

Other reasoning patterns used by strategic planners can be identified and modelled. The discussion here is not meant to be exhaustive. Rather, it is designed to illustrate that learning strategic management is more than just learning the task definitions given in Chapter 2. It involves learning how planners actually perform the tasks when making a wide range of decisions.

To better understand the reasoning processes involved in strategic management, it is also useful to understand the thinking (cognitive) processes underlying them.

Figure A-14: Segment of a Knowledge-Based System Worksheet: Identifying Opportunities and Keys-to-Success

Object	Attributes	Values	Controlling Concept	Implications	Implied Keys to Success or Opportunities
Customer	Age	Infant Teen Young Adult Middle-Age Older	Experimental, Growing, etc.	Fashion conscious Frequent brand changes, etc.	Provide current, even faddish products
	Income	Under $12,000 $12,000 - $24,000 $24,000 - $48,000 etc.	High Disposable	Higher living standard High discretionary income	High-quality product needed Price not a barrier
	Education	High School College Graduate	Well-Educated	Perception of being informed, more sophisticated but sometimes naive	Provide new technology or image of new technology and value
	Sex	M/F			
	Location Other Demographic Information				

Confirmations and Combinations

Provide a product which appears to be high-tech, state-of-the-art, and in vogue or soon to be in vogue

SOME BASIC THINKING PROCESSES AND SKILLS INVOLVED IN STRATEGY FORMULATION

This section describes some of the basic decision-making processes involved in strategy formulation that are discussed throughout this book.

Some General Thinking Processes

Based on the studies done by cognitive scientists, some of which are noted at the end of this section, several general thinking processes useful in understanding strategy formulation decision making can be identified:

- ***Analysis***. Analyzing or diagnosing, that is, breaking a decision situation into components, is necessary in all phases of strategic management, for example, when identifying factors affecting a decision, such as those shown in Figure A-10.
- ***Evaluation***. Comparing and weighing, that is, evaluating, occurs at many stages in the decision process, for example, when determining the most and least important keys to success and opportunities or when comparing the relative strengths and weaknesses of competitors and the company in these critical areas or when deciding among alternative enterprise-wide strategies. The analysis and evaluation processes are most often identified with rational decision-making processes.
- ***Synthesis***. Synthesizing involves interrelating and bringing together various elements of a situation as when formulating alternative enterprise-wide strategies. While often explainable in rational terms, synthesizing also occurs on the intuitive and more creative (and so less definable) levels, as, for example, when Stew Leonard conceived an amusement park strategy for his $100 million supermarket [Wald 1989].

Specific Cognitive Processes, Tasks, and Associated Skills

Several other thought processes, tasks, and associated skills involved in strategic company management that are relevant to discussions throughout this book include:

- ***Conceptualization***. Conceptualization (or abstraction) and reconceptualization involve grouping specifics into "kind of" categories. The creation of the decision models shown in Figures A-4, A-5, and A-8 are an example of conceptualization.
- ***Inferential Reasoning***. An activity which deals with the future, such as planning, requires drawing inferences or implications from facts, events, or other situation factors. Inferential reasoning skills (whether inductive, deductive, or intuitive), are necessary, for example, to determine future opportunities and key-to-success factors during the structured competitive market analysis and to estimate potential risks and identify potential threats in the marketplace.
- ***Hypothesis Development***. Hypotheses are supposed or proposed ideas about such things as new

ways to do business in a specific competitive market, possible key-to-success factors, likelihoods of events occurring, alternative assumptions about possible competitor actions, and alternative enterprise-wide strategies to be evaluated.

- ***Associative and Intuitive Reasoning.*** Associative reasoning works on several levels. For example, the mind might develop patterns (conceptualizations) and look for analogous ideas in related fields. This can help stimulate alternative strategy formulation. For instance, an airline company can be viewed as being in the business of taking people to places of business and pleasure. From this viewpoint, an airline could be perceived as being in the business and vacation service business (reconceptualization). Within this associative perspective, an airline would be prompted to consider owning hotels, resorts, and rental car companies. One could go further and make associations that are not easily explained by rational processes, and so could be considered intuitive. As one expert has pointed out [Osborn 1963], success depends as much on applied imagination as on programmable rational thought processes. So-called creative and intuitive skills can, therefore, be significant contributors to effective strategic management decision making [Dennett 1988].
- ***Heuristics Guidelines or Rules of Thumb.*** A planner is constantly developing rules of thumb to guide and assist in decision making, as discussed earlier in this Appendix.
- ***Related Personality and Emotional Factors.*** While not directly within the scope of this Appendix, personality and emotional factors can have a substantial impact on decision making, as is seen in the discussions of strategy implementation in Chapters 12 and Appendix B.

These processes and skills are examined in more detail in earlier chapters, where relevant to the strategy management processes and applications discussed. For example, explicit techniques for doing the inferential reasoning and associative reasoning involved in identifying opportunities and keys to success are given in Chapter 4. And the hypothesis development and testing involved in creating alternative company strategies is described in Chapter 7.

Many useful exercises have been developed for stimulating creativity and idea generation. These include: use of metaphors, Crawford blue-slip writing, problem reversal or new perspectives, wishful thinking or brainstorming, and others. The idea behind many of these is to guide reconceptualization of problem definitions and situation factors, as shown in Figures A-4, A-5, A-7, and A-11 through A-14, in order to create new approaches and eventually new solutions.

Conceptualization stimulates associative and inferential reasoning which in turn helps transfer knowledge to new contexts. Many years ago, for example, BIC used the process depicted in the simple diagram shown in Figure A-15 to examine the product it made — pens — in conceptual terms to stimulate thinking about product line expansion. Its pens in conceptual (kinds of) terms were: mass-produced, disposable, for personal use, mass distributed, low cost, usable by a wide range of consumers of both sexes. As the company searched for products which fit the same pen-product concept categories, one that came to mind was razors and razor blades. The concept of razors and razor blades had all the characteristics identified for pens above, with the exception that razor blades had only comparatively limited use among women. BIC successfully entered this market. Another analogous product that was test marketed was women's panty hose; however, that product failed.

Figure A-15: Using Concepts to Stimulate Associative Reasoning

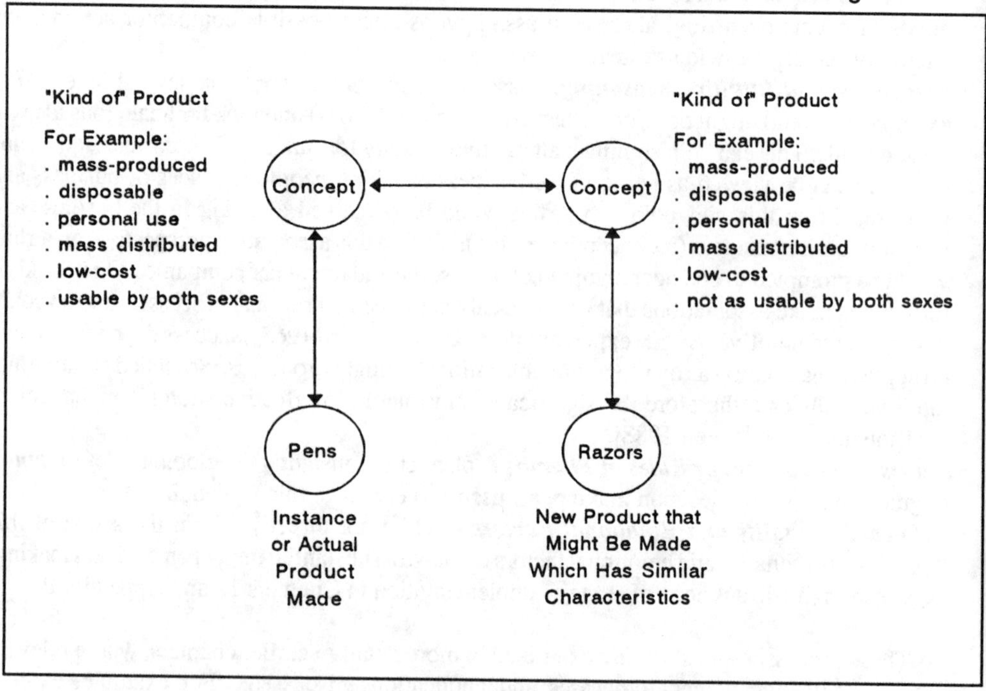

The discussion in this section is only a brief introduction to the subject. Cognitive scientists have been providing insights into and definitions of creative decision-making processes for over half a century [Dewey 1938; Einstein and Infeld 1938]. Much of the current research on more rational management decision-making processes grows out of work done at Carnegie Mellon University and MIT by such people as Simon, Cyert, and Licklider [Keen and Morton 1978, p. viii; Morton 1971; Simon 1960, 1969, 1976 and 1979], and other early researchers [Anderson 1983; Brightman 1980]. A major body of research also exists concerning creativity and decision making [Amabile 1983; Besemer 1981; Brogden 1964; Bruner 1968; Couger 1990; Jackson 1965; Keil 1987; Miller 1987; Rhodes 1961; Rickards 1985; Roberts 1988; Rothenberg 1976; Udell 1977]. Those wishing to explore the subject further might want to consult the author's monographs on the subject [Mockler 1992(B&D)] and other works which are listed in the References at the end of this Appendix.

AN INTEGRATED STRATEGIC MANAGEMENT PROCESS

It is important to understand how the strategic management tasks outlined in Figure A-1 and discussed in Chapter 2 are carried out in an integrated way in the formulation and implementation of business strategies. Figure A-2 outlines such a context-specific integrative process in simplified form, based on the strategic management tasks and processes identified and discussed so far in this Appendix.

In the process outlined in Figure A-2, a planner:

- Bases his/her reasoning on an analysis of basic situation elements, such as *industry* and *competitive market factors*, and *competitor factors*
- Moves through intermediate reasoning steps, such as *comparative competitive market position analyses*
- Ultimately makes a wide range of strategy decisions, such as the *general strategy direction*, *strategic focus*, and *strategic approach*, which very often become more precise as the study progresses

The decision-making model in Figure A-2 differs from the task model in Figure A-1 in that it traces reasoning relationships among model components and details the reasoning involved in doing strategic management tasks. It is an extension and amplification of the process outlined in Figure A-3.

The strategic management process shown in Figure A-2, and its many amplifications and variations given throughout this text, is both adaptive to individual situations and structured to some degree. For this reason, it replicates practical experience in strategic management and so is useful for teaching and learning purposes. Such a context-specific strategic management process model also has a sound theoretical basis in cognitive psychology and in management and planning sciences. It is not a complete model of the process, however, nor is it the only way to model or describe it — anymore than there is one *single* way that *all* strategic planners make *all* their decisions in *all* strategy formulation situations. This is shown in Figure A-7 where the intermediate conceptualization phase as depicted allows for considerable freedom in the way problems are reconceived and solved. In addition, the process is not a rigid procedural one, in which one goes sequentially from step to step. Rather it is a continuing, freely flowing adaptive process within which the mind moves about in a variety of ways.

The reader should also remember that, as has been pointed out throughout the book, a strategy infrequently first appears in its final form. A strategy more often emerges through a succession of approximations. Sometimes alternatives must be considered — that is, hypotheses must be tested and sometimes rejected. At other times, as more information about competitors and markets is obtained, initial ideas are reformed, reformulated, revised, amplified, and sketched out in more detail. This emergent process, which moves through gradually more specific conceptualizations, is modelled in Figure A-7 and described in Chapter 12.

The context-specific processes outlined in the figures in this Appendix and elsewhere in this book provide a useful framework, however, for understanding and learning strategy formulation. They are also useful and necessary for building more complex and varied contingency models and processes, as well as for developing knowledge-based and other computer systems and manual tools that help in learning and doing strategic management.

QUALITATIVE, QUANTITATIVE, SYSTEMS, AND COMPUTER TECHNIQUES AND TOOLS USEFUL IN STRATEGY FORMULATION

While this book focuses primarily on the contingency processes involved in formulating and implementing strategies, some attention is given to the many qualitative, quantitative, systems, and computer tools and techniques useful in doing strategy formulation and implementation.

Since these tools and techniques are understandable only within the context of strategic management applications, the discussion of them is for the most part limited

- To the sections where the basic strategy formulation and implementation processes and tasks these tools and techniques support are discussed, and
- To the discussions at the end of each chapter after basic strategic management processes and tasks in different areas have been discussed.

One type of computer system aid, *knowledge-based systems*, is a computer system that replicates one way expert planners think or reason. Knowledge-based systems can be consulted for assistance in doing strategy formulation; some of them can actually make strategy recommendations in specific situations [Mockler 1989(A&B) and 1992(C)].

Examples of knowledge-based systems that make use of rules have been discussed in this

Figure A-16: Sample Segment of Knowledge Base Questions and a User Query (Initial Concept Testing Prototype)

question(potential-obsolescence) =	'How would you characterize the potential for technological obsolescence in this industry segment [very low, low, average, high, very high)?'
question(demand-uncertainty) =	'How would you assess the uncertainty of future demand in this industry segment (very low, low, average, high, very high)?'

The first question above, which is stored in the system's knowledge base, causes the system to print the following query on a user's computer screen:

> How would you characterize the potential for technological obsolescence in this industry segment (very low, low, average, high, very high)?
>
> >> (A user types an answer in here.)

Figure A-17: Dependency Diagram for Strategy Planning System - General Strategy Directions Subsystem

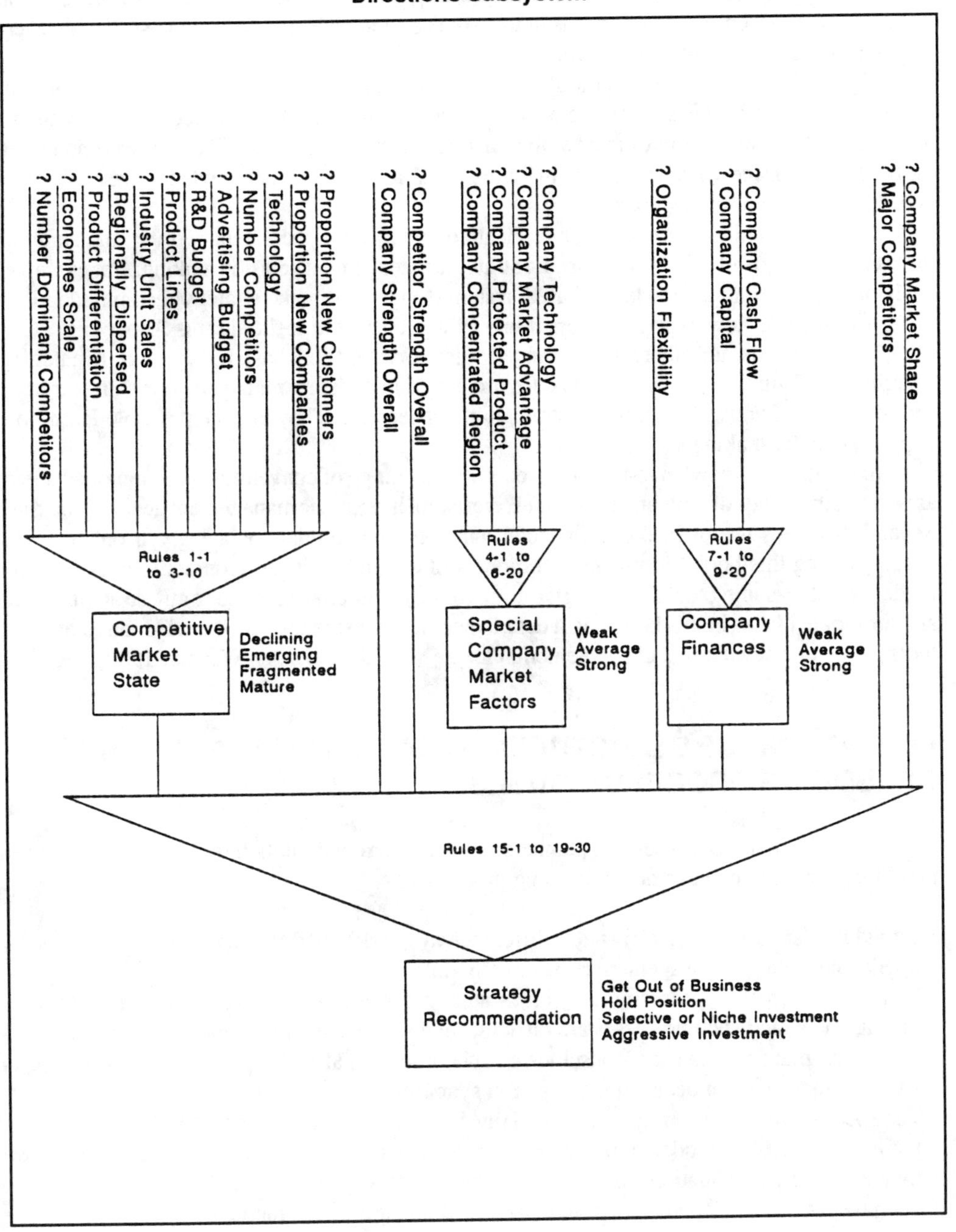

Appendix. For example, Figure A-9 is an example of a rule from one of these systems, and Figure A-10 is an example of a decision chart summarizing rules from another segment of that system. Figure A-16 gives one of the questions in that same system, which a user of the system answers during a consultation with the system.

Figure A-17 diagrams a simplified knowledge-based system prototype. Examples of expanded versions of this system and of other strategic management knowledge-based systems are given in the final sections of most of the earlier chapters in this book. The disk accompanying the book contains the system modelled in Figure A-17, as well as other knowledge-based systems described elsewhere in this book.

Since knowledge-based systems replicate one way strategic planners think, the study of them is especially useful for those learning strategic management decision making. For example, analyzing the rules in a knowledge-based system designed to make strategy recommendations gives insights into how expert planners think, as was discussed earlier in this Appendix.

These systems, and other more advanced object-oriented ones based on the pattern matching described in Figures A-11, A-12 and A-13, are useful in assisting managers in making strategy formulation decisions, that is, doing strategic management. They also help people learn how experts go about making such decisions.

In addition to knowledge-based systems, a wide range of conventional computer systems, as well as other kinds of tools and techniques, are useful in strategic management decision making. Several key ones useful in doing financial analyses and simulations are given on the disks accompanying this book. Mathematical models of a firm and its environment are also useful model-based reasoning tools in strategy formulation. Additional examples of these are included at appropriate places in this book and a detailed comprehensive review of a wide range of these tools is given in several useful supplemental texts [Mockler 1992(A); Webster 1989].

LIMITATIONS OF STRUCTURED STRATEGIC MANAGEMENT REASONING PROCESS MODELS

As can be seen from observing planners at work, inherent limitations exist in structuring and modelling strategic management reasoning processes:

- Individual planners can reason in many different ways, making it difficult to develop universally applicable strategic management reasoning models
- Intuitive and creative processes, as well as more rational processes, are involved in strategic management, and such processes are difficult (but not always impossible) to structure
- Individual manager's biases, conscious or subconscious, also can play a significant role in strategic management decision making [Buksyar 1990].
- The specific processes can vary substantially from situation to situation and from planner to planner, so that the models replicate only in a general or semi-structured way how expert planners deal with situations; they do not represent the only expert way
- The process itself is inherently complex and, in some areas, unstructured

- In practice, seasoned planners are unlikely to be able to articulate how they make decisions, since they have been doing it for so long they are no longer conscious of how they do it

To illustrate, Stew Leonard broke with many traditional ways of doing business in his industry when he opened his supermarket in Norwalk, Connecticut. His store was not part of a grocery store chain, carried only a few hundred items (most supermarkets carry more than 25,000 items), and relied mainly on showmanship — making shopping fun — and low prices to attract customers. The store combined butcher shop, bakery, and fish and produce market, with a small selection of other items, such as detergents. Its annual sales were in the $100 million range, and its sales per square foot run $3,100 a year compared with an average of $300 to $500 in the industry [Wald 1989]. Creatively breaking, not following, the rules made for success at Stew Leonard's store. The specific thought processes through which Stew Leonard reached decisions about his strategies were not that clearly definable, although they could generally be described as resulting from a shrewed analysis of specific company, competitor, and competitive market situation requirements.

As The Games Gang experiences in Chapter 1 and the Stew Leonard examples show, strategy formulation is applied creative decision making, that is, decision making which strikes a balance between intuition and creativity, within a disciplined framework of rational processes focused on successfully serving a competitive market given one's available resources.

Strategy formulation is ultimately still a relatively unstructured kind of decision making, since it involves dealing with future, and therefore uncertain, events and since it can involve creativity and intuition. This does not mean that it is impossible to structure how strategic management decisions are made and so model the contingency processes involved in making these decisions. As seen in the discussions in the chapters in PARTS TWO and THREE and in this Appendix, it is possible to define and structure *many* strategic management reasoning processes in ways useful for learning and doing strategic management. It simply means that people working in the field of strategic management have not yet fully identified and defined how a wide range of their decisions are made in business.

One final limitation to keep in mind is that the material in this Appendix is only one of many ways to understand strategic management and acquire strategic management skills. The previous chapters in this book present a variety of learning perspectives useful to a wide range of readers, some of whom, because of their background, training, experience, or the educational institution they are attending, may not need the kind of detailed explanations given in this Appendix.

BUSINESS STRATEGIC AND CONCEPTUAL THINKING

Understanding what business strategy is requires understanding conceptual thinking. A business strategy is a *concept*, an articulated idea of the *kind* of business activity to be engaged in. This concept is often clearly defined in the mind of the strategy formulator; at the outset it may seem more a vision statement to others.

A more precise definition of that vision may emerge quickly or over a period of time. This process of defining the visionary strategy concept may involve studying the context of the activity more carefully, making plans to carry it out, carrying it out, and, as required, continually defining and redefining the initial strategy concept.

Much of the confusion about strategic management arises from not accepting the basic conceptual nature of strategy formulation and the interaction of the strategy concept with reality and flexible, adaptive implementation actions, during which time the initial concept can evolve or even change.

REVIEW QUESTIONS

1. Describe the integrated adaptive context-specific process involved in strategic management decision making that is outlined and discussed in the Appendix. What are some of its limitations as a descriptive model?
2. What is cognitive modelling? Describe different ways in which strategic management thinking or cognitive processes have been outlined or modelled in this text.
3. Describe the IF-THEN heuristics that are used by strategic planners in making strategy formulation decisions.
4. Describe the ways in which solutions can emerge in strategic management.
5. Describe some of the situations in which pattern matching reasoning processes can be useful in making strategy formulation decisions.
6. Describe situations in which a planner might reason directly from the situation facts to a conclusion, and situations in which a planner might bypass this reasoning and use past analogous experience to come to a decision.
7. Describe some of the basic cognitive processes and skills involved in strategy formulation. Discuss some of the strategic management areas where they are put to work usefully.
8. What are the limitations of cognitive models of strategic management decision processes? What are some of their uses?
9. Describe the usefulness of quantitative systems and computer techniques and tools in strategy formulation decision making. Also, describe their limitations.
10. Describe the distinctions between the strategic management tasks and general contingency processes described in Chapter 2 and some of the more advanced strategic management contingency processes described in this Appendix.

EXERCISES

1. Read recent issues of the periodicals referred to in the references at the end of the Appendix, or other related periodicals of your choice and find examples of

   - A well-developed company strategy formulation. Write a report which traces how the company matched competitive market success requirements in opportunity areas with available company resources in formulating these enterprise-wide strategies.

- A strategy that went wrong, paying special attention to the ways in which an incomplete or incorrect initial diagnosis of competitive market forces and competitors caused the problems.

2. Read the *Superb Biscuits* company study in the Case Study Section of this book. Write a report describing major opportunity areas and critical factors affecting success in the industry involved. In addition, identify the major company strengths and weaknesses, as well as major competitor strengths and weaknesses.

3. Write a similar report on another case study at the end of this text or any company of your choosing.

4. The disks accompanying this book contain several prototype knowledge-based systems. Follow the directions accompanying the disks to run a consultation using the system with the filename PLANNING.REV or any of the other seven knowledge-based systems on that disk which you have not already run. For this consultation, you might want to use the information contained in one of the company studies in the Case Study section of this book (whose title contains an actual company name). If you wish, print out the knowledge base and study it while you are running the system and restudying this Appendix, in order to get a fuller picture of how basic strategy formulation decisions are made.

REFERENCES

Amabile, T., *The Social Psychology of Creativity*, New York: Springer Verlag, 1983.

Anderson, John R., *The Architecture of Cognition*, Cambridge, MA: Harvard University Press, 1983.

Berg, Eric N., "At Fuller Brush, New Ways to Get Foot in Door," *The New York Times*, May 18, 1989, pp. D1, D2.

Bernstein, Aaron, *Grounded: Frank Lorenzo and the Destruction of Eastern Airlines*, New York: Simon & Schuster, 1990.

Besemer, S.P., and D.J. Treffinger, "Analysis of Creative Products: Review and Synthesis," *The Journal of Creative Behavior, 3,* November 15, 1981.

Brightman, H.J., *Problem Solving: A Logical and Creative Approach,* Atlanta, GA: Business Publications Division, Georgia State University, 1980.

Brogden, H.E., and T.B. Sprecher, "Criteria of Creativity," in Taylor, E.W., (ed.), *Creativity Progress and Potential,* New York: McGraw Hill 1964.

Bruner, J.S., *Toward a Theory of Instruction*, New York: Norton, 1968.

Buksyar, Edward William, *Strategic Management and the Perception of Order*, Doctoral Dissertation, University of Arizona, 1990.

Couger, J. Daniel, "Ensuring Creative Approaches in Information Systems Design," *Managerial and Decision Economics*, Volume 11, 1990, pp. 281-295.

Dennett, Daniel C., *Brainstorms*, Cambridge, MA: Bradford Books (MIT Press), 1988.

Dewey, J., *Logic: The Structure of Inquiry,* New York: Putman, 1938.

Einstein, A., and L. Infeld, *The Evolution of Physics*, New York: Simon and Schuster, 1938.

Forsythe, Jason, "Systems Give Pepperidge Farm Freshness," *InformationWEEK*, March 20, 1989, pp. 29-31.

Hamermesh, Richard G., *Making Strategy Work*, New York: Wiley, 1986.

Jackson, P., and S. Messick, "The Person, the Product and the Response: Conceptual Problems in the Assessment of Creativity," *Journal of Personality, 33*, 1965.

Keen, Peter G.W., and Michael S. Scott Morton, *Decision Support Systems: An Organizational Perspective*, Reading, MA: Addison-Wesley, 1978.

Keil, J.M., *The Creative Corporation*, Homewood, IL: Dow Jones-Irwin, 1987.

Kleinfield, N.R., "Even for J. Crew, the Mail-Order Boom Days Are Over," *The New York Times*, Business Section, September 2, 1990, p. 5.

Miller, W.C., *The Creative Edge*, Reading MA: Addison-Wesley 1987.

Mockler, Robert J., *Computer Software to Support Strategic Planning Decision Making*, New York: Macmillan, 1992(A).

Mockler, Robert J., *Contingency Approaches to Strategic Management*, Research Working Paper, New York: Strategic Management Research Group, 1992(B).

Mockler, Robert J., *Knowledge-based Systems: An Introduction to Expert Systems*, New York: Macmillan Publishing, 1992(C).

Mockler, Robert J., *Structured Industry/Competitive Market Analysis*, Research Working Paper, New York: Strategic Management Research Group, 1992(D).

Mockler, Robert J., *Knowledge-based Systems for Management Decisions*, Englewood Cliffs, NJ: Prentice Hall, 1989(A).

Mockler, Robert J., *Knowledge-based Systems for Strategic Planning*, Englewood Cliffs, NJ: Prentice Hall, 1989(B).

Mockler, Robert J., *Structuring and Analyzing Competitive Groups Within an Industry or Competitive Market*, Research Working Paper, New York: Strategic Management Research Group, 1991.

Morton, Michael S. Scott, *Management Decision Systems: Computer-Based Support for Decision Making*, Cambridge, MA: Division of Research, Harvard, 1971.

Osborn, Alex, *Applied Imagination*, New York: Scribner, 1963.

Porter, Michael E., *Competitive Advantage*, New York: The Free Press, 1985.

Porter, Michael E., *Competitive Strategy*, New York: The Free Press, 1980.

Rhodes, M., "An Analysis of Creativity," *Phi Delta Kappan*, April, 1961.

Rickards, T., *Stimulating Innovation: A Systems Approach*, New York: St. Martin's Press, 1985.

Roberts, E.B., "Managing Invention and Innovation," *Research-Technology Management*, January-February 1988.

Rothenberg, A., *The Creativity Question*, Durham NC: Duke University Press, 1976.

Rowe, Alan, "Expert Systems in Strategic Management," presented at the Decision Sciences Institute 20th Annual Meeting, New Orleans, November 20-22, 1989.

Simon, H.A., and S.K. Reed, "Modeling Strategy Shifts in a Problem-Solving Task," in *Cognitive Psychology*, Vol. 8, 1976, pp. 86-97.

Simon, H.A., "Information Processing Models of Cognition," *Annual Review of Psychology*, 1979, 30, pp. 363-396.

Simon, H.A., *The New Science of Management Decision*, New York: Harper and Row, 1960.

Simon, H.A., *The Science of the Artificial*, Cambridge, MA: MIT Press, 1969.

Udell, G.G., M.F. O'Neill, and K.G. Baker, *Guide to Invention and Innovation Evaluation*, Washington D.C.: Superintendent of Documents, U.S. Government Printing Office, 1977.

Wald, Matthew L., "Stew Leonard's, Believe It or Not!," *The New York Times*, May 25, 1989, pp. D1, D6.

Webster, James L., William E. Reif, and Jeffrey S. Bracker, "The Manager's Guide to Strategic Planning Tools and Techniques," *Planning Review*, November/December 1989, pp. 4-12, 48.

Weiner, Eric, "Lorenzo, Head of Continental Air, Quits Industry in $30 Million Deal," *The New York Times*, August 10, 1990, pp. A1, D8.

APPENDIX B

MANAGING A STRATEGY FORMULATION AND IMPLEMENTATION EFFORT

The objective of Appendix B is to introduce readers to the tasks involved in organizing and managing strategic management efforts, as well as in carrying out these tasks in specific situations. Such efforts, often referred to as strategic planning efforts in business, originally focus more on strategy and plan formulation and less on strategy and plan implementation.

As with other strategic management tasks, such efforts are organized and carried out in a variety of ways. In addition, based on surveys of several hundred large companies, it appeared that considerably less than half of U.S. companies had formal strategic planning efforts as of the late 1980s. Corporate strategy planning efforts seem to be reviving in the early 1990s, within a more context-specific orientation. For example, at a series of meetings with several dozen company planning officers and their CEOs, it was clear that their companies were creating and strengthening planning organizations and positions at the corporate level [McConahey 1992].

The discussion in the early sections of Appendix B provides general guidelines for planning, organizing, directing, staffing, and controlling formal strategic planning efforts. The factors affecting decision making, the use of situational factor analysis in making decisions in specific situations, and the relation of this strategic management task to the integration and implementation of strategies and related enabling plans are discussed in the final sections of Appendix B. The discussion also covers the relationship of these tasks to other strategic management tasks shown in Figure B-1, as well as to the fostering of *strategic thinking* — a critical aspect of strategic management.

While carrying out a formal planning effort is listed as a separate strategic management task in Figure B-1, it is not necessarily a discrete task. It is part of the continuing strategic management

Figure B-1: Strategic Management Tasks

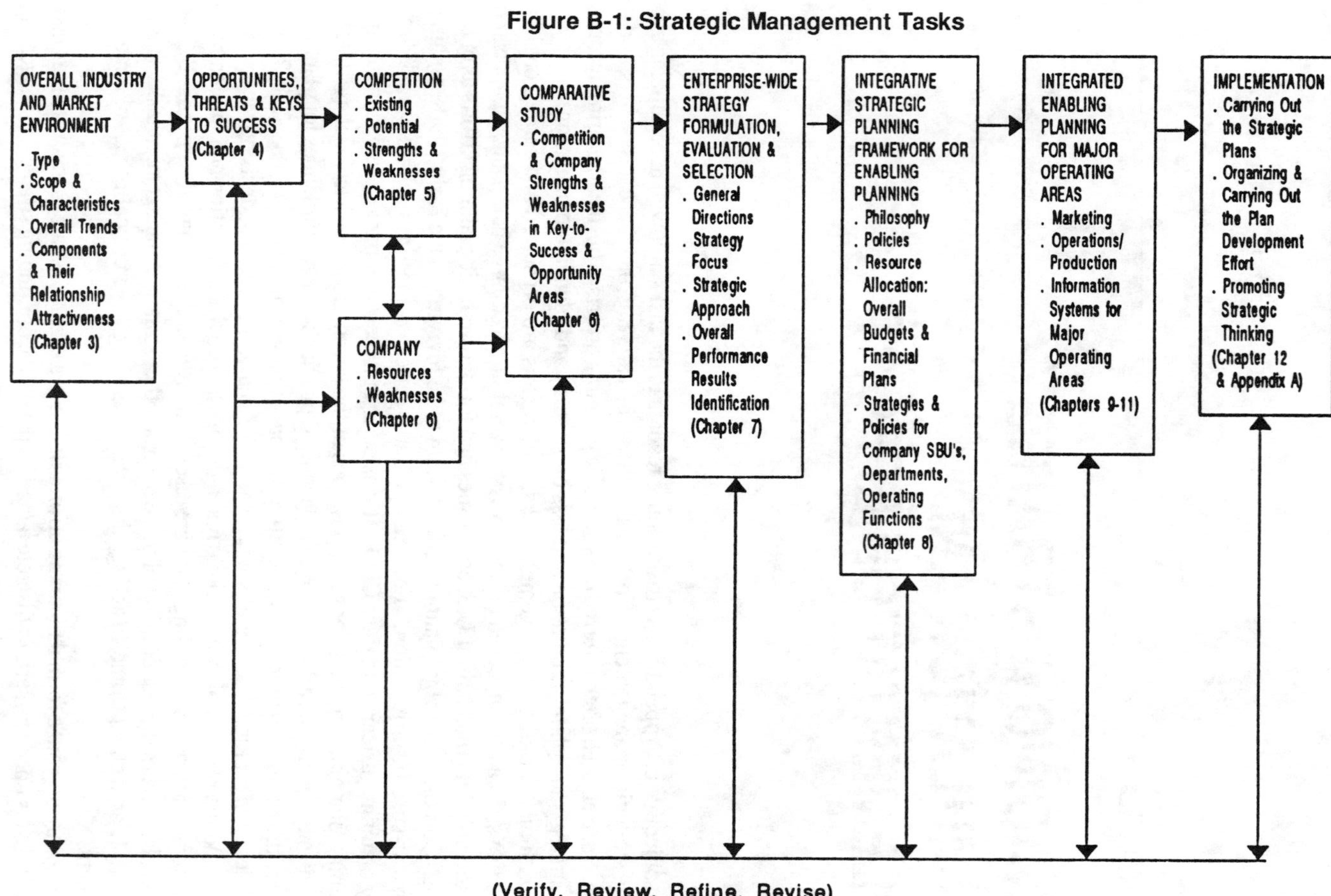

process designed to:

- Formulate and provide a strategic focus to guide operating managers
- Make use of the wealth of available operating manager experience in developing a strategic focus that is specific enough to be useful in helping to run a business more effectively from day to day
- Build consensus and commitment and promote strategic thinking

The process functions then not only to get strategies and related strategic plans formulated. It is also a critical step in ensuring that the strategies and plans themselves are integrated and operationally oriented, a task described in Chapters 8 through 11, and in helping promote and guide the subsequent implementation of the strategies and plans described in Chapter 12. In addition, it is not necessarily a formal step taken by most companies.

THE TASKS INVOLVED

The discussion in this section describes the tasks involved in organizing and managing strategic planning efforts, and provides guidelines for performing them.

Changing Function and Structure of Formal Planning Organizations

Many companies have formal planning departments [Hohn 1986; Prescott 1989; Stanat 1990]. The heads of many of these departments meet at The Conference Board's Strategic Planning Conference and at The Planning Forum's Conference each year to describe their operations and to discuss their problems and opportunities [Reimann 1988, 1989, 1990, 1991]. These planners also meet regularly at Planning Forum special interest group roundtables.

Some experts argue that while formal planning efforts expanded substantially during the 1970s and early 1980s, they declined in the late 1980s at major corporations. However, the more commonly held opinion is that strategic planning activities have not diminished. Rather, the locus of strategic planning has shifted from the corporate level to the level of those managers involved in implementing strategies and strategic plans, and for this reason has become less visible [Prescott 1989]. This shift coincides with the shift in emphasis from focusing on developing strategies and plans to a broader focus on strategy formulation and implementation, that is, strategic management.

Evidence exists to support this opinion. For example, the experiences of companies like Signode in organizing and carrying out its planning effort over the years illustrates the changing broadening focus of formal strategic planning efforts and the different ways these efforts can be organized and carried out [Noyes 1985]. The following is a brief history of Signode's planning organization:

> **Phase One:** Until 1972, Signode had no formal planning. Management decisions were made intuitively at the highest level of the organization in response to short-term challenges and

opportunities. The company was considerably smaller then, so such informal strategic planning was possible. This is the case at many smaller companies ["Survey" 1986].

Phase Two. In 1972, Signode began to develop a more formal planning process. In 1974, the company developed its first ten-year plan and two years later held its first formal strategic planning session. At this point, group-level executives and even some division-level executives became actively involved in shaping the strategic direction for the company. Still, top management controlled the planning process. During these early formal stages, strategic planning was largely numbers oriented and focused on financial concerns and accounting data. This seems to be somewhat typical of the early phases of formal strategic planning efforts.

Phase Three. From 1979 to 1981, the company's strategic planning began to emphasize issues rather than numbers. During this period, such concepts as the growth-share matrix, portfolio management, definition of business units, and market and competitive analysis were introduced into the formal planning process. Even though the system was in place and was fairly well-accepted and understood, line management's involvement remained minimal and gaps existed between the overall-company strategy and the way the business was run at the operational level. It is fairly common initially to experiment with new planning technologies and approaches as qualitative issues become more important. It is also common in less mature planning efforts for an integration gap to exist between operations and overall-company strategies, especially when strategic issues are emphasized.

Phase Four. In 1982, line managers — the people who implement the plans — became involved as full partners in company-wide planning processes. Such involvement can lead to a major shift in the function of a planning department, where one exists, especially as lower levels take on more and more of the actual planning work. This shift is occurring in many companies that have formal planning efforts.

The evolution of Signode's formal planning effort illustrates the shift that occurred in business in general during this period— from focusing on strategic plan development to a broader strategic management focus that emphasized implementation as the key to success. This shift led to the abolishment of many formal planning departments at the corporate level in the late 1980s.

Similar experiences at FMC Corporation, a conglomerate with a portfolio of operating divisions in diverse businesses, led to the development in stages over two decades of an even more flexible organization of the company's planning effort. The following is a summary of how that planning effort worked in 1990 [Early 1990].

The overall planning process at FMC began by identifying which businesses faced significant strategic decisions and which businesses had other reasons to benefit from going through the formal process during the year. The businesses not slated for a full-scale analysis would merely complete an update of their strategic actions and financial forecasts for use in corporate planning and for linkage to the other parts of the management system. The corporate planning department then scheduled the three major elements of the newly developed planning system for each business:

- An Issues and Alternatives Meeting
- The date that the Plan Summary would be due from the division managers
- An Optional Strategy Discussion

The *Issues and Alternatives (I&A) Meeting* gave corporate and top line management the opportunity to compile up-to-date information on significant changes in the business and to agree on which key issues must be addressed. It was a small meeting, involving the CEO, the COO, the division manager, the group vice-president, and a few members of top corporate management. It was generally held two to four months after the formal process in the division began and two months before the recommended strategy was due.

The meeting focused on questions, not answers. Not expecting answers freed corporate and line management to be more creative and open about their assessment of the business. For each issue, the division manager was expected to provide a few alternative responses, one of which later became the basis for the strategies. However, no strong recommendations were expected, because this would put the division manager in the position of selling and defending. This informal process allowed the division manager to float some trial balloons and get feedback from corporate management in a relatively low-risk environment. The early timing of the meeting also allowed corporate management's strategy suggestions to be accepted more easily by the division managers and their teams, and gave them the opportunity to develop the suggestions further. This meeting was designed to foster effective communication in a problem-solving environment.

The *Plan Summary*, the second element scheduled, was limited to 10-to-12 pages and included one required format summarizing the financial projections. It described the previous strategy, its implementation status, the situation analysis, recommended strategies, the key actions, risks, opportunities, and expected results. The general manager's cover letter briefly stated how the recommended strategies responded to the issues discussed at the I&A Meeting, pointed out why it was chosen over other alternatives, and raised any important implementation risks.

After receiving the Plan Summary, corporate management decided if they want to hold a *Strategy Discussion* with the division manager and, if so, what topics they wanted to cover. General managers who were able to devise responsive strategies with credible projections for adequate returns often were not required to attend a Strategy Discussion. If the meeting was held, the time available for preparation was limited to a couple of weeks, and the size of the meeting was kept small. Following acceptance of the proposed strategy, the Plan Summary was modified appropriately and sent to top corporate and line management to keep them up-to-date on the formal outcome of the strategic planning process.

Compared to the previous planning system (process) at FMC, the planning system in 1989 was less bureaucratic. Neither voluminous plans nor elaborate slide shows were permitted. Planners tried to answer letters and phone inquiries quickly to enhance communication and relevance. The focus was on issues, decisions, and shared understanding rather than on forms and presentations. The system gave corporate management an effective forum to maintain the enterprise-wide strategic emphasis on "becoming our customers' most valued supplier" by relating it to the specific businesses at FMC. The planning department functioned as coordinator and facilitator; it did not do the planning. Rather, the process enabled corporate management to constructively participate in the process of formulating business strategy from the beginning, before line management advocacy began. During the first several years after recapitalization in 1986 — while debt levels were quite high and repayment schedules were designed to be aggressive — flexibility and early input were quite important to successful strategic management.

What has been called the decline of formal corporate planning departments, then, can be perceived as the maturing of the discipline, as it moved from financial plans to strategic management issues and plans and as its execution moved closer to the implementation or user level. In addition to the experiences of companies such as Signode and FMC, broader surveys provide evidence of this so-called "downsizing" of the planning function in the 1980s. For example, one survey of 95 large companies [Prescott 1989] indicated that in more than half of the companies surveyed major strategic planning functions had been initiated by or taken over by operating departments during the preceding four years.

The shift to having users do functions formerly performed by a corporate group is not a phenomenon limited to the strategic planning area — it had been going on for a decade in the computer information systems area [Mockler 1992; Radding 1989]. It is much more natural and efficient to have lower level managers involved in strategy and related enabling plan development as much and as early as possible in the strategic management process, even to the point of having them prepare the plans. This is true at least in situations where they will be carrying out the plans.

Formerly having been considered a specialized corporate technical function (both from a financial and an information gathering and analysis viewpoint) at many companies, enterprise-wide strategy and related enabling plan development is now being done more and more by those who carry out the plan. As in the computer information systems area, technology has furthered this trend in the strategic management area, where managers, through on-line computerized databases and other computer software tools, now have direct access to massive amounts of information in a form useful for strategic management purposes. Under these new organizational approaches, where the situation dictates that line managers who implement plans become more involved in formulating them, the role of corporate planners is shifting from just doing planning to supporting and coordinating the planning effort.

The Emerging Importance of the Technical Support Function

Because of the wide range of situations encountered in business — from very large companies such as Volkswagen to the small candy company described in Chapter 7 — not everything discussed in this section is occurring at every company. For example, the following strategic information and planning services were provided by Volkswagen's corporate planning department in 1986:

- Managing the budgeting process, from corporate strategy formulation and long-range program development through sales forecasting, capacity planning, expense budgeting, earnings projections, and investment planning, to setting up result reporting systems and reviewing actual results

- Providing quantitative information (sales, shipments, income trends, etc.) on both the economic environment and the automobile industry from external databases
- Providing qualitative information on political trends, ecological trends, and technological trends
- Providing analyses of internally generated information on operations, including projections of trends indicated by this data and analysis of deviations from planned performance
- Developing scenarios of possible moves into new product concepts, manufacturing methods, and international locations, and providing strategic and financial analyses needed for personnel planning
- Performing value-added analyses [Hohn 1986]

Large industrial companies with relatively concentrated product lines, such as automakers and steel companies, will probably always have such formal planning departments, which are deeply involved in analyzing economic trends and in preparing comprehensive financial plans.

In industrial situations less dependent on major economic and industry movements, and in situations such as Signode where operating managers become more involved in doing the actual planning, a corporate planner, planning department, or planning executive is under increasing pressure to

- Allow actual strategic planning tasks be carried out by the departments which will be implementing the plans
- Provide technical support to those doing the strategic planning

For example, a survey of 95 programs existing in corporations to gather competitive intelligence information useful in both strategic and operational planning yielded the following results [Prescott 1989]:

- About half these programs were located in corporate and divisional planning departments and half in functional departments, such as marketing
- About half the programs were strategic in nature, and half were concerned with supporting tactical projects designed to assist in implementing business strategy
- The programs' annual budgets ranged from $15,000 to $6,500,000
- On average they had three fulltime employees, one part-time employee, and one clerical assistant
- About half were organized to provide a flow of interrelated intelligence for a particular set of industries and competitors on an on-going basis
- On average the programs were four years old
- Two-thirds of the companies had sales over one billion dollars and 20 percent had sales less than $250 million

These programs involved strategy formulation, data collection, data analysis to develop intelligence, dissemination of intelligence to appropriate managers on a timely basis, and data evaluation.

The implications of this study for formal strategic planning departments are

- Better and faster competitive market intelligence useful in strategic planning is needed and new technology is available for fulfilling that need
- If corporate planning departments do not fulfill that need, line mangers will create their own technical support units to provide strategic competitive market intelligence

Such studies illustrate how new strategic information needs, and new technologies to fulfill them, are arising in business. They also illustrate how companies and managers are moving to fulfill these needs. In some companies, formal corporate planning departments are meeting the needs and providing the technical support needed. At others, corporate planning departments have been eliminated and units are being formed within operating areas to fulfill the new strategic planning information needs. This is referred to as "downsizing" the strategic planning function, that is, moving it from the corporate to the operational level.

In addition to providing newly emerging technical services, formal planning departments are also providing more coordination and integration services, as additional management levels become more involved in strategic planning efforts. These coordination tasks are described in the following sections on direction and staffing.

An Emerging Role for Corporate Planning Departments

The following describes the author's study in mid-1992 of two dozen revived strategic planning departments at major U.S. corporations. In most instances these companies had hired or promoted new planning directors. In all instances their role was defined as:

- Working with the corporate CEO on special assignments such as mergers and acquisitions (in this role they were expected to initiate action and carry out special assignments), and
- Working with operating managers to provide assistance, mostly on an as-needed and as-asked for basis, in doing the planning required by the company's CEO.

In working with operating managers, their experiences were that they had to start with issues and tasks of specific interest to the operating managers in getting their jobs done (not overall corporate issues), and through helping in these interest areas prove their value and gain trust. Similarly, in working with CEOs they had to pay as much attention to current problems, such as cutting costs quickly, as to long-range problems. In fact, all the CEOs mentioned the problems at General Motors where the president was in effect demoted for not curing short-range operating problems [Lohr 1992]. The early 1990s were difficult times for many corporations, and surviving and prospering over the short run in very competitive markets was extremely important.

Direction: Personal Involvement and Leadership

While strategy formulation may be largely an intellectual activity, strategy implementation is in large measure a dynamic organizational process whose success depends on people.

The effectiveness of the strategic management effort, therefore, depends on the effectiveness of its initiator, leader, and guide — often referred to as its champion. According to the many planners and corporate executives who discuss their strategic planning experiences at annual conferences, championship of strategic planning efforts must initially come from the company's top management [McConahey 1992]. It must also come at other points in the strategic management process where critical resource allocation decisions are made.

The job of enterprise-wide strategy formulation and implementation is not delegatable [Reimann 1989, p. 43]. CEOs establish overall directions for a firm [Robert 1988]. This does not, however, preclude participation in the process — especially in formulating the strategic focus and approach — by lower level company managers responsible for carrying out strategic plans.

The impact of a CEO's personal leadership is evident in many of the situations cited in earlier chapters: Colman Mockler at Gillette [Chakravorty 1991], Lee Iacocca at Chrysler [Iacocca 1983], Michael Walsh at Tenneco [Hayes 1992], and Roger Penske at Detroit Diesel [White 1991].

The impact of the CEO's personality and leadership skills on all phases of the strategic management process was substantial in each company situation. The CEO was the critical driving force for effectively integrating enterprise-wide, strategic business unit, and operating plans. Their personal involvement was especially important in obtaining the commitment needed for successful plan implementation.

Through their involvement, these chief executives also helped promote *strategic thinking* and commitment throughout their companies, thus enabling managers to be continually more responsive to the changing competitive market environment.

Leadership and communication styles and techniques useful in strategy formulation and implementation were discussed in Chapter 12.

Direction: Oral Communications

Open and collaborative dialog helps the strategic management effort in many ways. In addition to reaffirming the personal involvement of top management, it provides a mechanism for

- Clarifying concepts during plan development
- Adapting overall-company plans to operational needs on a timely and detailed basis
- Helping those operating managers unfamiliar with strategic planning techniques to acquire strategic planning skills
- Generally involving those who will be carrying out the plans more directly and intimately in the development process
- Coordinating and controlling the planning effort

In these ways, greater integration of the overall-company and operating plans can be enhanced through greater reliance on oral communications [Povejsil 1989]. Without such integration, strategic plans become outdated before they are used. In the words of one corporate planner, "strategic thinking grows through dialog and dies through writer's cramp" [Reimann 1988, p. 43.].

Open and cooperative dialogue also enables the strategic management process to foster strategic thinking among key operating managers [Reimann 1988, pp. 42-44]. A strategic thinking orientation among company decision makers helps ensure that strategy formulation and strategic plan development will continue, as managers become more responsive and adaptable to their increasingly competitive external environments. Strategic thinking is also what facilitates the effective implementation of strategic plans. This is confirmed in Grinyer's study, which found that the amount of informal communications (for example, talking versus written memos) in firms studied was positively correlated with long-term profits [Reimann 1989, p. 42].

Staffing: Participation as a Way of Achieving Integration and Commitment From Those Carrying Out the Plan

The ability to integrate and eventually carry out strategic plans depends largely on the commitment to the plans by those operating managers who will be carrying them out. This can be partially achieved through top management's personal involvement and through reliance on oral communications. More important to effective planning in many situations, however, is the participation of those managers who will be carrying out the plans [Morton 1988(B)]. Wherever appropriate to the situation, strategic planning should be done at the lowest practical management decision-making level [Reimann 1989, p. 41].

The terms used by corporate planners to describe the ideal relationship between plan and plan user (implementer), such as "proprietary interest," "owning," and "buying in," are the same terms used to describe the relationship between expert computer systems and their users. In the case of expert systems, as with strategic plans, the solution is to involve the intended user in the actual development of the system wherever possible [Mockler 1992].

Using plan development participation as a means of obtaining line manager commitment is not always easy to accomplish. While the benefits are clear [Davidson 1986], doers are not always the best planners, either by nature or by training [Reimann 1986]. This obstacle can be partially overcome by the education and conditioning that comes through oral communication, coaching, participation, and inspirational leadership. It is an obstacle worth overcoming, since it is critical to imbedding the required strategic thinking so necessary for longer term, continuing strategic plan formulation and implementation.

The example described in Chapter 12 of how AT&T Credit, a $3 billion strategic business unit, let employee groups formulate and carry out enterprise-wide strategic changes illustrates how this participative approach can work [Deutsch 1991].

While participation in the development effort can help achieve integration of overall-company and operating plans, it is not the only way — nor necessarily the best way — in many situations.

The Non-Participative Approach

Many situations do not lend themselves to having wide participation in the development effort. For example, top management may have concluded that the change being considered is so radical that existing personnel will not be able to adapt to it and new staff will be needed.

According to published reports and personal interviews, this appears to have been the case at the investment banking firm First Boston Corporation when it merged with Credit Suisse, another financial firm, and went private in 1988. After the move was made, a large number of operating managers left or were asked to leave. This shakeup was viewed by many as an intentional part of the firm's new enterprise-wide strategy, since it permitted hiring "a new generation of senior managers" who were "moving in to run the business in a more cost-conscious way" that took into account difficult current market conditions [Bartlett 1989; Siconolfi 1990].

Non-participation can be a useful approach to formulating and carrying out new strategies in situations

- Where main segments of the existing organization are not to be part of an enterprise-wide strategic plan implementation, or
- Where existing personnel lack the perspective and skills needed to effectively formulate strategies or carry out strategic plans.

Many types of situations may be encountered when organizing a strategy formulation and implementation effort. While there are some general guidelines about what might often work, what will work ultimately depends on the specific situation context requirements.

Process as Important as the Plan to Encourage Strategic Thinking

The major benefit of effective strategic management often is not the plan itself. Frequently, it is the orientation developed by the participants during the process of formulating strategies — for example, through analyzing the markets, technological and other opportunities, competition, and relative company position.

These exercises in situational strategic thinking prepare division and line managers for doing strategic planning on a continuing basis, since participation in the development effort promotes strategic thinking throughout a company [Reimann 1989, 43]. Strategic thinking can be the greatest benefit of the process, because it helps ensure that strategic planning will continue to be done after the plan is prepared, thus readying decision makers to more quickly anticipate and exploit changing market conditions [Reimann 1988, p. 42]. In a sense, this is one form of future strategic management control. Controlling its effectiveness in the future is highly dependent in many situations on the capabilities and adaptability of those in a position to respond quickly to changes in market conditions — the operating line managers.

The objective of the strategic management process is not just to produce a plan in a book to be consulted by operating and other managers from time to time. While strategic management efforts have many of the characteristics of a project [Meredith 1989], they are not single events or efforts. Strategic management, or thinking, is a way of continually making decisions that are situationally oriented, especially in regard to the competitive market environment.

This is not the sole function of strategic management efforts, of course, since the strategic effort will produce strategies and strategic plans. It just means that other benefits accrue from the effort, and these benefits are especially important in markets that are rapidly changing, where strategic plans often become obsolete as they are being written. People, then, provide the best control of a strategic management effort.

Focus on Implementation

In carrying out a management effort, the ideal focus — based both on research and anecdotal evidence — is on the output and results of the plan [for example, Morton 1988(A) and Chakravarthy 1987] — not on plan books and the formality of the plan development effort. In fact, according to one expert, the more flexible and informal the process, the less inhibiting and therefore the more effective it is likely to be [Reimann 1989, p. 42]. Many planning directors believe that the planner's role is that of facilitator, or "activator," who functions to energize the organization to overcome obstacles that threaten to come between strategic plans and their realization [Reimann 1988, p. 43].

Special Problems of Smaller Companies

While much of the discussion in this appendix can be useful in any strategic management effort, the orientation of the discussion has been on strategic management in companies sufficiently large to have their own planning department or planning director, or to hire outside consultants to help formulate enterprise-wide strategies and strategic plans.

Strategic management in smaller companies does not require all these formal mechanisms. The problems in these smaller companies are more likely to be finding the time to do planning, to gather information needed for planning, and to understand how to do planning effectively and efficiently [Curtis 1983].

These more limited planning efforts vary greatly from company to company and depend to a great degree on the owner/manager's personality, work habits, and experiences.

For example, William K. Harris, President of Bernard C. Harris Publishing Company, Inc., has described his experiences in establishing a formal strategic planning process at his relatively small firm. His family's firm was growing rapidly toward the $40 million mark in sales and faced a transition from his father's entrepreneurial leadership to more professional management. Its core business of education publishing, where the company had a 65 percent market share, was maturing and seemed unable to support its historic growth. Thus, the company's reactive and highly centralized management was no longer adequate.

A systematic process of strategic management was implemented with the help of outside consultants. This process involved all senior managers as well as several key long-term middle managers. In 1988 this team's four off-site meetings for planning the company's future produced a strategic plan. Four major product extension projects were launched, but they all did not move along as fast as originally hoped. A Fall 1989 follow-up identified shortcomings and developed controls to deal with them.

Several lessons were learned from Harris Publishing's experience about differences between small and large company strategic management. First, the planning process is much less formal in a smaller firm since fewer people and levels are involved. Also, plans can be much less detailed — a ten-page document is long. The downside is that the greater informality affected Harris' ability to reach its goals. Oral communication was not enough at Harris; a certain amount of writing was necessary.

Second, a champion was needed, just as at a large firm. If nothing is done to adjust their already heavy workload, managers can be overwhelmed by additional duties like planning. They must be given both the time and proper incentives to motivate them to do the job right. Also, clear-cut responsibilities must be delegated. The job cannot be split between two people, or each will assume the other is taking care of things. Those responsible for strategic planning must also be provided with clear, written objectives and be held strictly accountable.

While managers may realize the value of planning, they often cannot find the time to do a good job. In addition, managers are rarely inclined to delegate their regular duties to make room for new ones. Finally, according to William Harris, if their incentives are based on their on-going business responsibilities, it is even less likely that they will relinquish any of these [Reimann 1990].

In another situation, Stew Leonard's supermarket in Norwalk, Connecticut, is a family operation generating some $100 million in revenues from a single store location [Wald 1989]. Leonard, along with his two sons, manages the operation — he even occasionally dresses up in a cow suit to entertain customers' children in the store. Indications are that strategic planning is done mostly in Mr. Leonard's head, with reference to his intimate knowledge of his own store operations and the many industry and market information sources he encounters daily in his reading and travelling.

While this example may seem extreme, it is nonetheless typical of how a planning effort is often organized and carried out in a small owner/manager or entrepreneurial venture. Normally only as a company grows, does it begin to develop more formal organization structures and procedures for its planning effort, as at Harris Publishing and Signode.

AN APPROACH TO MAKING DECISIONS IN SPECIFIC READER SITUATIONS

The difficulties encountered in developing a general approach for creating an effective planning effort arise from the wide range of possible situations. At one extreme, these situations can involve on-going formal departments for very large companies, such as those at major automobile companies described elsewhere in this Appendix. At the other extreme, they may involve closely-held, small businesses, such as Stew Leonard's supermarket, where the owners are the overall operating managers and so the strategy formulation and implementation does not require elaborate organization steps [Wald 1989].

The following discussion, therefore, covers a wide range of factors which might be examined in organizing and carrying out a planning effort. The exact combination of these situation factors and their impact on a reader's organization and management efforts will depend on the situation requirements.

Critical Factors Affecting Decisions in This Area

As shown in Figure B-2, those factors affecting the organization and implementation of a plan development effort can be grouped into the following eight categories.

Existing plans and planning organization and processes. As indicated in the discussion in Chapter 2, a good starting point in organizing for strategic management is to analyze the existing planning situation. This involves examining existing formal and informal planning processes and procedures, participation in and attitudes towards strategic planning and integrated enabling planning, and the preparation, communication, and use of formal and informal strategic planning statements [Hax 1990].

Nature of the company, industry, and competitive market. The first situation factor affecting decisions about organizing and carrying out a strategic planning effort is the nature of the company, industry, and competitive market involved.

For example, Hohn describes the market and business factors analyzed in planning for a major company in the automobile industry [1986]. The industry and market themselves are such that formal planning efforts are needed to deal with the massive amount of detailed information and analysis involved. The major home appliance industry, segments of the food and beverage industry, the surgical and medical instruments industry, and the heavy farm machinery industry are examples of other industries where the business requirements can dictate considering having major formal corporate planning efforts. Regardless of the size or complexity of the industry, however, a small company in a major industry operating within a limited region may not have either the resources or need for formal corporate planning efforts. The special problems of organizing small company planning efforts were discussed earlier in this Appendix.

The size, scope, and nature of the company and its relation to the industry also can affect a company's formal planning effort. For example, the planning process at FMC described earlier in this Appendix provides an example of how a large conglomerate with a portfolio of operating divisions in diverse businesses organized its strategic planning effort to meet the needs of its special organization requirements.

The phase of a company's growth and the company's experience with formal planning efforts can also influence the effort. For example, a company may decide to focus initially on the financial aspects of strategic planning. Later, it may decide that its effort should focus on strategic issues. Signode focused on different kinds of strategic plans — financial and strategic-issue oriented — and had a different kind of strategic planning organization at different phases of its growth.

Other overall situation factors, such as the phase an industry is in, can also influence decisions involving a strategic planning effort. An emerging industry in a yet-to-be defined market, such as high-definition television, will require a major planning effort to deal with the uncertain and unstructured nature of the problem, and to provide a basis for a half-billion-dollar research and development investment. An entirely different effort (less formal and more decentralized) may be appropriate for strategic management in a mature or declining industry, where the environment is stable and well-structured, and information is more readily available.

Who initiates or champions consideration of a planning effort. As discussed earlier, the

Figure B-2: Decision Making in Strategic Planning Development Efforts

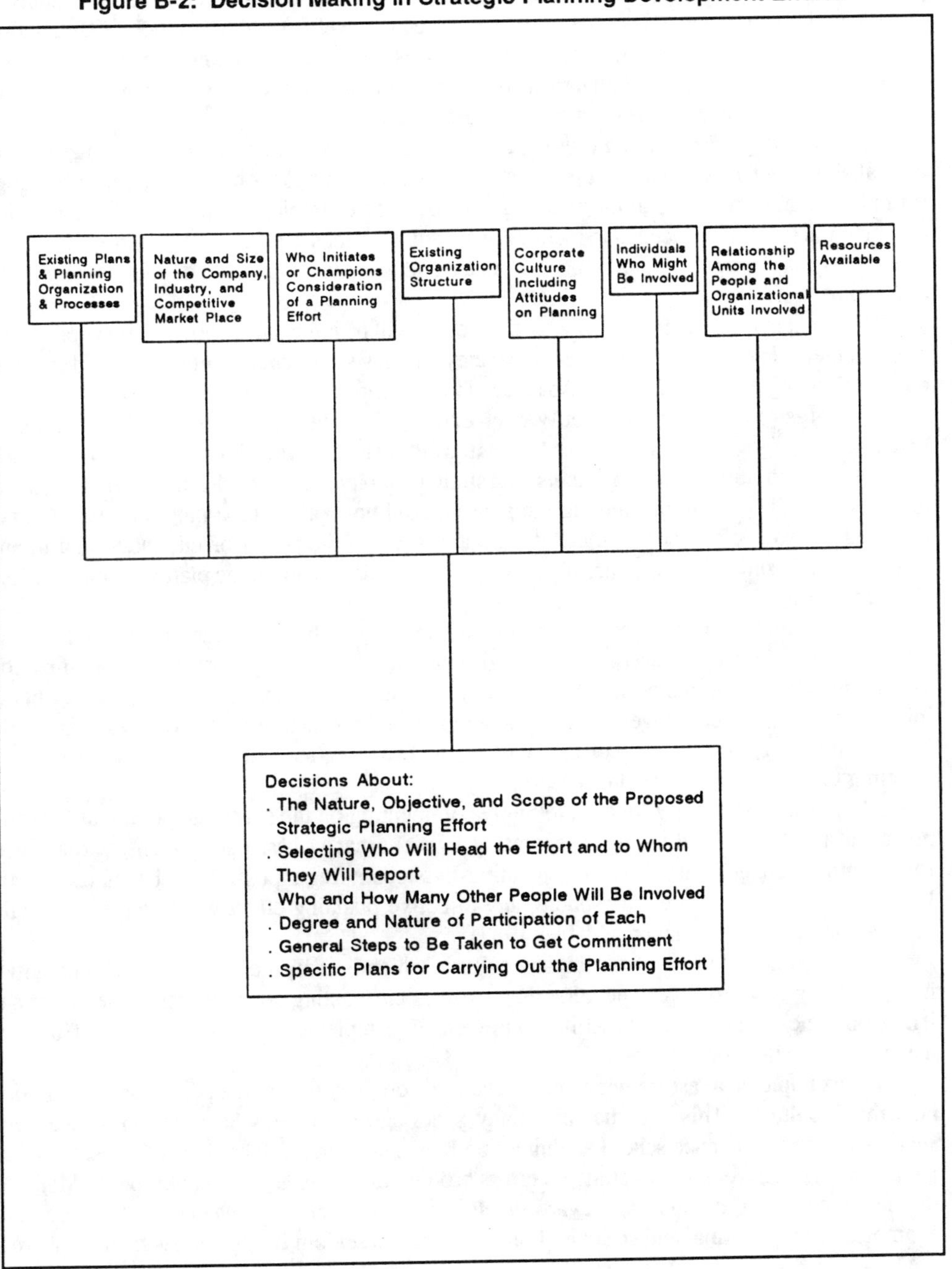

personal interest of the CEO in a planning effort, when consistently demonstrated, can have a significant impact on what resources will be devoted to the effort and how much organizational support it will receive. This factor then, especially as related to the organizational power of the champion and the amount of mutual trust and respect company leaders have, can often impact the design and execution of a formal strategic planning effort.

Existing organization structure. The existing organization structure, like many other critical situation factors studied in this section, can have an impact on carrying out the strategy formulation and implementation planning efforts. For example, an analysis of the existing organization structure is needed to identify operating divisions and functions that are significant to the enterprise-wide strategies being formulated and so should be considered for inclusion in the development effort.

Inherent in any existing organization structure will be informal or formal centers of power. These centers of power are examined to see if they will have an impact on organizing and carrying out the planning effort. They can also affect a plan's implementation.

S. Morgan Morton, President of Warner-Lambert Canada in 1988, described how earlier in his career at a large consumer product business the failure to involve a division manager very early in strategy formulation created problems with strategy implementation. The division manager had total responsibility for implementing the plan, but did not believe it would work and was not involved in its development. Failure to take into account the power of this individual in any strategic plan's success was apparently a major contributing factor in the plan's eventual failure [Morton 1988(B)].

Organization considerations are important since, in addition to mutual trust and respect among company managers, successful strategic planning efforts require fostering an organization environment which promotes strategic thinking and action appropriate to the strategies being implemented. This can cover: creating an organization structure that promotes teamwork, creative thinking, and faster decision making; and making staffing changes [Anders 1991; "Getting to Prime" 1991; Freedman 1991].

Corporate culture. Ed Mahler, jokingly commenting on the corporate culture at DuPont, noted that a feeling existed among the operating divisions that the best management approach was for corporate management to leave the operating divisions as free as possible to do their own thing. In such a corporate culture atmosphere, any effective planning effort would have to heavily involve the operating managers [Mahler 1987].

Each company has its own company culture, which is analyzed to determine its potential impact on any new project or operation that involves the existing organization. Whether or not it is an obstacle or can be used to facilitate more effective implementation of a planning effort will depend on the situation.

For example, in a fast-growing entrepreneurial company the culture is often a "we-can-do-no-wrong" culture. This was the case many years ago at Famous Schools, initially a very successful correspondence school selling art and writing courses. Planning was a seat-of-the-pants affair until several major strategic errors brought the company into bankruptcy. Many of the newly emerging computer software giants which flourished during the 1980s were also examples of this. Formal and structured planning efforts seldom flourish in such atmospheres, no matter how important they may be to the success of a venture. One of the major initial tasks faced by Louis Gerstner when he became head of RJR Nabisco and by David Johnson when he became president of Campbell Company was overcoming existing corporate culture obstacles [Anders 1991; Freedman 1991].

Individuals who might be involved. In addition to the CEO and planning director, other managers will often be involved in the planning effort. These individuals can affect the planning effort organization and staffing. For example, at a Chase Manhattan bank strategic business unit, the Municipal Bond Division, an analysis of individuals who might be working under the new strategic plan led to the conclusion that they should not be included in the planning effort because they were unlikely to be involved in the eventual plan implementation [Doran 1989].

As for the qualifications of individuals to do effective planning, many people are doers — not planners [Davidson 1986; Reimann 1986]. While they may be very effective at making and selling products, they may not be the best people to formulate strategies and strategic plans. In some situations, then, while it may be desirable in theory to have certain people participate in a planning effort, these people may not possess the qualifications to do strategic planning effectively.

Relationships among the people and organization units involved. Both the formal and informal existing organizational and people relationships influence the effectiveness of the strategy development effort. These factors affect the kind and degree of integration possible while carrying out the planning effort, or alternatively the amount and kind of resistance that must be overcome.

In the baked goods company discussed in earlier chapters, the new president was 29 years-old, recently graduated from an MBA program, and the son of the retired founder. For these reasons, many of his ideas met with considerable resistance from older and more experienced department heads. This organizational setting prevented any formal integrated strategic planning effort.

Available company resources. In addition to the dollar and people resources, in today's environment the amount of telecommunications and computer information systems resources can also have an impact on formal planning efforts. This is especially true at smaller companies.

Making Decisions Based on These Critical Situation Factors

As discussed in the preceding section, these critical situation factors are used to make decisions about the strategic planning effort in a variety of ways in many decision areas. Four of the six decisions listed at the bottom of Figure B-2 are discussed in this section.

The nature, objective, and scope of the proposed strategic planning effort. Just because a company is of a certain kind and in a certain industry does not necessarily mean it will inevitably have the same kind of planning effort as every other company in the same position.

For example, the personal feelings of the *planning director* and *individual board members* towards the value of strategic planning and what it involves, their preconceived notions about what the strategy should be, and their individual skills can dictate how the planning effort is organized and carried out. This will be especially true in small owner-managed companies, but can also influence decisions in very large companies, as was seen during the fight for control of

Time Inc. in mid-1989 [Fabrikant 1989]. *Available resources*, the *existing organization* and *culture*, and the *size of the company* and its *phase of growth* (as at Signode) can also effect the nature and scope of the planning effort.

Many leadership and organization factors may be examined in determining the nature and scope of the strategic planning effort. For example, when Louis Gerstner, the former head of American Express Company, was brought in to head RJR Nabisco Holdings Inc., he had a fairly clear vision of overall strategy for Nabisco which involved remaking the company [Anders 1991]. One of his first steps was establishing mutual trust and respect among and for top managers in the company. Another was providing an organization that would encourage movement in new directions. The organization environment changes introduced included: bringing in new staff; creating a cooperative organization structure that promoted more teamwork, creative thinking, and faster decision making; and modifying the corporate culture. These same step were also important for David Johnson when he took over as president of Campbell Soup Co. in January 1990 [Freedman 1991]. The importance of these initial steps in the planning effort can vary from company to company and are part of the decision as to the nature and scope of the planning effort ["Getting to Prime" 1991].

Selecting who will head the planning effort and to whom they will report. This is not necessarily an explicit decision in every situation. For example, in smaller companies, CEOs such as Stew Leonard simply go ahead and do the planning where they decide to do any at all. In many large companies, such as at Westinghouse, the planning director was selected by the CEO based on available personnel and the relationship of their skills and personalities to the organization's requirements [Povejsil 1989]. Since success of the planning effort depends so much on the effectiveness of its director and champion, this can be the most important decision made.

Who and how many other people will be involved. Where the initial thrust of the planning effort is to make major changes in company direction, that planning effort may involve corporate management only and not the operating managers whose jobs might be threatened by these changes. This seems to have been the case at Chase Manhattan, where major strategic changes in the Municipal Banking and Bond strategic business unit were made at the very top, without the participation of the operating managers, since the new plan involved bringing in new division managers from the outside and major dislocations of existing personnel [Doran 1989]. In this situation, the predetermined *nature and scope of the planning effort* and the *individuals* and *organization* being planned for dictated how the planning effort was organized and carried out.

Degree and nature of participation. Similar decisions are made about the nature of the participation of those selected to be involved in the planning effort. The *scope of the plan*, that is, the importance of different areas to the plan, will in part dictate the degree of participation desired for each area. This is then balanced with other factors, such as the *qualifications and availability of individuals* in those areas to do planning effectively, the availability of resources such as communication facilities and money needed to fund the planning effort, and the willingness and availability of the strategic planning effort's *champion and director* to do what is necessary to obtain that participation.

REVIEW QUESTIONS

1. Discuss the differences and relationship between doing enterprise-wide strategy formulation — developing the plans through a formal planning effort — and implementing the plans through company operations.
2. Why do you think a gap sometimes exists between enterprise-wide strategies and actual company operations?
3. Describe some of the basic individual and organizational behavior tasks and skills involved in the formulation and implementation of strategies.
4. Describe the evolution of formal strategic planning efforts, such as the one at Signode discussed in Appendix B.
5. Discuss some of the new technical support requirements for those doing strategic planning which are arising from competitive market pressures. Describe some of the approaches companies are using to meet these requirements.
6. Discuss the importance of personal leadership, or the championing of strategic planning efforts, on the success of planning efforts.
7. Describe the importance and function of oral communications to the effective implementation of a strategic planning effort.
8. Describe the importance of the participation of those who will be carrying out strategic plans in the plan development effort.
9. Describe those situations in which such participation is not desirable.
10. What is strategic thinking, why is it important to the success of a company, and in what ways can the strategic planning effort help to foster strategic thinking within a company?
11. Describe the critical factors affecting decisions about organizing and carrying out the planning effort, and the kinds of decisions that are made when planning for the formal strategic planning effort.

EXERCISES

1. Read the *Superb Biscuits Company* case study, as well as one of the studies which has extensive industry background discussions, from the final section of this book. Write a report describing the different approaches to carrying out the strategic planning development effort which might be most effective in each situation.

2. From the Case Study section of this book, choose a company study about which you have written a report in earlier chapters, and describe the steps that might be taken to obtain the maximum participation of operating managers in strategy formulation and implementation. Pay particular attention to steps that could be taken to promote strategic thinking and so create an organization environment for dealing effectively with major changes in the competitive market affecting the company.

3. Read recent issues of the periodicals referred to in the References section at the end of this Appendix, or other related periodicals of your choice, and find examples of successful or unsuccessful strategy formulation efforts. Write a report describing the lessons you learned about strategy implementation which might be useful to you if faced with a similar situation.

REFERENCES

Anders, George, "Old Flamboyance Is Out as Louis Gerstner Remakes RJR Nabisco," *The Wall Street Journal*, March 21, 1991, pp. A1, A6.

Bartlett, Sarah, "As First Boston Shifts, Defections Continue," *The New York Times,* June 27, 1989, pp. D1, D9.

Chakravarthy, Balaji S. "On Tailoring a Strategic Planning System to Its Context: Some Empirical Evidence," *Strategic Management Journal,* November-December, 1987, pp. 517-534.

Chakravorty, Subrata, "We Changed the Whole Playing Field: Triumph for Gillette's Colman Mockler — Technology as a Marketing Tool," *Forbes*, February 4, 1991, pp. 82-86.

Curtis, David A., *Strategic Planning for Smaller Businesses,* Lexington, MA: D.C. Heath, 1983.

Davidson, Mike, "Doers as Planners," *Planning Review*, September 1986, pp. 4, 44.

Deutsch, Claudia H., "Workers Get to Redesign Organization's Structure," *International Herald Tribune*, July 4, 1991, p. 11.

Doran, John J., "Ready for the Next Decade: Chase Manhattan Securities Inc. Revamps Its Municipal Banking and Bond Operations," *The Bond Buyer*, April 7, 1989, pp. 1-2.

Early, Stewart, "Issues and Alternatives: Key to FMC's Strategic Planning System," *Planning Review*, May/June 1990, pp. 26-33.

Fabrikant, Geraldine, "Divestiture is Planned by G&W," *The New York Times*, April 10, 1989, pp. D1, D4.

Freedman, Alix M., "Campbell Chief Cooks Up Winning Menu," *The Wall Street Journal,* February 15, 1991, pp. B1, B5.

"Getting to Prime," *Inc*., January 1991, pp. 27-33.

Hax, Arnaldo C., "Redefining the Concept of Strategy and the Strategy Formulation Process," *Planning Review*, May/June 1990, pp. 34-41.

Hayes, Thomas C., "Behind the Iron Hand at Tenneco," *The New York Times*, January 6, 1992, pp. D1, D6.

Hohn, Siegfried, "How Information Is Transforming Strategic Planning," *Long Range Planning*, August 1986, pp. 18-30.

Iacocca, Lee, *Talking Straight,* New York: Bantam Books, 1988.

Lohr, Steve, "Rubber Stamp Is Tossed Aside by G.M. Board," *The New York Times*, April 8, 1992, pp. A1, D19.

Mahler, Ed, "Developing Expert Systems at DuPont," *Expert Systems: Getting Business Results From Applied AI*, Randall Davis Seminar, New York: Decision Support Technology, October 26-28, 1987.

McConahey, Steve, Corporate and International Development (Planning Condition), Kemper Financial Services Inc. *The Emerging Role of the Strategic Planner in the 1990s: Key Elements*, New York: Planning Forum's Strategic Planning Special Interest Group, April 8, 1992.

Meredith, Jack R. and Samuel J. Mantel Jr., *Project Management: A Managerial Approach,* New

York: Wiley, 1989.

Mockler, Robert J., *Knowledge-Based Systems: An Introduction to Expert Systems,* New York: Macmillan Publishing Company, 1992.

Morton, S. Morgan, "Consultants," *Planning Review,* May/June 1988(A), p. 44.

Morton, S. Morgan, "Whose Plan Is It Anyway?", *Planning Review,* May/June 1988(B), p. 45.

Noyes, Thomas E., "The Evolution of Strategic Planning at Signode," *Planning Review,* September 1985, pp. 10-13.

Povejsil, Donald J., *Setting Strategic Direction: The Design of the Business Vision,* Seminar, New York: The Planning Forum, February 8, 1989.

Prescott, John E., and Daniel C. Smith, "The Largest Survey of 'Leading Edge' Competitor Intelligence Managers," *Planning Review,* May/June 1989, pp. 6-13.

Radding, Alan, "Technology Issues in Downsizing," *Computerworld,* June 12, 1989, pp. 69-78.

Reimann, Bernard C., "Doers as Planners," *Planning Review,* September 1986, pp. 5, 45.

Reimann, Bernard C., "Getting Value from Strategic Planning," The Conference Board's 1988 Strategic Planning Conference, *Planning Review,* May/June 1988, pp. 42-48.

Reimann, Bernard C., "Getting Value from Strategic Planning: The Encore," The Conference Board's 1989 Strategic Planning Conference, *Planning Review,* March/April 1989, pp. 40-47.

Reimann, Bernard C., "Getting Value from Strategic Planning," The Conference Board's 1990 Strategic Planning Conference, *Planning Review,* March/April 1990, pp. 28-33, 48.

Reimann, Bernard C., "Shareholder Value and Executive Compensation," *Planning Review,* May/June 1991, pp. 41-48.

Robert, Michael, *The Strategist CEO,* Westport, CT: Quorum Books, 1988.

Siconolfi, Michael, and William Power, "Hennessy Feels Heat as CS First Boston Fails to Gain Ground," *The Wall Street Journal,* September 19, 1990, pp. A1, A13.

Stanat, Ruth, editor, *The Intelligent Corporation,* New York: Amacon, 1990.

"Survey," *The Wall Street Journal,* October 31, 1986, p. A1.

Wald, Matthew L., "Stew Leonard's, Believe It Or Not," *The New York Times,* May 25, 1989, pp. D1, D6.

White, Joseph B., "How Detroit Diesel, Out from Under GM, Turned Around Fast," *The Wall Street Journal,* August 16, 1991, pp. A1, A8.

Appendix C

INTRODUCTION TO THE CONCEPTS UNDERLYING THE BOOK

Success in business comes from being able to do whatever is needed to get the job done, within well-defined legal, moral, and ethical limits.

Managers formulate visions and objectives (concepts) that seem fairly precise in their minds. They may even formulate specific tentative plans. Realizing these visions or carrying out these plans, however, often requires a greater or lesser degree of improvisation — in dealing effectively with a series of events and problems that were not, or often could not have been, anticipated.

This book is designed to help readers do these strategic management jobs more quickly, easily, cheaply and effectively. There is very little in this book — in fact in all business school courses — that readers could not learn on their own at work, if they had the time, occasion, money, energy, and dedication needed to do so. This book is, therefore, designed to supplement the lessons learned from experience, rather than replace them.

For these reasons, the focus of this book is on structured context-specific situation management in strategy formulation and implementation situations. The integrating concept underlying this focus is based on two premises:

- A diverse range of strategic management situations exist in business. They can differ substantially from industry to industry and from company to company. Large and small, service and product, domestic and global, mature and emerging industries and companies all have special requirements.

- At the same time, common underlying strategic management processes — thinking (cognitive) and behavioral — seem to characterize effective managers in these situations. These processes are situation-oriented, individually useful management processes because of the situational nature of strategic management.

This book attempts to identify both the underlying common processes or structures, as well as their wide range of applications, in specific strategic management situations.

This book's focus grows out of the author's work in five areas:

- Starting and running his own successful multimillion-dollar business ventures
- Identifying, studying, and writing about strategic management processes (general and situation-specific) useful in business, starting with his works published in *Harvard Business Review* in 1969 and 1971 and continuing through his current work in user-oriented strategic management theory
- Case research, development, and use, which began with his case studies published at Harvard Business School's Intercollegiate Case Clearing House in 1972 and which continues with the case studies included in this and other recent books
- Cognitive modelling of strategic management processes needed for developing expert knowledge-based systems, starting with his work in 1985 on knowledge-based systems to support strategic management decision making, which is described in this and several other books
- Developing innovative teaching methods, which led to several publications and a national innovative teaching award in 1990

Various skills and knowledge are needed to do strategic management well:

- Thinking (cognitive) skills, especially those needed in analyzing and structuring competitive market situations, in drawing inferences about possible future events, in synthesizing this material to make effective decisions, and in determining the most effective ways to implement strategies
- Organizational and interpersonal behavioral skills, especially those needed in promoting strategic thinking and reengineering business processes when formulating and implementing strategies
- Leadership skills of all kinds
- Facility in strategic management processes, techniques, and tools
- Knowledge of how different specific industries, competitive markets, business processes, and organizations function, and of how decisions are made and actions taken in specific business situation contexts
- Judgment and intellectual maturity, which come from experience, rather than from books
- Quantitative and computer information systems and other technical skills and techniques useful in doing strategic management

As indicated by the above list, both behavioral and rational thinking skills are important in strategy formulation and implementation. According to Peter Drucker, today's business school graduates are lacking in these skills [Levine 1992; Drucker 1992]. This book is designed to help students overcome these deficiencies.

While all of the skills listed above are useful in general for strategic management, they are not all needed to the same degree and in the same way in all strategic management situations. Not only do strategic management situations vary widely from industry to industry, but individual company characteristics also affect the process. The strategic management problems of mature and newly formed companies, large and small ones, and domestic and international ones can vary considerably.

Essentially one needs to learn to do what is necessary to succeed in his/her own specific strategic management situation, within well-defined moral, legal, and ethical parameters. In a book such as this one, this requires a *structured context- specific management orientation* — that is, an orientation which focuses on helping individual managers solve their own business situation/context problems, not one which focuses just on learning concepts, processes, techniques, and theory, or just on listening to stories of how others do strategic management. The second half of each chapter of this book provides guidelines for doing this when formulating and implementing strategies. These situation-specific approaches are part of an emerging strategic management theory based on contingency models of individual expert manager thinking patterns [Mockler 1992].

While this book has a singleness of purpose — to help readers learn how to formulate strategies and effectively carry them out in specific business situations, readers' backgrounds will be diverse. They may range from undergraduates with little or no meaningful business experience, to MBA students with or without work experience, to working executives of varying ages with some management experience. While some of these readers will have had specific industry, professional, or functional work experience, few readers will have had actual experience in making strategic management decisions for an entire business enterprise.

Given the diversity of reader age, experience, education, and training, the level of proficiency in the skill areas useful in strategic management will vary as well. For example, some readers will need to work on improving their systematic rational thinking processes, others on improving their interpersonal, leadership, and organizational skills, others on expanding their knowledge of how different businesses work, and others on acquiring skills to put general strategic management processes to work in context-specific business situations.

For these reasons, the methods used in this book to help readers learn to do strategic management in their individual situations are varied. They include:

- Information on what strategic management is and how it is done, through descriptions of core concepts and of decision-making and human resource management processes and skills used in strategic management, as well as through examples of actual business situations.

- Practical exercises and tools to help readers learn how to do strategic management tasks in specific situations through:
    - Case study exercises involving actual business experiences

  - Guidance on how to do industry and competitive market studies
  - Structured situation-specific decision-making and behavioral models that replicate the specific thought processes and interpersonal actions of experts
  - Conventional and knowledge-based computer aids that assist in strategic management practice in specific situations

- Guidance on how to access industry data sources through both manual and computer techniques, in order to obtain information on specific industries and companies under study

- Exercises and guidance in learning how to integrate enterprise-wide strategy formulation with other company operational strategy formulation and implementation within a specific company under study

- A variety of actual business situation exercises to help improve a reader's judgment as related to strategic management situations

- A variety of exercises and examples to help readers learn how to more effectively carry out strategies, that is, to put them to work to improve operations and profits

- Coverage of strategic management in increasingly important business areas in the 1990s, such as those involving environmental and social issues, international operations, and computer information systems

This book's integrated situational management orientation has also shaped the support material accompanying this book. Bound into the back of the text are computer disks which contain:

- Eight knowledge-based (artificial intelligence) systems for helping to do and to understand strategic management processes

- Spreadsheet models and databases for doing financial analyses and simulations, as well as other kinds of analyses, useful in making strategic management decisions in the company case studies in this book

These computer tools are provided for those who feel comfortable using them; the text can be used without these and other computer aids, since they are not appropriate for all teaching and reader learning situations. Their greatest contribution to this text is the descriptions they provide of how experts handle specific strategic management situations.

Each chapter is designed to move the reader from theory to practice. In line with this, most of the chapters in the book first present strategic management tools, techniques, theories, and concepts. The second half of these chapters give practical guidance on applying the material from the first half to actual situations which the reader might encounter. During these context-specific discussions, processes are modelled which experts have found useful in providing a disciplined, integrative, adaptive semi-structured approach to strategic management, which is at the same time focused on the individual manager's specific situation requirements.

Extensive explicit references to academic research has generally been omitted from the text, since this is an introductory text. Those wishing such detailed coverage of research references can consult the author's multivolume book, *Strategic Management Research Resources.* It covers books, monographs, articles, presentations, academic and professional conferences, training seminars and programs, doctoral dissertations, audio and video cassettes, corporate research, and other research sources in the field. A copy may be obtained by writing the author c/o Strategic Management Research Group, 114 E. 90th Street (Suite 1B), New York, NY 10128.

A great deal has happened in the field of strategic management since the author's first book on the subject in 1969, *Business Planning and Policy Formulation.* In fact, except for some core ideas on situational decision-making processes, this is an entirely new book, so great have been the changes over the quarter century since the first book was written.

REFERENCES

Drucker, Peter, *Managing the Future,* New York: Truman Talley Books/Dutton, 1992.

Levine, Michael, "How Will We Ever Manage?" *The New York Times Book Review,* April 18, 1992, pp. 18, 20.

Mockler, Robert J., *Contingency Approaches to Strategic Management,* Research Working Paper, New York: Strategic Management Research Group, 1992.

Appendix D

USING ONLINE DATABASES FOR MARKET RESEARCH

The following reprints a short article, "Market Research: The Online Connection," from *Online Access* (Spring 1992, pp. 18-21), written by Marydee Ojala, an information consultant based in Overland Park, Kansas. The final section is written by Al Henderson. The article is reprinted with permission.

All successful businesses make use of marketing research, whether they call it that or not. Observing the market, watching what competitors do, listening to customers, noticing changes that might affect the business — all these obvious procedures are done by business owners and managers every day. Systematizing the process, however, is another story.

According to the American Marketing Association, market research involves systematically gathering, recording, and analyzing data about problems related to marketing a product or service. Common market research areas include: Determining market characteristics, measuring market potential, analyzing market share, tracking business trends, identifying competing products, determining new product acceptance and determining ideal pricing mechanisms.

This can sound quite intimidating. Indeed, textbooks on marketing research display a fascination with gathering heavy-duty statistics, with focus groups, and with other primary research techniques.

ONLINE ADVANTAGES

But you can garner much of the same data more quickly and economically by conducting market research online, tapping into so-called "secondary information" such as technical reports, trade papers, and newsletters. Information consultants do this all the time.

For example, Gerry R. Cain, president of Trade Intelligence Professionals (TIP), Kansas City, Missouri, researches markets for a wide variety of companies, both large and small. A typical situation, he says, is: " A company that knows what they want to sell but needs to know who will buy."

Cain's main ally in research is the PTS MARS database, which he accesses through Dialog. "When I use MARS, I'm often looking for trend data. I want supporting information to reinforce a client's belief that a market exists. Of course, sometimes the answer is negative. I report this to the client, but I do it carefully. People want their ideas to be confirmed, but if they need to be blown out of the water, it's better for it to happen before a market launch bombs."

One of Cain's customers wanted to know about the security attitudes of apartment dwellers, since he wanted to sell home alarm systems for apartments. Cain checked several databases, including PTS MARS, PTS PROMT, and ABI/Inform. He discovered that changes in the economy, the rising number of working women living alone and an increase in criminal activity had in fact, made people more aware of safety issues. Cain's recommendation: Market home alarm systems not just to apartment dwellers but to lower income families in general, whether they were living in a house or an apartment.

CONSUMER TREND DATA

Trend data is an important part of a researcher's discovery process. You can find trend data in several online databases, depending on the product under consideration.

For example, if you want to know about the market for a consumer product, search databases that cover general periodical literature. Such databases as Information Access Co.'s Magazine Index or H.W. Wilson's Reader's Guide Abstracts provide valuable information. Newspapers—available online through Vu/Text, DataTimes and Dialog—are another window to popular tastes and how they're changing.

Knowing what the general public thinks about an issue or a product can be vital to good marketing research. Public Opinion Online (POLL on Dialog) is a comprehensive full-text collection of public opinion surveys. Data is collected by the prestigious Roper Center for Public Opinion Research.

Another search area might be newsletters devoted to tracking market research data. Among these are Affluent Markets Alert, Minority Markets Alert, Youth Markets Alert and The Boomer Report. Their coverage areas are evident from their titles. Perhaps not so obvious are Green Marketing Report (environmentally aware advertising, results of public opinion polls regarding the environment and health claims), Video Marketing News (trends in the home entertainment market) and American Marketplace (statistical information on consumers).

All of these are searchable via Newsnet, and several can be found as part of the PTS Newsletter database.

OTHER TREND DATA

Market research on non-consumer items — those used by business and industry — require searches in general business files. PTS PROMT is one excellent source for tracking usage of office machinery, demand for industrial products and production of components.

Individual industries are covered by many separate databases. For example, say you're interested in the defense industry, like Suzanne Swenson, manager of market research for Paramax, a subsidiary of Unisys. Her research generally focuses on the defense electronics industry, so she relies on Dialog and McGraw Hill's Aerospace Online.

"Because government contracts are so important to us," Swenson says, "I search Dialog's file 588, DMS/FI Contract Awards, quite frequently." The database is a comprehensive file of all non-classified U.S. government prime contract actions of $25,000 or more. Dialog also offers a specialized Report function on this file called Crosstab. It allows searchers to cross-tabulate and analyze numeric data in the file.

Swenson explains her normal methodology: "I usually start with a company name. I find PTS PROMT very useful for identifying recent actions of a company: Where are they focused? What are they doing? Another important database is Papers. Sometimes I search the entire OneSearch category to include all possible newspapers. But, if I know the company is located on the West Coast, for example, I limit my search to just those papers. The Los Angeles Times by itself might give me enough information."

Before she began online searching, Swenson used to spend a great deal of time calling investment analysts to ask their views. "Now I go online to Investext," she says. "It's such a time savings. It eliminates calls to the analysts. Plus, I don't have to wait to get the entire report in the mail. The full text is online."

Swensen relies on Investext both for specific company information and for industry trends. One strong point of investment reports is their reporting of market share figures for divisions of affiliates of large companies. Says Swenson, "It's easy to find overall market share statistics for defense electronics as a whole. Breaking it down to the smaller niches is very difficult. But Investext helps a lot."

For the international arena, ICC Business Research Reports performs a similar function. Of particular interest to European market research is ICC Keynotes database on Data-Star. Keynote Reports are also included in Dialog's ICC Business Research Reports database.

Another favorite of Swenson's is DMS/FI Market Intelligence Reports. Produced by Forecast International/DMS, the same guys who do DMS/FI Contract Awards, Market Intelligence Reports provides full-text access to industry-specific (such as aerospace and defense) reports.

DMS/FI Market Intelligence Reports is just one in a growing number of online databases that cover market research reports.

FIRST, SEARCH FOR RESEARCH

This is an excellent first step in a research project: See if someone else has already done it for you. Dialog recently added DataMonitor Market Research and EuroMonitor Market Research, previously available only on Data-Star. The Financial Times Business Reports database on Data-Star gives comprehensive coverage of worldwide markets for major industry sectors. Arthur Little's non-exclusive publications are online via Dialog.

Full-text market research reports can also be found in M.A.I.D. Although British in origin, it contains reports from several U.S. research outfits, such as Packaged Facts.

As a guide to market research reports already published, try the Frost & Sullivan database on Data-Star or Market Research Review on Newsnet. Industry Data Sources used to be valuable in locating published market research reports. However, the file has not been updated in over a year and should be used with caution.

INDUSTRY-SPECIFIC DATABASES

Don't overlook databases that are specific in content. Any database, technical or business, can yield rewarding market research results.

One who has learned this lesson is Susan Detwiler, president of S.M. Detwiler & Associates, which specializes in market research for health-care companies. Her searches start in PTS PROMT and PTS Newsletter databases but quickly move to specialized files. "My immediate second step is searching PJB for the Clinica newsletter and FDC Reports for the Orange Sheet. This indicates market size and points up any potential regulatory problems." When a product is regulated, as so many pharmaceutical products are, Detwiler researches the ramifications, searching Diogenes to see if the product is under investigation and how far along it is in the approval process. She moves on to government databases as indicated by the results.

From there, she searches specific areas, Detwiler explains: "For example, when I researched rubber gloves, I searched Rapra, which is a technical database for the rubber industry. For diapers, I checked both PaperChem and Textile Technology. The engineering databases are marvelous sources of market research information. This is where you really find information on upcoming products, long before it hits the business press. Engineers are just so proud of what they've done."

Often the key questions are: What is the competition? And who are the major players? At this point, Detwiler turns to Dun & Bradstreet Information Services databases. "Both Electronic Business and Dun's Market Identifiers contain very useful estimates of sales and employees. Dun's Financial Records gives information on backgrounds of the people running the company."

Detwiler has become a fan of CompuServe, as well. "They have real databases." she enthuses. "I just found a database on orphan drugs and rare diseases there. It's called Nord."

Although Detwiler does most of her searching direct with Data-Star (a host particularly strong in pharmaceutical industry information) and Dialog, she notes that many databases are available on CompuServ through IQuest.

Compuserve's PRSIG, a forum where market researchers hang out online, includes a section labeled Research. Here you can ask questions about methodology and receive detailed, informed answers. Furthermore, some very savvy searchers can guide you to some of the more offbeat market research databases.

How frequently do researchers go online? Laughs consultant Lan Sluder: "Seems like all my research projects start with online searches. Dozens, hundreds of them. Like: What are funeral directors spending on advertising? or Why is The Body Shop opening 1,000 stores in the U.S.? or What's the top-grossing steakhouse in the country?"

When you're going online for market research data, consider the motivation for publishing the information in the first place. If it's to sell a product, the data might be skewed. The same goes for organizations that are engaging in self-promotion or propagandizing. The trade press, as represented online in PTS PROMT or Trade & Industry, is particularly vulnerable to this. On the other hand, government data is much less suspect.

Other factors to consider are the consistency and quality of data. Often an online search will reveal contradictory information.

Says Cain of TIP: "I always explain carefully where my information came from and why it appears to contradict other information." Detwiler's approach is to rely on government data first, then to consider newsletters. She feels the scientific data in engineering and industry databases are reasonably trustworthy.

In spite of potential drawbacks, secondary research is the first step in conducting market research. Researchers may discover, as a result of online searching, that primary research is called for. However, it's obviously not cost-effective to spend $5,000 on a focus group only to find the same information online for a fraction of that.

For market researchers, online databases have become a vital tool. Not only do the databases help researchers find needs, they show ways to fill them. The following are two actual market research experiences.

TWO MARKET RESEARCH CASE STUDIES

John Kuranz and Heather May have very different types of jobs. But they both need information quickly to do their jobs well, so both turn to online market research for informative reports in a hurry.

Kuranz is president of Triactor North America, Inc. Based in Wilmington, Delaware, Triactor holds North American rights to a combustion technology that "inhibits the formation of polyaromantic hydrocarbons in the early stages of combustion." In short, you get a dramatic savings in fuel consumption.

The technology can be used in everything from the food industry to power plants. That broad range of potential applications makes trying to pitch these services a real problem: How do you make the pitch? With such diverse needs, how do you "talk their language"?

Kuranz is simply too busy to do the research on his own. And with only 10 employees, no one else has either the time or expertise. That's where Find/SVP comes into play. Kuranz calls on Find/SVP, one of the world's largest information brokers, to conduct online market research on his target markets. International industry and market studies provide the business intelligence he needs.

For example, recently Kuranz needed to know everything he could on how the paper corrugating process works and what kinds of energy it uses, so he could prepare a sales proposal and talk knowledgeably with potential customers.

"Thanks to Find," says Kuranz, "I got real smart about the industry in about a week's time. In any kind of a sales environment, if you can get yourself smart quick, you're at a distinct advantage."

Heather May works for a considerably larger company. She's manager of corporate information services for Dun & Bradstreet in New York.

Hey wait a minute! Isn't Dun & Bradstreet itself a purveyor of online information? Correct. So why does a nice manager of corporate information services like May need an information broker?

Well, May's "customers" are internal departments: Public Relations, Economic Analysis, the Office of the Chairman. When they need information, says May, they need it NOW. The answer: Resources and people who know an industry, people who know where to find esoteric information. Find/SVP, says May, supplements her reference collection and adds new resources to her Rolodex.

Kuranz and May are among the many business users of "competitive intelligence," the current buzzword in market research. Actually, competitive intelligence is much more encompassing than traditional market research.

According to the New York-based Conference Board: "Competitive intelligence is both the product and the process of collecting various kinds of data—anything from trade rumors and financial statistics to product specifications and news of plant construction—and then selecting, interpreting and presenting the data as information to be used in decision making."

"What generally separates competitive intelligence from basic market-share and product-tracing information is that it has strategic import. That is, the analysis not only describes the company's present position but also suggests what should be done to advance it."

CASE STUDIES

BIO-REFERENCE LABORATORIES INC.: THE CLINICAL LABORATORY TESTING INDUSTRY

Bio-Reference Laboratories, Inc. — a small, publicly-owned company — offered personalized and efficient clinical laboratory testing services through the use of various chemical diagnostic tests, including a wide range of routine and specialty tests supervised by respected physicians and scientists. The company operated in the local four-state area of northern and central New Jersey, New York, Pennsylvania, and Connecticut. From October 1989 to October 1990 the company's patient count increased 38% to 539,109 [Form 10-K 1991].

Bio-Reference faced several problems as it tried to compete with larger competitors in the clinical laboratory testing market. From February 1987 through July 1989 the company lost $3,125,202, primarily because of an unprofitable mobile-testing division. After selling that division in the middle of 1989, the company's sales volume grew steadily. However, while gross profits increased 191% from 1989 to 1990, the cost of services rose 144%. In 1990 the company was still operating in a deficit while paying off long-term debt [Form 10-K 1991].

Several strategic trends were expected to affect Bio-Reference's future profitability. These trends include projected changes in demographics and illnesses which would affect the quantity and quality of available staff and the types of services offered to customers; increasing government regulations (some leading to the closing of private doctor office and hospital labs and hence changing the potential customer base growth); and technological advancements in equipment. In 1992, management was contemplating how to take advantage of the changing clinical laboratory environment and strategic forces which were causing many small laboratories to downscale, close, or consolidate.

THE INDUSTRY AND COMPETITIVE MARKET

THE CLINICAL LABORATORY TESTING INDUSTRY

The clinical laboratory testing industry was a $20 billion national industry according to 1990 estimates, $5 billion of which was earned by independent laboratories [SmithKline Beecham, 1990 Annual Report]. The industry, which had high fixed costs, was fragmented, with regional laboratories coordinating the efforts of smaller testing laboratories. By requiring these labs to be licensed in order to operate in their geographic area of business, government requirements made it difficult for regional laboratories to completely decentralize testing.

The testing services offered to hospitals, doctors, clinics, private employers, and Health Maintenance Organizations (HMOs), were of two types: routine and specialty testing. These two differed in the complexity of the testing procedures involved. Routine tests were simple blood, urine, or blood chemistry tests. Specialty testing involved the use of more specialized equipment and reagents (testing chemicals), as well as more labor time. Skilled technicians were essential for providing either type of service because even the most routine testing procedures required formal training and proficiency testing.

The industry was dependent on certain controlling forces, for example, changing services and customer requirements, changing profit structure, increasing government regulations, Medicare and Medicaid reductions, low availability of laboratory staff, technological developments, and competition. The following section discusses the impact of these factors on anticipated trends in the competitive environment.

The competitive environment of clinical lab testing evolved as the country entered a new era of consumerism in which customers and legislators evaluated clinical services in the same manner as they evaluated market services: on the basis of quality, value, and return on investment. The outcome was patient protection legislation resulting in many regulations aimed at standardizing methods of quality measurement in healthcare services.

TESTING SERVICES

Laboratories received specimens for testing in several ways: directly from physicians, through the mail, or via company couriers. After getting samples, the laboratory then used sophisticated equipment in the actual testing procedure. Laboratory results could be hand-delivered or relayed by direct computer links. Test results were usually available within 24 hours, although specialty tests sometimes took longer. In emergencies, lab technicians reported results over the phone. By combining routine and specialty testing capabilities, some companies were able to offer thousands of different tests.

Routine Testing

Major types of routine tests included: blood and urine analysis; blood chemistry tests (which yielded complete profiles of chemical components, such as cholesterol, glucose, and potassium, that reflected chemical functions elsewhere in the body); hematology services (testing the state of the blood itself to diagnose anemia, etc.); serology (testing the clear yellow fluid that separates from clotted blood); and toxicology (testing for poisons). Routine testing procedures required the laboratory and technicians to obtain a license from the state in which the tests were performed. Equipment was not highly specialized and could often run a variety of simple tests simultaneously.

Specialty Testing

Specialized laboratories required unique equipment, specific licenses, and an extensively trained technical staff to become proficient at conducting sophisticated testing procedures. The specialty test portfolio of services included PAP smear testing, AIDS testing, drug abuse screening, endocrinology (hormone) testing, rheumatology testing, and the Elisa test (originally designed to diagnose AIDS, but now used to detect Lyme Disease). Since labs charged higher prices for specialty test procedures, this sort of work generated more revenue.

In order to project future possibilities of laboratory medicine and the variety of tests that labs might perform, Bio-Reference planners considered changing demographics and society healthcare trends. This meant taking into account current trends, for example, the growing number of elderly people, the expected increase in the number of people who will contract AIDS, and stronger efforts to combat substance abuse.

Total Demand Increase

The laboratory testing market was growing for many reasons such as increased demand for testing geared toward diseases prevalent in older people, the development of tests to determine health and fitness levels, the development of diagnostic tests such as those for monitoring AIDS, and tests for substance abuse screening.

Tests for the Aging Population

In 1876, average life expectancy was 40 years. A child born in 1990 could expect to live 75.6 years. Life expectancy in 1960 was 69.7; experts expected this to increase by 8.2% to 77.9 years in 2010, as shown in Figure 1. The proportion of Americans 65 and older rose from 4% of the total population in 1900, to 8.1% in 1950 and 12.5% in 1989. Experts expected this trend to continue, with percentages reaching 12.9 in 1995, 13.0 in 2000, and 13.9 in 2010. Projections suggest that by the year 2050, 21.8% of the population will be over 65 years old, as shown in Figure 2. Therefore, while the overall population will double from 1950 to 2050, the number of Americans over the age of 65 will triple [*Statistical Abstract of the United States*, 1991].

As the population ages, the clinical laboratory testing industry expects to see an increase in demand for tests focusing on diseases prevalent in the over 65 population segment.

Figure 1: United States Life Expectancies

Source: Information obtained from the *Statistical Abstract of the United States*, 1991, p. 73.

Figure 2: The Increasing Elderly Population

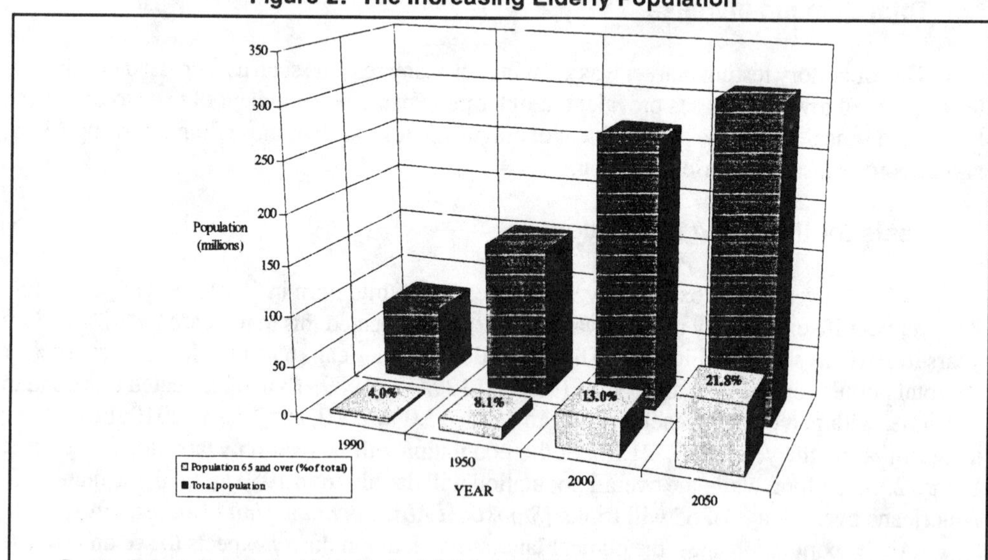

Source: Information obtained from Statland, *MLO*, July 1989, p. 80 and *Statistical Abstract of the United States*, 1991, p. 16.

Health and Fitness Tests

With many individuals enjoying good health well into their 80s, labs expected interest in health and fitness programs to increase, with new laboratory tests being sought to demonstrate the benefits of physical activity. For example, tests might conclude that running a certain distance daily increases production of enzymes that are beneficial to the runner's health. Labs also expected increased emphasis on proper diet and nutrition. This should cause an increase in nutritional assessment tests such as those measuring cholesterol, blood glucose, and vitamin D levels [Statland 1989].

AIDS Testing

The threat and spread of AIDS also led to increased testing. In 1991 alone, 43,389 AIDS cases were reported in the United States [*Morbidity & Mortality Weekly Report*, January 3, 1992]. According to the Center for Disease Control, as of 1991 more than 195,000 AIDS cases had been reported in the United States, and the disease had claimed more than 126,000 lives. Figure 3 shows reported AIDS cases in the United States from 1984 to 1991. According to the World Health Organization, the number of documented AIDS cases was expected to climb from 1.5

Figure 3: Reported AIDS Cases: United States, 1984-1991

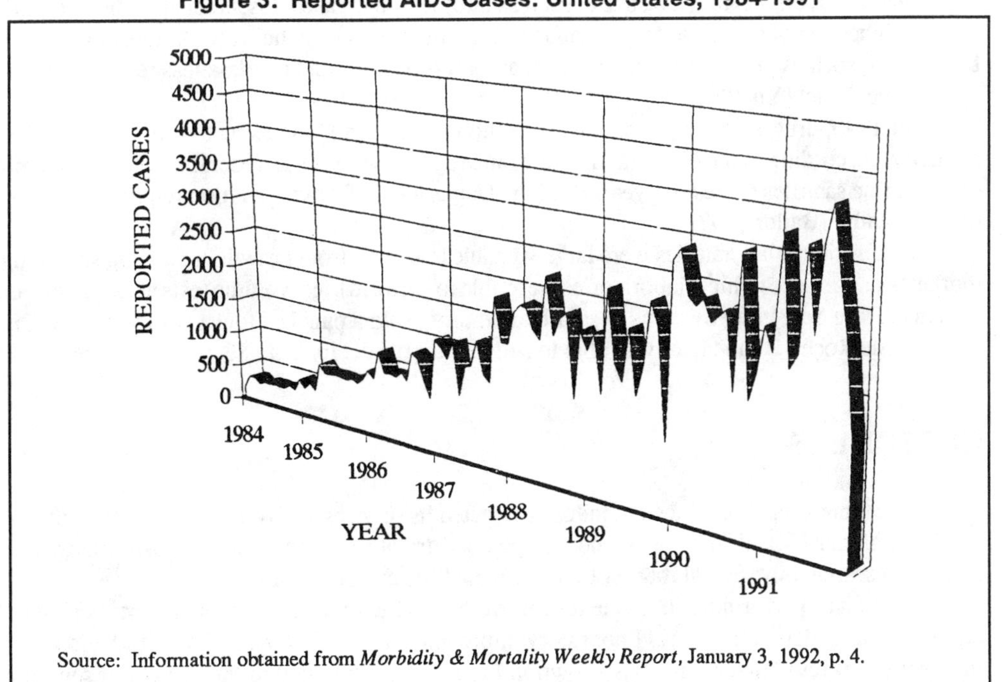

Source: Information obtained from *Morbidity & Mortality Weekly Report*, January 3, 1992, p. 4.

million in 1991 to 12-18 billion by the end of the century [Savitz 1991]. Although there was inconsistency in figures regarding the number of documented AIDS cases, there was consistency in the perception that cases would continue to increase.

AIDS-related life and health insurance claims jumped more than 17% in 1990 — a significantly smaller rate of increase than the 37% and 56% growth rates reported in 1988 and 1989 respectively. These claims cost insurers nearly $1.28 billion. The declining rate of increase indicated that the period of 100% growth for laboratories performing such tests had passed. Through awareness and education, more people may have begun taking measures to protect themselves from acquiring AIDS. Of the states, New York ranked second, New Jersey seventh, and Pennsylvania ninth in AIDS-related insurance claims [Best Review, 1991].

Many private institutions, such as life insurance companies, required policy applicants to undergo blood and/or urine tests to screen for certain diseases. In addition to this explosive growth, the larger clinical laboratories introduced other tests which allowed the labs to experience continued growth [Asinof 1989].

Substance Abuse Screening

There had been increasing awareness and concern in America's public and private sectors towards the adverse affects of substance abuse in the workplace. Due to illegal drug use and alcohol abuse, companies experienced losses ranging from decreased productivity to theft. Substance abuse effects may be subtle, such as tardiness, increased absenteeism, a slower work pace, a higher rate of defective output and less time spent per day at the work station, or they may be obvious, such as personality changes, behavioral problems, and carelessness resulting in on-the-job accidents [Yu 1991].

In 1990, drug screening was a $216 billion market and was expected to grow by 25% annually. According to the National Institute on Drug Abuse (NIDA), federal employees submit 40,000 urine samples for testing yearly and the Department of Transportation requires 8 million tests annually [Bailer 1992].

Small clinical laboratories were largely unable to benefit from growth in the drug screening market because large clinical laboratories were able to perform high-volume tests at less cost. For instance, Drug Screening Systems, a small laboratory, sold a panel of four tests for over $12 in 1990, while Roche Biomedical was able to sell similar panels for only $3.

CUSTOMERS

The clinical laboratory testing industry targeted its services at physicians, hospitals, clinics, HMOs, pharmaceutical and insurance companies, private and government institutions, and medical researchers. Several market trends affected the customer base.

Physicians performing in-office testing were faced with an increase in government standards — as a result of the Clinical Laboratory Improvement Act of 1988 (CLIA)—and a decrease in government reimbursements. As shown in Figure 4, this resulted in the growth of send-out

Figure 4: Physicians' Office Total Test Volume

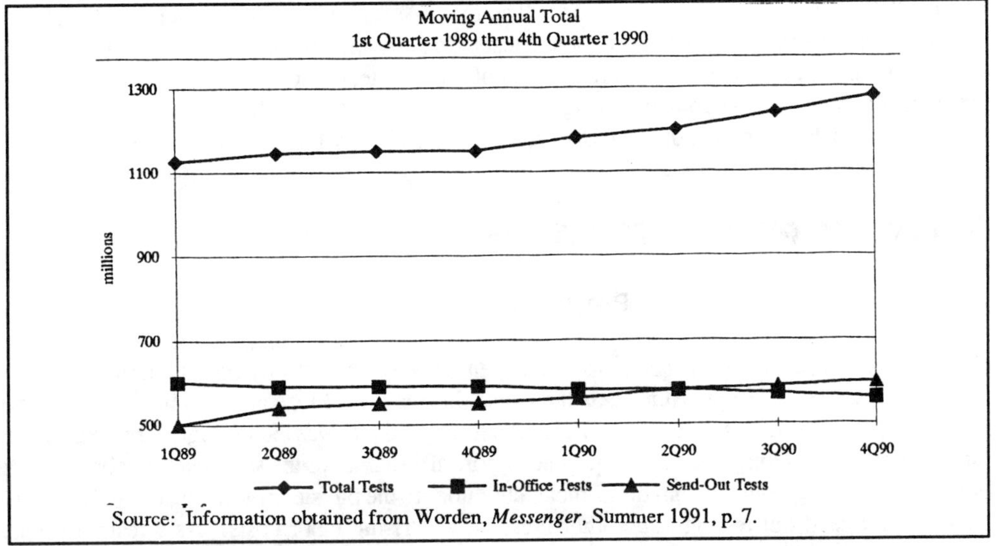

Source: Information obtained from Worden, *Messenger*, Summer 1991, p. 7.

testing and the decline in in-office testing.

The nation's approximately 6,000 hospital laboratories captured $13 billion of the $20 billion testing market. Hospitals had been concerned primarily with in-patient testing, but in the late 1980s they began recognizing business opportunities in their laboratories and many began aggressively marketing clinical testing to outside customers. However, large, independent laboratories were better prepared to handle large contracts such as those for drug screening for employers or government agencies.

The proliferation in substance abuse and AIDS-related diagnoses resulted in the growth of specialized high-profit, non-routine testing. Government institutions, private industry, and physicians were increasingly demanding these types of tests. For example, insurance carriers required certain medical tests in order to avoid paying millions of dollars in AIDS-related health insurance claims. Large clinical laboratories met the demand for tests by using technological innovations to perform specialized tests in large volumes.

The accelerating rise of healthcare costs had increased the popularity of managed health care programs such as HMOs. HMOs contract with healthcare providers such as physicians and hospitals for services to HMO subscribers, who pay a fixed premium for access to the affiliated providers. A laboratory that contracted with an HMO provider or was used often by one or more of them, could count on a large percentage of its income to be steady and sizable. HMO membership quadrupled in 10 years — from only 9.1 million in 1980 to 34.8 million in 1990. From 1990 to 1991, membership increased by another 1.7 million, to 36.5 million. HMO physicians often compared laboratory fees when choosing a laboratory for testing services [Freudenheim 1991].

Government, insurance companies, and large corporate employers paid most patient's medical costs. Consequently, normal market forces that would typically serve to drive down prices in other markets were not at work. The fee-for-service basis of payment for physicians provided an incentive to expand diagnostic tests. In addition, the demographic implications of an aging population, as well as the rising cost of medical technology, were expected to require more health subsidies, all contributing to healthcare cost escalation. The strengthening of HMOs gave clinical laboratories additional opportunities to seek new business arrangements.

CHANGING PROFIT STRUCTURE

Rising Costs and Price Pressures

The attempts by many labs to reduce expenses were thwarted by several current industry pressures. One of these pressures was the increasing staff workloads caused by a small supply of laboratory technicians entering the field. Another pressure was technological breakthroughs in microprocessors that have made equipment more affordable for the smallest test labs resulting in a shift of testing volume from the clinical laboratory to the physician's office thus reducing the demand for send-out testing. One other pressure was rising labor costs. As a result of these pressures, per-unit cost rose. This per-unit testing costs increase caused many laboratories to increase volume and others to consolidate in an effort to drive unit costs down.

The market environment changed in 1986 when Medicare imposed an outpatient fee schedule, thus limiting how much clinical laboratories could be paid for their services. Other insurance carriers adopted variations of the Medicare fee schedule in order to limit how much they would pay for laboratory services. HMOs and other prepaid health plans put lab services out to bid. Some health plans even insisted that physicians use a single or select group of labs. This trend exerted pressure on laboratory reimbursement, which led to a decline in per-test revenue.

Payment Plans

Customers could choose to be billed monthly by an itemized invoice showing the date, patient's name, specimen I.D. number, test performed, and the fee. Alternatively, customers could choose to have their patients billed directly for laboratory services. Third-party billing to Medicare and Medicaid programs, as well as to insurance companies, was another billing method.

GOVERNMENT REGULATIONS

Technological changes in the laboratory industry, the increasing number of large-scale commercial laboratories, greater workloads, and quick turnaround times called for new industry standards. The increase in government regulations forced the clinical laboratory testing industry to be more careful in its attention to detail. The regulation of labs under the CLIA of 1988 shifted the focus from personnel qualifications alone to the accurate performance of clinical laboratory proficiency testing. These regulations were introduced during a period of shrinking budgets, escalating costs, and increased competition. In addition, government regulations also required operating clinical laboratories to have licenses in every state in which they operated. According to one report in *Medical Laboratory Observer* (*MLO*), after several changes in Massachusetts law, the price of one battery of blood tests reportedly dropped from $14.00 to $2.30 [*MLO*, 1988].

If past trends were any indication, the 1990s would bring about more protectionist legislation for the laboratory field. Changes in government regulations were expected to cause clinical laboratories to pool their resources in order to overcome revenue limits, escalating costs, and excess testing capacity [Hirsch 1989]. As standards became more stringent and reimbursement rates decreased, many small laboratories were faced with the possibility of going out of business.

The Healthcare Financing Administration (HCFA)

The CLIA was passed to ensure the accuracy of the 4 to 6 billion medical tests that were performed annually in the United States [United States Code Annotated, 42263a, 1991]. Before 1990, there were no federal standards for proficiency testing programs, staffing, and medical lab maintenance. In 1990, the Healthcare Financing Administrator (HCFA) began setting such standards. The new HCFA rules affected 4,500 independent labs and 6,600 hospital-based labs that participated in Medicare and were subject to standards set by the federal government or by private organizations that accredit facilities. Physician labs which performed more than 5,000 tests annually had to be monitored for compliance with Medicare standards. The HCFA had determined that expanded regulations under CLIA could increase the numbers of laboratory sites it oversaw from 12,000 to 300,000. Inspected labs were charged a licensing fee of between $2,000 and $5,000, depending on the scope of laboratory operations, in order to absorb additional costs [Wagner 1989].

States that did high-volume PAP smear testing were also studying ways to tighten regulation of clinical labs. Laboratories that performed examinations and analyses of PAP smears had been subject to increased liability due to misdiagnosis. New York was the only state that required testing of PAP technicians [Bogdanich 1988].

Fees

Laboratory fees were also under scrutiny. Fees had been escalating mainly because of outpatient testing, which remained largely free from caps under Medicare ruling Part B. Indications were that the 1990s would bring more protectionist legislation from Washington, D.C.

If proof of accuracy could not be obtained, more and more customers would in all likelihood be willing to take their cases to court. The danger of consumerism in healthcare was that it created increasing emphasis on litigation as a means of defining or challenging standards of quality in delivered service [Sisk 1989].

MEDICARE/MEDICAID REDUCTIONS

Since July 1966, the federal Medicare program had provided two coordinated plans for nearly all people aged 65 and over. These were a hospital insurance plan and a voluntary supplementary medical insurance plan, financed partially by monthly premiums paid by participants [*U.S. Industrial Outlook*, 1991]. Under Medicaid, all states (except Arizona) offered basic health services to certain people with low incomes [*Statistical Abstract of the United States*, p. 91, 1991]. In 1988, 7,579,000 people received Medicaid for laboratory bills totalling $543,000 [*Statistical Abstract of the United States* , 1991, No. 149].

Medicare was faced with budgetary cuts in the early 1990s, which had adverse effects on those clinical labs that received substantial revenues from Medicare or Medicaid payments. In a key step toward enactment of Medicare spending cuts for fiscal 1990, the House Ways and Means Committee approved reducing clinical laboratory payments by $95 million. Savings would be achieved in two ways. First, laboratory fee caps were reduced by 5%, down from 100% of the national median of local fee schedules. Second, the lab fee consumer price index (CPI) annual update would be limited to 2 percent, rather than the previously projected 4.7% [*Medical Laboratory Observer*, vol. 21, 1989]. Medicare payments for testing services had declined since the early 1980s. For instance, as shown in Figure 5, laboratories were reimbursed $18.00 for glucose testing in 1983. By 1989 that amount had dropped to $6.27.

Figure 5: Sample Reduction in Medicare Payments (for outpatient glucose testing services)

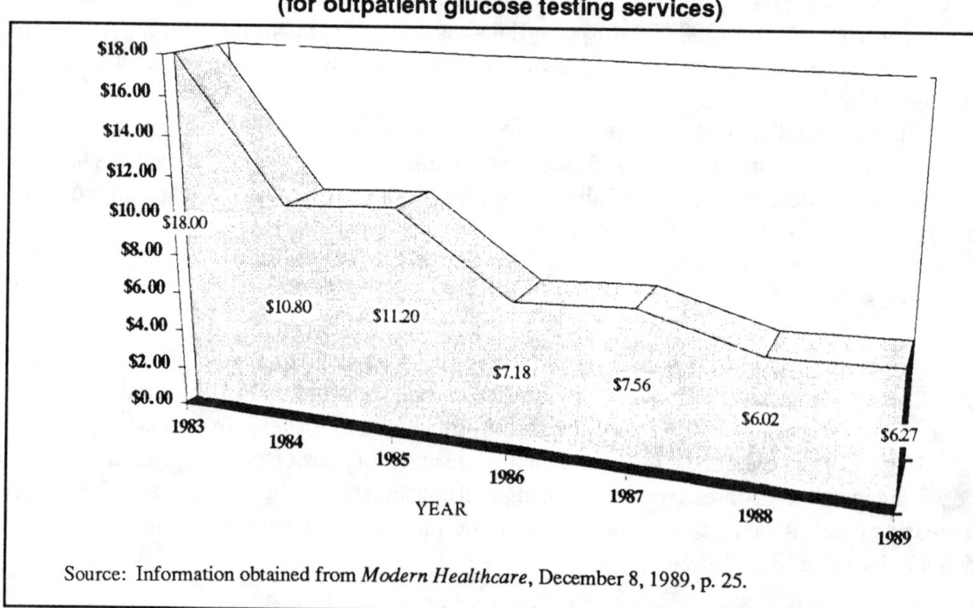

Source: Information obtained from *Modern Healthcare*, December 8, 1989, p. 25.

President Bush's healthcare reform proposal in 1992 mentioned Medicaid spending caps and included suggested reductions in Medicare and Medicaid spending. However, federal Medicaid spending was projected to reach $84.5 billion in 1993 — a 16.6% increase over 1992 [Wagner and Weissenstein 1992].

STAFFING

Although there was no absolute documentation pertaining to a shortage in clinical laboratory staff or the reasons for it, informal surveys of laboratory managers and educators across the country in 1989 indicated that it was a trend resulting from declining school enrollment [Sisk 1989].

Also in 1990, the BLS projected that employment for clinical laboratory technologists and technicians would increase by 19% from 1988 to 2000. Technicians and related support occupations were among the three major occupational groups requiring the highest levels of education. These three groups — managers, professionals, and technologists — were projected to increase their relative shares of employment at the expense of groups with lower levels of education [*Outlook 2000*, 1990].

Although the number of clinical laboratory technicians was projected to grow, Figure 6 shows that the graduate and education programs producing them had been decreasing significantly since 1982.

A key reason for declining program enrollment was demographic, that is, fewer available 18-year-old students who would normally enter such programs. This decline was expected to continue through the mid-1990s. Other basic reasons for the decline in laboratory personnel included low salaries, high stress, lack of status and recognition [Barros 1988], and a fear of contracting diseases such as AIDS. Even with declining school enrollment in the 1980s, it was predicted that there would be approximately 288,000 clinical laboratory technicians and technologists in the year 2000. This number would be 46,000 more than in 1988.

The employment rates suggested that the market was absorbing new graduates as quickly as they were produced. For clinical lab technicians and technologists, finding a job in their field would not be very difficult because of the many available positions projected. However, for employers, finding qualified and affordable technicians could be challenging.

TECHNOLOGICAL DEVELOPMENTS

Clinical laboratories were being pressed on two fronts. On one hand, a shortage of medical technologists made it increasingly difficult to process all of the work. On another hand, growing financial pressures demanded that labs become more productive. Laboratory automation offered a partial solution. "Intelligent" test packs were developed to perform multiple dissimilar tests simultaneously [DeCrese 1989]. As a result, labs were expected to become increasingly

Figure 6: The Decline of Laboratory Education Programs

		1982	1983	1984	1985	1986	1987	1988
	Total programs	639	638	615	584	516	509	464
MT	Enrollment	8,783	8,296	8,883	8,150	6,691	6,371	5,706
	Total graduates	5,996	5,318	5,199	4,862	4,477	3,979	3,432
	Total programs	187	206	221	225	214	216	212
MLT-AD	Enrollment	5,039	5,504	6,934	6,115	5,662	5,665	4,725
	Total graduates	1,746	1,860	2,437	2,275	1,930	1,898	1,568
	Total programs	73	66	57	56	47	46	44
MLT-C	Enrollment	1,778	1,743	1,683	1,340	1,409	1,231	1,480
	Total graduates	1,079	1,305	1,517	1,003	817	635	802
	Total programs	50	49	47	43	41	41	40
HT	Enrollment	199	250	263	196	218	203	202
	Total graduates	139	141	146	132	126	115	119
	Total programs	69	66	61	58	51	47	47
CT	Enrollment	351	343	318	279	260	215	189
	Total graduates	261	256	233	200	193	156	131

Source: Information obtained from Castleberry, *Medical Laboratory Observer*, 1989.

Programs covered here are medical technologist (MT), medical laboratory technician-associate degree (MLT-AD), medical laboratory technician-certificate (MLT-C), histologic technician (HT), and cytotechnologist (CT).

automated in non-traditional ways in the near future, especially in the areas of robotics and computers.

Robotics

Clinical laboratories have housed a wide selection of affordable and flexible robotic systems. Robots are mechanical devices programmed to perform a variety of tasks with human-like dexterity. They have always been an integral part of fully-automated analyzers where they are used for such tasks as pipetting (siphoning) specimens and reagents. These types of robots had restricted motion and limited programmability; they were usually dedicated to a single function. In contrast, the newer stand-alone robots were fully programmable and had a wide range of three dimensional motions.

These devices conferred several real benefits on the clinical laboratory. They cut costs by allowing unattended operation, eliminated risks associated with handling bio-hazardous materials, performed repetitive or complex tasks in the same way each time, reduced the errors that tend to plague relatively boring tasks, and were fast and flexible.

The ultimate step in robotics will be full automation of specimen flow from start to finish. Bar-coded specimens will move along conveyor belts and be shunted to the proper location as they pass transfer points. Once the specimens reach their intended location, they would be lined up for aliquoting (portioning of a solution) into the appropriate tube for an instrument. The instrument would then be loaded automatically by a robot, and the completed tray of specimens removed to make room for the next.

Robots will take over many of the mundane tasks of laboratory technicians. This change would be expensive initially, since most of the equipment would be custom-developed, but in time standard systems will become available. Installation would be driven by the need of laboratories to lower costs and to recruit and retain skilled staff. The bio-safety aspects, such as the fear of acquiring AIDS, would lend additional urgency to the acquisition of robots. Robots will enable the technologist of the future to spend more time monitoring sophisticated instruments and less time mixing supplies and pouring specimens [Lifshitz 1989].

Computers

Computers, more than any other technology, were responsible for advances in clinical laboratory automation, including the many features that made instruments easier to operate. These features included automatic rerun and dilution, on-line trouble shooting, reagent inventory, management, bi-directional interface with a host computer, extended calibration, and real-time quality control.

Computers were expected to continue to simplify the user interface and operation of clinical laboratory analyzers in the 1990s. Knowledge-based expert systems were expected to provide computer-assisted support for troubleshooting, maintenance, and quality control activities. New patient data could be interpreted in light of historical data to determine what follow-up action to take. An instrument could also be linked via modem to the manufacturer's central computer in order to compare data from other laboratories.

These systems were expected to permit instruments to make decisions that generally would require multiple interpretive steps by a human. As knowledge-based expert systems became more accurate and commonplace, many of the common interpretive procedures in the laboratory would be replaced.

Knowledge-based systems technology based on artificial intelligence will enable instruments to order appropriate follow-up tests based on first test results. Rather than wait for the clinician to review the result and essentially come to the same conclusion, the instrument — in consultation with its own expert system or the laboratory's expert system — would be able to order the next test.

Computers would no longer produce only numeric reports; instead, graphic representation of data would be the norm. Predictive values would appear alongside the numeric values to guide the interpretation. Where necessary, interpretive and diagnostic data would advise the clinician of his/her choice and possible conclusions [Lifshitz 1989].

COMPETITION

Some of the largest firms in the clinical laboratory testing industry that operated within the four-state area were SmithKline Bio-Science Laboratories, Metpath, Inc., Roche Biomedical Laboratories, and National Health Laboratories. These companies were experienced in the field, had wide customer bases, and owned highly expansive and advanced facilities.

SmithKline Bio-Science Laboratories

With 26 major clinical laboratories and 350 patient service centers this division of SmithKline Beecham Corporation provided services to physicians, hospitals, government, and industries under the name SmithKline Bio-Science Laboratories [SmithKline Beecham, 1990 Annual Report]. In 1990, its clinical laboratory service sales were $917 million and accounted for 10% of sales from SmithKline Beecham continuing operations. It conducted tests for 50,000 clients and controlled 17% of the nationwide independent laboratory market. Unlike most independent laboratories, SmithKline Bio-Science had a separate research and development facility. The ability to enhance service levels and increase productivity while developing new diagnostic tests for markets were areas that SmithKline Beecham considered its keys to success.

Metpath, Inc.

Metpath, Inc. was a division of Corning Glass Works. In 1988, Metpath, which was located in a 230,000-square-foot building in Teterboro, New Jersey, had a net income of more than $30 million, while paying off most of its $140 million debt. Metpath's major competitor was SmithKline, which, through acquisitions, had bypassed Metpath as the leader in the clinical laboratory testing industry [Chithelen 1989].

Roche Biomedical Laboratories

This subsidiary of Hoffman-La Roche, Inc. offered a complete range of routine and specialty testing procedures for physicians, hospitals, clinical laboratories, and researchers. The division had five regional clinical laboratories, with one located in Raritan, New Jersey, and it offered more than 1,500 separate test procedures. Roche Biomedical's parent company had been developing a drug to prevent the spread of AIDS in infected individuals [Starr 1991]. With research in such important fields, Hoffman-La Roche was able to keep Roche Biomedical informed of any new developments that may have warranted upgraded specialty testing equipment.

National Health Laboratories

National Health Laboratories, Inc., incorporated in Delaware in 1971, was one of the leading clinical laboratory companies in the United States in the early 1990s. The company consisted of 16 major laboratories — including a national reference laboratory for "esoteric" (specialty) testing and for testing drugs of abuse — 65 central offices and 341,341 collecting stations and immediate turnaround laboratories serving customers in 42 states. The company processed approximately 96,000 specimens and ran approximately 281,000 laboratory tests daily. In 1991 net sales reached $603.9 million. Two potential new markets for National Health Laboratories were hospital reference laboratories and substance abuse programs certified by NIDA in 1989 [Form 10-K 1991].

Local Market

The market for clinical laboratory testing within the four-state area (New York, New Jersey, Connecticut, and Pennsylvania) was so good that a small company could become profitable by providing quality service and on-time delivery. Large firms were in direct competition because they were competing at a much higher level, focusing more on test volume than on small-volume, high priced tests.

THE COMPANY

HISTORY

Bio-Reference Laboratories, Inc., was organized under the laws of New Jersey in December 1981 as Med-Mobile, Inc. The Company had marketed and developed mobile medical screening facilities ("Med-Mobiles") that were capable of conducting medical examinations at work sites and other locations. In February 1987, the company diversified through the acquisition of a licensed clinical laboratory (Bio-med Clinical Laboratory, Inc.), which it expanded through further acquisitions and development into a full service clinical laboratory [*Standard & Poor's*, October 10, 1991].

The acquisition of Bio-med was designed to enable the company to immediately offer laboratory services and avoid the delays associated with independently licensing, equipping, and staffing a laboratory. The company also gained access to the existing clientele of Bio-med and was able to use Bio-med's name and goodwill to expand business.

The company's primary business objective became the operation of Bio-med Clinical Laboratory, Inc., a corporation that owned and operated a clinical laboratory in Wayne, New Jersey. The company further developed Bio-med's operations and expanded the laboratory's services through the March 1988 acquisition of Cytology and Pathology Associates, Inc. (CPA), a clinical laboratory located in Englewood, New Jersey. The company consolidated and relocated the Bio-med and CPA operations to its modern laboratory facility in Elmwood Park, New Jersey, and continued to expand and develop the operations and marketing of the Laboratory [Form 10-K 1991].

In July 1989, the company sold substantially all of the assets of its mobile-testing division and all such activities ceased, except for the rental of vans and medical equipment to third parties. The company no longer provided any additional support services. The purchase price was paid in cash less approximately $90,000, which was used to exercise certain lease purchase rights of the assets sold. The purchasers were not affiliated with the company nor with any officer or director of the company.

The company underwent a major transformation after completing its initial public offering of stock in September 1986. On December 1, 1989, the company changed its name from Med-Mobile, Inc., to Bio-Reference Laboratories, Inc. The major focus of the company became its clinical laboratory divisions; these names also changed. Bio-med Clinical (acquired in 1987) became Bio-Reference Laboratories; Cytology and Pathology Associates became Cytology Bio-Reference. Managers at Bio-Reference Laboratories felt that the specialty testing field was an important area to break into; two of the most important and fastest growing areas in clinical laboratory services were rheumatology and cellular immunology testing. So two new laboratories were established in 1989: Rheumatology Bio-Reference and Cellular Bio-Reference. The former specialized in tests ordered by rheumatologists (joint disease specialists); the latter concentrated on specialty testing primarily designed to monitor the care of AIDS patients. The laboratory structure is shown in Figure 7.

COMPANY'S LABORATORY SERVICES

By 1992, the company was composed of several testing divisions: Bio-Reference Laboratories, Cytology Bio-Reference, Cellular Bio-Reference, and Rheumatology Bio-Reference.

Bio-Reference Laboratories

Bio-Reference offered a comprehensive list of chemical diagnostic tests to physicians

Figure 7: Bio-Reference Laboratories, Inc.

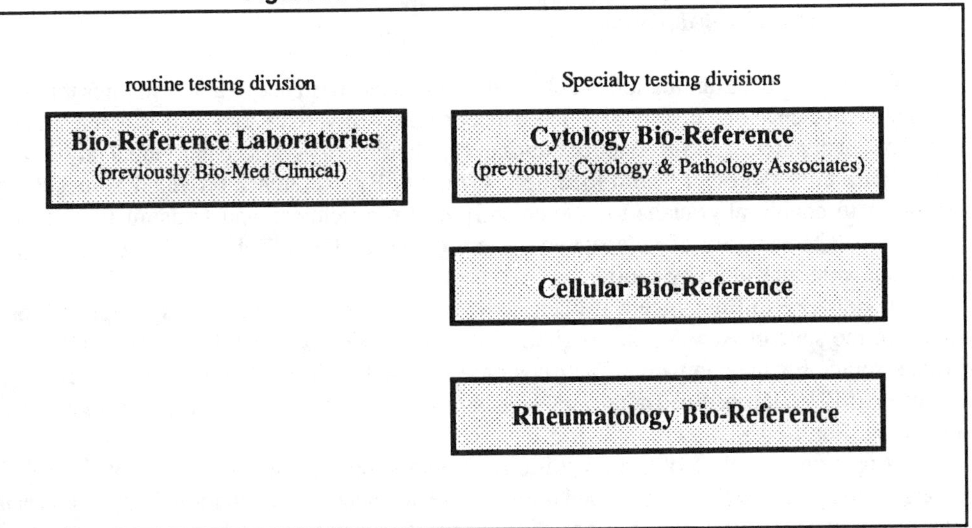

performing routine examinations of their patients. The broad categories of testing included complete blood and urine analysis, blood chemistry tests, hematology services, serology, and radio-immunology analysis and toxicology. Under these categories over 100 individual tests, ranging from cholesterol testing to drug screening, were offered. Tests were performed for 20,000 patient profiles or 60,000 individual tests per month. The company was operating at only 50 percent of its full capacity; the major testing equipment maintained by Bio-Reference had the capability to perform approximately two times the number of tests currently being run.

Operations. Bio-Reference accepted specimens primarily from New York and norther New Jersey. Specimens were either dropped off at the Company's laboratory or picked up by company couriers. All test results were compiled by Bio-Reference's computer system and computerized results were generally furnished to the physician within 24 hours either by courier or direct computer connection. All billing was computerized with tape-to-tape submission to Medicare and medicaid allowing for the easy processing of claims. The Company employed 17 full-time couriers who used Company vehicles to pick-up specimens and drop off test results that were not transmitted electronically. There were three shifts of workers, with the majority of the work processed on the midnight to 8:00 am shift. Bio-Reference had the capacity to perform immediate turnaround results in the event of an emergency.

Licensing. Bio-Reference was licensed by the states of New York and New Jersey and the City of New York. To maintain its licenses, it was required to participate in proficiency testing programs by the licensing authorities. Bio-Reference was enrolled in proficiency programs sponsored by each authority with whom they were licensed, as well as the Centers for Disease Control and the College of American Pathologists.

Cytology Bio-Reference

Cytology is the examination of cells to determine the existence of abnormalities that may indicate the presence of a disorder such as cancer or infertility. Cytology Bio-Reference is the second major division of Bio-Reference Laboratories. It primarily serviced individual physicians, clinics, hospitals, and other health facilities. Cytology Bio-Reference provided all necessary containers to enable physicians to conveniently obtain specimens and transmit them to the laboratory. The majority of its specimens were delivered through the mail, although some specimens were picked up by courier.

Cytology Bio-Reference was licensed by the state of New Jersey and had applied for a license in the state of New York. In 1988, Cytology Bio-Reference sales represented a new revenue source for the company. The division accounted for 29% of the company's revenue increase. In 1989, it processed approximately 16,000 patients per month at an average of $9.81 per patient [Form 10-K 1991].

Approximately 95% of Cytology Bio-Reference's business was the examination of PAP smears. The cytotechnologist is trained to recognize and analyze any abnormal appearances in cells. This analysis reveals the presence of outside infectious agents such as herpes, fungus, or the presence of an abnormality that could suggest cancer. The cytotechnologist then evaluates each sample on the basis of a classification system that ranges from Class I, which indicates negative results, to Class V, which indicates a malignancy.

The company limited the number of PAP smears that any cytotechnologist could review in one day to 85 because of misdiagnosis liability created through the national standards for quality assurance in cytology services [United States Code Annotated, Title 4. 263a, (f)4B, 1991]. The company's fulltime cytotechnologists were paid hourly wages while part-time cytotechnologists were paid per case. Cytotechnologists were not required to perform a minimum number of reviews per day. The company also employed two fulltime pathologists to assist the cytotechnologists and encouraged referrals of difficult or questionable slides to the laboratory supervisor.

Cytology Bio-Reference followed the same procedure as Bio-Reference, generally transmitting test results to referring physicians or healthcare facilities within 24 to 48 hours.

New Laboratory Services: Cellular Bio-Reference and Rheumatology Bio-Reference

In 1989, the Company embarked on a business strategy to create two specialized laboratories: Cellular Bio-Reference and Rheumatology Bio-Reference. By concentrating on specialty tests, the average revenue per patient increased from $20.81 in 1989 to $24.82 in 1990.

Cellular Bio-Reference was established to concentrate in the areas of cellular immunology and offer an analysis of T-cell subsets, beta-2 micro-globulins and the P-24 antigen. These tests were useful in monitoring the status of AIDS patients. This laboratory required unique equipment and specific licensure and was not licensed to begin accepting specimens until early

Figure 8: Selected Financial Data (Years Ended October 31)

	1990	1989	1988	1987	1986
Operating Data:					
Revenues Net	$13,380,004	$8,110,590	$4,171,198	$1,002,215	$ —
Operating Expenses	$14,889,293	$9,633,867	$5,351,226	$1,224,758	$227,966
[Loss] from Operations	($1,509,289)	($1,523,277)	($1,180,028)	($222,543)	($227,966)
[Loss] from Continuing Operations	($2,074,323)	($1,923,775)	($1,373,952)	($253,153)	($244,270)
[Loss] from Discontinued Operations	$—	($132,971)	($541,092)	($822,086)	($54,270)
[Loss] on Disposal of Segment	$—	($323,979)	$—	$—	$—
Net [Loss]:	($2,074,323)	($2,380,725)	($1,915,044)	($1,075,239)	($298,540)
Net [Loss] Per Share					
Primary	($0.80)	($4.06)	($4.37)	($2.85)	($1.21)
Fully diluted	($0.80)	($4.06)	($4.37)	($2.85)	($1.21)
Cash:					
Dividends Per Common Share	$None	$None	$None	$None	$None
Finance Sheet Data:					
Cash (Overdraft)	($206,882)	($139,027)	$412,453	$182,904	$1,215,865
Total Assets	$7,957,791	$7,011,703	$6,033,977	$2,653,455	$1,916,487
Total Long Term Liabilities	$755,289	$2,598,673	$866,870	$1,160,921	$195,853
Total Liabilities	$6,588,411	$6,842,147	$4,386,386	$2,286,482	$606,110
Working Capital (Deficiency)	$833,910	($743,280)	($1,408,617)	($422,506)	($1,020,145)
Shareholders' Equity	$1,369,380	$169,556	$1,647,591	$366,973	$1,310,377

Source: Information obtained from Bio-Reference Laboratories, *Form 10-K, 1991*.

1990.

Rheumatology Bio-Reference was started by individuals who had directed the specialty lab at the Hospital for Joint Disease in New York, and was designed to serve rheumatologists. It provided testing such as complement, DNA, immunoglobulins, anti-cardiolipin, Lyme assay, and other analyses used in the diagnosis and treatment of arthritis and connective tissue disorders. This laboratory required specialized equipment and extensive training of technical staff in order to become proficient at conducting sophisticated testing procedures.

Cellular Bio-Reference and Rheumatology Bio-Reference were originally conceived and developed as separate profit centers, with separate staff, medical directors, and equipment. These laboratories began to accumulate costs in 1989 mainly because the company accelerated the amortization of start-up costs over a 6-month period rather than a 12-month period. In 1990, the company merged the specialty laboratories into the main laboratory in order to cut costs (promote savings). Cellular Bio-Reference and Rheumatology Bio-Reference no longer operated as separate profit centers. However, much of the $5 million sales increase in 1990 probably was attributable to these new divisions.

FINANCE AND REVENUES

The company had been able to finance its growth through loans and common stock offerings to the public. The financial success of the business was dependent on the success of its operations to generate sufficient revenue to pay its debts and finance new investments.

Finances

Gross profits increased from $2,117,431 during the period ended October 31, 1989, to $4,045,475 for the year ended October 31, 1990. This was a 191% increase in gross profits. However, as shown in Figure 8, the company had shown a loss from continuing operations in 1990 and the previous 4 years.

The working capital deficit increased by more than $90,000 between 1989 and 1990 (from $743,280 to $833,910) [Form 10-K 1991]. The company continued to have serious cash-flow problems: it had a cash overdraft of $67,855 in 1990. To help offset the use of cash for continuing operations, in addition to the cash overdraft the company raised $1,162,747 by issuing stock and an additional $892,669 through short- and long-term financing. After repaying $553,911 in existing debt the proceeds resulted in a net increase in cash from debt (equity) financing of $1,569,360.

Dividends had not been paid on the company's common stock since its inception, and by reason of its contemplated future financial requirements and business plans (such as the expansion of its specialty testing service), the company did not contemplate or anticipate paying any common stock dividend in the foreseeable future.

Prior to being sold, the mobile-screening division lost more than $2,000,000 from its inception through July 1989. From February 1987 to July 1989, Bio-Reference Laboratories lost a total of $3,125,202. Starting virtually from scratch in 1990, the company was on the verge of $1,000,000 per month of revenues, a level at which the company would have had profitable operations. (Financial data necessary to determine the percentage of total revenue from each division of Bio-Reference Laboratories was not available.) The company did not plan any major capital expenditures for 1991 and approximated that $75,000 would be spent for equipment purchases and computer upgrades.

Revenues

Revenues were recognized at the time of service performance rather than when payments were received. A majority of the payments received for services rendered were derived as third-party payments from Medicare programs for the elderly, Medicaid programs for the medically indigent, HMOs, and other health plans. The remainder of the company's payments were derived directly from doctors, individuals, unions, employers, and others.

The company was certified by Medicare and Medicaid to receive payments for services rendered. The company submitted invoices to the government and received payments based on rates determined by the government. Their rates were generally lower than the retail rates charged by the company and were subject to change based on the determination of the administering authority. Other third-party payments were based on rates set by state authorities, negotiated rates with insurers, or the Company's retail rates. The company's laboratory operations derived approximately 13.5% of its revenues from Medicare, 17.5% from Medicaid, 15.25% from insurers, and 53.8% from direct payments [Form 10-K 1991].

In July 1990, the Company, in response to an increase in outstanding self pay accounts — which are paid directly by the patients — over 120 days, altered its billing procedures on self-pay. Rather than billing for services twice within 75 days from the date of service and producing bills weekly, the company began billing five times within 75 days (with the last letter coming from an attorney employed by the company) and producing bills on a daily basis. Subsequent to fiscal year 1990, the company instituted other procedures to enhance collection of self-pay accounts, i.e., following up daily on bad addresses or returned mail bills, visiting physicians' offices to compare billing information, and discontinuing service to physicians' offices with large percentages of unpaid self-pay accounts. In addition, the company embarked on a point-of-sale collection program.

MARKETING AND SALES

The company primarily used direct marketing and, to a lesser degree, brochures, magazines, newspapers, or electronic media to gain new business.

Marketing

The company's marketing staff increased from 10 employees in 1989 to 17 in 1990. A majority of the company's marketing efforts were devoted to the expansion of its laboratory business. The acquisition of Cytology Bio-Reference not only increased the laboratory's services offered, but also supplied a significant list of physicians and other medical facilities (hospitals and clinics) to which the company marketed its line of testing services.

In 1990, Bio-Reference began to emphasize marketing to physicians whose patients pay the laboratory directly for services (self-pay) rather than billing insurance companies, government agencies (Medicare and Medicaid), or the physicians themselves. Self-pay accounts were typically billed for services at list price and therefore represented a higher profit margin business. In fiscal 1990, the company had increased its self-pay accounts 71% from 1989 [Form 10K 1990, p 13].

The company marketed its laboratory services through sales representatives who received base salaries plus commissions. Company sales representatives contacted physicians, hospitals, and HMOs to solicit business. These sales representatives were also responsible for promoting the company to clients and providing efficient client service.

Sales

Bio-Reference Laboratories had shown a steady growth rate in its sales volume. Sales increased by $5,269,414 between 1989 and 1990. That same year its patient count increased 38% — from 389,734 to 539,109. The increase in these figures was mainly attributable to the start-up of its two newest divisions: Cellular Bio-Reference and Rheumatology Bio-Reference. Management believed that the trend would continue [Form 10-K 1991, p 12].

GOVERNMENT REGULATIONS

Government regulations affected laboratory operations in two ways: licensing and waste disposal.

Licensing

The company's laboratory operations required licensing in each jurisdiction of operation. Bio-Reference and Cytology Bio-Reference each had an interstate license which was a necessary prerequisite to obtaining a license in any jurisdiction outside the city or state in which the laboratory was located. Bio-Reference was licensed in the states of New York and New Jersey and in the city of New York. Cytology Bio-Reference was licensed only in New Jersey. The laboratory technicians also had to qualify for laboratory employment under state and city regulations. There was no assurance that the laboratory would maintain necessary licenses, and in the event the laboratory lost its license in a particular jurisdiction, it was required to cease all activities in that jurisdiction.

Waste Disposal

The company was also subject to federal and state regulations governing the transportation and disposal of medical waste, including body fluids. Federal regulations required licensing of interstate transporters of medical waste. In New Jersey, the company was subject to the Comprehensive Medical Waste Management Act (CMWMA), which required registering as a generator of special medical waste. The CMWMA mandated the sterilization of certain medical waste and provided a tracking system to ensure disposal in an approved facility. Due to recent events involving the ocean dumping of medical waste, new regulations — which could have a material effect on the company's day-to-day business — were being drafted.

All of the company's medical waste was transported away and disposed of by a licensed interstate hauler. The hauler provided a manifest of the disposition of the waste products, as well as a certificate of incineration which was retained by the company. Additional regulations governing the disposal of medical waste were under consideration by federal, state, and local authorities.

MANAGEMENT AND ORGANIZATION

In 1989, the Company implemented the College of American Pathologists (CAP) Workload System, modified for commercial laboratories. This system was to be implemented to allow the Company to identify staffing inefficiencies and to control costs. At the end of 1990, the Company had 268 employees, none of whom were represented by a union or covered by a collective-bargaining agreement. The company considered its relations with employees to be satisfactory. A hiring freeze and price increases were instituted effective November 1, 1991, in an effort to increase revenues; senior staff had taken voluntary salary reductions of 8%, payroll was further reduced with the termination of more than 30 employees during February 1991; and overtime was reduced by 50%. It was anticipated that these actions, in conjunction with the changes in the company's collection procedures, would increase cash flow by approximately $45,000 per month. Management believed, but could not ensure, that the company would have sufficient cash to fund its operations for at least the next 12 months [Form 10K 1991].

TOWARDS THE FUTURE

Several strategic problems faced Bio-Reference Laboratory owners and needed to be addressed to meet the challenges of the 1990s. Strategic areas of concern were expansion of test services offered in light of changing market needs, staffing deficiencies, government regulations, and technological developments.

Some executives felt that Bio-Reference Laboratories should concentrate on specialty tests performed through its Cellular and Rheumatology divisions which may have been responsible for much of the 38% patient increase in 1990. Batteries of sophisticated specialized tests were likely to be needed more frequently since the over 65 age group was expected to make up 13% of the American population by the turn of the century, and people will continue being tested for AIDS.

Rheumatology Bio-Reference employed a specialized team of technologists proficient at conducting sophisticated tests in its state-of-the-art laboratory. Cellular Bio-Reference had acquired necessary licensure to operate in 1990. Its laboratory had unique equipment designed to run specialty tests. Unlike routine testing laboratories, it was able to test for AIDS as well as monitor the progress of the AIDS virus in patients. New York, New Jersey, and Pennsylvania were all among the top 10 states for AIDS insurance claims, and since the number of people infected by the disease was expected to increase, it was likely that the large market which Bio-Reference served would continue to increasingly need AIDS testing and monitoring.

Anticipating arguments about the early unprofitability of the divisions, these executives pointed out that the first year's projections for the divisions were unrealistic, especially since the company had sped up its amortization from 12 months to 6 months. These executives also felt that Bio-Reference's routine testing division alone was not strong enough to compete against larger laboratories performing low-margin, routine testing — such as urine analysis for drug use — less expensively and at higher volume than the company. Many competitors had government or hospital contracts or contracts with large corporations which frequently required routine tests.

Other Bio-Reference managers felt that routine testing alone would lead to longer-term strategic success and that specialty testing divisions were not needed and should be sold. Executives supporting this strategy felt that too much money and energy had been supporting the two specialty divisions which began losing money at their inception in 1988. Money from the sale of these divisions could pay off most of the company's debt and enable it to continually upgrade routine equipment and recruit highly qualified technologists or technicians. Managers felt that due to underutilized equipment and the possibility of overestimated AIDS projections, there would not be enough work to warrant the separate specialty testing divisions. They also worried that larger clinical labs would capture most of the specialty testing market, since some of the major competitors were owned by much larger corporations that also had medical and pharmaceutical research and development facilities. These companies would be better able to develop new tests for specialty areas.

Moreover, managers in favor of routine testing felt that theirs was a reasonably predictable and growing market: There would always be a need for routine testing and the country was spending $216 billion on drug abuse screening alone in 1990. Specialty testing requirements, on the other hand, were constantly changing, necessitating funds for upgraded equipment and for research and development.

Management was exploring these and other strategic decisions as they sought ways to gain on their major competitors.

REFERENCES AND BACKGROUND READINGS

Asinof, Lynn, "Insurance Testing Keeps Medical Labs Growing," *Wall Street Journal*, November 30, 1989, p. A1.

Bailer, Michael, Telephone interview, National Institute on Drug Abuse, Drug Testing Section, March 23, 1992.

Barros, Annamarie, "Strategies to Achieve Recognition and Status," *Medical Laboratory Observer*, Vol. 22, February 1989, pp. 17-18.

Bests Review, "AIDS-Related Claim Survey Results," 1991, pp. 10, 14.

Bogdanich, Walt, "AMA to Study Quality Control in Pap Testing," *Wall Street Journal*, January 14, 1988, p. 4.

Castleberry, Barbara M., "Who Will Staff the Laboratory of the '90s?," *Medical Laboratory Observer*, Vol. 21, July 1989, pp. 59-66.

Chithelen, Ignatius, "Clinical Case," *Forbes,* Vol. 143, Iss. 6, March 20, 1988, pp. 178, 180.

Clinical Laboratory Observer (1989), 16th edition, pp. 117, 118.

"Congress Expanding Scrutiny of Clinical Labs," *Medical Laboratory Observer*, Vol. 20, May 1988, pp. 21, 22.

DeCresce, Robert P., Lifshitz, Mark S., "Drug Abuse Screening: Get Your Lab's Share of a Booming Market," *Medical Laboratory Observer*, Vol. 19, October 1987, pp. 31-34.

DeCresce, Robert P., "The Impact of the New Technology," *Medical Laboratory Observer*, Vol. 21, July 1989, pp. 41-46.

Form 10-K, Bio-Reference Laboratories, *Securities and Exchange Commission,* August 20, 1991.

Form 10-K, National Health Laboratories, *Securities and Exchange Commission*, 1991.

Freudenheim, Milt. "In a Stronghold for HMOs, One Possible Future Emerges," *New York Times*, September 2, 1991, pp. 1, 28.

Glaser, Vicki, "AIDS Crises Spurs Hunt for New Tests," *Technology Business*, Vol. 8, Iss. 1, January 1988, pp. 34-39.

Hirsch, Thomas P., "New Lab Consolidations: Competing on a Cost Basis," *Medical Laboratory Observer*, Vol. 21, July 1989, pp. 69-71.

"House Panel Approves $95 Million Cut in Lab Payments for 1990," *Medical Laboratory Observer*, Vol. 21, August 1989, pp. 23-24.

Lifshitz, Mark S., and Robert P. DeCresce "Automation: Trends in Instrumentation, Robotics, Computers," *Medical Laboratory Observer*, July 1989, pp. 73-77.

"Making Medical Labs Measure Up," *Technology Review*, Vol. 92, July 1989, pp. 13, 14.

Medical Laboratory Observer, Washington Report, May 1988, pp. 21-22.

Morbidity and Mortality Weekly Report, Vol. 40, January 3, 1992, Vol. 41, January 24, 1992.

Outlook 2000, "Projections of Occupational Employment, 1988-2000," U.S. Department of Labor, Bureau of Labor Statistics, April 1990, pp. 41-63.

Savitz, Eric J., "No Magic Cure," *Barron's*, December 16, 1991, pp. 10, 11, 22-29.

Sisk, Faye A., "Trends in Regulation and Reimbursement," *Medical Laboratory Observer,* Vol. 21, July 1989, pp. 49-55.

SmithKline Beecham Corporation, 1990 Annual Report, p. 21.

Standard and Poor's, "Industry Surveys," Vol. 52, No. 19, Sec. 2, October 10, 1991, pp. 9671, 9672.

Starr, Cynthia, "Roche Mounts Three-Pronged Attack on AIDS Virus," *Drug Topics*, July 22, 1991, pp. 25-27.

Statistical Abstract of the United States, 1991, pp. 16, 73, 91.

Statland, Bernard, "How Illness Demographics Will Affect the Lab," *Medical Laboratory Observer*, July 1989, pp. 79-86.

United States Code Annotated, The Public Health and Welfare, Title 42, 263, 1991, pp. 593-608.

U.S. Industrial Outlook, Health and Medical Services, Chap. 44, 1991.

Wagner, Lynn and Eric Weissenstein, "Bush Healthcare Reform Plan Gets a Mixed Reaction," *Modern Healthcare*, Vol. 22, No. 6, February 10, 1992, pp. 4, 5.

Wagner, Mary, "Labs Test Positive for Profits," *Modern Healthcare*, Vol. 18, Iss. 50, December 9, 1988, pp. 36-41.

Worden, Lawrence J., "Market Facts," *Messenger: The Newsletter of the Biomedical Marketing Association*, Vol. 18, No. 2, Summer 1991, p. 7.

Yu, Joanna, Pei-Jun Chen, Edward J. Harshman and Eugene G. McCarthy, "An Analysis of Substance Abuse Patterns, Medical Expenses and Effectiveness of Treatment in the Workplace," *Employee Benefits Journal*, Vol. 16, No. 3, September 1991, pp. 26-30.

BLAKESTON & WILSON COMPANY: A SMALL REGIONAL CANDY COMPANY

Blakeston & Wilson of Chicago, Illinois, was a manufacturer of medium-price, high-quality chocolate candy. Its chocolates, sold under the brand name Perfection, were distributed through company-controlled stores and by candy wholesalers (usually called jobbers in the candy trade).

The company was organized in 1938 when it purchased the assets of the bankrupt Sidwell Wilson Company. Mr. Wilson, who had been president of the defunct company, was instrumental in securing necessary capital and in organizing the new firm, of which he also became president. Whereas the original company had an unsuccessful profit record, Blakeston & Wilson achieved immediate financial success. Profits were earned each year from 1938 through 1946. Mr. Wilson believed that the failure of his first company resulted from excessive sales costs; in turn, he believed that the success of the new company resulted from the fact that lower sales costs had been achieved. Profits for the first quarter of 1947 were the highest in the firm's history.

During 1947, Blakeston & Wilson planned to double the number of Perfection Chocolate Shops which marketed its candy. This expansion in retail store operations was the outgrowth of a policy adopted in 1943. Prior to that time, the company had sold its chocolates solely to wholesalers and large chain buyers. Mr. Wilson stated that his company had entered the retail sales field in 1943 to assure a stable, profitable postwar market for a part of his factory's manufacturing capacity. The opening of these Perfection Chocolate Shops was a real innovation

Case material of the Harvard Graduate School of Business Administration is prepared as a basis for class discussion. Cases are not designed to present illustrations of either correct or incorrect handling of administrative problems.

in the company's distribution procedures; Blakeston & Wilson executive personnel had not had previous experience in retail store operation. Operating results from 1943 through April of 1947, however, had convinced Mr. Wilson of the success of the policy as well as of the wisdom of further retail sales expansion.

Predecessor Company

The Sidwell Wilson Company, incorporated in 1923, had sold packaged and bulk chocolates under several brand names. Sales volume had averaged $700,000 annually with selling expenses of approximately $100,000 (see Exhibit 1). The company had employed eight salesmen who, under the direction of Mr. Wilson, served wholesalers and buying syndicates in the Middle West and the East.

Stock ownership had been originally divided between Mr. Wilson (25%) and the majority stockholders (75%). By borrowing money from a company supplier, Mr. Wilson had purchased complete ownership of the company in 1926. Serious losses during the early thirties made repayment of the loan impossible and, in 1937 company assets were sold to satisfy creditor claims.

"The company failed," Mr. Wilson stated, "primarily because our selling expenses were too high. Moreover, we were selling to wholesalers who played one manufacturer against another to force prices down. We worked and sweated to make a few dollars manufacturing candy while the wholesalers and retailers took large margins for distributing and selling our products. Conse-

Exhibit 1: Predecessor Company — Sidwell Wilson Company

Profit and Loss Statement for the Year Ending December 31, 1935

		Percentage of Net Sales
Net sales	$623,069.97	
Less: Cost of Sales	520,616.71	83.56%
Gross profit	$102,453.26	16.44
Less: Selling, general, and administrative expenses		
Freight and cartage outward	$ 22,618.72	3.63
Shipping wages and supplies	10,505.42	1.69
Advertising	4,373.97	0.70
Selling expenses	40,536.91	6.50
Administrative expenses1	9,740.40	3.17
Miscellaneous expenses	9,015.74	1.45
Total expenses	$106,791.16	17.14
Net loss for period	$ 4,337.90	0.70

Source: Company records

quently, the consumer paid a high price for candy on which we did not make profits." The company had also been troubled by shortages in working capital. "We had just $3,000 plus equipment when we started in 1923, and when we did occasionally make money, the stockholders took it all out in dividends."

Formation of Blakeston & Wilson

After analyzing the difficulties which he had encountered in his first business, Mr. Wilson concluded that by reducing sales expense he could successfully compete in the candy business. To secure capital for his new enterprise, Mr. Wilson approached Mr. Blakeston, a director and operating executive of a large midwestern variety chain. Mr. Blakeston and three of his associates furnished the minimum amount required, $30,000. They received 500 shares of preferred stock; in addition, when all preferred stock had been retired from earnings, they were to be issued 48% of the company's authorized common stock. For services rendered, Mr. Wilson was then to receive 52% of the common stock.

By March of 1938, necessary machinery had been installed and production was initiated. Company offices, located in the factory building, were furnished simply; all administrative and overhead expense was kept to a minimum. The executive organization of the new company consisted of two men: Mr. Wilson, president and general manager, who was in charge of sales and promotion work, financial administration, and supervision of administrative personnel; and Mr. Herman Smith, production manager, who directed manufacturing, purchasing, and cost accounting work, in addition to performing some other miscellaneous duties.

Product

Blakeston & Wilson in 1947, manufactured quality boxed and bulk chocolates. The company's boxed chocolates were packed in attractive, but inexpensively designed, paper boxes. All Blakeston & Wilson candy was hand-dipped, a process normally used only for expensive packaged chocolates; medium-price and some expensive chocolates were usually dipped by machine. Hand-dipping was reputed to create thicker, creamier chocolate coatings over the candy center — qualities which the company believed were recognized and appreciated by consumers. Mr. Wilson stated that his chocolates (75 cents per pound) were equal in quality to those sold in the high-price range ($1.00-$2.50) and superior in quality to other medium-price chocolates ($0.75-$1.00). "The difference in price between medium- and high-price chocolates lies primarily in expensive boxes and decorations and in large promotional expenditures, not in the quality of the candy," he stated.

Prior to World War II, the company had manufactured some standard hand-dipped chocolates for variety chains and grocery chains. Shortages of raw materials had forced the company to reduce sharply production for these outlets during the war years.

Original Sales Plan of Blakeston & Wilson

Blakeston & Wilson, until 1943, sold chocolate candy under a variety of brand names only to wholesalers and to two large chains. The company sold to 121 wholesalers in an area bounded by Madison, Wisconsin, Rock Island, Illinois, Louisville, Kentucky, and New York City. Wholesalers were given usual trade discounts and exclusive sales rights for a specified area. A typical wholesaler's sales varied in volume from $4,000 to $25,000, with an average of $8,000. He, in turn, sold to outlets such as drug and department stores, clubs, and grocery stores. Wholesalers did not carry other brands of chocolates in a competitive price range. They did, however, carry both lower-price and higher-price chocolates.

"My theory was that there were more people who would buy our product because of its quality value than there were people who would have to be coaxed into buying it by expensive sales efforts," said Mr. Wilson. In carrying out his policy to cut sales expenses, Mr. Wilson personally handled all sales work; he had no salesmen or sales representatives. Mr. Wilson periodically visited wholesalers and syndicate buyers, determined credit policies, supervised sales accounting work, selected candy items, and designed candy packages. "My selling costs for the wholesale and syndicate trade vary between 1.5% to 2% of gross sales." Mr. Wilson stated, "whereas usually costs in the industry for selling to that trade amount to 6%." He attributed the industry's high selling costs to its use of numerous salesmen, expensive missionary sales work, and high promotional expense. "We do very little promotional work for our wholesalers, and the wholesalers do not do any promotional work on our candy. They have recognized our effort to shave expenses and therefore place the best box of candy in the consumer's hands at the lowest price." Company sales promotional material initially consisted of circulars describing candy manufacturing processes and counter display cards. "The quality of our candy will sell these chocolates without sales promotion," Mr. Wilson emphasized.

Mr. Wilson had personally selected his wholesalers when the new company was first organized. Thereafter, he visited each distributor approximately three times a year. These visits were informal and frequently amounted to a game of golf with the executives of the concern. Mr. Wilson knew each executive personally, and all business relations were on a first name basis. During World War II, his visits to company wholesalers became more infrequent, since selling at that time consisted of allocating scarce supplies of candy among these firms.

In 1947, commenting on the excellence of his original wholesaler selection, Mr. Wilson noted, "We haven't gained or lost a new account in over nine years." Shortages of candy as well as a heavy personal workload had prevented Mr. Wilson from returning to his prewar schedule of visits to wholesalers.

Entrance into Retail Sales Operations

During the depression years of the early 'thirties, the candy industry had been described as "sick"; its chief symptom was overcapacity with its attendant pains of price cutting, secret rebates, and overextension of credit. Since the incorporation of Blakeston & Wilson in 1938, however, candy production — as well as the price per pound received by the manufacturer — had increased substantially (see Exhibit 2). Company sales, following the general industry pattern, increased from $286,000 in 1938 to $909,000 in 1942. Though wartime sugar rationing had hampered production, this difficulty had been partially eliminated through the increased use of nonrationed substitute materials. Moreover, manufacturers of medium- and high-price packaged chocolates

Exhibit 2: Average Wholesale Value per Pound of Confectionery Sold by Manufacturer-Wholesalers and Manufacturer-Retailers, 1925-1945

	Manufacturer-Wholesalers		Manufacturer- Retailers	
Year	Number of Firms	Average Value Per Pound	Number of Firms	Average Value Per Pound
1925	386	$0.229	96	$0.392
1926	386	0.226	96	0.396
1927	369	0.222	113	0.348
1928	381	0.224	118	0.319
1929	394	0.210	123	0.335
1930	405	0.196	113	0.386
1931	404	0.174	114	0.366
1932	337	0.136	81	0.340
1933	301	0.131	44	0.376
1934	354	0.137	44	0.387
1935	308	0.142	48	0.385
1936	308	0.143	40	0.420
1937	265	0.153	33	0.451
1938	265	0.144	33	0.453
1939	244	0.143	29	0.449
1940	244	0.144	29	0.436
1941	224	0.153	24	0.468
1942	235	0.188	29	0.489
1943	258	0.218	26	0.414
1944	258	0.232	40	0.490
1945	353	0.244	51	

*In 1945 total sales of candy were candy bars 55%, package candy (primarily boxed chocolates) 20%, bulk candy 15%, and specialty candies 10%.

Source: Department of Commerce, 19th Annual Report on Confectionery Sales and Distributions, 1946, p. 23.

had benefited greatly from the sharply increased national income. Consumers were willing to buy these more expensive candies, on which the manufacturer realized excellent margins, instead of cheaper bulk candy formerly purchased in variety stores.

Mr. Wilson, despite his firm's prosperity, was apprehensive over future prospects for sales to the wholesaler trade. On the basis of the experience with his former company, he believed that competition would first appear and be most severe on sales made to wholesaler organizations. Manufacturers selling through wholesalers, Mr. Wilson stated, could never be certain how much they could sell, and they had little control over prices received for their products. Mr. Wilson believed that a market for at least a part of his productive output could be secured at a controlled price by opening company-operated candy stores. He was not sure of making profits in these stores. "If we could just break even on store operations, our profits would come from manufacturing the candy."

Mr. Wilson, although he had worked in the candy industry since 1909, had not had any experience in retail sales work or in retail store management. He therefore discussed his idea for retail candy stores with his board, company bankers, and associates in the industry; they were unanimous in their disapproval of his plan. Despite these objections, Mr. Wilson announced that he planned to open a retail store, if necessary by supplying funds from his personal resources. The board of directors, after this statement, reluctantly approved the new policy.

Perfection Candy Stores, Inc., was organized to finance operations of the new retail store; the necessary capital was subscribed by Mr. Blakeston and his associates. They received the preferred stock of the new corporation plus 48% of its common stock. Mr. Wilson received the remaining 52% of the common stock for "services rendered." The 6% cumulative preferred stock did not have voting power unless three consecutive annual dividend payments were passed. The new corporation had the same management and board of directors as did Blakeston & Wilson; it was a separate corporate entity only for tax purposes and as a method of limiting the financial liability of Blakeston & Wilson.

The first Perfection Chocolate Shop was opened in Chicago in the fall of 1943. At that time all former brand names of the company, with the exception of those used for the syndicate trade, were abandoned, and the name "Perfection" was adopted for chocolates sold to the company store and to the wholesale trade.

Operation of Retail Stores

Success in the operation of the first Perfection shop led to further expansion during 1946. Between January and August of that year, five additional Perfection shops were opened in the business section of Chicago. Each new shop was organized, financed, and individually incorporated as was done in the case of the original store.

Perfection Chocolate Shops were located in sections of Chicago where pedestrian traffic passing each store was heavy, as well as where the possibilities that passers-by would purchase candy were high, i. e., near hotels, department store shopping areas, and financial districts. Shops featured Perfection packaged chocolates in 1/2-pound, 1-pound, and 2-pound boxes in addition to Perfection bulk chocolates; they sold only Blakeston & Wilson products and did not handle accessory lines such as nuts and novelties. Most chocolates were 75 cents a pound or $1.45 for a two-pound box. A few specially packed boxes of chocolates retailed at higher prices — $1.25 to $1.50 a pound.

Each shop had a manager and, usually, four clerks. These were all girls and they were selected with regard to their appearance, character, and education. Starting weekly wages were $30, which were advanced to $35 after three months' service; competing firms started their sales girls at $22 a week. Managers were paid between $40 and $50 a week. In addition, both clerks and managers were paid a bonus if each girl sold over $480 of candy per week; clerks averaged between $2 and $14 per week in bonuses. Managers were eligible for an additional supervisors' bonus.

Mr. Wilson believed that any Perfection Chocolate Shop was in a strong competitive position because (1) it sold high-quality, reasonably priced candy, (2) all stores were efficiently operated, and (3) each store had a large sales volume.

Perfection chocolates were superior in quality to other medium-price chocolates. They were five cents less per pound, however, than chocolates sold by the leading competitor of Perfection Candy Shops — a seminational chain of retail candy stores. Savings resulting from reduced retail selling costs and efficient manufacturing operations were passed on to the customer through the use of highest quality candy ingredients, Mr. Wilson stated.

Perfection Candy Shops were operated more efficiently than competitive shops, Mr. Wilson said, because of several unique operating features which he had developed. He had designed all Perfection shops with a small display window in which several boxes of candy were high-lighted. Traditionally, retail candy stores had large display windows which, he believed, took several hundred dollars of display stock as well as many hours of time for decoration. Furthermore, Perfection bulk chocolates were packed in specially designed five-pound boxes at the factory; these boxes fit into display cases in the retail stores without rehandling. Competitive stores, said Mr. Wilson, packed their candies in stock boxes at the factory and the candy had to be repacked for store display. Moreover, he continued, through the operation of the bonus payment plan for store clerks, there was an incentive upon their part to keep store personnel at a minimum — the fewer clerks in a store, the higher the individual bonus payments to each girl.

He believed that Perfection sales volume per store (1947) was substantially higher than the sales volume of competitive candy outlets.

Mr. Wilson originally (1943 through August of 1946) personally directed all retail store operations. He visited each store daily to check on operations and to assure himself that everything was being handled satisfactorily. He hired all store personnel, supervised advertising and promotion campaigns, and determined details of operating procedures. Daily reports of cash and sales as well as a weekly report of inventory constituted his formal check on store operations. "It worked out beautifully," said Mr. Wilson. The primary management difficulty during this period was to find sufficient supplies of candy to meet the accelerated wartime demand for quality products.

To secure critically short materials, such as butter, sugar, and chocolate, which were necessary for the manufacture of Perfection chocolates for his retail trade[1], Mr. Wilson reduced production of all low-margin chocolates sold to chain buyers; this sharply diminished sales to those two customers. Sales to wholesalers were maintained at varying percentages of their 1941 purchases. These material sources were not sufficient, however, to fill the retail store demand for Perfection chocolates, and a wartime customer ration of one pound per day was instituted. In April, 1947, the improved materials situation permitted the removal of this wartime customer ration in all shops.

Retail Management Corporation

To relieve a heavy personal workload, as well as to prepare for intensive postwar

[1]Sugar rationing for candy manufacturers was first set at 70 percent of the 1941 base use period; this quota was increased to 80 percent in July, 1942. The highest level of ration was reached from August, 1943, to December, 1944, when the sugar ration was 80 percent of the 1941 base, plus a 10 percent bonus. The lowest ration level was 50 percent for the last six months of 1945. In 1947 the ration was 75 percent, but was expected to end in October.

competition, Mr Wilson organized the Retail Management Corporation; that company was to supervise the operations of all Perfection Chocolate Shops. "My usual business day was 15 hours long," he stated. "With conditions in the industry returning to normal I knew that more intensive management efforts were going to be required. I did not have the time to supervise retail store operations in addition to my regular work." Retail Management Corporation was incorporated on August 1, 1946; it was organized and financed in the same manner employed in the incorporation of Perfection shops. Mr. Wilson, as president of Retail Management Corporation, made all major decision for the new concern.

Exhibit 3 shows the intercorporate relationships among Blakeston & Wilson, Retail Management Corporation, and the several Perfection Chocolate Shop companies.

Mr. Wilson appointed his son Kenneth as manager of the new company. Kenneth upon graduation from college in 1937, had been employed by the Sidwell Wilson Company as a salesman. He was assigned to develop wholesale business in the Michigan area. After a six months' trial period, this attempt had been abandoned as unprofitable. Kenneth later worked in the leather industry until his induction into the army. He returned to work for his father in November of 1945. At that time Mr. Wilson planned to have his son handle sales to wholesalers in the Middle Atlantic states. "Sugar rationing continued during 1946, however, and selling to wholesalers was still primarily a matter of ordertaking," said Mr. Wilson, "so we placed Kenneth in charge of the Retail Management Corporation." Kenneth's experience with retail sales and with the candy industry was limited to his earlier work with his father. "I wanted to give my son a chance at the business. He doesn't know much about it, but the way I look at it, I would have to teach either a stranger or my son. I might as well gamble on my son."

The staff of Retail Management Corporation consisted of four persons in addition to Kenneth Wilson. A supervisor of stores inspected (weekly) the appearance of store property, displays, and personnel and filled out an inspection report which noted the results of his investigation; this report was given to the store manager with a duplicate copy forwarded to Kenneth Wilson. To correct any inadequacies noted on the inspection report, each manager checked her Perfection Operating Manual. This manual, written by Sidwell Wilson, outlined in detail approved operating procedures to be used in his retail stores. He believed that, through the use of this manual, store operations and activities were so systematized that necessary supervision was limited to an occasional check by the supervisor of stores, Kenneth Wilson, or himself. Sidwell Wilson's daughter, Thelma, was director of merchandising and purchasing. She determined inventory requirements for the shops and purchased supplies of chocolates from Blakeston & Wilson. A commercial artist developed display and counter card promotional material; radio and newspaper advertisements were prepared by a Chicago advertising agency. A bookkeeper kept necessary accounting records. Neither of the Wilson children had previous experience in retail sales work.

Retail Management Corporation, in supervising the management of all Perfection Chocolate Shops, hired personnel, inspected the appearance of stores and store personnel, kept necessary accounting records, purchased candy and supplies, and furnished necessary financial service and advice. It received 10% of the gross sales of all Perfection shops as a management fee. Retail Management agreed to spend at least one-half of this sum for advertising purposes, the exact amount to be determined by Blakeston & Wilson.

Exhibit 3: Blakeston & Wilson Intercorporation Relationships

BLAKESTON & WILSON
Location: Chicago, Illinois
Board of Directors: Wilson, Blakeston, and Munson
President: Mr. Sidwell Wilson
Function: To manufacture chocolates for wholesale trade and for company-controlled stores.

RETAIL MANAGEMENT CORPORATION
Location: Chicago, Illinois
Board of Directors: Wilson, Blakeston, and Munson
President: Mr. Sidwell Wilson
General Manager: Mr. Kenneth Wilson
Function: To supervise the management of all Perfection Chocolate Shops for Blakeston & Wilson

PERFECTION CHOCOLATE SHOPS, INC.
(Each company was individually incorporated)
Locations: Various cities
Board of Directors: Wilson, Blakeston, and Munson
President: Mr. Sidwell Wilson
Manager: Appointed for each store
Function: To operate shops selling Perfection

Note: Stock ownership of all companies was held by Mr. Wilson, Mr. Blakeston, and Mr. Blakeston's associates. Overall management of all companies was handled by Mr. Sidwell Wilson

The number of Perfection Chocolate Shops supervised by Retail Management increased from 6 to 17 between August, 1946, and April, 1947. Store sales averaged $90,000 per unit. Store rentals ranged from $5,000 to $20,000 a year, with an average payment of $8,000. Overhead costs were approximately 3% of gross store sales. Invested capital, per store, varied from $10,000 to $15,000. All shops were successful financially.

Eight of the eleven new shops had been established in towns within a 200-mile radius of Chicago, e.g., Gary, Indiana, and Peoria, Illinois. Perfection shops in all eight non-Chicago cities came into competition with retail outlets such as drug and department stores which also sold Perfection packaged chocolates distributed by company wholesalers. This created a great deal of resentment on the part of the wholesalers who felt their market was being usurped.

Price

Perfection chocolates had originally retailed at 65 cents a pound; by 1946, as had been previously stated, the retail price had been increased to 75 cents a pound or $1.45 for the two-pound box. Retail prices were the same at both Perfection Chocolate Shops and retail stores supplied by company wholesalers. In 1947, Blakeston & Wilson sold Perfection chocolates to its wholesalers at 40 cents a pound and to Perfection shops at 42 cents a pound.

Manufacturing costs had increased 17 cents per pound between 1943 and 1946. Furthermore, prices of chocolate and other raw materials had continued to increase during the first quarter of 1947, and the possible removal of sugar rationing in October of 1947 was expected to raise the price of that important commodity.

Despite rising material costs, retail price reductions were already appearing among some brands of packaged chocolates. One leading chain competitor of Perfection had reduced the price of its two-pound box of candy from $1.55 to $1.50 in March of 1947. Mr. Sidwell Wilson did not plan to reduce the retail price of his candy to meet this competitive development. Any price reduction, he believed, would first have to be made to the wholesaler trade since he was well acquainted with the extremely competitive aspects of wholesaling.

When material prices returned to normal, Blakeston & Wilson planned to use any savings resulting from lowered costs to improve the quality of Perfection chocolates. "Our chocolates, which we sold for 65 cents a pound in 1943, were of better quality than chocolates which we now sell for 75 cents a pound," Mr. Wilson stated. The company had been forced to reduce product quality, as had its competitors, to take care of increased raw material prices.

Advertising

"We spent over $100,000 in 1946 advertising Perfection chocolates, said Mr. Wilson. Two-thirds of this money was expended for radio advertisements, the remaining one-third for newspaper advertisements. Blakeston & Wilson financed but a small part of the Perfection advertising fund; most of the money had been supplied by the Retail Management Corporation with assistance from individual Perfection stores. Radio and newspaper advertisements were concentrated in the Chicago area and in cities where Perfection shops were located. These advertisements stressed the quality of Perfection chocolates but did not mention that Perfection candies were hand-dipped; this was in conformity with industry advertising practices. By mutual agreement candy manufacturers did not advertise whether their chocolates were hand-dipped or machine-dipped.

Advertising expenditures for Perfection chocolates, among packaged and bulk chocolate manufacturers, were second only to those of the Stephen F. Whitman & Son Company in Philadelphia. That company manufactured nationally advertised and distributed Sampler chocolates which retailed at $1.75 for a 20-ounce package. Mr. Sidwell Wilson said that expenditures for advertising in 1947 would be substantially higher than 1946 totals.

Manufacturing

The Blakeston & Wilson factory originally occupied the first three floors of a warehouse; the company had recently expanded into two floors of an adjoining building. Manufacturing operations and storage facilities were located on each floor so that raw materials would be in close proximity to the production activities in which they were used. All manufacturing departments were air conditioned, and the plant was equipped with cold storage facilities capable of holding

300,000 pounds of finished candy. Candy-making machinery was old but in good repair. In 1947 the plant was producing approximately 22,000 pounds of candy per day, five days a week. Capacity plant production was 30,000 pounds per day.

Mr. Sidwell Wilson believed that company manufacturing operations were efficient because: (1) he personally owned and operated his business, which gave him a close check on all operations; (2) he had invented a continuous process production line which enabled him to hand-dip chocolates at a lower cost than other competitive hand-dip chocolate manufacturers; and (3) his labor force was more efficient and effective than employee groups in other companies.

Mr. Wilson did not believe that any company could secure a significant advantage over its competitors as far as raw materials purchasing was concerned. Sugar and chocolate prices, he said, were normally set by the New York City and foreign exchanges, and the price for a specified type of product was identical to all large-scale purchasers. Sugar, the primary ingredient of candy, was purchased by most companies on a day-to-day basis. "The only way normally to secure bargain sugar prices would be to gamble on futures—we tried that once and lost." Manufacturers of medium-price candies, however, could and did make some savings on minor items by using substitute or average quality fruit centers, cream, and butter. Perfection chocolates, contrary to this practice, were always made from the highest grade ingredients obtainable.

Mr. Smith, production manager, was assisted in factory supervision by four foremen and two floor ladies. He believed this number was the minimum staff required. In fact, when one of these assistants was ill, Mr. Smith had to take over temporarily his or her duties. He received two weekly production reports, which were also available for Mr. Wilson's use. They listed production by department, the number of manufacturing employees and total hours worked, and indirect factory expenses. He believed, however, that his most effective control technique was close personal supervision over factory operations. Mr. Smith was completely responsible for all manufacturing activities; Mr. Wilson did not concern himself with production problems unless some major change in policy was contemplated.

Hand-dipped chocolates were more expensive to produce than machine-dipped candies primarily because of substantially increased labor costs. Mr. Smith estimated that machine-dipping resulted in savings of from four to five cents a pound in labor and material costs over Blakeston & Wilson's hand-dipping process. "We can afford to hand-dip our chocolates only because of the savings effected by our low sales cost."

Mr. Sidwell Wilson, in 1937, had developed and patented his continuous production line process for dipping, cooling, and packing varied selections of chocolates. This process, he believed, enabled Blakeston & Wilson to hand-dip chocolates for three cents less per pound than competing hand-dip chocolate manufacturers. He had installed four of these units in his factory in 1938 at a cost of $4,000 per unit. In 1947 two units were operating at capacity (7,500 pounds per unit a day); the other two units because of material shortages, were operating at partial capacity. Mr. Wilson had attempted to sell the process to other manufacturers for $100,000 per unit, but only one sale had been made to a small Evanston, Illinois, chocolate manufacturer.

The company's labor force was composed of 200 employees, most of whom were women engaged in dipping and packing chocolates. Labor and management relations were excellent; the company had never been organized. Wages equalled those of competing firms in the Chicago area; in addition to their base pay, all employees who had been with the company more than five years (96) participated in a profit-sharing plan which company officials believed stimulated employee interest and productive efficiency.

Wages of employees had risen steadily since 1938. At that time dippers were paid 30 cents an hour; in 1947 they started at 87 cents an hour. In addition to base pay, dippers were eligible for a bonus of from one to nine cents an hour if they approached or reached the maximum production rate (24 pieces a minute); in 1947 most dippers were earning the maximum bonus. Mr. Smith awarded the bonus to dippers by occasionally checking production operations. "The bonus is based on my judgment as to how well they are doing," he said, "not on time or motion studies." The bonus system, which had been in effect for four years, had not been extended to other employees.

Mr. Smith personally handled the limited amount of cost accounting work done on all manufacturing operations. He had established standard costs on materials and direct labor for producing one hundred pound lots of each type of candy included in the Perfection selection. Standards for burden had not been established, he said, since these charges were fairly constant from year to year. Standard costs were occasionally checked against actual costs when Mr. Smith believed this necessary. Though many of the company's standard cost sheets were obsolete because of changes in materials prices, Mr. Smith did not believe revisions were necessary so long as the company secured a 28% gross manufacturing operating profit (exclusive of burden charges). Exhibit 4 lists standard cost information on a typical chocolate item manufactured both for bulk and package sale.

Chain Store Customers

By April, 1947, increased sales of bulk and packaged chocolates were again being made to the variety chain with which Mr. Blakeston was associated. Mr. Wilson had not re-established sales relations with the retail grocery chain to which he had sold chocolates prior to World War II. That company was building its own large candy factory and was installing candy departments in all its retail outlets. "We don't want to sell to any customer who is in competition with us in

Exhibit 4: Blakeston & Wilson — Standard Costs for 100-Pound Mix of Chocolate-Covered Cream Candy

Materials	$26.97
Direct Labor	7.65
	$34.62

Source: Company records.

the manufacture of candy," Mr. Wilson declared. He had not yet attempted to secure another large grocery chain outlet since a shortage of raw materials still hampered production. Such an outlet would be necessary during normal times, he felt, to insure his plant of capacity operations during the entire year.

Control

In conformity with Mr. Wilson's desire to keep administrative expenses to a minimum, only a few reports were prepared for his use. He received a monthly balance sheet and profit and loss statement from all corporations as well as daily reports on Blakeston & Wilson production and sales made by individual Perfection Chocolate Shops.

Mr. Sidwell Wilson, in addition to the investigations made by Retail Management Corporation, inspected several Perfection shops on one day each week. "As far as store operations are concerned, our best indicator of trouble is when customers begin to complain — then we start action," he said.

Mr. Sidwell Wilson personally checked wholesaler relations on his visits to those concerns. "That gives me all the control I need over those operations. I believe this system will be effective as long as I am personally running the business; it may not prove effective under other operating conditions." He further believed that the widespread advertising campaign for Perfection chocolates would provide an incentive both for his wholesalers to continue to carry the line and for the retailers supplied by these firms to hold to the advertised price.

Executive Organization

The executive organization of Blakeston & Wilson in April, 1947, was substantially the same as in 1938. An assistant treasurer had been engaged in 1946 to take charge of all detailed accounting work with the exception of cost accounting records. Mr. Sidwell Wilson, 56 years of age, was still actively engaged in all company operations. "I can do anything from firing a boiler to selling packaged chocolates," he stated. He personally approved all major policy and operating decisions made for Blakeston & Wilson, Retail Management Corporation, or any of the 17 Perfection Chocolate Shop corporations.

At quarterly meetings of the board of directors, Mr. Wilson discussed general company problems with the board. All Perfection Chocolate Shops were operating at a profit, and Mr. Blakeston and his associates were convinced that the decision to enter the retail sales field had been a wise one. All Blakeston & Wilson preferred stock had been retired by this time, and Mr. Wilson owned 52% of the outstanding common stock.

Mr. Smith, 45 years of age, had been an accounting instructor before becoming associated with the company. The office staff of the company, excluding secretarial help, consisted of three women who handled all sales and production records as well as payroll accounts. "Other companies of comparable size have large administrative organizations - up to 25 persons. By keeping a small stable customer list and using a minimum of expensive records, our administrative section can be kept to a minimum size," said Mr. Smith.

Expansion

Mr. Wilson was planning to expand his chain of retail shops. Four additional store leases had been signed, and before the end of 1947 the company planned to operate between 25 and 30 shops. "If I were a younger man, we would open 500." He believed that Perfection shops should expand immediately: (1) to get as many consumers as possible familiar with Perfection chocolates and (2) to become established in the retail candy business during 1947, a time when raw material shortages prevented other companies from entering this field. In 1947 about one-third of Blakeston & Wilson production was being sold through company-controlled stores, and Mr. Wilson wanted to increase substantially that amount.

Among the potential sites for new Perfection shops were Cleveland and Detroit. Retail candy shops, both locally owned and chain stores, were already in operation in these towns. Previous expansion had placed Perfection shops in direct competition with a seminational chain of retail candy stores. That company, incorporated in 1919, operated several hundred stores in the Middle West and along the East Coast which sold medium-price hand-dipped chocolates and salted nuts. Mr. Wilson believed that company's sales volume averaged only $50,000 per store. "We know how to sell in volume at low costs."

Competition for Perfection chocolates sold by company wholesalers came from hundreds of locally and regionally promoted packaged chocolates as well as from several brands of nationally distributed candies.

Mr. Wilson estimated that the productive capacity of the candy industry had expanded by 30% since 1939. Industry sales in 1939 were approximately $308 million; in 1944 they were $658 million and in 1945 they were $620 million. During the period plain candies had increased 30% in volume whereas packaged candies, primarily boxed chocolates, had risen 310%. As of 1947, numerous companies were planning or were already in the process of plant expansion; for example, the Kraft Cheese Company, which had entered the caramel business before the war, planned erection of a $750,000 candy plant in Kendallville, Indiana. An interesting development was the rapid rise in chain grocery store candy sales. As one writer put it (in 1946) "Grocery stores now sell a larger volume of candy than of coffee or butter."

In Exhibits 5 and 6 are shown the income and balance sheet data of Blakeston & Wilson for the years 1938 - 1946 inclusive. In Exhibit 7 are shown the combined balance sheet data of the Perfection Chocolate Shops for the year 1946.

Exhibit 5: Blakeston & Wilson Income Statements — 1938 through 1946 (in Thousands)

	1938	1939	1940	1941	1942	1943	1944	1945	1946
Net sales	$286	$562	$668	$799	$909	$1,160	$1,239	$1,110	$1,349
% of sales	100.0%	100.0%	100.0%	100.0%	100.0%	100.0%	100.0%	100.0%	100.0%
Cost of sales	231	470	561	663	762	877	906	867	1,041
% of sales	80.8%	83.6%	84.0%	83.0%	83.8%	75.6%	73.1%	78.1%	77.2%
Gross profit on sales	$ 55	$ 92	$107	$136	$147	$ 283	$ 333	$ 243	$ 308
% of sales	19.2%	16.4%	16.0%	17.0%	16.2%	24.4%	26.9%	21.9%	22.8%
Selling, general and administrative expenses:									
Shipping	$ 13	$ 33	$ 44	$ 45	$ 37	$ 40	$ 44	$ 40	$ 44
% of sales	4.6%	5.9%	6.7%	5.6%	4.1%	3.5%	3.5%	3.7%	3.3%
Advertising, travel, entertainment, commissions, and other selling expenses	6	11	13	20	11	17	21	34	23
% of sales	2.1%	2.0%	1.9%	2.5%	1.2%	1.5%	1.7%	3.0%	1.7%
Executive and office salaries	12	18	19	26	40	40	40	45	50
% of sales	4.2%	3.2%	2.8%	3.2%	4.5%	3.3%	3.3%	4.0%	3.7%
Contributions to profit-sharing plan						19	21	27	
% of sales						1.5%	1.9%	2.0%	
Miscellaneous	6	5	11	16	16	23	25	25	30
% of sales	2.0%	0.9%	1.6%	2.1%	1.7%	2.0%	2.0%	2.3%	2.2%
Total expenses	$ 37	$ 67	$ 87	$107	$104	$ 120	$ 149	$ 165	$ 174
% of sales	12.9%	12.0%	13.0%	13.4%	11.5%	10.3%	12.0%	14.9%	12.9%
Net profit before federal taxes on income	$ 18	$ 25	$ 20	$ 29	$ 43	$ 163	$ 184	$ 78	$ 134
% of sales	6.3%	4.4%	3.0%	3.6%	4.7%	14.1%	14.9%	7.0%	9.9%
Provision for estimated federal taxes on income and excess profits	$ 3	$ 4	$ 3	$ 8	$ 18	$ 131	$ 150	$ 50	$ 60
% of sales	1.0%	0.7%	0.4%	1.0%	2.0%	11.3%	12.1%	4.5%	4.4%
Net profit carried to surplus	$ 15	$ 21	$ 17	$ 21	$ 25	$ 32	$ 34	$ 28	$ 74
% of sales	5.3 %	3.7%	2.6%	2.6%	2.7%	2.8%	2.8%	2.5%	5.5%

Note: Totals from 1943 through 1946 include sales made by Blakeston & Wilson to company-controlled Perfection shops.
Source: Company records

Exhibit 6: Blakeston & Wilson Balance Sheets - 1938 through 1946 (in Thousands)

ASSETS	1938	1939	1940	1941	1942	1943	1944	1945	1946
Current Assets:									
Cash in Bank and on Hand	$ 11	$ 10	$ 13	$ 8	$ 32	$161	$202	$134	$227
Accounts Receivable	21	24	33	26	54	73	60	61	26
Inventories at Cost or Market, Whichever is Lower	9	21	24	90	44	36	36	62	118
Total Current Assets	$ 41	$ 55	$ 70	$124	$130	$270	$318	$257	$371
Cash Surrender value of Life insurance policy	1	2	8	9	9	10	11	16	17
Together	$ 42	$ 57	$ 78	$133	$139	$208	$329	$273	$388
Postwar Refundable Portion of Estimated Excess Profits Tax					12	26			
Fixed Assets	13	39	45	45	38	34	38	33	39
Deferred Charges	8	13	19	11	10	9	17	17	14
TOTAL ASSETS	$ 63	$109	$142	$189	$187	$335	$410	$323	$441
LIABILITIES AND CAPITAL									
Current Liabilities:									
Note Payable at Bank			$ 7	$ 37	$ 7	$ 7	$ 6		
Accounts Payable and Accrued Expenses	$ 15	$ 19	31	25	20	29	67	$ 41	$ 58
Reserve for Federal and State Taxes	3	5	5	10	21	139	200	133	160
Total Current Liabilities	$ 18	$ 24	$ 43	$ 72	$ 48	$175	$273	$174	$218
Postwar Refund of Estimated Federal Excess Profits Tax						$ 12	$ 26		
Capital Stock:									
Preferred Stock:									
Authorized and issued - 500 Shares of $6 Cumulative Without Par Value	$ 30	$ 50	$ 50	$ 50	$ 50	$ 50	$ 50	$ 50	$ 50
Less: Held in Treasury						18	50	50	50
Common Stock:									
Authorized, issued, and Outstanding 1,000 Shares Without Par Value							104**	104	104
	$ 30	$ 50	$ 50	$ 50	$ 50	$ 32	$104	$104	$104
Earned Surplus:									
Balance, January 1		$ 15	$ 35	$ 49	$ 67	$ 89	$116	$ 7	$ 45
Add: net Profit	$ 15	21	17	21	25	32	34	28	74
Postwar Refund of Excess profits Taxes								26*	
Less: Dividends Paid		1	2	3	3	3	39	16	
Amount Transferred to Capital Stock Account							104*		
Under Accrual of Prior Years' Taxes, etc.			1						
Balance, Dec. 31	$ 15	$ 35	$ 49	$ 67	$ 89	$116	$ 7	$ 45	$119
TOTAL LIABILITIES AND CAPITAL	$ 63	$109	$142	$189	$187	$335	$410	$323	$441

300 shares of preferred issued and outstanding December 31, 1938

**Stated value of $100 per share of common voted by board of directors

* Treated as deferred income in prior years, transferred to earned surplus December 31, 1945

**Exhibit 7: Blakeston & Wilson Balance Sheet as of December 31, 1946
Perfection Chocolate Shops (Combined) (in Thousands)**

ASSETS		
Current Assets:		
Cash		$130
Inventories (at cost)		18
Total Current Assets		$148
Fixed Assets		41
Deferred Charges:		
Improvement to Leased Premises	$56	
Unexpired insurance premiums	7	
Total Deferred Charges		63
TOTAL ASSETS		$252
LIABILITIES AND CAPITAL		
Current Liabilities:		
Accounts Payable		$ 32
Reserve for state and Federal Taxes		52
Total Current Liabilities		$ 84
Capital Stock and Surplus		
Capital Stock:		
Preferred	$ 47	
Common	19	66
Earned Surplus:		
Balance, December 31, 1945	$ 20	
Net Profit, 1946	113	
	$133	
Less: Dividends Paid	31	
		102
TOTAL LIABILITIES AND CAPITAL		$252

Source: Company records

CATV ENTERPRISES, INC.: THE CABLE TV INDUSTRY

CATV Enterprises, Inc., has a permit from New York City and State to operate a cable TV system in Riverdale (an affluent section of the Bronx, one of the five boroughs in New York City). The area is comprised of approximately 25,000 dwelling units: 2,500 of these are private homes and the remainder are mostly large apartment houses [Management 1992]. At the end of 1991, CATV had more than 10,100 subscribers who paid $12.95 monthly for basic cable service [CATV 1992].

In early 1992, CATV was a privately-held corporation with 51 percent of its stock owned by Group W Satellite Communications, Inc. (Group W Cable) and 49 percent owned by the estate of the company's founder, Theodore Granik. Since 1967, the company has been managed by Westinghouse Electric Company, of which Group W is a subsidiary. From 1967 to 1987 no capital investments for improving the system were made. This was largely because of difficulties with New York City in obtaining a permanent operating permit, known as a franchise. A franchise is typically granted for 10 to 15 years; without one there was no guarantee of a minimum life for the system.

From 1967 to 1987, the loudest complaints from Riverdale residents centered around the desire for more programming. In 1987, CATV partially addressed these complaints and replaced two public broadcasting stations with two popular cable channels. In 1988 and again in 1989, further changes and technical improvements were made. All of these upgrades were funded internally.

Additional internally funded upgrades were made during 1991 to address FCC regulations which prohibited signal leakage. These upgrades required the rewiring of 80 percent of

Riverdale's private homes and 50 percent of its apartment buildings. The result was a dramatic increase in picture quality and a 37 percent increase in subscribers.

From 1982 to 1985 Westinghouse owned and operated over 150 cable systems across the nation under its Group W Cable subsidiary [Weinstein 1986, p.12]. In 1984, Group W Cable was the third largest multisystem operator (MSO) in the United States, with as many as 2,000,000 subscribers. However, Figure 1 shows that by 1991 Group W Cable was not even one of the top 30 MSOs nationally.

CATV is still owned by Westinghouse only because of difficulties encountered with New York City in selling it. In 1984, a franchise for the entire Bronx, including Riverdale, was awarded to Cablevision Systems Corp., a large MSO. Since New York State regulations forbid the granting of exclusive franchises, the status of CATV Enterprises was unclear [Plunkett & Zacks 1989]. As of early 1992, CATV's status still had not been clarified, as both state and city authorities had not moved to address the issue. The general belief was that both the city and state would like to see a competitive cable environment in the Bronx [Medzon 1991].

When the franchise for the entire borough of the Bronx was awarded to Cablevision, Group W decided it would be easier to sell CATV to Cablevision than to worry about possible difficulties with the government. Cablevision, while initially interested in purchasing CATV, backed out of the deal in 1991 [Medzon 1991]. Cablevision claimed the deal fell through because of its declining stock value and the resulting inability to raise the needed funds (approximately $20 million). However, according to CATV managers, the real reason Cablevision backed out of the deal was three-fold:

- Cablevision realized it could quickly wire Riverdale from adjoining sections of the Bronx. This meant Cablevision could be in Riverdale and in competition with CATV by January 1993. Cablevision felt CATV would be unable to upgrade its system in this time to compete effectively.
- CATV did not have a franchise and it would cost in excess of $1 million to meet the city's requirements to obtain one. Cablevision knew that without the franchise it would be very difficult for CATV to sell to another major system operator.
- Group W desired to get out of the cable system operating business, so Cablevision knew Group W would be reluctant to finance any CATV plant upgrades.

In short, Cablevision realized it could wire Riverdale and hoped to force CATV out of business by some time in 1994 [Management 1992]. In early 1992, CATV's management needed to reach a decision on the disposition of the company. Issues to discuss included:

- Will conditions, politically and legally, change to allow for CATV's sale? In the past, the sale of CATV has been prohibited by the City of New York.
- Could the owners of CATV receive a franchise instead of a temporary operating permit if systems are upgraded? The State refuses to grant a franchise since the system does not meet its technical standards.
- Would anyone buy CATV without a franchise? Anyone buying CATV would be gambling on

Figure 1: Top Cable System Operators, 1991
(Ranked by number of basic subscribers)

System operator	Basic subscribers (000)	System operator	Basic subscribers (000)
TCI	12,334	Century	884
ATC	4,700	Falcon Cable TV	874
Continental	2,800	Paragon	838
Warner	1,677	Telecable	641
Comcast	1,665	Scripps-Howard	630
Cox	1,661	KBLCOM	559
Cablevision Sys.	1,651	Cencom	552
Storer	1,616	Tele-media	531
Jones Intercable	1,493	Lenfest Group	510
Nehouse	1,267	Multivision Cable	477
Adelphia	1,146	TCA Group	450
Cablevision Ind.	1,132	Post-Newsweek Cable	444
Times Mirror	1,126	Maclean Hunter Cable	404
Viacom	1,084	Wometco Cable	382

Source: Adapted from "Operating Gains Continue," *Standard and Poors Industry Surveys,* February 13, 1992, pp. M29-30.

getting a franchise after rebuilding the system at a cost of $1 million.

- Could CATV compete with Cablevision? Cablevision, one of the largest and most aggressive cable system operators, offered a multitude of pay-TV services and cable programming.
- Will the growth trend in the cable industry continue? Cable television historically has been an industry which has found new avenues for profit. A U.S. Commerce Department study, however, stated that "steady growth in the cable universe will continue to cut down potential new subscriber revenue and lead to single-digit cable growth throughout the 1990s, replacing the typical double-digit growth of the 1980s" [Sukow, p. 6].
- Would Cablevision rethink its decision if CATV emerged as a viable competitor? CATV is able to offer the same services as Cablevision at better rates.

If the legal conditions surrounding CATV's sale change, the company could be a very valuable acquisition for another system operator (by increasing market share and generating incremental revenues). If cable growth continues then CATV's revenue potential increases, making continued operations a viable alternative. If this should occur Cablevision may decide that CATV is a viable competitor and renew its efforts to purchase CATV.

THE INDUSTRY AND COMPETITIVE MARKET

THE CABLE TELEVISION INDUSTRY

The cable television industry brings a variety of programs into people's homes through the use of a cable, or wire. It consists of four segments: programmers, cable system operators,

Figure 2: The Growth of Cable Television: Number of Subscribers

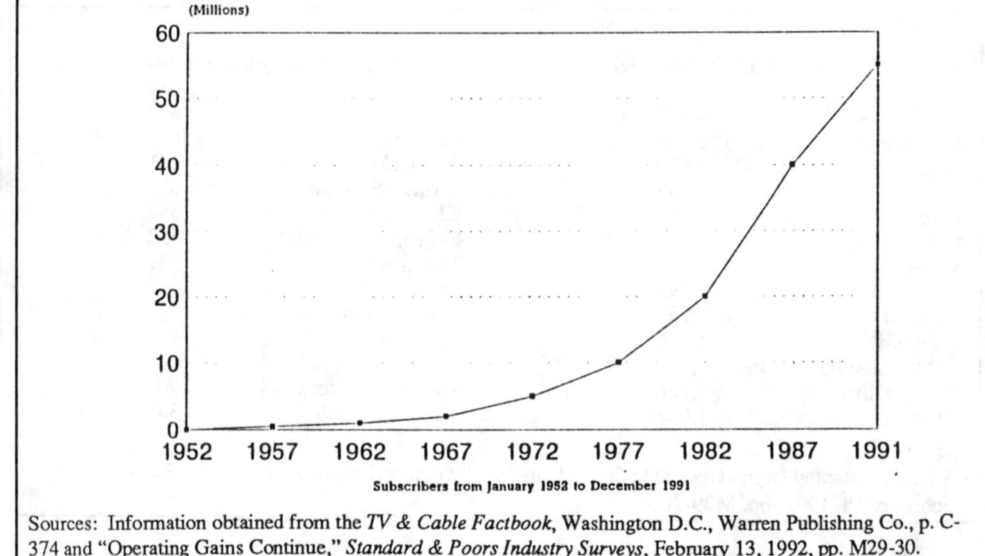

Sources: Information obtained from the *TV & Cable Factbook*, Washington D.C., Warren Publishing Co., p. C-374 and "Operating Gains Continue," *Standard & Poors Industry Surveys*, February 13, 1992, pp. M29-30.

distributors of programs to cable system operators, and equipment manufacturers.

Programmers are businesses that are involved in the production of programming, such as the Cable News Network (CNN), Home Box Office (HBO), Showtime, or Music Television (MTV). They sell programs to the cable system operator who in turn sells them to the residents of the area in which it does business. The programmers receive revenue from advertisers, but this does not generate enough profits to pay for quality programming. Many times, programming networks just starting up operations will *pay* operators a per-subscriber fee for the first few years just to get on to the system. Once established, they then *charge* the systems per subscriber. These charges generally range from five cents to 25 cents depending on the system size. Programming distributors use satellite or microwave relays to get the programming from the programmer to the operating systems. They sell their services to the programmer.

Because of the variety and uniqueness of some of cable TV's programming, as well as its growing ability to bid for exclusive productions or sporting events, it has been steadily growing in importance. Many states, such as New York, have passed legislation guaranteeing residents the right to receive cable TV services. Landlords cannot stop tenants from receiving cable any more than they can interfere with their obtaining telephone service [New York State 1984].

Figure 2 depicts cable TV's growth, in number of subscribers, from 1952-1991. In 1962 there were fewer than 800 cable systems in the United States, with a total of 850,000 subscribers [Weinstein 1986 p.1]. In 1991 more than 90 percent of the homes in the U.S. were able to subscribe to cable TV, and approximately 54 percent of them did for a total of 54,900,000 customers ["Operating Gains Continue" 1992].

Figure 3: The Elements of a Cable System (Plant)

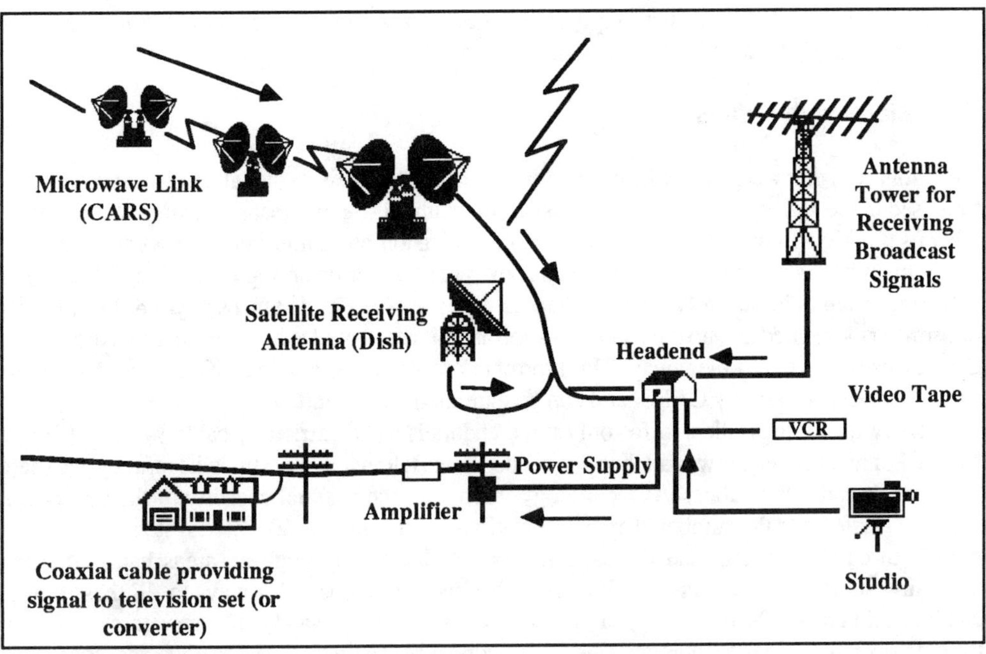

Its Origins

The cable TV industry began in the late 1940s as a means of bringing television to people living in areas that had difficulty with reception. These areas included locations that were too far from transmission sources and others that were obstructed from receiving signals, for example, by a hilly terrain or large masses of buildings. The early systems were more of a community antenna than what 1991 viewers would consider cable TV. The first cable systems picked up local television signals. Later, they utilized microwave relays to get stations that were further away. These microwave relays eventually were used to transmit programming dedicated to cable TV, such as Home Box Office (HBO). As technology advanced and a need for simultaneous distribution became important, satellites were used for program distribution.

The "Community Antenna"

Resourceful entrepreneurs, or sometimes the communities themselves, would erect a tower in the highest area and install an antenna on it. By retransmitting the amplified signals along a coaxial cable (an electrical conduit capable of carrying as many as 70 television channels), they were able to supply the community with television reception. However, while the coaxial cable was capable of carrying 70 channels in the early days, the electronics at the reception point were not. Cable TV is also known as the CATV (Community Antenna Television) industry. The electronics, cable, and antennas supplying service to a community, as shown in Figure 3, are commonly called the cable system or cable plant.

Microwave Relays

For areas that were too far from a television source to receive a signal, microwave relays — first used in the 1950s — provided a means of importing distant broadcast signals. A microwave relay uses a high-frequency signal to retransmit television programs from one point to another. The transmitter is mounted on a specially constructed tower or on top of a tall building. The receiving antenna is similarly located up to 25 miles away. For distances beyond this, another transmitter — located next to the receiver — retransmits the signal to another microwave receiver that can also be up to 25 miles away. This type of microwave link is called a "Community Antenna Relay Service," or simply CARS, and can be extended almost indefinitely.

Early technology allowed for only three channels to be carried by cable systems [Simon 1989]. For most areas this was all that was needed since television was still in its infancy and there were few broadcast stations. As technology improved, the channel capacity of the equipment increased faster than the number of available stations. By the mid-1950s cable systems were being built with equipment that had the capacity for 12 channels (though no areas had that many television stations) [Weinstein 1986, p.1.]. Cable operators looked for ways to fill these empty channels. In the 1960s availability of microwave links increased and cable operators used them to bring distant stations to their systems. This occurred even when the operators were located in large urban markets with several local television broadcasters.

Home Box Office

Early visions of cable TV were of a bright future because of the many imagined possibilities. These included interactive capabilities with banks, shopping, and the like. The problem was that the technology had not arrived yet. The industry languished for years awaiting the arrival of the prophesy. Then along came Home Box Office and the industry soared. Home Box Office, commonly called HBO, was the first premium cable service. With this unique product, which was introduced in November of 1972, a subscriber could watch first-run movies and special events in their entirety for an extra monthly fee [Brand 1987, p.64].

HBO was a small subsidiary of Sterling Manhattan Cable, a company controlled by Time, Inc. At first HBO was distributed to other cable systems by videotape and then in 1974, through microwave links. At this time they served almost 60,000 subscribers in 42 cable systems [Weinstein 1986, pp.2,3].

Satellite Distribution

HBO was important to the industry, not for the product but for the method in which it was

Figure 4: Satellite Distribution

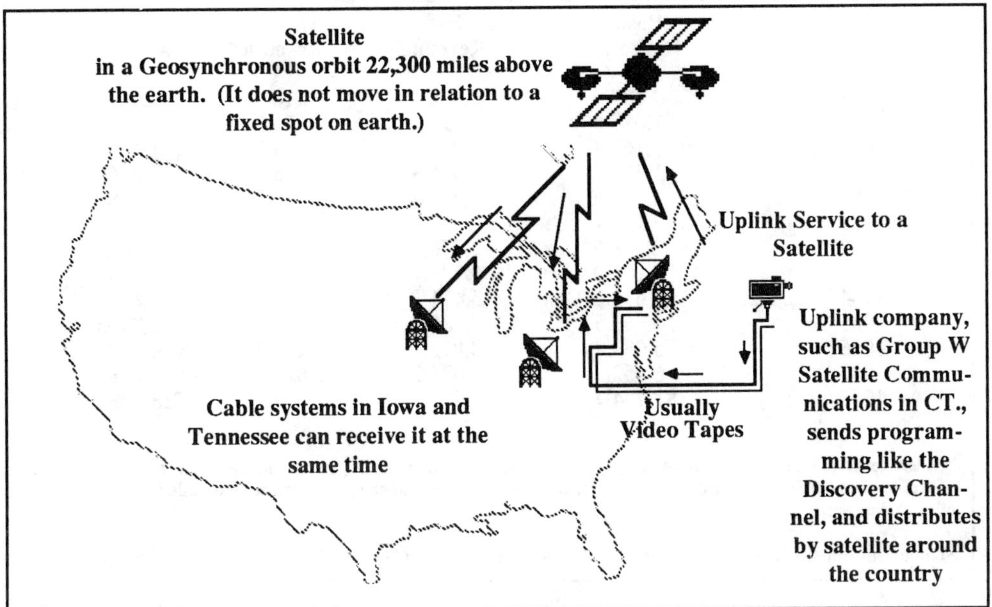
Satellite
in a Geosynchronous orbit 22,300 miles above the earth. (It does not move in relation to a fixed spot on earth.)
Uplink Service to a Satellite
Uplink company, such as Group W Satellite Communications in CT., sends programming like the Discovery Channel, and distributes by satellite around the country
Cable systems in Iowa and Tennessee can receive it at the same time
Usually Video Tapes

delivered to cable systems. While microwave links could serve local systems, it was not economically feasible for Time to set up its own network nationwide. Time, Inc. needed a method for delivering HBO to cable systems across the country simultaneously. With a large paying audience, it was reasoned, HBO could afford to buy programming good enough to attract new subscribers. With that in mind, Jerry Levin, a middle-level executive of Time, came up with an idea that changed the industry: satellite distribution [Brand 1987, p.31]. Suddenly, distance was no longer a concern of programmers.

Satellite distribution is a method of sending a signal to a satellite which is in a stationary, or geosynchronous, orbit above the earth. By sending a signal from the earth to a satellite, having the satellite increase its strength with electronic amplifiers, and transmitting the signal back to Earth, it became possible to send programming anywhere in the country. Figure 4 shows a satellite distribution system.

In 1989 nine satellites carried cable TV programming: each was capable of retransmitting up to 24 different signals. RCA Corporation, Hughes Aircraft Company, and AT&T were the principal owners of these communications satellites [*TV & Cable Factbook* 1989, p. C-374].

When HBO decided to use satellites for program distribution in 1975, no cable system had the $100,000 worth of equipment needed to receive the signal [Brand 1987 p.65]. Time took the chance that good programming would persuade operators to buy HBO and this paid off. The success of pay programming, such as HBO, can be seen in Figure 5, which compares industry revenues for basic and pay-TV services from 1976-1988. Only 22 percent of basic subscribers purchased a pay-TV service in 1976; the number had climbed to almost 70 percent five years later.

Figure 5: Cable Revenue From Subscriber Services: 1976-1988 (In millions)

Year	Basic Revenue	Pay Revenue	Other Revenue*	Total Revenue
1976	$887.0	$66.1	$16.4	$969.5
1977	1,024.8	123.6	71.5	1,219.9
1978	1,167.4	242.7	89.3	1,499.4
1979	1,355.4	435.5	115.5	1,906.4
1980	1,648.5	781.4	168.7	2,598.6
1981	2,100.1	1,332.8	280.7	3,713.6
1982	2,578.6	2,076.4	437.6	5,092.6
1983	3,101.0	2,786.7	630.9	6,518.6
1984	3,632.2	3,411.1	855.4	7,898.7
1985	4,366.5	3,788.7	1,084.8	9,240.0
1986	5,083.7	3,872.4	1,424.2	10,380.3
1987	6,552.7	4,074.2	1,621.7	12,248.6
1988 (est.)	$7,724.7	$4,278.9	$1,819.7	$13,823.3

*Other Revenue includes: pay-per-view, home shopping, expanded basic, installation, advertising, and miscellaneous (such as: security, remote control, converters, second sets, etc.) For more detailed data, please refer to the source.

Source: Information obtained from Paul Kagan Associates, Inc., Cable TV Investor, Nov. 29, 1988, p.9.

For the same period, industry revenues from pay-TV services increased from seven percent of total revenues to 36 percent. By 1991 these figures had risen to 85 percent and 43 percent, respectively. The ability of satellites to distribute programming unique to cable television led to the industry's success [Weinstein 1986, p.4.]. With the addition of pay programming, the regular programs included with a subscription to cable TV became known as "Basic Service."

The initial cost of the receiving antenna necessary to get satellite programming was expensive. The antenna, a familiar site on the American landscape, resembles a large dish. The dish is needed to gather the relatively weak signals and focus them on the receiving antenna, which sits slightly above the dish. Early dishes were 30 feet wide (as specified by the FCC). By the late 1970s the FCC had relaxed its requirements, allowing for a 15-foot dish. Equipment cost was also reduced by the size reduction. The price dropped to $15,000, bringing satellite reception to almost all cable systems [Weinstein 1986, p.4.].

CAPITAL GAINS: MOTIVATION FOR CABLE SYSTEM GROWTH

The cable industry developed because of a need. Fueled by its promise, it grew quickly. Early investors believed this industry was going to soar. Cable franchises were bid for and systems were built in a wild frenzy. The idea was to build a system and then sell it in order to realize a capital gain of intangible goodwill. After most areas in the country were wired, investors tried a new approach for obtaining capital gains from their systems — maximizing their cash flows.

Forecasts of the vast variety of programming and the interactive possibilities of cable

Figure 6: Construction Expenditures: 1975-1988

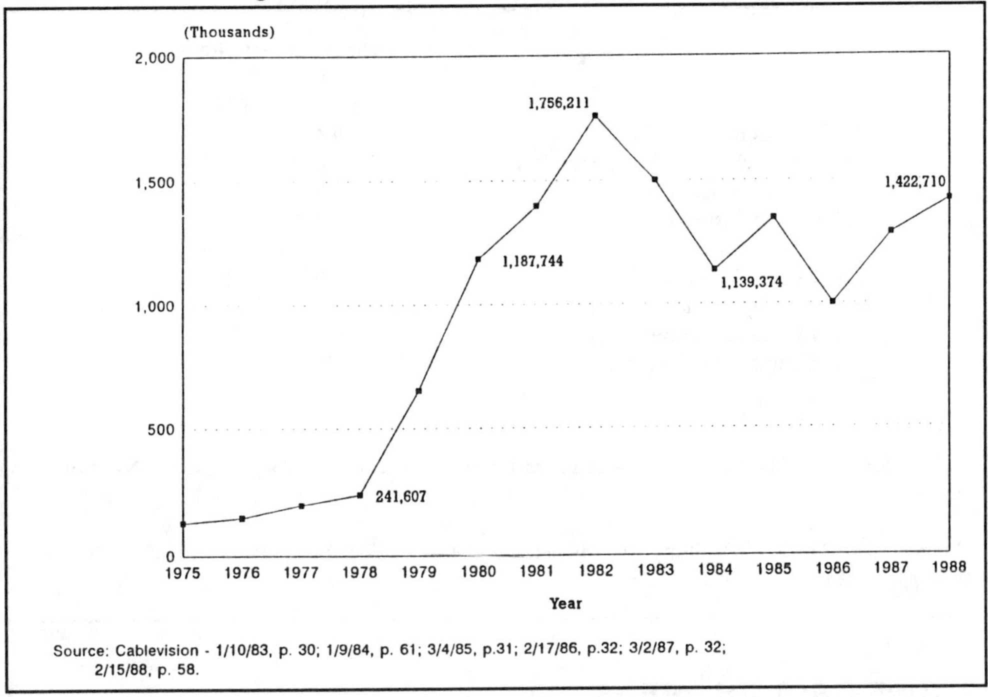

Source: Cablevision - 1/10/83, p. 30; 1/9/84, p. 61; 3/4/85, p.31; 2/17/86, p.32; 3/2/87, p. 32; 2/15/88, p. 58.

spurred the early entrepreneurs to wire the country. They saw, besides programming, alarm systems, pay-per-view (a method of charging for a single program), communication with your bank from your TV set, and other exciting possibilities for making money [Brand 1987, p.65; Weinstein 1986, p.52]. The cable TV industry grew rapidly in the 1970s. Although most newly formed cable companies took heavy losses, mostly from early lack of public enthusiasm, the industry's potential attracted investors. Prudently bidding for cable franchises from communities, these early investors hoped to build cable systems then sell them at substantial profits. As can be seen in Figure 6, in the late 1970s and early 1980s there was a steady increase in the construction of new cable systems.

When most areas were wired for cable, investors — still spurred by capital gains — bought smaller cable systems and formed large MSOs. A Salomon Brothers report on the future of the cable industry predicted that consolidation of cable system ownership during the early 1990s would result in 24 MSOs controlling 90 percent of total subscribers, compared with 74 percent of total subscribers currently under the control of the top 25 MSOs. This consolidation would be fueled by the decreased amount of leverage among the large MSOs — shown in Figure 7 and resulting from strong revenue growth in 1990 and 1991. Such consolidation would allow the MSOs to raise the funds necessary for purchasing smaller, under-capitalized firms [Moshavi 1991(B), p.14].

Figure 7: Leverage Decreasing for Top MSOs

	Debt times cash flow*	
	1990	**1991**
Adelphia Communications	9.1	8.9
American Television & Communications	1.6	1.1
Cablevision Industries	9.9	8.8
Cablevision Systems	9.0	8.3
Comcast Corporation	5.9	5.4
Continental Cablevision	8.0	7.5
Heritage Communications	7.1	6.6
Storer Communications	7.6	NA
Tele-Communications, Inc.	NA	6.4

*Cash flow is EBITDA: earnings before interest, taxes, depreciation and amortization. NA-Not available.

Source: "Top 25 MSO's Will Increase Ownership Over Next Four Years, Predicts Study," *Broadcasting,* December 30, 1991, p.14.

FUTURE GROWTH AREAS

With few areas remaining to bring cable to, the industry placed emphasis on developing cable systems to their maximum potential. In 1991, the normal industry price tag for a cable system was 12 times the annual cash flow less capital expenditures [Management, 1992]. This translated into an average price of more than $2,000 per subscriber ["Establishing a Value for Your System" 1988; Sukow 1991]. Fueling the desire to fully develop all means of revenue was the fact that a system's value increased by $12 for every $1 of increased profit.

In the late 1980s the industry was concerned with increasing marketing efforts, improving programming quality, obtaining programs that fit market demographics, maximizing programming revenue, and developing revenue from advertising insertion. Other avenues of growth looked to take advantage of the break-through technologies of the 1990s, such as video-on-demand, pay-per-view, and interactivity television, as discussed later in this case study [Coe 1991, p. 58]. Cable operators, as a means of retaining customers and maintaining a positive image, also looked to improve the quality of service.

Marketing To New Subscribers

Cable systems aggressively market the services they provide. All people living in the cable company's franchised areas are made aware of the benefits cable TV offers. With programmers' help, cable operators promote stations that can be seen only on cable TV.

Marketing is done at both local and national levels. Locally, cable systems utilize telemarketing campaigns, door-to-door sales, and direct mail to solicit new subscribers. Some cable systems will not allow a person to sign up for service over the phone. Rather, they insist a company representative make a personal visit to acquaint the prospective subscriber with the various services available [DeCourt 1989].

National and regional advertising is usually done by the programmer, who sometimes works in conjunction with the operator. Operators have been joining forces, such as by creating advertising cooperatives. The catch phrase, "dial 1 800 OK Cable," is from an operator-formed advertising cooperative used to deliver the message that if you don't have cable, then you're missing something you can't get anywhere else. Marketing aims for 85 percent penetration in a given market, that is, 85 percent of the households will subscribe to cable TV.

Programming

To add to the growing subscriber base, the industry attempts to offer better and more specific programming. Offering what broadcast TV does not is a powerful advertising tool of cable TV. Programming originated by cable operators, such as premium pay programming channels, network broadcasts, pay-per-view, and shopping channels, are some of the types of programming offered.

Many of the larger cable operators have been deeply involved with developing their own programming. They originally did so because not enough programming existed to fill channel space. Now they are becoming adept at it and are making it a successful business.

Most cable systems, especially the larger ones, offer programs of local origination. This type of programming originates in the studio of the cable system. It is geared towards the community and may consist of community board hearings, local high school sporting events, and the like. Local access, which provides air time to community members on the channel, is similar to local origination. Cable systems commonly also provide tailor-made programming for community areas with large ethnic concentrations. In the New York City area, for example, there are several Hispanic programs, as well as Indian, Greek, Korean, and Chinese.

Programming is also provided by the broadcast networks. Generally, these network broadcasts (NBC, CBS, ABC, and Fox) are provided as a part of the basic cable service.

A number of pay premium program channels, such as Showtime, Cinemax, The Disney Channel, and The Movie Channel, were developed after HBO's success. The pay channels provide programming to cable operators, usually for a fee which is passed on to subscribers. HBO's sister channel, Cinemax, was created to compliment HBO by showing different movies during the month. Showtime, which is not affiliated with HBO, markets itself as HBO's perfect companion. Showtime has the exclusive rights to the movies of two Hollywood studios.

In 1990, U.S. consumers spent an estimated $4.8 billion on subscribing to pay cable channels. This revenue was split between the cable system operators and the program operators. According to industry research firm Paul Kagan Associates, the leading pay-TV service is Time Warner's HBO, with about 17.5 million subscribers. Other major channels include Viacom's

Showtime (7.4 million), Time Warner's Cinemax (6.3 million) and The Disney Channel (5.5 million). The aggregate number of subscribers for these four services rose about 8 percent from 1988 to 1990, with the greatest increase (roughly 28 percent) registered by The Disney Channel ["Networks Still Losing Ground" 1991].

In addition, other programmers in the past provided cable operators with programming which was included in a subscriber's basic service, such as CNN, MTV, TNT, AMC, and ESPN. At times, cable operators pay a fee for these programming services; at other times they received fees from the programmers or got the programming free.

The increased number of pay premium channels offered, coupled with popular basic programming, however, has led many system operators to employ another revenue-generating tactic called tiering. *Tiering* involves the "unbundling" of the various programs originally offered as part of a cable operator's basic service, such as ESPN, MTV, TNT, etc., and moving them to a new cable category for which the subscribers must pay a premium over the basic cable rate. This tactic was also employed to diffuse calls for re-regulation of the industry, since cable operators felt that tiering would allocate the costs of the various channels among the viewers who most desired them ["Operating Gains" 1992, p. M29].

Pay-per-view is a premium service which allows the subscriber to select certain individual programs for a fee. Subscribers dial a phone number and are billed only for the desired program.

Pay-per-view services have taken advantage of new technologies. A unique added feature is video-on-demand which possesses pause and rewind functions similar to those of video cassettes. Unlike standard pay-per-view, where a film can be watched only at the time designated by the cable system, video-on-demand pay services can be viewed at the customer's convenience [Moshavi 1991(C)].

Shopping channels were developed for people who find shopping at home convenient. The cable systems receive a percentage of the sale as a commission, usually five percent [Management 1992].

Producers of programming are acutely aware of their ratings. While channel capacity was in abundance in cable's infancy, in 1991 43 percent of cable systems had the capacity for less than 30 channels and so programming space was limited. To attract and maintain subscribers, cable operators look for the best programming available. Such competition keeps programmers scrambling to create a better product. Before taking on a new program, operators must decide whether the benefits will outweigh the cost. Gaining new subscribers and retaining existing ones are an operator's major concerns [Boyle 1989].

This channel availability situation is changing. By late 1991, for example, in New York City a 150-channel capacity system had become available to 10,000 homes in Queens, New York. This expanded channel menu was expected to be offered throughout Queens and into Brooklyn. It was heralded as "the most historic event in television since HBO went up on the satellite" by the president of Time Warner's New York City Cable Group [Moshavi 1991(A)].

ADVERTISING AS A SOURCE OF REVENUE

Advertising is an area of great opportunity for the cable operator and the programmer. Programmers are competing with the networks for national advertising revenue. As shown in

Figure 8, total cable advertising revenue increased from $213 million in 1982 to $1.46 billion in 1988. This figure had increased to roughly $2 billion by 1990.

Local cable systems can insert their own local advertising into programs such as basketball games on The Madison Square Garden Network. This form of advertising may be the most effective for many local merchants. The systems themselves can also sell time to regional advertisers. Some systems are linking with other cable systems to form larger advertising bases. The potential for increasing revenues from advertising has barely been tapped. Advertisers are beginning to look at cable systems as a way to tailor their ads for different areas. It is now possible for national commercials to have local flair [Stump 1989]. Also, local merchants advertising on a cable channel whose demographics closely match their product lines can receive a high return on their advertising dollars.

Some of the growth in advertising revenue has resulted from technological advances. In New York, for example, the new technology being utilized is the "interconnect system" which allows for the satellite delivery of advertisements to individual cable systems. The interconnect

Figure 8: Cable Advertising Revenue 1980-1988 (In Billions)

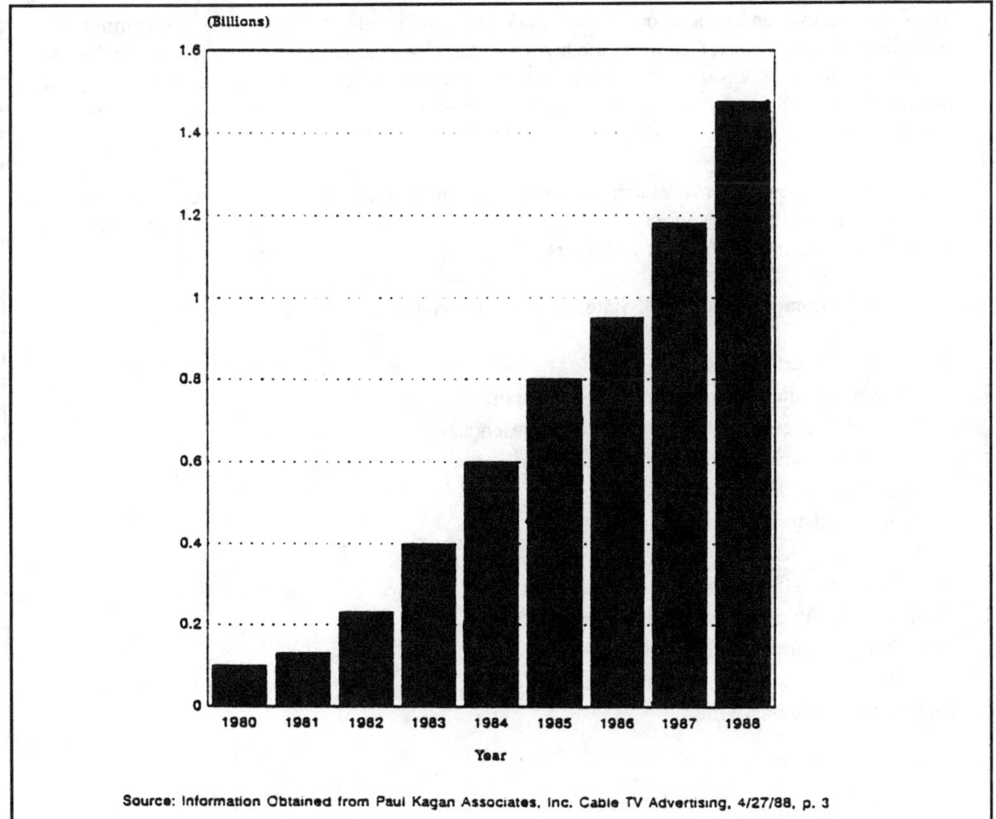

system eliminates the need for hand-delivered videotapes to individual cable systems, reduces the paperwork load of advertising agencies, and eases verification of ad placement. "The interconnect will do wonders for the New York market," says Thomas McKinney, president, Cabletelevision Advertising Bureau. Cable operators should be able to cut costs and increase revenues by using the interconnect system [Moshavi 1991, p. 24].

SERVICING

Part of maximizing revenues is customer retention. What was taken for granted in the past has become a prime area of concern for cable operators. Many operators, such as Tele-Communications Industries (TCI), the largest multiple system operator (MSO), believe service is the key to getting up to 85 percent of potential customers to subscribe to cable [Pasdeloup 1989

Figure 9: The Cable Customer's Bill of Rights

The Cable Television Association of New York, Inc., and its member companies are committed to providing cable television customers the highest level of professional service possible. To that end, we are committed to ensuring that our customers receive quality programming, reliable, superior quality signals and prompt, courteous service every time the customer is in contact with any cable system employee.

Recognizing that customer satisfaction can best be achieved through excellence both of product and service, the Association has adopted the following Cable Customer Bill of Rights, which underscores our industry's commitment to its customers.

As a cable customer in New York State, you have the right to:

1. Prompt and courteous service provided by helpful and knowledgeable sales, installation, construction and customer service representatives.
2. Convenient access to customer service representatives.
3. Prompt response to requests for installation and service repair and convenient appointment opportunities.
4. Prompt response in the event of system outages.
5. Prompt response to any billing inquiries.
6. Diligent investigation and timely resolution of all disputes.
7. Knowledgeable and informed response to all inquiries.
8. Reliable, clear and high quality television signals.
9. A description of all programming services offered and all subscription options available.
10. Fair and competitive rates.

Source: Cable Television Association of New York

(A)]. Providing the best picture possible and making service and installation calls at the customers' convenience are some of the areas that are being addressed. They are also some of the areas for which the industry is most criticized. Figure 9 shows a document from the Cable Television Association of New York that assigns a "Bill of Rights" to the customer. The document was assembled by New York cable operators.

NEW TECHNOLOGIES

Future growth in revenues will also hinge on new technologies in the 1990s, such as video-on-demand (already covered in the pay-per-view section), digital audio, and interactivity.

Digital Audio. Digital audio takes up no video bandwidth, yet subscribers who opt for it pay an average of $10 a month, according to Hal Krisberg, president, Jerrold Communications, which owns one of three digital audio services currently in the market. With CD-quality sound and a multitude of commercial-free formats, there "is no reason cable can't do to broadcast radio what it did to broadcast TV" [Moshavi 1991(C)].

Interactivity. Subscriber interactivity with a cable system, especially for non-entertainment uses, is another potential avenue of growth in the cable business. One company, Insight Telecast Inc., with backing from companies as diverse as Viacom, PBS, Spelling Entertainment, and Sumitomo, is creating an interactive electronic program guide that offers everything from automatic VCR recording to selecting programs by genre. Technology experts continue to talk of ways to use interactivity for other functions, including information services, banking, and educational programs, as well as for entertainment purposes.

COMPETITION

CATV Enterprises has competitors from four major areas: telephone companies, other cable companies, video rental stores, and Satellite Master Antenna Television (SMATV). The threat of another cable company is CATV's greatest possible competitor. However, with regulatory agencies and consumers clamoring for increased competition, phone companies — through the use of "video dial tones" — may move to the forefront. Video rental stores do not have the impact of the above, but do provide a video-on-demand service which CATV does not yet offer.

Telephone Companies

FCC regulations have thus far prohibited telephone companies from entering the cable business. However, with consumer complaints rising against cable system operators, the FCC may allow phone companies to enter the cable television business soon. Phone companies have the cash flow required and, more importantly, wires to nearly every home in America — making them a natural for the TV business.

The FCC proposes to allow phone companies to provide a video dial tone, by which they relay menus of TV programs from other sources to consumers. The FCC plan would give viewers more program choices since cable operators often refuse to carry a program that might steal viewers from another program that they own or control. Phone companies, in contrast, would be common carriers, obligated to transmit for a standard fee any program that someone wants to send. In order to compete CATV would have to provide additional programming, thus making system upgrades which could be quite costly. To CATV's advantage, the phone companies likewise would be required to spend a great deal of money in upgrading their current fiber optic networks, an expense which many phone companies do not want to incur.

Other Cable Companies

On June 1, 1983, Cablevision of New York City, a part of Cablevision Systems Corp., was awarded the franchise for the entire borough of the Bronx. Because CATV Enterprises possessed only a permit, the city included Riverdale in the franchise agreement. The status of CATV Enterprises is unclear since, as stated previously, there are no exclusive franchises in New York State. Conceivably, if the system was built according to state and local requirements, a franchise could be granted to replace the current permit [New York State 1988].

Cablevision Systems Corp., with more than 1,650,000 subscribers, was the seventh largest MSO in the country in 1991, as shown in Figure 1. It is establishing a cable system in the Bronx in four phases; Riverdale is scheduled for the third phase which should take place in 1993 [Management 1992]

Video Rental Stores

The video cassette rental industry has become a competitor of premium cable channels such as HBO. Video stores obtain recently-released films six months or more before cable TV receives them, so they have been able to take a share of the market from the cable operator. One large MSO, Cox Cable Communications, is venturing into the video store business to offset revenue losses to such outlets [Schley 1989 (A)]. The home video market reaches almost 70 percent of all TV households. Home video rentals and sales were expected to reach $9 billion in 1989 [Schley 1989 (A)]. While several video stores exist in Riverdale, their actual impact on CATV Enterprises is unknown. Management does not regard competition from video rental stores as a problem deserving of attention.

Satellite Master Antenna Television (SMATV)

SMATV is a method used to serve large multiple-unit dwellings. An apartment complex with over 400 units is a prime target for this type of service. A satellite receiving dish is placed on the property and then a distribution system is constructed to provide service to those residents desiring it. This system is, in effect, a miniature cable system. SMATV utilizes the same equipment, only on a smaller scale. It has the advantage of being able to provide service to areas that are not near a cable plant. In a cabled area usually a favorable arrangement is made between the SMATV operator and the owner or cooperative, in the form of remuneration. Since they are on private property, SMATVs are not subject to state and local jurisdiction. They do not pay franchise fees to the city or state [Weinstein 1986, pp. 161-165].

The disadvantage of this type of system is the service. Unless it is an unusually large complex, immediate home service is not always available for subscribers, who may wait days or even weeks for service to be restored in the case of an outage. Also, SMATV systems generally do not offer the number of channels that a cable system does due to space limitations for the satellite receiving dishes and their cost. These companies also require a long-term contract with the landlord to assure that they recover their capital outlays and realize a profit.

In CATV Enterprises' area two companies have been trying to provide buildings with service: Satellites Unlimited, located in Queens, New York, and Amsat, headquartered in Connecticut. As of December 1991, no buildings in Riverdale were serviced by SMATV companies.

GOVERNMENT REGULATION

The force with the greatest possible impact on the cable TV industry is the government. It regulates competition, allocates use of frequencies, protects markets, and at times controls profits. All of these affect the quality and number of programs, as well as the extent to which homes are serviced. New technologies can be advanced or impeded by the government. CATV Enterprises answers to the federal, state, and city governments. At the federal level it is regulated by the Federal Communications Commission. It answers to the New York State Commission on Cable Television and New York City's Office of Telecommunications. Since 1984, by legislative act, the functions of the three have been fairly well defined.

The Federal Government

The federal government impacts on the cable industry through establishing controlling commissions and enacting communication laws, such as those discussed below.

The Federal Communications Commission (FCC). The FCC was created by Congress from the Communications Act of 1934, several years before the first cable TV system. Since cable systems used CARS microwave links, which were already under the domain of the FCC, regulation of the cable industry fell under the FCC's jurisdiction also [Weinstein 1986, p.1.]. Since there were no provisions for cable TV, the industry found itself regulated at the discretion of the commission.

In the 1960s, the FCC did not look upon cable TV favorably. With constant pressure from the broadcasters, who feared loss of their markets from the importation of distant signals, the FCC took restrictive measures against cable. In 1966 it forbade importing signals into the 100 largest markets in the U.S. on the premise that they had ample coverage. In 1968 the FCC actually forbade new construction in these markets [Weinstein 1986, p.1.]. While some of the restrictions were relaxed in 1972 when the FCC issued new rules for cable, they were still quite rigid. For example, they prevented cable companies from showing movies that were between two and eight years old.

In 1989 FCC Chairman Sikes supported "adaptive regulation." He defined this as "effective, but adaptive, communications regulation, while continuing to remove outmoded, or unnecessary rules" [Mooney 1989]. Sikes viewed the FCC's role as that of a facilitator in speeding up the introduction of new technologies universally in the marketplace. As of 1991, the FCC's posture had not significantly changed. However, this does not necessarily bode well for the cable industry. As stated previously, the FCC is proposing allowing telephone companies into the television business.

The Cable Communications Policy Act of 1984. Congress enacted this act to allow cable to peacefully coexist with public authorities. It clearly spelled out the role of the FCC and the local governments. Of prime concern to cable operators was the removal of rate regulation by local authorities. This meant financial salvation for many systems, who, in their overexuberance to obtain a franchise, had agreed to provide basic service at unprofitable rates [Weinstein 1986, p.124-126.].

New York State

The New York State Commission on Cable Television is responsible for the technical adherence of systems to required specifications. These specifications are set by the FCC but enforced by the state. The agency collects a franchise tax of two percent of total receipts from the cable companies. In addition to technical audits, they also concern themselves with all aspects of customer satisfaction. They are the citizens' watchdog, making certain that everyone is able to receive cable service. State law forces landlords to allow cable entry and, conversely, forces cable systems to provide service to buildings that they, for some reason, find undesirable to service.

The City of New York

The City of New York decides what companies will have franchises in the five boroughs. Franchises in New York City are awarded on the basis of submitted bids. With investors enthusiastic to obtain franchises and with the city's power to award them, corruption and bribery were prevalent. New York City was blemished by corruption scandals in the late 1970s and mid-1980s. The leaders of the ruling political party of the Bronx were brought to trial in 1986 [Gaglia 1988]. Though the case was dismissed, it delayed Cablevision's construction of the Bronx and Brooklyn, its franchised areas, for years.

The Office of Telecommunications is part of the Bureau of Franchises of the City of New York. It performs functions almost identical to those of the state agency. CATV Enterprises files quarterly reports with them. Although the city is also involved with technical standards, the state is the predominant watchdog. The city receives five percent of the total receipts of the business as a franchise fee.

THE COMPANY

HISTORY

In 1965 Theodore Granik, a politically well-connected entrepreneur, obtained a permit to build a cable television system in Riverdale, a small but affluent section of the Bronx borough in New York City. Along with Riverdale, the city granted two other permits in the borough of Manhattan. Each of the three systems had two years to be up and running, at which time they would be reviewed for the granting of a franchise by the Board of Estimate of the City of New York. At the end of that time both Manhattan systems were in operation, Riverdale was not. As a result, a franchise was not granted to CATV Enterprises, Inc., the cable TV company formed by Granik. Instead, CATV was granted a two-year extension on its permit.

Granik ran into difficulties and needed financial and technical help. In July 1967 he sold a 49 percent interest in his cable company to Westinghouse Broadcasting Company. Westinghouse was familiar with cable TV since it owned two systems in the southern United States. From the beginning of the alliance until 1983, Bachman — a Westinghouse manager — was the general manager.

Granik died in 1968. His estate was administered by his brother, an attorney practicing in New York City. His wife and son, who lived in Washington D.C., took a passive role in the company's operation, as did the executor of the estate. In 1968 CATV Enterprises, Inc. was fully operational. However, additional efforts to secure a franchise were denied. The Board of Estimate, under Mayor Lindsay, granted additional two-year permits. In 1967 Mayor Lindsay had appointed Fred Friendly to head a team to investigate the city owning and operating a cable system, presumably in Riverdale [Gent 1967].

PLANT

In 1968 CATV had more than 3,000 subscribers. Most of these were in private homes which, because of hilly terrain, were obscured from direct reception. For the most part, those living in apartment buildings received good quality reception, due to the height of the buildings' antennae. New York City had the advantage of receiving many over-the-air broadcast stations. The advantage CATV Enterprises offered at this time was clear reception. While the company carried UHF channels that it converted to unused UHF channels, it did not pick up any distant signals. In 1986 the system still had the same electronics with the same limitations.

CATV Enterprises' subscription rate in 1968 was $5 for basic service and $6 in 1986. In the later part of 1985 the company increased the rate by five percent to $6.30, the amount permitted annually by its operating permit.

In 1991 CATV, in response to FCC regulations governing signal leakage, rewired the bulk of the residences it serviced. This rewiring had the additional benefits of dramatically increasing picture quality and allowing CATV to offer additional channels. Figure 10 shows CATV's much-

Figure 10: Rate Card

Monthly rates for first sets:

Basic Service . . . $ 12.95

(May require a converter, at an additional charge, if your set is not cable ready.)

Premium Service

Premium services available:

Home Box Office
Showtime
The Disney Channel
Sportschannel

All Premium Services are provided a la Carte.

First Pay Service .... $ 10.95
Second and third .... $ 9.95 each
The Disney Channel... $ 6.95

Monthly rates for Additional Sets:

Basic Service .... $ 3.75 each

Premium Service:

HBO .... $ 4.00 each
SHOWTIME .... $ 4.00 each
SPORTSCHANNEL..... $ 4.00 each
DISNEY CHANNEL ... $ 3.00 each

INSTALLATION CHARGES

WEEKDAYS:

First Set $35.00
Second Sets (done at the same time as First set)..... $17.50
Additional sets (if a separate trip is required.......... $35.00
Relocation or reconnection of sets.......................... $35.00

WEEKENDS:

There is an additional charge of $10.00 per installation.

For complete information regarding our policies please ask for a copy of our "Subscriber Policy."

CATV ENTERPRISES RATE CARD APRIL, 1991

Source: CATV Enterprises, Mr. Bill Rella, General Mgr.

expanded 1991 rate card [Management 1992]. Through deregulation CATV was able to raise its rates to a more realistic level of $12.95 per month.

Additional Channel Capacity

Even though state-of-the-art equipment was used to build CATV Enterprises in the 1960s, cable TV was in its infancy at that time and the system could transmit only 14 channels. Through internal funding, some of the outdated equipment was replaced. This additional channel capacity resulted in eight channels being added to the basic lineup as well as two pay services. In order to obtain a permanent franchise from New York City, CATV was required to expand its channel capacity to 100 channels. This would cost CATV approximately $1 million.

PRODUCT

In 1978 CATV Enterprises added Home Box Office. The system increased by 500 subscribers over the next few years [Management 1992]. In 1980, SportsChannel and The Madison Square Garden Network were added, sharing one channel. CATV now had about 4,000 subscribers, and for the first time, showed a profit.

In April 1987, CATV Enterprises replaced two UHF channels with satellite programs, Cable News Network (CNN) and Turner Broadcasting System (TBS). Another UHF channel was dropped and Madison Square Garden (MSG) was put on its own channel along with Financial News Network (FNN). These program channels, FNN and MSG, did not conflict with each other since FNN was on during the day and MSG began programming in the evening. These program changes led to an increase in subscribers of almost 30 percent in six months. By 1991 CATV had over 10,000 subscribers and a revenue base which could support an increase to the 100 channels required for a franchise.

MARKETING

Until 1986 CATV marketed only through the local newspaper, *The Riverdale Press*. There was no sales staff and no direct contact with apartment building managers to gain entry so CATV could service its residents. In 1987 a marketing campaign was begun with limited funds. One full-time and two part-time salespeople were hired. When additional channels were added in 1988 extra efforts were made to obtain sales, but a large expenditure was not in keeping with Group W's policy since they were committed to selling the cable system.

CUSTOMERS

The company had almost 3,000 customers in the early years. It saw only incremental

Figure 11: CATV Enterprises, Inc.
Statement of Operations 1984-1991

	1984	1985	1986	1987	1988	1989	1990	1991
SUBSCRIBER COUNTS								
Basic	4,100	4,167	4,474	5,418	6,450	7,400	8,800	10,188
HBO	unavailable	2,487	2,376	2,759	3,765	3,552	4,224	4,368
Sportschannel	unavailable	900	950	1,100	1,750	1,702	1,840	1,804
Showtime	N/A	N/A	N/A	N/A	400	955	1,135	1,633
Disney	N/A	N/A	N/A	N/A	280	466	554	927
REVENUE								
Basic	323,400	349,812	364,643	487,500	742,800	1,121,100	1,178,400	1,657,600
Installation	14,205	15,154	19,320	38,000	49,200	57,000	74,100	89,000
HBO	242,320	281,331	315,875	353,900	460,200	491,400	552,300	577,900
Sportschannel	80,773	101,201	128,146	153,500	193,900	223,100	219,100	252,300
Showtime	0	0	0		12,800	80,600	137,800	202,200
Disney	0	0	0	0	7,300	31,400	48,900	64,100
Misc	0	364	0	2,200	17,100	22,500	14,900	45,700
Total Revenue	660,698	747,862	827,983	1,035,100	1,483,300	2,027,100	2,225,500	2,888,800
EXPENSES								
Employee related	115,436	135,973	132,365	168,181	221,375	369,000	403,500	601,900
Vehicle expense	7,395	6,874	7,216	9,600	22,750	22,200	15,709	25,800
Repair & Maintenance	33,839	37,983	24,732	9,500	45,962	36,100	126,900	139,200
Duct and Pole rental	27,684	26,416	27,747	24,000	26,600	25,800	39,100	28,000
Headend rental	7,300	7,800	7,800	7,800	9,000	10,200	10,200	8,160
Outside contractor	31,847	31,083	29,856	66,700	67,698	119,600	263,100	315,400
Marketing	0	0	0	9,916	32,313	18,000	4,300	14,000
Programming	117,523	119,500	145,102	217,900	304,168	364,746	704,200	920,500
General & Administrative	78,995	57,773	103,757	124,800	151,215	240,107	313,610	596,082
Operating Taxes, fees	65,754	63,157	66,783	92,900	124,336	180,669	212,781	268,158
Total Expenses	485,773	486,559	545,297	731,297	1,005,417	1,386,421	2,093,400	2,917,200
Profit (loss)	174,925	261,303	282,626	303,803	477,883	640,679	132,100	(28,400)

Figure 12: 1990 Neighborhood Demographics Report
Zip Code: 10471
Bronx County, New York

	1980	1990
TOTAL POPULATION	30653	31544
TOTAL NUMBER OF HOUSEHOLDS	11992	13118
AVERAGE AGE	41.4	43.6
AVERAGE HOUSEHOLD INCOME	$ 27087	$ 41297

AGE GROUPS:

0-4	3.8%
5-11	6.1%
12-16	4.8%
17-21	6.9%
22-29	11.1%
30-44	22.7%
45-54	11.7%
55-64	11.0%
65+	22.0%
	100.0%

OCCUPATION:

EXECUTIVE	16.9%
PROFESSIONAL	26.7%
TECHNICAL	3.0%
SALES	11.0%
CLERICAL	22.2%
PRIVATE	0.7%
SERVICE	8.3%
FARMING	0.2%
CRAFT	5.5%
OPERATOR	4.2%
LABORER	1.3%
	100.0%

RACE:

WHITE	84.2%
BLACK	4.9%
OTHER	10.9%
	100.0%

HOUSEHOLD INCOME:

$ 0-14999	15.7%
$15000-24999	14.4%
$25000-34999	16.3%
$35000-49999	20.5%
$50000-74999	16.6%
$75000+	16.4%
	100.0%

TYPES OF HOUSEHOLDS:

SINGLE PERSON	30.3%
MALE	11.3%
FEMALE	19.0%
FAMILY	66.4%
NON-FAMILY	3.3%
	100.0%

OCCUPIED HOUSING UNITS:

OWNED	16.8%
RENTED	83.2%
	100.0%

AVERAGE HOME VALUE	$112856
AVERAGE RENT	$ 358

OCCUPIED HOUSING BUILT IN:

1975-1980	0.8%
1970-1974	4.5%
1960-1969	36.6%
1950-1959	24.2%
1940-1949	13.2%
PRE-1940	20.7%
	100.0%

Important:
1. Percentages for age, household income and race reflect 1990 updates. All other percentages are based on 1980 information.
2. 1980 income figures are expressed in 1979 dollars. 1990 income figures are expressed in 1989 dollars. Home value and rent are expressed in 1980 dollars.

Source: Information obtained from Mr. Bill Rella, G.M., CATV Enterprises **

increases until HBO was introduced in 1978. The subscriber count increased over the next few years to over 4,000. As changes were made to programming beginning in 1987, the system realized a steady increase in customers, as can be seen in Figure 11. In September 1991 CATV had approximately 10,100 subscribers to basic service.

Figure 12 shows the demographics of Riverdale in 1990. Average annual household income was more than $41,000 and 33 percent of Riverdale's population were over 55 years of age. From 1988 to 1993, Riverdale's population was expected to increase 4.6 percent with an increase of more than 30 percent in household income.

FINANCES

CATV was unprofitable until it added Home Box Office, first showing a profit in 1980 [Management 1992]. The addition of other premium channels, such as SportsChannel and The Madison Square Garden Network, helped CATV capture additional revenues and increased profits.

The technical changes required by the state and completed in December 1989 cost approximately $150,000. The company generated high enough profits to fund the expenditure. The only additional cash outlay the system had was in the form of interest to Westinghouse of $85,000 per year from a long-standing loan [Management 1992].

The additional technical improvements made in 1991 increased CATV's subscriber base by an additional 30 percent and increased revenues to approximately $2.9 million. Rising expenses over this time were one-time expenses associated with the system upgrade (i.e., outside contractors, employee-related overtime, etc.). Even though 1991 showed a net deficit, projections through 1993 showed a surplus of roughly $800,000 based on a 30 percent increase in revenues (current growth rate) and the stabilization of expenses through the elimination of one-time items [Management 1992].

TOWARDS THE FUTURE

The company is operated by Group W Cable, a division of Westinghouse reporting to the Broadcast Division. It had been Group W's intention for many years to sell the system. Because of the problems in the past with the city granting CATV a franchise, the company was leery of selling to anyone but a large MSO. Since the franchise for the entire borough of the Bronx was awarded to Cablevision Systems, Group W initially decided that it would be easier to sell to Cablevision than to worry about possible difficulties with the government. Cablevision, while initially interested in purchasing CATV, backed out of the deal in 1991. Cablevision claimed the deal fell through because of declining stock value and the resulting inability to raise approximately $20 million in funds. However, New York City had given Cablevision a franchise for the entire Bronx borough since the law permitted more than one cable company to service the area. Cablevision apparently intended to wire the Riverdale section of the Bronx, and so force CATV out of business by some time in 1994.

With the Cablevision alternative gone, CATV management had to rethink its strategy. A possible alternative was to sell CATV to a smaller, independent system operator. Other system operators had expressed interest in purchasing CATV. Selling CATV would meet Group W's objective of getting out of the system operating business, while recouping some of the Granick family's investment. It would not require extensive system upgrades (if the current levels of interest are maintained), and it would make the headache of dealing with Cablevision someone else's problem. The disadvantages all stem from the lack of a permanent franchise for CATV. Such a sale could be disallowed by the city or CATV could fail to receive "fair-value" for the system without the permanent franchise. Obtaining a permanent franchise would require expanding to 100 channels at a cost of $1 million. This could be internally funded through CATV's current revenue stream as well as by raising basic cable rates to $16.95.

Another alternative would be to continue operations. Plant enhancements such as "local signal origination" and "interdiction" could be internally funded through an increase in the basic service price of $4 to $16.95. These plant upgrades would result in programming on-par with Cablevision while not requiring converter boxes. (The $16.95 price is also $2 cheaper than what Cablevision currently charges.) On the down side, these upgrades were not guaranteed to be completed in time to compete with Cablevision in early 1993, possibly resulting in the loss of customers. Another positive sign for continuing operations was the doubling of CATV's revenues since 1987 after only minor upgrades to the system were made. Offsetting this were U.S. Commerce Department projections that growth in the cable industry would taper off during the 1990s. Underlying all of this was the lack of a franchise without which CATV's license could be taken away.

Management had to choose between selling the system or continuing operations. Since selling the system without a franchise would most likely result in CATV not receiving fair value, was this a chance management would want to take? Since making the upgrades to qualify for a franchise may not be completed in time, would making the additional upgrades necessary for allowing CATV to compete with Cablevision still make sense? If it decided to continue operations, what steps could it take to survive and prosper?

REFERENCES AND BACKGROUND READINGS

Bachman, Herb, *Telephone interview*, November 1, 1989.

Boyle, Joseph, R., "Channel Shelf Space Heats Up," *Multichannel News*, October 9, 1989, p.32.

Brand, Stewart, *The Media Lab Inventing the Future at MIT*, New York, N.Y., Viking Penguin Inc., 1987.

Cable Television Developments, Research & Policy Analysis Department, National Cable Television Association, Washington, D.C., January 1989.

Carnevale, Mary Lu, "Congress Seeks to Rein in Cable TV," *The Wall Street Journal*, December 11, 1989, pp. B1, B6.

CATV Enterprises, Inc., *Company Records*, Mr. Bill Rella G.M., 1992.

Coe, Steve, "Interactivity Seen as Key to Future Growth," *Broadcasting*, November 25, 1991, p. 37

Coy, Peter, "Cable TV: For a Better Picture, Try Competition," *Business Week*, December 23, 1991, pp. 58-59.

Cunningham, John, E., *Cable Television*, Indianapolis, Indiana, Howard W. Sams & Co., 1985.

DeCourt, Bruce, Manager of New Developments for Cablevision of New York, from August 1989, *Interview*, November, 1989.

"Digital Audio," *Broadcasting/Cable*, June 5, 1989, p. 3.

Edlitz, Karen, "State Associations Adopt Broader Roles," *Cable World*, December 4, 1989, p. 10.

"Establishing a Value for Your System," *National Cable Television Cooperative, Inc.*, March 1988. pp. 4-6.

"Foster and Franco Out at Microband," *Broadcasting*, December, 4, 1989, p. 86.

Gaglia, Leslie, "Cable Picture Gets Larger," *The Riverdale Press*, August 25, 1988, pp. 1, B2.

Gent, George, "Westinghouse Enters CATV Company in Bronx," *The New York Times*, July 28, 1967, p5.

Grover, Ronald and Lieberman, David, "In the Race for Viewers the Networks Fall Further Behind," *Business Week*, January 9, 1989.

Haugsted, Linda, "ESPN Gets First Baseball Advertiser, Seeks Others," *Multichannel News*, October 9, 1989, p. 9.

Kerver, Tom, "What Lies Ahead for Cable," Cable Television Business, pp. 21-24.

"Local Ad Sales Becoming Big Cable Business," *Broadcasting*, September 11, 1989, pp. 122-124.

Management of CATV Enterprises, Inc., *Statements*, February 1992, Rella, William, C., General Manager

Maskian, George, "City May Get Into Cable TV Game," *Daily News*, July 26, 1967, p. 40

Medzon, Karyn Miller, "Cable Deal's Off So 2 Companies May Vie for TVs," *The Riverdale Press*, September 26, 1991, p. A1-2

Mooney, Jim, *NCTA Presidents Report*, September 15, 1989, Washington, D.C., National Cable Television Association.

Moshavi, Sharon D., "NY Operators Connect to Interconnect," *Broadcasting*, February 3, 1992, p. 24

Moshavi, Sharon D., "Cable's Search for New Revenue Possibilities," *Broadcasting*, October 7, 1991(C), p. 51

Moshavi, Sharon D., "Time Warner Unveils 150 Channels," *Broadcasting*, December 23, 1991(A), p. 18

Moshavi, Sharon D., "Top 25 MSO's Will Increase Ownership Over Next Four Years, Predicts Study," *Broadcasting*, December 30, 1991(B), p.14.

"Networks Still Losing Ground to Cable," *Standard and Poors Industry Surveys*, March 14, 1991, pp. L38-41

"New CATV Owners Pledge Best Possible Picture Here," *The Riverdale Press*, August 3, 1967, p. 1.

New York State Commission on Cable Television, Albany, New York, "Order Granting Temporary Operating Authority," September 8, 1988.

New York State Commission on Cable Television, Albany, New York, "Notice of Intention to Install Cable Television Facilities and Service," March 21, 1984.

Nostalgia Market Profile: The 45Plus Age Demographic, A Summary For Cable TV, The Nostalgia Channel, 1988.

"Operating Gains Continue," *Standard and Poors Industry Surveys*, February 13, 1992, pp. M29-30.

Pasdeloup, Vincente, "TCI Takes Up Service Banner," *Cable World*, September 4, 1989, p. 4 (A).

Pasdeloup, Vincente, "Targeted Viewers, Low Cost Cited as Major Cable Benefits," *Cable World*,

December 4, 1989, p. 17 (B).

Paskowski, Marianne, "Cable Beats Out Stations for Movies," *Electronic Media*, October 9, 1989, pp. 1, 43.

Plunkett, Bob and Zacks, Richard, "Hook Up Hang Up," *Daily News*, April 9, 1989, pp. Business 1, 6, 7.

Reregulation of Cable Television Rates Would Choke Off Investment in New Programming and Improved Cable Technology, Publication of the National Cable Television Association, November 1989.

Schley, Stewart, "Cox's Video Plunge," *Cable World,* September 25, 1989, p. 24 (A).

Schley, Stewart, "Customer Coddling, TCI Style," *Cable World*, December 11, 1989, p. 6 (B).

Simon, Ronald, Phd. Electronic Engineering, Pnresident, AVT, Carteret, New Jersey, *Interview*, November 1989.

Stein, Lisa, "Satan and Salvation for Wireless Cable," *Cablevision,* November 7, 1988, pp. 46 and 48.

Stoddard, Rob, "Mapping Cable's Future," *Cable Television Business*, November 15, 1988, pp. 26-30.

Stoddard, Rob, "The End of Compulsory License," *Cable Television Business*, November 15, 1988, p.16.

Stump, Matt, "Local Ad Sales Becoming Big Cable Business," *Broadcasting*, September 11, 1989, pp. 122-124.

Sukow, Randy, "Cable Growth to Level Off, Commerce Study Says," *Broadcasting,* December 30, 1991, p. 6.

Taylor, Hal, "Cable Rate Up About 8 Percent Over 12 Months," *Multichannel News*, September 25, 1989 p.5.

"Testing the Limits of Basic Penetration," *Marketing New Media*, August 21, 1989, p. 4.

Thompson, Racel, W., "NATOA Urged to Take Stance on Rate Regulation," *Multichannel News*, September 25, 1989, p.25

TV & Cable Factbook, Washington, D.C., Warren Publishing, Inc., 1989.

"USTA Girds Its Loins for Fight With Cable Over Telco Entry," *Broadcasting*, December 11, 1989, pp. 35-37.

Verhovek, Sam Howe, "For Many New York Areas, Wait for Cable TV Ends," *The New York Times*, November 9, 1989, pp. B1, B6.

Wale, Steve, K., "Non-Cable Plan to Bring Boros Six More Channels," *New York Post*, April, 23, 1985, p. B6.

Weinschenk, Carl, "Jerrold Lasers, 'Converter-Phone' Herald New Vision," *Cable World,* December 4, 1989, pp. 1, 8.

Weinstein, Stephen, B., *Getting the Picture*, New York, The Institute of Electrical Engineers, Inc., 1986.

COOPER TIRE & RUBBER COMPANY: THE TIRE INDUSTRY

Cooper Tire & Rubber Company specializes in the manufacturing and marketing of rubber products for consumers and industrial users. Its products include automobile and truck tires, inner tubes, vibration control products, and specialty seating components. It markets its products nationally and internationally through well-defined distribution channels.

Cooper's profits reached a record $79.4 million in 1991, up 19.5 percent from 1990's profit of $66.5 million. Net sales reached a record $1.001 billion for the year, an 11.7 percent increase over the previous record of $896 million set in 1990 ["Cooper Tire Sets Sales.." 1992]. Between 1985 and 1990, Cooper's share in the tire replacement market grew annually by an average of 19.2 percent while overall market growth averaged only 1.6 percent annually. Cooper sold 23 million car and truck tires in 1990, in supplying about 12 percent of the entire replacement market [Hymowitz 1991].

In the deeply troubled tire industry, Cooper Tire & Rubber had consistently increased its share of the market as well as its net income in the replacement market niche. Other than Goodyear, it was the only U.S.-owned tire company among the big eight companies. Though it had often been cited as a possible takeover target by European tire makers, it was unlikely that such an attempt would be successful because these European companies were in debt.

The niche strategy that Cooper followed methodically had served the company well. Would this, however, continue to be the case? As the auto industry continued to shrink, major suppliers in the original equipment manufacturers (OEM) market were looking to the replacement market in order to maintain sales levels. Increased competition would mean lower prices and less profit. Cooper had the lowest research and development and advertising costs per sale of tires and had a higher profit margin than any of the big firms. However, it had never been a trendsetter, nor had it been the first to develop a new product. In an industry where new specifications and better performing tires were required to meet the consumer's interest in new technology, would Cooper maintain its advantage, or would it be forced to spend more money on R&D to keep up with industry developments?

THE INDUSTRY AND COMPETITIVE MARKET

TIRE AND RUBBER PRODUCTS INDUSTRY

The U.S. tire industry consists of multinational firms as well as U.S-owned independent manufacturers and distributors of radial and bias tires sold in the original equipment and replacement markets for passenger cars, light trucks, heavy trucks and buses, motorcycles, bicycles, aircraft, farm machinery, and industrial equipment. A diagram of the components of the

Figure 1: How the Tire Industry Works

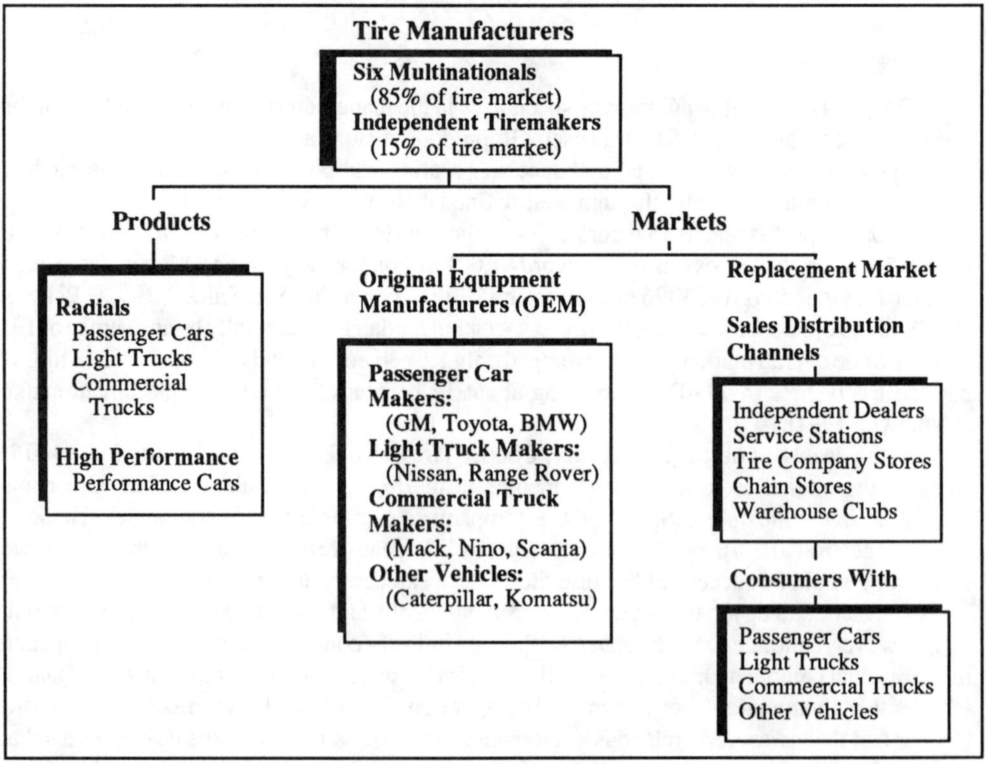

Tire Manufacturers

Six Multinationals (85% of tire market)
Independent Tiremakers (15% of tire market)

Products

Radials
Passenger Cars
Light Trucks
Commercial Trucks

High Performance
Performance Cars

Markets

Original Equipment Manufacturers (OEM)

Passenger Car Makers: (GM, Toyota, BMW)
Light Truck Makers: (Nissan, Range Rover)
Commercial Truck Makers: (Mack, Nino, Scania)
Other Vehicles: (Caterpillar, Komatsu)

Replacement Market

Sales Distribution Channels

Independent Dealers
Service Stations
Tire Company Stores
Chain Stores
Warehouse Clubs

Consumers With

Passenger Cars
Light Trucks
Commeercial Trucks
Other Vehicles

Figure 2: U.S. Tire Industry 1991
(Domestic and Import — Units in Millions)

Segment	Repl.	% of Segment	OEM	% of Segment	Total	** (Imports)	% Total	Exports
Passenger	152.0	78.0%	43.0	22.0%	195.0	(39.0)	76.7%	21.5
Med & Heavy Truck	10.5		2.6		25.0		5.1%	
		84.8%		15.2%		(7.0)		4.4
Light Truck	21.8		3.2		13.1		9.8%	
Farm	3.8		1.5		5.3		2.1%	
Other *	16.0				16.0		6.3%	
Total	204.1		50.3		254.4	(46)	100%	25.9

* Industrial, Aircraft, Motorcycle, Bicycle   ** Imports are included in totals

SOURCE: Information obtained from "Facts/Directory," *Modern Tire Dealer* 26th Ed., Jan 1992.

tire and rubber industry is given in Figure 1.

U.S. tire production grew at an average rate of 1.5 percent annually from 1987 to 1991. In 1991, an estimated 233.1 million tires were shipped in the U.S., not including those for farm machinery and industrial equipment. Forty-six million of these were imported, with Canada and Japan combining to supply 55 percent of the imported tires. The above figures do not include the 25.9 million exported tires, of which about 40 percent were shipped to Canada ["Facts/Directory" 1992]. This information is given in Figure 2.

The two markets in the tire industry are the original equipment manufacturers (OEM) market and the replacement market. The OEM market consists of all the vehicle manufacturers in the world, while the replacement market consists of all the vehicles already in use. In 1991, an estimated 22 percent of the passenger tire market shipments in the U.S., and 15 percent of the truck tire shipments went to the OEM segment of the market. An estimated 78 percent of passenger tires and 85 percent of truck tires were shipped to the replacement market. Approximately 10.6 million passenger tires came into the U.S. on imported vehicles. Some of these tires had been built in the U.S. and shipped overseas to be mounted on cars which were eventually exported to the U.S. As seen in Figure 3, the markets for both passenger and truck tires were declining. By 1992, the combination of longer lasting radials, consumer preference for imported vehicles (many of which came mounted with tires produced overseas), high market penetration by manufacturers of imported tires, and an economic recession had left their marks on the industry.

Original equipment manufacturers received shipments at their auto assembly plants. The replacement market was serviced through a distribution network of independent dealers, tire company stores, service stations, chain stores, discount and department stores, outlets, warehouse clubs, and other channels. Fast delivery, professional training, good service, the continuous feedback of information to customers, as well as effective promotion and advertising campaigns

Figure 3: Tire Industry Market
The Trend in Shipments in the U.S. (Domestic & Imports - Excluding Exports)

A. Passenger units in millions

Replacement		Original Equipment	
1986	144.30	1986	54.40
1987	151.90	1987	52.90
1988	155.30	1988	54.10
1989	153.80	1989	51.30
1990	152.30	1990	47.20
1991	152.00	1991	43.00

B. Truck units in millions

Replacement		Original Equipment	
1986	32.40	1986	6.90
1987	34.50	1987	7.80
1988	33.80	1988	8.60
1989	32.90	1989	8.10
1990	34.40	1990	7.30
1991	32.30	1991	5.80

SOURCE: Information obtained from "Facts/Directory," *Modern Tire Dealer,* 26th Ed., Jan 1992.

through media and other channels were critical requirements for success in this industry.

The 1980s were a period of consolidation and globalization for the major tire companies, many of which became fully integrated. In 1980, Firestone, Uniroyal, BF Goodrich, General Tire, Armstrong, and Mohawk were U.S.-owned and, along with Goodyear and Cooper Tire, held a majority of the North American market. By 1990 only two, Goodyear and Cooper, were U.S.-owned and the rest of the tire industry in North America was dominated by foreign-owned companies based in the U.S. In 1985, 13 producers owned 80 percent of the world-wide tire market. By 1991, approximately 82 percent of the world tire market was shared by six multinational manufacturers.

Horizontal integration was prevalent among tire manufacturers. In 1986, BF Goodrich and Uniroyal merged their tire operations in order to take advantage of one anothers' strengths. Uniroyal had strong OEM sales, while Goodrich was strong in the replacement market. Sumitomo of Japan purchased Dunlop in 1983 in order to expand into North American markets. Continental AG of Germany purchased General Tire in 1987. Michelin of France purchased Uniroyal/Goodrich in 1990, and Pirelli of Italy purchased Armstrong Tire in 1988. The tire industry experienced a decline in the number of plants due to the flurry of mergers and acquisitions. Employment in the tire industry fell consistently from 246,900 in 1977 to 180,700 in 1986, an average annual decline of 3.5 percent.

Many of the leading tire companies were also vertically integrated. For example, Goodyear produced its own synthetic rubber, manufactured tires, and then retailed them through its own outlets. Advantages of this strategy included technical benefits from producing raw materials, stability of supply, improved production coordination, and control of final markup.

Five important trends were shaping the development of the tire industry in the late 1980s: (1) the development and increased use of radial tires, (2) the reduction of tire aspect ratios (rubber used per tire), (3) the increased use of all-season and high-performance tires, (4) improvements in tire performance and reliability, and (5) rubber material research.

The tire industry faced a number of problems in the U.S. The tire industry was an oligopoly, that is, several firms accounted for the majority of output. Firms needed tremendous financial assets to compete in the market, which had high advertising and R&D costs. Also, the market was mature and faced declining unit volumes and low profit margins.

Among the main issues tire makers and markets would be dealing with in the 1990s were the economic slowdown in the U.S., the impact of oil prices and supply on production costs and consumer driving mileage, declining tire demand, severe price competition in the replacement market, and tire recycling and disposal. In addition, auto sales were expected to continue a slow to no-growth pattern. For example, auto sales in the first two months of 1992 increased only 1 percent over the first two months of 1991 [Patterson 1992]. These problems, coupled with the technological excellence and tread life of the modern radial tire, suggested flat growth in the tire industry in the 1990s.

PRODUCTS

The tire industry used three types of tire construction: radials, bias-ply, and bias-belted. In 1991, radials accounted for 187.9 million of the 195 million passenger tires shipped in the U.S. and the trend towards radials was still growing. Figure 4 shows the passenger tire construction types and their respective market shares from 1988 to 1992.

Radial Tires

The development of the radial tire revolutionized tire manufacturing. Radial tires were the indisputable leaders in the industry because of their durability, quality, and performance characteristics for passenger cars and for commercial use [Marshall 1989].

Radial tires offered improved wear, traction, steering response, ride quality, and reduced rolling resistance. The low-heat generation of radial tires and the use of highly reinforced compounds drastically reduced tread wear. Radial tires had an average life of 45,000 miles — compared to 25,000 miles for bias-belted tires and 18,000 miles for bias-ply tires. The average turnover rate of 1.5 tires per car a year in 1989 was expected to decrease to 0.5 by the mid-1990s [Griffiths 1989].

Tires are categorized into three main segments based on size: passenger, light truck, and heavy truck and bus tires. The passenger segment was further subdivided by tread design and

Figure 4: Passenger Tire Market Share by Construction Types (Tires shipped in the U.S. markets)

		% OE	% Replacement
1992**	Bias & bias-belt		0.9%
	Radial	100%	99.1%
1991*	Bias & bias-belt		1.2%
	Radial	100%	98.8%
1990*	Bias		1.0%
	Bias-belt		2.0%
	Radial	100%	97.0%
1989*	Bias		1.0%
	Bias-belt		3.0%
	Radial	100%	96.0%
1988*	Bias		3.0%
	Bias-belt		4.0%
	Radial	100%	93.0%

* These OE figures do not include bias-ply temporary spares but are included in total OE shipment numbers
** Projections
(Of the estimated 195 million passenger tires shipped in 1991: 7.1 million were bias-ply and bias-belted 187.9 million were radial)

SOURCE: Information obtained from "Facts/Directory," *Modern Tire Dealer,* 26th Ed., Jan 1992.

purpose of use, such as all-season, high-performance, and touring tires.

Passenger Tire Segment. *All-season* tires were the most popular passenger car radial tires in the U.S market. They performed well even under adverse weather conditions. In 1991, 145.4 million of the 195 million passenger tires sold were all-season tires. Only 7 million units were snow tires ["Facts/Directory" 1992].

High-performance tires were expected to be the radial product with the highest growth in market share. These were sporty-looking tires for use in high-speed driving. As consumer demand for performance vehicles grew, so did the OEM and replacement performance tire markets. Performance tires were higher priced and wore out about 30 percent faster than other passenger car tires, therefore requiring more frequent replacement. In 1991, performance tires accounted for over 31 percent or 61.1 million units of the entire passenger car tire market as compared to 14 percent in 1985. This market is projected to grow to more than 37.5 percent by 1995. Although performance tires had lower aspect ratios (they used less rubber per tire) and had improved lower rolling resistance, they were intended for high-speed performance vehicles, and auto manufacturers would be confronted with such issues as meeting rising fuel economy standards. Tire makers constructed high-performance tires to satisfy the increasing demand of higher specifications by the OEM market. European OEMs such as BMW, Mercedes Benz, Porsche, and others were requesting that tires meet as many as 50 specifications as compared to 10 specifications required 30 years ago. A breakdown of sales in performance tires by dealer and

Figure 5: Percent of Performance Tire Sales (By Vehicle Type)

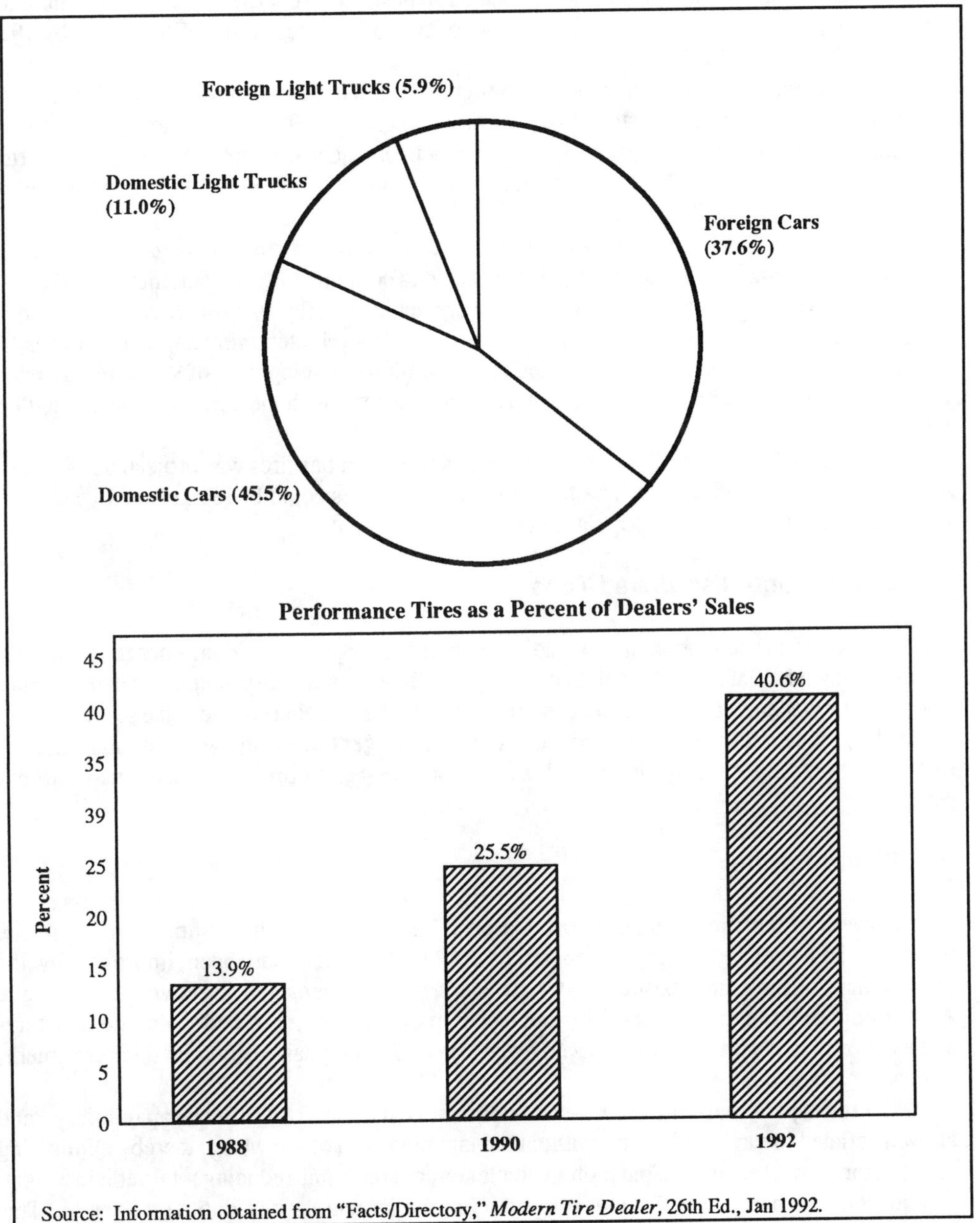

Source: Information obtained from "Facts/Directory," *Modern Tire Dealer*, 26th Ed., Jan 1992.

vehicle type is given in Figure 5.

Touring tires were intended to combine the look and some of the handling capabilities of a performance tire with the ride and noise characteristics of a luxury tire. This subsegment of the performance tire market was expected to grow to 25 to 30 percent of the OEM market by 1994 [*Modern Tire Dealer* 1990].

The tire industry expected to see more high-performance tires, more touring tires, and an increase in the use of V-and Z-rated all-season tires [Kaufman 1990, p.32]. V and Z performance tires were designed for up to 150 mph driving. Michelin intended to supply Mustang with the first all-season Z-rated tire in 1992. Larger diameter tires, that is, 18- and 19-inch OEM fitments, were to be introduced on the Corvette.

Light Truck Tires. The light truck tire market, already showing an annual growth rate of 10 to 12 percent since the early 1980s, was expected to continue to grow well into the 1990s. In the early 1980s the light truck was primarily a work vehicle, but by 1990 other vehicles could be classified under the light truck category, such as sport utility vehicles, minivans, and mini-trucks. The greatest change to come was expected to be the future development of speed-rated tires in light truck sizes to combine the features of a performance tire with the durability and strength of a light truck tire.

Truck and Bus Tires. The demand for radial truck and bus tires was projected to increase to 58.1 percent by 1996. Radial tires for commercial vehicles could be retreaded twice and this made radial tires increasingly popular in this market segment.

Bias-Ply and Bias-Belted Tires

Bias tires had been supplanted by radial-ply tires to a large extent. Numerous tire plants that closed during the 1980s involved tires of bias-ply or bias-belted construction. Except for bias-ply temporary spares, radials have accounted for all tires installed on new passenger cars as original equipment for many years. Since bias-ply passenger tires comprised less than 1 percent of the total passenger market in 1991, bias-ply and bias-belted tires were combined into one category.

Future Trends

Success in the tire business depended on reliability and quality. Improvements in tire reliability had been a primary emphasis of R&D. Reliability had been improved by the development of puncture-resistant materials and sealing systems and improved tire strength. Apart from providing maneuverability and isolation of vibration, tires had to endure punctures and wear from road surfaces. Future R&D was expected to emphasize continued improvements in tread wear and quality.

Flat run capabilities for tires were an important goal in tire R&D. Such capabilities would allow a deflated tire to be driven on without damaging the rim of the wheel, thereby eliminating the need for a spare tire, increasing motor vehicle storage space, and reducing total vehicle weight. Continental Tire had successfully developed a flat run system — its Conti-Tire System. This inverted rim system required the use of a differently shaped rim, which made its commercial adoption difficult as rim production techniques would need to be changed. This system was available in limited supply for one of the top cars in the world, the Mercedes Roadster, as optional equipment.

Inroads were also being made into the development of non-pneumatic tires. The non-pneumatic tire contained no pressurized air, so it could not go flat. Uniroyal/Goodrich had already reached an agreement with a Canadian manufacturer to produce and sell such tires worldwide for airport ground handling equipment.

MARKETS

Tires were sold in two primary markets: the original equipment and replacement markets. Various sizes and types of tires were produced according to automakers' specifications for the original equipment market. Foreign tire makers had a substantial share of the OEM market, since 25.6 percent of the cars sold in the U.S. were imported. Imported cars required 10.6 million tires in 1991, down almost 14 percent from 1990 figures. The bulk of tires produced were sold in the larger replacement market, which included the retreading segment of the tire industry. The retreading market was dominated by truck and bus tire customers who benefitted from cost savings and longevity of tire use.

Original Equipment

Original equipment tire demand was directly related to motor vehicle output. In 1991, 43 million passenger tires were shipped to new vehicle manufacturers. This represented 22 percent of the total passenger tire market. Original equipment represented 15.2 percent of the truck and bus tire market, or 5.8 million units. Research showed that 40 percent of customers replaced their original equipment tires with an identical brand of tires. Consumer loyalty related directly to product satisfaction.

Tire manufacturers had to keep current with advances in technology and customer needs to obtain and retain OEM business. Only those who were at the forefront in technology would continue to increase OEM market share.

OEM demand was also affected by the number of tires used per vehicle. Passenger cars required five units per vehicle. Commercial vehicle requirements, which varied with vehicle size, ranged from five units per vehicle for vans to more than 22 units for large industrial trucks.

Demand from automakers required tire makers to maintain adequate R&D facilities to keep current with technological breakthroughs. Increased price competition among suppliers and increased demand for improved technology on tire fitments were expected in the 1990s.

Replacement Tire Market

The U.S. replacement tire market has declined slightly. Of the total passenger market of

195 million units in 1991, 152 million were replacement tires, down from 155 million in 1990. In 1991, Americans spent $15.3 billion on new replacement tires. The total value of the replacement passenger tire market in the U.S. was $8.6 billion (56.2 percent of the overall replacement market). Passenger replacement tires accounted for 78 percent of all passenger tires shipped in 1991. In 1991 32.3 million replacement light truck, and truck and bus tires were shipped versus 16.5 million in 1970. The total value of light truck, and truck and bus replacement tires in 1991 was $6.2 billion or 40.5 percent of the total value of the replacement market. Replacement demand was expected to average 4 percent annually through 1995.

Tire replacement rate is affected by tire quality and tire construction. As the trend moved away from bias tires to radials replacement rates decreased. With the change from radial to high-performance tires, however, the replacement rate would once again increase, until improvements in durability increased the tread wear for performance tires too.

Retreading

Retreading tires adds longevity to their wear and use; it also provides a valuable service to society by reducing the number of scrap tires in landfills. However, the level of retreading also affects the replacement rate, since the replacement market is measured in terms of new tires, not retreads. Retreaded tires are less expensive and generally provide reduced tread life. Retread use

Figure 6: Market Size of Retreaded Tires in the U.S. in 1991

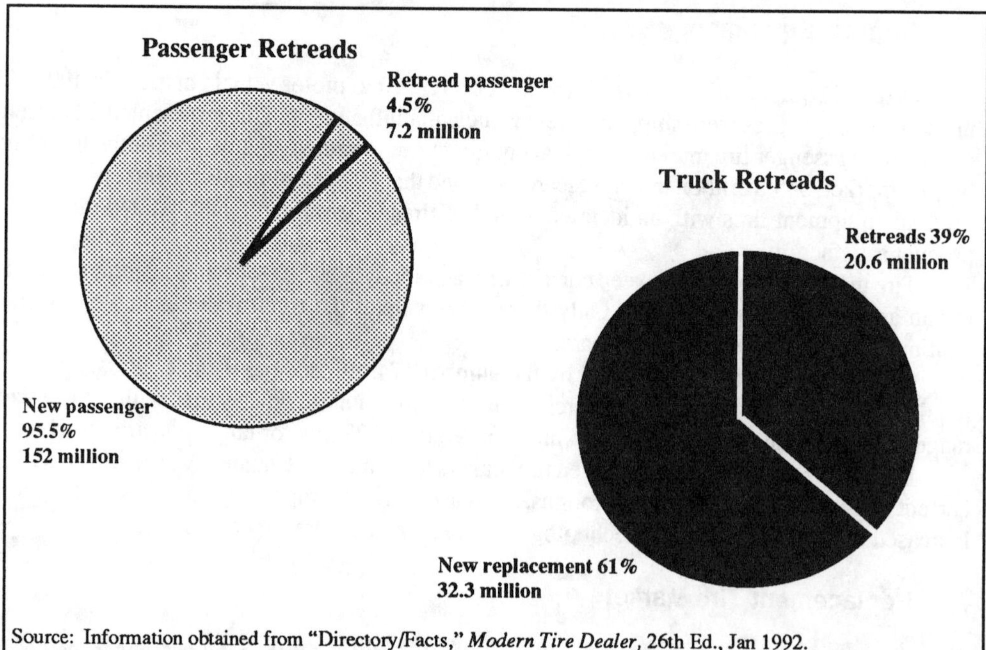

Source: Information obtained from "Directory/Facts," *Modern Tire Dealer*, 26th Ed., Jan 1992.

tends to decline with buyer affluence, especially in the passenger car market. Retreading is most popular in the commercial vehicle market because of the substantial cost advantages.

In the trucking industry, retreads outsold new tires. Therefore, manufacturers were working at making their new tires more durable, with improvements in belt and bead strength and casing liner compounds to ensure a tire's retread ability. In 1991, as shown in Figure 6, 7.2 million retreaded passenger tires were produced, while 20.6 million retreaded truck tires were produced ["Directory/Facts" 1992]. Since radial tires can be retreaded twice, the number of medium truck tires retreaded was increasing. Of the retread passenger tires in 1991, over 87 percent were radials.

Success in the retreading business entailed maintaining a delicate balance with the new replacement tire dealers within the retreader's area who purchased retread tires for inventory. Retreaders needed to be knowledgeable of manufacturers' tire specifications as well as vehicle manufacturers' recommendations for tire fitments. Retreaders were expected to continue to work with tire manufacturers in the 1990s on improving the quality of truck tires and their retreadability as well as passenger tire quality. Concerns with the environment were expected to encourage the American Retreaders Association to more actively educate government agencies, tire dealers, and retreaders on scrap tire disposal.

DISTRIBUTION

In the OEM market tires were distributed directly from tire plants to auto manufacturing plants. Replacement tires were distributed through independent tire dealers, tire company stores, department stores, service stations, warehouse clubs, and discount chains. The number of tire discounters and warehouses that sold at lower prices than dealer outlets grew substantially in the late 1980s. The percentage of sales by type of distributor in the replacement market for 1986 through 1991 is shown in Figure 7.

The role of the independent tire dealer in the distribution network was critical. The bulk of tires reached the market via independent dealers. In 1991 these dealers sold an estimated 101.8 million passenger tires for 67 percent of the replacement passenger car market ["Directory/Facts" 1992]. In 1990, independent dealers purchased 47 percent of their inventory directly from tire companies, down from 54 percent in 1987. Their purchases from warehouse distributors increased to 43 percent from 38 percent in 1987. A survey in 1990 of independent dealers showed that 34 percent carried one major tire brand and approximately 22 percent carried 2 to 3 brands. In the private brand market, 36 percent of the dealers carried one brand while 22 percent carried 2 to 3 brands. Quality was the number one criteria for purchasing a tire, followed closely by price. Seventy-two percent of the dealers advertised in newspapers while 81 percent used direct mail and radio ["Tire Dealer Profile" 1990, p.21].

The tire dealer's function was to help the consumer make the most appropriate tire purchase. Consumers appreciated a knowledgeable dealer who understood the performance capabilities of the wide variety of tires. Tire manufacturers provided for a strong support network to keep tire dealers up-to-date on tire technology. The best way for dealers to sell the product was by knowing the product better than the competitor, and by offering a better price.

Figure 7: Sales By Distributor Type

WHOLESALE AND RETAIL
How passenger tires reach the market - Distribution Channels

	1991	1990	1989	1988	1987	1986
Independent Dealers	67%	67%	67%	68%	68%	68%
Oil Companies	2%	2%	2%	2%	2%	3%
Tire Company Stores	12%	13%	14%	13%	13%	13%
Chain Stores, Dept. & Disc. Stores, Warehouse clubs	19%	18%	17%	17%	17%	16%

ESTIMATED SHARE OF THE PASSENGER TIRE RETAIL MARKET

	1991	1990	1989	1988	1987	1986
Tire Dealerships	54%	54%	54%	56%	56%	56%
Service Stations	6%	7%	7%	7%	8%	8%
Tire Company Stores	12%	13%	13%	12%	11%	11%
Misc. Outlets	1%	1%	2%	2%	2%	3%
Auto Dealerships	1%	1%	2%	2%	2%	2%
Chain Stores, Dept. Stores	19%	18%	17%	17%	17%	17%
Warehouse & Disc. Clubs	7%	6%	5%	4%	4%	3%

SOURCE: Information obtained from "Facts/Directory," *Modern Tire Dealer*, 26th Ed., Jan 1992

In 1934, tire makers operated 3,040 tire company stores in the U.S. By 1963 that number had climbed to 8,977. In the 1980s that number declined and by 1991 only Goodyear and Firestone owned a significant number of tire stores, about 2,800 outlets combined. In 1991, 12 percent of tire sales (or roughly 22 million units) were generated at company-owned tire stores. By operating their own stores, tire makers had an assured distribution source and could control the pricing and advertising of their products. However, tire stores generally showed a poor rate of return. These chains were saddled with the high overhead costs of a big corporation.

Department stores, discount chain stores, and warehouse clubs accounted for 19 percent of tire sales in 1991. The number of warehouse membership clubs increased from 296 to 504 between 1990 and 1991 as their market share increased to six percent from three percent in 1986.

Independent manufacturers such as Cooper Tires had to maintain close relationships with independent dealers, and offer fast delivery, technical assistance, good quality, inventory control, and competitive prices. The tire dealer determined what brand of tires was sold more than 50% of the time. When buying from a warehouse club or mass merchandiser, the customer asked for the brand advertised at a specific price in the newspaper and bought it. However, the independent dealer could change the mind of prospective consumers [Hone, 2/92].

MARKETING AND ADVERTISING

The top ten tire advertisers spent $36.2 million on TV ads in 1989. Goodyear, BF Goodrich, and Michelin accounted for two-thirds of these expenditures ["Goodyear tops TV.." 1990]. In 1990 Goodyear spent $178.7 million on ads in the U.S. — $35 million of which were spent on TV ads ["100 Leading.." 1991]. Tire companies had to establish an aggressive industrial marketing stance in order to remain viable competitors. Instead of producing a tire and then trying to market it, tire companies had to learn to analyze demand and then supply the market. The U.S. economy, consumer lifestyles, and the performance of various end-use markets had influenced the marketing strategies chosen.

Advertising campaigns were intended to reinforce tire brand loyalty. Studies showed that more than 40 percent of consumers replaced their original tires with identical brands. Manufacturers knew that the consumer subconsciously picked a tire because of the way it looked. For example, surveys had found that 85 percent of motorsport fans tended to purchase the same type of performance tire within three years. Apart from tread design, specific features such as price and tread life had to be stressed in marketing. Comfort, quality, and conservation were also key elements in advertising campaigns. Luxury car and image car owners showed the greatest brand loyalty. The lowest degree of loyalty existed in the less affluent, price-conscious buyer ["Motorsports" 1990].

One form of advertising in the tire industry was the auto show, where tire manufacturers as well as automakers exhibited new products and educated both industry tire dealers and the general public about the available features. Also, specialized industry journals and magazines sponsored by the industry covered news of the industry and analyzed industry outlook. Furthermore, most of the tire makers maintained their own publications to inform clients on a continuing basis of new technological findings and opportunities.

DISPOSAL AND RECYCLING

Entrepreneurs tried to implement new ways to dispose of the estimated 2 to 2.5 billion scrap tires in dumps and landfills in the U.S. and to deal with the nearly 270 million scrap tires entering the system annually. Roughly 85 percent of scrap tires wound up in dumps, four percent were exported or sold as used tires, eight percent were burned for fuel, and three percent went into processed rubber products. A growing awareness of solid waste problems and a growing number of state laws regulating tire dumping in landfills and the percentage of recycled rubber to be used in specific products were indications of potential federal legislation on disposal. Many states had mandated deposits on tire purchases; the deposit would be refunded when the tire was turned in. Others had limited the number of tires on any one disposal site. Taxes and fees on each tire sold had been imposed by over 30 states — the money was allocated toward research into new alternatives for disposal and recycling. Government agencies, the construction industry and tire manufacturers were seen as potential major customers of recycled tires.

Scrap tires could be used in (1) the utilities industry as supplemental fuel, (2) rubber modified asphalt concrete in road pavement, (3) other rubber and rubber-associated products, and (4) artificial reefs, breakwaters, and road mats. Some entrepreneurs have found unusual ways to use tires, such as in irrigation and drainage, road bases in swamps, and even in the building of homes [Ondrusch 1990].

COMPETITION

In 1991 the top six world leaders in tire manufacturing controlled 82 percent of the world market: Michelin (including Uniroyal/Goodrich), $10.4 billion in sales; Bridgestone/Firestone, $9.8 billion; Goodyear $8.5, billion; Continental/General $3.9 billion; Pirelli/Armstrong, $3.7 billion; and Sumitomo/Dunlop, $3.5 billion.

In North America, Goodyear led in market share of passenger replacement tires with 15 percent, followed by Michelin with 14.5 percent, Cooper with 10 percent, General with 9 percent and Firestone with 8 percent. Goodyear also led in the original equipment market with 36.5 percent, followed by Firestone and Uniroyal both with 17 percent, Michelin with 15 percent, and General with 12 percent. Estimated brand shares in the replacement and OEM tire markets for 1991 are shown in Figure 8.

Estimated tire production capacity as of January 1, 1992 totalled 829,300 units per day in the U.S., a 1.7 percent decrease over 1990. A breakdown of tire manufacturers' production capabilities is as follows:

Michelin	48,000 units/day
General	69,140 units/day
Cooper	83,600 units/day
Firestone	96,500 units/day
Kelly/Springfield	112,500 units/day
Uniroyal	118,500 units/day
Other	145,060 units/day
Goodyear	156,000 units/day

Plant capabilities in 1991 decreased by nearly 14,000 tires/day or 3.51 million units from 1990. Over 75 percent of U.S. tire plants were located in the South and Southwest. Most of these plants were antiquated and needed upgrading.

Goodyear Tire and Rubber Company (U.S.)

Goodyear was the largest tire manufacturer in the U.S., and second in the world. As of 1991, it had a 15 percent market share in passenger replacement tires and a 36.5 percent share in the OEM passenger tire market. It supplied General Motors with 33 percent of its tires, Chrysler with 83 percent, and Honda of America with 30 percent. Tire brands in the U.S. included Goodyear, Lee, and Kelly-Springfield.

In order to match its competitors' investments and maintain its strong presence in the tire

Figure 8: Estimated 1991 Brand Shares (Replacement Passenger Tire Market)

Goodyear	15.0%
Michelin	8.5%
Firestone	7.5%
Sears	5.5%
General	4.5%
BFGoodrich	3.5%
Bridgestone	3.5%
Cooper	3.5%
Kelly	3.0%
Multi-Mile	3.0%
Sentry	2.5%
Uniroyal	2.5%
Cordovan	2.0%
Dayton	2.0%
Dunlop	2.0%
Pirelli	2.0%
Armstrong	1.5%
Falls Mastercraft	1.5%
Hercules	1.5%
Monarch	1.5%
Montgomery Ward	1.5%
Remington	1.5%
Summit	1.5%
Yokohama	1.5%
Atlas	1.0%
Centennial	1.0%
Cornell	1.0%
Delta	1.0%
Jetzon	1.0%
Laramie	1.0%
Lee	1.0%
Mohawk	1.0%
National	1.0%
Regul	1.0%
Sigma	1.0%
Spartan	1.0%
Star	1.0%
Stratton	1.0%
Toyo	1.0%
Other	2.5%

Tire Marketers

TBC	6.0%
Del-Nat	2.0%
Jetzon-La	2.0%
Private B	2.0%
Falken	1.5%
Reliable	1.5%
Reynolds	1.0%

U.S. Market Share of OEM Tires in 1991

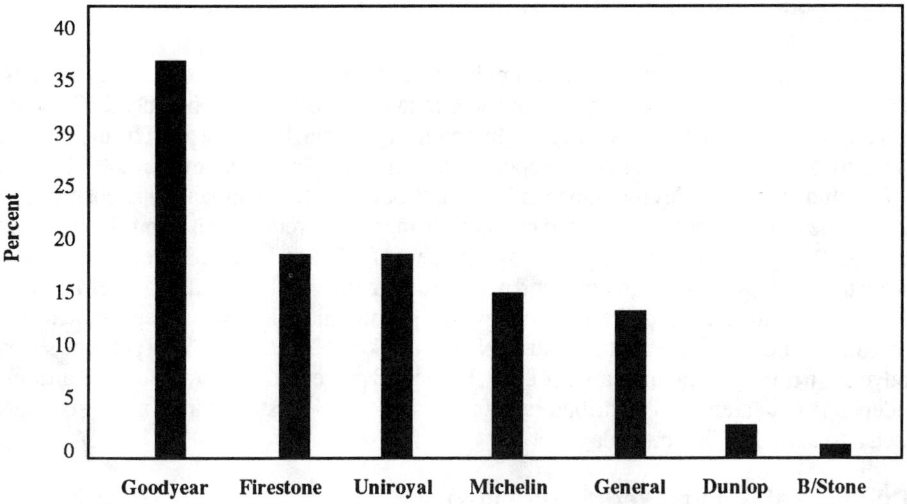

Source: Information obtained from "Facts/Directory," *Modern Tire Dealer*, 26th Ed., Jan 1992.

industry, Goodyear Tire & Rubber increased its capital expenditures to $760 million in 1989. However, over the next three years it decided to hold capital expenditures at less than $440 million to reduce debt. In addition, Goodyear spent $300 million on R&D in 1989, $331 million in 1990, and $330 million in 1991 ["Annual Report" 1991].

Goodyear had 10 tire plants in the U.S., seven under the Goodyear name and three under the Kelly-Springfield name, with a total capacity of 268,500 units/day in 1991.

In addition to continuing operations of company-owned stores, especially in areas where market share was weak, Goodyear was experimenting with "Just Tires" stores in test areas.

Goodyear announced in early March 1992 that it would sell Goodyear brand tires through Sears. Sears controlled 10 percent of the replacement market and this move could give Goodyear an additional three million units of sales a year. However, there was concern that this move could backfire by alienating Goodyear's 2,500 independent dealers, who might be undercut by Sears and thus turn to other name brands [Milbank 1992].

Michelin et Cie (France)

After its acquisition of Uniroyal/Goodrich in 1990, Michelin had won the number one spot among tire manufacturers. The company was one of the largest industrial organizations in France, and one of the largest privately-owned firms in the world. Michelin, including UGTC, had a market share of 14.5 percent of the passenger replacement tire market in the U.S. and 32 percent of the OEM passenger market. It supplied Ford with 23.5 percent of its tires, Chrysler with 17 percent, and Volvo and Subaru with 100 percent of their tires.

In the U.S., Michelin (including UGTC) had eight plants which produced a total of 166,500 units/day.

Bridgestone (Japan)

Bridgestone, the largest tire manufacturer in Japan, derived 70 percent of its sales from tires and related products. As its share of the domestic Japanese tire market approached 50 percent, the company entered the U.S. market in 1982 by acquiring a radial truck tire plant from Firestone. The company's U.S. presence was largely concentrated in the replacement tire market (11 percent in 1990) with distribution through independent retail outlets. The company was positioned to expand into the OEM market as Japanese automobile manufacturers increased production in the U.S. In 1991 Bridgestone/Firestone supplied 40 percent of OEM to Toyota, 35 percent to Nissan, 85 percent to Mazda, 40 percent to Ford, and was the exclusive supplier of OEM for GM's Saturn car. Bridgestone/Firestone's marketing strategy was to combine sales from independent dealers and company-owned stores. Firestone had a U.S. tire market share in OEM of 17 percent, second to Goodyear. In the replacement market, of which it held 8 percent, tires were sold by retail stores and independent dealers and distributors. In the U.S., Bridgestone/Firestone's six plants produced a total of 115,000 units/day.

Continental Gummi-Werke (Germany)

Continental was the fourth largest tire company in the world. In 1987 it acquired General Tire and Rubber Company in the U.S.

Tires accounted for about 75 percent of General Tires' total sales; rubber-related products such as rubber roofing products and tennis balls accounted for the other 25 percent. General Tires sold replacement tires through its system of franchised automotive service centers where it controlled 9 percent of the passenger segment. In the OEM market, General was a major supplier to General Motors and Nissan, supplying 12 percent of the OEM passenger tire market in North America.

Continental AG made 80 percent of its sales in the world tire market. Thirty-three percent of the company's tires were sold to Mercedes Benz, BMW, Volkswagen, and Porsche. Continental management decided to diversify operations, and by 1991 had acquired 800 independent retailers in the U.S, the U.K., Germany and Canada. These outlets were run by entrepreneurs who were more successful than big corporations in that market. However, Continental's efforts to obtain a direct share in the replacement market had been unsuccessful as of the early 1990s.

General Tires' estimated capacity in the U.S. as of 1991 was 69,000 units/day from four plants.

Pirelli (Italy)

Pirelli was the world's sixth largest tire company. In 1988 Pirelli purchased Armstrong Tire Co. in the U.S. in order to increase its sales in the OEM and replacement markets in the U.S. Pirelli placed one of its three major R&D facilities in Massachussets. Pirelli Armstrong Tire had three plants with an estimated capacity of 47,600 units/day. Exports from the U.S. were mainly light truck tires.

Sumitomo Rubber Industries (Japan)

Sumitomo Rubber, Japan's second largest tire producer, was a subsidiary of Sumitomo Electric Industries. Tires and related products represented nearly 80 percent of its sales in 1991. Sumitomo acquired the manufacturing facilities and distribution systems of Dunlop Holding in 1983. Dunlop marketed a full line of tires in the U.S. and had three plants in the U.S. with an estimated capacity of 45,000 units/day.

CHANGING COMPETITIVE ENVIRONMENT

Globalization and consolidation had created a highly competitive environment in the tire industry in the early 1990s. In Europe, a price war to maintain market shares had companies such as Michelin and Continental AG reducing prices by 17 percent in 1990 to keep their position against Bridgestone. This price reduction resulted in a decrease of profitability [Baldo 1990]. A price increase in September 1991, led by Continental AG, was partially successful, and Goodyear announced a increase of three to five percent effective May 1992. Dealers, however, feared they would be unable to pass on the increase to consumers despite the fact that the replacement market was showing signs of picking up [Milbank 1992].

Figure 9: U.S. Tire & Rubber Industry Statistics

	1987	1988	1989	1990	1991	1992*
Sales ($ mill)	11,537	12,608	12,815	13,376	13,000	13,700
Operating Margin	13.0%	11.1%	11.4%	9.1%	9.0%	10.0%
Net Profit	552.1	494.6	450.6	129.7	110	250
Net Profit Margin	4.8%	3.9%	3.5%	1.0%	0.9%	1.8%

*projection

SOURCE: Information obtained from "Value Line Investment Survey" December 20, 1991, p.123.

In the U.S. the consolidation process created several problems, primarily financial gaps caused by investment and spending in the joint ventures of the big six competitors. All the major companies had heavy losses in 1990, except for Cooper Tire whose profits rose by 14 percent. Figure 9 shows actual sales in the U.S. market from 1987 to 1990, and projected sales for 1991 and 1992 showed that demand would be constant for that period.

Worldwide competition among tire makers had created an overcapacity problem. Industry analysts expected an increase of 20 percent in the production capacity of the American tire industry. A number of plants would have to shut down permanently to maintain high productivity levels without incurring overcapacity.

Consolidation had not worked in the short term and the big five producers had begun to realize it. Continental AG dropped plans to pursue a merger with Pirelli in 1991. Increases in the prices of raw materials meant that production costs would also increase. Figure 9 shows an average of nine percent operating profit margin for 1991.

FUTURE TRENDS

Increasing market share appeared to be a central plan of tire companies. However, maximizing market share entailed building plants and equipment to produce enough tires to meet the most optimistic demand. This had resulted in chronic overcapacity for the industry. This overcapacity was one of the main reasons tire prices were low and the industry suffered from low return rates. Another problem caused by overcapacity was that in order to operate efficiently, the firms produced tires for private label retailers. These private label marketers competed with tire manufacturers for replacement sales [Byrne 1990].

In an effort to break loose of their dependency on the troubled OEM market, the large tire makers were expected to diversify into new markets, especially the replacement market that for so long had been left almost exclusively to the smaller independent tire makers. Customers in the U.S. replacement market were loyal to the local and regional manufacturers and distributors because independent distributors offered lower prices, higher quality, and better service.

Diversification into new geographic markets was a new strategy for tire makers. Eastern Europe, Latin America, and the newly industrialized Asian nations seemed to offer tremendous opportunities. Concentrating their efforts on getting a larger share of the American market appeared to have been an expensive mistake for many companies. These new overseas regions offered opportunities in both resources and markets.

THE COMPANY

HISTORY

Cooper Tire & Rubber Company was founded in 1914 by John F. Schaeffer and Claude H. Hart and was named The Giant Tire Company. In 1930 it merged with Cooper Corporation and moved its headquarters to Findlay, Ohio, under the direction of Ira J. Cooper. In 1946, the firm changed its name to Cooper Tire & Rubber Company because of the great contribution of Mr. Cooper to the company.

In the 1960s Cooper Tire & Rubber went public and its stocks began to be traded on the New York Stock Exchange (NYSE) under the symbol CTB. The 1960s and 1970s represented a great period of expansion for Cooper and its principal lines: tires and rubber industrial products [*Annual Report* 1989].

The economic expansion of the industrial world affected Cooper positively during the 1980s. In 1983, Cooper joined the ranks of "Fortune 500," a listing of the largest American industrial corporations. The company had also begun an aggressive period of expansion of plant and equipment, and new capital investment was made in plants in Findlay, Ohio; Texarkana, Arkansas; and Tupelo, Mississippi between 1980 and 1985. Within this period, the company developed an efficient distribution center for all its product lines. The company financed all its capital spending from sales, which surpassed a half billion dollars by 1985 [*Annual Report* 1985].

From 1985 to 1989, the company performed very successfully. Cooper's sales force was named the best sales team by *Sales & Marketing Management* magazine in 1986. In the same year, the company was listed in "The 101 Best Performing Companies in America" and the *Wall Street Transcript* named Chairman Ed Brewer and President Ivan Gorr best chief executives in the rubber industry [*Annual Report* 1989]. In 1991, *Financial World* magazine selected Gorr as winner of the silver award in the chemicals industry in its CEO of the Year competition [Hone 1991].

Because of the company's success, Cooper's management invested in several of its plants to increase production capacity. The company continued to improve its products, service, technology, distribution and warranty coverage — keys to success in the company's niche of the replacement tire segment [Hone 3/92].

PRODUCTS

Cooper's line of business was tires and rubber industrial products. The tire product line of the company included passenger tires, light truck and RV tires, medium truck tires, and inner tubes for the American replacement market [*Annual Report* 1990]. Rubber industrial products included vibration control products, hoses and hose assemblies, automotive sealing systems, and specialty seating components for the automotive components segment of the OEM market.

In the late 1980s, Cooper focused on the development and introduction of high-performance tires designed for larger engines and performance cars. Cooper introduced its first performance tire in 1987 and by 1991 offered six performance tire lines. The V-rated, 50-series Cooper Cobra VR50 Radial G/T was introduced in 1990 with an innovative center groove design that represented a significant departure from competitive performance tire tread patterns. The company was in the process of developing a V-rated all-season radial tire and an H-rated metric radial for the performance market [*Annual Reports* 1989 & 1990]. Cooper production and market strategies closely followed the trends of the replacement market — the principal source of Cooper's sales.

Cooper produced more than 1,000 rubber industrial products for OEM customers on a made-to-order basis using the processes of molding, extrusion, and rubber-to-metal bonding. The majority of these products were made for application on motor vehicles in the principal product categories of vibration control, hoses and tubing, body sealing, and interior seating. Because of the integral nature of vehicle design, the company worked closely with OEM in developing automotive components of this line. The company's sales of approximately $179.2 million in rubber industrial products in 1991 represented 20 percent of total company sales. New opportunities existed in this market as a major competitor had departed the ranks of automotive component suppliers, and Cooper had expanded supply contracts [*Annual Report* 1990].

MARKET

Cooper's principal market was the U.S tire replacement segment. The economic conditions in the U.S. in the early 1990s presented a unique opportunity for growth at Cooper. The conditions included an estimated population of 250 million, which was growing at an annual rate of one percent. U.S vehicle registrations were approximately 189 million passenger cars and trucks in 1990 and the growth rate of vehicle use was approximately twice that of population growth. American households averaged between two and three vehicle users or owners, and each passenger vehicle had an average life of 7.6 years. Passenger vehicles averaged 10,100 miles annually, with overall traffic mileage estimated at over three trillion miles annually ["Statistical Abstract .." 1991].

The American replacement market offered a total opportunity of $15.3 billion in 1991. Of this figure, replacement passenger tires accounted for $8.6 billion in sales while replacement truck tires accounted for $6.2 billion.

Between 1985 and 1990 Cooper's share of the replacement market had grown by 19.2

percent. Cooper Tire & Rubber Company held a 5 percent share of the world market and a 10 percent share of the U.S. market, and was the tenth largest tire manufacturer [Benway 1990]. In 1990, the company sold approximately 23 million car and truck tires, and supplied about 12 percent of the U.S. replacement market.

With the shift from bias-ply to longer lasting radials since the 1970s, consumers bought tires more infrequently and brand loyalty declined. Alan Reinhardt, Cooper's CEO, said that "tires are bought the way life insurance is bought. Someone asks a dealer or an agent they trust, 'What do you recommend?" Cooper's understanding of the way tires were sold was reflected in Cooper's low wholesale prices. According to *Modern Tire Dealer* magazine, dealers said their average gross margin on a Cooper tire was 33 percent. Cooper was able to offer value-hungry customers high-quality tires at a moderate price [Hymowitz 1991].

FACILITIES

The company had eight facilities, one each in Albany, Georgia; Clarksdale, Mississippi; Piedras Negras, Mexico; Auburn, Indiana; El Dorado, Arkansas; Bowling Green, Ohio; Findlay, Ohio; and Tupelo, Mississippi for the production of tires, inner tubes, and rubber industrial products [*Annual Report* 1990].

Regional distribution center facilities were located in strategic geographic areas to provide the best service to customers. Cooper's regional centers were located in Albany, Georgia; Dayton, Ohio; Los Angeles, California; Texarkana, Arkansas; Chicago, Illinois; Findlay, Ohio; New York, New York; New Brunswick, New Jersey; Dallas, Texas; Kansas City, Kansas; Tacoma, Washington; and Tupelo, Mississippi. Cooper's properties, plants and equipment were valued at $520.9 billion according to 1990 figures [*Annual Report* 1990].

Cooper spent approximately $100 million in capital investment in 1990. The principal acquisition was the Albany, Georgia plant where the company planned to start production of radial tires. The manufacturing and warehousing facility consisted of a 1.8 million square foot building on 325 acres of land [*Annual Report* 1990]. Cooper also continued upgrading its other eight facilities. The company planned new capital investment of $130 million in 1991 to maintain its then current competitive production position [Benway 1990].

The company's headquarters in Findlay had no frills. The lobby was adorned with Cooper tires encased in glass and resting on pedestals. The executive offices featured heavy metal desks and cheap panelling. The company's rock-bottom costs and no-frills approach, which extended even to the executive suite, allowed it to capture an ever-increasing share of the replacement market.

TECHNOLOGY

Cooper had an indisputable leadership role in developments of new technology in materials, compounds, production methods, and advanced equipment. The technological advances had led the company to high standards of quality and productivity in the production of tires, inner tubes, and industrial products. According to the "101 Best Performing Companies in America," Cooper was a highly productive and cost-efficient specialist in the rubber industry.

Automation of tire finishing had been introduced to improve productivity rates. The automation system sorted, trimmed, tested, buffed, and balanced a tire in a fraction of the time conventional methods took. The company was a leader in the practical use of finite element modelling, the mathematical process that allowed development engineers to analyze new product designs on computers against several tire performance variables. The application of this method permitted the company to speed up the process of bringing new products to market and increased the success rate of the selected designs [*Annual Report* 1990].

Cooper Tire closely followed trends in the replacement market and formulated its production strategies accordingly, but it had never developed a completely new product. The company's R&D facilities concentrated on minimizing production costs and improving productivity rates.

DISTRIBUTION

Cooper traditionally had distributed its products through independent dealers and distributors. The company's most important brands, Cooper and Falls Mastercraft, were distributed through 1,600 independent dealers who typically sold several other brands. Unlike other tire makers, such as Goodyear, Cooper didn't control its own network of company-owned stores. Chairman Ivan Gorr noted that "as independents they are motivated to be successful for themselves" [Hymowitz 1991]. Cooper did not undercut its dealers by selling the Cooper brand to mass merchandisers.

The company also manufactured tire products under private labels such as Hercules and Atlas and supplied them through other channels of distribution such as dealer and distributor buying groups, large retail chains, and oil companies. These products accounted for half of the company's output. Some of these customer relationships had been on-going for as long as 40 years [*Annual Report* 1990].

Cooper had developed a modern network distribution system to provide customers with top-of-the-line service. The network distribution center was linked by computers to inform customers of the available products and help them locate any product in the system. The main interest of Cooper's management was to fill customers' orders quickly and completely.

In order to provide better service, the company had renewed and extended its industry-leading warranty coverage on selected premium passenger radials. Although all tires had standard coverage for materials and workmanship, Cooper featured a "free replacement" limited warranty for the life of the tire on its premium products; Cooper also offered a limited warranty up to 60,000 miles on its touring radial tire. The company used and compared its products with a federally mandated program, the Uniform Tire Quality Grading (UTQG), which provided consumers with comparative information on tire treadwear, traction, and heat resistance [*Annual Report* 1990].

Cooper held fast to old-fashioned notions of loyalty towards employees, customers and suppliers. It promptly returned phone calls to dealers and listened to suggestions. It also flew disgruntled dealers to its Ohio headquarters on the company jet to iron out problems.

PROMOTION AND ADVERTISING

Cooper had successfully used the press, particularly *USA TODAY*, to maintain a national advertising program. The newspaper had been very effective in keeping consumers aware of the brand names used by Cooper and for the efforts of Cooper's management to promote dealers in their local markets. The company also had used radio as another channel of promotion and advertising. However, the company spent just five cents to sell $1 of its goods, compared to 20 cents for competitors such as Goodyear.

Technical information focusing on product knowledge, retailing, and telephone sales techniques were provided to independent dealers and other distributors. The company offered video courses, seminars, direct market assistance, and information bulletins to provide permanent feedback in regard to information concerning Cooper's distribution network [*Annual Reports* 1989 & 1990].

EMPLOYEES

In 1991 Cooper Tire Company employed more than 6,000 employees, most of them of long standing with the company. The company provided its employees with a stock purchasing plan, and some of them had become millionaires through it. In addition to this, the company provided a pension plan for retirees. By 1991, employee shareholders as a group owned more than 15 percent of the company.

The gulf between white-collar and blue-collar workers was lessened by caps on the salaries of senior management. There were also frequent golf outings where managers and factory workers mixed freely.

Company loyalty was also encouraged by Cooper's longstanding tradition of having employees stick labels printed with their names inside each finished tire. This practice was even highlighted in an ad campaign [Hymowitz 1991].

FINANCIAL RESULTS

Cooper Tire & Rubber Company reported record sales and earnings for the fourth quarter and full year ended December 31, 1991. Figure 10 shows Cooper's Statements of Income and Balance Sheets for 1990 and 1991. Net income for1991 reached a record $79.4 million, up 19.5 percent from $66.5 million in 1990. Per share earnings were $1.61 in 1990 compared with $1.42 in 1989. Net sales also reached a record $1.001 billion for 1991, an increase of 11.7 percent over the previous record of $896 million in 1990. Figure 11 shows the company's Summary of Operations and Financial Analysis for 1985 through 1991.

Cooper's chairman and chief executive officer, Ivan W. Gorr, attributed the 1991 performance records to Cooper employees, who emphasized superior levels of quality manufacturing

Figure 10: Cooper Tire & Rubber Company Statement of Income and Balance Sheet

STATEMENT OF INCOME

	Quarter Ended December 31		Twelve Months Ended December 31	
	1991	1990	1991	1990
Revenues:				
Net Sales	254,039,195	$212,815,315	$1,001,070,670	$895,896,295
Other Income	190,089	78,282	509,896	919,603
	254,229,284	212,893,597	1,001,580,566	896,815,898
Costs and expenses:				
Cost of products sold	201,630,986	170,481,944	820,639,025	740,004,455
Selling, general, administrative	12,520,958	11,222,019	51,936,400	47,177,222
Interest and debt expense	493,103	942,402	4,540,305	4,760,720
	214,645,047	182,646,365	877,115,730	791,942,397
Income before income taxes	39,584,237	30,247,232	124,464,836	104,873,501
Provision for income taxes	14,080,000	10,860,000	45,030,000	38,410,000
Net Income	$25,504,237	$19,387,232	$79,434,836	$66,463,501
Net Income per share	$0.62	$0.47	$1.92	$1.61
Weighted average shares aoutstanding	41,460,225	41,230,231	41,368,881	41,195,255

BALANCE SHEET

	December 31	
	1991	1990
Assets		
Current assets:		
Cash, including short-term investments	$24,431,564	$10,124,470
Accounts receivable	152,696,454	126,990,269
Inventories	77,964,996	121,404,034
Prepaid Expenses	6,633,878	9,272,195
Total current assets	261,726,892	267,790,968
Property, plant and equipment - net	388,557,001	334,794,268
Other assets	20,287,823	13,872,371
	$670,571,716	$616,457,607
Libailities and Stockholders' Equity		
Current Liabilities:		
Trade payables and accrued liabilities	103,275,165	89,881,376
Income taxes	8,028,166	3,916,266
Current portion of long-term debt	6,139,000	6,702,000
Total current liabilities	117,442,331	100,499,642
Long-term debt	53,512,205	91,026,532
Other long-term liabilities	21,097,000	22,192,000
Deferred Federal Income taxes	38,872,000	33,736,000
stockholders' equity	439,648,180	369,003,433
	$670,571,716	$616,457,607

SOURCE: Information obtained from "Cooper Tire Sets Sales..", Cooper Tire & Rubber Company, Feb 1992.

Figure 11: Cooper Tire & Rubber Company
Summary of Operations and Financial Analysis

INCOME DATA (000'S)	1991	1990	1989	1987	1986	1985
Net Sales	$1,001,071	$895,896	$866,805	$748,032	$665,775	$577,517
Gross Profit	180,432	155,892	139,482	106,419	93,877	81,515
Operating Income	128,495	108,715	94,188	66,575	56,031	46,432
Net Other Income & Expense	4,030	3,841	1,564	1,663	2,941	3,294
Pretax Income	124,465	104,874	92,624	64,912	53,090	43,138
Income Taxes	45,030	38,410	34,380	23,850	22,410	20,120
Net Income	79,435	66,464	58,244	41,062	30,680	23,018

BALANCE SHEET	1991	1990	1989	1987	1986	1985
Current Assets	$261,727	$267,791	$249,215	$229,227	$250,518	$227,615
Net Property & Fixed Assets	388,557	334,794	262,445	212,923	162,447	139,721
Total Assets	670,572	616,458	519,893	442,582	413,306	367,715
Current Liabilities	117,442	100,500	98,930	86,125	96,235	74,077
Long-Term Debt	53,512	91,027	65,727	67,790	70,059	76,795
Stockholders' Equity	439,648	369,003	310,064	257,756	221,566	195,151

PER SHARE *	1991	1990	1989	1987	1986	1985
Shares Outstanding (000's)						
(1) Average Shares	41,369	41,195	41,038	40,791	40,629	40,432
(2) Year-End Shares	41,481	41,259	41,130	40,911	40,692	40,576
Sales(1)	24.20	$21.75	$21.12	$18.34	$16.39	$14.28
Assets(2)	16.17	14.94	12.64	10.82	10.16	9.06
Equity(1)	10.60	8.96	7.56	6.32	5.45	4.83
Earnings(1)	1.92	1.61	1.42	1.01	0.76	0.57
Dividends	0.26	0.21	0.17	0.14	0.12	0.10
Cash Flow(2)		2.28	1.99	1.49	1.21	0.98
Price:Low	15.75	12.38	11.25	7.07	5.57	4.32
High	52.50	21.00	19.50	13.63	9.94	7.19
Average P/E(X)	17.80	10.30	10.80	10.30	10.30	10.10
Average Yield(%)		1.30	1.10	1.40	1.50	1.80

RATIO ANALYSIS	1991	1990	1989	1987	1986	1985
Operating Margin(%)		12.13	10.87	8.90	8.42	8.04
Pretax Margin(%)	12.40	11.71	10.69	8.68	7.97	7.47
Effective Tax Rate(%)	36.20	36.63	37.12	36.74	42.21	46.64
Net Margin(%)		7.42	6.72	5.49	4.61	3.99
Return on Beg. Assets(%)	12.90	12.78	13.16	9.94	8.34	7.80
Return on Beg. Equity(%)	21.50	21.44	22.60	18.53	15.72	13.10
Retention Rate(%)		86.98	87.84	86.09	84.77	81.99
Asset(Beg.) Turnover(X)		1.72	1.96	1.81	1.81	1.96
Financial Leverage(X)		1.68	1.72	1.87	1.88	1.68

SUPPLEMENTAL DATA	1991	1990	1989	1987	1986	1985
Capital Expenditures (000's)	$85,954	$100,141	$73,182	$70,621	$41,507	$26,548
Depreciation & Amortization (000's)	31,969	27,615	23,393	19,873	18,436	16,666
Wages, Salaries, Benefits (000's)	266,683	255,350	233,257	217,062	189,045	165,458
Number of Employees	6,545	6,225	6,041	6,031	5,720	5,398
Number of Stockholders	4,492	4,459	3,871	3,627	3,516	3,138

* Per share data reflects two-for-one stock splits in 1990, 1988.

SOURCE: Information obtained from "Annual Report", Cooper Tire & Rubber Company, 1991

and excellence in responding to the service needs of customers. "The Cooper team receives full credit for our achievements in 1991. Our employees produced more and sold more products than at anytime in our history. This was an outstanding performance considering the economic environment in which we operated. Demand for tires and engineered rubber products remained strong as our team developed new market opportunities," he concluded ["Cooper Tire Sets..." 1992].

TOWARDS THE FUTURE

Management at Cooper was optimistic about the company's future. It had the lowest R&D and advertising costs per sale in the industry and a higher profit margin than any of the large competitors.

Cooper's marketing strategy was to differentiate itself from the other big firms by avoiding the OEM market for tire sales and concentrating on selling various brand names to independent retail outlets in the replacement market. The company achieved a reputation for being a reliable supplier with up-to-date plants and with very few competing retail outlets of their own [Hicks 1990]. In addition, it had provided employees with strong participation plans that had allowed many factory level employees to become millionaires.

Industry analysts in 1992 were concerned that the shrinking of the auto industry and the globalization of the tire industry would increase competition in the replacement market and would result in price cuts and very low profit margins for tire makers such as Cooper.

Some managers at Cooper feared that despite the strong showing of the company in 1991, the increased number of competitors in the replacement market would hurt Cooper, which concentrated exclusively in this niche. In addition, industry figures had shown that in 1991 the replacement market had declined as compared to 1990 — a trend these managers feared would continue.

They argued that Cooper should expand outside the replacement market and increase its sales to the OEM market. Cooper was already supplying the OEM market with rubber industrial products for the automotive components segment. These products accounted for 20 percent of Cooper's sales. New business opportunities existed here as Cooper had gained expanded contracts and a major competitor had left the automotive components market. Cooper could increase its share of this market and at the same time use its reputation to sell its tire product line. It was estimated that in 1991, 43 million passenger tires and 5.8 million truck tires had been shipped to the OEM market. Cooper, some managers argued, would benefit from participating in that market.

To compete in the OEM market, tire makers had to be innovative and follow market trends and developments in the auto industry closely. Cooper had consistently increased its capital expenditure year after year and had upgraded all of its existing facilities. The acquisition of the Albany plant in 1990 increased the production capacity of the firm, and long-term expansion plans were in place at several of the other plants. Cooper had developed a unique method of tire finishing that was extremely precise and took a fraction of the time needed by conventional methods. This allowed Cooper to produce tires at lower costs than its competitors, which gave the company an edge in the OEM market where profit margins were slim. Its R&D team had been extremely strong in improving production methods and cutting costs. It had also earned high quality ratings from customers for its rubber industrial products, and worked closely with them to meet customer performance, quality, and cost goals. If the company decided to enter the OEM market its R&D team could apply its expertise for product innovation and new product development to match the requirements of the auto industry. This was proven by the fact that Cooper had successfully developed an innovative design for performance tires in 1990.

Another argument used by these managers to support entry in the OEM market was that the competition could strengthen customer loyalty to their brands through advertising campaigns. Should Cooper not participate in this market it could eventually lose its customers in the replacement market, 40 percent of whom were known to remain loyal to their original tire brands.

Other managers argued that to enter the OEM market for tires would put Cooper in a precarious position. To compete in the OEM market, tire makers needed to spend large amounts of money for R&D, and had to constantly keep up with developments in the auto industry. The OEM market could demand and set its own price, which meant that profit margins on sales to this market could be slim. Further, these managers argued that it would be difficult for Cooper to compete in this market against the big multinational firms that had huge investments in R&D departments around the world and were well entrenched in the OEM market. The OEM segment was contracting, and it was unlikely that competitors would make it easy for any new entrants in this market.

In addition, Cooper's plants were already operating at full capacity, unlike the rest of the industry. In order for Cooper to enter the OEM market, the company would have to expand its existing facilities and/or acquire new ones so as to be able to supply its expanded market. In its efforts to satisfy its new customers it might alienate its independent dealers by not being able to supply them with sufficient inventory on time.

On the other hand, these managers argued that instead of expanding into new OEM markets the company should strengthen its position in the replacement market. Cooper would continue to show the strong results that it had consistently shown in recent years, since it was well-established in the replacement market as a reliable supplier, and encouraged dealer loyalty by offering them a gross margin of 33 percent. Cooper, unlike Goodyear, did not sell to large discount stores or warehouses, and this was a strong point in its favor. Profit margins in the replacement market were much more rewarding and if Cooper continued to improve its computerized distribution network and maintained its reputation as an efficient supplier the company was expected to be able to keep its advantage in this market.

Cooper could also increase its market share by expanding its line of light truck tires. Light trucks were being used in new ways and were no longer confined to material transportation use. This was the fastest-growing segment of the replacement market. It could also penetrate this market through innovative product improvements in the performance, touring, and all-season product areas, as Cooper was now doing.

An estimated 152 million passenger units and 32.3 million truck tires were sold in the replacement market in 1991. Even though these figures were lower than those of 1990, motorists were retaining their vehicles for longer periods and continued to increase their use. In addition, the fact that high-performance tires were gradually replacing radials would mean increased replacement rates in the future since high-performance tires wore out 30 percent faster than radials.

Any price cuts that might ensue in the replacement market because of increased competition would affect Cooper the least of all the competitors, since it had the highest profit margin in the industry. Cooper could also count on the support of its dealers. The company maintained a good relationship with them, never undercut them by selling through warehouses or discount stores, and offered them the highest gross margin of profit. Cooper served them through an efficient computerized distribution network that ensured prompt delivery, and promoted these dealers through advertising campaigns in regional newspapers and radio spots. Cooper even flew disgruntled dealers to its headquarters in Ohio to correct problems. Cooper could capitalize on Goodyear's move to supply Sears with its brand tires by approaching Goodyear's independent dealers who felt threatened by this move.

Cooper was the indisputable leader in the American replacement market and it would be difficult for competitors to unseat it from its position. Its knowledge of this particular market would enable it to meet any new strategies developed by competitors and would allow Cooper to retain the clear advantage in its niche.

Should Cooper change its conservative policy and move away from its traditional and familiar market? Would the replacement market continue to experience flat sales, and should Cooper be looking at alternative markets? Management at Cooper in early 1992 was faced with answering these and many other strategic questions as they planned for the future.

REFERENCES AND BACKGROUND READINGS

"Annual Report," *Cooper Tire & Rubber Company*, 1989.

"Annual Report," *Cooper Tire & Rubber Company*, 1990.

"Annual Report," *Cooper Tire & Rubber Company*, 1991.

"Annual Report," *Goodyear Tire & Rubber Company*, 1991.

Anonymous, "The Tire Industry's Costly Obsession With Size," *Economist*, June 8, 1991, pp. 65-66.

Ballen, K., "Flat Tire Markets (Shrinking Demand for New Tires)," *Fortune*, December 3, 1990, pp. 14-15.

Baldo, Anthony, "Cooper Tire:Under Some Pressure," *Financial World*, July 10, 1990, p. 18.

Baldo, Anthony, "The Big Skid," *Financial World*, October 16, 1990, pp. 29-31.

Ballman, Barbara, "New Uses for Old Tires that Pay," *Chemical Week*, December 2, 1987, pp. 46-49.

Benway, Stuart J., "Tire and Rubber Industry," *Value Line Investment Survey*, December 20, 1991, p. 123.

"Bounce for Synthetic Rubber: Tires are Back in the Fast Lane", *Chemical Week*, April 19, 1989.

Bremner, Brian and Schiller Zachary, "Three who Bucked the Urge to Merge and Prospered", *Business Week*, October 14, 1991, p. 94.

Byrne, Dennis, "The Tire Superstore," *Tire Review*, July 1991, p. 9.

Byrne, Dennis, "Tire Review CEO Report," *Tire Review*, January 1992, p. 13.

"Cooper Tire Sets Sales and Earning Records for 1991," *Cooper Tire & Rubber*, February 11, 1992.

Davies, Jim, "Light Truck Tires," *Tire Review*, July 1991, p. 11.

Dewolf, R. "The Scrap Tire Problem Hangs in There," *Tire Review*, February 1991, pp. 24-26, 59-62.

Duke, Paul, "Economic Data are Repeating Fourth Quarter," *The Wall Street Journal*, February 19, 1991, p. A2.

"Facts/Directory 1991," *Modern Tire Dealer*, 26th Ed., January 1992.

Gibson, Richard, "Marketer's Mantra: Reap More with Less," *The Wall Street Journal,* March 22, 1991, pp. B1-B2.

Goldbaum, Ellen, "Pirelli Likes its Second Choice," *Chemical Week*, April 27, 1988, pp. 13-15.

"Goodyear Tops TV Tire Ad Spenders," *Modern Tire Dealer,* June, 1990, p. 59.

Griffiths, John, "Survival of the Biggest," *Financial Times Survey*, December 15, 1989, p. D1.

Hicks, Jonathan P., "Tire Company's Uphill Struggle," *New York Times,* June 13, 1989, p. D1.

Hicks, Jonathan "Chasing Few Buyers with Too Many Tires," *New York Times*, February 3, 1991, p. 5 (Business Section).

Hone, Jack, "Tire Talk," *Tire Review*, April 1991, p. 15.

Hone, Jack, "Doing the Right Things", *Tire Review*, March 1992, p. 15.

Hone, Jack, "Feeling Branded," *Tire Review*, February 1992, p. 15.

Hymowitz, Carol and O'Boyle, Thomas, "Cooper Tire and Dillard Stores Pinch Costs, Earn Loyalty and Keep up with Consumers," *Wall Street Journal*, May 29, 1991, pp. A1;A6.

Kaufman, D. "Which of These is your Performance Customers," *Tire Review*, March 1991, pp. 23-27.

"100 Leading National Advertisers," *Advertising Age*, September 25, 1991, pp. 70-75.

Marshall, Stuart, "Conflicting Demand of the Car Tire," *Financial Times Survey,* December 15, 1985, pp. C4;C5.

Milbank, Dana, "Goodyear Lifts Prices on Certain Tires on Signs that Demand is Picking Up," *Wall Street Journal,* March 3, 1992, p. A2.

"Motorsports", *Modern Tire Dealer*, May 1990, p. 17.

Nathans, Leah, "Anatomy of a Japanese Takeover," *Business Month,* June 1987, pp. 46-48.

Nevin, John J., "The Bridgestone-Firestone Merger: An Insider's Account, *Journal of Business Strategy,* July/August, 1989, pp. 26-30.

Ondrusch, Anthony, "Scrap Tires," *Tire Review,* February 1990, pp. 70-78.

"Our History", *Cooper Tire & Rubber*, 1989.

Patterson, A. Gregory, "U.S. Car Sales Rose Briskly Early in Month," *Wall Street Journal,* February 14, 1992. p. B1.

Paul, Ronald N., *The 101 Best Performing Companies in America,* Probus Publishing Co., Chicago Ill., 1986.

"Plastic and Rubber," *U.S. Industrial Outlook* 1990, pp. 14.4-14.5.

"Plastic and Rubber," *U.S Industrial Outlook* 1991, pp. 14.4-14.5.

"Plastic and Rubber," *U.S Industrial Outlook* 1992, pp. 14.4-14.5

Schiller, Zachary, "Can Bridgestone Make the Climb?", *Business Week,* February 27, 1989. pp. 78-79 (A).

Schiller, Zachary, "So Far, America is a Blowout for Bridgestone," *Business Week,* August 6, 990, pp. 82-83 (B).

"Statistical Abstract of the United States 1991," *Bureau of the Census,* 111th Ed., 1992.

Stewart, Tay and Schiller, Zachary, "That Screeching is Michelin Doing A U-Turn," *Business Week,* October 9, 1989, p. 50.

"25th Silver Anniversary Edition," *Modern Tire Dealer*, January, 1991.

Templin, Neal, "Sales of U.S.-Built Vehicles Slide 23.5%; Both Foreign, Domestic Showing is Poor," *The Wall Street Journal,* February 14, 1991, p. A2.

"Tire Dealer Profile," *Tire Review*, September 1990, pp. 21-31.

"Tires and Tubes Spend for Advertising Data, 1990," *Advertising Age,* August 13, 1990, p. 24.

Treece, James, B., "Detroit Could Use an Airbag Itself," *Business Week*, January 14, 1991, p. 67.

Wallace, Joseph, "All Tires Out," *Across the Board*, November, 1990, p. B1.

"World Statistics in Brief," *United Nations Statistical Pocketbook,* Thirteenth Edition, 1990.

Zagor, Karen, "U.S. Seen as Key to Global Market," *Financial Times Survey,* December 15, 1991, p. 3.

HARLEY-DAVIDSON INC.: THE MOTORCYCLE INDUSTRY

Harley-Davidson Inc. is a publicly-held, employee-owned manufacturer of motorcycles, recreational and commercial vehicles, military defense items, and small engines. In 1992, Harley's motorcycles were sold through a network of 600 franchised dealerships that emphasized quality and customer service. Recreational vehicles were also sold through a similar network, while contractual manufacturing was done on an individual basis with the government and other corporations. This case study concentrates on Harley-Davidson's motorcycle division and the motorcycle industry in general.

Harley-Davidson derived almost 70 percent of net sales and almost 100 percent of profits from motorcycle sales. As of 1992, sales of motorcycles and recreation vehicles were steadily increasing. However, the profit margins earned on motorcycles was greater. Harley-Davidson reported sales of $237.7 million in the fourth quarter of 1991. When combined with $702 million in sales for the first three quarters, as shown in Figure 1, this resulted in total sales of $940 million for 1991 — an increase of 8.8 percent from 1990. Sales were expected to increase through 1995 as Harley-Davidson capitalized on unprecedented brand loyalty and a vast untapped international market.

In the early 1990s, Harley-Davidson operated with a smaller budget and higher production costs than its competition. Despite these financial constraints, motorcycle sales steadily increased. In addition, other manufacturers frequently copied Harley's unique styling which appealed to American motorcyclists.

In looking to the future, Harley-Davidson was considering many strategic options. What opportunities could Harley-Davidson explore to continue its remarkable turnaround from near

Figure 1: Harley-Davidson, Inc.

Consolidated Statements of Income 1989-1991
(In Thousands)

INCOME STATEMENT	1989	1990	1991
NET SALES	$790,967	$864,600	$939,863
OPERATING COSTS AND EXPENSES:			
COST OF GOODS SOLD	$596,940	$635,551	$706,140
SELLING, ADMINISTRATIVE, AND ENGINEERING	$127,606	$145,674	$165,078
TOTAL OPERATING EXPENSES	$724,546	$781,225	$871,218
INCOME FROM OPERATIONS	$66,421	$83,375	$68,645
INTEREST INCOME	$3,634	$1,736	$950
INTEREST EXPENSE	($17,956)	($11,437)	($8,262)
LAWSUIT JUDGMENT	($7,200)		
OTHER, NET	$910	($3,857)	($3,239)
INCOME FROM CONTINUING OPERATIONS BEFORE INCOME TAXES AND EXTRAORDINARY ITEMS	$53,009	$62,617	$58,094
PROVISION FOR INCOME TAXES	$20,399	$24,309	$21,122
INCOME FROM CONTINUING OPERATIONS BEFORE EXTRAORDINARY ITEMS	$32,610	$38,308	$36,972
DISCONTINUED OPERATIONS, NET OF TAX:			
INCOME (LOSS) FROM DISCONT. OPERATION	$154		
GAIN ON DISPOSAL OF DISCONT. OPERATION	$3,436		
INCOME BEFORE EXTRAORDINARY ITEMS	$36,200	$38,308	$36,972
EXTRAORDINARY ITEMS:			
LOSS ON DEBT REPURCHASES, NET OF TAXES	($1,434)	($478)	
ADDITIONAL COST OF 1983 AMF SETTLEMENT	($1,824)		
NET INCOME	$32,942	$37,830	$36,972

SOURCE: Information obtained from HARLEY-DAVIDSON, INC., *1990 Company Report.* Information obtained from HARLEY-DAVIDSON, INC., *FORM 10-K*, December 31, 1991.

Figure 1: Harley-Davidson, Inc. (Contd.)

Consolidated Balance Sheets 1989-1991
(In Thousands)

	1989	1990	1991
ASSETS:			
CURRENT ASSETS:			
CASH AND EQUIVALENTS	$39,076	$14,001	$30,919
ACCOUNTS RECEIVABLE, NET	$45,565	$51,897	$71,517
INVENTORIES	$87,540	$109,878	$106,683
DEFERRED INCOME TAXES	$9,682	$14,447	$19,047
PREPAID EXPENSES	$5,811	$6,460	$8,677
ASSETS OF DISCONTINUED OPERATIONS			
TOTAL CURRENT ASSETS	$187,674	$196,683	$236,843
PROPERTY, PLANT, AND EQUIPMENT, NET	$115,700	$136,052	$163,686
GOODWILL	$66,190	$63,082	$59,894
DEFERRED FINANCING COSTS	$2,356		
OTHER ASSETS	$7,009	$11,650	$13,810
NONCURRENT ASSETS OF DISCONTINUED OPERATION			
TOTAL NONCURRENT ASSETS	$191,255	$210,784	$237,390
TOTAL ASSETS	$378,929	$407,467	$474,233

	1989	1990	1991
CURRENT LIABILITIES:			
NOTES PAYABLE	$22,789	$22,351	$39,526
CURRENT MATURITIES OF LONG-TERM DEBT	$4,143	$1,508	$1,563
ACCOUNTS PAYABLE	$40,095	$50,412	$55,412
ACCRUED EXPENSES AND OTHER LIABILITIES	$69,334	$72,260	$76,130
LIABILITIES OF DISCONTINUED OPERATION			
TOTAL CURRENT LIABILITIES	$136,361	$146,531	$172,631
LONG-TERM DEBT	$74,795	$48,339	$46,906
ACCRUED EMPLOYEE BENEFITS	$5,273	$9,194	$10,449
DEFERRED INCOME TAXES	$6,253	$4,628	$6,247
TOTAL NONCURRENT LIABILITIES	$86,321	$62,161	$63,602
TOTAL LIABILITIES	$222,682	$208,692	$236,233
STOCKHOLDER'S EQUITY			
PREFERRED STOCK			
COMMON STOCK	$92	$183	$183
ADDITIONAL PAID IN CAPITAL	$79,681	$87,115	$87,730
RETAINED EARNINGS	$77,352	$115,093	$152,065
FOREIGN CURRENCY TRANSLATION ADJUSTMENT	$508	$995	$1,566
	$157,633	$203,386	$241,544
LESS:TREASURY STOCK			
(539,694 SHARES) AT COST	($112)	($771)	($984)
LESS:UNEARNED COMPENSATION	($1,274)	($3,840)	($2,560)
TOTAL STOCKHOLDER'S EQUITY	$156,247	$198,775	$238,000
TOTAL LIABILITIES & STOCKHOLDER'S EQUITY	$378,929	$407,467	$474,233

SOURCE: Information obtained from HARLEY-DAVIDSON, INC., *1990 Company Report.*
Information obtained from HARLEY-DAVIDSON, INC., *FORM 10-K,* December 31, 1991.

bankruptcy? Should Harley-Davidson widen its existing motorcycle line, or diversify into other market niches such as dirt bikes? Should Harley-Davidson concentrate solely on North American sales, or expand forcefully into Europe or Asia? These were some of the decisions to be made if Harley-Davidson was to continue as the preeminent American manufacturer of motorcycles.

THE INDUSTRY AND COMPETITIVE MARKETS

THE MOTORCYCLE INDUSTRY

As shown in Figure 2, the motorcycle industry includes mopeds, lightweight, heavyweight, and sport motorcycles. The U.S. motorcycle industry was based on only a handful of manufacturers, each of whom differentiated itself from the others more or less through one distinguished product or design. Harley-Davidson was the only major U.S. motorcycle manufacturer; its competition came mainly from Japanese companies such as Honda, Suzuki, Yamaha, and Kawasaki. Most companies market their motorcycles and accessories on a worldwide basis, handling international trade through foreign distributors and domestic sales through franchised outlets. Tariffs and trade barriers have made entering foreign markets more difficult, thus limiting foreign sales.

Industry sales of motorcycles shrunk from 515,000 units in 1985 to 462,000 in 1991. One of the reasons for this decline was the recession. Historically, consumer durable goods have been sensitive to the economy because they are highly affected by consumer spending trends, or disposable income. Recessions meant less disposable income was available to consumers coupled with a decrease in the demand for high-priced leisure goods such as RVs and motorcycles [Kapusta 1991, pp. 6]. Another reason for shrinking sales was that computers and electronic products were competing for consumers' discretionary dollars. The most favorable segments for growth were highway motorcycles and off-road motorcycles, with a dramatic slowing in the market for dual-purpose motorcycles. Companies with fragmented product lines were expected to find themselves in an unfavorable position compared to those with a loyal customer base and highly visible and distinguishable product lines.

PRODUCTS

Three types of products or services are offered in the motorcycle industry: motorcycles, accessories, and financing services. All are intrinsically related to the sale of the main product: motorcycles. The motorcycles themselves vary extensively in design and function, and most producers specialize in a specific area. Manufacturers attempt to keep their customers loyal by producing add-on accessories matched to their motorcycles. Accessories, which can take the form of saddle bags, chrome handlebars, and other customized items, boost manufacturers' incomes because of their low production costs. Financing services were the newest area for motorcycle

Figure 2: Motorcycle Industry Breakdown

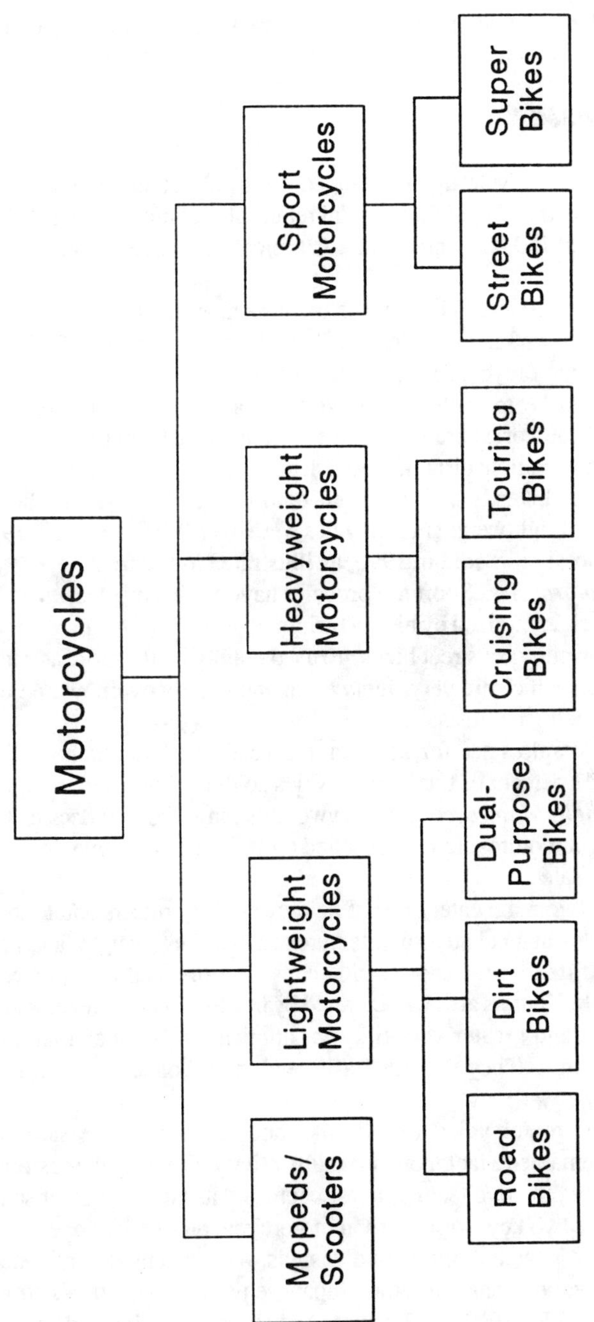

makers to explore. Previously, customers secured outside loans for purchasing motorcycles; they now had the convenient option of financing with the dealer at market rates.

Motorcycles

In 1992, motorcycle models ranged from 50cc (cubic centimeters) scooters to 1500cc heavyweights. In the United States, total retail sales of motorcycles in 1990 reached $1.8 billion and totalled over 450,000 units sold. A typical full scale product line would encompass the following:

Mopeds or Scooters. These are characterized by small engines (under 125ccs) and are used as an alternative to walking. Wholesale sales in 1990 were about 64,000 units and represented 17.3 percent of total motorcycle sales, as shown in Figure 3.

Lightweight Motorcycles. Lightweights have engine displacements ranging from 125ccs to 449ccs. Subcategories are road bikes, which are used mainly for city street driving and as alternative transportation; dirt bikes, which are recreational motorcycles used on off-road terrain; and dual-purpose bikes, which are used both in the city and on other types of terrain. Total wholesale sales of lightweight motorcycles were over 190,000 units in 1990 and represented 51.3 percent of the total units sold in 1990, as illustrated in Figure 3.

Sport Motorcycles. Sport motorcycles have engine displacements ranging from 450ccs to 749ccs and are characterized by highly fashionable and aerodynamic bodies and trim areas. They are classified by purpose: street bikes are used mainly by the more advanced rider of city streets, while superbikes which are very lightweight and greatly overpowered by larger motors, are for advanced and racing enthusiasts.

Total wholesale sales for sport motorcycles in 1990 reached 47,000 units in 1990 and represented 12.7 percent of total motorcycles sold, as illustrated in Figure 3.

Heavyweight Motorcycles. Heavyweights range from 750ccs to 1500ccs. In 1990 wholesale heavyweight motorcycle sales reached 69,000 units, as shown in Figure 3. This represented 18.7 percent of sales.

There are two main categories of heavyweights: cruisers and tourers. Cruisers are heavy, large motorcycles that balance such features as handling, weight, and appearance. These bikes are usually outfitted with custom saddlebags, chrome, and other accessories to create a truly customized look. Tourers are characterized by more defined style lines and offer a smoother ride, easier handling, and greater versatility in applications such as long-distance riding or cross-country motor trips. They are less flashy and more concerned with function or purpose than cruisers.

Internally, motorcycles are all alike and function in the same manner, so sales for a particular line remained a factor of buyer subjectivity. Offering the customer a diversified product line was a highly effective technique for capturing as large a market share as possible.

There were two keys to success in motorcycle production: one was a company's ability to create and patent new and innovative designs, motors, and components; the other key, in the absence of innovation, was imitation. Japanese producers used this strategy when they cloned Harley Davidsons. By 1992, the Japanese had stopped cloning and had begun introducing items

Figure 3: New Motorcycle Wholesale Sales by Major Types, 1986-1990

			Units										
			Model Type				Engine Type		Displacement Size (cc)				
	Wholesale $ Volume	Est. Retail $ Volume	Total Units	On-Highway	Off-Highway	Dual Purpose	Two-Stroke	Four-Stroke	Under 125cc	125-349cc	350-449cc	450-749cc	750 cc & Up
1986 (% of Total Units)	$1,790.247	$2,206.015	853.426 (100.0%)	273.148 (32.0%)	555.419 (65.1%)	24.859 (2.9%)	142.586 (16.7%)	710.840 (83.3%)	136.176 (15.9%)	383.572 (44.9%)	77.269 (9.1%)	153.533 (18.0%)	102.876 (12.1%)
1987 (% of Total Units)	$1,728.223	$2,125.598	728.042 (100.0%)	237.200 (32.5%)	465.051 (63.9%)	25.791 (3.5%)	141.577 (19.4%)	586.455 (80.6%)	116.774 (16.0%)	332.303 (45.7%)	60.094 (8.3%)	117.409 (16.1%)	101.462 (13.9%)
1988 (% of Total Units	$1,445.607	$1,769.990	483.005 (100.0%)	198.342 (41.1%)	257.658 (53.3%)	27.005 (5.6%)	104.825 (21.7%)	378.180 (78.3%)	69.240 (14.3%)	194.218 (40.2%)	38.265 (7.9%)	78.609 (16.3%)	102.673 (21.3%)
1989 (% of Total Units	$1,168.059	$1,434.965	405.679 (100.0%)	179.743 (44.3%)	208.333 (51.4%)	17.603 (4.3%)	115.737 (28.5%)	289.942 (71.5%)	82.934 (20.4%)	107.340 (42.0%)	28.380 (7.0%)	54.289 (13.4%)	69.736 (17.2%)
1990 (% of Total Units)	$1,180.242	$1,448.056	369.967 (100.0%)	138.010 (37.3%)	211.941 (57.3%)	20.016 (5.4%)	99.382 (26.9%)	270.585 (73.1%)	64.075 (17.3%)	160.960 (43.5%)	29.038 (7.8%)	46.855 (12.7%)	69.039 (18.7%)

Notes: Includes all-terrain vehicles and nopeds (limited speed, motor-driven cycles under 50 cc's without fully operative pedals). Scooter shipments included for 1989 and 1990. Excludes mopeds.

SOURCE: Adapted from the *Manufacturers Shipment Reporting System.* Annual Statistical Report, Motorcycle Industry Council, Inc., Irvine, California.

such as belt drives and automatic transmissions.

Accessories and Parts

Other products in this industry included many aftermarket accessories such as saddlebags, higher windshields, and customized seats. All of the leading motorcycle manufacturers either produced or contracted to have these items produced because of the high profit margins realized on them. Aftermarket sales remained a viable area for producers to explore and exploit because people wanted something to differentiate their bikes from others. As can be seen in Figure 4, sales of accessories and parts made up 35.5 percent of total retail sales in the motorcycle market in 1990.

Financing Services

One of the fastest-growing service areas in the motorcycle industry was consumer financing. Previously, motorcycles were seen as a cheap means of transportation. By 1992, they had taken on a new role. They came to be viewed as a recreational or luxury item at the high end of the market. This new perception of motorcycles led to the introduction of more expensive models with prices higher than those of some cars. As the prices of many motorcycles climbed well out of the reach of many motorcycle enthusiasts, motorcycle manufacturers began to set up consumer credit arrangements similar to those for new car purchasers. As a result, more motorcycles were sold on credit than ever before. Not only were people buying the higher priced models on credit, they were also purchasing the lower priced models on credit.

Many large manufacturers, for example Kawasaki, set up their own finance companies to meet this emerging demand. Harley-Davidson, however, lacked the capital to finance its own subsidiary, so the company entered into arrangements with an established finance company — Ford Motor Credit Company.

CUSTOMERS

The customer was the driving force behind the motorcycle industry. Motorcyclists tended to be a small close-knit community that told one another of their experiences with various products. This meant that one dissatisfied customer had the potential to dissuade many others from using the same product. Riders also tended to be very brand loyal and getting them to try something different could be as difficult as getting a smoker to try a different brand of cigarettes. Bikes were purchased with a specific use in mind, and, as seen in Figure 5, motorcyclists were growing more affluent. According to the Motorcycle Industry Council, in 1991 a typical motorcycle purchaser was a 33-year-old male with a household income of $40,000, as opposed to a 27-year-old male with household earnings of $17,800 in 1981 [Deutsch 1991, p. 4].

This change in customer characteristics was important. A key to success in the industry was carefully monitoring the typical motorcycle buyer and furnishing appropriate products. As companies attempted to expand their market shares, more nontraditional riders were targeted.

Figure 4: Motorcycle Outlet Retail Sales

	1990 Estimated Retail Sales by U.S. Motorcycle Outlets					
	Franchised M/C Outlets	% of Total	Non-Franchised M/C Totals	% of Total	All Motorcycle Retail Outlets	% of Total
New Motorcycles, Scooter & ATVs	$1,837,800,000	51.9%	$ 0	0.0%	$1,837,800,000	39.5%
Used Motor Cycles, Scooters & ATVs	$506,400,000	14.3%	$ 104,400,000	9.4%	$610,800,000	13.1%
Parts, Accessories & Riding Apparel	$853,400,000	24.1%	$ 802,200,000	72.2%	$1,655,600,000	35.5%
Service Labor	$276,200,000	7.8%	$ 177,800,000	16.0%	$454,000,000	9.8%
Other M/C Related Sales	$67,200,000	1.9%	$ 26,700,000	2.4%	$93,900,000	2.0%
Total M/C Related Sales	$3,541,000,00	100.0%	$1,111,100,000	100.0%	$4,652,100,000	100.0%

NOTES: Comparisons can not be made with prior years due to revisions in new vehicle sales estimates and differences in dealer list sources.

SOURCE: Adapted from the *1990 Motorcycle Retail Outlet Audit.* Motorcycle Industry Council, Inc., Irvine, California, August 1990 and the *1990 Motorcycle Retail Outlet Profile.* Motorcycle Industry Council, Inc., Irvine, California, May 1991.

Figure 5: Owner Profile: Income

HOUSEHOLD INCOME FOR PRIOR YEAR	% OF TOTAL OWNERS '90	'85	'80
UNDER $10,000	3.3%	10.6%	9.1%
$10,000-$14,999	4.2%	9.0%	13.0%
$15,000-$19,999	7.8%	11.2%	13.9%
$20,000-$24,999	10.6%	8.5%	12.9%
$25,000-$34,999	21.1%	17.8%	12.5%
$35,000-$49,999	19.8%	13.9%	5.9%
$50,000 & OVER	19.7%	6.8%	2.4%
DON'T KNOW	13.5%	22.0%	30.3%
MEDIAN	$33,200	$25,900	$0

Note: The owner is defined as the primary rider.

SOURCE: Adapted from the *1980 Survey of Motorcycle Ownership and Usage*, conducted for the Motorcycle Industry Council by Burke Marketing Research, Inc. Cincinnati, Oh., April, 1981. Adapted from the *1985 Survey of Motorcycle Ownership and Usage,* conducted for the Motorcycle Industry Council by Burke Marketing Research, Inc. Cincinnati, Oh., February 1986. Adapted from the *1990 Survey of Motorcycle Ownership and Usage,* conducted for the Motorcycle Industry Council by Burke Marketing Research, Inc. Cincinnati, Oh., February 1990.

Many younger riders were attracted to the speed and power associated with superbikes, while older riders often were attracted to luxury touring bikes. Women were targeted by companies seeking to change the image of motorcycling with smaller, easier-to-handle entry-level motorcycles.

Motorcycle purchasers can be classified into seven groups, based on age and riding habits:

- *Under 18* - This age group was largely made up of students who used mopeds or scooters for transportation to and from school. This group represented 11.1 percent of all sales in 1990, but rarely purchased motorcycles again later since they were perceived as a temporary, alternative form of transportation.
- *18-24* - This group of buyers used motorcyclesas a primary means of transportation or recreation. In 1990, it reperesented 15.6 percent of all sales and future purchases were likely for many of these customers. Within this age group, many types of motorcycles were purchased, based as much on advertising as on the riders' intent or usage. Of the types of motorcycles, entry-level lightweight road bikes and the more advanced superbikes were purchased most often. They were used for transportation, while dirt bikes were purchased for recreational riding.
- *25-29* - This was the largest user group, accounting for 16.0 percent of all purchases in 1990. Many of the buyers in this group were riders from the previous group who had advanced to

motorcycles requiring a higher degree of riding ability. Most motorcycles sold in this group were intermediate sport or heavyweight cruiser motorcycles. Rider stratification became more prominent in this group as buyers decided what type of riders they were and wanted to become.

- *30-34* - By the time buyers entered this age group they had owned, on average, a minimum of three motorcycles and new purchases were made within a strictly defined rider intent. This group made up 15.8 percent of buyers in 1990. The motorcycles most frequently purchased were the heavyweight cruisers used for transportation. Recreational purchases were limited to other types of road bikes, with dirt bikes experiencing declining sales as riders became more safety conscious and in some cases too large for the smaller engines powering dirt bikes.
- *35-39* - Motorcycle sales in this age group accounted for 13.7 percent of sales in 1990. This group's buying habits were influenced by many factors: other major purchases, such as homes, took precedence over motorcycles; and increased responsibilities at work and home resulted in a lack of time for recreational activities such as motorcycling.
- *40-49* - Purchases by this age group showed an upswing from the previous group to 15.0 percent of total purchases, but the use and type of motorcycle changed. Many buyers in this category were looking for motorcycles with heavy recreational possibilities, but not as aggressive as dirt bikes. The answer for many in this group was the easy-to-handle heavyweight tourer, which provided a smooth ride made enjoyable by the additions of AM/FM radios, trunks and other options. Many buyers were married couples looking for an alternative to taking the car out for weekend drives to the country.
- *50 and Over* - In 1990, this group accounted for 10.6 percent of motorcycle sales. Sales were concentrated in the heavyweight touring class and middleweight road bike categories.

As baby boomers approached middle age, the customer base expanded and motorcycle designs revolved around the needs of older riders. Older riders did not want the top superbikes, but rather a more comfortable and less complicated machine.

MARKETS

Although motorcycles are a worldwide product and sold internationally, three main geographic markets comprised the bulk of new motorcycle sales: North America, Asia, and Europe. Each of these markets was consumer-driven and customer-oriented along varying lines that included age, gender, and intended use.

North America

Of the three main markets, the North American market was by far the largest and most diverse. The United States and Canada, when combined, accounted for more than 60 percent of world motorcycle sales in the early 1990s. Most of the products offered in the North American market were targeted at the middle-aged male recreational rider, who, according to research, accounted for over 75 percent of motorcycle sales.

With the baby-boom generation aging, opportunities existed for the targeting and penetration of new markets, for example, designing bikes for older riders looking for a softer ride or for younger riders looking for entry-level motorcycles. New designs emphasizing more feminine lines and quieter engines were a key to winning over the incipient female market segment.

Although the U.S. economy was in a slight downturn in the early 1990s, increasing production levels and decreasing import levels were expected to sustain growth in the demographic markets mentioned above.

Asian

The Japanese market was the largest market untapped by foreign motorcycle producers largely because of Japan's protectionist trade policies. Heavyweight motorcycle sales increased in the 1980s due to the country's infrastructure. In Japan, motorcycles are not recreational or luxurious, but rather, a more convenient form of transportation in heavily congested cities.

Target markets in Japan range from young children to the elderly. Japanese companies were concerned more about competition from cheaper gray market goods than foreign competition from abroad.

The Japanese market was a strong, untapped one for foreign manufacturers. Young Japanese grew up with more disposable income than their parents and were the prime target for an American company like Harley-Davidson. This was because of their fascination with American 1950s pop culture, an era brought back to life by the reminiscent styling of Harley-Davidson's line of bikes. Success in the Japanese market would be hard to achieve unless the government opened up its doors to free trade.

Although Japan was the largest Asian market, possibilities existed elsewhere. Most Asian countries considered the motorcycle a basic, everyday means of transportation; the company that infiltrated this segment of the market with transportation motorcycles would gain significant market share in Asia. China, Korea, Taiwan, and Vietnam were among the major target markets.

Europe

Another market with high potential, but lackluster performance, was the European market. The key to success here was to establish a company within a member country of the European Economic Community (EEC) before 1992 in order to avoid being charged with the protective tariffs that were erected. Though sales in Europe were not as high as those in North American or Asian markets, they accounted for a fair portion of some companies' sales figures. Twenty percent of Harley Davidson's sales came from motorcycles and related items to European markets. Due to higher standards of living and higher disposable incomes after the formation of the EEC, motorcycle sales increased.

Russia, Poland, and Czechoslovakia had the potential to become great sources of revenue for many industries, including the motorcycle industry. Though the political environment was unstable, many companies were exploiting Central Europe's population by selling them a little piece of capitalism. McDonald's, Pizza Hut, and Pepsi were doing well in their Russian experiments. As for the motorcycle industry, where goods cost a bit more than food items, the philosophy was "wait and see."

GOVERNMENT REGULATIONS

Most government regulations involving the *production* of motorcycles came from the federal government. They controlled motorcycle imports by using tariffs and, in some cases, trade restrictions. The latter had been used once in the early 1980s to protect the last American producer — Harley-Davidson. Government regulations regarding the *use* of motorcycles, however, came from many of the state and local governments.

Federal Safety Standards

The National Highway Transportation Safety Act stipulates that a motorcycle manufacturer must produce a motorcycle that meets with all provisions of applicable federal safety standards and regulations. All motorcycles must meet these regulations before they can be sold, and if a defect is found after the sale the manufacturer may be forced to recall the motorcycle. Motorcycle manufacturers readily comply with these regulations and most voluntarily recall their products in the event of defects.

Despite these regulations, safety aspects of many of the new Japanese superbikes have become the subject of controversy. Due to the large number of fatalities and accidents occurring on these sport bikes, the federal government has considered limiting imports of these bikes or banning them altogether (as had been done with three-wheel all-terrain vehicles). Since many Japanese manufacturers specialized in their production, such restrictions would drastically affect their exports.

Trade Agreements

Another aspect of government regulation with international effects were trade agreements, or tariffs. The United States had an open trade agreement with Japan on the import of motorcycles into the U.S. In contrast, Harley-Davidson found it difficult to export its motorcycles to Japan. This imbalance of trade created a business arena whereby the Japanese could start dumping motorcycles in an attempt to lower their prices to the point where no one could compete with them. This was the case in early 1983 when Harley-Davidson was in the midst of its restructuring program and could not afford to compete with the Japanese on that level. President Reagan levied protective tariffs on all Japanese motorcycles for a period of five years under the built-in Escape Clause of the 1974 Trade Act. Harley-Davidson asked for the tariff to be lifted in mid-1986 — two and a half years before it expired — since it felt that it was no longer needed.

State and Local Safety Standards

Motorcycle operator licensing programs and procedures involve written tests similar to those given for automobiles, and driving tests to assess the operator's handling capability. These tests are geared towards either on- or off-road motorcycling. Furthermore, most states require the rider to wear a helmet and some sort of protective clothing. Other equipment regulations govern the usage or placement of rear view mirrors, foot pegs, and other safety gear. Each state has separate requirements for on-and off-road motorcycles.

COMPETITION

In the early 1990s, competition in the motorcycle industry consisted of only a handful of producers worldwide. The Japanese producers — Honda, Kawasaki, Yamaha, and Suzuki — produced a full line of motorcycles ranging from scooters to heavyweights, and together controlled the largest share of the market, as seen in Figure 6. Their success began with copying other products, but evolved to depend on innovative designs and technology. Other producers relied on targeting market niches. BMW, for example, produced only heavyweight motorcycles emphasizing shaft drive design technology, while Harley-Davidson produced heavyweight motorcycles emphasizing nostalgic design and detail. Figure 7 lists the six major U.S. motorcycle manufacturers.

Honda Motor Company

Honda was the largest of Harley-Davidson's competitors in both size, financial backing, and — most importantly — reputation. With huge finances backing the company, it repeatedly entered the market with something new or innovative. Honda's product line ranged from small scooters to tourers to custom bikes, with the latter two categories giving Harley-Davidson its biggest

Figure 6: New Motorcycle Registrations by Leading Brands

	1990		1989		1988	
Make	Rank	Market Share	Rank	Market Share	Rank	Market Share
Honda	1	27.4%	1	28.9%	1	39.0%
Yamaha	2	23.2%	1	25.7%	2	23.0%
Harley-Davidson	3	17.4%	5	14.0%	5	9.4%
Kawasaki	4	15.9%	3	15.7%	3	13.9%
Suzuki	5	15.3%	4	14.2%	4	13.3%
BMW	6	1.1%	6	0.9%	6	0.8%

	1987		1986		1985	
Make	Rank	Market Share	Rank	Market Share	Rank	Market Share
Honda	1	50.8%	1	55.0%	1	58.5%
Yamaha	2	19.8%	2	17.8%	1	15.7%
Harley-Davidson	5	6.3%	4	5.0%	5	4.1%
Kawasaki	4	10.2%	4	9.7%	3	10.4%
Suzuki	3	11.6%	3	11.1%	4	10.0%
BMW	6	0.7%	6	0.9%	6	0.8%

Notes: the market share for other brands was less than 0.5%.
R.L. Polk new registrations include the three most current model years. Some off-highway motorcycle and all-terrain vehicle new registrations are included. California 1990 statistics are derived from sales records, rather than registrations. Oklahoma new registrations first became available in 1987.
Source: Adapted from *New Motorcycle Registrations*, R.L. Polk & Co., Detroit, Michigan.

Figure 7: Profile of Major U.S. Motorcycle Manufacturers and Distributors

Brank	U.S. Motorcycle Distributor	Mcycle Manufacturer	Year of U.S. Incorporation	Oher Products Sold in U.S.
BMW	BMW of North America Inc. 300 Chestnut Ridge Road. Woodcliff Lake, NJ 07675 (201) 307-4000	BMW Motorrad GmbH & Co. Triebstrasse 32 8000 Munich 50 Germany	1976	Automobiles
Harley-Davidson	Harley-Davidson Motor Co. Inc 3700 W. Juneau Ave. P.O. Box 653 Milwaukee, WI 53201 (414) 342-4680	Same as distributor	1907	Motorcycle accessories recreational and specialized vehicle and related products
Honda	American Honda Motor Co. Inc. 1919 Torrance Blvd. Torrance, CA 90501-2746 (213) 783-2000	Honda Motor Co. Ltd. No. 1-1, 2 Chome, Minami Aoyama Minato-Ku, Tokyo 107 Japan Honda of America Mfg. Inc. 24000 U.S. Route 33 Marysville, OH 43040 (Engine Manufacturing Facility) 12500 Meranda Road Ana, OH 45302	1959	Automobiles, all-terrain vehicles, motor scooters, accessories for motor-cycles and products above, power products (generators , rototillers, outboards, lawnmowers, riding lawnmovers, lawn tractors, snow throwers, water pumps.)
Kawasaki	Kawasaki Motors Corp., U.S.A. 9950 Jeronimo Road Irvine, CA 92718-2016 (714) 770-0400	Kawasaki Heavy Industries, Ltd.,1-1, Kawasaki-cho Akashi 673, Hyogoken, Japan Kawasaki Motors Manufacturing 6600 N.W. 27th St. Lincoln, NE 68524	1967	All-terrain vehicles, Jet Ski, Jet Mate Watercraft, utility vehicles, acces-sories for motorcycles and products above, small engines, generators, watercraft trailers.
Suzuki	American Suzuki Motor Corp. 3251 East Imperial Hwy. Brea, CA 92621 (714) 996-7040	Suzuki Motor Corp. Hamamatsu-Nishi, P.O. Box 1, 432-91 Hamamatsu, Japan	1963	Automobiles, all-terrain vehicles, outboard motors, generators, accessories for motorcycles and products above.
Yamaha	Yamaha Motor Corp., U.S.A. 6555 Katella Ave. Cypress, CA 90630 (714) 761-7300	Yamaha Motor Co., Ltd. 2500 Shingai, IwataShi Shizuoka-Ken, 438 Japan	1960	Snowmobiles, go cart engines, go carts, golf carts, scooters, all terrain vehicles, outboard engines, water vehicles, stern drives, outdoor power products (gener-ators, snowblowers, lawn-mowers), accessories for motorcycles and products above.

Source: Information obtained by Motorcycle Industry Council from the U.S. distributors above.

challenge. Honda had changed its image of a Japanese company making toy bikes to that of a high quality producer of heavyweight motorcycles. In the heavyweight division its main models were the Honda Goldwing touring motorcycle and GL series sport bikes. Honda's line offered the widest selection of styles, classes, and sizes within the heavyweight category. Prices were similar to those set by the market, with an import tariff added on.

Honda had clearly emerged as a leading motorcycle manufacturer, but had also developed some problems along the way. Most significantly, Honda simply manufactured too many products to provide the amount of service that the serious motorcycle enthusiast wanted and deserved. Its dealerships carried everything from generators to scooters to snow-throwers, and salespeople had limited knowledge of each product. This strategy proved costly since customers had begun to place service ahead of technology. It was this trend that set Harley-Davidson apart from Honda and won customers.

Kawasaki

Kawasaki was Japan's second largest exporter of recreational products. Its products included a full line of motorcycles, all-terrain vehicles (ATVs), jet-skis and other variations on these, such as wetbikes. Leading technology and design concepts catapulted Kawasaki to the top of the highly profitable superbike market with entries such as the Ninja line of heavyweight sport motorcycles. An early entrant into this market, Kawasaki held a commanding lead in it. However, that lead was threatened by U.S. legislation limiting the number of sports bikes allowed into the U.S. for safety reasons. Unscrupulous dealers sold these superbikes to overeager beginners or thrill seekers without fully explaining to them that it takes a seasoned rider to handle a bike with these capabilities.

One area that Kawasaki had begun to explore was consumer financing. Through a financing company subsidiary, Kawasaki introduced the "Let the Good Times Roll" financing plan on its products for consumers who wanted to finance their purchases. The plan required a 10 percent down payment and allowed the purchaser to choose the time period and the interest rate for the loan. Since most American consumers viewed financing as an alternative way to purchase goods, the success of the plan seemed likely. Interest rates were manipulated to emphasize low monthly payments, allowing consumers to fit payments into their budgets instead of shopping around for low rates.

Although it was a well-diversified company, Kawasaki could experience a downturn in sales with the passage of restrictive legislation on superbikes. It exploited this market at the expense of some of its other lines, and other products — such as ATVs —which were of too limited use to offset losses in the event of a superbike market collapse.

Yamaha

Yamaha, the first Japanese company to hit Harley-Davidson right in its own markets, produced Harley clones. Yamaha's line of heavyweight motorcycles included the Virago and V-Max series, both of which looked so much like a Harley that it was hard to tell the difference. While Yamaha motorcycles had the distinctive appearance of a Harley, they lacked the Harley image.

Harley-Davidson was not the only company that Yamaha had cloned; a quick look at the product line showed imitation Kawasaki superbikes, Honda street bikes, and the like. Yamaha kept up with market trends, waited for new technology to emerge, and capitalized on hits by copying them. A market follower rather than a leader, Yamaha was destined to swing with the highs and lows of the industry. Other companies seeking protection from tactics such as Yamaha's sought to patent new technology before it could be reproduced.

Other Producers

In the heavyweight motorcycle market other producers included BMW (German), Moto-Guzzi (Italian), and Cagiva/Ducati (Italian). Most of these producers specialized in one area. BMW, for instance, was the first producer of the shaft drive motorcycle (most other motorcycles were driven by chains like bicycles). The two Italian firms specialized in racing bikes with innovative aerodynamic European styling. Markets for these motorcycles were somewhat limited due to their high prices and limited availability in the biggest market, North America.

In Harley-Davidson's market perhaps the only real competitor was BMW, which was limited in the amount of market share it could capture due to its high prices and low unit sales. Manufacturers in this group produced fewer bikes which appealed to a narrower range of buyers. Niche manufacturers did not have the market scope of the Japanese and so relied only on sales of a product line aimed at one type of demographic customer base while missing out on sales of bikes for other and more profitable market segments.

THE COMPANY

HISTORY

Harley-Davidson Motors Inc. was founded in 1903 as a manufacturer of small engines and parts. Gradually the transition to producing motorcycles took place. The first motorcycles produced were of varying sizes and weights. Once the company's sales of large street bikes increased, the company shifted to produce only heavy-weight motorcycles.

In 1969, after struggling to raise capital, Harley-Davidson Motors was bought by American Machine and Foundry Corporation (AMF) to bolster its position in the expanding sports and recreation markets. Sales improved until the late 1970s, when product quality was low, sales were lagging behind the newer Japanese bikes, and more of Harley's customer base switched to the newer and more dependable Japanese bikes. After years of losses and dismal market performance, AMF was investigating the sale of Harley to outside investors in late 1980 when a group of 11 top managers decided that the employees could turn the company around. As a result, a leveraged buyout of Harley-Davidson Motors Inc. took place to form the new Harley-Davidson Inc. that exists today.

COMPANY MISSION

Since the leveraged buyout in 1981, the mission statement of Harley-Davidson Inc. was one word — "quality." Other corporate objectives included establishing Harley-Davidson as a major competitor for contractual manufacturing work, such as government contracts, and as a subcontractor for other manufacturers in the areas of engines, parts, or any other product that fit with existing factory capabilities. Harley-Davidson won defense contracts for 500-pound metal bomb casings seven years in a row, and began producing small two-stroke engines for Briggs & Stratton. Growth in this area was slow, but the contracts guaranteed cash flow and working capital.

Harley Davidson applied its strategic ideal of quality to everything it did. Its shaky acquisition of Holiday Rambler Corp., an RV and commercial vehicle maker, led to an upgrade of all of its product lines and heavy investment in research and development for future products.

The key shift at Harley, according to Robert W. Hall, a professor at the Indiana University School of Business, was the decision in the early 1980s to emphasize customer satisfaction — regardless of the effect on short-term profits. This quality vision more than doubled Harley-Davidson's market share in five years. This was done at the expense of Honda, whose market share dropped from 39 percent in 1985 to 14 percent in 1990.

Harley executives come up with ideas for customizing their bikes during weekend rides with the Harley Owners Group. According to Steve Anderson, Editor of *Cycle*, "The executives ride a lot more than the Japanese and they listen incredibly hard to what customers want" [Holusha 1990, pp. 5].

Finally, dealerships that sold Harley-Davidson motorcycles and accessories must have certified motorcycle mechanics working for them and an appropriately trained sales force of Harley-Davidson professionals.

ORGANIZATIONAL STRUCTURE

Harley-Davidson Inc. had a centralized form of management with very loose lines of authority. The company's upper management was adamant about having the workers themselves serve as the unofficial middle management. By giving them more say in their jobs, management increased productivity without having to substantially increase wages. Workers dictated the quantity of materials needed to do their jobs, and determined what to do when sales lagged. Upper executives were able to concentrate on such things as planning.

Vaughn L. Beals, chairman of Harley-Davidson Inc., was credited with many of the positive changes that occurred at Harley-Davidson. Immediately upon taking office, he sent his senior officers to bike conventions to talk with the customers, to see what they liked, what their needs were, and what they were willing to pay for. This strategy is still embraced today with positive results for both the company and the consumer.

CUSTOMERS

In 1991, one in three Harley-Davidson buyers was a professional or manager. About 60 percent had attended college, up from 45 percent in 1984. The median age of buyers was 35, and the median household income rose sharply to $45,000 from $36,000 five years earlier. While this target market had supported the entire industry in the past, times had changed and Harley-Davidson and others had to start targeting other market segments. One segment that had been overlooked continually was the female segment of the population, and tremendous opportunities awaited the first company to penetrate this market. The number of female riders has steadily increased over the past few years. More women are working than ever before and as a result have their own disposable incomes. Also, motorcycling has shed its image of dirty, beer swilling, biker gangs to that of a legitimate recreational activity. Unfortunately, the recession dampened actual sales to this group.

Success in the women's market does not depend on marketing machines built for a man's body to female audiences — a whole new bike emphasizing design for female ergonomics had to be developed. Harley-Davidson offered machines like the XLH 883 Hugger, which boasted both a slimmer seat and reduced riding height, or the Heritage Softail Classic, which featured wide sweeping fenders, leather saddlebags, gas-charged shock absorbers, and a smoother clutch.

Another emerging target market was younger riders looking to buy their first motorcycles. This market had the added advantage of introduction, and the number of repeat customers was high once a manufacturer got them on its machine. Harley-Davidson's advantage here was that its bikes were some of the safest on the market, a strategy that would be extremely effective if the ban on Japanese super-bikes took place. Keys to success for the younger market were state-of-the-art technology, sleek aerodynamics, and radical styling.

PRODUCTS

Harley-Davidson served the heavyweight segment of the motorcycle industry by producing motorcycles with engine displacements of 850ccs or greater. Harley-Davidson manufactured three different size engines: 883ccs, 1200ccs, and 1340ccs. Of these, the company had two major product lines: touring motorcycles and cruiser motorcycles.

Touring motorcycles, designed for long-distance riding, featured windscreens, touring saddles, and trunks. As can be seen by the descriptions in Figure 8, some even had radios, cruise control, and other car-like features. Tourers were the most expensive of all motorcycles produced and offered the greatest convenience to the rider and the greatest profit to the manufacturer.

Cruisers were styled after early motorcycles and were the kind most often associated with Harley-Davidson. Harley, however, added modern technology such as accelerator pumps and constant velocity carburetors. These included the XLH 883 Sportster, Harley's least expensive model, which was the most frequently bought motorcycle in the U.S. in 1989. Harley hoped to increase ridership by providing a comfortable bike that the owner could enjoy until trading up to a bigger Harley. Harley-Davidson made virtually no profit on the 883 Sportster, but gambled that

Figure 8: Full-Dress Tourers

HARLEY-DAVIDSON FLSTC
HERITAGE SOFTAIL CLASSIC **$11,195**

The Heritage Softail Classic exemplifies the style that's made the Milwaukee firm famous. H-D took basic FLST Heritage Softail and added a king-size windscreen, chrome headlight and passing lamps, studded leather saddlebags and seat, two-tone fenders and gas tank, black chrome power train and staggered dual fishtail style mufflers. The 16-inch wire-spoked wheels and fat MT90 tires add to the distinctive 50's-style looks. Instrumentation is basic, but there's an imporved speedometer back-lighting system for 1990, making the gauge easier to read at night. And like all the 1990 1340cc Evolution engines, this one gets the new carb and clutch.

a-c 4-st V-twin 1340cc 1,40mm 5-sp 4.2gal 710lb

HARLEY-DAVIDSON FLTC **$13,345**
TOUR GLIDE ULTRA CLASSIC

Added to the Tour Glide's already legendary touring package are removable fairing lowers, cruise control with accelerate and resume features, a four-speaker sound system with remote controls for the passenger and a complete CB radio and intercom system. The FLTC has the new 40mm carb that eases starts and improves on the-road performance. Features include a large 5-gallon tank, 32-amp alternator, quiet, clean belt final drive, air assisted suspension at both ends and a full Harley King TourPak which lets you bring it all with you while traveling. A large touring saddle and rider and passenger footboards will keep you in comfort while you're on your way.

a-c 4-st V-twin 1340cc 1,40mm 5-sp 5.0gal 765lb

HARLEY-DAVIDSON FLTC TOUR GLIDE CLASSIC **$11,300**

The Tour Glide Classic features a frame-mounted fairing, chrome-trimmed engine, saddlebags complete with bag guards and a 20-watt-per-channel AM-FM stereo cassette. Like the rest of the FLT series, the classic has a rubber-isolated power train, 32-amp alternator, air-adjustable anti-dive, self-canceling turn signals, 16-inch wheels and raider and passenger footboards. The 1340cc power plant gets a new carb and clutch, and the bike rides on big MT90 16-inch tubeless tires. The King TourPak trunk features an adjustable antenna, carpeted interior and wraparound lights, and instrumentation includes a voltmeter and oil-pressure guage.

a-c 4-st Vtwin 1340cc 1,40mm 5-sp 5.0gal 741lb

Source: Adapted from the *Motorcyclist*, "1990 Buying Guide to Street Bikes", March 1990, p. 53.

Figure 9: Cruisers

HARLEY-DAVIDSON FLSTF FAT BOY **$10,995**

Harley's all-new Fat Boy is a member of the Softail family, but it has a distinctive look. It incorporates a disc front wheel wrapped with a new custom-steel fender, wide FLH-style handlebar, classic shotgun-style dual exhausts, wide textured-leather seat insert, hand-laced tank strap, a seal valance and a custom silver paint scheme with bright yellow accents on the tank logo, ignition lock, rocker boxes and primary cover. Along with the other 1340cc Evoloution engines in the Milwaukee company's lineup, the Fat Boy incorporates a new 40mm constant-velocity carburetor, a new better performing clutch and silent clean-running belt drive.

a-c 4-st V-twin 1340cc 1,40mm 5-sp 4.2gal 650lb

HARLEY-DAVIDSON FXSTC SOFTAIL CUSTOM **$10,445**

With pullback buck-horn handlebars, disc-style aluminum rear wheel and color-matched frame paint, this is truly a custom machine. The fork is raked out to a radical 33 degrees and carries a classic, wire-spoked, 21-inch front wheel and drilled disc brake. The tool controls are forward-mounted. The Softail Custom is powered by a solid-mounted Evolution V-twin equipped with a new, improved clutch and a constant velocity 40mm carburetor for quicker starting and enhanced low-speed performance. High-rpm operation is improved as well. And there's plenty of chrome every where, from the horseshoe oil tank and staggered dual exhausts to the handlebar, headlamp and fender brackets.

a-c 4-st V-twin 1340cc 1,40mm 5-sp 5.2gal 618lb

HARLEY-DAVIDSON XLH 1200 SPORTSTER **$5,845**

The largest of the Sportster lineup is also the only Harley-Davidson to carry a 1200cc V-twin Evolution engine. The four-speed Sportster 1200 features a low-rise buck-horn handlebar, dual handlebar-mounted instruments, a wide, plush stepped saddle, shorty dual mufflers, a higher trim level and a truckload of chrome. The V-twin breathes through a 40mm Mikuni constant-velocity carburetor equipped with an accelerator pump. A chain drives the cast, nine-spoke rear wheel. A 39mm telescopic fork holds the 21-inch cast front wheel and a single disc brake. A pair of chromed long-stroke shocks control the rear end's 3.6 inches of travel where a single disck handles the stopping chores.

a-c 4-st V twin 1200cc 1,40mm 4-sp 2.3gal 457lb

HARLEY-DAVIDSON XLH 883 SPORTSTER **$4,250**

Harley's most Spartan and least expensive motorcycle features a low handlebar, single seat, speedo-only instrumentation and cast-aluminum wheels. For 1990, the 883cc air-cooled V-twin's single 40mm carburetor breathes trough a new high-efficiency paper air filter with a dust-capturing ability that's 33 percent greater than that of foam filters. And it's still unmistakably Harley, from its teardrop tank to its heavily chromed dual exhausts. The 883's stretched-out twin-craddle steem frame rides on a 19-inch front and a 16-inch rear rim stopped with a disc brake at each end, and the low 28.5-inch seat height helps keep the Sprotster maneuverable and lets you get both feet on the ground easily.

a-c 4-st V-twin 883cc 1,40 mm 4-sp 2.3gal 461lb

Source: Adapted from the *Motorcyclist*, "1990 Buying Guide to Street Bikes", March 1990, p. 65

once you sat on a Harley, you'd stayed on a Harley. Harley-Davidson owners benefitted from higher resale value on their motorcycles as compared to Japanese bikes — an important consideration in a time of shrinking dollars and continued recession. Figure 9 describes some of Harley-Davidson's most popular cruisers.

The 1991 model year marked an evolutionary change in the company's entry-level motorcycle. For the first time since the model's introduction in 1957, the Sportster had a five-speed transmission as standard equipment. In addition, the Sportster Deluxe and 1200 came standard with a low-maintenance belt drive. These two new standard features normally were found only on the company's larger and higher priced custom and touring bikes. These enhancements allowed better penetration into the entry-level heavyweight motorcycle market, and the redesigned Sportster spurred sales of the company's higher priced products in the normal two- to three-year ownership cycle.

Harley-Davidson had shied away from the superbike category because of the safety issues surrounding these bikes. The company felt that by offering the consumer a safe, reliable product that would last years instead of one that would go out with the next generation or legislation, it could reasonably assure itself of developing a loyal customer.

Other products included a new line of riding and fashion apparel bearing the Harley-Davidson insignia. Introduced in late 1989, this line appeared to be a success. Though initially limited to Harley retailers, the company had begun to explore new outlets in the retail clothing market. Stores such as J.C. Penney and Sears added Harley apparel to their catalogs and many retail stores followed their lead. The only apparent drawback was that some faddish clothing lines disappear as fast as they appear.

MARKETING

Analyst Daniel Kapusta maintained that Harley-Davidson's classic styling created a mystique synonymous with motorcycles. In fact, the Harley-Davidson nameplate was one of the strongest brand names in America — an immeasurable asset. Harley-Davidson's brand loyalty was among the highest among products sold in the United States.

In a 1989 study conducted by Harley-Davidson, over 90 percent of the Harley-Davidson owners surveyed indicated that their next motorcycle would be a Harley [Kapusta 1991, pp. 5]

Industry analysts felt that the international market represented untapped potential, given that Harley-Davidson's domestic heavyweight market share was over 70 percent and its international market share was less than 15 percent. Analysts anticipated a future international market as large as the U.S. market [Kapusta, 1991, pp. 4]. Harley-Davidson was prepared to devote more attention to the foreign market, having signed up new distributors and expanded its dealer network from 120 to nearly 300. Early results had indicated that this strategy was a key to successful sales, particularly in Japan.

Harley-Davidson encouraged dealers to redesign their independently-owned stores to increase parts and accessories sales. Before modernization, some stores had a dark, menacing atmosphere. By creating a more inviting shopping environment and using innovative merchandising techniques, the dealer network had increased parts and accessories sales.

Harley-Davidson had kept consumer demand for its motorcycles up by using many incentive programs. For instance, younger markets were being targeted by special incentive programs such as the guaranteed trade-in value of $3,995 for 883 owners that bought their bikes new and were trading up to a 1340ccs model. This program not only gave the customer a guaranteed resale value on his/her bike, but also locked the customer into becoming a repeat customer.

Demo Rides

This part of Harley's marketing program started as a result of market data gathered at motorcycle events. Company officials brought new motorcycles to these events and had customers try them, use them, compare them to others, and rate them. This concept of marketing became so successful that demo rides have become expected by customers as the industry norm.

Road Rallies

Road rallies were a way to show consumers the long-term benefits of owning a Harley. They were usually held in large areas or through several states to let riders adjust to a Harley on a long ride. These programs, which started out with minimal expectations, turned out to be a huge advertising media that allowed riders to experience what their Harley-Davidsons could do that the other bikes couldn't.

Harley Owners Group

The Harley Owners Group was established to unite and solidify the existing base of Harley customers while encouraging new purchasers to feel that they were joining a fraternity of riders. The group, which was composed of Harley-Davidson owners worldwide, sponsored its own events, such as charity races, road trips, motorcycle vacations, and other related functions. The Harley Owners Group set a trend in the industry and other companies quickly established their own users' groups. However, none had the devotion to its products that Harley owners/members had.

FINANCING PLANS & STRATEGIES

Financing arrangements can be broken down into three categories: consumer financing, dealer financing, and corporate financing. The first two are external arrangements with established finance companies and the last one is internal corporate financing.

Consumer Financing

Consumer financing arrangements were done under a joint venture with Ford Motor Credit Company (FMCO), a wholly-owned subsidiary of Ford Motor Company Inc. Through this arrangement, customers borrowed the money to purchase a Harley through FMCO, which in turn gave a percentage of the interest payment to Harley-Davidson as a kind of commission or finder's fee. This not only gave consumers what they wanted — easy payment plans — but also gave Harley extra cash.

Another profitable solution to the problem of consumer credit was for companies to start their own finance companies, as Ford did. The benefits of such methods included controlling the interest rate and the receipt of monthly payments to increase cash flow. Other manufacturers, such as Kawasaki and Honda, started their own finance subsidiaries.

Since Harley-Davidson had enough cash flow to develop its own financing company, and given the fact that the subsidiary would pay for itself while providing steady income even in harsher financial climates, this was definitely an alternative for Harley-Davidson to consider.

Dealer Financing

Dealer financing is the process through which dealers paid for their Harley-Davidson purchases. Frequent refinancing and loan arrangements were required to allow dealers to keep a sufficient stock of current models on hand. Dealer financing was more difficult than consumer financing since capital requirements were greater and the transactions frequently involved more than one loan or type of loan. Because of the complex nature of dealer financing and the large sums of money involved, a company of Harley-Davidson's relative size usually did not become involved in that aspect of financing. If they were to become involved in dealer financing, Harley-Davidson would not need franchises because it would be financing its own inventory.

Harley-Davidson had an agreement with ITT International Finance Company to service its network of franchises. The arrangement was similar to the one with FMCO in that Harley received a commission on all loans made through ITT International Finance to franchised Harley-Davidson dealers.

Corporate Financing

Internally, Harley-Davidson's corporate financial strategies were as solid as its motorcycles. When extra cash was needed, Harley factored (sold) its accounts receivables — most of which were dealer accounts to ITT for the going rate on a dollar — and then at a predetermined date bought back the receivables. This convenient arrangement gave Harley an almost unlimited supply of credit.

As seen in Figure 1, earnings were up in 1991 as sales continued to rise and unprofitable operations were sold off. This led management to cancel some of its revolving credit lines and retire some debt early. This seemed to indicate that management felt confident about Harley's market position and future motorcycle sales.

TOWARDS THE FUTURE

In 1992, the future for Harley-Davidson looked just as promising as the recent past had been successful. Although current economic conditions did not warrant increased motorcycle sales, future sales were expected to be relatively stable as market share was gained. Competition from Japanese superbikes seemed to be declining as safety issues continued to make headlines.

Consequently, the Japanese firms were freed to take on Harley Davidson and unseat it from the top spot in its own U.S. market — something that will be very difficult to do.

Harley-Davidson's astonishing comeback in the heavyweight segment of the motorcycle market was looked upon as a miracle in the industry. However, management decided not to rest on its laurels, and opted to look for future success. Many company managers felt that while dominating a selected market niche was good, the company was overlooking lucrative markets for other types of motorcycles. Honda and Kawasaki offered a full line of motorcycles and scooters that appealed to customers of all ages and riding experience, while Harley limited itself to one. Some managers felt that Harley should offer other models.

As illustrated in Figure 6, Harley-Davidson's overall market share in 1990 was 17.4 percent, up from 4.1 percent in 1985. This put Harley-Davidson in third place behind Honda and Yamaha — an impressive achievement since Harley competes only in the heavyweight segment of the motorcycle market. To maintain momentum, Harley-Davidson could develop an introductory lower-displacement motorcycle to attract the beginning rider. Others in the company, however, felt that producing anything other than heavyweights would tarnish the Harley mystique and reputation.

Quality and service were becoming increasingly important as people looked towards their dealers for after-sales service and support. Harley-Davidson clearly had the Japanese beat in dealer service and was expected to continue to do so. The first company to locate a plant in Europe before the official commencement of the EEC in 1992 would have a distinct advantage since it would circumvent restrictive tariffs. It has yet to be determined how stiff the tariffs will be and if the market is sufficient to justify a major investment in manufacturing efforts, but the opportunity to sell products in Europe is appealing.

Those who opposed the idea of motorcycle diversification believed that emphasis on motorcycle accessories was necessary. Some company managers felt that any expansion in product line should come from high-margin items such as clothing. Harley-Davidson has achieved success in its apparel business with Harley-Davidson MotorClothes. Harley's Parts and Accessories reported record sales of $110 million in 1990, a 28 percent increase from the previous year. It would be reasonable to assume that as motorcycle sales increased, accessory sales would do likewise. Some company executives felt that sales of replacement parts were a guaranteed revenue source. The apparel segment and its continued success is still an issue to be determined. As styles and fashion change rapidly, it was difficult to determine if Harley clothes would become an industry mainstay or just another passing fad.

Many managers felt that Harley had never fully explored consumer financing although the agreement with Ford was a good one and customers who previously could not afford to consider purchasing a motorcycle were becoming Harley-Davidson customers. Kawasaki saw a marked improvement in sales after embarking on its financing program. Harley considered starting its own financing subsidiary when its contract with Ford expired in early 1992. Larger durable goods companies, like car manufacturers, often used their financing subsidiaries to carry them through difficult times and to finance further projects like research and development.

Harley-Davidson may not be able to afford to have its working capital jeopardized by consumer financing. Managers were concerned that getting into consumer financing would restrict the capital necessary to cover manufacturing costs and damage Harley's outstanding credit rating. There was also the possibility of new FASB regulations which would require nonfinancial corporations to include the earnings of financial subsidiaries in their income statements.

Harley-Davidson had been doing everything right — costs were down, sales were up, and so were profits. Some strategic decisions, however, still needed to be made.

REFERENCES AND BACKGROUND READINGS

1991 Motorcycle Statistical Annual, Motorcycle Industry Council, Irvine, California, 1991.

Allyn, Maureen F., "Fortune Forecast: The Great American Spending Spree Is Winding Down," *Fortune,* October 24, 1988, pp. 41-42.

Allyn, Maureen F., "Shoppers Will Keep Spending, But with a Little Less Gusto," *Fortune,* February 17, 1989, pp. 25-26.

Anderson, Steve, "Lean and Mean," *Cycle,* September 1991, p. 9.

Annual Report on Form 10-K, 1989, Harley-Davidson Inc.

Bairstow, Jeffrey, "Small Engines: Packing More Punch," *High Technology,* August, 1986, pp. 29-30.

Beals, Vaughn L., "Harley-Davidson: An American Success Story," *Journal for Quality and Participation,* June, 1988, pp. A19-A22.

Beals, Vaughn L., "Operation Recovery: How Customers Helped Us Turn Around Harley-Davidson," *Success,* January/February, 1989, p. 16.

Beals, Vaughn L., "Quality and Productivity: The Harley-Davidson Experience," *Survey of Business,* Spring, 1986, pp. 9-11.

Beels, Gregory, "Strategy for Survival," *Quality,* April, 1985, pp. 16-22.

Brockman, Michael, "The Three Faces of Harley," *Motor Trend,* March 1991, pp. 93-95.

Butler, Jeremy J., *Harley-Davidson, Value Line Investment Survey,* December 6, 1991, pp. 1761.

Cayer, Shirley, "Harley's New Manager-Owners Put Purchasing Out Front," *Purchasing,* October 13, 1988, pp. 50-54.

Deutsch, Claudia H., "Selling Bikes After the Wild Ones Have Settled Down," *The New York Times,* December, 1991, p. 4.

Gelb, Thomas, "Overhauling Corporate Engine Drives Winning Strategy," *The Journal of Business Strategy,* November/December, 1989, pp. 8-12.

Hackney, Holt, "Easy Rider," *Financial World,* September 4, 1990, pp. 48-49.

Hann, Peter, "Gambling Pays Off Big for Japanese Business," *International Management,* June, 1986, pp. 70-72.

Harley-Davidson Inc., *1990 Annual Report.*

Harley-Davidson Inc., *1989 Annual Report*

Harley-Davidson Inc., *Form 10-Q,* September 29, 1991.

"Harley's Hogs Are Doing Wheelies," *The New York Times,* April 17, 1988, p. F1.

Holusha, John, "How Harley Outfoxed Japan with Exports," *The New York Times,* August 12, 1990, p. 5.

"How Harley Beat Back the Japanese," *Fortune,* September 25, 1989, pp. 155-164.

"Japan Holds 50% World Share in Motorcycle Market," *Business Japan,* July, 1986, pp. 114-115.

"Japan Still Leads in World Production of Motorcycles / Diversified Product Lines and Innovative Thinking Pay Off Well / Suzuki Motor Co. Aims to Satisfy Riders' Diverse Needs / Kawasaki Introduces

High-Performance Street Bike," *Business Japan*, July 1985, pp. 126-133.

Kapusta, Daniel J., *Harley-Davidson Inc., Robert W. Baird & Co. Inc.*, February 22, 1991.

Katayama, Frederick, "Japan's Prodigal Young Are Dippy About Imports," *Fortune*, May 11, 1987, p. 118.

Kern, Richard, "Where Consumers Spend Their Money," *Sales & Marketing Management*, January, 1988, pp. 38-43.

Kolbenschlag, Michael, "Harley-Davidson Takes Lesson from Arch-Rivals' Handbook," *International Management*, February, 1985, pp. 46-48.

Ludlum, David A., "Good Times Roll for Kawasaki," *Computerworld*, August 7, 1989, pp. 51, 56.

Marvel, Mark, "The Gentrified Hog," *Esquire*, July 1989, pp. 22-26.

Moody's Industrial Manual, 1991.

"Motorcycle Makers Shift Tactics," *The New York Times*, Doron P. Levin, September 16, 1989, p. 17.

"Motorcycle Makers Turn to KD Sets for Exports," *Business Japan*, July, 1987, pp. 112-114.

Muller, E.J., "Harley's Got the Handle on Inbound," *Distribution*, March, 1989, pp. 70, 74.

"Now Harley-Davidson is All Over the Road," *The New York Times*, Claudia Deutsch, April 17, 1988, pp. 12.

Okubo, Toshihiko, "Motorcycle Production Recovers from Slump," *Business Japan*, July, 1989, pp. 103-105.

Perryman, M. Ray, "A Long-Term Perspective on the National Economy," *Baylor Business Review*, Winter, 1989, pp. 18-19.

Reid, Peter C., *Well Made in America: Lessons from Harley-Davidson and Being the Best*, McGraw Hill, New York, N.Y., 1990.

Roman, Monica, "Target Marketing: The Teen Market Is Growing Up," *Madison Avenue*, December, 1984, pp. 52-54.

Rose, Robert L., "Vrooming Back," *The Wall Street Journal*, August 31, 1990, p. A1.

Ryan, John, "Vaughn L. Beals: The Man Who Made the Eagle Soar," *Quality Progress*, May, 1986, pp. 84-88.

Saiki, Junichi, "Motorcycle Sales Continue to Stagnate," *Business Japan*, July, 1988, pp. 66-68.

Scott, Carlee R., "Harley-Davidson Posts Profit Jump," *The Wall Street Journal*, February 21, 1992. p. B2.

Shalofsky, Ivor, "Research for Global Brands," *European Research*, May, 1987, pp. 88-93.

Sopohri, Mehran, "Manufacturing Revitalization at Harley-Davidson Motor Co.," *Industrial Engineering*, August, 1987, pp. 86-92.

Standard & Poor's Industrial Guide, August, 1991.

Sterngold, James, "American Business Starts a Counterattack in Japan," *The New York Times*, February 24, 1992 p. A1.

Tanzer, Andrew, "Create or Die," *Forbes*, April 16, 1987,pp. 52-57.

Taylor, Alex III, "The Economy of the 1990s: What Sober Spenders Will Buy," *Fortune* February 2, 1987, pp. 35-38.

"The Opening of Japan," *The Economist*, December 17, 1988, pp. 69-70.

U.S. Industrial Outlook, U.S. Department of Commerce, 1991, pp. 39-10, 39-11, 39-12.

U.S. Industrial Outlook, U.S. Department of Commerce, 1990, pp. 40-10, 40-11.

Van Hooydonk, Tyrone, "The Rise and Fall of the Japanese Cruiser," *Cycle*, August 1991, pp. 35-69.

"Vrrrooom: The Battle Over Harley Davidson," *Financial World*, December 12, 1989, p. 15.

Willis, Red, "Harley-Davidson Comes Roaring Back," *Management Review*, March, 1986, pp. 20-27.

"Zero to Sixty in Less Than Three Seconds," *Journal of American Insurance*, First Quarter, 1988, pp. 17-20.

HEWLETT-PACKARD COMPANY: THE COMPUTER WORKSTATION MARKET

Hewlett-Packard Company (HP) is a publicly-held company that designs, manufactures, and services electronic products and systems for measurement and computation. HP provides the capabilities and support needed to help customers worldwide improve their personal and business effectiveness. In 1990, HP was in second place behind Sun Microsystems in the workstation segment of the computer industry, with a 21.2 percent market share. In 1991, the company had more than 11,000 products and employed 89,000 people worldwide. Its net revenues were $14.4 billion, with international sales accounting for just over 55 percent of that amount. HP had 600 sales and support offices, as well as distributorships in 110 countries. Slightly more than half of the company's 1991 product revenues were derived through the efforts of its own sales organization.

Figure 1 shows the overall structure of the computer industry. Experts projected worldwide sales of over $19 billion in the workstation segment by 1992, up from $6.4 billion in 1989 [Standard and Poor's 1991]. To achieve success in this rapidly growing market in an ever-changing competitive environment, HP was examining several strategic issues.

Hewlett-Packard needed to integrate its various commercial and technical lines of workstations in order to reduce market confusion. In order to attract new customers, HP's management was also considering new uses and applications for its workstations. In addition, the company, in response to the shift in the selling function to resellers, was considering ways to restructure its distribution channels. An increasing number of customers were buying their products from value-added resellers (VARs), to whom HP granted discounts. This lowered selling prices and increased HP's sales costs. In addition, HP had continued its longstanding strategy of promptly positioning

Figure 1: Computer Industry Structure

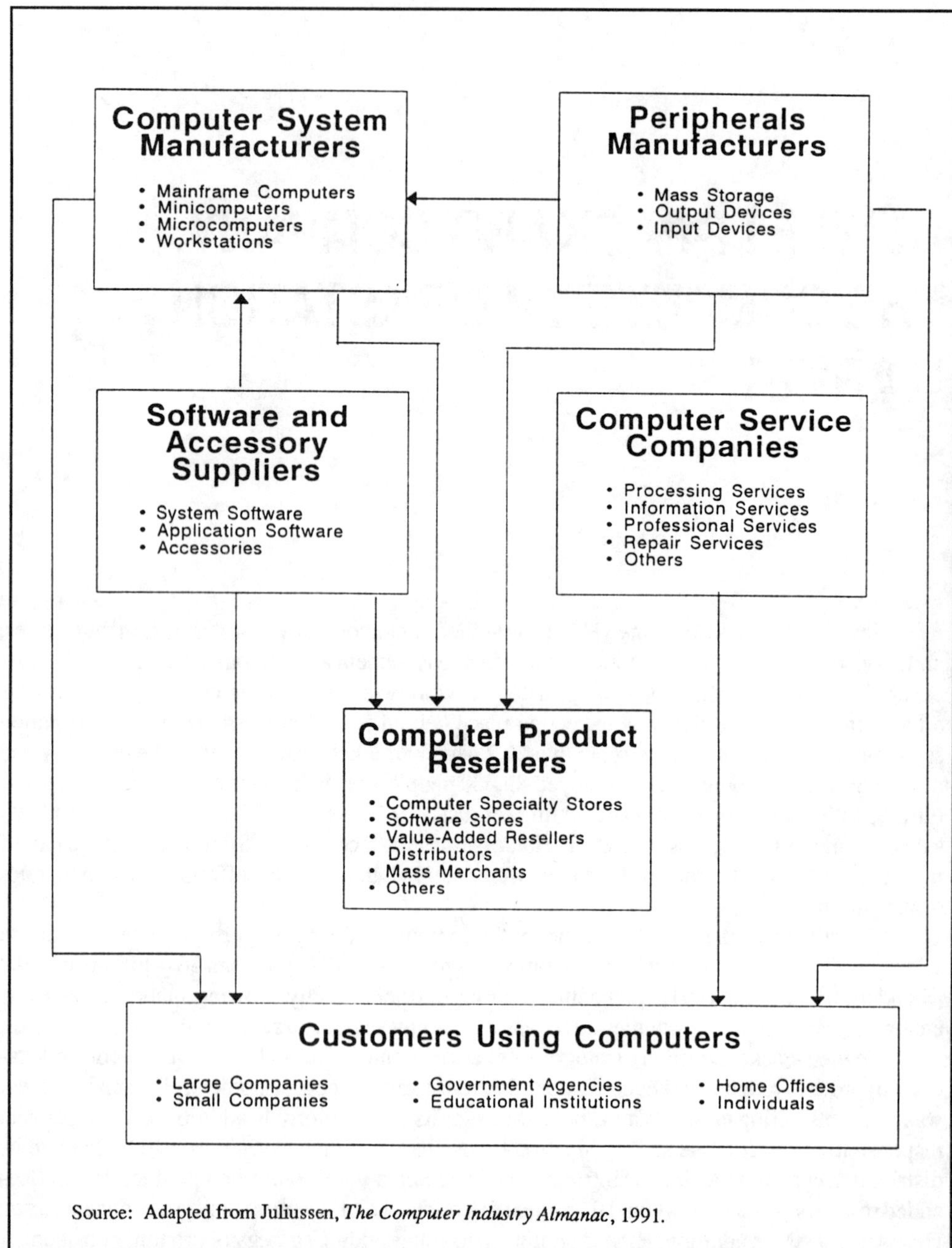

Source: Adapted from Juliussen, *The Computer Industry Almanac*, 1991.

itself in emerging markets by entering into joint ventures in Asia and Central Europe. HP was wondering how to extend this strategy to new areas overseas.

THE INDUSTRY AND COMPETITIVE MARKET

THE WORKSTATION SEGMENT OF THE COMPUTER INDUSTRY

Workstations were similar in appearance to the single-user general-purpose personal computer (PC) in that they both had a terminal and a console or keyboard. However, their internal designs were different. The single-user, general-purpose PC had a disk drive, a single microprocessor chip with a resident operating system, and local programming capability; hence, they were called "stand-alone" systems. The original workstations were diskless "dumb terminals" without resident operating systems and local programming capabilities. Instead, they were connected to a mainframe computer that provided central processing and file storage capabilities. Today, workstations are single-user, stand-alone computer systems which can perform scientific calculations at extremely high speeds. Workstations use one or more high-performance microprocessors and special-purpose hardware to achieve very advanced graphics capabilities. Compared to the PC, modern workstations offer users greater processing power and at least four million bytes of random access memory (RAM). They also feature high-resolution monitors and sophisticated software capable of handling multi-tasking (more than one task at a time) and of communicating via networks with other computers, such as PCs, workstations, and mainframes.

In 1991, the workstation segment was one of the fastest growing areas in the overall computer industry. Created in 1981 by Apollo (now a division of Hewlett-Packard) and legitimized in 1985 by Sun Microsystems, workstation sales of U.S.-based vendors soared by a compound annual rate of more than 110 percent between 1986 and 1988. Growth slowed in 1990, as overall revenues advanced 21.5 percent, down from 40.3 percent in 1989. [Standard and Poor's 1991]. Contributing to the sluggishness of the overall computer industry were the U.S. recession, deep price cutting, the transition from proprietary to open-based systems, maturation of traditional technical markets, and the lengthening of sales cycles. However, U.S. workstation vendors nonetheless enjoyed another year of strong demand for their systems from both domestic and foreign customers in 1991. U.S. suppliers stimulated demand by offering new products with substantially improved price/performance ratios, and by slashing prices as much as 25 to 40 percent on selected existing entry-level and high-end systems. The battle for market share among leading manufacturers and their efforts to displace personal computers in certain commercial accounts, drove the price per millions of instructions per second (MIPS) for a low-end workstation to less than $300 retail. This translated to less than $240 after volume discounts [U.S Department of Commerce 1992].

The workstation segment, like the entire computer industry, was characterized by extremely high levels of competition, the rapid development of new products and technologies, and a strong dependence on foreign suppliers for computer memory chips. This segment was still in the early stages of its growth cycle, and presented opportunities for future growth in the 1990s. Workstations were projected to account for only three percent of the entire computer industry's sales in 1992, as seen in Figure 2; however, this segment had great potential. Figure 3 compares price and performance of different computer product segments.

Since their introduction in the early 1980s, workstations had been used primarily for computationally intensive engineering and scientific applications. In the late 1980s and early 1990s, however, U.S. manufacturers aggressively moved into such commercial markets as electronic publishing, business graphics, financial services, and office automation. This move was facilitated by having application software developers transfer a number of PC-based business software to workstation systems, and the commitment by software firms to develop more applications for workstation systems. The joining of workstation performance with the personal computer's vast software base and networking capabilities lured dozens of computer manufacturers and software developers into this emerging market. The raw data processing power of the PC vied with that of low-end workstations, and the technological features that once distinguished PCs from workstations began to converge. As a result, the PC and workstation segments began to consolidate.

Workstation manufacturers such as Sun Microsystems, HP, Digital Equipment Corporation (DEC), and IBM were targeting business and commercial users in addition to their traditional engineering and scientific markets. More business applications were being modified to run on UNIX operating systems, a system widely used on workstations. PC companies such as Apple and Compaq were planning to build more powerful desktop machines using Reduced Instruction Set Computing (RISC) microprocessors borrowed from the world of engineering workstations.

Distribution patterns were also changing in the workstation market. Traditionally, workstations had been sold primarily by direct sales forces or through value-added resellers (VARs). Increasingly, workstations were being offered by the same computer dealers and retail outlets that served the PC market. Some workstation suppliers had begun to use mass distribution channels for their products.

As workstations entered the business market, a conflict between PC and workstation software standards arose. While Microsoft's DOS and IBM's OS/2 operating systems dominated the PC world, UNIX (in its various forms) was the operating system of choice for workstations. Members of the Advanced Computing Environment (ACE) initiative, an industry consortium of 84 companies, supported both a future unified version of UNIX and a future version of the OS/2 operating system. This strategy suggested that members were hedging their bets until it became clearer which direction the business workstation market would take.

THE PRODUCTS

There were three major types of workstations on the market in 1991. The first was the personal workstation, which bore the greatest resemblance to the PC. These low-end workstations were similar to high-end PCs. These models offered the workstations' increased capabilities, as well as ease of use and the ability for future expansion. The second type of workstation was the

Figure 2: Computer Industry World Market in 1992* — By Segment

Segment	Market Share (%)	Market Share ($ Billions)
Services andOther Software	38.5	249.9
Peripherals	19.0	123.3
PCs	16.5	107.1
Minis & Mainframes	13.5	87.6
PC Software	5.5	35.7
Datacommunications	4.0	26.0
Workstations	3.0	19.4
	100%	$649 Billion

* Projected by Price Waterhouse

Source: Information obtained from Standard and Poor's *Industry Surveys*, 1991.

Figure 3: Computer Product Segments

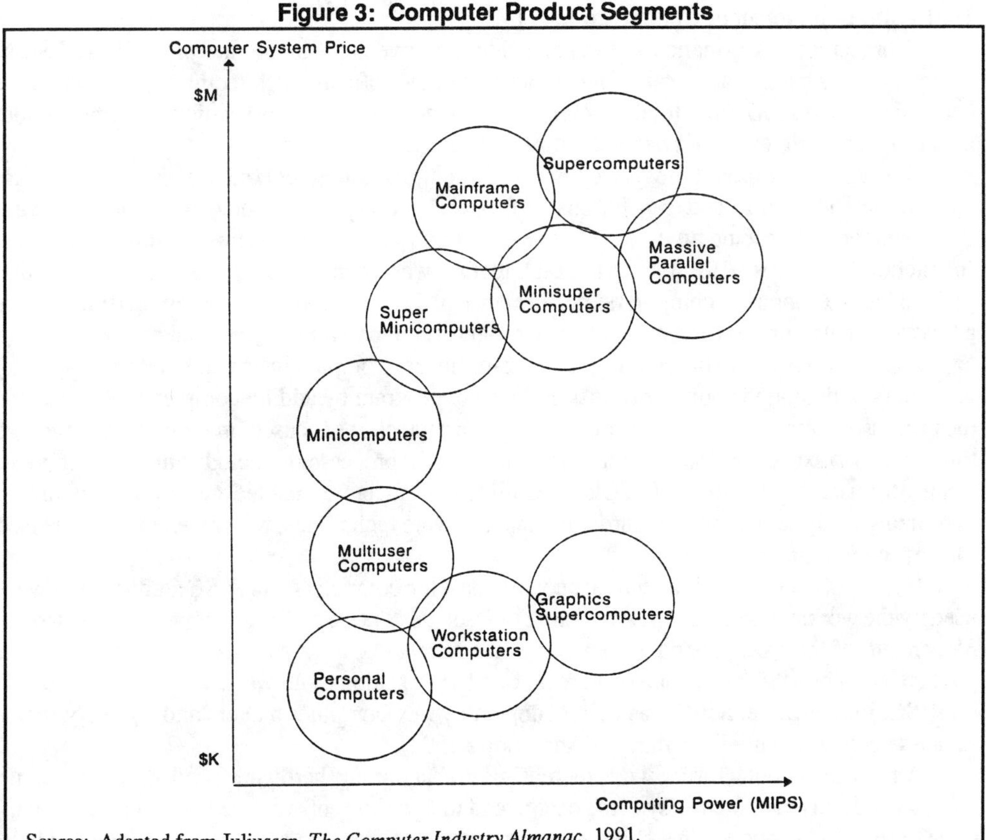

Source: Adapted from Juliussen, *The Computer Industry Almanac*, 1991.

graphic workstation. These models were usually middle-of-the-line workstations which could create and manipulate images and/or text. The third type was the high-end design workstation used by engineers, scientists, and architects for computer-aided design, manufacturing, and engineering (CAD/CAM/CAE) applications.

The price and performance distinctions between workstations and other types of computer systems blurred at both the low and high ends of the market in the early 1990s. At the low end, personal workstations had experienced a price reduction of more than 60 percent since 1981 and had added features which made them more accessible and user friendly. Units had an internal memory of 400-840 megabytes (MB) which could be expanded to 4.4-9.45 gigabytes (GB). Performance speeds ranged from 13.7-50 MIPS. These improvements placed the entry-level, low-end workstation in the cost range of the PC, which also featured improved operating speeds and increased storage capabilities. At the high end, design workstations offered the greatest amount of memory, typically around 800-2.6 GB, expandable to 26.5-236 GB. These units achieved operating speeds ranging from 28.5-76.7 MIPS. Systems with up to eight central processing units (CPUs) operating at 230 MIPS were introduced for approximately $200,000 in 1991 [U.S. Department of Commerce 1991].

Workstation performance was enhanced by improvements in the internal design of workstation systems and the acceptance and adoption of new software architectures. Manufacturers had been able to reduce the total number of components used in workstation systems without adversely affecting the unit's dependability and performance.

Software is required by every computer system, including workstations. Since software applications add value and can be cost effective, as compared to new hardware, software development had become an essential component of workstation systems. The new Reduced Instruction Set Chips (RISC) software architecture was an approach to computer design that yielded breakthroughs in computers' performance and price. Computer system performance is a function of the number of instructions in a program and the average time it takes a processor to execute an instruction. In order to improve performance, Complex Instruction Set Chips (CISC) focused on reducing the number of instructions per program by adding complex instructions to the processors' instruction set. In contrast, RISC architectures focused on reducing the average time needed to execute an instruction by streamlining the processor to include only simpler, more frequently used instructions. RISC's streamlined architecture enabled more effective use of optimizing compilers, powerful hardware, and software techniques, which generally decreased total execution time.

CISC had been the architecture of choice in desktop computers, but RISC architectures were used by the workstation industry. According to Dataquest Inc., RISC workstations accounted for 35 percent of the value of and 25 percent of the number of units shipped in 1989. Dataquest predicted that by 1993 more than 60 percent of all workstations sold worldwide would be based on RISC. Furthermore, RISC was being adopted by minicomputer makers and by every major Japanese computer supplier [Standard and Poor's 1991].

American manufacturers were increasingly abandoning hardware production to pursue value-added activities such as systems design and integration, software development, and after-sales service and support. This shift in emphasis resulted from the comparative advantage held by the U.S. in this area, as opposed to Japan's advantage in hardware production.

Technological innovations in workstation products were expected to continue in the future. The rapid pace of product introductions had reduced the product life cycle of traditional 32-bit workstations to only one year. Industry analysts projected that by 1994 workstation products would be 10 to 15 times more powerful than the units of 1989. This meant the major workstation producers would have to continue to devote significant portions of their sales revenue to the improvement of their products in order to remain competitive.

The majority of the new systems used RISC microprocessors as their central processing units and UNIX as their operating system environment. Low-end models introduced in 1991 had average performance speeds of 32.8 MIPS and a minimum of 4 GB total disk capacity. Models introduced at the high end had average performance speeds in excess of 50 MIPS and a minimum of 26.5 GB total disk capacity. Some workstations featured superscalar architectures in which several instructions could be executed simultaneously per clock cycle, significantly boosting system performance over that of competitive products. A number of suppliers marketed models with three-dimensional graphics capabilities for under $10,000. At the high end, some graphics supercomputer systems with up to eight central processing units had performance speeds of over 200 MIPS and up to 2.6 GB of main memory. Workstation manufacturers would not be able to continue to compete on the basis of technological advantage alone. Their ability to develop products that could be easily modified to take advantage of future technological developments, as well as be more compliant with industry standards, would be one of their keys to success. Giving the customer the freedom to mix and match hardware and software was commonly referred to as "open systems."

CUSTOMERS

The workstation industry targeted its products worldwide to a broad range of customers, including organizations and individual users. Organizations included high-technology and business corporations of all sizes, government agencies, and nonprofit organizations. In addition, workstations were designed to meet the needs of the ultimate or actual users of the machines: technical users (scientists and engineers), business/ commercial users (analysts, controllers, and programmers), and individual users.

Technical users, or traditional customers, provided manufacturers with more than half of their workstation revenues. Revenue growth from technical users of workstations was expected to remain steady throughout the mid- to late 1990s. Technical users worked for engineering and high-technology firms, government research laboratories, and nonprofit institutions such as hospitals and educational institutions. The common characteristic of this group was its need to solve complex computing and research problems. This demanded the increased capabilities and applications of the workstation, rather than the traditional PC. Technical users generally used high-end design workstations for their CAD/CAM/CAE applications. Compared to other users of workstations, technical users were not very price-sensitive. They desired substantial memory and graphics capabilities, and often utilized add-on components, such as graphics accelerators, to increase their hardware's flexibility.

Business and commercial users traditionally used mid-range computer systems which supported individual terminals for office automation, financial services, electronic publishing, graphics design, and animation. The increased price/performance ratios offered by workstations had caught the attention of business and commercial customers. These users needed additional software applications and placed greater emphasis on high levels of after-sales service and support. This group of users had become an important source of revenue to the workstation industry by 1992, and the trend was expected to continue.

The declining price levels of the low-end models made the individual user very important to the workstation segment. As the PC's life cycle matured, the individual user continued to look for ways to increase efficiency and effectiveness at work. These needs were increasingly being fulfilled by the personal workstation and the development of software packages for individual applications. Individual users purchasing workstations would demand a high level of service and competitively priced systems from workstation manufacturers.

SALES AND DISTRIBUTION

In the domestic market, workstation manufacturers sold their products directly to computer users or through a variety of resellers. Generally speaking, open-based system hardware was essentially a commodity and application software ran on such systems without modifications. Gross margins on a mainframe sale could be 70 percent or more, while gross margins on open-based workstations could be as low as 30 percent. These margins were too small for manufacturers to rely solely on an extensive direct sales force [Standard and Poor's 1991]. Therefore, workstations were commercially distributed through a variety of channels, mainly direct sales forces, value-added resellers (VARs), and other resellers such as computer specialty stores.

In the early stages of the industry, direct sales was the primary channel used to sell workstations. This method was appropriate because it offered the customer — usually a large corporation, government agency, or nonprofit institution — who was investing large sums of money in the product, a higher degree of individualized attention and technical support. This consideration was particularly important when trying to sell government contracts and large corporate accounts. However, as the personal workstation gained the attention of the individual customer, workstation manufacturers diversified their distribution channels in the U.S. to compete with high-end PC manufacturers.

The workstation sales function had shifted from direct sales to value-added resellers (VARs). Value-added resellers were vendors who specialized in narrow segments called vertical markets. They assembled hardware components into a computer system and "added value" to it by installing customized software before selling the complete package to the final consumer. This method of sales met the needs of price-sensitive small-to-medium sized firms and institutions.

Although VARs were the principal sellers of workstations between 1989 and 1991, U.S. manufacturers had broadened their distribution channels to include other resellers — such as computer specialty shops — in order to lure commercial customers away from PC suppliers into traditional workstation markets. Computer specialty stores, which focused on selling personal computers and related products, were the most important sales channel for such computers — especially to individual users. Workstation manufacturers were attracted by the success of this channel and were establishing footholds in computer specialty stores. These stores were fast becoming important sales channels for workstations and related products. Almost 250 specialty shops/dealers distributed workstation products in the U.S. in 1990, according to a report from Summit Strategies, a Boston-based consulting firm [U.S. Department of Commerce 1991].

In the international market, a mixed distribution strategy that included direct sales and value-added reselling was used. Selling in foreign markets had certain inherent problems: foreign currency risks, import/export controls and duties, and economic and political risks. The European market, with a population of 320 million, was expected to continue to be a major source of revenue for U.S. producers. An appropriate mix of direct sales and value-added reselling was expected to be a successful strategy for this market.

THE WORKSTATION MARKET

The major companies operating in the workstation segment of the computer industry produced a wide range of workstation models which were distributed both domestically and internationally.

The Domestic Market

The domestic market for workstations was approximately $5 billion in 1990, and was expected to grow to over $11.4 billion by 1992 due to continued expansion of product lines and the customer base [Juliussen 1991 and Standard and Poor's 1991]. By 1993, sales in this segment were expected to account for almost 30 percent of all computer revenues and 76 percent of computer industry growth [Juliussen 1991]. Given the lingering recession, the U.S. computer equipment industry expected moderate domestic growth over the short term. A majority of this growth was expected to come from traditional workstation users (scientists and engineers) who worked for engineering and high-technology firms. However, the number of business/commercial users and individual users was also expected to increase rapidly, as the number of software applications and support programs for these two groups continued to expand.

Workstation manufacturers were attempting to reach an agreement on the standard operating format for workstations. In 1990, the dominant system in the U.S. was the UNIX system (and its derivatives, POSIX and XENIX). However, some workstation manufacturers had adopted alternative formats such as Apple's A/UX and IBM's AIX formats. Furthermore, some manufacturers were using the OS/2 format found in the high-end PCs as a base for their workstation systems. Reaching an agreement on which standards to use was a risk that could produce unsatisfactory results for U.S. manufacturers. On the one hand, an agreement could lead to lowered prices, expanded potential markets, and increased consumer choice. On the other hand, it could benefit foreign producers by allowing them to use their high-volume, low-cost production methods to capture market share.

Figure 4: Worldwide Workstation Market (In Billions)

Market Segment	1989	1990	1992*
U.S.	$4.1	$5.0	$11.4
Foreign	2.3	2.8	8.0
Total	$6.4	$7.8	$19.4

* Projected by Price Waterhouse

Sources: Information obtained from Standard and Poor's *Industry Surveys*, 1991, and Juliussen, *The Computer Industry Almanac*, 1991.

The Foreign Markets

The foreign markets, most notably Europe and Japan, were expected to grow at a much faster rate than the U.S. market, and as such, were expected to become significant revenue sources, as shown in Figure 4. In recent years, several U.S. firms had either established new production facilities or expanded existing ones in Europe and Asia to more effectively serve these rapidly growing markets.

U.S. companies accounted for roughly 93 percent of the 76,850 units produced in Europe during 1990, according to estimates by Dataquest Inc. The size of the European market and the 1992 unification of Europe in particular, could have long-term impacts on the workstation industry's future. With the formation of a "United States of Europe," there would be few, if any, restrictions on travel between member countries. There would also be a unification of the major tax rates, technical and operating standards, and possibly a common currency. By adopting uniform standards and eliminating individual duties and tariffs, the production and marketing of new products would become less costly for U.S. manufacturers. A real danger, however, was that a united Europe could increase protectionist policies aimed at U.S. manufacturers and their products. In anticipation of this possibility, many U.S. firms had acquired or entered into joint ventures with European firms in order to establish a European base. This was not a perfect solution, however, because 80 percent of a company's production would have to take place within Europe, with no more than 20 percent of parts and labor coming from outside of its borders. In spite of these restrictions, U.S. firms expected to manufacture locally more than half of what they sold to European users by 1994, up from only 22 percent in 1992 [U.S. Department of Commerce 1992].

The U.S. led Japan in the workstation industry and had been active in the Japanese market since the mid-1980s. The U.S. presence in the Japanese market was largely through original equipment manufacturer (OEM) marketing arrangements with major Japanese consumer electronics and computer suppliers, or through contracts assigning production to Japanese partners. OEMs are vendors who assemble computer systems from components originally manufactured by other suppliers. In 1990, Sun Microsystems, Silicon Graphics, and Hewlett-Packard/Apollo opened plants in Japan [U.S. Commerce Department 1992].

The Japanese market had grown annually at an average rate of 61 percent from 1988 to 1990, to almost $1.5 billion in 1990. In Japan, workstations were used primarily for software development, but computer-assisted design (CAD) and artificial intelligence (AI) were also important applications. In 1990, U.S. suppliers garnered a 75 percent share of this market and generally enjoyed price and performance advantages over Japanese manufacturers [U.S. Department of Commerce 1992].

MATERIALS SUPPLIERS

The two main resources used in the U.S. workstation industry were raw materials or commodities, and semiconductors and other electro-mechanical subassemblies. The first group of materials included aluminum, copper, brass, steel, plastic resins, silicon, and gold. The materials and supplies necessary for manufacturing operations were available in the required quantities from several suppliers, in addition to the commodities market. Thus, shortages in materials and delays in shipment did not adversely affect production schedules.

Figure 5 lists the top ten semi-conductor suppliers by sales in 1980 and 1990. As shown in Figure 6, Japanese and Far Eastern manufacturers had been the major suppliers of these chips since overtaking the U.S. in 1986. Of the second type of materials (semi-conductors) necessary for the production of workstations, dynamic-random-access-memory chips (DRAMs) were in sufficient supply, though problems were expected in the future. As shown in Figure 7, Japan's top four memory chip manufacturers captured 49 percent of worldwide DRAM production in 1989. In fact, Texas Instruments and Micron Technology were the only two U.S. producers of DRAMs in 1990. At full capacity, these two firms combined could satisfy only 25 percent of the U.S. demand in 1989.

The continued low output of U.S.-made DRAMs drove up prices and forced U.S. manufacturers to delay the introduction of several new product lines until 1991. This strategic weakness contributed to the erosion of profit margins for U.S. companies. It was feared that in the near future the Japanese could demand the licensing of proprietary design information from U.S. producers, in exchange for increased supplies of these chips. This would permit the Japanese to make great strides in the development of their workstations, which were considered to be about two generations behind the U.S. products.

Because of these anticipated problems, some U.S. manufacturers decided to take action. Seven companies, including IBM, DEC, and HP, decided to help U.S. Memories raise $1 billion to form a start-up DRAM manufacturing company. This effort later collapsed because of an unforeseen overcapacity in the open DRAM market which led to saturation in the computer industry. This resulted in the unwillingness of major industry players (notably Apple, Compaq, and Sun) to contribute funds to the venture. In addition, the lack of involvement from the federal government ensured the demise of U.S. Memories in January 1990.

Figure 5: Top Ten Semiconductor Suppliers Worldwide Sales (In Millions)

1980		1990	
TEXAS INSTRUMENTS (U.S.)	1580	NEC (Japan)	4952
MOTOROLA (U.S.)	1110	TOSHIBA (Japan)	4905
PHILLIPS	935	HITATCHI (Japan)	3927
NEC (Japan)	787	MOTOROLA (U.S.)	3692
NATIONAL	747	INTEL (U.S.)	3135
TOSHIBA (Japan)	629	FUJITSU (Japan)	3019
HITACHI (Japan)	622	TEXAS INSTRUMENTS (U.S.)	2574
INTEL (U.S.)	575	MITSUBISHI (Japan)	2476
FAIRCHILD	566	MASTSUSHITA (Japan)	1945
SIEMENS	413	PHILLIPS	1932
TOTAL	**$7,964M**	**TOTAL**	**$32,557M**

Source: Information obtained from *Sematech, Annual Report 1991*.

Figure 6: Estimated Worldwide Semiconductor Market (As Percentage of Total Market)

Region	**'82**	**'83**	**'84**	**'85**	**'86**	**'87**	**'88**	**'89**	**'90**	**'91**
Japan	33	38	39	42	47	49	51	50	47	47
U.S.	56	54	52	48	42	40	38	38	40	39
Other	11	8	9	10	11	11	11	12	13	14
Total	**100**	**100**	**100**	**100**	**100**	**100**	**100**	**100**	**100**	**100**

PURCHASERS OF SEMICONDUCTORS IN 1991 [$ BILLIONS]

Region	**1991**
Japan	$20.9
U.S.	$15.4
Europe	$10.1
Other	$ 8.2
Total	$54.6

Source: Adapted from Pollack, *New York Times*, 1992.

Figure 7: DRAM Market Leaders
(Estimated 1989 Market - $9,200 million)

Firm	Country	Sales ($ millions)	Percentage of Market
Toshiba	Japan	1,525	16.6
NEC	Japan	1,100	11.9
Hitachi	Japan	1,000	10.9
Samsung	S. Korea	950	10.3
Mitsubishi	Japan	900	9.7

Source: Information obtained from *Electronic Business,* April 16, 1990.

THE COMPETITIVE MARKET

The workstation industry was highly concentrated and was dominated by U.S. manufacturers. Increasing levels of competition were expected in the workstation segment of the computer industry, which was projected to grow from $6.4 billion in 1989 to more than $30 billion by 1995. This meant that each producer would be vying for market share [U.S. Department of Commerce 1991]. More U.S. personal computing firms were expected to branch into business workstation manufacturing. Large, vertically integrated Japanese electronic companies (as well as manufacturers in South Korea and Taiwan) were expected to use their strengths as low-cost, high-volume hardware and semi-conductor producers to offset their current lack of software offerings and distribution channels in the U.S.

The major computer manufacturers (both foreign and domestic) were expected to increase their market presence by introducing new software packages, as well as dramatic pricing strategies. Some industry observers were expecting that by 1993, an onslaught of low-priced clone manufacturers in Japan and the Far East would force U.S. vendors to rethink their research and development and marketing strategies. Industry observers predicted that by the mid-1990s several U.S. firms might leave hardware design and manufacturing to concentrate on software development or systems integration, or to market foreign-made workstations on an OEM basis, while others might produce only the more profitable, higher performance systems [U.S. Commerce Department 1992].

Competition in this industry could be divided into two categories: domestic producers (competitors) who led in the development of new technologies, and foreign producers who specialized in the production of clone products and the development of computer memory (DRAM) chips. In general, U.S. manufacturers were developing increasingly complex workstations, networked systems, and support software, while foreign producers were involved mainly in the development and production of computer memory chips (DRAMS) and clone products. However, Japanese manufacturers were expected to begin concentrating on the development of low-end workstations, improved software packages for workstations, and the creation of software applications in the Japanese language — an area traditionally ignored by U.S. manufacturers. There was no major effort to create software applications in the various European languages since the character set used by the Romance and Slavic languages of Europe were easily adaptable to the Roman characters used in English.

Domestic Competition

Apollo Computers, which was acquired by Hewlett-Packard in 1989, was the pioneer of the early stand-alone workstations. Founded in 1980, Apollo's first offering was a fully configured (set-up) system with a price tag close to $60,000. In 1985, Sun Microsystems entered the market with a competitive UNIX workstation which sold for roughly $30,000 in full configuration. From the very beginning the workstation market had been characterized by fierce competition among a number of small, young, innovative companies that were leading the industry.

Domestic competition consisted of an assortment of well-known firms, and some lesser-known firms. These included Apollo, Compaq, Control Data, Data General, DEC, HP, IBM, Intergraph, NCR, NeXT, Stardent, Sun Microsystems, and Unisys. These firms intended to move aggressively in order to become the market leader while the segment was young, so they could capitalize on its future growth. HP's acquisition of Apollo was an example of this aggressive strategy. Other major competitors were also acquiring smaller firms, especially software development firms. This gave the acquiring firm access to complicated new supporting software without the heavy development costs. This in turn freed up companies' research and development budgets for the creation of new hardware. Despite the many players in the domestic workstation market, only Sun, Hewlett-Packard, Digital Equipment Corporation, and IBM had captured significant market shares as of 1990, as seen in Figure 8.

Sun Microsystems dominated the workstation market with a 32.4 percent market share and sales of $4.8 billion in 1990. Sun's Sparc RISC-based microprocessor and its SunOS version of UNIX attracted several licensed clone manufacturers who offered Sun-compatible computers. The company's strategy was to establish Sparc as the industry standard, and, due largely to the success of its other products, it was succeeding.

Hewlett-Packard, with a 21.2 percent market share and $3.1 billion in 1990 workstation revenues, was the number two workstation vendor. HP's position was expected to be strengthened by the introduction of its HP Apollo Series 700 workstations in 1991. Using an enhanced version of the RISC architecture upon which its minicomputers were based (called Precision Architecture), HP made a technological leap by producing systems that greatly outperformed its competitors' comparably priced systems. HP claimed that its new Series 700 Model 730 workstation was twice as fast as IBM's fastest workstation, and offered three and a half times the

Figure 8: RISC-Based Workstation Market Share (%)

Firm	1990[1]	1992[2]
Sun	32.4	35.0
HP	21.2	16.0
DEC	16.2	12.0
IBM	6.7	9.0
Other	23.5	28.0
	100%	**100%**

Note: The figures for 1992 were from projections made in 1991 before release the of HP's Series 700 workstations.

Sources: Adapted from [1] Standard and Poor's *Industry Surveys*, 1991, and [2] Radding, *Computerworld*, 1992.

performance of Sun's Sparcstation 3.

Digital Equipment's share of the workstation market declined from 23 percent in 1989 to 16.2 percent in 1990. Sales for 1990 were $2.4 billion. DEC was aggressively supporting the ACE consortium and planned to upgrade its DECstation product line with new workstations based on the powerful R4000 RISC microprocessor from MIPS Computer Systems.

IBM has made a resurgence in the workstation market since its 1990 introduction of a range of products based on its own RISC design. Sales of its RS/6000 workstations totaled $1 billion in 1990, resulting in a market share of 6.7 percent. Sales of its workstation products were expected to total $2 billion in 1991, up from $1.7 billion in 1990. IBM made moves to aggressively challenge Sun Microsystems. According to International Data Corp., Sun and IBM was expected to tie for first place among workstation vendors by 1993.

Japanese Competition

The major Japanese competitors in the workstation market were Fujitsu, Matsushita, NEC, Sony, and Toshiba. During 1988 and 1989, the Japanese attempted to penetrate the U.S. workstation market by targeting CAD/CAM/CAE users and increasing software development. They concentrated on the price-sensitive, low-end market in order to take advantage of high-volume, low-cost production methods. However, they had few established distribution channels and lacked applications software.

Early on, the Japanese had adopted a somewhat different strategy, which was to design better chips for initial use in their own machines, and as such became innovators in the industry. This was because the Japanese had some major technological advantages since workstations required large amounts of DRAMs (which they produced) and so could be built without buying microprocessors from Intel or Motorola (U.S. companies). By mid-1989, the Japanese had begun to offer RISC-based clone workstations in the U.S.

Japanese firms were expected to intensify their challenge to U.S. firms both in the U.S. and foreign markets. They planned to expand their operations in the United States as had NEC, Oki, and Toshiba by following Matsushita in establishing new plants. In addition, workstation shipments from Japanese facilities for U.S. consumption and exports were expected to more than double, surpassing 80,000 units by the end of 1992 [U.S. Department of Commerce 1992].

THE COMPANY

Hewlett-Packard was incorporated in 1947 as the successor to a partnership founded in 1939 by William Hewlett and David Packard, developers of the audio oscillator. The company became the leading manufacturer of electronic testing and measuring instruments for the science, telecommunications, and aerospace industries. In the early 1960s, this expertise and technology was applied to the analytical chemistry and medical fields.

HP went public in 1961, and introduced its first computer in 1966. This computer was designed to gather and analyze the data produced by the company's electronic instruments. In 1972, HP developed the first scientific hand-held calculator. In the mid-1970s, the company branched into the business computing segment with the HP 3000 Series. The HP 9000 and Vectra Series were added in the 1980s. The 1989 acquisition of Apollo Computers helped HP become the number one producer of computer workstations. HP acquired Avantek, Inc., a company whose product line expanded and complemented the radio- and microwave-frequency segment of HP's business, in November 1991. In 1991, Hewlett-Packard had 89,000 employees worldwide. As shown in Figure 9, gross sales for 1991 were $14.4 billion and net earnings were $755 million. Gross sales of $16 billion and net earnings of $955 million were projected for 1992 [Niemond 1992].

CORPORATE STRUCTURE AND PHILOSOPHY

In 1991, David Packard served as chairman of the board, John Young served as president and chief executive officer, and Dean O. Morton served as executive vice president and chief operating officer. In October 1990, HP implemented a major change in its management structure. This reorganization was undertaken to simplify structure, to streamline decision making, and to give managers more direct control over the technologies and sales activities required for the company's success.

The company's new structure consisted of three main organizations, as shown in Figure 10; each of these contained several groups and divisions. The Computer Systems Organization brought together the workstation and multiuser systems businesses. Executive Vice President Lew Platt was in charge of this group. The Computer Products Organization combined the PC and

Figure 9: Consolidated Statement of Earnings
Hewlett-Packard Company and Subsidiaries

For the years ended October 31 In millions except per share amounts	1991	1990	1989
Net revenue:			
Equipment	$11,019	$10,214	$ 9,404
Services	3,475	3,019	2,495
	14,494	13,233	11,899
Cost and expenses:			
Cost of equipment sold	5,634	5,072	4,513
Cost of services	2,224	1,921	1,578
Research and development	1,463	1,367	1,269
Selling general and administrative	3,963	3,711	3,327
	13,284	12,071	10,687
Earnings from operations	1,210	1,162	1,212
Interest income and other income (expense)	47	66	65
Interest expense	130	172	126
Earnings before taxes	1,127	1,056	1,151
Provision for taxes	372	317	322
Net earnings	$ 755	$ 739	$ 829
Net earnings per share	$ 3.02	$ 3.06	$ 3.52

Source: Information obtained from *Hewlett-Packard, Annual Report - 1991.*

Figure 10: Organizational Structure
Hewlett-Packard Company

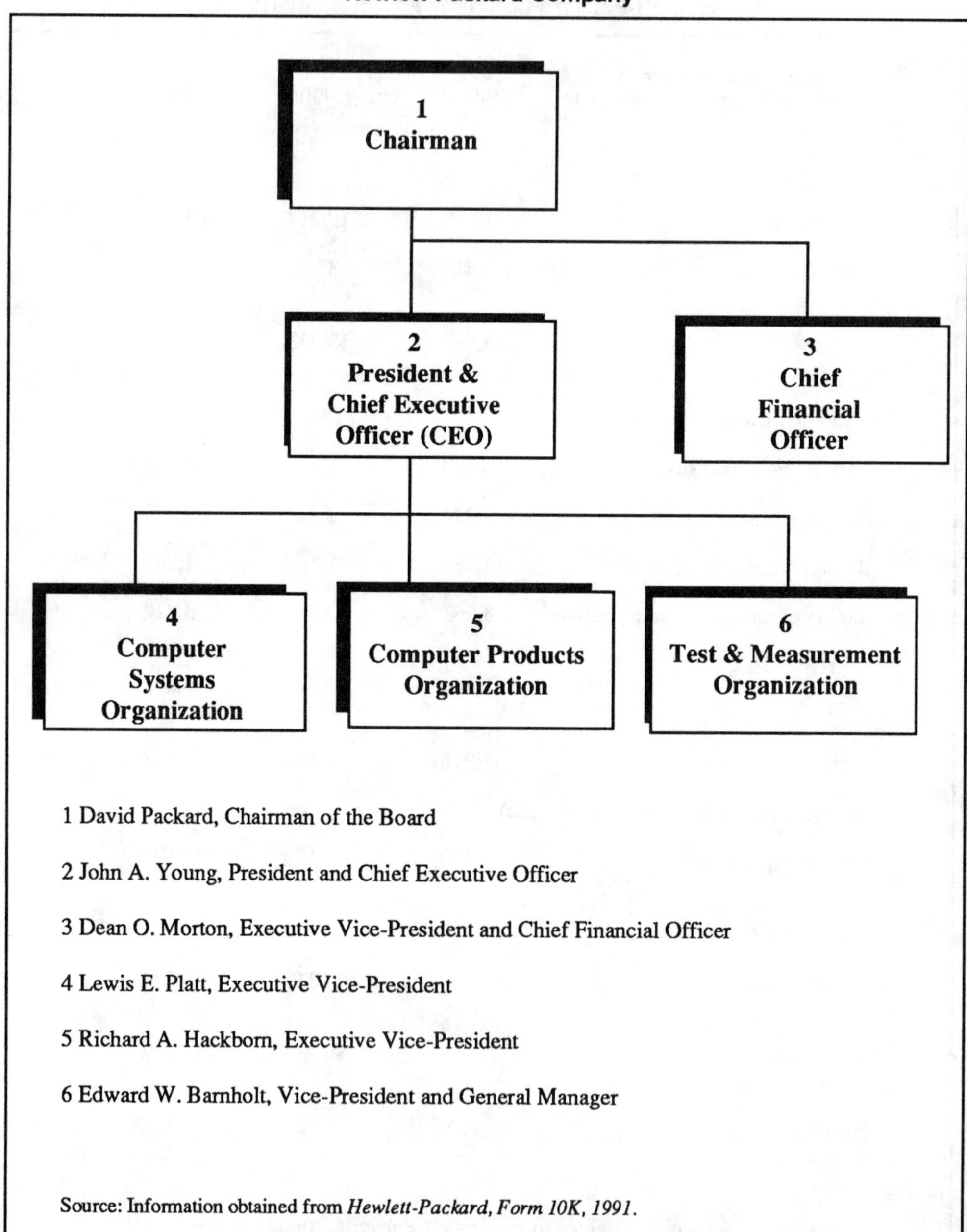

peripherals business and was headed by Executive Vice President Dick Hackborn. The Test and Measurement Organization, under Vice President Ned Barnholt, combined the activities of the Electronic Instruments and Microwave and Communication Groups. All three groups reported to Young through the respective vice presidents.

The company's reputation as a good employer was legendary in the industry. HP fostered an innovative, nonauthoritarian atmosphere that encouraged employees to develop their own ideas, while at the same time stressing the importance of teamwork and co-operation. To this end, the company practiced management by objectives (MBO). This policy was based on seven written corporate objectives which provided a framework for individual and group goal setting. These objectives are shown in Figure 11.

Under the direction of Young, HP had become more computer systems oriented. This was evidenced by a 31.2 percent annually compounded increase in computer sales from 1982 to 1991. In 1991, computer sales accounted for 65.5 percent of HP's revenue, with 34.4 percent of that amount coming from computer information systems, and 31.1 percent coming from the sales of peripheral devices such as printers, disk drives, and networked products.

The company's computer systems, personal peripheral products, and other peripherals were used in various applications, including engineering and scientific computation and analysis, instrumentation and control, and business information management. HP's core computing products and technologies included its PA-RISC architecture for systems and workstations, and software infra-structure for open systems. Key products included the HP 1000, designed for factory automation and real-time data acquisition; the HP 3000 Series of computer systems designed for commercial applications; the HP 9000 Series, which runs HP-UX — HP's

Figure 11: Hewlett-Packard's Corporate Objectives

Profit: To achieve sufficient profit to finance our company's growth and to provide the resources we need to achieve our other corporate objectives.

Customers: To provide products and services of the highest quality and the greatest possible value to our customers, thereby gaining and holding their respect and loyalty.

Fields of Interest: To participate in those fields of interest that build upon our technology and customer base, that offer opportunities for continuing growth, and that enable us to make a needed and profitable contribution.

Growth: To let our growth be limited only by our profits and our ability to develop and produce innovative products that satisfy real customer needs.

Our People: To help HP people share in the company's success which they make possible; to provide employment security based on their performance; to ensure them a safe and pleasant work environment; to recognize their individual achievements; and to help them gain a sense of satisfaction and accomplishment from their work.

Management: To foster initiative and creativity by allowing the individual great freedom of action in attaining well-defined objectives.

Citizenship: To honor our obligations to society by being an economic, intellectual, and social asset to each nation and each community in which we operate.

Source: Adapted from Hewlett-Packard, *Corporate Objectives, 1990.*

implementation of the UNIX operating system — consisting of workstations with powerful computational and graphics capabilities, as well as multiuser computers for both technical and commercial applications; the HP Vectra Series of IBM-compatible personal computers for use in business, engineering, manufacturing, and chemical analysis; and the new HP 95LX palmtop personal computer. The company's peripheral products included a variety of system and desktop printers such as the industry-leading HP LaserJet family and the HP DeskJet family. The company also produced measurement systems for use in electronics, medicine, and analytical chemistry.

Hewlett-Packard continued to demonstrate its ability to combine measurement and computation, and to provide service for its equipment, systems, and peripherals. The company promoted industry standards which recognized customers' preferences for open systems in which different vendors' products could work together. The company often based its product innovations on such standards.

WORKSTATION PRODUCTS

The HP Apollo Series 700 workstations were HP's high-end products. Based on price/performance, standards, networking, and graphics capabilities, HP had the best RISC-based workstations in the industry. Designed for power, the Series 700 products were the fastest PA-RISC desktop and deskside workstations on the market [Radding 1992]. Before the Series 700, performance like this could be obtained only with mainframe systems. HP's commitment to open systems and standards was inherent in the Series 700 family. The UNIX-based HP-UX operating system provided a path to OSF/1, the industry-standard operating system of the 1990s. In addition, HP's client/server and transparent networking technologies allowed the user to build a distributed cooperative computing environment.

Models 720, 730, and 750 were on the market in 1991. According to HP's technical literature, the 720 was the industry's best price/performance expandable workstation in a desktop. Integrated graphics included the leading-edge X11, 2D/3D vector performance, and outstanding 3D-color modeling and rendering. The 730, which used a 66 MHz PA-RISC processor, was the industry's highest performance desktop workstation. It boasted the industry's fastest X11, 2D/3D vector performance, and 24-plane solids performance on a desktop. The Model 750 offered the industry's leading performance and expandability in a deskside system. Large random access memory (RAM) and disk capacities made the 750 ideal for server applications. This model supported all the graphic options available on the 720 and 730.

In January 1992, Hewlett-Packard introduced additions to the Series 700 line of workstations as well as more than 16 multiuser systems and servers. HP demolished existing standards in low-price RISC workstations when it announced two new machines: the Series 700 Model 705 for $4,990 and the Model 710 for $9,390. Based on 11 benchmark tests run by the Systems Performance Evaluation Cooperative (SPEC), a consortium involving about 24 RISC vendors, HP's new machines came in at a price/performance rating of $147 per "SPECmark." This performance catapulted HP past the previous low-price RISC market leaders: Sun ($246 per

SPECmark), DEC ($245 per SPECmark), Solbourne Computer, Inc. ($300 per SPECmark), and Data General ($434 per SPECmark) [Radding 1992]. This HP announcement lessened enthusiasm for IBM's January announcement of its RISC System/6000 Model 220, a 25-SPECmark machine with a $6,345 base price and a rating of $254 per SPECmark. Other HP hardware introductions included a line of X-terminals, which are low-cost alternatives to workstations.

HP had already started to warm up for the next round of workstation wars by announcing its next-generation Precision Architecture-RISC microprocessor. The superscalar PA-RISC 7100 chip which was to show up in new HP computer systems in late 1992, would reportedly deliver 50 percent more performance over current HP 9000 and 3000 mid-range systems. Company officials said that full compatibility would be guaranteed with previous PA-RISC chips. The next generation of chips was expected to have clock speeds doubling the current 50-100 MHz and a performance rating of 120 SPECmarks. According to Jack Jeffers, quality assurance manager at Quaker Oats Co. in Jackson, Tennessee, where HP's workstation systems were used to run a statistical process control system, "Anything that gives us faster response time for people on the factory floor is welcome." This was a testament as to the effectiveness of HP's research and development program in helping to keep the firm competitive. The company's product developments were expected to continue to fulfill the market's demand for decreased price and increased performance standards — helping to make the company the dominant player in the workstation market.

CUSTOMERS

Hewlett-Packard offered its products to technical, business/commercial, and individual customers in a variety of settings, for example, high-tech and industrial corporations, business firms, government agencies, and educational institutions. In 1991, with the exception of the U.S. Government, no single account represented more than five percent of the company's orders. Compared to its major competitors, HP had fewer extremely large customers.

Most of HP's workstation revenues were earned by supplying technical users with graphic and design workstations. Technical users, including scientists and engineers, were the traditional mainstay of the workstation market. Orders from this group were expected to grow at a steady pace.

Business/commercial users, as a group, accounted for the next highest portion of HP's workstation revenues. These users constituted a relatively new target customer base, as they traditionally utilized mid-range computer systems which supported individual terminals for office automation, financial services, and electronic publishing. The improvement in the price and performance competitiveness of workstations, compared to mid-range systems, persuaded many customers to switch to workstation systems. The performance, network, and connectivity features that workstation systems offered were expected to lead to a steady increase in the number of business/commercial users abandoning mid-range computer systems in favor of personal and design workstation systems.

Individual users, such as the business/commercial users, constituted a new target customer.

The high cost of workstations in the past had proved unattractive to the individual user who traditionally purchased PCs. But the improved performance, coupled with intense price competition, had made personal workstations very attractive to the individual user. As the differences between high-end PCs and personal workstations became less well-defined, individual users were expected to purchase more workstations and to be significant customers for the industry to target.

SALES AND DISTRIBUTION

Slightly more than half of Hewlett-Packard's product revenue was derived through the efforts of its own sales organization selling to end users. The remaining revenue was derived through value-added resellers (VARs) and other resellers such as computer specialty stores. In 1991, a higher proportion of net revenue was generated from products such as personal peripherals, which were sold mainly through outlets such as mass merchandisers. Mass merchandisers included stores such as consumer electronics stores, department stores, and discount stores such as Sears and Montgomery Ward. Sales operations were supported by a 34,000 strong team comprised of field service engineers, sales representatives, and service and administrative personnel.

As shown in Figure 12, the company's total orders originating from outside the U.S. increased steadily since 1986 to $8.2 billion in 1991. International orders accounted for 53 percent of total orders in 1989, 54 percent in 1990, and 56 percent in 1991 [*Hewlett-Packard Annual Report* 1991]. The majority of these international orders were from customers other than foreign governments. Approximately 66 percent of HP's international orders from 1989 to 1991 originated in Europe, with others coming mostly from Japan, the Far East, and Canada. Most of the sales in international markets were made by foreign sales subsidiaries. Other sales were made directly from the parent company in the U.S. For international markets with low-volume sales, sales were made through various representative and distributorship arrangements.

Hewlett-Packard's international business was subject to risks customarily encountered in foreign operations, including fluctuations in monetary exchange rates, import/export controls, and political risks. However, the company believed its international diversification provided stability to its worldwide operations and reduced the impact of adverse economic shocks in any single country. In 1991, HP expanded its presence in Eastern Europe and the Commonwealth of Independent States by a variety of means, including formation of various joint ventures and sales and support subsidiaries.

During 1991, the company sold its products through a mix of direct sales and value-added resellers. Direct sales were the largest channel in previous years; however, HP began selling its low-end workstations through independent resellers in 1988. In 1991, HP began offering its entire workstation family through a new direct-mail unit.

Figure 12: Selected Financial Data
Hewlett-Packard and Subsidiaries

For the years ended October 31 In millions except per share amounts and employees	1991	1990	1989	1988	1987	1986
U.S. orders	$6,484	$6,143	$5,677	$4,780	$4,262	$3,826
International orders	8,192	7,342	6,483	5,290	4,117	3,375
Total orders	$14,676	$13,485	$12,160	$10,070	$8,379	$7,201
Net revenue	14,494	13,233	11,899	9,831	8,090	7,102
Earnings from operations	1,210	1,162	1,212	1,084	905	752
Net earnings	755	739	829	816	644	516
Per share:						
Net earnings	3.02	3.06	3.52	3.36	2.50	2.02
Cash dividends	.48	.42	.36	.28	.23	.22
At year-end:						
Total assets	11,973	11,395	10,075	7,858	8,547	6,770
Employees	89,000	92,200	94,900	86,600	82,300	82,300

Source: Information obtained from *Hewlett-Packard, Annual Report - 1991.*

HEWLETT-PACKARD'S COMPETITIVE POSITION

The company encountered aggressive competition in all areas of its business activities. Its competitors were numerous, ranging from some of the world's largest corporations to many relatively small and highly-specialized firms. Hewlett-Packard competed primarily on the basis of technology, performance, price, quality, reliability, distribution, and customer service and support.

Several important strategic strengths had helped HP become a serious contender in the workstation segment. The company was financially strong and compared favorably to other firms in its industry. The company had extensive, well-developed distribution networks, and a large and highly-trained sales force which served both domestic and international markets. HP also maintained complete and competitive product lines with good price/ performance ratios. Workstation models utilized the UNIX operating system, the de facto industry standard. In 1991, HP had an experienced management team and a solid research and development program in place. Research and development expenditures were 10.1 percent of net revenues [*Hewlett-Packard 10K Report* 1991]. HP's excellent research and development program enabled the product developers to maintain a current and competitive product line. New products were essential in this industry in which technology and success went hand-in-hand. More than half of HP's 1991 orders were for products that had been introduced since 1989 in the preceding two years.

HP had some weaknesses to correct before its overall competitive position could be improved, especially in the workstation market. Market research suggested that HP had fallen behind some of its competitors in providing satisfactory after-sale service and support. The company lagged in the development of software that could take advantage of its improved hardware systems designs. The two families of computer systems — the HP 9000 UNIX-based computers and the HP Apollo 700 Series — were at times competing with each other and creating confusion in the market and among customers. Furthermore, the improved price/performance of its own PC line was beginning to compete with its low-end workstations.

TOWARDS THE FUTURE

The challenge for all workstation companies was to maintain profit margins as average workstation prices fell and to adjust to new distribution channels as the market for workstations expanded. In 1992, Hewlett-Packard was considering strategies that recognized the importance of balancing efforts to improve the effectiveness of the firm in the workstation segment. There was universal agreement that HP should continue to aggressively offer its wide product line to both domestic and foreign markets. In addition, HP should continue to compete on the basis of technology, price, performance, quality, distribution, and customer service and support. However, there was disagreement on the specific strategies the company should pursue.

One manager suggested the best strategy would be to concentrate on the high-end of the proprietary workstation market. HP's proprietary RISC-based Precision Architecture had allowed the company to surpass its competitors. The company's workstations had superior price/performance ratios coupled with the high quality for which HP was legendary. By focusing on this niche, it was argued, the company could realize high margins while expanding its domestic and foreign customer base.

John Young, the president and CEO of Hewlett-Packard, did not agree with this strategy. He felt the company had to compete in both the low- and high-ends of the workstation market. He suggested that HP manufacture both proprietary and open-systems hardware for its entire line of workstations. HP's workstation segment had not gotten high marks for customer service and support, compared to the rest of the computer industry. Young wanted to continue matching product quality with marketing quality for HP's workstations while maintaining a lead position in workstation price/performance against Sun, DEC, and IBM. Although proprietary system platforms carried greater profit margins than did open, or nonproprietary, systems, the trend toward open systems was unstoppable.

Given the dynamic nature of the industry and its intensely competitive environment, management was considering what it should do about these and other major strategic problems facing the company.

REFERENCES AND BACKGROUND READINGS

Alster, Norm, "Drowning in DRAMs," *Forbes*, November 11, 1991, p. 41.

Anthens, Gary, "Bush Trip Yields High-Tech Silver Lining," *Computerworld,* January 20, 1992, p. 85.

Bayer, Tony, "Open Systems Slowly Gaining Steam in Factory," *Computerworld*, October 28, 1991, p. 78.

Burrows, Peter, "A 'Single Industry Voice' Gets Results in Chip Wars," *Electronic Business,* May 6, 1991, p. 11.

David, Bernard J., "ACE Promises Unity and Fragmentation," *Systems 3X/40 0,* Vol. 19, Iss. 10, October 1991, pp. 90-94.

Electronic Business, April 16, 1990, p. 48

Francis, Bob, "Workstations Enter the Third Dimension," *Datamation*, Vol. 37, Iss. 17, September 1, 1991, pp. 34-38.

Handleman-Sagan, Julie, *Electronic Business*, March 30, 1992, p. 23.

Hewlett-Packard, *Annual Report - 1991,* Hewlett-Packard, 3000 Hanover Street, Palo-Alto, California, 94304.

Hewlett-Packard, *Corporate Objectives - 1990*, Hewlett-Packard, 3000 Hanover Street, Palo Alto, California, 94304.

Hewlett-Packard, *Form 10K, 1991*, Securities and Exchange Commission, Washington, D.C. 20549.

Hughes, David, "Hewlett-Packard, Digital and IBM Race to Create Faster Workstations," *Aviation Week & Space Technology*, Vol. 135, Iss. 7, August 19, 1991, pp. 103-107.

Johnson, Maryfran, "HP Announces Next-Generation PA-RISC Chip," *Computerworld,* February 24, 1992, p. 8.

Johnson, Maryfran, "Sun Storage Prices Plummet," *Computerworld*, March 30, 1992, p.16.

Juliussen, Karen, and Juliussen, Egil, *The Computer Industry Almanac, 1991*, Computer Industry Almanac Inc., Dallas, Texas, 1991.

Mockler, Robert J., *Strategic Management: An Integrated Situational Management Orientation,* D & R Publishing Company, Yorkville Station, NY, 1990.

Niemond, George A., "Hewlett-Packard," *Value-Line Investment Survey*, 1991, p. 1095.

Pollack, Andrew, "U.S. Chip Makers Stem the Tide in Trade Battles with Japanese," *New York Times*, April 9, 1992, p. A1.

Radding, Alan, "RISC Desktop Machines: PCs in Disguise?," *Computerworld*, March 23, 1992, pp. 85-87.

Sematech, Annual Report 1991, Sematech, 2706 Montopolis Drive, Austin, Texas, 78741.

Standard and Poor's, *Industry Surveys*, October 17, 1991, pp. 75-83.

U.S. Department of Commerce, *U.S. Industrial Outlook,* Washington, D.C., 20549, 1991.

U.S. Department of Commerce, *U.S. Industrial Outlook*, Washington, D.C., 20549, 1992.

Verity, John, "From Mainframes to Clones, a Trickery Time," *Business Week,* January 13, 1992, pp. 97-98.

LUMEX, DIVISION OF LUMEX, INC.: THE HEALTH CARE PRODUCTS INDUSTRY

Lumex, a division of Lumex, Inc., was part of one of the largest and fastest growing industries: healthcare. Lumex experienced consistent sales and profit growth during the late 1960s and 1970s due to the legislation that created Medicare and Medicaid. Unfortunately, in the late 1980s federal budget reductions dramatically altered the way Lumex was reimbursed for purchases of its products. As shown in Figure 1, Lumex had consistent sales growth between 1986 and 1991. Profits dipped in 1987 as a result of changes in healthcare reimbursement legislation, but increased again in 1988 due to management's ability to cut costs and increase sales.

During the early 1990s there was increased legislation for integrating the handicapped into society. For example, in July 1990 President Bush signed an act banning discrimination on the basis of a physical or mental handicap in employment, public accommodations, ground transportation, and telecommunication services. As a result of this legislation, businesses such as supermarkets, restaurants, and theaters were expected to restructure their facilities to accommodate the disabled, for instance by widening aisles for wheelchairs and installing ramps and automatic doors [Holmes 1992, p.1]. In addition, the Air Carriers Access Act, scheduled to be passed in 1992, required airlines to make all lavatories accessible to the handicapped [Metzger 1991, p.62]. These laws were expected to increase the market for specialty wheelchairs and other medical products at an unprecedented rate.

Demographics was another reason why this market continued to expand: the elderly population was expected to increase as the baby-boom generation aged. Also, increased AIDS cases and new market opportunities overseas added to the demand for these products. The trend toward integrating the handicapped into society presented many expansion opportunities for

Figure 1: LUMEX Division's Sales and Profits (in Thousands of $)

YEAR	SALES	PROFIT
1987	$35,918	$2,756
1988	$38,051	$2,142
1989	$40,448	$2,344
1990	$44,560	$2,646
1991*	$45,897	$2,912

* estimated

Source: Based on information from Lumex Annual Report, 1990.

Lumex in homecare product marketing, as did the newly emerging consumer product market composed of people who wanted healthcare products for their home to increase their comfort and convenience.

In light of the changing market forces, management was seeking answers to several critical questions: What will customers needs be in both the long-term care and the homecare market and how can Lumex products meet those needs? What products and/or product lines will build on Lumex's brand equity and generate acceptable sales and gross profits? What will be the best distribution method for the market? What will be the best long-term source of reimbursement (payment) for Lumex products? What will be the best way to compete in the international market?

THE INDUSTRY AND COMPETITIVE MARKET

THE MEDICAL PRODUCTS INDUSTRY

The size of the healthcare market (goods and services) in 1992 was $738 billion; it absorbed 13 percent of the gross national product ["Healthcare Spending Climbs Upward in '92," 1992, p.2]. By the year 1995 spending was expected to exceed one trillion dollars and by the year 2000 healthcare was expected to account for 15 percent of the gross national product. As a comparison, military spending peaked at 6 percent during the Reagan Administration and by 1990 accounted for approximately 5.5 percent of the GNP [Freudenheim 1990, p. D1]. The political trends of the 1990s suggested that in the future less money would be allocated for military spending and more money would flow into the healthcare sector.

The medical product industry supplied products to the institutional market, which included acute-care facilities (hospitals) and long-term care facilities (nursing homes and congregate care centers) and to the homecare market (consumers using medical products in a home setting). Products ranged from a simple cane used by a homecare patient to a complex imaging machine used by an institution.

Figure 2: Medical Product Sales Projection 1989-1994 (Overall Industry)

YEAR	SALES
1989	$27,302
1990	$29,609
1991	$31,998
1992	$34,596
1993	$37,418
1994	$40,488

Source: Based on information from "Banking on Basics," *Health Industry Today*, January 1990.

Figure 3: U.S. Population (By Age Group Over 65) (Actual and Projected)

YEAR	AGE 65-74	AGE 75+	TOTAL 65+
1990	13,187	18,733	31,920
1995	14,934	18,930	33,864
2000	16,639	18,243	34,882
2010	18,323	21,039	39,362

Source: Based on information from *Statistical Abstract of the United States*, 1991, U.S. Department of Commerce, 111th Edition, January 1991, pp. 1002-1007.

The medical product industry estimated its sales at $31 billion in 1991 [Estimated from "Banking on Basics" 1990 pp.20-23]. As shown in Figure 2, sales of medical products were expected to grow at an annual rate of 8.5 percent through 1995 ["Banking on Basics" 1990, pp.20-23].

Healthcare spending and the expected growth in medical product sales were directly related to the growth of the elderly population. As shown in Figure 3, both the 65-74 age group and the over 75 age group were expected to grow at a steady rate. The total number of persons over the age of 65 was projected to reach 13.5 percent of the population by 1995 — almost 34 million people.

Healthcare professionals strongly influenced the type and brand of product patients took home. Typical referral sources for homecare products were physical therapists, occupational therapists, and discharge planners. The end user had little or no knowledge of the types of products available to them and, therefore, relied on the healthcare professional or the homecare dealer to select a product for them. Medical products used in the home usually were recommended by a healthcare professional while the patient was in an acute-care setting. Products sold to acute-care and long-term care facilities were sold either on a direct basis to the facility or through a medical-surgical dealer. There were approximately 540 med-surg dealers in the United States in 1991; most of them were part of large chains capable of a high level of service.

Medical products for use in the home were distributed through a network of home healthcare dealers who called on referral sources, such as physical therapists. Referral sources with the help of the dealers helped patients choose and order products for use in their homes. There were approximately 14,000 homecare dealers in the United States in 1991. Pharmacies entered homecare product distribution in the late 1980s but did not make major inroads due to the large space and inventory investment required.

One of the critical factors affecting sales and profitability in the medical product industry was the reimbursement system. The healthcare industry grew and developed rapidly during the mid-1960s when Medicare and Medicaid legislation was passed. Medicare is a federally funded program designed to provide healthcare for persons over the age of 65. In contrast, Medicaid is funded jointly by the individual state involved and the federal government. Part A of Medicare provides for hospital services while Part B covers homecare products and services. Reimbursement under Medicare was particularly important in the homecare market since medical products utilized in acute-care and long-term care facilities were not directly financed by the government, as they were in the homecare market. Figure 4 shows the large percentage of revenue that Medicare represented to a homecare dealer in 1991.

MARKETS

The market for medical products was divided into two well-defined segments: the homecare market and the institutional market.

Figure 4: Source of Homecare Dealer Revenue (Overall Industry)

SOURCE	PERCENT
Medicare/Medicaid	50.00%
Private Insurance	19.00%
Retail/Open Account	13.00%
Medicare Co. Payment	8.00%
Providers	8.00%
Cash/Bank Cards	2.00%

Source: Based on information from "Financial Survey for Homecare Dealers - 1991," *Health Industry Distributors Association*, p.32.

The Homecare Market

The traditional homecare market was those persons requiring care and treatment at home. This group included paraplegics, quadriplegics, stroke victims, arthritics, and the "frail" elderly. The homecare market (goods and services) was expected to double from $8.8 billion in 1988 to $16 billion in 1995 ["Aging Population to Fuel Growth of Homecare Market" 1990, p.1]. According to FIND/SVP, a New York market research and information consulting group, the home healthcare product market was expected to grow at an annual rate of 7 percent, to $1.96 billion by 1995.

The specific types of medical products used in the home depended on the status of patients as they were discharged from acute-care facilities. At the time of discharge, product suggestions were given to patients (the end users) by referral sources who were actually involved in the patient's recovery.

Due to increased costs, insurance companies encouraged patients to leave hospitals sooner. As a result of this, many patients finished the recovery process at home. In addition, the sharp increase in the rate of certain diseases, such as AIDS, was expected to directly increase the size of the homecare market.

Unlike long-term care facilities, homecare patients did not have the luxury of a maintenance department to service their equipment. The end user needed prompt delivery and quick service from the homecare dealer in case products failed or problems arose. For these reasons, relationships with referral sources and prompt delivery and service were keys to a successful homecare business. This was true for both the product manufacturer and homecare dealer.

A new homecare consumer market emerged in the late 1980s. This new market was composed of healthy consumers who wanted medical products to increase their convenience and comfort in the home setting. The new consumer showed interest in purchasing products such as safety bars for their bathtubs or specialty cushions for their favorite chairs. These products were distributed principally through catalog advertising — often on a cooperative basis with a mass merchandise retailer. This market was expected to grow at the same rate as other personal-care products.

Several consumer homecare products eventually made their way into retail stores such as Walgreen's and People's Drugs. Lechmere Stores, a division of Dayton-Hudson, had a 250 SKU (stock-keeping unit) assortment of home healthcare products — including wheelchairs, back massagers, and Eggcrate foam mattresses — designed for the mass market ["Good Prognosis for Home Health Care" 1991, pp. 66-68].

A key to success in the retail market was reaching the consumer through a nonmedical channel at a low cost. Catalog advertising was often done on a cooperative basis with mass merchandisers such as Sears or J.C. Penney. The mass merchandiser and the manufacturer shared the cost of advertising. Other keys to success included redesigning and repositioning existing homecare products to meet the needs of healthy consumers who wanted these products for comfort and convenience. Catalog advertising could be initiated by a manufacturer's sales representative calling on mass merchandisers. The formation of an internal consumer marketing group would be essential to implementing a successful strategy.

The Institutional Market

The institutional market consisted of those people requiring some type of institutionalized, supervised care. This market was divided into two segments: acute-care and long-term care facilities. Acute care facilities provided traditional hospital-based care offering one or more of the following services: (1) rehabilitation within a hospital based setting, (2) off site or out-patient ambulatory care, and/or (3) acute-care beds that could double as long-term care beds if necessary.

Products used in acute-care facilities were purchased or leased by the hospital's purchasing agents through institutional dealers, including manufacturers, and were paid for partially by Medicare/Medicaid and partially by the facility itself. Keys to success in this area were providing low-cost quality products and making sales calls to the hospital administration's purchasing agents.

Long term care facilities provided skilled intermediate and low-maintenance care. This segment included traditional nursing homes and congregate care centers, which continued to be an emerging industry segment. Congregate care facilities included several types of facilities, ranging from board-and-care homes — one to six elders living in boardinghouse style where a "landlord" handled the meals and housekeeping — to assisted living centers, which were a cross between a nursing home and a hotel with varying levels of personalized care in a homelike setting [Roffmann-New 1991, pp.57-78]. Congregate care facilities relied heavily on reimbursement sources other than Medicaid or Medicare, such as insurance payments or direct payments from those patients who were ineligible for other benefits. Therefore, supplying this type of institution with products was very profitable. However, the exact needs of each facility differed and it was difficult for medical product suppliers to determine each institution's precise needs.

In 1989 there were approximately 6,800 acute-care hospitals in the United States [*American Hospital Association Statistics* 1990]. This figure was down from a high of 7,200 facilities in 1975. In 1990 there were approximately 26,000 long-term care facilities with 1.52 million residents [*Lumex, Inc. Annual Report* 1990]. Figure 5 shows the number of persons expected to require long-term care beds between 1990 and 2050.

Although most medical product manufacturers have diversified into both the homecare and institutional markets, the most successful companies initially focused on one market and diversified only after achieving a major share of one market.

END USERS AND REFERRAL SOURCES

Patients, the end users for medical products, were highly dependent on healthcare professionals. In the homecare market, when purchasing medical products, most end users depended on the referral source to recommend a particular product or brand. Patients were sent to referral sources, such as physical and occupational therapists, by their physicians. In addition, as part of hospital procedure, patients going home were assigned a discharge planner who processed their

Figure 5: Long Term Care Resident Projection 1990-2050 (in Thousands)

YEAR	NUMBER OF RESIDENTS
1990	1,520
2000	1,932
2010	2,284
2020	2,629
2030	3,370
2040	4,340
2050	4,754

Source: Based on information from *National Nursing Home Survey: U.S. Administration on Aging*, Bureau of Census Population Projections, 1989, pp. 101-103.

release from the hospital. If a patient in need of medical equipment for home use was not referred to a physical or occupational therapist the discharge planner would order the equipment for them. The referral sources often consulted with homecare dealers to determine the best product for the patient in question.

End Users

Both the homecare and institutional medical products targeted several markets: the frail and well elderly, the disabled, and the healthy consumer.

The frail elderly were people who became disabled to such an extent that some type of in-patient care was required. They included victims of heart attacks, strokes, falls, debilitating arthritis, and potential surgical patients. These people resided in an acute-care setting for some length of time. In contrast, the well elderly were people with mild disabilities who did not require institutionalized care. They were taken care of at home by their family or a visiting nurse, or in many cases they were self-sufficient. Many suffered from a variety of mild disabilities, including arthritis, vertigo, and chronic back pain, or were out-patient surgical candidates.

The disabled category included those persons who were disabled as a result of a birth defect, accident, or service-related disability. These individuals usually began treatment in an acute-care setting but were sent home if their health was restored. If the injury caused a permanent disability, they were sent to a rehabilitation center or to a long-term care facility. This category also included temporary disabilities such as broken arms or legs.

Finally, as discussed earlier, healthy consumers wanted medical products in order to increase comfort and convenience in the home setting. They purchased products through retail catalogs distributed by stores like J.C. Penney and Sears.

Referral Sources

With the exception of the healthy consumer, most end users were brought to an acute-care facility due to an illness or injury. The amount of time each patient spent in the acute-care facility depended on the illness and diagnosis: a stroke victim might spend months while a person with a broken arm might be treated in several hours.

Patients contacted a referral source through a physician's recommendation. The referral source often consulted with the homecare dealer and then recommended and ordered a particular product or brand for the patient based on the individual's condition.

These products were then billed either to Medicare/Medicaid, to a third party —such as a patient's insurance company — or to the patient, if the patient was ineligible for other benefits. Most patients were unfamiliar with the brands and manufacturers of medical products and depended on the referral source to help make the best decision for their recovery. Due to their knowledge of the industry, referral sources were considered very credible and most patients relied on their decisions.

By indirectly linking the end user and the manufacturer, referral sources were a key factor in the sales and distribution process. Referral sources often worked with the homecare dealer who represented the manufacturer's products. Because of the strong influence of the referral source, it was critical for them to be part of the manufacturer's representative's sales call pattern until consumer and brand awareness was created. Because the health of their patients was their primary concern, the referral sources were more concerned with quality products than prices. These individuals did not officially make a profit from suggesting a manufacturer's products, yet their recommendation enhanced the product's credibility.

PRODUCTS

Medical products were divided into five categories. The two primary segments were surgical and medical instruments and surgical appliances and supplies. These two broad product categories comprised almost 71 percent of medical product sales in 1991. The categories below are based on the Standard Industrial Classification Coding System (SIC). The actual products represented within each category are not necessarily defined accurately by the category name.

Surgical and Medical Instruments

In 1991 this segment represented approximately 33 percent of medical product sales. Sales in 1990 were $9.5 billion [*U.S. Industrial Outlook 1991*]. Products in this category were used in surgical procedures and testing. Testing, diagnostics, and disposables were typical high-volume surgical products. This category was expected to grow by 8 percent through 1995 ["Banking on Basics," 1990, pp.20-23]. Since patients and physicians depended on correct diagnosis, a key to success in this area was providing safe, quality products that gave accurate results.

Surgical Appliances and Supplies

In 1991 this segment was the largest of the medical product industry. Sales in 1990 were $10.7 billion — 37 percent of medical product sales [*U.S. Industrial Outlook 1991*]. Products

Figure 6: Medical Product Sales Projection 1989-1994 (in millions)

PRODUCT CATEGORY	1989	1990	1991	1992	1993	1994	ANNUAL GROWTH RATE
Surgical Appliances	$10,485	$11,593	$12,752	$14,023	$15,431	$16,947	10.00%
Surgical & Medical Equip.	$ 9,315	$10,154	$10,966	$11,844	$12,791	$13,814	8.00%
Dental Equipment	$ 1,580	$ 1,662	$ 1,745	$ 1,832	$ 1,924	$ 2,020	5.00%
ElectroMedical	$ 4,158	$ 4,400	$ 4,708	$ 5,038	$ 5,390	$ 5,768	7.00%
X-Ray Apparatus	$ 1,764	$ 1,800	$ 1,827	$ 1,854	$ 1,882	$ 1,912	1.50%
TOTAL	$27,302	$29,609	$31,998	$34,596	$37,418	$40,483	
Cumulative Percent Growth		8.45%	8.07%	8.12%	8.16%	8.20%	

1989 are actual figures
1990-1994 are estimated

Source: Based on information from "Banking on Basics," *Health Industry Today*, January 1990.

in this category included medical equipment such as wheelchairs, hospital beds, orthopedic supplies, and respiratory products. The U.S. wheelchair market's sales were estimated at approximately $480 million in 1991. Reimbursement for custom wheelchairs depended primarily on third-party reimbursement either directly from patients or from insurance companies, rather than government funding [*Sunrise Medical Annual Report* 1991]. The surgical appliances and supplies category was expected to grow at a rate of 10 percent annually through 1995 ["Banking on Basics," 1990, pp.20-23]. Keys to success in this area were providing quality products that were constantly being upgraded to create patient comfort or surgeon convenience.

Other Categories

The remaining three categories included dental equipment, electro-medical products and X-ray apparatus. In 1990 these categories combined for $9.5 billion in sales. Figure 6 gives a growth projection by product category. Although the market for these products was large, this industry segment was dominated by several major players. In addition, there were very high barriers to entry, including the intricate technology needed to create these products. Keys to success in this area were innovative research and development and fast delivery and product service by the dealer.

SALES/SERVICE/DISTRIBUTION

The homecare and the institutional markets used different product distribution channels. The environment surrounding the homecare market required quick product delivery to the patient, immediate service on equipment, and efficient billing. Medical products sold for use in the home were sold through a distribution network of home healthcare dealers who called on and worked closely with referral sources to decide which products best met patients needs. The referral source ordered the products for patients and then billed Medicare/Medicaid. When the patient was ineligible for these benefits a third party such as an insurance company was billed. Patients were almost always left out of the purchasing loop since Medicare/Medicaid patients were never required to pay for the products and were not required to fill out a barrage of paperwork.

Redistributors were sometimes used by homecare manufacturers who were interested in wider product distribution. However, due to the capital-intensive nature of institutional product purchases, there was little room for a redistributor in this market segment.

In the institutional market, products were sold to central buying locations of institutions in order to facilitate contracting directly with the manufacturer. Products for the institutional market were sold either on a direct basis to the facility or through a medical-surgical dealer. Figure 7 shows the distribution channels for medical products.

Homecare Product Sales/Service/Distribution

Homecare products were distributed primarily through homecare dealers. According to *Homecare* magazine, there were over 14,000 homecare dealers in the U.S. in 1990 [Segedy 1990,

Figure 7: Medical Product Distribution

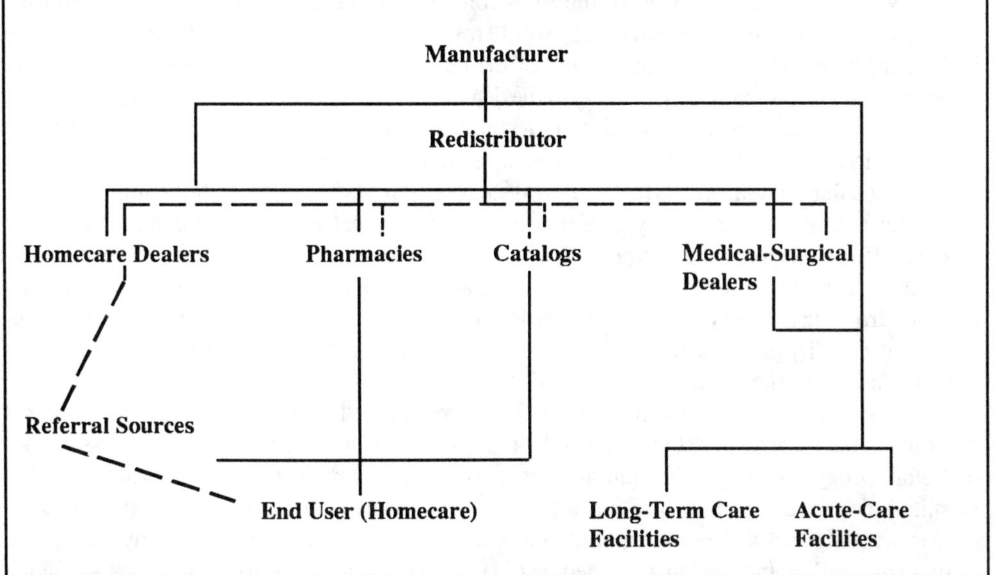

p.30]. Homecare dealers worked very closely with physical or occupational therapists who served as product referral sources within acute care facilities. If the physician did not refer the patient to a physical or occupational therapist, but the patient needed equipment for use in the home, the discharge planner ordered it for the patient.

After evaluating the patient's condition, the referral source often consulted with the homecare dealer as to the equipment needs of that particular patient. The referral source would then order the product from the homecare dealer and bill Medicare/Medicaid, the patient's insurance company, or the patient. The insurance company usually covered only a certain percentage of the cost and the remainder of the payment was the patient's responsibility. The homecare dealer delivered and assembled the equipment in the patient's home. Depending on the type of equipment, after-sale service was sometimes provided. Unlike in long-term care facilities, homecare patients did not have a maintenance staff available to repair broken products. Instead, they called the homecare dealers. If the service was prompt and dependable, they would be more likely to discuss this with their referral source and repurchase the product when it was necessary. Both the referral source and the patient would be more likely to be brand loyal to new products from the same manufacturer. The key to a successful dealership was the ability to service homecare patients on demand. Servicing the dealer and the patient efficiently and effectively was also important to product manufacturers whose products were represented by these dealers.

Homecare dealers ranged in size from small independents to large national chains. Approximately three-fourths of the homecare dealers had retail showrooms where referral sources and acute-care purchasing managers could view products. The patient was almost completely left out of the purchasing loop, accentuating the fact that retailing in the homecare market was in its infancy. Instead, the sales force called on referral sources and established relationships with them in hopes that they would refer products to their patients. A recent change in the distribution channel was the advent of the redistributor. Redistributors provided a wider selection of products, same-day delivery to the dealer, and delivery of smaller orders. While most homecare products were still sold directly to the homecare dealer, sales through redistributors continued to grow. The key to creating a successful base of homecare dealers was to bring the homecare dealer in on sales calls to the referral sources who worked either at the hospital or in their own offices. Depending on the type of product, either the dealer or the manufacturer would be responsible for servicing the product. When the manufacturer serviced a product or called on referral sources, the homecare dealer who accompanied the manufacturer received the bulk of the referrals from that facility or office. Additionally, a major key to success in this market was providing a quality product. Referral sources, who did the actual ordering, were more concerned with the quality of the products than the price.

In 1990, pharmacies also played a role in the sale and delivery of homecare products. Although there were over 35,000 independent drug-stores according to the National Association of Retail Druggists, only 6,000 pharmacies were actively involved in the homecare market. Despite being in the perfect position to come into contact with persons requiring homecare products, the high service levels required to succeed with these products caused many pharmacies to avoid the market. In addition, most people did not purchase products for themselves — referral sources did it for them.

While most pharmacies stocked canes and walkers, few aggressively marketed these products. People who purchased these products in pharmacies were not referred by a physical or occupational therapist. Rather, they decided on their own that this product would help their condition and paid for it directly, with no reimbursement from Medicare/Medicaid or an insurance company since benefits such as these were given only to patients who were referred to the products by medical personnel.

The emergence of the healthy consumer was beginning to change the way medical products were marketed at the retail level. This new consumer purchased products through retail outlets, including large drugstores such as Walgreen's, People's Drug, and Eckerd Drug.

According to a study conducted by Discount Merchandiser, outlets other than homecare dealers were selling an increasing amount of home healthcare products to consumers who simply wanted to take better care of themselves. There was strong interest in bathroom products, such as bathtub safety rails, and personal-care products, such as lumbar neck and back supports.

Institutional Product Sales/Service/Distribution

Products sold to acute-care or long-term care facilities were sold directly or through a dealer. When selling directly, the manufacturer sold to the facility with its own sales force. This type of distribution was typical for large, capital-intensive purchases. The sales force called on purchasing agents or hospital administrators who were responsible for making purchasing decisions. In contrast, some manufacturers sold to the facility through a dealer. This type of dealer was classified as a medical-surgical dealer. They differed from homecare dealers in that med-surg dealers called on directors of nursing, operating room nurses, administrators, and materials managers. While some med-surg dealers were small independents, most were part of large chains.

In either case, the manufacturer's sales force was required to call on the facility to generate product demand. A major key to success in the institutional market was supplying services and product information. This included setting up and frequently servicing equipment and educating both management and staff. Institutional buyers were interested in cutting costs while maintaining quality, so price was important. Another key to success in this area was offering turn-key packages. These included evaluating facilities' particular needs, setting up entire systems of installed equipment, and educating senior management about the systems.

REIMBURSEMENT PROCEDURES

Medicare is a federally funded program designed to provide healthcare for persons over the age of 65. Medicaid is funded jointly by the individual state involved and the federal government.

Furnishings and other products used in the care and treatment of a patient within an institutional setting were not reimbursed directly by Medicare or Medicaid. Rather, these purchases were paid for by the facility. Financing and leasing programs were important to institutions who wanted to purchase large quantities of medical products at the lowest cost possible. Medicare provided physician and hospital services under Part A, and homecare products and services under Part B.

Part A

Until 1983 when the Prospective Payment System (PPS) was implemented, a cost plus billing system was used by most providers. The cost of a product or service was simply passed on to Medicare. The PPS legislation dramatically altered this by setting up a series of Diagnostic Related Groups (DRGs). Each DRG gave hospitals a set fee for each diagnosis. Any expense incurred during treatment that was in excess of the amount specified by the DRG had to be absorbed by the facility. If the facility was able to care for the patient within the DRG limit, any leftover funds were considered profit. This resulted in patients being discharged from facilities faster than ever. Studies have shown that the changes in the reimbursement system have resulted in elderly people often being discharged in unstable condition [Gilbert 1990, p. 22.].

Healthcare providers immediately focused on the cost of every product and service purchased by the hospital. These changes caused the price of a product or service to be the most important factor when acquiring a product. Products that have proven to be most successful despite the cutbacks in reimbursement are those products that provide a "treatment" that can be billed each time the product is used. An example of such a product is a an air bed which is often used in the treatment of pressure ulcers. Every day the bed is used to treat a patient, the facility can bill Medicare. Despite varying reimbursement levels among Medicare carriers, an air bed can quickly become a source of revenue for the facility.

Part B

Until 1983, Medicare beneficiaries who needed a homecare product usually rented the product from a local homecare dealer. Depending on the disability, a referral source often suggested that the patient rent a product rather than have Medicare pay for its purchase. This did not make a difference to the patient, as Medicare absorbed the expense of either a rented or purchased product. However, this appealed to homecare dealers as products such as wheelchairs, walkers, commodes, and beds could be rented for long periods allowing for revenues that more than covered the original purchase prices of these products. In 1983, legislation was enacted so that products costing less than $120 could be billed only as a purchase and could not be rented. More expensive items could be rented only up to the purchase price at which time a final payment was made and the beneficiary then owned the equipment. Legislation passed in 1988 further limited the amount and type of equipment that was reimbursable under Medicare. These changes had a profound effect on the homecare product market. The quality of the product was now of secondary importance and homecare dealers maximized their profit by providing the cheapest "acceptable" product. Homecare dealers looked for ways to decrease their dependence on Medicare patients and to increase their private insurance claims and cash sales from patients who were not covered by Medicare.

Although many groups, including The National Association of Medical Equipment Suppliers and Health Industry Managers, continued to lobby for better reimbursement processes, the Medicare and Medicaid system continued to change for the worse. Developing alternate sources of funding was a key to success for both institutions and homecare dealers. All healthcare providers needed to quickly take advantage of the fact that most of the disposable income in the United States continued to be held by those 55 years of age and older.

Based on the various changes in the reimbursement environment, product development on the part of most manufacturers was divided into two areas:

1. **Developing cost-reduction programs**: This included developing standardization programs that reduced the cost, hence, the price of the product to the homecare dealer. This reduced price then increased the spread (profit) between the price paid by the homecare dealer and the amount reimbursed by Medicare and/or Medicaid.

2. **Developing innovative products**: The benefits of developing a unique and patentable product were great. If the product was capable of reducing the cost of treatment, there was a good chance that the product would receive a separate billing code for Medicare reimbursement. Because the product was unique, only that product could be billed under that specific code. This resulted in a virtual monopoly, limited only by the number of persons who were medically required to receive that particular product. A similar situation existed within the pharmaceutical industry.

COMPETITION

Lumex had four major multiproduct competitors. A large number of single product companies competed with Lumex on a local or regional basis but were not major threats to Lumex's long-term growth. Figure 8 compares the sales growth and profits of Lumex and its four major competitors.

Everest and Jennings (E&J). E&J was once the largest manufacturer of wheelchairs in the world, holding a 90 percent share of the wheelchair market in the late 1970s. Since then, E&J has seen its market share erode dramatically, due to the company's inflexible research and development strategy. E&J did not encourage the development of new products to meet market changes. The company felt that there was no reason to change, since it was the market leader with a reputation for quality. Its failure to keep up with and to respond to the aggressive pricing programs and innovative products of its largest competitor, Invacare, caused E&J to loose its position as market leader.

In 1988, E&J introduced a line of patient-care products to augment its wheelchair product line and to be more competitive with Invacare's one-stop shop strategy. This attempt failed. Late in 1989, E & J announced its intent to stop selling patient-care products and to concentrate on its core business: wheelchairs. Unfortunately, this move hurt E&J. In late 1990, E&J announced a loss of $50 million on sales of $132 million [*Everest & Jennings Annual Report* 1990]. To eliminate this operating loss, E&J reduced its domestic workforce by over 20 percent [Segedy 1990, p.30].

In 1991, the Jennings family considered filing for bankruptcy, but before that happened E&J was bought out by a Hong Kong-based firm, IEP. Total restructuring took place in sales and marketing areas. E&J eliminated selling directly to any homecare dealer and elected to sell its product line through redistributors only. The effect of this change was not yet known in 1992.

E&J's primary strength was its name. Its reputation and product dependability were respected by both the institution and homecare dealers. E&J had an excellent reputation with referral sources. This reputation came about by utilizing a dedicated and aggressive "rehab" sales force. By increasing its sales efforts directly at the referral source level, E&J hoped to shift the buying influence away from the homecare dealer, who could suggest a competitor's product [Segedy 1990, p.30]. If E&J was to remain a major factor in this market, its operating profit needed to be improved quickly.

Invacare. By 1990, Invacare was the largest single source homecare company in the United States. Invacare manufactured a wide array of homecare products including wheelchairs, beds, seating products, respiratory products, and passive motion devices used in physical therapy and patient care.

Invacare's strategy was to earn market share at any cost. This, combined with their one-stop shop concept, allowed Invacare to experience a dramatic sales increase in the late 1980s and early 1990s. In 1989 a major shortfall in profits from the homecare division put severe pressure on Invacare's management to change its strategy and start selling to the long-term care market. Invacare's first move was to raid Lumex's sales force and hire six Lumex people. With this as a core, Invacare also introduced a new bed specifically designed for the long-term care market.

Figure 8: Financial Comparison of Major Competitors (All figures are in thousands)

COMPANY	LUMEX DIVISION			E&J			INVACARE			TEMCO			SUNRISE MEDICAL		
LOCATION	BAY SHORE, NY			CAMARILLO, CA			ELYRIA, OHIO			PASSAIC, NJ			TORRENCE, CA		
FOR YEAR END:	12/31/89	12/31/90	% chg	12/31/89	12/31/90	% chg	12/31/89	12/31/90	% chg	12/31/89	12/31/90	% chg	12/31/89	12/31/90	% chg
SALES	$40,448	$44,560	10	$183,881	$132,782	-28	$186,100	$229,800	23	$23,400	$27,300	17	$172,069	$203,825	18
COST OF GOODS	$22,412	$24,361	8.7	$135,842	$ 99,020	-27	$129,200	$153,100	18	$13,000	$13,600	5	$111,311	$133,916	20
GROSS PROFIT	$18,036	$20,199	12	$ 48,039	$ 33,762	-30	$ 56,900	$ 76,700	35	$10,400	$13,700	32	$ 60,758	$ 69,909	15
OPERATING EXPENSES	$15,691	$17,553	12	$ 84,756	$ 80,329	-5.2	$ 48,100	$ 59,900	25	$ 9,600	$12,900	32	$ 46,787	$ 52,581	12
PROFIT B T &I	$ 2,344	$ 2,646	13	($36,717)	($46,561)	-26	$ 8,800	$ 16,800	91	$ 800	$ 100	-89	$ 13,971	$ 17,328	24

Note: The above financials are from the latest available documents.
Only Sunrise Medical has released 1991 financials.

Source: Based on information from Company Annual Reports.

From 1989 to 1990, Invacare's sales grew by 23 percent. The company announced an across-the-board price increase that took affect April 1, 1990. Invacare reported a net profit of $7.6 million on sales of $230 million for the year ending December 31, 1990 [*Invacare Annual Report 1990*, p.10].

In November/December 1991, Invacare expanded both its product offerings and its geographic base by acquiring a Canadian wheelchair company and a Canadian manufacturer of seating and positioning products [Invacare Annual Report, 1990, p. 5].

In 1992 the company planned to expand its medical-related product lines by introducing 75 new products and revamping its Action motorized wheelchair line to allow disabled persons to control and adjust wheelchairs on their own. Prior to this introduction, these adjustments could be made only by technicians and therapists. In an attempt to make medical equipment look less institutional, Invacare developed a new line of walkers in colors such as mauve and teal. The effects of this strategy were not yet known in 1992 ["Invacare Rolling Out 75 New Medical-Related Products" 1988, p. 12].

Invacare's primary strength was its broad product line which covered over 50 percent of products that most homecare dealers sold on a regular basis. In addition, Invacare had the most extensive warehouse network of any manufacturer — 31 in all. Invacare had an excellent reputation for having the best service of any manufacturer. Its extensive warehouse network enabled homecare dealers to reduce their inventory. Because of the slow payment of claims by Medicare, cash flow was critical to a dealer's business. By decreasing the on-hand inventory of the homecare dealers and increasing the inventory turnovers, Invacare's distribution system improved dealers' cash flows. Invacare was perceived as being the most supportive company in the industry from homecare dealers' perspectives.

Sunrise Medical. Sunrise manufactured both homecare and institutional products through five divisions: Bio-Clinic focused on pressure management products for decubitus ulcers; Guardian concentrated on patient-care products; Quickie Designs manufactured wheelchairs; Joerns focused on long-term care beds and furnishings; and Sunrise Medical Ltd. developed international sales. In fiscal year 1991, Sunrise had sales of $203 million and generated $8.0 million in net profit [*Sunrise Medical Annual Report 1991*, p.20].

The acquisition of Quickie wheelchairs in 1987 gave Sunrise technology for future product development that was previously lacking. Sales of custom wheelchairs were expected to continue to grow and Sunrise anticipated reaching a 23 percent market share by fiscal year 1995 [*Sunrise Medical Annual Report* 1991, p.5].

In December 1991, the company purchased Health Products, Inc. (HPI) of Houston, Texas. HPI manufactured air floatation therapy, including mattresses and specialty beds for decubitus ulcers. In January 1992, Sunrise acquired Sopur, a privately-held German wheelchair manufacturer with operations in Netherlands and Czechoslovakia. This acquisition gave the company access to the international market ["Sunrise Medical to Acquire German Wheelchair Maker" 1992, p.40].

One of Sunrise's success stories was its Bio-Clinic Eggcrate foam products. Originally used by acute-care facilities as a pressure management product, the product soon found its way into the home as a comfort product. As home use grew, mass merchandisers began to distribute the product in the housewares department of their stores and catalogs. Distribution in the consumer market gave Sunrise an edge over other competitors in terms of brand awareness and distribution through a nonmedical channel. Shortly after the company's initial success in this market, Sunrise began offering some of its other homecare products through these distribution channels.

Sunrise's primary strength was a quality image which was constantly being reinforced at the referral source level. In contrast to Invacare and Temco, the primary sales call for the Sunrise sales force was the referral source, which made Sunrise the brand of choice for many hospital-based referrals.

Temco. Temco's growth during the late 1980s was a direct result of changes in the Medicare/ Medicaid reimbursement system. By manufacturing a "me-too" product and selling it for up to 25 percent less than any other manufacturer, Temco initially was able to enjoy rapid growth. For fiscal year 1990, Temco had sales of $10.5 million and generated $100,000 in net profit. These profits were down 89 percent from the previous year, reflecting that the market was emphasizing quality products.

Temco's product lines included homecare pressure management products, ambulatory aids, and patient room products. Temco's products were traditionally less expensive than the other manufacturers and were originally judged to be adequate for the market. In 1990 Temco introduced a line of specialty seating products including recliners and rockers to be sold in the long-term care market. These products which were priced 15-21 percent below the average market price exactly duplicated Lumex products.

In June 1991, the company began using an integrated and targeted market approach for each market serviced by the company's products. In October 1991, Graham-Field Health Products purchased Temco's healthcare division ["Graham-Field Health Products Acquires Temco Healthcare Division of Temco National Corp." 1991, p.1]. The results of this acquisition were not yet known in early 1992. However, based on the fact that quality products and reputation were important in this industry, low-cost products, such as Temco's, in general, generated some suspicion among referral sources and purchasing agents. The manufacturer had the burden of proving that the quality of these products equalled that of the more expensive brands.

THE COMPANY

HISTORY

Lumex was started in 1947 by Charles Murcott. The first products manufactured by Lumex were lights, light stands, and a combination projection screen and portrait backup. Other tubular products were added, including the first medically-oriented product — a floor-to-ceiling intravenous stand.

In 1950, a golf cart with a folding seat and several marine accessories were added to Lumex's product line. Needing more space to manufacture, the company moved in 1952 to Valley Stream, New York. In 1965 the company moved to a 50,000-square-foot facility in Bay Shore, New York to expand its manufacturing capacity, which was an important key to success in producing a variety of products. During this time frame, the company gradually phased out nonmedical products and focused on ambulatory aids, commodes, footstools, intravenous (I.V.) stands, and physician equipment. Innovative research and new product development fostered the company's growth.

A major development in the financial growth of Lumex occurred in 1969 when the company went public and was traded on the over-the-counter market. In 1979, Lumex shares were listed on the NASDAQ.

In 1970 Lumex acquired the patent rights to isokinetic devices for testing, rehabilitation, and exercise. The Cybex division of Lumex, Inc. was formed around these patented products and in December of 1980, this division set up a separate manufacturing facility in Ronkokoma, New York. In 1983, Cybex acquired Eagle Performance Systems, a manufacturer of variable resistance weight machines in Owatonna, Minnesota. In 1985, Cybex introduced the first computerized isokinetic equipment designed to test and rehabilitate back injuries.

In 1986, the Lumex division acquired two companies. The first was Swedish Rehab, an importer of high-quality accessories to daily living such as cervical and lumbar supports used by people with chronic arthritis. The second company was the Akros Company of Gloversville, New York. Akros manufactured a line of pressure management products designed to prevent and treat pressure sores.

As a result of Lumex division's growth, a 130,000-square-foot facility was built in 1989 next to the present facility in Bay Shore, New York. Later that year the Lumex division acquired the assets of Contemporary Health Systems, of Gardena, California. Contemporary imported and distributed a line of stainless steel wheelchairs manufactured in Taiwan.

By the 1990s Lumex was operating at close to maximum capacity; any major expansion of sales would require the expansion of production facilities. In 1991, the company acquired exclusive distribution rights to Stema Bathing Systems, a French line of hydrotherapy products. Division sales in 1991 approached $46 million — up 3 percent from 1990. Profits for 1991 were estimated to be $2.9 million — up 10 percent from 1990. Lumex division's products accounted for 50 percent of the company's sales in 1990 and 1991 [*Lumex Financial Statements* 1991, p.3].

The company believed its success depended on product quality, innovative research and development, customer service, and pricing.

PRODUCTS

Through its Lumex division, the company manufactured and distributed over 400 products in 1990 for the homecare market and the institutional market. The Lumex product line was categorized by its primary market, although some cross over existed between the homecare and the institutional market. This occurred primarily with homecare products that were sold in acute-care facilities for training purposes. Lumex products were used by disabled patients and elderly individuals at home and in health care facilities. The continued growth in the elderly population was expected to increase the need for products which offered mobility, independence, comfort, and safety. In addition, the Lumex product mix changed in the early 1990s to include products designed to aid healthy consumers in their daily living.

All of the company's product lines were advertised in trade and professional journals and were supported by extensive literature and audio-visual presentations which were developed company's marketing department. Products were also displayed and exhibited at numerous trade shows.

Homecare Products

Lumex's homecare products were divided into five major categories: bathroom safety products, ambulatory aids, patient-room products, pressure management products, and personal-care products.

Bathroom safety products were primarily safety oriented. They were used to assist people while toileting, moving about the bathroom, and bathing. Products in this category included grab bars, toilet safety frames, bathtub safety rails, bath seats, raised toilet seats, transfer benches, and shower hoses. This product line was also being repositioned in the healthy consumer market, as a means of providing comfort and convenience. Lumex expected this product area to grow steadily throughout the 1990s.

Ambulatory aids assisted people with varying degrees of walking difficulties. Products included in this category were canes, crutches, quad-canes, folding walkers, and wheeled, walkers.

Patient room products were used primarily by those patients who were confined to a bed. Products in this category included bedside commodes, bed rails, trapeze bars and overbed tables.

Homecare pressure management products were used by patients who were susceptible to skin ulcerations caused by sitting or lying for long periods of time. Products in this category included cushions, mattresses and alternating pressure pads. The company was scheduled to introduce its Akros line of low air mattress for the homecare market in 1992.

Personal care products were designed to assist with daily tasks. These products were also used by people with chronic arthritis and back/neck pain. Products in this category included cervical and lumbar supports, eating and drinking aids, dressing and grooming aids, and other daily living accessories.

Institutional Products

Five major categories of institutional products were: specialty seating products, wheelchairs, conventional products, casework and beds, and pressure management products.

Specialty seating products were designed for use by persons who sit for long periods of time (up to 12 hours per day). Products included in this category were recliners, rockers, and geriatric chairs.

Wheelchairs were designed for transporting and mobilizing patients. An array of wheelchair types and shower chairs were designed to meet the particular requirements of the patient and caregiver. Specialty wheelchairs—including extra-wide and reclining models — were expected to continue to be popular in the future. The wheelchair product line was sold in the homecare market as well as the institutional market.

Conventional products, used primarily by acute-care facilities, were utilized by the caregiver rather than by the patient. Products in this category included intravenous (I.V.) stands, hampers, linen carts, and patient controls.

Casework and beds were used to furnish the patient's room in a long-term care facility. They were available in a wide array of wood and plastic finishes to meet the specific design requirements of a facility. Products in this category included bedside cabinets, wardrobes, luggage racks, overbed tables, and beds.

Institutional pressure management products were used by people who were immobile for long periods of time and who were at risk for skin ulcerations. Products included in this category were mattresses for intensive-care and critical-care beds, and operating room table pads.

PRODUCT DEVELOPMENT AND QUALITY

Lumex emphasized innovative product research and development. The company employed eight people in its program to upgrade and expand product lines by upgrading existing products and developing new products internally. One major consideration in this area was modifying existing homecare products, such as bathroom safety lines and specialty seating products, to make them less medicinal so they would appeal to the healthy consumer market. The cost of the company's product development activities — including salaries and employee benefits, materials used, and allocated facility expenses — was $4,602,799 in 1990 [*Lumex 10-K* 1990, p.15].

The company remained committed to investing in the development of new products and enhancements for its product lines. Lumex's management acknowledged competitor's moves toward lower prices due to the uncertain reimbursement surrounding Medicare/Medicaid benefits and reacted by offering some reductions in their pricing strategy and by stressing their products' reputation for quality.

SALES/SERVICE/DISTRIBUTION

Lumex division's homecare products continued to be sold throughout the United States, Canada, and other countries through its own sales force to approximately 4,500 dealers and to smaller dealers and pharmacies through large wholesalers [Lumex Annual Report 1990, p.10]. In 1990, Lumex expanded its distribution channels by hiring a specialized group of account representatives to focus solely on homecare dealers and referral sources who the company felt were keys to product recommendations and sales.

Most of Lumex's institutional business was done on a direct basis. Lumex continued to sell directly to hospitals, nursing homes, and alternate site facilities on a regular basis. However, direct sales accounted for only 10 percent of total institutional sales with the remaining 90 percent coming from med-surg dealers. The importance of selling directly to the customer either through retail mass merchandiser or catalog advertising was increasing due to the radical change in product mix that took place in the late 1980s and early 1990s.

Lumex contracted with several large long-term care chains on a direct basis. In addition, Lumex sold several products on an exclusive basis to the acute-care market through other manufacturers whose presence in that market was greater than Lumex's.

In 1989, Lumex's single largest customer was the Veteran's Administration. Sales to the VA, which were almost $4 million in 1989, impacted the homecare product line as well as the institutional product line. In 1990, the company's institutional sales division consisted of 31 sales people who called on hospitals, nursing homes, clinics, and dealers to demonstrate products. The company sold its homecare products through an extensive dealer network.

In early 1992 sales of Lumex's products in Canada were managed through an exclusive distributor who warehoused the division's products and sold them throughout that country. International sales, excluding Canada, were handled through a network of 45 dealers, primarily in Europe, Australia, and Japan. As in the past, foreign sales remained subject to normal risks such as protective tariffs and export/import controls. However, since most of these sales were expected to be made in countries with stable political environments, and since payments remained in U.S. dollars, the effects of these instability factors were expected to be minimal [*Lumex Annual Report* 1990, p.10].

FINANCES

In 1990, gross profit margins improved, as a percentage of sales compared to 1989, due to changes in the product mix and company-wide programs to improve manufacturing productivity and efficiencies. These improvements in efficiency and productivity helped to offset lower margins from international shipments and competitive pricing in the durable medical equipment market.

The sales of Lumex division's products continued to grow steadily, benefitting in 1989 from the newly acquired line of stainless steel wheelchairs and the Akros pressure management products. However, in the fourth quarter of 1989, the wheelchair line added $150,000 to administrative expenses.

In 1990, the company's financial condition remained strong with working capital in excess of $23.8 million, including cash, cash equivalents, and temporary investments of $2.2 million and with a current ratio of 2.6 to 1. Cost-reduction programs, combined with lower capital spending and planned reduction of inventories, provided a substantial improvement in earnings and cash flow during the second half of 1990. Short-term borrowing under the company's bank line of credit, which had risen to 5.5 million in 1989, was reduced to $2.25 million at the end of 1990.

TOWARDS THE FUTURE

The growth of the population segment that needs and uses medical products represented an unprecedented opportunity for Lumex in 1992. Opportunities existed in both the homecare market and the long term care market. While the demand for medical products was growing, most medical product manufacturers were experiencing reduced profits as a result of changes in the Medicare/Medicaid reimbursement system. In an attempt to adapt to this increasingly uncertain reimbursement environment, companies began aggressively cutting product prices in hopes of winning more market share. In addition, some of Lumex's competitors were expected to have greater financial resources and larger facilities with state of the art machinery, equipping them to better handle the pressure of industry price cuts. Invacare, one of Lumex's major competitors, reported sales of $230 million in 1990 vs. the Lumex division's $46 million in sales for that same period. Manufacturers and dealers who concentrated on products and markets that depended solely on Medicare and Medicaid were headed for trouble if they did not find additional sources of revenue. The marketing directors for Lumex's homecare and institutional divisions were discussing many strategic alternatives.

For example, homecare industry analysts emphasized that a new healthcare consumer was emerging and that this market was no longer limited to homecare patients who depended on referrals from professional sources to make their purchases. The new consumer was someone who wanted healthcare products to increase his/her comfort and convenience. Research showed that one of the best customers in this area was a working mother who purchased a safety bar for her bathtub so that her elderly mother would have something to hold on to when getting in and out of the tub, or so that her young children could grab on to it while playing at bath time. According to a study conducted by *Discount Merchandiser*, stores other than homecare dealers were selling an increasing amount of home healthcare products to consumers who simply wanted to take better care of themselves. This market created its own demand for these products.

Some managers at Lumex argued that a strategic opportunity existed for Lumex to become a consumer goods company with products designed to meet the needs of this newly emerging market. To achieve success in this area, Lumex would have to modify and reposition existing products, such as their bathroom safety line, walking aids, and seating products, to target the everyday consumer. The least expensive way to enter this market was to sell products to consumers through retail store catalogs. This strategy would require only one salesperson to service the national catalog offices. Traditionally, retailers like J.C. Penney and Sears participated in cooperative catalog advertising which allows the vendors to keep costs at a minimum.

Additional advertising in geriatric magazines such as *Modern Maturity*, or consumer magazines such as *Better Homes and Gardens*, would reach the desired target market, but this was expensive—almost $113,000 for a black-and-white, one-page ad. This type of advertising would be a second step once the products in this market began bringing in revenues. One competitor, Sunrise Medical, had already established distribution channels in this area, almost by accident, because this new consumer group originally began buying these products from traditional medical product dealers. Sunrise had made the selection process easier for consumers by offering products in retail catalogs. The Lumex homecare management thought there was still an opportunity for Lumex to emerge as a major medical products consumer goods company since Sunrise had only begun to tap this market.

While other managers agreed, they pointed out that an effort to restructure the company as a consumer goods manufacturer was premature and expensive for a company grossing only $46 million in sales. Consumer marketing is very different from institutional marketing since it costs a great deal more and requires an additional internal marketing team with consumer goods experience. Because only one company had approached the market this way, Lumex had no way of predicting potential success. In addition, although Lumex's cash position remained strong, it appeared that Lumex's plant was working at close to maximum capacity. These managers emphasized that industry analysts studying the long-term care market were foreseeing inevitable growth because of continuing construction of additional long-term care facilities. These managers believed that the company could use existing lines of distribution to offer a much broader product line in the long-term care market. There was an opportunity to win over new institutions by providing quantity discounts and special packages of goods and services to meet long-term care facilities' needs. Since many of these facilities were just starting out, there would be an opportunity for Lumex to train its sales force to be more service oriented. If any area should be given more financial resources, these managers insisted it be the institutional market.

Those managers who favored selling directly to the healthy homecare consumer market argued that institutions depended heavily on Medicare and/or Medicaid payments which limited profits. In addition, Lumex had already invested a great deal in the long-term care market and future growth was limited. The best thing about positioning Lumex as a consumer goods company was that this new market segment depended mostly on third-party reimbursements which were not as restrictive as Medicare/Medicaid payments. These managers stressed that while the company was small now, it could not afford to miss this emerging industry segment. The company already had the products for this market, such as bathroom safety bars and seating products —it was simply a matter of redesigning and repositioning these products by making them look less "medicinal" and more attractive. Marketing existing products in a new and different way was also a key to success in this area. Investing in this emerging market segment on such a timely basis could ensure the division's future, as many competitors had not yet identified this niche. Lumex had to move quickly before the market became saturated.

In light of these arguments, the company was wondering which decisions Lumex should make about these and other strategic alternatives.

REFERENCES AND BACKGROUND READINGS

"Aging Population to Fuel Growth of Homecare Market," *Long-Term Care News*, February 1990, p.1.

American Hospital Association Statistics, 1990.

"Banking on Basics," *Health Industry Today*, January 1990, pp. 20-23.

"CBO Projects Stable Growth for Medicare DME Outlays," *Medical Product Sales*, May 1990, pp. 30 & 31.

Curtain, Leah and Carolina Zurlage, editors, *DRG's: The Reorganization of Health*, S-N Publications, Chicago, Illinois, 1984, pp. 1-20.

E&J Annual Report, 1989.

E&J Annual Report, 1990.

"Everest and Jennings Reaches Agreement on its Restructuring," *Wall Street Journal* September 11, 1991, p. A5.

Eubanks, Paula, "Chronic Care: A Future Delivery Model?," *Hospitals*, March 20, 1990, pp.42-46.

"Financial Survey for Homecare Dealers - 1991," *Health Industry Distributors Association*, p. 32.

Freeman, Anne, "The Energizer" *Medical Industry Executive*, February-March 1992, pp. 29-31.

Freudenheim, Milt, "A.T.& T.'s Plan to Slow Costs," *New York Times*, February 27, 1990, p. D2.

Freudenheim, Milt, "Job Growth in Health Care Soars," *New York Times*, March 5, 1990, p. D1.

Freudenheim, Milt, "Research Outlays to Aid the Elderly," *New York Times*, March 13, 1990, p. D2.

Gannon, Kathi, "Home Health-Care Products Thriving into the 1990's," *Drug Topics*, March 5, 1990, p. 26.

Gilbert, Susan, "Is America Abandoning Sick Patients?," *The Good Health Magazine*, April 29, 1990, p. 22.

"Good Prognosis for Home Health Care," *Discount Merchandiser*, July 1989, pp. 66-68.

"Graham-Field Health Products Acquires Temco Healthcare Division of Temco National Corp.," *PR Newswire*, October 3, 1991, p.1.

"Health Care Spending Climbs Onward in '92," *Medical Product Sales*, February 1992, pp.2(2).

Holmes, Stephen,"Sweeping U.S. Law to Help Disabled Goes into Effect," *New York Times*, January 27, 1992, pp. 1(2).

"Hot Markets for Home Healthcare," *Hospitals*, March 5, 1990, p. 16.

Invacare Annual Report, 1989.

Invacare Annual Report, 1990.

"Invacare Rolling Out 75 New Medical-Related Products," *Plain Dealer*, November 13, 1991, p. H1.

Lumex Annual Report, 1980.

Lumex Annual Report, 1989.

Lumex Annual Report, 1990.

Lumex Form 10-K, 1990.

"Lumex, Inc., Corporate Profile," *Medical Care Products*, December 1988, p. 12.

Medicare Manuals, U.S. Department of Health and Human Services, Healthcare Financing Administration, Publication 12, Print Date: June 1989, pp. 50-54.

Medical Healthcare and Marketplace Guide, 1990 pp. 113-115.

Metzger, Maureen, "From Hospital to Home - Medical Appliances Expand," *Appliance Manufacturer*, June 1991, pp. 62-64.

National Nursing Home Survey: U.S. Administration on Aging, Bureau of Census Population Projections, 1989, pp. 101-103.

"OBRA 89: New Reductions, Regulations, and Changes," *Ernst and Young*, January 1989, pp. 34-38.

Parver, Corrine Propas, "More DME Cuts Proposed," *Homecare*, February 1990, pp. 38-39.

Roffmann-New, Amy, "Elder Care: Alternatives to the Nursing Home," *Better Homes and Gardens*, September 1991, pp. 57-58.

Segedy, Andria, "E & J Turns to Independent Reps, Seeks Broader Product Line," *Homecare*, March 1990, pp. 30 & 122.

Statistical Abstract of the United States, 1991, U.S. Department of Commerce, 111th Edition, January 1991, pp. 1002-1007.

Sunrise Medical Annual Report, 1989.

Sunrise Medical Annual Report, 1991.

"Sunrise Medical to Acquire German Wheelchair Maker," *Modern Healthcare*, January 27, 1992, p. 40.

Temco Annual Report, 1989.

Temco Annual Report, 1990.

U.S. Industrial Outlook 1991, Health and Medical Services, U.S. Department of Commerce, 1991, pp. 54-60.

MARSHALL OIL COMPANY: EFFECTS OF STRATEGIC RELOCATION MOVES ON MINORITY EMPLOYEES

LOCATION OF MARSHALL OIL COMPANY IN MID-MANHATTAN

Marshall Oil Company, a multiproduct chemical and energy manufacturer with corporate headquarters at 15 Central Plaza, occupies five buildings throughout mid-Manhattan and employs 1,700 people. These five locations contain all of the accounting functions for the corporation's five divisions. The data center located at 1565 Broadway employs 450 people — mostly accountants, supervisors, and computer technicians. The Central Plaza address houses 123 employees — mostly top management, including Mr. John Lang, President of Marshall Oil Company. The remaining employees are mostly blue-collar workers — typists, teletype operators, and clerks who are located mainly at 909 Broadway where the five divisions of the company are headquartered. At this location, the division's daily transactions are received from the plants and then encoded onto special forms and entered into the automated accounting system.

ANNOUNCEMENT BY PRESIDENT LANG ABOUT RELOCATION TO DALLAS

In early 1990, it was rumored that Marshall was planning to relocate. In March 1990, President Lang announced that four of the company's five locations would be moved to Dallas and consolidated into one building. The relocation was to take place in stages, with the 909 Broadway location scheduled to move first, in the summer of 1990. Corporate headquarters, however, would remain at 15 Central Plaza for the immediate future. Also, Lang stressed that every effort would be made to facilitate the "uprooting" of employees. While he urged every employee to make the move, Lang assured employees that Marshall would aid those choosing to remain behind in every way possible. His announcement letter to employees ended by noting that details of the move would be made known once they were formalized.

HISTORY OF MARSHALL OIL COMPANY

In 1989, Marshall Oil Company had an after-tax profit of $263 million. In the third quarter of 1990, profits declined from $1.35 to $1.00 a share, a situation which the President attributed to general business decline. In general, the company was an innovator and is constantly seeking new products and business ventures.

Marshall was very careful of the image it projects in the media. The personnel department had the responsibility of keeping the corporate image untarnished. Recent strikes in the Wood Haven Refinery in Ohio and the Mortin Plant in Alabama were quickly ended with no adverse publicity. Marshall public relations personnel simply said that liberal increases were granted to the refinery workers. The company considered its fringe benefit package to be exceptional and a first in the oil industry. Its retirement fund was considered on par with Sears Roebuck and IBM.

MANAGEMENT'S REASONS FOR RELOCATION

Marshall's main reason for relocating was to reduce costs. Its five New York locations rent for $150,000 a month. Monthly operating costs will be more than cut in half once the initial outlay of capital for the construction of the Dallas office building was completed. Marshall has title to a two-acre parcel of land donated by the State of Texas. Another incentive for the relocation was a tax feature which allowed for reduced real estate taxes for the first ten years. Also, a construction loan of $40 million has been obtained through the Texas National Bank.

Management hoped to induce employees to relocate by emphasizing Dallas' lower cost of living compared with New York's. Dallas also had many of the social advantages of New York—a symphony, theaters, and fine restaurants. One of the drawbacks most discussed by personnel was the Texas "blue" law which restricts liquor sales in public places.

DETAILS OF RELOCATION ANNOUNCED BY THE PERSONNEL DEPARTMENT

A formal letter detailing the relocation move for employees was circulated in April 1990. The key factors contained in the letter were that

- Special emphasis would be given to technical and supervisory personnel in an effort to retain them.
- Other personnel who desired to relocate would have to request a transfer to Dallas from their supervisor. The decision as to whether the employee would be allowed to relocate would depend on the supervisor's recommendation and the company's needs.

The letter further said that key personnel would be sent to Dallas to train people at the plant and to provide a skeleton crew prior to the move. Every employee who chose to relocate would be entitled to a week's visit to Dallas to secure lodging. The company had secured the services of several real estate brokers in the area and their brochures would be made available. The letter ended by saying that, regardless of the differences in the standard of living, each employee would be paid the same as in New York.

MARSHALL'S PROGRAM OF "SELF-HELP" FOR "HARD-CORE" EMPLOYEES

During 1989, Marshall had initiated a program of "self-help" with the aid of the Harlem Employment Agency and the Congress of Racial Equality (CORE) to provide on-the-job training for people without high school diplomas and for some people on welfare. The two agencies placed 125 people at Marshall, most of them clerks and typists. Eight of these employees had been transferred from 909 Broadway to other locations as private secretaries as their skills improved. All of the people hired through the two agencies received a starting salary of $8.00 an hour. These employees were well-received by their fellow workers and were considered model employees by management.

Because they were not in supervisory capacities, these employees were not specifically being asked to relocate. Each would have to petition a supervisor if desiring to relocate.

PLANNING STRATEGY FOR "HARD-CORE" EMPLOYEES

At a secret meeting held by this group of employees after the announcement, Mr. John Bennington, a clerk in the Petrochemical Division, was elected group spokesperson. These employees felt that due to their lack of seniority and education, their chance to be chosen to relocate was slim. They decided to combine their grievances and contact Mr. Ray Kent—the head of the Harlem Employment Agency who was responsible for placing most of them at Marshall.

Mr. Bennington met with Mr. Kent the next day and aired the employees' complaints. Since most of these employees had been employed by Marshall for less than one year, their inexperience would exclude them from the possibility of relocating. Mr. Bennington pointed out that a clerk with experience could be hired in Dallas for $7.65 an hour, 35 cents less an hour than these employees were getting in New York. Mr. Kent ended the meeting by saying that the workers should do nothing until he contacted them.

The next day Mr. Kent contacted Mr. John Soames, the personnel assistant at Marshall with whom he had a good working relationship. It was mainly through Mr. Soames' effort that Mr. Kent had been able to place so many employees at Marshall. Mr. Soames said that he had learned that this group of employees felt that the company was taking advantage of them. "No one likes to lose a good job," he added. However, he assured Mr. Kent that a committee of personnel experts was working on the severance package, and everyone would be paid what the company felt was adequate to compensate them for their loss. He ended the meeting by saying, "Don't worry, Marshall will take care of its employees."

ANNOUNCEMENT OF TERMINATION PACKAGE BY MR. JOHN O'NEILL

One week after this conversation, Marshall made public its termination package. In a letter to each employee, Mr. John O'Neill, Vice-President of personnel and Chair of the Relocation Committee, announced the company's policy towards those employees electing to remain in New York. Marshall would offer:

- One week's pay for every year of service
- Pay for unused vacation time
- A lump-sum payment of all retirement fund money donated by employees

Mr. O'Neill stated that he highly recommended that each employee carefully consider the move to Dallas. He added, however, that the company would not penalize those who chose to remain behind.

After reading the letter, Mr. Bennington consulted with employees in his group to obtain their reactions to O'Neill's letter. The unanimous decision was that Mr. Kent should be contacted again.

The next day Mr. Kent was asked to attend a meeting that evening at Mr. Bennington's home. At the meeting the employees aired their feelings about the move and the severance pay.

Mrs. Melva Jones, a typist, said, "Marshall is just trying to cut costs. They don't want us to relocate. They haven't even asked us."

Mr. John Mix, a clerk, said, "I'm not a high school graduate and have been working for Marshall for only two months. How can they place me at another company at the same pay? It's impossible considering the business recession."

The majority of employees felt that Marshall did not want them to relocate, that it would be impossible to obtain a similar job, and that they would probably be forced back on welfare.

After hearing from the workers, Mr. Kent said that he sympathized with them and would do everything possible to help them. The next morning, Mr. Kent contacted Mr. Soames and set a meeting with Mr. O'Neill for two o'clock that afternoon.

DEMANDS OF "HARD-CORE" EMPLOYEES

At the meeting attended by Mr. Kent, Mr. Bennington, Mr. Soames, and Mr. O'Neill, the opinions of the minority employees were aired by Mr. Kent. He said that 119 of the employees had worked for Marshall for less than one year and would, therefore, be ineligible for severance pay. He said that Marshall, who at first had tried to help these people, was now turning its back on them in an effort to reduce costs. Since most of these workers did not possess high school diplomas, placing them at other companies would be almost impossible. He felt that Marshall would simply be laying these people off. Most of them would have no recourse but to return to welfare.

Mr. Kent felt that, in view of the circumstances, Marshall should make a special severance payment of $2000 each to these employees. This money would be used while seeking other employment.

Mr. O'Neill and Mr. Soames both expressed deep feelings for the welfare of all of Marshall's employees. Mr. O'Neill promised to convey these feelings to Mr. Lang and the executive committee. He assured them that a decision would soon be made.

MR. O'NEILL MAKES DEMANDS KNOWN TO PRESIDENT LANG AT DAILY EXECUTIVE MEETING

The next morning at the daily meeting between the vice presidents and the president, Mr. O'Neill made the situation known to all present. He expressed his fear that media attention to the situation would be damaging to Marshall's image.

The executive committee decided that Mr. O'Neill would be given the authority to reach an "understanding" with Mr. Kent. Since he was considered a very good labor negotiator and had settled many wildcat strikes quickly, the general consensus was that Mr. O'Neill would have no trouble in this situation.

Mr. O'Neill accepted the job somewhat apprehensively. He mentioned that Mr. Kent was a headline-seeker and often used pressure by the news media to force acceptance of his demands. He added that Mr. Kent was the leader of a rent strike in Harlem a few years ago.

The unanimous decision was that Mr. O'Neill would quickly reach an "understanding" with Mr. Kent and that Marshall's capital outlay would be as low as possible.

Mr. O'Neill left the meeting unsure of how to deal with Mr. Kent. He decided to "sleep on it" and contact Mr. Kent in the morning. What should Mr. O'Neill's position be and how should he proceed?

THE MCA MUSIC ENTERTAINMENT GROUP: THE PRERECORDED MUSIC INDUSTRY

During the early 1980s, the MCA Music Entertainment Group of MCA Inc. experienced sluggish growth, mainly because of strong competition in the industry. In 1983 the MCA Music Entertainment group began growing rapidly after being rejuvenated by Irving Azoff, its new president. The group experienced growth in the mid to late 1980s, but some industry experts attributed this growth to its diversification and expansion into other music-related operations, such as concerts halls and merchandising. MCA Music Entertainment was, however, also finding and developing creative, talented artists who had strong audience appeal. In addition, the technological evolution of music formats had challenged MCA to exploit these new technologies in the prerecorded music industry.

During 1990, major strategic moves were made by MCA Music Entertainment and its parent company, MCA Inc. MCA Music Entertainment acquired two smaller record companies and entered into joint distribution ventures with both German and Japanese firms. MCA Inc. was acquired by the Matsushita Electric Industrial Company of Japan; this merger gave MCA Music Entertainment creative and strategic control of its operations while increasing the financial resources available to the division.

In the early 1990s, MCA faced many additional strategic decisions involving overseas markets, the types of music it wanted to provide, and the consumers it wanted to target both here in the U.S. and abroad.

THE INDUSTRY AND COMPETITIVE MARKET

THE PRERECORDED MUSIC INDUSTRY

Using the talents of thousands of artists and musicians, record companies record music on vinyl records, cassette tapes, and compact discs (CDs) for music listeners. Since 1983 the music business has snapped out of what only a few years earlier seemed like a terminal case of the post-disco blues. In an industry that thrived on novelty, the comeback drew on a combination of new talent, new sounds, new technology, and a remarkable shift in customers' tastes.

The prerecorded music industry was dominated by six diversified international companies with large resources to promote their music. These companies had discovered that recorded music was not only a major business in itself; it also could be the catalyst for expanding into other entertainment business such as motion pictures, videotapes, video disks, and cable TV.

U.S. prerecorded music industry sales of $3.8 billion in 1983 almost doubled by 1990. As shown in Figure 1, U.S. consumers spent $7.5 billion on prerecorded music in 1990. This represented a 14.6 percent increase from 1989. This dramatic increase occurred even though total unit sales had increased only slightly more than 50 percent since 1983. The higher cost of CDs was the most significant reason for this rise in sales volume. In 1990, the average suggested price for CD albums was $11.53, compared with $7.46 for cassettes [*Standard & Poors Industry Surveys* 1991 (A)].

Figure 1: Total U.S. Prerecorded Music Sales

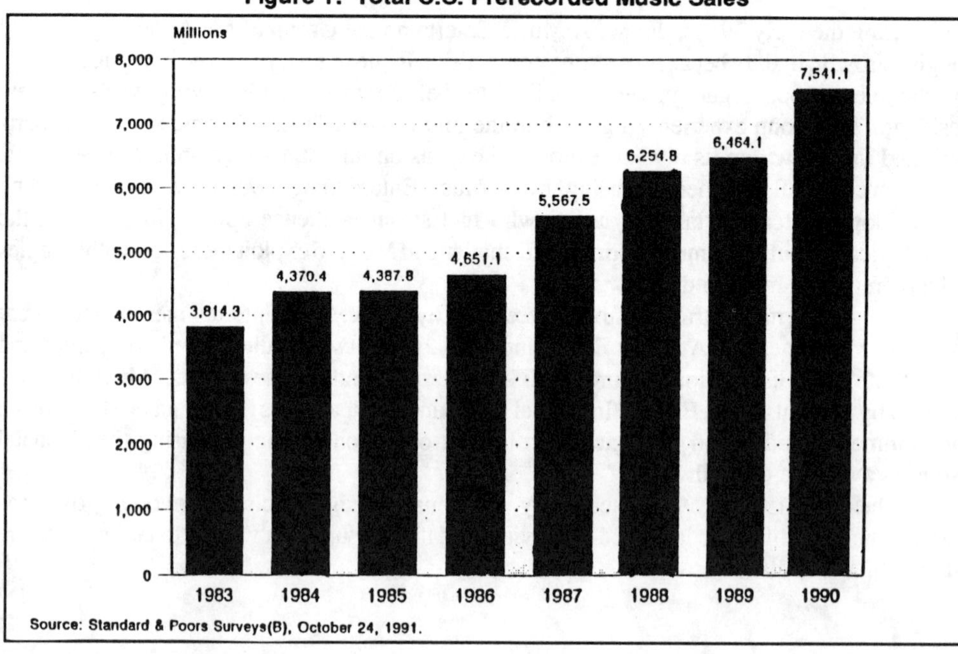

PRERECORDED MUSIC

The recording industry is one of the most energetic, creative, and exciting industries in the world. The music performed and recorded by thousands of artists and musicians entertains millions of people worldwide. From a strategic viewpoint, the emotional impact of music is what propels consumers to purchase a given record. If music does not succeed emotionally, it ultimately fails to attract the listener. This stimulates record companies to find and develop what consumers want to hear.

Artist & Repertoire

During the 1980s, the heart of a record company was the Artist & Repertoire (A&R) department. A&R was responsible for finding new artists and songs which appealed to music listeners. Various genres of music were discovered and developed by A&R departments: rock, pop, Black/urban, country, classical, jazz, gospel, and miscellaneous. Figure 2 shows respective percentages of dollar volume purchased for each genre by music listeners for 1985-1989. In 1989, rock music (42.9 %) and pop or "Top Forty" music (14.4 %) were the two top types of music purchased. Black/urban music continued to grow in popularity, capturing 14 percent of the market in 1989. Miscellaneous saw the most growth in the early 1990s largely because of the popularity of rap music. The M.C. Hammer album *Please Hammer Don't Hurt Em* sold more than eight million units in 1990 [*Standard & Poors Industry Surveys* 1991 (A)].

Figure 2: Types of Music Purchased

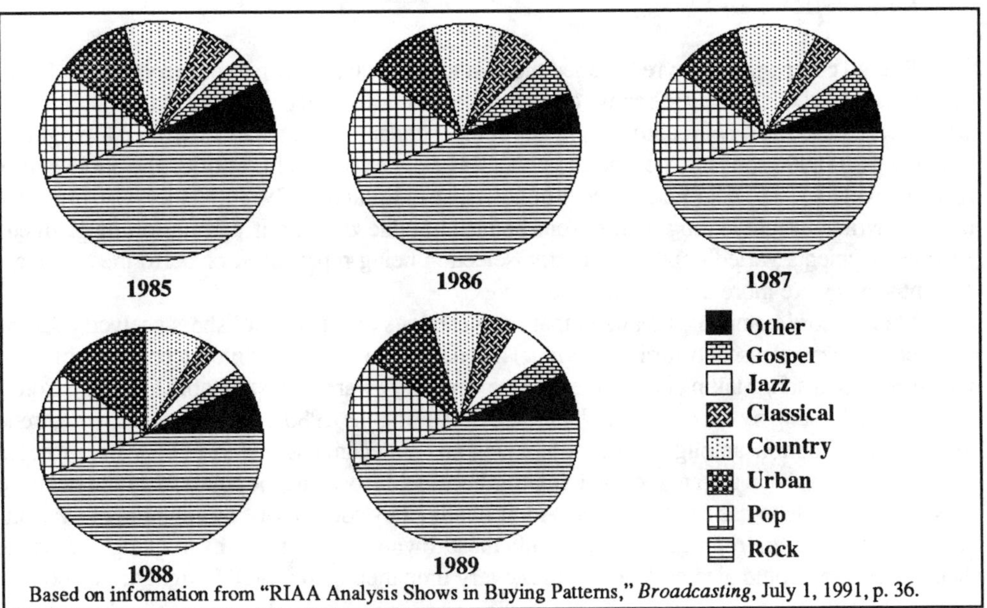

Based on information from "RIAA Analysis Shows in Buying Patterns," *Broadcasting*, July 1, 1991, p. 36.

During the 1980s, record companies' A&R departments faced the task of finding new talent and developing this talent to make it salable. A&R executives had to be aware of consumer tastes, because the reservoir of songwriting and recording talent was diverse, but limited. Artists, whether prospective signings or superstars, needed constructive musical criticism and career guidance in order to remain successful as consumer tastes changed.

A&R departments carefully searched for artists outside the mainstream of music genres, but risks were involved in developing talent whose music might have limited appeal. Although record companies profited from new genres, such as rap and electric music, these uncommon sounds probably would have survived only short term had they not been developed in the appropriate manner.

Artists were sometimes transferred from a less popular genre of music (such as gospel or country) into a mainstream genre of music (such as pop or rock). These were crucial decisions because of the substantial cost of promotion and exposure that was required to bring about such a transition. If the transferred artist did not attain success within the mainstream, heavy losses could be sustained.

The deliberate transfer of performers from outside the mainstream to within the mainstream was one reason for the international attraction of American pop and rock stars. Music is less dependent upon language than other forms of entertainment. In 1990, 25 percent of the $3 billion of music sold in Japan had English lyrics [*Newcomb* 1991]. In addition, American pop and rock music stars were inimitable; American music had characteristics that were not duplicated elsewhere. For these reasons, an artist who was steered into the pop or rock music genre could capture larger audiences in both the United States and internationally.

Music Publishers

Record companies often researched the past to re-release older popular recordings. Music publishers assisted in getting the songs of songwriters recorded and performed. Music publishers, which were subsidiaries of record companies or independent entities, had the ownership rights to as many as 100,000 songs in their possession. These ownership rights entitled the publishers to receive royalties from songs performed in concerts, on radio, and on TV. Publishers also protected the songwriter by preventing songs from being reproduced without permission or payment. Royalty payments varied depending on the selection being reproduced or performed — more current songs were more costly than older songs.

Many record companies realized that song catalogs of music publishers shelved over the years could be re-released to attract additional listeners. This was done quite successfully in 1991, with re-released songs taking home many of the Grammy awards, most notably Nat King Cole's *Unforgettable*, sung by his daughter Natalie Cole. During the 1980s, there was a growing trend toward consolidation among record companies and independent music publishers. Record companies saw special advantages in doing this because, by owning the rights, they did not need outside permission to use certain songs. Additionally, they could profit by encouraging various artists to perform or reproduce songs with these ownership rights: by owning the songs themselves, they could also collect royalties every time their songs were bought or played.

PROMOTION

When a music recording is complete, the project moves into a promotional phase. Promotion is the most important means used by record companies to profit from a recording. To attract the music listener, record companies use a variety of sources: music television (MTV), radio, motion pictures and videocassettes, corporate sponsorship, and trade publications.

Music Television

Music videos became a vital component of the industry in 1981, with the introduction of the Music Television channel. MTV reached more than 45 million households in 1991. However, expenses for the production of a music video were substantial for a record company. The production of videos such as Michael Jackson's *Remember The Time* (1992) and M.C. Hammer's *Too Legit To Quit* (1991) cost more than $1 million. During the early existence of MTV, video clips were expected to evolve into a commercial product line of their own. A market never developed, but with the evolution of the videodisc (a compact disc which incorporates sound and video) such a line could become profitable. Most major record companies had home video divisions, but the output and sales of these divisions were usually modest. Nevertheless, music videos were an important factor in a record company's promotional mix.

Radio

During the 1980s, radio was the primary means by which music was promoted. Radio promotion exposed new and old music, so a record company had to maintain a good working relationship with a radio station to insure successful promotional support. Radio airplay was important, since more frequent airplay resulted in greater exposure and sales. Record companies sought radio's cooperation not in playing the songs of established performers, but also in providing adequate airplay to new performers. However, a dilemma existed because radio programmers felt they should respond to the desires of the audience which usually meant playing the songs of familiar artists. The same problem was also found on the Music Television channel: MTV programmers tended to air established acts more frequently than new acts.

Record companies were hurt by this practice since it limited the exposure of up-and-coming artists. Some record companies offered incentives to radio stations in return for playing their music. They sponsored radio contests with prizes such as concert tickets, jackets, and t-shirts. Such promotional tools were used quite often by major record companies because they could better afford the costs involved.

A more recent trend in radio broadcasting offered some relief to record companies trying to air their new acts. Radio stations targeted a particular audience when playing music. Approximately 12 different types of music genres were being broadcast over the radio. The most popular genres were adult contemporary, top 40, album rock, country, and urban. In 1988, there was a proliferation of new radio stations which, while still targeting a particular audience segment, began playing a wider selection of songs within each particular genre instead of airing the music which listeners were accustomed to hearing. Album rock stations, for example, began to play entire record sides of seldom-heard groups rather than popular hits. This practice, if continued, would give record companies the needed exposure for new acts.

Movies

Motion pictures became an effective tool for promoting artists and their soundtracks in the 1980s, as soundtracks had benefitted from the popularity of the movies they accompanied. On some occasions, the soundtrack helped the motion picture capture a larger audience. For example, when "Dirty Dancing" was released in 1987 it was a low budget film with an appealing soundtrack consisting of a few new songs plus old hits. The film became a hit as a result of its soundtrack and its later released videocassette followed in this success. Synergism of the motion picture and recording industries helped stimulate sales in both. For this reason, mergers between the two were profitable and occurred frequently.

Corporate Sponsorship

Another means of promotion by record companies was corporate sponsorship of an artist. A corporation would sponsor an artist by underwriting expenses for his/her concert tours or by paying him/her a hefty salary in exchange for product endorsements. In exchange, the artist allowed his/her name and photograph to be affiliated with the product in magazine, billboard, video, and TV advertisements. Such arrangements were usually made with artists who were well-established and very popular—normally artists in mainstream music. This type of agreement was very costly for the corporation but well-liked by record companies because the advertising campaign was paid for by the corporation. Also, this type of campaign was almost always shown nationally and sometimes internationally resulting in exposure in numerous markets. Therefore, sales could be augmented without a large expense on the part of the record company.

One popular sponsorship was taken on by Pepsi in 1987 with Michael Jackson, in conjunction with his new album release. This campaign increased Pepsi's market share considerably. On the other hand, in 1989 Pepsi sponsored Madonna's newly-released album *Like A Prayer*. Madonna's title song offended many groups and individuals and was taken off the air on some radio stations. As a result, Pepsi suffered from bad publicity and its market share declined. Corporations and record companies have been more careful with these types of arrangements since this occurrence.

Trade Publications

Hit songs are the lifeblood of the record industry. Charting the hits is the task of the industry's trade publications, the most reliable of which is *Billboard Magazine*. Most publications gather information from radio stations and retail outlets to determine which releases are currently most popular with the public.

During the 1980s these weekly charts served a variety of purposes. Radio stations used them to measure a record's national performance and factored this information into their programming decisions — such as whether to add or drop a record, or increase or decrease its rotation. Record companies used chart information in promoting their releases to radio stations and retail stores. Convincing a station or retailer to add a record on the basis of its national chart performance or regional air-play activity would, in turn, fuel the record's momentum the following week.

Trade publications did more than publish charts. Each covered the overall industry by reporting news, trends, and business developments. A number of publications also made charts available via on-line database systems. Record companies which effectively referred to these publications developed a keen sense of the industry, thereby successfully promoting their music.

DISTRIBUTION

Distribution of prerecorded music in the U.S. was done through several outlets — record stores, tape/record clubs, mail-order establishments, and department stores. As shown in Figure 3, record stores historically have been the most profitable distribution outlet for prerecorded music. Retailers received the product directly from the record company or through a wholesaler.

In the late 1980s more than 60 percent of the dollar volume of prerecorded music was sold

Figure 3: Place of Purchase—Percentage of $ Volume

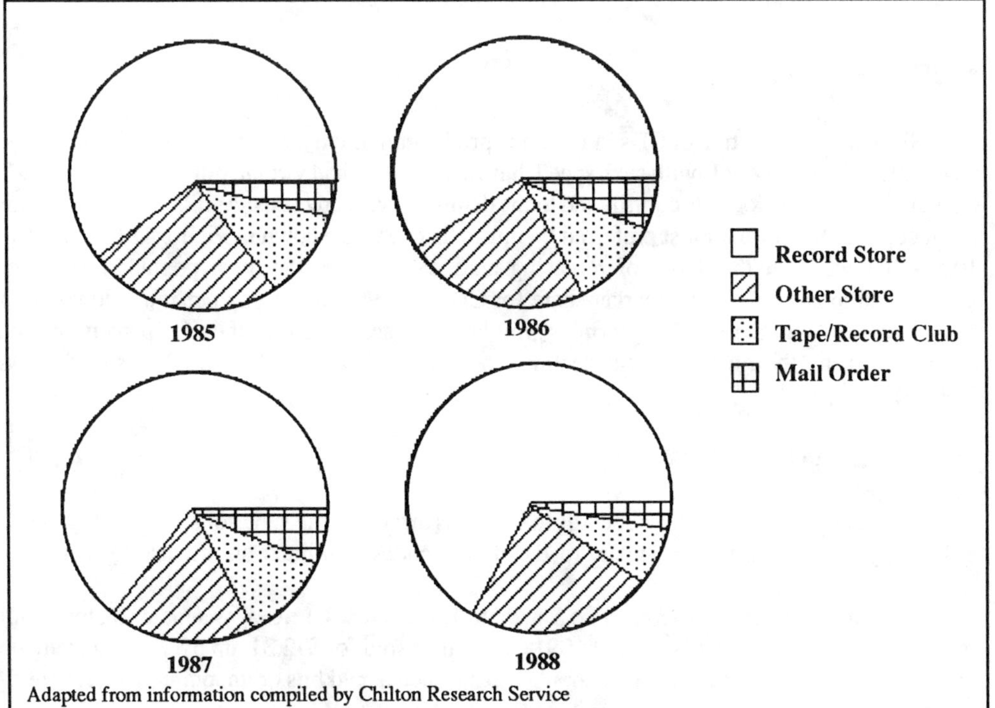

Adapted from information compiled by Chilton Research Service

through record stores. These stores ranged from national retail chains with hundreds of outlets, to one-store (mom and pop) enterprises. Large record stores relied on strong promotion and creative services by record companies for increased sales. Creative services included designing the proper packaging to get retail shelf space for any release, in addition to producing merchandising aids (point-of-purchase product display pieces) which consisted of in-store posters, rack cards, storage racks, browser bins, and displays. Consolidation at the retail level continued in the late 1980s with the two largest retailers, Musicland (680 stores) and Transworld Music Corporation (440 stores), growing through acquisition.

Department stores and discount chains accounted for a somewhat smaller percentage of sales. They sold only familiar hits rather than music by new or obscure artists. Record companies with established pop artists sold through these outlets.

Small record shops tended to be successful when they carried specialty music not found in the larger record stores. For this reason, they focused on consumers who did not have a mainstream music preference, and carried jazz, classical, rap, and reggae. Record companies which had developed artists within such uncommon genres distributed to these outlets.

Wholesale operations owned by major record companies sold directly to large-volume retailers which bought centrally for their stores. Major record companies also provided distribution services for a number of smaller record companies. Smaller retailers bought from independent wholesalers, known as one-stops, which carried major record labels and independent label recordings.

MUSIC FORMATS

Since the introduction of CDs in 1982, the production of vinyl records has declined rapidly. CDs replaced vinyl records with such speed that vinyl records had virtually disappeared by 1991. Other popular music formats contributed to the demise of vinyl records. Audiocassette tapes, for instance, were the format most preferred by music listeners, as shown in Figure 4. However, in 1990, CDs were on the verge of replacing audiocassettes as the most popular format for prerecorded music. The total market share for CDs in 1990 was only .2 percent below that of audiocassettes. Of the remaining formats, vinyl records accounted for only 1.1 percent of total market sales in 1990, a 68 percent decline from 1989 [*Standard & Poors Industry Surveys* 1991(B)].

Compact Discs (CDs)

The rapid switch from vinyl records to CDs was driven by the superior audio quality of CD technology in which a laser scanner "reads" digital codes imprinted on the disc to reproduce sounds.

CDs ranged in size from 3-inch, to 5-inch, to 12-inch discs. Price was a major factor in full acceptance of CDs. In the first half of 1991 CD albums sold for $12.31, up 6.8 percent from the first half of 1989. CD prices for less popular music such as old hits or uncommon genres (mid-

Figure 4: Formats Purchased—Percentage of $ Volume

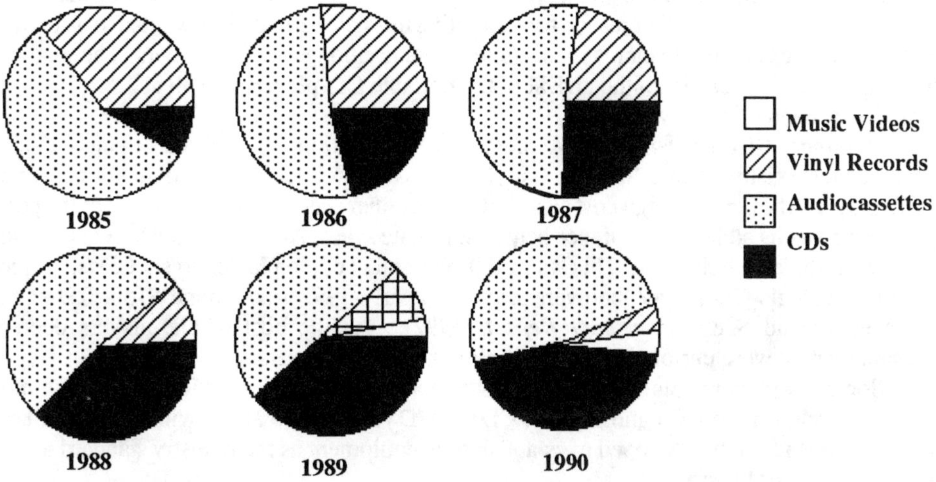

1985 1986 1987 1988 1989 1990

Music Videos
Vinyl Records
Audiocassettes
CDs

Based on information from Standard & Poors Survey(B), October 24, 1992.

line CDs) were, on average, $11. Retail prices on CDs steadily dropped, prior to 1991, reflecting price cuts from manufacturers/suppliers and an increasing availability of older, previously released hits. In comparison, the average suggested retail prices for audiocassettes and vinyl records remained relatively stable ($7.52 - $8.05).

However, lower prices for CDs didn't mean lower profits for music companies. Manufacturing costs had dropped dramatically in the late 1980s, reflecting competition from new plants joining the industry, higher manufacturing volumes, and increased familiarity with manufacturing the new format. CDs sold at wholesale for approximately $8 per disc. After paying $3 in manufacturing costs and $1 in royalty fees, record companies still retained a profit of $4 per disc sold.

Increases in production efficiencies had grown throughout the industry in the late 1980s. General Electric's plastics division introduced a plastic resin in 1988 that reduced the molding process by as much as five seconds. This new resin enabled CD manufacturers to produce CDs at a much faster rate without additional plant capacity. The biggest benefit of this new technology was the speed at which manufacturers were able to respond to market demand.

This rapid growth of CD sales in the first ten years of its existence demonstrated that the quality of the sound of the music was the most important factor to the consumer.

CD-3 Inch Single. The CD-3 inch was introduced by many record companies in the late 1980s. The CD-3 plays up to 20 minutes of music compared to 75 minutes for the 5-inch CD. The

CD-3 cost less than the 5-inch CD and allowed consumers to buy a particular song, album cut, or mini-album. Mini CDs retailed at prices ranging from $3.49 to $5.98, and accounted for only about .2 percent of the total sales in the singles market. The industry trend to manufacture CD-3s was due to the smaller disc's greater portability — similar to the portable cassette player. Also, record companies had another reason for promoting this new format: they wanted to offer the CD-3 at a lower price in order to increase consumer demand among non-CD owners. The smaller disc was expected to benefit from the arrival of the portable CD-player, as well as from an expected increase in standard CD ownership.

Compact Disc Player. In 1990 most of the population still resisted buying CD-players because their existing music libraries (vinyl records and audiocassettes) could not be played on a CD-player. The player's high cost also slowed consumer acceptance. The arrival of the portable CD-player and its added convenience helped stimulate sales. Another innovation to CD-players was the multiple CD-changer. This was a CD-player that could play up to six CDs in sequence.

For a single CD-player the average price in early 1992 was around $150; CD-changers averaged around $385 [*Consumer Reports* 1992]. As the cost of CD-players decreased, consumers who were curious about CD quality purchased players.

Some CD-player manufacturers introduced combination players which could accommodate 3-inch, 5-inch, 8-inch CDs and 12-inch CDVs (CDVs combine audio with video similar to a videotape). Manufacturers hoped to establish such equipment as the industry standard to further attract CD-player buyers.

Audiocassettes

As of early 1992 audiocassette tapes were the prerecorded format most favored by music listeners. Sales of 171 million audiocassettes represented about 46 percent of the industry's dollar volume in 1991. The huge sales of portable tape players during the 1970s and 1980s helped audiocassettes remain the format of choice. The popularity of audiocassette tapes was usually a matter of convenience: they could be played in a home stereo system, a portable cassette player, or a car stereo while other formats, such as vinyl records, allowed no such flexibility. However, the advent of smaller CD-players and discs affected audiocassette sales [*Standard & Poors Industry Surveys* 1991(A)]. In the 1980s, audiocassette tapes cost less than CDs and offered a larger selection of music — two reasons for their continued popularity.

In 1988, a new format resulted from the popularity of album-length cassettes: the cassette single, which consisted of just one or two songs with roughly 20 minutes of playing time. In 1991, the cassette single format accounted for 4.6 percent of sales by total dollar volume. The cassette single became popular by carrying hit songs, particularly in rock and pop, and also because of its low cost — an average price of $2.99 as of 1989. Record companies had even test-marketed oldie hits on the cassette single because of its success. There were an estimated 325 million cassette players in the U.S. in 1991.

NEW TECHNOLOGY

During the 1980s, technological developments promised to provide better quality recordings and hardware players, thereby contributing to industry growth over the long term. With superior computer-based technology making CDs so popular, industry participants had begun to focus their resources on other digital formats. Two new formats were released in 1992 — Digital Compact Cassettes (DCC), and Mini Discs [*Standard & Poors Industry Surveys* 1992]. Market introduction of these new formats was slow, but the opportunities attached to their successful entry should more than compensate the industry for its time and patience.

Concerns over copyright infringement and the higher cost of the new players were the two major factors affecting success. To resolve the copyright issue, the recording and consumer electronics industries have endorsed legislation which would compensate the recording industry for every machine and blank tape sold by the consumer electronics industry [*Standard & Poors Industry Surveys* 1992].

Digital sampling also is changing the way music is produced. Any sound or voice can be transformed into a series of numeric codes and stored on a compact disc. These encoded sounds can then be slightly altered by changing the numeric codes. This breakthrough in technology has created several copyright problems as musicians can create new sounds from other artists' previously recorded works.

Digital Audiotape (DAT)

This new technology combined CD-quality sound with the ability to record and erase on an audiocassette tape. This innovation resembled an audiocassette tape in appearance, but the smaller size made it more portable. The only drawback was DATs wear after long periods of usage. The DAT player originated in Japan but was not very popular there due to its high price and the limited availability of prerecorded tapes. Sony Corp. introduced DAT machines into the U.S. in 1990, but the machines experienced difficulty in gaining market acceptance [*Standard & Poors Industry Surveys 1991*(B)]. This most likely resulted from increasing consumer uncertainty as to the standard industry medium; consumers were reluctant to purchase hardware which could become obsolete in the near future.

Because of DAT's excellent recording capabilities, many record companies worried that its introduction might increase the fidelity of home taping and significantly hurt prerecorded music sales. Also, copyright infringement could result if reproduction royalties were withheld from record companies. Record companies would not encourage the introduction of DAT technology unless legislation was enacted which would require players to be equipped with an anti-copying device.

Digital Compact Cassettes (DCC)

This tape recorder/player recorded digitally and could play the older analog audiocassette format. This added feature meant that consumers would not need to replace their existing music libraries immediately.

Prior to its introduction in the early 1990s, the DCC format had generated support among the major recording companies. They were actively involved in its development and planned to introduce DCC prerecorded music of major recording artists simultaneously with the DCC player/

recorder in an attempt to attract consumers into sampling the new format.

Recordable Compact Disc

To stimulate acceptance of the CD as the industry standard for the prerecorded medium, in 1988 Tandy Corp. developed an erasable compact disc with possible applications in both computer and audio equipment. Although an audio CD recorder-player was not yet available, it was likely that such an introduction would also cause uncertainty in the industry as to what consumers should buy. Again, introduction of this recordable CD would hurt prerecorded music sales through an increase in home taping.

CONSUMERS

In the 1980s, record companies made an effort to appeal to customers by offering them the music they desired. The most lucrative markets were teenagers and baby boomers. These two groups combined purchased more than half of all prerecorded music. As the U.S. market matured,

Figure 5: Consumer Profile by Age: Percentage of $ Volume

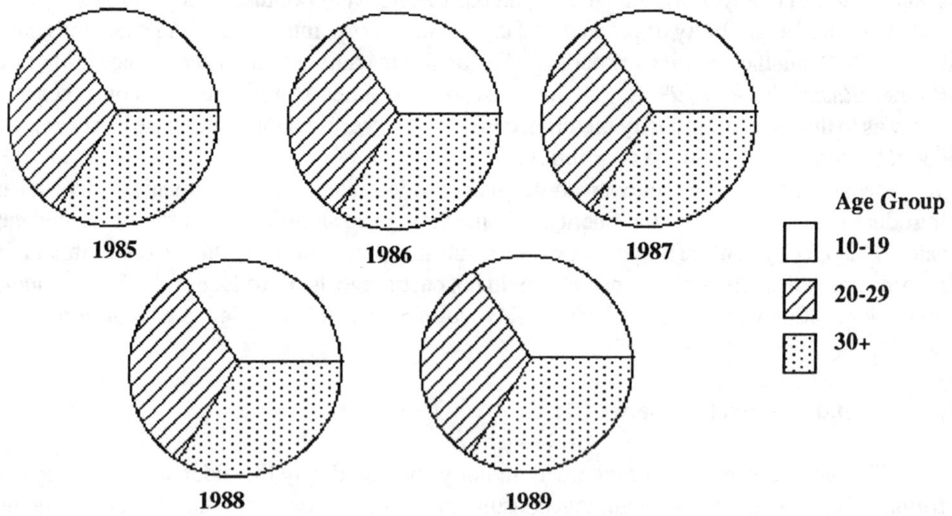

1985

1986

1987

1988

1989

Age Group

10-19

20-29

30+

Adapted from information compiled by Chilton Research Service and *Broadcasting*, July 1, 1991, p. 36.

the ability to attract older music fans was important since the number of U.S. teenagers was declining. Figure 5 shows the consumer profile by age for 1985 to 1989.

With the emergence of the CD, new buyers were attracted in the U.S., as well as in international markets.

Teenagers and Young Adults

Teenagers and young adults (10- to 29-year-olds) accounted for 64.5 percent of industry sales in 1989. This group had historically been a crucial market for sales of prerecorded music. Record companies targeted this market by offering rock music and pop music. Because audiocassette tapes and players were less expensive than CDs and their players, they were purchased more frequently by this cost-conscious market. To take advantage of this market, record companies expanded their audiocassette single offerings with a broader range of music. The success of the audiocassette spurred at least three record companies to look "back to the future" by marketing oldie titles in this format [Rosen 1989].

Baby Boomers

In 1989, baby boomers (30- to 39-year-olds) accounted for 35 percent of industry sales. These highly educated, high-income, older folks preferred classical, big band, jazz, and soft rock. Many of these baby boomers were visiting music stores more frequently since the emergence of CDs. They initially helped popularize the format because they liked its superior sound quality and because they were able to afford the high initial investment in CD players. Baby boomers, who had previously stopped buying music, returned to the market with the advent of CDs. Many were interested in replacing their existing music libraries with the CD format.

Record companies introduced new strategies to attract baby boomers. The music had to appeal to these listeners — new versions of music they knew, loved, and perhaps already owned on a different format. Record companies found that music catalogs that had been shelved in recent years could be re-released in CD format to increase revenues.

International

In 1990, worldwide sales of prerecorded music reached $24 billion. As the U.S. market matured during the 1980s, new markets were necessary for additional revenues. Substantial growth was expected in the international market due to a rising standard of living, the success of the CD in most industrialized countries, and the expansion of world demand for prerecorded music. This market was potentially very lucrative. To be successful record companies would have to develop desired music, mainly rock and pop music. Record companies which became familiar with international markets and had strong international promotion and distribution channels could successfully reach and exploit this market. International sales figures in 1990 were as follows: Japan, $2.9 billion (12%); U.K., $2 billion (8.3%); Germany, $2.3 billion (9.6%); France, $1.7 billion (7.1%) [*Standard & Poors Industry Surveys* 1991(B)].

COMPETITIVE ENVIRONMENT

During the past decade, the recording industry was dominated by six major international companies. These companies were very diversified in other entertainment operations such as movies, home videos, music publishing, television, and manufacturing of various formats. There were strong links among these operations and synergy made them profitable.

One major company, Warner Communications, was U.S.-based. The others were Sony (Japan), Philips N.V. (the Netherlands), Thorn/Emi (United Kingdom), Bertelsmann A.G. (West Germany) and Matsushita MCA (Japan). Collectively, these six accounted for over 80 percent of the $7.5 billion in revenues in the U.S. market in 1990 [*Standard & Poors Industry Surveys* 1991(B)]. Figure 6 lists the major record companies and their music labels, and major artists along with their 1991 revenues. These competitors are summarized below.

Sony (CBS Records): Sony led the industry in superstars and international distribution, but depended too much on big hits. Music labels included Columbia, Epic, and CBS. In 1991, Sony's music-related sales revenue was $3.6 billion. Sony's 1991 performance reflected the strong sales of its new act, C&C Music Factory, along with the continued strength of such performers as Michael Bolton, Mariah Carey, and Michael Jackson.

Warner Communications: In 1991, Warner was the leader in U.S. sales with a roster of diversified acts, and was still building overseas. Music labels included Electra and Atlantic. Revenue in 1991 was $3 billion. Warner became one of the world's leading music publishers with the 1987 acquisition of the Chappell Group. Its top performers included the New Age music group R.E.M., and Natalie Cole, the 1991 Grammy award winner for best song.

Philips N.V.: In 1991, Philips was popular abroad; U.S. operations were growing but distribution costs were high. Music labels included Polygram, Mercury, Deutsche Grammonphon, and the 1992-acquired A&M Records. Revenue in 1991 was $3.7 billion and its top performers included Amy Grant and Sting.

Bertelsmann: In 1991 Bertelsmann was popular in country and pop music. Music labels included RCA and Arista. Revenue in 1991 was $2.2 billion. This privately-owned company was involved in a scandal in 1990 when its multi-million-dollar artists Milli Vanilli were exposed as frauds. Other top performers were Whitney Houston, Clint Black, and the rock group the Grateful Dead.

Thorn/EMI: In 1991 Thorn/EMI was in transition; Britain's biggest label was struggling to rebuild in the U.S. Music labels included Capitol and EMI Manhattan. Revenue in 1991 was $1.7 billion. In 1989 the company become a leader in music publishing with the acquisition of song catalogs which included the CBS music catalog. Thorn/EMI was able to greatly increase its U.S. sales as a direct result of the tremendous success of superstar rap performer M.C. Hammer and country superstar Garth Brooks.

Major record companies designated different labels for each genre of music: rock, pop, country, Black music, etc. By segmenting the company into divisions, and by employing separate staffs, record companies were able to nurture relationships with recording artists and, at the same

Figure 6: Major Competitors in Record Industry

COMPANY MAJOR LABELS	REVENUE BILLIONS	TOP ARTISTS
CBS RECORDS/SONY Epic Columbia CBS	$3.6	C&C Music Factory, Michael Bolton, Mariah Carey, Michael Jackson
WARNER COMM. Electra Atlantic	$3.0	Genesis, R.E.M., Natalie Cole, Phil Collins, Van Halen
PHILLIPS N.V. Mercury A&M Records Polygram	$3.7	Sting, Amy Grant, Elton John, Janet Jackson, Bryan Adams
BERTELSMANN Arista RCA	$2.2	Grateful Dead, Aretha Franklin, Whitney Houston, Clint Black
THORN/EMI Capital EMI Manhattan	$1.7	Garth Brooks, Sinaed O'Conner, M.C. Hammer, Vanilla ICE
MCA * Motown Geffen	$0.551	Reba McEntire Guns'n Roses Jody Watley

*MCA'S 1991 breakdown unavailable; revenues is 1990 total.

SOURCE: *Standard and Poors Industry Survey* March 12, 1992 Pages 32-33.

time, focus on the tastes of music listeners in that particular genre.

Label categorization was used for promotional reasons, such as to obtain radio air-time. If a radio station were playing 30 records and five were of one label, it was difficult to get them to play additional songs with the same label [Grein 1988].

In the U.S. in 1990, 20 percent of industry sales were by smaller independent record companies which had succeeded by catering to a particular segment of the market with a specific genre, such as gospel, blues, reggae, and rap. Their diminutive size and iconoclastic spirit aided them in breaking ground in new, non-mainstream music styles.

Independents were able to respond quickly to the rapidly changing tastes of the market and their initiatives frequently directed the way for later successes by major record companies. On the other hand, independents were weakened by tight budgets, small staffs, and low profiles. They often felt threatened when major companies stepped into uncommon genres, since they lacked the necessary funds to compete with the major companies' promotional efforts.

The acquisition trend of the 1980s that saw CBS acquired by Sony, and RCA by Bertelsmann, continued in 1990 with the acquisition of MCA by Matsushita. Foreign companies stood ready to buy when U.S. entertainment companies became available. Foreign companies were attracted to U.S. companies for several reasons. American pop performers were heard worldwide and contributed the most to the global talent pool. Foreign companies were eager to recruit talent because it was difficult for foreign companies to imitate such music.

In spite of their advantages in the talent area, U.S. entertainment companies found it difficult to compete with foreign firms. Weakened by a devalued dollar and vulnerable to the dynamics of a free market, U.S. companies had been increasingly squeezed between Japan and the Pacific Rim countries, as well as the prospect of a united and economically reinforced post-1992 Europe. Along with this, U.S. firms were unfamiliar with many international markets. As a result, some U.S. entertainment companies were prime candidates for all types of cooperative ventures with foreign companies, including mergers.

THE COMPANY

HISTORY

MCA Inc. was founded by Jules C. Stein in 1924, mostly as a talent agency representing big name stars such as Jimmy Stewart and Bette Davis. By the early 1930s, Stein had a flourishing national talent agency. In 1936, he signed on Lew Wasserman as national director for advertising and public relations. Wasserman became MCA's top agent and had worked his way up to CEO of MCA Inc. by 1973.

In 1946, Wasserman convinced Stein to move into television and MCA soon became the nation's biggest producer of television shows. Incorporated in Delaware in 1958, MCA bought Paramount's pre-1948 film library of over 750 films to rent to television. MCA also bought Universal Studios' production lot which, during the 1980s, was turned into one of the all-time great publicity attractions when the public was invited to tour studio operations. In 1960, MCA started producing films for theater; it had been on the edge of the motion picture industry for years.

In 1966, MCA took the final entry into theater films when it merged with Decca Records. By this time MCA had completely abandoned its function as a talent agency and was heavily involved in movie production.

In 1967, MCA acquired Kapp Records and solidified its position in the music business. In 1988, business activities of MCA Inc., including its subsidiaries and divisions, consisted of seven major business segments: filmed entertainment; music entertainment; video rentals and mail-order sales; book publishing; toy products; broadcast and cable television; and miscellaneous operations.

In 1990, MCA Inc. entered into negotiations with Matsushita Electric of Japan. MCA's chairman, Wasserman, felt the acquisition of MCA by Matsushita would provide global growth opportunities for MCA. Matsushita agreed to pay $6.59 billion for MCA and assumed MCA's long-term debt of $1.36 billion. The president of Matsushita, Akio Tanii, stated that managerial and creative decisions for MCA would continue to be made by MCA.

MCA MUSIC ENTERTAINMENT GROUP

In 1990, the Music Entertainment Group included such divisions as the Universal Amphitheater, MCA Concerts, Facility Merchandising, Winterland Concessions, MCA Event Marketing, MCA Records, MCA Distribution, and MCA Music Publishing, as shown in Figure 7.

In 1990, MCA Records added two additional labels, Geffen and GRP. Its seven other music labels each represented certain genres of music: the Universal and Island Records labels served country; Motown & MCA Records served Black music; Uni and Chrysalis served rock; and IRS Records served pop music. Island Records and Chrysalis Records were labels distributed primarily in Canada.

The Music Entertainment Group provided 22.6 percent of total revenues for MCA Inc. during 1989. Figure 8 shows that revenue for the Music Entertainment Group increased from $477,496,000 in 1987 to $1,075,496,000 in 1990. During this time operating costs rose considerably.

The Music Entertainment Group was broadly diversified in the music industry. In the early 1980s, MCA placed less emphasis on MCA Records as the main source for profit generation. However, synergy among all operations stimulated profits. Therefore, in the late 1980s MCA Inc. attempted to make MCA Records and its related operations of primary importance.

In 1990, MCA Records manufactured, marketed, and released compact discs, records, and tapes on the MCA Records label and other labels, and was a 20 percent owner of Motown Records. MCA Distribution distributed recorded music for MCA Records, Motown Records, and others. In foreign countries — other than Canada and the U.K. — MCA compact discs, records, and tapes were distributed principally by Warner International. Videotapes and videodiscs for the MCA Home Video division were also distributed through these channels. The following describes several other subdivisions:

Universal Amphitheater and MCA Concerts: These were concert stadiums and amphitheaters (open-air facilities) which hosted a wide variety of talent from performers to sport competitions.

Facility Merchandising: This division held the exclusive novelty vending rights to over 45 concert facilities nationwide. It also handled major outdoor dates for such concert tours as U2 and Guns 'n Roses in 1992.

Winterland Concession: Acquired in 1988, it is the concert industry's largest full-service

Figure 7: The Subdivision of MCA Entertainment Group

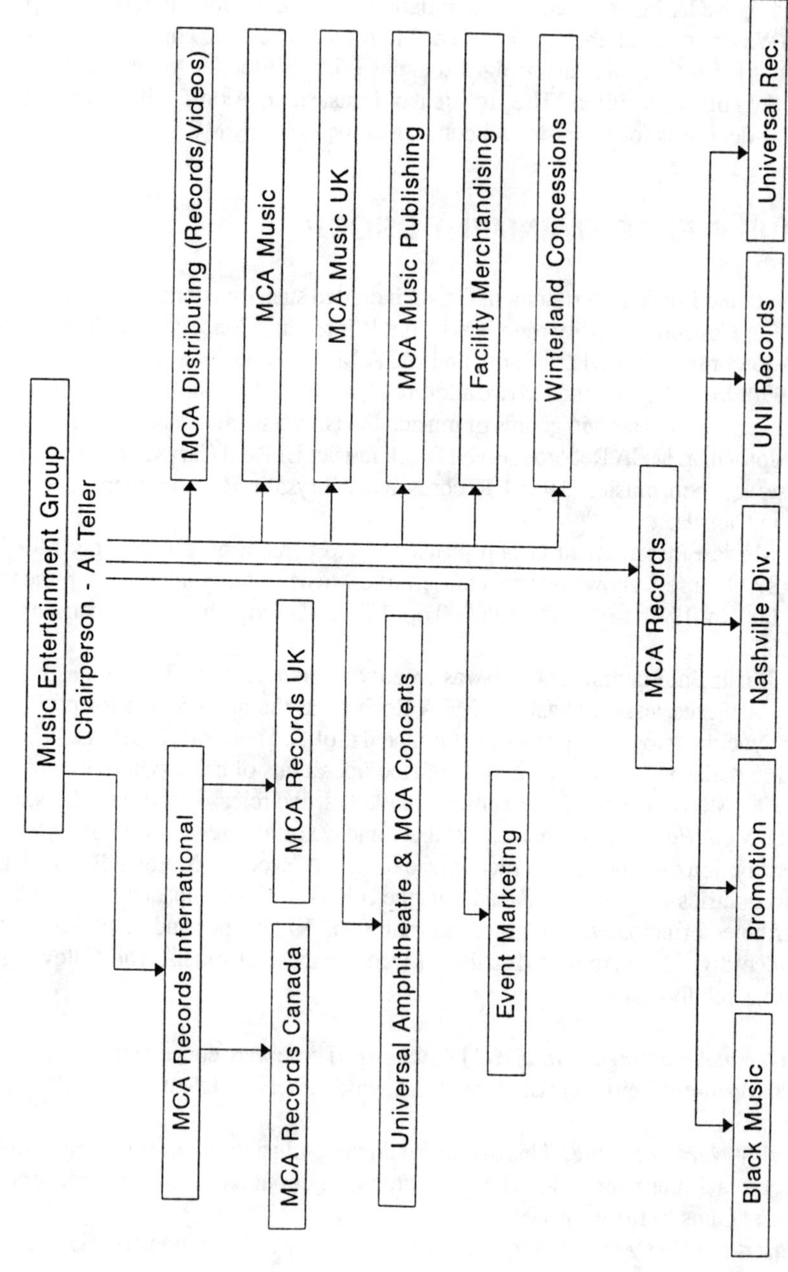

Figure 8: MCA Music Entertainment Group Financial Summary

($ in thousands)	1990	1989	1988	1987	1986
Revenues	$1,075,496	$764,718	$661.028	$477,496	$386,171
Operating Income (Loss)	$95,699	$56,516	$60,480	$40,863	$33,753
Not Allocated to Operations					
Corp. General Administration	$33,387	$29,681	$20,041	$16,057	$14,133
Investment Loss (income)	($16,225)	($13,777)	$4,092	($21,991)	($16,562)
Interest Expense	$71,989	$85,126	$74,565	$43,436	$7,032
Income Before Taxes	$291,433	$388,460	$238,916	$190,854	$203,704
Income Taxes	$107,773	$143,700	$74,000	$53,600	$52,800
Net Income **	$183,660	$244,760	$164,916	$137,254	$150,904

**Omitted are revenues from MCA's six other divisions so total will not sum correctly

Based on Information from: *MCA Inc. 3rd Quarter Report* 1990

merchandiser. It designed and marketed custom-printed t-shirts, sweatshirts, and other merchandise which was sold principally at concert and sports facilities nationwide as well as to retailers.

Event Marketing: This division presented and promoted the company's operations in shopping malls, theme parks, fairs, and other alternative venues. Plans for event marketing included customizing alternative venue promotions for major corporations.

MANAGEMENT

When Irving Azoff took over as president of the Music Entertainment Group in 1983, the record and publishing operations expanded aggressively into record distribution, artist selection and promotion, and merchandising. The record and publishing operations turned around from a loss of $7 million in 1983 to operating income of more than $95 million in 1990.

Upon taking over, Azoff fired 41 of the 46 acts on the music roster and hired some of the top executives in the industry. He negotiated a deal with Motown to distribute its records in the U.S., a move that more than doubled MCA's market share. In 1990, MCA's U.S. market share was roughly 4.5 percent.

Azoff's major strategy was summed up in this statement: "We're in the music business, not the record business." This concept stressed vertical integration, or obtaining talented recording artists — a move which emulated the industry's general trend. Although MCA does not provide figures solely for its record division, analysts estimated it grew eight percent in 1990.

In August 1988, Al Teller of MCA Records (the subsidiary) was promoted to chairman of the Music Entertainment Group after Azoff's resignation. Teller's major concerns were finding new talent, increasing MCA's rock and roll repertoire, and expanding overseas. Artist development involved breaking in new acts, establishing these acts, and sustaining these artists' careers. Teller focused on strengthening the overall artist roster and refining the artist acquisition strategy, as well as on aggressively finding talent on the streets.

Since 1988, the record division has undergone major restructuring and cost cutting plans. Thirty principal staff members were discharged from MCA's A&R and sales department, its jazz and classical division, Unicity Music (a music publishing affiliate), and Uni Records (a subsidiary label).

The strategy behind restructuring was to foster a more effective working relationship between the A&R centers of MCA Records and the company's marketing and promotion team. This would, it was hoped, result in stronger, more creative artist development strategies and new marketing campaigns. This restructuring strategy was not surprising since in the early 1980s MCA had experienced difficulties in breaking in and developing new pop talent, with new acts coming mostly from the Black music genre. However, this restructuring would eventually prevent MCA's jazz and classical division's music publishing catalog from capitalizing on CD sales. Understaffing also could mean a lack of thorough research in choosing the right music for the right market.

In the 1980s, MCA Inc. received many acquisition offers from outside companies, domestic and foreign. This was due to its great accumulation of assets (such as Universal Studios), its substantial film library, and many other diversified activities. In late 1990 MCA was acquired by Matsushita Electric of Japan's for more than $6.5 billion.

MAJOR EVENTS

In 1989 and 1990, the Music Entertainment Group continued to diversify activities. Some of the highlights are listed below:

Movies

MCA sold many records as the result of movie soundtracks. Some movies that had contained popular music soundtracks were "The Breakfast Club," "Beverly Hills Cop," and "Dirty Dancing." Another popular soundtrack was from the movie "The Commitments," which told the story of a struggling music group in Ireland. Sales of the soundtrack were so good that an album release by the group was seen as a strong possibility in late 1993.

Music Publishing

MCA's music publishing operations, with a collection of over 50,000 songs, earned sizable royalties from foreign operations. Superstars such as Michael Jackson and Whitney Houston had borrowed MCA's songs. In the 1980s, MCA acquired several foreign and domestic music catalogs and expanded its European operations. With the acquisition of Geffen Records, MCA increased its catalog with many songs by leading artists. Such moves helped MCA to remain the number two music publishing company in the early 1990s.

Acquisitions

MCA's biggest acquisition event was its own by Matsushita Electric of Japan. This acquisition cost more than $8 billion after MCA's debt was consolidated. Virgin Records, the largest surviving independent record company, was being considered as a possible MCA acquisition in early 1992. The Bertelsmann Music Group and the Sony Music Group were also in competition for the company.

In 1990, MCA acquired GRP Records Inc. and the David Geffen Company. GRP had an extensive catalog of songs while Geffen had major rock acts under contract and was one of the largest independents. Joint ventures were formed with both the Victor Company of Japan Ltd. and Bertelsmann Music Group of Germany. Distribution in these two countries previously had been handled by Time Warner Inc. The agreements created new companies, with 50 percent owned by each of the firms in each case. The new companies were responsible for the distribution of existing labels and allowed MCA to develop its own artists in these countries. This had strategic importance because in many parts of Europe, 30 to 60 percent of record sales were by local artists. In Japan this figure was about 70 percent.

Hit Records

In 1991 MCA Records set an industry record for advance album sales, largely due to the album releases of its heavy metal rock group Guns 'n Roses. The prerelease demand was for over four million copies. Other leading records were released by Tom Petty and the Heartbreakers and by the contemporary group Bel Biv Devoe. Another album release that had potential to become successful was "Achtung Baby" by the rock group U2.

MARKETING STRATEGY

In the early 1990s MCA was creating new strategies for the development and marketing of new and old artists. These strategies focused on Black, country, and pop music by creating new promotional devices and developing the music for wider appeal domestically and internationally. MCA was also making greater use of radio.

Black Music

MCA's Black music label, Motown, enjoyed much success during 1989 and 1990. It introduced new talent and re-established old talent. Jheryl Busby, the newly installed president of Motown, was expected to continue to emphasize artist development. Motown would continue to run operations on its own but would interface with MCA for services such as distribution and creative work. Busby wanted to maintain Motown's unique sound through artist development. He also wanted to plan a larger artist crossover into pop and rock music for foreign appeal.

Country Music

In country music, MCA had two of the top female vocalists on the charts — Patty Loveless and Reba McEntire. Patty Loveless had terrific talent, but it had taken MCA some time to establish her as one of the top country singers. MCA's country division ran a major advertising campaign for Patty Loveless' video which aired on cable television along with a CD single from her album in 1991. Some other promotional devices were also used. MCA had Ms. Loveless call up radio stations, autograph posters, and even arrange an endorsement deal with Justin Boots. This promotion was augmented by boot giveaways on the radio and through retail outlets, as well as a grand prize of an all-expense paid trip for two to see Ms. Loveless perform. Ms. Loveless's face was highly visible throughout industry conventions, on television, and in newspapers. These strong promotional activities established her as the number one country female act in the early 1990s.

In 1991 Reba McEntire was still the number one female country recording star. Her album sales accounted for much of the success of MCA's country division. Her appearance on the NBC sequel to *The Gambler* in 1991 increased her exposure and helped boost her record sales.

Pop Music

MCA used a different approach to develop and market teenage superstar Tiffany. Since Tiffany was only 15, her image was difficult to establish. MCA thought it had a talented individual, but radio stations were reluctant to play her music. So instead of targeting radio stations, MCA brought Tiffany's performances to the audience via shopping malls. She was a smash hit in Salt Lake City, where 4,000 people filled the mall to hear her. As word travelled, people started calling radio stations to request her songs, and records started selling. This strategy launched the top 40 radio career of this teenage superstar.

Radio

MCA's success could also be attributed to the radio market, where feedback from listeners was an important measuring device. Listeners' preferences came through request lines to radio stations and they, in turn, played what listeners requested. For MCA, radio was an indicator of events and therefore supporting radio was a high priority. Using promotional devices such as contests had been a priority of MCA [Freeman 1989].

TOWARDS THE FUTURE

In the 1980s, the prerecorded music industry had extraordinary year-to-year growth. This was a direct result of new technological advances and successful new recording stars. This trend was expected to continue into the 1990s and the potential for even greater growth existed as even newer technologies were being developed, expanded, improved, and made more affordable.

Even with such potential looming, the record companies saw the U.S. market as peaking out and felt that any further increases in sales would mainly be the result of consumers updating their music libraries as formats changed.

In light of these anticipated trends, in early 1992 MCA executives were exploring several alternatives to keep the company competitive.

Al Teller, chairman of the MCA Music Entertainment Group, was determined to increase MCA's market share. Matsushita Electric, MCA's new parent company, was the twelfth largest industrial power in the world and owned a large market share of the music hardware industry worldwide. Matsushita was eager to acquire additional prerecorded music software to insure a steady supply of material for its music hardware. MCA had retained a high degree of autonomy after this merger and was expected to look for new sources of musical property rights.

One alternative under consideration to increase MCA's market share was to adopt a policy in which MCA concentrated solely on dominating one genre of music. A genre that was a good choice for MCA to exploit was the rock music genre. To succeed in this genre, the company would have to have a majority of that genre's top performers. With the acquisition of Geffen Records, MCA had added the popular rock band Guns 'n Roses to its list of music performers, which also included the successful rock band U2. This gave MCA two of the most popular bands within the rock music genre. To succeed in this genre, it was also important to be able to promote the available music to the proper consumer. MCA had a history of creative promotion in regard to pop music, using mall concerts to expose artists to a large group of its consumers — teenagers. This creative ability of MCA in regard to promotion suggested it knew what consumers to target and where to find them. No other major recording company would be able to accomplish this genre specialization feat as easily as MCA. Because of its size and diverse activities in the entertainment industry, MCA's competitors are simply too large to specialize in one genre.

Such a strategy had disadvantages, however. A one-genre policy would limit MCA's ability to acquire other labels. Also, if sales were to decline or if MCA failed to promote an artist successfully, the setback could severely damage MCA.

Another alternative for increasing the company's market share was to continue to expand company operations into all genres of music and seek increased international sales. To accomplish this, a company would need to have either a separate label already established in the target country or establish a joint venture with an existing local firm. MCA had begun one such venture in 1991 in Japan, where MCA, JVC Corp., and VMI of Japan had created a record label to be called MCA Victor, which was to distribute records from all the labels under the MCA umbrella [Newcomb 1991].

This alternative presented opportunities for large gains in international sales. By acquiring or establishing completely localized record companies, MCA would have people familiar with this market running the business. Also, potential artists who wished to work with their own people in producing a record would not be frightened away. Another benefit from this alternative was that by seeking to maintain a diverse selection of music performers the company could seek growth in a number of directions and not worry about slow growth in one area. Another key to success was MCA's financial state since being acquired by Matsushita. With the resources and international presence of its parent company, MCA's ability to accomplish such deals would be increased.

However, this policy could have disadvantages for MCA in the long run. If a company was acquired to make available a release of one of MCA's artists, what would happen when those sales leveled off? Would a company with limited abilities be retained on the off-chance that it would sell another "hot" album later? Also, ventures that could be very profitable over a number of years may not be consummated because returns are not immediate.

These and other strategic questions affecting MCA's long- term future were being explored by management.

REFERENCES AND BACKGROUND READINGS

Burr, Ramiro, "Obscenity Charges Dropped in Texas," *Billboard Magazine*, December 22, 1990, p. 11.

Consumer Reports, March 1992. p. 187.

Cox, Meg, "Music Industry Composes Counterpoint as Demands to Censor Lyrics Increase," *The Wall Street Journal,* October 19, 1990, p. B1.

de Cordoba, Jose, & Harlan, Christi, "Rap Group's Acquittal Seen as Warning to Prosecutors," *The Wall Street Journal,* October 22, 1990, p. B3.

DiMartino, Dave, "3-Inch CD Gets Big Play as Majors Start Ball Rolling," *Billboard Magazine*, March 26, 1988, p. 1 & 76.

Dow Jones Wire Service, "Backed by Matsushita's Money, MCA Plans to Seek Acquisitions," *The Wall Street Journal,* November 28, 1990.

Dow Jones Wire Service, "Japan's JVC to Form Joint Record Company In Japan," October 1, 1990.

Dow Jones Wire Service, "MCA, Bertelsmann Music in Distribution, Licensing Pact," November 12, 1990.

Dow Jones Wire Service, "Matsushita Plans to Borrow $4.8 Billion For MCA Buyout," November 30, 1990.

Dow Jones Wire Service, "Matsushita President Says MCA to Keep Creative Independence," November 29, 1990.

Dubler, Steven, "Hit-Driven MTV Irks Majors," *Billboard Magazine,* April 2, 1988, p. 1, 66.

Fabrikant, Geraldine, "$6.13 Billion MCA Sale to Japanese," *Wall Street Journal*, November 27, 1990, p.D1

Fabrikant, Geraldine, "New Products Help to Bolster Music Sales," *The New York Times*, October 22, 1990.

Fabrikant, Geraldine, "The Record Man With Flawless Timing," *The New York Times*, December 9, 1990, p. 4.

Fantel, Hans, "As More Companies Make Compact Disks, Flaws Increase," *N.Y. Times*, September 25, 1988, p. 30.

Farhi, Paul, "Compact Discs Turn Tables on Vinyl Record Sales," *Washington Post*, March 1, 1989, p. F1, F2.

Freeman, Kim, "Steve Meyer and The Secret of MCA's Success," *Billboard*, February 20, 1988, p. 18.

Gold, Gerald, "MCA Draws on Some Famous Old Names," *New York Times*, May 22, 1988, p. h26.

Goodman, Fred, "Record Industry Preparing to Bury the LP," *Rolling Stone*, March 10, 1988, p. 24.

Greene, Michael, "Music/Radio Marriage on the Rocks," *Billboard Magazine*, February 23, 1991, p. 6.

Grein, Paul, "Uni Records Knows What It Wants to Be," *Los Angeles Times*, May 5, 1988, p. 28.

Hoffman, Bill, "Milli Vanilli Phoni Baloni," *New York Post*, November 16, 1990, p.3.

Holland, Bill, "RIAA Looking to Congress for Performance-Right Bill," *Billboard Magazine*, February 23, 1991, p. 4.

Hughes, Kathleen, "Uncertain Role Japan's Ventures in Hollywood Mostly Are Less Than Stellar," *The Wall Street Journal,* November 27, 1990, p.A3&A8.

Hunter, Nigel, "Key Global Markets Love That CD," *Billboard Magazine*, March 11, 1989, p. 1.

Jeffrey, Donald, "Defying Labels," *New York Newsday,* November 12, 1990 p.2,3,8,& 9.

Katz, Raymond, L. "Media/Leisure Time Weekly," *Shearson Lehman Brothers*, October 15, 1990.

Landro, Laura, "Time Warner Drops Stein Suit, Signs New Pact With the Sire Records Head," *The Wall Street Journal,* November 20, 1990, p. B6.

Lerner, Michael, "The Hit Man of Record Biz," *Newsweek*, February 8, 1988, p. 48.

Lieberman, David, "Now Playing: The Sound of Money," *Business Week*, August 15, 1989, p. 86-90.

Lieberman, David, "They're Playing Whose Song?"*Business Week*, January 23, 1989, p. 42.

Matsushita Electric, *1990 Annual Report,* 1990.

Mayfield, Geoff, "Front-Line CD Price Cuts Continue," *Billboard Magazine*, April 9, 1988, p. 1 & 97.

MCA Inc., *1987 Annual Report*, 1987.

MCA Inc., *1988 Annual Report*, 1988.

MCA Inc., *1989 Quarterly Reports*, 1989.

MCA Inc., *1989 Annual Report*, 1989.

MCA Inc., *1990 Quarterly Annual Reports*, 1990.

MCA Inc., 3rd Quarter Report to Shareholders, September 30, 1990.

"MCA's Music Unit, Bertelsmann Sign Distribution Pact," *The Wall Street Journal,* November 13, 1990, p. B7.

"MCA Nears Accord on Rights to Music Distribution Rights," *The Wall Street Journal*, December 10, 1990, p. B7.

McGowan, Chris, "Pioneer's Combo Player May Lure New CD Buyers," *Billboard Magazine*, May 27, 1989, p. 57.

Meyer, Marianne, "Take Two," *Marketing & Media Decisions*, September 1987, p. 46-54.

Morris, Chris, "Al Teller Is New President of MCA Records," *Billboard*, September 3, 1988, p. 1, 76.

Morris, Chris, "MCA Layoffs Cut Broad Swath," *Billboard Magazine*, December 3, 1988, p. 1, 73.

Morris, Edward, "Copyright Society of the South Meet Focuses On New Technology," *Billboard Magazine*, February 23, 1991, p. 79.

Morris, Edward, "Recent Album Success Cements MCA's Love Affair With Loveless," *Billboard Magazine*, Sept. 8, 1989, p. 44.

Murr, Andrew; Shwartz, James, "Solid Gold for Cool Cash," *Newsweek*, March 26, 1990, p. 34.

Nathan, David, "For Red-Hot MCA, Senior A&R VP Silas is Golden," *Billboard Magazine,* May 21, 1988, p. 26.

"New-Artist Development Pays Off," *Billboard Magazine,* December 24, 1988, p. 11.

Newcomb, Peter, "Homegrown Stars," Forbes, August 19, 1991, p. 131.

Penzer, Erika, "Making Music With CD's," Incentive, May 1989, p. 110-112.

Recording Industry Assoc. of America Inc., *Inside the Recording Industry: A Statistical Overview 1989 Update.*

Recording Industry Assoc. of America, Inc., *Inside the Recording Industry: An Introduction to America's Music Business*, 1988/89.

"RIAA Analysis Shows Changes in Buying Patterns," *Broadcasting*, July 1, 1991, p.36.

Robins, Wayne, "No Future?," *New York Newsday*, February 17, 1991, p. 4&5.

Rosen, Craig, "New AACTion Against Pirates," *Billboard Magazine*, December 15, 1990, p. 84.

Rosen, Craig, "3 Labels Test Future of Oldie Cassette Singles," *Billboard Magazine*, April 15, 1989, p. 1, 76.

Ross, Sean, "Labels Praise Rockin' Top 40s," *Billboard Magazine*, May 6, 1989, p. 1, 19. A.

Ross, Sean, "AC is No. 1 in New Format Ratings," *Billboard Magazine*, September 16, 1989, p. 1, 20. B.

Sanger, David, "Matsushita Shifts Stance on MCA," *The Wall Street Journal*, November 30, 1990, p. D5.

Sanger, David, "Politics and Multinational Movies," *The Wall Street Journal*, November 27, 1990, p. D1&D7.

Sanger, David, "Tanii-san Goes Fishing in Hollywood," *The New York Times*, November 25, 1990, p.1&6.

Schlager, Ken, "Midyear Chart Recap: WEA Is the One," *Billboard Magazine*, August 5, 1989, p. 1, 76-77.

Schwartz, James; Murr, Andrew; Taliaferro, John, "Geffen Goes Platinum," *Newsweek*, December 10, 1990, p. 44-46.

Shapiro, Eben, "Philips Offers Its Challenge to Sony Digital Tape Player," *The New York Times*, January 12, 1991, p. 31&32.

Standard & Poors Industrial Surveys "Leisure," McGraw Hill Publishing Co., March 14, 1991 (A), pp. 42-44.

Standard & Poors Industrial Surveys "Leisure," Mc-Graw Hill Publishing Co., October 24, 1991 (B), pp. 6-8.

Standard & Poors Industrial Surveys "Leisure," Mc-Graw Hill Publishing Co., March 12, 1992 , pp. 31-33.

Terry, Ken, "Labels Divided Over How to Program, Market CD-3s," *Billboard Magazine*, October 10, 1988, p. 1, 103. A.

Terry, Ken, "Industry Oversupply Puts Squeeze on CD Pressers," *Billboard Magazine*, December 3, 1988, p. 1 & 70. B.

Tomsho, Robert, "As Sampling Revolutionizes Recording, Debate Grows Over Aesthetics, Copyrights," *The Wall Street Journal*, November 5, 1990, p. B1.

Verna, Paul, "Video Outlets Embracing Longforms," *Billboard Magazine*, February 23, 1991, p. 42 & 44.

Walley, Wayne, "From Shopping Mall to Superstar," *Advertising Age*, June 6, 1988, p. 28.

White, Thomas, "Industry Growth Requires Better A&R," *Billboard Magazine*, April 23, 1988, p. 9.

Winans, Christopher, "The LP Fades," *Wall Street Journal*, March 23, 1989, p. A(1)E col 5.

Zimmerman, Kevin, "CD's Spark Show Tune Reissues," *Variety*, June 8, 1988, p. 77 & 81.

Zimmerman, Kevin, "WEA, Warner Record Division a Multi-Label Hydra," *Variety*, March 8, 1989, p. 4.

MERCER'S CHOICE: GOING INTO BUSINESS FOR ONESELF

The following are thoughts written by Betty Mercer on the events which led her to think seriously about going into business for herself.

I liked being a sixth grade teacher. The children were adorable. One morning, I was looking out the window of my classroom, watching the parents drop off their little darlings. They all looked the same— the parents I mean. The fathers all thought they looked great in their $200 business suits, on their way to the subway. The mothers were young and attractive. They tried to dress nicely but they couldn't because they always needed the money for the kids. Most of the parents worked, dads happy to get their 7 percent raise each year climbing up that "corporate ladder" and moms helping by bringing in that little "extra income."

As I looked out the window, I wondered if I was headed in the same direction. I decided to do something about my situation. I wanted to insure that my destiny wouldn't be the same as those parents.

BACKGROUND

I started my undergraduate liberal arts program in 1980 at a large nearby university. I graduated cum laude in three years. The following year I began the MBA program fulltime as a graduate assistant.

I had many different jobs during this time period. Freshman year, I got my real estate salesperson's license and worked weekends in a realty firm. Sophomore year, I worked as a student worker at the university and kept that position until graduation. It was during these first years of employment that I realized that working for other people made them money, not me. Over the summer, I looked at the possibility of being an entrepreneur.

In the summer of 1982, I sold various specialty items. I made about $2,000 for the summer. The following summer, I expanded my operations—having already established a reputation and customers I did much better and made about $8,000. There seemed to be a good potential for growth, but the product lost its appeal.

During the summer of 1984, I found a new opportunity. I was at Point Lookout and it was sweltering. There were boys selling icecream for $1.00. This seemed reasonable because the walk to the concession stand was so far that it could cause heat stroke. I bought some icecream from one of the boys and my girlfriend and I asked the boy questions about where he bought his inventory and how much money he made in a day. He told us all about the business. Well, that was the mistake of his life, because the following weekend we were out there with our cooler selling icecream. We made about $400 each on weekends and took the rest of the week off. There wasn't enough business on weekdays and we wanted to enjoy our summer.

I became engaged the following Christmas and a June 1985 wedding was planned. My fiance and I started out looking for an apartment to rent in Forest Hills. The rents were very high—between $700 and $800 per month for a one-bedroom apartment. We began looking for a place to live in our spare time. We decided to look at co-ops and condos and found that for the same $800 per month we could own the apartment rather than make some landlord rich!

We spent months looking around. Finally, we found our first co-op for $61,600. We were thrilled, but there was one problem. We needed to put 20 percent down, and that came out to $12,320. Between the two of us we had only $2,320, and we needed another $10,000. We begged and borrowed from every friend and relative we had and we raised the money. Within six months the value of the co-op had increased so much, we decided to sell. The selling price was $79,000. After all closing and other costs our profit was about $12,000.

Rather than paying people back right away, we kept the original $10,000 and added our $12,000. This gave us a more substantial amount to invest. We bought two reasonably priced co-ops in the next building. Again we intended to live in one, but the prices were skyrocketing. At this point, we knew the market very well. We were able to seek out good deals, but again we didn't have the capital necessary.

The first partner we took in was a friend who had some extra cash to invest but didn't know where to invest it. The deal was that he put in all money needed and we set up the deals, a 50/50 partnership. This worked well. He was making a lot more money than he had been with his cash in a money market fund, and he had a lot of tax write-offs. We were making money setting up deals, and not putting a cent of our own money in. After that, we did the same with three other people.

This went well for a period of about two years. We finally saved up enough cash to put down on a business. I knew that I wasn't going anywhere teaching and I wanted a cash business of my own. It was at this point that the search had begun.

THE SEARCH FOR A BUSINESS TO BUY

I had literally no idea what type of business to enter into. I had no real experience in any type of business. I had no friends or relatives who owned businesses. I just knew that I wanted to make as much money as I could with the least amount of investment possible. I didn't even know where to begin looking for a business. I did make one decision at this point though, taking my lack of experience into consideration.

I decided to buy an already established business rather than start one from scratch. I knew the investment costs would be higher, but I felt that I couldn't afford the risk of starting my own. If I started my own, I would take the risk of losing all the money we worked so hard to get, although if it were successful my ROI would probably be much greater. The way I looked at it, I'd first buy a going business to learn everything about it. The businesses to follow, I could start on my own.

Now that that decision was made, I could begin my task of finding out which type of business I'd like to go into. I started out by looking at the business opportunity section of local newspapers. I began by eliminating those businesses that were completely out of the question for a young girl to enter into, such as bars, restaurants, landscaping, auto repair, butcher shops, and gas stations. Then, I eliminated businesses that didn't appeal to me at all, such as delis, diners, coffee shops, fast food, fish markets, floor covering, hair salons, pizza places, tanning salons, taxi cabs, and video stores. This narrowed my search down considerably.

The first business that appealed to me was the nail salon business. I got manicures every week and could see that money was being made. The problem was that there weren't any salons for sale. I kept it in mind, but decided to look at other types of businesses.

My next selection was laundromats. There seemed to be an opportunity to make money and invest almost no time. Perhaps once or twice a week I would have to stop by to pick up quarters and make sure that all machines were working properly. Laundromats have service contracts generally, and this would mean that if a machine was malfunctioning I would make a phone call. I couldn't believe that laundromats could make $50,000 to $100,000 per year on quarters.

I looked at many laundromats advertised in the paper and I almost bought one. The woman who was selling had been widowed recently and she just wanted to get rid of it. I don't think that she realized the value of it. I spent some time investigating the business, and while I was doing this someone else beat me to it.

The First Promising Opportunity

While going through the paper again, I became interested in stationery stores, so I spent my weekends and evenings looking at them as well. As I answered ads or went looking at businesses, I learned what types of questions to ask and I learned a little about the industry I was questioning each time. Each owner tells you bits and pieces, and so you learn.

While looking at these businesses, I called some brokers. Some ads are listed with brokers so you call them to find out further information. They gave me additional listings to check out, and called me when they had something they thought I might be interested in. This process went on for months. I had seen and investigated over 50 businesses at this point.

One day, I stopped in to see a broker I had seen many times before. He asked if I would be interested in a specialty candy and toy store. I usually looked at everything that sounded good, so I went.

He gave me the address and I went to the store. The owners did not know that I was a potential buyer. I spent about one-half hour inside looking at the merchandise and watching the goings-on. The store was busy. Two nicely dressed women were helping customers choose gifts and I thought the store seemed cute. Although I was inside the store a short time, I decided that I liked it and that I would do further research into the possibility of buying such an establishment.

Studying The Factors Affecting Success

My next step was to look the area over to find out about the location and the competition.

The store was located on the main street of the town, adjacent to many other stores. Across from the store was the town's L.I.R.R. station. The location seemed prime, with people inevitably passing by all day long. I walked in and out of the other stores up and down the block to get a feel for the area. There was plenty of parking — the railroad parking lot across the street, a parking lot in back of the store, and street parking along the block.

My next step was to check out the competition. I went through the phone books to see if there were similar listings in the area. The following day I went back to the store to look at it again. I walked around again and asked people on the street about the store. I asked them where I could find a similar store. I liked the answers I heard. There didn't seem to be any competition at all. Was that possible? It was too good to be true. I decided that I liked this type of store although it wasn't on my original list of types of stores to consider.

I called the broker and told him that I liked the store, and that I wanted to proceed to the next step. He set up a meeting with the owners and I went with my husband to look at the store again.

The First Interview

The owners' names were Mary and Brian. He was an equipment salesman. She basically owned and ran the store on her own. We had many questions to ask them.

The first question was "Why are you selling?" The answer was that Brian's job was taking him to Florida. He was already down there and flew up on weekends. They had purchased a house in Florida and were being forced to move down there permanently. They were a couple in their late forties with two grown children. It was obvious that Brian was an excellent salesman which made him a very likable person, and it worried me. He could sell the Brooklyn Bridge. I decided to proceed with extreme caution. We asked other questions as well, such as:

What is the rent?	$1,200 per month
How long is the lease?	7 years left
How long have you owned the store?	4 years
How much is telephone per month?	Approx. $100
Who are main suppliers for candy?	Associated, Grand, Mark and Mel

Who are toy suppliers?	Reeves, Woods of America, Smallworld, Nikko, Nubrite
Is giftwrap free?	Yes
Who is competition?	No one
Is parking convenient?	No problem
What holidays do you close for?	None

The questions were countless. The price was $240,000 with $60,000 down. Brian said that the business grossed $240,000 annually and that the net was about $107,000. The next step was trying to substantiate these numbers to the best of our ability. Mary and Brian, of course, did not show us their income tax returns. My husband, who is a CPA, went through all of their books. Books can be phony, of course, so he went through all purchases made, the invoices, their checking account, etc. This showed how much they purchased, which gave a good picture of their business volume. We could tell just by looking at the merchandise in the store and checking the prices marked against the invoices that the markup was a minimum of 100 percent. We were satisfied with the numbers and called our lawyer, Ralph, to check out the store, its previous owners, etc. Sales and expenses were as follows:

Annual Sales	$245,000
Cost of Goods Sold (35% of sales)	87,750
Gross Profit (65% of sales)	159,250
LESS Operating Expenses:	
Rent (includes taxes, gas water)	14,400
Telephone	1,200
Payroll (includes payroll taxes)	17,000
Insurance	1,080
Advertising	300
Alarm	120
Miscellaneous Supplies	2,000
Net Income, before Notes	$123,000
Repayment of Notes signed to cover new cash portion of purchase price ($1,316 per month)	15,792
Net Income**	$107,208

**Note that there is no tax provision set up. The corporation is formed as a Subchapter S Corporation and the taxes flow through the owner's personal return.

The Negotiation

Brian wouldn't budge on the down payment, but he did seem very anxious to sell. Flying back and forth was getting to him, and we knew it. He seemed to expect some negotiating anyway. We haggled on numerous occasions, and the selling price was finally reduced to $190,000, $60,000 down.

As I investigated the situation more seriously, I went to the store each day after school and all day Saturday and Sunday for three weeks. At first, it seemed so overwhelming. I wanted to see if I would be able to handle the operations of the business and exactly what was expected of me. There was so much to learn and Mary was very helpful.

First of all, there were many suppliers that Mary had to deal with. I had to learn about each company, what they supplied, who was the best person at the company to speak with, how their prices and merchandise compared to other companies, and what the terms on goods were. I needed to know phone numbers, addresses, and how long it took an item to come in from a particular company. For example, everything ordered from Woods of America in Ohio is on backorder and takes at least three months to get in.

Next, I had to familiarize myself with every item in the store. I had to know what merchandise we did and did not sell. This was very time-consuming and at the time it was very overwhelming.

I had to learn how to giftwrap properly using cellophane. It sounds very simple, but it took time and practice. I had to learn how to deal with customers, to make suggestions for them, to help them make decisions and to make sure they left the store happy. I learned how to make suggestions, give options, and push the items with higher markups.

I had to learn how to operate the cash register, make out order forms and credit card slips. Again, it sounds so simple, but I was overwhelmed by all of these things being thrown at me at once.

During this time period I also attended an annual toy fair and a semiannual giftfair. Mary, Brian and I went together so they could show me what type of items to buy and what companies they had dealt with previously. They showed me how to make deals, and how to bargain. They showed me who not to bargain with as well. I had to open new accounts and establish my own credit. I knew I had enough information to make my decision on whether or not to buy the business.

MICHAEL JEWELERS, INC.: THE GOLD JEWELRY MANUFACTURING INDUSTRY

Michael Jewelers, Inc. was a publicly-held gold jewelry manufacturer founded in 1975 by two brothers, Michael Paolercio and Anthony Paolercio, Jr. The family run business originated in a basement and was financed using contributions from relatives. In 1982, the brothers leased space in a building in Manhattan's jewelry district. By 1984, they owned a six-story building on W. 46 Street; it was eventually sold in 1989 for $2.2 million. They also purchased a factory building in Westchester County, New York. After 10 very successful years of business, the company went public in October 1986.

Following these events, Michael Jewelers, Inc. was in an acquisition mode; it purchased two earring manufacturers and a gold chain manufacturer. During this period, the company's main products were 14 karat gold, diamond-cut pendants, rings, and bracelets. Michael Jewelers, Inc. pioneered the use of the diamond cutting procedure, a hand-crafted art by which a diamond cut bit is used to cut designs onto a finished product. The name of this process is derived from the illusion of diamonds appearing on the product.

As noted in Figure 1, net sales had increased from $38.6 million in 1984-85 to $106 million in 1987-88. At this point Michael Jewelers experienced its first loss. While sales increased by 40%, income decreased from $2 million to a loss of $.9 million during the same period. Michael Jewelers and the industry embarked upon implementing cost-reduction programs aimed at reducing overhead expenses. Michael Jewelers chose to aggressively reduce its total number of employees as part of this cost-cutting program. As of June 30, 1990, there were 348 employees, a 20% reduction from the 416 a year earlier [*Moody's Industrial Manual* 1990].

Since implementing these cost reductions in 1988-89 Michael Jewelers had been profitable,

Figure 1: Michael Jewelers, Inc.
Net Sales and Net Income by Fiscal Year (Thousands of Dollars)

Fiscal Year	Net Sales	Net Income
1984	38,553	2,062
1985/86	60,593	2,926
1986/87	75,874	3,098
1987/88	106,624	(891)
1988/89	95,468	926
1989/90	85,388	2,206
1990/91	120,194	2,131

Source: Information obtained from *Moody's Industrial* 1992.

with net profits reaching $2.1 million in 1990-91.

Company executives believed that they were no longer in danger of bankruptcy and wanted to position themselves to grow in the 1990s. Michael Paolercio, President of Michael Jewelers, stated in the late 1980s that business had been enhanced by the recession because people turn to popularly priced jewelry in difficult economic times. However, with tough economic times predicted for the 1990s, the competition was expected to be tough, with companies fighting hard for market share. Company executives had to make several strategic decisions about the company's future. Should a new higher priced product line be created to increase profit margins? Should the company distribute its finished products to wholesalers, retailers, or both? Should new items in their current price range be produced? Should other small companies that were in the same market be acquired to increase market share? These were just some of the questions that Michael Jewelers' management had to answer in order to remain competitive and maintain market share in the 1990s.

THE INDUSTRY AND COMPETITIVE MARKET

GOLD JEWELRY MANUFACTURING

Major product groups in the gold jewelry manufacturing industry included pendants, chains, bracelets, earrings, rings and watches. Some of the products contained small precious or semi-precious stones.

Gold jewelry has always been considered a luxury item, as well as a status symbol. Therefore, much of the historical market has included the population sectors with high disposable income. More recently, technological changes enabling the production of less expensive items have targeted a new market with a low-to-medium level of disposable income.

Gold jewelry accounted for 20% of jewelry industry sales. Gold jewelry quadrupled from

1969 to 1990, while sales in the rest of the industry only tripled.

Money was made in this industry in two major ways: by selling a company's manufactured product; or by selling and marketing products manufactured by other companies. Some money could also be made through gold speculation.

The gold jewelry manufacturing industry involved the purchasing and alloying of the gold, manufacturing it into different products, and selling the products to various customers. Manufacturers purchased 24 karat gold bars from banks and other financial institutions, gold refiners, and traders. This was done via consignment and other short-term credit methods. For this reason, the manufacturer needed good credit in order to obtain the raw material.

The manufacturers then used alloys in their production process to transform the 24 karat gold into the various karats used for the finished product. Gold-tone metal or fake gold (called fashion jewelry) was seldom utilized by these companies; the inventory problems were too great. The gold was then manufactured into various finished products by machine or hand processes.

The finished products were then sold to wholesalers, retailers and other customers, often through catalog showrooms and televised home shopping clubs since jewelry manufacturers rarely sold directly to the public. Until 1987, much of the marketing and actual selling of these products took place on a highly personalized basis so strong salesperson-customer relations were necessary. More recently, the emphasis on catalog selling meant that many sales took place over the phone rather than in person.

The remaining sales and marketing took place through advertisements in industry journals and at trade shows. Two major trade shows took place annually in New York in February and August. The February show provided approximately 20% of the sales that the August show did. During the August show, the main objective was to prepare for the Christmas season. The main ordering did not take place until October or November, but the majority of the product line needed to be in at least sample form for the August show.

Industry revenues came primarily from finished product sales. The sale price generally was based on a gold price component in conjunction with the cost of labor component and other materials used. An additional charge was added when stones and other raw materials were involved.

Cost efficiency was a major key to success in the finished product area, especially when selling to wholesalers. Manufacturing and labor were the major cost components that needed to be evaluated. As such, many manufacturers had begun to use creative methods to minimize these costs. Some examples included:

- Reducing the number of hours worked per employee, rather than relying on seasonal labor which yielded high training costs for labor intensive jobs, as well as increased severance costs. According to unemployment guidelines, these seasonal employees were eligible to collect unemployment insurance worth 50% of their pay.
- Consolidating operations into smaller areas, or leasing space rather than owning it.
- Using offshore production.

The last major area where money was made was through the marketing of other companies'

Figure 2: Historical Gold Prices 1975-1991

Month	Price Per Ounce	Month	Price Per Ounce
Jan-75	176.8	Jan-83	479.9
Jul-75	165.7	Jul-83	423.1
Jan-76	125.3	Jan-84	370.9
Jul-76	118.0	Jul-84	346.4
Jan-77	132.9	Jan-85	302.8
Jul-77	144.0	Jul-85	317.8
Jan-78	173.7	Jan-86	345.5
Jul-78	189.3	Jul-86	348.9
Jan-79	227.6	Jan-87	408.3
Jul-79	295.3	Jul-87	450.8
Jan-80	680.0	Jan-88	476.6
Jul-80	643.3	Jul-88	437.6
Jan-81	557.4	Jan-89	404.0
Jul-81	408.8	Jul-89	375.0
Jan-82	384.1	Jan-90	410.0
Jul-82	340.1	Jul-90	362.5
		Jan-91	384.0

Source: Information obtained from *CRB Commodity Yearbook* 1991.

products. Jan Bell Marketing, Inc. was one of the first major companies to sell other companies' products almost exclusively. In 1989, they had $177 million in annual sales, with a net income from operations of $9.3 million, or $.30 per share [*Standard and Poors Corporation Records* 1990]. Their company strategy was to supply popular jewelry, watches, and other products which were purchased from jewelry manufacturers at exceptional price/quality values. Jan Bell's growth coincided with the increase of wholesale membership clubs, which on average marked up items only 10% over cost. Another important factor was the fluctuation in gold price during this time period as shown in Figure 2.

Four main components interact in the day-to-day workings of the gold jewelry manufacturing industry. They were the customer/distribution channel — where manufacturers distributed their finished product, the product itself, the labor force used to manufacture the product, and the inventory control method.

CUSTOMER/DISTRIBUTION CHANNELS

Customers included jewelry wholesalers, jewelry retail stores, and other channels of distribution, such as catalog showrooms, department stores, and home shopping clubs.

Jewelry Wholesalers

As of December 1990, there were 4,268 wholesalers in the jewelry industry. Most of these wholesalers were located in New York or California [*U.S. Dept. of Commerce, Bureau of the Census County Business Patterns* 1990]. They comprised the largest customer by weight of gold (based on conversations with key industry employees). Wholesalers acted as the middlemen or brokers between manufacturers and other types of customers. Since a great deal of this business was done by consignment, the wholesaler's risk could be minimized. However, this was an extremely competitive market. As a result, a wholesaler's profit margins were limited.

Two wholesalers were Metal Market and Rainbow's End. Metal Market was a national concern whose market was primarily in New York, Californi,a and Florida. Rainbow's End was a smaller wholesaler that distributed its products in the Northeast.

The wholesaler customer group was not expected to grow, but rather, to remain stable over the next five years. Success in selling to this area depended on the ability to produce a popular, competitively priced product that would be inexpensive to distribute. In addition, success depended on having relationships with a number of different wholesalers. These could be strengthened through incentives, awards, or bonuses.

Jewelry Retail Stores

There were 29,257 retail stores that sold jewelry as of December 1990. The largest concentration of these stores was in California, Florida, New York, Pennsylvania and Texas ["The Retail Jewelry Industry in 1986" 1989]. They comprised the second largest customer by volume in gold ounces. According to the U.S. Department of Commerce's 1982 Census of Retail Trade, 72% of the stores did 97% of the business. Retail stores had a much higher failure rate than did wholesalers in this risky market with wide fluctuations in profits. These jewelry retail stores were either classified as single location neighborhood stores or chain stores that might be found in a shopping mall, on a main street in a town, or in a flea market. The markup on the cost to the end consumer was usually considerable, ranging from 200% to 300%.

About one-third of jewelry sales took place in November and December, the Christmas selling season. The next largest month was May, largely Mother's Day sales.

A manufacturer might have many retail store customers, but they generally would not buy in large quantities other than during the Christmas season. They were more likely to first order display pieces and then order stock as necessary.

Success in this area depended on maintaining close personal contact with the buyers and helping retailers to determine appropriate stock levels based on demographics and seasonality. In addition, the manufacturer needed to have a good inventory and customer record-keeping system (which can be part of a management information system) to be able to determine retailer's purchases amounts and good credit standings.

Others

Catalog showrooms, department stores, mass merchandising/discount stores, and home shopping clubs comprised other customer distribution channels.

Catalog showrooms were similar to mail-order stores; some samples might be displayed on the floor, but the ordering was done mainly through catalogs. Many, such as Service Merchandise and Consumers Distributors, were chain operations with a high flow of merchandise. Extremely popular in the 1970s they remained as one of the manufacturer's larger customers. Much of the merchandise was low-to-medium priced, and was theoretically sold to the consumer at below-retail prices. As such, a key to success was the ability to provide a line that matched these needs at a cost-effective level. In addition, since these stores bought in such large quantity, it was important to have an effective method of shipping, with a quick turnaround time after the initial order.

Jewelry markups were generally highest in department stores, due to high overhead expenses. These chain or single location stores, like Macy's and Bloomingdales, generally sold medium to higher priced merchandise. While department stores historically had been the mainstay for U.S. consumers, some of the larger department store chains declared bankruptcy during the late 1980s. Such conditions might limit opportunities in this area. Some merchandise was sold through store catalogs, for example, Sears and J.C. Penneys. Keys to success included providing the appropriately priced merchandise and having an efficient distribution system to send the product to different locations if necessary.

Home shopping clubs became popular in the later 1980s, as cable television reached more and more homes. These were generally 24-hour television shows which displayed an item for a limited period of time at below-market price. Special segments were aired with only one manufacturer's products shown.

Home shopping clubs generally purchased in great volume, and had the opportunity to return unsold merchandise. They were generally broadcast on cable television channels. The number of homes that could receive cable transmissions was expected to grow 5% to 10% annually during the early 1990s. The number of home shopping clubs and their sales declined in the late 1980s, so, while their short-term future seemed certain, the market was not as prosperous as it had been and could not be expected to grow substantially.

Keys to success in this area included the ability to provide a large quantity of merchandise on short notice, the ability to provide a large variety of items should a special segment be aired, and a market sense of currently popular items. This was especially important since merchandise on these shows would initially be sold within a few days of purchase by the club.

PRODUCT

In 1990, sales in the gold jewelry market accounted for approximately $2.3 billion of the $12.2 billion in the gem and gold industry ["What the $12.2 Billion-a-Year Retail Industry Sells" 1990]. The gold jewelry category consisted of wedding bands, other rings, chains and necklaces, earrings, pins, pendants, and watches. Other fad items, such as earcuffs, were produced and distributed in metropolitan or college areas.

Gold Wedding Bands

In 1990, gold wedding bands comprised approximately 14% of total gold jewelry sales, or $322 million. As shown in Figure 3, the bulk of demand peaked during the summer months, reaching a high point of almost 12% in June. This meant that wedding band production took place largely in March and April with lows in January and February. This was almost counter-cyclical to the demand for other gold jewelry, which peaked in November and December, with the bulk of production taking place in August and September. Keys to success included advertisements in various brides and wedding magazines, the ability to target and manufacture new types of wedding bands, such as the tricolor bands that were popular in the mid-1980s, and the ability to do the fine engraving and detail work that these bands required.

One significant trend was that people were marrying later. In 1981, the average bride and groom were two years older than their counterparts 15 years earlier ["The Changing Customer" 1985]. While the brides and grooms were getting older, marriage rates were higher than in the previous 10 years. An opportunity existed in that the income level for married couples was also expected to rise thus enabling the purchase of more expensive rings.

Other Gold Rings

The main purchasers of gold rings were men. They spent an average of $112 per piece, compared with women who spent an average of $86 dollars per piece. Rings were generally sold

Figure 3: Percentage of Year's Weddings Per Month, 1988 & 1989

	1988	**1989**
January	5.0	5.8
February	5.2	5.8
March	7.3	7.0
April	7.6	7.9
May	9.3	9.5
June	11.6	11.7
July	9.4	9.5
August	10.2	9.7
September	9.6	9.4
October	9.0	8.3
November	7.4	7.2
December	8.4	8.2
	100.0	**100.0**

by weight, as described above. Some of the rings might have small precious or semiprecious stones, however this category did not include diamond engagement rings.

The rings were targeted toward different age and ethnic groups. There were assortments of rings for under $50 as well as rings for under $500. Most rings were sold in the Northeast, where the population was not expected to grow as quickly as in other regions ["Jewelry Store Sales - 1988" 1989].

Keys to success included the ability to quickly produce popular items, as well as the ability to maintain a current inventory using computer systems to monitor item production.

Other Gold Jewelry

This category consisted of chains and necklaces, earrings, earcuffs, pins, pendants, and watches.

Gold chain imports from Italy fell more than 24% in the late 1980s. Demand did not decrease, rather more U.S. companies were producing their own chains. Most gold watches were sold in the Central and Western U.S. This was in contrast to other types of jewelry, which were sold mainly in the Northeast.

Pendants accounted for the highest volume of items sold, followed by chains and earrings. Most of this merchandise was sold to wholesalers, and then distributed to retailers and others.

Opportunities existed in the number of commercial ventures that promoted licensed items. This included the manufacturer making a gold pendant out of another company's logo or trademark. These licensing agreements were popular and lucrative during the 1980s. Keys to success were similar to those of gold rings.

LABOR FORCE

The production and professional staff had different requirements in terms of skill levels, hiring, and compensation. The production staff included skilled craftsmen and unskilled laborers. The professional staff included salespeople, managerial personnel, accounting personnel, and other financial personnel.

Production Staff

Two factors were important when analyzing the production staff:

- The seasonal nature of the industry, and
- The need for skilled labor.

One-third of a company's sales took place in November and December. As such, extra labor was required from August through November. Very little work was done in the first quarter of a calendar year, so manufacturers had several options to consider. They could hire seasonal labor

— thus minimizing the fulltime crew to manufacture for inventory during slow periods or reduce work hours for regular staff during slow periods, or combine the two approaches.

The problem with having seasonal staff during peak periods was that a great deal of the finishing work was done by hand (e.g., diamond cutting, stone placement). Skilled craftsmen were needed, and they could generally command better positions and wages than seasonal or temporary jobs provided. However, other levels of handwork could be performed by seasonal workers, or by workers with reduced hours.

In addition, several alternatives existed with remuneration: hourly wages, straight salary, profit sharing, and bonuses. In the past, straight salary with some form of profit sharing and bonuses had been used for craftsmen. Less skilled production laborers had been paid on an hourly basis. Another possibility was to base employees' pay on the number of finished products. While this seemed to be a return to the sweatshop environment of the early 20th Century, it was a viable alternative for a skilled craftsman.

More recently, manufacturers had the unskilled portion of their production done offshore, for example in Barbados or Jamaica, where lower labor cost outweighed the increased transportation, inventory, and security costs.

Professional Staff

This group of personnel had to possess financial skills and obviously could not be hired on a seasonal basis. The major issue with the professional staff was the type of remuneration. The professional staff was paid a base salary, unlike the salesperson, who received a base salary in addition to commission.

INVENTORY CONTROL

Monitoring inventory was one of the most complex tasks in the manufacturing process. A simplified version of the route that purchased gold takes is shown in Figure 4.

As shown in Figure 4, the gold arrived, was checked in, and was sent to the refinery, where the various karats of gold were alloyed. From there, it was either sent to the wax department to be made into pendants, earrings, or rings, or to the assembly department to be made into coil for various types of chains. Once the base product was completed, it was sent to the various finishing departments for satin finish, diamond cutting, and stone placement. The finished products were sent to the showroom or finished goods inventory, depending on the customer order. Next, the customer orders were sent to the inventory control department to be priced. From there the product/order was sent to the shipping department and on to the customer distribution channel. In the case of returns, the product was either cleaned in the finishing department and returned to the showroom or finished goods inventory, or melted down in the refinery and sent to the various production departments.

Inventory management tracked the gram weight of gold in each department on a daily basis. In the past, this process was tracked and monitored by hand through daily inventory control

Figure 4: Inventory Movement Cycle

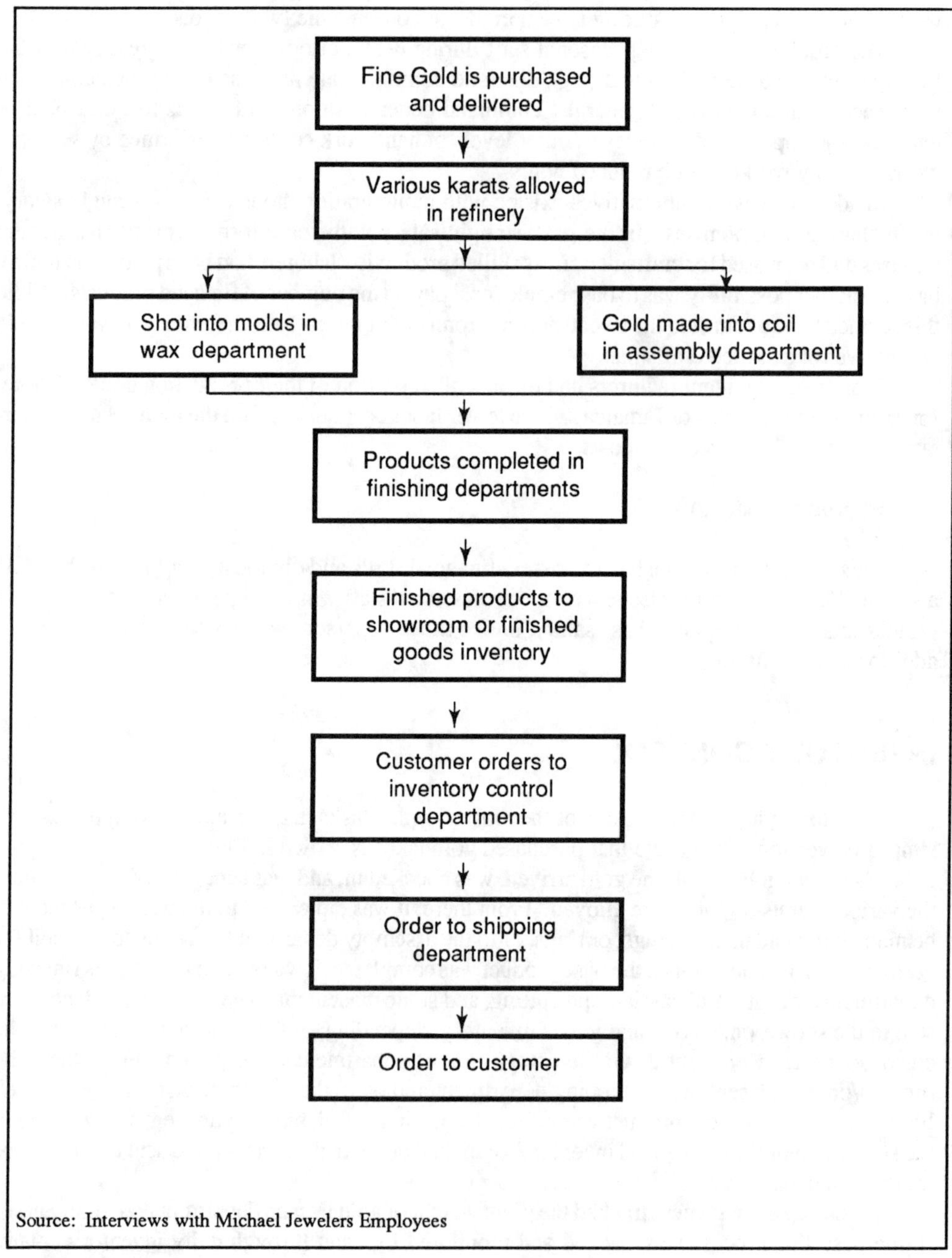

Source: Interviews with Michael Jewelers Employees

records. Today, more companies have management information systems (MIS).

A physical inventory was done on a monthly basis in each department. This included weighing each piece of gold in trays or plastic bags to obtain the gross weight. Much of this work was done by hand. This process was also becoming more sophisticated, especially with the use of bar codes, or UPC type codes ["Bar Codes Tagged as the Future of Speedy Inventory Control" 1989]. Using this process, a tray was placed on a scale, weighed, and facts — such as excess weight — were entered into a computer. A bar code tag was then produced and attached to the tray. The bar codes were read by a hand-held portable bar code reader. Not only was the physical inventory performed faster and labor costs saved, accuracy was also greatly improved.

Major inventories took place at the end of December, after the Christmas season, and at the beginning of July, when the jewelry industry closes down. In addition, bank auditors conducted quarterly inventories to examine the amount of gold owned and on consignment for credit and reporting purposes. Significant variances in the physical inventory as compared to the "paper" or MIS indicated inventory, could result in a reduced credit rating and would require an immediate follow-up inventory.

GOLD SPECULATION

Gold speculation went hand in hand with a company's daily management in this industry. Manufacturers attempted to purchase raw materials at the lowest possible price. In the gold jewelry manufacturing industry, the most expensive raw material was the actual piece of gold. Buyers in this market monitored trends and bought gold at the lowest possible price.

Gold purchases were carried out on a daily basis to take advantage of lower gold prices when prices were expected to increase in the future (as per conversations with employees at Michael Jewelers, Inc.). A manufacturer was also expected to own a certain percentage of the gold in its inventory.

Jewelry manufacturers could purchase gold through various markets. The major, more stable markets were banks and other financial institutions which based the gold price in relation to a London fix (the price of gold per ounce on the London Market). These institutions charged a premium for providing this type of brokerage service. The monthly price per gold ounce for the period 1975-1991 is shown in Figure 2. During this time, the price of gold generally ranged between $110 and $676 dollars per ounce, displaying wide fluctuations. Its low was $110 in August 1976 and its high was $676 in September 1980 *[CRB Commodity Yearbook* 1991].

THE COMPETITION

The jewelry manufacturing business was highly competitive, with competitors ranging from small regional suppliers of jewelry to manufacturers with national distribution capabilities. The principle competitive factors in the market were price, quality, design, and customer service [*Michael Jewelers 10K* 1988].

Figure 5: Sales and Profits for Jewelry Manufacturers (Millions of Dollars)

Company	1991 Sales	1991 Profits	1990 Sales	1990 Profits	1989 Sales	1989 Profits
Designcraft	20.3	(2.8)	31.5	0.1	45.6	(7.1)
Harlyn	29.3	1.6	31.3	1.9	24.8	1.5
Jewelmasters	46.1	(1.5)	52.8	(1.0)	65.3	1.0
Michael Jewelers	120.2	2.1	85.4	2.2	95.5	.926
Richton	20.7	(1.2)	22.2	0.4	30.5	(3.0)
Swank	130.0	5.4	137.7	6.8	143.6	10.1
Totals	**366.6**	**3.6**	**360.9**	**10.4**	**405.3**	**1.4**

Source: Information obtained from *Moody's Industrials 1992.*

1991 sales and profits of the six major publicly-held competitors in the gold jewelry manufacturing industry in early 1992 — Michael Jewelers, Harlyn, Jewelmasters, Richton, Swank and Designcraft, are shown in Figure 5.

Harlyn Products

Harlyn Products was headquartered in Los Angeles, California, In 1991, Harlyn had $29 million in sales—a 6% decrease from 1990. Net profit decreased by 15% during the same period. The stock price fluctuated between 2 1/4 to 2 3/4 from 1987 to 1991, which was similar to Michael Jewelers' stock price fluctuations. In 1991, another year of record earnings was reported with net income of $1.6 million.

Harlyn's main business and strength was the special-order manufacture and sale of various types of gold, silver, and precious and semiprecious stone jewelry to retail jewelers and department stores throughout the U.S. Their customers included Sears, J.C. Penney, Kay Jewelers, WalMart, and Saks. The company's weaknesses were the production of low-priced items and a lack of specific licenses.

In late 1989, Harlyn acquired George Hoffman Jewelry Manufacturing, a Beverly Hills-based manufacturer and marketer of fine diamond jewelry, in the hopes of broadening its product line and enhancing its reputation.

The company had followed the trend towards offshore production and operated a production facility in Bangkok through which it planned to increase foreign sales. Therefore, Harlyn had strengths in both the manufacturing and sales ends. The company had 185 employees and felt that employee morale was good.

In 1988, the company instituted a cost-reduction program to cut shipping, selling, general and administration expenses. By 1990, it had achieved its goal of a 25% reduction. Management also had a goal to increase sales by 50% from 1989 to 1991. This goal was not achieved; sales increased only by 18%.

Jewelmasters

Jewelmasters' headquarters and manufacturing facility were located in West Palm Beach, Florida. Company sales decreased from \$65.3 million in 1989 to \$46.1 million in 1991. In 1990 and 1991, Jewelmasters experienced net losses of \$1.0 million and \$1.5 million respectively. The total number of employees as of February 1991 was 441.

Jewelmasters also manufactured fine gold jewelry, but its distribution channels differed from its competitors. It leased departments in stores — such as Wanamakers, May Company, Bonwit Tellers, and Woodward and Lothrops — in 147 locations. Over 43% of its retail sales were attributable to the leased locations in May Company. However, restructuring within May Company caused four of nine departments in May's Goldwater chain to close. Products sold included those manufactured by Jewelmasters, as well as those manufactured by competitors.

Merchandise was sold at retail prices ranging from \$250 to \$2,800 for gold rings with and without semiprecious gems, and \$35 to \$8,500 for miscellaneous gold jewelry. These prices exceeded those of Michael Jewelers since Jewelmasters had a strong background in higher priced jewelry, but minimal experience with lower to medium priced items.

The company's marketing strategy was to offer exclusively designed, fine jewelry reflecting the latest trends and styles in fashion at competitive prices. This effort was aimed primarily at female customers, who were the primary purchasers through its retail outlets.

The company believed that its success was largely dependent on its manufacturing capability, which enabled it to closely monitor the quality of workmanship of its fine jewelry, and on its quick response to market intelligence which allowed it to respond to the latest fashion and style trends. Its goal for the 1990s was to continue to increase cost efficiency. The company was also committed to improving upon and achieving the full potential of its MIS.

Richton

Richton's main office was in New York City. 1991 sales were \$20.7 million — a 32% decrease from 1989. The company attributed its "soft sales" to a decreased demand for fashion jewelry starting in the fourth quarter of 1988. The total number of employees as of April 1990 was 367.

Richton was an international concern, which manufactured and marketed its Canadian products through Coro Inc., and its European products through RIL. Approximately 95% of its products were sold in Canada. The company had more than 10,000 items, some of which were sold under the Oscar de la Renta brand name, in addition to Dicini and Pavanne labels. The company felt employee relations, which were covered primarily by a collective bargaining agreement, were good.

The company had strengths in foreign distribution, but a weakness in U.S. distribution. It also had a strength in its trademarked items. Most of Richton's merchandise was medium to high priced; the company offered very little lower priced merchandise.

Swank

Swank Inc. was headquartered in Massachusetts. It manufactured and distributed jewelry as well as other gift and accessory items. Net sales for 1990 were \$138 million with profits of \$6.8

million. Swank's jewelry line accounted for approximately 35% of sales.

The company operated 19 factory outlet stores and 8 production and distribution facilities in Massachusetts, Arkansas, Connecticut, Missouri, and the Caribbean. It distributed its product under the Anne Klein label in Canada, Singapore, Australia, New Zealand, and Europe.

The company's strengths included knowledge and use of specialty and outlet stores and ownership of the Anne Klein label. Some weaknesses included the lack of concentration on a jewelry line.

Designcraft

Designcraft's main office was in New York City. Designcraft manufactured and sold a wide range of stamped and cast precious metal products for large-volume customers in the U.S. Finished goods were sold to wholesalers, catalog houses, large chain stores, and mass merchandisers. Sales had declined since 1988, from $46 million in 1989 to $20 million in 1991. This represented a reduction in sales of 57% in only two years.

In April 1989, Designcraft sold all of the assets of Namdur Inc. for approximately $696,000 and in January 1990, sold substantially all of the assets of Howard H. Sweet & Sons Inc. for approximately $4,530,000. These were Designcraft's two major holdings. In early 1990, Designcraft filed for Chapter 11. As of 1991, there were only 14 employees in the corporation. The future of Designcraft was unknown. They no longer, however, posed a threat as a competitor.

THE COMPANY

Michael Jewelers was incorporated as an S Corporation in 1975 by two brothers, Michael and Anthony Paolercio. Its initial locations included basements, backyards, bedrooms, and closets in the homes of various friends and relatives. Capital and financial advice was also provided by these friends and relations.

Michael Jewelers' design of a diamond-cut, lightweight gold charm was a major breakthrough. These charms were designed to sell for "in between" occasions, such as presents for Mom, Dad, the boss, and the like ["Michael Anthony Goes for Rope," 1989]. Michael Jewelers' strength was identifying what the consumer was willing to spend and designing an affordable and attractive product line. One of the products that helped bring the company to prominence was a simple #1 Mom charm that sold for $15 to $20. Now its #1 line included #1 hairdresser, #1 godmother, and the like. The growth in the company was also linked to the strong general economic conditions during the 1980s.

In 1984, the company branched into a new product type: the licensing of bunny charms for Playboy Enterprises. By 1986, its licensed product line included major league baseball, basketball, Ghostbusters, Peanuts, Garfield, and Popeye. At that point, sales had doubled. Other licenses included Batman, Nintendo, and Disney characters.

The company's products were sold to over 600 customers throughout the U.S. Sales were made mainly to wholesalers, and also to retail stores, catalog showrooms, department stores, mass

Figure 6: Michael Jewelers, Inc.
Organization Chart

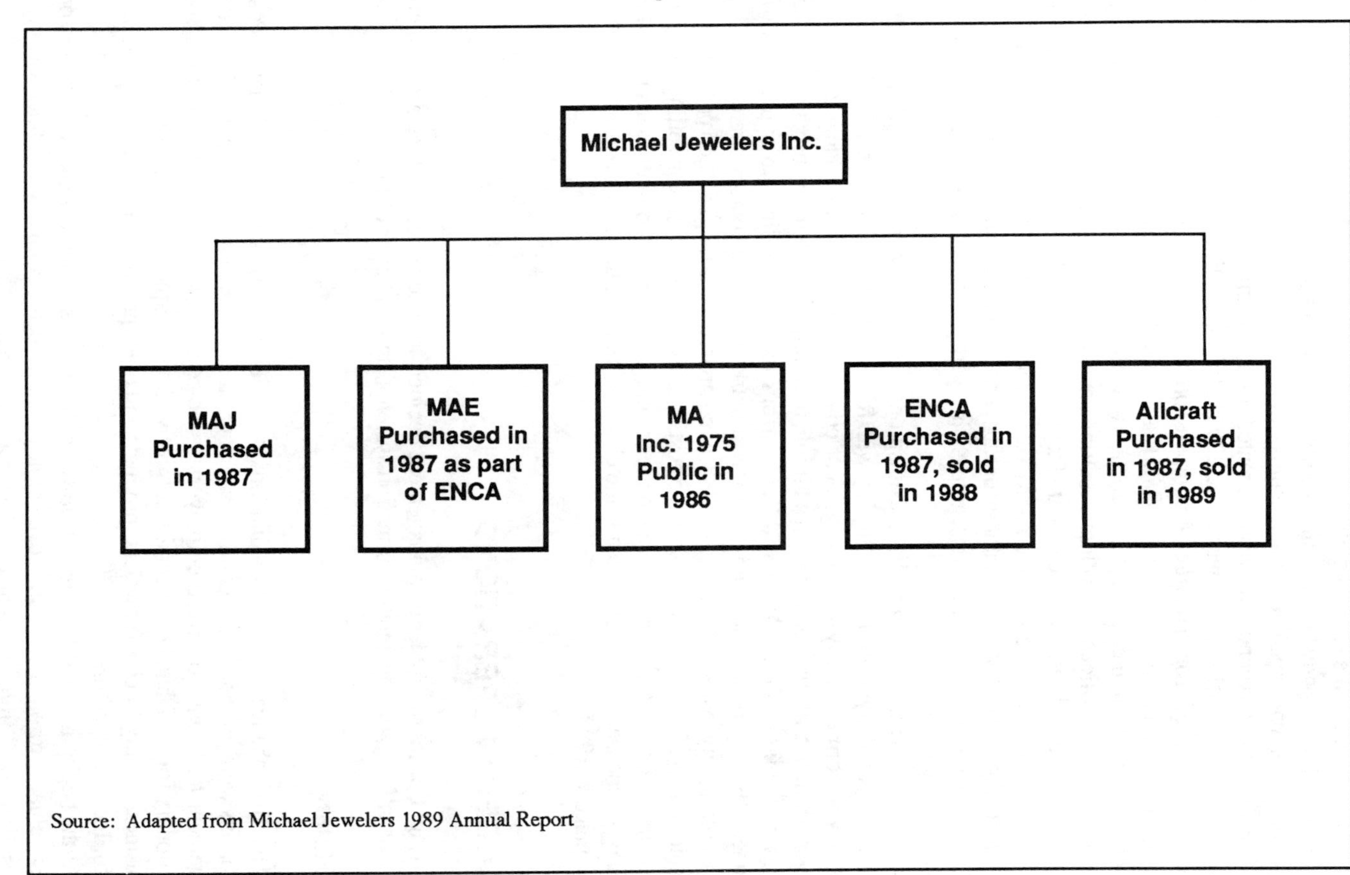

Source: Adapted from Michael Jewelers 1989 Annual Report

merchandisers, and home shopping clubs.

In 1986, the company raised $8 million dollars through a public offering and earmarked this money for equipment expenditures and acquisitions.

The equipment expenditure was designated for a cadcam computer used to design lighter weight, more detailed charms. It was especially useful for the licensed items where a potential charm could be traced from a picture. A computer process could build the charm up into a three-dimensional form and create the mold. While this required a high capital expenditure, the return on investment was favorable. The cadcam products were fairly inexpensive to produce, and sold well.

Figure 6 shows Michael Jewelers' resulting acquisitions. These included the purchase of MAJ, a rope chain and bangle bracelet manufacturer in 1987; ENCA, a manufacturer of earrings in 1987 (sold in 1988, one division — MAE — retained); and Allcraft charms in 1987 to complement the original Michael Anthony product line. Michael Anthony later sold this division in 1989. Until MA was purchased, most gold chains were purchased in Italy. By 1992, there was almost no Italian activity.

One problem that arose from those acquisitions, however, was that the expansion was much too fast. The company went from a company with fewer than 300 employees in 1985, to over 400 in 1987. The former family-led management could not adapt to this change and hired new managers from outside the company. In addition, the company added new product lines, such as earrings and rope chains, that were different from its previous lines to appeal to different consumers. Each product line required different marketing and inventory strategies.

The company lost $.22 per share in 1988, as compared to earnings of $.66 per share in 1987. The main causes of the loss were a rise in the cost of sales, and an increase in selling, general, and administrative expenses. These cost increases could be attributed to poor management of the company's expenses. It was clear that some changes, many in the manufacturing segment, had to take place in 1988.

CHANGES IN OPERATIONS

In light of these problems, management decided to take action in three areas to control expenses: staffing, management information systems, and higher priced product lines.

Staffing

The first change was a re-evaluation of top employees and their salaries. Position descriptions were provided for second tier staff and salaries were based on tasks performed. The management team gave overpaid employees a choice of a pay cut or termination. This was revolutionary for what had been a family company. Some employees were terminated and went into business selling Michael Jewelers' products and other products themselves. Others went to work for local competitors.

At the beginning of 1990, Michael Jewelers felt that its remaining employees were one of its most valuable resources. To improve employee morale, the company instituted weekly cash lotteries along with frequent company picnics and parties.

Figure 7: Michael Jewelers, Inc.
Comparison of Financial Data 1990 to 1991 (Thousands of Dollars)

	1990	% of 1990 Sales	1991	% of 1991 Sales
Net Sales	85,388		120,194	
Cost of Sales	71,452	83.68%	96,646	80.41%
Gross Profit	13,936	16.32%	23,547	19.59%
SG&A Expenses	8,702	10.19%	15,727	13.08%
Operating Income	5,234	6.13%	7,820	6.51%
Net Income (Loss)	2,206	2.58%	2,131	1.77%

Source: Information obtained from *Moody's Industrial* 1991.

Management Information Systems

Another step toward expense control was the introduction of a computer-based management information and inventory control system. A computer department was created and staffed to develop this system, which replaced much of the work that had been done by hand. A mainframe computer and PCs were used to track costs, prices, and invoices, and to perform other tasks. In addition, many of the remaining staff members were trained to use computers.

Higher Priced Product Line

The management team decided to diversify its product line and offer higher priced jewelry. The Maurice Katz line, acquired in 1989, was composed of heavier, more artistic and more expensive merchandise than the company had dealt with before. The production and sale of these products required skilled craftsmen and different product processes, as well as different marketing approaches. The company trained employees to handle these special new product requirement. By 1992, sales of this line had not developed as hoped and plans were made to drop the new line.

As a result of action in these three areas, the company's financial picture improved in 1991, in spite of the problems with the Katz line. Figure 7 compares financial data for 1990 and 1991. Specific reductions were made in general, selling, and administrative expenses.

The company's stock prices fluctuated between $2 and $4 for the 1991 fiscal year. Financial advisors at Prudential-Bache felt that this was more a reflection of the stagnant stock market than an indication of the company's strength.

THE PRODUCT LINE

Michael Jewelers' product line generally ranged in wholesale price from $10 to $700, with an average item selling for approximately $20 [*Michael Jewelers 10K* 1989].

Type of Product

A breakdown of the product line in 1989 is given in Figure 8. Charms and pendants accounted for half of net sales in 1989. The next largest line was chains, which represented approximately one-fifth of total sales. This was a turn around from 1988, when charms and pendants had represented 35% of total sales, and chains 41%. In 1990 Michael Jewelers' mainstay products — charms and pendants — represented more than half of the company's sales.

Licensed Products

The company's licensed products in 1992 came from Playboy Enterprises, Major League Baseball, National Football League Properties, National Basketball Association, National Hockey League Services, Nintendo, and Disney (including Muppets). The sports charms had proven to be successful, especially for catalog showroom stores.

Figure 8: Michael Jewelers Product Line
Percent of Net Sales, 1989

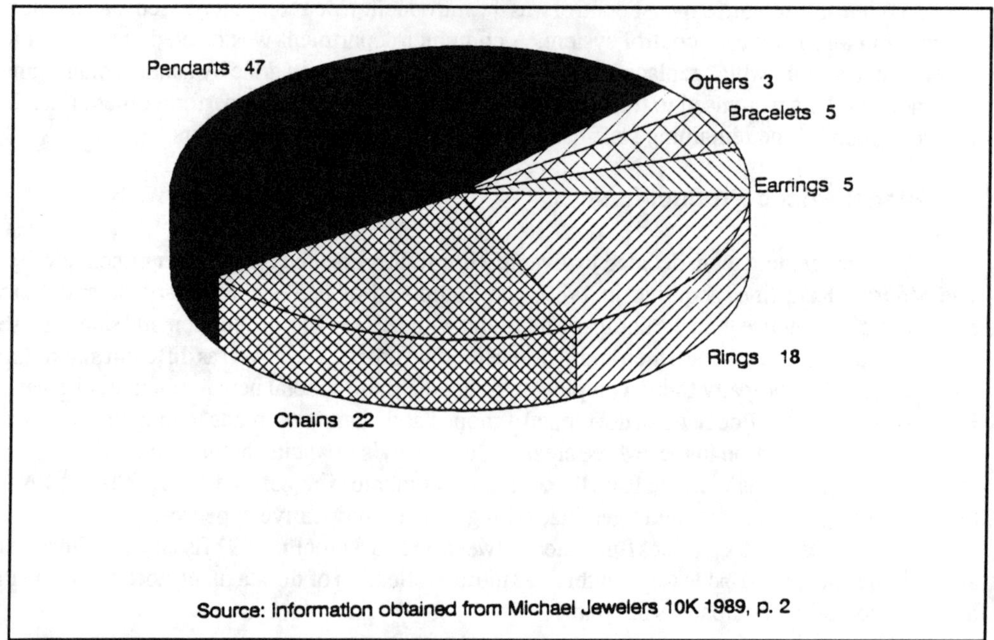

Source: Information obtained from Michael Jewelers 10K 1989, p. 2

SALES AND MARKETING

Marketing and sales were carried out by the company's in-house sales force, primarily at the showroom in Mount Vernon, New York, and through the use of product catalogs.

In 1988, Michael Jewelers sponsored a Marketing Seminar for retail jewelers. The topics included trends in marketing, sales training display, and management. The company also discussed setting and meeting goals, collecting demographic information, and telemarketing. The sales staff was able to provide a great deal of this information to Michael Jewelers' retail customers, which helped to build a good relationship.

Michael Paolercio retained involvement in many of the larger accounts. Five of the company's largest customers (out of 600) accounted for close to 20% of 1990 sales. One customer alone counted for more than 5%.

Foreign sales were slightly higher than 1% of total sales for 1989. This had been targeted to increase through the 1990s, especially in the European markets. Figures 9 and 10 give a more in-depth view of the financial position of the company.

Figure 9: Michael Jewelers, Inc.
Income Statement 1989-1991 (Years Ended Jun. 30)
(Amounts in Thousands)

INCOME STATEMENT	1989	1990	1991
NET SALES	$95,468	$85,388	$120,194
COST OF GOODS SOLD	$83,472	$71,452	$96,646
GROSS PROFIT	$11,996	$13,936	$23,548
SELLING, GENERAL, & ADMINISTRATIVE EXPENSE	$8,734	$8,702	$15,727
OPERATING INCOME BEFORE DEPRECIATION	$3,262	$5,234	$7,821
GOLD CONSIGNMENT FEE, NET	$818	$849	$1,405
OPERATING PROFIT	$2,444	$4,385	$6,416
INTEREST EXPENSE	$1,605	$1,171	$1,559
LITIGATION SETTLEMENT	($535)		
GAIN ON SALE OF DIVISION ASSETS		$445	
GAIN ON SALES OF REAL PROPERTY	$995		
OTHER EXPENSE, NET	$179	$571	($1,194)
PRETAX INCOME	$1,478	$4,230	$3,663
TOTAL INCOME TAXES	$552	$2,025	$1,532
INCOME BEFORE EXTRAORDINARY ITEMS & DISCONTINUED OPERATIONS	$926	$2,205	$2,131
INCOME ON DISPOSAL, NET	($183)		
DISCONTINUED OPERATIONS	($84)		
NET INCOME	$659	$2,205	$2,131

Source: Information obtained from Moody's Industrial, 1991.
Information obtained from Moody's Industrial, 1992.

**Figure 10: Michael Jewelers, Inc.
Balance Sheet 1989-1991 (Years Ended Jun. 30)
(Amounts in Thousands)**

	1989	1990	1991
ASSETS:			
CURRENT ASSETS:			
CASH & EQUIVALENTS	$3,297	$5,761	$634
NET RECEIVABLES	$10,571	$9,335	$14,399
INVENTORIES	$29,735	$5,843	$14,494
PREPAID EXPENSES & OTHER CURRENT ASSETS	$1,703	$1,144	$779
TOTAL CURRENT ASSETS	$45,306	$22,083	$30,306
MACHINERY & EQUIPMENT, NET	$5,150	$5,935	$7,991
INTANGIBLES	$1,360	$1,253	$1,125
OTHER ASSETS	$836	$1,501	$2,484
TOTAL NONCURRENT ASSETS	$7,346	$8,689	$11,600
TOTAL ASSETS	$52,652	$30,772	$41,906
LIABILITIES & EQUITY			
	1989	1990	1991
CURRENT LIABILITIES			
ACCOUNTS PAYABLE-GOLD SUPPLIER	$24,529		
ACCOUNTS PAYABLE-TRADE	$468	$717	$878
LOAN PAYABLE	$1,689		
CURRENT PORTION OF LONG TERM DEBT	$595	$1,235	$1,202
TAXES PAYABLE	$177	$831	$53
ACCRUED EXPENSES	$1,792	$1,644	$3,488
DEFERRED TAXES			$203
TOTAL CURRENT LIABILITIES	$27,561	$4,427	$7,513
LONG TERM DEBT	$10,570	$9,658	$8,456
DEFERRED TAXES	$117	$1,627	
TOTAL NONCURRENT LIABILITIES	$10,570	$9,775	$10,083
TOTAL LIABILITIES	$38,131	$14,202	$17,596
EQUITY:			
PREFERRED STOCK			
COMMON STOCK	$5	$5	$7
ADDITIONAL PAID IN CAPITAL	$12,681	$12,681	$21,888
RETAINED EARNINGS	$1,835	$4,041	$6,172
DEFERRED COMPENSATION			$3,600
LESS: TREASURY STOCK		$157	$157
COMMON EQUITY	$14,521	$16,570	$24,310
TOTAL EQUITY	$14,521	$16,570	$24,310
TOTAL LIABILITIES & EQUITY	$52,652	$30,772	$41,906

Source: Information obtained from Moody's Industrial, 1991.
Information obtained from Moody's Industrial, 1992.

INTERNAL STRENGTHS AND WEAKNESSES

Conversations with and surveys completed by the top management indicated the following strategic strengths and weaknesses for Michael Jewelers in early 1992:

Strengths:

- A high-quality product with a low production cost. This was improved by use of cadcam technology — a mainstay for Michael Jewelers, whose motto was "Quality and Style are our only constants." The company's cadcam technology enabled it to provide a wide range of licensed and other items with a quick turnaround.
- A workforce with a low turnover and high level of reliability. This was reinforced through incentives, employee newsletters, as well as morale builders, such as parties and raffles. There was never any question of unionizing the shop.
- An efficient group of major distribution channels.
- A wide variety of licensed items.
- Good relationships with a variety of customers. No one customer accounted for the bulk of the company's sales.

Weaknesses:

- The lack of a strong management team. This happened in part because Michael Jewelers was a family business, with a lack of professionally trained top staff. This weakness was minimized in 1989, when more outside professionals were brought in.
- Low gross margins in general in the jewelry industry, which Michael Jewelers felt could not be improved upon.
- A mature market; there was limited growth in the company's market.
- Little to no experience with retail operations.
- Little experience with high priced jewelry.

CORPORATE PHILOSOPHY

Michael and Anthony felt that fiscal 1989 was when the company rebounded from its earlier problems. Reductions in workforce and operating expenses were implemented. Also product prices were increased, and less profitable accounts were reduced. The major events were as follows:

- Significant reduction of selling, general and administrative expenses
- Significant reduction of workforce
- Increased productivity
- Divestiture of unprofitable manufacturing operations
- Closing of unprofitable showroom operations

In 1992, the company wanted to take advantage of its strengths: good products and dedicated people [*Michael Jewelers, Inc. Annual Report* 1989].

TOWARDS THE FUTURE

The jewelry industry is highly cyclical, and is affected by changes in disposable personal income and consumer confidence. During the first two quarters of 1990, the rate of increase in disposable personal income and expenditures slowed in the U.S. The University of Michigan's Consumer Sentiment Index had declined steadily from 1989 to a 17-year low of approximately 45 in 1991. Historically, falling consumer spending has resulted in a drop in consumer spending on discretionary items such as jewelry. As the recession continued into 1992, economists predicted a slow and gradual climb with total GDP expected to increase at an annual rate of 1.0% to 1.5% over the next few years. One of the problems, economists said, was "a heavy consumer debt load" [*U.S. Industrial Outlook* 1991].

Michael Jewelers' management was exploring a variety of strategic directions for the company to pursue in the 1990s in light of economist's prediction. One alternative was to modify the product line to contain more medium- to high-priced merchandise, a market segment which Michael Jewelers had not been able to penetrate. Marketing management believed this was a sound strategy because analysis pointed to increased demand in this market segment. One manager cited an industrial outlook survey which stated, "the bulk of the baby boom generation is now middle aged and approaching their highest income years." Their homes have already been purchased, leaving substantial discretionary income. As they age, their disposable incomes will increase even further, fueling purchases of high-quality, luxury products such as jewelry" [*U.S. Industrial Outlook* 1991]. The marketing group believed that even though Michael Jewelers had little experience in this market segment, the company would capitalize on the "Michael Jewelers" brand image and success in the low-medium priced market. Michael Jewelers' competition was not as widely known and did not have the same brand image and consumer loyalty. There would be little additional cost since Michael Jewelers already had experienced artisans.

Other key managers thought that this alternative would not work. They thought that this strategy was too radical and would require a major marketing campaign involving a sizeable investment. They argued, "why enter a new market, especially when we have little to no experience in it?" A senior executive at Michael Jewelers cited the fact that the company had failed at a medium- to high-priced jewelry line and stated that the company should focus on its existing customer base and expand their existing product line. The low-end price of the jewelry business would thrive as a result of the 1990-1992 recession because people turn to popularly priced jewelry in difficult economic times. Their alternative was for the product line to continue to represent its area of expertise: a low- to medium-priced assortment of this type of product, with a small selection of higher priced merchandise. Historically, Michael Jewelers had created a respected name for this type of product: its production methods were considered to be state-of-the-art, and its quality was recognized as being high. The competition did not have the same customer distribution channels and brand loyalty as Michael Jewelers. The executive added, "We know we're the best in this market — let's use our established name and dominate by increasing the product line with similar low priced products of high quality." One manager also cited a recent *Business Week* article which contradicted the marketing organization's position [*Business Week* 1992]. The article stated that businesses will change in the 1990s and improve their competitive position by eliminating an entire layer of management — middle management. Many of these jobs are currently occupied by "baby-boom" executives, thus reducing the affluence and influence of that group. A less affluent and more price-conscious market for jewelry could, therefore, be expected.

In light of these arguments, management was wondering what to do about these and other pressing strategic options.

REFERENCES AND BACKGROUND READINGS

"Bar Codes Tagged as the Future of Speedy Inventory Control," *Jewelers' Circular-Keystone*, October 1989, pp 141-142.

Business Week, "Downward Mobility," March 23, 1992, pp 56-63.

"Companies use temps to cut costs," *Jewelers' Circular-Keystone Directory*, July 1989, p. 901.

CRB Commodity Yearbook, 1991.

Edelstein, Cindy, "A 1990's Kind of Goldrush," *Jewelers' Circular-Keystone*, May 1989, pp. 56-60.

"Financial Embarassments in the Jewelry Industry," *Jewelers' Circular-Keystone Directory*, July 1989, p. 912.

Flickinger, Bruce, "Public jewelry retailers strong, suppliers mixed in 1988," *Jewelers' Circular-Keystone*, August 1989, pp 334-353.

"Gems and Gold: The Jeweler's Sales Winners", *Jewelers' Circular-Keystone Directory*, July 1989, p. 900.

"Gold and Silver Prices," *Jewelers' Circular-Keystone Directory*, July 1989, p. 951.

Harlan Products Annual Report, 1989.

Harlan Products Form 10K, 1989.

Holmes, Deborah, "The Changing Customer," *Jewelers' Circular-Keystone*, September Part II, 1985, p. 182.

"How Jewelry Stores Divide Up the Sales," Jewelers' *Circulary-Keystone Directory*, July 1989, p. 902.

"Industry Demographics", *Jewelers' Circular-Keystone Directory*, July 1989, p. 900.

"Interactive TV Shopping Still Growing Slowly", *Jewelers' Circular-Keystone Directory*, July 1989, p. 900.

Jan Bell Marketing Inc. Annual Report, 1988.

Jan Bell Marketing Inc. Form 10K, 1988.

Jan Bell Marketing Inc. Form 10Q, 1988. Jewelmasters, Inc. Annual Report, 1989.

Jewelmasters, Inc. Form 10K, 1989.

"Jewelry Store Sales - 1988," *Jewelers' Circular-Keystone Directory*, July 1989, p. 905

"Manufacturers Need to Raise Quality," *Jewelers' Circular-Keystone Directory* , July 1989, p. 904.

"Marketing Should Leave Nothing To Chance," *Jewelers' Circular-Keystone*, December 1988, pp 56-58.

"Michael Anthony Goes for Rope," *American Jewelry Manufacturer*, February 1989, pp. 34-39.

Michael Jewelers' Inc. Form 10K, 1988.
Michael Jewelers' Inc. Annual Report, 1989.
Michael Jewelers' Inc. Form 10K, 1989
Michael Jewelers' Inc. Form 10Q, 1989
Mockler, Robert J., *Business Planning and Policy Formulation*, 3rd Edition, New York, NY, D and G Publishers, 1983.
Mockler, Robert J., *Strategic Management and Implementation, An Integrated Decision Making Approach*, Harrisburg, PA, Merrill Publishing, 1992.
Moody's Industrial Manual, 1990.
"Precious Metal Jewelry Manufacturers in 1986," *Jewelers' Circular-Keystone Directory*, July 1989, p. 906.
Richton International Corporation Annual Report, 1989.
Richton International Corporation Form 10K, 1989.
"Shared Work," *Kilogram*, April 1990, p. 1.
Shore, Russell, "Gold Demand Jewelry Booms, Investors Yawn," *Jewelers' Circular-Keystone*, May 1989, pp. 68-71.
Shore, Russell, "Jewelry Costs Could Rise With Proposed Sanctions", *Jewelers' Circular-Keystone*, January 1990, p. 200.
Standard and Poors Corporation Records, 1990. "Summer at the JA: Show Me Something New," *Jewelers' Circular-Keystone*, September 1989, p. 48.
"Ten Demographic Myths," *Jewelers' Circular-Keystone*, September Part II, 1985, pp. 200-202
"The Best Small Companies," *Business Week*, May 22, 1989, pp. 101-104.
"The Retail Jewelry Industry In 1986," *Jewelers' Circular-Keystone Directory*, July 1989, p. 906.
"Total Jewelry Businesses," *Jewelers' Circular-Keystone Directory*, July 1989, p. 912.
"What the $12.2 Billion-a-Year Retail Jewelry Industry Sells," *Jewelers' Circular-Keystone Directory*, July 1990, p. 900.
"When Couples Marry," *Jewelers' Circular-Keystone Directory*, July 1989, p. 910.
U.S. Department of Commerce, Bureau of the Census Country Business Patterns, 1990.
U.S Industrial Outlook, 1991.

NORDSTROM INC.: THE RETAIL WEARING APPAREL INDUSTRY

Wallin and Nordstrom, a shoe store, opened its doors in 1901. During the early part of the century business flourished, and in 1923 a second store was opened. After half a century of increased shoe sales, Wallin and Nordstrom expanded into apparel. Today the company's name is Nordstrom. In 1991, the company had 69 stores with sales of $2.89 billion and a net income of $115.8 million [Sack 1991].

The retail apparel industry changed dramatically in the early 1990s. R.H. Macy's, the industry's leading retailer, filed for bankruptcy protection in 1992. Alexander's, a major New York retailer, was also seeking bankruptcy protection in early 1992 [Silverman 1992]. On the other hand, The Gap, a San Francisco-based specialty retailer, posted $2.5 billion in sales and $100 million in earnings in 1991 [Mitchell 1992].

Nordstrom had survived and prospered in this turbulent environment. To remain in this position in the 1990s the company had to answer many strategic questions: What customers did it want to serve and what products would these customers want? How could Nordstrom improve its customer services? How quickly and how far could Nordstrom expand and still maintain its formula for success?

THE INDUSTRY AND COMPETITIVE MARKET

THE RETAIL WEARING APPAREL INDUSTRY

The retail industry involves the selling of goods, in a retail store location, to the ultimate consumer for personal or household consumption. A segment of the retail industry, the retail wearing apparel industry, consists of companies which sell clothing, accessories, and shoes to women, men, and children through retail stores.

Companies operating within the retail wearing apparel industry are involved in sourcing (finding manufacturers to produce goods), buying, shipping and storing, unpacking and ticketing, promoting and advertising, and selling.

Companies in the retail wearing apparel industry sell merchandise through several types of outlets. Department stores sell a wide variety of moderately- to high-priced merchandise. Specialty stores sell specific types of merchandise and target specific groups of customers. Mass merchandisers sell a wide variety of goods, at prices lower than most department stores. Discount stores sell fashionable apparel at lower prices than department stores. Catalog retailers sell their merchandise through mail order. Off-price stores sell quality, fashionable merchandise at discount prices. Boutiques and small shops sell various styles of apparel in many price ranges, with inventory levels varying widely from store to store.

The 1987 stock market crash caused a slowing of sales, earnings, and return on sales for major retail companies. As a result, 1987 sales only marginally surpassed 1986 sales [Marsh 1989]. Figure 1 shows apparel retail store sales for 1989 and 1990. Apparel sales are included in two categories: general merchandise stores and apparel and accessory stores.

As illustrated in Figure 1, sales in the apparel and accessory category increased only 3.3 percent from 1989 to 1990, compared to a 3.8 percent increase in the general merchandise category. Consumer spending on clothing continued to rise in 1990, although the approximately 1 percent increase recorded was considerably less than the 4.8 percent increase recorded from 1988 to 1989 [U.S Department of Commerce 1991]. Many factors contributed to this slow growth — the lack of fashion direction in women's apparel, consumer resistance to higher prices, and rapid over-expansion by retailers.

Retailers, nonetheless, planned to open as many stores in 1992 as they had in 1991 — with one exception: stores were expected to be even larger. With this strategy, stores were attempting to maximize sales, raise market share, and capitalize on the concept of one- stop shopping. However, many analysts believed that this was not the answer to the problems plaguing the overall retail industry. The main problem, according to a study conducted by Smith Barney Harris Upham, a New York investment firm, was that the growth rate of sales per store had slowed in the last decade and so size did not matter. The report showed that in 1987 dollars sales per store grew at an average annual rate of 3 percent between 1948 and 1977. Since 1977, the average annual growth rate of sales growth has slowed to six-tenths of 1 percent. In one analyst's opinion, the answer to the retail industry's problems was increased efficiency. One suggested solution was using technology more effectively to automate backroom operations and to allow customers to serve themselves [Barmash 1992].

During 1991 and 1992 an increasing number of retailers, including Macy's, filed for bankruptcy protection. Another popular retailer, the Oklahoma-based Street's, closed its doors after the 1991 Christmas selling season. Street's, which operated 10 stores, had been in operation since the 1930s, but heavy competition from outlets such as Dillard's Department Stores, The Limited Inc., and Wal-Mart Stores, forced the 51-year-old chain to shut down [Helliker 1991].

Other retailers who filed for bankruptcy between 1988 and 1992 included Federated

Figure 1: Sales of Retail Stores By Kind of Business 1990 and 1989

(Millions of dollars) **Kind of Business**	**1990**	**1989**	**%change**
Retail trade, total.	1,826,293	1,747,804	+4.5
Total (excluding automotive group)	1,441,204	1,363,653	+5.7
Durable goods stores, total	661,594	652,739	+1.4
Building materials, hardware, garden supply, and mobile home dealers	95,132	92,700	+2.6
Building materials, supply, hardware stores	82,117	79,612	+3.1
Building materials and supply stores	69,703	67,045	+4.0
Hardware stores	12,414	12,576	-1.2
Automotive dealers	385,089	384,151	+0.2
Motor vehicle and miscellaneous automotive dealers	352,892	353,765	-0.2
Motor vehicle dealers	334,859	335,278	-0.1
Motor vehicle dealers (franchised)	312,983	309,714	+1.1
Auto and home supply stores	32,197	30,386	+6.0
Furniture, home furnishing and equipment stores	91,937	91,493	+0.5
Furniture and home furnishing stores	50,420	51,082	-1.3
Furniture stores	27,436	29,720	-7.7
Floor covering stores	12,979	12,136	+6.9
Household appliance, radio and TV	32,561	32,387	+0.5
Household appliance stores	9,071	9,462	-4.1
Radio and television stores	23,490	22,925	+2.5
Sporting goods stores and bicycle shops	13,936	13,531	+3.0
Book stores	7,356	6,492	+13.3
Jewelry stores	14,667	14,049	+4.4
Nondurable goods store, total..	164,699	1,095,065	+6.4
General merchandise group stores	212,140	204,387	+3.8
Dept. stores (excl. leased depts)	169,681	164,358	+3.2
Dept. stores (incl. leased depts)	175,684	169,506	+3.6
Conventional dept. stores (incl.) leased depts.)	53,149	52,844	+0.6
Discount dept. stores (incl. leased depts.)	84,494	78,744	+7.3
National chain dept. stores (incl. leased depts.)	38,041	37,918	+0.3

Figure 1: Sales of Retail Stores By Kind of Business 1990 and 1989 (Contd.)

(Millions of dollars)

Kind of business	1990	1989	%change
Variety stores	7,410	7,356	+0.7
Miscellaneous general mdse. stores	35,049	32,673	+7.3
Food stores	371,580	349,120	+6.4
Grocery stores	348,243	328,075	+6.1
Meat, fish (seafood) markets.	6,517	6,709	-2.9
Retail bakeries	6,745	5,753	+17.2
Gasoline service stations	130,200	117,791	+10.5
Apparel and accessory stores	94,455	91,426	+3.3
Men's & boys clothing furnishings	8,976	9,548	-6.0
Women's cloth., spec. stores, furriers	33,450	32,637	+2.5
Women's ready-to-wear stores.	30,194	29,260	+3.2
Family clothing stores	27,407	25,768	+6.4
Shoe stores	17,839	17,163	+3.9
Eating and drinking places	186,162	175,344	+6.2
Eating places	173,086	163,645	+5.8
Restaurants, lunchrooms, cafeterias	93,809	89,076	+5.3
Refreshment places	76,893	72,189	+6.5
Drinking places (alcoholic bev.)	13,076	11,699	+11.8
Drug and proprietary stores	69,169	62,495	+10.7
Liquor stores	21,618	20,033	+7.9
Nonstore retailers	48,285	45,247	+6.7
Mail order houses (department store merchandise)	4,669	4,676	-0.1
Other mail order	26,172	24,173	+8.3
Miscellaneous shopping goods stores	65,938	64,025	+3.0

Source: Information obtained from U.S. Department of Commerce, "Retail Trade:1990," *Current Business Report,* 1992, pp. 1-29.

Department Stores (1990), Allied Stores (1990), Carter Hawley Hale (1991), Revco Department Stores (1988), Ames Department Stores (1990), and Hills Department Stores (1991) [Norris 1992].

Mergers, acquisitions, and corporate restructuring were also on the rise during the early 1990s. As earning potential lessened, companies acquired or merged with other companies. This trend in the retail wearing apparel industry was expected to continue [Norris 1992].

Retail square footage increased dramatically during this period. In 1990, 15 square feet of retail space existed for every woman, man, and child in the country. This growth surpassed consumer population growth and created a buyer's market. Retail apparel stores were attempting to gain market share by expanding geographically. Malls especially were becoming overcrowded

Figure 2: Retail Industry Customer Segment 1990

CUSTOMER	% OF APPAREL MARKET SALES
Women	
18-34	20
35-54	35
55 & over	30
Total	85
Men	10
Children	5
Total	**100%**

Source: Levin, Gary, "Boomers Leave a Challenge," *Ad Age*, July 1991, pp. 1 and 14.

with specialty and department stores, resulting in market saturation in many areas.

CUSTOMERS

The retail wearing apparel industry has a wide range of customers. For purposes of this study, these customers can be grouped according to sex and age, as shown in Figure 2.

Women

Women, who accounted for more than 75 percent of the apparel market in 1990, spent money on themselves as well as other family members. As shown in Figure 1, retail apparel stores' 1989 sales of women's apparel and accessories were $61.9 billion. This number increased to $63.6 billion in 1990, a 2.8 percent increase. These figures included sales of new merchandise as well as items held in inventory. The sales of this segment reportedly increased by approximately the same margin for the following year [U.S. Department of Commerce 1992]. The value of merchandise shipped from manufacturers to retail apparel outlets for major category items such as blouses, dresses, suits, and coats was $14.3 billion in 1990. Two-thirds of all retail apparel sales for 1989 and 1990 were purchases by women of shoes, accessories, and apparel for women.

As shown in Figure 2, 18- to 34-year-old women accounted for 20 percent of sales in the U.S. apparel market in 1990. This group responded quickly to changes and trends within the wearing apparel industry and frequented stores that responded likewise. Retailers like The Limited had grown rapidly and became very profitable by targeting this group [Koselka 1991]. However, this group was expected to shrink 11 percent — to 62.4 million — by the year 2000 [Donston 1991]. Even so, this category was expected to continue to be especially important because its members' habits were not formed [Levin 1991]. Another group characteristic is that these women prefer fashions that are contemporary rather than traditional. They wish to purchase contemporary styles at outlets which are known for selling such merchandise, often returning to these outlets for repeat purchases.

Another trend which had developed was the dramatic increase in the number of women in the work force. This group, the 35-54 age group, accounted for 35 percent of sales in the overall apparel market and was expected to become the most important demographic group in this industry. This segment, unlike the 18- to 34-year-old segment, was expected to grow during the 1990s. Members of this age group are more likely to spend a large proportion of their disposable income on wearable apparel [U.S. Department of Commerce 1992]. Individuals in this group spent an average of $2,000 on apparel in 1991. Members of this group sought reasonably-priced clothing that was sophisticated and career oriented [U.S. Department of Commerce 1991].

The fastest-growing population segment is the over 55 age category. This group made about 30 percent of apparel purchases in 1990. As a whole, this group was at its peak spending capabilities and was expected to be a strong market for many types of career, casual, and active wear apparel. This group had been known to spend $13 billion on apparel in a single year [U.S. Department of Commerce 1992].

Special Markets

A special market — known as the large-size market — was an increasingly important segment of the women's market. In 1990 more than $10 billion was spent on apparel by the 40 million American women wearing size 14 or larger. This was expected to continue to be a lucrative market since demand was high, but supply was low.

"This is a great market to be in because customers' appreciation is so high," said Susie Phillips, vice-president of marketing at Lane Bryant. Large-sized women had faced extremely limited choices in selection, quality, and fashion in the past so opportunities existed in select or diverse lines of large-size apparel [Adams 1988].

Petite women, those under 5'5" tall, also found it difficult to purchase apparel that fit. Petite customers frequently encountered ill-fitting sleeves and hem lengths. This segment at times was ignored because of the belief that these customers could alter the clothes to fit. However, this was costly. The popular catalog merchandiser Clifford & Wills was one of several marketers to offer a select group of merchandise that could be purchased in petite sizes at the same cost as the similar regular size items [*Clifford & Wills Spring Catalog* 1992].

Historically, women have spent more than any other demographic group on wearable apparel and they were considered to be the number one target of apparel merchants. Women favored department stores, discounters, and factory outlets for apparel, although specialty stores seemed to be gaining in popularity in the late 1980s. Women tended to purchase apparel that was moderately priced and had a designer look. Stores which offered designer-look, quality apparel at low prices were the most suitable for their shopping needs [Lee 1992].

Men

Men accounted for only a small portion of retail apparel industry sales — about 10 percent. Men's dollar sales totalled only $8.9 billion in 1990. In general, men devoted less time to shopping. When they did find time, chain stores such as The Gap were the most popular for sportswear items such as shirts, sweaters, and trousers, according to 47 percent of the men interviewed in a nationwide fashion study. Department stores were the preferred sales outlet for suits and business attire by 37 percent of those interviewed ["Upfront" 1991]. Men also shopped more often at stores that were conveniently located.

Children

The children's market accounted for the smallest portion of retail sales within the apparel industry in 1990: 5 percent of the market. This segment's customers were under the age of 18 and for the most part relied upon other family members to purchase or fund their apparel. The industry generally divides this category based on sex and combines market data with that for men and women.

PRODUCTS

The range of products offered in the retail wearing apparel industry were vast. Items included outerwear products (blouses, jackets, and trousers), accessories (belts, hats, and scarves), and shoes. Retailers offered all of these products at various prices and in many types, styles, colors, and sizes for men, women, and children. Figure 3 lists several merchandise categories and their values in 1988, 1989, and 1990.

Price

Price was determined by many factors: the cost of labor and shipping; the fabrics used to make a garment; the length of time it took to produce a garment; and the fashion or style of the garment. In 1991, sales of higher priced fashions slowed and sales of moderately priced products rose as demand increased for reasonably priced apparel. Shoppers spent the largest amounts on inexpensive apparel in 1991 ["Retail Apparel Industry" 1992]. Major retailers, such as Wal-Mart, were planning on cutting out middlemen. These retailers wanted to deal directly with the manufacturer instead of a wholesale broker or merchandise representative. The 2 to 3 percent saved on wholesalers' commissions would result in savings for the consumer since this amount normally would be added to the price of a retailer's merchandise [Barmash 1992].

Type and Style of Clothing

The type of clothing offered by the apparel industry included accessories, shoes, outerwear, and undergarments. As shown in Figure 3, shipments of men's/boys' trousers — the number one men's category for 1990 — were valued at $5.915 billion. Men's/boys' neckwear, the smallest men's category, was valued at $501 million in 1990. Sales in all men's categories except suits/ coats and work clothing declined from 1989 to 1990.

Figure 3: Value of Apparel Shipments From Wholesalers to Retailers 1990 (Select Merchandise Categories)

(in millions of dollars except as noted)

Item	1988	1989	1990	Percent Change 1988-89	Percent Change 1989-90
Industry Data					
Value of shipments	15,101	15,468	15,288	2.4	-1.2
Men/boys' suits/coats	3,169	3,102	3,137	-2.1	1.1
Men's and boys' shirts	4,031	4,170	4,101	3.4	-1.7
Men's and boys' neckwear	500	502	501	0.4	-0.2
Men/boys' trousers	5,767	6,061	5,915	5.1	-2.4
Men/boys' work clothing	1,633	1,633	1,634	0.0	0.1
Value of shipments	14,315	14,288	14,307	-0.2	0.1
Women's/misses' blouses	3,573	3,810	3,691	6.6	-3.1
Women's/misses' dresses	6,037	5,771	5,908	-4.4	2.4
Women's suits/coats	4,705	4,707	4,708	0.0	0.0
Value of shipments	3,884	3,921	3,904	1.0	-0.4
Women/child's underwear	2,621	2,716	2,669	3.6	-1.7
Bras & allied garments	1,263	1,205	1,235	-4.6	2.5

Source: Information obtained from U.S. Department of Commerce, "Apparel," *U.S. Industrial Outlook* 1991, pp. 34-1 to 34-7.

Under the women's category, women's/girls' dresses — the number one category in 1990 — were at $5.195 billion — an increase of 2.4 percent from 1989. The value of shipments in the women's/girls' suits/coats category did not change from 1989 to 1990 [U.S. Department of Commerce 1991].

Styles of apparel included casual, traditional/classical, and contemporary. Casual apparel, items such as denim jeans, knit stirrup pants, and sweaters, was worn as leisure clothing by all age categories. These items were not usually worn to the office or at a formal affair. Casual clothing appeared to be gaining popularity in the early 1990s. Classical or traditional apparel was simple and sophisticated clothing worn for formal occasions. Traditional style apparel was usually designed with standard colors and patterns, to enable the customer to use the items for more than one season. Classical items included traditional silhouettes, such as A-line skirts and button-up blouses and shirts, in basic colors such as black, navy, and beige. Such items also included beaded cocktail dresses and elegant evening wear with special details such as jeweled buttons. Contemporary clothing was unique and original in design. Fabrics usually featured bright colors and abstract patterns.

INVENTORY MANAGEMENT

Advances in technology can benefit retailers of wearing apparel in terms of inventory management. Technology permits tracking sales of popular sizes and styles and allows for fast reordering. Two types of technology which aid in the inventory management process are bar coding and Electronic Data Interchange.

Bar coding uses various symbols to identify vendor item markings, price, department, and style number. This system has led to automated replenishment of merchandise, improved merchandise information, and speedier checkouts [Robins 1988(A)]. In 1991, J.C. Penney had converted 40,000 point-of-sale registers to bar-code scanners in order to decrease supplier response time for reorders.

Electronic Data Interchange (EDI) is a computerized system which records inventory, as well as items and styles sold. When the need arises, a reorder can be placed automatically by the computer system. An added benefit of this system is decreased inventory costs [Robins 1988(C)].

ADVERTISING AND PROMOTION

Advertising and promotion was an integral part of operations for an apparel retailer. The target market dictated the method of advertising and/or promotions used by the retailer. Firms developed positioning strategies, strategies aimed at specific market segments, since retailers who know their clientele can choose the medium that best suits their products. Magazines such as *Vogue*, for example, are geared towards the designer market. Therefore it is very unlikely that a discount retailer would advertise there.

A study of media involvement conducted by Audits & Surveys Inc. for the Magazine Publishers of America Association found that in 16 of 19 areas of interest, print was the prime media source for working women, young adults, and the affluent. The study also indicated that 60 percent of newspaper readers were professionals with annual incomes of $60,000 or more [Schwartz 1991]. Readers found printed advertisements to be far more responsive to their needs and interests than television. Sixty-three percent of men and 64 percent of women believed that print was the medium that best suited their personal needs. Only 29 percent of men and 28 percent of women had the same feelings about television advertising [Schwartz 1991]. A Time/Seagram study concluded that as little as four weeks of advertisement exposure in print could increase a product's use by 75 percent and its purchases by nearly 300 percent [Schwartz 1991].

Television ranked second to newspapers with a 21 percent share of overall advertising revenues. Television advertising involved four different areas: network, national, local, and cable. Local advertising spots were used primarily by retailers such as department stores. Due to the intense competition among department stores, it was necessary for them to reach the local population to inform it of upcoming sales or promotions [Boone 1989].

CUSTOMER SERVICE

In the 1990s department stores were realizing what specialty stores had practiced all along — good customer service was important to success in the retail apparel industry. Personalized attention was being stressed in both types of stores to lessen the focus on the increasing price of apparel. This was especially important due to the increase in the older population which demands this type of service and attention.

Many department stores had problems implementing good customer-service programs, possibly due to their lack of experienced and trained personnel. In contrast, specialty stores had a definite competitive edge. These smaller stores offered personalized and specialized services, such as phoning customers when a new item arrived.

SPECIALIZATION

Companies in the retail wearing apparel industry once strove to be "all things to all people." The increasing cost of catering to diverse customers, however, led many companies to specialize by product or market segment [Gill 1989]. Many department stores even subdivided into mini-boutiques to capture a variety of market segments. According to some industry authorities, "specialization and market segmentation strategies will soon replace population growth as a means to boost sales. The strategy of serving a broad customer base is no longer viable: specialty stores now dominate virtually every category in retailing" [Sack 1988].

COMPETITORS

The retail wearing apparel industry was in the maturity stage of its life cycle in 1992. Both the number of customers and the amount of money they were spending on apparel were slowing. In addition, a large number of firms were competing in the same market. The increase in the number of stores selling apparel had caused the supply of goods to exceed demand in an already saturated market. Competition in this industry came from a variety of sources, including department stores, specialty stores, mass merchandisers, catalog retailers, discount stores, and off-price stores, as well as numerous boutiques and small shops. Figure 4 lists the top retailers within each of these segments.

Department Stores

Department stores sell a wide variety of merchandise, including apparel, accessories, and cosmetics, in a convenient shopping atmosphere. Department stores carry a wide range of merchandise and cater to customers' many needs. However, department stores did not achieve the same levels as specialty stores in terms of ambiance and customer service, nor did they compete with off-price chains which carried designer clothes at lower prices [Sack 1989]. Department stores' sales totalled more than $70 billion in 1990. The top five department stores and their sales volumes in 1990 are shown in Figure 4 [Top 100 Department Stores 1991].

To improve sales, many department stores targeted their merchandise at higher income

Figure 4: Retail Apparel Industry
1990 Major Outlets Ranking

Department Stores	
J.C. Penney	$14.6 Billion
Marvin's	4.1 Billion
Dillard's	3.6 Billion
Macy's Northeast	3.1 Billion
Nordstrom	2.89 Billion
Specialty Stores	
The Limited	$5.5 Billion
Marshalls	2.2 Billion
T.J. Maxx	2.0 Billion
Gap Inc.	2.0 Billion
Mass Merchandisers	
Wal-Mart	$3.26 Billion
K-Mart	3.21 Billion
Sears	3.20 Billion
Catalog Retailers	
Best Products	$2.30 Billion
Lands' End Inc.	1.40 Billion
CML	0.74 Billion
Luria & Sons	0.33 Billion
Discount Stores	
Rose's Stores	$ 2.0 Billion
Dollar General	1.2 Billion
Jamesway Corp.	1.1 Billion
Off-Price Stores	
Ross Stores	$1.65 Billion
Burlington Coat Factory	1.62 Billion
Dress Barn	0.60 Billion
Syms Corp.	0.45 Billion

customers. Also, many stores developed the "store within a store" format, dividing apparel departments into separate sections based on design and fashion.

Specialty Stores

Specialty stores offered ambiance, strong fashion statements, and good customer service. They took advantage of the growing segmentation of the mass market by targeting merchandise at distinct market segments. Specialty stores carried apparel which was targeted mainly at upscale customers.

Specialty stores usually were distinguished from competitors by merchandise selection and presentation. They often offered a unique type of quality merchandise. Total 1990 sales were more than $35 billion — an increase of 7.3 percent from the previous year. The top four apparel specialty outlets and their sales volumes in 1990 are shown in Figure 4 [Top 100 Specialty Stores].

Mass Merchandisers

Mass merchandisers offered customers a wider variety of goods, increased convenience, and lower prices than most department stores. The wearing apparel sold in mass merchandise stores was generally less fashionable and usually of lower quality than that sold in other types of apparel stores. Unlike specialty and department stores, mass merchandisers were not known throughout the industry as leaders in service. Total sales for this segment were $85.5 billion in 1990. The top three mass merchandisers and their sales volumes in 1990 are listed in Figure 4 [Top 100 Department Stores].

Catalog Retailers

Catalog retailers were a growing force in the retail wearing apparel industry. The number of mail-order catalog retailers has exploded since 1980, aided primarily by the low start-up costs associated with them. In an effort to compete directly with catalog retailers, many department stores increased catalog mailing in the 1980s. However, the saturated market and increased postal rates have caused many department stores to discontinue their catalogs.

Catalog retailers took advantage of demographic changes affecting the retail industry. These changes include the two-income family, rising disposable incomes, customers' limited shopping time, the increased use of credit cards, and Americans' fondness for dialing toll-free numbers. In 1990, total mail order sales volume was $200.7 billion, a 9.49 percent increase from 1989 ["Mail Orders Top 250+" 1991]. The top four catalog retailers and their sales volumes for 1990 are listed in Figure 4 ["Retail Apparel Industry" 1991].

Discount Stores

Discount stores offered lower prices and more convenience than mass merchandisers and off-price stores. However, one problem was that consumers sometimes perceived lower prices to mean lower quality and less service. Discount stores were shifting their attention away from selling a broad assortment of goods, to selling large selections of targeted products such as lower priced apparel. Total discount store sales for 1990 were $85.5 billion, a 7.3 percent increase from 1989. The top discount stores and their sales volumes in 1990 are listed in Figure 4 [Retail Apparel Industry" 1991].

Off-Price Stores

This type of apparel store attracted the price-conscious, fashion-conscious customer. They carried designer fashions at lower prices than department or specialty stores. The major disadvantage of off-price stores was a lack of available capital to invest in their stores. Total sales for 1990 were over $5 billion. The top four off-price stores and their sales volumes for 1990 are listed in Figure 4 ["Retail Apparel Industry" 1991].

THE COMPANY

HISTORY OF THE COMPANY

In early 1992, Nordstrom Inc. operated 69 retail stores. The stores were located mainly in the northwestern and western regions of the country with the exception of its newest stores, which were located in Virginia, Washington D.C. and New Jersey.

During World War I, business was slow and it was difficult to sell shoes, the company's original product. Wallin and Nordstrom worked very hard to keep the business flourishing. In 1923, the newly found post-war prosperity caused business to boom. During this time Wallin and Nordstrom opened their second store. They were dedicated to keeping the business a family-run business, with each partner employing family members. In 1928, John W. Nordstrom sold his share of the partnership to his three sons, who had started with the company as stock boys.

Nordstrom continued to prosper throughout the decades, first increasing the size and locations of stores, and then expanding the product line to include wearing apparel and accessories [*Nordstrom, Inc. Annual Report* 1988].

PRODUCTS

Nordstrom began as a retailer of high-quality, good-value shoes in a wide variety of styles and sizes for men, women, and children. In 1992, Nordstrom was still dedicated to selling quality merchandise at a good value. However, in addition to shoes, products now included women's, men's, and children's wearing apparel and accessories. They sold a limited number of styles, considered classic rather than trendy, since Nordstrom targeted customers who preferred traditional apparel. Nordstrom aimed at broad customer appeal and based its stores' inventories on geographic location.

Figure 5: Percentage of 1990 Nordstrom's Sales By Merchandise Category

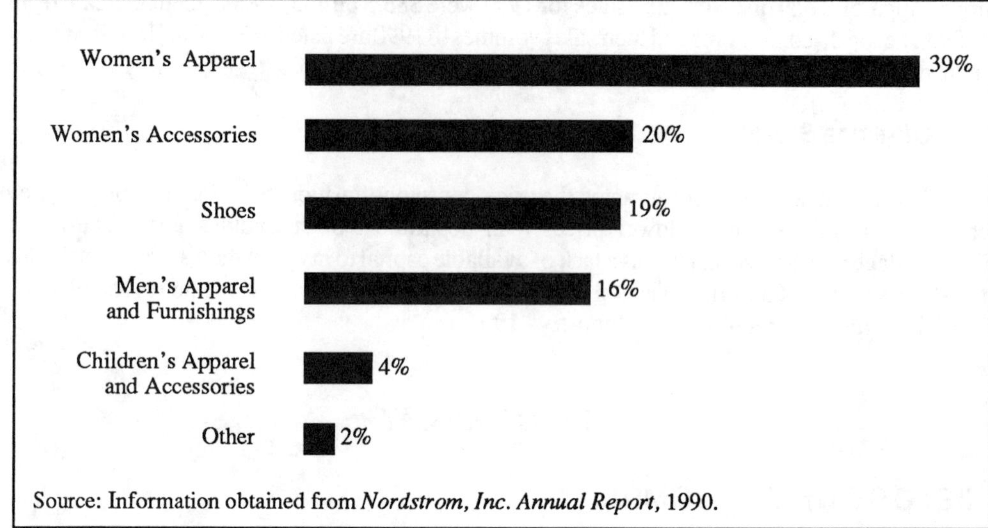

Source: Information obtained from *Nordstrom, Inc. Annual Report,* 1990.

Figure 5 shows Nordstrom's sales by major merchandise category.

CUSTOMERS

Nordstrom offered high-priced items for customers with above-average incomes. It targeted customers who were unwilling to purchase fashion-forward apparel and carried only classic merchandise. Nordstrom's stores were equipped with large traditional designer areas, as well as departments that offered basic items such as bluejeans.

Nordstrom entered existing population centers rather than "blazing new trails." It served mainly "upwardly mobile" markets. For example, Nordstrom's new store in Paramus, New Jersey, was located in an upscale neighborhood. This store included the standard valet parking and piano music which Nordstrom insisted its customers wanted.

Decisions regarding Nordstrom's merchandise purchases were made by regional buyers. The theory was that individual buyers knew the actual needs of their customers and were experienced enough to select appropriate inventory needs. New stores opening in East Coast areas were expected to be geared towards career-oriented individuals. Therefore, a new Washington D.C. store was expected to offer a selection including more than ladies' suits [*Nordstrom, Inc. Annual Report* 1990]. Nordstrom was convinced that customers wanted wearable fashions at good values, and targeted merchandise buys accordingly [*Nordstrom, Inc. Annual Report* 1990].

CUSTOMER SERVICE

The basic philosophy of the Nordstrom organization was to provide superior customer service, selection, quality, and value. Customer service has been a distinguishing characteristic for Nordstrom Inc. throughout its history. For Nordstrom, customer service did not stop with a cheerful smile and an available salesperson. Its stores were known for their elaborate attempts to please their customers. Many Nordstrom stores did not play recorded music, but provided live piano music. Coat checking services were available so customers were not burdened with carrying extra loads while shopping [Schwadel 1989].

In an age of incompetent and elusive sales service, shopping had become a chore for most customers. Nordstrom, with its legendary reputation for customer service, had an edge over its competition. Its commitment and dedication to customer service had built a strong base of loyal customers in an age when store loyalty was a thing of the past [Schwadel 1989].

Nordstrom provided sales training sessions and motivational seminars for its staff. Salespeople were expected to make merchandise suggestions to customers, ring up sales, and assist customers with returns and exchanges. Nordstrom employed more floor staff people than any other store chain. Sales staff were also expected to call loyal customers and thank them for their patronage, as well as send personal notes to alert them as to new lines and special incentive sales. Nordstrom's experienced sales staff even went to new stores to train new customer-service personnel [Schwadel 1989].

The strong dedication to customer service did not always have good results. Many salespeople felt too much pressure to sell and "put on a happy face" at all times. They were expected to follow a dress code, resulting in a loss of individuality for some employees. This caused some problems, and in 1991 Nordstrom was accused of unfair labor practices. Employees reported that they were not being compensated for overtime and extra duties performed. The State of Washington Department of Labor and Industries issued an order against Nordstrom, directing it to change its practices. Also, a lawsuit was filed on behalf of the employees seeking damages. These lawsuits were pending in early 1992 [Solomon 1992].

Nordstrom's excessive expansion may also cause customer service problems in the future. Only a limited number of the employees were willing to relocate and train future employees at new locations [Schwadel 1989]. As a result, Nordstrom may find it difficult to maintain standards.

EXPANSION

Nordstrom Inc. has undergone many expansions since the company's earliest days. John W. Nordstrom, the founder of Nordstrom Inc., started the expansion in the early part of the century when he and his partner opened their second shoe store in 1923. In 1961, Nordstrom owned and operated eight shoe stores and had 600 employees. Gross sales were $12 million that year. This success led Nordstrom to expand its business to include wearing apparel, so the company bought an existing chain store and offered a full range of apparel to appeal to customers' needs.

Nordstrom opened its first store outside the Northwest region in Southern California in 1978,

Figure 6: Square Footage by Market Area at End of 1990

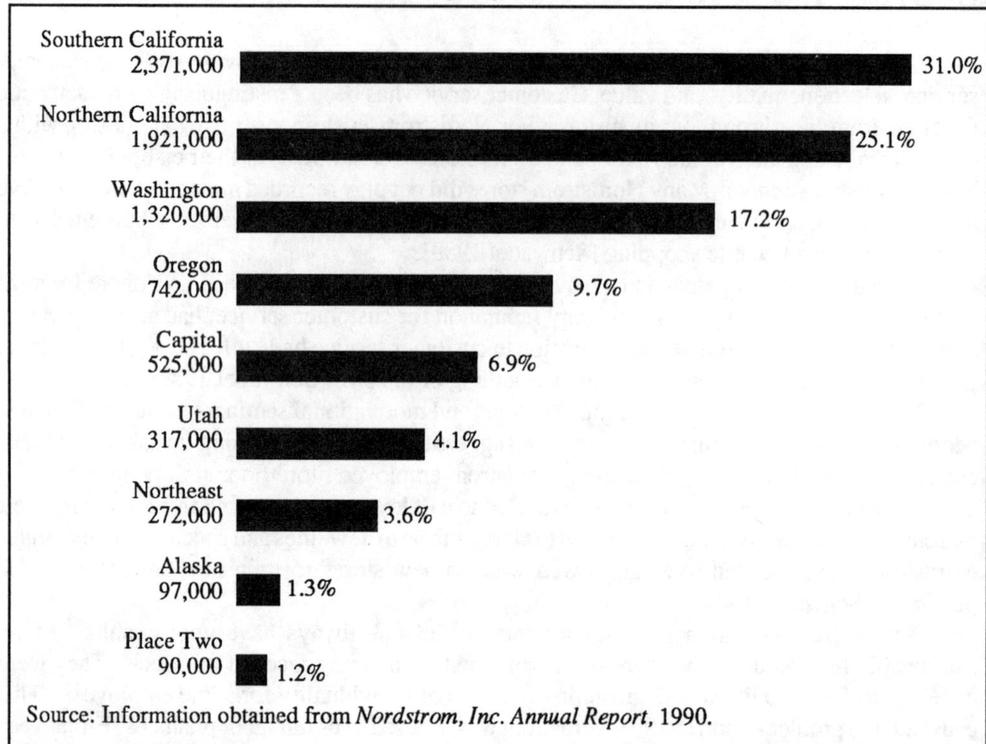

Source: Information obtained from *Nordstrom, Inc. Annual Report,* 1990.

and by 1990 its stores were located in six states. Figure 6 shows the geographic concentration of Nordstrom stores in 1990.

When Nordstrom opened a new store in Sacramento in 1980, the crowds were so overwhelming that the company was forced to request merchandise shipments from its other California stores in order to meet customer demand. Rather than predicting customer needs in this geographic area, Nordstrom executives decided to put everything in the store and let the customers decide what should be stocked [Ginsberg 1989(B)].

The drive to expand nationally was largely due to the fact that Nordstrom had been successful in all of its store openings. This success drove company executives to try their expertise in picking locations on a national level [Stevenson 1989]. At first, Nordstrom stores were located only in the northwestern and western regions of the U.S. In 1988, it opened its first East Coast store in McLean, Virginia. This suburban Washington D.C. store was an instant success. Due to Nordstrom's decentralized management structure, the apparel buyers for this store were able to test the market prior to the store's opening and choose merchandise they felt would be successful in that area of the country. This method of buying was successful and sales for the store's first year were in excess of $100 million [Born 1989].

In the third quarter of 1989, another East Coast store opened in the Pentagon area of Washington, D.C. Again, the store was stocked with the traditional apparel deemed appropriate for Nordstrom's up-wardly mobile, affluent customers. Also, trained staff members were transferred to the Washington, D.C. area to train new employees in the Nordstrom philosophy of selling and customer service. Long-term success was predicted for this store, which was located directly above the Metroliner train service. This location was expected to serve customers who stopped and shopped on a whim, as well as tourists visiting Washington, D.C. [Schwadel 1989].

By 1992 Nordstrom had built four stores in the Eastern U.S. and had opened 12 clearance stores called Nordstrom Rack in Washington State, Oregon, California, and Maryland. Nordstrom also leased shoe departments in stores in Hawaii [*Nordstrom, Inc. Annual Report* 1990].

MANAGEMENT STRUCTURE

Nordstrom, Inc. has continued to be a family-owned and -operated business. In 1992, 40 percent of the company's stock was owned by Nordstrom family members. Two brothers, John and Jim, and a cousin, Bruce, were co-chairs of the company. Another cousin, Jack McMillan, was president, and a friend of the family held the position of senior vice-president. These top five executives shared decision-making power: all had equal votes concerning policy and store location, and each member was allowed to veto any decision, at any time. Each executive oversaw and operated a different segment of the company [*Nordstrom, Inc Annual Report* 1988].

The family ownership of the business was said to have had an extraordinary stabilizing effect on the company during times of industry turbulence, caused by the increase of mergers and acquisitions in the retail wearing apparel industry and the "revolving door" ownership in many companies [Schwadel 1989].

Most decisions regarding the daily operations of the stores were made at the local store level because Nordstrom had a decentralized management structure. Corporate executives did not offer much direction in this area, but rather allowed regional and store managers decision-making control.

The decentralization of buying operations could cause problems. Some buyers could become overzealous when shopping for their stores, causing an overabundance of merchandise in inventory. This, in turn, could cause a large number of unnecessary markdowns. This was the case during the second quarter of 1989, when more markdowns occurred than were predicted [Schiffman 1989].

Although it is a family-oriented business, with future executives in the Nordstrom family currently working their way upward (three store managers, three buyers, and one management trainer), there are still great opportunities for other dedicated employees. Nordstrom has always promoted from within its organization [Schwadel 1989].

COMMUNICATIONS

Nordstrom relied on electronic mail for intercompany communications. Because the firm was a specialty retailer with an unusually large number of buyers (900 versus 60 to 100 at regular department stores) and vendors (27,000), its lines of communication needed to be constantly flowing to obtain the latest information.

In the spring of 1992, Nordstrom — in conjunction with MCI Communications Corp. — planned to set up what it called V.I.P. Express (Vendor Information Partnership) using a product called Lotus Express. Nordstrom intended to connect its five-year-old internal e-mail system via a proprietary gateway to MCI's forward network and then to MCI Mail. In the summer of 1991, 40 of Nordstrom's vendors were put on a pilot system and another 2,000 were expected to be on the voluntary system by the end of the following year [McCusker 1991].

FINANCIAL

Nordstrom was expected to borrow external capital in order to continue its expansion. Between 1988 and 1991, Nordstrom spent $328.9 million on expansion and improvements and

Figure 7: Nordstrom, Inc.

Income Statement 1988-1991 — Years ended Jan. 31 (Dollars in Thousands)

	1988	1989	1990	1991
NET SALES	$1,920,231	$2,327,946	$2,671,114	$2,893,904
OPERATING EXPENSES:				
COST OF SALES	$1,300,720	$1,563,832	$1,829,383	$2,000,250
SELLING AND ADMINISTRATIVE	$477,488	$582,973	$669,159	$747,770
TOTAL OPERATING EXPENSES	$1,778,208	$2,146,805	$2,498,542	$2,748,020
OPERATING INCOME (LOSS)	$142,023	$181,141	$172,572	$145,884
OTHER INCOME (EXPENSES):				
SERVICE CHARGE INCOME	$53,662	$57,268	$55,958	$84,660
INTEREST EXPENSE	($32,952)	($39,977)	($49,121)	($52,228)
TOTAL OTHER INCOME (EXPENSES)	$20,710	$17,291	$6,837	$32,432
EARNINGS BEFORE INTEREST AND TAXES	$162,733	$198,432	$179,409	$178,316
PROVISION (CREDIT) FOR INCOME TAXES				
INCOME (LOSS) BEFORE MINORITY INTEREST	$162,733	$198,432	$179,409	$178,316
MINORITY INTEREST IN INCOME (LOSS)				
INCOME FROM CONTINUING OPERATIONS	$162,733	$198,432	$179,409	$178,316
TAXES	$70,000	$75,000	$64,500	$62,500
NET INCOME (LOSS)	$92,733	$123,432	$114,909	$115,816

Source: Adapted from *Nordstrom, Inc. 1989 Annual Report*
Adapted from *Nordstrom, Inc. 1990 Annual Report*

Figure 7: Nordstrom, Inc.

Balance Sheet 1988-1991 — Years ended Jan. 31 (Dollars in Thousands)

CONSOLIDATED BALANCE SHEET	1988	1989	1990	1991
ASSETS:				
CURRENT ASSETS:				
CASH AND EQUIVALENTS	$4,949	$16,058	$33,051	$24,662
ACCOUNTS RECEIVABLE NET	$404,615	$481,580	$536,274	$575,508
INVENTORIES	$312,696	$403,795	$419,976	$448,344
PREPAID EXPENSES	$7,922	$22,553	$21,847	$41,865
TOTAL CURRENT ASSETS	$730,182	$923,986	$1,011,148	$1,090,379
PROPERTY, PLANT AND EQUIPMENT, NET	$502,661	$594,038	$691,937	$806,191
INVESTMENTS IN UNCONSOLIDATED AFFILIATES				
INTANGIBLE ASSETS (NET)				
OTHER NON-CURRENT ASSETS	$1,424	$3,679	$4,335	$6,019
TOTAL NON-CURRENT ASSETS	$504,085	$597,717	$696,272	$812,210
TOTAL ASSETS	$1,234,267	$1,521,703	$1,707,420	$1,902,589

LIABILITIES AND STOCKHOLDER'S EQUITY	1988	1989	1990	1991
ACCRUED INCOME TAXES	$17,085	$20,990	$12,491	$24,268
NOTES PAYABLE	$88,795	$95,903	$102,573	$149,506
ACCOUNTS PAYABLE	$166,524	$190,755	$195,338	$204,266
ACCRUED EXPENSES, SALARIES, & TAXES	$101,204	$120,821	$151,687	$163,365
CURRENT PORTION OF LONG TERM DEBT	$21,091	$19,696	$27,799	$10,430
TOTAL CURRENT LIABILITIES	$394,699	$448,165	$489,888	$551,835
LONG-TERM DEBT	$215,300	$356,471	$418,533	$457,718
OBLIGATIONS UNDER CAPITALIZED LEASES	$23,952	$23,049	$22,080	$21,024
DEFERRED TAXES	$67,107	$54,077	$43,669	$45,602
OTHER NONCURRENT LIABILITIES				
TOTAL NON-CURRENT LIABILITIES	$306,359	$433,597	$484,282	$524,344
TOTAL LIABILITIES	$701,058	$881,762	$974,170	$1,076,179
STOCKHOLDER'S EQUITY				
PREFERRED STOCK:				
COMMON STOCK:	$146,317	$147,629	$148,857	
PAID IN CAPITAL				
RETAINED EARNINGS	$386,892	$492,312	$584,393	
TOTAL STOCKHOLDER'S EQUITY	$533,209	$639,941	$733,250	$826,410
LESS: TREASURY STOCK (520,000 SHARES) AT COST				
TOTAL STOCKHOLDER'S EQUITY	$533,209	$639,941	$733,250	$826,410
TOTAL LIABILITIES & EQUITY	$1,234,267	$1,521,703	$1,707,420	$1,902,589

Source: Adapted from *Nordstrom, Inc. 1989 Annual Report*
Adapted from *Nordstrom, Inc. 1990 Annual Report*

planned to spend another $500 million over the following three years. As seen in Figure 7, Nordstrom Stores Inc. consolidated balance sheet for 1990-1991, Nordstrom should be able to handle the increased debt needed for its expansion mission [Schiffman 1989].

Steadily increasing sales had reached $2.9 billion by the end of 1991 — a substantial difference from the $10,000 earned in 1901, the year Nordstrom opened its first store. Figure 8 shows Nordstrom's sales in millions for 1981 through 1990, while Figure 9 shows net earnings for the same 10-year period.

TOWARDS THE FUTURE

In early 1992, Nordstrom management was considering strategic alternatives for the company's future. Nordstrom had a reputation among industry members and customers for providing outstanding customer service and quality apparel. In a saturated industry where consumers were spending less on wearing apparel, Nordstrom was looking for ways to expand the company.

Some Nordstrom executives argued that the company should enter markets in other regions of the U.S. These executives argued that the affluent Nordstrom customer bought traditional style apparel and was looking for a conveniently-located outlet. These executives wanted to search out upscale markets because they knew this was where to find the Nordstrom customer. They

Figure 8: Nordstrom Stores, Inc. Net Sales 1981-1990

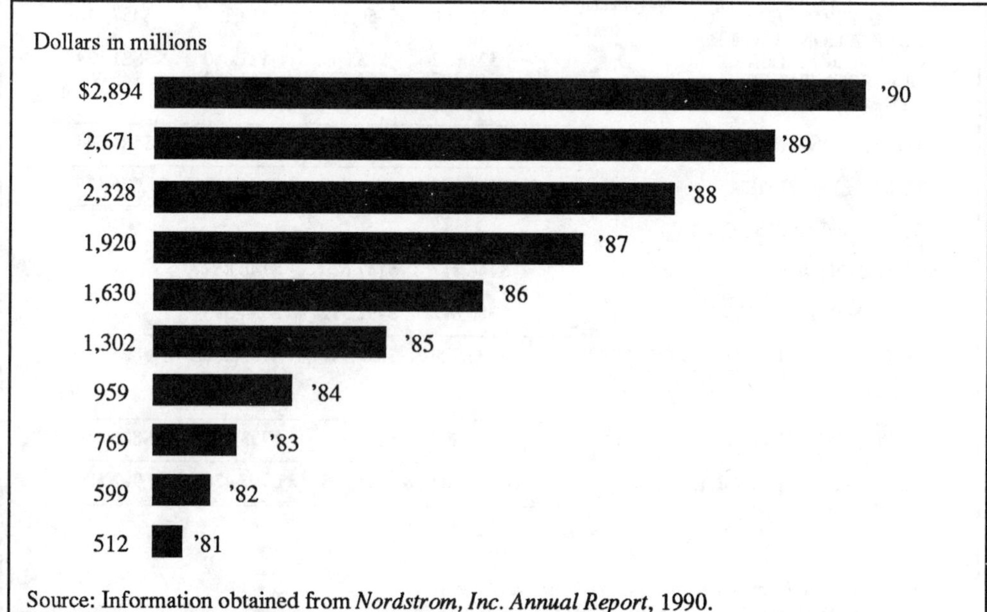

Source: Information obtained from *Nordstrom, Inc. Annual Report*, 1990.

Figure 9: Nordstrom Stores, Inc. Net Earnings 1981-1990

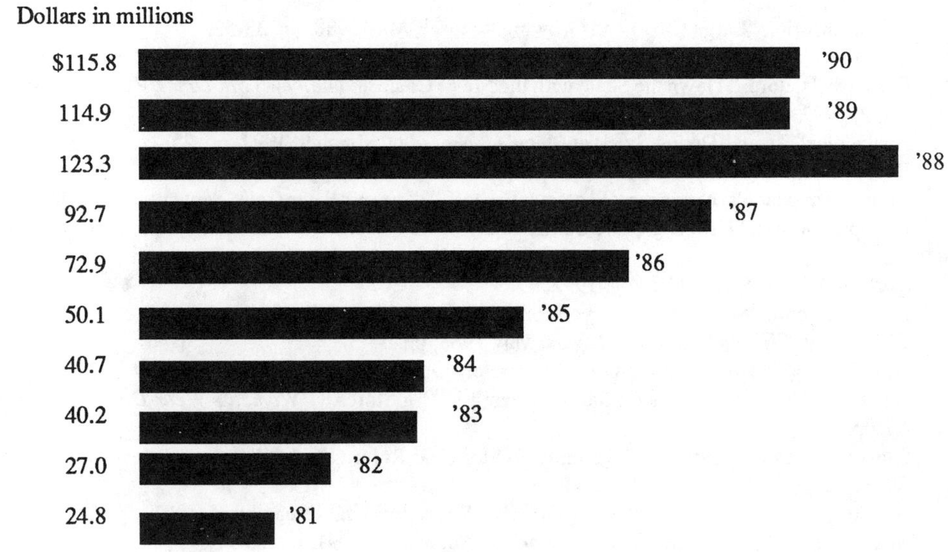

Dollars in millions

'90	$115.8
'89	114.9
'88	123.3
'87	92.7
'86	72.9
'85	50.1
'84	40.7
'83	40.2
'82	27.0
'81	24.8

Source: Information obtained from *Nordstrom, Inc. Annual Report*, 1990

believed that if they approached their expansion efforts in this fashion they would obtain more customers, as indicated by past efforts. For example, a study showed that 23 percent of the residents of Riverside and Monroe Valley — cities that attracted affluent and upwardly mobile population segments — shopped in other areas. This study also indicated that these residents would prefer shopping at more convenient locations, thus representing potential Nordstrom markets.

However, other managers believed this approach was not justifiable during those times. They wanted to put plans for expansion on hold until there were definite signs of an economic recovery and a long-term increase in consumer spending. They felt that since company earnings had declined over the past two years and stock had dropped 13.5 points, it would be unwise for the company to expand. These executives felt customers were balking at Nordstrom's moderate to high prices. They believed customers were not just waiting for an economic recovery before spending, rather that the trend toward lower prices was a long-term trend which would cause these customers to turn to Nordstrom's competitors.

In view of this debate, Nordstrom was considering the above alternatives as well as many other strategies and their long-term effects on the company.

REFERENCES AND BACKGROUND READINGS

Adams, Muriel, "Large (Size) and Growing," *Stores*, May 1988, pp. 33-52.

Baldo, Anthony, "Nordstrom: Success Has Its Price," *Financial World*, July 25, 1989, pp. 15.

Barmash, Isadore, " Down the Scale with the Major Chains," *The New York Times*, Business Section, February, 2, 1992, p. 5.

Benkelman, Susan "Taking Stock at Macy's," *Newsday*, March 9, 1992, pp. 25-27.

Boone, Kurtz, *Contemporary Marketing*, Fifth Edition, 1989, pp. 404-425.

Born, Pete, "Macy's, Nordstrom: Pentagon Faceoff," *Women's Wear Daily*, September 28, 1989, p. 11.

Ciampi, Thomas, "Dec. Big-Store Sales Mostly Weak," *Women's Wear Daily*, January 6, 1992, pp. 19.

Clifford & Wills Spring Catalog, 1992.

Donston, Scott, "Media Reassess as Boomers Age," *Ad Age*, July 1991, pp. 12.

Gill, Penny, "Who's Counting," *Stores*, May 1988, pp. 33-52.

Gill, Penny, "Moderate Sportswear: Moderately Optimistic," *Stores*, January 1989, pp. 19-32.

Ginsberg, Steve, "Commission Sales Growing in Big Stores," *Women's Wear Daily*, January 4, 1989(A), pp.16.

Ginsberg, Steve, "Nordstrom's Sacramento Store Has Robust Start, "*Women's Wear Daily*, October 24, 1989(B), p. 16.

Helliker, Kevin, "Final Markdown," *The Wall Street Journal*, December 4, 1991, pp. A1, A6.

Koselka, Rita, "Fading Into History," *Forbes*, August, 19, 1991, pp. 70-71.

Lee, Georgia, "Lower Prices Key at Atlanta Show," *Women's Wear Daily*, February, 12, 1992, pp. 8.

Levin, Gary, "Boomers Leave a Challenge," *Ad Age*, July 1991, pp. 1 and 14.

"Mail Orders Top 250+," *Direct Marketing*, July 1991, pp. 30-49.

Marsh, Lisa, "Analysis of Retail Performances for Fiscal 1988, "*Women's Wear Daily*, August 24, 1989, pp. 4-5.

McCusker, Tom, "The Message Is Integration," *Datamation*, August 15, 1991, pp. 31-32.

Mitchell, Rissell, "Inside the Gap," *Business Week*, March 9, 1992, pp. 58-64.

Nordstrom, Inc. Annual Report, 1990.

Nordstrom, Inc. Annual Report, 1988.

"Nordstrom Plugs Tyler Leak," *Chain Store Age Executive*, September, 1989, pp. 40-42.

Norris, Floyd, "Win or Lose, Buyouts Do It Big," *The New York Times*, January 28, 1992, pp. D1, D8.

"Retail Apparel Industry," *Value Line*, February 28, 1992, pp. 1601-1711.

Robins, Gary, "Auto ID," *Stores*, September 1988(A), pp. 1-16.

Robins, Gary, "Automating Reorders," *Stores*, November 1988(B), pp. 20-27.

Robins, Gary, "EDI: Closing the Loop," *Stores*, April 1988(C), pp. 53-62.

Sack, Karen J., "Nordstrom Inc.," *Standard & Poor's Corp.*, October 2, 1991, pp. 4793-4794.

Sack, Karen J., "Retailing: A Basic Analysis," *Standard & Poor's Industry Survey's*, April 20, 1989, pp. 75-112.

Sack, Karen J., "Retailing: An Industry at the Crossroads," *Standard & Poor's Industry Surveys*, December 22, 1988, pp. 61- 63.

Schechter, Dara, "Howell Says J.C. Penney Is Ready for Big Growth; Cites Technology as Aid," *Women's Wear Daily*, October 27, 1989, p. 10.

Schiffman, Michael, "Nordstrom, Inc.," *Value Line*, September 1, 1989, p. 1651.

Schneider, Bart, "Retail Store Industry," Value Line, September 1, 1989, pp. 44-45.

Schwadel, Francine, "Nordstrom's Push East Will Test Its Renown for the Best Service," *The Wall Street Journal*, August 1, 1989, p. A1(col. 6), p. A4(col. 4).

Schwartz and Kraft, "Managing Consumer Diversity: The 1991 American Demographic Conference," *American Demographics*, August 1991, pp. 22(6).

Silverman, Edward R., "Supplier Trouble for Alexander's," *Newsday*, March 7, 1992(A).

Silverman, Edward R., "Macy's Cutbacks Coming," *Newsday*, March 8, 1992(B), pp.7.

Soloman, Charlen-Marmer, "Nightmare at Nordstrom," *Personnel Journal*, September 1990, pp. 76-83.

Stevenson, Richard W., "Watch Out Macy's Here Comes Nordstrom, "*The New York Times Magazine*, August 27, 1989, pp. 34-40.

"Top 100 Department Stores," *Stores*, July 1991, pp. 31-43.

"Top 100 Specialty Stores," *Stores,* August 1991, pp. 25-41.

"Upfront: Salon International, Mode Masculine," *Stores*, March 1991, pp. 14.

U. S. Department of Commerce, "Retailing," *1989 U.S. Industrial Outlook*, January 1989(A), pp. 54-1 - 64-3.

U.S. Department of Commerce, "Apparel," *1989 U.S. Industrial Outlook*, January 1989(B), pp. 41-1 -41-6.

U.S. Department of Commerce, "Apparel," *U.S. Industrial Outlook 1991*, pp. 34-1 -34-7.

U.S. Department of Commerce, "Retail Trade: 1990," *Current Business Report 1992*, pp. 1-29.

Yang, Dori Jones and Laura Zinn, "Will the Nordstrom Way Travel Well?," *Business Week*, September 3, 1990, pp. 82-83.

REEBOK INTERNATIONAL LTD.: THE ATHLETIC FOOTWEAR INDUSTRY

With sales increasing from $1.3 billion to $2.7 billion in only four years, Reebok International was one of the top competitors in the branded U.S. athletic shoe market in 1990 [Tedeschi 1992(A)]. This Stoughton, Massachusetts company was the superstar of the 1980s in athletic footwear.

Reebok formed in 1979 with four employees and delivered 200 pairs of running shoes that year. The company's unorthodox marketing style and creative thinking led to an increase in its earnings to over $165 million by 1987, and its stock exploded from 5 3/8 when it went public in 1985 to a high of 35 in 1992 ["Reebok International Ltd." 1992]. In the 1980s, Reebok's sales increased more than 400 percent. Figure 1 compares Reebok's income statements for mid-1988 through 1991, while Figure 2 compares balance sheets for the same period. Sales volume climbed upward from 1988 through 1991, reaching a high of more than $2.7 billion in 1991. In 1990 Reebok employed more than 3,000 people and delivered more than 270 million pairs of athletic shoes worldwide [Reebok 1990(A); Tedeschi 1992(A)].

In 1992, Reebok was surpassed as the industry leader in athletic shoe sales by Nike Inc., its major competitor. Management was looking at ways to regain the number one position. Major strategic decisions included determining the kinds of products to emphasize (performance versus fashion) and the most effective ways to promote them, as well as selecting the most effective distribution channels selection and sales outlets.

**Figure 1: Reebok International, Inc.
Consolidated Income Statements 1988-1991 (Amounts in Thousands)**

	1988	1989	1990	Nine mos. ended Sept. 30, 1991
NET SALES	$1,785,935	$1,822,092	$2,159,243	$2,147,867
OTHER INCOME (EXPENSE)	($1,351)	$11,377	($893)	$4,681
TOTAL REVENUES	$1,784,584	$1,833,469	$2,158,350	$2,152,548
COST AND EXPENSES:				
COST OF SALES	$1,122,226	$1,071,751	$1,288,314	$1,302,312
SELLING EXPENSES	$260,891	$278,939	$353,983	$347,838
GENERAL & ADMIN. EXPENSES	$149,195	$174,972	$202,352	$167,266
AMORTIZATION OF INTANGIBLES	$14,216	$14,427	$15,646	$12,248
INTEREST EXPENSE	$14,129	$15,554	$18,857	$14,043
INTEREST INCOME	($6,633)	($12,953)	($15,637)	
TOTAL OPERATING EXPENSES	$1,554,024	$1,542,690	$1,863,515	$1,843,707
INCOME BEFORE INC. TAXES	$230,560	$290,779	$294,835	$308,841
INCOME TAXES	$93,558	$115,781	$118,229	$123,845
NET INCOME	$137,002	$174,998	$176,606	$184,996

Adapted from: *Reebok International, Inc. 1991 Quarterly Reports*
Reebok International, Inc. 1990 Annual Report
Reebok International, Inc. 1989 Annual Report

THE INDUSTRY AND COMPETITIVE MARKET

THE ATHLETIC SHOE INDUSTRY

In 1990, there were over a hundred different companies which sold more than 1 billion pairs of shoes annually, and athletic footwear had become the driving force behind the overall shoe industry. The different construction and kinds of shoes sold included leather, synthetic leather, rubber, and plastic; dress, casual, and athletic. Athletic shoes accounted for more than one-third of all shoes sold.

Twenty years ago, only one pair of sneakers was needed to run, jump, and play. In the 1980s sneakers were replaced by athletic shoes. Athletic footwear consisted of many types of shoes, such as shoes for running, walking, aerobics, basketball, tennis, and bicycling. The number of athletic footwear companies increased as shoe categories increased. Some of the athletic footwear companies competing in the industry included Adidas, Converse, L.A. Gear, Nike, Puma, and Reebok.

Sales in the overall shoe industry grew to $11.2 billion in 1992, as shown in Figure 3. This growth was attributed, in part, to the increased number of people who participated in athletic activities and fitness programs. In addition, a more casual style of dress became increasingly

Figure 2: Reebok International, Inc.
Consolidated Balance Sheets 1988-1991 (Amounts in Thousands)

	1988	1989	1990	Nine mos. ended Sept. 30, 1991
CURRENT ASSETS:				
CASH AND EQUIVALENTS	$99,349	$171,424	$227,140	$34,398
ACCOUNTS RECEIVABLE NET	$276,204	$289,363	$391,288	$549,716
INVENTORY	$301,920	$276,911	$367,233	$355,095
DEFERRED INCOME TAXES	$26,293	$34,845	$31,673	$33,406
PREPAID EXPENSES	$9,905	$11,735	$12,328	
TOTAL CURRENT ASSETS	$713,671	$784,278	$1,029,662	$972,615
PROPERTY & EQUIPMENT	$92,546	$136,776	$160,132	$195,137
LESS ACCUMULATED DEPREC. & AMORT.	$18,419	$30,542	$49,017	$55,004
TOTAL PROPERTY & EQUIPMENT	$74,127	$106,234	$111,115	$140,133
OTHER NON-CURRENT ASSETS:				
INTANGIBLES,NET	$264,506	$261,398	$255,051	
OTHER NON-CURRENT ASSETS	$11,145	$14,457	$7,397	
TOTAL NON-CURRENT ASSETS	$275,651	$275,855	$262,448	$278,331
TOTAL ASSETS	$1,063,449	$1,166,367	$1,403,225	$1,391,079

	1988	1989	1990	Nine mos. ended Sept. 30, 1991
CURRENT LIABLILITIES:				
NOTES PAYABLE	$75,208	$1,651	$68,660	$28,803
CURRENT MATURITIES OF LONG-TERM DEBT	$404	$598	$1,411	$5,358
INTEREST BEARING ACCOUNTS PAYABLE				
A/C PAY AND ACCRUED EXPENSES	$105,247	$148,360	$166,061	$284,150
INCOME TAXES PAYABLE	$34,634	$43,834	$49,071	$69,427
DIVIDENDS PAYABLE	$8,490	$8,538	$8,576	$6,816
TOTAL CURRENT LIABILITIES	$223,983	$202,981	$293,779	$394,554
LONG-TERM DEBT, NET OF CURRENT MATURITIES	$112,662	$110,302	$105,752	$221,516
DEFERRED INCOME TAXES	$4,224	$8,788	$6,965	$6,968
TOTAL NON-CURRENT LIABILITIES	$116,886	$119,090	$112,717	$228,484
TOTAL LIABILITIES	$340,869	$322,071	$406,496	$623,038
STOCKHOLDERS' EQUITY:				
COMMOM STOCK	$1,129	$1,139	$1,144	
ADDITIONAL PAID-IN CAPITAL	$266,564	$275,336	$281,478	
RETAINED EARNINGS	$424,002	$564,987	$707,336	
UNEARNED COMPENSATION	($2,808)	($524)	($191)	
FOREIGN CURRENCY TRANSLATION ADJUSTMENT	$1,815	$3,358	$6,962	
TOTAL STOCKHOLDERS' EQUITY	$690,702	$844,296	$996,729	$768,041
TOTAL LIABILITIES & STOCKHOLDERS' EQUITY	$1,031,571	$1,166,367	$1,403,225	$1,391,079

Adapted from: *Reebok International, Inc. 1991 Quarterly Reports*
Reebok International, Inc. 1990 Annual Report
Reebok International, Inc. 1989 Annual Report

Figure 3: Composite Statistics: Show Industry Sales, 1987-1992

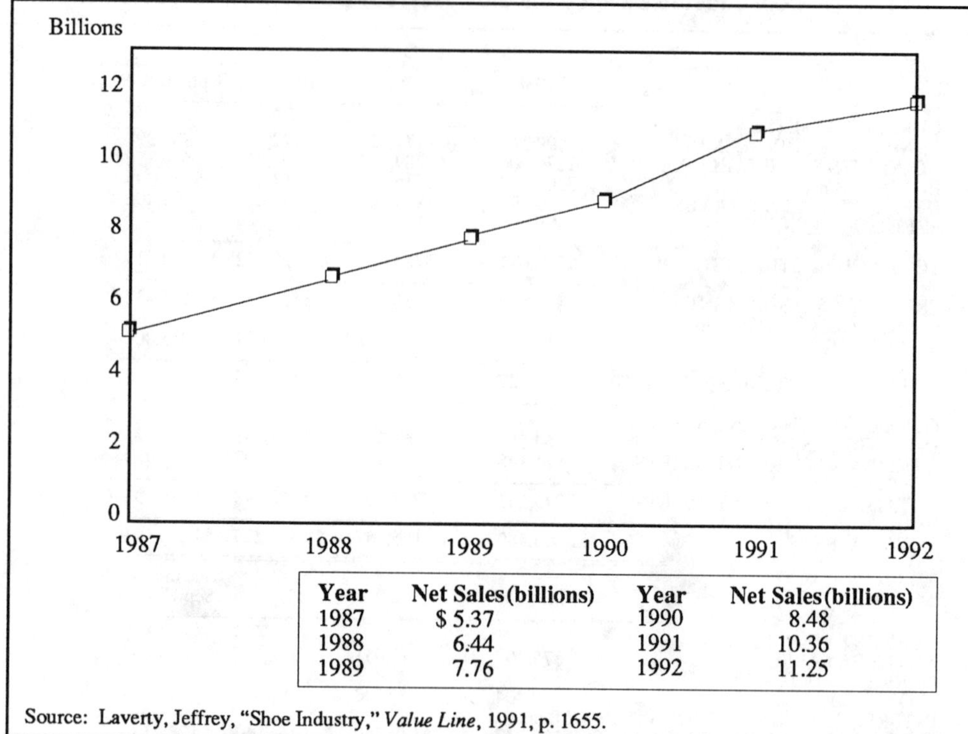

Year	Net Sales (billions)	Year	Net Sales (billions)
1987	$ 5.37	1990	8.48
1988	6.44	1991	10.36
1989	7.76	1992	11.25

Source: Laverty, Jeffrey, "Shoe Industry," *Value Line*, 1991, p. 1655.

popular and acceptable in work situations. Consumers of all ages wore athletic shoes instead of other casual and dress shoes.

Historically, the athletic shoe industry had not been kind to industry leaders. By introducing products at the right time or within the proper niche, any athletic shoe company could achieve a high market share. However, market leaders typically turned over about once every five years.

Most athletic shoe manufacturers relied on intense advertising to persuade fickle consumers to buy their brand products. Each competitor had to establish a distinct image for its athletic shoes. Many types of retail outlets were used to sell and distribute athletic footwear. The peak sales seasons in the athletic footwear industry were the spring and fall, which coincided with spring break and back-to-school periods.

PRODUCTS

A variety of shoes were sold in the athletic footwear industry. Some products emphasized function, while others tended to be more fashionable. These products sold at high prices, even though manufacturing costs were low.

Figure 4: Market Share for U.S. Athletic Shoes, 1990

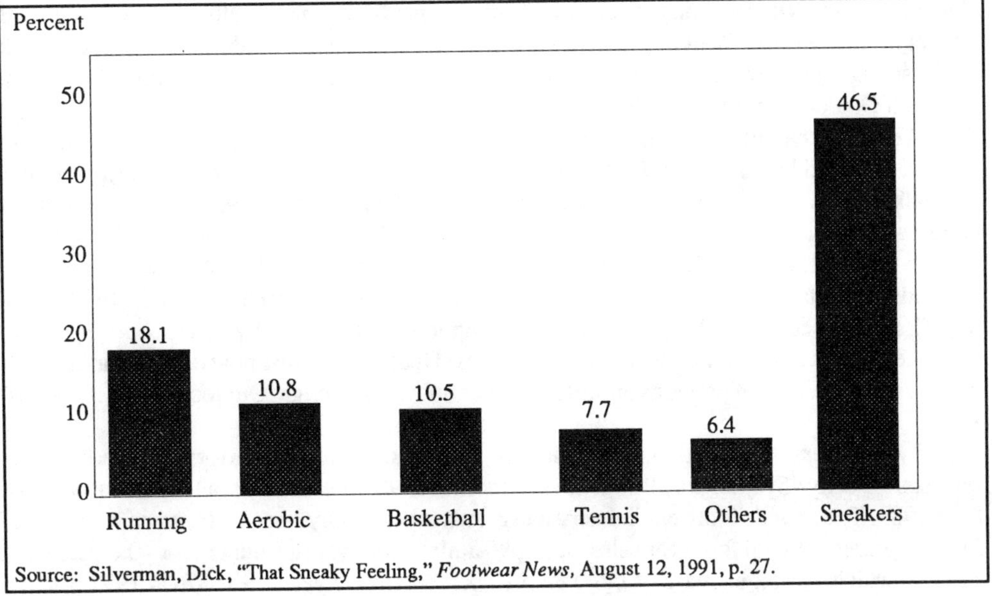

Source: Silverman, Dick, "That Sneaky Feeling," *Footwear News*, August 12, 1991, p. 27.

Types of Shoes

Most different athletic shoes produced in the industry were developed with a particular athletic activity in mind. Some shoes were made for a specific team sport, while others were made for individual activities. Figure 4 shows market shares for the major categories of athletic shoes in 1990.

In the 1970s, the nation's increasing interest in becoming physically fit and active led sneaker manufacturers to develop different types of athletic shoes. The first specialized shoes to be offered were for running, tennis, and basketball. The more popular of the three, the running shoe, was made with extra sole cushioning.

The aerobic shoe was created in 1982 in response to a growing interest in exercising, especially among women. The aerobic shoe, with less heel cushioning, differed from the running shoe.

In 1988, bicycling shoes were developed. They offered special features which allowed the user to gain more momentum in competitive bicycling. Also cross trainers, athletic shoes which could be used for multiple athletic activities, were constructed. These lightweight and flexible shoes were used for aerobics, basketball, and running, as well as other sports in which lateral movement was important. Bicycling was expected to become the second largest participatory sport of the future. For example, runners and aerobic participants were switching from running in marathons to bicycling.

By 1991, walking shoes had become popular — largely because of the increased number of older people who were walking for exercise. This fast growing athletic activity became a growth market for many firms. Walking attracted a wide range of people, including young participants, but its strength remained in the huge walking market of people older than 45 ["Super Show Puts Focus on Outdoor Activities" 1992].

Walking shoes differed from running shoes in that they were designed with a lower mid-sole and had more padding in the inside of the shoe. A custom fit and proper cushioning were required for walking shoes since comfort had become a major factor in the development of footwear products ["Super Shoe Puts Focus on Outdoor Activities" 1992].

In late 1991, a market for outdoor athletic footwear emerged. Outdoor shoes were developed for outdoor sports — primarily hiking, trail running, and mountain biking [Ferrara 1992 pp.64-67]. Consumers considered the outdoors a very important part of their lives, as people of all ages and fitness levels looked outdoors for their activities. Outdoor footwear now featured fashionable looks without the bulk of previous products ["Super Show to Highlight Outdoor, Value Athletics" 1992].

By 1990, less than half of the entire athletic shoe market was non-performance footwear, or "sneakers." Only 45 percent of all athletic shoes sold in 1990 were sneakers, a 1.9 percent decrease from 1989. The athletic footwear industry had grown substantially since 1986, when it accounted for 29.2 percent of total footwear sales. By 1990 athletic footwear accounted for 40.6 percent of sales — which was an increase of more than 39 percent in five years [Silverman 1991 p.27].

The Importance of Technology and Fashion

Technological advances were important to product diversity and product integrity. Athletic shoes were very sophisticated and offered state-of-the-art features such as air-cylinder suspension systems, superfoam inner soles, dual density bottoms, anatomically molded ankle collars, and adjustable support straps. Technology was one of the keys to the rapid growth of the athletic footwear industry. New technology was introduced frequently and existing technology was fine-tuned to develop new features ["Super Show Puts Focus on Outdoor Activities" 1992]. Nike was specialized in high-performance and technologically advanced athletic shoes with the invention of a specialized sole for running shoes called Nike Air. A gas-filled sack embedded in the shoe's heel provided a better bounce when running. Reebok followed Nike's emphasis on performance and technology by introducing the Pump basketball shoe. The Pump featured a round button on the shoe's tongue which could be pushed to inflate a chamber. This conformed the athletic shoe to an individual's foot. The Pump was eventually introduced in nine sport categories ["Reebok Rebounds With the Pump" 1991; Reebok 1991(B)].

Footwear was initially developed for specific athletics since participants were sophisticated about their athletic footwear needs and would not accept nonperformance substitutes, cheap imitations, or footwear designed for multi-sport activities. A good technological design addressed a major consumer concern. For example, sprinters' concerns about getting fast starts in races were answered with a redesigned, specialized running shoe which provided lightness, support, and cushioning [Reebok 1992 *Running*].

Even though technology was important in establishing the credibility of manufacturers, the majority of athletic shoes were not purchased for the particular function or sport for which they were designed, but rather for the fashion aspects. The industry estimated that 80 percent of the athletic shoes purchased were not worn for the activity for which they were designed. In other words, some running shoes never ran a mile, few basketball shoes ever made jump shots, and some aerobics shoes never made it to exercise class.

Statistics on retail outlets suggested the growing importance of the fashion aspect of the business. In 1989, high-end specialty retailers maintained their market share while that of department stores grew from 9 percent in 1987 to 10 percent in 1989 ["The Numbers Game" 1990]. The fashion industry also influenced footwear since consumers demanded that styles be changed frequently. Athletic shoes were updated twice a year [Arthur 1990 pp. 84-88] and street looks were added to the athletic shoe in response to these demands ["Super Show Puts Focus on Outdoor Activities" 1992].

Athletic shoes were worn everywhere: on the trains and buses, in shopping centers, and even in formal restaurants. Sixty percent of the running shoes purchased were used for commuting to and from work. As a result, some manufacturers began to offer athletic footwear based on fashion and appearance rather than performance. Rather than the basic white sneaker of the past, athletic footwear companies concentrated on producing colored shoes, as well as ones incorporating prints such as floras or a denim-look. Footwear was considered part of the wardrobe and blended with the wardrobe. For example, Asics thick soled wrestling shoe came in brilliant colors and was popular with casual users ["Super Show Puts Focus on Outdoor Activities" 1992].

Fashion and function appeared to be integrating in the 1990s. Athletic footwear firms were innovators and produced new technological products that catered to all athletic categories. The footwear contained technology enabling the athlete to be competitive. At the same time, companies also produced athletic shoes which appealed to fashion-oriented consumers.

Pricing

New technological features increased the price of athletic shoes. As Keri Christenfeld, analyst at New York's Needham & Co., said, "It's all a matter of value perception, customers have been led to believe they are getting more for their money." Performance-oriented customers purchased the higher priced athletic shoes. The importance of fashion and complimenting one's wardrobe led the customer to buy athletic shoes at any price. Prices varied among the different athletic footwear manufacturers. One of the highest priced athletic shoes was Reebok's The Pump which retailed for $170 [Reebok 1991(B)].

By 1991, recession weary consumers took a back-to-basics approach and the popularity of products became more price sensitive. Median price levels were in the $50 to $80 range, with the shoes maintaining as many technical features as possible ["Super Show Puts Focus On Outdoor Activities" 1992].

Product Sourcing

Most athletic footwear products were designed in the United States but were usually produced overseas — generally in the Far East. During the early 1990s, athletic footwear companies imported and sourced largely from South Korea, Taiwan, the Philippines, China, Thailand, and Indonesia because of cheaper labor costs.

The unusual aspect of this industry was that manufacturing costs were extraordinarily low in relation to the product's price. For example, at the low end a shoe might cost $7 to manufacture and sell for $30; at the high end a shoe might cost $30 and sell for as much as $175.

CONSUMERS

The U.S. and international markets for athletic footwear were divided into five segments: children, teenagers, men, women, and the older market.

Domestic Market (U.S.)

In 1990, athletic footwear domestic sales were divided as follows: 18 percent for children and teenagers, 42 percent for men, and 40 percent for women [Lee 1990]. Companies could effectively position their products by fully understanding consumer needs and wants, and by carefully following the market trends. For example, in tennis the young consumer was brand conscious and desired light weight and color, while the mature consumer was price-sensitive and comfort-oriented. Yet, both wanted advanced technology ["Tennis Shoe Firms..." 1991].

Children. Athletic shoes commanded 43 percent of all footwear purchases for children, with functional athletic and sport shoe styles dominating the boys' market and fashionable low heels and flats dominating the girls' market. Footwear purchases for girls were about 1.3 times greater than those for boys. Children were known throughout the industry as the ultimate cross-trainers, since they lived in their athletic shoes. Opportunities emerged for companies that provided more fashion-oriented athletic shoes. In 1992, the children's market was expected to grow as companies focused on flexibility and comfort to aid children in their developmental years.

Teenagers. Virtually all teenagers owned at least one pair of sneakers. The most frequent buyers of athletic footwear, teenagers, purchased new athletic shoes almost every three months. An Athletic Footwear Association (AFA) study also found that teenagers paid more for athletic shoes and were more influenced by styles and trends than comfort and fit. In addition, athletic shoes represented 38 percent of a typical teen's shoe wardrobe, with basketball shoes as the favorite. Companies that provided current, even faddish products, would gain with this group, since teenagers were fashion-conscious and frequently changed brands.

Men. Men evaluated their athletic shoes on performance and technical value. Athletic shoes represented 32 percent of the average man's shoe wardrobe. Fifty-three percent of those who worked out with exercise equipment, and more than 50 percent of bicyclers, were men.

Companies such as Nike and Reebok were successful in targeting this segment of the functional athletic footwear market in the late 1980s and early 1990s. In 1992, men were purchasing fewer pairs of athletic shoes but were paying more for each purchase. Many experts felt that a decline in the growth rate of this market and the high promotional budgets required to sell to it made this segment less desirable [Freeman 1991].

Women. Women preferred their shoes to be comfortable and fashionable [Sloan 1989(A)]. Athletic shoes comprised 22 percent of the average woman's shoe wardrobe. The fastest growing segment of the athletic business, the women's market, exceeded the size of the men's market by more than 30 million pairs annually ["The Numbers Game" 1990]. Women purchased over 10.6 million pairs of walking shoes in the 1990s. More than 85 percent of the 23 million participants in the aerobics market were women, and they also represented 42.7 percent of the running market [Lee 1990; "The Numbers Game" 1990]. Companies were developing technologies to target this growing women's market. With the success of Reebok's "Step Reebok" aerobic workout program in 1991, it was expected that athletic footwear companies would be producing more functional athletic footwear product lines for women, as women began showing a greater interest in sports participation. [Reebok 1990(A) *Annual Report*].

The Older Market. In 1990, the 75-84 age group and 85 plus age group had increased 21 percent and 51 percent respectively [Schewe 1991 pp. 59-66]. Even those with no prior exercise experience adopted walking as their primary workout. Consumers in this group were looking for an athletic shoe with more function and less fashion. Opportunities existed for companies that could accommodate this group, even though this group was expected to form only 7 percent of the population in the 1990s ["Current Population Reports" 1990].

International Market

In the early 1990s, athletic footwear companies like Reebok, Nike, and L.A. Gear actively pursued the international market.

In 1990, Reeboks were sold in more than 120 countries. Reebok was the number one sports and fitness performance brand in many of these countries. Reebok's international sales totalled 19 million pairs for $725 million in sales. In 1991, international sales increased by 51 percent.

In 1990, Nike was the second most-recognized American brand to foreign consumers — second only to Coca-Cola. Nike marketed its products in approximately 66 countries. International sales increased 80 percent in 1991 and accounted for 29 percent of total revenues. In contrast, U.S. sales increased only 22 percent in 1991 — compared to 29 percent in 1990.

In 1989, international sales for L.A. Gear surged to $52 million from $20 million in 1988. The company planned to sell its products in 100 foreign countries, including the Soviet Union. With declining U.S. sales, L.A. Gear had to turn to the international market for survival.

Athletic footwear companies targeted the same consumers in the international market as they did in the domestic market. Consumers in Europe, Latin America, and Japan wanted functional athletic footwear that was also fashionable. Price was not a major factor because consumers purchased American brand athletic footwear even when the dollar was strong and prices were rising [Bannon 1989 p. 20].

Europeans were fascinated with U.S. products. American athletic footwear products had strong appeal in this market [Reichlin 1991 pp. 56,60]. Europeans were preoccupied with performance when they purchased athletic shoes, but fashion was still important. Lars Samuelson, the European managing director for New Balance, believed that most European consumers based purchases on function, such as running and tennis shoes for associated activity. These consumers later developed strong interests in aerobic and walking shoes. There was also a shift from all-white athletic shoes to bold-colored shoes.

Consumers in certain Latin and South American countries, for example, Mexico and Brazil, demanded American athletic shoes—especially for soccer. This was due, in part, to the popularity of the sport in these countries. Japanese consumers also wanted more U.S. athletic footwear. Prior to 1990, Japanese consumers increased their purchases of American brand athletic footwear, especially purchases of athletic shoes with many technical features.

ADVERTISING AND MARKETING

Advertising and marketing played a major role in the success of athletic footwear companies, and companies used various techniques to promote their brands.

Marketing was essential in the promotion of any new technological features or trendy styles of athletic shoes. Athletic footwear companies spent millions of dollars in advertising in order to increase brand loyalty. This included television and magazine advertisements, trade shows, billboards, and point-of-purchase displays. Reebok's advertising budgets for 1989 through 1992 are shown in Figure 5.

Each product line and category was advertised and marketed differently. Athletic footwear companies used different themes, with some describing a product's specific function while others focused on a specific consumer segment to develop brand recognition.

Professional athletes and famous singers and actors were used to endorse products. Professional basketball players like Michael Jordan and Kareem Abdul-Jabbar endorsed basketball shoes. Other athletes, for example, Bo Jackson, endorsed the cross-trainer which emphasized the importance of total fitness and exercise. Famous singers and actors such as Michael Jackson and Belinda Carlise endorsed the more stylish and fashionable athletic shoes, while Sinbad endorsed the Blacktop, which was targeted at inner city youth. In addition, opportunities to increase brand awareness and image across the entire product line existed through the use of professional endorsements. These endorsements were believed to increase sales in the performance and fashion-oriented markets.

In 1991, as professional endorsement costs increased, companies were turning to sentimental advertisements using unknown performers. This method could prove successful in positioning a company's image and brand name in relation to its competitors [McCarthy 1990]. Examples of this type of advertisement theme were Nike's "Just Do It," Reebok's "Life is Short, Play Hard," and L.A. Gear's "Get In Gear".

DISTRIBUTION OUTLETS

Most athletic footwear was distributed through department stores, athletic specialty shoe stores, and sporting goods stores. Some other types of outlets were pro shops, discount stores, mail-order catalogs, and showrooms. Some athletic footwear companies also maintained their

Figure 5: Reebok International Ltd. Advertisment Budgets, 1989-1992 (in Millions)

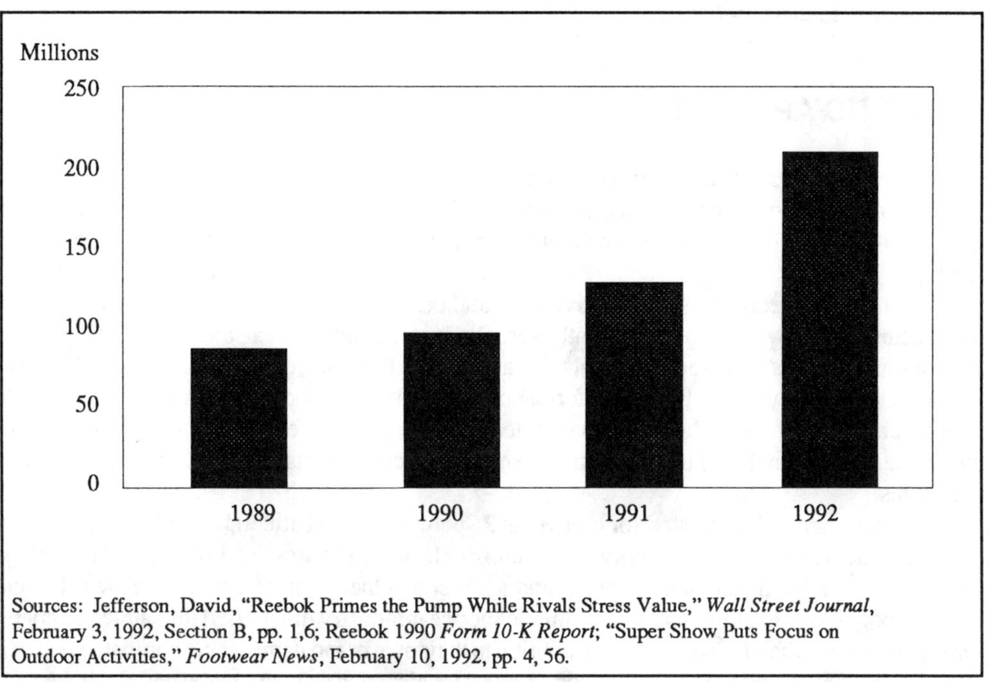

Sources: Jefferson, David, "Reebok Primes the Pump While Rivals Stress Value," *Wall Street Journal*, February 3, 1992, Section B, pp. 1,6; Reebok 1990 *Form 10-K Report*; "Super Show Puts Focus on Outdoor Activities," *Footwear News*, February 10, 1992, pp. 4, 56.

own retail outlets.

Department Stores

Department stores captured the largest percentage of sales for all types of athletic shoes. Department stores emphasized the fashion aspects of athletic footwear through colorful displays. Many department stores had separate departments for athletic footwear so they could add newer classifications and styles. Some department stores leased their athletic shoe departments to specialty athletic footwear franchises. Function-oriented athletic footwear companies could increase exposure of their products by selling through department stores, which emphasized the fashion aspect of athletic footwear.

Specialty and Sporting Goods Stores

Specialty and sporting goods stores carried very high-performance or technically oriented footwear. These athletic footwear specialty shops increased in number as new technological designs were added to different shoes. Some specialty stores sold exclusively one product category, for example, running and walking shoes. The salespeople in these stores were well-trained and well-educated about both the athletic activity and the athletic shoe. Fashion oriented athletic footwear companies could sell products in specialty and sporting goods stores by adding functionality to their footwear.

ATHLETIC APPAREL

Sales of athletic apparel had increased steadily since 1986. A study by the Sporting Goods Manufacturing Association (SGMA) showed that the sports apparel market by 1989 had become a $23 billion industry, more than twice the size of the athletic footwear industry [Finkelstein 1990].

Athletic apparel consisted of active wear and performance wear. Active wear was sought by consumers who wanted to look like athletes. Products included sweatsuits, shorts, long-sleeve fleece shirts, t-shirts, tank tops, light jackets, and socks. Preference for this casual style of dress increased noticeably in the 1980s. Performance wear was marketed to the serious athlete and to those persons who wanted clothes that reflected their active lifestyles. The various lines of performance wear included tennis shirts and shorts, bicycling shorts and tops, and running shorts and pants.

Athletic apparel accounted for more than 25 percent of most athletic footwear manufacturers' total sales revenue. Consumers were looking for head-to-toe dressing in one brand so athletic companies merchandised their footwear and apparel together in an effort to increase sales and brand recognition. Competitors in the athletic footwear industry diversified into athletic apparel on the strength of their brand names. In addition to their own brand name, some companies carried clothing lines featuring the names of sports professionals , such as Ivan Lendel and Boris Becker.

In this large and growing industry, opportunities existed for athletic footwear companies that could effectively merchandise their footwear and apparel together on the strength of their brand name. The combination of footwear and apparel could result in increased sales for both products as well as in strengthened brand recognition.

COMPETITION

Major competitors in the athletic footwear industry in 1990 included Nike, Reebok, L.A. Gear, Converse, and Adidas.

The top three competitors, Nike, Reebok, and L.A Gear, controlled 64 percent of the athletic footwear market. Nike was the leader with 30 percent market share, followed by Reebok with 24 percent and L.A Gear with 13 percent [Pereira 1991(B) p.1]. The 1990 market shares of U.S. athletic shoe manufacturers are shown in Figure 6.

Market positions changed often as demonstrated by the industry's history and as dictated by its fashion basis. Low barriers to entry existed for new competitors due to low entry costs and the volatility of the athletic footwear market. Athletic shoes were sourced overseas at low cost, then promoted with a brand name and sold at high prices.

Figure 6: Manufacturers' Market Shares for U.S. Athletic Shoes, 1990

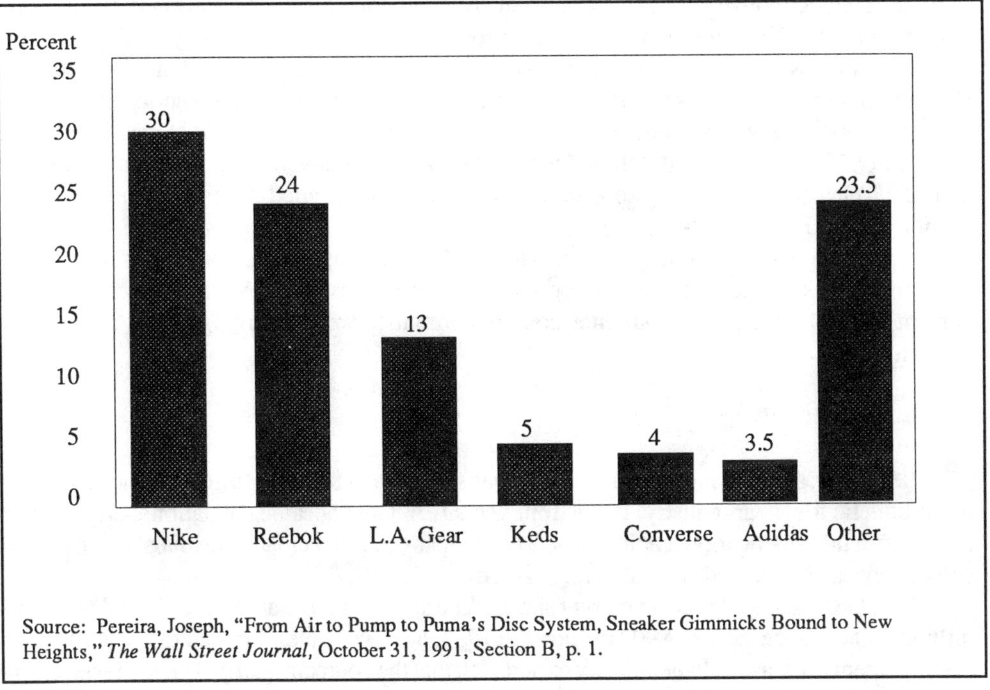

Source: Pereira, Joseph, "From Air to Pump to Puma's Disc System, Sneaker Gimmicks Bound to New Heights," *The Wall Street Journal,* October 31, 1991, Section B, p. 1.

Nike

Nike, a publicly-owned company based in Beaverton, Oregon, was incorporated in 1968 by Philip Knight and Bill Bowerman. The company's principal business activity involved the design, development, and worldwide merchandising of high-quality sports footwear and apparel.

In 1991, Nike was the number one U.S. athletic footwear company. That year Nike set an earnings record in the athletic footwear industry with a net income of $287 million on sales of $3.0 billion. High-tech footwear comprised most of Nike's sales. Nike had maintained its edge in the athletic footwear market by maintaining its image as the athlete's sport shoe company [Tedeschi 1991(A)].

Over the years Nike became a status symbol in athletic footwear. The company had a reputation for being innovative and customer-driven. Researching new technologies became the company's strategy for success. Nike's Sport Research Lab studied all functions and forms of activities providing vital information for shoe design and construction. In 1990, Nike spent $8.4 million on research and development [Yang 1990].

Nike had strengths in all athletic shoe categories. The Nike Air technology had been incorporated into all shoe categories and Nike was the first company to introduce the cross-trainer shoe and subsequently defined the look. Nike believed that form followed function.

Nike targeted both men and women, but sold more men's shoes. It led the industry in sales of men's athletic footwear, but had long been criticized for its lack of attention to the women's market. In 1989, Nike introduced women's shoes targeted for the physically active woman.

Nike aggressively promoted its products. It focused on brand positioning through heavy sales promotions and endorsements, mainly using professional athletes to endorse its products. Nike also placed advertisements in publications such as *Runner's World, Sports Illustrated, Vogue, GQ, Mademoiselle* and *Rolling Stone*. Nike was the top advertising spender in the industry in 1989. Television advertising totalled $19 million, while printed advertisements cost $13.2 million [Bagot 1990 pp. 61-65].

Nike marketed its products in approximately 66 countries. International sales increased 80 percent in 1991 and accounted for 29 percent of total revenues. As U.S. sales increased only 22 percent in 1991, it appeared that enormous opportunities were emerging in the international market.

L.A. Gear

L.A. Gear, a fast-rising company which was started in 1985, posed threats in the fashion end of the athletic footwear industry. In just four years L.A. Gear became the nation's number three company in the athletic footwear industry. The company initially created an image using brightly colored shoes and sexy ads aimed at teenage girls.

L.A. Gear held a 13 percent market share of the athletic shoe market in 1990 and netted $31 million in income on sales of $902 million. In 1991, however, sales dropped to $618 million — a 31.5 percent decrease. Many industry experts felt that the company had grown too fast. Internal controls had gotten out of hand and blurred the company's image. The winning formula had weakened as L.A. Gear lost touch with its fickle female teenage crowd. Quality also declined, as was demonstrated when L.A. Gear's functional athletic footwear fell apart in television athletic contests.

L.A. Gear implemented different strategies for men's, women's, and children's athletic footwear. L.A. Gear focused on fashion rather than function for women since the company believed that 80 percent of athletic shoes were purchased for casual wear, not for sports. In the late 1980s and early 1990s the majority of L.A. Gear's products were made for women. Men's athletic footwear consisted of improved versions of competitors' functional athletic footwear. New product development was based on reverse engineering, that is, taking apart a competitor's product to copy its design. Children's shoes initially were downsized versions of adult athletic footwear, but in 1991 L.A. Gear developed, "Bendables," a new product line, for functional developmental shoes.

L.A. Gear had trouble shedding its image as "the teenager's athletic shoe." It marketed its product to young women by highlighting attractive styling. However, men's shoes constituted only 23 percent of sales — compared to 60 percent of sales for competitors.

In 1988, L.A. Gear expanded to produce apparel and accessories. The company felt that the products could easily be cross-merchandized with athletic footwear. However, after experiencing low profit margins in its apparel division in 1988 and 1989 and losses in 1990 and 1991, L.A. Gear withdrew from this market.

In 1989, L.A. Gear's international sales jumped to $52 million from $20 million in 1988. The company planned to sell its products in 100 foreign countries, including the Soviet Union. The international market appeared to be a growth market for L.A. Gear.

The company spent millions of dollars in establishing a brand image for all consumer segments. The California "valley girl" look was used to promote casual shoes and famous basketball players endorsed basketball shoes. In order to enter and compete in the men's segment of the market, L.A. Gear signed superstar Michael Jackson to endorse its new line of "Michael Jackson" shoes. [Rottman 1989 p. 1]. L.A Gear spent a total of $21.5 million on athletic shoe advertising in 1989 [Bagot 1990 p.1].

Converse

In 1990, Converse held a four percent share of the athletic footwear market. The company had built a solid reputation with its basketball shoes and sales exceeded $340 million. Converse's canvas athletic basketball shoes were extremely popular in the European market because of their appearance and comfort.

Converse repositioned itself from a basketball shoe firm to a diversified company through footwear development programs for tennis, running, and field sports. It also developed mid-sole technology called the New Wave Energy System, which was expected to be implemented in its shoes in the 1990s.

Adidas

Adidas USA was a subsidiary of a West German corporation until 1992. Adidas was the international market leader of athletic footwear until the mid-1980s. The company had over 100 worldwide distributors, giving it an extensive amount of business in foreign countries.

Adidas had a strong athletic apparel focus and, as a result, constantly introduced and promoted new leisure wear. Athletic apparel accounted for almost 45 percent of Adidas' athletic sales, in the early 1990s. Adidas introduced athletic shoes with a new technological design — the Torsion Bar — which provided lateral stability. Adidas devoted most of its advertising budget to its athletic apparel line, especially its Mr. Adidas leisure wear.

THE COMPANY

REEBOK'S HISTORY

Reebok was created for one reason — men wanted to run faster. With this in mind, Joseph William Foster of Bolton, England, made himself a pair of track shoes in 1890. His company, J. W. Foster, became one of the world's first athletic shoe manufacturers. In 1958, Joseph and

Jeffrey Foster, two of the founder's grandsons, started a second company which was called Reebok after the African gazelle. Reebok eventually was combined with J.W. Foster to form one organization. Over the next 20 years Reebok continued to produce these famous elite running shoes and marketed them by mail throughout the world.

Reebok was virtually unknown in the United States until 1979 when Paul Fireman, an American marketer of outdoor sports equipment, saw Reebok shoes at an international trade show in Chicago. Within several months, he obtained an exclusive North American license from the family-owned company which permitted him to sell Reeboks in the United States. Paul Fireman immediately introduced three running shoes into the U.S. shoe market in hopes of capitalizing on the recreational running craze. He had problems entering the running shoe market because Reeboks were the most expensive running shoes at that time.

In 1981, after running out of money, Fireman approached Pentland Holding Industries, a British shoe distributor, for backing. Pentland Holding gave him $77,500 in cash in exchange for a 55.5 percent ownership of his operation. The shoes started to sell, and by the end of the year Reebok had $1.5 million in U.S. sales. Even though this was a substantial showing, Fireman was not satisfied. He felt that the running craze had peaked and that he should concentrate his efforts elsewhere.

He found success in the neglected aerobics market. At that time, women demanded no specific aerobic shoe from retailers. In 1982, Reebok introduced the first aerobic shoe, the Freestyle. This shoe combined a comfortable, colorful, stylish ballet-slipper top with a durable rubber sole [Sedgewick 1989 pp. 28-34]. It was shipped to stores in the early spring of 1983 and just collected dust on the shelves for three or four months.

In a brilliant marketing ploy, Fireman targeted aerobics instructors by offering discounts and giveaways. He felt that students might mimic their aerobic instructors or at least ask them for advice on aerobic shoes. Reebok also sponsored a certification program for aerobics instructors. Suddenly, retailers were ordering 200 pairs of aerobic shoes at a time. By the end of 1983, Reebok had sales of $13 million, mostly from its aerobic shoe line where Reebok came close to earning a 100 percent share of the market [Stern 1987 p. 23]. This led Reebok to expand from domestic manufacturing plants to production facilities in Korea and Taiwan.

Paul Fireman and Pentland Holding Industries bought Reebok, along with the rest of its worldwide licensing rights, from the Foster family in 1984. Pentland Holding then reduced its holdings to 41 percent of Reebok. In 1985, the company went public, with stock selling at 5 3/8. In 1991, Reebok reduced Pentland Holding's ownership to about 13 percent by re-purchasing approximately 24.5 million shares of its own outstanding stock [Reebok 1991(B)].

IMAGE

When Reebok first entered the athletic shoe market, the market was one dimensional. Consumers purchased athletic shoes for their ability to improve and enhance performance. Almost all other influencing factors, for example, fashion, color, style, and fabrication, were ignored. Then Reebok developed its aerobic shoes, which received attention for more than just comfort and performance. Their brilliant colors and soft garment leather made them an overnight success [Therrien 1986 pp.89-90] and these stylish athletic shoes became standard equipment for trendy young consumers. Reebok's shoes became the fashion footwear for the 1980s, luring consumers of more conventional casual footwear.

Reebok's shoes almost replaced traditional street shoes. Social commentators said that America's love affair with the sneaker was just another indication of how society was declining, and how consumers were making do with less. As one of the first to introduce fashion and color to athletic footwear, Reebok's image was that of a fashion-oriented athletic shoe company.

By concentrating on style rather than performance, Reebok originally found that consumers would pay high prices for its shoes. While Reebok offered price-conscious consumers aerobic shoes for as low as $29.95, Reebok also offered shoes at five different price points up to $53.99. This strategy was equally successful in other shoe categories. By 1991, Reebok had introduced many athletic shoes which had focused on performance.

MAJOR PRODUCT LINES

During its first 11 years of operations, Reebok grew into a billion-dollar corporation that produced all types of athletic footwear and apparel under various brand names. It achieved this position primarily through acquisitions.

Reebok Brands

Reebok brands included various lines of shoes and apparel. Reebok footwear includes men's, women's, and children's athletic and casual footwear. Athletic shoes were produced in all sports categories. Reebok targeted consumers with active lifestyles as its primary base. In addition, it had a line of full-support infant and toddler shoes called Weeboks. Metaphors, Reebok's line of women's casual shoes, combined fashion and athletic shoe technology.

Reebok introduced the Pump technology into athletic shoes in November 1989. The technology included an internal air-bladder system that addressed the long-standing challenge of ankle support with an air-cushioned custom fit [Reebok 1989 Annual Report].

The company entered the apparel market in 1985 on the strength of the Reebok name, with a line of men's and women's performance wear, activewear, and sportswear. This athletic apparel was targeted at the more affluent consumer. The company also sold general sportswear like warm-up suits and sweatshirts to a broader market.

Boks, Reebok's casual shoe line, was spun off into its own division in 1992. The line focused on casual footwear with the latest technology. The footwear, which ranged from street hikers to bucks with lug soles, was targeted at men and women aged 18 to 34 ["Boks to Feature Casual Line..." 1992].

Rockport

Reebok decided to diversify and expanded into specialized footwear through the acquisition of Rockport, a well-known manufacturer of dress, casual, and walking shoes. Rockport was a leader in the development of bio-mechanically designed shoes structured for the walking motion of the foot. The division was consolidated with John A. Frye Company, a well-known producer of high-quality dress shoes and boots.

In 1989, the Rockport division had a banner year, achieving significant sales growth and an earnings increase of more than 150 percent. In 1989, the Rockport boating shoe, the Walking Pump, the Signature Collection, and the DressSports line were introduced [Reebok 1990(A) *Annual Report*].

In 1990, while the U.S. dress and casual footwear market had a no-growth year, Rockport posted gains of 21 percent in sales [Reebok 1990(A) *Annual Report*]. New growth channels for 1991 included the expansion of Rockport footwear in European markets and the introduction of apparel which capitalized on Rockport's strong brand appeal [Reebok 1991(B)].

Avia

In 1987, Reebok purchased Avia Inc., an athletic footwear manufacturer known for producing high-performance and technological shoes. Avia's specialized athletic footwear products included shoes for aerobics, running, basketball, and tennis. Avia added a cycling line to its mix of athletic footwear to meet the increased demand for these shoes. A new technology, called ARC, which enhanced the sole by improving cushioning and stability, was incorporated into these shoes.

Ellesse USA

In 1988, Reebok purchased Ellesse USA and all North American rights from Ellesse International, an Italian sports apparel company. Ellesse was well known for designing and marketing men's and women's sportswear. It had also produced athletic footwear with its own brand name targeted at the young trendy consumer.

Ellese believed in "the Beauty of the Sport" and its name became synonymous with innovative and classic elegance. In the first nine months of 1991, sales grew to $53 million — a 60.8 percent increase over the same period in 1990 [Reebok 1991(B)].

Boston Whaler

Boston Whaler was acquired by Reebok in October 1989, adding another respected brand name to the company. Boston Whaler, a noted leader in recreational boating, was noted for exceptional quality, durability, safety, and stability. This division brought in sales of $47 million in 1989 [Reebok 1989 Annual Report] and sales of $37 million in a recession-afflicted industry in 1990.

SALES/DISTRIBUTION OUTLETS

Reebok's philosophy was that distribution helped determine a consumer's perceptions. Therefore, most of its brands were sold through department stores, athletic specialty stores, and sporting goods stores. Even though the majority of Reebok's products were distributed through these retailer outlets, other types of outlets were also used, depending on the brand. For example, the Weebok line of shoes was distributed through department stores, family shoe stores, and juvenile shoe stores. Each major division had its own separate sales force.

Reebok operated several retail outlet stores which sold footwear, apparel, and accessories bearing the Reebok, Weebok, Metaphors, Rockport, Avia, and Ellesse brand names. These outlets were located so as not to interfere with normal distribution channels.

SOURCING

Reebok sourced its footwear primarily in South Korea and Taiwan, with these two countries accounting for approximately 61 percent and 20 percent respectively of the company's total footwear production. Reebok purchased an average of 18 million pairs of footwear per month.

Each of the company's operating units dealt with a manufacturer on a purchase order basis. Asia's 10 factories produced athletic footwear to Reebok's specifications; these shoes were then shipped to Reebok's main warehouse in Stoughton, Massachusetts. All manufacturing was supervised by Reebok's management, located in Massachusetts. Daily FAX transactions to Reebok's development people in the Far East who worked with the local manufacturers facilitated communications.

The principal materials used in the company's footwear products were leather, nylon, rubber, ethylvinyl acetate, polyurethane, and pigskin. Most of these materials were obtained from a number of sources so that the loss of a supply source would disrupt production only temporarily. Reebok believed that it had adequate substitute supply sources for the products obtained from foreign suppliers.

Reebok developed a computer-based matrix in its Canton, Massachusetts, headquarters to coordinate manufacturing and marketplace needs more efficiently. Its computers reduced production lead times by 25 percent. It had developed plants in Thailand and mainland China in anticipation of Koreans leaving shoe factories for better-paying jobs in electronics factories.

Even with Korean currency rising against the dollar and payments of tariffs which ranged from 8.5 percent to 37.5 percent, Reebok still benefitted greatly from having all its shoes made abroad. By selling shoes, which cost only $7 to manufacture and distribute, at $30 a pair wholesale, Reebok profited enormously. The company's reliance on others' production had kept its own debt to a minimum.

MARKETING POLICY

The company's marketing policy consisted of influential and segmented marketing. The strategy of influential marketing was based on psychographics which examined how consumers perceived themselves, what they valued, and how they spent their leisure time. Segmented marketing emphasized marketing to numerous consumer segments rather than a homogeneous population.

Influential Marketing

Reebok grew by defying conventional marketing wisdom, which tended to rely on demographics, market research, and mass-media advertising. It used influential marketing in order to understand the athletic footwear consumer.

Reebok asked two important questions: what appeals to consumers and what motivates them to buy a product? The company's marketing strategy was based on answering these questions, as well as on providing all the support necessary to make its consumers feel comfortable with their purchases. For example, the Blacktop had a street-level image which emphasized "Performance with a human face" and contained the message that regular guys played outdoor ball [Megel 1991].

Segmented Marketing

In many ways, Reebok created segmented marketing for the athletic footwear industry. In 1983, Reebok discovered a large but ignored market segment — women — and became the first company to make athletic footwear for women. The company quickly and aggressively tapped a new marketing opportunity by identifying aerobics and making a name for itself in that market.

Reebok continued to influence and maintain its involvement in the aerobics movement. It published aerobics newsletters, sponsored aerobics seminars, and provided discounts to instructors. Reebok also helped organize and sponsor the National Aerobics Championships. Through these efforts, Reebok achieved an 85 percent market share of a sport that appealed mostly to women. It was the first time a company ever made athletic footwear targeted at women.

Reebok constantly explored and developed new market segments or expanded and reinforced old ones. Reebok divided the athletic footwear market into different consumer segments, and, for every consumer segment identified, the company either sponsored or became involved in promotional and public relations activities and events that were influential and important to that segment.

Established trust and confidence in one consumer segment often helped Reebok enter another segment. For example, a large percentage of the women purchasing Reebok's aerobic shoes were mothers; therefore the company also marketed it children's shoes to them. These women felt comfortable about buying Weeboks for their children since they trusted the brand. To popularize this shoe, Reebok created a stuffed animal called Willoughby Weebok. It also produced puppet shows in major malls featuring the stuffed animal and his friends.

In an effort to appeal to teens, Reebok became the official shoe company of the nationwide Six Flags Theme Parks. The company sponsored several of the rides and offered free shoes to the parks' employees. Reebok also helped underwrite the Human Rights tour, Now! — a world music tour during the fall of 1988 which featured some of the biggest names in rock music.

To attract older people, Reebok became involved in fitness walking. By acquiring Rockport, the company was able to build on an established brand name known for its casual and performance walking shoes. To promote the benefits of fitness walking, Rockport sponsored Rob Sweetgall's 50-state, 50-week walk around the United States and funded technical and biomedical research at the Rockport Walking Institute.

Reebok's marketing philosophy gave it an awareness of changes within each consumer segment. For example, after noticing that former runners were entering both the walking segment and the cycling segment, Reebok quickly developed products to appeal to these consumers.

ADVERTISING POLICY

The advertising approach developed by Reebok in the early 1980s continued into the 1990s. Reebok advertised heavily in specialty periodicals and more lightly in broad-based general interest magazines. The media promoted use of products by a select group of successful athletes and celebrities.

Reebok's first advertisements were targeted at the serious athlete via magazines like *Tennis, Shape and Fit,* and *New Body*. Reebok concentrated on advertisements in specialty magazines, for example *Runner's World,* to create a bond with specific consumers. Advertisements were placed in magazines like *Esquire* and *Glamour* to promote awareness among people who had an influence in terms of brand referencing and leadership.

Another key feature in Reebok's advertising strategy was celebrity endorsement. The company focused not only on professional athletes for endorsements but also on actors and singers who were considered heroes or leaders for different consumer segments. Past endorsers included Bill Cosby, Mick Jagger, Michael J. Fox, and Bruce Springsteen. Actress Cybil Shepard even accepted her 1985 Emmy award while wearing a pair of tangerine-colored Reebok high-tops. Sports professionals such as tennis stars Hana Mandlikova and Ken Flach, and basketball players Danny Manning and Dennis Johnson, also endorsed or wore Reebok's athletic shoes.

Reebok reorganized its Reebok brand business in the U.S. into two units — performance and lifestyles. The lifestyles division offered fashion statement shoes for females and teens. The performance unit had a number of sports celebrity spokespersons: Atlanta's Dominique Wilkins, basketball coach Pat Riley, tennis champs Michael Chang and Arantxa Sanchez, and the PGA pro tour's Greg Norman [Bagot 1990 pp. 61-65].

In 1990, the company budgeted $70 million for advertising and promotion. New advertisements highlighted the company's best shoes by focusing on performance and enhanced features such as the Energy Return System, Hexalite, and Energaire [Bagot 1990 pp.61-65]. In 1991, the company budgeted $140 million for advertising and promotion to get its message "Life is Short, Play Hard" to the consumer. Worldwide, $220 million was budgeted for 1992 advertising [Jefferson 1992 pp. 1,6].

MANAGEMENT

Reebok's high-flying founder and chairman, Paul Fireman, was said to have a knack for pushing a concept to its limits [Sedgewick 1989 p. 31]. To him there was no good or bad or even effective or ineffective. There was only the exciting and the dull.

Reebok's top executives had no experience in the shoe business when they joined the company. Its chief operating officer, C. Joseph LaBonte, was the president of Twentieth Century Fox when it produced "Star Wars" and "Chariots of Fire." The president of Reebok Brands formerly was the highly successful chief executive of HBO Video whom LaBonte knew from his days in the movie business. Mark R. Goldston, chief marketing officer, was once the president of Faberge USA. While many competitors emphasized performance and design of high-priced athletic shoes, Goldston believed that Reebok should continue to sell image.

During 1989, Fireman handed the day-to-day control of operations over to LaBonte, while he attended to the big picture. "It's not that I'm glad to get the day-to-day stuff off my back," he said. "It's that I only have one back." He kept his hands in designing products. Aside from some new high-profile marketing talent in upper management, associates still believed that Fireman had the best sense in the company for which athletic shoes would sell. Around Reebok, he was known for controlling meetings and turning everyone in the same direction. For these skills, Fireman received a combined salary and bonus of $14.6 million in 1989. In a move towards cost control, Fireman agreed to take one of the biggest pay cuts ever by reducing his annual compensation to $4.8 million in 1991 [Reebok 1990(B)].

Reebok's management's team contributed to the company's success in a time of rapid change [Morgenson 1988 p. 119]. It was a young company, with relatively young executives. This, in effect, helped produce exciting and innovative products. Throughout the 1980s, Reebok's management implemented a three-prong diversification strategy. First, the company acquired firms with products that appealed to the trendsetting 18- to 45-year-old age group. Reebok also planned to develop internally and expand internationally. According to Fireman, Reebok's success was attributed to the following: its effective marketing style, its risk-taking approach, a dedicated staff, product development through teamwork and a focus on the consumer. The company strongly believed in customer satisfaction, finding out exactly what they want and then delivering it to them.

TOWARDS THE FUTURE

What will the 1990s have in store for Reebok International? Management at Reebok was currently looking at alternative strategies for the company to regain the number one industry position. One of the main strategic questions it faced was whether and how to emphasize and balance fashion or function in its product lines.

Some executives felt that if Reebok focused on manufacturing technologically advanced athletic shoes for all sports categories it could seize industry leadership from Nike. The assumption was based on the past performance of Reebok's technically advanced high-performance shoes. Although Nike led in overall market share in 1989, Reebok's $170 shoe, the Pump, ran the $175 Nike Air Pressure shoe off the court [Pereira 1989].

Management believed that more superior shoes like the Pump would re-energize the entire Reebok brand line. Their argument went like this: Reebok had initially built its reputation on performance-oriented footwear with the introduction of the aerobic/fitness shoe in 1982. In 1989, the Pump technology was introduced and became an immediate sales success. Continued success came from the availability of Pump technology in all of Reebok's athletic footwear. One of the most important technological developments in industry history, the Pump technology was expanded to five chambers and used in nine sport categories [Reebok 1991(B)]. This technology led to a two percent increase in market share for Reebok in 1990. However, even with this increase, Nike still maintained a six percent lead over Reebok in market share. In 1991, Reebok again introduced new technology with the Blacktop, a more rugged outdoor basketball shoe. The Blacktop added over $100 million to Reebok's total sales [Megel 1991]. However, Nike's sales still surpassed Reebok's. A major commitment to technology-based products seemed to be needed to increase in market share. This meant greater research and development at Reebok [Reebok 1991(B)].

Some executives argued that if more of Reebok's research and development budget had been devoted to the development of functional components of products and less towards upgrading fashion components, Reebok would have kept its number one position. They felt that Reebok had lost its position to Nike when the company began to focus on marketing fashionable, rather than functional, shoes.

On the other hand, some executives argued that Reebok would regain its position more effectively by focusing on the fashion aspects of athletic shoes. They based their assumption on the fact that 80 percent of athletic shoes purchased were not worn for the activity for which they were designed [Bagot 1990]. In 1991, when Reebok had record sales of $2.7 billion the Pump had accounted for only 16 percent of Reebok's sales [Foltz 1992 pp. 1,5]. This was an indication that performance was not driving the industry [Tedeschi 1992(A)]. Since the introduction of the Pump in 1989, the Blacktop was the only big technological innovation by Reebok. These executives feared that as the Pump matured, sales growth would slow.

These executives argued that in the past several years Reebok had spent too much on research and development for technically advanced shoes and, with the exception of the Pump and Blacktop, had not been successful. Moreover, the focus on technical performance over the past several years had caused Reebok to lose its fashion-conscious consumers. They argued that athletic shoes that were more fashion oriented would yield greater sales in the larger fashion oriented market, and that added technical features made shoes too costly to manufacture. Moreover, fashion-oriented shoes could be marketed more easily with coordinated fashion sportswear, such as the "Life Styles" line that Reebok was developing. Consumers were looking for head-to-toe dressing in one brand. With head-to-toe dressing, consumers would want to own many pairs of athletic shoes to accent their wardrobes, instead of the usual one pair of athletic shoes. These executives felt that a shoe without added technology could be sold if properly promoted. To keep customers interested, especially teenagers, Reebok had to continually redesign shoes [Foltz 1992 pp. 1,5].

Executives supporting the fashion-focused product strategy argued that a study showed that the athletic apparel segment was a $23 billion industry, more than twice the size of the athletic footwear industry [Finkelstein 1990]. In combination with fashionable athletic shoes, this was the market segment that held the most promise.

In light of these arguments, management was studying how to answer these and other strategic questions.

REFERENCES AND BACKGROUND READINGS

Arthur, Charles, "Fashion's Fancy Footwork," *Business* (UK), July 1990, pp.84-88.

Bagot, Brian, "Brand Report: Shoeboom!," *Marketing & Media Decisions*, June 1990, pp.61-65.

Bannon, Lisa, "Demand for Top U.S. Athletics Still Strong Among Europeans," *Footwear News*, September 18, 1989, pp. 2, 20.

Bayor, Leslie, "Shoe Marketers Prep for Workout," *Advertising Age*, March 11, 1991, p. 12.

Benoit, Ellen, "Lost Youth," *Financial World*, September 20, 1988, pp. 28-31. "Boks by Reebok Gets Independent Div. Status," *Footwear News*, December 9, 1991, p. 19.

"Boks to Feature Casual Line With Performance Influence," *Footwear News*, February 3, 1992, p. 62.

Buell, Barbara, "Nike Catches Up With the Trendy Frontrunner," *Business Week*, October 24, 1988, p.88.

Burkeley, William, "Reebok Posts a 39% Rise in Earnings; Sales Surge Pressures Nike, Other Rivals," *Wall Street Journal*, July 23, 1991, Sec. A, p. 5.

Colter, Gene, "Are Athletics Makers Serving Stale Products?," *Footwear News*, October 28, 1991, pp. 2, 24.

"Current Population Reports," *U.S Bureau of the Census, 1990*, series P-25, Nos. 519,917, 1045, and 1057, p. 13.

"Distribution: Better Customer Service Justifies New Center," *Modern Materials Handling*, March 1989, pp. 14-15.

Dumaine, Brian, "Design That Sell and Sells and...," *Fortune*, March 11, 1991, pp. 86-94.

"Economy, Timing Hurt Shoe Shows," *Footwear News*, December 9, 1991, pp. 1, 16.

Ferrara, Dan, "Happy Trails," *Men's Health*, April 1992, pp. 64-67.

Finkelstein, Anita, "The Newest Team, Footwear and Apparel Step Up To Bat," *Footwear News*, July 1990, p. 72.

Freeman, Laurie, "Flat-Footed: Ad Campaigns Try to Spark Sales as Sport Shoes Hit Plateau," *Stores*, Aug 1991, pp.67, 68.

Foltz, Kim, "Reebok Fights to Be No.1 Again," *New York Times*, March 12, 1992, Sec. D, pp. 1,5.

"Into The Rough," *The Economist*, March 15, 1991, p. 71.

Jefferson, David, "Reebok Primes the Pump While Rivals Stress Value," *Wall Street Journal*, February 3, 1992, Sec B, pp. 1, 6.

Jereski, Laura, "Can Paul Fireman Put the Bounce Back in Reebok?," *Business Week*, June 18, 1990, pp. 181-182.

Jereski, Laura, "Paul Fireman Pulls on His Old Running Shoes," *Business Week*, Nov 6, 1989, pp. 46-47.

Laverty, Jeffery, "Shoe Industry," *Value Line*, 1991, p. 1655.

Lee, Sharon, "Athletic Sales Hit $3.5 billion," *Footwear News*, May 16, 1988, pp. 1,22.

Lee, Sharon, "Athletic Styles Walking Tall," *Footwear News*, April 1990, p. 10.

Lee, Sharon, "The Price is Right," *Footwear News*, July 15, 1991, pp. 26, 28.

Martinez, Angel R., "Two CEO-Driven Improvement Programs," *Management Review*, November 1988, pp. 15-18.

McAllister, Robert, "Avia Looks to Bolster Its Aerobics Business," *Footwear News*, September 30, 1991.

McCarthy, Michael, "Changes Brewing at Coke," *The Wall Street Journal*, April 20, 1990, Sec. B, p. 1.

McKay, Deirdre, "Walk This Way," *Footwear News*, September 9, 1991, pp. 14-15.

McNally, Pamela, "Casualties of Change," *Footwear News,* January 27, 1992, p. 40, 42.

Meeks, Fleming, "The Sneaker Game," *Forbes,* Oct 22, 1990, pp.114-115. Megel, Archie, "The Blacktop Is Paving Reebok's Road to Recovery," *Business Week,* August 12, 1991, pp. 27.

Morgenson, Gretchen, "Has the Runner Stumbled?," *Forbes,* August 1988, pp. 118-119.

Nike 1990 Annual Report.

Pereira, Joseph, "Pumped-Up Reebok Runs Fast Break With New Shoe," *The Wall Street Journal,* December 20, 1989, Sec. B, p. 1.

Pereira, Joseph, "Athletic-Shoe Sales in Coming Months Are Expected to Be Sluggish in the U.S.," *The Wall Street Journal,* April 1, 1991(A), Sec. B, p.6.

Pereira, Joseph, "From Air to Pump to Puma's Disc System, Sneaker Gimmicks Bound to New Heights," *The Wall Street Journal,* October 31, 1991(B), Sec. B, p. 1.

Pulda, Ellen, "LaBonte Leaves Reebok," *Footwear News,* October 30, 1989, pp. 1,18.

Ramirez, Anthony, "The Pedestrian Sneaker Makes a Comeback," *The New York Times,* October 14, 1990, p. 17.

Reebok 1989 *Annual Report.*

Reebok 1990(A) *Annual Report.*

Reebok 1990(B) *Form 10-K Report.*

Reebok 1991(A) *Quarterly Reports.*

Reebok 1991(B) *Backgrounder.*

Reebok 1992 *Running.*

"Reebok International Ltd.," *Corporate Industry Research Reports,* 1990(A).

"Reebok International Ltd.," *Corporate Industry Research Reports,* 1991(A).

"Reebok International Ltd.," *Market Guide Report,* 1992.

"Reebok International, Ltd.," *Moody's Industrial Manual,* 1990(B).

"Reebok International Ltd.," *St. John's University -Disclosure Compact Disk,* 1991(B).

"Reebok Rebounds With the Pump," *The New York Times,* June 7, 1991, Sec D, p. 6.

"Reebok Sees Net Earnings Falling Below Projections," *Womens Wear,* November 30, 1988, p. 27.

Reichlin, Igor, "Where Nike and Reebok Have Plenty of Running Room," *Business Week,* March 11, 1991, pp. 56,60.

Rigg, Cynthia, "Buying Gets Hot," *Advertising Age,* Nov 12, 1990, p. 24.

Rooney, Ellen, "Athletic Retailers Find Classics Are Surest Route in B-T-S Season," *Footwear News,* July 31, 1983, pp. 56,60.

Rooney, Ellen, "Can High Tech Shoes Pass the Test," *Footwear News,* July 1990, p. 66.

Rottman, Meg, "Michael Jackson Signs Mega L.A. Gear Contract," *Footwear News,* September 18, 1989, pp. 1, 19.

Rudolph, Barbara, "Foot's Paradise," *Time,* April 1989, pp. 54-55.

Ryan, Thomas, "Some Firms Shine in Bleak '90 Market," *Footwear News,* July 8, 1991, p. 28.

Schewe, Charles, "Strategically Positioning Your Way into the Aging Marketplace," *Business Horizons,* May/June 1991, pp. 59-66.

Sedgewick John, "Treading on Air," *Business Month,* Jan. 1989 pp. 28-34. Silverman, Dick, "Athletic Firms See More Growth Via Technology," *Footwear News,* Febuary 14, 1989, pp. 1,18.

Silverman, Dick, "That Sneaky Feeling," *Footwear News,* August 12, 1991, pp. 27.

Sloan, Pat, "Reebok Rethinks U.B.U.," *Advertising Age,* March 17, 1989(A), pp. 1, 80.

Sloan, Pat, "Reebok Responds to Nike," *Advertising Age,* Feb 1989(B), pp. 2, 72.

Sloan, Pat, "Reebok Chief Looks Beyond Nike," *Advertising Age,* Jan 29, 1990, pp. 16, 57.

Sloan, Pat, "Reebok Double Pump Courts Interest," *Advertising Age,* November 4, 1991(A), p. 12.

Sloan, Pat, "Reebok Laces Up Chiat Ads," *Advertising Age,* July 8, 1991(B), p. 4.

Sohng, Laurie, "Active Casual: Turning Up the A.C.," *Footwear News*, February 12, 1992, pp. 8-9.

Stern, Aimee, L., and Anne Hollyday, "Reebok: In for the Distance," *Business Month*, August 1987, pp. 22-25.

"Super Show Puts Focus on Outdoor Activities," *Footwear News*, February 10, 1992, pp. 4, 56.

"Super Show to Highlight Outdoor, Value Athletics," *Footwear News*, January 27, 1992, pp. 1, 52.

Tedeschi, Mark, "Bob Meers Plays to Win," *Footwear News*, July 15, 1991(A), pp. 2, 28.

Tedeschi, Mark, "Reebok Building Walking Line," *Footwear News*, July 15, 1991(B), p. 24.

Tedeschi, Mark, "Reebok Earnings, Volume Topple 4th Qtr. Records," *Footwear News*, February 13, 1992(A).

Tedeschi, Mark, "Reebok to Play Up Running More," *Footwear News*, January 27, 1992(B), p. 49.

"Textiles, Apparel, & Home Furnishings," *Standard and Poor's Industry Surveys*, 1991, pp. 86-94, 164-166.

"Tennis Shoe Firms See Age, Attitude the Great Divide," *Footwear News*, October 14, 1991, p. 2.

"The Numbers Game, Keeping Score of Athletic Footwear," *Footwear News*, July 1990, p. 64.

Therrien, Lois, and Amy Borrus, "Reeboks: How Far Can a Fad Run?," *Business Week*, February 24, 1986, pp. 89-90.

Tracy, Diane, "Well, at Least One Annual Report Has an Eye-Catching Bottom Line," *The Wall Street Journal*, Apr 2, 1991, Sec B. p.1.

Udis, Howard, "L.A. Gear, Inc," *Value Line*, 1991(A), p. 1660.

Udis, Howard, "Nike, Inc," *Value Line*, 1991(B), p. 1661.

Udis, Howard, "Reebok International Ltd.," *Value Line*, 1991(C), p. 1662.

"Wall Street: Reebok International Ltd.," *Money*, February, 1992.

Weinschenk, Carl, "Sports/Leisure" *Setting*, 1986, p. 35.

Weinstein, Fannie, "Youth Marketing: 'Time to Get Them in Your Franchise'," *Advertising Age*, February 1, 1988, pp. 86-87, S25.

Williams, Lisa. "Big 3 Athletic Companies Jockey for Markey Share," *Footwear News*, September 4, 1989, pp. 1,27.

Witt, Clyde, "Reebok's Distribution on Fast Track," *Material Handling Engineering*, March 1989, pp. 43-48.

Yang, Dori, "Step by Step with Nike," *Business Week*, Aug 13, 1990, pp. 116-117.

Zipser, Andy, "Mutual Choice: Pumping Up Profits," *Barron's*, Oct 21, 1991, pp. 46-47.

THE SEVEN-UP COMPANY: THE SOFT DRINK INDUSTRY

The Seven-Up Company is an operating subsidiary of Dr Pepper/Seven-Up Companies, Inc. It manufactures, markets, sells, and distributes soft drink extracts and concentrates (basic flavoring ingredients for soft drinks), and fountain syrups (extract or concentrate with added sweetners and water) within the United States. The Seven-Up Company sells its products principally to independent licensed bottlers who package carbonated beverages for resale. In 1990 the soft drink business industry reached $27.5 billion in sales and sold 7.9 billion cases. Figure 1 shows soft drink consumption in total sales and cases sold from 1983 to 1990.

In 1990, The Seven-Up Company and the lemon-lime segment of the soft drink industry both experienced decreased market share. Market share for The Seven-Up Company dropped to 4.0 percent in 1989, the third consecutive year of decline. Market share for the entire lemon-lime segment of the soft drink industry dropped to 11.7 percent, the fourth decrease in five years. Figure 2 compares major soft drink competitors' market shares and product consumption for 1985-1990, while Figure 3 compares the same information for soft drinks by flavor.

In 1991, The Seven-Up Company named Frances I. Mullin as its third chief operating officer in four years. Faced with a fourth straight year of declining sales volume, Mullin needed to consider Seven-Up's product line, as well as its bottling and distribution infrastructure.

THE INDUSTRY AND COMPETITIVE MARKET

THE SOFT DRINK INDUSTRY

Soft drinks have existed since the early 1800s when many U.S. druggists concocted blends of fruit syrups and carbonated soda water to sell at their soda fountains. The formulas for Coca-

Figure 1: Production and Consumption of Soft Drinks

Year	Wholesale Revenue	Cases Sold (192 ounces)
1990	27,511,300,000	7,914,000,000
1989	26,710,000,000	7,680,000,000
1988	26,060,000,000	7,530,000,000
1987	25,750,000,000	7,155,000,000
1986	21,333,499,000	6,770,000,000
1985	19,990,816,000	6,500,000,000
1984	18,896,814,000	6,130,000,000
1983	17,427,168,000	5,780,000,000

Source: Information adapted from "Soft Drink Trends," *Beverage Industry Annual Manual 91/92*, March 1991, pp. 14-34.

Figure 2: Major Soft Drink Competitors 1985-1990

MARKET SHARE (IN PERCENTAGES)

Year	Coke	Pepsi	Seven-Up	Dr. Pepper	Dr Pepper/Seven-Up Companies, Inc.
1985	38.6	29.8	5.9	4.9	10.8
1986	39.9	29.8	5.1	5.3	10.4
1987	40.3	30.2	5.3	5.4	10.7
1988	40.5	30.7	4.9	5.6	10.5
1989	40.0	31.7	4.2	5.6	9.8
1990	40.4	31.8	4.0	5.8	9.8

CASES SOLD (IN MILLIONS)

Year	Coke	Pepsi	Seven-Up	Dr. Pepper	Dr Pepper/Seven-Up Companies, Inc.
1985	2509.0	1937.0	383.5	318.5	702.0
1986	2694.0	2071.6	338.5	324.9	663.4
1987	2854.8	2203.7	372.0	357.8	729.8
1988	2997.0	2356.8	353.9	399.0	752.9
1989	3072.0	2434.5	322.5	430.0	752.5
1990	3197.0	2516.6	316.5	459.0	775.5

Source: Information adapted from "Soft Drink Trends," *Beverage Industry Annual Manual 91/92*, March 1991, pp 14-34.

Figure 3: Soft Drink Product Type Consumption, 1985-1990

MARKET SHARE

	1985	1986	1987	1988	1989	1990
Colas	67.5%	68.8%	69.0%	69.1%	69.5%	69.9%
Lemon-Lime	12.2%	11.3%	10.6%	10.4%	12.0%	11.7%
Pepper Type	4.9%	4.6%	4.7%	5.1%	5.3%	5.6%
Juice Added	3.9%	4.9%	4.5%	3.6%	—	—
Root Beer	2.3%	2.2%	2.4%	2.4%	2.6%	2.7%
Orange	0.8%	1.4%	1.0%	0.8%	2.4%	2.3%
All Other	8.4%	6.8%	7.8%	8.4%	8.2%	7.8%
TOTAL	100.0%	100.0%	100.0%	100.0%	100.0%	100.0%

CASES SOLD
(IN MILLIONS)

	1985	1986	1987	1988	1989	1990
Colas	4387	4657	4937	5203	5337	5532
Lemon-Lime	793	765	758	783	921	926
Pepper Type	318	311	336	384	407	443
Juice Added	253	331	322	271	—	—
Root Beer	149	148	172	181	200	214
Orange	52	95	71	60	184	182
All Other	546	460	558	632	630	617
TOTAL	6498	6767	7154	7514	7679	7914

COLAS: DIET AND CAFFEINE-FREE
MARKET SHARE

	1985	1986	1987	1988	1989	1990
Diet	23.1%	24.0%	24.8%	25.9%	27.9%	29.4%
Caffeine-Free	4.7%	N/A	N/A	N/A	5.2%	5.9%

COLAS: DIET AND CAFFEINE-FREE CASES SOLD
(IN MILLIONS)

	1985	1986	1987	1988	1989	1990
Diet	1500.2	1622.7	1771.4	1951.0	2140.0	2330.5
Caffeine-Free	307.4	N/A	N/A	N/A	402.1	466.2

Source: Information adapted from "Soft Drink Trends," *Beverage Industry Annual Manual 91/92*, March 1991, pp.14-34.

Cola, Pepsi-Cola, and Dr Pepper were all developed in this way. Soft drink products were categorized by flavor, such as cola or lemon-lime, or by ingredients, such as juice added. Soft drinks were distributed through many outlets and sold in various product forms and packages.

Three major groups were involved in the production and distribution of soft drinks: concentrate and syrup producers, bottlers, and retailers [Christensen 1987]. Concentrate and syrup producers manufactured basic flavors and sold them to independently franchised or company-owned bottlers. Bottlers added carbonated water and sweetener to the concentrate and packaged the resulting soft drink. Retailers then sold the soft drinks to the customer.

Two major groups competed in the soft drink industry. The first group consisted of the large diversified soft drink companies: The Coca-Cola Company, PepsiCo, Inc., and The Dr Pepper/ Seven-Up Companies, Inc. The second group consisted of the smaller companies such as Royal Crown Cola, A&W, and the like. Figure 4 shows the chronology of major soft drink brand introductions since 1885.

In 1968, soft drink consumption stood at 21.4 gallons per person per year, fourth highest on the U.S. beverage chart behind milk (23.3 gallons), coffee (37 gallons) and tap water (69.4 gallons). By 1989, consumption of soft drinks had more than doubled. During the 1980s alone, soft drinks had an average annual growth of 3.6 percent. By 1990, soft drink consumption had reached 47.5 gallons—up almost a gallon from the 46.6 gallons consumed in 1989. The trends in soft drink consumption per capita for 1985-1990 are shown in Figure 5.

Soft drink sales increased 3.0 percent in 1990. John C. Maxwell Jr., the beverage industry's director of research/statistics, predicted a similar 3.0% sales increase for 1991 with per capita consumption expected to reach 49.0 gallons. In addition, international prospects for the soft drink industry were very attractive. Expanding operations overseas represented a significant opportunity for the soft drink industry. Although soft drink consumption abroad was generally less than in the United States — less than one-half according to 1990 estimates made by Coca-Cola—growth potential was considered great.

CUSTOMER

According to the U.S. Bureau of the Census, in 1990 the population of the United States was 250 million. Of these people, 90 million were below the age of 25, 117 million were between the ages of 25 and 60, and 43 million were above the age of 60. Soft drink industry analysts realized that people between the ages of 25 and 60 represented the greatest opportunity for market growth because of the group's size, income, and expenditures. In addition, analysts observed that this particular group was becoming concerned with making more health-oriented purchases and that these customers were looking for products that offered more and cost less. These consumers were also more willing to switch brands in order to save money.

Size

The population of the United States in 1960 was 180 million. Of these people, 42.2 percent,

Figure 4: New Soft Drink Brand Introductions

Year	Brand	Company	Description
1885	Dr Pepper	Dr Pepper	Regular pepper
1886	Coca-Cola	Coca-Cola	Regular cola
1898	Pepsi-Cola	Pepsi-Cola	Regular cola
1920	7UP	Seven-Up	Regular lemon-lime
1934	Royal Crown Cola	Royal Crown	Regular cola
1961	Sprite	Coca-Cola	Regular lemon-lime
1962	Diet Rite Cola	Royal Crown	Diet cola
1962	Diet Dr Pepper	Dr Pepper	Diet pepper
1963	Tab	Coca-Cola	Diet cola
1964	Diet Pepsi	Pepsi-Cola	Diet cola
1964	Mountain Dew	Pepsi-Cola	Hillbilly flavor
1970	Diet 7UP	Seven-Up	Diet lemon-lime
1971	S. F. Dr Pepper	Dr Pepper	Diet pepper
1972	Mr PiBB	Coca-Cola	Regular pepper
1974	Welch's Grape	Welch's *	Regular grape soda
1974	Diet Sprite	Coca-Cola	Diet lemon-lime
1977	Pepsi Light	Pepsi-Cola	Diet with lemon
1978	Sunkist	General Cinema	Regular orange soda
1979	Mello Yello	Coca-Cola	Hillbilly flavor
1980	RC 100	Royal Crown	Diet caffeine-free
1980	Diet Sunkist	General Cinema	Diet orange
1982	Decaffeinated RC	Royal Crown	Reg. caffeine-free
1982	RC 100 Regular	Royal Crown	Reg. caffeine-free
1982	LIKE	Seven-Up	Reg. caffeine-free
1982	Pepsi Free	Pepsi-Cola	Reg. caffeine-free
1982	S. F.Pepsi Free	Pepsi-Cola	Diet caffeine-free
1982	Diet Coke	Coca-Cola	Diet cola
1982	Sugar Free LIKE	Seven-Up	Diet caffeine-free
1983	Pepper Free	Dr Pepper	Reg. caffeine-free
1983	S. F. Pepper Free	Dr Pepper	Diet caffeine-free
1983	Caffeine Free Coke	Coca-Cola	Reg. caffeine-free
1983	C. F. Diet Coke	Coca-Cola	Diet caffeine-free
1983	Caffeine Free Tab	Coca-Cola	Diet caffeine-free
1983	7UP Gold	Seven-Up	Spice-flavored

* Brand acquired by Dr Pepper in 1982

Source: Information adapted in part from "New Soft Drink Brand Introductions," *Jesse Meyer's Beverage Digest*, April 1983, p. 61.

Figure 5: Per Capita Soft Drink Consumption, 1985-1990

Year	Cases Sold (In Millions)	Percentage Change	Per Capita (In Gallons)
1985	6,500	6.0	40.8
1986	6,770	4.2	42.1
1987	7,155	5.7	44.1
1988	7,530	5.4	46.0
1989	7,680	2.0	46.6
1990	7,914	3.0	47.5

Source: Information adapted from "Soft Drink Trends," *Beverage Industry Annual Manual 91/92*, March 1991, pp. 14-34.

or 76 million, were between the ages of 25 and 60. In 1980, the general population grew 26 percent to 227 million while the group of people between the ages of 25 and 60 grew at a 28 percent rate to 98 million. This age group now comprised 43.2 percent of the overall population. By 1990, the population stood at 250 million, up 10 percent from 1980. The population of 25 to 60 year-olds had grown another 20 percent and was 117 million. This group now accounted for 46.8 percent of the total U.S. population.

Income

According to the United States Bureau of Labor Statistics, members of the 25 to 60 year-old age group had an average annual income, before taxes, of $33,665. In comparison, the under 25 age group's average annual income was $14,827, while those over the age of 60 averaged $17,205 annually.

Expenditures

According to the U.S. Bureau of Labor Statistics, in 1990 consumers between the ages of 25 and 60 accounted for more than half of all expenditures. The average total of all expenditures by people living in the United States was $23,950, while the average total of all expenditures by consumers in the 25 to 60 year-old age group was $29,455. In addition, the U.S. Department of Agriculture, Economic Research Service, reported that .6 percent of all expenditures was for soft drink purchases. In other words, the average person spent $144 ($23,950 x .006), on soft drinks in 1990. This meant that, on average, consumers were purchasing 192 12-ounce servings per year.

PRODUCTS

All soft drinks consisted of a flavor base, sweeteners, and carbonated water, with some containing caffeine and artificial coloring. In 1990, cola-flavored drinks accounted for approximately 69.9 percent of the soft drink industry's sales or $19.2 billion. Lemon-lime drinks accounted for approximately 11.7 percent or $3.21 billion, and all others, including niche brands, accounted for approximately 18.4 percent or $5.06 billion in sales. Dollar amounts are wholesale amounts and are based on total sales divided by the number of cases sold in 1990 ($27.5 billion/ 7.9 billion cases = $3.47 per case). Colas were clearly the first choice of Americans, as is shown in Figure 3.

Colas

In 1990, colas (primarily Coke and Pepsi) drove industry growth with the largest increase in sales volume. Coke increased its volume sold by 123 million cases for $426 million in revenue while rival Pepsi recorded an increase of 84 million cases for $291 million. This combined increase of 207 million cases, or $717 million, out-paced the rest of the industry's 190 million case or $659 million increase.

In 1990, colas accounted for approximately 69.9 percent or $19.2 billion of the total market, up from 1989's 69.5 percent or $18.6 billion, and were bolstered by strong diet and caffeine-free soft drink sales.

By 1990, diet soft drinks were taking a growing share of the market. From 1989 to 1990, diet soft drink sales increased 8.9% and accounted for 29.4 percent or $8.08 billion of all soft drink sales. Better than any other food or beverage category, the soft drink industry had successfully mainstreamed its diet category. Throughout 1990, bottlers and most franchises made diet soft drinks a major part of their marketing plans.

In 1990, caffeine-free soft drink sales increased by 15.9 percent and case volume reached an all-time high of 466.2 million cases or $1.62 billion ["Soft Drink Trends" 1991]. With these gains, the category now accounted for 5.9 percent share of the soft drink market — the highest percentage since 1985. According to Michael Bellas, president of Beverage Marketing Corp. and a beverage industry analyst, "Caffeine-frees benefitted from the consumer trend of purchasing 'good for you' products and this trend would continued into the '90s" [Sfiligo 1989]. The trends in market share and cases sold of diet and caffeine-free cola products for 1985-1990 are shown in Figure 3.

Considering the motivations of the consumer, health concerns and changing purchasing patterns, diet and caffeine-free colas appeared to be a growing opportunity for soft drink companies.

Lemon-Lime

From 1985 to 1990, the lemon-lime segment of the soft drink industry experienced a decline in market share in every year except 1989. While market share decreased in 1990, sales increased by .4 percent over 1989. Unfortunately, industry analysts did not see this as a positive trend, as the sales increase was attributed primarily to price increases. While the cases of lemon-lime drinks sold increased, these sales were outpaced by the rest of the industry.

Increases experienced were not evenly distributed among all competitors. With the exception of Coca-Cola and Dad's Root Beer Company, companies that manufacture lemon-lime products Sprite and Bubble-Up respectively, all of the participants in the lemon-lime segment lost market share. The Seven-Up Company, a long-time leader in the segment with the 7UP brands, lost 1.1 percent in 1989. PepsiCo, a company that entered the segment with Slice in 1989, lost a 10.8 percent market share in 1990. For companies that had been in or recently entered the market, such as PepsiCo, success was expected to come from aggressive marketing and advertising campaigns and the increased availability that could be achieved through additional fountain or vending outlets. The trends in percentage market share and cases sold in the lemon-lime segment of the soft drink industry for the period 1985 to 1990 are shown in Figure 3.

Others

In 1990, the combined other segment of the soft drink industry captured 18.4 percent or \$5.06 billion of the total market. This segment consisted of pepper-type (5.6% or \$1.54 billion), root-beer (2.7% or \$742.5 million), orange (2.3% or \$632.5 million), and niche brands (7.8% or \$2.145 billion). Of all the product types in this segment, niche brands appeared to be the most promising. For example, in 1990 Dr Pepper's Welch's, a grape soft drink, increased sales by 10 percent, 41.8 million cases or \$144 million — compared to 38.0 million cases or \$131 million in 1989. This marked Welch's fourth consecutive year of increased case sales. A major reason analysts gave for Welch's success was consumers' increased interest in "new age" sparkling, carbonated health-oriented juice drinks. By 1991, the value of this type of soft drink and other niche brands approached \$1 billion and analysts expected this type of soft drink to grow 15 to 20 percent annually and represented a significant opportunity ["Bottled and Canned Soft Drinks" 1992].

MARKET

In 1990, the soft drink industry captured more than 50 percent of total beverage gallonage in the domestic market ["Per Caps" 1992], but by 1992, the soft drink industry was beginning to evaluate new opportunities. The industry looked overseas for growth opportunities and found that the international market was primed for accelerated growth.

Domestic Market

For much of the 1980s, the soft drink industry experienced an annual growth rate averaging 5 percent. By 1989, sales and cases sold reached \$26.7 billion and 7.6 billion respectively. However, this growth rate was not expected to continue. According to industry analysts, soft drink consumption would grow at a 2 to 3 percent rate for the next five years rather than at the substantial rates of the 1980s ["Bottled and Canned Soft Drinks" 1992]. Analysts gave the following reasons for this slowed growth rate: (1) health concerns of the consumer, (2) more frequent eating away from home, and (3) demographic shifts.

Industry analysts expected growth opportunities to come from product extensions and innovations. Analysts were keeping an eye on the soft drink segment such as all natural sodas and sparkling, carbonated juices. The segment had already reached $1 billion in sales and analysts estimate the value of shipments to grow 15 to 20 percent annually ["Bottles and Canned Soft Drinks" 1992].

International Market

The international market, in particular Western Europe, was opened during World War II when Coca-Cola followed American G.I.s overseas. In the years that followed Coca-Cola built a powerful bottling system that allowed it to dominate Western Europe for 50 years. In 1959, Pepsi was introduced in Eastern Europe during an international trade show and by 1973 PepsiCo had an exclusive agreement to sell Pepsi in the Soviet Union. In the 1990s, beginning with the fall of the Berlin Wall, other soft drink companies began to venture overseas. By 1991, the value of U.S. soft drink exports had reached about $121 million, an increase of 14% over 1990 ["International Competitiveness" 1992]. Analysts said that this increase was the result of three important factors: (1) an increase in personal income, which allowed for more discretionary spending, (2) the wider availability of refrigeration, and (3) an increase in the worldwide use of vending machines. Analysts also contended that, along with the above reasons, a 290-million customer base in Eastern Europe made international markets a tremendous opportunity for soft drink companies to exploit. Analysts suggested that a presence in international markets would be a key to success in many companies.

BRAND NAME

A strong brand position and the consumer loyalty it generates have numerous benefits: pricing flexibility and leverage, improved chances of success for new products and brand extensions, and production efficiencies.

Pricing flexibility is perhaps the greatest factor. If brand loyalty exists and if it is substantial, prices could be raised without jeopardizing volume or market share. In addition, strong market share can affect pricing leverage. Retailers cannot afford to bargain for price, because they cannot go without having their shelves stocked with a brand that has a strong loyalty.

Products that display a strong position in the market and offer good margins for the retailer can improve the chances of success for a product line extension or new product, both of which offer important growth potential. Many new products fail not because of poor customer acceptance but because of poor visibility in supermarkets and/or grocery stores.

Lastly, well-known brands generate production efficiency as market share and volume expand. Greater volume reduces overhead costs of unit production and distribution, while benefitting operating margins. In addition, greater volume could lead to lower prices, which in turn could lead to greater growth in volume.

MARKETING, PROMOTIONS, AND ADVERTISING

In the 1990s marketing, promotions, and advertising were expected to reflect the changes occurring in the aging baby-boom market. For reasons mentioned earlier, companies were expected to emphasize "new age" products as well as conduct business as usual for their respective core brands.

Marketing and Promotions

In 1990, marketing and promotional departments were waiting for the national recession to end. In 1991, they were still waiting for a recovery. By 1992, these departments stopped waiting and decided to make the economy and environment work for them. Through research they realized that consumers were no longer concerned with status brands. In fact, consumers were health-conscious and, more than ever, interested in receiving something of value. As a result marketers and promoters began planning for a product that would appeal to aging baby boomers by promoting health. This point was not lost on advertisers, since it emphasized what they were doing in the early 1990s.

Advertising

In 1990, according to the Television Bureau of Advertising from figures supplied by Leading National Advertisers Inc./Arbitron Multi-Media Service, carbonated soft drink makers spent $20.3 million in radio advertising — a 17 percent increase from $17.3 million spent in 1989. Also in 1990, national spot radio advertising increased 15 percent—from 1989's $16.2 million to $18.7 million — and network radio advertising spending totalled $1.5 million in 1990, compared to $1.1 million the previous year. Carbonated soft drink ad dollars totalled $498 million in 1990, up 12 percent from $444 million in 1989.

The number one advertising medium for carbonated soft drink makers, spot television spending, totalled $198.8 million in 1990. Figures 6 and 7 show the dollars spent on radio and television advertising by various companies and for various products.

Industry analysts sought recovery for the slumping lemon-lime segment through aggressive advertising. Advertising was perceived as a crucial element in differentiating a company's products from those of competitors.

PRIMARY PACKAGING TRENDS

Supported by strong multipack sales and successful recycling efforts, cans continued to outpace other types of primary packaging. According to estimates of 1990 primary packaging shipments made by Beverage Industry magazine, only the number of returnable glass bottles sold declined but this trend was expected to change. Analysts gave two reasons for possible reversal:

Figure 6: Radio Advertising Spending (In Millions)

Company	1989 Network	Spot	1990 Network	Spot
Coca-Cola Co.	606.6	4,548.0	403.6	7,312.6
Cherry Coke		126.6		79.3
Coke Classic Caffeine-Free			5.4	10.7
Coca-Cola Gen. Promotion		14.0		
Coca-Cola				1,379.7
Coca-Cola Classic	227.2	1,768.7	133.8	2,680.5
Coca-Cola Cultural Events				53.7
Coca-Cola Sports Events				7.7
Mello Yello Soft Drink		127.5		139.2
Minute Maid	50.4	248.2	6.4	424.3
Sprite	78.6	722.3		776.2
Diet Cherry Coke			88.2	20.4
Diet Coke		1,445.6		1,567.2
Sprite Sugar Free	57.4	6.9		7.8
PepsiCo Inc.		7,276.0		6,208.7
Mountain Dew		1,101.9		683.2
Mug Root Beer		477.3		497.3
Pepsi-Cola		3,275.1		2,601.6
Pepsi-Cola General Promotion		160.5		
Slice Regular		500.7		696.8
Mountain Dew Diet		36.6		24.0
Pepsi Free Diet		130.0		40.8
Pepsi Light Sugar Free				76.5
Slice Diet				0.9
Seven-Up & Dr. Pepper Cos.	484.1	1,624.2	363.0	1,511.9
7UP		686.5		499.8
Cherry 7UP		345.7		187.2
Dr. Pepper	447.8	433.2	303.0	535.8
Diet 7UP		66.3		219.5
Dr. Pepper Sugar Free	36.3	85.2	60.0	69.6

Source: The Television Bureau of Advertising from figures supplied by Leading National Advertisers/ Arbitron Multi-Media Service as reprinted in "Radio Waves," *Beverage Industry*, August 1991, p. 4.

Figure 7: Television Advertising Spending
Top 10 Carbonated Soda Advertisers on TV

Company	1989 Network	Spot	1990 Network	Spot	%Chg
Diet Pepsi	21,244,200	33,980,500	36,363,400	37,598,200	+34
Diet Coke	23,603,300	23,906,500	27,084,000	25,377,400	+17
Coca-Cola Classic	35,093,300	23,675,000	26,979,900	22,055,500	-8
Pepsi-Cola Regular	20,370,500	34,700,100	27,992,500	30,554,200	+6
7UP Regular	17,789,000	1,074,300	18,822,000	826,200	+13
Dr. Pepper Regular	10,286,000	6,095,100	14,487,900	7,496,500	+36
Sprite	9,159,900	8,900,200	6,331,500	9,868,800	-4
Minute Maid	5,418,400	3,695,900	5,172,300	3,890,200	+11
Diet 7UP	1,807,400	310,900	7,353,300	203,600	+108
Slice Regular	1,291,900	9,122,100	29,400	8,471,400	-18

Source: Television Bureau of Advertising from figures supplied by Leading National Advertisers/Arbitron Multi-Media Service as reprinted in "Radio Waves," *Beverage Industry,* August 1991, p. 4.

Figure 8: Soft Drink Sales by Package Type
(Units: Billions of 12-oz. Equivalents)

	1988	% Market	1989	% Market	1990	% Market
Cans	44.9	44.5	49.4	48.0	53.3	52.0
PET	32.0	31.7	31.5	30.5	32.0	30.1
NR Glass	13.2	13.1	13.2	12.8	13.8	11.9
R Glass	10.2	10.7	9.0	8.7	6.7	6.0
Total	100.9	100.0	103.1	100.0	106.2	100.0

Source: Information adapted from "Primary Packaging Trends," *Beverage Industry Annual Manual 91/92,* March 1991, pp. 70-72.

(1) resealability, an option cans do not have, and (2) growth of "new age" products, the sparkling, carbonated juice drinks mentioned earlier, which need the image of glass bottles to attract upscale consumers. Figure 8 compares soft drink sales by package type for 1988-1990 ["Primary Packaging Trends" 1991].

PRODUCTION AND DISTRIBUTION

Three major groups were involved in the production and distribution of soft drinks: concentrate and syrup producers, bottlers, and retailers. Concentrate and syrup producers made the basic flavors and sold them to independently franchised or company-owned bottlers. Bottlers added carbonated water and sweetener to the concentrate and packaged the resulting soft drink. Retailers sold soft drinks to consumers. In the soft drink industry, the breakdown of cost per $1 sale was manufacturing $0.48, marketing $0.27, distribution $0.21, and profit $0.04 [O'Neil 1987].

Concentrate and Syrup Producers

There were more than 50 concentrate producers in the United States. Of these many were regional and private producers who manufactured and sold extensive lines of soft drink flavors, such as grape, orange, and ginger ale. Coca-Cola and PepsiCo totally dominated the industry with a combined market share of more than 70 percent. Some functions exhibited by concentrate and syrup producers were (1) suggesting and setting operating procedure standards for their bottlers, and (2) negotiating directly with major suppliers, particularly sweetener and packaging suppliers in order to encourage reliable supply, faster delivery, and lower prices for their bottlers.

Bottlers

Bottling was a capital-intensive process involving a high-speed bottling line where each package type required separate bottling equipment. By 1990, ten years of vertical integration had reduced the number of franchised soft drink bottlers significantly. Even more dramatically, the industry, through vertical integration, witnessed a decline in the number of soft drink producing plants. The nation's soft drink industry was reshaping. Consolidations occurred and bottling companies became larger and fewer [Gatty 1989]. By 1992, Coca-Cola Company owned 55 percent of its bottling operations, while PepsiCo, Inc. owned 51 percent of its operations. In addition, PepsiCo had large equity interests in five of its top ten independent bottlers ["Bottlers Grade Their Parents" 1991].

Retailers

Industry analysts divided retail outlets for soft drinks into four categories: (1) food stores, (2) fountains, (3) vending, and (4) others. Figure 9 shows some other soft drink outlets.

Figure 9: Soft Drink Outlets

Where it's sold today	Soft Drink
Chain supermarkets	41.2%
Independent	14.5%
Mass merchandisers	5.7%
Convenience stores	11.2%
Drugstores	3.6%
Beverage stores	4.7%
Bars/restaurant	2.9%
Gas stations	3.7%
Other	12.5%

Source: Information adapted from "Mega-Markets Boost Supermarket Strength," *Beverage Industry*, May 1989, p. 36.

Food Stores. In 1989, food stores were again the fastest growing and primary soft drinks outlet. Statistics from Beverage Market Corp. showed that supermarkets, in relation to other retail outlets, steadily increased their market share throughout the 1980s. In 1982, supermarkets accounted for 48.2% of packaged volume — a figure that had climbed to, 50.2 percent by 1987 [Hemphill 1989]. Lower prices and larger soft drink aisles were two factors contributing to increased supermarket sales. The other important factor was that supermarkets were consumers' choice for most of their planned soft drink purchases.

Fountains. Fountain soft drinks accounted for more than 25 percent of total U.S. soft drink consumption in 1990 — an increase of 3 percent over 1989 ["Fountain/Foodservice Trends" 1991].

How had this second largest channel for soft drinks managed to be so successful going into the 1990s? According to Charles S. Frenette, senior vice president of Coca-Cola U.S.A., this was due to changing lifestyles, mainly "the increasing popularity of soft drinks — evidenced by continued growth in per capita consumption figures — with the trend toward greater mobility on the part of the consumers and a higher incidence of dining away from home," said Frenette ["Fountain and Foodservice Trends" 1991].

In 1990, Coke controlled almost 60 percent of the fountain segment, compared to Pepsi's 32 percent. Dr Pepper/Seven-Up accounted for 8 percent of fountain sales.

Vending. In 1990, vending accounted for 11 to 15 percent of soft drink sales. With the increase in sales and profits, beverage franchise companies were coming up with more efficient marketing programs and financial incentives to help bottlers attract vending consumers. PepsiCo, Coca-Cola Company, and Dr Pepper/Seven-Up all offered programs to help bottlers succeed in the "power channel."

Others. Convenience stores made up the remaining 10 to 14 percent of the market. These stores differed from supermarkets in that they sold 1,500 cases or fewer per month, while supermarkets sold 1,500 to 10,000 cases per month.

LEGAL ENVIRONMENT

One of the biggest challenges for the soft drink industry was solid waste, according to E. Gifford Stack, vice president of National Soft Drink Associates (NSDA) [Gatty 1989]. By 1990, bottlers and state soft drink associations were beginning to provide assistance in dealing with the problem. Fortunately, it was determined that only four out of the 50 states would face serious difficulties within the next five years. In recognition of the impending crisis, the soft drink industry and the government were beginning to develop strategies that would directly affect the beverage industry's practices and profits. In addition, Congress and the Environmental Protection Agency (EPA) were considering plans that included both management and reduction elements. The active participation of the industry would be an important part of both strategies [Blacock 1989].

GENERAL COMPETITIVE MARKET TRENDS

In 1990, soft drinks captured more than 50 percent of the total beverage market in gallonage (soft drink 53%, beer 27%, fruit juice 7%, bottled water 10%, wine 2%, spirits 1%). Soft drinks continued their upward climb with a 3.0 percent sales increase. Bottled water, at 10 percent growth, remained the industry juggernaut. Juice and fruit drink consumption gained as discounting wars returned to the segment. Spirits sales declined for the eleventh consecutive year, but the category showed signs of leveling off. Wine suffered its second consecutive year of shrinking consumption for the first time since prohibition was repealed, and appeared to be an industry in crisis. Beer sales showed a 1.9 percent gain in 1990 but per capita consumption fell another 0.1 percent. The beverage industry market share for 1990 is shown in Figure 10.

The Coca-Cola Co. and PepsiCo, Inc. together controlled more than 70 percent of the U.S. soft drink market. Their tremendous brand name strength enabled the companies to spread out their marketing and advertising expenses over an ever-increasing stream of revenues. In 1990, America's top 10 soft drinks were

Figure 10: Beverage Industry Market Share, 1990

	Market Share %
Soft Drinks	53
Beer	27
Fruit Juice	7
Bottled Water	10
Wine	2
Spirits	1

Source: Information adapted from "Per Caps," *Beverage Industry*, February 1992, p. 15.

Figure 11: Soft Drink Brand Consumption Market Share (Cases in Millions)

	1988		1989		1990	
	Mil. Cases	% Market	Mil. Cases	% Market	Mil. Cases	% Market
Coke Classic	1501.0	19.9	1501.0	19.5	1532.5	19.4
Pepsi-Cola	1382.0	18.4	1368.0	17.8	1370.0	17.3
Diet Coke	612.0	8.1	673.2	8.8	723.6	9.1
Diet Pepsi	393.0	5.2	440.0	5.7	490.0	6.2
Dr Pepper	325.6	4.3	351.0	4.6	382.2	4.8
Sprite	267.5	3.6	277.0	3.6	285.8	3.6
Mountain Dew	255.0	3.4	280.0	3.4	300.0	3.8
7UP	235.0	3.1	230.8	3.0	229.9	2.9
Caf-Free Diet Coke	148.0	2.0	186.3	2.4	207.4	2.6
Royal Crown	122.0	1.7	109.0	1.4	107.0	1.4

Source: Information adapted from "Soft Drink Trends," *Beverage Industry Annual Manual 91/92*, March 1991, pp. 14-34

1. Coca-Cola Classic	19.4%	7. Sprite	3.8%
2. Pepsi-Cola	17.3%	8. 7UP	2.9%
3. Diet Coke	9.1%	9. Caffeine-Free Diet Coke	2.6%
4. Diet Pepsi	6.2%	10. Caffeine-Free Diet Pepsi	1.4%
5. Dr Pepper	4.8%		
6. Mountain Dew	4.8%		

In terms of corporate growth, 1990 was again led by the cola giants. The Coca-Cola Company — with one of the best-known worldwide brand images — was the first soft drink company to employ the franchise bottler system and was the industry leader in both domestic and overseas markets. On the other hand, PepsiCo, Inc., employed excellent offensive marketing strategies, including use of catchy advertising slogans, for example, "Pepsi, the choice of a new generation" and "You've got the right one baby." In addition, PepsiCo's management understood the importance of product diversification. Figure 11 illustrates the market shares and case sales of major competitors.

Figure 12: Market Share by Major Brand Name

	1988 Market	1989 Market	1990 Market
Coca-Cola			
Classic	19.9	19.5	19.4
Diet Coke	8.1	8.8	9.1
Sprite	3.6	3.6	3.6
C.F. Diet Coke	2.0	2.4	2.6
Coca-Cola	1.3	0.9	0.7
Diet Sprite	0.7	0.8	0.8
Cherry Coke	0.9	0.7	0.6
Diet Cherry Coke	0.3	0.3	0.2
C.F. Coke	0.2	0.2	0.5
Pepsi-Cola	18.4	17.8	17.3
Diet Pepsi	5.2	5.7	6.2
C.F. Diet Pepsi	1.0	1.2	1.4
Slice	1.1	1.0	0.9
C.F. Pepsi	0.9	0.9	0.9
Diet Slice	0.7	0.6	0.4
Dr Pepper	4.3	4.6	4.8
Diet Dr. Pepper	0.4	0.4	0.4
C.F. Dr Diet Pepper	0.1	0.1	0.1
C.F. Dr Pepper	—	—	—
Welch's	0.5	0.5	0.5
Subtotal	*5.3*	*5.6*	*5.8*
7UP	3.1	3.0	2.9
Diet 7UP	1.0	0.9	0.9
Cherry 7UP	0.5	0.3	0.2
7UP Gold	0.1	—	—
LIKE	—	—	—
Others	—	—	—
Subtotal	*4.7*	*4.2*	*4.0*
Total	**10.0**	**9.8**	**9.8**

Source: Information adapted from "Soft Drink Trends," *Beverage Industry Annual Manual 91/92*, March 1991, pp. 14-34

MAJOR COMPETITORS

Competition within the soft drink industry was composed of two distinct groups. The first was the two large, internationally diversified soft drink companies, The Coca-Cola Company and PepsiCo, Inc. The second group was the smaller brand name companies such as A&W.

The total market shares of Seven-Up Companies and its two major competitors are shown by product for 1988-1990 in Figure 12.

The Coca-Cola Company

In 1990, Coca-Cola Company's soft drinks brands owned 40.4 percent of the soft drink market. In the fast-rising diet segment, Coke brands achieved a 44.3 percent share—well ahead of Pepsi's 28.8 percent.

Coca-Cola was focusing on strengthening its bottling operations in order to create greater consumer demand. In the past, local bottlers, especially in Europe, handled the marketing and distribution of soft drinks, but — with recent acquisitions and joint venture agreements— companies were regaining control of their marketing, bottling and distribution functions. With company-controlled marketing and distribution systems, companies were capable of low-cost soft drink delivery which in turn supported a flexible pricing policy. In light of this, Coca-Cola Company had been rapidly buying up independent soft-drink bottlers and was spinning its bottling operation into a separate but controlled company, thereby gaining greater control of its production and distribution operations. As of 1991, The Coca-Cola Company owned 55 percent of its bottling and distribution plants, while PepsiCo, Inc. owned 51 percent of its bottling and distribution plants and had larger equity interests in five of its top 10 independent bottlers.

In 1990, Coke's package, logo, taste, and even its advertising did not change much from Tibet to Tahiti. Not only did this approach save money; it also helped Coca-Cola cultivate a worldwide image as a leading consumer product. Unfortunately, this decision by Coca-Cola led to unhappiness among its bottlers. The remaining independent bottlers, with whom Coca-Cola had 45 percent of their business, had one common complaint: Coca-Cola lacked the willingness to venture into new product development. Some bottlers believed this unwillingness was due to the following reasons: (1) Coca-Cola did not want to get burned again like it did with "New Coke," and (2) Coca-Cola did not want to compete in markets that were small or that required them to manufacture at small volumes since the company considered this to be economically infeasible. Bottlers also had similar complaints about PepsiCo, Inc.

PepsiCo, Inc.

Total volume for PepsiCo, Inc. rose by more than 3.4 percent in 1990. This was achieved without adding major divisions, unlike in 1986 when Pepsico acquired Kentucky Fried Chicken and Seven-Up International.

In 1990, the beverage industry reported that PepsiCo brands accounted for 31.8 percent of all soft drink sales — a gain of .1 percent over the previous year. Pepsi also gained ground on Coke in the diet soft drink market. Diet Pepsi's market share increased from 28.7 percent to 28.8 percent, while Diet Coke declined from 45.1 percent to 44.3 percent.

A trio of fast food chains — Kentucky Fried Chicken, Pizza Hut and Taco Bell — gave PepsiCo the largest worldwide restaurant system. In all, 16,500 restaurants featured Pepsico products. Kentucky Fried Chicken alone contributed $4.1 billion of the reported $11.5 billion of PepsiCo's worldwide sales.

THE COMPANY

HISTORY

The Seven-Up Company, first called the Howdy Company by founder C. L. Griggs, has been in business since 1920. In 1929, the St. Louis-based Howdy Company introduced 7UP as a carmel-colored, lemon-lime soda, with an advertising slogan of "A glorified drink in bottles only. Seven natural flavors blended into a savory, flavory drink with a real wallop." In 1936, Griggs changed the name of the Howdy Company to The Seven-Up Company. From 1936 to 1946, 7UP was the third largest selling soft drink in the world. In 1967, The Seven-Up Company became publicly-owned and in 1968 the company introduced its legendary "Uncola" marketing campaign. In 1970, Diet 7UP was introduced. In 1978 the company was acquired by Phillip Morris, Inc., which in 1986, failed in an attempt to negotiate the sale of Seven-Up to PepsiCo, Inc. In 1987, an investment group headed by Hicks and Haas bought Seven-Up (in a separate transaction Hicks and Haas also bought Dr Pepper; the total figure reported for both purchases exceeded $400 million). Later in 1987, Hicks and Haas named John R. Albers CEO of both Dr Pepper and Seven-Up, and moved Seven-Up's operations base from St. Louis, Missouri to Dallas, Texas. In 1988, the holding companies Dr Pepper and Seven-Up merged, forming the Dr Pepper/ Seven-Up Companies, Inc. In 1991, The Seven-Up Company named Frances I. Mullin as its president and chief operating officer.

MANAGEMENT

In connection with the 1986 leveraged buyout of Seven-Up, the Dr Pepper/Seven-Up Companies, Inc. entered into a management agreement with Seven-Up. This management agreement, which was amended in connection with the acquisition, stated that Dr Pepper would perform management services for Seven-Up consisting of those services normally performed by senior management personnel of a corporation. The management agreement provided that the CEO of Dr Pepper would also serve as, and discharge the duties of, the CEO of Seven-Up — to the extent that the rendering of these services for Seven-Up by such an officer did not adversely

Figure 13: The Seven-Up Company and Subsidiaries
Consolidated Statement of Operations
Three Years Ended December 31, 1990 (In Thousands)

	1988	1989	1990
Net sales	$ 265,978	246,877	229,844
Cost of sales	68,482	63,114	47,502
Gross profit	197,496	183,763	182,342
Operating expenses:			
Marketing	136,378	117,585	119,513
General & Admin.	45,426	21,805	20,995
Amortization of intangible assets	4,662	4,651	4,650
Total oper. Exp	186,466	144,041	145,158
Operating profit	11,030	39,722	37,184
Other income (Exp):			
Interest Exp	(31,306)	(37,824)	(32,029)
Other, net	(1,483)	109	127
Total other Inc/(Exp)	(32,789)	(37,715)	(31,902)
Income (loss) before income taxes & extraordinary items	(21,759)	2,007	5.282
Income taxes (benefit)	(3,281)	1.931	2.940
Income (loss) before extraordinary items	(18,478)	76	2,342
Extraordinary items:			
Benefit from utilization of net operating loss carryforwards		(1,637)	(2,585)
Debt restructuring chrg	5,293		
Net Income (Loss)	(23,771)	1,713	4,927
Preferred Stock dividend requirement	14,812	23,262	27,478
Net loss attributable outstanding common stock	$(38,583)	(21,549)	(22,551)

Source: The Seven-Up Company, *Annual Report, 1990*

affect the responsibilities of the officer to fulfill his obligations as chief executive officer of Dr Pepper. As a result, the manufacturing, general and administrative operations, as well as certain market research and support functions, fountain-food service sales activities, and sales administration activities of Seven-Up and Dr Pepper were integrated.

The general and administrative operations of the two companies that had been integrated were: legal, human resources, treasury, accounting, purchasing, corporate communications, and executive management. The primary sales and marketing operations of the two companies, including advertising and promotional activities, had been and remained separate. Accordingly, it was anticipated that Dr Pepper would not provide any managerial or administrative services to Seven-Up in connection with Seven-Up's primary sales and marketing operations. Seven-Up and Dr Pepper would continue to operate as separate companies and there were no plans for Dr Pepper to merge with, acquire, or be acquired by Seven-Up. In return for providing management services to Seven-Up, Dr Pepper received a fixed annual fee of $7.5 million (subject to a 5 percent annual increase beginning in 1996) and a contingent fee based on Seven-Up's annual performance but not to exceed $2.5 million.

The management agreement also provided for the allocation of capital expenditures and all operating expenses between Dr Pepper and Seven-Up. The primary term of the management agreement was 25 years, subject to earlier termination in certain circumstances.

Prior to their formal merger in Spring 1988 — a transaction valued at $1.3 billion—Dr Pepper and Seven-Up combined certain administrative and manufacturing functions to cut costs. The merger was expected to lead to further economies of scale. Financial results for Seven-Up from 1988-90 are shown in Figure 13. John R. Albers, who served as chairman of both Dr Pepper and Seven-Up, assumed the position of President/CEO of the newly-formed parent company and of each division. Seven-Up President James Harford resigned in May and was replaced by Frances I. Mullin in 1991.

Overall, the Dr Pepper/Seven-Up merger linked two well-known brands under an aggressive management team committed to gaining market share in the intensely competitive $40 billion soft drink market.

PRODUCTS

The Seven-Up Company manufactured, marketed, sold, and distributed soft drink extracts and concentrates, and fountain syrups in the United States. The Seven-Up Company's principal products were 7UP, Diet 7UP, Cherry 7UP, and Diet Cherry 7UP. In 1990, 7UP, Diet 7UP, Cherry 7UP, and Diet Cherry 7UP concentrates and syrups accounted for approximately 57.7 percent, 32.6 percent, 3.1 percent, and 3.1 percent, respectively, of Seven-Up Company's sales revenue.

Other Products

In 1990, Seven-Up marketed Howdy brand soft drink concentrate on a regional basis, as well as caffeine-free colas under the brand names of LIKE and Sugar-Free LIKE. These brands accounted for less than 1% of 1990 sales revenue. As of 1992, spurred by the success of Dr Pepper's Welch's and Nautilus, Seven-Up was investigating the feasibility of new product development or brand extension.

MANUFACTURING AND TECHNICAL FACILITIES

The Seven-Up Company owned a 168,000-square-foot, state-of-the-art production facility in Overland, Missouri. In early 1992, the facility was operating at full capacity on an eight-hour shift five days a week. It was management's belief that Seven-Up could manufacture and produce profitably in small volumes, in particular, a 25 to 50 million case range.

SALES AND DISTRIBUTION

Concentrates and extracts manufactured by The Seven-Up Company were sold to independent bottlers for packaging and resale. In addition, these independent bottlers produced syrups under one or more of the trademarks owned by Seven-Up for distribution to fountain outlets. These licensed bottlers, who produced the finished soft drink product by adding sweetner and carbonated water, were generally granted the exclusive right to sell and distribute the licensed product in bottles and cans and the non-exclusive right to sell and distribute fountain syrups within a certain territory. 7UP brand products were distributed in 379 licensed territories in the United States. The Seven-Up Company, in addition, sold fountain syrups directly to fountain outlets and to licensed bottlers and wholesale distributors for resale to fountain outlets. The company also engaged in sales of finished products for distribution to overseas military installations.

EMPLOYEES

As of December 31, 1990, Dr Pepper/Seven-Up Companies employed 873 persons — 320 in sales activities, 172 in administrative activities, 117 in financial activities, 110 in marketing activities and 154 in production activities. Employees in production, administrative, and financial activities had dual responsibilities to both Dr Pepper and Seven-Up. No company employees were represented by a union and the company considered its employee relations to be good.

MARKET

Sales volume and market share slipped for the company's major brands in the late 1980s. Total market share for all Seven-Up brands was 5.9 percent in 1985, but had dropped to 4.2 percent in 1989. Sales woes continued into 1990, with Seven-Up's market share, falling another .2 to 4 percent.

ADVERTISING

According to Senior Vice-President of Marketing Russ Klein, "Growth in the diet category is coming from younger consumers and male consumers who are finding diet soft drinks an acceptable alternative to sugared soft drinks" [Hemphill 1989]. In response, Seven-Up increased television advertising for Diet 7UP 108 percent in 1990, a strategy geared towards improving bottler confidence. In 1992, after a nine-year absence, the "Uncola" advertising theme was expected to return with a heavy emphasis on Diet 7UP. Seven-Up planned to spend 43 percent of its 1992 marketing dollars on Diet 7UP. Three new commercials scheduled to air in April of 1992 were expected to help 7UP brands differentiate themselves from the competition and help them battle for the 30 percent of the time consumers opt for non-colas in their soft drink selection ["Franchise Player" 1991].

PROMOTION

In the early 1990s the company supported its brands with a variety of promotional activities, including a salute to 100 years of basketball. In 1992, Seven-Up gave away one hundred $10,000 scholarships in an under-the-cap promotion and promoted the Seven-Up Shoot-Out, a double-header basketball event that was televised nationally from St. Petersburg, Florida. TV advertising slated for March of 1992 supported the scholarship giveaway promotion and in addition to the scholarships, consumers won $100 gift certificates from Foot Locker and/or mini-basketballs from Spalding.

The new Diet 7UP advertising followed in April, and the summer Turn-Un promotion ran from June through Labor Day. The aim of the contest promotion was to drive consumer demand for all forms of can packages and 2-liter bottles as well as to extend the Uncola message.

The company also worked to take advantage of the growth surge in Cherry 7UP, which had seen an average sales increase of 26 percent in 196 markets in 1992. The unique taste of this brand and its diet counterpart were emphasized in all major promotions and radio advertising.

LEGAL ISSUES

Prior to the 1987 Seven-Up leveraged buyout, Phillip Morris sold the international franchise operations of Seven-Up to PepsiCo, Inc. Accordingly, PepsiCo, Inc. holds the right to produce and sell soft drinks under the 7UP and certain associated trademarks internationally. The terms of the sale prohibit Seven-Up from distributing any of its soft drink products existing at the time of such transaction, as well as any products developed thereafter that are marketed under the 7UP trademark outside of the United States and its territories and possessions.

On October 29, 1991, The Federal Trade Commission denied Pepsi/Canada Dry New York bottler Harold Honickman's request to acquire Seven-Up's Brooklyn distributorship. The FTC ruled the merger as "anti-competitive" on these grounds: (1) the acquisition would make Harold Honickman one of the leading soft drink bottlers in New York, (2) competition would be lessened by reducing the number of competitors (Nassau and Suffolk Counties would be down to three bottlers while Brooklyn and Queens would have only two), and (3) ties between Pepsi and Seven-Up would be heightened. Seven-Up filed for judicial review, and the case was expected to come before a federal appeals court in March of 1992 ["7UP: Down and Out in New York" 1991].

On Wednesday, February 26, 1992 Seven-Up Company filed a lawsuit against Coca-Cola Company in a Dallas federal court. Seven-Up asked for $500 million in punitive damages and accused Coca Cola Company of trying to corner the lemon-lime market by stealing away 7Up bottlers with "lies" and "coercion." Seven-Up claimed Coca-Cola was using illegal means to persuade independent bottlers to abandon 7Up and sell Coca-Cola's Sprite instead. It was believed that Coca-Cola's motivation stemmed from 30 years of frustration in the lemon-lime segment of the soft drink industry.

TOWARDS THE FUTURE

In 1992, company management was considering the future. By late 1993 the company, would be completely out of bank debt and future funds freed from that obligation could be put to new strategies. Over the years, Seven-Up had watched the 7UP trademark deteriorate while the industry expanded overseas and vertically integrated. Management's job was to restore the luster of the trademark by considering various strategic alternatives for the company.

One of the key decisions that Seven-Up management faced was brand extension. Some managers felt that producing a new line of products under the 7UP brand name, such as an All-Natural Diet Grape 7UP, would put Seven-Up in a better position to compete with Coca Cola Co. and PepsiCo. Some managers wanted this brand extension because "new age" products were a major part of a growing $1 billion a year market. In addition, these managers argued that such a product would appeal to consumers, particularly those between the ages of 25 and 60, because of its health and dietary features. Operationally, these managers felt that this sparkling carbonated juice drink could be produced profitably in a 25 to 50 million case range, a range considered by analysts to be unprofitable and uninviting to Coca-Cola and PepsiCo. These managers also felt that if they sacrificed some of the profit in order to reduce the price they would capitalize on the consumer characteristic of switching brands to save money. In addition, these managers felt confident in their decision to go ahead with a brand extension because Coca-Cola Co. and PepsiCo were reluctant to develop new products.

Last, these managers argued that Seven-Up could produce a product such as Grape 7UP better than Coca-Cola Co. or PepsiCo because (1) Seven-Up had a lawsuit pending against Coca-Cola Co. so Coca-Cola would most likely stay away from competing unprofitably for the sake of avoiding negative press, and (2) Seven-Up's sister company Dr Pepper, with whom Seven-Up had an integrated management structure, had already experienced success with a grape soft drink and securing market information regarding pitfalls could be easy and legal.

In contrast, some managers felt that new product development was too risky and that Seven-

Up had never read a market correctly. In support of this, these managers pointed to the failure of 7UP Gold and suggested that their bottlers had long memories and would not welcome nor support a new product. In addition, these managers argued that the appeal of "new age" products was a fad ready to die. As for capitalizing on the consumer characteristic of switching brands for the sake of saving money, these managers argued that too was remote. In support of this belief, they argued that since Coca-Cola and PepsiCo had the ability to discount their products more effectively, Seven-Up would be priced out of the market. As for the lawsuit, negative press would not deter Coca-Cola Co. from a $1 billion a year market. Last, these managers argued that Seven-Up did not have a sufficient sales force to make its new products accessible to a mass market. Their feelings were based on the fact that Seven-Up did not have its own sales administration. Although primary sales functions remained independent, sales administration for Seven-Up had been integrated with Dr Pepper ever since the 1986 management agreement.

In light of the above situation, the company was wondering what to do about these and other strategic decisions.

REFERENCES AND BACKGROUND READINGS

"7UP: Down and Out in New York," *Beverage Industry,*December 1991, p. 1.

"A Frantic Search for New Products," *Standard and Poors Industry Surveys,* June 27, 1991, p. F4.

Blacock, Cecelia "Congress Zeros in on Waste Problem," *Beverage Industry,* March 1989, p. 6.

"Bottled and Canned Soft Drinks," *U. S. Industry Outlook 1992,* October, 1991, p. 35.

"Bottlers Grade Their Parents," *Beverage World,* October 1991, pp. 26-36.

Brownstein, Vivia "Consumers Will Help the Economy Stay in Shape Next Year," *Fortune,* October 1989, p. 31.

Christensen, Andrews etc., *Business Policy,* Sixth Edition, 1987, pp. 60, 278 and 306.

Cohen, William A., *Market Management,* Macmillian Publishing Co. N.Y., 1988, p. 442.

Davis, Tim "Cans Prove Their Mettle," *Beverage World,* June 1989, p.33.

Donaton, Scoot, "Media Reassess as Boomers Age," *Advertising Age,* July 15, 1991, p. 13.

Farlander, Lee K., "Valued-Added Promotion Build Sale," *Beverage Industry,* August 1989, p. 16.

Farlander, Lee K., "Franchise Programs Spur Vending Growth," *Beverage Industry,* January 1989, p. 21.

"Fountain/Foodservice Trends," *Beverage Industry Annual Manual 91/92,* March 1991, pp. 67-69.

"Franchise Player," *Beverage Industry Annual Manual 91/92,* September 1991, pp. 1, 24-26

Galvin, Andrew, "Beverage Market Index for 1989," *Beverage World,* May 1989, pp. 22-25.

Gatty, Bob, "Reed the Helm the Challenge Consolidations," *Beverage Industry,* January 1989, p. 13.

Gatty, Bob, "Solid Waste Dominates List of Industry's Legal Issues," *Beverage Industry,* May 1989, p. 10.

Hemphill, Gary A., "Diet Do It Up Big," *Beverage Industry,* December 1989, p. 1.

Hemphill, Gary A., "Mega-Markets Boost Supermarket Strength," *Beverage Industry,* May 1989, p. 36.

"Industry Timeliness," *Value Line,* 1989

"International Competitiveness," *U. S. Industry Outlook 1992,* October, 1991, p. 37.

Konrad, Walecia, "Cola Wars: All Noisy on the Eastern Front," *Business Week,* January 27, 1992, p. 94.

Lany, Nancy A., "Hoisting the Glass," *Beverage World,* June 1989, p. 36.

Levan, Gary, "Changing Markets: Boomers Leave a Challenge," *Advertising Age*, July 8, 1991, pp. 1, 14.

Levandoski, Robert C., "Niche Beverages: After the Thrill is Gone," *Beverage Industry*, August 1992, p. 1.

Liesse, Julia, "Brands in Trouble," *Advertising Age*, December 2, 1991, pp. 16-18.

"Liquid Consumption Trends," *Beverage Industry Annual Manual 91/92*, March 1991, pp. 10-12.

"New Soft Drink Brand Introductions," *Jesse Meyer's Beverage Digest*, April 1983, p. 61.

"Per Caps," *Beverage Industry*, February 1992, p. 15.

"Primary Packaging Trends," *Beverage Industry Annual Manual 91/92*, March 1991, pp. 70-72.

"Radio Waves," *Beverage Industry*, August 1991, p. 4.

"Seven-Up Goes After Coca-Cola," *New York Newsday*, February 28, 1992, p. 39.

Sfiligo, Eric, "Caffeine-Frees," *Beverage Industry*, June 1989, p. 2.

"Special Report," *Beverage Industry*, March 1989, pp. 16-18.

"Soft Drink Trends," *Beverage Industry Annual Manual 91/92*, March 1991, pp. 14-34.

"Soft Drink Report," *Beverage Industry*, June 1989, p. 33.

The Seven-Up Company, *Annual Report*, 1990.

"Top 50 Beverage Companies," *Beverage World Databank* 1991-92, October 1991, pp. 24-27.

"Vending Trends," *Beverage Industry Annual Manual 91/92*, March 1991, p. 65.

SUPERB BISCUITS, INC.: A REGIONAL COOKIE AND CRACKER COMPANY

Crackers and cookies bearing the Superb name appeared on the shelves of about 80 percent of all retail food stores in the four-state area of Illinois, Michigan, Indiana, and Ohio. Superb Biscuits, Inc., of Chicago produced and distributed a wide line ranging from simple, square salt crackers to filled chocolate-coated cookies sold in foil-wrapped assortments. More than 80 different items and package sizes were available, and company sales reached $7.6 million in 1956. (For financial statements, see Exhibits 1 and 2.)

Competitive Situation

Superb encountered competition of two types. Most important were the "Big Three" — National Biscuit Company, Sunshine Biscuits, Inc., and United Biscuit Company, with combined sales of almost $700 million in 1956 (see Exhibits 3 and 4). According to Superb's estimates, National Biscuit reached 90% of all outlets and had about 40 percent of the market, while Sunshine sold to about 70 percent of the outlets and held about 25 percent of the market. Superb was believed to run a good third in its own territory, with about 22 percent of total sales.

Competition also came from about six medium-size or small companies, either local or regional in character, operating in part or all of Superb's territory. Several dozen such firms were scattered throughout the United States.

Product lines of the big companies were essentially the same as Superb's although they put more emphasis on crackers and on offering a wider variety of items. The smaller companies generally specialized in high-priced fancy cookies, custom recipes, or accessories like ice cream

This case was made possible by the cooperation of a business firm which remains anonymous. It was prepared by Mr. Erich A. Helfert, Research Assistant, under the direction of Harvard Business School and Professor George Albert Smith, Jr., as the basis for class discussion rather than to illustrate either effective or ineffective handling of an administrative situation.

cones.

In contrast to Superb and most other smaller companies, the three large firms were to some extent both horizontally and vertically integrated. Together they had acquired almost 50 small baking or supply companies during the last 30 years, which were either operated as divisions, or supplied large portions of the parent companies' flour and packaging requirements. Furthermore, two of the large firms had divisions making bread, fresh cakes, cake mixes, dried fruits, potato chips, or similar foods.

Most crackers and a few sweet cookies were standardized high-volume products that carried a low margin and required large-scale automatic production to return a profit to the producer. Most sweet cookies, on the other hand, were specialized products or assortments commanding better prices at lower volumes. Their manufacture called for special machinery or hand operations, while shorter runs necessitated frequent changeovers, especially in single-plant companies. An industry spokesman indicated that the large companies favored the high-volume items that were better suited to their automatic production lines.

There was little differentiation among the high-volume products offered by various makers, except for package design. Significant price differences appeared only during special promotions. Specialties, on the other hand, were claimed to be new and different. Superb officials said new products had to be introduced periodically in order to "show new faces in the market." The large companies were active in this respect, and one of them was reported to have introduced about 10 new items over a six-month period. If a new product proved highly successful, however, competitors would probably develop similar items; fig bars, for example, had started out as specialties of two companies. On the other hand, according to Superb officials, many specialties showed a tendency to be "fads" that "went flat" after 90 days or so.

It was customary among the large- and medium-size companies, including Superb, to employ a sales force charged with order-taking in the food stores, and with arranging fresh stock on the shelves or in special displays featuring price reductions or new products. In most stores the salesmen checked stocks and replenished merchandise entirely on their own responsibility. In these cases they had developed a relationship with the storemanagers, who trusted them to keep the right amounts of salable products on hand. The men also exchanged stale, unsalable packages, and rotated the stocks according to age-dates on the cartons.

These services were considered important to keep the good will of the store and its customers. Industry spokesmen indicated that volume in a given store depended a great deal on the personality and aggressiveness of the biscuit salesman, and they considered it unlikely that independent brokers or jobbers would give similar attention to service. Supermarkets and larger stores generally assigned fixed shelf space to each of the important firms in the area, and rotated special promotion privileges among them. Nevertheless, the relationship of the salesman to the store personnel influenced any preferential treatment the company might receive.

Two of the Big Three carried on national advertising programs, using magazines, radio, and television. Smaller companies had to rely more heavily on advertising allowances to retailers, store promotions, and limited local radio, television, and billboard displays. Expenditures proportional to those of the large competitors were considered by Superb officials to be less than proportionately effective.

History and Organization

Superb Biscuits, Inc. was founded at the turn of the century; it thrived for 25 years, expanding its product line through new items. The depression, however, hit the company hard, and after experiencing severe losses Superb changed hands in 1936. The new majority stockholder was Earl T. Kingsbury, father of the current president, Richard F. Kingsbury. Although the plant was equipped with modern machinery, the previous management had allowed the quality of the product to slide when reverses set in, and Earl Kingsbury was faced with the task of upgrading standards and recovering the acceptance of Superb biscuits in the trade. He believed that poor sales service and lack of freshness-control had created considerable ill will.

Bringing with him a number of new executives, Earl Kingsbury attempted to reorient the company to his philosophy of giving high quality for the lowest possible price. Working against heavy financial odds, he effected changes in the production and sales departments, and sales and profits increased. Mr. Kingsbury was characterized by company officials as a shrewd financial operator whose frugality and determination were the main driving forces behind Superb's recovery. They said he had assumed close personal direction of the business and continually made decisions on both details and policy. His door was always open to subordinates, with whom his contacts were many and varied. Many who had worked under Mr. Kingsbury spoke of him as "wonderful" and "smart." When his health deteriorated seriously in 1954, Mr. Kingsbury was forced to resign all duties, and his son Richard, then 26, was elected president. Richard Kingsbury had served under his father for two years in production and traffic.

The company was organized into four departments — sales, production, finance, and legal and personnel. Each was headed by a vice president (see Exhibit 5). The president met monthly with this group of officers. The board of directors consisted of the president and four members representing some 300 stockholders; the Kingsbury family held a majority of the shares. These board members were the company's banker, an investment broker, and vice presidents of two suppliers. Meetings were held regularly every month, usually after the officers' meeting, and the board maintained a close interest in operating results and major capital expenditures.

Sales and Promotion

The company's sales organization, under James V. Cannon, vice president, aimed at three different markets. The first was composed of food stores in the company's four-state home territory. These were called on by 110 salesmen supervised by 10 district managers. Deliveries were made by company trucks, either from the plant or from eight scattered warehouses. William R. Stewart, territorial sales manager, personally administered the large chain store accounts where formal authorization by central buying offices was required for sale of products in the stores. This market accounted for about 60 percent of sales.

The second market, accounting for about 15 to 20 percent of Superb's volume, was outside the home territory in scattered centers of population like Milwaukee, Kansas City, and even Washington, D. C. Five company salesmen, working directly under Mr. Cannon, called on the 10 independent distributors who served these areas.

The third market consisted of various private and governmental institutions to which special types of biscuits were supplied on a contract basis. Competition was keen in this field, and bids were negotiated individually. While the first two markets showed only moderate seasonal fluctuations, the third required its heaviest volume during the first four months of the year. Institutional sales were managed by Robert Decker, who had 21 years of service with Superb.

Mr. Cannon had joined the company in 1936 after spending 14 years in the sales department of Scott Paper Company. A relative of Earl Kingsbury, he started as a Superb route salesman and rose to his present position after serving as district manager and territorial sales manager for a number of years.

Mr. Cannon commented that he believed one of the company's bigger problems was the high cost of distribution for the home territory. "Bill Steward and I wonder about the merits of the present system, which is the most expensive form of selling," he said. He indicated that costs in the home territory totaled about 35 percent of sales in 1956. This figure included sales salaries and commissions, trade discounts, advertising, delivery, and sales administration expenses, all allocated on the basis of dollar volume. In the large cities outside the territory, where limited advertising was carried on, total costs averaged about 31.5 percent of sales, while sales costs on institutional business averaged about 20 percent of net sales. Mr. Cannon said that while institutional accounts were the most desirable in terms of selling costs, their seasonal character and competitive nature prevented the company from taking on a higher volume. In general, Mr. Cannon foresaw even higher selling costs for all types of accounts. He mentioned, for example, that drivers' wages were bounding upward along with rail rates.

In the home territory, company salesmen averaged about 175 accounts each, on which they called weekly. It was estimated that one-fourth of these stores purchased as little as $5 to $10 per month. On an average, it required at least one hour per month to service even the smallest account. Salesmen received a base salary of about $300 per month. On an average, it required at least one hour per month to service even the smallest account. Salesmen received a base salary of about $300 per month, plus graduated percentage bonuses for sales in excess of the quotas set with their cooperation by Mr. Stewart. Salesmen generally exceeded their base quotas, and yearly contests were held for the best salesman. The men kept detailed records of calls made, new accounts opened, and sales volume by accounts. From this information, weekly summaries were prepared for the district managers and the home office. All salesmen worked from route books and timetables prepared by the district managers. Turnover among salesmen was low, according to Mr. Stewart.

The president commented that he felt the need for increased volume on present routes. He believed that his big competitors had an advantage in terms of selling costs. He estimated that their volume per salesman was from one and one-half to two times that of Superb, owing to larger territories or wider product lines. Furthermore, he estimated that Superb's delivery costs per sales dollar ran about 20 percent higher than competitor's costs, and sales administration about 10 percent higher. Advertising and promotional costs he considered about equal percentagewise (see Table 1 below).

Mr. Cannon was weighing the pros and cons of changing from direct selling in the home territory to independent distributors, as used in the extra-territorial market. These middlemen,

Table 1: Superb Biscuits, Inc. — Comparative Breakdown of Sales Dollar Superb vs. Large Companies (Estimates)

	Superb	Estimate for Biscuit Operations of Large Competitors
Gross sales	110.0%	110.0%
Trade commissions	8.0	8.0
Returned merchandise	2.0	2.0
	10.0	10.0
Net sales	100.0%	100.0%
Raw materials and supplies	52.8	50.0*
Director labor	9.3	9.5
Manufacturing overhead	6.5	7.5
	68.6	67.0
Gross margin	31.4	33.0
Selling expense:		
Advertising and promotion	2.8	3.0
Sales salaries and commissions	5.8	4.6
Other	1.1	.8
	9.7	8.4
Delivery, warehousing	3.3	2.3
Freight	5.1	4.5
General and administrative	10.7	11.2
Interest	.1	.1
	19.2	18.1
Total expenses	28.9	26.5
Net income (before taxes)	2.5	6.5
Federal income taxes	1.2	3.2
Net income	1.3%	3.3%

*Lower because of vertical integration.

Source: Company records and estimates of company officers.

located in the large cities, generally received a flat 25 percent discount off list price. Mr. Cannon stated that they had been very successful in selling Superb products and he was considering adding several more to the present 10 to enlarge the field. He stated that selling through these channels was "hard selling" but "good selling," explaining that distributors generally asked for "special deals" in terms of price concessions or free goods (e.g., one carton free for every dozen), but at the same time they assumed all risks and the company was not forced to stand behind them with a guarantee to take back unsalable stock. "Selling direct through salesmen is almost like selling on consignment," he said, "while distributors have no recourse. But then, distributors take on only 'good sellers' — which in a way is an advantage. Why clutter a store with slow-selling items?" Mr. Cannon stated that the company's rate of returned goods was not quite 2 percent of net sales.

He added that selling through distributors required strong men "able to say no" to the many demands for special favors. Furthermore, he said, the company would be subjected to greater price pressures, since distributors generally carried more than one brand of biscuits and would tend to push the brand most profitable to them.

Another change weighed by Mr. Cannon was modification of salesmen's compensation. He said, "We are considering the possibility of putting our men on straight commission, which would also cover their expenses. At the moment we have two or three of our district managers stewing over the problem. If they think it is a good idea, we shall tell the other managers, and in turn have them sell it to the salesmen."

Mr. Kingsbury thought the company might well be forced to change its distribution system in the long run. He stated that National Biscuit and some small firms had experimented with a split arrangement, putting salaried men in charge of large chain accounts, while paying the salesmen who covered independent stores on straight commission. "Under such a system," he said, "we would be better set for the eventual transition in food marketing to complete predominance of the large supermarket."

Mr. Kingsbury visualized, as a long-term possibility, the institution of direct delivery of biscuits to chain warehouses, eliminating the individual would be served by driver-salesmen carrying the necessary stocks in their trucks. This would reduce the number of men required to one-third or less, he said.

Mr. Cannon indicated that the company's resources were insufficient for the extensive market research carried on by its large competitors. The company used an outside firm to supply monthly reports on relative market shares. "Everyone is in research," he said, "but when you are small you must sell hard instead, get more outlets, and keep them well stocked." He said that Superb had to rely on its sales force to bring back information about competitive developments. The district managers held regular monthly meetings with their men, and occasionally all salesmen and sales personnel were brought together to discuss advertising or promotional problems. During 1956 there had been four such meetings, a considerable increase over previous years.

New product and promotional ideas at times greatly stimulated sales according to Mr. Cannon. For example, during 1955 Superb had introduced three products aimed at different nationality groups, using authentic recipes; sales had jumped as much as 35 to 50 percent in outlying centers of population where these groups were heavily represented. Mr. Cannon believed that such specialties helped to promote regular sales by making the Superb name better known. Promotional ideas of the present year included handing out sample cookies, with an advertising message attached, in the elementary schools of Kansas City. The expense of the samples was borne by the distributor. "We must make little things pay," commented Mr. Cannon, and stated that he was glad the company had begun moving toward such new product ideas and promotions.

Advertising had undergone changes and was still being modified. Before 1936 the company had spent up to 10 percent of net sales on advertising, especially when sales began to slip. Earl Kingsbury had drastically cut expenditures to an average of $100,000 to $115,000 per year, including cooperative advertising for the home territory which amounted to about 40 percent of the total. In the recent past, most of the budget was spent on billboards (35%) and on some radio spots (25%). Magazine advertising was negligible. In 1956 the company initiated spots on local television and signed up for another billboard campaign (30% of budget) during the summer. Furthermore, the advertising agency was asked to come up with a suitable slogan tying the product line to reasons for consumer preference for Superb biscuits. The 1957 advertising budget was set at almost $250,000, an increase of about 24% over past years.

Richard Kingsbury believed that during his father's management the lines of authority in the sales department had become blurred because district managers were allowed to carry their problems directly to the president. "This custom resulted in nobody knowing who was to tell what to whom," he said, adding that it was not until five years ago that the sales vice president had begun to spend most of his time in the central office. Prior to that time he had been mainly occupied with extraterritorial sales. Mr. Kingsbury commented that, except for approving the size of the advertising budget, he made it a point not to interfere in the sales department. He wanted to foster the rebuilding of authority for the department head. He believed that morale and turnover among sales personnel had improved greatly in the last five years, especially because there were no longer numerous hirings and firings.

Production

Increased efficiency and better mechanization were the main problems that concerned the vice president of production, Alfred Kingsbury, an uncle of Richard Kingsbury. He believed that it was vital for the company to increase productions without increasing labor costs. "We have not been able to pass on increased costs to the consumer — competitors have not been able to do this either. Automation is the ultimate answer, and we are compelled to go into it, but in the intermediate period we must buy better and produce better. If I could schedule longer runs, for instance, I could double our tonnage output, but our sales force needs variety," he said.

Alfred Kingsbury was made a vice president when Earl Kingsbury took over the company. He had been a sales representative with another biscuit company and had run food stores before that. Reporting to him were Steven R. Miller, plant superintendent, and William T. Pugh, head of scheduling. Mr. Miller, a chemist and former head of the laboratory, was placed in his present position early in 1956 by Richard Kingsbury, who explained that he had fired two men formerly serving as joint superintendents because they were unwilling to delegate authority and accept new ideas. Mr. Miller, aged 30, was in charge of production, efficiency control, the laboratory, and maintenance. Mr. Pugh, a man of 18 years' experience in the biscuit industry, was in charge of scheduling, hiring of production workers, and related personnel services.

The plant, together with the offices, was located in a four-story building in a suburban area and was served by a spur track of the Rock Island Railroad. The ground floor was used for warehousing and shipping, while the second and third floors contained offices and manufacturing area. The fourth floor was rented to another firm. Major items of equipment were four 200-foot continuous band ovens, a battery of dough mixers that handled about 400,000 pounds of flour and shortening per week, several kneading machines, packaging lines serving the ovens, and three icing, sandwiching, and coating lines. Most of the equipment had been of very advanced design at the time of installation and had been kept in good condition, according to Mr. Kingsbury. Several conveyor arrangements allowed continuous product-flow.

Production operations were divided into four sections, mixing, baking, icing, and packing. The plant worked in two shifts and the work force totaled close to 400 men and women. Labor relations were peaceful and all workers were unionized. Both Mr. Kingsbury and Mr. Miller indicated that they made sure to consult with union representatives before making any change in operations that affected the workers, and they thought this policy was one of the foundations of labor peace. "We have to build the strength of the union for our own good," said Mr. Miller, who indicated that union stewards attended the monthly meetings of foremen and production management.

Mr. Miller was considered by Alfred Kingsbury to be aggressive, smart, and progressing well in his new job. Mr. Miller said he made it a point to rebuild the authority of his foremen who had been undermined by his predecessors. He indicated that he allowed them more freedom to make operating decisions and required workers to see their foremen first before bringing complaints to him. At the same time he was concerned with quality and efficiency. "Every Friday I get together with my foremen and discuss what we mean by quality — I prefer to call it constancy — and analyze systematically how to do better in it. I also look for savings; just recently we cut expenses $400 per month by using paper towels instead of cloth to clean machinery." To avoid costly stoppages of the continuous production lines, Mr. Miller insisted on extensive preventive maintenance.

Mr. Miller shared the president's concern about introducing better machinery, and kept a file of new developments. He had joined Richard Kingsbury on an extended trip to machinery suppliers in the United States and Europe, and had assisted in selecting several new packaging machines.

Scheduling was described as complicated owing to the large variety of products offered. Both Alfred Kingsbury and Mr. Pugh spent most of their time working out the daily and weekly programs for the four sections. A minimum run of two hours was required for any one product, and the problem was to dovetail inventories and current requirements of the eight warehouses and the extra-territorial markets.

New product development had historically been concentrated in the production area, where one specialist was spending his full time on trying out new recipes. Several years ago a committee had been formed which consisted of Messrs. Alfred Kingsbury, Cannon, Perry (vice president and treasurer), Stewart, as well as the new products specialist, and the company's part-time art director. According to the president, the committee produced little and met very infrequently until about a year ago when it was realized that more new products were needed. Since that time six new items had been developed and approved, and the committee now met three times per month. Of the six items which had been introduced through in-store promotions, only two showed continued success, two were "slowly dying," after a three-month life, while two never "went off the ground," he said. One of the successful items was a medium-priced assortment, while the other was a new form of cookie. Mr. Kingsbury believed that there were "too many thumbs" in the new product field and said that he was still looking for the best possible method of "hatching ideas" and accelerating their utilization. He said the majority of new ideas actually came from jobbers and distributors, while a few original ideas had emerged from production personnel. "There are not many ideas that are completely new in this field," he said, and told of an instance where a new cookie had been developed by mistake when a worker used the "wrong" spices.

Alfred Kingsbury stated that new products had to meet high turnover requirements in addition to being different. "In the recent past all biscuit companies have lost five to ten items each due to stores wanting products with faster turnover. More and more items are competing for the available shelf space in a market." He believed that the industry would have to stimulate the basic demand for biscuits if it wanted to grow further.

Finance and Control

Donald T. Perry, vice president and treasurer, had spent his entire career in varying positions in the biscuit industry. Previously plant manager for a medium-size biscuit manufacturer, he had joined Superb as assistant to the president in 1936, and was appointed vice president soon thereafter.

Mr. Perry was in charge of finance and purchasing. The general office manager, Mr. Banister, supervised the office and accounting staffs. The company employed a product-cost system that traced labor and materials costs for each product, based on the daily runs through the four production departments. At least four times per year the average costs for each product were compiled and compared to current sales prices, and the gross margin was determined to see whether the product was profitable. Costs, except labor costs, were not recorded by department, but were allocated on the basis of weight of the finished product. Other data collected included average weight of output, barrels produced per hour, percentage yield from raw materials, and cost of finishes. Small variations in coatings, for instance, could prove very costly, according to Mr. Perry. Richard Kingsbury indicated that he favored several changes in the accounting area, particularly an attempt to establish basic standards of output on which to base a "more realistic" allocation of burden. He also wanted a more detailed breakdown of departmental expenses and reorganization of the company's monthly financial reports.

Inventories were taken weekly in each warehouse and the central office maintained close control over the ordering procedures which were based on four-week moving averages. Owing to the semiperishable nature of the products, no more than one week's inventory of finished goods was kept on hand. Similarly, raw materials were kept down to four weeks' supply at the most. The company's spoilage experience was less than 1/4 of 1 percent of sales, according to Mr. Perry.

The treasurer considered his most serious problem to be "how to balance the budget." He worried over increased costs due to a rise from wage negotiations which were to start in the spring of 1957. Costs of raw materials and freight showed an upward trend. "There is no end to increases," he said, "and the Middle East troubles have sent commodities way up." He said that the biscuit industry had made general price advances in early 1957, but that this had been just enough to offset some of the cost increases of 1956, leaving no room for the expected 1957 rise. "Price advances are generally made uniformly by the whole industry with the large companies taking the lead," he said, "and only occasional reductions on single products are made individually."

Mr. Perry believed that the company was too small to do any hedging in the commodity markets, which he considered a special field in itself, not even tackled by the large companies. Superb generally bought flour requirements for about 120 days ahead, under standard millers' contracts, and once in a while ventured to buy six months' supplies. The latter action involved a risk of paying storage charges to millers should the company be unable to take delivery within the stated period; thus the advantage of lower prices might be eliminated. The purchasing agent, Mr. Sanders, who had 35 years' experience in procurement, believed that Superb paid essentially the same prices for its raw materials as the large competitors, owing to the fact that the large companies generally bought on the plant level rather than centrally.

Quarterly budgets were tentatively prepared, focused mainly on the cash flow required to meet seasonal swings. The president commented that since about one year formal budgeting procedures had "all but gone out of the window," because of the difficulties of forecasting demand and costs.

Every year, to meet seasonal needs, Mr. Perry borrowed several hundred thousand dollars in short-term funds on a line of credit. Superb was still saddled with arrears of $71,000 on its preferred stock, but the president hoped to be able to pay this off within the next year and then start paying dividends on the common.

Proposals made by the production department or the president for expenditures on new machinery were analyzed by Mr. Perry. On the basis of his calculations, Mr. Richard Kingsbury decided on the merits of the purchase and defended it before the board, which passed on every expenditure over $2,000. The board gave its approval on almost all projects presented by him, he said. Richard Kingsbury spent most of his time on finding new ways to mechanize the processes of manufacture.

In the past, many special machines had been developed and built by Superb, but this had become increasingly difficult in recent years, said Mr. Perry. In the early years, Earl Kingsbury had economized greatly and held back on capital expenditures where possible. Up to 1956 Superb had relied solely on internally generated funds for capital outlays and had not considered outside money. The president now felt it was high time the company started looking for long-term loans to finance more machinery.

Mr. Perry also assisted in setting product prices based on cost data, but he said the company had little leeway in pricing standard products where prices tended to be industry-wide. "We must find more specialties on which we can put a price tag of our own," said Mr. Perry, "but still most of the volume is done with a limited number of standard varieties that you must have in order to be competitive. If we withdrew these low-margin products, the customer in the store might not pick up the specialty items either, and our display space would be cut. Moreover, our factory would have greatly reduced volume which would shift burden costs onto other products."

Personnel and Legal

Frank J. Newman, vice president and secretary, was in charge of the legal affairs of the company and also directed personnel policies. He hired all personnel except production workers. A lawyer by training, Mr. Newman left private practice in 1936 to join Earl Kingsbury first as counsel, later as secretary and clerk; he was made vice president in 1954. Mr. Newman obtained leases for district warehouses, appraised distributors' contracts, and gave advice on provisions of the Pure Food and Drug Act. Furthermore, he negotiated union contracts with the teamsters and bakery worker locals.

Mr. Newman also prepared the agenda for officers', directors', and stockholders' meetings. He said that about a year ago the officers' meetings had "petered out" and Richard Kingsbury had temporarily stopped them altogether. About six months later they were resumed and had been kept up regularly to date. Mr. Newman said that in these meetings the officers considered "matters of over-all policy," which included items like group insurance coverage, the problems of uniform package design, and the volume of institutional sales desirable.

Traffic

Superb maintained a shipping and receiving department under Mr. Thomas McNamara, who had spent 20 years with the Great Northern Railroad before joining the company in 1936. Mr. McNamara supervised the compilation of truck and rail loads of finished products and determined the best possible routing. He worked closely with the sales department.

Organizational Developments

Before becoming president, Richard Kingsbury had worked in two functional departments looking for improvements. His interest in efficiency had led to substantial labor savings in shipping. He said it had been easier to convince the teamsters' union of the need for changes than some of the foremen, and he believed that resistance to new ideas had been fostered by the centralized control of his father. Mr. Kingsbury described the two plant superintendents he had fired as uncooperative, hard-headed, antilabor, and as standing in the way of improvements. He said he had fired three additional foremen showing similar attitudes. Mr. Kingsbury felt he now had the right men in the superintendents' positions, those who could lead the foremen and look for better manufacturing methods.

Soon after becoming president, Richard Kingsbury had issued a directive that prohibited on-the-spot firing by foremen. He said his father had never agreed to this change while he was in control, but Richard Kingsbury believed the exercise of firing authority was inconsistent with good supervision. The directive stated that written requests for the release of a worker should be sent by the foreman to Mr. Newman and be approved by Alfred Kingsbury and Mr. Miller.

Mr. Kingsbury stated that his own youthful age had been a "small powderkeg" at the time of his father's resignation. "There was not much doubt in the minds of the directors about the succession," he said, "but the other executives did not share that certainty as they had little contact with the board. It became a question of whether I was taking over in name or in fact, and at least two of the officers had aspirations. Many lingering animosities came into the open at that time, and I finally had to stop the officer's meetings in early 1956 because nothing could be accomplished in them."

"Coordination was lacking between the departments," he continued, "and I stuck my neck out to cut bottlenecks. But the people involved had to cool down first, and I did not resume the meetings for about half a year."

Richard Kingsbury commented on the current meetings as follows: "We are now operating with the vice presidents as heads of functional line departments. Actually we never act as a management group. The only real cooperative efforts occur if two department heads have an overlapping problem like priority schedules of production. But other matters are treated separately and will likely continue to be treated as such. For instance, advertising policy is handled solely as a sales problem. Actually, the vice presidents have been used to operating this way since my father's time. There was even a terrific interdepartmental animosity; each department tried to push the other around," he said. Mr. Kingsbury explained that there had been so-called "policy meetings" under Earl Kingsbury, but although ideas were debated collectively, Earl Kingsbury personally set policies.

"It is my prerogative to set policies which are self-governing, as contrasted with day-to-day affairs. I mainly concern myself with interdepartmental matters, or with weaknesses in any one department. For instance, I felt I had to take action in the production area — but I take action only if initial suggestions do not bring results," he explained.

In speaking of interdepartmental cooperation, Mr. Cannon said that until recently coordination between his department and the factory had not always been the best. During 1956, however, William Stewart had the idea of forming a production planning group to consist of Mr. Cannon, Alfred Kingsbury, the heads of scheduling and sales service, and himself. The group began by working on the problem of slack periods caused by seasonal demand for certain high-volume products, especially institutional biscuits. An attempt was made to forecast such fluctuations and schedule appropriate substitute products to keep the factory operating at capacity. Similarly, the group helped to schedule production on products for which demand was especially heavy. Mr. Cannon stated he felt this group had helped both his department and the production area.

Richard Kingsbury also thought the group was a good idea, as it taught certain sales personnel "the physical facts of life about the factory." He said that salesmen tended to push certain items too hard, thinking they could have more supplies immediately. This resulted in temporary but embarrassing shortages, during which the home territory was generally neglected in favor of outside areas. "This was quite contrary to the natural emphasis required — I still believe that our home territory is our mainstay," he said. "On the other hand," he added, "the factory was tempted to produce items that best fitted its production schedules."

The older executives commented that Richard Kingsbury showed great insight and capabilities, especially for his age. They said his interest in new machinery foreshadowed promising developments. Mr. Perry remarked: "Richard can do a lot of things with people who of themselves would not think of changing their old ways. By being in a position of authority he can spark new thought and urge its acceptance." Alfred Kingsbury said that no major steps were taken either by the president or by the officers without mutual consultation. "Dick is naturally more dependent on the department heads because his experience is shorter. He would not think of doing something without bringing it up with one or all of us. Likewise, we talk to him about our problems and listen to his views."

TOWARDS THE FUTURE

Mr. Kingsbury visualized a need for stricter cost controls and a more unified sales promotion. "I consider our present product line a hodge-podge in terms of appearance," he said, and indicated that, as one step toward improving package design and uniformity, Superb had asked its paper and cardboard suppliers to analyze current packages and suggest changes. This practice was common among small biscuit companies that were unable to afford large sums for professional designers.

The question of product diversification had arisen several times during the past three years. The idea of going into cereals and cake mixes had been discarded owing to the difficulties envisioned in competing with nationally advertised brands. Mr. Kingsbury stated that he and some of his officers felt the company should expand its line "if and when the right opportunity comes." New products might be added either through subcontracting of production or through utilizing the present plant. Mr. Kingsbury felt that the potential of the present sales force might be more fully realized with additional compatible products.

Exhibit 1: Superb Biscuits, Inc.
Income Statement, Years Ending December 31 (Thousands of Dollars)

	1956	1955	1954	1953	1952	1951	1950	1949	1948	1947	1946	1945
Net sales	$5,555	$7,001	$7,156	$7,508	$6,829	$6,374	$5,311	$4,841	$4,676	$4,933	$3,825	$3,704
Cost of goods sold	5,182	4,800	5,002	5,229	4,763	4,516	3,647	3,321	3,398	3,471	2,519	2,434
Gross profit	$2,373	$2,201	$2,154	$2,279	$2,066	$1,858	$1,664	$1,520	$1,278	$1,462	$1,306	$1,270
Selling, delivery and administration	2,199	2,029	1,990	2,036	1,814	1,672	1,469	1,389	1,289	1,148	946	899
Operating profit	$ 174	$ 172	$ 164	$ 243	$ 252	$ 186	$ 195	$ 131	$ <11>	$ 314	$ 360	$ 371
Other income	23	29	10	10	4	17	14	15	13	4	9	<11>
Total income	$ 197	$ 201	$ 174	$ 253	$ 256	$ 203	$ 209	$ 146	$ 2	$ 318	$ 369	$ 360
Interest expense	11	5	10	20	22	13	16	22	21	7	8	19
Income before income tax	$ 186	$ 196	$ 164	$ 233	$ 234	$ 190	$ 193	$ 124	$ <19>	$ 311	$ 361	$ 341
Federal income tax	$ 91	$ 95	$ 82	$ 119	$ 121	$ 95	$ 73	$ 47	$ <5>	$ 119	$ 140	$ 246
Net profit	$ 95	$ 101	$ 82	$ 114	$ 113	$ 95	$ 120	$ 77	$ <14>	$ 192	$ 221	$ 95
	$ 40	$ 41	$ 42	$ 42	$ 43	-	-	-	-	$ 43	$ 21	-
Percentage Analysis												
Net sales	100.0%	100.0%	100.0%	100.0%	100.0%	100.0%	100.0%	100.0%	100.0%	100.0%	100.0%	100.0%
Cost of goods sold	68.6	68.5	69.9	69.6	69.7	70.9	68.7	68.6	72.7	70.4	65.9	65.7
Gross profit	31.4	31.5	30.1	30.4	30.3	29.1	31.3	31.4	27.3	29.6	34.1	34.3
Selling, delivery and administration	29.1	29.0	27.8	27.1	26.6	26.2	27.6	28.7	27.5	23.3	24.7	24.3
Operating profit	2.3	2.5	2.3	3.3	3.7	2.9	3.7	2.7	<0.2>	6.3	9.4	10.0
Other income	0.3	0.4	0.1	0.1	0.0	0.3	0.2	0.3	0.3	0.1	0.2	0.3
Total income	2.6	2.9	2.4	3.4	3.7	3.2	3.9	3.0	0.1	6.4	9.6	9.7
Interest expense	0.1	0.1	0.1	0.3	0.3	0.2	0.3	0.4	0.5	0.1	0.2	0.5
Income before income tax	2.5	2.8	2.3	3.1	3.4	3.0	3.6	2.6	<0.4>	6.3	9.4	9.2
Federal income tax	1.2	1.4	1.1	1.6	1.8	1.5	1.4	1.0	0.1	2.4	3.6	6.6
Net profit	1.3	1.4	1.2		1.5	1.6	1.5	2.2	1.6	<0.3>	3.9	5.8 2.6
Preferred dividends	0.5	0.6	0.6	0.6	0.6	-	-	-	-	0.9	0.6	

Bracketed figures are negative
Source: Company records.

Exhibit 2: Superb Biscuits, Inc.
Balance Sheets, December 31 (Thousands of Dollars)

Assets	1956	1955	1954	1953	1952	1951	1950	1949	1948	1947	1946	1945
Cash	$ 189	$ 160	$ 188	$ 134	$ 199	$ 120	$ 123	$93	$98	$ 149	$ 180	$ 268
Receivable - net	274	241	234	281	273	256	192	182	156	155	175	105
Inventories	983	753	608	572	449	518	375	326	317	332	306	205
Investments - restricted	-	-	-	119	109	100	92	82	74	64	56	52
Total current assets	$1,446	$1,154	$1,030	$1,106	$1,030	$ 994	$ 782	$ 683	$ 645	$ 700	$ 717	$ 630
Land, building & machinery	1,487	1,432	1,327	1,229	1,141	1,085	995	947	926	892	473	454
Reserve for depreciation	710	636	574	495	463	410	379	351	302	259	236	254
Net property	$ 717	$ 796	$ 753	$ 734	$ 678	$ 675	$ 616	$ 596	$ 624	$ 633	$ 237	$ 200
Prepayments	80	75	53	41	34	76	42	26	42	28	53	25
Goodwill	-	-	-	-	-	-	-*	450	450	450	450	450
Organization expense	-	-	-	-	-	-	-	-	-	-	88	88
Total assets	$2,303	$2,025	$1,836	$1,881	$1,742	$1,745	$1,440	$1,755	$1,761	$1,811	$1,545	$1,393
Liabilities												
Notes payable	$ 570**	$ 150	$ 75	$ 113	$ 38	$ 19	$ 22	$ 22	$ 11	$ 75	$ 30	$ 30
Accounts payable	206	235	205	175	173	238	139	124	232	158	104	89
Accruals	209	217	229	188	156	146	119	82	82	73	98	68
Federal income taxes	64	223	178	241	245	238	264	278	241	268	288	
Total current liabilities	$1,049	$ 825	$ 687	$ 717	$ 612	$ 641	$ 544	$ 506	$ 566	$ 574	$ 520	$ 538
Notes payable - long term	-	-	-	281	319	356	244	266	289	300	150	180
Cumulative preferred stock ($ .50 div. rate)	419	419	419	428	428	428	427	428	428	428	428	428
Common stock	122	122	122	122	122	122	122	122	122	122	122	122
Earned surplus	723	669	610	340	269	198	103	433	356	387	325	125
Total stock and surplus	$1,264	$1,210	$1,151	$ 890	$ 819	$ 748	$ 652	$ 983	$906	$ 937	$ 875	$ 675
Less: reacquired pref. stock	10	10	2	7	8	-	-	-	-	-	-	-
Net stock and surplus	$1,254	$1,200	$1,149	$ 883	$ 811	$ 748	$ 652	$ 983	$ 906	$ 937	$ 875	$ 675
Total liabilities	$2,303	$2,025	$1,836	$1,881	$1,742	$1,745	$1,440	$1,755	$1,761	$1,811	$1,545	$1,393
Net current assets (thousands of dollars)	$ 397	$ 329	$ 343	$ 389	$ 418	$ 353	$ 238	$ 177	$79	$ 126	$ 197	$92
Current ratio	138:1	140:1	150:1	154:1	168:1	155:1	144:1	135:1	114:1	122:1	138:1	117:1
Number of shares- pref.(1,000)	41	41	42	42	42	43	43	43	43	43	43	43
Earned per share - preferred	$ 2.26	$ 2.47	$ 1.98	$ 2.72	$ 2.70	$ 2.23	$ 2.81	$ 1.79	$-	$ 4.49	$ 5.18	$ 2.24
Dividends per share - preferred	$ 1.00	$ 1.00	$ 1.00	$ 1.00	$ 1.00	$-	$-	$-	$-	$ 1.00	$ .50	$-
Arrearages per share- preferred	$ 1.75	$ 2.25	$ 2.75	$ 3.25	$ 3.75	$ 4.25	$ 3.75	$ 3.25	$ 2.75	$ 2.25	$ 2.75	$ 2.75
Total arrearages (thousands of dollars)	$71	$92	$ 115	$ 136	$ 158	$ 182	$ 160	$ 139	$ 118	$96	$ 118	$ 118
Number of shares -common(1,000)	122	122	122	122	122	122	122	122	122	122	122	122
Earned per share - common	$ 0.44	$ 0.66	$ 0.51	$ 0.76	$ 0.75	$ 0.60	$ 0.81	$ 0.45	$<0.29>	$ 1.39	$ 1.63	$ 0.61
Net tangible assets per share - common	$ 6.31	$ 5.70	$ 5.02	$ 2.67	$ 1.89	$ 1.13	$ 0.53	-	-	-	- -	
Per cent return on net worth (after tax)	7.5%	8.4%	7.2%	12.9%	13.9%	12.5%	18.4%	7.8%	<1.6%>	20.3%	25.3%	14.1%

*Goodwill was written off against earned surplus - now carried at $1. **Short-term funds of $500,000 for seasonal inventory needs included.
Bracketed figures are negative. Source: Company records.

Exhibit 3: Superb Biscuits, Inc. — Per Cent Changes in Sales and Profits
Three Large Biscuit Companies* and Superb Biscuits, Inc.

	Three Large Companies*				Superb Biscuits, Inc.			
Year	Sales (Millions)	% Change from Past Year	Net Profit (Millions)	% Change from Past Year	Sales (Millions)	% Change from Past Year	Net Profit (Millions)	% Change from Past Year
1956	$698.1	+ 9/8%	$31.1	+11.9%	$7.6	+ 8.6%	$ .095	- 6.0%
1955	635.9	+ 3.8	27.7	-	7.0	- 2.8	.101	+21.9
1954	612.8	+ 2.6	27.7	- 2.1	7.2	- 4.0	.082	-28.1
1953	597.4	+ 4.8	28.3	+ 1.4	7.5	+10.3	.114	+0.9
1952	570.2	+ 2.5	27.9	+ 3.7	6.8	+ 6.2	.113	+18.9
1951	556.1	+13.5	26.9	-19.7	6.4	+20.8	.095	-20.8
1950	489.9	+ 2.0	33.5	- 3.7	5.3	+10.4	.120	+57.9
1949	480.1	- 1.3	34.8	+32.3	4.8	+ 2.1	.077	- negative basis
1948	486.5	+10.9	26.3	+ 4.4	4.7	- 4.1	<.014>	-
1947	438.5	+22.6	25.2	- 5.3	4.9	+28.9	.192	-13.1
1946	357.4	+ 8.4	26.6	+26.0	3.8	+ 2.7	.221	+132.6
1945	329.6	-	21.1	-	3.7	-	.095	

*National Biscuit Company, United Biscuit Company, Sunshine Biscuit Company, Inc.
Bracketed figures are negative.
Source: Compiled by Harvard Business School Research staff from Moody's company records.

Exhibit 4: Superb Biscuits, Inc. — Per Cent Return on Net Worth over 12 Years
Typical Industry Performances and Superb Biscuits, Inc.

	Per Cent Return											
Company	1956	1955	1954	1953	1952	1951	1950	1949	1948	1947	1946	1945
National Biscuit Company	11.5%	10.7%	11.9%	11.5%	11.6%	10.8%	14.2%	15.3%	10.7%	12.4%	10.2%	15.9%
United Biscuit Company	8.2	8.1	4.2	9.8	11.2	12.3	14.7	17.2	26.7	32.4	37.4	15.7
Sunshine Biscuits, Inc.	12.5	12.0	12.2	12.8	12.8	14.3	17.9	20.6	20.4	15.4	24.0	11.2
Average of six large and medium companies (weighted average)	10.7	10.1	10.3	11.0	11.3	11.1	14.3	15.4	12.8	13.6	14.2	14.9
Superb Biscuits, Inc.	7.5	8.4	7.2	12.9	13.9	12.5	18.4	7.8	<1.6>	20.3	25.3	14.1

Relative Volume of Three Largest Biscuit Companies
(Selected years; Millions of Dollars)

	1956		1954		1951		1948		1945	
Company	Sales	%	Sales	%	Sales	%	Sales	%	Sales	%
National Biscuit Company	$410.4	59.0%	$376.4	61.5%	$329.9	59.5%	$296.2	61.0%	$205.0	62.2%
United Biscuit Company	137.1	19.7	117.2	19.4	107.2	19.1	87.7	17.9	50.6	15.4
Sunshine Biscuits, Inc.	150.6	21.3	119.2	19.1	119.0	21.4	102.6	21.1	74.0	22.4
Total	$698.1	100.0%	$612.8	100.0%	$556.1	100.0%	$486.5	100.0%	$329.6	100.0%

Note: Comparability is limited by the fact that the large companies have diversified or integrated their operations to some extent. For instance, NBC produces 80% of its own flour requirements and 50% of packaging supplies. NBC also produces bread and cake in the East. Similarly, Sunshine Biscuit and United Biscuit are engaged in comparable fields.

Bracketed figures are negative.

Source: Prepared by Harvard Business School Research staff.

Exhibit 5: Superb Biscuits, Inc.
Organization Chart

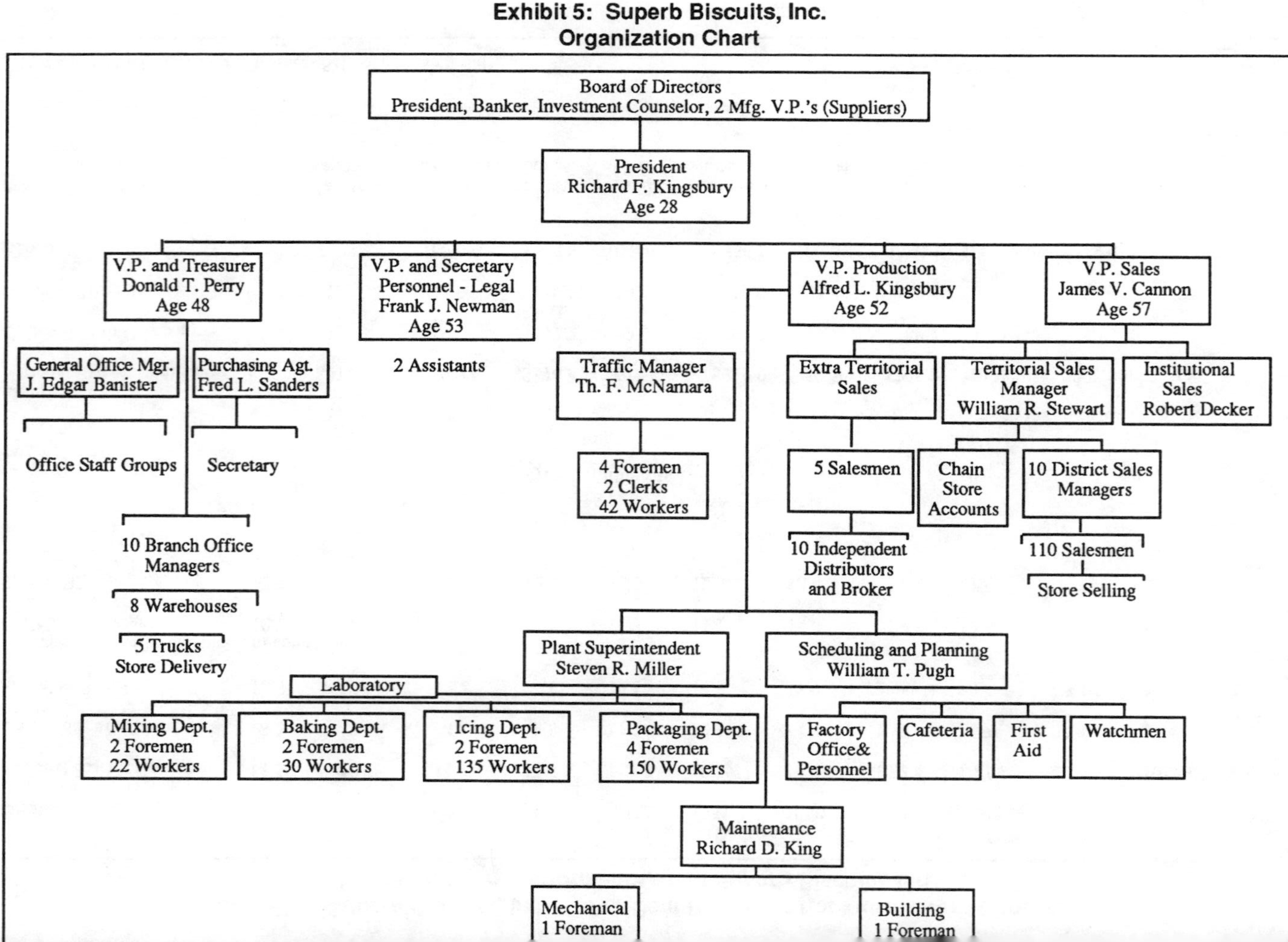

TELE-COMMUNICATIONS INC.: THE CABLE OPERATOR INDUSTRY

Cable TV (Community Antenna Television or CATV) is a system through which television and other signals are picked up by a single high antenna and then relayed to subscribers' televisions by a cable. CATV grew out of a need to bring difficult-to-receive television signals to towns that were too far away from the signal's point of origin or that had signals which were obstructed by mountainous terrain.

The cable television industry underwent phenomenal growth and large-scale changes in the first 40 years of its existence. The largest increases in subscribers, revenue, and market penetration occurred between 1978 and 1988. The industry's growth, in 10-year increments, is shown in Figure 1.

As of the end of 1990, Tele-Communications, Inc. (TCI)—along with its subsidiaries and affiliates—was the largest cable TV operator in the United States. In 1990, the company operated cable television systems throughout the continental U.S. and Hawaii, and almost one out of every four cable viewers was a TCI subscriber. Cable accounted for about 90 percent of TCI's operating income in 1989. In addition, the company also owns a majority of outstanding common stock in United Artists Entertainment Company (UAE) which, as of March 1990, operated 624 movie theaters with a total of 2,699 screens nationwide ["Tele-Communications Inc," *Prospectus*, July 13, 1990, p.5].

Dr. John Malone, the CEO of Tele-Communications Inc., acknowledged in 1992 that his company and the entire cable industry faced the challenge of finding new ways to compete. The threat of re-regulation, competition from telephone companies, the use of fiber optics, and the development of alternate transmission services were forcing cable operators to reconsider their

Figure 1: Cable Growth Over the First 43 Years

	1948	1958	1968	1978	1988	1991
SUBSCRIBERS	0	450,000	3,500,000	12,817,190	47,042,470	56,072,840
PENETRATION	0	1.1%	6.4%	17.5%	52.8%	61%
REVENUE	$0	$36,690	$240,000	$1,500,000	$13,000,000	N/A

Adapted from "Mileposts on the Road to 40" *Broadcasting*, Nov 21,1988 pp. 46-49 and from "By the Numbers" *Broadcasting*, Nov. 11, 1991, p. 84.

business definitions and strategies in 1992. Potential growth strategies included market penetration, product line extensions, and product or service diversification. Finding ways to attract more subscribers in already-wired franchise areas, generating more revenue through aggressive advertising, or expanding into new areas such as programming and high-definition television were examples of such strategies [Carter 1989 (E)].

THE INDUSTRY AND COMPETITIVE MARKET

THE CABLE TELEVISION INDUSTRY

The Beginning

In 1948, John Walson, one of the founders of the cable television industry, started a CATV system in Mahanoy City, Pennsylvania, by erecting a pole and stringing twin lead wire to his warehouse at the foot of a mountain. From there, the wire was strung along Pennsylvania Power and Light poles to his appliance shop where he held television demonstrations [Jessell 1988]. These demonstrations led to a great demand by the townspeople not only for television sets, but also for inclusion in the system that would allow them to receive these outside stations.

With informal permission from the power company, Walson connected town residents who purchased his TV sets to the antenna on top of the mountain, via twin lead wire. The initial hook-up fee was $100 and, after the first year, he charged a $2 monthly maintenance fee. Within the next six months Walson had included over 700 homes in his system. The homeowners were called subscribers and the money that they paid to be included in the system were called subscription fees. Over the next few years entrepreneurs in surrounding communities started services similar to Walson's. These services were known as community antenna television systems and the owners of these systems were known as cable operators [Whiteside 1985(A)].

The 1950s

In the early 1950s, the commercial broadcasting industry, television stations, and television networks were not opposed to cable operators since these operators provided a means of extending commercial broadcasters' signals, thereby increasing the number of available viewers. This allowed broadcasters to charge more for advertisements. However, as the number of CATV systems increased in the late 1950s, broadcasters became uneasy about the increasing competition.

By 1955, about 400 CATV systems, with more than 150,000 subscribers, were in operation. These operators were beginning to import, via commercial microwave relay systems[1], programs from distant stations. The operators made these programs available to their subscribers, sometimes omitting local broadcasting signals [Whiteside 1985(A)].

The 1960s

In the 1960s, the first major pay-cable service, Subscription TV (STV), was developed by Matthew Fox. A one time vice president of Universal Pictures turned wheeler-dealer, Fox saw a chance to make money by offering viewers programming that they could not receive over commercial television. Programming included movies and "events" such as sports or entertainment. One of Fox's goals was to get the rights to major league baseball games away from commercial broadcasters and charge audiences to see them via STV [Whiteside 1985(A)].

Competition and regulation trends during this decade were unfavorable towards cable operators. Commercial broadcasters and movie theater owners attempted to curtail the growth of the cable television industry, and the United States Federal Communications Commission (FCC) took steps to assist them by:

1. prohibiting the supply of programs from distant points via microwave relay systems,
2. restricting the showing of movies that were less than 10 years old and sporting events that were less than 5 years old, and
3. imposing "must-carry" rules which required cable operators to carry all local broadcasting signals on their systems.

In addition, Proposition 15, which made STV illegal in California, was passed in 1964. This decision was later overturned, but not before STV declared bankruptcy. At the same time, telephone companies were making it very difficult for cable companies to use their poles in the wiring of towns. They often charged disproportionately high rates to lease their poles. Nevertheless, the cable industry continued to grow.

[1] Microwave relay is a system used to move broadcast signals from one location to another without the use of land lines. Land lines are the actual cables that are strung on telephone poles and which transport signals to individual homes.

The 1970s

During the 1970s government regulations and technological improvements helped the cable operators. The FCC enacted rules which allowed the importation of distant signals and which allowed pay-cable services to show newly-released movies. This led to a substantial increase in the building of new systems and the upgrading of old systems. Upgrading—increasing the number of signals that could be delivered to subscribers—was necessary because of the increased channels that were available to subscribers.

Both basic service channels and pay-service channels increased in number during the 1970s. Basic services were advertiser-supported channels that assembled and sold programming to cable operators. The operators offered these services as their core package of entertainment, and costs were included in the subscription price of signal delivery. These basic services included local broadcasts, as well as community service and other independent channels. Pay-cable services, on the other hand, were initially commercial free. Pay services mostly depended on revenue from subscriptions. Consumer demand for increased services led to the creation, in late 1970 and early 1980, of other narrow-based basic programming channels, such as Music Television (MTV) and Cable News Network (CNN). The most popular basic services in 1988, based on subscriber

Figure 2: Top 20 Basic Cable Programming Services, 1988

NETWORK	SUBSCRIBERS (000'S)	AFFILIATES
Arts & Entertainment Network (A&E)	38,000	3,000
Black Entertainment Television (BET)	22,228	1,800
Cable News Network (CNN)	50,293	11,860
CBN Family Channel	44,277	8,303
C-SPAN	41,500	3,100
The Discovery Channel	40,642	5,000
ESPN	50,902	9,500
Financial News Network (FNN)	33,412	3,500
Headline News	35,774	3,410
Lifetime	42,757	3,800
MTV	46,070	5,405
The Nashville Network (TNN)	44,835	7,741
Nick At Nite	39,600	3,440
Nickelodeon	45,500	6,600
Superstation TBS	49,190	9,426
Turner Network Television (TNT)	26,500	1,512
USA Network	47,296	10,100
VH-1	32,139	2,530
The Weather Channel	38,174	3,600
WGN-TV	24,900	11,415

Source: *Cablevision*
Adapted from "Media Current Analysis," *S&P Industry Surveys,* June 22, 1989 p. M4.

Figure 3: Top Pay Cable Premium Programming Services, 1990

SERVICE	SUBSCRIBERS (000'S)	SYSTEMS
Home Box Office	17,000	7,400
American Movie Classics	20,000	1,700
Showtime	6,600	6,000
Cinemax	6,600	3,650
The Disney Channel	4,337	5,700
The Movie Channel	2,700	3,250
Bravo	2,500	375

Source: *Cablevision*
Adapted from "Media Current Analysis," *S&P Industry Surveys*, Jan. 11, 1990, p. M30.

levels, are shown in Figure 2. Figure 3 lists the most popular pay-cable services in 1990.

Home Box Office, the pay-cable service that revolutionized the industry, was the idea of Charles Dolan, CEO of Cablevision Systems Corporation. Dolan was attempting to prevent the financial ruin of Sterling Manhattan Cable [Lieberman 1989], a cable system in lower Manhattan which he headed and which was partly owned by Time Incorporated. Dolan decided to offer programs—mainly of live sporting events and uncut versions of movies—at an additional cost to subscribers. In November 1972, HBO's first signals were transmitted via microwave transmitters from the top of the Pan Am Building in New York City.

It wasn't until 1975, when HBO changed from using a commercial microwave relay system to using two transponders leased on RCA's Satcom I satellite, that the pay-cable service really caught on. Figure 4 illustrates how the flow of programming went from a programmer such as HBO (Program Uplink) to the satellite, down to the cable operator (Earth Station) and into the subscribers' homes. Cable operators received signals via satellite dish. These dishes initially cost about $100,000, an unaffordable price for smaller operators. However, as technology increased, smaller dishes became available for roughly $20,000. The combination of increased availability of lower cost satellite dishes and decreased restrictions on the part of the FCC caused dynamic growth in the entire cable industry [Whiteside 1985].

The 1980s

The rush to wire the U.S. with cable led to the creation of multiple system operators (MSOs)—cable operators who owned franchises in various cities and areas around the country. Franchises were specific geographic locations where the cable operators had exclusive rights to supply cable. Though constructing the systems was expensive, the cable operators recouped their investment through the sale of basic and pay-cable subscriptions. During this period of renewed growth, cable operators targeted potential customers in cities or suburbs who had available to them several commercial broadcast signals. Areas such as Long Island, New York, had initially

Figure 4: Illustration of Satellite Transmission

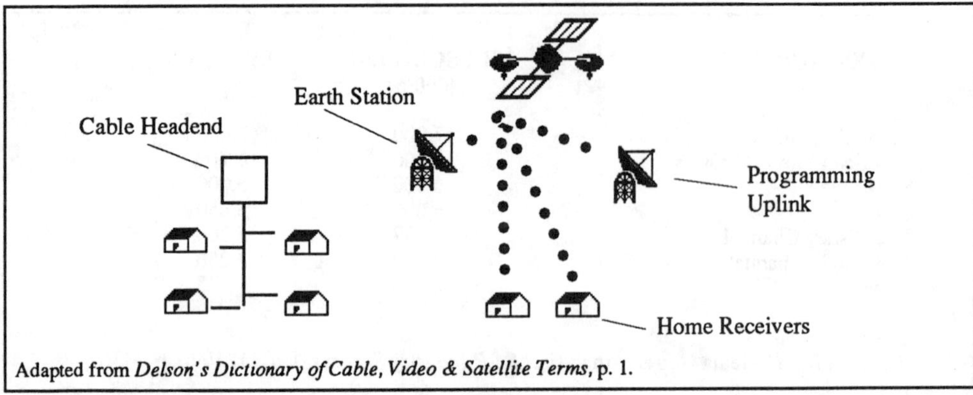

Adapted from *Delson's Dictionary of Cable, Video & Satellite Terms*, p. 1.

been viewed as bad investments for cable operators, but were proving to be lucrative. Long Island is now one of the largest cable franchises in the country.

In the 1980s, regulations again assisted cable operators. The U.S. Court of Appeals imposed "must-carry" rules that required cable systems to carry local broadcast signals, and the Cable Communications Policy Act of 1984 was passed allowing each city to collect a five percent annual franchise fee from operators' gross revenues. However, it prohibited these cities from regulating cable operators' subscription fees or contracts [Jessell & Stump 1988]. Following the passage of the Cable Act of 1984, horizontal and vertical integrations rapidly increased. Cable operators had huge amounts of cash and increased amounts of borrowing power which enabled them to acquire cable operations and invest in plant and programming.

In 1989 Nielson statistics indicated that total cable subscribers numbered about 50 million. About 55 percent of all U.S. households subscribed to basic services and approximately 29 percent of all U.S. households had pay-cable services. Each cable operator's franchise was a virtual monopoly, as homes desiring service were forced to subscribe to the operator with the franchise in that area.

SERVICES

In the late 1980s, the cable operator acted as a middleman between households and original programmers, and between advertisers and households. Figure 5 estimates the flow of revenue for the cable industry from 1989-1992. The operators made money in five ways:

- fees paid by subscribers who wanted to receive basic cable service
- fees paid by subscribers who wanted to receive pay-cable service
- fees paid by advertisers who bought time on basic channels which had been allocated from the basic services for sale by the cable service operators

- fees paid by home shopping networks
- fees paid by subscribers for pay-per-view movies, special events, and sporting events.

Subscriber Fees for Basic and Pay-Cable Service

Cable operators offered subscribers different cable "packages" which could include basic cable service along with one or more pay-cable services. For example, customers in Farmingdale, Long Island subscribing to basic cable service (30 channels) plus five premium services (HBO, Showtime, The Movie Channel, Cinemax, and The Disney Channel), could get a package from their local franchise operator (Cablevision) called "Rainbow Gold" for about $65.95 per month.

Cable operators then paid both the basic and the pay-cable services (programmers) on a per-subscriber basis. Each operator negotiated with each programmer as to the terms of payment and the amount paid per subscriber. Exceptions to this general rule were some network channels which did not receive payment, and home shopping services. Although these were considered basic services, they paid the operators for including their channels in the basic service package. Larger operators had more bargaining power with each of the basic and pay services. The ever-increasing number of services entering the market allowed the big MSOs to negotiate low rates and also to be allocated time to sell to advertisers on the basic channels.

Figure 5: Cable Industry Revenue (estimated)

	1989	1990	1991	1992
Basic Cable Revenue (mil $)	$9,300	$10,575	$11,530	$12,730
Pay Cable Revenue (mil $)	4,751	4,828	5,080	5,240
Other Revenues* (mil $)	4,830	5,990	6,650	7,300
TOTAL CABLE REVENUE	$18,881	$21,393	$23,260	$25,270
Basic Cable Subscriptions** (mil)	51.5	53.7	56.1	58.6
Pay Cable Subscriptions** (mil)	43.8	45.6	46.0	46.0
Average monthly basic rate	$15.50	$16.75	$17.50	$18.50
Average monthly pay rate	$9.25	$9.00	$9.25	$9.50
Annual cap investment (mil $)	1,825	2,000	1,400	1,500
Depreciation & Amort. (mil $)	2,400	2,928	3,210	3,575
Net Income (mil $)	2,344	2,680		
Operating Cash Flow*** (mil $)	7,890	9,410		

* Includes: advertising, installation, converter rentals, pay-per-view, expanded basic service, and other revenues
** At year end
***Includes operating income before depreciation and amortization, interest or taxes

Sources: Cable Advertising Bureau; *Cablevision*; Standard & Poor's
Adapted from "Media Current Analysis," *S&P Industry Surveys,* Feb. 7, 1991, p. M29

Advertiser Fees

Cable operators sold time to advertisers who wanted to place "spot ads." Spot advertisements were targeted towards specific audiences in specific geographic areas. They differed from national advertisements placed with the basic services which were shown over all systems carrying that basic channel regardless of the geographic location.

Home Shopping Service Fees

Home shopping services were part of operators' basic channel packages. Home shopping services sold consumer goods through presentations and commercials. Viewers could then telephone to place orders, charge orders to their credit cards, and have the merchandise shipped to them. These home shopping services typically paid the appropriate cable operators—as determined by the purchasers' ZIP codes—a percentage, usually about five percent, of their gross sales. Paul Kagan Associates projected revenues for home shopping services could reach $1.8 billion in 1989 and $2.8 billion in 1990. This translated into $90 million in revenue for cable operators in 1989 [Solomon 1989, p. 22].

Pay-Per-View Service Fees

Pay-Per-View (PPV), in its basic form, was a way for subscribers to purchase individual programs rather than pay for a monthly premium subscription. Pay-Per-View was one way for cable operators to compete with the popular videocassette recorder. Typically, the operator made a deal with original programmers such as Columbia, Warner, or an event organizer, and then offered a particular movie, sporting event, or other form of entertainment during a specific time. The subscriber then signed up, either by calling the cable operator or by pressing a button on his/her remote control, and the movie or the event was then "piped into" that person's television set. The operator then paid the original programmer the agreed-upon price per subscriber and kept the balance.

CURRENT MARKET CONDITIONS

The phenomenal growth and changes within the cable industry during the 1980s changed the focus on how operators made money. To increase subscription dollars and to attract additional advertisers, cable operators were trying ways to capture new customers within their franchises. Advertisers had become a primary focus, as the cable industry (both operators and programmers) were finding new ways to sell their programming services as an advertising medium.

CUSTOMERS

Cable operators had two sets of customers. Their first set of customers were the subscribers who purchased access to programming (basic, pay, or pay-per-view). Their second set of customers were the advertisers who were buying access to the subscribers in order to market their products.

The "Community Industry Forecast," a survey released in June 1989 by Veronis, Suhler & Associates, predicted that cable television's compound annual growth would drop from the late 1980s' double-digit performance to 7.7 percent through 1993. The survey predicted that half of future cable subscriber growth would stem from price increases [GM 1989].

Subscribers

Even with the slowing of the economy, cable subscriptions were expected to increase five percent annually through the mid-1990s since cable is a relatively inexpensive source of entertainment [*Gruntal Investment Research,* August 24, 1990, p.1]. Operators explored new ways to attract people who had not subscribed to services in the past. To attract new subscribers, operators and programmers were distributing coupons, offering joint venture promotions—such as HBO and Continental Airline's half-fare companion ticket program with a sign-up of at least three months of HBO— and giving away traditional promotional items such as shirts and clocks. These intense marketing strategies were geared toward the specific target audiences that programmers had determined were the most likely to subscribe. Morgan Stanley analyst John Tinker estimated in 1989 that it cost an operator $670 to enlist a subscriber and $2,500 per subscriber to buy a system [Knowlton 1989].

Operators also made efforts to retain their subscribers. During 1989, several cable operators introduced new customer service programs to increase customer satisfaction. Such programs attempted to have customers identify the programming they liked with the operators who provided it. Cable operators were aware that many customers felt that the growth of the cable industry had led to "unresponsiveness."

Advertisers

Advertisers purchased access to subscribers in order to market their products. These advertisers purchased spot ads targeted toward specific audiences in certain geographic areas. In March 1990, *Advertising Age* reported that cable TV reached about 57.1 percent of American households, compared to only 48.1 percent in 1987. However, the cable industry had not captured a comparable amount of available advertising revenues. A 1986 study by DDB Needham Worldwide analyzed various cable/broadcast network television commercial combinations to determine advertising reach and impression. The study concluded that "an advertising impression will be unaffected whether viewed on a network channel or a cable channel." One of the obvious drawbacks for advertisers was that they were not provided with adequate information/data on the cable industry and its audience [Katz 1989].

In 1988, advertisers spent about $14.6 billion on spot advertising, but only a little over $400 million went to cable operators [Reece 1989, p. 58]. Advertising agencies selected which advertising mediums to use and one drawback often dissuaded them from choosing cable: purchased advertising spots were not always run. To overcome this problem, a system was developed to verify spot ad runs. The system, called an addressable headend, worked as follows: An agency would send one tape of a commercial to a service center where it was uplinked to a satellite and brought down in just those markets where it was supposed to run. The spot would run and then a telephone call would send the data back through a phone line to a laser printer. An affidavit would then be typed to confirm the run.

A service called Cable Audience Profile from Nielson also addressed the same problem. It was a diary-based, meter-adjusted, fairly accurate set of books. Cable-Trak from Arbitron was another service that measured audiences in the cable market. These methods could only estimate, but both companies (Arbitron and Nielson) were working on ways to more accurately measure cable audiences [Reece 1989, p. 59].

COMPETITION

During the early years, competition in the cable industry came from several areas. Bill Daniels, one of the industry's pioneers, described the attitude of the media and entertainment industry towards cable from the start:

> ENEMIES...You start with the three networks - ABC, NBC, CBS - local stations, local theater owners, movie producers, the FCC, AT&T, most cities, states and counties, the Congress, and because of the political clout that the broadcasters had with senators and congressmen, 99% of Washington lawyers, any lobbyist in Washington that represented a broadcaster, and the power companies... [Jessell & Stump 1988, p. 35].

In the early 1990s, cable operators encountered intense competition at three different levels [Fabricant, 1990]. The first level of competition was with other cable operators and was referred to as franchise competition because it occurred primarily when local and city governments franchises were awarding franchises. However, in the mid-1980s, franchise competition took on an additional meaning as cable operators began to compete with each other in the area of programming. The second level of competition was with other forms of signal transmission and was commonly referred to as distribution competition. This competition generally occurred after franchises were awarded and was growing more intense as technology advanced. Finally, the third level of competition came from various broadcast and media sources as cable operators competed with these other sources for subscribers and advertising revenues.

Franchise Competitors

Operators encountered franchise competition while bidding for new areas in which to operate (franchises) and when renewing expired franchise agreements. Franchise competitors included both large MSOs and small independent operators. Since most of the available franchises had been awarded by the late 1980s these franchise competitors met only when franchises were up for renewal. These operators, either by themselves or through the media companies that owned them, began to invest in programming. Hence, franchise competitors were gradually evolving into competitors for programming. Figure 6 lists the cable operators (and the media companies that owned them) with the largest investments in programming in 1989. The companies that competed with TCI for franchises and for programming interests were American Television & Communications and Warner Cable, Cablevision, and Viacom.

American Television & Communications and Warner Cable. In the summer of 1989, Time Inc. and Warner Cable Communications merged to form the largest media and entertainment company in the world. The company's estimated 1989 revenue was $10.6 billion and operating income was $1.7 billion. This conglomerate brought cable into the homes of about 5.6 million customers—approximately 12 percent of the total U.S. cable market in 1989. The company incurred $14 billion in debt to merge and the cost to service the debt was approximately $100 million per month.

In addition to its cable holdings, Time-Warner was the country's largest magazine publisher and one of the largest book publishers. Its film and programming division included Home Box Office, Cinemax, HBO Video, and Warner Brothers Films. Time-Warner also carried several of the most popular music and record labels.

Cablevision Systems Corp. Headed by CEO Charles Dolan, Cablevision had the eighth largest franchise in the U.S. and the third largest investment in programming by a cable company. In 1989, Dolan was concentrating on the operation of cable franchises and the provision of programming. Cablevision had grown through the acquisitions of $549 million in franchises from Viacom Inc. in early 1989; and an $18 million regional sports channel in Los Angeles, with

Figure 6: Media Companies with a Stake in Cable Programmers

Telecommunications Inc.	Time-Warner Inc.	Cablevision	Viacom
American Movie Classics	Black Entertainment Tel	American Movie Classics	Cable News Network
Black Entertainment Tel	Cable News Network	Bravo	Cable Value Network
Cable News Network	Cable Value Network	Cable News Network	Fashion Channel
Cable Value Network	Fashion Channel	Cable Value Network	HeadlineNews
Discovery Channel	Headline News	CNBC	Lifetime
Fashion Channel	Home Box Office	Fashion Channel	Movie Channel
Headline News	Movietime	Headline News	MTV
Home Sports Entertainment	Shop Television Network	Shop Television Network	Nickelodeon
Rocky Mountain Sports Net.	Travel Channel	Sports Channel America	Showtime
Showtime	Turner Broadcasting System	Travel Channel	Turner Broadcasting System
Think Entertainment	Turner Network Television	Turner Broadcasting System	Turner Network Television
Turner Broadcasting System	Viewers' Choice	Turner Network Television	VH-1
Turner Network Television			Viewers' Choice

Source: National Cable Television Association
Adapted from Bill Carter, "With America Well Wired, Cable Industry is Changing," *The New York Times*, July 9, 1989, p. 20.

another planned for Ohio. Cablevision's two film networks, Bravo and American Movie Classics (a partnership with TCI), faced increased competition with the introduction of Turner Network Television (TNT) in the late 1980s.

In mid-1990, Cablevision served over 1.1 million subscribers and had the highest revenues and cash flow per subscriber of all publicly traded cable companies [Gruntal Investment Research, March 5, 1990, p.3]. Cablevision's Class A shares went public in 1986 at $14.50 and in June 1989 sold at about $41. Dolan's family owned nearly all of the Class B shares, which gave him the power to pick 9 of the 13 members of Cablevision's board of directors.

Viacom International Inc. Viacom had approximately one million subscribers in mid 1989 and the fourth largest investment in programming by a cable operator. Viacom owned Showtime, a popular pay-cable movie channel and MTV, a basic service music channel. In mid-1989, Viacom was in the process of suing Time-Warner for monopolistic activity. Viacom felt that Time's cable operators, ATC and Warner, showed an unfair preference for Time's pay-cable services [Carter 1989(C)]. Even more interesting would be the result of Tele-Communications, Inc.'s October 1989 purchase of a 50 percent share of Viacom's Showtime. Time-Warner was proposing a countersuit to block this deal as of the end of 1989.

Distribution Competitors

Distribution competitors, the second level of competition that the operators encountered, were other forms of transmission services. These services included Direct Broadcast Satellite (DBS), Multi-point Microwave Distribution Service (MMDS), Satellite Master Antenna Television (SMATV), and videocassette recorders (VCRs).

Direct Broadcast Satellite (DBS). A DBS is a high-powered satellite system that works like a cable satellite. However, since a DBS operated with more power than cable satellites, its signal could be received with much smaller, and therefore more affordable, Earth stations. A DBS transmitted several signals directly to homes for pickup by way of a small roof-top dish antenna. These satellites would, in effect, bypass the need for the cable operators and for the current expensive home satellite dishes. Programmers could lease or sell small dishes to households that could pay these programmers directly for their monthly services. As of 1989, the dishes that had to be attached to the houses in order to receive the service were still relatively expensive—between $500 and $1000. In addition, not enough programmers participated in providing this type of service, perhaps due to the high initial capital investment.

Multi-point Microwave Distribution Service (MMDS). An MMDS is, by definition, an over-the-air, super-high-frequency service providing omnidirectional transmission to selected customer location within a 10 to 20 mile radius. These were licensed by the FCC as common carriers which meant that they had to lease their transmission facilities to service providers. Generally, they leased most of the station time to pay movies services, which provided programming to hotels and apartment buildings. The MMDS operators could also transmit video, data, text, and other services to customers who had special antennas and converters. Although MMDS was expensive and utilized on a limited scale, this was expected to change due to the licensing of a majority of markets, the approval of increased transmitter power, and the expansion of frequency availability [*Securities and Exchange Commission Form 10K*, 1990, pp. I-8].

Satellite Master Antenna Television (SMATV). SMATV operators used satellite dishes to deliver cable programming to multi-unit dwellings. In 1989 approximately 800,000 to 1 million people subscribed to SMATV, and another 800,000 or so used SMATV when they watched TV in one of the 3,000 hotels that used the system. SMATV or "Private Cable" was considered a niche business, with prices for systems reaching $700 per subscriber in 1989. One of the problems that SMATV encountered was the higher prices they had to pay for programming—roughly 15 to 20 percent more than the cable operators. Another problem was that some cable channels, including HBO, A&E, and SportsChannel, refused to be shown on SMATV [Pearce 1989].

Videocassette Recorders (VCRs). VCRs were instruments used to play videocassettes that contained programming. VCRs had the ability to record, play back, and erase. In the mid-1980s this industry segment experienced phenomenal growth—a 65 percent penetration of the 90 million U.S. television households in 1989. This occurred as people, trying to escape long lines, overcrowding, and higher priced movie theaters, discovered the joy of viewing current movies in the comfort of their own homes. However, VCRs could not offer live entertainment and sporting events. In addition, the customer had to leave home in order to rent or buy a tape containing programming.

Other Competitors. To some degree, cable TV competed with other media for both subscribers and advertisers. The networks, for example, were losing both advertisers and viewers to cable. Initially, movie theaters also lost customers to cable TV, as well as to other TV broadcasting.

PROGRAMMING

Programming could mean one of several activities. Original programmers were the movie makers and the event coordinators. Pay-cable programming involved the showing of newly-released movies and some original programs. Such services normally did not carry advertising. Basic programming was the showing of television network shows and reruns, news, and some special-interest programming such as all-music channels. Basic services normally carried advertising. The situation became even more confusing in the 1990s when some cable operators began including some "pay" services, such as the American Movie Classics channel which carried no advertising, as basic services included in the basic cost of service.

Cable operators had become more vertically integrated by the 1990s. Investment in programming was a way for operators to gain increased control over what could be offered to their customers by gaining access to sources such as film libraries and movie companies. It was also a way for them to share in the revenues generated from that segment of the industry. Some analysts thought that the cable operators were eager to acquire investments in programming partly because of the fear of increased government regulation which would limit their revenue generating capacity [Fabricant 1989(C)].

Pat Fili, Lifetime's senior vice president, programming and production, described the trend towards basic programming in the late 1980s:

> Pay was the big trend eight or nine years ago...but now...everyone is trying to get into basic,...operators love it because their strategy is to sell choice; they can sell differentiation,...advertisers...what they're buying on basic is much cleaner. They know what they're getting [Carter 1989(C), p. 36].

Time-Warner (owner of ATC and Warner Cable) started its own basic service in 1989. Previously the company had invested only in established basic services. In the spring of 1989, HBO announced its intention of becoming a basic programmer. The Comedy Channel, with an all comedy-clip format, would be a direct competitor with the "HA" channel, a Viacom product which was to debut just months after The Comedy Channel.

TECHNOLOGY

The cable industry was very sensitive to developments in the technology related to transmission (distribution), programming (movie making), or hardware (televisions). There were two developments that could change the way the entire industry operated: fiber optics and high-definition television.

Fiber Optics

Fiber optics, a single thin strand of glass fiber that could carry pulses of laser light that contain hundreds of thousands times more information than traditional copper wire, represented the future in the communications industry. In 1989 projected expansion of fiber optics into homes by 1992 was about 225,000 [Markoff 1989]. Fiber optics had the potential for rendering obsolete virtually all of America's existing cable TV wiring infrastructure [Slutsker 1988, p. 176].

As of mid-1989 fiber optic cables were already widely used in long-distance lines and between local telephone exchanges. But extending them into the home could create vast markets for residential electronic information services. These services ranged from on-line shopping to delivery of newspapers electronically and the creation of a new generation of smart home appliances that could combine the functions of televisions, computers, FAX machines, and telephones. Visionaries foresaw such things as home banking, electronic mail, picture telephones, and customized television feeds becoming standard home fare [Markoff 1989, sec. 3, p. 1].

Fiber optics gave the cable companies one distinct advantage. With fiber optic transmissions, the cable companies could eliminate the theft of signals. The use of copper coaxial cables to transmit programming allowed theft (as high as 30 percent of programming) since converter boxes could be used to descramble the signals. With fiber optics, programming would be under software control at a central office and would become virtually impossible to steal [Slutsker 1988, p. 177].

High-Definition Television

The introduction of high-definition television (HDTV), which offers 35mm-like pictures, paved the way for new technologies and business opportunities. With the introduction of this product came a need for increased capabilities in the methods used to transmit the signals. This presented a problem with the existing transmission capabilities as the HDTV signal needed 30 megahertz (Mhz) of signal bandwidth, whereas the regular TV bandwidth was only 6 Mhz in early 1990 [Broad 1989, p. C1]. Nevertheless, the FCC initiated an inquiry into whether it should adopt a standard for HDTV and, in conjunction with a further Notice of Inquiry, decided to adopt an HDTV over-the-air standard by September 1993 [*Securities and Exchange Commission Form 10-K*, 1990, pp. I-7].

Experiments using digital transmission, which allowed HDTV signals to be carried on 6 Mhz bands by filtering out signals that were not in motion on the screen and sending only the changes, were taking place in late 1989. These methods would allow the cable operators to utilize existing cable systems. However, fiber optic transmission would totally eliminate the problem of capacity because of the enormous amounts of signals that it could handle.

LEGAL

Several legal aspects of the cable industry threatened to change how the operators did business. It was possible that legislation allowing the telephone companies to compete with the cable companies in the supply of programming would pass by the early 1990s. In addition, Congress was threatening to regulate in areas such as the pricing of subscriptions, on the cable operators. Other regulations regarding programming were to become effective in January 1990.

Telephone Company Crossownership

In 1970 the FCC, in an attempt to protect the infant cable industry and to promote new technology, ruled that telephone companies were forbidden to operate cable television systems. This rule was called the crossownership ban and was the basis of the Cable Communications Policy Act of 1984. The FCC, in setting the regulations, was attempting to establish a competitive market through which an independent cable industry would be able to deliver innovative service to its customers. Congress felt that the telephone companies, who were in a monopoly position both as a telecommunications provider within local areas and also as owners of the pole lines, could and would prevent the development of an independent cable industry.

The FCC did allow the telephone companies to file for waivers of the crossownership rule in rural communities where Community Antenna Television (CATV) services could not exist except through an affiliate of the local telephone company. These applications, however, proved to be quite costly—mainly due to the requirement for extensive supporting documentation—and were too costly for the telephone companies.

On September 22, 1988 the FCC proposed to eliminate the rules that it had instituted almost 20 years prior. In order to do this, it had to submit a legislative proposal to amend the Cable Act of 1984. Before anything could be proposed, several issues had to be examined: whether the rules would still be necessary to maintain a competitive environment; whether the rules had hindered the development of new services; and whether equal access to pole lines and conduit space for independent cable operators could be ensured. The FCC used the results of these inquiries as its basis for a legislative proposal to remove the crossownership rule.

To circumvent existing restrictions in the late 1980s, the telephone companies formed strategic alliances with cable operators. For example, GTE, a telephone company in California, formed an agreement with Apollo Cablevision, the operator who had the cable television franchise in Cerritos, California. GTE provided the local telephone service and was separately contracted to install either coaxial cable—which television used—or fiber optic cable to all 16,000 homes in the town. Apollo would then lease access to the cables so that they in turn could provide 36-channel service to the homes [Markoff 1989].

As of late 1990, the mood within governing bodies (FCC and Congress) was once again shifting against telephone company entrance into the cable industry. On July 26, 1990, the FCC's review of the cable industry was released. It stated that additional competition was desirable but did not specifically endorse the telephone companies' entrance into the cable industry. Then, on July 31, 1990, the Senate Commerce Committee approved a compromise bill regarding the telephone company crossownership issue. The bill would allow telephone companies to lease their facilities only and further restricted them from having any control over programming content. ["Cable TV Industry," March 5, 1990, p. 1]. The approval of this compromise bill eased the minds of many cable operators who feared intense competition from telephone companies because of their vast amounts of capital, resources, and experience in communications.

Re-regulation

In the late 1980s, political momentum turned against the cable industry. Deregulation brought about large price increases for basic cable services as operators passed on increased programming costs to the subscribers. An example of this practice was when ESPN entered into its agreement to air NFL games on Sunday nights. ESPN then charged the operators an additional 9 to 10 cents per subscriber per month [Friedman 1989; Brown 1989]. In turn, the operator raised basic subscription prices to cover their additional costs.

Critics accused the cable industry of being monopolistic and anti-competitive, citing a 30 percent increase in the basic subscription rate between 1984 and 1989. More than a dozen bills to re-regulate the industry were pending in Congress at the end of 1989. Senator Al Gore (D-Tenn) was perhaps the cable industry's chief critic on Capitol Hill. He wanted to either regulate the cable industry or permit the phone companies to operate cable systems as competitors. The suits between the cable operators themselves (Viacom and Time-Warner) added weight to the argument that monopolistic practices existed [Carter 1989(B)].

However, 1990 turned out to be a very positive year for the cable industry in terms of this pending regulatory issue. Although both houses of Congress proposed legislation to re-regulate the cable industry under bills named the "Cable Television Consumer Protection Act of 1990," these bills were "out of committee" in both houses and therefore would not be voted upon until 1991 at the earliest. [*Gruntal Investment Research,* August 1990, p. 2]. In addition, these bills were significantly revised from the more restrictive earlier versions and thus harsh penalties are not likely ["Cable TV Industry," March 5, 1990, p. 2]. Therefore, a strict re-regulatory environment is not expected even if this legislation is passed.

Syndication Exclusivity

Syndication Exclusivity (SNYDEX) was the right of a broadcaster to require a cable operator to delete from its menu a particular show that the broadcaster had exclusive rights to, within 35 miles of their studios. The cable operator could not show the program on any broadcast station at the same time as the broadcaster. This rule, which was scheduled to be implemented by the FCC in 1990, would cause scheduling complications for the cable operators. It was expected to cause periods when certain stations would have no programs to air due to the lack of available substitute programs or errors in scheduling.

Robert Sachs, senior vice president at Continental Cablevision, noted that some TV stations might have been willing to waive their SYNDEX rights in exchange for better channel positioning by the operators. The operators had the right to place the channels anywhere on their system. For example, TCI could make the NBC affiliate channel #28 on its system whereas ATC could make the NBC affiliate channel #4 on its system.

THE COMPANY

BACKGROUND

In 1964, a group of investors and partners formed Community Television, Inc. (CTV). The purpose of the company was the same as all cable television companies at that time — to bring television into the homes of customers living where terrain and/or long distances interfered with reception. This company was the forerunner of what is now Tele-Communications Inc. (TCI).

The chief executive officer of TCI as of the end of the 1980s was Dr. John Malone, who was viewed by some as being the most powerful man in the cable industry at the time. Malone was a magna cum laude Yale graduate with two MBAs and a PhD in operations research. He joined TCI in 1973 after working as a economic planner in Bell Lab's R&D department for AT&T; as a management consultant at the blue-chip New York firm, McKinsey & Co.; and then as president of General Instrument's Jerrold Division [Ainslie 1989]. Malone turned down a more lucrative offer from Warner Cable in order to work at TCI.

Malone was brought to TCI by Bob Magness, the company's founder and chairman of the board since 1989. The Oklahoma native Magness, born in 1924, was a graduate of Southwestern State College in Oklahoma. His philosophies: "Keep it simple," and "We'd rather pay interest than taxes," shaped TCI from the start [Knowlton 1989].

In 1973 TCI was a small, primarily rural multiple system operator with $92 million in revenues. Burdened with a floating rate debt, it was in the middle of a liquidity crisis. Malone spent his first four years fending off bankers who were trying to foreclose [Ainslie 1989]. By 1977 TCI was in a stronger financial position, allowing Malone and Magness to pursue their portfolio strategy. "Forget about earnings," Malone said. "What we really wanted was appreciating assets. Our goal was to own as much of the assets as possible, finance them in the most efficient way, and therefore build wealth."

From 1973 to 1989 Malone completed 482 deals, an average of one every two weeks. A map of TCI's more than 1,000 local cable systems would show a speckling across the U.S., with dense concentrations in the Rocky Mountain region, the Northwest, Texas, the Southeast, the San Francisco area, and Chicago [Knowlton 1989].

FINANCE

At the end of 1989 revenues of $3.3 billion were projected and TCI's operating cash flow was $1.3 billion annually. This was more than any other communication company and more than the three networks combined. TCI's stock split 24-to-1 between 1974 and 1989. A $1,000 investment in 1974 yielded $913,350 in 1989. There were secretaries at TCI worth over $1 million compliments of the stock in the company's retirement plan. In 1988 TCI paid more than $700 million in interest on its debt and most remaining revenue was earmarked for capital expenditures and acquisitions [Knowlton 1989]. Between 1988 and 1989, TCI's cable television revenues increased 38 percent and revenues from theater operations increased 16.6 percent [*Annual Report*, 1989, pp. 2-4]. Growth in cable revenues was attributed to increases in subscriber levels, higher service charges, and further acquisitions. Increased theater revenues were attributed to higher ticket sales and prices as well as further acquisitions and stable operating costs. In addition, the company sold certain investments and assets for a pre-tax gain of $61 million in 1989 [*Securities and Exchange Commission Form 10-K*, 1990, pp. II-5].

However, in 1989, operating expenses also grew at a higher rate than normal due to certain one-time charges and increased programming costs. Interest expenses on loans for further acquisitions also increased [*Annual Report*, 1989, pp. 2-5]. At the end of 1989, the company had $4.9 billion (or 60 percent) of fixed-rate debt with a weighted average interest rate of 10.6 percent and $3.3 billion (or 40 percent) of variable-rate debt with interest rates approximating the prime rate [*Securities and Exchange Commission Form 10-K*, 1990,, pp. II-5]. In addition, TCI recorded a loss of $26 million in 1989 due to early extinguishment of debt and a net loss of $257 million in 1989 because of decreased gain on sales of assets, increased interest expense, and increased losses by affiliates [*Annual Report*, 1989, p.2-5]. Furthermore, TCI's purchase of 42.5 percent of indirect interest in SCI Holdings, Inc. (SCI) and the merger of United Cable Television Corporation and United Artists Communication, Inc. (UAIC) had a negative impact on the company's earnings due to the cost of servicing the debt incurred to finance these transactions, as well as the resulting increase in depreciation and amortization [*Securities and Exchange Commission Form 10-K*, 1990, pp. II-6]. Figure 7 shows TCI's Financial Statements for 1989. In the figure previous years of data are shown for comparative purposes.

These results reflect only one period of operations and not the company's overall, long-term financial position—many of the negative effects are primarily short term. In fact, 1989 was a positive year for TCI: new sources of capital funding were cultivated, higher cost debt was retired, and continued growth through acquisition was funded [*Annual Report*, 1989, pp.I-4]. In addition, revenue growth is expected to continue due to increases in subscribership levels, higher

**Figure 7: Tele-Communications, Inc.
Consolidated Balance Sheets 1987-1989
(Amounts in Millions)**

CONSOLIDATED BALANCE SHEET	1987	1988	1989
ASSETS			
CASH	$79	$20	$19
TRADE AND OTHER RECIEVABLES,NET	$135	$197	$255
PREPAID EXPENSES	$28	$46	$53
INV. IN AFFIL.,OTHER CO. AND RELATED RECE	$1,071	$1,818	$1,925
PROPERTY AND EQUIPMENT, AT COST:			
LAND	$118	$170	$182
CABLE DIST. SYST.	$2,179	$2,843	$3,996
THEATRE BUILDINGS AND EQUIP.	$490	$651	$706
SUPPORT EQUIP. AND BUILDINGS	$207	$258	$397
	$2,994	$3,922	$5,281
LESS ACCUMULATED DEPRECIATION	$549	$781	$1,102
	$2,445	$3,141	$4,179
FRANCHISE COSTS NET OF AMORTIZATION	$2,375	$3,144	$4,649
OTHER ASSETS, AT COST, NET OF AMORT.	$164	$208	$352
TOTAL ASSETS	$6,297	$8,574	$11,432
LIABILITIES AND STOCKHOLDERS EQUITY			
ACCOUNTS PAYABLE	$84	$89	$148
ACCRUED INTERESTS PAYABLE	$79	$83	$142
ACCRUED LIABILITIES	$190	$218	$292
DEBT	$4,905	$6,202	$8,176
DEFERRED INCOME TAXES	$105	$148	$113
OTHER LIABILITIES	$92	$143	$325
TOTAL LIABILITIES	$5,455	$6,883	$9,196
MIN. INTERESTS IN EQUITY OF CONS. SUBSID.	$55	$485	$1,328
STOCKHOLDER'S EQUITY:			
CLASS A COMMON STOCK,$1 PAR VALUE	$129	$154	$307
CLASS B COMMON STOCK,$1 PAR VALUE	$24	$24	$48
ADDITIONAL PAID IN CAPITAL	$536	$865	$648
RETAINED EARNINGS(DEFICIT)	$140	$196	($75)
	$829	$1,239	$928
LESS TREASURY STOCK, AT COST	($42)	($33)	($20)
TOTAL STOCKHOLDERS EQUITY	$787	$1,206	$908
TOTAL LIABILITIES AND STOCKHOLDER'S EQUITY	$6,297	$8,574	$11,432

Figure 7: Tele-Communications, Inc. (contd.)
Consolidated Income Statements 1987-1989
(Amounts in Millions)

INCOME STATEMENT	1987	1988	1989
REVENUE	$1,709	$2,282	$3,026
OPERATING COSTS AND EXPENSES:			
OPERATING	$713	$930	$1,287
SELLING, GENERAL AND ADMINISTRATIVE	$346	$464	$632
DEPRECIATION	$230	$304	$410
AMORTIZATION	$62	$93	$128
TOTAL EXPENSES	$1,351	$1,791	$2,457
OPERATING INCOME	$358	$491	$569
OTHER INCOME (EXPENSE)			
INTEREST EXPENSE	($353)	($564)	($817)
SHARE OF EARNINGS(LOSSES) OF AFFILIATES,NET	($4)	$7	($89)
GAIN ON SALES OF ASSETS	$42	$194	$61
LOSS OF EARLY EXTINGUISHMENT OF DEBT		($17)	($26)
COMPENSATION RELATING TO STOCK APPRECIATION RIGHTS		($32)	($75)
MINORITY INTERESTS IN LOSSES (EARNINGS)	($9)	$1	$33
OTHER, NET	$16	$20	$42
TOTAL OTHER INCOME (EXPENSE)	($308)	($391)	($871)
EARNINGS (LOSS) BEFORE INCOME TAXES	$50	$100	($302)
INCOME TAX EXPENSE (BENEFIT)	$44	$44	($45)
NET EARNINGS (LOSS)	$6	$56	($257)

Source: *Tele-communications, Inc. 1988 Annual Report.*

service charges, increased sale of spot advertisements, additional programming revenues, more satellite subscribers, and increased pay-per-view activity. TCI's management believes that the available lines of credit, net cash provided by operating activities, proceeds from the sale of assets, and the company's ability to obtain additional long-term financing will provide adequate sources of short-term and long-term liquidity in the future [*Annual Report,* 1988].

ORGANIZATIONAL STRUCTURE

TCI's regional operating divisions were structured as stand-alone entities. Each division was separately incorporated and fully staffed in all areas at that level. This decentralization took place in early 1987. The company was organized as follows:

1. *West Marc Communications, Inc.* was a subsidiary of TCI which became involved in cable TV in 1986 and served over 500,000 basic subscribers and 300,000 pay subscribers [*Annual Report*, 1989, pp. I-24]. Prior to this time, West Marc primarily operated microwave communications [*Annual Report*, 1989, p. I-24]. West Marc increased cable TV operations through acquisitions and in 1988 it also entered into a multiyear agreement with MCI Telephone to construct and maintain a 1,500-mile digital microwave system from Seattle to Denver.

2. *United Artists Entertainment Company* was the result of the merger between United Cable Television and United Artists Communications in February 1989. This subsidiary controlled approximately 2,700 screens in 628 movie theaters as of December 1989. During 1990, the theater division relocated its headquarters from East Meadow, New York to Denver, Colorado, in order to reduce costs and consolidate operations with UAE's overall corporate headquarters [*Annual Report*, 1989, pp. I-22].

3. *X-Press Information Services, Ltd.* was a wholly-owned subsidiary of TCI which had operated exclusively as a cable information programmer. In mid-1989, X-Press shifted its focus from providing cable-delivered news and information to delivery of consumer- based entertainment software and services [*Annual Report*, 1989, pp. I-18].

4. *Cabletime, Inc.* was a subsidiary of TCI that put out monthly program guides for cable TV subscribers. In April 1989, the Cabletime guide changed its digest format to a full- sized magazine named "TV Entertainment" [*Annual Report*, 1989, pp. I-21]. In addition, Cabletime distributed other related guides to specific subscribers.

5. *Heritage Communications, Inc.* was a TCI subsidiary that in 1990 made a transition from being an independent company with an emphasis on acquisitions, to being an operating company with an emphasis on internal growth, financial performance, and operating controls.

TCI had been attempting to acquire established producers of programming as well as programming distribution services so that it would not be dependent on rival operators who charged unfavorable prices. TCI's investments in programming of 1988 are shown in Figure 8. In addition to those shown, TCI purchased a 50 percent interest in Showtime in late 1989.

Malone and Magness shared voting control at TCI; together they owned 65 percent of the Class B stock, which had 10 times the voting power of the more widely traded Class A shares.

Figure 8: Tele-Communictions' Programming Investments (1988)

Programming Investments:

Turner Broadcasting System, Inc	24%
Black Entertainment Television	14%
Home Sports Entertainment	60%
American Movie Classics	43%
The Discovery Channel	14%
Think Entertainment	25%
Cable Value Network	17%
QVC Network, Inc.	19%

Source: *Tele-Communications Inc. 1988 Annual Report*

The three man executive committee composed of Malone, Magness, and an outside director (*Salt Lake City Tribune* publisher, Paul J. O'Brien) made all policy decisions and could act speedily on deals without convening or, in many cases, consulting the board of directors. TCI's management style had prevailed with long-term focus, effective decentralization, lean management, and aggressiveness [Knowlton 1989].

CUSTOMER SERVICE

In September 1989 TCI announced a 20-point customer service campaign aimed at limiting churn (disconnects), boosting penetration, and quieting TCI's (and the cable industry's) critics in and out of government. Bob Thomson, TCI vice president, Government Affairs, highlighted four of the 20 points as follows:

1. Give better trained customer-service representatives the authority to make decisions, particularly small adjustments to bills.
2. Set up regional phone centers so that a "TCI person," not an answering service operator, would be available to answer calls on a 24-hour-a-day basis.
3. Call customers after they had had work performed in their homes to make sure all work was satisfactory.
4. Promise to respond to all service calls within 24 hours under "ordinary business conditions."

Other programs included expanded training programs for managers and employees who had direct contact with customers, a 30-day money-back guarantee for new subscribers; and expanded office and service hours.

Reaction from Capitol Hill to TCI's announcement was mixed. Aides to Senator Al Gore declared that the program highlighted points which should have been covered all along. Others, for example, Congressman Al Swift (D-Wash), said that the program was a "smart move." He felt that because TCI was the industry leader, other cable operators would follow by implementing similar programs. Swift also felt that by successfully dealing with concerns over rates and customer service, the issues of vertical integration, re-regulation, and other various "broadcast-cable issues" might be dropped.

OPERATIONS

In early 1990, TCI, along with a group of nine other cable operators and GE American Communications, formed a joint venture called K-Prime Partners in order to bring programming to rural communities and other special niche subscribers [*Annual Report,* 1989, pp. I-25]. This project enabled the group to offer a satellite-to-home broadcasting service by using GE's Satcom K-1 satellite and consisted of several superstations and a few pay-per-view services. The service was intended primarily as an alternative means of delivering distant broadcast signals. The signals were intended for subscribers who lost programming as a result of the syndicated exclusivity rules (SYNDEX) enacted on some signals (broadcast stations such as WWOR-NY) to avoid the administrative and technical burdens involved in scheduling around the blackout periods. However, if successful and well-accepted this project might initiate fast paced growth in the KU-Band satellite industry.

The satellite signals were scrambled so that the cable operators could charge subscribers. To receive the service, each subscribing home needed an Earth station with a dish at least one meter wide and an addressable receiver descrambler. Figure 4 shows how signals previously went from a programming uplink to a satellite and then down to an Earth station. It was now possible to place an Earth station and descrambler in the home, thereby allowing the programming to be directly transmitted [*Cable Operators Look,* 1989].

Some critics viewed TCI's (and other operator's) interest in the Satcom K-1 as defensive. In 1989 it was far superior to other satellites for broadcasting to homes. If the cable operators controlled the available transponders on the Satcom K-1, they would not have to worry about others launching a service that would bypass conventional cable systems. CEO Malone insisted that TCI's main reason for using the satellite was to compensate viewers for loss of programming due to SYNDEX.

John Sie, senior vice president, pointed out another strategic reason for use of the Satcom K-1: the satellite could allow cable operators to offer high-definition television service if the FCC adopted a HDTV transmission standard that was incompatible with cable systems.

TOWARDS THE FUTURE

Dr. Malone had been called upon several times by the federal government to state his company's position on high-definition television (HDTV). He stressed that TCI supported the development of processed digital HDTV (and was, in fact, a partner with others in conducting experiments in this area). TCI's managers felt that the future of television belonged to cable, broadcast, and some elements of the home satellite dish industry, who—by working together—would provide the best that feasible technology had to offer the television viewer. TCI intended to continue to upgrade its plant using the most cost-effective technologies available, in order to maintain its position as the primary video provider to the home [TCI 1988 *Annual Report*]. The impact of proposed legislation would be a major determining factor for the future of the cable industry.

In light of the current trends, some of TCI's managers felt in 1990 that the company should pursue a vertical integration strategy. Dr. Malone and Martin B. Davis of Paramount Communications had discussed a possible merger. This strategy stemmed largely from the Time-Warner merger, as a way to compete with that newly-formed media giant [Fabricant 1989]. TCI's large customer base could easily market Paramount's large library of programming. In addition, TCI had the financing capabilities to allow for different types of mergers, whether it be a friendly takeover or a stock swap.

Other TCI managers felt that diversification into other cash-rich business was the right way to go. They pointed out that other cable companies, such as COMCAST, were diversifying into other heavy cash generating industries such as cellular telephones [Knowlton, 1989]. This industry experienced rapid growth in the late 1980s with some companies adding up to 750 new subscribers per month. This growth rate was higher than the cable industry at the end of 1989. While TCI has the potential ability and resources to accomplish this course of action due to its size, nationwide locations, technical competence, and financing capabilities, such an option would be very expensive and risky. The company would need an enormous amount of capital to acquire existing cellular operators with franchise rights, a substantial customer base, access to distribution outlets, and a knowledgeable sales force. Furthermore, TCI would be directly competing with the largest cellular operators, who possessed vast amounts of capital, resources, and experience in the communications area. At the end of 1990, TCI management was still uncertain whether or not this alternative should be explored further.

Still other TCI management felt that the company should focus on attracting new subscribers either through acquisitions or within its own franchises. Subscribers represented various revenue sources to the company, through additional subscription fees, increasing service charges, and higher prices that could be paid for advertisement. In the next three to five years, industry analysts predicted that subscribers, as well as service charges, would continue to increase at five to seven percent per year while advertising and pay-per-view activity was expected to increase 15 to 50 percent annually [*Gruntal Investment Research*, August 1990, p. 1]. TCI had the capabilities needed to attract new subscribers: price flexibility, various basic and pay service packages, an improved customer-service program, and promotional joint ventures and giveaways.

Many managers, however, were very concerned about upcoming legislation regarding regulation and the telephone industry's entrance into the cable TV industry. These managers felt the company could make better use of its resources by diversifying into alternative distribution forms such as direct broadcast satellite (DBS). DBS had growth potential because it could be received by a large number of subscribers without the need for a cable hookup, and had the potential to transmit over 100 channels. Also, several new DBS satellites were being launched. Competition in the area of DBS was expected to intensify as more cable operators become involved in DBS service and further technological developments reduced system costs. In addition, DBS was still relatively more expensive to subscribers than cable TV, required high initial capital investments by operators, and as of yet programmers were still reluctant to provide this type of service.

Taking all this into consideration, TCI management was still somewhat confused and unsure as to which of the several potential alternatives the company should pursue in the future.

REFERENCES AND BACKGROUND READING

"A Cable TV Company Promotes Its Image," *The New York Times*, Oct. 10, 1990, p. D21.

Ainslie, Peter, "Malone Along," *Channels*, June 1989, pp. 30-36.

Alexander, Charles, P., "A Deal Heard Round the World," *Time*, March 20, 1989, pp. 55-56.

Andrews, Edmund, "Goals of TCI in Cable Spinoff," *The New York Times*, August 28, 1990, pp. D8.

Benson, Jim, "One-stop Shopping Causes Furor," *Advertising Age*, April 10, 1989, pp. S26-S30.

Broad, William J., "U.S. Counts on Computer Edge in the Race of Advanced TV, *The New York Times*, November 28, 1989, pp. C1, C13.

"Broadcast / Cable TV Industry," *Value Line Investment Survey*, June 29, 1990, pp.379-389.

Brown, Merrill, "Awakening Cable," *Channels*, June 1989, p. 28.

Burgi, Michael, "Cable Turns On to Tune-In Promotion," *Channels*, April 1989, pp. 60, 61.

"CAB Conference Promotes Cable's Growth," *Broadcasting*, April 17, 1989, pp. 52, 53.

"Cable Operators Look to Heavens for New Homes," *Broadcasting*, June 19, 1989, pp. 62, 63.

"Cable TV Industry," *Gruntal Investment Research*, March 5, 1990, pp. 1-5.

"Cable TV Measure is Dead: Sponsor," *Newsday*, Oct. 20, 1990, (B), pp. 13.

"Capital Hill Ultimatum," *Broadcasting*, May 29, 2989, p. 34.

Carter, Bill, "Cable Channels Bite Hands That Feed Them," *The New York Times*, May 29, 1989(A), p. 35.

Carter, Bill, "Cable May Get Its Wings Clipped," *The New York Times*, July 10, 1989(B), p. D1.

Carter, Bill, "No Laughing Matter," *The New York Times Magazine*, November 5, 1989(C), pp. 50-58.

Carter, Bill, "Technology Adds Choices and Programming Needs," *The New York Times Magazine*, July 24, 1989(D), p. D8.

Carter, Bill, "With America Well Wired, Cable Industry Is Changing," *The New York Times*, July 9, 1989(E), pp. 1, 20.

Dreyfuss, Joel, "The Coming Battle," *Fortune*, February 13, 1989, pp. 104-107.

Emshwiller, John, R., "Prying Open the Cable-TV Monopolies," *The Wall Street Journal*, August 10, 1989, p. B1.

Fabrikant, Geraldine, "Cable Operators Worry About Feeling Too Good," *The New York Times*, May 22, 1989(A), p. D8.

Fabrikant, G., "For Cable Networks, the Road Gets a Little Steeper," *The New York Times*, February 26, 1989(B), p. F6.

Fabrikant, G., "Cable Giant Hungry for Programs," *The New York Times*, February 26, 1989(C), p. F6.

Fabrikant, G., "Fighting For Visibility in a Proliferating Industry," *The New York Times,* Business Section, February 4, 1990, p. 10.

Friedman, Wayne, "Getting Into Scoring Position," *ADWEEK Special Report*, April 10, 1989, pp. 39, 40.

GM, "Economic Indicators," *Broadcasting,* June 19, 2989, p. 43.

Goldman, Kevin, "Broadcasters, Cable Enter 'Era of Blur'," *The Wall Street Journal,* September 28, 1989, p. B1.

Greenwald, John, "Tune In, Turn On, Sort Out," *Time,* May 29, 1989, p. 68.

HAJ, "Fiber Gets Closer to Home," *Broadcasting,* October 16, 1989, p. 34.

Huff, Richard, "Cable Upfront Sales a Smash; May Double Last Year's Bucks," *Variety,* July 19-25, 1989, pp. 41, 42.

Jessell, Harry, and Stump, Matt, "CABLE, the First Forty Years," *Broadcasting*, November 21, 1989, pp. 35-49.

KM, "GAO Cable Rate Survey to Debut at August 3 House Hearing," *Broadcasting,* July 24, 1989, p. 79.

Katz, Helen E., and Lancaster, Kent M., "How Leading Advertisers and Agencies Use Cable Television," *Journal of Advertising Research,* Feb/Mar 1989, pp. 30-37.

Kleinfield, N.R., "Stung by Cable Audience Claims, Networks Retaliate," *The New York Times,* January 9, 1989, p. D6.

Knowlton, Christopher, "Want this Stock? It's Up 91,000%," *Fortune,* July 31, 1989. pp. 97, 100, 104.

Landro, Laura, "Comcast Leapfrogs Its Rivals With Acquisition Binge," *The Wall Street Journal,* March 2, 1989(A), p. A8.

Landro, Laura, "MSG Wins Victory in Fight to Remain Basic Cable Service," *The Wall Street Journal,* March 10, 1989(B), p. A8.

Lieberman, David, "A Cable Mogul's Daring Dance on the High Wire," *Business Week,* June 5, 1989, pp. 133-136.

Luxenberg, Stan, "Why Cable Stocks May Keep Rising," *The New York Times*, June 25, 1989, Sec 3, p. 8.

Markoff, John, "Here Comes the Fiber-Optic Home," *The New York Times,* November 5, 1989, pp. 1, 15.

MS, "Gillette Says Customer Service is Key to Success," *Broadcasting*, August 28, 1989, pp. 33-34.

MS, "Cable Networks On a Roll With Upfront Sales," *Broadcasting,* July 17, 1989 pp. 75-76.

"Media Current Analysis," *Standard & Poors Industry Surveys,* June 22, 1989, pp. M1-M4.

"Media Current Analysis," *Standard & Poors Industry Surveys,* February 23, 1989, pp. M1-M4.

"Notice of Annual Meetings of Stockholders," *Tele Communications, Inc*., June 28, 1990, pp.1-11.

Pearce, Kevin, "SMATV, Still Kicking," *Channels, Field Guide 1989,* p. 118.

Phillips, Graham, H., "TV Ads Must Sell, as Well as Build Brands," *ADWEEK*, April 17, 1989, p. 30.

Reece, Chuck, "Cable Sellers Learn the Buyer's Lingo," *Channels,* April 1989, pp. 58, 59.

"Register of Corporations, Directors, and Executives," *Standard and Poors,* Vol. 1, 1990, p. 2637.

Rudnitsky, Howard, and Cone, Edward, "Make Way for John Malone," *Forbes,* April 6, 1987, pp. 124-132.

Sapporito, Bill, "The Inside Story of Time Warner," *Fortune,* November 20, 1989, pp. 164-210.

Schultz, Lou, "A Cable Television Advertising Commentary," *Broadcasting*, June 26, 1989, p. 23.

"Sie Labels Telco Plan For Cable Entry Lose, Lose, Lose Proposition," *TCI Newsletter,* April 18, 1990, pp.1-3.

Sims, Calvin, "Wireless' Challengers Nipping at Cable Operators," *The New York Times,* June 12,

1989, pp. D12.

Slutzker, Gary, "Good-bye Cable TV, Hello Fiber Optics," *Forbes,* September 19, 1988, pp. 175-179.

Solomon, Harvey, "Making CVN Different," *Channels,* November, 1988, p. 22.

Stein, Lisa, "Why Your Screen Might Be Blank," *ADWEEK Special Report,* April 10, 1989, pp. 33-34.

Stevenson, Richard, "In Hollywood Big Just Gets Bigger," *The New York Times,* October 14, 1990, (F), p. 12.

"TCI Tackles Customer Service Problems," *Broadcasting,* September 25, 1989, p.36.

"TV in 1995: Looking Good," *Broadcasting,* January 2, 1989, pp. 39-40.

Tele-Communications Inc. *1988 Annual Report.*

Tele-Communications Inc. *1989 First Quarter 10K Report.*

"Tele-Communications Announces Possible Spin-Off," *TCI Newsletter,* Jan. 18, 1990, p. 1.

"Tele-Communications,Inc.," *Annual Report, 1990.*

"Tele-Communications, Inc.," *Donaldson, Lufkin & Jenrette Action Recommendation,* April 5, 1990, pp. 1-18.

"Tele-Communications, Inc.," *Gruntal Investment Research,* August 24, 1990, pp. 1-3.

"Tele-Communications, Inc.," *Prospectus,* July 13, 1990, pp. 1-15.

"Tele-Communications," *Securities and Exchange Commission Form 10 K,* March 26, 1990, pp.I-1 - II-30.

"Tele-Communications," *Securities and Exchange Commission Form 10 Q,* August 13, 1990, pp.I-1 - II-3.

"Tele-Communications, Inc.," *TCI Newsletter,* August 14, 1990, pp. 1-3.

"TCI, Fox Agree on White Area Service," *TCI Newsletter,* Sept. 6, 1990, pp. 1-6.

"TCI Reports First Quarter Results," *TCI Newsletter,* May 16, 1990, pp. 1-3.

"The Big Chill on Capital Hill," *Broadcasting,* April 17, 1989, pp. 27-29.

Whiteside, Thomas, "Onward and Upward with the Arts," *The New Yorker,* May 20, 1985, pp. 45-87.

"Words of Warning from Mooney," *Broadcasting,* May 29, 1989, pp. 35-36.

Ziegler, Peggy, "It's Tie-In Time," *ADWEEK Special Report,* April 10, 1989, pp.4-6.

Zoglin, Richard, "Heady Days Again for Cable," *Time,* May 30, 1989 pp. 52-53.

UNI-MARTS INC.: THE CONVENIENCE STORE INDUSTRY

In 1992 Uni-Marts Inc. was a leading operator of convenience stores located in Pennsylvania, New York, New Jersey, Delaware, Maryland, and Virginia. Two types of products were sold: inside products (traditional merchandise) and outside products (gasoline and heating oil). The inside product mix accounted for 65.2 percent of sales in 1990. As shown in Figure 1, this included food and food-service items and non-food items. The outside product, gasoline, accounted for 34.8 percent of total sales at convenience stores in 1990.

The convenience store industry faced a host of demographic, financial, and competitive developments in the early 1990s. Overall industry profits increased an average of 13.2 percent annually during the 1980s, and reached $74.1 million in 1990. This growth was due primarily to increased gasoline sales. Traditional convenience store operators — stores like Dairy Mart began as convenience stores offering food and merchandise — were plagued with increasing debt and bankruptcy filings, leaving them vulnerable to intensifying competition from 24-hour supermarkets and gasoline convenience stores.

As market conditions changed, Uni-Marts was faced with many strategic decisions. Should it expand its targeted customer base, widen its line of offered merchandise and services, or expand within or beyond its present region of operations?

Figure 1: Convenience Store Industry
Inside Products Percentage of Merchandise Sales, Gross Margin

FOOD ITEMS	Percentage of Merchandise Sales 1990	Gross Margin Percent 1990	Percentage of Merchandise Sales 1989	Gross Margin Percent 1989
Beer/Wine/Liquor	15.1	28	14.9	28
Prepared Foods	7.4	46	8.8	47
Fountain Drinks	3.5	59	3.7	61
Drinks/Juices	11.5	37	11.8	37
Milk/Dairy Products	5.4	25	6.3	24
Grocery Products	2.9	33	3.9	34
Candy & Gum	5.4	45	5.3	44
Salty Snacks	4.5	37	3.6	38
Breads/Cakes/Cookies	4.1	34	4.1	33
Frozen Items	4.5	43	3.3	43
Packaged Deli	0.9	35	0.7	32
NON-FOOD ITEMS				
Health & Beauty	2.5	39	2.3	38
Tobacco	24.0	26	23.3	26
Publications	4.2	21	3.4	21
Auto/Motor Oil	0.7	38	0.8	33
General Merchandise	3.4	40	3.8	41
TOTAL	**100.0**		**100.0**	

Source: Information obtained from "Industry Averages by Product Category," *National Petroleum News Factbook*, July 1991, p. 130.

THE INDUSTRY AND COMPETITIVE MARKET

THE CONVENIENCE STORE INDUSTRY

The convenience store industry is a segment of the retail industry. A convenience store is a retail business which provides the public with a convenient location to quickly purchase various consumable products [State 1989, p. 5]. Convenience store companies are categorized as either traditional operators or petroleum marketers. Traditional operators are companies that began with the purpose of operating convenience stores, whether or not gas was included in the product mix. Petroleum marketers had their roots in the petroleum industry, either as independent oil jobbers or as franchisees of major oil companies [Ebel 1989, p. 10].

As shown in Figure 2, the convenience store industry competes with other segments of the retail industry, such as the grocery, petroleum, and food-service industries. In 1990 convenience stores accounted for 20.8 percent of total retail food sales, 26.4 percent of total retail gasoline sales, and 54.8 percent of total retail food-service sales.

Figure 2: Convenience Store Industry's Percentage of Sales of Other Retail Industries — 1990

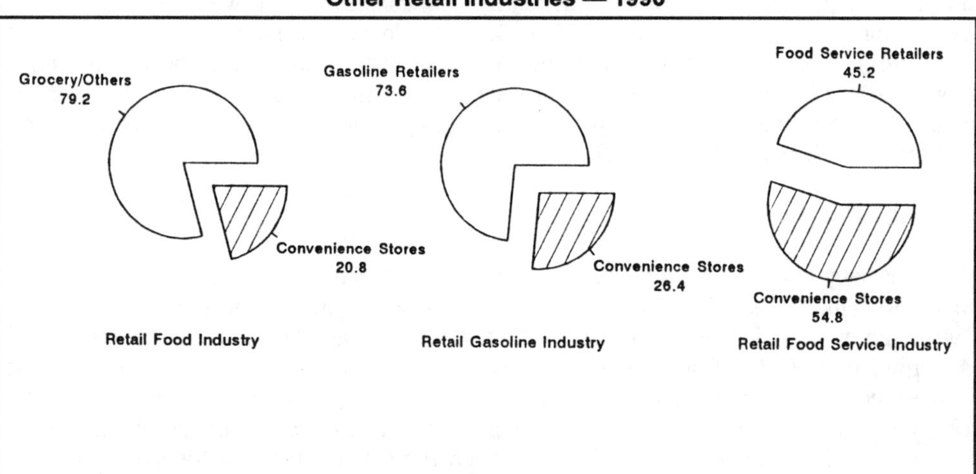

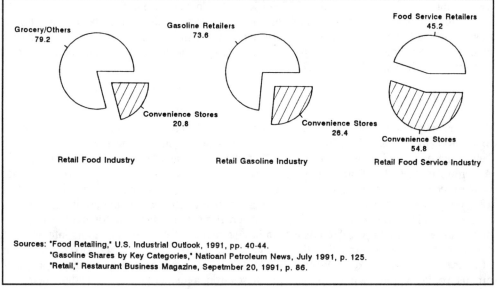

Sources: "Food Retailing," U.S. Industrial Outlook, 1991, pp. 40-44.
"Gasoline Shares by Key Categories," Natioanl Petroleum News, July 1991, p. 125.
"Retail," Restaurant Business Magazine, Sepetmber 20, 1991, p. 86.

CUSTOMERS

Traditionally, convenience store customers were blue-collar, 18- to 34-year-old males. During the 1980s, this group's size had begun to shrink in proportion to the rest of the U.S. population. For this reason, convenience stores expanded their product lines to target customers in need of the time-saving benefits that convenience stores supplied. These people were better-educated, of a wider age group, and had a broader income base. The consumer base now included working women, two-income families, aging baby boomers, single-parent families, and diversified ethnic groups.

Working Women

The number of employed women, aged 16 and over, increased 10 percent from 1975 to 1990. This figure was expected to increase another six percent over the next 15 years [Fullerton 1991, p. 33]. This trend translated into an increase in disposable income and a decline in time availability. To appeal to women and to help alleviate the time constraints facing them, convenience stores needed to offer products and services normally found at supermarkets and other outlets.

Two-Income Families

The percentage of dual-income couples with children remained constant from 1970 to 1990.

Conversely, single-income households declined dramatically over this same period. As a result, the purchasing power of the two-income family grew substantially between 1970 and 1990, as average family income grew from $38,700 to $49,600. Convenience stores needed to analyze the changing composition of the household and the implied behaviors of its members. Women were now equal bread-winners, so retailers could no longer target their products at males. Such research could help determine the relationships between these individuals' purchase patterns and product consumption [Schwartz 1991, p. 22].

Aging Baby Boomers

The baby-boom generation males, who grew up with convenience stores and were aged 18 to 35 during the 1970s and 1980s, were this industry's most loyal customers. As they entered the 1990s, these individuals were in their peak working years and beginning to feel burned out. According to the Gallup Poll, 43 percent of employed women and 33 percent of employed men were expected to reduce their job commitments within the next five years [Edmondson 1991, p. 17]. Many baby boomers were expected to emphasize family values and spirituality as they approached middle age. A decline in baby boomer participation in the work force could mean less disposable income and possible changes in buying habits. Taking these factors into account, convenience stores were expanding their product strategies to include the needs of other segments of their surrounding markets. Women would be more attracted to a clean facility, and ethnic groups would be more inclined to make purchases from a retailer that stocked ethnic items.

Single-Parent Families

This market segment showed significant gains in income and market share between 1970 and 1990. The majority of single-parent families were headed by women with relatively low incomes, even though these incomes increased by an average of $4,000 in this 20-year period [Green 1991, p. 40]. Heads of these families would demand quick, convenient locations from which to make purchases. The convenience store was in a position to offer these customers ease of accessibility and a wide variety of products from which to choose.

Ethnic Groups

Hispanics, one of the fastest-growing ethnic groups, were largely responsible for America's increasing ethnic diversity [Schwartz 1991, p. 23]. This segment made up 7.7 percent of the labor force in 1990 — a figure that was expected to increase to 11 percent by 2005. Asians and others, the smallest of ethnic groups, were expected to grow to 4.8 percent, up from 3.3 percent in 1990. The black labor force of 10.8 percent was the majority ethnic group and was expected to grow one percent. Given the increased participation and concentration of these groups, convenience stores were developing merchandising niches to cater to these markets' individual tastes and needs.

Changing Markets

Demographic diversity created growth opportunities which convenience stores could take advantage of. Convenience stores could take advantage of the time constraints that families faced by offering a wide assortment of convenience and impulse items. Ethnic groups were emerging in mass numbers, creating another window of opportunity. Studying a convenience store's surrounding demographics and further segmenting its market by age, sex, and income could aid in the selection of appropriate products and services. A store located in a primarily two-income earner environment would do better to stock merchandise that appealed to both men and women. Food that could be consumed within 10 minutes of being taken home, grocery items that would normally be purchased at supermarkets, and services that would provide time savings were all items in demand by these convenience store customers.

PRODUCTS

Convenience stores offered two major types of products: inside products (merchandise) and outside products (gasoline). Inside products were divided into three categories: food items, non-food items, and services. Outside products were petroleum products. Total industry sales for 1990 were $74.5 million. As shown in Figure 3, inside (non-gasoline) products accounted for $40.4 million or 54.2 percent and outside (gasoline) sales accounted for $34.1 million or 45.8 percent of total sales.

Figure 3: Convenience Store Industry
Total Non-Gasoline vs. Gasoline Stores

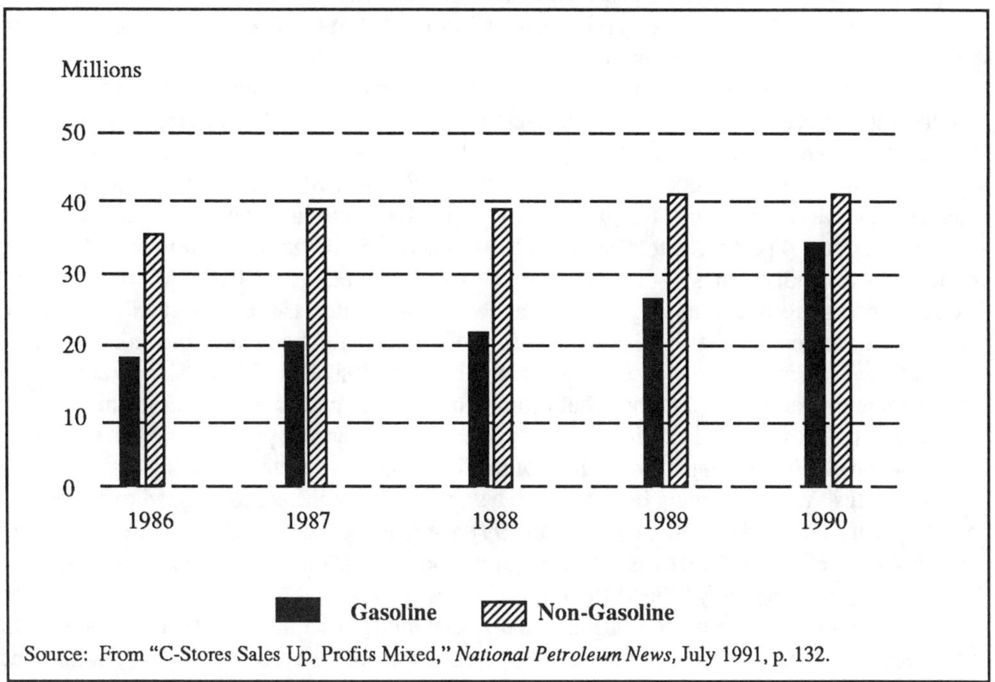

Source: From "C-Stores Sales Up, Profits Mixed," *National Petroleum News*, July 1991, p. 132.

Inside Products

In 1990, convenience stores introduced to their stock more than 3,000 new grocery items, including new candies, gums, snacks, soft drinks, beers, and tobacco items. This brought the average number of items offered per store to approximately 6,200 [Elliot 1991, p. 60]. Store size was increasing and traditional operators had streamlined inventory by offering basic merchandise and concentrating on high turnover items rather than a wide selection of slow-moving items. The increased emphasis on food service meant that more store space was allocated to food preparation and cooking equipment. Also, a growing number of convenience stores were providing seating for eat-in customers. Petroleum marketers, on the other hand, were expanding their store size in order to increase the number of items offered.

While traditional operators stocked only 33 percent more items than petroleum marketers, their inventory value was 75 percent higher since they invested more heavily in high-ticket items such as health and beauty aids, deli items, and self-service fast food. Store inventory turned over an average of 13 times annually for the traditional operator and 16 times at the smaller petroleum marketer locations.

Food items. The top four food items listed in Figure 1 represented 37.5 percent of inside merchandise sales in 1990 and generated 42.5 percent of total profits. Two of these product groups, alcoholic beverages and bottled/canned soft drinks/juices, were the products most successfully merchandised in the past for convenience stores whereas food service was the growth product of the 1980s. The food-service category consisted of prepared foods, fountain sodas/drinks, fresh juices/drinks, and frozen drinks.

In 1990, beer, wine, and liquor accounted for 15.1 percent of total merchandise sales. These products generated most of the petroleum marketers' sales because they carried a more limited product mix than traditional marketers.

Since the mid-1970s, convenience stores had introduced fast-food services in an attempt to increase sales and gross profit margins. In 1977, fast-food sales at convenience stores totalled $382 million or 4.4 percent of total sales. In 1991, this figure rose to $6.5 billion or 15.5 percent of total merchandise sales — an increase of over 1600 percent ["Retail..." 1991, p. 86]. Convenience store operators aggressively added fast-food items in an effort to broaden the convenience store customer base and increase profit margins. As a result, convenience stores' share of food service sales increased substantially between 1987 and 1991 to 54.8 percent. Fast-food programs varied widely from chain to chain. Several chains had opted to initiate joint ventures with fast-food chains, while others had developed their own programs. Also, supermarkets — in an effort to recoup a larger share of the food market — were increasing their prepared food offerings. While spending for food eaten away from home increased, expenditures for food purchased at supermarkets remained flat. In 1991 at-home food and beverage consumption was expected to stabilize or increase, and spending for food and drink outside the home was expected to decrease proportionately ["Food Retailing..." 1991, p. 40-5].

Convenience store operators began to realize that food service attracted more females, older customers, and those with higher incomes. Food-service items also provided higher margins and profits per square foot than other inside products and drew customers from fast-food and supermarket competitors [Williams 1991, p. 38a]. More significantly, with gross margins of 46 percent in prepared foods and 59 percent in the fountain area, these areas contributed 18.8 cents per profit dollar on average. Petroleum marketers also were involved in food-service on a smaller, but just as profitable scale.

Non-Food Items. Non-food items included tobacco products, periodicals, health and beauty aids, and other non-food items, such as school supplies, housewares, pet supplies, photo supplies, and automotive products. Sales in the first three non-food categories shown in Figure 1 increased slightly in from 1989 to 1990.

Services. Services were introduced in an attempt to build store traffic, to appeal to broader customer segments, and to differentiate a convenience store chain from its competition. Services that were offered successfully by convenience stores included:

Service Areas

ATMs	Prescriptions
Dry Cleaning/Laundry	Video Rental
Film Processing	Entertainment/TV and Sales
Post Office/UPS	Floral Services
Travel/Airline Reservations	Lottery Tickets
Car Wash	Appliance Drop
Shoe Repair	Communication Services
Tool Rental	

The services offered by individual stores depended on the characteristics of surrounding communities and the presence of other specialty stores such as video and food-service retailers. Lottery tickets were more profitable in lower income areas and were big traffic builders, especially when jackpots reached high levels. Video rentals were most successful in less-populated areas without big video chains in the vicinity ["C-Store..." 1990, p. 52].

No specific formula for services would be most profitable for all marketers. The key to success was to find the right merchandising mix for the particular area in which the store was located. Each department and product category in the store was closely scrutinized for its individual performance as a "profit center" within the store's overall operation ["C-Store..." 1990, p.52].

Outside Products

Outside products were different types of petroleum products: regular unleaded gas, premium unleaded gas, leaded gas, midgrade unleaded diesel, and blended gas. As shown in Figure 4, the number of convenience stores selling gasoline declined slightly in 1988 and 1990. This decline was related to an overall disposition of units by traditional operators [Smedley 1991, p. 36]. The steady increase of sales from 1986 to 1988 was caused by the increased participation of oil companies in the convenience store industry. At the same time, traditional operators

Figure 4: Total Number of Convenience Stores, 1986-1990: With Gasoline and Without Gasoline

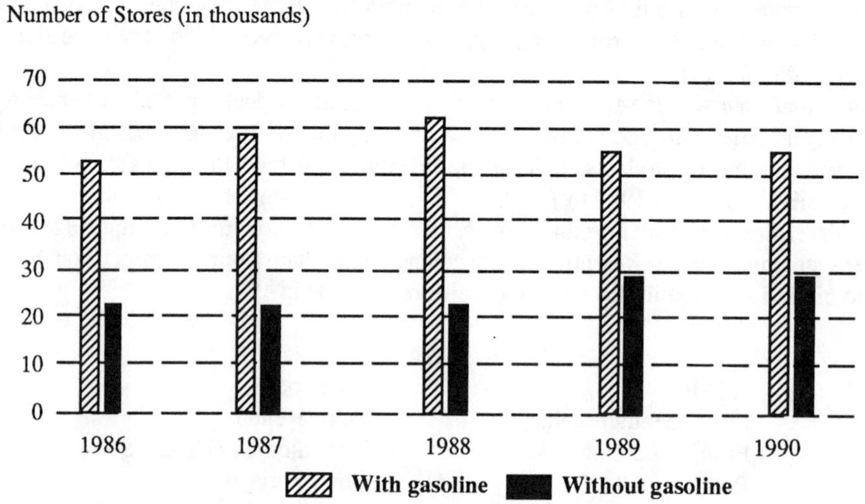

Number of Stores (in thousands)

70
60
50
40
30
20
10
0

1986 1987 1988 1989 1990

With gasoline Without gasoline

Source: From "C-Stores Sales Up, Profits Mixed," *National Petroleum News*, July 1991, p. 132.

expanded their gas facilities to attract more customers.

The introduction of self-service gasoline was the most significant development within the convenience store industry in the 15 years prior to 1989. Consumer acceptance of self-service gasoline gave convenience stores a pricing advantage over full-line service stations and accelerated the addition of gasoline to the product mix offered by convenience stores.

The number of service stations nationwide declined dramatically between 1972 and 1989. However, at the end of 1990, this figure had increased from 110,000 in 1989 to 210,000 in 1990. This growth in the number of service stations resulted from the inclusion of all places where motorists could buy gasoline for their cars in the 1990 figures ["Gasoline..." 1991, p. 125]. During the late 1980s, the number of service stations declined by approximately 3,000 per year. This decrease in traditional service stations created opportunities for convenience stores to increase their shares of total gallons sold and number of outlets. The convenience store industry's share of retail gasoline volume reached 46.4 percent in 1990. Total gasoline sales rose from $17.9 billion in 1986 to $34.1 billion in 1990 ["C-Store Sales..." 1991, p. 132].

Traditional operators were expected to continue to add gasoline to their product mix in order to compete with petroleum marketers. Self-service gasoline attracted consumers and triggered impulse purchases.

COMPETITION

Two generic competitors existed within the convenience store industry: traditional operators and petroleum marketers. They had been rivals ever since petroleum marketers began to convert service stations situated on prime real estate into convenience store/super pumpers. The convenience store industry was a fast growing industry between 1986 and 1990. While the convenience store industry was expected to continue to grow, several signs indicated that the industry was reaching maturity and that future growth would be much slower.

Changing Competitive Markets

Declining sales and unit growth, downsizing by traditional operators, oversaturation in urban markets, the impact of pending legislation, contracting profit margins, and increasing market segmentation were all factors leading to an increasingly difficult competitive environment in the industry.

Declining Sales and Unit Growth. Total convenience store sales grew at an average annual rate of 10 percent from 1986 to 1990, compared to a rate of 27.2 percent annually in the early 1980s. New unit expansion also slowed to approximately two percent annually between 1987 and 1990.

Downsizing by Traditional Operators. The 1980s were years of consolidation, mergers, and leveraged buyouts as big companies grew even bigger. Throughout the early and mid-1980s, Circle K and Dairy Convenience Mart experienced explosive growth, however, by the end of the decade both companies had experienced cash flow problems and were losing money. After rapid expansion, Southland and Circle K began selling off stores through acquisitions financed by junk bonds. Convenience store chains were examining their markets and abandoning "poor performers," while investing more time and money in their prime locations ["C-Stores, C-Stores..." 1991, p. 36].

Oversaturation in Urban Markets. Increased expansion in the 1980s by both traditional and petroleum marketers led to an oversaturation of urban markets. Competition was also intensified by the presence of supermarkets and specialty service stores. As a result, rural areas were beginning to be invaded by those convenience store chains looking for new markets outside of metropolitan areas [Smith 1990, p. 49].

Pending Legislation. Pending legislation would have a significant impact on the industry if passed. The primary issue was proposed legislation that would require petroleum marketers to have underground storage tank liability insurance. Also, the Americans with Disabilities Act would affect the industry with its employment-related requirements and guidelines for providing equal access to facilities [Williams 1991, p. 38A]. Both issues would entail increased costs and could force convenience stores to consolidate.

Margin Contraction. As an industry matures and competition intensifies, profit margins often contract. The convenience store industry posted a $149 million loss in 1990 compared to a $271 million profit in 1989. This loss largely resulted from heavy losses by the industry's two largest chains, Southland Corp. and Circle K. The average gross margins of convenience stores decreased from 26.2 percent to 21.8 percent in 1990 ["C-Stores Sales..." 1991, p. 132].

Market Segmentation. A much more competitive operating environment arose for the convenience store industry in the 1990s. In 1989 multiple convenience store chains were located within the same vicinity so operators had to give customers a compelling reason to enter their store rather than the competitor's. This led many convenience stores to adopt a market segmentation strategy. By segmenting the market, companies tried to differentiate themselves from the competition and, in doing so, achieved dominance in a specific consumer segment. Improving food-service programs and adopting branded ideas, such as 7-Eleven's "Slurpee," were expected to be the future avenue for maintaining market segmentation in the convenience store industry.

Overall, in 1989, convenience store chains expanded considerably, but all that the chains had to show for thousands of new stores were sharply reduced profits. As they entered the 1990s, convenience store chains were trying desperately to attract customers with a new generation of products and services. They were realizing that life simplification and product diversity were what consumers wanted. Chains such as 7-Eleven and Stop & Go were offering not only gas pumps, but also car washes, deli counters, video rentals, automatic teller machines, and fast food. Retailers also adopted niche marketing ideas to target local market needs. Fresh buffets, breakfast pizzas, and specialty sandwiches were just a few of the products offered to cater to customers' needs and to create opportunity niches.

In 1991, the petroleum marketers had nicer stores in better locations, and so were faring better than the traditional operators. Traditional convenience stores were being forced to increase their petroleum offerings and improve existing facility appearances.

The new oil company stores did not resemble the tiny cigarette-and-soda kiosks maintained by gas stations for so many years. Unlike the larger traditional operators, Chevron, Shell, Ashland Oil, and many others were putting up spacious, brightly lighted stores. Broad canopies shielded pumps, stores, and customers from the weather. Smoothly contoured buildings, slick signs, tile floors, and brick or enameled aluminum exteriors welcomed customers to stores where grime had been permanently banished [Deutsch 1989].

Competitors

The traditional convenience store chains were plagued with huge debt, poor locations, inappropriate ideas, and inadequate leadership in the early 1990s. As shown in Figure 5, 15 chains filed for Chapter 11 bankruptcy protection or Chapter 7 liquidation between 1989 and, early 1991. As a result, many convenience stores opted to downsize by closing or disposing of some locations. This trend was expected to continue over the next few years because of the emphasis placed on improving existing locations and exiting from low-performance markets.

The largest ten convenience stores in 1990 are listed in Figure 6. The two largest convenience store chains, Southland Corp., and Circle K, focused on solving debt problems created through extensive acquisitions and on improving cash flows. They disposed of many poor performing locations and exited from certain markets. Factors considered when making these decisions included demographics, market size, and store concentration. Due to debt diversions, both companies were unable to put resources into remodeling and marketing and gave ground to competitors.

National Convenience Stores emphasized major markets and new merchandising strategies while turning a $7.5 million loss in 1989 into a $383,000 profit in the third quarter of 1990. This company restructured its retail network to mirror that of the major oil companies, concentrating

Figure 5: Traditional Convenience Store Chains That Filed for Chapter 11 Bankruptcy Protection of Chapter 7 Liquidation Since 1989

COMPANY	HEADQUARTERS	KEY CHAINS	TOTAL STORES
The Southland Corp.	Dallas	7-Eleven/High's Quick Mart	6,190
Circle K	Phoenix	Circle K	4,783
Krauser's Food Stores	New Jersey	Dairy Stores	136
Majik Market Corp.	Florida	Majik Market	367
Plaid Pantry	Oregon	Plaid Pantry	107
Convenient Food Mart, Inc.	Chicago	Convenient Food Mart	550
Kwik Stop	New York	Kwik Stop	60
Sami Quik Stop	Ohio	Sami Quik Stop	15
Crouch C-Stores	Kansas	Crouch's	4
Tyler & Simpson	Oklahoma	N/A	N/A
Q n'E	Georgia	Quick N'Easy	15
Micky's C-Stores	Texas	Micky's C-Stores	20
Wickland Oil	California	Regal Stations	2
JFM, Inc.	Arkansas	Jr. Food Mart	80
Farm Stores, Inc.	Florida	Farm Stores	260

Source: Information obtained from Dwyer, Steve, "Traditional Chains Struggle Financially," *National Petroleum News*, March 1991, p. 22.

Figure 6: 1990 Top 10 Convenience Store Companies

COMPANY	HEADQUARTERS	KEY CHAINS	TOTAL STORES
The Southland Corp.	Dallas	7-Eleven/High's Quick Mart	6,190
Circle K	Phoenix	Circle K	4,783
Dairy Mart	Connecticut	Dairy Mart	1,189
Cumberland Farms	Massachusetts	Cumberland Farms	1,100
Silcorp	Canada	Mac's Convenience Stores/ Mike's Marts	999
National Convenience Stores	Houston	Stop N Go	1,091
Casey's	Iowa	Casey's Gen'l Stores	769
Kampgrounds	Montana	Kampgrounds of America	650
Little Chef	Florida	Little Champ Food Stores	560
The Pantry	North Carolina	The Pantry	448

Source: Information Obtained From Smedley, Peggy, "C-Stores, C-Stores...Where Are they?...Who Are They," *National Petroleum News*, September 1991, p. 50.

on those markets where it had a strong presence and abandoning low-performance markets [Dwyer, 1991, p. 22]. Unable to overcome its grave debt situation, however, NCS was forced to file for bankruptcy in late 1991.

Dairy Mart, with 1,189 units, experimented with its food-service menu by opening a "Sub Station" in 1991 at its store in Connecticut. The Sub Station offered a limited line of hot and cold made-to-order subs. After a trial period, Dairy Mart planned to roll this concept into other stores.

Wawa, Inc., an operator of 484 units, also emphasized its food-service line. Its biggest sales category and profit center was the delicatessen. Wawa's strong food-service operation was credited with attracting more female customers. Although the company built its food-service business around local favorites, it also catered to health-conscious consumers. The "Fresh Buffet," a selection of refrigerated entrees and desserts, was designed to appeal to working men and women who were looking for something quick and healthy [Hussey 1991, p. 130].

A mid-size convenience chain, QuikTrip Inc, installed automated teller machines in most of its 281 stores. These machines dispensed scrip — rather than cash — that could be used to purchase merchandise or gasoline, with the customer receiving any unused portion in cash. The use of scrip generated impulse purchases.

Smaller convenience store chains (those with fewer than 200 units) were more successful in the early 1990s than their larger counterparts. Some mid-size chains, such as Huck's Convenience Stores (Illinois) and Town & Country Food Stores (Texas), narrowed the gap on their gasoline-to-merchandise ratios. This put them in a position to combat the increased

Figure 7: Number of Convenience Stores Traditional vs. Petroleum Marketers

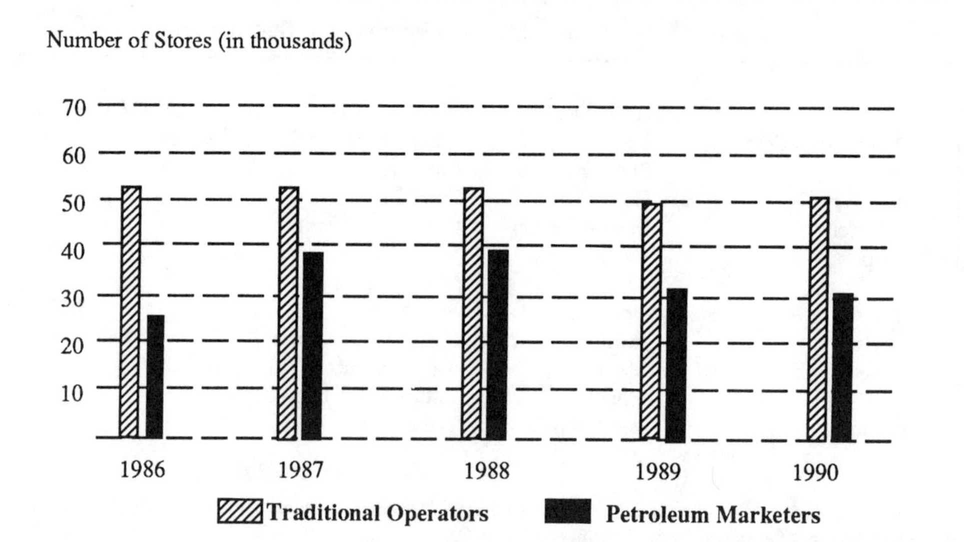

Source: From "Gasoline Fuels Growth of Convenience Store Industry," *Chain Store Executive*, August 1991, p. 37a.

participation of the major oil companies in the convenience store industry. The major oil companies were the biggest competitors for the traditional operators. The big oil companies and their smaller counterparts owned many prime locations — the corner sites in high traffic zones — and had converted these locations into convenience store/pumper combinations.

The major oil companies were willing to spend large dollar amounts on new locations [Dwyer, 1991, p. 21]. Gasoline convenience stores capitalized on everything the traditional stores lacked: cleanliness, convenience, safety, friendliness, and an appeal to men and women alike [Williams 1991, p. 38a]. The oil companies were also more experienced in adapting to the changing marketplace. As shown in Figure 7, store growth in the industry had come mainly from petroleum markets from 1986 to 1990.

THE COMPANY

Uni-Marts Inc., a traditional operator, was founded in 1972 and completed its initial public offering of common stock in December 1986. As of December 1, 1991 the company operated 339 convenience stores in rural areas of Delaware, New Jersey, New York, Pennsylvania, Maryland, and Virginia. In addition to its convenience stores, Uni-Marts owned and operated Meadow Pride Dairy — a processor of milk and ice cream products which accounted for approximately eight percent of corporate sales in 1991 — and State Gas & Oil divisions.

Uni-Mart's convenience stores offered everything from packaged foods and household items to gasoline to videocassettes to pizza, so they often became "town stores," or social centers for the community. Uni-Marts' small-town strategy gave it growth potential higher than the normal convenience store chains. About 160 small convenience chains were trying to make it big in Uni-Mart's territories. Half of Uni-Mart's growth came from acquiring some of these smaller store chains and half from constructing new ones. Between 1988 and 1991, sales grew 89 percent, from $136 to $258 million.

As shown in Figure 8, for the fiscal year ended September 30, 1991, Uni-Marts, Inc. recorded net sales of $257.6 million, a six percent increase over 1990 net sales of $242.8 million. However, net earnings decreased 10 percent to $2.45 million versus $2.85 million in 1990.

In fiscal year 1991, Uni-Marts constructed eight stores and closed or otherwise disposed of eight stores. In December 1991, they acquired 141 GettyMart convenience stores located in Pennsylvania and Virginia from Getty Petroleum Corp. This acquisition expanded the number of states in which Uni-Marts operated to six. In 1992, they planned to open approximately five new stores within or adjacent to Uni-Marts' current market area as part of an overall expansion strategy.

With the purchase of Foodcraft Inc., in 1988, Uni-Marts also obtained Valley Farms Dairy. This acquisition resulted in a 220.1 percent increase in dairy sales to affiliates in 1990. Uni-Marts struggled with the idea of restructuring or possibly selling its assets in early 1991. This prospect was later abandoned, leaving industry analysts wondering about the company's future. Although Uni-Marts' net sales had steadily increased from 1985 to 1990, net earnings were unchanged in 1989 and 1990.

Figure 8: Uni- Marts, Inc. — 7 Subsidiaries' Selected Financial Data for 1987-1991, Year Ended September 30

	1991	1990	1989	1988	1987
Statement of Earnings Data					
Net Sales by the Company and its Franchises:					
Merchandise	$141,082	$137,159	$128,906	$86,532	$78,614
Petroleum	94,592	81,449	68,523	46,412	37,434
Other	21,902	24,211	18,586	3,867	4,264
Total	257,576	242,819	216,015	136,811	120,312
Cost of Sales	189,597	176,753	155,262	97,836	85,970
Gross Profit	67,979	66,066	60,753	38,975	34,342
Selling Gen'l. and Admin.Expenses	53,056	51,275	47,866	30,977	27,784
Depreciation & Amortization	6,297	5,918	4,907	2,831	2,519
Intrest Expense	4,956	4,680	3,630	895	787
Earnings Before income Taxes	3,670	4,193	4,350	4,272	3,252
Provision for Income Taxes	1,186	1,338	1,499	1,419	1,410
Net Earnings	2,484	2,855	2,851	2,853	1,842
Earnings Per Share	0.35	0.40	0.40	0.41	0.30
Dividends Per Share	0.45	0.10	0.08	0.08	0.08
Operating Data Convenience Stores Only:					
Average Sales, per Store Operating a Full Year:					
Merchandise Sales	$418	$414	$383	$374	$341
Petroleum Sales	$429	$390	$371	$333	$318
Gallons of Petrolem Sold	399	413	420	426	472
Gross Profit per Gallon of Petroleum	$0.131	$0.130	$0.134	$0.121	$0.101
Total Gallons of Petroleum Sold	83,280	80,423	72,736	55,185	51,655
Number of Stores Open at Year End	339	339	342	240	234
Stores Added by New Construction	8	8	25	10	14
Stores Added by Acquisition	-	-	89	-	13
Stores Closed	8	11	12	4	1
Balance Sheet Data					
Working Capital (Deficiency)	$3,028	$3,698	$3,295	$4,288	$2,822
Total Assets	95,111	97,703	90,756	48,044	38,034
Long-Term Obligations	45,985	46,543	38,545	15,041	7,155
Stockholders' Equity	26,221	27,096	25,966	21,469	19,866

Source: Information Obtained From Annual Report on Form 10-K, 1991, Uni-Marts, Inc.

CUSTOMERS

Convenience stores changed dramatically in the five years prior to 1991, and as a result, consumers' perceptions of convenience stores changed. In the mid-1980s, most consumers would not have gone into a convenience store to purchase lunch or to rent a video. Consumers viewed convenience stores primarily as a place to quickly purchase grocery items. In contrast, according to Henry B. Sahakian, president and chief executive officer of Uni-Marts, consumers viewed convenience stores as a place to buy gas, buy deli items, have lunch, cash a check, or rent a video, as well as to quickly purchase grocery items.

Uni-Marts researched store demographics to profile each location's customer base. While most people shop at convenience stores, the frequent shoppers had historically been men between the ages of 18 and 35. Management believed that America's shifting life-styles and demographics were changing the profile of the frequent convenience store shopper. There were increasing numbers of working women, two-income households, single-parent households, and ethnic groups. These consumers valued their time and appreciated businesses that allowed them to save time.

PRODUCTS

Uni-Marts Inc. had continued to update its inside and outside products to meet customers' changing needs. Uni-Marts felt that opportunities for new products and services existed ["Operators" 1989, p. 168]. In 1991, increased sales caused merchandise gross margins to increase 3.1 percent over those in 1990. Petroleum products also contributed strongly to net earnings.

In 1991, convenience store petroleum gross margins were $.131 per gallon, $.01 higher than 1990 gross margins. This margin increase, combined with the increased number of gallons sold, significantly affected earnings. In 1991, merchandise sales accounted for 54.7 percent of total sales, a 2.8 percent increase over 1990. This rise was primarily attributable to higher sales levels per store.

Inside Products

Uni-Marts' product mix consisted of more than 3,500 items. Typical in-store merchandise was food items, non-food items, and services. Food items consisted of items such as dairy products, beverages, tobacco products, groceries, frozen foods, candies, and snacks. Non-food items consisted of items such as health and beauty aids. In addition, nearly all stores offered deli items, fresh-baked goods, and self-service fast food. Management believed that fast-food products would be an opportunity area for the future. Uni-Marts had a greater emphasis on groceries than the industry primarily because of its small town locations [*Annual Report* 1991, p. 7].

Food Items. Changes in the product mix carried in convenience stores resulted in increased sales of higher margin products. Uni-Marts hoped to refine fast-food product offerings and introduce new ones since fast foods were an important customer traffic builder and generally had higher gross profit margins than traditional product segments. Each store's fast-food selection was specifically designed to satisfy its particular market's demands. The fast foods offered included coffee, fountain soda, hot dogs, meatball sandwiches, nachos, pizza, chicken, soup, fresh deli sandwiches, muffins, doughnuts, and breakfast sandwiches [*Annual Report* 1991, p. 7].

Fast foods had great potential for Uni-Marts because of its small town and rural locations. In these areas, they were often the only outlets which offered fast food. This was in stark contrast to urban areas where competition between fast-food restaurants and convenience stores was intense.

Services. Sahakian felt that customer services were excellent traffic builders. They were also labor-intensive and required efficient procedures so they could be performed quickly. He thought some companies would scale back on their services and others would continue to test and introduce new services to their stores. Success depended on how well companies trained their employees to perform the services. Uni-Marts supplied services such as video rentals, lottery tickets, money orders, and free check cashing.

Video rentals were predicted to have a mixed future in the convenience store industry, depending on store's locations and the efficiency of its program. Uni-Marts rented videos in nearly all of its stores and intended to offer them in future stores. Uni-Marts had great success with video rentals since many of its stores were located in small towns and rural areas. Other chains, with stores in more metropolitan areas, had not been as successful because of greater competition.

Outside Products

Outside products—principally petroleum products—were the largest single product category at Uni-Marts' stores, accounting for 36.7 percent of total sales in 1991. As of December 1, 1991, gasoline was offered at 315 locations, or 92.9 percent of Uni-Marts' stores [*Annual Report* 1991]. Although petroleum sales carry a gross margin of only about 12 percent, operating expenses were minimal and, as a result, this category was an important contributor to company profits, as well as being one that built traffic. The company generated above-average margins on petroleum because 205 of the company's stores were in small towns where price competition was not intense.

Gasoline was expected to continue to be a very important component in the product mix of many stores. Increased competition by major oil companies in some market areas could hurt some companies' gasoline profits and deter future growth in those areas. Uni-Marts, however, intended to offer gasoline at every new location when possible ["Four..." 1989, p. 170]. As a result of a contract with Getty Petroleum Corp., all Uni-Marts stores were to begin offering Getty brand products in fiscal 1992. This was expected to give Uni-Marts a competitive advantage because of Getty's strong brand recognition and reputation for distributing only the highest quality petroleum products.

GEOGRAPHICAL AREA

Uni-Marts operated in six states, which were among the nation's least saturated per capita by convenience stores according to the most recent convenience store market analysis performed by CACI, Inc. New York was the second least-saturated state in the nation. New Jersey, Pennsylvania, and Delaware were the nation's sixth, seventh, and eleventh least-saturated states, respectively. In Uni-Marts' market areas, there were 160 convenience store chains that each owned fewer than 150 convenience stores [*Annual Report* 1991]. For this reason, Uni-Marts had no plans to become a national operation ["Uni-Marts" 1989, p. 80].

DISTRIBUTION

Most of Uni-Marts' merchandise was ordered directly from one wholesale distributor in order to take advantage of cost efficiencies. Merchandise inventory was ordered at the store level to ensure that each market's demands were met. Gasoline inventory was ordered at the corporate level because of its complexity. Optimal order quantities and delivery dates were determined by the petroleum department. These methods of inventory replacement were implemented to handle significant expansion without requiring extensive modification.

FINANCES and MANAGEMENT

Management required each store to supply it with timely reports that showed sales, inventory purchases, gross profits, and operating expenses. Stores were evaluated by comparing performance to detailed budgets and prior-year performance. Uni-Marts felt that its management team, headed by ten officers with an average of 15 years in the industry, was more than capable of running a much larger chain. Short-term credit facilities in the amount of $10 million and operating leases were to be the primary sources of funding for future acquisitions.

TOWARDS THE FUTURE

In 1992, Uni-Marts' management team was contemplating future growth strategies. The company had experienced a period of rapid expansion since going public in 1986. What was once a small convenience store chain with less than 150 stores had more than doubled in size in less than three years to 339 stores. Management hoped that this expansion rate could be maintained and that Uni-Marts would become a substantial player in the industry.

The changing competitive environment in the convenience store industry affected all future growth strategies. Uni-Mart's success was based on it ability to offer courteous service and the products demanded by its customers, as well as easily accessible locations and clean facilities. Management did not want to jeopardize these strengths while moving in new directions in the future.

Uni-Marts, with a good mix of urban and rural locations, had a geographic advantage over may of its competitors. One alternative for Uni-Marts was to concentrate future expansion within or adjacent to the rural areas of current six-state region. In early 1992, some managers argued that this would be to Uni-Marts' advantage because this would keep them out of direct competition with the major convenience stores since the saturation level in these areas was lower.

Concentration in rural locations was an opportunity area that most food retailers ignored. Urban markets were becoming overpopulated by the large convenience store chains and carried higher start-up and operational costs. The costs of opening the average rural store costs were about one-third less than those of opening a comparable urban store [Benish 1991, p. 62]. With only 160 small chains as competitors, Uni-Marts' current region of operation was one of the least populated and least competitive.

Henry Sahakian, Uni-Marts' President, saw many opportunities for additional expansion within or adjacent to Uni-Marts' current market area. Many small towns were still viable markets for Uni-Marts' convenience stores. Also, Sahakian believed that increased competitive pressures in urban markets and proposed legislation would cause the convenience store industry to consolidate, providing Uni-Marts with attractive acquisition candidates [*Annual Report* 1990].

However, national expansion was also a lucrative strategic alternative for Uni-Marts because of heavy debt burdens of the larger convenience store chains. Their concentration on restructuring and downsizing meant that they would not be pursuing opportunities available in many of the less-saturated markets around the nation. Because the cost of acquisition and operations in rural areas was cheaper than in urban areas, the amount of financing required would not be too extensive, so national expansion was feasible for Unimarts.

The required financing would come from short-term credit facilities and operating leases, increasing Uni-Marts' debt-to-equity ratio. Debt payments and operating costs would thus be dependent upon future sales if no plans were made to raise equity. Gasoline competition proved to be unyielding in rural areas. With petroleum marketers as the dominant players in these markets, gasoline facilities were very important to the success of any convenience store. The cost of these facilities was a major consideration in light of the compliance with federal and state environmental regulations that was required. Rural locations usually serviced larger territories so extensive research was required before site locations were selected. If not strategically placed in central locations, these sites would not be very prosperous.

Taking all of these factors into consideration, Uni-Marts executives were contemplating regional and national expansion alternative strategies for the 1990s, as well as other possible strategic moves which might take advantage of competitive market trends and competitor situations.

REFERENCES AND BACKGROUND READINGS

Annual Report on Form 10-K, 1990, Uni-Marts, Inc.

Annual Report, 1991, Uni-Marts, Inc.

Benish, Dave, "Thriving , Not Surviving, in Rural America," *National Petroleum News,* January 1992, p. 62.

"C-Store Profit Boosters," *National Petroleum News,* September 1990, pp. 38-55.

"C-Stores Sales Up, Profits Mixed," *National Petroleum News Factbook,* July 1991, p. 132.

"C-Stores, C-Stores, C-Stores... Where Are They?...Who Are They?," *National Petroleum News,* September 1991, pp. 34-50.

Deutsch, Claudia H., "Rethinking the Convenience Store," *The New York Times,* Business Section,

October 8, 1989, pp. 1 and 15.

Dwyer, Steve, "C-Stores Are Catching the Wave in Target Marketing Techniques," *National Petroleum News,* May 1991, pp. 26-30.

Dwyer, Steve, "Traditional Chains Struggle Financially," *National Petroleum News,* March 1991, pp. 21-22.

Ebel, Chris, "Industry Report 1989," *Convenience Store News,* May 31-June 25, 1989, Vol. 25, No. 7, pp. 7-39.

Edmondson, Brad, "Burned-Out Boomers Flee to Families," *American Demographics,* December 1991, p. 17.

Elliot, Coney, "Getting the Edge Over Competition," *National Petroleum News,* May 1991, p. 60.

"Food Retailing," *U.S. Industrial Outlook 1991,* pp. 40-4 - 40-5.

"Four C-Store Officials Predict the Industry's Future Money Makers," *ConvenienceStore News,* September 26 - October 15, 1989, pp. 170-171.

Fullerton Jr., Howard N., "Labor Force Projections: The Baby Boom Moves On," *Monthly Labor Review,* November 1991, pp. 31-44.

"Gasoline Shares by Key Categories," *National Petroleum News Factbook,* July 1991, pp. 124-125.

Green, Gordon, and Edward Welniak, "The Nine Household Market," *American Demographics,* October 1991, pp. 36-41.

Grondin, Barbara, "Major Oil Companies Keep Growing While Many Traditionals Scale Back - Top 50" *Convenience Store News,* Vol. 25, No. 9, July 17 - August 9, 1989, pp. 38-83.

Grossfield, Sandra, "Grocery Store Industry," *Value Line,* May 26, 1989, pp. 1498 and 1591.

Hazelton, Lynette D., "Fast Food and Mini-Marts Bite Into Grocers," *The New York Times,* June 18, 1989, p. F11.

Howard, Theresa, "C-Stores Intensify Foodservice Buildup," *Nation's Restaurant News,* January 6, 1992, pp. 1 and 77.

Hussey, Anita, "C-Store Competition: Fighting for the Foodservice Dollar," *Progressive Grocer,* February 1991, pp. 130-133.

"Industry Averages by Product Category," *National Petroleum News Factbook,* July 1991, p. 130.

Lang, Joan, "Retail," *Restaurant Business,* September 20, 1989, pp. 98 and 99.

Manges, Michele, "Convenience Stores Woo Women, Yuppies," *The Wall Street Journal,* Market Place, July 11, 1989, p. B1.

"NACS Convenience Store Customer Purchasing Patterns Research Report," *The National Association of Convenience Stores,* 1989, pp. 1-75.

"Operators Reveal Strategies for the '90s," *Convenience Store News,* September 26 - October 15, 1989, pp. 154-168.

Proval, Cheryl, "Demographics," *Premium Incentive Business,* November 1989, pp. 41-43.

"Retail," *Restaurant Business Magazine,* September 20, 1991, pp. 86-87.

Schwartz, Joe, and Susan Krafft, "Managing Consumer Diversity: The 1991 American Demographics Conference," *American Demographics,* August 1991, pp. 22-29.

Slovak, Julianne, "Uni-Marts Inc. (Company to Watch)," *Fortune,* April 10, 1989, v119, p. 90.

Smedley, Peggy, "C-Stores, C-Stores, C-Stores...Who Are They?...Where Are They?," *National Petroleum News,* September 1991, pp. 34-68.

Smith, Donald M., "The Rural American Market: How are Marketers Coping?," *National Petroleum News,* November 1990, pp. 49-53.

"State of the Convenience Store Industry 1989," *National Association of Convenience Stores,* 1989, pp. 1-34.

"Uni-Marts: Big Profits in Small Towns," *Convenience Store News,* Vol. 25, No. 7, May 31 - June 25, 1989, pp. 1 & 80-83.

Williams, Teresa, "Gasoline Fuels Growth of Convenience Store Industry," *Chain Store Age Executive,* August 1991, pp. 37A-38A.

U.S. HEALTHCARE: THE HEALTH CARE INDUSTRY

U.S. Healthcare (USHC), with more than 1.3 million members in 1992, was the largest for-profit health maintenance organization (HMO) on the U.S. East Coast. USHC operated primarily in three Northeastern locations: the Mid-Atlantic (Pennsylvania, New Jersey, and Delaware), Greater New York (Northern New Jersey, New York, and Connecticut), and New England (Massachusetts).

A major trend supporting the continued success of USHC was persistent medical inflation. Health spending in the United States was projected to be 13.4 percent of GNP in 1992. Under traditional fee-for-service health insurance plans, doctors and hospitals often inflated their bills to patients. Health Maintenance Organizations, in contrast, managed health care spending by limiting a patient's choice of doctors and hospitals. Under this system, doctors' fees were based on the number of patients selecting that particular doctor. Because the HMO set a physician's fees, it was in the best interest of the physicians to keep the number of medical procedures performed and the related costs to a minimum.

Many opportunities existed for the managed health care industry: the opportunity to expand, because experts felt that HMOs would be a building block for a national health care system; the opportunity to build provider networks, because of growing federal limitations on medical care reimbursements; the trend towards providing different medical product lines and service options at several price levels to consumers; and the trend towards the proliferation of mega-HMOs.

The managed health care industry was also faced with many threats: the proliferation of new HMOs that offered members flexibility in selecting out-of-network providers; the trend among employers to limit the number of health care plans offered to employees; state laws regulating premium rate increases; and increasing competition in a crowded market.

In light of industry trends, U.S. Healthcare's management faced many difficult decisions in 1992. One alternative for improving market share was geographic expansion beyond the present three regions of operation. Management was also considering the type of provider network that should be developed in each of these new locations. In addition, management was considering whether to offer out-of-network options and increase costs, or whether to maintain existing provider networks and keep costs low. In 1992, the company realized that HMO enrollment in general was growing rapidly and that the company needed to develop service plans to attract new members. Management felt the $500 million in assets on their balance sheet would make the company a powerful competitor. In 1992, however, USHC was not certain of the best uses for this capital.

THE INDUSTRY AND COMPETITIVE MARKET

THE HEALTH CARE INDUSTRY

The managed health care industry can be divided into two segments: traditional health care

Figure 1: Comparison of Traditional Health Care and Managed Care Providers

	Traditional Health Care	Managed Care
Physician	selection of your own	selection from a network of physicians or panel of providers
Coverage	traditional insurance company	HMO or PPO
Out-of-Pocket Expenses	payment of deductibles, then a percentage of claims (usually 20%)	no deductibles small per-visit co-payment (usually less than $10)
Claim Forms	yes	no

Source: Information obtained from "Oxford Health Plan," *Oxford Plan company brochure,* August 1988, p.4.

providers, and managed care providers. Traditional health care providers are the physicians and hospitals normally associated with a traditional indemnity insurance plan. Managed care providers are physicians and hospitals who have contracted with a Health Maintenance Organization (HMO) or Preferred Provider Organization (PPO). Figure 1 compares types of providers.

Traditional Health Care Providers

Employees of many companies receive health care delivered through traditional health care providers such as physicians and hospitals. Employees choose their own providers, are covered by a traditional insurance company, and receive benefit payments from this insurance company.

Selection of provider. In order to receive health care, employees select and receive services from any physician or hospital. Choices are normally based on the provider's geographic location or local reputation. Employees may receive care from as many different providers as they want.

Coverage and benefits. Coverage for traditional provider services is through a traditional insurance company. When an employee receives care, s/he completes a claim form to be sent to the insurance company. The insurance company reimburses both the provider and the employee after the employee has paid a deductible, usually in the range of $100 to $300. The employee pays a percentage of the medical charges (usually 20 percent) after satisfying the deductible. In such cases, traditional insurance coverage then reimburses the provider for 80 percent of the medical charges.

Managed Care Providers

There are two types of managed care providers: Health Maintenance Organizations and Preferred Provider Networks.

Health Maintenance Organizations. An HMO is characterized by an organized health care system of physicians and hospitals, serving an enrolled member population, often for a prepaid fee.

These health care providers contract with HMOs to create networks of hospitals, doctors, and other health care providers that provide services for certain fixed fees. These fees are based on a per patient or fee-for-service schedule. Providers receive payment for their services on a monthly basis according to the number of patients that have selected that HMO physician. Whether a physician received a fee-for-service or capitation payment, incentives existed to minimize costly procedures.

Preferred Provider Organizations. A PPO is similar to an HMO in that it is based on provider networks. However, PPO participants may use either network or out-of-network providers. When an out-of-network provider is selected, that member's premium costs are higher.

On January 1, 1990, 575 HMOs and 773 PPOs existed in the United States. PPOs have grown faster than HMOs because PPOs cost less than indemnity plans and do not have the rigid structures of traditional HMOs. Experts predicted that enrollment in PPOs would be approximately 73 million by 1993 [Agovino 1991]. As of June 30, 1991, the largest PPO was Blue Cross & Blue Shield Plan PPOs, with 13.9 million members. Aetna Health Plans, the tenth largest PPO, had two million members [Geisel 1991].

HMOs and PPOs differed from traditional health care providers in provider selection, type of coverage, and benefits received.

Selection of provider. In order to receive health care, members must select a physician from a network of HMO physicians or a panel of PPO physicians. A PPO member can also elect to use an out-of-network provider. These networks and panels are set up based on the employer's geographical location. During the early 1990s, health maintenance organizations also developed point-of-service plans. Under this arrangement, members could choose out-of-network providers, something they had been unable to do in the past.

Coverage and benefits. With managed care providers, there were no claim forms and no deductible was paid unless the member chose an out-of-network provider. In such cases, the member incurred out-of-pocket expenses, such as payment of a deductible and a substantial co-payment. In all other cases, the member would be responsible to the provider for a minimal co-payment (usually less than $10).

HEALTH MAINTENANCE ORGANIZATIONS

Three aspects of HMOs are discussed in this section: the provider network, types of HMOs, and premium determination.

Physician Network System

The HMO provider network consists of physicians, hospitals, and other outpatient treatment facilities that work together to provide members with medical services. The network has the following characteristics:

- It limits hospital care and associated costs by promoting the use of alternative treatment settings, whenever possible. These alternative settings include outpatient surgical centers, home health care, and diagnostic or laboratory centers.
- It promotes continuity of care so members know where to go for care and so providers work together.
- It assures the member has access to appropriate health care providers. A member in need of treatment from a specialist is referred to an appropriate provider.
- It monitors the amount and kind of care provided, via a central record-keeping service.
- It allows providers to communicate with each other to avoid duplicating services or a failure to provide needed services.

Types of HMOs

Members can receive services at one of two types of HMO locations. Staff HMOs are clinic sites where the physicians are salaried employees. Medical treatments are performed in a central location. In contrast, Independent Practice Associations (IPAs) are individual physicians who contract with HMOs to provide services to members in their own offices. Of these two types of HMOs, the IPA model is the most attractive alternative since most patients prefer to receive care in the physician's own office.

Determining Premiums

HMO premiums are determined by community rating, a method that calculates premiums based on the claims of members within the HMO's geographic location. This is different from traditional insurance carriers which calculate their premiums based on the demographic experience and actuarial trends of a particular employer or organization.

GROWTH OF HEALTH MAINTENANCE ORGANIZATIONS

Figure 2 shows the growth in HMO enrollments from 1983 to 1991. HMO enrollment more than tripled in this time period. The largest increase in HMO enrollment, as shown in Figure 3, occurred in the Mountain/Pacific region [Geisel 1990]. According to the *1990 HMO Directory*, HMO enrollment reached 38 million in 1990. The directory listed HMOs in 49 states plus Puerto Rico, Guam, and the District of Columbia.

The growth of HMOs in the 1990s was expected to continue due to the factors discussed below.

Figure 2: Growth of HMOs, 1983-1991

YEAR	ENROLLMENT IN MILLIONS	PERCENTAGE OF U.S. POPULATION ENROLLED
1983	12	5.3
1984	18	6.4
1985	19	7.1
1986	21	8.8
1987	28	10.7
1988	32	12.0
1989	34	13.0
1990	37	14.1
1991	38	14.9

Source: Information obtained from the U.S. Department of Health and Human Services; Commerce Department

Figure 3: HMOs Boom in the West

More than one-third of all HMO enrollees live in the Mountain/Pacific region. In contrast, New Englanders comprise less than one-tenth of all HMO enrollees.

REGION	RATE INCREASE (%)
Mountain Pacific	36.4
California	
Oregon	
Washington State	
Idaho	
Nevada	
Montana	
Wyoming	
Utah	
Colorado	
Arizona	
New Mexico	
West Central	12.4
Texas	
Oklahoma	
Kansas	
Nebraska	
South Dakota	
North Dakota	
Louisiana	
Arkansas	
Minnesota	
Iowa	
East Central	19.2
Wisconsin	
Michigan	
Indiana	
Tennessee	
Kentucky	
Missouri	
Alabama	
Ohio	

REGION	RATE INCREASE (%)
Mid Atlantic	13.7
New York	
Pennsylvania	
New Jersey	
New England	7.4
Maine	
Massachusetts	
New Hampshire	
Rhode Island	
South Atlantic	11.0
West Virginia	
Delaware	
Maryland	
South Carolina	
North Carolina	
Georgia	
Florida	

Source: Adapted from Geisel, Jerry, "HMO Enrollment Grows, Despite Fewer Plans," *Business Insurance*, 16 April 1990, p.2.

Impact of Medical Inflation

As a means of controlling health care costs, employers were expected to continue to offer HMOs to their employees. In the 1980s, total national health care expenditures rose from $250 billion to $660 billion. Additionally, corporate medical expenses increased 20.4 percent in 1990, with medical plan costs per employee amounting to $3,161 versus $2,600 in 1989 and $2,160 in 1988.

HMO Act of 1973

Very few HMOs existed before the HMO Act of 1973. This act encouraged the growth of HMOs by creating a favorable regulatory climate. Regulations went into effect describing the circumstances under which corporations employing 25 or more persons in an HMO's geographical area were obligated to offer employees a choice of medical coverage through a traditional insurance company or an HMO.

As a result of the act, HMOs gained popularity in the early to mid-1980s with the number of HMOs growing approximately 18 1/2 percent from the early 1980s. At the end of 1990, 22 percent of insured Americans under 65 were enrolled in an HMO plan. This was good news for HMOs since total premiums increased as HMO enrollment grew. Industry experts projected that by 1995, almost half of the total U.S. population would be enrolled in a managed health plan [*Standard & Poors* 1990.]

Resolution of Image Problem

Until 1989, the industry faced a "bad image" problem. This stemmed from the huge financial losses incurred by many of the newer HMOs, as well as by well-established HMOs.

As a result of this bad image, HMOs implemented more restrictive underwriting criteria when determining their premium rates. These criteria helped HMOs to once again establish themselves financially through minimal annual premium increases. Figure 4 categorizes HMOs by the percentage of average annual premium increases. In 1992, HMO premiums were expected to increase by 11 percent, while traditional insurance plans' rates were expected to increase by 18 percent. This meant that HMOs could stay ahead of inflation, remain competitive and show profits.

For-Profit Status

The shift among HMOs from nonprofit status to for-profit status was another indication of industry growth. Many for-profit HMOs were owned by profitable insurance companies which gave the HMO the added benefit of being affiliated with a well-known company. In 1991, 68 percent of HMOs were for-profit organizations.

Figure 4: Distribution of HMOs by Average Annual Premium Increase — January 1990

Average % Increase	Percentage of Plans
10 or less	12
10.1-15	45
15.1-20	29
20.1-25	12
25.1-30	0
30.1 or more	2

Source: Adapted from Landes, Jennifer, "HMOs See Better Performance, Competitive Position," *National Underwriter,* February 12, 1990, p.41.

HMO Plan Design

Many employees found HMO plans, with their low premiums, an attractive health care option. As employers began to shift benefit plan costs to employees, employees did not want to incur additional out-of-pocket expenses. Promoters of HMOs argued that HMO plans provided more comprehensive coverage per premium dollar than comparable traditional insurance company plans, and that HMOs were able to accomplish these economies of scale without compromising health care quality.

Geographic Expansion

Geographic expansion by many major HMOs increased as many of the larger, well-known HMOs expanded their networks. This expansion contributed to the impact of HMOs in the marketplace. Although HMOs had started out on the West Coast, particularly in California, they rapidly moved into the Northeast. The HMO with established networks in different areas of the country would be more successful than its competitors.

RECENT LEGISLATION

Federal and state governments had enacted various statutes that regulated HMOs. These laws governed premium rates, quality assurance procedures, enrollment requirements, corporate governance policies, provider relations, licensure and financial reserves and conditions.

An amendment to the *HMO Act of 1973*, the *Health Maintenance Organization Act of 1988* was signed into law on October 24, 1988. This amendment gave employers greater flexibility in determining the amount of employer premium contributions toward an HMO plan, thus changing the premium-setting structure of the HMOs.

According to the *HMO Act of 1973*, an employer's contribution to an HMO plan (i.e., the amount of an employee's health care premium paid by the employer)had to equal the largest contribution the employer made to a traditional health care plan. This is illustrated in the following example:

	HMO PLAN	TRADITIONAL PLAN
Monthly premium per employee	$110	$135
Employer contribution	$102	$102
Employee contribution	$ 8	$ 33

Because the employer's contributions for both plans had to be equal, the employee contribution would vary—most likely in the HMO's favor since its premiums were usually lower than traditional plan premiums.

This equal contribution rule was repealed in 1988. The new law, which required the employer's contributions to an HMO plan not be "financially discriminatory," allowed employers to determine the amount of their premium contributions. This eliminated employees' preference for one plan over another based on the amount of their contributions. In the future, employees probably would not automatically choose the HMO plans because they had to contribute the least to it. Instead, the costs to employees for a traditional health care plan versus an HMO plan would be very close.

This new law was favorable because it allowed HMOs to set group premium rates based on the revenue requirements needed to provide service to a particular group. This offered employers incentive to promote wellness among their employees. If a particular employer's claims were low, premium rates for that group would also be low. This new law was referred to as the "adjusted community rating."

During 1992, President Bush offered Congress a proposal to initiate a tax credit for those people receiving no health care insurance. Had Congress passed this legislation, HMOs would have benefitted from the national health care reform enactment.

CUSTOMERS

The customers of the managed care industry consisted of the employers who offered the HMO to their employees, and employees who joined the HMO. These employers included business and government organizations. During 1992, managed care organizations were beginning to offer their services to Medicare recipients. Industry executives envisioned a role for managed health care in the reformation of national health care [Faltermayer 1992].

Employers

In 1991, 62 percent of all U.S. employers offered an HMO to their employees as a result of the *HMO Act of 1973*, which required employers to offer a managed care plan to their employees. In most cases, the employer was approached by a specific HMO and decided to offer that particular

HMO's plan as a result.

Of the 38 percent of employers who did not offer an HMO, many had not been approached by any specific HMO. This percentage was expected to decrease as more HMOs began to aggressively pursue these employers. This would lead to competitive selling as HMOs tried to increase employer enrollment.

HMOs were expected to work harder both at attracting and keeping employers since employers had more corporate bargaining power due to the *Health Maintenance Organization Act of 1988*. This act resulted in more flexibility for employers when determining how much they should contribute to each health plan offered to their employees. Since HMO premiums were now required to reflect the health care claim experience of the specific employer, marketplace chaos had been created. Many employers faced higher premiums under this new premium-setting structure because of the bad claim experience of their employees, and as a result had shifted the higher costs to their employees. As a result, employees did not automatically choose the HMO plan because it was the least costly. Since the costs of a traditional insurance plan and an HMO plan were now very similar, employees were reconsidering their options when choosing between an HMO or a traditional health care plan. Employees had to determine whether they really wanted to be enrolled in a plan with designated physicians [Norman 1989].

Employees

According to an extensive data project completed by A. Foster Higgins & Co., Inc., a benefits consulting firm, HMOs tended to enroll younger-than-average employees and enrollment percentages varied with dependent characteristics such as individual versus family coverage.

Enrollment patterns indicated that younger employees tended to choose HMOs as their benefit plans. HMOs had become an increasingly popular choice with younger employees for various reasons. Younger employees, most of whom had not chosen their own physicians, were usually willing to select a physician from the limited HMO provider network in order to have the HMO plan features.

While young families had high HMO enrollment rates, enrollment rates declined dramatically as the families matured. Individuals, on the other hand, had lower HMO enrollments at younger ages and higher enrollments at older ages. The enrollment pattern for families was higher at younger ages, with dramatically decreased participation as the family matured. This may have been due to the heavy medical expenses incurred during child-bearing years, and because these families no longer had small children. The enrollment pattern for younger employees suggested that as they grew older and experienced more health problems they began to favor HMOs.

New Customer Segments

In 1992, new customer segments emerged for health maintenance organizations to target. These segments included Medicare recipients and the 37 million uninsured citizens of the United States. During the 1992 election campaign, President Bush suggested low-income families should receive a $3,700 tax credit to help offset the lack of medical benefits. The managed-care companies would benefit as low cost, quality medical care prevailed in health care reform [Ginzberg 1992].

COMPETITION

Two types of competition existing in the managed care industry were traditional health care providers and other managed-care providers.

Traditional Health Care Providers

Traditional health care providers were managed care providers' biggest competitors because they did not require subscribers to use an HMO physician network. Many employees were willing to pay a deductible as well as a percentage of their actual health care costs in exchange for the freedom to choose their own health care providers. These traditional providers monopolized the health care industry until the early 1970s, when HMOs first appeared on the health care scene. During the early 1990s, traditional insurance companies were not competing successfully with HMOs. Traditional insurers were facing the highly competitive pricing from HMOs. Also, some large insurance companies were encountering problems in the development of their own HMO-type plans.

HMOs

Figure 5 shows the top ten HMOs ranked by U.S. member enrollment as of December 18, 1991. The largest HMO, Kaiser Permanente, had approximately 5.9 million members while number ten, Sanus Corp. Health Systems, had approximately 661,000 members.

USHC operated as a regional health maintenance organization. Competition existed from many additional HMOs operating in the same regions as USHC. The number of USHC's HMO competitors in 1990 and their regions of operation are shown on the following chart:

REGION (marketplace)	# of HMO Competitors
Mid-Atlantic	21
New York	32
New England	10

On a national level USHC competed with large HMOs with substantial financial resources, growing memberships, and strong provider networks. The top three HMOs listed in Figure 5 are discussed below.

Kaiser Permanente. The largest HMO in the country in 1992 was Kaiser Permanente which originated on the West Coast. Kaiser had 5.9 million members and was rapidly expanding on the East Coast, where it operated in several large cities.

Figure 5: Top 10 General Service HMOs

Plan/Sponsor	Number of Participants (in Millions)
Kaiser Permanente	5.90
Blue Cross/Blue Shield	5.20
CIGNA Healthplan	2.20
United Healthcare Corp.	1.40
Aetna Health Plans	1.30
U.S. Healthcare, Inc.	1.20
HIP of New York	.99
Prudential Health Plans	.97
Health Net	.82
Sanus Health Systems	.66

Source: Geisel, Jerry, "HMO Enrollment Grows, Despite Fewer Plans," *Business Insurance*, December 18, 1991, p. 40.

Competition from other health plans could force Kaiser to make some changes. In response to the 1988 amendment to the 1973 HMO act, Kaiser had to adjust premiums for some of its employers who argued that their employees cost less to serve since their claim experience was good. This was something Kaiser traditionally had not done.

Kaiser had also never had to launch a major advertising campaign. For the first time in 1989, the company felt the need to advertise via a sophisticated television, radio, and print campaign that personalized the program's physicians. Kaiser had other concerns: management was worried that changes implemented by competitors could raise the company's costs and cause it to deviate from its winning formula. For example, other HMOs in mid-1991 had begun to allow members to use out-of-network physicians. Many of the physicians in the network feared that such a move would break up the tightly-knit group practices that had made HMOs successful in controlling service costs and quality [Agovino 1991].

Blue Cross/Blue Shield Plan HMOs. The Blue Cross/Blue Shield nonprofit plans which operated independently on a regional basis had also gained a prominent position in the HMO marketplace. In early 1983, Blue Cross/Blue Shield launched a national HMO network to attract large multi-state employers. This network, which was composed of approximately 94 regional HMOs, attained popularity because of the familiar Blue Cross/Blue Shield name. Empire Blue Cross/Blue Shield served nearly 10 million customers in 28 counties of New York State.

During 1991, Blue Cross/Blue Shield Plan HMOs introduced a flexible service plan called Empire BlueChoice. This service offered members low-cost premiums without compromising the quality of health care. Because of efficiency improvements in 1990, Empire spent only 7.4 cents of every premium dollar on administrative costs.

Figure 6: Comparative Size of Eastern Regional HMO Organizations

HMO	MEMBERS (Millions)	REVENUES
U.S. Healthcare	1,300,000	1,300
HIP of New York	893,837	260
Harvard Community Plan	368,158	482
Physicians Health Service	135,482	210
Empire Blue Cross/Shield	132,000	60
Cigna Health Plan (NY)	122,537	49
Sanus Health Plan (NY/NJ)	60,000	17

Source: Information obtained from Agovino, Theresa. "Agressive HMO Polishes Act in N.Y." *Crain's New York Business*. August 26, 1991, p. 15

CIGNA. In 1990, CIGNA Corporation marketed its services in all 50 states. CIGNA's HMOs served approximately 2.1 million members. CIGNA also used IPA networks to offer prepaid dental coverage in 29 states serving 1 million members as of December 31, 1990. Revenues from prepaid services in 1990 were $2.1 billion.

In the early 1990s, CIGNA acquired EQUICOR from the Equitable Life Assurance Society. This move brought CIGNA 450,000 more HMO enrollees, and the purchase of COMED of New Jersey added 86,000 enrollees.

An HMO competed mainly with those firms operating in the same region. HMO competition could be intense in a given geographic area. U.S. Healthcare had large competitors who were well-established in their existing markets. Figure 6 lists total members and revenues for 1990 for USHC and its major competitors.

Changing Competition

Establishing new provider networks, developing flexible new health care plans, and intensifying selling strategies were the areas which would provide HMOs with the greatest challenges and opportunities in the future. New service plan development relied on the network of hospitals, physicians, laboratories, and nursing homes the HMOs had contracted with and ultimately marketed to their customers. HMOs needed to increase the number of employers offering their plans to employees. Those HMOs which could introduce a new plan in a particular area would probably achieve a competitive advantage.

Although cost containment would lead to the continued growth of HMO enrollment, those companies that could provide flexibility in their existing plans would be the most attractive to current and potential users. Traditional insurance providers offered indemnity plans which gave employees flexibility in selecting a provider. HMOs were at a disadvantage because they did not operate as insurance companies and had to evaluate whether they should align themselves with insurance companies by offering indemnity features. HMOs needed to enter new markets to increase membership growth. One possible market was government Medicare recipients who received health care from HMO provider networks. The industry viewed government partnership as a means to increase membership but were concerned about the competitive pricing which would result to achieve this business.

THE COMPANY

HISTORY

U.S. Healthcare, Inc. received its license to operate in 1977 — four years after the passage of the *HMO Act of 1973*. The company's first HMO was the Health Maintenance Organization of Pennsylvania (HMO-PA), which was one of the top five IPA model HMOs in the U.S. in 1992. The company's nonprofit status changed to for-profit in 1982.

Since the late 1970s, the company had expanded into other geographical locations in the Northeast including the Mid-Atlantic, Greater New York, and New England. By January 1992, total membership was 1.33 million.

SERVICES

The company provided comprehensive health care services to members through an extensive physician network composed of independent family physicians, specialists, and medical facilities such as hospitals and outpatient treatment facilities [*Annual Report* 1990]. Key features of these services are listed below.

Physician Coordination

U.S. Healthcare contracted individually with its 3,500 physicians and specialists who serviced employers in various geographical areas. When special care was needed, the member was referred free of charge to a participating specialist in the HMO network. The specialist then worked with the member's primary physician to manage the member's case. Members who required treatment for a rare or complicated illness had access to some of the country's elite medical facilities at no additional cost. Such integration illustrates one of the key features of HMO plans.

During 1992, the company began to limit the number of providers who could offer services in a given geographic location. It achieved this by imposing stricter qualifications on physician providers. Only doctors who provided 24-hour service, scheduled no more than five patients an hour, and kept good medical records could join the HMO. Physicians had to be board certified with established hospital privileges. This meant that younger physicians just out of residency were not qualified to join USHC. USHC believed such restrictions would enable the company to review each provider's costs and quality of care [Rice 1991].

Physician Reaction

In February 1992, several U.S. Healthcare physicians were interviewed about their experiences as USHC providers. Two different perspectives of the company are represented by the opinions of a pediatrician and a specialist in obstetrics and gynecology.

The pediatrician was pleased with USHC. His practice was primarily comprised of USHC members, and as a primary care physician his fees were prepaid by the plan on a capitation fee schedule. He said doctors who had large USHC practices could earn about $20,000 a month from HMO patients. However, patients were not limited to the number of visits they could make to this doctor. This challenged the doctor to make proper diagnoses and promote wellness at his clinic.

The obstetrician was less pleased with USHC. As a specialist he was compensated by a fee-for-service arrangement. However, limitations were set up by the company for certain medical procedures. This meant that on certain patients he could lose money. He felt that incentives were not there to deliver quality care. This doctor was also displeased with the USHC system which required him to employ two assistants to handle the claim forms required by the company.

IPA Model

USHC operated as an IPA HMO, which meant members were able to receive care from a physician in a private office setting. Most members preferred to receive care in this type of setting instead of a less personalized "clinic" atmosphere. Members could receive care from the same physician during each visit rather than be treated by any available physician in a clinic.

Service Philosophy

The company's services were based on the philosophy that quality health care could be made more affordable by emphasizing patient management, preventive care (including routine physicals and eye exams), and early treatment. In most cases, members were fully covered for preventive care, a specialist's care, hospitalization, surgery, home care, and maternity care. Members paid a $2 charge for each physician office visit [*Annual Report* 1990].

Current Services

According to the *1990 U.S. Healthcare Member Handbook*, USHC offered the following services:

1. Primary and Preventive Care
2. Outpatient Care
3. Inpatient Hospital and Extended Care
4. Maternity Care
5. Mental Health and Substance Abuse Treatment
6. Emergency Care

The company provided special care and wellness programs which included the following:

1. Prenatal Care
2. Healthy Eating Program
3. Fitness Club Reimbursement
4. Routine Vision Care
5. Cancer Detection Program

MARKETING POLICIES

U.S. Healthcare's marketing policies focused mainly on the company's geographical location, customers, and sales efforts.

Geographic Location

The company predominantly serviced the East Coast from Boston to the Delaware area. When questioned about extending operations beyond the Northeast corridor, Leonard Abramson, president, CEO and founder of USHC, responded that "the company had carved a niche in the Northeast, and that population on the East and West coasts was highly concentrated." While he did not say the company planned to expand into the Northwest, he implied that a future market may exist in that area.

One reason for the company's decision to concentrate on Northeastern expansion was that many of the nation's largest employers had regional offices in New York, Boston, and Philadelphia. If the license to operate in Boston was not granted, the company would not be able to say it was servicing the entire East Coast. According to Abramson, the Boston area provided the company with the ability to attract physicians and hospitals to set up a "very, very good" network. In order to set up an attractive network, there had to be a substantial number of new potential providers in each service location.

Customers

The company's first group of customers was the employer groups with which it contracted to offer its services. The company offered these employers the chance to reduce their health care costs by using an HMO. Some employers bristled at the company's aggressive use of state and federal laws under which HMOs could insist that companies offer their services to employees [Rice, 1991]. The company's second group of customers was the provider networks which elected to participate in USHC's plans. The company had also begun to contract with government agencies. As of late 1991, six percent of revenues were derived from this market.

USHC planned to focus on its employer base by selling to the more informed benefits coordinators who viewed the company as a friend rather than as an adversary trying to negotiate every contract. Once the company had developed substantial networks in each of its existing geographic areas, it could invest in the development of provider networks in other geographical areas.

Sales Efforts

The company's sales efforts were conducted through a direct sales force of 183 representatives and 44 marketing management personnel. The marketing effort was supported by an extensive database which was used to identify prospects and to establish enrollment goals. Marketing efforts were also conducted through various media forms. During 1991, the company spent $4.3 million on its print and television campaigns. During 1992, advertisement expenditures were expected to increase 50 percent to $6.4 million.

During 1992, USHC was preparing to handle more national accounts. The company had become affiliated with regional HMOs across the country, and during 1991 14 regional HMOs were added to the network. Executives at USHC did not anticipate that many companies would require employees to use a specific health insurer. They believed employers wanted health insurers to compete against each other so they could offer quality insurance at the best possible price [Rice 1991].

FINANCIAL MANAGEMENT

During 1991, USHC's earnings nearly doubled to $151 million. Due to a stock split, shareholders received a 116 percent return on their investments. Experts felt USHC had done an excellent job holding down medical costs. For a typical publicly-held HMO medical costs were usually about 800 percent of premium income. During 1991, USHC brought this ratio down to 78 percent, freeing up millions of dollars for expansion. Businesses accounted for 98 percent of revenue and their premiums had increased merely 13 percent annually, on average, since 1986, compared with an average increase of 20 percent for traditional insurance plans. The monthly premium for a typical family of three ranged from $265 to $344 in 1991. Financial information on U.S. Healthcare is provided in Figures 7 and 8.

CONTRACT MANAGEMENT

USHC also managed an HMO for Blue Cross of St. Louis which was very interested in building an HMO patterned after the U.S. Healthcare model. Blue Cross owned 100 percent of this HMO and provided all the required financing. U.S. Healthcare received $2 million to $4 million for its management services. However, if certain performance criteria were not met by Blue Cross, U.S. Healthcare would purchase 100 percent of that HMO's stock and financially support it.

When Abramson was questioned about anticipated capital spending for the company, he responded that the company planned to generate any money needed for these expenditures from its own internal operations and by withdrawing from its cash reserves. In 1991, the company did not have any long-term debt nor any plans to acquire such debt.

Figure 7: U.S. Healthcare, Inc.
Income Statements 1987-1991 (Amounts in Thousands)

INCOME STATEMENT	1987	1988	1989	1990	1991
REVENUE:					
PREMIUMS	$597,567	$719,523	$972,781	$1,287,205	$1,659,667
INVESTMENT INCOME	$13,857	$13,762	$21,835	$33,164	$44,101
OTHER, PRINCIPALLY ADMIN. SERVICES FEES	$15,700	$5,568	$5,591	$9,669	$4,733
TOTAL REVENUE	$627,124	$738,853	$1,000,207	$1,330,038	$1,708,501
EXPENSES:					
MEDICAL CLAIMS AND CAPITALIZATION COSTS	$554,030	$641,706	$843,515	N/A	N/A
ADMIN. AND MARKETING COSTS	$77,547	$87,711	$110,861	N/A	N/A
TOTAL EXPENSES	$631,577	$729,417	$954,376	$1,209,193	$1,462,683
INCOME (LOSS) FROM OPERATIONS	($4,453)	$9,436	$45,831	$120,845	$245,818
LITIGATION SETTLEMENT		($2,750)		$2,000	
(LOSS) FROM U.S. BIOSCIENCE INC.	($649)	($1,543)	($1,197)	$1,219	$1,485
INCOME (LOSS) BEFORE INCOME TAXES	($5,102)	$5,143	$44,634	$124,064	$247,303
PROVISION FOR (BENEFIT FROM) INCOME TAXES	($6,150)	$1,515	$16,252	$46,544	$96,203
NET INCOME	$1,048	$3,628	$28,382	$77,520	$151,100

Sources: Adapted from U.S. Healthcare, Inc., *1988 Annual Report*.
Adapted from U.S. Healthcare, Inc., *1989 Annual Report*.
Adapted from *Standard & Poor's Corporation Records*, 1991.

ACQUISITIONS

In regard to potential acquisitions, Abramson stated in 1989, "We're always looking. We'd like to stay in the health care service industry. The company has management who will want to stay long term and become an integral part of the future of the company. I'm looking for companies where we can be synergistic and potentiate what we do. I don't want something out there removed from what we do; I want something that fits into our overall philosophy and structure. We have the money, we have the will and we have the drive to make these things happen so we are talking to investment bankers and we are in search for companies, and we are constantly involved in looking at opportunities." Abramson also stated that no future plans existed for any

Figure 8: U.S. Healthcare, Inc.
Consolidated Balance Sheet 1987-1991(Amounts in Thousands)

CONSOLIDATED BALANCE SHEET	1987	1988	1989	1990	1991
ASSETS:					
CURRENT ASSETS:					
CASH AND EQUIVALENTS	$756	$6,491	$30,082	$33,424	$56,590
MARKETABLE SECURITIES	$129,296	$74,851	$176,258	$280,868	$33,511
RECEIVABLES	$34,070	$45,799	$66,287	$66,733	$72,104
REFUNDABLE INCOME TAXES		$1,943			
OTHER CURRENT ASSETS	$23,497	$3,194	$5,502	$9,702	$12,729
TOTAL CURRENT ASSETS	$187,619	$132,278	$278,129	$390,727	$174,934
LONG-TERM MARKETABLE SECURITIES	$41,168	$106,022	$91,123	$148,291	$500,539
PROPERTY AND EQUIPMENT-NET	$21,227	$22,376	$35,003	$66,679	$73,998
INTANGIBLE ASSETS-NET	$8,940	$8,499	$7,624	$7,462	$8,426
OTHER LONG-TERM ASSETS	$1,650	$2,013	$2,425	$307	$321
TOTAL ASSETS	$260,604	$271,188	$414,304	$613,466	$758,218
LIABILITIES AND STOCKHOLDER'S EQUITY					
CURRENT LIABILITIES:					
MEDICAL AND CAPITALIZATION COSTS PAYABLE	$94,668	$111,073	$212,731	$313,061	$336,200
UNEARNED PREMIUMS	$4,722	$6,247	$7,845	$10,900	$19,823
ACCOUNTS PAYABLE AND ACCRUED LIABILITIES	$17,054	$10,691	$17,987	$24,247	$28,489
INCOME TAXES PAYABLE	$1,670	$160	$6,491	$25,609	$16,456
TOTAL CURRENT LIABILITIES	$118,114	$128,171	$245,054	$373,817	$400,968
LONG-TERM LIABILITIES		$3,058	$5,328		
COMMITMENTS AND CONTINGENCIE					
DEFERRED CHARGES	$2,665				
OTHER LONG-TERM LIABILITIES	$1,066			$6,112	$10,356
TOTAL LIABILITIES	$121,845	$131,229	$250,382	$379,929	$411,324
SHAREHOLDER'S EQUITY:					
COMMON STOCK, $.005 PAR VALUE	$231	$233	$238	$242	$368
CLASS B STOCK, $.005 PAR VALUE	$27	$26	$24	$24	$36
ADDITIONAL PAID IN CAPITAL	$108,086	$109,605	$114,392	$121,894	$136,101
RETAINED EARNINGS	$100,905	$97,407	$116,037	$177,620	$303,454
TREASURY STOCK-AT COST	($69,346)	($65,813)	($65,713)	($65,713)	($91,292)
UNEARNED PORTION OF RESTRICTED STOCK	($1,144)	($1,499)	($1,056)	($530)	($1,773)
SHAREHOLDER'S EQUITY	$138,759	$139,959	$163,922	$233,537	$346,894
TOTAL LIABILITIES & SHAREHOLDER'S EQUITY	$260,604	$271,188	$414,304	$613,466	$758,218

Sources: Adapted from U.S. Healthcare, Inc., *1988 Annual Report.*
Adapted from U.S. Healthcare, Inc., *1989 Annual Report.*
Adapted from *Standard & Poor's Corporation Records,* 1991.

spinoffs. However, he did not state that he would oppose a possible merger to become affiliated with a traditional insurance company [Norman 1989].

Abramson was particularly concerned with weak HMO management of insurance companies. He stated, "Big insurers are good at processing paper and handling money. But medical management is not their forte. We took over two Travelers HMOs for $1 each — and we overpaid. They were in terrible shape, overpaying physicians and hospitals, not negotiating good contracts" [Norman 1989].

U.S. BIOSCIENCE

U.S. Bioscience, a company formed by USHC in 1987, was a developer and marketer of agents used in the treatment of cancer. In 1989, Marion Merrell Dow Laboratories invested $15 million in this company. The arrangement with Dow resulted in profitable operations for this segment of USHC in 1991. On February 3, 1992, the FDA refused to recommend approval of the company's highly touted cancer drug, Ethyl. USHC still owned 17 percent of Bioscience, but planned to distribute those shares to its stockholders as a special dividend. In 1992, Schering Plough Corporation entered into an agreement to market and sell U.S. Bioscience products.

TOWARDS THE FUTURE

What will the 1990s have in store for U.S. Healthcare? In 1992, USHC management was exploring possible strategies for the company. It was seeking a strategy that would enable the company to increase membership by 50 percent by the year 2000.

The industry trend was towards geographic expansion of HMO services and the coordination of health care plans that were flexible, yet able to contain health care costs.

Geographic Expansion

Several executives favored regional expansion into new adjacent geographic markets. They considered Baltimore, MD., Washington,D.C. and Richmond, VA. prime target markets because of their large municipal and private employer bases and favorable demographics, as well as the proximity and attractiveness of medical providers.

These executives argued that expansion would be achieved by selling the company's plans to benefits managers throughout those areas. Such regional growth was favored because of the continuing rise in health care costs. Employers that used networks of doctors and hospitals had reduced their health care costs by one third. The executives felt by targeting the largest employers in each region, U.S. Healthcare could out perform its competitors because of its strong management skills in developing and controlling quality and efficiency for provider networks. They felt that USHC could succeed with a regional expansion strategy because of lower premium costs and the attractive feature of no claim forms. They also supported regional expansion because of the company's recent success in developing flexible service plans. Because traditional health insurance companies were not well managed, their administration costs continued to increase. As employers found traditional health care plans too costly to offer their employees, managed care plans would see a continued increase in enrollment.

Other executives argued against geographic expansion. They preferred for the company to focus on becoming an HMO management company. Because national health care reform would be on the mind of many Americans, USHC would be better suited to become a mega-HMO that would focus on providing consulting services to other HMOs, PPOs, insurance companies, and government agencies. Because these organizations were purchasers of health care, these executives felt that USHC could provide management expertise and support functions to help these organizations grow. This group of executives believed the company should rely on its recently acquired sophisticated computers to analyze, track, and process an abundant amount of information. Many USHC competitors had not yet realized the benefits of a "paperless" medical office. Although the company had improved its operating efficiency, many IPA members did not appreciate the burden of claims processing that was being shifted to them. Because patients did not need to fill out insurance forms, doctors and their staffs were now required to do so. Executives felt U.S. Healthcare was ahead of the competition in terms of automating claims processing at the physician level, and looked toward the new trend of complete techno-management of all medical procedures, claims, and administration which the company was positioned to exploit. The technical improvements the company had made could be utilized by other organizations to improve operations. Executives had anticipated the growth of managed care and advocated that high fixed costs associated with this rapid growth would be burdensome for many managed health care organizations. Because other HMOs were smaller and did not have the capacity to finance such technological improvements, executives viewed the opportunity to provide managed-care management services for other companies as an opportunity for those companies to leverage their profits through such management services offered by U.S. Healthcare.

REFERENCES AND BACKGROUND READINGS

Agovino, Theresa, "Aggressive HMO Polishes Act in N.Y.," *Crain's New York Business,* August 26, 1991, p.13.

Annual Report on Form 10-K, 1990, U.S. Healthcare, Inc.

Cox, Brian. "Know Competition in Marketing HMOs, PPOs," *National Underwriter,* April 29, 1991, p.11.

Faltermayer, Edmund. "Let's Really Cure the Health System," *Fortune,* March, 23, 1991, p.46.

Geisel, Jerry, "HMO Enrollment Grows, Despite Fewer Plans," *Business Insurance,* April 16, 1990, p.3.

Ginzberg, Eli. "Managed Care Hasn't Lived Up to its Promises," *The New York Times,* February 20, 1992, p.A28

Koco, Linda. " Competition Spurs Growth Point-of-Service HMOs," *National Underwriter,* April 29, 1991, p.7.

Koco, Linda. "Point-of-Service HMOs Are Growing Rapidly," *National Underwriter,* June 10, 1991, p.15.

Koenig, Richard. "U.S. Healthcare, Its Profits Strong, Seeks Added Clout in New York HMO Market," *The Wall Street Journal*, February 4, 1991

Landes, Jennifer, " HMOs See Better Performance, Competitive Position," *National Underwriter*, February 12, 1990, p.41

New Jesey HMO Association, *Presentation before the Governor's Commission on Health Care Costs,* June 12, 1990.

Norman, James R., " Can Insurers Nurse Their HMOs Back to Health?" *Business Week*, January 16, 1989, p. 80.

Oxford Freedom Plan, " *Oxford Health Plan company brochure*, August 1988, p.4.

Rice, Faye, "America's Hottest HMO," *Fortune*, July 15, 1991, p.94.

Standard and Poors *Industry Surveys - Health Care*, August 22, 1991, p.H 72.

Waldholz, Michael, " U.S. Bioscience..." *The New York Times*, February 4, 1991 Sec. B4.

Paine Webber Investment Research Report U.S. Healthcare, February 19, 1991, p. 375.

UNITED PARCEL SERVICE: THE AIR CARGO INDUSTRY

"We run the tightest ship in the shipping business."
"When your package absolutely, positively has to be there overnight."

The demand for delivery of letters and packages has increased greatly over the last few years, with parcels now going from Palo Alto, California to London, England, overnight.

As shown in Figure 1, from 1986 to 1989, the air cargo industry grew steadily. Approximately 230 carriers in the commercial airline industry logged 15.5 billion ton-miles in 1989 compared to 12.7 billion ton-miles in 1988 ["Aerospace & Air Transport Industry Surveys," June 21, 1990]. A ton-mile is defined as transporting a ton (2000 lbs.) of freight a distance of one mile.

Businesses and individuals increasingly want packages and letters delivered as quickly as possible. This is why, in the 1990s, most parcels are not delivered by trucks alone, but by airplanes and trucks combined.

To keep up with this emerging trend, United Parcel Service (UPS), mainly a ground transporter of packages until 1982, entered the air cargo market. UPS held second place in the domestic air cargo market in 1989 with a market share of 26 percent.

UPS was faced with many problems in the early 1990s. It was clear that the real growth of the air cargo industry was outside of the U.S. Its major competitor in the U.S., Federal Express, entered the international market by purchasing Flying Tiger Line —an international carrier — as well as a number of small European carriers. For UPS it was not a question of global expansion, but rather a question of which market to enter: the European market, the Asian market, or the South

Figure 1: Air Cargo Movement for U.S. Carriers

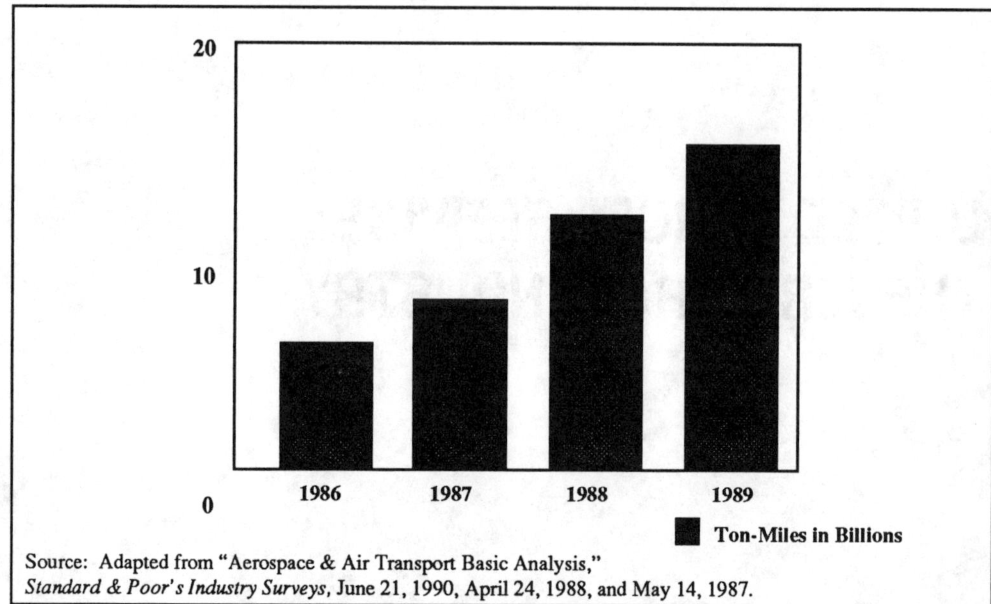

Source: Adapted from "Aerospace & Air Transport Basic Analysis," *Standard & Poor's Industry Surveys*, June 21, 1990, April 24, 1988, and May 14, 1987.

American market? UPS was exploring strategic decisions in areas such as the markets to be served and how to enter those markets.

THE INDUSTRY AND COMPETITIVE MARKET

THE AIR CARGO INDUSTRY

The air cargo industry transports parcels through air freight forwarders via airplanes. Air freight forwarders are firms which use airplanes and trucks to pick up and deliver parcels. The air cargo industry became very important because the parcel delivery business emphasized speed and reliability, rather than solely reliability.

The air cargo industry is one segment in the freight transportation industry, as illustrated in Figure 2. Other segments of the freight transportation industry are the shipping industry, the on-ground transportation industry, and government-operated mail service. This case study focuses mainly on the air cargo industry.

The Early Phases

In the early phases of the freight transportation industry, letters and small packages were

Figure 2: Competitive Segments of Freight Transportation Industry

Freight Transportation Industry

Air Cargo Industry

Government Mail Service

On-Ground Transportation Industry

Shipping Industry

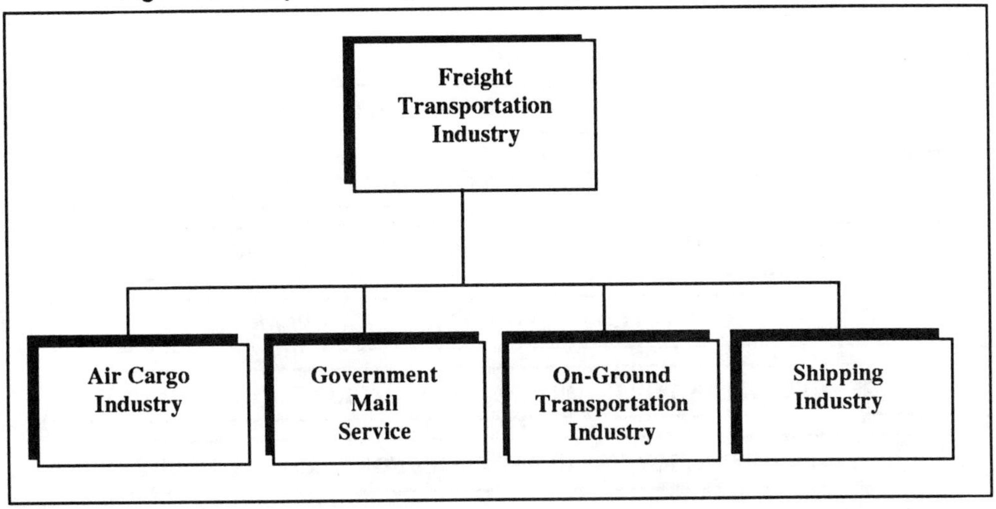

shipped through the U.S. Post Office or through freight forwarders who primarily used trucks or trains to move bulk mail. Delivery time averaged a week for distances greater than 500 miles. This process consisted of a customer dropping off a package with a courier or the courier picking up the package from the customer, and then transporting the parcel by truck to another depot. At the final terminal, the packages were loaded into delivery vans at night and delivered the following day.

Before 1977, packages sometimes were shipped in the bellies of passenger airliners. Freight forwarders contracted with passenger airlines to transport parcels to destinations along their routes.

In 1977, the Air Freight Deregulation Act created an entirely new industry: firms were allowed to use airplanes for the sole purpose of transporting parcels. With deregulation came an increase in the number of companies in the air cargo sector, and by the late 1980s the market was saturated.

The Central Hub

The air cargo industry changed drastically due to the creation of the central hub system, which makes nation-wide overnight deliveries possible. As shown in Figure 3, air couriers now pick up packages and letters from customers and send them to a nearby airport terminal. From the terminal, the parcels are flown to the hub, re-routed, and loaded into the respective planes. This all occurs in the early morning hours. This choreography is so precise that a one-minute delay can make as many as 20,000 packages miss their guaranteed delivery time [Dumaine 1986, p. 101]. Delivery vans were integrated into the air cargo market to handle the last phase—delivery to the customer's residence.

Figure 3: How the Central Hub System Operates

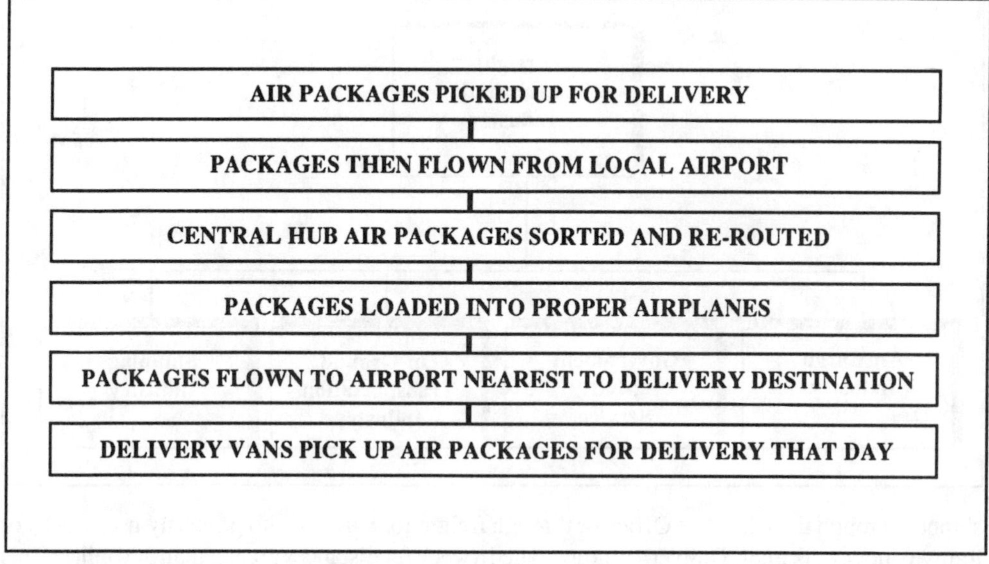

Because demand and volume were so large, most major air freight forwarders established regional hubs on the East and West coasts to avoid overloading the central hub and to increase delivery effectiveness in regional areas. To better serve the increased growth in the international market, carriers began setting up hubs in foreign countries, especially in Europe.

CUSTOMERS

Two basic customer segments that air carriers catered to in the late 1980s were the business sector and the individual sector.

The Business Sector

Businesses were the heaviest users of air freight forwarder services in the 1980s. According to one estimate, at least 80 percent of the air carrier industry's $11 billion in 1988 revenues came from businesses ["Aerospace and Air Transport Basic Analysis" 1989]. The exact number of businesses using air freight forwarders was unknown since this was considered privileged information. However, it is assumed that most businesses are an existing or potential user of air freight service.

Air couriers established contracts with businesses, such as mail-order firms, wholesalers, retailers, and other companies that needed high-volume shipment of goods. These contracts bound firms to specific couriers which handled all shipping orders. Air courier services also offered volume discounts and bulk rates to attract businesses.

Businesses which used air couriers and found them to be reliable increased the use of air cargo services since it meant decreased warehousing costs and efficient delivery times of raw materials and finished goods, as well as improved customer service.

The Individual Sector

The individual segment—the smaller of the two customer segments — was important nevertheless. Individuals sent packages and letters to other people and firms. Gifts and other types of parcels were increasingly being sent through air freight forwarders, especially at holiday periods and for special occasions, because of the increased reliability and speed.

Perception

As consumers' perceptions of the availability, convenience, and reliability of air freight forwarders increased, the industry was expected to grow. The cargo outlook was good for a number of reasons: the persistent expansion of many national economies; the increasing acceptance and desirability of air freight distribution methods; and the booming popularity of overnight and second-day delivery services ["Aerospace and Air Transport Basic Analysis" 1989].

Since the services offered by various air carriers were almost identical, success was based on customers' perceptions of image and reputation. Freight forwarders strived to offer the fastest, friendliest, and cheapest service available. A loss in customer confidence could be disastrous to a courier. This is why air carriers continuously seek to increase available services and expand their customer base.

GROWING OVERSEAS MARKET

Growth in the international arena is expected to be strong in the 1990s ["Aerospace & Air Transport Basic Analysis," June 21, 1990]. In response to continued progression towards globalization, air carriers are trying to meet shippers' needs worldwide. A need exists not only for overnight deliveries within the U.S., but for overnight deliveries to Europe and to Asia.

The European Market

The European market has been growing at an annual rate of 20.5 percent. This percentage reflects increased international trade and expansion of many national economies. In 1988, air carriers transported 4.53 billion ton-miles overseas, resulting in a gain of 16.4 percent in overall international freight carriage ["Aerospace & Air Transport Basic Analysis" 1989].

In 1992, the 12-member European Economic Community unified to create a single transportation market and air carriers had to establish their presence prior to this time to benefit from this growth [*Transportation and Distribution* January, 1990]. Thus, several freight forwarders established European hubs, acquired European carriers, set daily transatlantic flights with extensive feeder flights, and built ground distribution networks.

The Asian Market & The Pacific Rim

The Asian air express cargo market is expected to grow even faster than the European market in the 1990s. Asian traffic accounted for an estimated 35 percent of world air freight volume in 1986; this number is expected to grow to about 47 percent by the year 2001 ["Aerospace and Air Transport Basic Analysis" 1989].

An estimated 60 percent of the total worldwide tonnage moved by sea-air connections originates in Japan. Two of the most important factors affecting the continued growth of sea-air transportation are airfreight capacity and U.S. government restrictions.

SERVICES

Services provided by air freight couriers include overnight and second-day air service, full-service air express counters, same-day pickup service, and guaranteed overnight deliveries.

Overnight and Second-day Air Service

Overnight and second-day air service were largely responsible for the air cargo industry's expansion. The ability of couriers to pick up and deliver a package or letter overnight was hailed as a great invention. Second-day air service was basically the same as overnight delivery, except that delivery was made two business days after pickup.

The popularity of overnight and second-day air service was so great that by the late 1980s the U.S., Canada, parts of Europe, and a few countries in the Pacific Basin were using these services. As the concept of overnight delivery caught on, air freight carriers expanded their operations to untapped European and Asian markets, while keeping an eye on South American and African markets.

From 1983 to 1986, some air freight forwarders experienced 50 to 80 percent growth in their overnight and second-day air services. Growth rates are expected to remain in the 10 percent range throughout the 1990s ["Aerospace & Air Transport Basic Analysis" 1989].

Full-service Air Express Counters

The full-service air express counter was another service air cargo couriers were expanding. These counters, where packages can be delivered or picked up for overnight delivery or for second-day air service are usually located in the heart of the business district in major U.S. cities. This service caters primarily to businesses, but individuals are also encouraged to use it. The number of and demand for these types of facilities have continued to increase in the 1990s.

Same-day Pickup Service

Another service air carriers provide is same-day pickup service. This service is for businesses and individuals who want their packages picked up for delivery the next day. This service provides flexibility to customers who urgently need shipments made. When a customer calls in, the courier contacts its drivers to inform them of a pending pickup. Usually within two or three hours after the customer's call, an air courier makes the pickup. Couriers which offer same-day pickup service fill a market niche because customers often do not have advance shipping notice. The increased convenience to the customer makes same-day pickup service desirable.

UPS and Federal Express are the only companies that offer this service in the U.S. Federal Express offers it in most cities, while UPS phone-in-pick-up service is now available in 41 metropolitan markets around the country.

Guaranteed Overnight Deliveries

Guaranteeing overnight deliveries by 10:30 a.m. the following day quickly became an industry standard. This forced air freight forwarders to place special emphasis on the delivery of air express parcels, because delivery not made on time would cost the air courier a refund and the possible loss of customer goodwill.

TECHNOLOGICAL ADVANCES

Technological advances were an integral factor affecting the air cargo market in the late 1980s. Industry leaders were using and expanding communications and data processing networks for tracking packages, delivery equipment, and delivery routes.

Tracking Packages En Route

The increased use of technology was at first specifically applied to the tracking of packages en route. The use of bar-coded labels on every package, along with computerized communication networks, was a major advancement in enabling the tracking of customer packages. These bar-coded labels enabled the air courier to identify a package's receiver and sender by scanning it electronically. Couriers placed scanners at several check points throughout their distribution network to scan for missing packages. There appear to be no drawbacks to the use of bar-coded labels.

Using bar-coded labels on packages helps customers find their packages and enables air freight forwarders to know a package's location within half an hour. Another advantage of bar-coded labels, besides consumer satisfaction, is that the labels reduce the number of claims against a courier on lost or misplaced packages because both customers and couriers have an idea of every parcel's location within the distribution network.

Tracking Equipment

Tracking equipment for use by air couriers was implemented in 1989. Electronic monitoring of delivery vans, truck engines, and transmissions avoids costly vehicle breakdowns and delays in parcel delivery or pickup.

Tracking Delivery Routes

Another future technological capability available to couriers involved the tracking of delivery routes. Using electronic networking to map roads and air routes would improve delivery and pickup service by allotting time more efficiently to delivery van drivers and pilots. This type of system would minimize traffic tie-ups and help guide air courier employees to alternative routes. In the early 1990s, the tracking of delivery routes was still in the developmental stage.

Freight Inventory, Release and Shipment Tracking (FIRST)

FIRST is an innovative program which enables customers to expedite and consolidate the inventory and release of international shipments, while producing the necessary data for air bills, commercial invoices, and custom's clearance simultaneously. All of the activities of FIRST are aimed at improving speed — an increasingly important concern in the movement of cargo.

Figure 4: Competition in Air Freight Transportation Industry Components of Competition

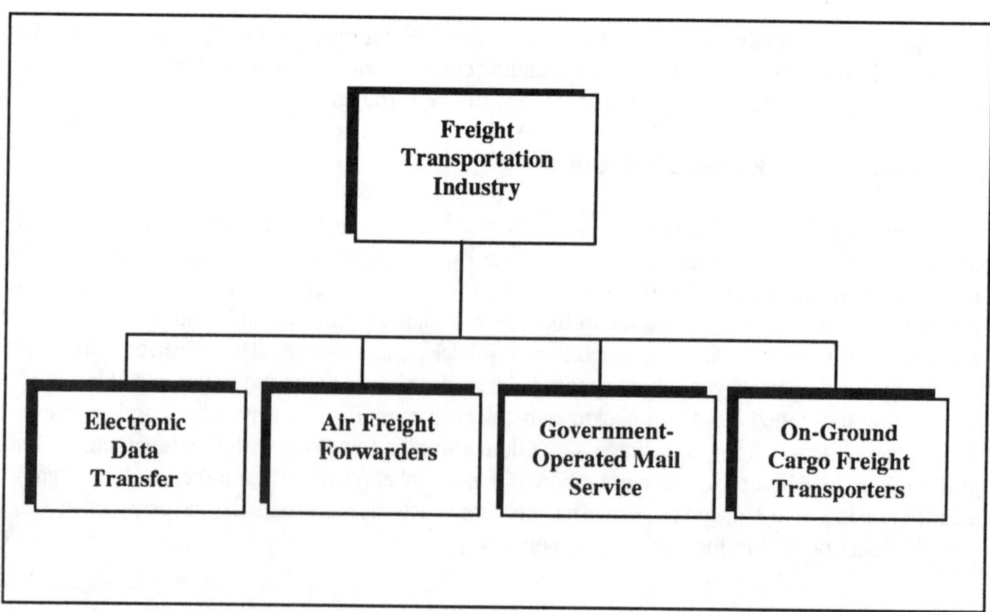

COMPETITION

Within the air cargo industry, competition falls into four groups: electronic data transfer — such as facsimile (FAX) machines; air freight forwarders, such as Federal Express; government-operated mail service, the U.S. Post Office; on-ground cargo freight transporters, such as the trucking industry. Figure 4 illustrates these competitive sectors.

Electronic Data Transfer: Facsimile Machines

The emergence of electronic data transfer in the mid-1980s severely hurt the air cargo industry, especially its overnight letter delivery service.

The development and improvement of the facsimile (FAX) machine was threatening the air cargo market, especially overnight and second-day air services. Overnight FAX document transfer grew in the 50 to 60 percent range in 1986. As the market became saturated, growth slowed to about 10 percent in 1988, and industry experts — such as Standard and Poor's — expect the annual growth rate to remain stable at about 10% ["Aerospace & Air Transport Basic Analysis" 1989].

Other Air Freight Forwarders

Air freight forwarders are declining in numbers but increasing in strength. The three most

Figure 5: Market Share in Domestic Air Express Market (1988)

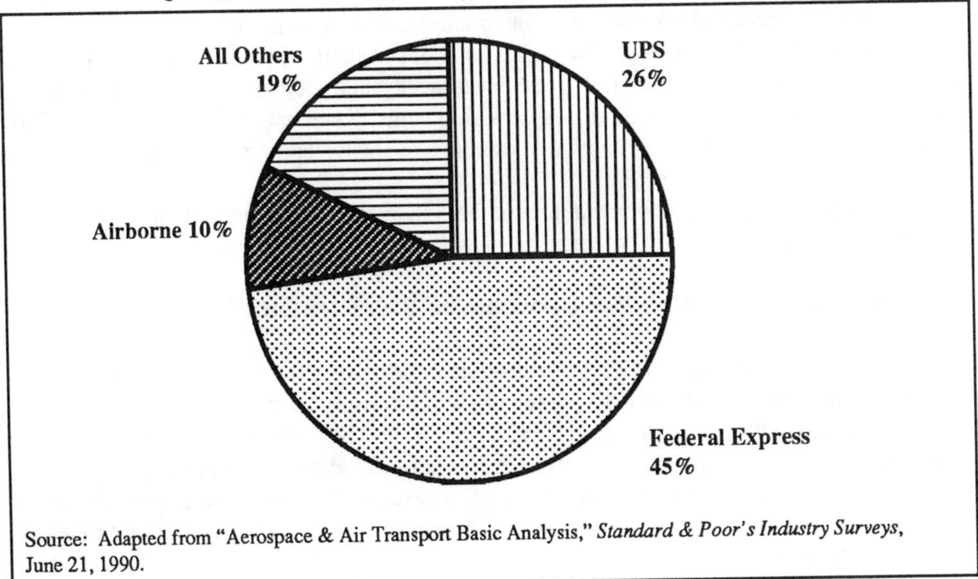

Source: Adapted from "Aerospace & Air Transport Basic Analysis," *Standard & Poor's Industry Surveys*, June 21, 1990.

competitive air freight couriers in the 1990s, besides United Parcel Service, are expected to be Federal Express, DHL, and Airborne Freight.

Federal Express. Federal Express clearly dominates the U.S. market, and is expected to remain a major competitor in all air cargo services. Federal created the overnight market 15 years ago and used its vast technology base to capture nearly half of the overnight market in 1988, as seen in Figure 5. Federal Express is so prominent in the air cargo market that when someone ships a package overnight he is likely to say "I'll Federal Express it to you" regardless of which service is being used [Dumaine 1986].

In 1990, Federal was using 384 planes in its air cargo operations. To take advantage of the international market, Federal established a hub in Brussels, Belgium, and hoped to spread its domination in the overnight market abroad. Through several acquisitions, mainly Tiger International, Inc., the company's strategy is to penetrate the international market and expand its services. Air routes and assets acquired have enabled the company to provide express delivery service to previously unserved areas and offer heavyweight air cargo services worldwide.

Federal experienced a major defeat in 1985 and 1986 when the development of the Fax machine caused its Zap-Mail service to fail. This attempt to corner the electronic data transfer market backfired, and Federal wrote off $350 million in losses in 1986 and 1987 [Foust 1987].

DHL. DHL did not appear capable of making major inroads in the U.S. market in 1990 because of industry saturation. DHL's net operating revenue was $473 million in 1989.

Even though DHL is not a major competitor in the U.S., it controls more than 40 percent of the international market—by far the largest share of any company ["Aerospace & Air Transport Basic Analysis" 1989]. DHL is based in California and integrates an established ground delivery network with its airplanes. DHL, with its 105 planes, was expected to be a force in the international marketplace in the 1990s. The services DHL offered in the early 1990s were limited to overnight and second-day air service, both domestic and international.

Airborne Freight. Airborne Freight is a smaller competitor in the U.S. market and seems anxious to expand overseas. In 1987 it achieved a substantial coup by winning an exclusive contract to carry IBM's domestic air express shipments ["Aerospace & Air Transport Basic Analysis" 1988]. Airborne's strategy is to establish exclusive contracts with large companies which require air express services.

Airborne, which held a 10 percent share of the U.S. overnight market in 1988, operates a fleet of 76 airplanes, and offers only domestic overnight and second-day air service.

Government-operated Mail Service: The U.S. Post Office

Government-operated mail service holds a major position in the air cargo industry, since air couriers are prohibited from providing certain types of delivery services.

The U.S. Post Office is a threat in the air cargo market because it has a monopoly on first-class mail. No other firms, including air freight carriers, can transport first-class mail. Therefore, letters, of which the first-class mail market mostly consists, are excluded from air courier delivery services. The Post Office also has express airmail services which guarantee overnight and second-day air deliveries.

The U.S. Post Office has been in the air express field for 11 years, and has a domestic overnight market share of seven percent. Because the U.S. Post Office — as a branch of the U.S. government — is not a profit-making organization, its services cost more and consumers' perceptions of the quality and reliability of its services are not as high as for privately-owned companies. As a result, its overnight market share seemed to be falling in the early 1990s. There is some feeling in the industry that the Post Office operates inefficiently and unprofitably, but that a reorganization could pose a substantial threat to the air cargo market and related services.

On-ground Cargo Transporters

With the successful development and acceptance of the FAX machine, many air cargo couriers deemphasized letter transport and expanded delivery of boxes and other bulk packages. This placed air couriers in direct competition with on-ground cargo transporters, such as trucks, railroads, and passenger buses.

The trucking and railroad industry. Most heavy bulk packages are transported via the trucking and railroad industries. Roadway and Carolina are the main truck cargo carriers. Roadway had a net income of $80.2 million in 1988, compared to Carolina Freight Corp.'s net income of $10 million. In 1989, Roadway captured 27 percent of the ground freight transportation market share, while Carolina held a 17 percent market share ["Railroad & Trucking Basic Analysis" 1989]. Roadway offered same-day pickup service, but did not have guaranteed overnight delivery service.

As air cargo carriers have begun handling bigger packages, analysts expect the freight trucking industry to decline steadily. In the railroad freight transportation operating revenues have changed little — from $26,661 million in 1985 to $27,123 million in 1988 ["Current Statistics," 1989]. The dominant railroad freight carrier is Consolidated Rail Corp., which earned $349 million in operating revenues in 1988 and had a net income of $3.06 million. Small freight parcels seem to be of minor interest to railroads, which concentrate mainly on transporting larger cargo such as coal, metals, and ores.

Passenger bus companies. Other notable rivals in the air freight transportation market are passenger bus companies. The most visible competitor is the Greyhound Bus Line, which offers similar services as air cargo carriers, plus Greyhound Same-Day Service, for trips under 250 miles. The one problem Greyhound has is that most customers dislike going to a bus depot to pick up and deliver parcels. Unlike air cargo carriers, bus companies have no delivery and pickup network to reach customers' residences.

CONSOLIDATION

As profits continued rising and competition became greater in the air cargo industry, mergers and acquisitions caused the number of competitors to decrease. For example, in 1987 Purolator Courier was acquired by Emery Air Freight. However, Emery sustained large losses in 1988 and early 1989, and was bought out for $240 million by Consolidated Freightways (CF Air Freight).

Figure 6: The Number of Firms Involved in U.S. Freight Transportation Market (1978 vs. 1989)

U.S. DOMESTIC AIR FREIGHT CARRIERS 1978

American Airlines	Eastern	United
Braniff	National	Western
Continental	Northwest	Flying Tiger
Delta	TWA	Airlift International

U.S. DOMESTIC AIR FREIGHT CARRIERS 1989

Airborne Express	Burlington	DHL
Federal Express	UPS	

Source: As reproduced from "Aerospace & Air Transport Basic Analysis," *Standard & Poor's Industry Surveys*, 1982 & 1988, which in turn obtained the data from Cargo Facts.

Towards the end of 1989, Consolidated was rumored to be a takeover possibility for Airborne. Also in 1988, Federal Express purchased Tiger International for $800 million. Tiger was the largest all-cargo air carrier for heavy shipments and its purchase was part of Federal's expansion program.

At the beginning of 1990 UPS acquired seven European transport companies to strengthen its operations in Europe and the Pacific. This included the purchase of the London-based IML Air Service Group Ltd. — a document and parcel delivery company which serves 37 countries.

With deregulation in 1977, passenger airlines gradually eliminated air cargo services as seen in Figure 6. With the exception of Northwest Airlines, which operated air freighters on transpacific routes, none of the U.S. airlines appeared capable of or desirable of re-entering the air cargo industry.

Industry experts were predicting in 1989 that two or three air cargo firms would survive this consolidation and be viable competitors in the international air cargo market in the 1990s.

PROBLEMS

A few problems that could affect the future of the air cargo market were a shortage of freighter aircraft, rising fuel prices, and the threat of a price war.

Shortage of Freighter Aircraft

The average growth rate in the air cargo industry was 20 percent in the 1980s and air freight forwarders were finding it difficult to obtain the necessary aircraft ["Aerospace & Air Transport Basic Analysis" 1989]. Many air carriers had placed orders with aircraft manufacturers, such as Boeing, to expand their fleets, but a large backlog of passenger-plane orders was expected to delay delivery of these freighter aircraft until the early to mid-1990s.

Firms tried to lease cargo airplanes, but a shortage existed in this area too, and air freight forwarders were forced to bid up prices on used passenger aircraft and refit these planes for cargo transport. This cost over $18 million per plane, and such costs pushed air freight rates even higher.

Rising Fuel Prices

The threat of rising fuel prices is a major concern for many air freight forwarders, since services charges would have to rise to cover such increases. During the 1990s, fuel prices are expected to rise 20% to 30% above 1989 price levels. The average price per gallon of fuel in 1989 was $1.13, according to Standard & Poor's.

THE COMPANY

United Parcel Service of America, Inc., is a holding and management company, the principal subsidiaries of which provide specialized transportation services, primarily through the delivery of small packages and parcels [*Form 10K UPS* 1988]. In 1989 UPS delivered 2.7 billion packages; by comparison, the U.S. Post Office delivered 1.4 billion packages. UPS achieved the status of being the largest private freight transportation company in the U.S. through its ground transportation services. In the early 1980s UPS entered the air cargo market.

UPS is a privately-held company in which the managers and supervisors own all common stock. UPS's stock is not listed on any exchange and there is no public market for its shares. Managers and supervisors receive shares as compensation earned. When a shareholder leaves the company, he has to sell all stock back to the company at the current price set by UPS, and when he retires he has up to 10 years to sell his stock.

HISTORY OF UPS

UPS began as a messenger service 83 years ago in Seattle, Washington. James E. Casey, its founder, declared, "the company must be owned by its managers and managed by its owners" [Labich 1988]. His philosophy was that what was good for the customer would ultimately pay off for the company. Through this kind of thinking, UPS transformed itself into a profitable U.S. transportation company.

UPS has been known primarily for its ground transportation services, and has built its excellent reputation through this service. Those boxy brown UPS trucks are such an integral part of the American landscape that they fit into the urban scene like so many telephone poles or fire hydrants [Labich 1988]. In 1989, UPS owned and operated 103,700 vehicles — from panel vans to tractor trailers—in its extensive ground network delivery service.

UPS's goal is to provide the best possible service at the lowest possible cost to its customers. UPS is one of the most envied companies in the U.S. because it provides outstanding service with stable prices. During the 1980s, UPS expanded by carrying the company's philosophy into the air cargo industry.

SERVICES OFFERED

The services UPS offers are broken down into two categories ground service and air service. The air service category is further subdivided into domestic overnight and second-day air service, international overnight and second-day air service, same-day pickup service, air express centers, and guaranteed overnight deliveries.

Ground Service

Ground service is simply the movement of freight by trucks or railroad cars to a specific destination. UPS provides ground service to every address in the U.S., Canada, and Germany.

A parcel for UPS delivery can weigh up to 70 pounds and can be up to 130 inches in length, width and height combined. UPS's ground rates have increased only 6.5 percent since 1982. Consumers' perceive UPS service to be flawless, and industry experts rate UPS as one of the top service firms in the U.S.

The company is considering expansion of its ground network overseas, because it contracts out local ground transportation companies to complete its air services abroad, except in Germany.

Air Services

UPS entered the air freight transportation market in 1982. Air service entailed the integration of its ground network system with airport terminals and hubs.

Domestic overnight and second-day air service. When UPS entered the overnight and second-day air markets, they did so with "UPS Next-Day Air" and "UPS Second-Day Air" services. For both of these, UPS provided pick up service with a one-day advance notice for new customers, or customers dropped off their parcels at a business air express center. Delivery was made by noon on the following day and by the same time two days later for second-day air parcels.

UPS established a central hub in Louisville, Kentucky, and regional hubs in Philadelphia, Pennsylvania and Ontario, California to serve the east and west coasts, respectively.

These air services were available anywhere in the U.S. and by 1988 UPS had cornered 15 percent of the overnight market share. In March of 1990, UPS raised its rates for the first time since establishing overnight delivery service in 1982.

International overnight and second-day air service. UPS provides international overnight and second-day air services to 39 countries, including Canada, all of Western Europe, 14 countries in Asia, and 57 cities in the People's Republic of China. In 1988 UPS opened its international hub in Cologne, West Germany, and had 2,700 regular shippers who sent daily shipments of approximately 220,000 packages.

Outside of West Germany, UPS has yet to establish its own ground delivery network to provide final delivery of international overnight and second-day air service to customers. To remain competitive in the international market UPS will need more hubs. In the Pacific Rim area, UPS has not designated a country or city to act as its central hub, and it also has no ground delivery network system in the Far East.

Same-day pickup service. UPS offers same-day pickup service to regular customers, who get daily pickup service regardless of whether they have a parcel. By the end of 1988 UPS drivers made 933,000 automatic daily stops for pickups. However, if a new customer calls for a pickup, the company needs a day's advance notice to arrangeit.

Air express centers. UPS had set up 19 air express centers in the U.S. by the end of 1988. These express centers catered mainly to businesses and were located in the heart of business districts in major metropolitan cities throughout the U.S. At these centers, overnight and second-day air packages could be picked up or dropped off to make air services more convenient for businesses. UPS was contemplating the expansion of these air express centers throughout the U.S. and in several major cities abroad.

Guarantees of overnight deliveries. On January 1, 1988, UPS introduced a money-back guarantee on domestic packages sent by UPS Next-Day Air service. This guarantee stated that UPS would refund the price of the delivery to the sender if delivery was not made by noon. Guaranteed overnight delivery for international parcels and other services offered was being considered by UPS management.

OVERSEAS EXPANSION

UPS has expanded overseas with its international overnight and second-day air services. International air service is now offered in countries and territories throughout the UPS service network, an increase of over 135 countries and territories since December 31, 1988, when it was available in only 39 countries. This expansion was achieved largely through the acquisition of IML Service Group Ltd. — a British-based company which serves over 100 countries. In addition, UPS acquired six other European companies which serve as freight forwarders in Belgium, Denmark, Finland, France, the Netherlands, and Switzerland [*The New York Times*, January 22, 1990].

The idea of establishing a hub in an Asian country, probably in Japan, is under consideration by UPS top management. The ability to capitalize on the fast-growing international air freight transportation markets could establish UPS as a leader in global air freight transportation.

UPS CREATES ITS OWN AIRLINE

In order for UPS to offer these new and expanded services they needed the aircraft to ship parcels cross country and overseas. In 1981, UPS purchased its first Boeing 727; since then the company has, in essence, created its own airline.

With deregulation, passenger airlines were free to change routes and curtail flights, and so

Figure 7: United Parcel Service Owned Air Fleet as of December 31, 1989

Description	Number Owned	Number Leased
McDonnell Douglas DC-8-71	20	
McDonnell Douglas DC-8-73	23	
Boeing 747-100		6
Boeing 757-200	15	
Boeing 727-100	32	
Boeing 727-200	8	
Fairchild SA227-AT	11	
Other		241
Total	**109**	**247**

Source: Information obtained from United Parcel Service, *10-K Report, 1989.*

became unpredictable in their schedules. Out of necessity, UPS began to assemble its own airline so that it would not have to rely on others to meet delivery guarantees. By 1988 UPS owned 107 aircrafts and leased another 247 airplanes. Figure 7 shows the types of airplanes in UPS's owned air fleet.

The pride of the fleet was the 757-PF. UPS bought 20 of these cargo aircraft with an option to purchase 15 more. In March 1989, UPS exercised the option for 10 more 757-PFs. These planes were newly designed freight carriers that were extremely quiet and economical. Quiet planes are expected to become the future in the aircraft industry, since people living near airports have demanded that available technology be utilized to reduce noise levels. The 757-PF was also the most cost-efficient freighter, which helped lower UPS's operating costs. The rest of UPS's fleet varied in model and size.

TECHNOLOGY

UPS was in the midst of the largest technological advancement in its history at the time of this case study. "If you went into our information services facility in 1985, you went into 1975 in terms of technology," said Francis Erbrick, UPS's vice president for information services. UPS had to greatly expand its technology base in order to compete in the air cargo industry. Starting in 1988 and continuing through 1991, UPS planned to spend $1.4 billion to equip, house, and staff what it claims will be one of the most advanced computer operations in the transportation industry [King 1988]. Figure 8 illustrates UPS's planned expenditure on technology.

Since UPS wanted the capability to make same-day pickups, it planned to install tracking

Figure 8: United Parcel Service Technology Budget Projection (1986-1991)

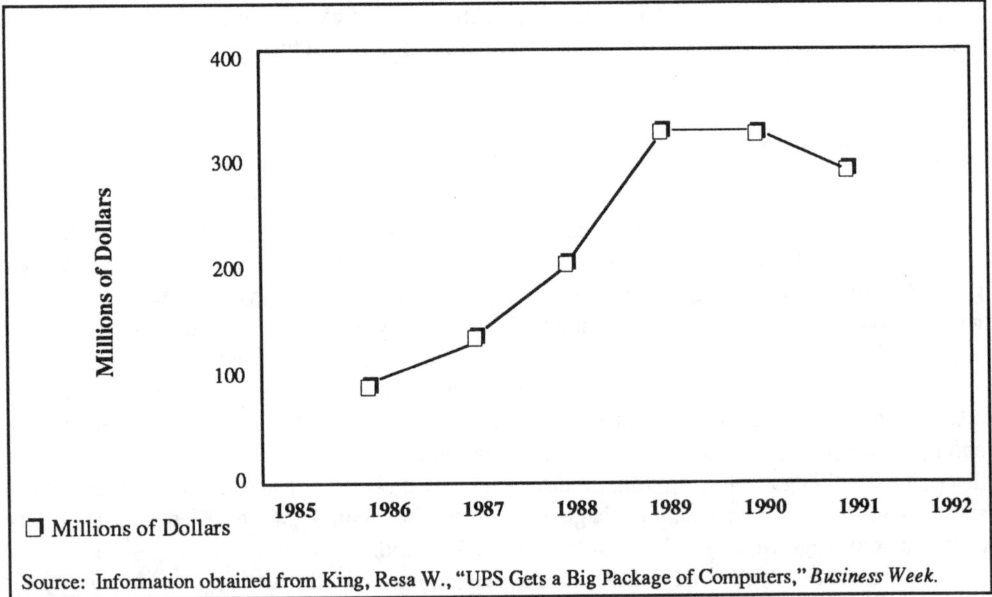

Source: Information obtained from King, Resa W., "UPS Gets a Big Package of Computers," *Business Week.*

systems and communications in its vehicles. In an effort to bridge this technology gap, UPS acquired two small computer firms. One company, Roadnet Systems Corporation, was acquired in 1986 for its expertise in computerized mapping, scheduling, and tracking systems. UPS may become the first company to map the entire U.S. for purposes of vehicle routing and tracking ["Big Changes at Big Brown Ready It for Future Growth 1989"]. The other company UPS took over was II Morrow, a manufacturer of on-board engine monitoring computer systems that keep constant surveillance on engine and transmission components. UPS hoped to use this technology to improve vehicle performance and reduce costly road breakdowns. UPS planned to have all of its trucks computerized and monitored by 1991. These plans were included in the $1.4 billion expansion strategy. Other than Federal Express, no other competitor has contemplated or used such sophisticated technology.

Another system UPS was developing was the Delivery Information Acquisition Device (DIAD). The DIAD was being tested to replace the delivery record where customers signed a sheet of paper to prove they had received their packages. Instead, the DIAD scanned bar-coded labels for shipper and package identification numbers. It also captured signatures for deliveries when the recipients received their parcels.

Another technological improvement that UPS developed in the international transport of packages was a link between the company and the U.S. Customs Services Automated Brokerage Interface. In April 1988, UPS became the first air carrier to connect custom brokers directly to Customs Services.

All of these technological improvements provide better service, such as same-day pickup, and improve the accuracy and timeliness of parcel deliveries and pickups. UPS is not only trying to match its competition in the technology field, but also, to move ahead of others and become a leader in technological aspects of the air freight transportation industry.

MANAGEMENT

UPS managers and supervisors want the company to succeed because they own it. Most of the top managers have come up through the ranks, which means they started as drivers and then gradually advanced to higher levels. The employees, therefore, have a very strong identification with the company. The closely-held nature of the company frees executives to make long-range strategic decisions without worrying about Wall Street's reaction [Labich 1988].

One area of concern for UPS management is volume discounts. The idea of offering discounts to high-volume customers does not appeal to management, which believes rates are low enough. Due to the air cargo market becoming saturated and competitors offering volume discounts, UPS began offering volume discounts on October 17, 1988. Previously customers spent $8.50 to mail a two-pound package; now it costs between $7.50 and $7, depending on the customer's average weekly volume over a 13-week period.

On February 12, 1990 UPS increased its interstate rates for domestic ground service by 4.4 percent and for second-day air service by 6.3 percent. In addition, it increased its next-day air letter rates by 50 cents for daily pick-up customers. This rate hike offset the volume discounts given to high-volume customers.

UPS has the ability to attract, develop, and keep talented people. In the Greenwich, Connecticut headquarters, hourly employees, vice presidents, and the chairman and chief executive dine and search for parking spaces together. Everyone is on a first-name basis. This management style and philosophy accounts for industry experts rating UPS with IBM.

MARKETING

UPS was one of America's most publicity-shy corporations until 1988. The company does not volunteer much information about itself and it is difficult to retrieve data from the firm. In 1988, UPS moved strongly into the advertising field with a slogan that said, "We run the tightest ship in the shipping business." This campaign was launched with $35 million dollars and UPS planned to continue advertising to make its name even more visible.

Marketing the UPS name was not difficult since the company had been ranked first in *Fortune's* corporate service reputation survey for five consecutive years. Industry opinion of the company is very high since customers believe they are getting great service for their money. This perception has created a vast amount of customer goodwill and loyalty towards the company.

FINANCE

UPS is in excellent financial shape with heavy cash flow and a successful sale of $700 million in debentures to the public. These debentures which represent UPS's first public offering of taxable debt, received a AAA rating by Moody's Investor Service and by Standard & Poor's. At the end of 1989 UPS had operating revenues of almost $12.4 billion and a net income of more than $693.4 billion, as shown in Figure 9.

MAINTENANCE

If UPS could add another letter to its name, it would be M for maintenance. The company is maintenance mad about its 111,258 trucks and vans, and its fleet of airplanes. All vehicles are washed every day and are placed on a computerized maintenance schedule. This is the main reason why UPS's package cars remain in service for an average of 22 years and its feeder vans log two million miles or more. The airplanes receive the same attention, and a very substantial effort is made to avoid breakdowns and delays.

Figure 9: United Parcel Service

CONSOLIDATED INCOME STATEMENT

INCOME STATEMENT	1987	1988	1989
NET REVENUES	$9,682,155	$11,032,075	$12,357,918
COST OF SERVICES SOLD	($5,874,211)	($6,728,010)	($7,392,182)
GROSS PROFIT	$3,807,944	$4,304,065	$4,965,736
EXPENSES:			
SELLING, GENERAL, AND ADMIN. EXP	($2,837,255)	($3,228,828)	($3,750,466)
INTEREST EXPENSE	($3,734)	($5,443)	($14,833)
OTHER INCOME:			
NON-OPERATING INCOME	$45,704	$16,258	$2,671
INCOME BEFORE TAXES	$1,012,659	$1,086,052	$1,203,108
PROVISION FOR INCOME TAXES	($387,913)	($327,329)	($509,684)
NET INCOME BEFORE EXTRAORDINARY ITEM	$624,746	$758,723	$693,424
EXTRAORDINARY ITEM (LOSS)	$159,404	$0	$0
NET INCOME	$784,150	$758,723	$693,424

SOURCE: Information obtained from United Parcel Service, *10-K Report, 1989*.

Figure 9 (Cont.): United Parcel Service Consolidated Balance Sheet

CONSOLIDATED BALANCE SHEET	1987	1988	1989
ASSETS			
CURRENT ASSETS:			
CASH AND EQUIVALENTS	$135,547	$28,237	$41,594
MARKETABLE SECURITIES	$421,900	$381,551	$463,209
ACCOUNTS RECEIVABLE NET	$210,011	$358,106	$753,901
INVENTORIES	$267,584	$238,461	$298,553
OTHER CURRENT ASSETS	$593,113	$460,601	$465,906
TOTAL CURRENT ASSETS	$1,628,155	$1,466,956	$2,023,163
PROPERTY, PLANT AND EQUIPMENT, NET	$3,943,795	$4,792,310	$5,429,464
INVESTMENTS IN UNCONSOLIDATED AFFILIATES	$344,609	$0	$0
INTANGIBLE ASSETS (NET)	$0	$0	$0
OTHER NON-CURRENT ASSETS	$85,105	$444,360	$435,500
TOTAL NON-CURRENT ASSETS	$4,373,509	$5,236,670	$5,864,964
TOTAL ASSETS	$6,001,664	$6,703,626	$7,888,127

CONSOLIDATED BALANCE SHEET	1987	1988	1989
LIABILITIES AND STOCKHOLDER'S EQUITY			
CURRENT LIABILITIES:			
ACCOUNTS PAYABLE	$391,095	$500,083	$575,087
CURRENT PORTION OF LONG-TERM DEBT	$1,964	$10,169	$4,281
ACCRUED EXPENSES	$981,370	$1,279,875	$1,144,127
INCOME TAXES	$24,375	$95,755	$100,556
OTHER CURRENT LIABILITIES			
TOTAL CURRENT LIABILITIES	$1,398,804	$1,885,882	$1,824,051
LONG-TERM DEBT	$293,825	$140,009	$848,036
DEFERRED CHARGES	$1,281,513	$1,496,963	$1,627,305
OTHER LIABILITIES	$38,459	$18,785	$31,347
TOTAL NON-CURRENT LIABILITIES	$1,613,797	$1,655,757	$2,506,688
TOTAL LIABILITIES	$3,012,601	$3,541,639	$4,330,739
STOCKHOLDER'S EQUITY			
PREFERRED STOCK:			
COMMON STOCK:	$16,887	$16,187	$16,187
PAID IN CAPITAL	$271,844	$293,936	$296,371
RETAINED EARNINGS	$2,700,332	$2,851,864	$3,244,830
TOTAL PAID IN CAPITAL	$2,989,063	$3,161,987	$3,557,388
LESS: TREASURY STOCK (# SHARES) AT COST	$0	$0	$0
TOTAL SHAREHOLDER'S EQUITY	$2,989,063	$3,161,987	$3,557,388
TOTAL LIABILITIES & EQUITY	$6,001,664	$6,703,626	$7,888,127

SOURCE: Information obtained from United Parcel Service, *10-K Report, 1989.*

LABOR

By the end of 1989, UPS had approximately 241,000 employees. This number included the pre-loaders, loaders, truck washers, mechanics, pilots, eighteen-wheel haulers, and delivery drivers. Several aspects of UPS's labor force are explained in more detail below.

Drivers

The drivers are the backbone of the company because they establish and maintain a friendly one-on-one relationship with customers. The drivers are the real heroes of the company: living, breathing, Norman Rockwell portraits. Their attitude and appearance are important because goodwill towards the company is transmitted at this level. Drivers try to conform to customers' desires even if it means changing their normal schedules.

Part-time College Students

A labor tactic that UPS employs is hiring part-time college students. In 1988 the company had 40,000 part-time college students in its sorting centers. It is the "greatest recruiting ground imaginable" says Joseph R. Mederow, a UPS service vice president. This allows the company to see young upcoming talent so it can include some of them in the management team, as well as instill the company's winning philosophy in them.

Hard Work

The work is very hard, from the sorting and loading of packages to delivery to the customers. Time and motion studies have been applied to every position in UPS to get the most out of employees. The company expects much from its employees, and most employees respond with a passionate commitment to and strong identification with the company. Employees are not afraid of hard work, and up to 80 percent of the work force turns up for voluntary workshops. The company's labor turnover ratio is only four percent. Many employees talk about the company's mystique and want to see the company succeed.

Unions

Most of UPS's employees are unionized. On August 13, 1990 the union approved a three-year contract to replace the one that expired on August 1, 1990. This was achieved only after bitter negotiations and the help of federal mediators in a series of court battles between the union leaders and dissident groups. The new contract includes a wage increase of 50 cents an hour each year for the three-year pact, cost of living increases, new wage tiers for new employees, bonuses, and an employer contribution into the UPS health and welfare and pension funds totalling 35 cents an hour.

Presently, the threat of a strike or walkout is not great, but future employee dissatisfaction could cause major disruptions in service. Most unionized employees belong to the International Brotherhood of Teamsters.

TOWARDS THE FUTURE

With industry experts predicting slow growth in the domestic market, increased growth in the international market, the unification of Europe as one transportation segment, increased volume of transportation from Japan, and as a number of small carriers disappear from the air cargo business, UPS is faced with some difficult decisions.

As a result, UPS's management is exploring a variety of strategic directions for the company to pursue in the 1990s.

UPS battled to reach its labor contract agreement with its employee union. Some managers feel that a change in ownership style to an employee-held organization would be helpful. They argue that a great deal of employee motivation could be achieved by giving out a small percent of company ownership.

The company is exploring ways to overcome Federal Express's dominance in the domestic market. Should UPS offer all services available in the industry and can its low-cost structure remain intact with rising fuel prices?

Many in the industry agree that the greatest growth will take place in Europe, Asia, and the Pacific Rim. Most UPS managers are certain that they have to enter these markets to survive in the 1990s. But, management is divided as to the best method of market entry: acquisitions, direct expansion, or joint ventures. Managers who argue for acquisitions argue that UPS will be able to gain the new market experience and brand reputation of the new companies that they are buying. But others point out the need for high investment and the difficulty of integration. Those who believe in direct expansion argue that UPS can extend its low-cost structure to its new markets through this method. Others point out the time needed to develop these routes. Those who believe in joint ventures are certain this is the easiest and quickest way to enter these markets. But others are not ready to share these lucrative markets with other companies. Senior management decided to evaluate all of the alternatives before making a decision for any market segment.

Industry experts are predicting that UPS can be at the top or near the top in technology-enhanced delivery services. UPS has to be the most technologically advanced freight transportation company in the world in order to stay ahead of the competition. Some insiders think that UPS cannot maintain its low-cost structure since it has just signed an expensive contract with its employees. In short, management is considering ways in which it can differentiate itself from its competitors and improve its strategic position in the long run.

REFERENCES AND BACKGROUND READINGS

"Aerospace & Air Transport Basic Analysis," *Standard & Poor's Industry Surveys*, May 4, 1989.

"Aerospace & Air Transport Basic Analysis," *Standard & Poor's Industry Surveys*, 1988.

"Aerospace & Air Transport Basic Analysis," *Standard & Poor's Industry Surveys*, 1982.

"Aerospace & Air Transport Current Analysis," *Standard & Poor's Industry Surveys*, August 10, 1989.

"Battle for Overnight Skies: UPS Zooms to No. 2," *Advertising Age*, June 20, 1988, p. 80.

"Big Changes at Big Brown Ready It For Future Growth," *Distribution*, May 1989, pp. 16.

Bohman, Ray, "UPS to Offer New Cost- Cutting Opportunities," *Traffic Management*, December 1987, pp. 21-22.

Bradsher, Keith, "Cargo Boom Causes Plane Shortage," *New York Times*, Business Section, October 9, 1989, pp. D1 and D3.

"Corporate Performance Data," *Fortune*, January 19, 1987, p. 31.

"Current Statistics," *Standard & Poor's Statistical Service*, November 1989.

"Developments in Industrial Relation," *Monthly Labor Review*, October 1987, pp. 47-49.

Dumaine, Brian, "The Turbulence Hits the Air Couriers," *Fortune*, July 21, 1986, pp. 101-106.

Feazel, Michael, "Emery, UPS Expand Package Service Into European, International Markets," *Aviation Week & Space Technology*, October 6, 1986, pp. 44-49.

"Financial Ranking Data," *Fortune*, June 8, 1987, pp. 212-213.

Form 10-K UPS, December 31, 1989.

Fotos, Christopher P, "UPS Establish Its Own Airline to Simplify Flight Operations," *Aviation Week & Space Technology*, October 3, 1988, pp. 108-109.

Foust, Dean, "Why Federal Express Has Overnight Anxiety," *Business Week*, November 9, 1987, pp. 62-66.

"Ground Service Chart," *UPS* 1989.

"International Air Service Guide," United Parcel Service, August 1989.

King, Resa W, "UPS Gets a Big Package - of Computers," *Business Week*, July 25, 1988, p. 66.

Labich, Kenneth, "Big Changes at Big Brown," *Fortune*, January 18, 1988, pp. 56-64.

Lopez, Ramon, "United Parcel Service Creates Its Own Airline With the 757PF," *Aviation Week & Space Technology*, October 3, 1988, p. 107.

Mecham, Michael, "UPS Introduces 757 Freighters To Expand Service, Constrain Noise," *Aviation Week & Space Technology*, September 14, 1987, pp. 49-52.

"Pragmatic PACS Prefer Incumbents," *Fortune*, November 7, 1988, p. 12.

"Railroad & Trucking Basic Analysis," *Standard & Poor's Industry Surveys*, October 19, 1989, pp. 49-58.

"Rates for UPS Domestic Air Service" *UPS* 1989.

"Stars Of The Service 500," *Fortune*, June 5, 1989, pp. 54-62.

"UPS Company Profile," *St. John's Library Computer* 1989.

"UPS Expands Hub System to Keep Pace With Demand for Courier Services," *Aviation Week & Space Technology*, October 3, 1988, p. 109.

"UPS Grabs for a Bigger Share of the International Market," *Distribution*, November 1988, p. 26.

"UPS Offers Volume Discounts On Certain Deliveries," *Wall Street Journal*, October 25, 1988, Section C, p. 12.

"UPS Plans to Boost Some Rates, Making Price War in Deliveries Unlikely," *Wall Street Journal*, January 5, 1989, Section C, p. 15.

"What's the Best Way to Send Presents?," *Consumer Reports*, November 1987, pp. 662-66

Subject & Company Name INDEX*

---

* For Chapters 1 through 14 and for Appendices A and B only.

THE STRATEGIC MANAGEMENT RESEARCH GROUP

The Group and its Center of Knowledge-based Systems (KBS) Center for Business and its Center for Case Development and Use were formed in 1985 by its two principals, Dr. Robert J. Mockler and Dr. D.G. Dologite. The Group continues work done since 1969 by Dr. Mockler on cognitive modelling of strategic management and other management decision processes. The objective in forming the Group and its Case Development and KBS Centers was to promote not only research in the strategic management area, but also development of knowledge-based systems (KBS) and case studies for strategic management decision making, as well as teaching methods related to these areas. The Group and its Centers have done pioneering work in cognitive modelling of strategic management decision processes and developing knowledge-based systems (KBS), case studies, and related teaching techniques.

As part of the KBS project, for example, over 200 non-technical and technical business managers, most of them working full-time during the project, developed over 160 KBS prototype systems in conjunction with MBA courses in strategic management over a four year period. Based on replies to a survey of a sample test group, 28 percent of the survey respondents reported their KBS were used at work, 21 percent reportedly received promotions, pay raises or new jobs based on their KBS development work, and 12 percent reported their work led to participation in other KBS development projects at work. All but two of the survey respondents reported their work on their KBS development project led to a substantial increase in their job knowledge or performance. To give an idea of the scope of the project, a doctoral dissertation at University of Oregon during the same time period was reportedly based on a similar project in an accounting course involving seven students for one semester.

In a second project area, over a four year period some 100 case studies were prepared mostly by working managers. In constructing these case studies an effort was made to balance the need to have models of effective structured competitive market and company analyses in the cases, and at the same time ensure that the cases were able to give practice in cognitive remodelling or reconceptualization of strategic management situations and in formulating and evaluating alternative enterprise-wide strategies and implementing them more effectively. The first phase of the project involved guiding some 150 younger working executives in the modelling of company strategy formulation and implementation problems. Each executive participant in the study wrote an original case study on a company with which they worked or otherwise knew well enough to get first hand information from. At the same time, they limited the material presented in the case study to public domain information to avoid confidentiality problems. These case studies were revised and updated several times during the project. The subsequent phase of the study involved having a similar group write and present business planning studies and reports using the company studies developed during the first phase of the project.

The third Group project area extended work in the first two areas to developing innovative teaching techniques based on both case study and KBS development and use in conjunction with undergraduate, graduate, and executive business training programs. This work has led to national and regional awards for innovative teaching and research.

The fourth Group project area involves more formal work in strategic management theory development. In addition to the studies mentioned above, this work covers topics such as: modelling cognitive and behavioral (individual and group) processes involved in strategic management; change management; integrating the diverse approaches to strategic management theory and research; a wide range of application areas, including international and entrepreneurial situations and situations involving environmental/social factors; computer information systems supporting strategic management and their impact on different strategic management areas, including organization design, business process reengineering, leadership styles, and creativity; and using group decision support systems and environments to stimulate and guide management decision making and actions. In keeping with the applied nature of business management, special attention has been given to micro contingency theories related to management decision making in general and strategic management decision making in particular; this work focuses on theory useful to individual managers working in specific company situations.

These studies are the basis of much of the work described in the publications of the Group's two principles. This work includes over 40 books and monographs, over 150 articles and presentations, 100 case studies in strategic management, and several awards for innovative teaching and research.

AUTHOR BIOGRAPHY

Dr. Robert J. Mockler is a Professor of Business at St. John's University's Graduate School of Business. He is director of the Strategic Management Research Group and its Centers of Knowledge-Based Systems for Business and of Case Study Development. He has authored 30 books, 100 case studies and more than 120 articles and presentations covering such areas as strategic management, case study development and use, computer information systems, modelling of cognitive and behavioral management processes, business process reengineering, expert knowledge-based systems, competitive market analysis, management decision making, new venture management, multinational planning, group decision support systems for management, innovative teaching and business ethics. His first articles on strategic management and situational decision theory were published in *Harvard Business Review* in 1970 and 1971. His first book on strategic management was published in 1969 (Prentice-Hall). His latest books include two on expert systems development in 1992 (Macmillan) and two on strategic management in 1993 and 1994 (Addison Wesley, Simon and Schuster). He has lectured and consulted worldwide, and received national awards for innovative teaching. He has also started and run his own multi-million dollar business ventures.